1980 Craftworker's Market

where to sell your crafts

Edited By
Lynne Lapin

Assistant Editor
Leslie Wilson

Writer's Digest Books

Writer's Digest Books
Cincinnati, Ohio

About this Book

This is the first edition of *Craftworker's Market* produced on a computerized word processing system recently installed in the Writer's Digest Books editorial offices. Developed by the Quadex Corporation, Boston, the system is designed to store all the material in the book on a magnetic disk, which allows for easy and immediate access to information. Thus we have a master file of the most current markets information available. The market listings are read—and updated—on a video display terminal—much like a TV screen.

The text of the book was set in Times Roman, a type face designed by Stanley Morrison at the turn of the century for the *London Times*. It is a practical "work-horse" type which, because of its legibility, allows us to pack a generous amount of type onto the page, thus keeping *Craftworker's Market* to a convenient size.

The book is printed on a blue-white shade of Madison Superset, an uncoated groundwood paper, and is adhesive bound and attached to a hard case.

Barron Krody, a Cincinnati freelance artist, created the interior book design using supergraphic letters and numbers to contrast with the text. He chose a two-column layout for the articles in the front of the book and the market section introductions so as to visually separate this material from the market listings.

The book jacket showcases tools of the crafts trade and an 1890s brass cash register. The jacket was designed and photographed by Lawrence Zink Inc.

Craftworker's Market. Copyright© 1979. Published by Writer's Digest Books, 9933 Alliance Rd., Cincinnati, Ohio 45242. Publisher/Editorial Director: Richard Rosenthal. Managing Editor: Douglas Sandhage. Assistant to the Managing Editor: Connie Achabal. Printed and bound in the United States of America. All rights reserved. No part of this book may be reproduced in any manner whatsoever without written permission from the publisher, except by reviewers who may quote brief passages to be printed in a magazine or newspaper.

International Standard Serial Number 0161-0554
International Standard Book Number 0-89879-004-2

Contents

The Profession

How to Use Your
Craftworker's Market 1
The Craft Market Today 4
Working With the Retailer 10
Promoting Yourself and
Your Work 16

The Markets

Architectural and Interior
Design Firms 21
Colleges and Universities 30
Companies and
Manufacturers 49
Shops and Galleries 67
Shows and Fairs 413
Apprenticeships 643

Glossary 649

Index 651

The Profession

How to Use Your Craftworker's Market

We have gathered the wealth of information enclosed within the pages of this book to help you best sell your crafts as a craftworker. *Craftworker's Market* is the only directory available that gives specific details on thousands of markets for your work, and the only one geared strictly toward the purpose of helping you make money and get exposure by providing markets that are actively seeking crafts.

Start using this book by reading the marketing articles that follow. They give you the basic—and some not so basic—information you will need to successfully sell your crafts. Tips on pricing, promotion, determining what to produce and just plain selling your work are included as well as a piece on marketing and fashion trends.

Once you feel you know the "how-to's" you're ready to move on to the "where to's." Listings in The Markets section of this book are the bulk of *Craftworker's Market*. The information supplied in each listing covers the who, what, when and where of each market, and is supplied directly from the buyer/exhibitor.

There are six major sections in The Markets: Architectural & Interior Design Firms; Colleges & Universities; Companies & Manufacturers; Shops & Galleries; Shows & Fairs; and Apprenticeships. Architectural firms are best for craft professionals seeking the highest possible payments; companies are ideal outlets for persons who have products that lend themselves well to mass-production and appeal to a large number of people; shops and galleries are interested in a wide number of styles and degrees of crafts; and shows and fairs are great for the beginner as well as others looking for recognition and sales.

Within each listing in each section is included such information as who the contact person is, what type of crafts are desired and how to submit them, exactly what is desired, what to expect in terms of payment and fees, and other information the craftworker may want or need to know. Read each listing thoroughly before contacting a buyer or exhibitor. Is your craft medium welcome? Does your work fall within the price range offered? Is your craft of the right style, and would it fit in with the decor of the outlet?

Two especially important listing factors the retailer urges the craftworker to take note of are: (1) How should you contact this outlet? and (2) What type of work do they need? As a craftworker you will also want to look at prices, method of doing business (consignment vs buying outright) and the Profile subhead. *Studying the markets before submitting anything to them cannot be stressed enough.* We often hear complaints from craft buyers saying craftworkers don't pay close enough attention to the instructions provided in the listings. Not reading or ignoring instructions often ends in rejection of your work.

The following is additional advice and information we have compiled to help you use your *Craftworker's Market* to its best advantage:

• Read each listing thoroughly. A market may only want to work with craftworkers from a certain ethnic origin, or they may only consider those artisans who send a specified number of slides covering specific angles of the work. Also, take note that many of the listings do *not* want to receive unsolicited crafts in the mail—these buyers usually prefer to see the craftworker's resume or slides of the work first.

• The year in which a show or business was established will give you some idea of its reliability—a gallery established in 1953 is less likely to fold than one founded last year. But, while the risk is greater when working with a new firm, the buyers are usually more open to new names.

• If you don't recognize a name or term you read in a listing, chances are it will be defined in the glossary at the back of the book. For example, SASE means self-addressed stamped envelope—and this should be included with *all* correspondence with buyers.

• Information contained in the Profile subhead found in many listings will give you some idea of the type of atmosphere the buyer sells under, the best selling times, who the customers are, and other information concerning the type of work you'll have to produce for that particular outlet. Occasionally you will come across a listing with a How To Break In or Sales Tip subhead in which buyers give tips on how to sell to their particular market.

• A firm, publication or organization may not be included in *Craftworker's Market* for any one of the following reasons: (1) It asked to be omitted. (2) It did not return a questionnaire. (3) It does not buy crafts.

• If you know of a good market for crafts which is not included, please let us know. Send the name and address of the firm, what type of establishment it is (craft shop, gallery, kit manufacturer, show, etc.) and any other information you have. We will then contact them about a free listing in our next edition.

• If you have any problems with a particular market listed in this book—they have not returned your material after requesting it, you have not been paid, etc.—contact us by letter telling the nature of the complaint and what you've done in an attempt to settle it yourself first.

• You'll find your *Craftworker's Market* is put together alphabetically by name in some sections, and alphabetically by name within state in others. We have done this to help you find local markets more easily if you prefer to work locally. But, for those of you who want to use our marketing guide to its fullest potential and market your work nationally, we have listed the markets for other states.

Craftworker's Market can save the selling craftperson a great deal of time and money if used as a guide to marketing original handcrafted work. It is the most complete and useful tool of its kind, and will give you all the information you need to contact both buyers and exhibitors of craftwork. We would be glad to hear from you if you have suggestions or questions on using this volume of marketing leads.

State Abbreviations

Each listing in this book uses the US Postal Service's two letter state abbreviations in the address line. They are as follows:

AK	Alaska	LA	Louisiana	OK	Oklahoma
AL	Alabama	MA	Massachusetts	OR	Oregon
AR	Arkansas	MD	Maryland	PA	Pennsylvania
AZ	Arizona	ME	Maine	PR	Puerto Rico
CA	California	MI	Michigan	RI	Rhode Island
CO	Colorado	MN	Minnesota	SC	South Carolina
CT	Connecticut	MO	Missouri	SD	South Dakota
DC	District of Columbia	MS	Mississippi	TN	Tennessee
DE	Delaware	MT	Montana	TX	Texas
FL	Florida	NC	North Carolina	UT	Utah
GA	Georgia	ND	North Dakota	VA	Virginia
HI	Hawaii	NE	Nebraska	VI	Virgin Islands
IA	Iowa	NH	New Hampshire	VT	Vermont
ID	Idaho	NJ	New Jersey	WA	Washington
IL	Illinois	NM	New Mexico	WI	Wisconsin
IN	Indiana	NV	Nevada	WV	West Virginia
KS	Kansas	NY	New York	WY	Wyoming
KY	Kentucky	OH	Ohio		

The Craft Market Today

By Lynne Lapin

There is a listing in this book for the Appalachian Festival, which takes place annually for four days in the Cincinnati Convention and Exposition Center. I have gone to that show faithfully for the past three years to talk to craftworkers about their work and sales. The first two years it was crowded. The 1979 show was jam-packed. I walked through the festival aisles with my nose on the collar of the person in front of me, moving slowly two steps at a time.

Talking with the promoters of the Appalachian Festival after its close, I learned the 1979 show was the most successful thus far in terms of attendance as well as actual dollar sales at the booths. One craftworker reported he was able to make more than $3,000 in over-the-counter sales and more than $1,000 in after-show orders. He believes he would have earned much more if he had not run out of merchandise.

Why were attendance and sales up so much in 1979? There didn't seem to be an increase in the amount of advertising in relationship to previous years; it was held at the same location; there were about the same number of booths; and the types of crafts were similar to those of the earlier festivals. What happened at the 1979 Appalachian Festival is representative on a very small scale of what is happening throughout the country. People are flocking to craft fairs and shows to buy quality handcrafted merchandise—for decorative as well as functional purposes.

Even with growing inflation and threats of recession, sales today are better than they have ever been for craftworkers producing quality work. Not only are there more markets devoted strictly to crafts, but new areas, such as antique shops and florists are starting to seek craftwork.

A jeweler from Evanston, Illinois, reports her gross sales are up 40% over last year, and adds that "I would say a good craftsperson can make $20,000-50,000 per year, depending upon the craft and their designs and skill."

Bill and Kathie Ureda of Los Altos, California, opened a co-op called Down Home in 1976. Since that time their success has enabled them to grow seven-fold.

"Our business has doubled since January," says Luann Cohen of the Ursuline Gallery at San Antonio, Texas. She feels this is a reflection of the promotion the craft field is receiving, thus generating an increased interest in handcrafted work.

Quality Sells

Just as sales and sales outlets are increasing for craftspeople, so are the number of people working in the craft field. They range from parents raising a family on their craft income, to people getting a hedge on retirement, to housewives who sell their work to support their hobby craft. All these people are competing for a portion of the dollar market. The buying public has only so many dollars to spend, and with inflation taking a bigger and bigger chunk out of their incomes, that money will be less and less.

"It will be the craftspeople who can get their share of that dollar amount who will be able to survive," says Irene "Rae" Partridge, an Illinois show promoter/artist. "If a show puts in X number of additional exibitors, they better have X number of additional patrons or the craftsperson can never expect to get the amount of sales he got the year before. He ends up getting a smaller percentage of the dollar market."

Top-selling craftspeople report they have risen to their present positions by producing only top-notch work. "The average potter is dying," says Partridge. "People are looking for something special. Artists in pottery with sculptural additions or unusual glazes are doing very well."

Likewise, in other media it is the craftworker who is producing unusual, fine handcrafted workmanship that is prospering, while those people trying to push shoddy work go out of business.

Doug Rowe, a leatherworker from the Ft. Mitchell, Kentucky area, has been selling full-time at shows for two years. Like all beginning professional craftworkers, he has seen rough times financially, but has consistently followed the advice of a jeweler friend to "produce quality," and is now in a position where he receives more than enough orders to keep him producing from 8 a.m. to 1 a.m. many days. His customers keep returning because they realize that even through his prices may be a little higher than the booth set up next to him where a leather exibitor sells hats with union labels and machine-sewn seams, it is worth it because it is quality in both workmanship and materials.

It would be easy for craftworkers like Rowe to give up the timely steps of hand sewing handcut components together and also use lesser grade materials. But in the case of this leatherworker, as well as thousands of others who have persisted in abiding by rigorous standards, quality workmanship is paying off.

"With inflation causing money to get tighter, people are taking more time to search out good crafts. They're more selective in how they are spending their money," observes Partridge at the shows she promotes.

"Craftspeople are doing much better than artists," she adds. "More so this year than in the past. This is because the price range of crafts is closer to what people can afford. Craftspeople usually have at least one item the public can pick up by outlaying just a little pocket money (in the $5-10 range). People can't justify a $150 painting like they can a small craft item."

Following Trends

Although quality is one of the most important aspects of a good craft, it needs to be something the consumer wants and is willing to pay money to have.

"Business is good if you have a quality item that the public wants," says Charlotte B. Herron, stained glass artist from Washington, Pennsylvania. "Listen to what the public says it wants."

If you are a potter producing a beautiful set of canisters, how many do you think you would sell in purple? The color just doesn't go in red, yellow and green kitchens. This is the type of common sense information you can pick up in your day-to-day living that will help you produce work that will sell. As you visit other people's homes, note color schemes; see what colors kitchen utensils and appliances come in. You will find this knowledge helpful in increasing sales.

Reading can also help you keep abreast of what is going on in the craft field. Entering into 1979, *China Glass & Tableware* magazine predicted the upcoming trend in dinnerware would be casual. Craftworkers aware of this new development in public taste could adapt their lines along simplistic patterns, therefore outselling competitors with more ornate pieces.

Craft publications such as those listed in your library's copy of *Ayer's Guide to Periodicals*, will give you an idea of what your competitors are up to, what is selling at which fair, and in which section of the country. It is a good idea to subscribe to at least one publication in your medium and a general craft publication. *The Crafts Report*, a recent merger of *The Working Craftsman* and *The Crafts Report*, is one of the better publications today that helps keep craftworkers up-to-date on the current state of the art.

If, for example, you read the January 1979 issue of *The Crafts Report*, you would have learned what trends were noted among the crafts submitted for screening for the Winter Market of American Crafts in Baltimore, Maryland (one of the largest and most influential craft fairs). The issue included information such as: clay dinnerware has become very popular, probably because of Rosalynn Carter's use of handcrafts at a 1977 White House luncheon; there was a Japanese influence with more sophisticated glazing; stick pins are being replaced by large brooches; honey pots are popular as the public rejects sugar for more pure sweetenings; and the energy shortage has caused craftspeople to produce more warm clothing. Knowing what other people are making should help you better sell your work since competition from them can have a direct effect on your business.

Although it is a good idea to read and keep abreast of what other craftworkers are doing, it is also important (but often difficult) to produce items that are different from what others are producing.

"Craftspeople spend as much time as possible when they are at shows talking to other craftspeople about style and techniques," says Maxine Brown, a founder of the National Association of Craft Retailers and former Washington, DC shop owner. "This is fine, except work starts being influenced by what they are seeing. People who have been together for years start looking alike—that is, their work does." For this reason she says it is very difficult for galleries to find people who have fresh ideas and who are not influenced by the work of others.

Banning together and discussing work is something that is very widely advocated by successful craftworkers. Not only do associations serve as a good place to go and talk "shop" with the other people working in your field, but also as an exchange for leads—what is needed and who is buying it. A good example of this is the crafts on the jacket of this edition of *Craftworker's Market*. While searching for pieces to use in the photo, we called Mary Klein, former president of the Cincinnati Craft Guild. She referred us to other members, and viola!, their work is being exhibited (photographically) in bookstores throughout the country.

From season to season you'll find the crafts that sell best change in accordance to those that are most in line with fashions of the day and the prices people are willing to pay. One way to keep abreast of this, aside from reading trade and consumer magazines, joining associations and following the other advice outlined above, is to actually interview those people who are selling to the ultimate consumer.

If you hadn't read in *The Crafts Report* that honey pots were selling well, the exhibitors at Summerfair in Cincinnati would have been happy to tell you these $8-12 items were among their bestselling items, and that low-priced work (such as Christmas ornaments, belts, salt and pepper shakers and other small gift-type items) sold best.

Rachel Maines of the Center of the History of American Needlework, Pittsburgh, Pennsylvania, confirms that small gift items are also what is selling most in her shop.

"I don't know if you've noticed, but people don't really buy needlework for themselves, but for gifts for other people's homes. They don't want to spend more than $10-15. Other items that are doing particularly well here are soft sculpture, soft toys and quilts (both traditional and contemporary—but not expensive)."

Luann Cohen of the Ursuline Gallery at the Southwest Craft Center in Antonio, Texas, also is noticing a resistance to price. "Items under $200 move fastest. After that there is considerable price resistance. The item selling best is pottery." Expensive weavings are not selling well in her gallery because she believes people don't realize what extensive work and money for materials goes into fiberwork.

These are just a few quotes on what is selling around the country. When conducting your own interviews you will be able to ask specific questions about the medium in which you work. If you are a potter, ask how pottery moves in a particular shop or gallery; what types of pieces are selling best; and which glazes are most popular. Also, don't limit your interviews to one area of the country and assume what is true for one is true for all. For example, "Rae" Partridge says macrame has been declining in popularity in her Chicago metropolitan shows for the past two years. A call to West Bend, Wisconsin, later told us that Bette Fehring of the Pik Place finds macrame to be a "natural bestseller."

Also, you can't expect prices to be the same in one area as they are in another. A fiberworker from Utah wrote that pieces in that state sell at such low prices to attract local buyers, that tourists who come across a show or fair load up on these fantastic craft bargains.

The Challenges of Today's Craftworker

If producing crafts was a business with no problems, it would attract many more than the 250,000-350,000 craftworkers that now produce. Every industry has problems, both big and small.

Here are a few complaints that keep resurfacing in interviews with both craftworkers and retailers, and some solutions being enacted to alleviate problems:

• There are too many craftworkers who are producing shoddy work with only profit in mind. Several fears have been voiced because of this saturation. Christopher S. Shepherd, goldsmith from Nehalem, Oregon, best voices the concerns when he says: "When someone who calls himself a 'craftsman' produces a poor product and manages to sell it, we are all hurt. The unhappy customer lumps all craftsmen into one group and will, in all probability, not purchase handmade products in the future." The best way to overcome this problem is to help educate the public through craft demonstrations, answering questions and supplying literature (labels and brochures) describing your work.

• It is still very difficult to make a living from craftwork. Possible, but difficult. Outlets are increasing, and high-paying architectural markets are joining those outlets that cater to the general consumer. Many craftworkers find they are still teaching workshops or working in other fields to subsidize their craft business.

"It's very difficult to make a living by producing and selling crafts. Virtually every painter, sculptor or craftsperson I know is forced to subsidize his/her income by teaching on a college, museum or high school level; selling shoes; laying brick; or doing anything else to survive," says Jan B. Statman, printmaker from Longview, Texas.

Pat and Paul Wilson, Sault Ste. Marie, Michigan, stoneware producers, add: "The hours are long and you had better love what you're doing or you simply won't make it. Chances are it will not be a living of $10,000 clear, but as demand and appreciation grow for what you are doing, this can give you the guts to stick with it."

• With the price of everything going up, the craftworker is having a harder and harder time keeping up. Suppliers, taxes and high commission rates charged by galleries and shops are tearing into incomes.

There are solutions to high cost problems. Many craftspeople have joined forces to form co-ops. Not only do these groups pool their marketing efforts, but they can buy supplies in bulk at discount, and obtain group permits for retailing and stuffing. A permit that once had to be paid for by each individual craftsperson working in a particular medium, can now be purchased by the group.

As for commission rates, there are two sides to the coin. Craftworkers claim rates are too high, while galleries and shops say craftspeople are unfair; they too need operating capital.

The best way to avoid what you feel to be unfair commission rates is to take time before signing any agreement to find out what you will get in return for the percentage being taken from each sale. Will the outlet promote your work? Is the gallery sponsoring an opening to introduce your exhibit? What are the hours the shop is open? Is it in a good location, and with adequate display space? Will your work be on exhibit the entire time it is on consignment, or will it be placed in the backroom for periods of time? You will be able to find shops and galleries taking commissions from as low as 20% (usually for charitable purposes) to as high as 60% (primarily at galleries). Most shops and galleries today have commission rates in the 35-40% range.

• It is difficult to come up with operating capital. Even if you have the time to produce and the customers who will buy your work, there is nothing you can do if you don't have money for supplies. Doug Rowe has overcome this problem by building a line of credit with a local bank. He explains how this can be done: "The first thing is to find a banker who knows your business. As a craftworker you may be a little late with a payment occasionally while you are waiting for payment from a customer, but at other times you may take out a loan one week and repay it the next after a really successful show. My banker understands this."

To build his credit line Rowe first took out a $300 90-day note costing him $7.82. He repaid it and borrowed $1,000, then $2,000; and as he continues to prove himself to his banker by repaying his debts, he is able to build up a credit line. "It's important to have a ready cash reserve like this. If I find a good buy on leather I can buy it if I have a source from which I can borrow money to pay for it," Rowe explains.

• Too many shops want material on consignment, instead of buying outright. Craftspeople have a tendency to point to gift shops, department stores and other outlets that buy wholesale, and ask why the craft shop doesn't do business the same way. With consignment there is a danger that your work may sit in a shop for months and never bring you a cent. And you are helping the shop keep free inventory. But, on the other hand, you have to consider the nature of crafts. A department store and gift shop buys mass-produced "proven" sellers. A craft shop is working with very unique and special merchandise, and he or she can't be assured that these items will move.

I'm not saying consignment is a good way for a craftworker to have to earn a living (and it certainly doesn't help cash flow problems), but it is a way to make money and yet help keep the craft outlets open. I do suggest this: If your work does sell in a particular outlet, and a reorder comes in, request the shop now buy your work outright. Beginning craftworkers may find consignment is the only way to break into the retail market and prove themselves.

What is Happening to the Craft Market?

If you bought last year's *Craftworker's Market*, compare it to this year's book. You'll notice several changes, most of which are indicative of changes being talked about across the country.

Shops and galleries and shows and fairs will probably always remain the biggest buyers and exhibitors of crafts. I have noticed in the past year, though, that we have received a greater increase in listings in the shops and galleries section of this book as compared to shows and fairs. This is interesting in light of Irene "Rae" Partridge's statement that "arts and crafts has flooded its own market. There are so many shows per area that the public just can't support them. It would be better to have one or two really good ones per area."

We lost some shop listings because they went out of business, others were closed because of the owners' illness, and others asked not to be included because the response from being listed in last year's book was more than they had expected. On the other hand, we gained more than 300 new shops and galleries in this 1980 edition.

The most exciting thing about this year's craft market is the increase in professional markets for craftwork. More and more coverage is being given to crafts in architecture. Buildings that once would have been decorated with paintings are now featuring fiber hangings, windows that would have been paned glass are now stained glass, and many accessories that were previously mass produced are now handcrafted. We mailed invitations to be listed in Craftworker's Market to the same list of architects this year as we did for the 1979 edition. The result is that we increased the Architectural & Interior Design Firms section from 10 listings to more than 3 times that amount.

In the Companies & Manufacturers section, we heard from more than twice as many of these firms than last year—some are so desperately seeking prototypes and crafts that they sought us, rather than waiting to be contacted by mail.

The 1970s was successful in promoting crafts as a recognized and established form of art. Now it is up to the craftworkers to fine-tune their marketing skills, techniques and design and prove to the business world that they are professionals.

For the craftperson who follows sound business practice and produces quality products the public is willing to pay to have, the markets will always be there.

"It's not difficult to find craftspeople. They're all over," says Maxine Brown. "But shops in business for years are going to shows and seeing the same faces over and over. They need new talent. For example, if a gallery has been working with a good-selling potter for six years, the market is bound to become saturated with that potter's work. Reluctantly the shop owner will have to give up that potter."

By using your creative abilities to develop new and exciting products, and by following sound and reliable business practices, you will be well on the way to becoming one of those craftworkers who earns a hefty share of the dollar market.

Working With the Retailer

By Jenet Hoffmann

There are more than 1,500 shops, galleries, museums, department stores and other retail outlets listed in this edition of *Craftworker's Market*, most of which will work with craftspeople from anywhere within the borders of North America. With so many markets, how do you choose which ones to work with? How do you approach these outlets? Can you protect yourself from situations that could be hazardous to your craft business?

The answer to operating a successful craft business is to practice sound marketing and business methods. Follow several important steps before even approaching a craft outlet, such as taking a careful look at the work to be presented, knowing what prices to offer and so forth. Then, after you feel comfortable about what you have to offer, and the price you are asking, it is time to decide on outlets and then approach them.

Settling on a Product

It is difficult to be objective about your own work. But careful evaluation is necessary in preparing yourself to introduce your craftsmanship into the marketplace. Here are a few things you can question yourself on to objectively evaluate the work you are producing:

Will your product perform the function for which it was designed? A teapot may be beautiful, but does it poor well? A belt made of leather that stretches will not hold up well. A wall hanging with no attachments for hanging it on the wall can't serve its decorative purpose.

Have you chosen a style, product and color that is in keeping with today's fashion? A quilt may be striking in design, yet executed in colors that are seldom used in the home. You may have designed your own line of beautiful thigh-length skirts, but if fashion magazines are showing ankle length, no one will wear them.

Is your product priced competitive with similar items retailing in stores, boutiques and craft fairs? It may be difficult, in some cases impossible, to compete with the prices at which mass-produced work is sold; but it is important to keep those sales tags in mind.

"Our products must be of a higher quality at an equal or lesser price in order to survive in the marketplace," said Christopher S. Shepherd, Nehalem, Oregon, gold smith. "This should be easily accomplished because their overhead and shipping are much higher than ours."

Ask yourself if you would spend that kind of money on the item if you were in the buying public's shoes, suggested Linda Beers-Aydlott, jewelry designer.

What supplies went into your work, and what were their costs? If producing your line depends on materials that must be special ordered, know how long it takes from order to delivery. Can you afford the space and tie-up of funds needed to keep extra supplies on hand? If so, maybe you can buy in bulk. Bulk prices are usually lower. For example, in buying yarns, some companies have a minimum wholesale order ($50-300), while others discount prices from 5-20% depending upon the total dollar amount ordered. Check with your suppliers. If you cannot afford to order in bulk, you may be able to pool orders with other craftworkers in your medium. The lower your supply costs, the less expensive your finished product will be, enabling more people to afford your work.

Learn other tricks to keep your prices at a salable level. If you are spending too much time producing an item, study your production process. Look for ways to save time. Can you batch your work? I know a weaver who produces handwoven shirts. She finds it saves time to do all weaving, cutting, sewing and finishing for five shirts at a time, rather than completing each shirt individually from start to finish.

What size businesss can you handle? It takes more space and money to produce large orders than small. You must have a firm idea of how much capital you have available to run your business. A new enterprise needs capital to keep it running until it is established. You must also be realistic about your income needs. Figure out whether you can produce enough items in the time you have available to meet those needs on a weekly or monthly basis.

Once you have evaluated your product or products and determined at what price or prices they should sell, you are now ready to go out and determine which retailers you should approach.

Study the Market

Your market and product(s) should be compatible. Visit department stores to study which items sell best and which appear on clearance racks. Also check trade and consumer publications to learn which items are highlighted. Don't ignore the local scene. Note items featured in local advertising. What are people wearing, using and decorating with?

When possible, visit shops to note the kind, quality and price of items carried. Also check to see if craftworkers' names are identified with their work. If not, ask the person tending shop who created a particular item. A shop attendant should know whose work is being carried. Keep a written personal account of the shops you visit.

To find shops in your area, or when traveling, use the Shops & Galleries section of *Craftworker's Market*, the yellow pages, and trade publications such as *The Crafts Report*. It is a bad idea to drop by a shop or gallery and expect the owner or manager to spend time chatting with you. A retailer has a responsibility to care for the customers who come to look at the products being carried. But, if the attendant is having a slow period and is willing to spend time answering questions, attempt to get a general feel for the store. What items sell best? Is there a type of work the retailer would like to carry, but can't find? Or, are there special products customers have been asking for? Whatever you do, don't drop by casually at a gallery or shop listed in this book that requests that you write or call or send samples. This is a sure way to hurt sales.

The Interview

Review your notes on the shops you visited and make a list of those you want to contact. For those listed in *Craftworker's Market*, be sure to follow their instructions on how they prefer to be contacted. Some may want you to make an appointment by phone or by letter; others have set aside a day of the week for craftspeople to "drop by"; and yet others want to review slides or samples by mail. If you call or write, address yourself to the person listed in the *Craftworker's Market* listing; or, in the case of other leads, ask to speak to the owner or manager.

A sales presentation should be prepared before your initial contact with a shop or gallery. An excellent way to practice your approach is to role-play. Ask a family member or friend to take the part of a shop owner and make a presentation. Give all information pertinent to your work. After the presentation, discuss with the "shop owner" how you can improve your performance. Repeat this process until you are comfortable.

Samples of your line, slides of your work or a combination of both should be incorporated into your presentation. Don't take only your best work—and definitely not your less desirable pieces—but take that which is representative of the quality of workmanship that can be expected from you. Make the most professional presentation possible. For example, if you sell jewelry, take a velvet pillow on which to display your work. Your products should be completely finished and ready to wear or use.

A 2x2 transparency is almost impossible to see without magnification, so take along a viewer. The slides should be tagged with all pertinent details, such as size, materials, price to store, suggested retail price, availability and delivery time. Each should be clear and of true color quality.

Your presentation will probably take place in the buyer's office or the store itself. The office or backroom is preferable because any customers who come in the store could interrupt in the front room. After listening to your presentation, the owner may give you an immediate response or say he/she will get back to you. Be assertive, but not pushy. If the retailer says he/she will get back to you, answer by saying something like, "Shall I call you next Wednesday?" or ask when you can expect to hear from him/her. If the owner wants to place an order, discuss terms, delivery dates, and other technicalities.

The Mail Approach
Working with shops and galleries by mail allows you to get national exposure and the best possible sales. Most listings in *Craftworker's Market* will consider crafts from almost anywhere within the United States and Canada.

Presentations by mail should include a cover letter stating your terms of business and a resume/business card for future reference. Most listings in this book will give instructions on how to approach them, but you will find that most often the prefered method of contact is with slides.

Slides should be sent in plastic viewing sheets, not boxes. Mark each slide with a complete description of the piece being shown—size, materials, price, availability and delivery time. Never send actual work unless it is specifically requested. No one will be impressed if you send them unrequested work that they have to go through the trouble to repack and return. You may actually have trouble retrieving those pieces.

Talk Terms
When you approach a retailer to carry your work, you should be aware of the different terms by which shops and galleries handle crafts. These include consignment, wholesale, guaranteed sale and commissions.

On *consignment*, the shop accepts your work on loan. When the store sells your work you receive the price it sold for minus the commission that is received by the gallery or shop. Commission rates vary from 20-60%. Galleries usually have the higher commission rates; charitable organizations, the lower.

If your work does not sell on consignment, the shop will return it to you or hold it until you pick it up. Usually the craftworker is responsible for delivering orders and the shop accepts responsibility for returning unsold items.

When you work on consignment you are tying up your inventory for a period of time, so attempt to gain the best possible exposure. Agreements concerning publicity for your work;

Working With the Retailer

amount of time work will be displayed; how and when payment will be made for sold pieces; and other arrangements should be outlined in a consignment agreement (Write the Artists Equity Association, 3726 Albemarle St. N.W., Washington DC 20016 for a copy of their sample Artist-Dealer Agreement).

Your agreement should also clarify how exclusive area representation and commission work will be handled—if at all. Exclusive representation means that one shop or gallery is the sole outlet for your work in a designated locale. If a shop wants an exclusive arrangement, find out exactly what they have in mind and what they are going to do to promote your work in order to earn that exclusive right.

It is a good idea to set a time limit on both consignment selling and exclusive representation when first dealing with a shop. This way your work is only tied up for a limited period of time if it does not move in a particular shop. Three months is a good amount of time for a trial period. This will give customers time to become acquainted with your work and the shop a chance to develop a market for your product.

If a shop or gallery does not routinely sign agreements with craftworkers, don't hesitate from presenting your own. A shop or gallery that refuses to sign a consignment agreement is probably not a good business risk. Remember you are doing business and you are responsible for your protection.

Be certain to keep clear and accurate records of the pieces you have in each shop, and those for which you have received payment. Visit local shops to see if your work is being exhibited or is lying in the backroom gathering dust. If work is not visible and you have not been paid, check to see if it has been sold or is gathering dust in the storeroom. For other retailers you can follow up by phone or letter to ask why you have not heard about the status of your work.

Wholesale means that the store purchases the item and marks up the price. You set the wholesale price, but not the retail price. The markup of the price of the work by the retailer is usually 100%, which is double your price to the shop. In some cases the markup may be higher.

A wholesale transaction begins with a purchase order (in duplicate) listing the shop or gallery's order, prices for each piece and delivery date. Each purchase order should be signed by the shop owner. Two other necessary forms are the packing slip and invoice. Each packing slip lists the contents of each individual box in the delivery and should be made in duplicate. One copy is included in each box, and another is for your files.

The invoice, (in triplicate) lists your name, to whom the order is sent, date of shipment, items sent, terms of business and total amount due. The invoice is mailed the same day a delivery is sent. Terms of business are usually "net 30 days" or "2/10/net 30." Net 30 days means the bill is payable within 30 days of receipt. 2/10/net 30 means the shop receives a 2% discount if the bill is payed within ten days, otherwise the full amount is due in 30 days. Enclosing a stamped addressed reply envelope often encourages prompt payment. You may also charge interest on past due accounts if this policy is clearly stated on the invoice—"Interest at the rate of 1½% per month charged on past due accounts."

The *guaranteed sale* mixes consignment and wholesale selling. Shops will buy your work outright if you agree to replace nonselling items after a fixed period of time with those more likely to sell.

In addition to consignment, wholesale and guaranteed sale agreements, a shop or gallery may be willing to accept *special orders* for you.

The commision rate for a special order to a shop or gallery may be different from the consignment rate. For instance, Incorporated Gallery in New York City takes 50% on consignment work and 33% on commissions. A craftworker should be paid one-third to one-half of the total price before beginning work, with the balance due upon delivery of the piece. In the event a client does not accept the finished piece, the craftworker has not lost all. Carol Beron, a New York fiber artist, also asks for a design fee of 10% of budget before she actually starts any work on a project.

A good way to check a shop's credit is to note some of the names carried by a shop. Call them and ask what their experience with that shop has been. For example does the store pay accounts promptly? Fellow craftspeople are generally happy to share such information.

"Be helpful to other craftsmen," said Terry Bedard, Anchorage, Alaska, craftworker producing feather, leather and metal work. "I don't mean give them your supply sources necessarily, but be willing to lend a hand, answer questions, etc. If you have your own style and do quality work, you don't have to be afraid of competition, and when you're working shows it's great to have someone to visit with or help out when you need an extra hand."

Once an order has been placed, discuss how your work will be displayed and identified. Well-displayed work sells better than poorly displayed merchandise. Some shops and galleries may be interested in your products, but would not be able to display them well because of inadequate space, lighting, etc. So, choosing a gallery or shop is not simply a matter of who will carry your work.

Inform the shop owner about your refill capabilities, the time needed from the time the order is placed until delivery time. If your work has been selling well on consignment in a particular shop, you may want to ask the store to buy future orders at wholesale. Reorders may be routinely placed by a shop when their stock runs low or the shop may expect the craftworker to call or visit. Ask about reorder policy. If you have developed a new line or added products to an exisiting line, you will want to make another sales presentation to the shop owner focusing on the new items. When you develop a new line it is wise to do a small marketing test. Test the items at local craft fairs or in one or two shops. If the response if favorable, build up your inventory and seek additional orders.

Much of the information above applies to galleries as well as shops, but galleries do have some very special ways of doing business. Galleries differ from shops in that, although they may represent many craft artists, they usually feature the work of one, two or three artists at a time. When a gallery wants to show your work ask if this is a one-time chance, or the beginning of an ongoing relationship. You may be able to participate in group shows on a regular basis and one-person shows at specific intervals. If you accept a show with a gallery it is important to get a contract specifying the dates of the show, delivery date of work, who pays for the printing and mailing costs of invitations, refreshments at the opening and advertising fees. Some galleries accept all costs involved with a show, while others may even charge a rental fee. Don't be afraid to ask why if a gallery accepts only a limited portion of the show's expenses. Ask if they give interior decorators and designers a 10-20% discount. If so, are you expected to share in this discount? When work is delivered to the gallery, like a shop, have the owner sign a consignment agreement.

Handling Rejections, Sticky Situations and Awkward Questions

If the owner refuses your work, ask what you can do to make your product more salable. Also, realize that a shop that refuses your merchandise may not be an appropriate outlet for you. Perhaps the owner realizes he/she doesn't have adequate display space to do your work justice, or maybe the clientele is wrong. Ask the dealer, perhaps other outlets can be suggested.

Sometimes an owner will show interest in your work, but ask you to change your price. You should know how you arrived at your price and be able to tell why or why not you are or are not able to change the fee. Don't accept an order if it means you will lose money.

It is not uncommon for a customer who sees work in a shop or gallery to track down the artist to get lower prices at that person's studio. This is a bad practice to submit to, and is considered by most galleries and shops to be unethical and unprofessional. When a craftworker sells work from the studio at lower prices than the retailer, this discredits the gallery or shop and its efforts to market your work. Many shops will drop a craftworker who does this. The retail price of your work should be the same regardless of whether you are selling at a shop, a gallery or a fair. At a crafts fair you are contributing your time and effort, not to mention transportation and display costs, and should be reimbursed for these costs.

Sometimes circumstances cause a shop or gallery to be late in sending payment. But, if you have sold items to a retailer wholesale, you should send a courteous reminder after 35-45 days. If payment has not arrived after 10 to 15 days from the time you send the reminder, send a more strongly worded note. A final notice should be sent after 60 days stating that the bill will be turned over to a collection agency if no payment is received. A collection agency will take a percentage of the bill, so you will lose some of your profits; but, in addition to that, the shop receives a bad credit rating.

It is wise to seek legal advice if you continue to have difficulty in receiving payment. Many communities have a Volunteer Lawyers for the Arts organization or a Legal Aid Society which offers services at a reduced rate. When you have a bad experience with a retailer, notify the source where you found the listing. *Craftworker's Market* and *The Crafts Report* welcome feedback, and you will be helping fellow craftworkers.

Jenet Hoffmann, a New York City craftworker producing weavings and fiber constructions, has studied art forms formally for more than ten years. To her name are numerous gallery exhibits, architectural commissions, lectures, freelance designs for women's magazines, and articles in The Crafts Report, Contract Interiors *and* Shuttle, Spindle and Dyepot.

Promoting Yourself and Your Work

Successful businesses advertise. Promotion helps them reach new customers and retain the old. As a craftperson involved in selling, you, too, need to plan a promotional campaign. Your program doesn't have to be expensive, just well organized.

The most basic and inexpensive form of advertising is word of mouth. So, the first key to building a successful craft business is to send customers off on a note of satisfaction. The satisfied customer boasts to friends about his wonderful craft find, and from this your customer list begins blossoming into a healthy clientele.

But, don't stop with word of mouth. Take action. Have a guest book on hand when exhibiting your work. This should provide a place for visitors' names and addresses. You can have buyers list their names in the book or provide a separate record for the names and addresses of people who have bought your work. Once you have accumulated the list, you may want to send them announcements of new lines, shows you are entering, galleries where your work is appearing, and other information that will remind them you are still around and producing. This is a key way to spur repeat sales.

Inexpensive Publicity

Another way to reach prospective buyers is through press coverage. When you feel you have something newsworthy or an item that may be of particular interest to the community, be sure to keep the local media informed by writing a press release.

Being the modest creatures we are it is often hard to "blow our own horn," but writing a press release and sending it off to the local newspaper or radio station doesn't have to be an ordeal. For example, imagine you are going to be giving weaving demonstrations in the area's newest mall. There is a very good chance the mall will send a release to the local media so they will receive the publicity. If this happened, and your name was used in the article and it helped your business you'd be happy, maybe even overjoyed, right? Then why not do the same thing yourself? You don't need to talk in adjectives, bragging about how beautiful the work is you do. Just give the facts—who, what, when, where and why.

The main keys to writing a publicity release are to keep it as brief as posssible without leaving out important details and to try to get all the important information near the beginning. An editor usually cuts copy from the bottom if the piece is too long for its topic or if space requires a shorter article.

The release should be typed double-spaced on 8½x11 paper. At the top of the page note when the information is for release (for example, For Immediate Release); the name of the person the release is coming from; and an address and phone number where that person can be called for additional information for a possible feature story. Also, in two or three words under this information, tell what the release is about (for example: pottery show opens).

Most newspapers welcome a good black and white photograph when available. They can run the illustration along with your release or they might elect to run the photo alone with only a caption.

Current photographs of you working with your craft are the best publicity illustrations to have on hand. You will notice in your local paper that pictures of artwork alone rarely are used. The human interest element is much more desirable. (Books that can help the craftworker wishing to learn to take his/her own photos are the *Here's How* books published by Eastman Kodak; *Encyclopedia of Practical Photography*, Time/Life Books; and Petersen Publishing books.)

Never send material to a newspaper without addressing it to a specific name. You can find the names and addresses of various editors by checking *Ayers Guide to Periodicals* in your local library. Or, call the newspaper and ask who you should send it to. Include the name whether you are sending an actual release or simply writing the press or electronic media to get them interested in developing their own feature on you and your work.

It is preferable that you make first contacts by phone or letter, but at some point it is a good idea to personally meet the person you'll be working with. People like to work with individuals they know; but be sure not to make a nuisance of yourself. A friendly attitude will be well-received, especially by the harried reporter who deals with a variety of "no comment" types each day.

Don't be discouraged if you send out releases that aren't used or are rewritten. The truth of the news world is that if it is a slow day and not much news is happening even a bad release might get used. On the other hand, if it is a really newsy day, a very good release might get passed over for a more newsworthy or timely article. Well written or not, almost all releases that are used are rewritten. If, though, you repeatedly submit releases and none are used, don't hesitate to contact the person to whom you've sent the materials. There may be a problem that you can very easily remedy, thereby increasing your publicity. Maybe your angle isn't local enough. Perhaps you have been omitting information that is vital to the story. Or, maybe the photos you sent aren't appropriate.

By asking questions and designing your release to conform to the needs of the press, both you and the newspaper will benefit. You will gain free publicity, while the paper will have interesting and informative material to include on its pages. Remember, this is a free service, don't abuse it by making demands.

Another low-cost means of attracting people to you and your work is to demonstrate your craft. Always do this at shows where it is permitted. One person comes to watch, then another, then another, until finally you have attracted a crowd. And a crowd attracts people's curiosity, making your work the center of attention. Not only do people watch demonstrations, but there is something in human nature that makes a person find something they actually saw being made more appealing. A friend of *Craftworker's Market* tells the story of how he visited a New York City craft show. At this exhibit was a glass blower shaping a fish. The piece of glass turned out to be probably the worst execution in the entire show, but he saw it produced and wanted that item and none other. He ended up buying the piece, even after the craftworker told him he wasn't very proud of the fish and would prefer not to sell it.

Don't limit your demonstrations to fairs in which you participate. Contact craft supply shops and malls. Not only are shop demonstrations good publicity for you, but they often pay. Remember, though, shops want demonstrations that promote the products they sell. If you want to "sell" a shop on a demonstration, use the products they carry.

Paid Advertising and Direct Mail

There are other forms of promotion

that are more costly than those mentioned above, but that are worth checking to learn the costs and what benefits might be gained. These include paid advertising and direct mail.

Paid advertising includes both classified and display ads. Prices vary greatly, depending upon the publication with which you are working. Most magazines and newspapers print the cost per word at the beginning of classified sections. Write magazines for their "rate card," and call newspapers and the electronic media for their costs.

Once you decide you are going to buy advertising space, take time to study different publications to decide which would be best for your type of product. Look at local papers. Are there craftspeople advertising there now? Are they buying display space or classifieds? Contact persons who advertise in the publications in which you are interested. Ask them how response has been to their ads. Have they monitored sales to learn how many individuals have come to them because of the ad?

Next, if you are willing to mail orders to people, you should check regional and national publications that appeal to the type of customer you are trying to reach. Study craft and gift trade publications, as well as those geared toward the general consumer. You will find a list of publications that might be of interest to you as a craftworker in *Ayer's Guide to Periodicals* in most libraries.

If you determine you want to place a display ad in a publication, one of the first questions you'll have to ask yourself is: "Where will I get the ad?" One expensive possibility is to commission an advertising agency to design one for you. A more desirable idea is to save time and money by developing your own or trading artistic talents with a friend. Copy will most likely be an important part of your promotion, so you will either have to use calligraphy or have this typeset (call local typesetting firms for estimates). And, you will usually want to include a photograph or line drawing of your work or other illustrations pertaining to the desired message. The ad should be prepared to the specifications outlined by the magazine or newspaper with which you are working. Another possibility is to request that the magazine have its art staff design an ad for you. The biggest problem with the latter method is that you may have little control over the end product because by the time you receive the dummy, deadlines may negate any chances of having it changed.

If you are planning to accept mail orders, there are several ways you can handle a display or classified ad. First, you can show one particular product or line of products in your advertisement, list the price or prices, and have customers mail in orders. If you choose this route, it is a good idea to incorporate a coupon into the ad. Key (code) the coupon so you will know where the order originated. For example, you may decide to place an ad for handcarved spoons in *American Crafts* and the same ad in a regional paper. Keying the ads will let you know if the sales are being originated from readers of one publication or the other. One idea you might want to incorporate is to add a line to the address of one ad telling readers to write to Department 1A, and a line to the other telling readers to write to Department 1B.

A second tactic you can employ in your advertising is to get people to write to you for your catalog. This way you aren't restricting yourself to a limited number of products—you can make them aware of all you have to offer through your catalog.

Direct mail is different from advertising you buy in a publication in that it is advertising that is directly sent through the Postal Service to potential buyers of your work. To promote your work by mail you need to have a list of names. A list you definitely want to use is the names and addresses of persons who have previously seen your work—those who have signed your guest book, for example. These people enjoyed your work earlier so they would be your most likely buyers.

Another way to get a direct mail list—aside from gathering names yourself—is to rent it. The average price of a direct mail list is $30 per 1,000 names. What you are doing when you order a specific list is renting name and address labels for a one-time use. You can learn what types of lists are available for lease (such as craft galleries/shops) by consulting your library's copy of *SRDS Direct Mail List Rates & Data*.

Code your direct mail advertising reply envelopes when using more than one list. This can be done by fanning any return envelopes you are supplying and placing a colored line on the sides. So, if you get an order returned in an envelope with a green line on the side, you might know it came from one list, while a red slash indicates a different list.

Although direct mail allows you to reach a specific audience, you may find the cost to be somewhat prohibitive. You will need envelopes with addresses or labels and a brochure or flyer to either mail in the envelope or to use as the entire piece. You will also have to pay the cost of postage to the consumer. The initial cost may be higher for this type of advertising, but if you have the right list you will probably find that this method of selling your work has cost you less than other advertising forms.

Here we come back to that ever-important advise: "Keep good records." Whether you are using publicity techniques or paid advertising you are using both time and money to get your craft known. Keep records on the response you are getting from each of these methods. If you don't watch how many orders you get from a particular ad or article, you may keep on working with a publication that is doing you little or no good, while you might stop advertising in a publication that is pulling very well for you. Treat advertising like a science and it will be a profitable tool. By spreading the word in this way you can best reach your maximum sales potential in your particular medium.

As a selling craftsperson, you should never let your guard down. Buyers can be found almost anywhere you meet people. For this reason always carry a few business cards in your wallet and some resumes in your brief case.

Biographical or Résumé Sheet

Most working people have had to design a resume to tell potential employers about their qualifications. Look at the outlets carrying your work as your employers. Not only do they want to know something about you before "hiring" you, but they also want to know about you and your work so they can answer questions asked by customers. All this relates heavily to the personal nature of crafts.

The resume will also help you work with reporters. Suppose someone from the media decides to do a write-up on you, what better way to fill in the gaps about your work in the craft field than to give him/her a resume for reference.

When writing your resume, stick to the facts. There are numerous formats for putting your particular information down on paper; but, the basic information should include the following:

• Personal data: name, address, phone number (of home and studio), media in which you work, and any

other data you feel helpful, such as age, marital status, etc.
• Educational background: list schooling as it relates to crafts.
• Professional experience: list jobs you have held in the crafts field; exhibitions and shows you have participated in; publications you have written for; and galleries and shops you sell to or have exhibits in.
• References: list two personal references along with the names and addresses of persons who have worked with you professionally. (It is always a good idea to ask a person ahead of time to be a reference.)

Try to keep your resume to one page of information. Most single-page resumes can be run off in a day's time by "quick" printers for approximately $5 per 100. If you are extremely active in the crafts field you may want to only have a few resumes printed at a time. This way you can periodically update your sheet and have new ones printed.

Business Cards/Labels

A business card allows you to always have your name, address, phone number and area of specialization available in a reduced printed form. It is small and can easily fit in a wallet or pocket-sized case. A plain, one-color business card can be printed for less than $10 per 100.

Give the cards to potential buyers of your work at shows and sales, as well as leaving them with retailers and other businesses you hope to be able to work with. And don't limit the cards to *buyers* of your work, distribute them to passers-by as well. They may get back to you for a purchase in the future.

Putting labels on your work is an inexpensive way to get yourself known and help improve sales. Design a tag that is distinctive and attractive, yet reflective of your personality or the nature of your crafts. Include copy telling about you and/or your work.

Try to answer the questions you've most often been asked by buyers and viewers of your craft.

While printed labels can be attached to most work, you may want to sew fabric labels to inconspicuous spots on soft items, such as clothing. Cards can be produced individually by hand, silkscreened or printed. The cost would be about the same as that of a business card, depending on the paper or material used.

For added benefits you may want to create a label that can double as a business card. If you do this, make certain your address and phone number can be easily removed by the retailer if he/she wishes to do so. (Although many shops and galleries may request that labels be placed on work, they do not want to encourage customers to leave the store and call the crafworker to attempt to get the work at discount.)

Markets

Architectural and Interior Design Firms

It's the fervor with which architectural and interior design firms are seeking crafts that is new—not the concept of using crafts in architecture. Almost every town has a section in which there are old homes with glittering stained glass windows and beautifully-carved facades.

Today we are experiencing a resurgence of the use of this art form in home and public building design. Not only are there stained glass windows, but there is a growing use of crafts in interior design. We see weavings in restaurants where once there were paintings; wooden sculptures replacing those of granite; and then there are pillows, furniture, desk paraphernalia and other accessories that are individually designed and executed.

Compare last year's *Craftworker's Market* to this. We have more than tripled the Architectural & Interior Design Firms section. The number of works to be purchased and commissioned during the next year is 1,000, as compared to about 200 in 1979. These range from exterior crafts such as stained glass and woodworking to indoor items such as design accessories.

To find architectural markets in addition to the listings in this book, consult the yellow pages of the phone book for other companies and keep up with the community building contractors' associations' construction reports found in the library. Your best bet when looking for an architectural firm to work with is to seek out those with an interior design department.

Most of the listings in this book ask to see brochures. Designing a brochure of your work and qualifications could well be worth the extra time and expense (approximately $250 for 500 1-page foldout color brochures; exact estimates can be obtained from printers in your area). In addition to creating a professional impression, a brochure can be easily filed for future reference. A. Dewitt Day, design director of A. Dewitt Day and Associates, tells us he keeps brochures on file for consideration for as long as five years.

When you seek interior design or architectural firms not listed in this book, you may want to call the head of the design department and make an appointment to show your work. If refused, don't be discouraged. Send slides, photos or your brochure, and a cover letter that says this is the type of work you do, these are your qualifications, these are your terms and your prices. Close by saying you will give them a call in a week or so to set up an appointment. Have your portfolio ready for personal interviews.

Not all architectural firms will report back to you immediately. Some will only contact you when they have a specific project for your craft. Every six months or so you should give them another call, reminding them of your work and bringing them up to date on your career.

You may also want to place small ads in trade publications such as *Contract Interiors, The Designer, Decor, Interior Design, Interiors* or *Residential Interiors*. Again, your brochure will be an asset in responding to these.

Don't limit your architectural assignments exclusively to architectural and interior design firms. Call the offices of some professionals—doctors, lawyers, etc. They are frequently interested in crafts not only for decorative purposes but as an investment.

Remember, salesmanship is involved as well as your craft ability. Try to educate and convince; gallery showings or competition awards are always impressive. Make the rounds, get exposure, take advantage of the resurgence of crafts in the building industry.

ADI (ASHWORTH DESIGNS, INC.), 10449 N. 25th Place, Phoenix AZ 85028. (602)992-6560. Contact: Dean Ashworth. Architectural and landscape architectural firm specializing in residential, institutional and commercial customers. Buys 100 craftworks and commissions 1-6 craft designs annually. According to Ashworth, craftperson can have a free hand and should think up something creative. "We recently designed a development that called for all the media listed below."
Acceptable Work: Considers wall hangings; pillows; self-standing statues; signage; umbrella stands; one-of-a-kind furniture; items for display on tables; renderings; and models. Acceptable media include ceramics; fiber art; glass art; leatherworking; metal sculpture; pottery; and wood sculpture.
Terms: Payment is made by cash within 45 days of acceptance. Send brochure of work and resume. SASE. Reports in 30 days maximum; keeps resume on file.

WILLIAM R. BAKER, 2322 Lincoln Park West, Chicago IL 60614. (312)549-0641. Design Director: William R. Baker. Architectural and interior design firm specializing in institutional, industrial and commercial clients. Designs 10-15 interiors; buys 200 craftwork pieces; and commisssions 5-10 craft designs annually from local and out-of-town craftworkers. Send brochure of work. Include return postage if samples sent. Reports when needed.
Acceptable Work: Considers wall hangings, pillows, ashtrays, umbrella stands, desk accessories and one-of-a-kind furniture in ceramics, glass, metal, pottery and wood.

BANK BUILDING CORP. OF AMERICA, 2200 Century Parkway NE, Atlanta GA 30345. (404)633-2971. Design Director: Erman Fortenberry. Architectural and interior design firm specializing in financial buildings and professional offices. Local and out-of-town craftworkers. Upon approval, purchase order is issued. Send brochure of work with resume. SASE. Files brochure permanently.
Acceptable Work: Considers wall hangings, self-standing statues, ashtrays, umbrella stands and desk accessories in ceramics, fiber, glass, leather, metal and wood.

CARL COX AIA ARCHITECT, 81-713 Hwy. 111, Indio CA 92201. Contact: Carl Cox. Architectural firm specializing in residential and commercial clients. Designs 20 interiors annually from local and out-of-town craftworkers. Send brochure of work and resume. Will return samples with SASE. Reports in 3 weeks.
Acceptable Work: Considers wall hangings and self-standing statues in ceramics, fiber, metal and wood.

Wudtke Watson Davis, Inc., San Francisco, California, an architectural and interior design firm, commissioned Frances Osburn, IBD, The Treadleworks, and Babette to design and fabricate mini-quilts and ceiling banners for Stack's, a restaurant they recently designed. The craftworker meets with the architect/designer to discuss the scope of the work, client preferences and designer input during fabrication of the project.—Photo by Dan Whitney.

MARIA RADOSLOVICH COX, 330 E. 59th St, New York, NY 10023. Design Director: Maria R. Cox. Interior design firm specializing in residential, institutional and commercial clients. Send brochure of work or call for appointment. *Do not* mail samples—will not be returned. Reports when needed. Keeps brochure on file.
Acceptable Work: Considers wall hangings, pillows, table accessories, ashtrays, umbrella stands, desk accessories and one-of-a-kind furniture in batik, ceramics, fiber, glass, leather, metal pottery and wood.

JUDITH WOLF CRUTCHER AIA & ASSOCIATES, 546 Grant Ave., San Francisco CA 94108. Contact: Judith W. Crutcher. Architectural firm specializing in residential, institutional and commercial clients. Commissions 2 craft designs annually from local and out-of-town craftworkers. Flat fee. Send brochure of work and resume. Does not return samples. Keeps resume on file for 2 years.
Acceptable Work: Considers wall hangings, architectural features and one-of-a-kind furniture in ceramics, fiber, glass, metal, pottery and wood. Recently hired a ceramicist to fabricate and install a slab construction fireplace.
To Break In: "Have photographic examples and references showing reliable completion of the work."

A. DEWITT DAY & ASSOCIATES LANDSCAPE ARCHITECTS & PLANNERS ASLA, 4566 Office Park Dr., Jackson MS 39206. (601)981-5524. Contact: A. Dewitt Day. Architectural firm. Designs 6 interiors; buys 10-20 original craftworks; and commissions 1-2 craft designs annually. Considers wall hangings, self-standing statues and display pieces for use in planning exteriors. Acceptable media include ceramics, some fiber art, glass art, metal sculpture, pottery and wood sculpture. "The craftsman sets his price—I see if the project's budget can

afford original artwork and how much." For past work has paid: $900 for wood sculpture for deck residential client; $17,000 for bronze work for a commercial client; $51,000 for stone work for a park; and $7,000 for steel work for a park. Mail resume; brochure of work with price list; and cover letter and slides of work. No samples returned. Reports to craftworker "only if I can sell their work to our clients or if we have projects where we can use their works." Keeps resume on file a maximum of 5 years. Recently commissioned a bronze sculpture to be completed for the Josh Halbert Gardens.
To Break In: "Include a brochure; price list; resume—anything that will help us sell your art to our clients."

DESIGN GROUP 3, 1349 Larkin St., San Francisco CA 94109. (415)673-8995. Design Director: Betty Blomberg. Interior design firm specializing in residential and commercial clients. Designs 50 interiors annually; buys 75 craftwork pieces; and commissions 10 craft designs annually from local and out-of-town craftworkers. Craftworker sets retail price. Price range of paintings: $200-2,000; tapestries: $400-1,000. Send brochure, cover letter and slides of work. "Design Group 3 will contact if interested." Include return postage with slides. Reporting time depends upon particular job requirements. Keeps brochure on file indefinitely.
Acceptable Work: Considers wall hangings, pillows, self-standing statues, table accessories in ceramics, fiber and glass. Recently "commissioned artwork for large condominium project public spaces, designating theme and giving free rein."
To Break In: Craftworker should have "excellent presentation techniques of work combined with thorough research of what firms are doing what, newspaper accounts of upcoming projects and real estate/home sections."

DEZIGN HOUSE III, 1701 E-12 Park Centre W., Cleveland OH 44114. (216)621-7777. Director: Ray Elias. Private design studio working primarily in interior design work. Estab. 1962. Represents 75 craftworkers who do custom work in all crafts. Price range: $100-10,000. Requires exclusive area representation. Craftworkers who are experienced in interior design work are asked to make personal inquiries by letter first.

EVA'S INTERIORS, 276D Rt. 2, Long Grove IL 60047. (312)634-1373. Buyer: Eva Homor. Craft/gift shop/interior design studio. Estab. 1978. Represents 100-150 craftworkers.
Acceptable Work: Considers batik, ceramics, glass art, pottery, scrimshaw, soft sculpture, tole painting, wall hangings, weavings, woodcrafting and pillows. Especially needs one-of-a-kind handcrafted furniture and accessory pieces. Specializes in natural materials, rustic and nautical articles. One-of-a-kind and handmade production-line items. Price range: $5-500; bestsellers: $5-150.
Terms: Works on consignment; 50% commission (exceptions made on pieces over $300). Retail price set by joint agreement. "Since we are a small community of approximately 60 shops, we have to have items exclusively in Long Grove. Do not contact me if anyone else in town has your work." Send slides with SASE. Reports in 2 weeks. Work may be shipped or hand delivered. Dealer pays insurance on exhibited work. Display time: 3 months maximum (except items over $300).
Profile: "We are located in a very old town in the country just minutes from downtown Chicago. The shop is rustic in nature with exposed wood beams and brick walls. Display areas are natural sisal or barnwood backed. Our customers come from the surrounding 6 states. Convention groups are bused here for the day. Also local homeowners (homes range in the $200,000+ price range." Best selling time: summer and Christmas.

FANTASY CREATIONS, 337 Glenn Ave., Lawrenceville NJ 08648. (709)883-7751. General Manager: Chomy Garces. Manufacturers accessories for dollhouses, mainly nursery items or toys in miniature (1"-1' scale) in bread dough and wood. Co-sponsors a miniature show, "Miniature Makers Society," and offers 2 seminars annually. Buys and commissions work. Buys about 200 designs annually. Pays $10-25 for dolls; 3 miniflowers for $1-3 each; and 30¢-50¢ for foods. "We also use ½" scale for Christmas tree decorations; submit by August." Send resume, sanples and/or actual work. Reports in 4 weeks.

FARMER—MANN INTERIORS, INC., 330 Clay Ave., Lexington KY 40502. (606)266-4881. Design Director: Irene Mann. Interior design firm specializing in residential and commercial clients. Buys original pieces of craftwork from local and out-of-town craftworkers. Considers wall hangings, pillows, self-standing statues, table accessories, ashtrays, umbrella stands, desk accessories and one-of-a-kind furniture. Acceptable media includes ceramics, glass, leather, pottery and wood. Send brochure and call for interview. SASE. Reports as soon as possible. Keeps brochures on file indefinitely.

FINCK, STOWELL & FROLICHSTEIN, INC., 222 W. Adams St., Chicago IL 60606. (312)641-6141. Design Directors: S.R. Frolichstein or Heather McTammany. Architectural firm working with all clients. Designs 20 interiors; buys 15 craftwork pieces; and commissions 10 craft designs annually from local and out-of-town craftworkers. Send brochure with cover letter. Does not return samples or report back. Keeps brochure on file for 2 years.
Acceptable Work: Considers wall hangings and self-standing statues in ceramics, fiber, metal and wood.

FISHER & SPILLMAN, 3204 Fairmount, Dallas TX 75201. (214)748-6488. Design Director: Jean Dahlgren. Architectural firm specializing in institutional and commercial clients. Designs 10-15 interiors, buys 15-20 craftwork pieces; and commissions 5-10 craft designs annually from local and out-of-town craftworkers. Send brochure and resume. Include return postage if samples sent. Reports in 1 week. Keeps resume on file indefinitely.
Acceptable Work: Considers wall hangings, pillows, self-standing statues, table accessories and one-of-a-kind furniture in ceramics, fiber, glass, metal, pottery and wood. "We meet with the craftsperson initially, set perameters for the job, design criteria, review designs, negotiate with the owner, finalize designs and have final installation and payment."
To Break In: "Get your designs to designers—in brochure form, in slide form or actual samples. Send show blurbs."

'Woodward's Mill,' this tapestry woven in earthtones, was commissioned by Bank Building Corporation of America, Atlanta, Georgia, for Gwinnett Federal Savings and Loan. Woodward's Mill is an actual historical site in Gwinnett County which makes it an ideal subject for the tapestry. The weaving, which took 4 months to complete, was designed by Lee Avery Catts and woven by Kathy Smith, both of Atlanta, Georgia. Bank Building Corporation of America commissions a variety of work from local and out-of-town craftworkers.

PERRY B. GOLDSTEIN ARCHITECT, P.C., 600 Old Country Rd., Garden City NY 11530. (516)741-5955. Contact: Perry B. Goldstein, AIA. Architectural firm dealing with residential, institutional and commercial clients. Specializes in bank branches, 'back office' spaces and computer spaces. Designs 50 interiors; buys only a few craftwork pieces; and commissions 2-3 craft designs from local and out-of-town craftworkers. Commissions directly with clients. Send brochure of work or call for appointment. If previously arranged and return postage included, will return samples. Reports when needed. Keeps brochure on file as agreed upon.
Acceptable Work: Considers wall hangings, self-standing statues, table accessories, ashtrays, umbrella stands, desk accessories and one-of-a-kind furniture in ceramics, glass, metal, pottery and wood. "Firm acts as third party between craftworker and client—craftworker has direct relationship with firm."

GRUZEN & PARTNERS, 1700 Broadway, New York NY 10019. (212)582-7040. Design Director: Peter Gumpel. Architectural firm specializing in residential, institutional and commercial clients. Send brochure of work. Include return postage if samples sent. Keeps brochure on file for 6 months-1 year.

Acceptable Work: Considers wall hangings and banners in batik, ceramics, fiber, glass, metal, pottery, and wood.

MARTINA HAMILTON ART DEALER, 1623 3rd Ave., New York NY 10028. (212)722-3311. Contact: Martina Hamilton. Estab. 1976. Art Dealer dealing with law firms, stockbrokers and corporations. Represents 60 craftworkers. Considers fiber art including weavings and wall hangings. Pays $75/square foot. Charges 33⅓% commission. Retail price set by joint agreement. Send resume with slides. SASE. "We prefer if the artist has done previous corporate installations." Work may be shipped or hand-delivered. "Slides of craftworkers' work are shown to the client. The artist selected is then asked to view the specific space, make 2 drawings and swatches ($100 fee paid to craftworker), and craftworker then makes the item."

HIGH POINT GLASS & DECORATIVE CO., Box 101, High Point NC 27261. (919)882-4519. Contact: A. W. Klemme, Jr. Manufacturer. Clients are residential, institutional and churches. Commissions approximately 75 craft designs annually. Considers stained and leaded glass craft items. "Cost depends upon the amount of work required to produce the product." Send "letter with resume of abilities and pictures of work available." SASE. Reports as to interest in work; keeps resume on file 3-5 years. "We work with designers either at our studio or freelance."

HUBBUCH IN KENTUCKY, 882 E. High St., Lexington KY 40502. (606)269-2306. Design Director: Barbara Ricke. Interior design firm dealing with residential and commercial clients. Designs thousands of interiors annually among all the branch firms; Hubbuch in Kentucky is one of the branches. Works with local and out-of-town craftworkers. Considers wall hangings, pillows, self-standing statues, table and desk accessories, ashtrays, one-of-a-kind furniture and all custom art work. Acceptable media include ceramics, fiber, glass, leather, metal, pottery and wood. Pays according to current market prices. Send brochure of work; call for interview; send cover letter and slides of work; or mail resume. SASE. Reports as soon as possible. Keeps materials on file.

INTRARC PLANNING CORP., 7370 NW 36th St., Miami FL 33166. Contact: John G. Dieckmann, ASID. Architectural/interior design firm specializing in residential, commercial and medical clients. Designs 10-20 interiors annually. Considers wall hangings; self-standing statues; ashtrays; desk accessories; and one-of-a-kind furniture. Acceptable media include metal sculpture; pottery; ceramics; and wood sculpture. Payment determined "by job budget allowance." Pays $10-200/assignment. Send cover letter and slides of work. SASE. Keeps resume on file for 1-2 years.
To Break In: "Contact designers, show examples of your work, and ask them for ideas or suggestions as to what you might be able to create for their needs—let them provide you with designs (originals) *they* can use."

JOVE/DANIELS/BUSBY, 909 W. Peachtree St. NW, Atlanta GA 30309. (404)892-2890. Interior Design Director: Karen League; Architectural Design Director: Henri Jova. Architectural and interior design firm dealing with residential, institutional, industrial and commercial clients. Designs 50+ interiors; buys 100+ craftwork pieces; and commissions 25+ craft designs annually from local and out-of-town craftworkers. 25% deposit, remainder after installation of item. "Send brochure, cover letter, slides and resume; follow up with a telephone call and perhaps an interview." Include return postage if samples sent. Reports when needed. Keeps resume on file indefinitely.
Acceptable Work: Considers wall hangings, pillows, self-standing statues, table accessories, ashtrays, umbrella stands, desk accessories and one-of-a-kind furniture in batik, ceramics, fiber, glass, metal and pottery.

JUNG & CLOYES, AIA, Box 340, Del Mar CA 92014. (714)755-2313. Design Director: Eugene H. Cloyes. Architectural firm dealing with residential, institutional, industrial and commercial clients. Designs 10 interiors annually with local and out-of-town craftworkers. Direct payment by client. Send brochure or call for appointment. Include return postage if samples sent. Does not report back or keep brochure on file.
Acceptable Work: Considers wall hangings, self-standing statues, one-of-a-kind furniture, draperies and lighting in batik, ceramics, fiber, glass, metal, pottery and wood.

MCCLOSKEY AND ASSOCIATES, 250 E. Short St., Lexington KY 40507. (606)252-3508. Architectural Design Director: Forrest G. McCloskey. Interior Design Director: Susan Rudd

McCloskey. Architectural and interior design firm deal with residential, institutional, industrial and commercial clients. Designs a variety of interiors. Works with local and out-of-town craftworkers. Considers wall hangings, self-standing statues, table accessories and one-of-a-kind furniture. Acceptable media include ceramics, glass, metal, pottery and wood. Price is set by craftworker. Pays $25-1,500/project. Send cover letter and slides or brochure of work. SASE. Reports as soon as possible. Keeps materials on file for as long as items remain stylish.
To Break In: Exhibit in as many craft, art and home shows as possible to become known."

MARGARET MCCORMICK INTERIOR DESIGN INC., 707 S. Brevard Ave., Tampa FL 33606. (813)251-0084. Design Director: Margaret McCormick. Interior design firm specializing in residential, institutional and commercial clients. Designs 80 interiors; buys 240 pieces of original craftwork; and commissions 80 craft designs annually from local and out-of-town craftworkers. Craftworker contracts directly with client. Pays $25 minimum for weavings; $10-400 for ceramics. Send cover letter with slides; brochure of work; or mail resume. Reports "if and when I have a job for them." Files brochure/material indefinitely. Recently commissioned tapestry for 2-story lobby. "We gave the weaver the colors and the approximate size, and she did the design. We approved it and got the commission from the client for her."
Acceptable Work: Considers wall hangings, pillows, self-standing statues, table accessories, ashtrays, desk accessories and one-of-a-kind furniture in batik, ceramics, fiber, glass, metal, pottery and wood.
To Break In: "Quality b&w single sheet flyer should be sent by mail to widest number of design professionals with a return mail card for response."

JAMES A. MARTIS JR., ARCHITECTS, 28790 Chagrin Blvd. 7250, Cleveland OH 44122. (216)831-0757. Contact: James A. Martis Jr. Architectural firm specializing in residential, industrial and commercial clients. Designs 5-10 interiors; buys about 10 pieces of original craft work; and commissions about 10 craft designs annually. Considers wall hangings; pillows; self-standing statues; items for display; ashtrays; desk accessories, and one-of-a-kind furniture. Acceptable media include batik; ceramics; fiber art; glass art; metal sculpture; pottery; and wood sculpture. Payment determined by "competitive market price; what the creator feels the work is worth." Call to arrange interview, or send brochure of work. SASE. Reports in 1 week; keeps resume on file permanently. Working process: "discuss concept of, or objective of work; designer submits sketches; reviewed with client; contract agreed upon for execution."

ANTHONY T. NAPPI, AIA, 66 Court St. Room 2302, Brooklyn NY 11201. Design Director: Anthony Nappi. Architectural firm specializing in industrial and commercial clients. Designs 10-20 interiors; and buys 30-40 craftwork pieces annually from local and out-of-town craftworkers. Price range of desks: $1,000-3,500. Send brochure of work. If previously arranged and return postage included, samples will be returned. Reports when needed. Keeps brochure on file until item is discontinued or improved.
Acceptable Work: Considers wall hangings and one-of-a-kind furniture in batik, glass, and wood.

NUCKOLS—GREELY INTERIORS, 106 E. Main, Midway KY 40347. (606)846-4521. Design Director: Mary Jane Nuckols. Interior design firm dealing with residential clients. Buys original craft work from local and out-of-town craftworkers. Considers wall hangings (no macrame), pillows, ashtrays, desk accessories and one-of-a-kind furniture. Acceptable media include ceramics, fiber and pottery. Pays according to current market prices. Send cover letter and slides or brochure. SASE. Reports as soon as possible. Keeps material on file for several years. "Make sure work is usable. Too many craft things look amateurish and are not saleable."

ABRAHAM ROTHENBERG ASSOCIATES, 16 Bridge Sq., Westport CT 06880. (203)226-7351. Design Director: Abraham Rothenberg. Architectural firm specializing in residential, institutional and commercial clients. Designs 10 interiors annually. Works with craftworkers, preferably local. Send brochure of work. Include return postage if samples sent. Reports back when needed. Keeps brochure on file.
Acceptable Work: Considers wall hangings, ceramics, fiber, pottery, and wood. "We are working on two restaurants and are interested in craftswork as decor."

SCHACHT—JOHNSON ASSOCIATES, INC., 120 S. Riverside Plaza, Chicago IL 60606. (312)236-7700. Design Director: Sven O. Johnson. Architectural and engineering firm dealing

with residential, institutional, industrial and commercial clients. Designs 30 interiors annually. Works with local and out-of-town craftworkers. Send brochure and resume. Reports by letter or phone. Keeps brochure on file as long as applicable.
Acceptable Work: Considers wall hangings, self-standing statues, table accessories, ashtrays, desk accessories and one-of-a-kind furniture in ceramics, glass, metal and wood.

LIZA SHERMAN CORPORATE ART, 19 W. 55th St., New York NY 10019. (212)581-1638. Contact: Liza Sherman. Specializes in selling large quantities of posters and limited edition original prints to international business clients. Considers large, colorful abstract images or landscapes; ethnic art; and especially weavings and tapestries. Clients are architects, corporations and space planners.

DIXON SMITH INTERIORS, 1655 Lobdell St., Baton Rouge LA 70806. Contact: Dixon Smith. Gallery/antique shop/interior designer. Estab. 1946. Represents 10 craftworkers.
Acceptable Work: Considers batik, ceramics, jewelry, pottery, quilting, wall hangings, weavings and woodcrafting. One-of-a-kind and handmade production-line items. Price range: no limit.
Terms: Buys outright and works on consignment. Dealer pays insurance on exhibited work. Requires exclusive area representation. Visit shop with actual work or call for appointment. Work may be shipped or hand-delivered.

DUFFY B. STANLEY, ARCHITECTS, 308 Bassett Tower, El Paso TX 79901. Contact: Duffy Stanley. Architectural firm specializing in institutional; commercial; and public clients. Designs 2-3 interiors annually. Acceptable media include glass art; leatherworking; metal sculpture; pottery; and wood sculpture. Mail resume and brochure of work.

CHARLES SZORADI, AIA, 1710 Connecticut Ave. NW, Washington DC 20009. (202)234-2155. Design Director: Barbara H. Szoradi. Architectural firm specializing in residential, institutional and commercial clients. Designs approximately 10 interiors; buys a maximum of 10 craftwork pieces; and commissions about 10 craft designs from local craftworkers. Send

This tapestry, made by Irene Pittman for Tampa Wholesale Company, is one of 80 craft designs commissioned annually by Margaret McCormick Interior Design Inc., Tampa, Florida. Specializing in residential, institutional and commercial clients, Margaret McCormick Interior Design designs 80 interiors and buys 240 pieces of original craftwork per year.

brochure. Does not report back but keeps brochure on file.
Acceptable Work: Considers wall hangings, weavings, banners, stained glass windows, wrought iron work and cabinet work.

TAPESTRY ASSOCIATES, 300 Central Park W., New York NY 10024. Director: Lee Naiman. Agent and consultant to architects and designers. Estab. 1970. Represents 12 craftworkers. Considers batik; wall hangings; and weavings. Fine one-of-a-kind designer pieces. Price range: $500 minimum; bestsellers: $1,000-2,000. Works on consignment; commission varies. Retail price set by joint agreement. Send slides, biography and return postage. Reports in 3 weeks. "One work of each artist is usually on display." Customers are corporate and institutional.

URBAN DEVELOPMENT CO., 1451 River Park Drive, Suite 125, Sacramento CA 95815. (916)920-4013. Design Director: William Marshall. Architectural and interior design firm dealing with all clients. Designs 200 interiors; buys substantial craftwork pieces; and commissions many craft designs from local and out-of-town craftworkers. Send brochure of work. Include return postage if samples sent. Reports as soon as possible. Brochure kept on file for 2 years. Direct commission with the architect.
Acceptable Work; Considers wall hangings, self-standing statues, desk accessories and one-of-a-kind furniture in batik, ceramics, fiber, glass, leather, metal, pottery and wood.

WAX—BEYMAN ASSOCIATES, 144 Grove Ave., Cedarhurst NY 11516. (516)569-6336. Design Director: Norman Wax. Architectural and interior design firm specializing in residential and commercial clients. Designs 5 interiors; buys 100 craftwork pieces; and commissions 3 craft designs annually from local and out-of-town craftworkers. Send brochure and resume. Include return postage if samples sent. Reports when needed. Keeps brochure on file for 1 year. "I set parameters of what I need and want and leave the design to the craftsperson."
Acceptable Work: Considers wall hangings, self-standing statues, table accessories, ashtrays, umbrella stands, desk accessories and one-of-a-kind furniture in fiber, glass, metal, pottery and wood.

HELENE WEISSNER DESIGNS, INC., 4330 NE 2nd Ave., Miami FL 33137. (305)573-6666. Works with local craft designers. Considers decorative wall hangings; pillows; self-standing statues; and items for display on tables, etc. Considers ashtrays, umbrella stands; desk accessories; and one-of-a-kind furniture. Acceptable media include batik; ceramics; glass art; metal sculpture; pottery; and wood sculpture. Send brochure of work. Keeps brochures indefinitely.

CLEVELAND A. WINGE, AIA, 9340 Culver Blvd., Culver City CA 90230. (213)839-3255. Architectural firm specializing in residential, institutional and commercial clients. Designs 3-4 interiors; and buys 2-3 craftwork pieces annually from local craftworkers. Send brochure with prices for basic budget estimate. Include return postage if samples sent. Reports as needed. Keeps brochure on file as required.
Acceptable Work: Considers wall hangings, inserts, and stained glass windows and doors in batik, ceramics, glass, metal, pottery and wood. Recently hired craftworker for installation of bronze casting in bank interior.

WUDTKE, WATSON, DAVIS, INC., 233 Sansome St., San Francisco CA 94104. (415)398-0200. Design Directors: Eric Engstrom and Larry Matarazzi. Architectural and interior design firm specializing in institutional, commercial, and restaurant products. Designs 20-30 interiors; buys 20-30 craftwork pieces; and commissions 10-15 craft designs annually from local and out-of-town craft workers. Payment and payment schedules determined by negotiation with artist/craftsman on price; payment generally at completion of total project of which craft piece is a part. Send brochure, cover letter and slides. Do not call. Include return postage if slides sent. Reports in 2-3 weeks. Keeps brochure on file for 2-3 years. "Discussions held regarding scope of work, client preferences, designer input. Craftsman's work reviewed during fabrication by architect and/or designer.
Acceptable Work: Considers wall hangings, pillows, stained glass and carved wood signs; projects in batik, fiber, glass and metal. Also paintings and mixed media wall pieces.

Colleges and Universities

If you've been limiting your concept of colleges and universities to the realm of educational opportunities, you're missing a growing market for your crafts. This section of *Craftworker's Market* lists more than 100 colleges and universities with money-making and exhibition opportunities for craftspeople from outside the campus community.

A growing number of the nation's more than 3,000 colleges and universities are exposing their students to crafts from outside their campuses. Included is Ohio State University, a school with more than 50,000 affiliates. Ohio State offers craftworkers an opportunity to sell and exhibit in their student activities center and gift shop. Other campus outlets you'll find in this section include bookstores; college organizations sponsoring craftworkers for a percentage of sales; bulletin boards where ads can be placed; galleries; and shows and fairs.

Although jewelry and personal items for students are popular, the college market by no means restricts itself to specific media. This is a market for items ranging from smoking paraphernalia to children's toys; media range from glass to fibers.

The eventual owner of campus-bought crafts won't always be the student. Members of the surrounding college community also come to buy, and students purchase gifts to take home to their family and friends during holiday breaks. Your on-campus location will be a boost to the student's holiday shopping—especially as vacations usually seem to be preceded by hard-to-get-away exam times.

Items under $20 are reported to sell best on college campuses, but a few will handle those marked as high as $50. Keeping this in mind, you should prepare to exhibit at schools by producing in volume. A number of high-quality, reasonably-priced production pieces will certainly outsell expensive one-of-a-kind work.

If there is a campus near you that isn't listed here, don't despair. There are also colleges listed under the Shops & Galleries and Shows & Fairs sections. Many of the schools we've included had just begun taking crafts; so, chances are the school near you has also recently joined this on-campus craft movement.

You can learn of additional colleges and universities in your vicinity by checking *Comparative Guide to American Colleges* (Harper & Row, Publishers, Inc., 10 E. 53rd St., New York NY 10022) or *Barron's Profiles of American Colleges* (Barron's Educational Series, Inc., 113 Crossways Park Dr., Woodbury NY 11797). Both books can be found in most libraries.

Once you find the school you'd like to work with, call the director of student activities and tell him/her you would be interested in promoting your work on his/her campus; offer to stop by and show your portfolio. Chances are you'll open doors to an entire new and exciting market for your crafts!

ADRIAN COLLEGE, Rush Union, Adrian MI 49221. (517)265-5161. Director of Student Activities: Garret Demarest. Write explaining qualifications. "Potential gross per day is not more than $100. Student residents on campus number only 600."
Shows: Student activities committee sponsors craft shows. Celebration of Spring is annually held outdoors for 1 day in May. Estab. 1979. Considers all crafts appropriate for college community. Entries accepted until show date. Work may be offered for sale; 10% commission. Craftworker or representative must attend show.
Bookstore/Gallery: Rush Union has exhibit space for craftworkers and sponsors craftworkers for a percentage of sales. Considers batik; baskets; candlemaking; carvings; sculpture; ceramics; decoupage; glass art; jewelry; macrame; metalsmithing; mobiles; pottery; wall hangings; and weavings. Charges 10% commission on sold works. Craftworker sets retail price. Bestsellers: items under $10.

Workshops: Student activities committee holds craft workshops. Average time period varies. Pays by flat rate. Considers all crafts.

ALDERSON-BROADDUS COLLEGE, Box 1397, Phillippi WV 26416. (304)457-1700. Director of Student Affairs: Carl Hatfield. Student Union sponsors annual Alderson-Broaddus College Arts and Crafts Fair ($5 entry fee); Art Department holds craft workshops. Craftworker sets retail price. Write explaining qualifications.
Acceptable Work: Considers baskets, candlemaking, carvings and sculpture, ceramics, children's toys, dolls, furniture, handbags and leather accessories, jewelry, lapidary, macrame, metalsmithing, needlecrafts, pillows, pottery, wall hangings, weavings and traditional Appalachian crafts. Bestsellers: $1-25.

AMERICAN INTERNATIONAL COLLEGE, 170 Wilbraham Rd., Springfield MA 01109. (413)737-5331. Coordinator of Student Activities: Patricia Kelly. Student activities committee sponsors craftworkers for percentage of sales and has bulletin board where craftworkers can advertise. Considers baskets; candlemaking; carvings; sculpture; ceramics; children's toys; dolls; glass art; handbags and leather accessories; macrame; pottery; wall hangings; and weavings. Charges 15% commission on sold items. Craftworker sets retail price. Bestsellers: $2-15. Write with resume and illustrations of work, or call for interview. "I would like to see some of the outside craftspeople have workshops for our students."

AQUINAS COLLEGE, 1607 Robinson Rd. SE, Grand Rapids MI 49506. (616)459-8281 (ext. 304). Director of Student Life and Activities: John J. Nichols. Student Activities Department sponsors craft shows; has exhibit space for craftworkers; and holds workshops. Considers all crafts. "We are interested in providing a facility for the artist to display his/her crafts but would also like to have the experience become an educational one for our students. Thus, we are most interested in people who can do demonstrations and/or lectures on their art." Craftworker sets retail price. Write explaining qualifications.

STEPHEN F. AUSTIN UNIVERSITY, Box 3056, SFA Station, Nacogdoches TX 75962. (713)569-3401. Craft Shop Director: Billie Elliott. Craft shop holds craft workshops and has bulletin board where craftworkers can advertise. "The craft shop is for all persons affiliated with the University. We provide free to low-priced materials and offer a variety of noncredit classes." Classes offered in batik; baskets; candlemaking; carvings and sculpture; ceramics; decoupage; furniture; handbags and leather accessories; jewelry; macrame; needlecrafts; pottery; wall hangings; and weavings. "We do not resale but always looking for employees." Write for personal interview.

AVERETT COLLEGE, 420 W. Main St., Danville VA 24541. (804)793-7811, ext. 214. Director of Student Activities: Kelsey Klime. Student Activities Association sponsors craft shows and craftworkers for a percentage of sales, holds craft workshops and has bulletin board where craftworkers can advertise. "What we would be interested in would be craftsmen to come to our campus once during the fall for a weekend or a day and once during the spring to show, sell and perhaps demonstrate their particular crafts." Considers batik; baskets; carvings; candlemaking; sculpture; decoupage; furniture; handbags and leather accessories; jewelry; macrame; metalsmithing; mobiles; needlecrafts; pottery; wall hangings; and weavings. Charges 15-20% mark-up on items purchased outright and sold in bookstore or gallery. Bestsellers: $2.50-40. Write with resume and illustration or samples or work.

AVILA COLLEGE, 11901 Wornall Rd., Kansas City MO 64145. (816)942-8400. Director of Student Life: Thomas R. Lease. Student Union Board sponsors craft shows; has exhibit space for craftworkers; holds craft workshops; and has bulletin board where craftworkers can advertise. Craftworker sets retail price. Write for personal interview explaining qualifications; include illustrations of work.
Acceptable Work: Considers carvings and sculpture, glass art, jewelry, macrame, mobiles and wall hangings. Bestsellers: $5-25.

BALL STATE UNIVERSITY, c/o Drawing & Small Sculpture Show, Art Gallery, Muncie IN 47306. (317)285-5242. Director: William E. Story. See Drawing & Small Sculpture Show.

BENTLEY COLLEGE, Forest and Beaver Streets, Waltham MA 02154. Contact: Women's Programming Board. Women's Programming Board sponsors craftworkers for 15% of sales. Prefers working with craftswomen. Considers batik, baskets, candlemaking, ceramics, glass art, handbags, jewelry, lapidary, macrame, metalsmithing, mobiles, pillows and pottery. Craftworker sets retail price. Bestsellers: $5-20. Write explaining qualifications and include illustrations of work.

BERRY COLLEGE, Box T, Mt. Berry GA 30149. (404)232-5374. Director of Student Activities: W. Rufus Massey Jr. Academy art department sponsors craft shows and student activities has exhibit space for craftworkers.
Show: "Exhibit and sale outdoor in spring during Berry Patch Festival." Annual outdoor show held 2 days in April. Entries accepted until 2-4 weeks before show. Work may be offered for sale; craftworker must attend. Considers all crafts. Requests entry fee. Craftworker sets retail price. Write with illustration of work.

BOWDOIN COLLEGE, Museum Shop of Museum of Art, Walker Art Building, Brunswick ME 04011. See Museum Shop, Bowdoin College Museum of Art.

BRADFORD COLLEGE, S. Main St. Haverhill MA 01830. Associate Dean for Student Services: Joseph Forgiano. Student activities office sponsors craftworkers for percentage of sales. "Exhibition limited to 8x10 table; 1 craftworker per day allowed to sell; some demonstration work is appropriate and valuable; and most crafts will be purchased by students for presents and/or room decoration." Considers batik, baskets; candlemaking; carvings and sculpture; ceramics; children's toys; decoupage; glass art; handbags and leather accessories; macrame; mobiles; pottery; wall hangings; and weavings. Charges 15-25% commission on sold items. Craftworker sets retail price. Bestsellers: $20 maximum. Write with illustrations of work.

BRIDGEWATER STATE COLLEGE, Student Union, Park Ave., Bridgewater MA 02324. (617)697-4825. Assistant for Program Development: Claire A. Scott. Student Union sponsors crafts shows; has exhibit space for craftworkers; and holds craft workshops. Considers all crafts. Charges 10% commission on sold items. Craftworker sets retail price. Write for personal interview explaining qualifications; include illustrations of work or samples.

CATAWBA COLLEGE, Hoke Student Union, Salisbury NC 28144. (704)637-4412. Dean of Students: K. Ann Toney. Write with resume and illustrations of work; if possible, send sample.
Shows: College Union Board sponsors craft shows. Christmas Crafts Fair is annually held indoors for 3 days in December. Estab. 1977. Considers all crafts. Entries accepted until 4 weeks before show. Work must be offered for sale. Craftworker or representative must attend show.
Gallery: College Union Board has exhibit space for craftworkers. Represents 1 craftworker. Considers all crafts. Bestsellers: $1-25. Charges commission on all goods sold. Craftworker sets retail price.
Workshops: "We have a Visiting Regional Artist Program in which we use 1 craftsman/month in our student union for 3 days. The craftsman is expected to demonstrate, display, and sell his craft. He also talks with students about his craft. We provide room and board plus $10/day to cover travel expenses." Artist also receives all profits from crafts sold. Considers all crafts.

CHATHAM COLLEGE, Woodland Rd., Pittsburgh PA 15232. (412)441-8200 (ext. 239). Contact: Coordinator, Office of Student Activities. Activities Board/Office of Student Activities sponsors craftworkers for percentage of sales; and Office of Student Activities has bulletin board where craftworkers can advertise. Charges 10-15% commission on sold items. Craftworker sets retail price. Write for personal interview explaining qualifications; include samples or illustrations of work.
Acceptable Work: Considers all crafts, especially "thematic/ethnic crafts to fit in with special spring weekend theme (changes yearly)". Bestsellers: $1-60.
Shows: Activities Board sponsors craft shows. Entry fee varies. Pre-Christmas show is annually held outdoors for 3 days in early December. Spring Weekend Show and Fair is annually held indoors for 3 days in late April. Work must be offered for sale. Craftworker or representative must attend show.
Bookstore/Gallery: Art Society has exhibit space for 1-2 craftworkers. Rental fee varies.
Workshops: Art Society/Office of Student Activities or Art Department holds craft workshops. Average workshop lasts 4 hours. Pay arrangements made through Art Department.

CHICAGO STATE UNIVERSITY, 9500 South King Drive, Chicago IL 60628. (312)995-2300. Coordinator, Student Development: Mary Arnold. Write with illustrations of work or call and describe work.

Shows: University Center/Programming Council sponsors craft shows. Cultural Arts Festival—Exhibit and Sale Fair is annually held indoors for 3 days in October. Estab. 1978. Considers batik, baskets, candlemaking, carvings and sculpture, ceramics, children's toys decoupage, dolls, glass art, handbags and leather accessories, jewelry, macrame, mobiles, needlecrafts, pillows, pottery, wall hangings and weavings. Entries accepted until 2 weeks before show. Work may be offered for sale. Craftworker or representative must attend show.
Bookstore/Gallery: See The University Gallery of Chicago State University.
Workshops: University Center holds workshops. Average workshop lasts 2-5 days. Payment negotiable. Considers pottery, jewelry, weaving and toy construction.

CLEMSON UNIVERSITY, Clemson University Student Union, Program Office, Clemson SC 29631. (803)656-2461. Assistant Program Director: Bill Mandicott. University Union sponsors craft shows. Contact by mail, phone, and/or personal interview.
Gallery: University Union has exhibit space for craftworker. Represents 1 craftworker. Considers baskets, candlemaking, carvings and sculpture, ceramics, decoupage, glass art, handbags and leather accessories, jewelry, macrame, metalsmithing, needlecrafts, pottery, wall hangings and weavings. Only exhibits crafts made by artists-in residence. Bestsellers: $2-10. Charges 15% commission on sold items. Craftworker sets retail price.
Workshops: University Union holds craft workshops. Average workshop lasts 2-5 days. No payment. Considers all crafts.

COLBY COLLEGE, Mayflower Hill, Waterville ME 04901. (207)873-1131. Director of Student Activities: Patrick Chasse, Jr. Colby Bookstore buys some small crafts outright for resale; Student Activities/Art Department sponsor crafts shows; Roberts Gallery has exhibit space for craftworkers; Student Center has bulletin board where craftworkers can advertise; and Student Activities Office holds craft workshops. Craftworker sets retail price. Bestsellers: $1-10. Write with illustrations of work or call for personal interview.
Show: Colby Craft Fair, annual indoor show established 1960. Held 2 days in October (Parents' Weekend). Entries accepted until 4-6 weeks before show. Work may be offered for sale. Craftworker must attend show.
Exhibit Space: "For 1-person or group shows in the gallery (710 square feet), we like to have workshops and/or demonstrations during that period by the exhibiting artists. We also arrange for mini-shows (1 or 2 days) with a workshop or demonstrations.
Workshops: The workshops are usually at the beginner level, so that professional crafspeople may not find them particularly challenging." Pays honorium fee of $25/day plus room and board and sales opportunity. Average length: 1½-3 hours. Interested in weaving and pottery.

COLLEGE OF NEW ROCHELLE, Campus Activities Office, New Rochelle NY 10801. (914)632-5300. Contact: Campus Activities Director. Social organizations sponsor guest exhibitions. Considers all crafts. Write explaining qualifications; include illustrations of work.

THE COLLEGE OF WOOSTER, c/o Functional Ceramics, Art Center Museum, Wooster OH 44691. (216)264-1234, ext. 388. Show coordinator: Phyllis Clark. See Functional Ceramics.

CONCORDIA TEACHERS COLLEGE, 7400 Augusta Ave., River Forest IL 60305. (312)771-8300. Show Director: Doug Mertz. Student Activities Committee sponsors craft shows. Concordia Christmas Craft Show is annually held for 2 days in December. Considers all crafts. Bestsellers: $30-3,000. Entries accepted until 5 months before show. Entry fee varies each year. Craftworker sets retail price. Work must be offered for sale. Craftworker or representative must attend show. Write with illustrations of work. "We have approximately 110 exhibitors from as far as Oklahoma with an expected attendance of 7,000-8,000 people."

CORNELL UNIVERSITY, Ithaca NY 14850. (607)256-5170. Director of the Craftshop: James E. Floyd. University Union sponsors 3 craft shows per year (fall, Christmas, spring); sponsors craftworkers for percentage of sales; and holds craft workshops. Considers all crafts. Fee depends on fair and time of year; table rental usually $20/day. Winter shows take place in Student Union. Craftworker sets retail price. Bestsellers: $5-10. Send SASE for entry blanks.
Workshops: Pays craftworker negotiable fee to present workshops in clay for 3 days-1 week.

DAKOTA STATE COLLEGE, Trojan Center, Madison SD 57042. (605)256-3551, ext. 274. Director of Housing and Activities: Robert J. Courtney. Coordinator of Student Activities: Kelly Johnson. "We are interested in craft demonstrations as well as the sale of craft products." Write with resume and illustrations of work.

Shows: Union Board sponsors craft shows. Union Board Crafts Fair is annually held indoors for 1 day in December. Considers all crafts. Entries accepted until 1 week before show. Work may be offered for sale. Craftworker or representative must attend show.
Bookstore/Gallery: Union Board has exhibit space for craftworkers. Considers all crafts. Charges $15 for 1 day; $25 for 2 days. Craftworker sets retail price.
Workshops: Union Board holds craft workshops. Average workshop lasts 1 day. Considers all crafts. Payment on a flat fee basis.

DAVIS & ELKINS COLLEGE, Elkins WV 26241. (304)636-1900. Crafts Coordinator: Margo Blevin.
Shows: Campus Activities holds show. Mountain Music & Crafts Festival is annually held indoors for 2 days in April. Estab. 1977. Considers all native mountain arts and crafts. Entries accepted until 1 week before show. Minimal entry fee. Work may be offered for sale; no commission. Craftworker or representative must attend show.
Workshops: Craft Coop/Informal Skills Sessions has working space for craftworkers; holds craft workshops; has bulletin board where craftworkers can advertise; and holds informal classes open to community. Considers baskets, dolls, pottery, weavings and particularly crafts native to Appalachian region. "Craftworker may use coop facilities (looms, potters' wheels) for a small fee. We hold classes for the community and the college, ranging from 1-day workshops to 8-week courses. These are on a coop basis, with collected fees going to artists." Write explaining qualifications.

DEL MAR COLLEGE, c/o National Drawing & Small Sculplture Show, Ayers at Baldwin Corpus Christi TX 87404. (512)881-6216. Chairman: Joseph A. Cain. See National Drawing & Small Sculpture Show.

DUQUESNE UNIVERSITY, Student Union, 1000 Vickroy St., Pittsburgh PA 15219. (412)434-6621. Recreation Director: William De Phillips. Call for personal interview.
Shows: Recreation Center sponsors craft shows. Rock & Gem Stone is annually held indoors for 5 days in fall. Estab. 1976. Considers lapidary. Entries accepted until 90 days before show. Work must be offered for sale. Craftworker or representative must attend show.
Bookstore/Gallery: Recreation Center buys crafts outright for resale; consigns crafts for resale and sponsors craftworkers for percentage of sales. Represents 1 craftworker. Considers all crafts marketable to students. Charges 10% commission on sold items. Program must be booked 6 months in advance. Craftworker sets retail price. Price range: $2-75; bestsellers: $6-25.
Workshops: Recreation Center holds workshops. Average time and payment varies. Considers all crafts.

FELICIAN COLLEGE, c/o Felician College Arts & Crafts Fair, 9476 E. Bay Harbor Dr., Bay Harbor Island FL 33154. (305)864-8725. Art Director: Iris G. Klein. See Felician College Arts & Crafts Fair.

FITCHBURG STATE COLLEGE CAMPUS CENTER, 160 Pearl St., Fitchburg MA 01420. (617)345-2024. Assistant Director, Campus Center: Victoria Angis. Write with resume and illustrations of work.
Shows: Campus Center sponsors craft shows. Holiday Crafts Sale is held annually indoors for 2 days in early December. Estab. 1976. Consider all crafts. Entries accepted until 1 week before show. Work may be offered for sale. Charges $15 table fee/day for craft sales. Craftworker or representative must attend show.
Gallery: Campus Center has exhibit space for craftworkers. Considers all crafts. Bestsellers: $1-20. Charges $15 table fee for craft sales. Craftworker sets retail price.
Workshops: Campus Center holds workshops. Average workshops lasts 1 day to 8 weeks. Pays $6.50-10.50/hour. Considers all crafts. "We sponsor noncredit craft classes and demonstrations for the college community taught by students and professional craftspeople."

FRAMINGHAM STATE COLLEGE, Student Activities Office—F.S.C., Framingham MA 01701. (617)620-1220. Contact: Program Advisor. Craftworker sets retail price. Bestsellers: $1-20. "The Student Union Activities Board sponsors various exhibits and sales for the college community. For the past three academic years, vendors and exhibitors have been setting up inside the college center and outside the facility. Vendors display their crafts from once a month to two weeks at a time. Work may be offered for sale; if so, the sponsoring organization (SUAB) receives 10% of sales income. Craftworkers' representatives must be present to

Colleges and Universities 35

exhibit/sell their own crafts. If an artist is not selling his work, but only exhibiting, his presence is not necessary. We are basically looking for anyone willing to come into our college center and exhibit and possibly sell their craftwork. Some crafts are taught in a mini-course program." Write explaining qualifications; include samples or illustrations of work. Considers jewelry, adult games, candlemaking, ceramics, glass art, handbags and leather accessories, macrame, mobiles, needlecrafts, pillows, pottery, smoking paraphernalia, wall hangings and weavings.

HOBART AND WILLIAM SMITH COLLEGES, Attention: Crafts Guild, Geneva NY 14456. (315)789-5500. Contact: Crafts Guild.
Acceptable Work: Considers batik, ceramics, leather accessories, jewelry, pottery and weavings. "We are interested mainly in pottery."
Shows: Crafts Guild sponsors craft shows. Spring Folk Festival is annually held outdoors for 2 days in May. Estab. 1977. Entries accepted until 1 week before show. Work may be offered for sale. Craftworker or representative must attend show. Considers all crafts.
Workshops: Crafts Guild holds craft workshops. Average workshop lasts 3 hours. Payment negotiable. Especially interested in ceramics and batik. "We're also looking for raku personnel to give a workshop. Our batik program is up and coming and we would welcome workshops in this medium also."

HOOD COLLEGE, Frederick MD 21701. Assistant Dean: Lois Geib. Chairman, Art Department: Alex Russo. Renaissance has bulletin board where craftworkers can advertise. Write to Alex Russo (for Hodson Gallery and workshops) or Lois Geib (for shows) with illustrations of work and samples.
Shows: Renaissance sponsors a craft show. Festival of the Arts is held annually outdoors for 1 day in April. Considers all crafts. Especially needs "those that the college students (all women) would be likely to buy." Entries accepted until show. "We prefer to see samples beforehand, but it's not necessary." Work may be offered for sale; charges table space fee. Craftworker or representative must attend show.
Gallery: Student organizations sponsor special one-person gallery shows. Considers baskets, candlemaking, handbags and leather accessories, jewelry, macrame, pillows, pottery, smoking paraphernalia, wall hangings and weaving. Charges 10% commission. Hodson Gallery is in Tatem Arts Center, and exhibits are mostly by professional artists or student exhibits.
Workshops: Average workshop lasts 1 day. Pays occasionally. Considers ceramics (wheel and hand built), jewelry, silk-screen, graphics and sculpture.

JUNIATA COLLEGE, Ellis College Center, Huntingdon PA 16652. (814)643-4310, ext. 84. Director of Programming: Wayne Justham. Write with illustrations of work, "then we will contact for interview."
Shows: Fine Arts Committee sponsors craft shows. Artist's on the Hill is held annually outdoors for 1 day in October. Estab. 1977. Considers all crafts. Entry deadline varies. Entry fee: $10-25. Work must be offered for sale. Craftworker or representative must attend show. "Craftsmen may sell, exhibit, or demonstrate their craft."
Gallery: Fine Arts Committee has exhibit space for craftworkers. "Basically we're interested in bringing quality craftsmen to the community to do one-person shows, selling throughout the year. There are no specific requirements except that the artist be interested in talking with the public as well as selling to them." Considers all crafts. Bestsellers: $2-50, any work in any price range is welcome, however. Gallery rental fee: $10-25, or mutually agreeable terms. Craftworker sets retail price.
Workshops: Fine Arts Committee holds workshops. Considers all crafts.

KEENE STATE COLLEGE, L.P. Young Student Union, Keene NH 03431. (603)352-1909, ext. 214. Contact: President of Distaff Club. Write for information. Distaff Club sponsors craft show. Keene State College Distaff Club Christmas Crafts Fair is held annually indoors for 1 day in December. Estab. 1977. Considers all crafts. Bestsellers: $2-30. Entries accepted until 2 weeks before show. Entry fee charged. Work may be offered for sale. Craftworker sets retail price. Craftworker or representative must attend show.

KENT STATE UNIVERSITY, Kent Student Center Offices, Kent OH 44242. (216)672-2554. Coordinator—Gallery and Crafts Center: Sylvia Koch. All Campus Programming Board/Kent Student Center Programming sponsors craft shows; Kent Student Center has exhibit space for craftworkers; various student organizations sponsor craftworkers for percentage of sales; and Kent Student Center Programming holds craft workshops and has bulletin board where craftworkers can advertise. Considers all crafts. Fees are variable. Craftworker sets retail price. Bestsellers: $15 maximum. "We have a gallery and are interested in different types of shows. We would like to sponsor competitions in the future. Write with slides.

KING'S COLLEGE, Wilkes-Barre PA 18711. (717)824-9931 (ext. 350). Director of Student Activities: James Doherty, CSC. Write for personal interview explaining qualifications.
Gallery: Student Center has exhibit space for craftworkers and sponsors craftworkers for percentage of sales. Represents 1 craftworker. Considers baskets, candlemaking, ceramics, glass art, macrame, metalsmithing, mobiles, pottery, wall hangings and weavings. Craftworker sets retail price.

KNOX COLLEGE, Box 79, Galesburg IL 61401. (309)343-0112. Director: Michael Murphy. Contact by mail, phone, and/or personal interview.
Shows: Student Union Gallery sponsors craft shows. Arts & Crafts Fair is annually held outdoors 1 day in early May. Estab. 1978. Considers all crafts. Entries accepted same day as show. Work must be offered for sale. Craftworker or representative must attend show.
Bookstore/Gallery: Student Union Gallery has exhibit space for craftworkers and sponsors craftworkers for percentage of sales. Considers all crafts. Craftworker sets retail price. Bestsellers: $2-50. "Gallery/lounge in Student Union has large display area for various crafts. We are not in this for the sale of products, but rather for the display of quality goods. Sales, as a bi-product, though, are OK."
Workshops: Student Union Gallery holds craft workshops. Considers all crafts. Average time and payment varies.

LA ROCHE COLLEGE, 9000 Babcock Blvd., Pittsburgh PA 15237. (412)913-9333, ext. 168. Director, Student Activities: Regina S. Battaglia. The Student Activities Committee sponsors craft shows, has exhibit space for craftworkers, sponsors craftworkers for percentage of sales and has a bulletin board where craftworkers can advertise. Considers all crafts. Charges 5% commission on sold items. Craftworker sets retail price. Bestsellers: $1-25. Write with resume and illustrations of work.

LA SALLE COLLEGE, 20th Street and Olney Avenue, Philadelphia PA 19141. (215)951-1370. Assistant Director, Student Life: Christine Lysionek. Student Life and Student Programming sponsor craft shows, have exhibit space for craftworkers and sponsor craftworkers for percentage of sales. Considers batik; baskets; candlemaking; ceramics; glass art; handbags and leather accessories; jewelry; macrame; needlecrafts; pottery; wall hangings; and weavings. Charges 20% commission on sold items. Craftworker sets retail price. Bestsellers: $5-50. Write with illustrations of work.

LADYCLIFF COLLEGE, Highland Falls NY 10928. (914)446-4747. Director of Tower Gallery: Mr. John E. Davis. Art Department/Art Therapy holds guest lectures and demonstrations; Tower Gallery sponsors craft shows and has exhibit space for 1-15 craftworkers; and Student Housing sponsors sales in jewelry. Considers all crafts. Especially needs batik, baskets, carvings, sculpture and ceramics. Fees vary according to individual and program. "We are primarily interested in exposing students and the community to high quality craftwork. We hold 11 shows a year in the Tower Gallery. One-person and group shows are scheduled 1 year in advance. We do not maintain a gallery for marketing, but have sold pieces from our gallery. We also run a work/study program in craft and museum studies."

LAURENTIAN UNIVERSITY, c/o Laurentian University Museum & Arts Centre, Department of Cultural Affairs, Laurentian University, Sudbury, Ontario, Canada P3E 2C6. (705)675-1151, ext. 400. Director: Pamela Krueger. See Laurentian University Museum & Arts Centre.

LAWRENCE UNIVERSITY, Wilson House, Appleton WI 54911. (414)739-3681, ext. 542. Associate Dean, Campus Activities: Tom Lonnquist. Union has bulletin board where craftworkers can advertise and a display case for exhibits. Write with illustrations of work.
Shows: Campus Life and Art Department sponsor craft shows. Christmas Arts & Crafts Fair is annually held indoors for 1 day during the first weekend in December. Estab. 1978. Considers all crafts. Entry deadline varies. Entry fee: $15-25. Work may be offered for sale. Craftworker or representative must attend show. Celebrate (Rites Of Spring) is held annually outdoors for 1 day in May (around Mother's Day). Estab. 1974. Considers all crafts. Entries accepted until 1 week before show. Entry fee: $15-25. Work may be offered for sale. Craftworker or representative must attend show.
Gallery: Art Department and S. Mudd Library have exhibit space for craftworkers.

Workshops: Average workshop lasts 2-5 days. Payment terms vary. Considers all crafts. Craftworker sets retail price.

LINCOLN UNIVERSITY, Lincoln University PA 19352. (215)932-8300 (ext. 221). Vice President for Student Affairs: Marie R. Vernon. Student Affairs—Residential Life and Development sponsors craftworkers for percentage of sales and holds craft workshops. Considers all crafts. "We are a small college and would like our students to become interested in crafts, hold craft workshops and hold craft shows." Write with samples or illustrations of work or call for personal interview.

LOYOLA UNIVERSITY, 6363 St. Charles Ave., Box 20, New Orleans LA 70118. (504)865-3622. Program Director: Diane Gulick. Arts and Crafts Center has bulletin board where craftworkers can advertise. Write with resume and illustrations of work.
Shows: Arts and Crafts Center sponsors shows. "We hold annual juried art shows; and arts and crafts sales twice a year." Considers all crafts. Bestsellers: $1-35. Charges 15% commission on sold items. Craftworker sets retail price.
Gallery: Loyola Union Art Gallery and Arts and Crafts Center consigns crafts for resale. Loyola Union Art Gallery Committee has exhibit space for craftworkers. Represents 1 craftworker. Considers all handmade crafts. Bestsellers: $1-35. Charges 15% commission on sold items. Craftworker sets retail price.
Workshops: Arts and Crafts Center holds craft workshops. Average workshop lasts 2-4 days. Payment terms negotiable. Considers all crafts. Especially interested in pottery and wood.

MACALESTER COLLEGE, 1600 Grand Ave., St. Paul MN 55105. (612)647-6297. Coordinator, Campus Programs: Tom Leviton. Art Department sponsors craft shows (entry fee); Art Department/Campus Programs has exhibit space for craftworkers (with rental charge) and holds craft workshops; Campus Programs sponsors craftworkers for percentage of sales and has bulletin board where craftworkers can advertise. Considers all crafts. Charges 10% commission on sold items. Craftworker sets retail price. Write explaining qualifications; include illustrations of work.

MANHATTAN COLLEGE, Box 16, Riverdale, Bronx NY 10471. (212)548-1400 (ext. 269). Director of Special Programs: Stephen Viscusi. Send samples.
Shows: Social Life sponsors Kaleidoscope, an annual craft festival held outdoors for 1 day in April. Estab. 1978. Considers all crafts. Craftworker sets retail price. Bestsellers: $1-15. No entry fee. Work may be offered for sale. Craftworker needn't attend show.

MARIETTA COLLEGE, Marietta OH 45750. (614)373-4643. Director, Campus Activities: Lew Yeager. Art Department sponsors craft shows and Student Center has exhibit space for craftworkers. "We have designated an 8x8 area in our Student Center for craftpersons to demonstrate, show and sell their creations. We have had a variety of such exhibits, some successful ($1,100 jewelry sales in 3 days) some not so successful ($200 macrame sales in 3 days). Our Art Department sponsors the annual Marietta College Crafts National competitive exhibition and is involved in the extensive Indian Summer Festival, a college/community show." Student Center considers all crafts. Charges 10% commission on sold items. Craftworker sets retail price. Bestsellers: $1-25. Write with resume.

MARION COLLEGE, Marion IN 46952. (317)674-6901. Book Store Manager: Nolan Hauser. Book store buys and consigns crafts for resale. Considers all crafts. Write with resume.

MARYMOUNT COLLEGE, Tarrytown NY 10591. (914)631-3200. Director of Student Activities: Sally Smith. Student Activities sponsors displays (with fee) and has bulletin board where craftworkers can advertise. Considers all crafts. "We do not hold individual craft displays, but will display their brochure. We set 1 day up for everyone. We will make promotional material available to the students to direct them to an individual who makes what they are looking for. Write with samples or illustrations of work.

MICHIGAN STATE UNIVERSITY, c/o Museum Gift Emporium, West Circle Dr., Michigan State University, E. Lansing MI 48824. Contact: Peg Dickman. See Michigan State University—Museum Gift Emporium.

MORAVIAN COLLEGE, Haupert Union Bldg., Bethlehem PA 18018. (215)865-0741. Union Director: Paty Eiffe. Haupert Union Program Board has exhibit space for craftworkers and holds craft workshop. Considers all crafts including carvings and sculpture, ceramics, glass art, jewelry, mobiles, pillows, pottery, kites, posters and woodworking. Bestsellers: $2-15. "We set up a room to accommodate the needs of the craftsperson for a 5-day period." Pays $100/day. Work may be offered for sale; craftworker sets retail price. Write with resume; illustrations of work; and samples.

MOUNT VERNON COLLEGE, Office of Student Activities, 2100 Foxhall Rd., Washington DC 20007. (202)331-3422. Director of Student Affairs: Kathleen Arveson. Student Activities Office sponsors craft shows, has exhibit space for craftworkers and has bulletin board where craftworkers can advertise. "We have a small exhibit of crafts for sale at reasonable prices to girls of Mt. Vernon College." Considers candlemaking; ceramics; handbags and leather accessories; needlecrafts; wall hangings; and weavings. Charges 10% commission. Craftworker sets retail price. Bestsellers: $3-25. Write with resume.

MOUNTAIN EMPIRE COMMUNITY COLLEGE, c/o Home Crafts Day, Big Stone Gap VA 24219. (703)523-2400. Director, Continuing Education: Patricia M. Collier. See Home Crafts Day.

MURRAY STATE UNIVERSITY, c/o Clara M. Eagle Gallery, Murray State University, Murray KY 42071. (507)762-3784. Director: Richard Jackson. See Clara M. Eagle Gallery.

NEW HAMPSHIRE COLLEGE, 2500 N. River Rd., Manchester NH 03104. Director of the Hobby Shop: Andrea Banchik. Write with resume and request for personal interview. Hobby Shop has bulletin board where craftworkers can advertise.
Shows: Hobby Shop sponsors craft shows. Arts & Crafts Festival is annually held indoors for 1 day in late winter. Estab. 1976. Considers all crafts. Bestsellers: 50¢-$10. Entry deadline varies. Work may be offered for sale. Craftworker or representative must attend show. Presents awards.
Bookstore/Gallery: Hobby Shop has exhibit space for craftworkers. Considers all crafts. Bestsellers: 50¢-$10. "We are looking mainly for craftspeople to demonstrate and/or exhibit their crafts at the Hobby Shop in return for free advertising. The Hobby Shop is an arts and crafts studio designed for recreational use by the students.
Workshops: Hobby Shop holds craft workshops. Average workshop lasts 3 hours. Payment varies. Considers all crafts.

NORTH PARK COLLEGE, Art Department, 5125 N. Spaulding, Box 21, Chicago IL 60625. Contact: Professor G. Bradley. Art department has exhibit space for 1 craftworker at a time. Considers batik, ceramics, glass art, jewelry, leatherworking, metalsmithing, pottery, soft sculpture, weavings and woodcrafting. Write with resume and slides of work.

NORTHWESTERN MICHIGAN COLLEGE, c/o Traverse Bay Outdoor Art Fair, 1701 E. Front St., Traverse City MI 49684. (616)946-7990. Contact: Sandy Beyer at 6839 Deepwater Point Rd., Williamsburg MI 49690. See Traverse Bay Outdoor Art Fair.

OAKTON COMMUNITY COLLEGE, c/o Starving Artists Arts & Crafts Fair, 7900 Nagle, Morton Grove IL 60201. (312)967-5120. Director: Jay Wollin. See Starving Artists Arts & Crafts Fair.

OHIO STATE UNIVERSITY, Earthtones, 1739 N. High St., Columbus OH 43210. (614)422-2325. Contact: Art Exhibit Coordinator or Gift Shop (Earthtones) Supervisor. Write or call to set up personal interview.
Shows: Art Exhibits sponsors craft shows. Renaissance Festival annually held outdoors (indoors for inclement weather) for 1 day in May. Considers all crafts representative of Renaissance or Medieval periods. Entries accepted until 2 weeks. Entry fee: $5-12. Work may be offered for sale. Craftworker or representative must attend show.
Bookstore/Gallery: Earthtones consigns crafts for resale. Art Exhibits has exhibit space for craftworkers. Represents 1 craftworker. Considers all crafts marketable to college students and staff. Suggested maximum price of consignment craft: $30. Bestsellers: $3-8. Maximum size: 3'x4'. Works on consignment; 30% commission. Craftworker sets retail price subject to sponsor agreement.
Workshops: Creative Arts Program holds craft workshops. Considers all crafts.

OREGON INSTITUTE OF TECHNOLOGY, Oretech Branch PO, Klamath Falls OR 97601.

(503)882-6321. Arts & Crafts Chairman: Chris Wallon. Arts and Crafts Department sponsors annual Arts and Crafts Show ($10-20 entry fee); has exhibit space for craftworkers; sponsors craftworkers for percentage of sales; holds craft workshops; and has bulletin board where craftworker can advertise. Considers all crafts. Charges 3-5% commission on sold items. Craftworker sets retail price. Bestsellers: $1-25. "We are interested in establishing workshops and seminars in all areas of arts and crafts for nominal charge to community and student participants." Call for personal interview or write explaining qualifications; include samples or illustrations of work.

OREGON SCHOOL OF ARTS & CRAFTS, 8245 SW Barnes Rd., Box 5784, Portland OR 97225. (503)228-4741. Sales Manager Gloria Baer-White. See The Oregon School of Arts & Crafts Gift Gallery & Craft Supply Store.

OTTUMWA HEIGHTS COLLEGE, c/o Ottumwa Heights Family Art Festival, Ottumwa IA 51501. (515)682-4551. President: Sister Bernadine Pieper. See Ottumwa Heights Family Art Festival.

PEPPERDINE UNIVERSITY, Campus Life, Malibu CA 90265. (213)456-4201. Social Development Coordinator: Thomas E. Gabbard. Campus Life/Art Department sponsors craft shows; Campus Life has exhibit space for craftworkers and has bulletin board where craftworkers can advertise. Craftworker sets retail price. Write explaining qualifications.
Acceptable Work: Considers baskets, candlemaking, carvings, sculpture, ceramics, children's toys, decoupage, dolls, glass art, handbags, leather accessories, jewelry, lapidary, macrame, metalsmithing, mobiles, needlecrafts, pillows, pottery, wall hangings and weavings. Bestsellers: 25¢-$25.

PITTSBURG STATE UNIVERSITY, Student Union, Pittsburg KS 66762. (316)231-7000, ext. 276. Program Director: Mike Sullivan. Student Union Board sponsors craft shows and craftworkers for percentage of sales. "Craftperson is set up in lobby near 2 cafeterias. Traffic is high for approximately 6 hours." Considers adult games; batik; candlemaking; ceramics; decoupage; glass art; jewelry; macrame; mobiles; wall hangings; and weavings. Charges 20% commission on sold items. Craftworker sets retail price. Best sellers: $1-20. Write with resume, illustrations of work or samples.

QUEENS COLLEGE, Charlotte NC 28274. (704)332-4121 (ext. 226). Student Activities Director: Donna Maloni. Student government will sponsor craft shows and craftworkers for percentage of sales. "We have never had a show, but might possibly have one in October." Considers candlemaking, carvings and sculpture, ceramics, glass art, jewelry, macrame, needlecrafts, pottery, wall hangings and weavings. Bestsellers: $2-20. Charges 10% commission on sales under $100; 15% commission on sales over $100. Craftworker sets retail price. Write with resume, illustrations of work and/or samples or call for information.
Workshops: Student government holds workshops. "We are interested in having workshops in leather, macrame, cross-stitch, jewelry, candlemaking, wicker-works, weaving, string art, carvings and sculpture, ceramics and pottery."

ST. ANDREWS PRESBYTERIAN COLLEGE, Laurinburg NC 28352. (919)276-3652, ext. 235. Chairman, Art Department: Anne Woodson. Write with resume and illustrations of work, or call or write for personal interview.
Shows: The Art Department, Art Guild, and the Special Events Committee sponsor craft shows. "We're open to the possibility of sponsoring a crafts festival." 1979 may be first year for St. Andrews Invitational Art Exhibit, an annual indoor show. Considers all crafts. Bestsellers: $5-100.
Workshops: Art Department, Art Guild and the Special Events Committee hold craft workshops. Average workshop lasts 3-5 days. Payment terms are negotiable. Interested in ceramics and weaving. "There is a possibility that a craftsman could be hired to teach craft the month of January."

ST. CLOUD STATE UNIVERSITY, Atwood Center, Craft Center, St. Cloud MN 56301. (612)255-2202. Program Director: Patricia A. Krueger. Write with resume. Craft Center, Art Department, has bulletin board where craftworkers can advertise.
Shows: Program Board and Atwood Center sponsors 5 annual craft shows. Other exhibits/shows are possible by arrangement. Fibers Invitational is annually held indoors for 30 days in March/April. Estab. 1978. Considers fibers only (weavings, quilting, soft sculpture, etc.).

Entries accepted until 21 days before show. Work may be offered for sale. Craftworker needn't attend show. Spring Festival of Arts is annually held indoors for 2 days in May. Estab. 1974. Considers all crafts. Entries accepted until 5 days before show. Work must be offered for sale. Craftworker or representative must attend show. Lemonade Fair is annually held outdoors (weather permitting) for 1 day in July or August. Estab. 1974. Entries accepted until 10 days before show. Work must be offered for sale. Craftworker or representative must attend show. Artists and crafters set up and sell work sidewalk style. Holiday Sale is annually held indoors for 2 days in December. Estab. 1971. Considers all crafts. Entries accepted until 5 days before show. Work must be offered for sale. Craftworker or representative must attend show. Quilt Exhibit is annually held indoors for 15-21 days in December. Estab. 1974. Considers all handmade quilts. No kits. Entries accepted until 21 days before show. Work may be offered for sale. Craftworker needn't attend show.

Bookstore/Gallery: Program Board and Atwood Center has exhibit space for craftworkers. "Students and professional artists are invited (or present resume/portfolio and request exhibit space)." Considers fibers, pottery, jewelry, wood and all fine art media. Craftworker sets retail price. "Those selected to exhibit may sell work, but must be able to deal directly with buyers. We do not act as sales agents and do not take commission." Ward's University Bookstore consigns and buys crafts outright for resale. Bookstore is private enterprise, contact separately.

Workshops: Craft Center and Atwood Center sponsors workshops and classes. Average workshop lasts 2-3 weeks, approximately 1-6 sessions. "Those hired as workshop instructors are paid either hourly or flat rate for workshop." Considers all crafts except pottery, "as the Craft Center is not equipped and lacks space for clay handling and firing."

ST. FRANCIS COLLEGE, 1901 Spring St., Fort Wayne IN 46808. (219)432-3551. Chairman, Art Department: Mr. Papier. Art department has exhibit space for craftworkers, holds craft workshops and has bulletin board where craftworkers can advertise. Considers batik; ceramics; jewelry; macrame; metalsmithing; pillows; pottery; wall hangings; and weavings. Charges 20% commission on sold items. Craftworker sets retail price. Bestsellers: $10-50. Write for personal interview.

ST. FRANCIS COLLEGE, JFK College Center, Loretto PA 15940. (814)742-7000, ext. 267. Director, Student Art: Donwick Peruso. Student Union Organization sponsors craft shows and craftworkers for percentage of sales, and workshops. "Basically an artist in residence program. We provide space and table. Hours usually 10 a.m. - 4 p.m." Considers baskets; candlemaking; carvings and sculpture; glass art; handbags and leather accessories; jewelry; macrame; metalsmithing; pottery; wall hangings; and weavings. Charges 10% commission on sold items. Craftworker sets retail price. Bestsellers: $2-15. Average workshop lasts 4 hours. Pays $50 and craftworker keeps profits from sold work. Especially interested in glass blowing, leatherworks and woodworking. Write with resume and illustrations of work.

ST. JOSEPH COLLEGE, c/o Arts & Crafts Fair, 1678 Asylum Ave., W. Hartford CT 06117. (203)232-4571. Contact: Alumnae office. See St. Joseph College Arts & Crafts Fair.

ST. MARY OF THE WOODS COLLEGE, St. Mary of the Woods IN 47876. (812)535-4141. Vice President for Student Affairs: Sue Weitz. Senate buys crafts outright for resale; Bookstore/Senate consigns crafts for resale; Art Department sponsors craft shows; and Art Department/Senate has exhibit space for craftworkers and holds craft workshops; and Student Affairs has bulletin board where craftworkers can advise. Considers all crafts. Fees are negotiated. Retail price set by joint agreement. Price range: $1-200; bestsellers: $1-20. Write with illustrations of work.

ST. MARY'S COLLEGE, c/o Moreau Gallery Three, Notre Dame IN 46556. (219)284-5717. Gallery Coordinator: Michele Fricke. See Moreau Gallery Three.

ST. MARY'S COLLEGE OF MARYLAND, St. Mary's City MD 20686. (301)994-1600. Contact: Director of Student Activities. Bookstore/student government consign crafts for resale; Fine Arts Guild sponsors craft shows and holds craft workshops; Bookstore has exhibit space for craftworkers; and Student Government has bulletin board where craftworkers can advertise. Considers adult games, carvings, sculpture, ceramics, jewelry, macrame, mobiles, wall hangings and weavings. Charges 10-15% commission on sold items. Craftworker sets retail price. Price range: $1-10; bestsellers: $2-15. Write with illustrations of work.

Colleges and Universities   41

SANTA FE COMMUNITY COLLEGE, c/o Spring Arts Festival, Box 1530, 3000 NW 83rd St., Gainesville FL 32602. (904)372-1976 or 377-5161. Director: Karen Beach. See Spring Arts Festival.

SHIPPENSBURG STATE COLLEGE, S. Prince St., Shippensburg PA 17257. (717)532-1532. Chairman of the Art Department: Harry Bentz. Art Department sponsors craft shows and has bulletin board where craftworkers can advertise. Write with illustrations of work.
Gallery: Art Department has exhibit space for craftworkers. Considers batik, baskets, carvings, sculpture, ceramics, children's toys, furniture, glass art, jewelry, macrame, metalsmithing, pottery, wall hangings and weavings. Bestsellers: $5-75. "We are looking for a diversity of craft items. Our gallery is 34x34 with grid track lighting, lunch rods for hanging, 12 portable panels and 3 floor display cases for exhibit of work. We welcome either designer or production craftspeople." Craftworker sets retail price. No charges or fees.
Workshops: Art Department holds craft workshops. Considers all crafts. Especially interested in basketry, weaving, ceramics, metal enameling and jewelry. Average workshop lasts 1-2 days. "Check on payment terms upon completion of workshop."

WILLIAM SMITH COLLEGE, c/o Crafts Guild, Hobart and William Smith Colleges, Geneva NY 14456. (315)789-5500. See Hobart and William Smith Colleges.

SOUTH DAKOTA STATE UNIVERSITY, Student Union Council, University Student Union, Brookings SD 57007. Student Union Council Arts and Exhibits Committee Chairman: Mike Collins. "All craftspeople should be willing to speak freely with students and answer any questions. All money earned from commissions and space rental is used to purchase original artwork for the SDSU Student Union." Write explaining qualifications; include illustrations of work.
Shows: Student Union Council Arts and Exhibits Committee sponsors craft shows. The Christmas Arts & Crafts Festival is held annually indoors for 3 days during the first week of December. Estab. 1975. Considers all crafts. Entries accepted 1 week before show. Work may be offered for sale. Craftworker sets retail price. Craftworker or representative must attend show. "Space rental is significantly reduced and qualified demonstrating craftspeople can be given space free of charge."
Gallery: Student Union Council Arts and Exhibits Committee has exhibit space for craftworkers. "We exhibit one-dimensional works in the Gallery Lounge, but purchases are limited at present to paintings and graphics." Charges 10% commission on sold items or $25/day, whichever is greater. Also see Agricultural Heritage Museum and South Dakota Memorial Art Center Shop.
Workshops: Student Union Council Arts and Exhibits Committee holds craft workshops. Average workshop lasts 1 day. Payment is on an individual arrangement. Considers all crafts.

SOUTHEAST MISSOURI STATE UNIVERSITY, Recreational Center/University Center, Henderson Ave., Cape Girardeau MO 63701. (314)651-2284. Recreational/Craft Center Coordinator: Jill Smyle. Craft Center/University Center has exhibit space for craftworkers; University Center has bulletin board where craftworkers can advertise. Considers all crafts
Shows: Craft Center/University Center sponsors craft shows. Arts & Crafts is held annually outdoors for 1 day prior to Christmas. Entries accepted until show date. Work may be offered for sale. Craftworker or representative must attend show. Considers all crafts.
Workshops: Craft Center/University Center holds craft workshops. Average workshop lasts 1 night or afternoon. Works on percentage basis. Considers all crafts.

SOUTHERN ILLINOIS UNIVERSITY, Student Center, Craft Shop, Carbondale IL 62901. (618)453-3636. Arts and Crafts Coordinator: Kay M. Pick Zivkovich. Write with resume, describing specific field of interest.
Shows: Museum Art Gallery Association (MAGA) sponsors craft show. MAGA "Harvest of Art" is annually held outdoors for 1 day in the fall. Considers all crafts by professional craftworkers. Entries accepted until 1 month before show. Prejudging by slides. Entries accepted until 4 weeks before show. Work must be offered for sale. Craftworker must attend show. Student Center sponsors 5 shows/year. All Center shows annually held indoors for 1 day in November and December and 2 days in February, March and April. Considers all crafts by professional craftworkers. Entries accepted until 2 weeks before shows. Work must be offered for sale. Charges $3-5/table space. Craftworker or representative must attend show.
Gallery: MAGA buys crafts for resale. Represents 5 craftworkers. Considers all crafts from Southern Illinois. "Individuals must install their own exhibits." Display cases are available

in the student center for exhibitions. Craftworker sets retail prices.
Workshops: The student center craft shop holds workshops for SIU students, faculty, staff and alumni only; has bulletin board where craftspersons can advertise. Average workshop lasts 6-8 weeks. Pays per hour; contract made and payment made at end of workshop. Considers all crafts.

SUNY COLLEGE OF ENVIRONMENTAL SCIENCE & FORESTRY, Syracuse Campus, Syracuse NY 13210. Contact: Assistant to Vice-President for Student Affairs. College has space for craftworkers, holds craft workshops and has bulletin board where craftworkers can advertise. Considers baskets; ceramics; candlemaking; handbags and leather accessories; macrame; mobiles; needlecrafts; pillows; pottery; wall hangings; and weavings. Craftworker sets retail price. Bestsellers: $35 maximum. Write with illustrations and/or samples.

TARKIO COLLEGE, Box 456 Tarkio College, Tarkio MO 64491. (515)322-3630, ext. 416. Director of Student Development: Patty Pangburn. Write explaining qualifications, write with illustrations of work or send samples.
Shows: Department of Student Affairs sponsors craft shows. Arts & Crafts Festival is annually held outdoors (weather permitting) for 1 day in April. Estab. 1979. Considers all crafts except adult games, children's toys, lapidary, mobiles and smoking paraphernalia. Bestsellers: $5-30. Entries accepted until 4 weeks before show. Entry fee: $7. Craftworker sets retail price. Craftworker or representative must attend show.

TEXAS CHRISTIAN UNIVERSITY, University Programs and Services, Ft. Worth TX 76129. Program Coordinator: Dottie Phillips. Write with resume.
Shows: Student Activities sponsors craft shows. Christmas Fair is annually held indoors for 2 days in December. Considers all crafts. Bestsellers: $1-35. Entries accepted until 3 days before show. Work must be offered for sale; 10% commission. Craftworker sets retail price. Craftworker or representative must attend show.
Gallery: "During the year a craftsman may set up but must be sponsored by a Programming Council committee." Represents 1 craftworker. Considers all crafts, primarily from Texas. Bestsellers: $1-35. Work may be offered for sale; 10% commission. Craftworker sets retail price.
Workshops: Student Activities holds craft workshops. Average workshop lasts 1-2 days. Would consider payment on percentage of student attendance.

TRINITY COLLEGE, Colchester Ave., c/o Director Student Activities, Burlington VT 05401. (802)658-0337. Director Student Activities: Linda Ready. Student activities may sponsor craft shows, has exhibit space for craftworkers and has bulletin board where craftworkers can advertise. "The college encourages local craftpeople to come to campus to sell their crafts. Generally only 1 craftsperson is here at a time and we set them up at meal times in the lounge near the cafeteria." Considers crafts "that college students would like and could afford." Daily fee: $5. Craftworker sets retail price. Bestsellers: $15-20 maximum. Write with resume.

UNION COLLEGE, Carnegie Hall, Schenectady NY 12308 (518)370-6118. Coordinator of Student Activities: Lorraine T. Marra. College Center sponsors craftworkers for percentage of sales and has bulletin board where craftworkers can advertise. Considers ceramics; handbags and leather accessories; jewelry; macrame; mobiles; needlecrafts; pottery; and wall hangings. Space charge for 1 day: $20. Craftworker sets retail price. Bestsellers: $3-30. Write with resume and illustrations of work.

UNIVERSITY OF ALABAMA, Ferguson Center/Alabama Union, Box CQ, University AL 35486. (205)348-7525. Program Director: Patricia C. O'Neill. Union sponsors craft shows, has exhibit space for craftworkers, sponsors craftworkers for percentage of sales, has bulletin board where craftworkers can advertise and plans to hold craft workshops in the future. Considers batik; baskets; carvings and sculpture; ceramics; dolls; furniture; stained and leaded glass; jewelry; lapidary; macrame; mobiles; needlecrafts; pillows; pottery; wall hangings; and weavings. Charges 10-25% commission on sold items. Craftworker sets retail price. Write with resume or call for personal interview.

UNIVERSITY OF CALIFORNIA AT DAVIS, M.U. Silo Craft Center, University of California, Davis CA 95616. (916)752-1475. Operations Technician: Jane Antee. Call for personal interview.
Shows: M.U. Craft Center sponsors craft shows. Christmas Craft Faire is annually held indoors

for 3-5 days during the first or second weekend in December. Estab. 1971. Considers all crafts. Entries accepted until 2 weeks before show. Work may be offered for sale; 25% commission. Craftworker needn't attend show.
Bookstore/Gallery: M.U. Craft Center consigns crafts for resale. Considers all crafts. Charges 25% commission on sold items. Craftworker sets retail price. Price range: $100 maximum; bestsellers: $10-40.
Workshops: M.U. Craft Center holds craft workshops. Average workshop lasts 1 day/week for 6 weeks. Pays $3.50-5/hour. Considers all crafts. Especially needs leather.

UNIVERSITY OF CALIFORNIA AT RIVERSIDE, 900 University Ave., Riverside CA 92521. (714)787-4571. Recreation Director: Butch Mayo. Send name, address and type of craft.
Shows: Campus Activities/Recreation Department sponsors craft shows. UCR Market Day is held semiannually outdoors for 1 day in December and May. Considers all crafts. No garage sale items. Bestsellers: $1-40. Entries accepted until 1 day before show. Entry fee: $7 for students other than UCR campus; $12 for nonstudents. Work may be offered for sale; no commission. Craftworker sets retail price. Craftworker or representative must attend show. Considers all handmade crafts.

UNIVERSITY OF CENTRAL ARKANSAS, Box W, Conway AR 72032. (501)329-6793. Dean of Students: Robert C. Dawson. Student Center sponsors craftworkers for percentage of sales. Considers batik; candlemaking; carvings and sculpture; ceramics; glass art; handbags and leather accessories; jewelry; macrame; metalsmithing; pottery; wall hangings; and weavings. Charges 10% commission on sold works. Craftworker sets retail price. Bestsellers: $5-20. Write with resume and illustrations of work.

UNIVERSITY OF CENTRAL FLORIDA (formerly Florida Technological University), Box 26000, Village Center, Orlando FL 32807. (305)275-2611. Program Director: Paul N. Franzese. Village Center Programming Department sponsors craft shows, has exhibit space for craftworkers and sponsors craftworkers for percentage of sales. "We like to sponsor individual craftspersons such as silversmiths; candlemakers; potters; etc., in our Village Center for 10% commission on sales."
Show: "We have an annual outdoor craft fair during 2 days of the fall quarter called 'Creations.'" Also a Village Center Annual Arts & Crafts Fair. Entries accepted until 1 week before show. Work may be offered for sale. Craftworker must attend show. Awards given. Considers all original crafts. $20 entry fee for annual craft fair; 10% commission in Village Center for sold items. Craftworker sets retail price. Bestsellers: $1-30. Write with photos or slides of work.

UNIVERSITY OF GEORGIA, Visual Arts Division, Student Activities Memorial Hall, University of Georgia, Athens GA 30602. (404)542-7774. Program Advisor: Rick Johnson. Student Activities Department has bulletin board where craftworkers can advertise. "From time to time, we like to have craftspeople come and demonstrate to the campus, possibly outside during warm weather. We have no special facilities for craftsmen yet, but will in future years when the New Student Center is built. We would like to establish a history of bringing crafts to UGA." Write explaining qualifications; include slides of work.
Shows: Student Activities Department sponsors craft shows. Gift Bazaar is held annually indoors for 5 days in December. Estab. 1970. Considers all crafts made for holiday decorations or gifts. Bestsellers: $10-100. Entries accepted until 1 month before show. Work must be offered for sale; 10-20% commission. Craftworker sets retail price. Craftworker or representative must attend show.
Gallery: Student Activities Department has exhibit space for craftworkers. Represents 1-3 craftworkers. Considers all crafts. Especially needs fabric and ceramics. Bestsellers: $10-100. Charges 10-20% commission on sold items. Craftworker sets retail price. "We have limited space (15x40) and security."
Workshops: Student Activities Department and Art Department hold craft workshops. Average workshop lasts 1-2 days. Payment covers travel and lodging, plus small honorarium or 100% profits if crafts are sold. Considers all crafts. Especially needs ceramics, jewelry, fabric, puppetry and mobiles.

UNIVERSITY OF IOWA, University of Iowa, Iowa City IA 52242. (319)353-3119 (IMU Craft Center). (319)353-5334 (Fine Arts Council—Thieves Market). Contact: Judy Gagliardi or Nancy Cook. Write to the Fine Arts Council—Thieves Market for more information. "Fine Arts Council is organizing an Artists Referral Center. More information will be available in the fall of 1979."

Shows: Thieves Market/Fine Arts Council sponsor craft shows. Thieves Market is held indoors throughout the year. Estab. 1965. Considers ceramics, sculpture, weavings, leathercrafting, metalwork, bookbinding and papermaking. Entries accepted until 1 month before specific show date. Work may be offered for sale. Craftworker or representative must attend show.
Bookstore/Gallery: IMU Craft Center consigns crafts for resale and has bulletin board where craftworkers can advertise; Fine Arts Council has exhibit space for craftworkers. Considers batik, baskets, carvings, sculpture, ceramics (not poured), leaded glass or copper foil glass art, leather accessories, jewelry, lapidary, macrame, metalsmithing, needlecrafts, pottery (not poured), wall hangings, weavings, calligraphy, natural dying, paper making and bookbinding. Charges $5-25 or 20% commission on sold items. Craftworker sets retail price. Bestsellers: $3-200.
Workshops: Fine Arts Council holds workshops. Average workshop lasts 2-3 days. Payment includes cash and boarding. Considers ceramics, sculpture, weavings, leathercrafting, metalwork, bookbinding and papermaking.

UNIVERSITY OF KENTUCKY, 203 Student Center, Lexington KY 40506. (606)258-8867. Program Director: John H. Herbst. Student Center Board sponsors craft shows; has exhibit space for craftworkers; holds craft workshops; and has bulletin board where craftworkers can advertise. Considers candlemaking, carvings, sculpture, ceramics, furniture, glass art, jewelry, macrame, metalsmithing, pottery, wall hangings and weavings. Fees negotiated. Craftworker sets retail price. Write explaining qualifications; include samples or illustrations of work.

UNIVERSITY OF MAINE AT FARMINGTON, Activities Office, Farmington ME 04938. (207)778-3501. Chairman, Crafts and Exhibits Committee: Kaye Edgett. Write with illustrations of work or send samples.
Shows: Student Activities Office sponsors craft shows. Held indoors for 1 day in December and March. Considers all crafts. Work may be offered for sale. Craftworker or representative must attend show.
Gallery: Student Activities Office has exhibit space for craftworkers. Considers all crafts. Rental charge: $2/table. Craftworker sets retail price.
Workshops: Student Activities Office holds craft workshops. Average workshop lasts 1 afternoon, possibly 2 days. Considers jewelry and weaving. "We have started this year holding workshops for small groups of students where we ask craftsmen to come demonstrate, instruct, and let students participate in making crafts."

UNIVERSITY OF MARYLAND, Room 1221, Student Union, College Park MD 20742. (301)454-4987. Crafts Center Director: Linda S. Sullivan. Student Union Program Office has exhibit space for craftworkers. "We also have an artist-in-residence program that craftworker may participate in." Write for applications.
Shows: Student Union Program Office sponsors 2 large craft fairs/semester (1 in April, 1 in December). Holiday Craft Fair is annually held indoors for 3 days during the first or second week in December. Estab. 1978. Considers all crafts. Entries accepted until 1 month before show. Work may be offered for sale. Craftworker or representative must attend show.
Workshops: Student Union Program Office holds workshops. "This is in the planning stages. We have a Craft Center opening with programs in the fall. I will be hiring some instructors at approximately $5-10/hour vs percent of class enrollment."

UNIVERSITY OF MASSACHUSETTS AT BOSTON, University of Massachusetts Harbor Campus, Boston MA 02125. Assistant Director of Information Services: Christopher S. Clifford. "We have a nontraditional student population with an average age of 25+; 50+% work full-time, and are heavy buyers in art works and jewelry." Write with illustrations of work.
Shows: Information Office sponsors 3-4 craft shows. Spring Arts—Spring Infofest is annually held outdoors for 2-3 days in April. Estab. 1974. Considers all crafts. Bestsellers: $2-100. Entries accepted until 7 days before show. Work must be offered for sale; 20% commission. Craftworker sets retail price, but needn't attend show. "Craftworker should have own display equipment and not more than 12' total table frontage."

UNIVERSITY OF MICHIGAN, UM Artists and Craftsmen Guild—2nd Floor, Michigan Union, Ann Arbor MI 48109. Director, UM Artists and Craftsmen Guild: Celeste Melis. Director, Union Gallery: Rita Bartolo. Director, Pendleton Arts Information Center: Shirley Smith. Program offers professional resources to develop art skills.

Shows: UM Artists and Craftsmen Guild and Union Gallery sponsors 4 craft shows. For information, see University Artists & Craftsmen Guild Summer Arts Festival, University Artists & Craftsmen Guild Christmas Art Fair, University Artists & Craftsmen Guild Fall Art Fair and University of Artists & Craftsmen Guild Spring Art Festival.
Gallery: Union Gallery has exhibit space for craftworkers. Represents 15-30 craftworkers. Considers all crafts. Bestsellers: $1-1,000. Charges 30% commission and $25 membership fee. Craftworker sets retail price. Send slides and resume for jury committee.
Workshops: UM Artists and Craftsmen Guild holds craft workshops. Average workshop lasts 1 weekend or 1 day/week for 8 weeks. Payment is on a cash basis. "We need teachers for special workshops; subjects are open to the artist's imagination and creativity."

UNIVERSITY OF MISSOURI-COLUMBIA, Museum of Anthropology Sales Desk, 104 Swallow Hall, Columbia MO 65201. See Museum of Anthropology Sales Desk, University of Missouri-Columbia.

UNIVERSITY OF NEBRASKA AT LINCOLN, Nebraska East Union, Suite 314, Lincoln NE 68583. (402)472-1776. Recreation Manager: Ray Koziol. Nebraska East Union has bulletin board where craftworkers can advertise. Write explaining qualifications or call.
Shows: University Program Council—East sponsors craft shows. East Union Holiday Craft Fair is held annually indoors for 2 days in fall. Estab. 1977. Considers all crafts. Entries accepted until 1 week before show. Work may be offered for sale. Craftworker or representative must attend show.
Bookstore: Nebraska East Union has exhibit space for craftworkers. Considers all crafts. Bestsellers: $5-40. Fees (if any) are minimal.
Workshops: Nebraska East Union holds craft workshops. Average workshop lasts 2 hours/session; 6 sessions. Payment ranges $3-10/hour. "We consider any crafts that are currently popular and will draw participants/students. The craft program is still in its initial stages. Small workshops using meeting rooms are planned until our craft facility itself is completed. For now, we are open to about any kind of presentation, workshop, etc."

UNIVERSITY OF NORTH CAROLINA AT CHAPEL HILL, Chapel Hill, Campus Y, Y Bldg. 151-A, Chapel Hill NC 27514. (919)933-2084. Director: Edith M. Elliott. Campus Y sponsors craft show. Crafts Bazaar is annually held indoors for 3-4 days during the first weekend in December. Considers batik, baskets, candlemaking, carvings and sculpture, children's toys, dolls, glass art, handbags and leather accessories, jewelry, lapidary, macrame, metalsmithing, mobiles, needlecrafts, pillows, pottery, wall hangings and weavings. Bestsellers: $3-75. Entries accepted until 3 months before show. Work may be offered for sale; 20% commission. Craftworker sets retail price. Craftworker must attend show. Write for applications before July 31.

UNIVERSITY OF NORTH CAROLINA AT GREENSBORO, Elliott University Center, Greensboro NC 27412. (919)379-5510. Assistant Program Director: Bruce Harshbarger. Assistant Director: Terry Weaver. Student Center Programming Board sponsors some craft shows; provides exhibit space for craftworkers at certain times; sponsors craftworkers for percentage of sale; and might hold craft workshops. Considers all crafts, especially folk-life works. Business Office sets retail price. "We use exhibits of this sort with regard to special outdoor weekends. Write explaining qualifications; include illustrations of work."

UNIVERSITY OF SANTA CLARA, c/o De Saisset Art Gallery & Museum—Gallery Shop, The University of Santa Clara, Santa Clara CA 95053. (408)984-4528. Manager/Gallery Coordinator: Georgianna Lagoria. See De Saisset Art Gallery & Museum—Gallery Shop.

UNIVERSITY OF SOUTH DAKOTA, c/o W.H. Over Museum, The University of South Dakota, Vermillion SD 57069. 9605)677-5228. Director: June Sampson. See W.H. Over Museum.

UNIVERSITY OF SOUTHERN CALIFORNIA, YWCA, Craft Center, University Park, Los Angeles CA 90007. (213)741-6208. Coordinator, USC Craft Center: Jo Ann M. Fried. Craft Center sponsors 2 annual craft shows. "We have 2 craft fairs each year with approximately 100 craftspeople. Commercially-manufactured goods do not qualify. The show is several years old and quite successful." Considers all crafts. Entry fee: $40. Craftworker sets retail price. Write with resume and illustrations of work or call for application.

UNIVERSITY OF THE PACIFIC, University Center, Stockton CA 95211. (209)946-2171. University Center Director: Gary Kleemann. Write with resume and illustrations of work.
Shows: Universiy Center sponsors 2 craft fairs (1 in early December and 1 in late April) and "allows occasional craftsmen to come sell their work in the University Center." Semiannual indoor/outdoor show held 4-5 days in November and April. Considers all crafts. Bestsellers: $2-15. Work may be offered for sale. Craftworkers or representative must attend show. Charges 10% commission on sold items. Craftworker sets retail price.
Workshops: University Center holds craft workshops. Average workshop lasts 1 day. Payment is mostly on volunteer basis. Considers stained glass and pottery.

UNIVERSITY OF VICTORIA, Maltwood Art Museum & Gallery, University of Victoria, Box 1700, Victoria, British Columbia, Canada V8W 2Y2. (604)477-6911 (6169 local). Director/Curator: Martin Segger. See Maltwood Art Museum & Gallery.

UNIVERSITY OF VIRGINIA, c/o Bayly Museum Shop, Rugby Rd., University of Virginia, Charlottesville VA 22903. Manager: Janice F. Bowen. See Bayly Museum Shop, University of Virginia.

UNIVERSITY OF WISCONSIN AT OSHKOSH, 748 Algoma Blvd, Oshkosh WI 54901. (414)424-2358. Art Director: Gail D. Floether. Write explaining qualifications; include illustrations of work.
Shows: Reeve Union sponsors craft shows. May Fair is held annually outdoors (indoors if rain) for 2 days in May. Estab. 1976. Work may be offered for sale. Craftworker or representative must attend show. Considers all crafts.
Gallery: Reeve Union has exhibit space for craftworkers. Considers all crafts. Bestsellers: $1-200. Charges 10% commission on sold items vs $22 room rental, whichever is greater. Craftworker sets retail price.
Workshops: Average workshop lasts 2 days. Considers all crafts. "If the craftworker gives a demonstration or holds a workshop, no commission is charged on items sold. If the craftwork and demonstration is unique—something different and educational—we have money available to pay the artist for doing the workshop."

UNIVERSITY OF WISCONSIN AT STEVENS POINT, Arts and Crafts Center, UC-UWSP, Stevens Point WI 54481. (715)346-4479. Student Manager: Sally Eagon. Arts and Crafts Center has bulletin board where craftworkers can advertise. Write with illustrations of work. "We would prefer craftspeople to give active demonstrations when selling."
Shows: Arts & Crafts Center/UAB sponsor craft shows. UAB Art Fair is held annually indoors for 2 days in spring. Estab. 1973. Considers all crafts. Entries accepted until 1 month before show. Work may be offered for sale. Craftworker or representative must attend show.
Gallery: Arts and Crafts Center has exhibit space for craftworkers. Represents 1-3 craftworkers. Considers all crafts. Bestsellers: $2-50. Charges 20% commission on sold items "from exhibit area only."
Workshops: Arts and Crafts Center holds craft workshops. Average workshop lasts 1-2 days. Payment terms negotiable. Considers all crafts.

VIRGINIA COMMONWEALTH UNIVERSITY, c/o Anderson Gallery, 907½ W. Franklin St., Richmond VA 23220. Director: Harriet Dubowski. See Anderson Gallery.

WELLS COLLEGE, Aurora NY 13026. (315)364-3300. Assistant Dean of Students: Mickie Cuevas-Post. Dean of Students Office holds workshops; Dean of Students Office and various student organizations have exhibit space for craftworkers; various student organizations sponsor craftworkers sor percentage of sales; and Communications Department has bulletin board where craftworkers can advertise. Considers all crafts. Write for information.
Shows: Dean of Students Office sponsors craft shows. Food/Crafts is annually held indoors for 1 day in January. Considers all crafts. Entries accepted until 1 week before show. Work may be offered for sale. Craftworker or representative must attend show.

WESTERN KENTUCKY UNIVERSITY, Gallery—Ivan Wilson Center For Fine Arts, Bowling Green KY 42101. (502)745-2345. Director: John Warren Oakes. Send resume and slides. Reports in 4 weeks.
Shows: Fine Arts Center sponsors shows. Considers batik, ceramics, glass art, jewelry, leatherworking, metalsmithing, needlecrafts, pottery, soft sculpture, wall hangings, weavings and woodcrafting.

Gallery: Fine Arts Center has exhibit space for craftworkers. Considers batik, ceramics, glass art, jewelry, leatherworking, metalsmithing, needlecrafts, pottery, soft sculpture, wall hangings, weavings and woodcrafting. One-of-a-kind pieces only. Displays for 3 weeks.
Workshops: Fine Arts Center holds workshops. Average workshop lasts 2-7 days. Payment negotiable. Considers all crafts.

WESTERN MARYLAND COLLEGE, Westminster MD 21157. (301)876-3752. Director of College Activities: Joan M. Nixon. Art department sponsors crafts shows and has exhibit space for craftworkers. College Activities sponsors craftworkers for percentage of sales and has bulletin board where craftworkers can advertise. "We sponsor a program with a working craftsman actually 'doing' his craft. Serves as demonstration in addition to sales." Considers all crafts. Charges 10% commission on sold items. Craftworker sets retail price. Bestsellers: $2-10. Write with illustrations of work.

WHITWORTH COLLEGE, Hardwick Union Bldg., Spokane WA 99218. (509)466-3276. Director of Student Activities: Lunell Haught. Union Building sponsors craft shows ($5-10 entry fee) and has exhibit space for craftworkers. Considers all crafts. Bestsellers: $1-10. Write for information.

WILKES COLLEGE, IDC Office, Wilkes Barre PA 18702. (717)825-3054. IDC President: Gary Toczycowski. Inner Dormitory Council sponsors craft shows; and Inner Dormitory Council/Student Government holds craft workshops. Considers all crafts. No charges or fees. Craftworker sets retail price. Bestsellers: $1-15. "We sponsor a day with all kinds of exhibits. At the same time, food and drink (soda, cider, etc.) are sold, music is playing and clowns walk around. We provide advertisement and people." Write or call for appointment.

WINSTON SALEM STATE UNIVERSITY, Box 13154, Winston Salem NC 27102. (919)761-2044. Assistant Director of Student Activities: Elaine P. Browne. Student Union has bulletin board where craftworkers can advertise. Write or call for personal interview.
Shows: Student Union sponsors craft shows. Montage is annually held outdoors for 1 day in fall. Estab. 1975. Considers batik, candlemaking, handbags, leather accessories, jewelry, macrame, needlecrafts and wall hangings. Entries accepted until 4 weeks before show. Work may be offered for sale; commission charged. Craftworker or representative needn't attend show.
Gallery: Student Union sponsors craftworkers for percentage of sales. Represents 45 craftworkers. Considers batik, candlemaking, handbags, leather accessories, jewelry, macrame, needlecrafts and wall hangings.
Workshops: Student Union holds craft workshops. Average workshop lasts 8 weeks.

WORCESTER POLYTECHNIC INSTITUTE, Worcester MA 01609. (617)753-1411, ext. 291. Associate Dean of Students: Bernard H. Brown. Student Affairs Office sponsors craft shows, has exhibit space for craftworkers, and sponsors craftworkers for percentage of sales. Considers all crafts. Charges 10% commission on sold items. "We only sponsor craftworker if prices are reasonable for students." Bestsellers: $2-10. Write with resume and samples or call for personal interview.
Workshops: Student Affairs Office holds craft workshops. Average workshop lasts 1-3 days. Payment terms are negotiable. Considers all crafts. "We have a January intersession period when we could have craftsmen do a 2-3 day workshop."

WORCESTER STATE COLLEGE, 486 Chandler St., Worcester MA 01602. (617)752-7700. Director, Student Center and Student Activities: Paul M. Joseph. Student Center sponsors craft shows, has exhibit space for craftworkers, sponsors craftworkers for percentage of sales and has bulletin board where craftworkers can advertise. "One of the goals of our Student Center is to provide an on-going exposure to crafts. We will encourage week-long craft demonstrations/sales and run 1 per month. Considers all crafts. Craftworker sets retail price. Bestsellers: $1-25. Write with resume and illustrations of work (if available).
Workshop: Student Center holds craft workshops. Average workshop lasts 4 hours to 2 days. Payment terms negotiable. Considers all crafts which can be demonstrated indoors.

XAVIER UNIVERSITY, Office of Student Development, Victory Pkwy., Cincinnati OH 45207. (513)745-3201. Assistant Dean of Student Development: Peggy Dillon. Student Development sponsors craft shows and craftworkers for percentage of sales. "We hold a craft show each year in late November or early December. Since we are a small school we can only give each exhibitor about 12x9 space. We normally supply table and chairs; but people with their own set-up are welcome as long as the display is no larger than specified above." Considers all crafts. Entry fee: $10/day or 10% commission on sold items. "We use a system of either a flat fee or a percentage." Craftworker sets retail price. Bestsellers: $2-10. Write with resume. Limited number of spaces available.

Companies and Manufacturers

"Crafts fulfill a need in each of us to personalize what comes into our lives. And as we become more and more industrialized, that need for handcrafted items will also increase."

If your motivation as a craftsperson is based on Julie Shafler of Julie: Artisan's Gallery's philosophy above, then the last place you may want to look for markets for your crafts is the mass-producing markets of this section.

But if you are interested in making more than $500 for a weaving kit design or model, read on. The listings in this section will buy about 13,000 craft designs in the next year. Buyers range from miniature firms seeking actual handmade merchandise to jewelry manufacturers seeking prototypes.

There are markets for every type of craftworker here—from the ceramacist to the metal sculptor. And, as public interest in crafts grows, there will be an increase in the number of items designed after original handicrafts, and a growing need for do-it-yourself craft kits.

The listings in this section have been designed to tell you who you should contact and by what means; how soon they'll report back to let you know if they're interested in your work; and by what means they pay.

Once you receive an assignment from a company or manufacturer it is always a good idea to get all dealings in writing. Handshakes and gentlemen's agreements are easier to obtain and more pleasant to work with, but a written agreement is the best way to avoid forgotten or broken promises.

Also, inquire as to whether your signature will appear on the product. Push for this as it is an excellent way to increase your exposure. Consumers who are pleased with the first piece they buy designed by you will watch for your future work—and so with other manufacturers. Some companies have policies against including signatures or names; others make information about the craftperson a standard item to be included—it gives the mass-produced pieces a bit of personal appeal.

Don't limit yourself to the markets in this section. If you feel you have a product that would have mass market appeal, keep your eyes open for the right company to produce it. An excellent place to find potential manufacturers for your work is by browsing through gift and stationery shops. Write the producer of products similar to your own; ask if they would be interested in working with you and send photos of your work as samples.

You can also find companies by sending a press release to publications, such as *Greetings*. Include a black and white photo, and ask the magazine to include your article in their New Products section.

ADAMSCO, INC., Box 1086, Tulsa OK 74101. (918)587-7591. President: G. F. Adams. Manufactures kits and components (ie. beads for macrame) using cast polyester. Buys and commissions 6-10 designs annually both to use as prototypes for products and to show creative uses for company products. Write explaining qualifications. Reports in 2 weeks.

AMERICAN MINIATURES, 102 2nd Ave. N., Mount Vernon IA 52314. (319)895-6371. President: Tim Morrissey. Manufacturer and distributor of miniature houses, furniture and accessories. Buys and sometimes commissions crafts to use as prototypes; and uses craftworkers to help with product distribution. Buys 10-20 designs annually. Pays $100 minimum for furniture; $25-50 for accessory items. Products are of metal and wood. Works on 1''-1' scale. Call or write with samples. Reports in 2 weeks.

ANGELIQUE JEWELRY, 7263 Engineer Rd., Suite B., San Diego CA 92111. (714)292-8300.

Contact: Jeff Elden. Estab. 1969. Manufacturer of porcelain, floral and feather jewelry for speciality and department stores; Angelique label. Buys 100-200 designs/year. Query with color drawings or photos. SASE. Reports in 2 weeks.
Needs: Uses artists for product design and illustration. Pays $5-25 for pendant designs.
To Break In: "Prepare a series based on a theme. Look for fashion trends and develop an original off-shoot. Themes submitted in February/March should tie into the following fall. Submissions during June/July must relate to the following spring."

AZTEX CORPORATION, Box 50046. Tucson AZ 85703. Contact: Elaine Haessner. Book publisher. Publishes nonfiction soft and hardback books, with a large format 6x9 or larger, not mass-paperback. Specializes in 'how to' for plastic modeling of airplanes, tanks, ships, etc; wargaming guides; and general military and transportation histories. Buys and commisisons designs to illustrate books. Send photos or slides of work done previously. Reports in 4 weeks.

C. J. BATES & SON, Rt. 9A, Chester CT 06412. (203)526-5381. Manager, National Accounts: Cliff Earley. Manufacturer of knitting needles; crochet hooks; embroidery hoops; and knitting and crochet accessories. Send resume. Reports in 1 week.
Needs: Buys crafts in bulk for resale; and commissions and buys designs to use as prototypes. Uses 40-50 designs annually. Payment for knitting, crocheting and embroidery based on garment.

BAUMGARTEN'S, 1190-A N. Highland Ave. NE, Atlanta GA 30306. President: H.J. Baumgarten. Estab. 1950. Publishes rice paper napkins to complement fine china. Commissions models. Assigns 6 projects/year. "We need a model maker who could make certain gift products for us which we would send as models to the Far East for manufacturing. Models are received more readily than drawings over there." Query with actual work or samples. SASE. Reports in 2 weeks.

THE BEADERY, Box 178, Canonchet Rd., Hope Valley RI 02832. (401)539-2432. Design Coordinator: Holly J. Smith. "We package our parent company's craft items and sell through mail, wholesalers, distributors and dealers." Produces craft kits, component parts for the jewelry industry and beads for the craft industry as well as a line of macrame rings and beads. Also sells bulk beads and spooled wire. Works in plastic. "We have the ability to metal-plate our plastic parts. Colors used in jewelry are seasonal and change each year, while the colors used in crafts are maintained and used year round with no usage boundaries." Write explaining qualifications or call requesting personal interview. Include photos of previously completed work or samples of actual work being offered. Reports in 2 weeks.
Needs: Buys 12 designs annually for use as prototypes for products. "We would publish the design using our product in the form of a sheet of instructions, or as the basis of a kit (ideas for use of our beads.)" Pays $10 for small ornaments or decorations; $15-35 for simple hanger or medium objects; $20-75 for elaborate hanger or design; $8-11/hour for design ideas with instructions; $4-7/hour for variation creations. "We will accept craft projects from the entire country—the beads used should be Beadery-brand or we will alter the bead used (no imported beads please). Christmas items should arrive by July 1, accompanied by brief directions."

BECKY'S CRAFTS, Western Shore, Rt. 3, Box 3T, Lunenburg County, Nova Scotia, Canada B0J 3M0. (902)627-2563. Contact: Hildred Vaughan. Craft factory. Manufactures clothing, dolls, needlecrafts, quilting and wall hangings. Buys and commissions designs and finished products. Send samples of work with SASE. Reports in 2 weeks.

BELMAR EDITIONS LTD., 1313 S. Killian Dr., W. Palm Beach FL 33403. (305)845-6075. President: M. Belford. Manufactures gold plated and porcelain thimbles. Specializes in custom designs. Buys crafts and designs outright for resale. Write explaining qualifications. Samples should be sent on request only.

EMILE BERNAT & SONS CO., Depot and Mendon Streets, Uxbridge MA 01569. (617)278-2414; "no collect calls." Craft Design Coordinators: Sydelle Byer or Laurel Horvat. Manufacturer of latch hook rugs and pillows; quick stitch; needlepoint; and stitchery—both stamped canvases and kits. "Our needlework line is very varied and includes contemporary, traditional, florals, geometrics, etc. with emphasis on texture and dimension. We purchase designs of all types to be used as printed canvases or kits." Pays minimum $150, rugs; $75, pillows; $75, needlepoint. Payment determined by size and complexity. Write explaining qualifications and send slides and drawings of work. Reports in 2 weeks.

Companies and Manufacturers 51

"The creative process is without end," writes the president of Open Door Enterprises, Inc. "We have continued to create fresh new product lines geared to the ever changing market we serve." Open Door Enterprises, Santa Clara, California, manufactures kits for string, wire and mosaic art, embroidery and color-it-yourself poster kits. Fresh ideas will be considered by writing to Fred Fortune explaining qualifications.

BERSTED'S HOBBY CRAFT INC., Box 40, Monmouth IL 61462. (309)734-7011. Sales Manager: Roger Bersted. Kit manufacturer and bulk supplies. Products are kits of plaster casting; papier mache; basketry; liquid rubber; and chair caning. Buys crafts in bulk for resale; commissions craftworkers; buys design outright; and sponsors Kiddy Kraft Klub craft show. Minimum payment is 5% of invoice price. Submit resume and specific pieces being offered; arrange personal interview. Reports in 2 weeks.

BGI CRAFTS INTERNATIONAL, 9712 Mirage Circle, Garden Grove CA 92644. (714)636-1570. President: Ilene Miller. Manufacturer of macrame and weaving supplies; porcelain beads; porcelain wind chimes; ceramic beads; and gift items. "We sell finished products, kits, and open stock." Buys and commissions "hundreds of designs annually" to use as prototypes, and buys crafts in bulk for resale. Payment varied; determined by originality and quality of workmanship. Write with samples for a personal interview. Reports in 3 weeks.

BIRD HOUSE ENTERPRISES, 110 Jennings Ave., Patchogue NY 11772. (516)654-1044. Contact: Gail Bird. Mail order firm. Estab. 1977. Represents 10 craftworkers. Buys outright (sometimes) and works on consignment; 25% commission. Retail price set by joint agreement. Send slides or call for appointment.
Acceptable Work: Considers batik, clothing, dollmaking, jewelry, needlecrafts, quilting, soft sculpture and wall hangings. "All artwork must contain miniature punch needle embroidery." Especially needs fashion accessories and decorative pieces. One-of-a-kind and handmade production-line items. Price range: $50-500; bestsellers: $75-150.
Profile: "The method of display is in traveling exhibits, such as fashion shows. These include lecturing, slide shows, demonstrating and teaching 17th century punch needle embroidery (Igolochkoy). I wholesale and retail the handcrafted needle to do this Russian peasant craft and sell finished products with this needle art on it." Customers: ages 10-adult; $5,000+ incomes; embroiderers. Best selling time: September-December.
To Break In: "Follow current trend ideas, fashion accessories and have excellent color sense."

BLUE DELFT CO. INC., 1201 Broadway, New York NY 10001. (212)679-7644. Manager: Henry Blumner. Manufactures jewelry in brass, silver and gold. Buys and commissions 24 designs annually to use as prototypes for products; and buys crafts in bulk for resale. Prefers craftworkers from northeastern part of US. Write explaining qualifications and send samples. Reports in 1 week.

BOYE NEEDLE CO., 916 S. Arcade, Freeport IL 61032. Contact: Jeff Anderson. Manufactures art/needlework accessories (hand sewing needles, scissors, crochet hooks, afghan hooks, cro-hooks, knit pins, knit accessories, latch hooks and canvas, embroidery hoops, applique looms, books and leaflets, frames and stands, knit stands and tote bags and weaving looms). Buys and commissions designs; also provides equipment. Specific instructions given for each job. Pays $50-5,000 for various jobs. Write explaining qualifications. Reports in 3 weeks.

KEN BROWN STUDIO, Box 637 CW, Hugo OK 74743. (405)326-7544. Contact: Ken Brown. Studio of calligraphic art. Sells parchment reproductions of calligraphic art, ink drawings and decals. Line includes poems, quotations and religious prints. Interested in made-ups of prints. Commissions craftworkers who are familiar with the work. Buys 40-50 designs annually. Pays $20 minimum for memory boxes and plaques. Call for personal interview. Reports in 2 weeks.

CAL-ACCESSORIES CO., INC., 1103 Front St., Uniondale NY 11553. (516)481-4422. President: Mark Frankl. Importer/Distributor. Handles doll houses, doll house furniture/accessories, thimble boxes and printer wall boxes in wood; and thimbles in porcelain. To be considered for inclusion in catalog, write for information.

THE CALICO DOLLHOUSE, Rt. 130 & Quarry Lane, North Brunswick NJ 08902. (201)297-4545. President: Rita Bianco. Deals in wooden miniature dollhouse furniture and accessories. "We offer a complete line of turnings and spindles for the craftsperson. A SASE is all they need to send for our complete list." Buys crafts in bulk for resale. Write with samples of work that is being offered for sale and explain qualifications. Reports on inquiries in 2 weeks.

CARDINAL CHINA COMPANY, Box D, High Street, Carteret NJ 07008. (201)541-5194. Director of Marketing: Stan Wahlberg. Manufacturer of doll house furniture and accessories. Works on a scale of 1"-1' in wood, metal, plastic and rattan. Buys crafts in bulk for resale and buys prototypes for products. Write for personal interview explaining qualifications and

Companies and Manufacturers 53

product. Present specific pieces being offered or photos at interview.

CAROUSEL CRAFTS COMPANY, Box 42549, Houston TX 77042. General Manager: Roy Adams. Manufacturer of needlecraft kits. Buys crafts/designs to use as prototypes for products. "We review sample before purchasing design." Payment is negotiable. Submit resume, samples and/or actual work. Reports in 3 weeks.

CHOCOLATE & VANILLA LTD., 460 W. 24th St., New York NY 10011. Contact: Peter Listro. Estab. 1977. Considers ceramics and sculpture. Special need for food reproduction. Fine handmade production-line items. Price range: (retail) $1-40; bestsellers: (retail) $2-10. Buys outright; pays royalty. Submit color slides. SASE. Reports in 2 weeks. Dealer pays insurance for exhibited work.
Profile: "We buy whimsical, unique, and functional items from craftworkers and resell to better gift and department stores on a national basis. We will also arrange for the limited manufacture of a sculptured item using an old world method and buy it outright or arrange a royalty for the craftworker; e.g. dinner bells, paperweights, magnets, pen holders, pencil sharpeners and bookends." Heaviest wholesale buying time: February-March and September-October; best selling time: January-February and November-December.

CLAPPER PUBLISHING CO., INC., 14 Main St., Park Ridge IL 60068. (312)825-2161. Assistant Editor: Nancy Tosh. Publishes craft magazine and books. Buys 80 designs annually, usually to create ideas for magazine articles. Send letter with photo of/or specific pieces being offered. Seasonal items should be sent 6 months prior to publication. Reports as soon as possible.

COLONIAL CRAFTSMEN, INC., Box 1644, Wayne NJ 07470. (201)696-7700. President: Robert Kunz. Manufacturer of wood craft kits; functional yet decorative designs. Buys and commissions designs to use as prototypes for products and orders demos or build-ups of products for use by dealers (furnishes raw materials). Pays $1-25 for tole painting and $10-50 for dollhouse assembly. Submit resume. "It is helpful for craftworker to be from local area." Reports as soon as possible.

CONNOISSEUR STUDIO, Box 7187, Louisville KY 40207. (502)426-6600. Manager of Administrative & Marketing Services: Carol Carrithers. Manufactures arts and crafts supplies and kits (paints, finishes, paper marquetry, scraper foil supplies, books). Buys and commissions designs to use as prototypes for products. Pays $15 minimum for original designs; sometimes pays on royalty basis. "We are open to new craft products, designs, kit ideas and book ideas. Payment is based accordingly on the merit of each." Write explaining qualifications; include photos of/or actual work. Reports in 2 weeks.

CRAFTS LTD., 295 Melville Rd., Farmingdale NY 11735. (516)249-0949. Manager: Wiliam N. Alter. Manufactures 3-dimensional needlepoint kits and ceramic macrame beads (featuring rainbow effects). Buys imported crafts in bulk for resale and crafts/designs outright. Uses about 25 designs annually. Payment for original gifts is open. Submit resume, samples or actual work. Reports in 4 weeks.

CREATE YOUR OWN, INC., Hickory Corner Rd., RD 2, Milford NJ 08848. (201)479-4015 or 766-7414. President: Catherine Knowles. "We manufacture needlepoint oriental rug kits (18 mesh printed in full color); crewel and embroidery kits for quilts, drapes, linens, pillows and pictures for miniatures; as well as carrying a complete line of regular size needlepoint pillows, pictures and accessories." Kits include canvas, linen or fabric printed in full color; yarn or floss; needle; and instructions. "We specialize in museum reproductions of Persian and Oriental art as well as adaptations of 17th and 18th century floral masterpieces."
Terms: Buys and commissions prototypes for products. Pays $200-400/design depending on complexity of design; and buys samples of the finished product (including instructions and diagrams). Write explaining qualifications or send samples or photos. Reports in 2 weeks.

CUSTOM HOUSE OF NEEDLE ARTS & DESIGN, INC., 76 Elm St., W. Townsend MA 01474. (617)597-6639. President: June S. Clark. Manufactures crewel embroidery kits silkscreened on linen. Buys and commissions designs. "We either purchase designs or work on royalty basis." Buys 10 designs annually. Rate of payment depends upon size and detail. Pays $25-100 or royalty of 5% of wholesale for embroidery designs and $15-50 for original design embroidery; must include yarn count and stitch instruction. Submit resume and samples of embroidery technique and/or photos of work done previously. Reports in 2 weeks.

CUSTOM-FOAM CRAFTS, INC., Box 712, 1001 N. Rowe St., Ludington MI 49431. (616)843-3401. Contact: Dick Mark. "We manufacture all basic shapes of Styrofoam for the craft and floral industries. We also make complete project kits, foam coat, glitter and accessories." Uses craftworkers to evaluate products and possibly make kit prototypes. "We welcome new designs and ideas." Pays royalty on sales, negotiable. Write with samples explaining qualifications. Reports in 3 weeks.

DESHANE MINIATURE GALLERIES, 6272 S. Jamestown, Tulsa OK 74136. (918)494-6710. Contact: Ann L. Nelson. Miniatures manufacturer. Produces decorative accessories for dollhouses and miniature rooms in wood, metal, paper, ceramics, clay, fabric, oil, and watercolor. "We do not specialize in a particular theme or style though we do have a number of Oriental items. All items must be 1"-1' scale." Buys crafts in bulk for resale; sometimes buys and commissions crafts. Pays 30% of wholesale price. Submit resume and samples of actual work being offered or photos of previous work.. Reports in 3 weeks.

DESIGN DIVISION-REGENCY/CENTURY GREETINGS, 1500 W. Monroe, Chicago IL 60607. (312)666-8686. Art Director: David Cuthbertson. Publishers of all styles Christmas cards—full-color reproduction, mixed media. Buys designs to use as prototypes for one-of-a-kind card reproduction. Buys 50 designs annually. Pays $100 for any media; original returned. Submit resume and photos or slides of work done previously. Reports in 3-4 weeks. "Format of designs should fit some standard rectangular size; prefer to work from slides of works."

DOLL HOUSE MASTER, 1650 3rd Ave., New York NY 10028. (212)534-1012. Manager: Joe Block. Manufactures all-wood dollhouses (live smoke out of chimney, electric wiring, and plumbing included). Buys crafts in bulk for resale. Write with samples explaining qualifications. Reports in about 3 days.

EDMOND SCIENTIFIC CO., 101 E. Gloucester Pike, Barrington NJ 08007. (609)547-3488. Contact: Director of New Products. Mail order catalog firm. Manufactures telescopes and optical devices. Product line in mail order includes microscopes, binoculars, magnifiers, rangefinders, lasers and holography, weather instruments, lab equipment, electrical equipment, tools, fiber optics, metal detectors, toys, games, hobbies and crafts. Specializes in space, astronomy and scientifically-oriented products. Buys crafts (ready for resale, packaged and priced merchandise only). Send actual work to New Products Office for consideration.

Replica Sea Craft Studios, Middletown, New York, produces life-size model fish kits and miniature model boat kits. Designer Richard Surving says that everyone enjoys creating things and that taking a box of materials and turning it into a close replica of a fish almost makes the fish seem alive again. "Models take from 20-30 hours to build; the artist must be sensitive to boat or fish models."

Companies and Manufacturers 55

BETH & BILL ETGEN FINE JEWELRY, 3600 Whitney Ave., Sacramento CA 95821. (916)481-3912. Contact: Beth Etgen. Jewelry shop. Estab. 1970. Considers jewelry and metalsmithing. "We now specialize in silver and gold jewelry by women artist jewelers. We need sterling silver prototypes or waxes suitable for modeling and replicating in limited editions. We presently pay $500 minimum for a good design or design group. A good design last year grossed its designer over $1,000 when royalties were included. One sterling silver piece paid a royalty of 35¢ on each piece sold. 6,000 were sold. Don't send items, just photographs, slides or 3x5 prints. SASE. We can then correspond for samples. If work looks good, we accept piece for production and advertise it in our mailer to our clients."

FIBREC, INC., 1154 Howard St., San Francisco CA 94103. (415)863-6150. General Manager: Mike Flynn. Manufactures and converts artist materials, primarily for textile artist (dyes, thickeners, batik kits, fabric paints, stencils, etc.). Buys designs annually to use as prototypes for products (new product ideas, new crafts, variations or improvements on existing crafts.) Craftworker receives royalty or commission based on gross sales of the product. Write with description of the idea or product. Reporting time varies.

FIBRE-FORM PRODUCTS, INC., 505 Hamilton Ave., Suite 107, Palo Alto CA 94301. (415)326-2760. President: Jay Pidto. Manufactures molded pulp forms (papier mache) and Christmas ornament kits. Buys and commissions 20 designs annually for publication and/or demonstration. Pays royalty for kit designs and $50-150 for original designs; $50/day for demonstrations. Send photos of work done previously and/or call for personal interview. Reports immediately.

FITZGERALD ENTERPRISES, INC., 1610 E. 12th St., Oakland CA 94606. (415)533-3727. Merchandise Coordinator: Penny Brown. Craft wholesaler/manufacturer/publisher. Sells beads, cords, rings and other accessories for macrame and weaving and publishes books for the craft market. Buys crafts in bulk for resale; offers advice to craftworker; adds and promotes new ideas to the industry; and buys and commissions work. Minimum payment: $50. Submit resume, samples, actual work and/or arrange interview. Reports in 2 weeks.

FLO-SCULPT STUDIOS, INC., 8 W. 19th St., New York NY 10011. (212)675-8892. Vice President: James Fobel. Kit-manufacturer. "We are manufacturers of Flo-Sculpt (TM), which is a pre-mixed, non-toxic acrylic substance for making 3-D appliques. Flo-Sculpt is placed in a standard cake decorating bag with decorative tip and squeezed onto waxed paper. The designs air dry overnight and are then painted with acrylic, spray paint or enamel and then glued onto accessories, furniture, walls, etc. Anything you can do with cake decorating you can do with Flo-Sculpt — and it will be permanent. We make special kits that include the Flo-Sculpt, all tips, designs and materials necessary to complete any designated project." Buys crafts in bulk for resale, and "need teachers of Flo-Sculpt. Must be experienced cake decorators; send photos." Works on commission and buys work outright. Pays $50 minimum/Flo-Sculpt design project; $50 minimum/day for teacher. Payment determined by job. Write explaining qualifications. Reports in 3 weeks.

GALLO MANUFACTURING CO., 1312 N. Memorial Dr., Racine WI 53404. (414)633-4281. President: Michael S. Gallo. Manufactures woodcraft hobby kits. Buys crafts in bulk for resale and buys crafts/designs outright. Write for personal interview. Reports in 1 week.

GEM ACCESSORIES & GIFTS, LTD., 44 Vark St., Yonkers NY 10701. (914)968-8295. President: Stanley Meyers. Manufactures bath accessories and gifts (towel bars, dishes, cup dispensers, waste baskets, mirrors). Buys designs to use as prototypes for products. Write explaining qualifications. Reports in 2 weeks.

GO FLY A KITE INC., Box AA-E, Haddam Industrial Park, East Haddam CT 06423. President: Andrea Bahadur. Manufactures, designs and imports kites. "We deal in kites and kite accessories on all levels from mass market $1.29 kites to handcrafted $500 kites in paper, cloth, plastic, dowels, etc. Birds, butterflies, airplaines—or anything one would expect to see in the sky—are particularly popular." Buys crafts in bulk for resale and commissions crafts/designs. Uses 20 single designs (30,000 pieces) annually. Payment varies. Submit resume, sample, actual work and/or arrange interview. Usually reports in 3 weeks.

GRAPHIC IDEAS, 3108 5th Ave., San Diego CA 92103. Art Director: Jill Timm. "We create new toys, crafts and products for other firms; also premiums, gifts and promotional items.

Sometimes we manufacture and sometimes we sell concept and idea. Whatever is created will need to be mass produced at a low cost. In the past we have produced a lot of paper items (card, calendar, games) but we are open to any good idea or product in any area." Buys 25-30 designs annually. Pays $150 minimum for product ideas; $100 minimum for designs and illustrations; and sometimes 2-5% royalties. Submit resume, rough drawings of ideas, slides and/or photos. Reports in 4 weeks.

GREENBERG PUBLISHING CO., 605 Gaither Rd., Sykesville MD 21784. (301)489-4029. President: Bruce Greenberg. Mail order house specializing in railroad-related publications, gifts and novelties. Works in wood and plastic (children's toys), metal (jewelry), pottery and embroidered patches—all railroad-related. Buys and commissions 10 designs annually suitable for mass production. "We need items that can be manufactured in a minimum of 100 of a kind." Send samples of specific pieces being offered. Reports in 1 week.

ERIC H. GREENE CO., 3431 E. Lapalma, Anaheim CA 92806. (714)632-7901. President: G.R. Driggers. Manufactures crewel and needlepoint kits providing 239 colors of yarn. Buys and commissions designs for mass production. Send samples or photos of designs. Reports in 1 week.

HARTSTONE INC., 3 Commerce St., Chatham NJ 07928. President: P. Hart. Ceramic manufacturer and importer. Manufactures dinnerware and gourmet cookware in stoneware and porcelain. Commissions 40-50 designs annually to use as prototypes for products. "We are interested in new items and designs." Pays $500 minimum for all designs. Write explaining qualifications and send samples/photo. Reports in 1 week.

D.E. HENRY & ASSOCIATES INC., 565 Covina Blvd., San Dimas CA 91773. (714)599-4839. Vice-President of Sales: Dave Archibald. Manufactures ceramic macrame items (owl and frog eyes, clock faces and works, beads, animals). Buys and commissions designs to use as prototypes for products. Pays $200-300 for instruction sheets; price varies on other items. Call for interview or send photos of work done previously. Reports as soon as possible.

HIGHLANDS & ISLANDS IMPORTS, INC., 300 E. Fourth St., Box 220-A, Royal Oak MI 48068. (313)547-5800. Importer and distributor for domestic, UK and Canadian consumer goods (exluding food and confectioneries, electrical and electronic items). "Products are either imported, manufactured for, or manufactured by Highlands & Islands Imports, Inc." Buys/commissions 20-30 designs annually; and buys crafts in bulk for resale. Pays $4-40 for silver jewelry; $6-120 for leather goods. "Many of the products and product lines marketed are manufactured and distributed under the trademark High-Isle Products. These trademark products are manufactured to High-Isle Products specifications by companies located in the United Kingdom, Canada and the United States." Write for personal interview explaining qualifications; include photos of work done previously. Reports in 2-4 weeks. "Sometimes we file the source for future reference."

HILL-LOONEY INC., Box 1533, Wewoka OK 74884. (405)257-2639. Contact: C.W. Hill. Manufactures stitchery, needlepoint, felt applique and tree ornament kits. Buys 20 designs annually to use as prototypes for products. Pays $25/design minimum; $100/design maximum. Call for interview. Reports in 4 weeks.

HOBE CIE. LTD., 138 S. Columbus Ave., Mt. Vernon NY 10553. (914)664-2640. Jewelry manufacturer. Commissions new product development. Uses 10,000 designs annually. Payment varies. Send samples and arrange interview. Reports in 4 weeks.

I.S.L.E. LABORATORIES, INC., Box 173, 8302 Sylvania Metamora Rd., Sylvania OH 43560. (419)882-7320. New Product Manager: David Gottschalk. Kit Manufacturer. Reproduces wood carvings or plaques in rigid foam or plastic resin. Buys 12-18 designs annually to use as prototypes for products (reproduction by molding). Write explaining qualifications and send photos of work. Reports in 3 weeks.

ISLAND'S IMPORTS, 12634 Monarch, Houston TX 77047. (713)433-8617. Contact: Ben McKinley. Mail order firm. Estab. 1978. Considers candlemaking, glass art, leatherworking, needlecrafts, quilting, wall hangings, weavings and woodcrafting. One-of-a-kind and hand-made production-line items. Price range: 50¢-$500; bestsellers: $10-150. Buys outright and works on consignment; 40% commission. Write to be considered for inclusion in catalog.

Companies and Manufacturers 57

SASE. Reports in 1 week. Work may be shipped or hand-delivered. Heaviest wholesale buying time: fall and summer; best selling time: fall.

JACQU MIN INC., 7601 Forsyth Blvd., St. Louis MO 63105. (314)726-0474. President: Jacqueline Schaefer. Manufactures miniature dollhouse accessories in wood, ceramics and tin pot metal. Submit resume and samples. Reports in 1 week.

J.D. ENTERPRISES, 581 W. 10th St., Pittsburg CA 94565. (415)432-0300. Contact: Jim Dolhanyk. Manufactures wooden craft products, mostly tole boards and plaques. Specializes in redwood; heavy demand for Christmas items. "We manufacture wooden plaques for decoupage; tole; and decorating and are open for new ideas." Write and call. Reports promptly.

JO-HAN MODELS, INC., 17255 Moran Ave., Detroit MI 48212. (313)366-2230. President: John Haenle Jr. Manufactures plastic scale model airplane and car kits and built-up promotional models for the automotive field. Submit resume. Reports in 1 week.

JOY ENTERPRISES, Box 375, Bethany WV 26032. Contact: Jim St. Clair. Mail order firm. Estab. 1974. Represents 25 craftworkers.
Acceptable Work: Considers dollmaking and woodcrafting. Only toy-related items. Especially needs new folk toys. One-of-a-kind and handmade production-line items. Price range: 75¢-$200; bestsellers: $3.75-10.
Terms: Buys outright. Shop sets retail price. Send samples. Reports in 2 weeks. Work may be shipped or hand delivered.
Profile: "Item is listed with picture or drawing in our mail order catalog and is shown in some shows. Be able to produce high quality wood working in quantity. Our toys sell to all ages and incomes as toys for both children and adults." Heaviest wholesale buying time: March-September; best selling time: Christmas.

J-S WOOD PRODUCTS, INC., 11309 Emerald St., Dallas TX 75229. (214)620-2006. Sales Manager: Jay Sharp. Manufactures plaques and specialty woodcraft items (mainly pine, some birch), designed for use in tole painting and decoupage. Buys designs to use as prototypes for products; buys crafts in bulk for resale and samples for trade shows. Pays $5-25 for tole sample. "Payment varies from sample to sample. Often trade for additional supplies. We are also seeking full or part-time permanent woodworkers." Call for interview. Reports in 1 week.

JUST ACCESSORIES INC., 112 W. 34th St., New York NY 10001. (212)564-5168. President: Richard N. Bloch. Fashion firm specializing in children's accessories. Buys and commissions 25 designs annually to use as prototypes; and buys crafts in bulk for resale. Write explaining qualifications and send samples, photos/slides or brochures. Reports in 1 week.

K&L CO., Box 52281, Tulsa OK 74152. Manufactures 20mm (HO-scale) figures in metal (tin and lead). "We manufacture the most complete line of metal American Civil War figures anywhere (cavalry, infantry, artillery, civilian)." Commissions only a few sculptings annually of new figures. "We need miniature model makers and sculptors." Write explaining qualifications. Reports in 2 weeks.

LAMOUREUX INC., 191 NW 71 St., Miami FL 33150. Contact: E. Lamoureux. Mail order firm. Estab. 1969. Considers kits and do-it-yourself items. Buys outright. Price set by joint agreement. Reports in 10 days.

LEISURE TIME PUBLISHING & CRAFT PRODUCTS INC., 2125 S. 48th St., Suite 110, Tempe AZ 85282. President: Bob Aufftet. Craft book publisher and latch hook pattern manufacturer. Commissions and buys 150 designs annually for publication. Pays $60-100 for macrame patterns; $75 for latch hook designs. Send actual work (for latch hook designs); Send photos and 1 set of instructions (for macrame patterns). Reports in 2 weeks.

LIFE-LIKE PRODUCTS INC., 1600 Union Ave., Baltimore MD 21211. Vice President, Marketing Services: Jay Kramer. Hobby/craft material manufacturer. Produces miniature trees and landscape materials. Buys and commissions designs to develop a line based on products. Submit resume and arrange interview. Reports in 1 week.

LION'S VALLEY STONEWARE LTD., 2450 Foothill Dr., Vista CA 92083. (714)726-2229.

President: Jack Young. Manufactures stoneware. Specializes in planters, cookware, clocks and picture frames. Buys and commissions 100 designs annually to use as prototypes for products. "We buy originals for models; therefore, originals should be of such a design as to be able to be casted." Write explaining qualifications. Reports in 1 week.

LOVE-BUILT TOYS & CRAFTS, 2907 Lake Forest Rd., Box 5459, Tahoe City CA 95730. (916)583-1555. Contact: Dale C. Prohaska Jr. Sells patterns to make wooden toys. Buys designs for custom-made wooden toys to be reproduced in woodworking pattern. Also buys craft project lesson plans for grades K-12 using toy-making supplies. Pays $25, depending on amount of work needed to complete the project.

MAGNUS CRAFT CORPORATION, 304-8 Cliff Lane, Cliffside Park NJ 07010. Managing Director: P.H. Brown. Manufactures handicraft kits and their components in wood, leather, beads and cold enameling. Buys crafts in bulk for resale. Send samples of specific pieces being offered. Reports in 4-6 weeks.

MAXWELL HOUSE MINIATURES, Box 653, Edinboro PA 16412. (814)734-4594. Contact: Sandy or Pam Maxwell. Miniature doors and window manufacturer. Produces wood windows and doors in Victorian, Federal, Colonial and modern styles. Sponsors craft show "Maxwell House Miniature Show and Sale."

ME ENTERPRISES, 2650 Country Club Dr., Glendora CA 91740. (213)963-1456. Managing Director: Allan Markowitz. Manufactures portable weaving looms, wind cords and yarns; imports jute; and wholesales wooden beads and metal rings. Buys and commissions designs to use as prototypes for customers who occasionally need made-ups. Buys 1-4 designs annually. Pays $25 minimum for macrame or weaving samplers. Craftworkers must be from local area. Call for interview. Reports in 3 weeks.

MIKASA, 25 Enterprise Ave., Secacus NJ 07094. Contact: J. Orshan. Manufactures tableware (china and stoneware dinnerware) and gifts. Works in ceramics, glass and brass. Specializes in high fashion shapes and colors. Buys designs and shapes outright to use as prototypes for products. Pays $100 minimum. Write for personal interview; include samples/actual work. Reports in 1 week.

MINIATURE REFLECTIONS, 409 S. 1st, Evansville WI 53536. (608)882-4682. Contact: Patricia Diedrich. Manufactures needlepoint kits for miniature rugs; supplies miniature-making supplies; hardwoods; and books and magazines about period decorating and miniatures. Specializes in period styling such as Victorian and Colonial. "We do our own design work but are interested in expanding and working with craftpersons." Submit resume and photos. Reports as soon as possible.

MINIS BY ME, 606 David St., West Hempstead NY 11552. Contact: Marilyn Davidson or Elaine Fleischman. Work with miniature furniture and accessories. Specializes in modern designs mostly in Lucite and/or related materials. Also interested in dried flowers, macrame, metals, etc. Work should be finished completely, 1"-1' scale. Buys crafts in bulk for resale; supports cottage industry. Commissions 20-50 designs annually. Pay for assembly of items to our specifications based on minimum wages. "Always interested in new ideas. Submit samples, resume and price per item." Prefer local craftworkers.

STEPHEN A. MINTZ COMPANY, 705 Scottsdale Rd., Westminster MD 21157. (301)876-6323. Secretary/Treasurer: Stephen Allan Mintz. Manufacturer of fine quality aluminum and stainless steel toys and jewelry. Specializes in railroad and geometric toys. Buys and commissions designs to use as prototypes. Buys 4 designs annually. Payment depends on size of object. Submit resume. Reports in 3 weeks.

MISS BOUTIQUE INC., 112 W. 34th St., Rm. 710, New York NY 10001. (212)564-5168. President: Richard N. Bloch. Fashion firm. Manufactures a variety of children's items in natural fibers. Buys and commissions designs to use as prototypes. Uses 200 designs annually. Submit resume and actual work or photos of previous pieces.

MORGAN LOOM FACTORY, Railroad Engine House, Guilford CT 06437. (203)453-6341. President: A. Licata. Kit manufacturer/loom manufacturer. Manufactures small hand looms and weaving kits. Buys and commissions designs to use as projects for weaving kits. Buys 4-6

Companies and Manufacturers 59

Handicraft kits and their components are manufactured by Magnus Craft Corporation, located in Cliffside Park, New Jersey. Craft kits, such as those projects shown, are produced for children. Magnus Craft Corporation buys crafts in bulk for resale and can be contacted by sending samples to P.H. Brown, its Managing Director.

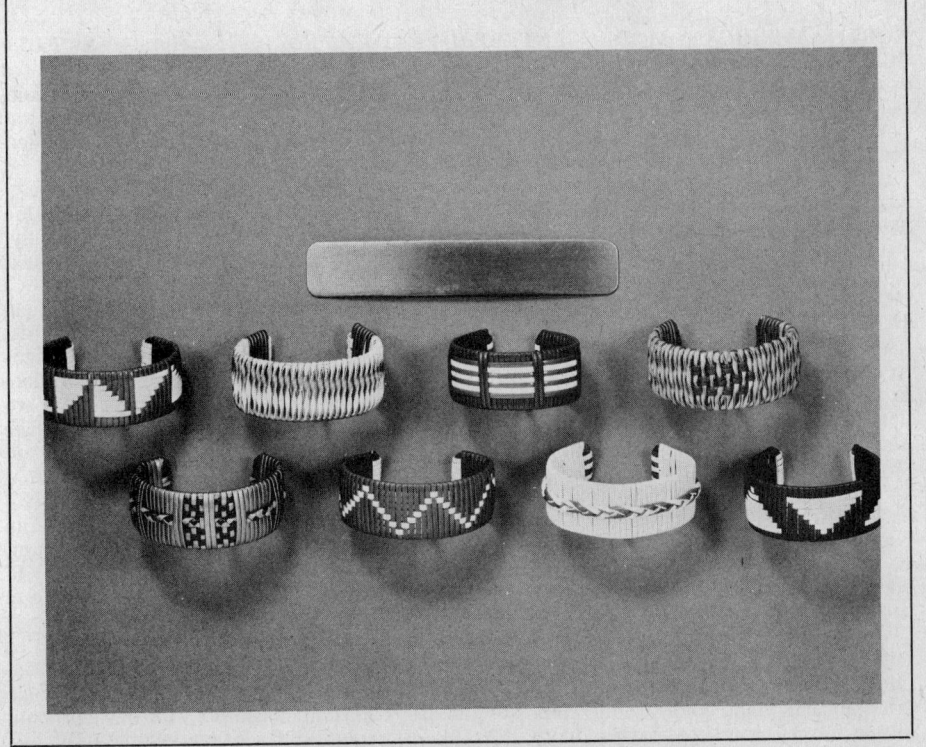

designs annually. Pays maximum of $15 for made-up loom samples and maximum of $250 for weaving kit designs. Submit resume, samples and/or actual work. Reports in 2 weeks.

NASHCO PRODUCTS, INC., 1015 N. Main Ave., Scranton PA 18508. (717)347-4210. Order Department: Linda Tibbitts. Manufactures decorated and undecorated toleware items in steel sheet—black or raw. Specializes in trays, wastebaskets, umbrella stands, silent butlers and canisters. Buys 3-6 designs annually. Submit samples. Reports in 4 weeks.

NATCOL CRAFTS, INC., Box 299, Redlands CA 92373. (714)795-2407. President: Thomas Blakistone. Manufacturer of candle molds, resin molds and products, liquid craft products, silk flowers, dough art and plaster molds. "We aim at producing whatever the consumer has a need for. Will consider any new product idea." Buys 5-10 prototypes annually. Pays $50 minimum/mold design; $100 minimum or precentage/new product idea; $15-50/flower arrangement. Call or write for personal interview. Christmas craft projects must be submitted by August 1. Usually reports in 1 week; "varies with need or workload."

NEEDLE IN THE HAYSTACKER, INC., 306 S. Lookout Mtn. Rd., Golden CO 80401. (303)526-1717. President: Ralph Loeff. Manufactures straight sewing, patchwork and applique kits; and finished items including placemats, kitchen accessories, stuffed toys, pillows, and Christmas stockings. Mostly works in fabric. Specializes in calico and country styles with some contemporary and innovative items. Buys and mainly commissions 50-100 designs annually to use as prototypes for products. Pays $150 minimum for crib quilts; $75 minimum for toys. Write explaining qualifications; include Polaroid pictures of items offered.

NICHOLAS PRESS, 132 Nassau St., New York NY 10038. Art Director: A. Goldson. Manufactures everyday greeting cards, seasonals, posters and notes. Style varies but specifically leans toward more modern design concept for Christmas lines. "Good possibility for buying designs to use as prototypes but have bought none to date. Since this is a new market for us, research and craftworkers themselves will have to aid us in defining proper minimum and maximum payment." Submit resume and photos of work done previously or similar work being offered, "also suggested price for designs and all other basic information." Reports in 4 weeks.

NORTH AMERICAN MODEL ENTERPRISES INC., Box 1473, Hurst TX 76053. (817)282-5735. President: Jim Simpson. Manufactures R/C model aircraft kits and related accessories in balsa wood, metal, plywood, Styrofoam, fiberglass and molded plastic. Commissions less than 6 designs annually. Pays 1-3% net sales for aircraft, electronics and component designs. "Submissions must be original, exclusive, functional and easily duplicated." Write for interview explaining qualifications. Reports in 4 weeks.

NORTHFIELD LOOMS, Box 258. Northfield MN 55057. (507)645-6952. President: Don Myers. Manufactures wooden weaving looms. Buys or commissions 10 craft designs annually. Pays $30-50 for weavings; hourly wage for woodworking. Submit resume. Reports in 1 week.

OCA CRAFTS CO., 852 Hawthrone Dr., Pittsburgh PA 15235. (412)241-7215. President: Jean Hennel. Manufactures OCA kits; silk-padded and painted pictures used for greeting cards; hanging pictures; fire screens; table tops; clothing; and purses. Buys and commissions designs to develop ancient Oriental art form found in museums. "Finished worked design/product prices higher according to design and size." Prices for design only are 5x7 sketch greeting card design, $2-5; 9x12-2'x2' design/sketch picture or table, $5-25; 2'x2'-3'x6' pictures for fireplace and regular screen, $25-100. "Craftworker must know art form and how it works." Submit resume. Reports in 2 weeks.

C. M. OFFRAY & SON INC., 261 Madison Ave., New York NY 10016. Creative Director: Ann Karas. Manufacturer and importer of woven edge fashion ribbons in polyester grosgrain, satin, velvet, jacquards, checks, plaids and polka dots. Colors and patterns updated seasonally to comply with fashion trends. Buys designs for new end uses for ribbons; only interested in original design concepts. Write for interview. Reports in 2 weeks.

OPEN DOOR ENTERPRISES, INC., 1201 Comstock St., Santa Clara CA 95050. (408)985-2660. Art Director: Fred Fortune. Manufactures kits for string art, wire art, mosaic art, embroidery and color-it-yourself poster kits. Buys and commissions 50-100 designs annually to use as prototypes for products. "We like to explore different marketable products.

Payment will depend on the useability of the product idea (i.e. degree of completion, sourced materials, and design finalization of product or idea submitted)." Write explaining qualifications. Reports in 3 weeks.

ORCHARD YARN & THREAD CO. INC., 524 W. 23rd St., New York NY 10011. (212)243-8995. Director of Marketing: David Blumenthal. Manufactures craft yarns. Buys and commissions 25 designs annually to use as prototypes for products. Pays $50 minimum. Write explaining qualifications.

PAPERCRAFT CORP., Papercraft Park, Pittsburgh PA 15238. (412)362-8000. Director of Merchandising: Ralph Marmo. Publishes Christmas giftwrap and cards printed on paper stock. Specializes in "traditional Christmas subjects done in interesting techniques." Buys and commissions about 150 designs to reproduce into giftwraps and cards. Pays $150-275 annually for giftwrap; $75-150 for greeting cards. Send actual work. Giftwrap designs must repeat on a 27" cylinder; greeting cards must be sizes 5"x7", 4¾"x6¾" and/or 4¼"x6¾" plus bleed. Reports in 2 weeks.

This rabbit clock is only one new item being featured by D.E. Henry and Associates of San Dimas, California. Besides clock kits, D.E. Henry produces ceramic and macrame crafts, specializing in different kinds of eyes, beads and animals. David Archibald, vice-president of sales, will pay $200-300 for instruction sheets for designs to use as prototypes for products.

HAZEL PEARSON HANDICRAFTS, 16017 E. Valley Blvd., Industry CA 91744. (213)968-4645. Products Manager: Virginia Ross. Kit manufacturer and how-to book publisher. Maintains open stock catalog, including materials such as jute, cords and other such supplies. Kits produced include needlework, latch hook, macrame, string art and other miscellaneous crafts.
Terms: Commmissions craftworkers to create projects for books and kits, and buys designs outright. A simple design assignment would pay $15-25, and prices would progress up with degree of difficulty, originality and type of craft. Write with snapshots and explain qualifications; or if you are interested in doing a book, send writing samples. Reports on inquiries in 2-4 weeks.

POT-POUR-RI, 204 Worcester St., Wellesley MA 02181. (617)237-1744. President: Susanne Knowles. Retails gift merchandise, including completed handcrafted articles for Christmas, cooking and table top, etc. Buys or works on royalty for use as prototypes for kits. Write explaining qualifications. Reports within 4 weeks.

QUILL ART, INC., 11762 Westline Dr., St. Louis MO 63141. President: Barbara Maddox. Manufactures quilling, sculpture and dimensional design kits in paper and cardboard of various grades. Specializes in decorative and functional pictures, ornaments and decorations. Buys and commissions 20-25 designs to use as prototypes for products. Pays $10-150 for original designs. "New items are introduced in January and June. We need new designs 4 months preceding." Write for personal interview and send samples of specific pieces being offered, photos or slides. Reports in 2-4 weeks.

RAINBOW WEST BATIKS, Box 661, Grand Junction CO 81501. (303)245-1963. Contact: Muffy Ferguson. Retail/wholesale batik outlet. Estab. 1977. Represents 3 craftworkers. Buys designs or ideas for batik. Reports in 3 weeks. Send slides or photos and wait for reply.
Profile: "Only outlet as far as I know that has only batik. We would like to establish full range of batik items including prints, fabric, wallpaper, toys, clothing, etc." Best selling time: summer.

REPLICA SEA CRAFT STUDIOS, Millpond Studios, RD 4, Millsburg Rd, Middletown NY 10940. Designer: Richard Surving. Manufacturer of model boat kits and model fish kits; supplies paper templates, plaster mesh and molding compound with kits. Fish are life-size (30"); boats are ½"-1' scale. Commissions craftworkers to create build-ups for in-store promotion. "Kits and materials are provided free for craftspeople that are given commission. Handicapped people will be given preference and special assistance where necessary." We will need about 200 units in the next 6 months." Pays $100-300/model. Write with photos or slides of work, explaining qualifications and requesting personal interview, or call for personal interview. "Applicants that qualify must build 1 model from kit, as directed, before contract is given. Models take from 20-30 hours to build; the artist must be sensitive to boat or fish models." Reports in 2 weeks.

SELEXOR DISPLAYS INC., 1916 Park Ave., New York NY 10037. (212)368-7791. Director of Marketing: R. McCarthy. Manufactures trade show/showroom exhibits and displays constructed in wood, Plexiglas and miscellaneous materials. Commissions designs to use for customer requirements. "We counsel the craftworker in use of materials." Submit resume and samples; write for interview. Reports in 1 week.

SHIVA, INC., 4320 W. 190th St., Torrance CA 90509. (213)542-5583. Vice President: Sheila W. Ross. Manufactures artists paints (oil, acrylic, casein, designers), printing ink, varnishes and oils. Produce tubes for open stock and kits. Commissions designs to use as prototypes for products. Provides brochures and technical advice. "Fees are always negotiated before a commission is offered on package designers and painting demonstrators." Write explaining qualifications. Reports in 2 weeks.

JUDITH SNELL LTD., Box 804, Oakville, Ontario, Canada L6J 5C5. (416)844-7662. Contact: Judith Snell. Wholesaler of macrame and bazaar craft ideas. ("Bazaar crafts use styrofoam, felt and other general craft items.") Buys and commissions 25-50 designs to use as prototypes for products. Pays $75-200 for macrame; $50-75 for bazaar crafts. Write explaining qualifications; include photos of work and written explanation. Reports in 3-4 weeks.

SPINNERIN YARN CO., INC., 230 5th Ave., New York NY 10001. (212)532-8426. Product Manager: Lynn Schroeder. Manufactures needlepoint, stitchery and rug kits. Produces in 100% wool and/or 100% cotton embroidery floss and 100% cotton needlepoint and rug canvas. Specializes in landscapes, naturals, moderns and florals. Buys 200 designs annually. Pays $50-150 for stitchery designs; $75-200 for needlepoint designs; and $50-150 for rug designs. Write explaining qualifications and send samples or call for interview. Reports in 4 weeks.

STENCIL-MAGIC, 8 W. 19th St., New York NY 10011. (212)675-8892. Vice President: James Fobel. Manufactures pre-cut stencils, stencil patterns, stencil kits, brushes, paints, stencil paper, books and instructions. Buys and commissions crafts to use as prototypes; and buys crafts in bulk for resale. "Designs must work as stencils, meaning the designer must have knowledge of stencil bridges or registration marks." Buys and commissions 10-15 designs annually. Pays $25-75/custom stencil design. Payment determined by job. Write explaining qualifications. Reports in 3 weeks.

STERLING/DRAKE PUBLISHERS, INC., 2 Park Ave., New York NY 10016. (212)532-7160. Contact: Charles Nurnberg. Publishes craft books. Commissions work for books. Write explaining qualifications or call for personal interview. Reports in 3 weeks.

THE STITCHERY, INC., 204 Worcester St., Wellesley MA 02181. (617)237-1744. President: Susanne Knowles. Produces needlecraft kits and retails through 8 mail order catalogs/year. Buys or works on royalty for use as prototypes for kits. Write explaining qualifications. Reports within 4 weeks.

SYMMOGRAPHY, INC., Rt. 3, Box 32, Strawberry Plains TN 37871. (615)933-1331. President: Jim Bartram. Manufactures string art kits, oak reproduction tables, book racks, upholstered solid foam youth chairs and ottomans. Buys and commissions designs to use as prototypes. "Ideas; designs; and new kits can be functional or decorative. We need simple designs for Plexiglas items or kits and small wood items to utilize oak scrap." Minimum payment is $50-100, negotiable. Submit resume. Reports in 1 week.

TEX-CRAFT CO. INC., 311 E. Park St., Moonachie NJ 07074. (201)440-2500. President: Arnold Epstein. Manufactures Schiffli embroidery emblems; sew on and iron on patches; iron on and embroidery initials; and belting design trimmings. Uses fabric, denim, cork, polyurethane, and velveteen in timely and age-old themes. Buys designs to use as design prototypes. Payment varies. Submit resume and copies of work done previously. Reports in 2 weeks.

TEXTURED YARN ARTS, INC., 1329 Aloha St., Seattle WA 98109. General Manager: Gary Haldane. Manufactures cord and yarns for weaving, macrame and other craft uses. Buys and commissions designs to use as prototypes. "We welcome suggestions for craft yarns and cord." Buys 12 designs annually. Pays $100-200 for new weaving or macrame designs. Submit samples. Reports in 8 weeks.

THORENS MUSIC BOXES, Division of Elpa Marketing Industries, Inc., Box 1050, Thorens and Atlantic Ave., New Hyde Park NY 11040. (516)746-3002. Marketing Manager: Edwin Lesson. Manufactures and imports musical movements for music boxes, mounting movements in wood, glass, and brass cases, and in jewelry boxes, figurines, and picture frames. Buys designs to use as prototypes; buys crafts in bulk for resale; and hires local casemakers to help expand present gift line. Buys 6-8 designs annually. Pays $50-150/box design. Submit resume and samples of actual work. Reports in 3 weeks.

Soap dolls appeared on the cover of the January/February issue of Crafts 'n Things, a craft magazine put out by Clapper Publishing Company, Inc., Park Ridge, Illinois. About 80 designs are bought annually, usually to create ideas for magazine articles. Seasonal items should be sent 6 months prior to publication.

E.J. TOWLE COMPANY, 760 Market St., San Francisco CA 94102. President: W.G. Lefort. Manufactures silver, gold, and gold-filled jewelry with particular emphasis on Northwest coast Indian designs and Hawaiian designs. Buys designs to use as prototypes. Buys 10-20 designs annually. Pay $25-200. Send resume and samples. Reports in 2 weeks.

UTEXIQUAL PRODUCTS, DIV., 125 Whipple St., Providence RI 02908. (401)831-6020. Office Manager/Sales Department: Gloria Fong. General Manager: Chip Richards. Manufactures miniatures, sculptures, plates, dishes, gift items, promotional items, belt buckles and some jewelry items in pewter, white metals and related materials. Specializes in belt buckles, nature items (small birds and animals), sports-related items (belt buckles, figurines) and western-theme items. Buys and commissions 2-5 designs annually ("but we are expanding and could use more") to use as prototypes for products. "We are always looking for new ideas and additions to our line, especially buckles and miniatures." Pays $75-500+ for model or die making; $25-200/artwork design. "Since we have never really commissioned items, we have no base for an estimate, but one could be worked out with the artist. These are very rough figures, as design and model making can involve different degrees of effort. Christmas items should be submitted as much as 8 months to a year in advance, unless they are finished products, which would need about 1-2 months. Size requirements would have to be worked out for production needs after we see sample or art." Send resume, samples, work, or call or write for interview. Reports in 2-3 weeks.

VESTA GLASS, INC., Box 1426, Corning NY 14830. (607)962-2870 or 962-2800. Vice President, Sales: August V. Titi. Sales Promotion: Peter Burke. Manufacturer of glass collectibles and giftware (Christmas ornaments, suncatchers, mirrors, crystal miniature animals and stained glass). Buys hundreds of crafts in bulk for resale. Pays $1 minimum or $35-70 maximum for glass engraving, lampwork, stained glass, etc. "The majority of our items are in the $1.50-3 areas; very little is done in areas over $35." Write with sample, explaining qualifications. Reports in 2 weeks. "We deal only with craftsmen able to supply large numbers of an individual item. We show our wares at over 20 wholesale shows (open to trade only) each year."

WALRUS FACTORY, INC., Box 4269, San Rafael CA 94903. President: Kathleen Madden. Manufactures string art and nail craft kits. Works in nails, colored threads and paint. Buys and commissions 8 designs to use as prototypes for products. Pays $100 minimum for finished designs; $50 minimum for rough designs; and 3-4% net sales for outstanding designs on a regular basis. "We talk about how to do our kits and decide what themes we want. We also supply raw materials. String art must be 16"x24" or 7"x11"; nail craft must be 7"x11". Write explaining qualifications. Reports in 3 weeks.

WILLIAM K. WALTHERS INC., 5601 W. Florist Ave., Milwaukee WI 53218. President: B.J. Walthers. Manufactures model railroad construction kits (including structures, electrical accessories and printed materials). Works on HO and O scale in wood, metal, plastic and diecast. Commissions 2-3 prototypes and samples of existing products annually. Pays $5+ for kit ideas; $25+ for complete designs; and $15+ for display models from existing kits. Write explaining qualifications. Reports in 3 weeks.

BETTY WIITA DECORATOR CRAFTS, INC., 500 W. Chestnut St., Clayton NJ 08312. (609)881-2218. Designer: Betty Wiita. Manufactures dried flower kits with dried natural materials. Specializes in floral arrangements; candle rings; and wall hangings. Buys designs; looking for new ideas. Payment is negotiable. Submit resume and photos. Reports in 1 week.

WOODRING CRAFT©, 35 W. 44th St., New York NY 10036. (212)575-0670. Director of Marketing: Dennis C. Hoff. Assistant to the Director of Marketing: Kathleen Keller Grgin. Manufactures premium quality wood products such as wood rings, tapestry rods, oval frames and plaques, miniature ring frames, latch hook rug poles, wood bracelets, Veneer Touch® wood inlay papers, Sand-Rite® sanding and finishing pads. Commissions crafts to show creative uses for products. Pays $10-150/craft in woodworking, woodburning, macrame or weaving; $10-75 for framing or general crafts; provides basic materials. "Our products must be clearly identifiable in sample (not covered in any way). When craftsperson makes inquiry, an approximate idea of time required to finish a sample should be given as well. Write explaining qualifications and send sketch of ideas. "Interested and qualified craftspeople could write to us for brochures showing products with which they would be working and then submit sketch of ideas." Reports in 2 weeks.

Companies and Manufacturers 65

These items show several crafts which Connoisseur Studio of Louisville, Kentucky has produced. "Because we manufacture a variety of arts and crafts products, it is difficult to narrow down what we accept," says Carol Carrithers, Manager of Adminstrative and Marketing Services. "We are open to new craft ideas."

X-ACTO, 45-35 Van Dam St., Long Island City NY 11101. (212)392-3333. Promotion Manager: Edward R. Lehman. Manufactures precision knives and tools. Exhibits only finished pieces for trade show displays. Does not commission or buy. Write explaining qualifications and ask for personal interview. Reports in 3 weeks.

YALEY ENTERPRISES, 145 Sylvester Rd., San Francisco CA 94080. (415)761-3428. President: Thomas Yaley. Manufactures candle crafting supplies, macrame supplies and bulk candle waxes. Buys designs. Call for personal interview. Reports in 2 weeks.

YE OLDE HUFF N PUFF, 4820 W. Whitehall Rd., Pennsylvania Furnace PA 16865. Contact: Shirley Koontz. Manufactures model railroad car kits, HO and O scale, wood with metal detail. Looking for ideas for new products in model railroading.

Jack Young, president of Lion's Valley Stoneware Ltd., Vista, California, uses a craftworker's original model as the cast for new stoneware pieces which the company buys or commissions. David Stewart, who has produced a pottery line for Lion's Valley Stoneware, said that such great care goes into the designing and making of the models that the cast pieces often look better than the original. Lion's Valley Stoneware Ltd. specializes in planters, cookware, clocks and picture frames.

Shops and Galleries

As a full or part-time craftworker you can make money selling your crafts in one of three ways: direct selling (see Shows & Fairs), wholesaling, or retailing your work. The latter two methods involve working with a some sort of craft outlet.

The markets in this section are primarily shops and galleries, ranging from those that carry crafts exclusively, to museum shops, gift stores, banks and other outlets that will consider the work of craftworkers for exhibit and/or sale.

These outlets usually request a commission of 30-60% on sales when work is handled on consignment. Others will buy outright (wholesale) and usually double the price at which you sell them the work. For more specific information on the methods by which shops and galleries work be sure to check Working With the Retailer in the front of this book.

As with any listing in *Craftworker's Market*, the requirements for each shop and gallery should be read carefully. For example, although many retailers accept all media, others are looking for specific items. Also, every listing tells you what the price range is of the goods being carried. This lets you know how your work fits in as far as price is concerned. In general, paying attention to details in the listing will make the task of selling your work an easier one.

There is no need for you to contact only those listings from your locale. Most shops and galleries do not place geographical limitations on the craftspeople with whom they work. It is always a good idea to include a self-addressed-stamped envelope (SASE) with all correspondence you do through the mail. This helps assure that you will receive a response. You will probably be asked at some point, especially when working with shops and galleries via the postal system, to send slides or photos of your work.

In addition to the markets listed in this section, don't overlook possibilities in your own community. Many florists, boutiques, antique shops and other businesses are supplementing their present lines with handcrafted items.

More information on markets and other craft-related happenings can be found by reading *The Crafts Report*, *Quality Crafts Merchandising* and the *Goodfellow Review of Crafts*. Check the Publications of Interest section of this book for a full list of periodicals that provide the names and addresses of new marketing outlets.

Alabama

THE GINGERBREAD HOUSE, 514 Cloverdale Rd., Montgomery AL 36106. (205)265-0415. Director: Kay D. Deal. Craft/gift shop. Estab. 1974. Represents 200 craftworkers.
Acceptable Work: Considers all crafts except decoupage and soft sculpture. No kits. Especially needs utilitarian pottery, quilts and unusual children's items. One-of-a-kind and handmade production-line items. Price range: $1-400; bestsellers: $1-50.
Terms: Works on consignment; 28½% commission. "We will consider buying outright in some cases. Craftworker decides on his price and the shop adds on to that so that we get 28½%." Send slides or samples. Reports in 1 week. Work may be shipped or hand-delivered.
Profile: "We are a medium size shop (operated by the Foothills Art and Craft Guild as a nonprofit corporation) located in a New Orleans-style mall in an old established neighborhood. The shop is divided up and treated as a little Southern-style house with divisions for a baby room, living room, bedroom and old-fashioned kitchen (with antique stove, piesafe, etc.). There's also a gallery area for 1-man shows. We try to display at least 1 of each item on consignment at all times. Duplicates are filed in a stock room by consignor's number. If item doesn't sell after a reasonable length of time, consignor is notified to pick it up and has 2 weeks to do so before it becomes property of the shop." Customers: middle to upper incomes. Heaviest wholesale buying time: October-December; best selling time: Christmas.

THE GREATER BIRMINGHAM ARTS ALLIANCE, Box 2152, Birmingham AL 35201. (205)251-1228. Director: Jack Horlacher. Nonprofit gallery. Estab. 1969. Represents 1 craftworker per month in one-man show. Considers glass art; jewelry; pottery; wall hangings, and weavings. One-of-a-kind designer pieces only. Price range: $15-500. Works on consignment; 25% commission. Craftworker sets retail price. Reports in 3 weeks.

THE LOLLIE SHOP, 2917 Linden Ave., Birmingham AL 35209. Contact: Christine Davis. Gift shop. Represents 30 craftworkers. Considers batik; candlemaking; ceramics; clothing; decoupage; dollmaking; glass art; jewelry; needlecrafts; pottery; quilting; tole painting; and woodcrafting. Also needs stained glass ornaments; ceramic mobiles; and pottery. Price range: $1-250. Works on consignment; 30% commission. Craftworker sets retail price. Reports in 4 weeks. Write before mailing work. "I send a list of what has been sold to each person between the first and tenth of each month along with a check for their share."
Profile: Work is displayed on rustic shelves and by hanging items on the walls. "We carry stained glass ornaments, handcrafted items of good quality; and needlepoint, crewel, cross stitch, knitting, crochet, smocking and tatting supplies and provide classes." Customers are in middle to high income bracket.

USS ALABAMA BATTLESHIP, Box 65, Mobile AL 36601. Manager: Alice Miller. Museum gift shop. Estab. 1964. Considers candlemaking; ceramics; decoupage; dollmaking; glass art; jewelry; wall hangings; weaving; and woodcrafting. Nautical theme preferred. Fine handmade production-line and one-of-a-kind items only; utilitarian and/or decorative. Price range: $5-60. Works on consignment; but prefers to buy outright. Shop sets retail price. Query.
Profile: "We buy mostly small items and sell in volume. We try to have something for everybody. We have 375,000 visitors a year." Best selling time: June-August.

THE WHITE ELEPHANT GALLERIES, c/o Frank M. Young III, 3624 Ridgeview Dr., Birmingham AL 35213. (205)252-8847. Craft shop/gallery located in Mentone, Alabama. Estab. 1976. Represents 15-25 craftworkers.
Acceptable Work: Considers dollmaking, jewelry, needlecrafts, pottery, quilting, soft sculpture, tole painting, toys, wall hangings, weavings and woodcrafting. Especially needs pottery, ceramics, decoupage, metalsmithing, leatherworking and glass art. "Many of our items are rustic mountain type, although we have crafts of all types on display." One-of-a-kind and handmade production-line items. Price range: 75¢-$350; bestsellers: $2.50-150.
Terms: Buys outright and works on consignment; 25%commission. "We have a consignment agreement and instructions for consignors available upon request." Craftworker sets retail price. Send resume and slides. Reports in 2 weeks. Work may be shipped or hand-delivered.
Profile: "Shop is located in an old historic hotel in Mentone, which is a resort area in north Alabama near Chattanooga, Tennessee. We have several rooms, each of which is devoted to a particular line of merchandise." Heaviest wholesale buying and best selling time: March-September.

WINDWARD CRAFTS, Rt. 1, Mentone AL 35894. (205)634-3819. Contact: Mildred Moerlins or Jill Howard. Estab. 1975. Represents 15-20 craftworkers.
Acceptable Work: Considers batik; candlemaking; dollmaking; glass art; jewelry; leatherworking; metalsmithing; needlecrafts; pottery; quilting; soft sculpture; wall hangings; weavings; and woodcrafting. Finished, one-of-a-kind or handmade production items; utilitarian and/or decorative. Price range: $1-300; bestsellers: $2-20.
Terms: Works on consignment and occasionally buys outright; 30% commission. Craftworker sets retail price. Write or query with color transparencies or b&w prints of work. Reports in 2 weeks. Dealer pays shipping from shop and insurance for exhibited work.
Profile: "Windward Crafts is an old 2-story log house which was originally a small inn for summer tourists. We are open only in the summer, with all items displayed all summer. Customers are a wide variety of people vacationing in the area."

Alaska

ALASKA CERAMIC SUPPLY, INC., 7901 Old Seward Hwy., Anchorage AK 99502. (907)344-2094. General Manager: Paul Jackson. Rental gallery/pottery classes/wholesale supply company. Estab. 1965. Represents up to 24 craftworkers in gallery. Considers ceramics; pottery; and soft sculpture. Price range: $10-800; bestsellers: $25-75. Works on consignment and buys outright; 25% commission. Retail price set by joint agreement. Rental gallery fee: $1/square foot. Reports in 1 week. Work may be shipped or delivered in person; dealer pays insurance on exhibited work.

Profile: "All one-time exhibits are displayed in a manner satisfactory to the craftsman and our High Fire Division manager. By being in conjunction with their supplier, our craftsmen are given special treatment, guidance, understanding, and their wares receive tender loving care. We treat amateurs and professionals alike, and we urge the professionals to help the others. Heaviest wholesale buying time: spring; best selling time: summer tourist season. "In Alaska, the interest in crafts during the last 5 years has tripled. The input of craftsmen from the other 49 states has helped tremendously. We are growing by leaps and bounds."

ALASKA FOUR SEASONS GALLERY, 408 7th Ave., Fairbanks AK 99701. (907)452-2413. Contact: Cherie Yates. Craft/gift shop with custom framing facilities. Estab. 1973. Represents 5 craftworkers.
Acceptable Work: Considers batik, ceramics, clothing, glass art, jewelry, leatherworking, metalsmithing, pottery, scrimshaw, soft sculpture, wall hangings, weavings and woodcrafting. One-of-a-kind and handmade production-line items. "We have a limited presentation area so crafts we select must each possess strong visual and tactile appeal." Price range: $1-300; bestsellers: $10-75.
Terms: Buys outright and works on consignment; 30% commission. Retail price set by joint agreement. Send resume and slides with SASE. Reports in 2 weeks. Work may be shipped or hand-delivered. Dealer pays insurance on exhibited work.
Profile: "We run a cottage industry, using framing as the strong financial base. Success with framing has lead to new endeavors with handcrafted stained glass, leather, calligraphy, photography and fiber arts. Customers are mobile, educated, art conscious 25-40 year olds with reasonably good to excellent incomes. They look for items that reflect high quality with a special interest in utilitarian/functional design."

ALASKA NATIVE ARTS & CRAFTS, 425 "D" St., Anchorage AK 99501. (907)274-2932. Contact: Mary Lou Lindahl. Estab. 1937. Represents hundreds of local craftworkers. Native art only. Primitive and finished one-of-a-kind items; utilitarian and/or decorative. Price range: $1.50-4,500; bestsellers: $40-110. Buys outright. Retail price set by joint agreement.
Profile: Heaviest wholesale buying time: winter; best selling time: summer. Shop is a native coop. Customers buy crafts for their artistic value and as an investment.

ART, INC., 700 E. Benson Blvd., Anchorage AK 99503. (907)278-1212. Manager: Georgia Blue. 3 areas with art suplies, custom frame sections and contemporary Alaskan art gallery. Estab. 1976. Represents 90-125 contemporary Alaskan artists and craftpersons.
Acceptable Work: Considers jewelry, metalsmithing, paints, pottery, prints, soft sculpture, wall hangings and weavings. Specializes in contemporary Alaskan arts. One-of-a-kind designer and fine art pieces only. Price range: $5-400; bestsellers: $10-250.
Terms: Works on consignment; 40% commission. "Craftworker primarily sets price, but it may be discussed." Send slides or call for appointment. Reports in 2 weeks. Work may be shipped or hand-delivered. Dealer pays insurance on exhibited work.
Profile: "Gallery space is open. It has off-white walls with black cubes to display paintings, prints, pottery, jewelry and sculpture. Separate jewelry cases are available as well. We have new exhibits every 2 weeks usually showing 2 artists' work. Since we do have 3 areas of businesses, our clientele varies. We seem to consistently sell throughout the year with the spring and late fall being our peak seasons."
To Break In: "It's most helpful to deal with a well-organized artist. Appointments made ahead insure my being in shop. I'm always interested in seeing new work but we do stay with handling contemporary works and not the more traditional or representational Alaskan art."

THE ART SHOP & STUDIO OF J. VAN HOESEN, Box 323, Haines AK 99827. Contact: Jack Van Hoesen. Summer gallery and studio. Estab. 1972. Represents 8-10 craftworkers. Works on consignment and buys outright; 30% commission. Retail price set by joint agreement. Reporting time varies according to season. Query first. Dealer pays insurance on exhibited work.
Acceptable Work: Considers jewelry; leatherworking; metalsmithing; pottery; and woodcrafting. All styles; utilitarian and/or decorative. "I am interested in Alaskan crafts or items oriented to the 'Last Frontier' motif. No trinkets please! I desire crafts not widely marketed in the state, but available only from the craftsperson directly and a very few other outlets (quality shops or galleries)."
Special Needs: Wants silver and woodcarving representative of the northwest coast Indian art. "I will consider some items of special quality or uniqueness for a traveling exhibit in the lower 48 states in conjunction with my own gallery shows of wildlife and nature paintings."

Profile: Open during summer only. "Items are usually grouped according to craftsman, but not always. A display blurb about the craftsman is used, so the craftsman should submit a summary of his background and/or unique quality of his particular craft if not readily evident when viewing the items." Heaviest wholesale buying time: spring; best selling time: summer. "Most of my market is the summer tourists visiting the state of Alaska or residents who purchase uniquely Alaskan gifts to send elsewhere."

ARTIQUE LTD., 314 G., Anchorage AK 99501. (907)274-4784. President: Jean Shadrach. Gallery. Estab. 1971. Represents 10 craftworkers, preferably Northern (from US), Canadian, Alaskan and Japanese.
Acceptable Work: Considers ceramics, jewelry, pottery, wall hangings and weavings. Specializes in fine one-of-a-kind and handmade production-line items. Price range; $5-500; bestsellers: $30-200.
Terms: Buys outright and works on consignment; 30% commission. Retail price set by joint agreement. Requires exclusive area representation. Send slides with SASE. Work may be shipped or hand delivered. Dealer pays insurance on exhibited work.
Profile: "We have a fairly large area with sculpture stands and large open windows for street viewing. We have a very good reputation for handling only the best art work. Since we're in downtown Anchorage, there's much foot traffic, both tourist and local. It's a crossroads—we have people from Japan, Europe and all parts of the US." Heaviest wholesale buying and best selling time: May-December.

THE ARTWORKS, 3055 College Rd., Fairbanks AK 99701. (907)479-2563. Contact: Gloria Fischer. Craft shop/gallery. Estab. 1974. Represents 25-30 craftworkers. Considers batik; candlemaking; glass art; jewelry; metalsmithing; wall hangings; weavings; Eskimo and Indian crafts; and handbound blank books. All styles; utilitarian and/or decorative. Price range: $1-1,000; bestsellers: $5-50. Works on consignment and buys outright; 30% commission. Retail price set by joint agreement. Prefers exclusive area representation. Reports in 2 weeks. Ship or hand-deliver work. Shop pays insurance on exhibited work.
Profile: "Emphasis is on uncluttered display in order to show each piece to its best advantage. Work is not necessarily grouped by craftperson." Minimum display time: 6 weeks. Best selling time: summer and pre-Christmas months; heaviest wholesale buying time: spring and fall. Shop is "located in a traditional log cabin, but nevertheless has a contemporary feel. Traditional native crafts are displayed side by side with contemporary pieces, all of which seem to blend harmoniously." Customers are primarily "in 20s and 30s, outdoors oriented, well-educated and have traveled widely. We're located near the University of Alaska."

BERING STRAITS ESKIMO ARTS & CRAFT, Box 948, Nome AK 99762. (907)443-2680. Manager: Jerome Trigg, Jr. Craft/gift shop. Estab. 1974. Represents 500 craftworkers.
Acceptable Work: "We deal in ivory carving, skin sewing, grass baskets, wood carving and skins. The shop has a large selection of ivory carvings, handmade Eskimo mukluks and slippers, a fine line of handcarved jewelry, which consists of earrings, necklaces, bracelets, tie tacs and cuff links. You will also see fine hand-woven jewelry done with grass and a fine selection of skins." Especially interested in new ideas. One-of-a-kind and handmade production-line items. Price range: $5-1,150; bestsellers: $5-150.
Terms: Buys outright. Shop sets retail price. Make appointment to show work. Work must be hand-delivered.
Profile: "The ivory carvings are kept clean by dusting and oiling each piece daily, if necessary. They are displayed in glass cases and spaced evenly to give them 'room to breathe.'" Customers are interested in Eskimo arts and crafts. "Both the rich and poor walk into our door with the desire to learn more about the Eskimo culture and its art." Heaviest wholesale buying time: winter; best selling time: summer.
To Break In: "The best way to sell to me is have nice but small items which don't cost too much. These are easier to sell."

DINJII ZHUU ENJIT MUSEUM, Box 42, Fort Yukon AK 99740. (907)662-2345. Coordinator: Virginia Alexander. Museum gift shop. Estab. 1976. Represents 10 craftworkers from the Yukon Flats area.
Acceptable Work Considers beadwork and birch bark baskets; specializes in Athabascan beadwork. Primitive and fine one-of-a-kind pieces only; utilitarian and/or decorative.
Terms: Price range: $3-600; bestsellers: $3-50. Works on consignment; no commission. Craftworker sets retail price. Reports in 1 week. Ship or hand-deliver work.

Profile: "All items are on display in 1 room of the Museum. They are not in glass cases. We display them until they are sold or the artists ask for them back. It is the only gift shop in Fort Yukon." Best selling time: June-September. "Most of our customers are middle-aged or older tourists. They generally have a rather moderate income."

KAILL FINE CRAFTS, 4 Marine Way, Merchants Wharf, Juneau AK 99801. (907)586-2880. Contact: Anne Kaill. Estab. 1976. Represents 75 craftworkers. Considers batik; candlemaking; ceramics; dollmaking; glass art; jewelry; leatherworking; metalsmithing; pottery; quilting; soft sculpture; toys; wall hangings; weavings; and woodcrafting. Finished one-of-a-kind items OK; utilitarian and/or decorative. Price range: 65¢-$2,000; bestsellers: $10-20 and $40-80. Buys outright or on consignment; 33⅓% commission. Retail price set by joint agreement. Requires exclusive area representation. All methods of contact OK. Reports in 2 weeks. "In Alaska, US Mail or air freight is our only means of shipment." Dealer pays insurance for exhibited work; negotiates shipping and in-transit insurance. "I rotate items and change the gallery weekly." Best selling time: Christmas.
Special Needs: Unusual, not necessarily expensive items, including kites, musical instruments, cards, prints, quilts and dolls.

SKAGWAY ARTISTS COOP, Box 116, Skagway AK 99840. (907)983-2487. Contact: Charlotte Irwin. Craft shop located at 5th and Broadway. Represents 7+ craftworkers. "We prefer Alaskan-made merchandise, although we buy and consign from the lower 48."
Acceptable Work: Considers all crafts. Especially needs small pieces such as jewelry or items easy to pack.
Terms: Buys outright but mostly works on consignment; 30% commission. Craftworker sets wholesale price; shop adds 30%. Profile: "We are now located in the newly established Klondike Gold Rush National Historic Park, in a small community (population 900). We have a resident potter, painter, goldsmith and silversmith, ivory carver and toymaker. We cater to a tourist trade of 160,000. Many come by cruise ship." Heaviest selling time: May-September.

Arizona

COB-WEB HALL, Box 2035, Prescott AZ 86302. (602)445-2262. Contact: Dick or Beth Jorgensen. Gallery. Estab. 1962.
Acceptable Work: Considers batik; ceramics; glass art; jewelry; leatherworking; metalsmithing; pottery; soft sculpture; woodcrafting; and limited clothing, needlecrafts, wall hangings and weavings. One-of-a-kind designer pieces only. Price range: $2-500: bestsellers: $10-50.
Terms: Works on consignment and buys outright; 33⅓% commission. Craftworker sets retail price. Requires exclusive area representation. Reports in 4 weeks (sometimes a little longer). Gallery pays return shipping to craftworker.

COLORADO RIVER INDIAN TRIBES MUSEUM, Rt. 1, Box 23-B, Parker AZ 85344. (602)669-9211, ext. 213. Director: Charles A. Lamb. Assistant Director: Curtiss Martin. Museum gift shop/tribal museum. Estab. 1956. Represents about 50 craftworkers from the Mohave, Chemehuevi, Hopi and Navajo tribes of the Colorado River Indian Reservation.
Acceptable Work: Considers clothing; dollmaking; jewelry; leatherworking; pottery; woodcrafting; basketry; beadwork; Kachina carving; and rug weaving. Everything must be Indian-made. Fine and primitive one-of-a-kind pieces. Price range: $6-800; bestsellers: $6-50.
Terms: Works on consignment and buys outright; 20% commission. Retail price set by joint agreement. Reports as soon as possible. Work may be shipped or hand-delivered. Work is displayed 30 days.
Profile: "Price list is sent out to dealers and other shops and customers when requested. We are owned and operated by the Colorado River Indian tribes and located on a reservation." Heaviest wholesale buying (prior to) and best selling time (during): Christmas, Easter, Fourth of July and Thanksgiving.

THE DEPARTURE, 1720 E. Speedway, Tucson AZ 85719. (602)327-5721. Contact: Julie Harding. Boutique selling clothing, gifts, jewelry and crafts. Represents 10-15 ethnic craftworkers.
Terms: Buys outright. Shop sets retail price. Write with SASE describing craft. Reports in 2 weeks. Work may be shipped or hand-delivered. Requires exclusive area representation.
Acceptable Work: Considers ceramics, clothing, dollmaking, jewelry, pottery and soft sculpture; "everything except pieces with an 'Americana' feel." One-of-a-kind and handmade production-line pieces. Price range: $5-100; bestsellers: $12-30.
Profile: "Although the emphasis is on clothing, I carry gifts, rugs, folk art from around the

world, plus American-made jewelry and other crafts. Ours is a colorful shop. Heaviest wholesale buying and best selling time: fall."

FAMOUS FRENCH GALLERY, 2402 E. Grant Rd., Tucson AZ 85719. (602)325-7464. Contact: Grace Dove. Gallery/gift shop with custom framing and interior arranging services. Estab. 1978.
Acceptable Work: Considers batik, ceramics, decoupage, pottery, quilting, tole painting, wall hangings, weavings and "any quality original work that lends itself to framing—custom or standard. Work must be unframed to be acceptable." Especially needs pottery and ceramics suited for planting. One-of-a-kind and handmade production-line items. Price range: $5-50.
Terms: Buys outright and works on consignment; 40% commission. Retail price set by joint agreement. Requires exclusive area representation. Call for appointment with samples; no mail answered. Reports immediately. Work must be hand-delivered. "If accepted on consignment, craftworker must sign gallery contract."
Profile: "There's no back stock. All items are on display at all times. We prefer some items on a 'take order' basis. Our principal business in is custom framing, sensibly priced original oils, and readymade frames. We have interior arranging on an outcall basis." Customers: "extremely varied, but tending toward middle to upper incomes, 30 years-old and up." Heaviest wholesale buying time: summer; best selling time: fall-winter.
To Break In: "Craftworker must keep inventory sheets in duplicate (1 for our gallery) and must check in with gallery at least once a month after being accepted."

FIVE NINETY THREE, Box 1425, 593 4th Ave., Yuma AZ 85364. (602)783-7977. Contact: Linda Lane. Craft, jewelry and jewelry supplies shop. Estab. 1973. Considers all crafts. Price range: $5-1,000; bestsellers: $5-75. Works on consignment and buys outright; 40% commission. Retail price set by joint agreement. Requires exclusive area representation. Submit slides and photos. SASE. Reports in 1 week.

THE FRANKLIN GALLERY, 105 N. Beaver, Flagstaff AZ 86001. (602)774-0183. Contact: David Franklin Menne. Gallery and frame shop. Estab. 1974. Represents 6-12 craftworkers. Considers bronze sculpture; and prints. One-of-a-kind designer pieces only; utilitarian and/or decorative. Especially needs bronze sculpture and prints. Bestsellers: $20-60. Works on consignment; 33⅓% commission. Retail price set by joint agreement. Reports in 3 weeks. Work may be shipped or hand-delivered. Work displayed a minimum of 90 days. Customers are 30-50 years old; middle to upper incomes. Best selling time: July-December.

THE FRONT ROOM, 215 W. Leroux, Prescott AZ 86301. (602)445-0249. Contact: Judy Sears. Gallery and educational facility in pottery and jewelry. Estab. 1976. Represents 15 craftworkers. "We work primarily with students and graduates of our program but will take some outside crafts on consignment, if of the same high quality."
Acceptable Work: Considers ceramics, jewelry, metalsmithing, pottery, wall hangings and weavings. All sytles; pottery exhibits consist of mainly stoneware and porcelain, jewelry exhibits consist of everything except Indian jewelry. Fine one-of-a-kind and handmade production-line items. Price range: $2-200; bestsellers: $5-50.
Terms: Works on consignment; 30% commission. Retail price set by joint agreement. Reports in 2 weeks. Work is displayed a minimum of 30 days.
Profile: "Craftworker's ideas are encouraged as to display ideas, etc. We are located in a mixed community of many retired people and a good deal of college age students. We also have a large tourist trade." Best selling time: summer and pre-Christmas.

GALLERY 3, 3819 N. 3rd St., Phoenix AZ 85012. (602)277-9540. Contact: Sherry Manoukian.
Acceptable Work: Considers batik, ceramics, jewelry, pottery, sculpture, wall hangings, weavings and woodcrafting. Specializes in contemporary and Southwest art. Bestsellers: $150-400.
Terms: Works on consignment; 40% commission. Price range: $25-1,000, oils and acrylics; $25-500, graphics. Retail price set by joint agreement. Requires exclusive area representation. Query with samples. SASE. Gallery pays insurance on exhibited work.

GILA RIVER ARTS & CRAFTS, Box 457, Sacaton AZ 85247. (602)562-3411. Project Director: Roland Stewart. Craft/gift shop and museum gallery. Represents 50 American Indian craftworkers.
Acceptable Work: Considers jewelry, leatherworking, pottery, wall hangings and weavings. Especially needs Southwestern traditional items. Specializes in primitive and contemporary

pieces. One-of-a-kind and handmade production-line items. Price range: $5.50-56; best sellers: $34-3,200.
Terms: Buys outright and works on consignment; 30% commission. Retail price set by joint agreement. Requires exclusive area representations. Send resume. Reports in 2 weeks. Hand delivered work only. Dealer pays insurance on exhibited items.
Profile: "The shop is owned and operated by the Gila River Indian community. We have cases, natural sand, rock, pottery and shard displays; a shadow box gallery." Customers: tourists. Heaviest wholesale buying time: November-April; best selling time: winter.

GRA WUN JEWELERS, LTD., 7122 5th Ave., Scottsdale AZ 85251. Contact: Margaret Graves. Considers ceramics, jewelry, metalsmithing and glass art. Price range: $14-75. Buys outright. Craftworker determines fee. Requires exclusive area representation. Send transparencies or b&w photos (12x12x24") or smaller) of work.

THE HAND & THE SPIRIT CRAFTS GALLERY, INC., 4200 N. Marshall Way, Scottsdale AZ 85251. (602)946-4529. Contact: Joanne Rapp and Star Sacks. Craft shop/gallery. Estab. 1973. Represents 200 craftworkers.
Acceptable Work: Considers basketry, ceramics, jewelry, metalsmithing, quilting, soft sculpture and weavings. Specializes in fine art and Appalachian American crafts. One-of-a-kind and handmade production-line items. Price range: $10-$5,000; bestsellers: $5, $50-150.
Terms: Buys outright and works on consignment; 40% commission. Retail price set by craftworker or joint agreement. Requires exclusive area representation. Send resume with SASE. Jurying in July. Reports in 4 weeks. Dealer pays return shipping and insurance for exhibited work.
Profile: "Each piece is treated as an individual object. The gallery has complete space devoted to 8 shows/year (lasting 1-2 months). They are 2 or more person or thematic shows." Heaviest wholesale buying time: fall-winter; best selling time: winter and spring.

HOPI ARTS & CRAFTS COOPERATIVE GUILD, Box 37, Second Mesa AZ 86043. (602)734-2463. Manager: Mark Lormayestewa. Estab. 1949. Represents 280 local craftworkers. Best selling time: summer. Customers are ages 50-60; they buy crafts for artistic value and gifts.
Acceptable Work: Considers basketweaving; dollmaking; jewelry; painting; pottery; and weaving. Finished, one-of-a-kind and handmade production-line items. Price range: $5-3,000; bestsellers: $7-150.
Terms: Buys outright; 40% commission. Retail price set by joint agreement. Requires exclusive area representation. Reports in 2 weeks. Dealer pays shipping from shop and insurance.

HUACHUCA HISTORICAL SOCIETY, Box 766, Fort Huachuca AZ 85613. (602)538-5736. Director: James P. Finley. Museum gift shop. Estab. 1977. Represents 6 craftworkers. Heaviest wholesale buying time: spring; best selling time: summer.
Acceptable Work: Considers ceramics, jewelry and art prints. One-of-a-kind designer pieces. Price range: $7.50-60; bestsellers: $7.50-10.
Terms: Works on consignment; 40% commission. Gallery sets retail price. Reports in 1 week. Hand-delivered work only. US government pays insurance for exhibited work.

KNOX CAMPBELL GALLERIES, 3015 N. Campbell Ave., Tucson AZ 85719. (602)326-5533. Administrator: Susan Shriner. Considers some sculpture and woodcrafting. Specializes in Western art, but is interested in any theme. Works on consignment; 40% commission. Price range: $85-2,000; bestsellers: $500-1,000. Retail price set by joint agreement. Requires exclusive area representation. Send slides of work or call or write for interview. SASE. 1 month minimum exposure.

LA GALERIA, Box 617, Sedona AZ 86336. (602)282-3580. Contact: Ernestine Nestler. Gallery/gift shop. Estab. 1960. Represents 8 craftworkers.
Acceptable Work: Considers batik; ceramics; pottery; woodcarving; and wood sculpture. Fine one-of-a-kind pieces; utilitarian and/or decorative.
Terms: Works on consignment and buys outright; 33⅓% commission. Retail price set by joint agreement. Requires exclusive area representation. Reports in 1-4 weeks. Return shipping is negotiable; dealer pays transit insurance if notified at time of shipment and dealer pays insurance for exhibited work.
Profile: "We are essentially an art gallery and we handle quality gift items as a special courtesy to our collectors."

MUSEUM OF NORTHERN ARIZONA, Rt. 4, Box 720, Flagstaff AZ 86001. (602)774-5211; call weekdays. Museum Curator: Dr. Robert G. Breunig. Gift shop considers Navajo rugs; jewelry; and pottery (all Indian). Price range: $1-5,000. Buys outright. Sponsors 2 annual art competitions: Hopi Craftsmen; Navajo Craftsmen.

THE PAVILION, 7150 Main St., Scottsdale AZ 85251. (602)994-9444. Contact: Bill Orovan. Craft shop/gallery/gift shop. Estab. 1972. Represents 35 craftworkers.
Acceptable Work: Considers ceramics; decoupage; glass art; metalsmithing; needlecrafts; pottery; quilting; soft sculpture; wall hangings; weavings; and woodcrafting. Price range: $2.50-2,000.
Terms: Works on consignment and buys outright; 40-50% commission. Craftworker sets retail price. Requires exclusive area representation. Reports as soon as possible. Work may be shipped or hand-delivered.
Profile: "We are a unique combination of craft gallery, gift shop and art gallery. Some of our displays are rather elaborate, others quite simple." Heaviest wholesale buying time: late summer-early winter; best selling time: late fall-spring.

THE PENDLETON SHOP, Box 233, Sedona AZ 86336. (602)282-3671. Contact: Mary Pendleton. Gift shop. Estab. 1958. Represents 8-10 craftworkers.
Acceptable Work: Considers clothing; jewelry; leatherworking; needlecrafts; pottery; wall hangings; weavings; and woodcrafting. Price range: 95¢-$200.
Terms: Works on consignment and buys outright; 40% commission. Retail price set by joint agreement. Requires exclusive area representation. Reports as soon as possible. Work may be shipped or hand-delivered.
Profile: "Consigned items get as much attention as purchased items. Customers are older, with upper income." Displays consigned work 3-6 months. Heaviest wholesale buying and best selling time: spring-fall.

PHOENIX ART MUSEUM SHOP, 1625 N. Central, Phoenix AZ 85004. (602)257-1222. Manager: Marsha Weiss. Museum gift shop. Estab. 1959. Represents 2-3 craftworkers.
Acceptable Work: Considers clothing; glass art; jewelry; soft sculpture; and soleri bells. Especially needs soft sculpture. Fine one-of-a-kind and handmade production-line items; utilitarian and/or decorative. Price range: $1-200; bestsellers: $1-40.
Terms: Buys outright. Gallery sets retail price. "Only photos or personal calls accepted." Reports in 2 weeks. Accepted work may be shipped or hand-delivered. Dealer pays return shipping.
Profile: "Work is displayed in cases with colorful backdrop for 6-12 months. Customers are winter tourists and local residents, 25-60 years old with an income of $25,000 per year." Heaviest wholesale buying time: January and July; best selling time: winter.

THE THOMPSON GALLERY, 2020 N. Central, Phoenix AZ 85004. (602)258-4412. Contact: John R. Thompson. Considers sculpture; pottery; and jewelry. Works on consignment; 40% commission. Prices from $100. Set by artist. Requires exclusive area representation. 2 weeks exposure.

VERDE VALLEY ART GALLERY, INC., Box 877, Jerome AZ 86331. (602)634-5466. Gallery/gift shop. Estab. 1977. Represents 20 craftworkers. Price range: $5-350; bestsellers: $5-30. Works on consignment; 33⅓% commission. Retail price set by joint agreement. Reports in 1 week. Work may be shipped or hand-delivered. Work displayed 30 days minimum.
Acceptable Work: Considers batik; ceramics; clothing; dollmaking; leatherworking; bead work; glass art; jewelry; metalsmithing; needlecrafts; pottery; wall hangings; weavings; woodcrafting; and macrame. Especially needs ceramic wind chimes that have accurate musical tones; soft sculpture; and wood-carved or wood-sculpted items. Fine one-of-a-kind and handmade production-line items.
Profile: Work is shown in "glass cases, wall space, shelving and other unique displays. Shop is located in an historic, bicentennial mining town." Best selling time: summer-Christmas.

YUMA ART CENTER, 281 Gila St., Yuma AZ 85364. (602)782-9261. Director: Mark Anderson. Museum gift shop/rental gallery. Estab. 1962. Represents 20-30 Southwestern and southern California craftworkers. Heaviest wholesale buying time and best selling time: October-May.
Acceptable Work: Considers ceramics, jewelry, prints, sculpture and textiles. One-of-a-kind designer pieces. Price range: $25-750.

Terms: Works on consignment; 33⅓% commission. Retail price set by joint agreement. Reports in 2 weeks. Work may be shipped if previously arranged. Dealer pays return shipping and insurance. Work is rotated every 3 months.

Arkansas

ARKANSAS ARTS CENTER ART RENTAL-PURCHASE GALLERY, Box 2137, Little Rock AR 72203. (501)372-4000. Director: Townsend Wolfe. Museum craft/gift shop. Estab. 1966.
Acceptable Work: Considers clay, ceramics, glass art, enamels, fiber art, jewelry, leathermaking, metalsmithing, soft sculpture and wooden accessories.
Terms: "Open to regional artists from Arkansas, Louisiana, Missouri, Oklahoma, Texas, Tennessee and Mississippi who have had one or more works accepted for any regional or national juried exhibition." 20% commission. Exhibitor receives half rental fee. Submit 3 works for review.

BARBARA'S TOLE SHOPPE, 9501 Rodney Parham, Little Rock AR 72207. (501)225-0989. President: Barbara Bates. Craft/supply shop. Estab. 1973. Represents 10 craftworkers. Considers tole painting only. Price range: 50¢-$70; bestsellers: $1-10. Buys outright. Teaches classes also. Heaviest wholesale buying and best selling time: fall.

BOOGER HOLLOW NOVELTY CO., N. Star Rt., Dover AR 72837. (501)331-3440. Contact: Charles Johnson. Craft/gift shop. Estab. 1963. Represents 12 craftworkers.
Acceptable Work: Considers ceramics, dollmaking, pottery and woodcrafting. Especially needs woodcrafting. Handmade production-line items. Price range: $1-40; bestsellers: $5-20.
Terms: Buys outright. Shop sets retail price. Send pictures and prices. Reports in 2 weeks. Work may be shipped or hand-delivered.
Profile: "We buy in large quantities, but usually put out a very limited quantity of each craft." Customers: tourists. Heaviest wholesale buying time: March-September; best selling time: June-October.

M. M. COHN CO., 510 Main St., Little Rock AR 72203. (501)374-3311, ext. 266. Gift and Dinnerware Buyer: Susan Deaton. Department store. Mens' gifts, and gift and dinnerware department buys and consigns baskets; dinnerware; pillows; pottery; silverwork; wall hangings; and weaving. One-of-a-kind and handmade production-lines OK. Retail price range: $5-150; set by joint agreement. Submit resume and illustrations of work or arrange interview. "We try to appeal to a carriage trade apparel customer who is interested in both quality and uniqueness."

CROWLEY'S RIDGE AREA FOLK TRADE, Rt. 7, Box 56, Paragoule AR 72450. (501)573-6879. Craft Coordinator: Alice Denham. Craft shop. Represents 50 elderly, low-income, handicapped and disadvantaged craftworkers. "Our coverage is the 6 counties we are currently serving: Jackson, Poinsett, Craigbead, Greene, Lawrence and Mississippi.
Acceptable Work: Considers candlemaking, ceramics, crocheting, decoupage, dollmaking, knitting, quilting, tole painting and woodcrafting. Handmade production-line items only. Price range: $1-100; bestsellers: $5-75.
Terms: Works on consignment; 25% commission. Craftworker sets retail price. Requires exclusive area representation. Send slides. SASE. Reports in 2 weeks. Work must be shipped or hand-delivered.
Profile: "We have outside displays in the tourist season." Customers: tourists. Heaviest wholesale buying and best selling time: summer-fall.

THE DULCIMER SHOPPE, Drawer E, Hwy. 14 N., Mountain View AR 72560. (501)269-8639. Contact: Lynn McSpadden. Estab. 1962. Represents 10-12 craftworkers. Considers dollmaking; dried arrangements; jewelry; pottery; shuckery; white oak baskets; and woodcrafting. Fine, one-of-a-kind and handmade production-line items; utilitarian and/or decorative. Price range: $1-200; bestsellers: $1-125. Buys outright. Shop sets retail price, usually twice wholesale. Prefers exclusive area representation. Query. Reports in 2-3 weeks. Dealer pays shipping to shop and in-transit insurance.
Profile: "We do instrument making where visitors can watch." Heaviest wholesale buying time: March-August. Tourist customers.

MEL MAR SHOPS, Rt. 1, Box 446, Eureka Springs AR 72652. (501)253-9557. Contact: Melvin J. Soderquist. Gift/woodwork shop. Estab. 1974.
Acceptable Work: Considers dollmaking, metalsmithing and woodcrafting. Specializes in

Ozark regional crafts. Price range: up to $150; bestsellers: 24-75 (free-hand sculpture, lanterns and tables).
Terms: Buys outright. Shop sets retail price. SASE. Work may be shipped or hand-delivered.
Profile: "We have a man and wife woodworking shop, making reproductions of furniture, lanterns and taking special orders. We have a gift shop of handcrafted items which we purchase and retail. Our shop is small with no mass production. Each item is handcrafted, no 2 items will be exactly the same. This year, we started another building to rent to other craftpeople. As this building is finished and rented, we will start 1 more unit and continue for a craft village on 20 acres of land." Customers: "tourists from all over the world (mainly here to visit the passion plays)." Heaviest wholesale buying time: spring; best selling time: June-August. "Since ours is a tourist season from April 15-November 1, we need merchandise by May 1."

MUSEUM SHOP OF THE ARKANSAS ARTS CENTER, McArthur Park, Little Rock AR 72203. Manager: Jeanne Kelley. Museum gift shop. Estab. 1962. Represents 5-6 craftworkers who are members of the American Designer Crafts Association.
Acceptable Work: Considers ceramics; dollmaking; glass art; jewelry; and pottery. Especially needs one-of-a-kind toys. One-of-a-kind designer pieces; utilitarian and/or decorative. Price range: $8-200; bestsellers: $15-50.
Terms: Works on consignment and buys outright; 30% commission. Retail price set by joint agreement. Work may be shipped or hand-delivered. Heaviest wholesale buying time: fall and spring; best selling time: fall, spring and Christmas.

NELSON LEATHER CO., 84-B Spring St., Eureka Springs AR 72632. (501)253-7162. Contact: Jim or Susan Nelson. Craft shop. Estab. 1974. Represents 24 craftworkers.
Acceptable Work: Considers leatherworking, belt buckles and woodcrafting. "Most of the leatherwork we sell is functional." One-of-a-kind and handmade production-line items. Price range: 75¢-$350; bestsellers: $2-50.
Terms: Buys outright. Shop sets retail price. Exclusive Eureka Springs representation. Send slides. SASE. Reports in 2 weeks. Work may be shipped or hand-delivered.
Profile: "Our store has oak and brick floors with alternating wall panels of rough western cedar and native tree sections which have been mounted on 4x8 plywood sheets painted flat black. We use antique and new display cases for leather accessories and expensive buckles. Track lighting is used throughout the shop." Customers: average to high incomes. Heaviest wholesale buying time: spring-fall; best selling time: summer-fall.

THE OZARK FOLK CENTER SALES SHOP, General Delivery, Mountain View AR 72560. (501)269-3851. Contact: Kay Blair. Estab. 1973. Represents 60 Ozark area craftworkers.
Acceptable Work: Considers candlemaking; dollmaking; leatherworking; needlecrafts; pottery; quilting; wall hangings; weavings; and woodcrafting. Primitive and finished, one-of-a-kind and handmade production-line items OK. Price range: 35¢-$500; bestsellers: 35¢-$20.
Terms: Buys outright. Gallery sets retail price. Query with transparencies or photos. Reports in 3 weeks.
Profile: "The period we are interested in is 1820-1920 Ozark. The merchandise is displayed in period settings at times and also on well-lighted display shelves or rustic 'islands.' Located in state park." Heaviest wholesale buying time: winter; best selling time: August and October.

OZARK FOOTHILLS CRAFT GUILD, Box 140, Mountain View AR 72560. (501)269-3896. Director: James H. Sanders. Craft shop. Estab. 1961. Represents 150 Arkansas craftworkers.
Acceptable Work: Considers all crafts except decoupage. Especially needs scrimshaw, quilting, direct surface-designed fiber pieces (silkscreen on cloth, photosensethized fabric or other dye related techniques) and wood lathed products. Price range: 59¢-$200; bestsellers: 59¢-$25.
Terms: Must be member craftworker. Buys outright; payment within 30 days. Retail price set by joint agreement. Write for information on on membership and standards committee jurying. SASE. Reports in 2 weeks of standards committee decision. Work may be shipped or hand-delivered.
Profile: "Each object demands its own type of displaying, whether under glass display case, hung on a wall, framed on shelving units, on bales of hay, in baskets, over parallel dowel rods, hung in front of glass window, according to color, media, design and color compatibility. There are special interest centers where groupings of crafts items are placed (these usually have a color scheme in common or a specific craftsperson is featured)." Customers: tourists; out-of-state buyers who purchase at retail prices and market in own areas at double retail price"; local trade from Mountain View and Northern Arkansas residents; small amount of mail order customers. Heaviest wholesale buying time: spring-summer; best selling time: spring-fall.

Shops and Galleries 77

Originally limited to 7 neighboring counties in Arkansas, the Ozark Foohills Craft Guild has expanded to attract state-wide participation of over 400 members. The Guild encourages traditional and contemporary crafts through education programs and marketing outlets, several of which are listed in this book.

OZARK'S CERAMIC CORNER, Hwy. 65 S., Clinton AR 72031. (501)745-2091. Manager: Betty Hatcher. Craft/gift shop/studio. Estab. 1964. Considers ceramics, decoupage, dollmaking and macrame hangings for planters. Specializes in contemporary and designer crafts. Works on consignment; 30-40% commission. Retail price set by joint agreement. Write or call. SASE. Work may be shipped or hand-delivered. Display time: 6 months to 1 year. Customers: mostly average and above average incomes. Heaviest wholesale buying time: spring-early summer; best selling time: summer to pre-Christmas.

JON SCHADEN UNLIMITED PRODUCTIONS, 14 W. Center, Fayetteville AR 72701. (501)443-5213. Gallery Coordinator: Stephen Lance. Gallery and interior design studio. Estab. 1978. Represents 30 craftworkers.
Acceptable Work: Considers batik, ceramics, glass art, metalsmithing, pottery, soft sculpture, wall hangings, weavings and woodcrafting. Especially needs woodcarvings. Specializes in contemporary designer crafts. Prefers small or large items, not medium size. Handmade production-line items in ceramics only. Price range: $20-1,200; bestsellers: $20-35, $500-750.
Terms: Works on consignment; 30% commission. Gallery sets retail price. Send resume and slides. Reports in 2 weeks.
Profile: "Crafts are exhibited during the Christmas season in our winter fair exhibition. Large craft items are sold in spring at designer and collector exhibitions. We have very small permanent display area; therefore, we show primarily exclusive showings of fine art works and have two crafts exhibitions a year. We are growing and hope to change this. We display on glass shelving and sculptor stands." Customers: young, middle class ($14-20,000), career oriented. Heaviest wholesale buying time: winter-spring; best selling time: winter.

SEVEN SPRINGS CRAFTS SHOP, Heber Springs AR 72543. (501)269-3896. Director: James H. Sanders III. Craft shop. Estab. 1962. Represents 100 craftworkers.
Acceptable Work: Considers all crafts except decoupage. Especially needs scrimshaw, quilting, direct surface-designed fiber pieces (silkscreen on cloth, photosensethized fabric or other dye related techniques) and wood lathed products. Price range: 59¢-$200; bestsellers: 59¢-$25.
Terms: Must be member craftworker. Buys outright; payment within 30 days. Retail price set by joint agreement. Write for information on on membership and standards committee jurying. SASE. Reports in 2 weeks of standards committee decision. Work may be shipped or hand-delivered.
Profile: "Shop doesn't have much room for larger pieces." Display is on shelves; building is rustic. "There are special interest centers where groupings of crafts items are placed (these usually have a color scheme in common or a specific craftsperson is featured)." Customers are tourists and transients. Heaviest wholesale buying time: spring-summer; best selling time: spring-fall.

THE SPRING STREET POTTERY, 65 Spring St., Eureka Springs AR 72632. (501)253-9380. Manager: David J. Foddrell. Gallery. Estab. 1971. Represents 10 local craftworkers. Price range: $3.50-5,800; bestsellers: $9-75. Works on consignment; 20-50% commission. Retail price set by joint agreement. Requires exclusive area representation. Reports in 1 week. Work may be shipped or hand-delivered. Dealer and craftworker share cost of shipping and insurance. Work is displayed 6 months minimum. Best selling time: summer and fall.
Acceptable Work: Considers wall hangings; weavings; and antiques. Fine one-of-a-kind and handmade production-line items; utilitarian and/or decorative.

THE STORE, ARKANSAS TERRITORIAL RESTORATION, Territorial Square, Little Rock AR 72201. (501)371-2348. Manager: Maxine Rowland. Museum gift shop. Estab. 1972. Represents 120 Arkansas craftworkers. Best selling time: summer and Christmas.
Acceptable Work: Considers all crafts except clothing. Price range: 25¢-$200; bestsellers: 50¢-$20.
Terms: Works on consignment; 25% commission. Retail price set by joint agreement. Reports in 2 months. Work may be shipped or hand-delivered. Displays work for 6 months.

SUGAR CREEK CRAFT SHOP, Main St., Hardy AR 72542. Director: James H. Sanders III. Craft shop. Estab. 1962. Represents 125 craftworker members of the Ozark Foothills Craft Guild.
Acceptable Work: Considers all crafts except decoupage. Especially needs scrimshaw, quilting, direct surface-designed fiber pieces (silkscreen on cloth, photosensethized fabric or other dye related techniques) and wood lathed products. Price range: 59¢-$200; bestsellers: 59¢-$25.
Terms: Must be member craftworker. Buys outright; payment within 30 days. Retail price set

by joint agreement. Write for information on membership and standards committee jurying. SASE. Reports in 2 weeks of standards committee decision. Work may be shipped or hand-delivered.
Profile: "All crafts must be made of natural materials (no synthetics). Work is "displayed in a 2,500 square foot shop, year-round, on walls, shelves, under glass, in windows, until sold. There are special interest centers where groupings of crafts items are placed (these usually have a color scheme in common or a specific craftsperson is featured)." Customers are middle-income tourists; 18-85 years old. Heaviest wholesale buying time: spring-summer; best selling time: summer.

SUNWISE LEATHER CO., 22 S. Main, Eureka Springs AR 72632. Proprietors: Vernon or Phyllis Gaylor. Craft/gift shop. Estab. 1977. Represents 20-40 craftworkers.
Acceptable Work: Considers batik, ceramics, jewelry, leatherworking, metalsmithing (buckles), pottery, wall hangings and woodcrafting. "We are interested chiefly in leather items, but also handle others on consignment. Our products try to reflect the spirit of the mountain craftsman (e.g., hats, belts, handbags, belt buckles)." One-of-a-kind and handmade production-line items. Price range: $5-150; bestsellers: $7.50-40.
Terms: Buys outright and works on consignment; 30% commission. Shop sets retail price. Requires exclusive Eureka Springs representation. Send resume, drawings, photos or slides. Reports in 2 weeks. Work must be hand-delivered.
Profile: "Eureka Springs is an historically restored Victorian Ozark town. 1979 celebrated its centennial. Our season is April-October generally. We stock in early April and usually let the last restocking (early October) carry us through the holidays."

SYLAMORE CREEK CRAFT SHOP, Box 140, Mountain View AR 72560. (501)269-3896. Director: James H. Sanders III. Cooperative craft shop. Coop estab. in 1962; shop estab. in 1975. Represents 150 Arkansas member craftworkers.
Acceptable Work: Considers all crafts, plus musical instruments and craft publications. No synthetic materials. Contemporary and traditional Ozark crafts. One-of-a-kind and handmade production-line items. Especially needs items that would sell within the price range of $2-12 wholesale. Price range: 25¢-$300; bestsellers: 25¢-$25.
Terms: "All participating craftpersons must be within the guild's membership and approved in their given categories by the standards committee. $10 membership fee. Must be Arkansas resident and submit 5 articles in any given media." Buys outright and sometimes works on consignment; 50% commission. Retail price set by joint agreement. Reports in 3 weeks. Membership application and work may be shipped or hand delivered. Dealer pays return shipping on consigned work and insurance on exhibited work.
Profile: "The shop is a cooperatively run organization with a 2 member full time staff and year 'round office operation. Work is displayed "till sold on various retail display tools (counters, shelves, walls); hung, draped, arranged. Basically middle class tourist trade." Heaviest wholesale buying time: spring and summer; best selling time: spring, summer and fall.

THE VICTORIAN HOUSE, 85 Spring St., Eureka Springs AR 72632. (501)253-8747. Contact: Ken and Meg Kimball. Craft shop/gift shop. Estab. 1968. Represents 20 Ozark area craftworkers.
Acceptable Work: Considers candlemaking, ceramics, pottery, quilting, wall hangings, weavings and woodcrafting. One-of-a-kind and handmade production-line items OK. Price range: $1.60-200; bestsellers: $2-60.
Terms: Buys outright. Retail price set by joint agreement. Requires exclusive area representation. Call for appointment. Reports in 1 week. Work may be shipped or hand-delivered.
Profile: "The Victorian House is a gift shop that caters to a large tourist trade. Our primary concern is to provide to the tourists a variety of fine quality handcrafted items which reflect the artistry and craftsmanship still prevalent today."

WHITE OAK POTTERY, Rt 2, Box 349, Eureka Springs AR 72632. (501)253-8196. Contact: Ruthann or Lowell Baker. Craft/pottery shop. Estab. 1972. Represents 10 craftworkers. Customers: tourists. Heaviest wholesale buying time: spring; best selling time: summer.
Acceptable Work: Considers glass art, jewelry, pottery, wall hangings and weavings. Specializes in Ozark contemporary work. One-of-a-kind and handmade production-line items. Price range: $1.50-75; bestsellers: $1.50-30.
Terms: Buys outright and works on consignment. Craftworker sets retail price. Call for appointment. Work may be shipped or hand-delivered. Sample work will not be returned.

WOOD-N-THREAD, 61 S. Main St., Eureka Springs AR 72632. (501)253-9312. Contact: Joanna Hanna. Craft shop. Estab. 1976. Represents 12+ craftworkers from the Ozarks (Arkansas or Missouri) using mainly local materials.
Acceptable Work: Considers candlemaking, ceramics, dollmaking, jewelry, metalsmithing, needlecrafts, pottery, quilting, tole painting, wall hangings, weavings and woodcrafting. Especially needs "more contemporary/modern work. I have a lot of 'old world' crafts. Interested mostly in work made with wood or thread (yarn, etc.)." One-of-a-kind and handmade production-line items. Price range: $1-300; bestsellers: $3-50.
Terms: Buys outright and may work on consignment 30% commission. Retail price set by joint agreement. Call for appointment. Reports in 2 weeks. Work may shipped or hand-delivered. Dealer pays insurance on exhibited work. Items bought outright are exhibited until sold; consignment pieces are exhibited 2 months. "If item on consignment does well, we will buy further orders."
Profile: Customers are "middle income families looking for local crafts and better buys than they can get at home—also retired and college-aged looking for things they have never seen before." Heaviest wholesale buying time: June-August; best selling time: June-October.

WOOL-ART, 422 E. Locust, Rogers AR 72756. (501)636-5892. Manager: Elpha Kindred. Estab. 1964. Represents 15 craftworkers, plus buys from 21 American Indian tribes. Heaviest wholesale buying time: after January 1; bestselling time: pre-Christmas and July-August.
Acceptable Work: Considers dollmaking, metalsmithing, pottery, woodcrafting, wall hangings, split oak baskets, copper enamel, iron work, brooms and pine needle baskets. Especially needs more work from Indian tribes (baskets). Specializes in quality pioneer work. Price range: $1-200; bestsellers: $2.35 (placemats)-$75 (throws).
Terms: Buys outright. Dealer sets retail price. Requires exclusive area representation. Work must be hand-delivered on first order; later orders may be shipped.

California

ACORN GALLERY, 93 S. Central, Campbell CA 95008. (408)374-2420. Contact: Jim or Eloise Bond. Gallery/gift shop. Estab. 1962. Represents 10 craftworkers. Send slides with SASE or call for appointment; reports in 2 weeks. Work may be shipped or hand-delivered.
Acceptable Work: Considers ceramics, glass art, fine jewelry (including diamonds, rubies, sapphires), crystal, metalsmithing, pottery and scrimshaw. Especially needs whales, dolphins, sea gulls and sea otters in sculptures and glass. Fine designer, one-of-a-kind and handmade production-line items. "Nothing freaky, no signs of zodiac or horoscopes." Price range: $4-195. Mostly buys outright, but also works on consignment; 40-50% commission. Dealer pays insurance on exhibited work. Retail price set by joint agreement. Requires exclusive area representation.
Profile: "Our shop has large timbers—woodsy. It is not high-brow but it is top class—probably the most beautiful gallery of its kind in the Bay area. Customers are mainly 18-50; from college students to persons with $50,000 a year income." Best selling time: October-June.
To Break In: "We don't want to be higher priced than others. If they sell the work themselves at local craft fairs for less money than what I would have to charge, I'm not interested. I prefer people seriously in business with realistic prices."

ADI GALLERY, 530 McAllister, San Francisco CA 94102. (415)621-0602. Contact: Stephen Foster. Gallery. Estab. 1968. Represents 250 artists, sculptors, weavers, printmakers and painters. Considers weavings and wall hangings. Fine one-of-a-kind decorative items only. Price range: $800-3,000, tapestries; bestsellers: $1,000-2,000. Works on consignment. Retail price set by joint agreement. Requires exclusive area representation. Send slides for preliminary viewing. Gallery pays insurance on exhibited work.
Profile: "Since we are a gallery, once we accept an artist, we take his/her work in our consigned inventory for an indefinite period of time. This is then shown to our clients by the owner or director. Corporate art consultants work with designers. There are commissions and fiberworks must work in large corporate spaces although we do have private collectors too."

ADI GALLERY, Pier 39, San Francisco CA 94102. (415)956-5727. See above.

AFTER THE GOLD RUSH, Box 999, Arnold CA 95223. (209)795-2593. Contact: Rene or Kim del Valle. Craft shop. Estab. 1978. Represents 25-35 craftworkers. Considers batik; candlemaking; ceramics; clothing; glass art; jewelry; leatherworking; metalsmithing; pottery; wall hangings; weavings; woodcrafting; and enamelcraft. Fine one-of-a-kind and handmade production-line items. Price range: $2-125; bestsellers: $10-20. Buys outright. Shop sets retail price. Reports in 1 week. Customers are middle to upper-middle class, 24-40 years of age. Best selling time: summer and Christmas.

AMERICAN MUSEUM OF QUILTS & RELATED ARTS, Santa Clara Valley Quilt Association, 114 El Paseo de Saratoga, San Jose CA 95130. (408)378-5533. Director: Sylvia Moore. Museum shop. Estab. 1977.
Acceptable Work: Considers needlecrafts, soft sculpture, weavings, and especially needs quilts and quilted items. Items submitted for monthly exhibit must be of high quality workmanship and design.
Terms: Works on consignment. Items submitted for sale must be accepted by the Museum Selection Committee. Send resume and sample of work or call in person. Membership in the Santa Clara Valley Quilt Association is open to anyone. (Apply October 1-September 30; $12 dues, $6 for members 62 years or older, $18 for affiliate memberships). Send résumé and sample of work or call in person.
Profile: Exhibits changed the first Friday of every month. Classes in quilting and various areas of needlework are held at the museum. Experienced craftsmen with high standards of workmanship are regularly welcomed to sell items. Full credit is given to exhibitors.

APPALACHIA: AMERICAN MOUNTAIN CRAFTS & CULTURE, 340 Village Lane, Los Gatos CA 95030. (408)354-6700. Contact: Owen or Wendy Nagler. Craft shop/gallery/gift shop. Estab. 1976. Represents about 100 craftworkers who deal exclusively in Appalachian folk art and crafts. Considers clothing; dollmaking; metalsmithing; needlecrafts; pottery; quilting; wall hangings; weavings; woodcrafting; broomcraft; basketry; and shuckcrafts. Price range: $1-400. Works on consignment and buys outright. Work may be shipped or hand-delivered.
Profile: "The interior of the shop is designed to lend an authentic country atmosphere. There are informational signs about crafts and craftspeople." Customers are affluent. Best selling time: Christmas.

ARTISANS' ALLEY, INC., 13271 Century Blvd., Garden Grove CA 92643. (714)530-8120. Artisans' coop. Estab. 1972. Represents 100-150 craftworkers. Considers all crafts. "Special need for wood, leather and scrimshaw." All styles. Price range: $1-2,500; bestsellers: $2-100. "Artisans join the Alley and rent booth space. Members often buy outright or take on consignment the works of others not wishing membership. Spaces rent from $10-150 per month." Craftworker sets retail price.
Profile: "We have 6,000 square feet of space; variety of crafts; person to person involvement; 2 classrooms; and we have a fascinating cultural center for northern and central Orange County."

BARTEL INTERIOR DESIGN, 161 N. Larchmont Blvd., Los Angeles CA 90004. (213)466-7727. Contact: Vera M. Sweeney. Gift shop. Estab. 1969. Represents 6-10 craftworkers. Best selling time: fall; heaviest wholesale buying time: July and January.
Acceptable Work: Considers batik; ceramics; glass art; jewelry; and pottery. Handmade production-line items only. Price range: $5-300; bestsellers: $5-100.
Terms: Buys outright. Gallery sets retail price. Requires exclusive area representation. Reports in 2 weeks. Work may be hand-delivered.

BAZAAR DEL MUNDO GALLERY, 2754 Calhoun St., San Diego CA 92110. (714)296-3161. Contact: Kori Boss. Gallery. Estab. 1972. Represents 40-50 craftworkers.
Acceptable Work: Considers batik, ceramics, clothing, jewelry, pottery, scrimshaw, wall hangings, weavings and ethnic folk art. Specializes in bright-colored folk art; "an adaptation of utilitarian items into playful expressions of life. We are looking for inventive crafts, where craftsmen have combined mediums to achieve the unusual—an approach to crafts that borders on Mexican folk art, the fun and the frivolous! We have primarily been a jewelry gallery that is branching out to include particularly ceramics and clothing." Price range: $5-200; bestsellers: $10-50, $250-350.
Terms: Buys outright and works on consignment; 40% commission. Retail price set by joint agreement. Requires exclusive area representation. Send slides with SASE. Reports in 2 weeks. Work may be shipped or hand-delivered. Dealer pays shipping for solicited work and insurance for exhibited work. "We do approximately 6-8 shows a year in our gallery. Rather than shows that concentrate on themes, we emphasize one man shows along with our regular gallery stock of crafts. If we don't have enough of 1 craftsman's work to make a statement, we group his/her work by category."
Profile: "We are a gallery surrounded by 11 international shops and 3 restaurants. Located in

Old Town San Diego, our site is a remodeled hacienda looking out on exotic gardens of fresh flowers and tropical plants. 50% of our customers are regular patrons who come back to us on a monthly basis. Then, because of our prime tourist location in Old Town, at Christmas and in the summer, we cater to international tourists. Incomes range from approximately $25,000-150,000; ages 28-55." Heaviest wholesale buying time: spring and fall; best selling time: summer and winter.

BEAUX ARTS GIFT SHOP OF FRESNO ARTS CENTER, 3033 E. Yale, Fresno CA 93703. (209)237-2070. Manager: Ann Buchanan. Gift shop/rental gallery. Estab. 1973. Represents 100 craftworkers. Best selling time: Christmas.
Acceptable Work: Considers batik; ceramics; glass art; jewelry; needlecrafts; pottery; soft sculpture; wall hangings; weavings; and woodcrafting. Primitive and fine pieces. Price range: $1-200.
Terms: Works on consignment and buys outright; 33% commission. Retail price set by joint agreement. Reports in 1-2 weeks. Work may be shipped or hand-delivered. Dealer pays shipping to shop and insurance.

BROCKMAN GALLERY PRODUCTIONS, 4334 Degnan Blvd., Los Angeles CA 90008. (213)294-3766. Program Coordinator: Helen Singleton. Considers batik; ceramics; dollmaking; jewelry; leatherworking; metalsmithing; mobiles; pottery; prints; sculpture; wall hangings; weavings; and woodcrafting. Maximum size: 5x7. Paintings must be ready to hang. Works on consignment; 40% commission. Price range: $10-1,500; bestsellers: $15-75. Retail price set by joint agreement. Send slides or photos or call or write for interview. SASE. Gallery pays shipping from gallery and insurance for exhibited work. Work displayed for 3-week period.

CABOT'S OLD INDIAN PUEBLO MUSEUM, 67616 Desert View, Box 1267, Desert Hot Springs CA 92240. (714)329-7610. Curator: Colbert Eyraud. Museum gift shop. Estab. 1968. Represents 6 craftworkers.
Acceptable Work: Considers candlemaking, ceramics, glass art, jewelry, leatherworking, metalsmithing, pottery, scrimshaw, wall hangings, weavings and woodcrafting. Specializes in primitive, Appalachian, natural and desert crafts. One-of-a-kind and handmade production-line items. Price range: $3-150; bestsellers: $3-25.
Terms: Buys outright and works on consignment. "We add museum commission to craftworkers' desired price, from 20% to whatever sells item best." Retail price set by joint agreement. Call for appointment—be sure buyer is in. Reports in 2 weeks. Work may be shipped or hand delivered.
Profile: Trading post in a historic Indian monument. The museum carries early day relics and Indian and Eskimo artifacts and crafts. Customers: ages 16-75 with varied income levels. Heaviest wholesale buying time: September-March; best selling time: November-May.

CALIFORNIA ARTISTS & CRAFTSMEN'S GUILD, 1131 State St., Santa Barbara CA 93101. (805)963-2424. Contact: Fran Doll. Coop/rental gallery. Estab. 1971. Represents 60 craftworkers. Price range: $3-600; bestsellers: $20-100. Works on 40/60 consignment or booth space rental; 40% commission. Craftworkers sets retail price. Requires exclusive area representation. Write. Reports in 1 week. Best selling time: summer. Customers are young college students and married couples with good incomes.

CALIFORNIA COUNTRY FURNITURE, 7761 Broadway, Lemon Grove CA 92045. (714)461-9100. Contact: Jim Frey or Rick Carter. Craft/furniture shop. Estab. 1972. Represents 15-20 craftworkers.
Acceptable Work: Considers ceramics, metalsmithing, pottery, wall hangings, weavings and woodcrafting.. Especially needs furniture accessories, wall decor lamps and woodcrafts. Contemporary handmade production-line items. Price range: $5-1000; bestsellers: $8-150.
Terms: Works on consignment; 30% commission. Consignment items should be prolific for custom orders. Craftworker sets retail price. Call for appointment. Reports in 2 weeks. Work may be shipped or hand delivered.
Profile: "We display basically handcrafted pine furniture with contemporary designs, which are put into room settings with handcrafted items for room decor and accessories." Displays on shelves. Customers: ages 25-40, middle incomes, and "looking for something different in household furnishings". Best selling time: Christmas.

CANDY STICK STUDIO ART GALLERY, Box 132, Ferndale CA 95536. (707)786-4600. Manager: Carol Lahe. Rental gallery. Estab. l965. Represents 1 craftworker.

Shops and Galleries 83

Acceptable Work: Considers glass art, jewelry, leatherworking, metalsmithing, pottery and soft sculpture. Specializes in fine art. One-of-a-kind items. Bestsellers: $200-300.
Terms: Works on consignment; 30% commission. Retail price set by craftworker or by joint agreement. Requires exclusive area representation. Send resume and slides. Reports in 2 weeks. Work may be shipped or hand-delivered.
Profile: "We have a large art gallery in front displaying paintings and sculpture, with a small room for pottery. Art supplies and fine greeting cards are in the back room. We also have some space and cases for hand-blown glass and jewelry. In summertime, there is a lot of tourist trade. Yearly business, however, comes from local business people in Humboldt County—business on reputation established over the last 13 years." Heaviest wholesale buying time: presummer; best selling time: summer.

CANYON GALLERY TWO, 804 N. La Cienega Blvd., Los Angeles CA 90069. (213)653-5090. Contact: Masaharu Ichino or Roberta Best. Craft/gift shop/gallery. Estab. 1963. Represents 50-70 craftworkers.
Acceptable Work: Considers batik, candlemaking, ceramics, clothing, dollmaking, glass art, jewelry, leatherworking, metalsmithing, pottery, scrimshaw, soft sculpture, wall hangings, weavings, woodcrafting and ethnic and folk arts and crafts. Especially needs woodcrafting, fine procelain, sculptural pottery, and jewelry. Specializes in primitive, fine and contemporary crafts. One-of-a-kind and handmade production-line items. Price range: $10-1,500; bestsellers: $15-600.
Terms: Works on consignment; 50% commission. Retail price set by joint agreement. Requires exclusive area representation. Send resume, slides or call for appointment. SASE. Reports in 4 weeks. Work may be shipped or hand-delivered after pre-arrangement. Dealer pays insurance on exhibited work. Displays consigned work 90 days.
Profile: "Items are either displayed on white walls, if they are hanging pieces, or on pedestals, most of which are grey (some lavendar, coral and blue). All items are color coordinated with one another, i.e., ceramics, glass, wood and paintings are grouped to create an environment. We do well with interior decorators. I require that arrangements for peak sales (December) be made by September." Customers: middle to upper middle incomes; mid-20's to mid-60's; well-traveled, educated; many collectors.

CARMEL WORK CENTER SHOP, Box 3547, Carmel by the Sea CA 93921. Contact: Wes or Fritzie Bonenberger. Craft and gift shop. Estab. 1955. Represents California craftworkers only.
Acceptable Work: Considers California-made ceramics and especially needs stoneware, raku, crystaline glazed art glass, weavings and sculpture. Fine one-of-a-kind and handmade production items. Price range: $5-150; bestsellers: $5-50.
Terms: Buys outright and works on consignment; 40% commission. Retail price set by joint agreement. Requires exclusive area representation. Reports in 2 weeks. Work may be shipped or hand-delivered.
Profile: "We have received mailings from all parts of the country of many fine items, but regret we can only accept handcrafted items created by California artists. This has been our policy since 1955." Best selling time: summer.
To Break In: "We would appreciate more care by craftspeople to check individual pieces for glaze flaws, cracks, chips and finished, smooth bottoms. No time in shop to do more than check superficially. It's embarassing when a customer points out flaws."

CHOICE INCORPORATED, 101 Kansas St., Suite 433, San Francisco CA 94103. (415)431-1172. President: Audrey S. Jarach. Gallery. Estab. 1977. Represents 100 craftworkers. Considers batik; ceramics; glass art; metalsmithing; quilting; soft sculpture; wall hangings; weavings; and woodcrafting. Fine one-of-a-kind pieces only; decorative. Open price range. Works on consignment. Retail price set by joint agreement. Reports in 4 weeks. Work may be shipped or hand-delivered. Dealer pays insurance for exhibited work. Works on 90 day consignment and sells (wholesale) to interior designers, architects and corporate collectors.

COAST GALLERY, Hwy. 1, Big Sur CA 93920. (408)667-2301. Contact: Gary or Vicki Koeppel. Craft/art gallery. Estab. 1958. Represents 40 craftworkers. "We feature Big Sur and California coastal craftsmen, but exhibit selective crafts from across the country. Professional full-time craftsmen only."
Acceptable Work: Considers ceramics, dollmaking, glass art, jewelry, leatherworking, metalsmithing, needlecrafts, pottery, quilting, scrimshaw, soft sculpture, wall hangings, weavings and woodcrafting. One-of-a-kind and handmade production-line items. Price range: $3-500; bestsellers: $7.50-75.

Terms: Buys outright and works on consignment; 40% commission. "We often consign first for experiment, then buy outright." Dealer sets retail price. Requires exclusive area representation. Send resume, slides, photos or call for appointment. SASE. Reports in 4 weeks. Work may be shipped or hand delivered. Display time: 60-90 days on experimental work; otherwise permanent.
Profile: "We are the only gallery on Big Sur Scenic Highway 1. The building is 2 connected 34 foot diameter water tanks." Customers: predominantly tourists. Heaviest wholesale buying time: May-August; best selling time: summer and fall.

COFFEE CANTATA, 2030 Union St., San Francisco CA 94118. (415)931-7043. Manager: Judy Honig. Gallery. Estab. 1967. Sponsors 1-person and group showings. Considers batik; quilting; soft sculpture; wall hangings; and weavings. Fine one-of-a-kind pieces only; decorative. Price range: $50-2,500; bestsellers: $50-375. "We only display art and take 30% commission on sales." Craftworker sets retail price. Bring work in personally for review. Dealer pays insurance for exhibited work.
Profile: Gallery is open 12-14 hours daily along with 100-seat restaurant. Displays work for 30 days. Customers are all ages; tourists and locals.

COMMON GROUND ARTISTS CO-OPERATIVE, 509 N. Harbor Blvd., Fullerton CA 92632. (714)879-0075. President: Mary Ann Taggart. Gallery. Estab. 1973. Represents 15 (preferably local) craftworkers. Considers all crafts except decoupage. Fine and primitive one-of-a-kind pieces. Price range: $3-600; bestsellers: $3-50. Works on consignment. Craftworker sets retail price. Rental gallery fee: $50/month. Books from 2 months to 1 year in advance. Work may be shipped or hand-delivered. Dealer pays insurance for exhibited work. Reports in 7-14 days.
Profile: Displays change every month. "Association artists take turns working in the gallery. We charge no percentage on works. We advertise in southern California publications and have monthly meet-the-artists open houses." Best selling time: Christmas.

THE COMPANY STORE, 93 S. Central Ave. 84, Campbell CA 95008. (408)866-0232. Manager: Debbie de Diego. Craft/gift shop. Estab. 1977. Represents 60 craftworkers.
Acceptable Work: Considers all crafts. Especially needs glass art and metalworking. Specializes in contemporary and fine art crafts. One-of-a-kind items only. Price range: $1-11,500; bestsellers: $3.50-200.
Terms: Works on consignment; 40% commission. Retail price set by craftworker. Call for appointment. Reports in 4 weeks. Work may be shipped or hand-delivered.
Profile: Shop has "excess of 10,000 square feet for display," and is located in historical area. "The artisan must supply his/her own display. The employees then take on the responsibility of keeping it looking nice. The artisan is contacted when more stock is needed and may remain in The Company Store until either the artisan or the manager thinks it is no longer profitable for either party to remain." Customers: homemakers and tourists. Best selling time: summer and Christmas.

COUNTRYWIDE CRAFTS, 3608 The Barnyard, Carmel CA 93923. (408)624-6511. Contact: Marion or Bill Williams. Gallery/gift shop. Estab. 1976. Represents 50-100 craftworkers. Considers ceramics; clothing; glass art; metalsmithing; needlecrafts; pottery; quilting; weavings; and woodcrafting. Especially needs wood turnings; wood carvings; and functional ceramics. Primitive and contemporary one-of-a-kind items. Price range: $5-400; bestsellers: $10-50. Buys outright and occasionally works on consignment; 40% commission. Retail price set by joint agreement. Requires exclusive area representation. Reports at end of month. Deliver work personally by prior agreement only. Dealer pays insurance for exhibited work.
Profile: Gallery shows handcrafted pieces from all over America; nothing imported; mostly functional. Customers have high incomes. Best selling time: June-December; heaviest wholesale buying time: May-September.

CRAFT & FOLK ART MUSEUM, (formerly The Egg & The Eye), 5814 Wilshire Blvd., Los Angeles CA 90036. (213)937-5544. Shop Manager: Ann Robbins. Museum gift shop. Estab. 1965. Represents 200 craftworkers.
Acceptable Work: Considers ceramics, dollmaking, glass art, jewelry, pottery and woodcrafting. Specializes in fine and contemporary crafts. One-of-a-kind and handmade production-line items. Price range: $3-500; bestsellers: $5-25, $50-100.
Terms: Buys outright and works on consignment; 50% commission. Retail price set by manager or joint agreement. Call for appointment. Reports as soon as possible. Work may be shipped or hand delivered. Dealer pays insurance on exhibited work. Display time: 4-6 weeks, or all year if sales justify.

Profile: "Each artist is visually separated from other artists, the name clearly with work." Heaviest wholesale buying time: summer-fall; best selling time: December.

THE CRAFT GALLERY, 126 San Jose Ave., Box 155, Capitola CA 95010. (408)475-4724. Contact: Carin Mudgett. Craft shop. Estab. 1970. Represents 100 craftworkers.
Acceptable Work: Considers batik; candlemaking; ceramics; glass art; jewelry; leatherworking; metalsmithing; pottery; and woodcrafting. All styles; utilitarian only. Price range: $2-200.
Terms: Works on consignment and buys outright; 40% commission. Craftworker sets retail price. Requires exclusive area representation. Reports in 3 weeks. Work may be shipped or hand-delivered. Dealer pays shipping and insurance for exhibited work.

CRAFT STREET, INC., 24164 Laguna Hills Mall, Laguna Hills CA 92653. (714)770-0144. Contact: Margaret Hogg. Craft shop. Estab. 1977. Represents 100 craftworkers.
Acceptable Work: Considers candlemaking, ceramics, jewelry, leatherworking, metalsmithing, pottery, scrimshaw and woodcrafting. Handmade production-line items only. Price range: 75¢-800; bestsellers: $10-50.
Terms: Works on consignment; 24% commission. Craftworker sets retail price. Rental gallery fee: $500-850/year. Reports in 2 weeks. Work may be shipped or hand-delivered.
Profile: Craftworker constructs own display. "We have attractive stores in enclosed malls such as Los Cerritos Center, Laguna Hills and Marina Pacifica. We supply storage space and will stock for craftsmen." Heaviest wholesale buying time: October-December; best selling time: November-December.

CRAFTSMAN'S GALLERY OF CARMEL, Box 1249, Carmel CA 93921. (408)624-8850. Contact: Sammy Crum. Craft and gift shop. Estab. 1977. Represents 40-50 California craftworkers.
Acceptable Work: Considers all crafts except clothing and quilting. Fine one-of-a-kind and handmade production-line items. Price range: $1-1,000; bestsellers: $5-75.
Terms: Crafts shop is on a membership basis. "Artists pay a membership fee of $400/year for a 4x2 space; or $250 for a 2x2 space. They work 1-2 days a month or pay a $24 workshift fee and receive 80% of the retail price of their work." Craftworker sets retail price. Exclusive Carmel representation. Work may be shipped or hand-delivered. Dealer pays insurance for exhibited work.
Profile: "Members of the Gallery design and build their own display using natural motif. They also provide back stock to replace items as they are sold."

CRAFTSMAN'S GALLERY OF CARMEL, c/o Craftsman's Gallery of Carmel, Box 1249, Carmel CA 93921. (408)624-8850. Contact: Sammy Crum. Craft and gift shop located in New Heritage Harbor Complex (near Fisherman's Warf and the Conference Center). Estab. 1979. Represents 100 California craftworkers.
Acceptable Work: Considers all crafts except clothing and quilting. Fine one-of-a-kind and handmade production-line items. Price range: $1-1,000; bestsellers: $5-75.
Terms: Crafts shop is on a membership basis. "Artists pay a membership fee of $500/year for a 4x2 space; or $300 for a 2x2 space. They work 1-2 days a month or pay a $24 workshift fee and receive 80% of the retail price of their work." Craftworker sets retail price. Exclusive Carmel representation. Work may be shipped or hand-delivered. Dealer pays insurance for exhibited work.
Profile: "Members will decorate the interior of their displays using natural motif. They also provide back stock to replace items as they are sold."

CREATIVE CORNERS, 10661 Ellis St., Fountain Valley CA 92708. (714)964-2715. Contact: Bill Dominguez. Craft shop/rental gallery. Estab. 1975. Represents 80 craftworkers at 3 locations. $516-876/year. Send resume and request further information. Work may be shipped or hand delivered.
Acceptable Work: Considers all crafts except clothing. Handmade production-line items. Price range: 50¢-$700; bestsellers: $5-60. Lease agreement; 27% commission. Dealer pays insurance on exhibited work. Craftworker sets retail price.
Profile: "We are a new type store designed to assist craftsmen in marketing their handcrafted items in regional shopping centers. Each craftsman has the opportunity to lease space for his own display of his own design on a yearly basis. Once the display is in position and stock provided, we take care of all merchandising, cleaning and selling of your merchandise which allows extra time for the craftsman to generate more of his craft." Heaviest wholesale buying time and best selling time: Christmas and gift occasions.

CUSTOM HANDWEAVERS, Allied Arts Guild, Arbor Road and Creek Drive, Menlo Park CA 94025. (415)325-0626. Contact: Kathy Davis. Craft shop. Estab. 1965. Represents 10 craftworkers. Considers ceramics; pottery; wall hangings; and weavings. Handmade production-line items only. Price range: $1-300; bestsellers: $5-30. Works on consignment; 40% commission. Retail price set by joint agreement. Reports in 1 week. Work may be hand-delivered. Dealer pays insurance for exhibited work. Best selling time: May-December.

DAVID, Glass Department, Ocean & Dolores, Carmel-by-the-Sea CA 93921. See Light Opera, San Francisco.

DE SAISSET ART GALLERY & MUSEUM—GALLERY SHOP, The University of Santa Clara, Santa Clara CA 95053. (408)984-4528. Manager/Gallery Coordinator: Georgianna Lagoria. Museum gift shop. Estab. 1970. Represents 5-10 craftworkers. "There is an attempt to restrain the craftworkers to local talent; however, the overriding goal is one of quality.
Acceptable Work: Considers candlemaking, ceramics, glass art, jewelry, pottery, scrimshaw, woodcrafting and anything unusual. Price range: $1-30; bestsellers; $2-17. "The items must be reasonable in price, as this is on a University campus and budgets are limited for most students."
Terms: Buys outright and works on consignment; 40% commission. "Both policies have been used, and it depends on how much of a 'sure thing' an item is." Retail price set by joint agreement. Send slides. Reports in 1 week. Work must be hand-delivered. Display time: less than 2 months.
Profile: "We are a non-profit organization selling catalogues and posters from past and present museum exhibitions, a large selection of art cards, craft items and one-of-a-kind antiques. Items are displayed to enhance their best features by being placed alongside other items that blend well. They are rearranged to give a fresh appearance if it is obvious that their potential is being spoiled." Customers: students, faculty, staff and visitors of the University. Heaviest wholesale buying time: August-October, pre-Valentine's Day and pre-Easter; best selling time: Christmas, Valentine's Day and Easter.
To Break In: "Information about crafts should be presented in a straight forward fashion, a sample is most helpful. Variety is welcomed, as we are striving to build up a following of customers who come here first for their special shopping. To date, we have been very successful."

DEL MANO GALLERY, 11981 San Vicente, Los Angeles CA 90049. (213)476-8508. Contact: Ray Leier or Jan Francis. Craft/gift shop and gallery. Estab. 1973. Represents 200-300 U.S. craftworkers.
Acceptable Work: Considers batik, candlemaking, ceramics, clothing, dollmaking, glass art, jewelry, leatherworking, metalsmithing, pottery, scrimshaw, soft sculpture, wall hangings, weavings and woodcrafting. Specializes in contemporary fine crafts. One-of-a-kind and handmade production-line items. Retail price: 60¢-$7,000; bestsellers: 60¢-$300.
Terms: Buys outright and works on consignment; 40% commission. Retail price set by joint agreement. Requires exclusive immediate area representation. Send slides/photos with SASE. Reports in 3 weeks. Work may be shipped or hand-delivered. "Artist pays shipping to us—we pay return shipping on consignment." Dealer pays insurance on exhibited work, except for petty theft.
Profile: "We are a comfortable mixture of well-made gift-oriented items and exquisite one-of-a-kind fine art pieces—all 3 dimensional. We carry only work done in the U.S.—no imports, and have particularly fine jewelry and woodwork. Pieces are held 25-50 days on consignment. If there is no movement, we return them. We display all consignment work—only storing duplicates. Items are treated as individual pieces, not merchandise. Our customers are upper middle class to upper class, well educated, 18-90. They are quite sophisticated." Heaviest wholesale buying time: summer; best selling time: Christmas.
To Break In: "Establish a realistic retail price. Sell wholesale at 50%; sell retail (at fairs) at the retail price. Be complete about billing and paperwork—have clear bills with your name on them (not necessarily pre-printed)—just legible with address."

DEL MANO GALLERY, 492 S. Lake Ave., Pasadena CA 91101. (213)577-2630. Contact: Ray Leier or Jan Francis. Craft/gift shop and gallery. Estab. 1973. Represents 200-300 U.S. craftworkers.
Acceptable Work: Considers batik, candlemaking, ceramics, clothing, dollmaking, glass art, jewelry, leatherworking, metalsmithing, pottery, scrimshaw, soft sculpture, wall hangings, weavings and woodcrafting. Especially needs well-made mens gift items under $50. Specializes

in contemporary fine crafts. One-of-a-kind and handmade production-line items. Retail price: 60¢-$7,000; bestsellers: $30-150.
Terms: Buys outright and works on consignment; 40% commission. Retail price set by joint agreement. Prefers exclusive area representation. Send resume and slides/photos with SASE or call for appointment. Reports in 3 weeks. Work may be shipped or hand-delivered. "Artist pays shipping to us—we pay return shipping on consignment." Dealer pays insurance on exhibited work except for petty theft.
Profile: "We are a gallery and shop in one, in that we carry many items that are gift oriented (wallets) and many that are fine gallery-type pieces (miniature ivory carvings). However, we present all the work of an artist together with name cards to identify the work. We use hardwood and glass display cases, some shelves and pedestals." Customers: ages 18-50 conservative, upper middle class incomes and 'looking for quality function.'" Heaviest wholesale buying time: summer (orders for Christmas); best selling time: Christmas.
To Break In: "Be professional, make appointments. Establish a realistic retail price. Sell wholesale at 50%; sell retail (at fairs) at the retail price. Be complete about billing and paperwork—have clear bills with your name on them (not necessarily pre-printed)—just legible with address."

DOVETAIL, 3027 Fillmore St., San Francisco CA 94123. (415)931-4949. Contact: Melva Christopherson or Carla Roth. Craft/gift/furniture shop. Estab. 1972. Represents 100 American craftworkers. "Most of our suppliers are from the West, but we want to change that."
Acceptable Work: Considers batik, ceramics, clothing, dollmaking, glass art, jewelry, leatherworking, pottery, quilting, soft sculpture, wall hangings, weavings and woodcrafting. "We're interested in modern or contemporary styles; classic, not faddy; no Eskimo or Indian crafts. Special emphasis is placed on wood. We're always looking for any new approach to handcrafted home furnishings." One-of-a-kind and handmade production-line items. Price range: $1-2,500; bestsellers: $5-100.
Terms: Buys outright and works on consignment; 40% commission. Retail price set by joint agreement. Requires exclusive area representation within "our shopping area within San Francisco." Shipping negotiable; dealer pays all insurance. Unsold consigned pieces returned after 6 months.
Profile: "We specialize in hardwood furnishings. The beautiful furniture is a very dramatic background to the other handcrafted home accessories we sell. We are a small crowded store which mades every attempt to show a craftsman's work to its best advantage." Customers: ages 20-50, upper-middle to upper income bracket. Heaviest wholesale buying time: pre-Christmas and pre-summer; best selling time: Christmas and summer.
To Break In: "Consistency of quality is very important. We trust our long distance suppliers to pick out and send us a good selection."

DOWN HOME, 4600 El Camino Real, Los Altos CA 94022. (415)941-0518. Contact: Bill or Kathie Ureda. Craft coop gallery; $550-275/year. Estab. 1976. Represents 100 craftworkers, mainly from California.
Acceptable Work: Considers all crafts. Especially needs bread dough. Specializes in "gift-oriented/home decorating items of a medium grade to high quality. Some almost border on the fine arts but most are crafts." Handmade production-line items. Price range: $1-350; bestsellers $5-65.
Terms: Leases space; 20% commission. Craftworker pays insurance on exhibited work and sets retail price. Write with SASE or call for appointment. Reports in 1 week. Work may be shipped or hand delivered.
Profile: "Our stores are open 7 days a week, year round, providing maximum exposure. Artists build their own displays with certain size and design criteria but need not be present in the store. They can be selling at the same time they are home working! The store charges a minimal fee of $35 a month for those artists who do not work two 8-hour sales shifts in the store each month. We provide cashiering, management, advertising—all that is required to run a store of this nature and size in a major shopping center with hundreds of daily customers." Customers: "In the Bay area, residents are in the upper middle class range. The Stanford store is in the upper upper class range and demand high quality and unusual items. The Serramonte store is in the middle income area, a high volume area—less expensive unsophisticated items move best. Oakridge and San Antonio and Hillsdale are medium to high income." Heaviest wholesale buying time and best selling time: Christmas.
To Break In: "We need serious craftspeople who work full time at their craft and need reliable, honest and consistent outlets in the Bay area."

DREAM MASTERS, A GALLERY OF FANTASY & SCIENCE FICTION ART, 6399 Wilshire Blvd., Los Angeles CA 90048. (213)933-7326. Contact: Gail Selinger or Harrison Rose. Gallery. Estab. 1978. Represents 15 craftworkers.
Acceptable Work: Considers all crafts except clothing. Will accept costumes, though. "We are a thematic gallery featuring only science fiction and fantasy. We accept jewelry to ceramics to tapestry to any craft whose theme corresponds to our gallery." One-of-a-kind and handmade production-line items. Price range: $20-250; bestsellers: $6-10,000.
Terms: Works on consignment; 50% commission. Gallery sets retail price. Send slides with SASE. Reports in 2 weeks. Work may be shipped or hand-delivered. Dealer pays insurance on exhibited work. "We have shows that last from as little as 3 weeks to as long as 3 months."
Profile: "Everything is displayed attractively from display cases or sculpture stands. Paintings are framed and hung on the walls. Jewelry is placed in locked cases as are other items made of precious metals and/or with precious to semi-precious stones. Customers are of all ages with $5,000 a year to millionaire incomes; science fiction and fantasy interests. Best selling time: pre-Christmas.

THE EMERSON GALLERY, 18676 Ventura Blvd., Tarzana CA 91356. (213)342-3777. Contact: Wayne LaCom. Gallery. Estab. 1962. Represents 10 craftworkers. Best selling time: fall-spring.
Acceptable Work: Considers ceramics, glass art and pottery. Price range: $20-300; bestsellers: $10-200.
Terms: Works on consignment; 40% commission. Retail price set by craftworker. Requires exclusive area representation. Send resume and slides. Reports on inquiries in 2 weeks. Reports in 1 week. Displays work 2 months.

ENLIGHTENED SIGHTS STAINED GLASS, 813 State St., Santa Barbara CA 93101. (805)962-3008. Contact: Mindy Rosenblatt or Judith Bijou. Gift shop and gallery. Estab. 1978. Represents 50-60 craftworkers.
Acceptable Work: Considers blown and stained glass only. "In stained glass, we accept panels and hangings from a few square inches up to 25 square feet. The style is the choice of the artist—contemporary to traditional, 2 or 3 dimensional—as long as it reflects good taste and good craftsmanship." Blown glass: paperweights, vases, lamps and goblets. "We want to expose people to the vast possibilities glass holds today so style can be very traditional or very experimental; it can be drawn from any theme, culture or abstract idea." One-of-a-kind and handmade production-line items. Price range: $5-1,300; bestsellers: $5-40.
Terms: Buys outright and works on consignment; 40% commission. Retail price set by joint agreement. "Most of the work is on consignment (from artists all around the country to our own work). Some work is purchased outright at wholesale prices, particularly the smaller items and much of the blown glass. Requires exclusive Piccadilly Square representation. Send slides or call for appointment. Reports in 1-2 weeks. Work may be shipped but prefers hand-delivered work to insure safe arrival. Dealer pays insurance on exhibited work. "Goods stolen, lost or irreparably damaged are treated as if sold." Display time: approximately 2-6 months.
Profile: "Located in a large open shopping mall in the main area of Santa Barbara, our store is a combination of a custom studio (at the back of the store) and a gallery. Special one-person exhibits for 2-3 weeks may be scheduled for each month in late 1979. Stained glass panels are hung against windows, walls and open spaces; lamps are suspended from attractive wood beams, or on shelves or desks; paperweights and blown glass creations are displayed on shelves against walls and in very attractive, contemporary display showcases. Our location is excellent, in that we receive a lot of foot traffic, and are frequented by tourists and residents of Santa Barbara (which also homes a large university). The general population of the area is quite well-to-do, with a good art-awareness and appreciation for quality work. Ages of customers vary from 15-70." Heaviest wholesale buying and best selling time: Christmas and summer.

FAMILY & FRIENDS, 900 N. Point St., San Francisco CA 94109. (415)885-1072. Manager: Terrence Gockman. Craft shop. Estab. 1974. Represents 100 regional craftworkers. Considers one-of-a-kind ceramics and soft sculpture. Especially needs low-fire ceramics and porcelain of colorful design and colorful cotton clothing. Utilitarian and/or decorative. Price range: $1-250; bestsellers: $3-15. Works on consignment and buys outright; 33% commission. Retail price set by joint agreement. Reports in 1 week. Work may be shipped or hand-delivered. Dealer pays insurance for exhibited work.
Profile: Best selling time: summer and Christmas; heaviest wholesale buying time: spring and fall.

THE FIBER & PRINT WORKS, 1030 Mission St., S. Pasadena CA 91030. (213)441-2368. Director: B. Anderson. Craft/gift shop/gallery/school. Estab. 1968. Represents 10-20 craftworkers.
Acceptable Work: Considers batik, ceramics, clothing, needlecrafts, quilting, soft sculpture, wall hangings, weavings and original prints. No kits. One-of-a-kind and handmade production-line items. Price range: $10-3,500; bestsellers: $10-500.
Terms: Buys outright and works on consignment; 25% commission. Rental space fee: 1/2 the price of exhibition costs. Retail price set by joint agreement. On large items, must have 30/60/90 day net. Requires exclusive area representation. Send resume, slides, SASE, call for appointment, or (prefers) portfolio presentation. Reports in 2 weeks. Work may be shipped or hand delivered.
Profile: "We are located in a refurbished grocery store on a busy street with many antique and fine handcraft stores within walking distance. The area is safe with a low crime rate. The gallery is spacious with good lighting and there are excellent window displays which can be seen from the street. The school is well-established and has a serious learning environment for students who wish to become professional weavers and printmakers." Customers: upper incomes, well educated. Heaviest wholesale buying and best selling time: fall.
To Break In: "Must have guaranteed production and be able to fullfill commitments. Artist must understand economics and maintain high degreee of professionalism."

FIBERWORKS, Center for the Textile Arts, 1940 Bonita Ave., Berkeley CA 94704. Contact: Gallery Committee. The gallery houses fiber-related art work, but is not restricted to this area. A gallery committee is responsible for selecting the subject matter, inviting the artists to exhibit and for scheduling. Interested artists may submit slides and photos, and a resume; the committee reviews the slides submitted 3-4 times a year. "Our gallery shows are announced in our brochure which is mailed several times yearly. If interested, please write to be put on our free mailing list."

FORGE PATIO ART GALLERIE, ASSOCIATION, 3420 Mt. Diablo Blvd., LaFayette CA 94549. (415)284-1080. Contact: Barbara Speck. Gallery. Estab. 1972. Represents 25 Bay area artists and craftworkers. Considers batik; ceramics; glass art; pottery; wall hangings; and weavings. "We would like to carry some ceramic or wood jewelry — unique and different in design." Fine one-of-a-kind items only. Price range: $3-400; bestsellers average $20. Works on consignment; 40% commission. Craftworker sets retail price. Reports on first or second Tuesday of each month. Work may be hand-delivered or mail slides, photos and biography. Dealer pays insurance on exhibited work.
Profile: "The gallery, a showroom for 6 professional artists, also exhibits works of Bay area craftsmen. We sell unique, one-of-a-kind items of local artists in a well-lighted, beautifully displayed gallery. It is located in the El Diablo Forge Guild—a complex of shops and restaurants, part of which was once an actual forge. Each month, part of the gallery is devoted to featuring one (or a group of) artists and/or craftsmen. The remainder of the gallery is always a representation of our affiliated artists and craftsmen." Best selling time: Christmas, spring and fall.

GALERIE DE TOURS, Box 4996, Carmel CA 93921. Contact: Robert J. Kaller. Gallery.
Acceptable Work: Considers sculpture. "Those we represent must have some previous record of achievement. Recently, our gallery has handled works more in a historical vein." Price range: $500-75,000.
Terms: Works on consignment; 40-50% commission. Requires exclusive area representation. Charges commission on art sold in area after exclusive representation. Gallery pays insurance on exhibited work. 4 weeks minimum exposure.

GALLERY 8, 7464 Girard Ave., La Jolla CA 92037. (714)452-3732. Co-Director: Ruth Newmark. Estab. 1973. Represents over 50 craftworkers.
Acceptable Work: "We offer a collection of traditional and contemporary crafts whose common denominator is good design." Displays feature jewelry, ceramics, glass, wood, textiles, basketry, some furniture. Offers diverse juried shows, lectures, and workshops throughout the year. Price range: $1-1,500; bestsellers: $15-30. Buys outright or on consignment; 40% commission. Retail price set by gallery or joint agreement. Write. Reports in 2 weeks. Dealer pays shipping from shop and insurance for exhibited work.
Profile: Heaviest wholesale buying time: fall; best selling time: October-December. Customers buy crafts for artistic value or gifts.

GARENDO GALLERY, 2955 Ventura Blvd., Studio City CA 91604. (213)783-1861. President: Masako. Craft and gift shop. Estab. 1972. Represents 18 craftworkers. Best selling time: Christmas. Gallery store hours are 11-6 Tuesday-Thursday.
Acceptable Work: Considers batik; candlemaking; ceramics; clothing; glass art; jewelry; pottery; wall hangings; weavings; and woodcrafting. Fine or primitive one-of-a-kind items. Price range: $1-500.
Terms: Works on consignment and buys outright; up to 50% commission. Retail price set by joint agreement. Requires exclusive area representation. Work may be shipped or hand-delivered. Reports in 2-3 weeks.

GIFTS UNIQUE, 860 Lancaster Blvd., Lancaster CA 93534. (805)942-2113. Contact: Steve Buffalo. Gift shop. Estab. 1976. Represents 4-10 craftworkers.
Acceptable Work: Considers candlemaking, ceramics, dollmaking, glass art, jewelry, leatherworking, pottery, soft sculpture and woodcrafting. One-of-a-kind and handmade production-line items. "We carry a large selection of Indian jewelry and crafts, handblown glass, wood, crystal, German figurines, Norman Rockwell prints, cards and, in general, gifts you won't find just anywhere." Price range: $5-800; bestsellers: $10-100.
Terms: Buys outright and works on consignment; 25% commission. Retail price set by joint agreement. Call for appointment or send photos with catalog or flyer to indicate quality of work. Reports in 3 weeks. Work may be shipped or hand-delivered.
Profile: Items displayed on wall shelving, gondolas and in specialized corners. Uses track lighting, glass and wooden displays in 1,500 square feet of space. Customers: teenagers-senior citizens. Heaviest wholesale buying and best selling time: fall. "25% of our business is done in November and December."

GLAD HAND, 203-203½ Ave. I, Redondo Beach CA 90277. (213)540-2221. Contact: Boni Erickson. Craft shop. Estab. 1969. Represents 6 craftworkers.
Acceptable Work: Considers ceramics; glass art; jewelry; pottery; wall hangings; and weavings. Fine one-of-a-kind and handmade production-line items. Price range: $15-600; bestsellers: $35-75.
Terms: Works on consignment and buys outright; 33% commission. Retail price set by joint agreement. Requires exclusive area representation for jewelry. Reports in 4 weeks. Work may be shipped or hand-delivered. Dealer pays insurance for exhibited work.
Profile: "Large collections are featured 1 month; small collections featured 2-3 months." Best selling time: spring and Christmas; heaviest wholesale buying time: spring-summer.

THE GLASS FACTORY, 906 Broadway, Alameda CA 94501. (415)523-1010. Contact: Clarine Sauza. Stained glass shop. Estab. 1974. Represents 5 craftworkers. Send resume or call for appointment. Reports in 1 week. Work may be shipped or hand delivered. Best selling time: Christmas.
Acceptable Work: Considers glass, etchings, panels and lamps. Especially needs stained glass. One-of-a-kind and handmade production-line items. Price range: $7.50-5,000. Works on consignment; 30% commission. Craftworker sets retail price.

THE GUILD STORE, 131 12th St., Sacramento CA 95814. (916)446-2395. Contact: John Reiger. Craft shop. Estab. 1972. Represents 20 Sacramento area craftworkers. Considers all crafts except decoupage; dollmaking; molded ceramics; and tole painting. Especially needs blown and leaded glass, and leather. All styles. Price range: 25¢-$500; bestsellers: $2-20. Works on consignment; 38% commission. "Most items in the store belong to Guild Store Coop members. Each member works in the store 1 day a week and pays a 16% commission on sales to the store." Craftworker sets retail price. Reports in 2 weeks. Strongly prefers hand delivery. "We like to keep consignment items in the store a maximum of 4 months." Best selling time: June-August and November-December.

HALLIE'S WEST GALLERY, 3045 Ventura Blvd., Studio City CA 91604. (213)986-3837. Contact: Hallie Katz. Gallery. Estab. 1976.
Acceptable Work: Considers ceramics; clothing; glass art; jewelry; metalsmithing; soft sculpture; wall hangings; weavings; and woodcrafting. Fine one-of-a-kind and handmade production-line items only. Price range: $10-3,500; bestsellers: $25-250.
Terms: Works on consignment; 40% commission. Retail price set by joint agreement. Work may be shipped or hand-delivered. Dealer pays return shipping and insurance for exhibited work.
Profile: "Work is displayed on pedestals and in acrylic dome showcases and cubes; arranged

with other artists' work, grouped together when possible or necessary.'' Best selling time: winter-spring.

HAPPY HANGUPS, 200 W. Olive Ave., Fresno CA 93728. Contact: Norma Bates. Craft/gift shop. Estab. 1977. Represents 50 craftworkers.
Acceptable Work: Considers batik, candlemaking, ceramics, decoupage, dollmaking, glass art, jewelry, metalsmithing, needlecrafts, pottery, quilting, soft sculpture, wall hangings, weavings and woodcrafting. Especially needs wall hangings and small unique pottery/clay items. "Colors seem to sell items; therefore, items should fit into the surroundings. Any item that lends itself toward antiques goes well. Handmade production-line items only. Price range: $1-100; bestsellers: $5-25.
Terms: Buys outright and works on consignment; 40% commission. Also leases display spaces for $10-25/month, plus 20% commission. Craftworker sets retail price. Send slides. SASE. Reports in 4 weeks. Work may be shipped or hand-delivered. Dealer pays insurance on exhibited work.
Profile: "Ours is the only craft shop on the street of 17 or more antique shops. People walk from one shop to another with a map. The shop is in a 50-year old house and has a homey feeling. The coffee pot is on, there's a fireplace, and you can wander from one room to another, sit down and have coffee and cookies. We change displays often and often have yard/sidewalk sales outside. There's no competition in the crafts market.'' Customers: "middle-agers, newlyweds, and a very few young teenagers. They buy for themselves and their homes. All are very interested in knowing how things are made and the background of the craftsperson." Heaviest wholesale buying time: summer (for Christmas); best selling time: Christmas.
To Break In: "It's a really big job to get people to buy crafts for gifts—they need to really look great, no room for imperfections. Craftspeople should purchase crafts to give as gifts. Once people receive handcrafted gifts as presents, they will start buying them for other people. Jewelry doesn't move well."

HIDE 'N' FREAK LEATHER WORKSHOP & CRAFTS BAZAAR, 437 E. Main St., Ventura CA 93001. Contact: Jeff. Craft and gift shop. Estab. 1970. Represents 10 craftworkers. Considers leatherworking. Price range: $3-150; bestsellers: $9-25. Buys outright. Gallery sets retail price. Work may be hand-delivered. Heaviest wholesale buying time: November; best selling time: December.

HORIZON GALLERY, 32 B Miller Ave., Mill Valley CA 94941. (415)383-1512. Director: Mr. Richard Tokar. Craft shop/gallery. Estab. 1975. Represents 20 craftworkers.
Acceptable Work: Considers ceramics, glass art, jewelry, metalsmithing, pottery, soft sculpture, wall hangings and weavings. Specializes in fine designer and contemporary items. One-of-a-kind and handmade production-line items. Price range: $5-2000; bestsellers: $5-500.
Terms: Buys outright and works on consignment; 40% commission. Dealer pays insurance on exhibited items. Retail price set by joint agreement. Sometimes requires exclusive area representation. Send resume, slides or call for appointment. Reports in 3 weeks. Work may be shipped or hand delivered.
Profile: "An item is displayed on the appropriate shelf to enhance the item best. Jewelry is displayed in special cases as is small sculpture. Our ceramic and glass displays are unique and finely-made. An item is usually on display for 30 days before being taken down. We often hold items on consignment for 60-90 days, especially if we are featuring the artist. We are located in a well-traveled area.'' Heaviest wholesale buying time: holidays; best selling time: Christmas, summer, and all major gift giving events.

THE IMAGE, 320 University Ave., Palo Alto CA 94301. (415)324-9178. Contact: David Midlo. Craft/gift shop/gallery. Estab. 1974. Represents 40 craftworkers.
Acceptable Work: Considers candlemaking, ceramics, glass art, jewelry, metalsmithing, pottery, photography, and graphics. No oil paintings. Especially needs one-of-a-kind jewelry ($100+). Specializes in contemporary pieces. Handmade production-line items. Price range: $4-300; bestsellers: $6-65.
Terms: Buys outright and works on consignment; 40% commission. Dealer pays insurance on exhibited items. Retail price set by joint agreement. Call for appointment. Reports in 1 week. Work may be shipped or hand delivered.
Profile: "The main floor displays crafts, gifts and jewelry. The lower level, photography and graphics. The prime displayers on both levels are redwood shelf jewelry display cases against redwood paneled walls." Customers: ages 13-65, high income groups. Heaviest wholesale buying time: summer-fall; best selling time: December.

IN THINGS, 1041 Swarthmore Ave., Pacific Palisades CA 90272. Contact: Judy Elliott. Gift shop. Estab. 1972. Represents 2-50 crafworkers.
Acceptable Work: Considers clothing, jewelry, pottery and soft sculpture. "Any of these is OK, but wall space is very limited. Size matters because the store is small." Especially needs infants' and men's gifts and custom work (names, sports, etc.). One-of-a-kind and handmade production-line items. Price range: 59¢ (will only sell inexpensive items in packages of 6) to $150 ("looking to raise this figure"); bestsellers: $2.50-35.
Terms: Buys outright and works on consignment; 25-35% commission. "We pay on a monthly basis if volume merits." Retail price set by joint agreement. Requires exclusive area representation. Send resume or call for appointment. Reports in 1 week. Dealer usually pays insurance on exhibited work.
Profile: "We produce a catalog and if an item is great, it will be shown. Custom work is shown in sample form with a common name (eg., 'Karen'). Orders are taken from sample; 50% advance payment from customer guaranteed. We are a tiny department store in 660 square feet carrying toys, gifts, clothing and jewelry from infants through adults." Customers: 37,000 people live in and/or visit beach community; well traveled; mean income of $38,000/year. (Average house sells for $250,000-500,000). "The community will travel to Beverly Hills to be seen and pay more for items we may carry. We are trying to become our own 'Gucci' so Beverly Hills will come to us." Heaviest wholesale buying time: spring (for test markets), and Christmas (½ of annual business); best selling time: Christmas and May-June.

INTERNATIONAL HANDCRAFT & SUPPLY, 1550 Westwood Blvd., Los Angeles CA 90024. (213)474-6557. Contact Barbara or Betty Wynn Paller. Craft/gift/supply shop. Considers wall hangings and weavings. One-of-a-kind pieces. "We display weavings and macrame pieces mostly, some baskets. We cater to people who want to make their own artwork. We give a 15% discount to artists and shop owners with a resale license." Best selling time: pre-Christmas.

IRIS, 894 Solano Ave., Berkeley CA 94707. (415)525-1043. Contact: Susan or Ira Klein. Craft shop. Estab. 1976. Represents 150 craftworkers.
Acceptable Work: Considers all crafts except decoupage and tole painting. Especially needs "all medias with the unicorn theme—the store specialty. Fine one-of-a-kind and handmade production-line items. Price range: 5¢-$890; bestsellers: 5¢-$50.
Terms: Works on consignment and buys outright; 40% commission. Retail price set by joint agreement. Reports in 1 week. Work may be shipped (UPS only) or hand-delivered. "Return postage and insurance must be included." Dealer pays insurance for exhibited work. Work displayed for 3-month period.
Profile: Shop is decorated with wall-to-wall carpeting, spot and fluorescent lighting and wooden fixtures. Display for consigned items is total responsibility of the craftworker. Strive to achieve creative displays, e.g., telephone booth changing room. Customers are primarily of a median income ($30,000/year) and are often U.C. Berkeley faculty and professionals. Heaviest wholesale buying time: fall-winter; best selling time: winter-Christmas.

I-YE-QUEE GIFT SHOP, Box 7, Hoopa CA 95546. Contact: Vivien Hailstone. Gift shop. Estab. 1951. Represents 4 northern California Indian craftworkers. Considers jewelry and pottery with contemporary American Indian design. Price range: $1-500; bestsellers: $3-200. Works on consignment and buys outright; 30% commission. Craftworker sets retail price. Reports in 4 weeks. Work may be shipped or hand-delivered. Dealer pays return shipping and insurance on exhibited work. Customers are mainly tourists. Heaviest wholesale buying time: May-June; best selling time: July-September.

KAURI SHELL GALLERY, 1023 H St., Arcata CA 95501. (707)443-9586. Director: Geraldine Serpa. Gallery. Estab. 1977. Represents 20 craftwomen. Retail price set by craftworker. Reports in 4 weeks.
Acceptable Work: Considers batik; clothing; jewelry; needlecrafts; quilting; soft sculpture; wall hangings; and weavings. Fine one-of-a-kind pieces only. Price range: $20-200; bestsellers: $20-100. Handles membership work only."We are a women's gallery; we show only fine crafts."

KLEIN ART GALLERY, 332 N. Rodeo Dr., Beverly Hills CA 90210. (213)274-8955. Contact: David Klein. Considers sculpture. Maximum size: 30x40. Buys outright or on consignment; 40% commission. Bestsellers: $300-3,500. Retail price set by joint agreement. Sometimes requires exclusive area representation. Send photos of work or call or write for interview. SASE. 2-6 months exposure.

Shops and Galleries   93

ESTHER LEWITTES DESIGN GALLERY, 8344 Melrose Ave., Los Angeles CA 90069. (213)655-7112. Contact: Esther Lewittes. Craft and gift shop. Estab. 1973. Represents 6 craftworkers. Heaviest wholesale buying time: Christmas; best selling time: spring and fall-winter.
Acceptable Work: Considers ceramics; glass art; pottery; wall hangings; weavings; woodcrafting; and enamels. One-of-a-kind designer pieces only. Price range: $10-1,500; bestsellers: $10-1,000.
Terms: Buys outright. Gallery sets retail price. Requires exclusive area representation. Reports in 1 week. Work may be shipped or hand-delivered. Dealer pays insurance for exhibited work.

LIGHT OPERA, 900 N. Point, #102, Ghirardelli Square, San Francisco CA 94109. (415)775-7665. Contact: Buyer. Craft shop/gallery/gift shop. Estab. 1969. Represents 50-100 craftworkers. Considers high-glazed ceramics; glass jewelry/cloissone; and other art incorporating glass. Fine one-of-a-kind and handmade production-line items. Price range: $1-10,000; bestsellers: $20-500. Buys outright. Gallery sets retail price. Send slides or arrange appointment before submitting work. Reports in 2 weeks. Dealer pays insurance for exhibited work.
Profile: "We have an area of the store which is a gallery space in which we have rotating shows for periods of 4-6 weeks. These shows focus on the work of a particular craftsman or craftsmen. The rest of the store displays various artists' works—usually in groupings. We change our displays a good deal. We specialize in blown glass, leaded glass, paper weights and other uses of glass as an artistic medium." Heaviest wholesale buying time: spring and fall; best selling time: summer and winter.

LIVING DESERT RESERVE, Box 1775, Palm Desert CA 92260. (714)346-5694. Contact: June M. Sheffet. Museum gift shop. Estab. 1971. Best selling time: January-April; heaviest wholesale buying time: September-May.
Acceptable Work: Considers jewelry; metalsmithing; pottery; woodcrafting; and stone paintings. "We are desert oriented." All styles. Price range: 10¢-$15; bestsellers: $1.75-5.
Terms: Buys outright. Retail price set by joint agreement. Requires exclusive area representation. Reports in 2 weeks. Work may be shipped or hand-delivered. Dealer pays insurance for exhibited work. Most items displayed in cabinets.

LONG BEACH MUSEUM OF ART BOOKSHOP/GALLERY, 2300 E. Ocean Boulevard, Long Beach CA 90803. (213)439-2119. Manager: Barbara Hendrick. Museum gallery/book/gift shop. Estab. 1972. Represents 25 craftworkers.
Acceptable Work: Considers batik, ceramics, clothing, dollmaking, glass art, jewelry, pottery, soft sculpture, wall hangings, weavings and woodcrafting. Specializes in fine contemporary, bright-colored and ethnic items. One-of-a-kind and handmade production-line items. Price range: $5-200; bestsellers: $5-25.
Terms: Works on consignment; 40-50% commission. Retail price set by joint agreement. Requires exclusive area representation. Send slides. SASE. Reports in 4 weeks. Work may be shipped or hand delivered. Dealer pays insurance on exhibited work. Display time in gallery: 2 months.
Profile: "The bookstore/gallery located in the Carriage House on the grounds of the museum building." Customers: students, local patrons and out-of-town visitors; middle incomes. Heaviest wholesale buying and best selling time: Christmas.

LONGPRE GALLERY, 846 Foothill Blvd., La Canada CA 91011. Contact: Mrs. Longpre. Gallery. Estab. 1971. Represents 50 craftworkers. Considers painting, all medias; etchings; batik; jewelry; pottery; soft sculpture; tole painting; wall hangings; weavings; and woodcrafting. One-of-a-kind decorative designer pieces only. Price range: $20-20,000. Works on consignment; 40% commission for gallery. Retail price set by joint agreement. Requires exclusive area representation. Reports in 2 weeks. High income customers.
Promotion: Public relations work is done "in conjunction with news release. Biography poster solo exhibit." Send photos or slides with biography.

LOS ANGELES COUNTY MUSEUM OF ART, MUSEUM SHOP, 5905 Wilshire Blvd., Los Angeles CA 90036. (213)937-4250. Manager: Patricia Caspary. Museum gift shop. Estab. 1965. Represents 12 craftworkers.
Acceptable Work: Considers batik, glass art, jewelry and soft sculpture. Price range: $5-2,000; bestsellers: $10-55.
Terms: Works on consignment; 50% commission. Retail price set by joint agreement. Call or

write for appointment. Reports immediately. Work may be shipped or hand delivered. Display time: 1 month (longer if selling well).
Profile: Provides full documentation of craft for customers. Shop has "1,800 square feet of selling area. Stock includes books, reproductions, gifts, jewelry and cards." Customers: ages 25-60, professionals, upper middle class. Heaviest wholesale buying time: summer; best selling time: fall.

JUDAH MAGNES MUSEUM GIFT SHOP, 2911 Russell St., Berkeley CA 94607. Buyer: Arlene Sarver. Museum gift shop. Estab. 1974. Represents 25 craftworkers; "most are Jewish or are of Jewish interest but there are no restrictions." Considers ceramics; clothing; glass art; jewelry; metalsmithing; pottery; woodcrafting; cards; notepaper; prints; and books. All styles. Price range: 10¢-$375. Works on consignment, buys outright and orders by catalog; 40% commission. Craftworkers can set price they wish to receive, or retail price set by joint agreement. Reports in 1 week. Accepts items by mutual agreement and signed contract; don't send samples without permission.
Profile: "We have a large number of loyal customers. We sell often by mail order and wholesale to other shops." Best selling time: June-January.

MANY HANDS CREATIVE ARTS COOPERATIVE, 6350 El Cajon Blvd., San Diego CA 92115. (714)287-7150. Contact: members. Craft shop/gallery/gift shop. Represents 50 member craftworkers; "must live in San Diego County so they will be able to work in the shop about 12 hours per month to fulfill membership requirements." Considers all crafts. All styles. Price range: $1.25/finger puppet-$700/clock; bestsellers: under $10. Works on cooperative arrangement. "Due to our low overhead the craftsman receives about 95% of the retail price—it varies due to amount sold." Craftworker sets retail price. "Craftsmen should come into the store for an application for membership. We have a large turnover of craftsmen and need new craftsmen all the time. We accept new members through a jurying process. We would like to have more *serious* craftsmen apply."
Profile: "We are a cooperative with no manager. Craftsmen share all the work. The store is huge and we carry a tremendous variety of items in all price ranges. Due to our wide variety of craft items, we attract all kinds of customers—students to very wealthy people. At Christmas time they bring their lists and do all their shopping in our store." Craftworkers may use floor, wall or shelf space throughout the store or set up own display for work.
Sales Tip: "Know your market. Accept the fact that 100 small inexpensive items will sell before 1 'good' piece. Be willing to experiment with new materials and techniques and grow. Don't keep making the same thing over and over. Take classes in design and art theory—not just how-to classes."

MENDOCINO ART CENTER GALLERY, Box 36, Mendocino CA 95460. (707)937-5818. Gallery Manager: Hilda Pertha. Rental/sales gallery. Estab. 1959. Represents many craftworkers.
Acceptable Work: Considers batik; ceramics; glass art; jewelry; metalsmithing; pottery; prints; soft sculpture; and wood, bronze and other sculpture. Size and number limitations. Fine one-of-a-kind items. Price range: $2-1,500; bestsellers: $2-200.
Terms: Members only. Works on consignment and buys outright; 40% commission. Retail price set by craftworker. Send photos or slides. Reports in 3 weeks. Hand-delivered work only. Dealer pays insurance for exhibited work. "We ask to return or exchange unsold consignment items after 3-4 months."
Profile: Work is displayed in open shelf or wall displays; locked cases for small precious items. Heaviest wholesale buying time: summer-fall; best selling time: July-November.

THE MILK CO., 34 Washington St., Venice CA 90291. (213)396-9697. Contact: Clabe Hartley. Gallery/gift shop. Estab. 1971.
Acceptable Work: Considers candlemaking, ceramics, glass art, jewelry, leatherworking, pottery, scrimshaw and woodcrafting. One-of-a-kind and handmade production-line items. Price range: 50¢-$2,000; bestsellers: $10-30.
Terms: Buys outright and works on consignment. Retail price set by joint agreement. Requires exclusive area representation. Call for appointment. Reports in 2 weeks. Work may be shipped or hand delivered. Dealer pays insurance on exhibited work.
Profile: Multilevel shop/gallery. Customers: ages 25-50; $12,000+ incomes.

MOUNTAIN WEAVER, 20 S. Santa Cruz Ave., Los Gatos CA 95030. (408)354-8720. Contact: Jill Altmann. Craft shop. Estab. 1974. Considers batik; clothing; soft sculpture; wall hangings;

weavings; and baskets. Primitive one-of-a-kind and handmade production-line items. Price range: $1.50 minimum. Works on consignment; 25% commission. Retail price set by joint agreement. Reports in 1 month. Work may be shipped or hand-delivered.
Profile: Customers are ages 19-40 of mid-upper middle class backgrounds—many art students from professional families. Heaviest wholesale buying time: Christmas (November-January); best selling time: October-March.

MUD IN YOUR EYE POTTERY STUDIO, (Incorporates The Art Affaire), 50 University Ave., Los Gatos CA 95030. Contact: Frank Howell. Estab. 1971. Represents 150 craftworkers. Considers candlemaking; glass art; jewelry; leatherworking; metalsmithing; pottery; and soft sculpture. Fine one-of-a-kind and handmade production-line items only. Price range: $2-150; bestsellers: under $30. Buys outright. Retail price set by joint agreement. Requires exclusive area representation. Reports in 2 weeks. Work may be shipped or hand-delivered. Customers are ages 25-40, and very oriented toward crafts. Best selling time: Christmas and summer; heaviest wholesale buying time: fall.
To Break In: "We deal with only those craftspeople willing and able to produce on a production basis. Establish prices that are based on research, not emotion or love of an item. Have invoices with name and address of craftsperson at top (a cheap rubber stamp is fine). Include packing slips with orders and have invoices *match* packing slips."

THE MUSEUM SHOP, 3119 Fillmore St., San Francisco CA 94123. (415)922-1789. Contact: John R. Iacometti. Museum gallery/shop. Estab. 1969.
Acceptable Work: Considers batik, ceramics, clothing, dollmaking, jewelry, leatherworking, metalsmithing, pottery, quilting, scrimshaw, wall hangings and weavings. Specializes in primitive and one-of-a-kind pieces. Price range: $1.50-5,000; bestsellers: $50+.
Terms: Buys outright. Dealer sets retail price. Call for appointment. Work must be hand-delivered.
Profile: "We include artifacts and handicrafts, primitive arts (Pre-Columbian, African, Indian, Oceanic), old and unusual jewelry (sapphires, amber, rubies, trade beads, emeralds, ivory, lapis lazuli), Elegant handwoven fabrics (Peruvian ponchos to Moroccan djellabas and kaftans), handknotted Moroccan rugs, rare etchings, prints and maps. Each item has been personally selected from every part of the world to interest the collector and discriminating shopper seeking the unique and the unusual."

MY HOUSE GALLERY, 1143 Westwood Blvd., West Los Angeles CA 90024. (213)477-4073. Contact: Barry Axelrod. Craft shop/gallery/gift shop. Estab. 1976. Represents 75-80 craftworkers.
Acceptable Work: Considers all crafts. Fine one-of-a-kind and handmade production-line items. Price range: $1-2,000.
Terms: Works on consignment, buys outright and leases spaces; 50% commission. Craftworker sets retail price. Charges fee for exhibit space. Reports in 3 weeks. Dealer pays insurance for exhibited work.
Profile: "Shop is located in a very exclusive, very crowded retail area in walking distance from UCLA." Best selling time: holidays and summer.

THE NEEDLE NOOK, 35157 Yucarpa Blvd., Yucarpa CA 92399. (714)797-3782. Needlepoint shop. Estab. 1977. Represents 10 craftworkers. Best selling time: fall.
Acceptable Work: Considers ceramics; clothing; needlecrafts; wall hangings; weavings; and especially needs quilting. Handmade production-line items only. Price range: $4-395; bestsellers: $10-30.
Terms: Works on consignment and buys outright; 20% commission. Retail price set by joint agreement. Reports in 2 weeks. Work may be shipped or hand-delivered. Dealer pays return shipping and insurance for exhibited work. Work displayed until sold.

NEW WORLD RESOURCE & SUPPLY CO., 6578 Trigo Rd., Isla Vista CA 93017. (805)968-5329. Contact: Janice Emmrich. General store. Estab. 1969. Represents 15-20 craftworkers.
Acceptable Work: Considers batik; candlemaking; ceramics; clothing; jewelry; leatherworking; needlecrafts; pottery; wall hangings; weavings; macrame; and beadwork. Price range: $3-400; bestsellers: $10.
Terms: Works on consignment; 20% commission. Retail price set by joint agreement. Work may be shipped or hand-delivered.
Profile: "We try to talk the crafts up and display them favorably. We have a quite a hodge-

podge of rural needs—crafts, housewares, on and on. Customers: 50% students, 50% country folks. Heaviest wholesale buying and best selling time: pre-Christmas.

NORTH POINT PIER, Box 73720, San Francisco CA 94119. (415)981-8030. Operations Manager: Nick Hoppe. "We are a specialty shopping center dealing primarily in crafts. There are 110 shops available and a large number are craft-workshops where the artisan is manufacturing his craft in full view of the public." Write for more information.

NORTHRIDGE GALLERY & SCHOOL OF ART, 8925 Reseda Blvd., Northridge, CA 91324. (213)349-85. Contact: Lynda Ward Saltzberg. Gallery, art school and gift/supply shop. Estab. l965. Represents 5 craftworkers.
Acceptable Work: Considers batik, candlemaking, ceramics, clothing, dollmaking, glass art, jewelry, wall hangings, weavings and small sculpture. "Would prefer a variety of subtle pieces." One-of-a-kind designer pieces. Price range: $2-1,500.
Terms: Buys outright and works on consignment; 50% commission. Dealer pays insurance on exhibited work up to $150. Retail price set by joint agreement. Send slides or call in person. Work may be shipped or hand-delivered.
Profile: "We are a gallery which sells original oils, graphics, stock frames, gifts, greeting cards, prints, and offers a custom framing service. The display time is 1-2 months to start. The artist and owner discuss possibilities for display." Customers: upper middle incomes.

OLD SASH MILL, Box 1332, Santa Cruz CA 95060. (408)425-8331. Contact: Leland Zeidler. Craft Shopping Center. Estab. 1973. Represents 20 craftworkers. Considers batik; ceramics; clothing; glass art; jewelry; leatherworking; metalsmithing; wall hangings; weavings; and woodcrafting. One-of-a-kind designer pieces only; utilitarian and/or decorative. Price range: $5-1,000. Each business in the center has its own systems, methods and requirements. Write with SASE for a directory of shops, then write individual shops for further information.
Profile: "Authentic turn of the century sash mill structures with diverse representation of businesses in an attractive surrounding." Best selling time: summer and Christmas.

ORLANDO GALLERY, 17037 Ventura Blvd., Encino CA 91316. (213)789-6012. Co-Director: Philip Orlando. Gallery. Estab. 1958.
Acceptable Work: Considers ceramics, glass art, jewelry, metalsmithing, pottery, soft sculpture, wall hangings, weavings and woodcrafting. Contemporary one-of-a-kind pieces only. Price range: $50+; bestsellers: $150-200.
Terms: Works on consignment; 40% commission. Retail price set by joint agreement. Requires exclusive area representation. Send slides. SASE. Reports in 4 weeks. Work may be shipped or hand-delivered. Dealer pays insurance for exhibited work.

PACESETTER GIFTS, (formerly the Added Touch), 1582 Mission, Solvang CA 93463. Contact: Irene Parks. Gift shop. Estab. 1971. Represents 15-20 craftworkers. Considers ceramics; decoupage; porcelain figurines; glass art; jewelry; metalsmithing; woodcrafting; and Lucite and metal etchings. One-of-a-kind and handmade production-line items. Price range: $5-250; bestsellers: $5-50. Buys outright. Gallery sets retail price. Requires exclusive area representation. "Send pictures and SASE." Reports in 1-2 weeks. Work may be shipped or hand-delivered if notified in advance.
Profile: "We give all items in our shop the best care possible. Signs are always posted to cut down on handling, etc. We are a tourist area that draws from around the world. Heaviest wholesale buying time: spring-summer; best selling time: summer.

PACIFIC BASIN SCHOOL OF TEXTILE ARTS, 1659 San Pablo Ave., Berkeley CA 94702. (415)526-9836. Contact: Director. Considers batik; soft sculpture; weavings; all fiber media for contemporary and historical/ethnic textiles; and other fiber media. Craftworker supplies and installs any special lights, stands or other special installation accessories. Works on consignment; 25% commission. Bestsellers: $25-300. Craftworker sets retail price. Write for interview. Gallery sponsors reception. 5-6 weeks exposure.
Promotion: Exhibit is listed on the Pacific Basin calendar and on the gallery's brochure distributed in the community. Press release is sent to all local papers and mailing list publications.

PALM SPRINGS DESERT MUSEUM SHOP, Box 2288, 101 Museum Dr., Palm Springs CA 92262. (714)325-7186. Contact: Marcia Barrett. Museum gift shop. Estab. 1976. Represents 60 Western craftworkers. Considers ceramics; glass art; jewelry; and pottery. Fine one-of-a-kind and handmade production-line items. Price range: $4-500. Works on consignment and buys outright; commission varies. Retail price set by joint agreement. Requires exclusive area representation. Reports in 2 weeks. Work may be shipped if photos are hand-delivered by appointment first. Dealer pays return shipping and insurance. Best selling time: December-February and March-April; heaviest wholesale buying time: early fall and January.

PHOENIX SHOP, Big Sur CA 93920. Manager: Jonathan Drake. Craft and gift shop. Estab. 1965. Represents 15 craftworkers. Considers batik; candlemaking; ceramics; clothing; dollmaking; glass art; jewelry; leatherworking; metalsmithing; pottery; quilting; soft sculpture; and woodcrafting. All styles. Price range: $5-400; bestsellers: $10-50. Works on consignment and buys outright; 40% commission. Retail price set by joint agreement. Requires exclusive area representation. Hand delivered work only. Dealer pays shipping to shop if outright purchase and insurance for exhibited work. Best selling time: summer.

PLACER COUNTY MUSEUM, 175 Fulweiler Ave., Auburn CA 95603. (916)885-9570. Contact: Cevera Ingraham. Museum gallery/gift shop. Estab. 1948. Represents 5-60 craftworkers. Considers dollmaking; glass art; needlecrafts; quilting; wall hangings; weavings; and woodcrafting. All styles. Price range: $3-7,000; bestsellers: $3-15. Works on consignment; commission varies. Retail price set by craftworker. Reports in 4 weeks. Hand-delivered work only.
Profile: "Shop is located in the gold county in a historical museum." Best selling and heaviest wholesale buying time: summer.

THE PLEBIAN, 834 Kline St., La Jolla CA 92037. (714)454-1888. Contact: David or Marji Nightingale. Craft shop. Estab. 1968. Represents 20 craftworkers. Considers jewelry; metalsmithing; enamels; and cloisonne jewelry. Fine one-of-a-kind and handmade production-line items. Price range: $25-1,500; bestsellers: $25-150. Works on consignment; 30-33% commission. Craftworker sets retail price. Requires exclusive area representation. Submit photos or slides. SASE. Reports in 2 weeks. Work may be shipped or hand-delivered. Dealer pays insurance for exhibited work.
Special Needs: "We would like to carry more cloisonne enamels—either in jewelry or in small functional or non-functional art pieces (e.g., boxes). Also interested in small enameled pieces and metalsmithed items—functional or non-functional, unique jewelry in gold or silver."
Profile: "We have glass showcases (all with locks). Every item on display can be easily seen by the customers. If we have enough pieces by 1 craftsman we will feature them in a special case. We have been located in La Jolla 8 years, and have built a reputation of good, personal service. We own and operate our own business (no employees) and know many of our customers. La Jolla is a very wealthy area. It is also an area of summer and winter resorting with many tourists. Tourists come from everywhere, including Europe and Canada. We have a mailing list of 2,000." Displays work 1-6 months. Heaviest wholesale buying time: late spring and late fall; best selling time: summer and Christmas.

POTTERS STUDIO, 1801 E. McKinley, Fresno CA 93703. (209)266-5508. Contact: Hazel Olsen. Gift shop. Estab. 1970. Represents 15-20 craftworkers. Considers ceramics; jewelry; pottery; wall hangings; and weavings. Fine one-of-a-kind and handmade production-line items. Price range: $2.50-300; bestsellers: $25-80. Works on consignment and buys outright; 40% commission. Craftworker sets retail price. Reports in 2 weeks. Work may be shipped or hand-delivered. Dealer pays shipping to shop. Best selling time: spring and fall.

PRISM CRESCENTS, 2047 Allston Way, Box 182, Berkeley CA 94704. (415)841-1155. Co-directors: John Beuttler and Glenn Cochran. Craft shop/gallery. Estab. 1974. Represents 100 craftworkers. Price range: $2.50-2,000. Works on consignment; 30-40% commission. Craftworker sets retail price. Reports in 1 week. Payment upon request. Dealer pays insurance for exhibited work.
Acceptable Work: Considers batik; ceramics; glass art; jewelry; leatherworking; metalsmithing; needlecrafts; pottery; quilting; soft sculpture; wall hangings; weavings; and woodcrafting. "Special need for blown glass and fine arts." Fine one-of-a-kind and handmade production-line items.
Profile: "We are not just a shop or gallery but a group of independent artists/craftspeople that have created this retail outlet for our work. It is an open ongoing creation. Our customers are mostly people that like very high quality art/craft items." Best selling time: Christmas.

THE RAINBOW, 434 North Camden Dr. Beverly Hills CA 90210. (213)271-5384. Contact: MeraLee Goldman. Craft/gift shop. Estab. l971. Represents 50-100 craftworkers.

Acceptable Work: Considers batik shirts, rainbow candlemaking, bright ceramics, jewelry, needlecraft banners, quilting, soft sculpture, wall hangings (banners) and woodcrafting. Especially needs dollmaking, and bright colored contemporary items with a rainbow or heart motif. One-of-a-kind and handmade production-line items. Price range: $1-500; bestsellers: $15-100.

Terms: Mostly buys outright, but works on consignment with very expensive or wildly experimental items; 50% commission. Dealer pays insurance on exhibited items. Retail price set by joint agreement or by craftworker. "We will take pieces at craftworker's price but caution him/her when we think it is excessive or will not sell at his/her price." Send slides, photos, samples of work or call in person, without appointment, first Wednesday of month (10 am.-5 pm.). Reports in 2 weeks. Work may be shipped or hand-delivered.

Profile: "We are a very special place because all profits earned go to a fund—a treatment center for children with cancer. With the aid of over 100 volunteers, 1,000 members of our organization, and about 6,000-10,000 loyal customers, we are now treating over 300 children per month, funding primary research, training doctors, teaching practicing doctors, and providing play therapy and psychiatric support for the children and their families. Products are displayed, adored, and quickly sold. If it doesn't sell, we don't reorder. On the other hand, when it sells well, we quickly reorder. Customers include all income levels—from young mothers who shop here because they care so much about our medical program and young kids who just love the look and warmth of the shop, right up to all the movie and TV personalities (Ali McGraw usually packs her own Christmas order that goes to an orphanage or Indian Reservation)." Heaviest wholesale buying time: September-Christmas. Best buying time: Christmas, Valentine's Day, June graduation/wedding season.

To Break In: "We need high quality merchandise, clever, imaginative, and bright! Work must be well packed and shipped; business end handled responsibly by the craftsperson (shipping invoice, proper billing invoice so that we can pay them promptly). There must be no concealed damage in shipment. This is the one and only major problem we have had in nearly 8 years of operation—and it was only 1 person so that's a pretty-free record for us in our relationship with our craftspeople."

THE RAKU, 224 Yale Ave., Claremont CA 91711. (714)626-8876. Manager: Stephanie Soldner. Craft shop. Estab. 1957.

Acceptable Work: Considers batik, candlemaking, ceramics, clothing, glass art, jewelry, leatherworking, metalsmithing, pottery, soft sculpture, wall hangings, weavings and woodcrafting. One-of-a-kind and handmade production-line items. Price range: 50¢-1000; bestsellers: $30-50.

Terms: Mostly buys outright, some work on consignment; 40% commission. Dealer pays insurance on exhibited work except for breakage/theft. Craftworker sets retail price. Requires exclusive area representation. Send resume with SASE and call for appointment. Reports in 1-2 weeks. Accepted work may be shipped or hand-delivered.

Profile: "We've been successful in the folk and handcraft business for 20 years and hope to have a few more shops within the next couple of years. We now have 2 in southern California." Heaviest wholesale buying time: pre-holidays; best selling time: holidays and November-December.

To Break In: "Keep creative spirit and quality up. Deliver at time when stated, at price agreed on and there'll be no problems."

THE RAKU, 924 State St., Santa Barbara CA 93101. (805)966-9950. Contact: Peggy or Jerry Martin. Craft shop. Estab. 1957.

Acceptable Work: Considers batik, candlemaking, ceramics, clothing, glass art, jewelry, leatherworking, metalsmithing, pottery, soft sculpture, wall hangings, weavings and woodcrafting. One-of-a-kind and handmade production-line items. Price range: 50¢-1000; bestsellers: $30-50.

Terms: Mostly buys outright, some work on consignment; 40% commission. Dealer pays insurance on exhibited work except for breakage/theft. Craftworker sets retail price. Requires exclusive area representation. Send resume with SASE and call for appointment. Reports in 1-2 weeks. Accepted work may be shipped or hand-delivered.

Profile: "We've been successful in the folk and handcraft business for 20 years and hope to have a few more shops within the next couple of years. We now have 2 in southern California." Heaviest wholesale buying time: pre-holidays; best selling time: holidays and November-December.

To Break In: "Keep creative spirit and quality up. Deliver at time when stated, at price agreed on and there'll be no problems."

RIVERSIDE ART CENTER & MUSEUM, 3425 7th St., Riverside CA 92501. (714)684-7111. Curator: Katrin Wiese. Members gallery: sales and rental. Estab. 1910. Represents 100 member craftworkers.
Acceptable Work: Considers batik, ceramics, clothing, glass, jewelry, metalsmithing, pottery, sculpture, soft sculpture, wall hangings, weavings and woodcrafting. Especially needs blown glass, clothing, jewelry and glass works. One-of-a-kind designer pieces only. Price range: 25¢-$800; bestsellers: $5-100.
Terms: Works on consignment; 33⅓% commission. Craftworker sets retail price. Send slides. Reports in 1 week after jurying (third Tuesday of each month). Work may be shipped or hand-delivered. Display time: 6 months.
Profile: "We have a broad spectrum of artists working in every medium. We attempt to create individual areas for each style craft (traditional to contemporary). We have locked glass cases for jewelry, glass and sculpture; walls for paintings and weavings; simple display pedestals for ceramics; and racks for our paper products, cards, calendars and bookmarks. The shop is very simple and contemporary. Our members' gallery is in the Riverside Art Center, a charming 2-story Spanish building. Classes are held upstairs, exhibit galleries and member's rental/sales gallery is on the ground floor." Heaviest wholesale buying time: November-December and May-July." Best selling time: Christmas and spring.

ROBINSONS' RED DOOR GALLERY, 2840 Main St., Morro Bay CA 93442. Contact: Anita or Roger Robinson. Gallery. Estab. 1966. Represents 5 craftworkers. Considers ceramics; glass art; pottery; wall hangings; and weavings. One-of-a-kind designer pieces only; decorative and/or utilitarian. Price range: $4-750; bestsellers: $15-225. Works on consignment; 40% commission. Retail price set by joint agreement. Requires exclusive area representation. Reports in 3 weeks. Work may be shipped or hand-delivered. Dealer pays insurance for exhibited work.
Profile: "Some items by each artist or craftsman are always on display on a pedestal or whatever is appropriate. Our new building was especially designed as a gallery. We like to have new work about every 90 days to replace what has been sold and/or to rotate stock."

ROSEVILLE ARTS CENTER, 424 Oak St., Roseville CA 95678. (916)783-4117. Director: Penelope Burnett. Museum gallery. Estab. 1968. Represents 10 craftworkers. Requires membership—$10/year. Send slides with SASE. Reports in 1 week. Work must be hand-delivered.
Acceptable Work: Considers batik, candlemaking, ceramics, decoupage, dollmaking, glass art, jewelry, pottery, quilting, soft sculpture, wall hangings and weavings. Specializes in primitive, fine art and contemporary work. One-of-a-kind and handmade production-line items. Price range: $3.75-350; bestsellers: $3.75-50. Works on consignment; 30% commission. Craftworker pays insurance on exhibited work. Retail price set by joint agreement. "As we have just opened for lunch 3 hours daily, we feel we could move a large number of quality craft items that are in a very low price range with our heavier daily traffic ($10 and under)."
Profile: "We are primarily an art gallery with month long rotating fine arts exhibits. A crafts boutique and a painting rental gallery are subsidiary. We are located in a 1906 house which has a great deal of charm and atmosphere. Items on consignment can stay 6 months if unsold, then new merchandise is requested. Customers are middle and upper middle class, largely senior citizen patrons—community and civic minded, generally college-educated and interested in encouraging and promoting younger artists and artisans." Best selling time: Christmas. "We have an all crafts Christmas Boutique for the entire month before Christmas."

RUG CRAFTERS, 777 Bridgeway, Sausalito CA 94965. (415)332-0808. Manager: Donn Lorenzo. One of 3 craft shops. Estab. 1971. Represents 5 craftworkers. Considers wall hangings; weavings; rugs; and tapestries. Handmade production-line items only. Price range: $25-500; bestsellers: $45-120. Works on consignment; 40% commission. Retail price set by joint agreement. Reports in 2 weeks. Work may be shipped or hand-delivered. Dealer pays return shipping and insurance for exhibited work. Best selling time: June-December; heaviest wholesale buying time: May-September.

THE RUSTIC SHOPPE, Box 953, 45098 Main St., Mendocino CA 95460. (707)937-5787. Contact: Richard Huckins. Gift shop. Estab. 1975. Represents "hundreds" of craftworkers. Considers candlemaking; ceramics; jewelry; leatherworking; metalsmithing; pottery; and especially woodcrafting. Fine one-of-a-kind and handmade production-line items. Price range: 50¢-$2,500; bestsellers: $1.50-30. Works on consignment but prefers to buy outright; 33⅓-40% commission. Gift shop sets retail price if bought outright; craftworker sets retail price if on consignment. Requires exclusive area representation. Reporting time varies. Work may be shipped or hand-delivered. Dealer pays shipping and insurance for exhibited work. Best selling time: summer; heaviest wholesale buying time: January-August.

SAN JOSE ART CENTER GALLERY, 482 S. 2nd St., San Jose CA 95113. (408)294-4545. Director: Dr. Delmar Kolb. Gallery. Estab. 1938. Represents 5-50 California (primarily Santa Clara County) craftworkers.
Acceptable Work: Considers batik, ceramics, clothing, glass art, jewelry, leatherworking, metalsmithing, pottery, quilting, soft sculpture, wall hangings, weavings, woodcrafting, cast metals, assemblages and stone carvings. One-of-a-kind designer pieces only. Price range: $15-3,000; bestsellers: $15-150.
Terms: Provides exhibit space; 25% commission. Craftworker sets retail price. Send resume and slides. Reports in 4 weeks. Work must be hand-delivered. Dealer pays insurance on exhibited work.
Profile: "We are a permanent sales and rental gallery including a sales room for 3-dimensional artwork and books. Standard pedestal/platform and shelving provided for sculptural works; hanging or platform display method for textiles; and plastic bubbles and cases for jewelry and small items. Our tradition is 1 month shows. We are a nonprofit exhibit and workshop organization funded by donations." Customers: ages 18-100; "we provide a variety of technical skills, medium and styles representing the Greater San Jose area thus apppealing to a cross-section of customers." Best selling time: fall and winter.

SANTA BARBARA MUSEUM OF NATURAL HISTORY, 2559 Puesta Del Sol Rd., Santa Barbara CA 93105. (805)682-4711. Contact: Laurel Johnson. Museum gallery/gift shop. Estab. 1916. All craftwork relates to natural history, anthropology, botany, astronomy, marine life, bird life or animal life. Considers batik; jewelry; metalsmithing; and woodcrafting. All styles. Price range: $1-100; bestsellers: $1-10. Works on consignment and buys outright; 30% commission. Retail price set by joint agreement. Reports in 3 weeks. Work may be shipped or hand-delivered.
Profile: "As our gift shop is still in planning stages we hope to have it ready within the next 5 years. In the meantime, crafts are displayed in the book shop. The museum building is Spanish in design, and set in a wooded area on Mission Creek in Santa Barbara. Customers are of all ages: numerous school groups, tourists and visitors from all over. Interests tend toward natural history-related subjects." Heaviest wholesale buying time: spring-summer; best selling time: summer and Christmas.

SEA GALLERY, 475 W. Channel Island Blvd., Port Hueneme CA 93041. (805)985-1062. Contact: Fayrene or Ted Parrish. Craft/gift shop. Estab. 1977. Represents 6 craftworkers.
Acceptable Work: Considers scrimshaw. "Finely designed sea-related items only. Must have ocean or sea life theme." Handmade production-lines only. Price range: $5-500; bestsellers: $10-150. "We require 3 months minimum display period."
Terms: Works on consignment (will buy when proven); 40% commission. Craftworker sets retail price. Requires exclusive area representation. Reports on inquiries in 4 weeks.
Profile: "We advertise, plus send out a newsletter every 2-3 months. We are not show-oriented. Customers are sea and/or sailing/boating lovers, age 25-50, who have incomes in the $18,000-40,000 price range." Best selling and heaviest wholesale buying time: spring and fall.
To Break In: "Please write or make appointment before coming to the shop. Keep records accurately. Be professional about consistent pricing."

THE SEA, 525 N. Harbor Blvd., San Pedro CA 90731. (213)831-1694. Contact: Y. Williams DeSchmidt. Shell and nautical gift shop. Estab. 1968. Considers ceramics; jewelry; metalsmithing; needlecrafts; pottery; soft sculpture; and woodcrafting. Must be nautical, shell designs or dealing with the ocean. One-of-a-kind, and handmade production-line items. Price range: 50¢-$900; bestsellers: 50¢-$25. Works on consignment and buys outright. Retail price set by joint agreement.
Profile: "Crafts are mostly nautical or shells from the sea or land." Best selling time: summer and Christmas.
Profile: "Newest items are always given window display and are placed in prime spaces in the store. Our shop has a warm, homey environment in which we are able to offer handmade goods at very reasonable prices." Heaviest wholesale buying time: May-December; best selling time: May, July and November-December (mostly Christmas).

THE SHOP, Box 133, Amador City CA 95601. (209)267-5438. Contact: Harold Dickey. Estab. 1968. Represents 7 craftworkers. Considers pottery; weaving; wood; and leather that is not tooled or stamped. Price range: $2-600; bestsellers: $4-125. Works on consignment; 40% commission. Requires exclusive area representation. Write. Reports in 1 week. Dealer usually pays shipping from shop; negotiates in-transit insurance. Related items are segregated. Best selling time: October-April.

SHOREBIRDS, on the Boardwalk, Belvedere CA 94920. (415)435-0888. Partner: Joanne Horton. Gallery/gift shop. Estab. 1969. Represents 100 craftworkers.
Acceptable Work: Considers batik, candlemaking, ceramics, glass art, jewelry, pottery soft sculpture, wall hangings, weavings and woodcrafting. "We exhibit most forms of handcrafts, but only of extra special quality." Specializes in fine arts, some primitive and country folk art; mostly earth tones. One-of-a-kind and handmade production-line items. Price range: $3-1,200.
Terms: Buys outright and works on consignment; 40% commission. Retail price set by joint agreement. Requires exclusive area representation. Reports in 1 week. Work may be shipped or hand delivered. Dealer pays insurance on exhibited work. Display time: 3-4 weeks (longer if selling well).
Profile: "We have 2 good-sized rooms. The front area contains pottery, baskets, woodenware and kitchen items. The back area is a more formal gallery with paintings, sculpture, blown glass, etc." Customers: teenagers for jewelry; good incomes. Heaviest wholesale buying and best selling time: Christmas, "but our business is fairly steady."

SILVERS-MI-THING, Berth 77, Ports O Call Village, San Pedro CA 90731. (213)831-6805. Owner: Richard Acosta. Gift shop. Estab. 1976. Represents 10 craftworkers.
Acceptable Work: Considers ceramics, glass art, jewelry, metalsmithing, scrimshaw, wall hangings and weavings. One-of-a-kind and handmade production-line items. Price range: $2-400; bestsellers: $2-20.
Terms: Buys outright (after initial test period of 2-4 weeks) and works on consignment; 40% commission. Craftworker sets retail price. Requires exclusive area representation. Send slides or photos. SASE. Reports in 2 weeks. Work may be shipped or hand delivered. Dealer pays insurance on exhibited work.
Profile: Shop has "rustic interior. It is located in a unique tourist location—alongside the Los Angeles Harbor area. This area represents the early New England period with approximately 75 shops built in old-style New England motif." Heaviest wholesale buying time: June 1-September 30; best selling time: summer.

SOME PLACE, 2990 Adeline St., Berkeley CA 94705. (415)843-7178. Contact: Jules Kliot. Craft shop. Estab. 1965. Considers contemporary and antique lace and textiles. Price range: $1-3,000; bestsellers: $1-250. Buys outright and works on consignment. Reports in 1 week.

SOMETHING SPECIAL IN SIERRA CITY, Box 174, Sierra City CA 96125. Contact: Eunice Banks. Craft shop/gallery/gift shop. Estab. 1976. Represents local and regional craftworkers.
Acceptable Work: Considers all crafts of natural materials, utilitarian and/or decorative. Also fine arts. Price range: $1-200; bestsellers: $1-35.
Terms: Buys outright and works on consignment; 40% commission. Retail price set by joint agreement. Reports in 2 weeks. Work may be hand-delivered. Dealer pays return shipping and insurance for exhibited work.
Profile: "We are high in the Sierra Nevada northern mining area on historic Highway 49. Interest in gold mining history is keen here as is fishing, hunting and backpacking. Local scene is what sells." Best selling time: summer and winter; heaviest wholesale buying time: spring and fall.

SOMETHING TO CROW ABOUT, 104 Town & Country Village, Palo Alto CA 94301. (415)328-1744. Contact: Marge Pidto. Gift shop. Estab. 1976. Represents 15-20 craftworkers.
Acceptable Work: Considers batik, candlemaking, ceramics, clothing, dollmaking, jewelry, quilting and soft sculpture. Specializes in contemporary and bright-colored items. "Our shop sells many items with humor (e.g., ceramic donuts and fried eggs, fat ladies). We also sell appliqued ladies clothing and handpainted children's clothing. We do not buy pottery mugs or items that look very crafty. We are looking for cleverly done items at reasonable prices." Some one-of-a-kind but mostly handmade production-line items. Price range: $6-110; bestsellers: $6-80.
Terms: Buys outright and works on consignment (expensive items); commission negotiable. Retail price set by joint agreement. Requires exclusive area representation. Send slides, then samples. Reports in 2 weeks. Work may be shipped or hand-delivered. Dealer pays insurance on exhibited work.

Profile: "We sell a great many handmade items, from clothes for women to mobiles. We are interested in clean design, good color and good quality." Customers: children to grandmothers; high incomes. Best selling time: fall.

SOURCE GALLERY, 1099 Folsom St., San Francisco CA 94103. (415)621-0545. Gallery.
Acceptable Work: Considers sculpture; soft sculpture; wall hangings; and weavings. Price range: $500 minimum, fiberworks.
Terms: Works on consignment; 50% commission. Retail price set by joint agreement. Requires exclusive area representation. "Visit gallery to see if artwork is appropriate and compatible," then, query or call for interview; if out-of-town, send resume and slides. SASE. Gallery pays insurance on exhibited work and shipping from gallery unless work is specifically requested by artist at an earlier date. 6 weeks minimum exposure.

SPILLIKIN CORNERS AT MAGIC MOUNTAIN, 26101 Magic Mountain Pkwy., Valencia CA 91355. (805)255-4752. Craft shop and amusement park. Estab. 1977. Represents 30 Magic Mountain craftworkers.
Acceptable Work: Considers candlemaking, ceramics, dollmaking, glass art, jewelry, leatherworking, metalsmithing, pottery, quilting, tole painting, wall hangings, weavings, woodcrafting, printing, lampwork, basketry and broom making. Especially needs woodcarvings, candles and leather goods. Exhibits old fashioned country handmade pieces. One-of-a-kind and handmade production-line items OK. Price range: 29¢-$2,000; bestsellers: $3-50.
Terms: Buys outright. Buyer sets retail price. Does not require exclusive area representation. Send resume, slides or call for appointment. Reports in 2 weeks. Work may be shipped or hand-delivered.

SPIN IT-WEAVE IT, 2621 University Ave., San Diego CA. (714)291-SPIN. Contact: Sharon Price. Craft/supply shop. Estab. 1973. Send samples. Reports in 2 weeks. Work may be shipped or hand delivered.
Acceptable Work: Considers anything handwoven. Especially needs handwoven clothing. Handmade production-line items. Price range: $5-500. Works on consignment; 30% commission. Craftworker pays insurance on exhibited work. Dealer sets retail price. Requires exclusive area representation.
Profile: "We are in a high tourist area teaching all kinds of classes and selling related merchandise. Items are set on clothing racks and in window displays." Heaviest wholesale buying time: September-March.

THE STUDIO, 210 N. Balsam St., Ridgecrest CA 93555. (714)375-7970. Contact: Barbara Battles. Craft and gift shop. Estab. 1977. Represents 50 craftworkers.
Acceptable Work: Considers batik; ceramics; dollmaking; glass art; jewelry; leatherworking; metalsmithing; needlecrafts; pottery; quilting; soft sculpture; tole painting; wall hangings; weavings; and woodcrafting. Especially needs one-of-a-kind jewelry pieces and good quality quilts. Price range: $1-50, with exception of quilts; bestsellers: $3-25.
Terms: Works on consignment and sometimes buys outright; 33% commission (also charges a $5 annual consignment fee which handles paperwork; insurance; mailing; etc.). Retail price set by joint agreement. Reports in 3 weeks. Send photos and good description of items. Send minimum amount of items before sending large shipment. Dealer pays shipping to shop; return in-transit insurance; and insurance for exhibited work. Unsold consigned pieces returned after 4 months.
Profile: "We are in a desert area that is growing rapidly." Customers are of middle to high income. Best selling time: September-May.

STUDIO 7, 552 San Anselmo Ave., San Anselmo CA 94960. (415)457-0860. Contact: June Lederman. Miniatures gallery. Estab. 1970.
Acceptable Work: Considers dollmaking, glass art, metalsmithing, needlecrafts, pottery and woodcrafting. Only those items in ½", ¾" or 1"-1' scales. "We will consider any media as long as it's in the proper scale, however only fine art works are accepted. We prefer limited editions of at least twelve in a series—signed, numbered and dated by the craftsperson." One-of-a-kind and handmade production-line items. Price range: $1-425; bestsellers $5-75.
Terms: Buys outright. Retail price set by joint agreement. Call for appointment, bring or send samples of work with SASE. Reports in 2 weeks; immediately if hand-delivered. Work may be shipped or hand-delivered; return postage must be included.
Profile: "This is a 'museum setting' shop. Since the miniatures and dollhouse business evolved from a quality arts and crafts gallery, the transition has been carefully attended to assure the

same high quality craftsmanship and artistic display. We have kits for furniture and miniature homes (including papers, carpets and fabrics) to one-of-a-kind crafted items from all periods in history displayed in proper settings. Individual miniature items are displayed in complete room settings as museum pieces or as 'limited edition' items cataloged for steady customers who are always seekng the new and unusual. Our customers are mostly adults of a higher income bracket—many retired husbands are building dollhouses for wives, children and even grandchildren. Much care is spent in furnishing them." Heaviest wholesale buying time: late summer and fall; best selling time: Thanksgiving-Christmas.
To Break In: "Use of fine woods is most desireable—we do not accept items of balsa wood or careless finishes or glueing. Careful attention to thickness of wood so it adheres to strict dimensions, is also a requirement. A little background is helpful—the collector is always interested in the craftsperson."

STUDIO SUENAGA, 1105 Camino Del Mar, Del Mar CA 92014. (714)755-7575. Contact: Nancy Suenaga. Jewelry shop. Estab. 1971. Considers jewelry. Fine one-of-a-kind designer pieces; decorative only. Price range: $3-4,000; bestsellers: $50-800. Works very little on consignment. Owner sets retail price and pays shipping and insurance.
Profile: "The shop is 2,000 square feet with a large inventory of custom designed pieces displayed on velvets, burl and grapevine wood. Nancy's own designs have won many awards from the California (Southern) Exposition." Customers are 20-60 years of age, mostly professional with average income of $15,000. Heaviest wholesale buying and best selling time: Christmas.

STUDIOS WEST—ENCINITAS, 167 Saxony Rd., Encinitas CA 92024. (714)753-8186. Director: Ralph Ritchie. Gallery Manager: Tanya Vint. Studio/gallery/sculpture garden. Estab. 1969. "Most of the work shown is done by Studios West associated craftspersons with occasional invitational shows." Considers some pottery, and architectural and garden sculpture. One-of-a-kind fine crafts only. Price range: $10-5,000; bestsellers: $100-1,000. Buys outright (materials and facilities supplied by the studio). "We rarely work on consignment; but when we do it's 20-50% commission." Retail price set by joint agreement. "Rarely respond to inquiries unless in-person visit or SASE." Best selling time: spring or Christmas for architectural work; April-May and August-October for other work. Customers are age 30 or older with above-average income.

SUNNYVALE CREATIVE ARTS CENTER, Box 607, Sunnyvale CA 94088. (408)738-5521. Creative Arts Coordinator: Linda Pedroncelli. Gallery. Estab. 1973. Represents San Francisco Bay craftworkers, sometimes other parts of California. Considers batik; ceramics; clothing; glass art; jewelry; leatherworking; metalsmithing; needlecrafts; pottery; quilting; soft sculpture; tole painting; wall hangings; weavings; and woodcrafting. Primitive and fine one-of-a-kind pieces. Price range: $3-1,000; bestsellers: $3-500. "We are purely an exhibit gallery; any sales are handled by craftworker and the buyer." Craftworker sets retail price. Hand-delivered work only.
Profile: "Works are displayed as part of a 1-3 man show or group show. Most shows run 3 weeks. Since the gallery is in the middle of the Creative Arts Center, which is part of a 4 building community center, we get a wide variety of people who would not normally go to a gallery."

SWEET EARTH SHOP, 609 High St., Auburn CA 95603. Contact: Suzanne Souza. Craft and gift shop. Estab. 1975. Represents 25 craftworkers. Considers batik; candlemaking; ceramics; glass art; jewelry; metalsmithing; pottery; wall hangings; weavings; woodcrafting; illustrated children's books; and illustrated cards. Primitive handmade production-line items only. Price range: 50¢-$38; bestsellers: 50¢-$30. Works on consignment and buys outright; 35% commission. Shop sets retail price if bought outright; craftworker sets retail price if on consignment. Work may be shipped or hand-delivered, but must have prior approval if shipped. Dealer pays return shipping and insurance for exhibited work. Reports "immediately."
Profile: This shop has "a large variety. We sell our own pottery as well as work by other craftspeople." Best selling time: Christmas; heaviest wholesale buying time: summer and fall.

TARBOX GALLERY, 1025 Prospect St., La Jolla CA 92037. (714)459-0442. Director: Norma McCue. Gallery. Estab. 1971. Represents 30 West Coast craftworkers. Considers batik; ceramics; glass art; jewelry; metalsmithing; wall hangings; and weavings. One-of-a-kind designer pieces only. Price range: $5-5,000. Works on consignment with new artists and buys outright from artists established in the gallery; 50% commission. Retail price set by joint

agreement. Requires exclusive area representation. Reports in 1 month. Work may be shipped or hand-delivered on advance notice.
Profile: Best selling time: summer. "The gallery reflects the West Coast scene and is divided into 2 rooms: fine art and crafts. On displays there is some intermingling when effective." Customers are "tourists and local customers in moderate to good income brackets."

TEMPLE OF GOOD THINGS, 6241 W. 87th St., Los Angeles CA 90045. (213)670-3772. Contact: Louis Nusinow. Gift shop. Estab. 1969. Represents 25 craftworkers. Considers candlemaking; ceramics; glass art; jewelry; wall hangings; weavings; and woodcrafting. Primitive and fine one-of-a-kind pieces. Price range: $2-250; bestsellers: $5-150. Works on consignment and buys outright; 30-40% commission. Retail price set by joint agreement. Requires exclusive area representation. Reports in 4 weeks. Work may be shipped or hand-delivered. Dealer pays shipping to shop and insurance on exhibited work.
Profile: Best selling time: Christmas; heaviest wholesale buying time: fall. Customers are "7-85 years of age and are in middle to upper income brackets."

TEXTILES BY DESIGN, 5519 College Ave., Oakland CA 94703. (415)654-1434. Contact: Mary Hendricks. Craft shop/gallery. Estab. 1977. Represents 15-25 craftworkers. Considers wall hangings; weavings; basketry; textile dolls and toys; and textile kitchen and household items. Fine one-of-a-kind and handmade production-line items. Price range: $5-700; bestsellers: $10-40. Works on consignment; 45% commission. Retail price set by joint agreement. Reports in 1-2 weeks. Work may be shipped or hand-delivered. Dealer pays return shipping and insurance for exhibited work.
Profile: Best selling time: fall-early spring; heaviest wholesale buying time: fall and spring. "We are the only shop that we know of anywhere out here which specializes in handmade fiber arts. We handle nothing else and are *the* place to shop for textiles!"

TIDEPOOL GALLERY, 22762 Pacific Coast Hwy., Malibu CA 90265. (213)456-2551. Partner: Jan Greenberg. Gallery/gift shop. Estab. 1969. Represents 100-125 craftworkers whose work relates to the ocean in some way. Prefers California or Western craftworkers. Considers batik; ceramics; glass art; jewelry; needlecrafts; pottery; soft sculpture; wall hangings; weavings; and woodcrafting. All styles utilitarian and/or decorative. Price range: $20-250; bestsellers: $25-50. Works on consignment and buys outright; 40% commission. Craftworker sets retail price. Requires exclusive area representation. Reports in 2 weeks. Work may be shipped or hand-delivered. Dealer pays insurance for exhibited work.
Profile: Work is displayed "for a period of 2 months, then removed and displayed again." Customers are all ages and incomes. Best selling time: summer-Christmas; heaviest wholesale buying time: Christmas, spring and fall.

TRITON MUSEUM OF ART, 1505 Warburton Ave., Santa Clara CA 95050. Director: Jo Farb Hernandez. Works with sculptors; jewelers; and glass and textile artists. Features work of San Francisco Bay area and Santa Clara Valley artists, but will consider work of artists from other areas as well. 25% commission. Send resume and photos or slides.

UPPER ECHELON, 777 Bridgeway, Sausalito CA 94965. Buyer: Sandy Younglove. Gallery/shop. Estab. 1962. Represents 75 craftworkers.
Acceptable Work: Considers batik; candles; ceramics; glass art; jewelry; metalsmithing; pottery; wall hangings; weavings; and woodcrafting. Especially needs distinctive notes and cards, hand thrown juicers, batter bowls and sugar and creamer sets. Fine one-of-a-kind and handmade production-line items. Price range: 65¢-$200.
Terms: Buys outright. Retail price set by joint agreement. Requires exclusive area representation. SASE. Reports in 2-3 weeks. Deliveries accepted on order only.
Profile: This shop represents "some of the nation's finest crafts from the foremost craftspeople." Best selling and heaviest wholesale buying time: spring-fall.

VALLEY ART GALLERY, 1641 Locust Ave., Walnut Creek CA 94596. (415)935-4311. Director: Dorothy Magoffin. Gallery/museum gift shop/rental gallery. Estab. 1941. Represents 40 craftworkers. Best selling time: November-December.
Acceptable Work: Considers ceramics; glass art; jewelry; pottery; and woodcrafting. Fine one-of-a-kind and handmade production-line items. Price range: $2-75; bestsellers: $5-25.
Terms: Works on consignment; 25% commission. Retail price set by craftworker. Work may be hand-delivered. Dealer pays insurance for exhibited work. Reports "immediately if it is something we can use."

Shops and Galleries 105

VAN DOREN GALLERY, 10 Gold St., San Francisco CA 94133. (415)392-0434. Gallery. Considers contemporary sculpture. Maximum size: 10x15. Price range: $100-15,000. Set by joint agreement. 50% commission. Requires exclusive area representation. Sponsors openings. Send resume and color slides. Exhibited art insured. Shipping costs shared.

VENICE PLACE ARTS CENTER, 1023½ W. Washington Blvd., Venice CA 90291. (213)399-0574. Contact: Charles Jaeger. Craft shop/gallery. Estab. 1970. Represents 10 craftworkers.
Acceptable Work: Considers ceramics; pottery; soft sculpture; sculpture; and paintings. Fine one-of-a-kind and handmade production-line items only. Retail price set by joint agreement. This is a "collection of galleries and studios around a central patio which is beautifully landscaped." Best selling time: December.

WALNUT CREEK CIVIC ARTS GALLERY, 1641 Locust St., Walnut Creek CA 94596. (415)935-3300, ext. 256. Museum/gallery. Estab. 1963. Considers all crafts. One-of-a-kind pieces only. Price range: $50-2,000. Works on consignment; 25% commission. Craftworker sets retail price. Submit slides for review by staff. The time period for the show is 8 weeks with a 2 week period for installation."

WEE LITTLES IN HOBBY CITY, W64 N713 Washington Ave., Cedarburg WI 53012. (414)377-6170. Contact: Doris Casey. Miniature and doll shop located at 1238 S. Beach Blvd., Anaheim CA 90680. See Wee Littles Shoppe, Cedarburg, Wisconsin.

WHICHCRAFT, 312 E. Ojai Ave., Ojai CA 93023. (805)646-8709. Contact: Lydia Marcus. Craft/antique shop.
Acceptable Work: Considers jewelry, needlecrafts, pottery, quilting and scrimshaw. Specializes in primitive work. Price range: 25¢-$500; bestsellers: 80¢-$45.
Terms: Buys outright and works on consignment; 33⅓% commission. Dealer pays insurance on exhibited work. Retail price set by joint agreement. Requires exclusive area representation. Call for appointment and bring samples. Work may be shipped or hand delivered.
Profile: "We specialize in unusual and one-of-a-kind imports, antiques and crafts unobtainable in other stores. We also carry collector books and craft books."

WICKERSHAM & SONS, INC., 963 Laurel St., San Carlos CA 94070. (415)595-1850. President: Larry Wickersham. Music/gift boutique. "We sell any items, decorative or useful, of musical nature or theme." Buys outright and sometimes commissions work. Send samples or catalog. Reports in 1 week.

WHOLLY COW, 813 State St., Santa Barbara CA 93101. (805)965-3545. Contact: Gina Lestrade. Estab. 1976. Represents 9 craftworkers.
Acceptable Work: Considers leatherworking. Finished, one-of-a-kind and handmade production-line items only. Price range: $1-125; bestsellers: $20-60.
Terms: Buys outright and works on consignment; 35% commission. Retail price set by joint agreement. Query with transparencies or photos. Reports in 2 weeks. Shop pays shipping to shop and insurance.
Profile: Items displayed in groups and rearranged weekly. Best selling time: Christmas; heaviest wholesale buying time: spring-Christmas. Customers buy crafts for artistic value.

THE WOOLMARK, 322 Fifth Street, Eureka CA 95501. (707)442-9272. Contact: Lori Goodman or Terry Hill. Gallery/supply shop. Represents 10-15 craftworkers.
Acceptable Work: Considers batik, clothing, wall hangings and rugs; handspun only. One-of-a-kind and handmade production-line items. Price range: $5-300; bestsellers: $15-80.
Terms: Works on consignment; 25% commission. Craftworker sets retail price. Send slides. Reports in 1 week. Work may be shipped or hand delivered.
Profile: "We have a weaving, spinning, dyeing, knitting and batik supply store and a separate gallery area where we display hangings, garments and local baskets. We carry no synthetic yarns, no kits, and no quilting supplies. We, of course, take excellent care of any item on display. Garments are hung or folded depending on what is appropriate. Hangings are kept on walls or suspended from the ceiling. Utmost care is taken to make all displays attractive. 2 month full exhibit time with 6 months for garments. Our customers are mostly between 20 and 40 and interested in natural well done items. The area income is not high." Heaviest wholesale buying and best selling time: Christmas.
To Break In: "Price under $50; small items under $20 (scarves, bags, pillows, small hangings)."

WORLDS OF WILDLIFE, Village Corner, Los Altos CA 94022. (415)948-WILD. Contact: Jinny Collins. Gift shop. Estab. 1976. Represents 2-3 craftworkers.
Acceptable Work: Considers ceramics, glass art, metalsmithing, pottery, soft sculpture, wall hangings, weavings, woodcrafting, porcelain and soapstone. Wildlife only. "Keep animals accurate—nothing cutsy." One-of-a-kind and handmade production-line items. Price range: $6.50-600; bestsellers: $7.50-180.
Terms: Buys outright and works on consignment; 45% commission. Dealer pays insurance on exhibited work. Retail price set by joint agreement. Requires exclusive area representation. Call for appointment. Reports in 2 weeks. Work may be shipped or hand-delivered.
Profile: "Items are put in open, prime displays and are moved each month to different shop areas. There is a trial period of 30-45 days. Customers are high income adults with an animal interest." Heaviest wholesale buying time: fall; best selling time: late fall and spring.

YOUNG GALLERY, 100 Park Center Plaza, San Jose CA 95113. (408)295-2800. Director: Edna Young. Gallery shop. Estab. 1971. Represents 12-15 craftworkers. Considers ceramics; dollmaking; glass art; jewelry; and soft sculpture. Fine and primitive one-of-a-kind pieces. Price range: $20-3,500; bestsellers: $20-500. Works on consignment; 40-50% commission. Retail price set by joint agreement. Requires exclusive area representation. Reports in 2 weeks. Work may be shipped or hand-delivered. Dealer pays insurance for exhibited work.
Special Needs: Seeking quality ceramics; soft sculpture; glass ornaments; game items; fabrics; and handmade paper items.
Profile: Gallery draws high income people. Best selling time: December and June; heaviest wholesale buying time: October-December. Send biography with slides or photos and price list.

ZARA GALLERY, 553 Pacific Ave., San Francisco CA 94133. (415)788-8696. Director: Joseph Chowning. Considers ceramics; sculpture; and soft sculpture. Maximum size: 12' square. Work must be ready for exhibition. Primarily interested in figurative work. Price range: $150-30,000, sculpture; bestsellers: $500-5,000. Works on consignment; 33⅓-60% commission. Retail price set by joint agreement. Requires exclusive area representation. Send slides and resume. SASE. Gallery pays insurance. 4-5 weeks exposure.

Colorado

ALBATROSS GALLERY, 1708 15th St., Boulder CO 80302. (303)449-6807. Contact: Amy-Beth, Joan or Marilyn Markowitz. Gallery. Estab. 1974. Represents 80 craftworkers.
Acceptable Work: Considers ceramics, fiber arts, prints and sculpture. One-of-a-kind art/craft work and unique functional wares. Price range: open (presently $10-2,000). "Monthly shows may feature media not listed above."
Terms: Works on consignment; 40% commission. Craftworker sets retail price. Prefers exclusive area representation. Submit slides/photos with description of work and personal background. SASE. Reports in 3-4 weeks.
Profile: "Some items are displayed by function, others by artist. Displays are changed weekly. Our gallery has been in Boulder for the past 5 years and has been primarily devoted to functional pottery. As new owners, we intend to keep fine selections of functional pottery as well as expanding into areas of nonfunctional pottery, sculpture, paintings and fiber arts. Average customer is 30-45 years old with approximate income of $25,000-35,000." Heaviest wholesale buying time: pre-Christmas (October-December); best selling time: December and May-June (wedding gifts).

BLUE DOOR TOO GALLERY, 3150-G S. Peoria St., Aurora CO 80014. (303)750-1031. Director: Jim Robischon. Gallery. Estab. 1976. Represents 5 craftworkers.
Acceptable Work: Considers ceramics, jewelry, metalsmithing, soft sculpture, wall hangings, weavings and woodcrafting. Especially needs sculptural fiber art, particularly wall pieces; metalsmithing; glass art; sculptural woodcrafting; and batik. Specializes in contemporary and fine art one-of-a-kind designer crafts. Price range: $40-1,500; bestsellers: $100-450.
Terms: Works on consignment; 33⅓% commission. Retail price set by joint agreement. Send slides or call for appointment. "A note of introduction with a follow-up phone call is the best way for an artist to get an appointment with the proper person—don't just drop in with all your work unannounced." Reports in 4 weeks. Work may be shipped or hand delivered. Dealer pays insurance on exhibited work. Display time: 3 months (larger works may stay until sold).
Profile: Displays sculpture on individual pedestals. Shop "has white walls and sharp clean displays to give as much importance to the piece as possible. Rotation of artists' works is stressed." Customers: ages 25-55, $10,000-40,000 incomes, college-educated professionals. Best selling time: November-January.

To Break In: "An artist should know what type of works, style, price ranges that a gallery offers before approaching any gallery."

BRECKENRIDGE GALLERIES INC., Box 650, Breckenridge CO 80424. (303)453-2592. Director: Gary Freese. Gallery. Estab. 1969.
Acceptable Work: Considers batik and woodcrafting. Price range: $150-6,000. Specializes in contemporary Southwestern art. One-of-a-kind pieces only. "I am not interested in production pieces. I want to set up a 'high end' quality craft/fine art shop."
Terms: Works on consignment; 40% commission. Retail price set by craftworker or joint agreement. Requires exclusive area representation. Send slides. Reports in 1 week. Work may be shipped or hand delivered.
Profile: "The gallery will be opening a subsidiary gallery in Breckenridge. We are looking for the highest quality crafts to make up our second gallery (the current gallery consists of original paintings and bronzes). We will also be establishing a Colorado fine arts gallery." Customers: 50% from Colorado, 50% from 47 states. Heaviest wholesale buying time: prior to selling season; best selling time: November 25-April and May 30-Labor Day.

COMMONWHEEL ARTISTS COOPERATIVE, 102 Canon Ave., Manitou Springs CO 80829. (303)685-1008. Chairman/Shop Manager: Richard Elliott. Craft shop/gallery/cooperative. Estab. 1976. Represents 35 member craftworkers.
Acceptable Work: Considers batik, ceramics, clothing, glass art, jewelry, leatherworking, metalsmithing, needlecrafts, pottery, soft sculpture, wall hangings, weavings and woodcrafting. Especially needs metalsmithing, silversmithing, stained or blown glass, leather and clothing. One-of-a-kind and handmade production-line items. Price range: $1-300; bestsellers: $1-75.
Terms: Must be member of Commonwheel Artists Cooperative and live in the Pikes Peak area. Works on consignment; 25% commission. Must work 1 day/month minimum or $15 pay option. Craftworker sets retail price. Send slides or stop in at shop. Work must be hand-delivered.
Profile: "The gallery is open for exhibition on a monthly basis by anyone of professional quality (fine art or fine crafts). Displays are a group and individual effort." Customers: ages 18-80; mostly tourists (in summer); local middle and upper middle class residents (in winter); some wholesalers. Best selling time: summer.

CONFLUENCE GALLERY, 1002 S. Gaylord, Denver CO 80209. (303)722-0308. Craft shop/gallery/cooperative. Represents 25 craftworkers. "Craftspeople should be professional, with a direction and several years experience. No beginners."
Acceptable Work: Considers batik, ceramics, clothing, dollmaking, glass art, jewelry, leatherworking, metalsmithing, needlecrafts, pottery, quilting, soft sculpture, wall hangings, weavings, woodcrafting and mixed media. Especially needs jewelry, wood and glass. Specializes in fine contemporary crafts. "The emphasis is on one-of-a-kind pieces and quality multiples." Price range: $2-2,500; bestsellers: $5-40.
Terms: Works on consignment, members only; 10% commission. Charges entrance fee, plus $25/month. Members must work 1-2 days/month in the store. Craftworker sets retail price. Call for appointment. Reports in 1 week. Work must be hand-delivered.
Profile: "We are a cross between an art gallery and craft shop." Shop has 2 floors; items are displayed on walls, floor, stands and cabinets. "Craftworker is encouraged to remove items after several months and replace with new items." Customers: middle to upper incomes; educated. Best selling time: Fall-Christmas.

THE CREWEL ELEPHANT, 124 E. 13th St., Silverton CO 81433. Contact: William M. Howell. Craft and gift shop.
Acceptable Work: Considers ceramics; clothing; needlecrafts; and quilting. Especially needs needlework with emphasis on traditions from all areas. Price range: $5-300; bestsellers: $2-30.
Terms: Buys outright. Retail price set by joint agreement. Requires exclusive area representation. Reports in 2 weeks. Work may be shipped or hand-delivered with prior contact. Dealer pays shipping and insurance for solicited work.
Profile: "We feature primarily embroidered items; our mail order section offers designs for needleworkers both traditional and original; we are interested in reproducible needlework designs and patterns." Heaviest wholesale buying time: winter; best selling time: summer.

DENVER MUSEUM OF NATURAL HISTORY GIFT SHOP, City Park, Denver CO 80205. (303)575-3931. Business Manager: Dudley Smith. Assistant Manager: Thielma Gamewell. Museum gift shop. Estab. around 1963. Represents 6 craftworkers.

Acceptable Work: Considers clothing, jewelry, toys, wall hangings, weavings and woodcrafting. "For a natural history museum, we can sell only items which have a nature design, motif or some connection with our exhibits." One-of-a-kind and handmade production-line items. Price range: $1.50-200; bestsellers: $5-50.

Terms: Buys outright and works on consignment; 30% commission. Craftworker sets retail price. Call for appointment. SASE. Work may be shipped or hand delivered. Dealer pays insurance on exhibited work. Display time: minimum 3 months with 3 display changes if necessary.

Profile: Shop has 3 sections: "gift shop with a total variety of items from lead crystal to stuffed animals; an Indian shop with turquoise jewelry, rugs, baskets, pottery, sandpaintings and novelties; and a small bookstore." Heaviest wholesale buying time: spring and fall; best selling time: summer.

To Break In: "Be consistent in quality. Don't put a good stone in a cheap mount or a fine print in a cheap frame. Good packaging always helps."

THE ENCOUNTER, Box 136, Boulder CO 95006. (408)338-3431. Contact: Rachel or Walt Bachrach. Craft and gift shop. Estab. 1967. Represents 200-250 craftworkers. Considers all crafts except tole painting. All styles; utilitarian and/or decorative. Price range: 75¢-$1,200; bestsellers: 75¢-$600. Works on consignment; 33⅓% commission. "Also works on functional consignment for some craftswork, which gives guaranteed sale to craftsperson." Retail price set by joint agreement. Requires exclusive Boulder Creek representation. Reports in 2 weeks if by mail, same day if in person. Work may be hand delivered by pre-arrangement only. Dealer pays insurance for exhibited work. Work displayed 60 days minimum. Best selling and heaviest wholesale buying time: Christmas.

FOOTHILLS ART CENTER, 809 15th St., Golden CO 80401. (303)279-3922. Director: Marian Metsopoulos. Art center. Estab. 1968. Represents 5-100 craftworkers.

Acceptable Work: Considers batik, glass art, jewelry, leatherworking, metalsmithing, needlecrafts, pottery, quilting, scrimshaw, soft sculpture, wall hangings, weavings and woodcrafting. One-of-a-kind pieces only.

Terms: Exhibits only; 25% commission, for members; 33⅓%, non-members. Exhibit fee: $10/gallery. Craftworker sets retail price. Work must be approved by the Exhibit Committee. Call for appointment. Work may be shipped or hand delivered. Foothills Art Center pays insurance on exhibited work. Display time: approximately 1 month.

Profile: "We are a nonprofit cultural center for the Denver area and beyond. We offer monthly exhibits of fine art and crafts, classes, workshops, music series, poetry readings and art trips. Different artists or themes appear in the 8 galleries and showcases, with the exception of some of our larger shows, which fill all galleries. Members have a show in 1 gallery almost every month." Best selling time: October-December (during Holiday Art Mart).

THE GLASS LANTERN, LTD., 1801 E. Belleview Ave., Denver CO 80237. (303)779-0865. Contact: Luce Shuler. Gallery/gift shop. Estab. 1971. Represents 12 craftworkers. Price range: $1.50-800; bestsellers: $4.50-350. Works on consignment and buys outright; 30% commission. Retail price set by joint agreement. Requires exclusive area representation. Reports in 2 weeks. "Must jury actual work in person." Work may be shipped or hand-delivered. Dealer pays insurance for exhibited work.

Acceptable Work: Considers stained and acid-etched and sandblasted glass. One-of-a-kind designer pieces; utilitarian and/or decorative.

Profile: The shop carries "all stained glass items, finished hangings, lamps and small suncatchers and all supplies for craftsmen." All items are immediately displayed and changed in location every 2-3 weeks. Best selling time: summer-winter.

THE GOLD & SILVERSMITHS OF VAIL, Box 385, Vail CO 81657. (303)476-3131. Contact: James Cotter. Craft shop. Estab. 1970. Represents 5 craftworkers.

Acceptable Work: Considers jewelry and metalsmithing. One-of-a-kind designer and primitive pieces. Especially needs sterling 14K gold earrings; custom polishing on a piece basis and fabricated construction on a custom basis in gold and silver. Price range: $15-200; bestsellers: $60-125.

Terms: Works on consignment; 40% commission. Retail price set by joint agreement. Requires exclusive area representation. Send slides or photos. Reports in 4 weeks. Work may be shipped or hand-delivered. Dealer pays insurance for exhibited work.

Profile: Work is "displayed prominently in well-lighted glass display case. Customers are 25-40 year old professionals." Best selling and heaviest wholesale buying time: summer and winter.

GREEN RIVER, Box 10220, Aspen CO 81611. (303)925-5742. Partners: George Janecek or Judy Pollock. Estab. 1974. Represents 10 craftworkers. Price range: $1.50-2,000; bestsellers: $25-100.
Acceptable Work: Considers jewelry; leatherworking; metalsmithing; knife-making; buckles and antique guns. One-of-a-kind and handmade production-line items.
Terms: Works on consignment and buys outright; 33⅓% commission. Retail price set by joint agreement. Requires exclusive area representation. Reports in 2 weeks. Work may be shipped or hand-delivered.
Profile: "Our best customers are doctors, dentists, lawyers and company presidents." Best selling and heaviest wholesale buying time: winter and summer.

GRYPHON GALLERIES, LTD., 2440 E. Third Ave., Denver CO 80206. President: Erin Potter. Gallery. Estab. 1970. Represents 8 craftworkers.
Acceptable Work: Considers ceramics, glass art, jewelry, pottery, wall hangings, weavings and woodcrafting. Specializes in contemporary crafts. Price range: $25-1,000.
Terms: Works on consignment; 40% commission. Craftworker sets retail price. Requires exclusive area representation. Send resume or slides. SASE. Reports in 1 week. Dealer pays insurance on exhibited work.
Profile: "We are a contemporary gallery dealing only with full-time, professional painters and craftspeople. No interest in part-time hobbyists. Craftsperson must have other out-of-state galleries and museum shows to his or her credit."

LAUGHING BAER'S ADVENTURES IN NOBLE METALS, c/o General Delivery, Placerville CO 81430. (303)728-3758. Contact: Mike Baer. Studio. Estab. 1976. Considers jewelry and metalsmithing. Primitive and fine one-of-a-kind pieces; utilitarian and/or decorative. Price range: $1-2,000; bestsellers: $1-4. Works on commision, buys outright and trades; 25% commission. Sells wholesale. Retail price set by joint agreement. Reports in 2 weeks. Shipping is negotiable. Insurance for exhibited work set by joint agreement. Best selling time: summer and winter. Visiting acceptable.

MEADOWFOUND GALLERY, 727 Manitou Ave., Manitou Springs CO 80829. (303)685-5783. Contact: Autumn Lewis. Gallery. Estab. 1973. Represents primarily Southwestern craftworkers. "Almost all our suppliers have college degrees in art and have been working professionally at least 5 years."
Acceptable Work: Considers batik, weaving, jewelry, soft sculpture, toys, wood sculpture, and especially needs blown glass, unusual pottery, small wall hangings (weavings) and clay sculpture. Specializes in fine contemporary crafts. Handmade production-line items and one-of-a-kind pieces. Price range: $4-600; bestsellers: $25-100.
Terms: Prefers to buy outright, but works on consignment for featured exhibits and very expensive items; 40% commission. Retail price set by gallery or joint agreement. Send resume and slides or call for appointment. Reports in 1 week. Dealer pays insurance on exhibited work. Display time: 1 month for gallery feature (advertised in Colorado Springs media); 3 months maximum on consignment items.
Profile: "We are in a restored red brick turn-of-the-century building with around 1,600 square feet of display area. One room displays work by a featured artist and two other rooms hold continuous displays. A 10-man potery studio is visible through picture windows from the gallery. There's carpeting, many plants, natural wood and skylights. Items are rotated around the display areas." Customers: young and middle age professionals (lawyers, doctors). "Manitou Springs is a mountain village 6 miles from Colorado Springs (300,000 population) and most of our customers are from this area. In additon, we have a large summer tourist business." Heaviest wholesale buying time: October, March and July; best selling time: June-September and December.

MOUNTAIN VALLEY GIFTS, Rt. 2, Livermore CO 80536. (303)484-4589. Contact: Larry and Eileen Ackerson. Craft/gift shop. Estab. 1977. Represents 25 craftworkers.
Acceptable Work: Considers candlemaking, ceramics, dollmaking, glass art, jewelry, leatherworking, metalsmithing, needlecrafts, quilting, rock finishing (rough and cut), rosemaling, soft sculpture, tole painting, wall hangings, weavings and woodcrafting. Especially needs Western-design crafts. "Most of our customers are travelers so items should be kept small to medium in size." One-of-a-kind items only. Price range: 79¢-$250; bestsellers: $1.25-50.
Terms: Works on consignment; 25% commission. Craftworker sets retail price. Send resume, slides, SASE, call for appointment or stop in at shop. Reports in 3 weeks. Work may be shipped or hand delivered. Dealer pays insurance on exhibited work; "craftworker may have extra

insurance on more expensive items." Display time: 3 months. Limited to 12 items of the same type at a time.

Profile: "We are located just off Highway 287 between Fort Collins, Colorado and Laramie, Wyoming. The shop was built to resemble an old western store. An old wagon is outside and there are old wagon wheels along the porch. Inside, there's an old Ben Franklin fireplace and 24' split logs overhead used for hanging items. Classes are given in tole painting and rosemaling." Heaviest wholesale buying time: April-November; best selling time: May-December.

NATIONAL CARVERS MUSEUM, 14960 Woodcarver Rd., Monument CO 80132. (303)481-2656. Contact: Harry Meech. Museum gift shop. Estab. 1969. Represents 200 craftworkers. Considers woodcrafting. All styles; utilitarian and/or decorative. Price range: $2.50-2,500; bestsellers: $2.50-75. Works on consignment and buys outright; 30% commission. Retail price set by joint agreement. Reports in 3 weeks. Work may be shipped or hand-delivered. Dealer pays insurance for exhibited work. "This is a national museum exhibiting over 5,000 woodcarvings." Heaviest wholesale buying time: spring; best selling time: spring-summer.

PANACHE, 2217 E. Mississippi Ave., Denver CO 80210. (303)778-0519. Director: Frances Koehn. Gallery. Estab. 1978. Represents 20 craftworkers.
Acceptable Work: Considers, batik, ceramics, clothing, dollmaking, glass art, jewelry, metalsmithing, pottery, wall hangings, weavings and woodcrafting. "We consider most high quality crafts." Especially needs lower priced crafts. Specializes in fine art, contemporary and bright colored pieces. One-of-a-kind and handmade production-line items. Price range: $6-1,000; bestsellers: $20-100.
Terms: Buys outright but mostly works on consignment; 40% commission. Craftworker sets retail price for items on consignment; gallery sets retail price for items bought outright. Sometimes requires exclusive area representation. Send resume, slides or call for appointment. Reports in 2 weeks. Work may be shipped or hand-delivered. Dealer pays insurance on exhibited work.
Profile: "We are a new and small gallery dedicated to living up to our name. Most of what we show is contemporary and elegant. We display our items on shelves, cylinders, hanging shelves, hung from the ceiling, on mirrors and, in general, try to display in an innovative manner most advantageous to the piece. Displays usually get changed every month whether we are featuring a new show or not." Customers: average age group of 35; average to upper incomes; art oriented. Heaviest wholesale buying time: summer-pre-Christmas; best selling time: pre-Christmas.

THE PUG MILL GALLERY, 665 S. Pearl St., Denver CO 80209. (303)778-6427. Gallery/studio. Director: Cathy Cohen. Gallery/pottery studio. Estab. 1977. Represents 11 craftworkers/artists. "I encourage those from the Denver and Colorado area."
Acceptable Work: Considers batik, ceramics, metalsmithing, pottery, wall hangings and weavings. Especially needs blown glass "to add a touch of elegance to fine pottery." Specializes in functional pieces in contemporary styles. Handmade production-line items. Price range: $4-300; bestsellers: $4-25.
Terms: Buys outright (in quantity) those items which are sure easy sellers and works on consignment; 33⅓% commission. Retail price set by joint agreement. Send resume and slides. SASE. Reports in 2 weeks. Prefers work to be hand-delivered. Dealer pays insurance on exhibited work. The gallery features temporary showings, for 1-2 compatable artists lasting for 1 month (opening reception and advertisting).
Profile: "Pottery has a prominent place at the Pug Mill Gallery in a contemporary setting on mahogany shelves covered with red clay tiles. The off-white walls carry other media. We're off the downtown circuit of galleries in a pleasant inner city neighborhood integrating residental and small business. Customers are basically middle class and proud of their homes." Heaviest wholesale buying time: pre-Christmas; best selling time: Christmas (November-December).
To Break In: "Have inventory of your work ready when mailing. Put tags on items (with numbers and their prices). Be reliable, professional and dependable."

THE ROCKY MOUNTAIN GALLERY & GIFT SHOP, Box 1474, 1438 Miner St., Idaho Springs CO 80452. (303)567-4254. President: Shirley Clark. Gallery/gift/craft shop. Estab. 1975. Represents 25-50 craftworkers.
Acceptable Work: Considers batik, candlemakng, ceramics, glass art, jewelry, leatherworking, metalsmithing, pottery, scrimshaw, soft sculpture, wall hangings and weavings. Needs specific crafts at specific times during the year (write for schedule). One-of-a-kind and handmade

production-line items. Price range: $25-1,000; $25-250.
Terms: Buys outright and works on consignment; 33⅓% to 50% commission. Pays the 10th of every month. Craftworker sets retail price. Requires exclusive area representation. SASE. Reports in 2 weeks. Work may be shipped or hand delivered. Dealer pays insurance on ehxibited work. Display time: 3 months for consigned work.
Profile: "The merchandise is rotated, put in the window and advertised. Displays are on antiques on an old brick floor. There's good window frontage and spot lights." Caters to ski and tourist season in the gift shop; year around in gallery. Customers: middle class to wealthy. Heaviest wholesale buying and best selling time: summer and Christmas. We need good Western oils and watercolors year round."
To Break In: "This is Colorado. A mountain is a mountain and the same with animals. A picture of New York for example would not sell here."

Located in a pleasant inner city neighborhood, The Pug Mill Gallery in Denver, Colorado, attracts middle income customers who are looking for new items to add to their homes. Pottery is prominent in this contemporary-designed gallery, but blown glass is being sought "to add a touch of elegance to fine pottery."

ROCKY MOUNTAIN PARK CO., 4155 E. Jewell #603, Denver CO 80222. (303)757-0871. President: Ted James Jr. Gift shop. Estab. 1935. Represents 100 craftworkers.
Acceptable Work: Considers ceramics; glass art; jewelry; leatherworking; metalsmithing; pottery; wall hangings; weavings; and woodcrafting. Handmade production-line items only; utilitarian and/or decorative. Price range: $2-100; bestsellers: $5-25.
Terms: Works on consignment and buys outright; 50% commission. Retail price set by joint agreement. Reports in 1 week. Work may be shipped or hand-delivered. Dealer pays return shipping and insurance for exhibited work.
Profile: "We are the only gift shop in Rocky Mountain National Park. We average 2 million visitors annually in the 4 months we are open." Heaviest wholesale buying time: winter; best selling time: summer. "Craftworker should be able to supply reorder merchandise quickly; in a 4 month operation, time is of utmost importance."

SEBASTIAN-MOORE GALLERY, 1411 Market St., Denver CO 80202. (303)534-5659. Contact: Christy Sebastian or Mimi Moore. Craft shop/gallery/rental gallery. Estab. 1977. Represents 20 craftworkers.
Acceptable Work: Considers ceramics; clothing; dollmaking; glass art; jewelry; metalsmithing;

soft sculpture; wall hangings; weavings; and woodcrafting. Decorative one-of-a-kind designer pieces only. Price range: $20-1,000; bestsellers: $15-75.
Terms: Works on consignment; 40% commission. Craftworker sets retail price. Requires exclusive area representation. Reports in 2 weeks. Work may be shipped or hand-delivered. Dealer pays insurance for exhibited work. Displays work 6 weeks-3 months.
Profile: "Work is displayed in glass exhibit cases, on pedestals and wall space; gallery is 4,500 square feet. Customers are 30-60 year old professional people and art related students and collectors." Heaviest wholesale buying time: Christmas and summer; best selling time: October-December.

SELF EXPRESSIONS, 900 S. Clermont, Denver CO 80222. (303)758-5221. Owner: Joanne M. Bircher. Fiber supply shop/gallery/gift shop/classes. Estab. 1978. Represents 10 craftworkers.
Acceptable Work: Considers batik; clothing; needlecrafts; wood; pottery; stained glass; soft sculpture; wall hangings; basketry, weavings; and fiber basketry. Especially needs craft wearables; unusual woven hangings; and fiber craft pieces done in one or more techniques, such as a wall hanging woven, macramed and coiled. Fine one-of-a-kind designer and hand-made production-line items. Price range: $10-400; bestsellers: $10-150.
Terms: Works on consignment; 33⅓% commission. Retail price set by joint agreement. Reports in 2 weeks. Work may be shipped or hand-delivered. Dealer pays return shipping and insurance for exhibited work. Displays work 90-120 days.
Profile: "We are situated on the first floor of a little old red house with a warm, rustic atmosphere. The front room displays a vast variety of natural and novelty fibers for weaving, basketry, macrame, stitchery, knitting and crochet, and a complete line of accessory supplies such as rustic treasures, rings, feathers, books, hooks, etc. Consignment items are displayed throughout the shop. In the back portion of the shop are 2 classrooms where our diverse selection of fiber classes are taught." Heaviest buying and selling time: Christmas.

SUN SIGN, 1738 Pearl St., Boulder CO 80302. (303)444-4280. Contact: Jerry Hodge. Craft shop. Estab. 1966. Represents 25 craftworkers.
Acceptable Work: Considers batik, ceramics, glass art, jewelry, metalsmithing, pottery, soft sculpture, wall hangings, weavings and woodcrafting. Especially needs jewelry retailing for $15-75. Specializes in contemporary work, with some primitives. Price range: $10-600; bestsellers: $15-75.
Terms: Buys outright and works on consignment; 45% commission. Retail price set by joint agreement. Prefers exclusive Boulder representation. Send resume or slides. Reports in 2 weeks. Work may be shipped or hand delivered. Dealer pays shipping and insurance for exhibited work. Display time: 90 days maximum.
Profile: "New work goes into the window display and then, after several weeks, rotated in the general stock. Customers: 15-70 years old; other craftspeople, young professionals, tourists; well-educated; middle to upper incomes." Heaviest wholesale buying time: summer and Christmas; best selling time: Christmas.

SUTTON-HOO GOLDSMITH, 22 E. Bijou, Colorado Springs CO 80903. (303)471-7075. Contact: Charles Lamouaux or Diana Newell. Craft shop/gallery. Estab. 1972. Represents 15-20 craftworkers.
Acceptable Work: Considers jewelry; metalsmithing; and pottery. Fine one-of-a-kind and handmade production-line items; utilitarian only. Price range: $8-2,600; bestsellers: $8-500.
Terms: Works on consignment and buys outright; 40% commission. Craftworker sets retail price on consigned items only. Requires exclusive area representation. Reports in 2-3 weeks. Work may be hand-delivered after showing slides or photos. Dealer pays shipping to shop and insurance.
Profile: Work is shown in lighted showcases. Consigned work displayed minimum 3 months. "We have largest display of handmade jewelry in Colorado." Customers are 35-50; middle income and up. Heaviest wholesale buying time: January, September and October; best selling time: September-December.

TAPESTRY, 2859 E. 3rd Ave., Denver CO 80206. (303)322-2441. Contact: Carolyn Fineran. Gallery. Estab. 1974. Represents 75-100 craftworkers.
Acceptable Work: Considers dollmaking; glass art; jewelry; leatherworking; needlecrafts; soft sculpture; wall hangings; and weavings. Especially needs soft sculpture (dolls, plants and animals); good, basic, well-priced jewelry; and wall hangings for commercial office space. Fine one-of-a-kind and handmade production-line items; utilitarian and/or decorative. Price range: $10-3,000; bestsellers: $15-350.

Terms: Works on consignment and buys outright; 40% commission. Retail price set by joint agreement. Requires exclusive area representation. Reports in 4 weeks. Work may be shipped or hand-delivered. Dealer pays return shipping and insurance for exhibited work. Displays consigned work 6 weeks.
Profile: We "usually rotate displays monthly. Craft is treated as art; shop has elegant appeal; we do a lot with great soft sculpture. Customers are sophisticated professionals; upper-upper middle class, relatively affluent with a great sense of style." Heaviest wholesale buying time: June and August; best selling time: November-December.

THINGS FOR LIVING, Marina Square, 8101 E. Bellview St., Denver CO 80237 (303)377-9780. Craft shop/gallery/gift shop. Estab. 1974. Represents 100 American craftworkers.
Acceptable Work: Considers batik; candlemaking; ceramics; glass art; jewelry; leatherworking; metalsmithing; needlecrafts; pottery; quilting; soft sculpture; wall hangings; weavings; and woodcrafting. "Open to all new ideas." Fine one-of-a-kind and handmade production-line items. Price range: $2-2,000; bestsellers: $2-75.
Terms: Works on consignment and buys outright; 33⅓-40% commission. Retail price set by joint agreement. Requires exclusive area representation. Reports in 3 weeks. Shop pays shipping to shop; in-transit insurance; and insurance for exhibited work. Dealer and craftworker mutually set consignment time.
Profile: "We have a complete selection of items from all types of crafts; we do not specialize in only a few items." Best selling time: Christmas.

Under the new ownership of Amy-Beth, Joan and Marilyn Markowitz, the Albatross Gallery, Boulder, Colorado is a showcase for contemporary fine arts and crafts. Ceramics, fiber arts, paintings, prints and sculpture are accepted and monthly shows are held, sometimes showing media not mentioned. Items may be priced from $10 to $2,000.

TRIMBLE COURT ARTISANS, 114 Trimble Court, Fort Collins CO 80524. (303)493-9579. Contact any member shopkeeper. Cooperative/craft school/outlet. Estab. 1971. Represents 80 craftworkers, area professionals prefered.
Acceptable Work: Considers all crafts except ceramic molds, kits and decoupage. One-of-a-kind and handmade production-line items. Price range: $1-$150; bestsellers: $3-20.
Terms: Works on consignment; 33⅓% commission (25% commission, if work ½ day/week). Charges $10 yearly membership fee. Craftworker sets retail price. "Bring in representative sample of work a few days prior to the first Monday of the month." Reports in 1 week. Work may be shipped or hand delivered. Dealer pays insurance on exhibited work.
Profile: "We are a non-profit cooperative outlet and crafts school located in Old Town Fort Collins. We have 4 rooms: 1) for pottery, paintings and a special 'Exhibit of the Month'; 2) for antiques; 3) for paintings and classroom; 4) for toys, Christmas ornaments and miscellaneous. We have display cases (for jewelry and miniatures), large windows and hardwood floors." Customers: many students from Colorado State University; many local elderly folk; mostly women. Best selling time: Christmas.

THE UNIQUE, 21½ E. Bijou St., Colorado Springs CO 80903. (303)473-9406. Contact: Eva Asher. Craft shop. Estab. 1966. Represents 50-60 craftworkers.
Acceptable Work: Considers batik; candlemaking; clothing; dollmaking; glass art; jewelry; leatherworking; metalsmithing; needlecrafts; quilting; tole painting; wall hangings; weavings; woodcrafting; and Christmas ornaments. Especially needs textiles and ceramics. Price range: $2-1,000; bestsellers: $2.50-200.
Terms: Works on consignment and buys outright; 40% commission. Retail price set by joint agreement. Requires exclusive area representation. Reports in 2 weeks. Work may be shipped or hand-delivered. Dealer pays insurance for exhibited work.
Profile: "Works are usually displayed in groups with constant rearranging. Customers are college students, local people of all ages and incomes and summer tourists." Displays work minimum 90 days. Heaviest wholesale buying time: May-June and September-October; best selling time: Christmas and summer.

URIAH HEEPS, Box 1362, Aspen CO 81611. Contact: Tukey Koffend. "We are always looking for new jewelry—silver preferably. We are desperate for one-of-a-kind clothing, dresses, wraps, jackets. Not too 'craftsy'." Price range: $10-2,000. 33% commission. Retail price set by joint agreement. Prefers exclusive area representation. Send transparencies or photos. Dealer pays insurance for exhibited work; shipping costs shared. Openings sponsored and items displayed 6 weeks minimum. Located at Hotel Jerome in Aspen.

THE WATER WHEEL, 429 Elk Ave., B11, Crested Butte CO 81224. (303)349-5626. Contact: Jill West. Craft shop/gallery. Estab. 1972. Represents 120 Rocky Mountain craftworkers. Price range: $2-250; bestsellers: $2-40.
Acceptable Work: Considers batik; candlemaking; ceramics; glass art; jewelry; leatherworking; metalsmithing; pottery; quilting; wall hangings; weavings; and woodcrafting. Especially needs quilting. Fine one-of-a-kind and handmade production-line items.
Terms: Works on consignment and buys outright; 33⅓% commission. Retail price set by joint agreement. Requires exclusive area representation. Reports in 2 weeks. Work may be shipped or hand-delivered. Shipping and insurance payment negotiated.
Profile: "Customers are 95% tourists to Colorado with middle to upper incomes." Best selling and heaviest wholesale buying time: July-September and ski season.

WHICKERBILL CONTEMPORARY, 212 N. Tejon, Colorado Springs CO 80903. (303)633-0518. Contact: John Eastham. Gift shop. Estab. 1957. Represents 40 craftworkers.
Acceptable Work: Considers candlemaking; ceramics; glass art; jewelry; pottery; and woodcrafting. One-of-a-kind and handmade production-line items. Maximum price: $100; bestsellers: $5-35. Buys outright.
Terms: Craftworker sets retail price. Requires exclusive area representation. Reports in 2 weeks. Work may be shipped or hand-delivered. Dealer pays return shipping and insurance for exhibited work. Heaviest wholesale buying time: May-December; best selling time: summer and Christmas.

WILD ROSE STUDIO, 1331 18th St., Denver CO 80202. (303)623-4366. Contact: Bruce Anderson. Gallery/stained glass studio. Estab. 1972. Represents 6-10 craftworkers.
Acceptable Work: Considers all crafts. One-of-a-kind designer pieces only. Price range: $12-2,500; bestsellers: $12-150.

Terms: Buys outright but mostly works on consignment; 35% commission. Retail price set usually by craftworker; set by joint agreement "if I think the artist's prices are unrealistic on either end." Requires exclusive area representation. Send resume, slides or call for appointment. Reports in 2 weeks. Work must be hand-delivered. Dealer pays insurance on exhibited work.
Profile: "Wild Rose Studio is a producing stained glass studio working mostly on commission, but we do have a gallery showroom out of which we (and other artists/craftworkers) also sell. Gallery space is small so most shows are 1-2 person shows; about 50% were given openings. The gallery is part of a group of art galleries located in the Market Street Mall. A large portion of our customers are architects and designers. The rest are people in the upper income brackets. We have more couples than singles." Heaviest wholesale buying time: October-November; best selling itme: December.
To Break In: "I want work ready to display and delivered promptly; b&w photos are nice for press releases, also a good resume. (I mean complete not necessarily impressive.)"

Connecticut

ALENA JEWELERS-DESIGNERS, 12 E. Putnam Ave., Greenwich CT 06830. (203)869-0934. Contact: Alena Zinn. Jewelry store. Estab. 1973.
Acceptable Work: Considers karat gold jewelry only. We need well finished and simple, elegant designs—wearable designs a must." Fine one-of-a-kind and handmade production-line items. Price range: $25-3,000; bestsellers: $25-300.
Terms: Buys outright and works on consignment; 40% commission. Retail price set by joint agreement. Requires exclusive area representation. Send slides/photos or call for appointment. Reports in 3 weeks. Work may be shipped or hand delivered. Dealer pays: return shipping; shipping to shop and transit insurance if outright purchase; and insurance for exhibited work.
Profile: "Our store is very spacious and elegant. We specialize in simple, unique non-arty designs." Customers: all ages, fairly conservative, and in mid to upper income bracket. Best selling time: May-June; November-December.

APPALACHIAN HOUSE, 1010 Boston Post Rd., Darien CT 06820. (203)655-7885. Co-managers: John or Dolores Potterton. Craft shop. Estab. 1971. Represents 35 Appalachian coops and 40 Appalachian craftworkers—senior citizens, handicapped and lower income families.
Acceptable Work: Considers candlemaking, ceramics, clothing, dollmaking, glass art, jewelry, metalsmithing, needlecrafts, pottery, quilting, tole painting, wall hangings, weavings and woodcrafting. Especially needs gift items for teenagers and men. Appalachian work only. One-of-a-kind and handmade production-line items. Price range: $1-225; bestsellers: $3.50-25.
Terms: Buys outright. Retail price set by joint agreement. Send resume, slides and price list. Reports in 2 weeks. Work may be shipped or hand delivered.
Profile: "The store is in an old house in the center of town. We are in business to provide a needed outlet for Appalachian handcrafts and are staffed by volunteers. Our markup is usually much lower than a normal retail store because we are non-profit and items stay in the store until sold." Customers: middle to upper middle class, 25-45 and "those helping to preserve the Appalachian culture." Heaviest wholesale buying and best selling time: September-December.

ARTISANS CORNER, 61 Whitfield St., Guilford CT 06437. (203)453-3122. Contact: Joan Carpentiere. Craft shop and gallery. Estab. 1975. Represents 100 craftworkers.
Acceptable Work: Considers all crafts. Specializes in fine and contemporary crafts. One-of-a-kind and handmade production-line items. Price range: $1-700; bestsellers: $5-150.
Terms: Buys outright and works on consignment; 35-40% commission. Retail price set by joint agreement. Requires exclusive area representation. Send slides/brochures with SASE or call for appointment. Reports in 4 weeks. Work may be shipped or hand delivered. Dealer pays insurance on exhibited work ("on premises insurance").
Profile: "We stand facing the historic Guilford Green in an old quaint building (set back from the sidewalk) with a brick walk and a small garden area. The interior is rustic with walls of white stucco and brick. Many things are hung from wooden beams. A bay window holds our displays. We attempt to display items continuously—a rotation method is applied as to the location an item gets in the shop. Each takes its turn in the most prominent spots. All our items can be seen—it is a neat orderly shop." Customers: 25-40, above average incomes. "We also appeal to the younger and older folks, due to our wide range of crafts and price ranges." Heaviest wholesale buying time: spring and fall; best selling time: summer and November-December.
To Break In: "Items should be ready for display, realistically priced and guaranteed workmanship under normal conditions."

ARTISTS' MARKET, 319 Main Ave., Rt. 7, Norwalk CT 06851. (203)846-2550. Contact: Nancy or Jeffrey Price. Craft shop/gallery/frame shop. Estab. 1972. Represents 30-50 craftworkers who reside in the US, preferably New England or Northeast.
Acceptable Work: Considers jewelry; blown and stained glass; and pottery. Fine one-of-a-kind and handmade production-line items; utilitarian and/or decorative. Price range: $10-500; bestsellers: $1-100.
Terms: Buys outright. Usually requires exclusive area representation. Shipping payments are negotiable.
Profile: "We have very unusual crafts; high quality; and fair prices. We combine the crafts with a gallery of framed and unframed limited edition graphics. Customers are generally 25-50 in age, averaging on the young side; mostly fairly affluent. We get a lot of New York executive families since we're only 1 hour from the city." Best selling time: fall-winter.

AUFRICHTIG'S POTTERY AND JEWELRY SHOP, 837 Federal Rd., Brookfield CT 06804. (203)775-0105. Contact: Mr. or Mrs. N. Aufrichtig. Craft shop. Estab. 1971. Represents 24 craftworkers.
Acceptable Work: Considers candlemaking, stained or leaded glass art, jewelry, leatherworking, metalsmithing, all pottery made by owners, scrimshaw, macrame and woodcrafting. "Pieces should be well designed and well made—no funk art." One-of-a-kind and handmade production-line items. Price range: $2-250; bestsellers: $10-50.
Terms: Buys outright and works on consignment; 40% commission. "Consignment may be considered for something that's quite expensive or new to the items we have had experience selling." Requires exclusive area representation. Send resume and catalog. Reports in 4 weeks, if interested. Work may be shipped or hand delivered.
Profile: "The shop is an 1830 Victorian-type home. The inside is beamed and stained wood with cedar shelving. Pieces are rotated and we always have something represented by a craftsman (several pieces grouped together)." Customers: middle income, 20-45. Heaviest wholesale buying time: July-December; best selling time: October-December.
To Break In: "Keep styles and designs fresh and work always up to a high standard of craftsmanship."

BITTERSWEET FARM, 777 E. Main St., Branford CT 06405. (203)488-9126. Contact: David Wallace. Estab. 1973. Over 50 rental working/selling studios and specialty shops available. Studios available for craftworkers working in batik; weaving; silkscreening; pewter; macrame; and calligraphy. Monthly rents from $50-250. Utilities included. Write. Reports in 2 weeks.

MOLLY BRODY MINIATURES, 177 W. State St., Westport CT 06880. (203)226-5116. Contact: Molly Brody. Miniature shop. Estab. 1969. Represents 200-300 craftworkers.
Acceptable Work: Considers miniatures and dollhouses; size restriction 1"-1'. Special need for silversmith doing top quality sterling pieces. Fine one-of-a-kind and handmade production-line items. Price range: $1-1,200.
Terms: Works on consignment and buys outright; 33⅓% commission. Retail price set by joint agreement. Requires exclusive area representation. Reports in 4 weeks. Shipping payments negotiable; dealer pays insurance on exhibited work.
Profile: "We put most of our merchandise behind glass for protection. Customers range from 6-91 years. Generally high middle income fanatics about collecting miniatures. The field of miniatures is growing every year. We see a 10 year period of high sales and expect to develop a million lifetime collectors nationally."

THE CANVAS PATCH, 28 Broad St., Milford CT 06460. (203)878-7505. Manager: Marti Reed. Specialty shop. Estab. 1977. Represents 20 craftworkers.
Acceptable Work: Considers dollmaking, glass art, jewelry, needlecrafts, pottery, scrimshaw, soft sculpture, tole painting, wall hangings, weavings and woodcrafting. Also considers handpainting and monogramming on canvas handbags. One-of-a-kind items only. "We accept only items not seen at church fairs, craft fairs, etc., and only quality work which we feel will fit in with the theme of our shop." Price range: $1-250; bestsellers: $5-25.
Terms: Buys outright and works on consignment; 33⅓% commission. Retail price set by joint agreement. Requires exclusive area representation. Call for appointment or hand-deliver samples. Work may be shipped or hand delivered.
Profile: "We are a quality canvas shop specializing in all kinds of canvas bags, totes, purses and custom work and repairs. As well, we are a 'nautical country store' with many nautical decorative and gift items from all over the world as well as locally. Items are placed in groupings to show them off the best and are moved frequently. Like items are clustered to help customers.

Customers are people who appreciate fine work and out-of-the-ordinary pieces. They are boaters who dock in our harbor and walk to the green. People from surrounding areas, who have no shop like ours in their area, enjoy browsing in our nautical-country atmosphere as well as summer folk who live on the shore." Heaviest wholesale buying time; early spring and fall; best selling time: Christmas and summer.

COQUI GALLERIES, 20 Church Lane, Westport CT 06880. (203)227-5234. Contact: Rona Cohen or Gayla Halbrecht. Gallery. Estab. 1977. Represents 100 mostly contemporary American craftworkers; but would consider artists in other media in limited amounts.
Acceptable Work: Considers ceramics; hand-woven articles including clothing; glass art; jewelry; metalsmithing; needlecraft; quilting; soft sculpture; weavings; wall hangings; and woodworking. "Special need for more macrame; unusual functional items; seasonal items; jewelry; and clothing (art to wear for fashion shows and special exhibits). The interior design studio has been expanded and grown so much during the last year that we find we need more decorative arts (furniture, lamps, wall hangings, and large unusual sculpted pieces)." One-of-a-kind decorative items and quality production items; quality is stressed. Price range: $4-3,600; bestsellers: $15-60.
Terms: Mostly works on consignment and buys some outright; 40% commission. Retail price set by joint agreement. Requires exclusive area representation. Reports as soon as possible. Shipping payment negotiable; dealer pays insurance on exhibited work. Exhibited items are displayed for 30 days.
Profile: "We are the only gallery shop of its kind in the area. We are actually 2 galleries in 1 store—artisan gallery as above and separate design studio which specializes in interior design and commissions many works from artisan gallery for design clients (accessories, glass, furniture, etc.). We do monthly exhibits featuring well-recognized, as well as new, artisans. We do a great deal of PR on all exhibits. Customers are of all ages; highly educated; knowledgeable; and with large disposable income." Best selling time: spring and fall-Christmas.

COUNTRY BAZAAR, 451 Main St. S., Woodbury CT 06798. (203)263-2228. Contact: Jerry Madans. Antique and craft shop. Estab. 1968. Represents 6 craftworkers. Considers jewelry; metalsmithing; pottery; and woodcrafting. Primitive handmade production-line items; utilitarian and/or decorative. Price range: $1-100; bestsellers: $5-25. Works on consignment and buys outright; 33⅓% commission. Craftworker sets retail price. Reports in 2 weeks.

CRAFTS END, 26 Isaac St., Norwalk CT 06850. (203)853-9920. Contact: Marie LeFevre. Craft/gift shop and gallery. Estab. 1977. Represents 80 craftworkers.
Acceptable Work: Considers decoupage, dollmaking, glass art, jewelry, leatherworking, needlecrafts, pottery, soft sculpture, tole painting, wall hangings, weavings and woodcrafting. One-of-a-kind items only. Price range: $3-125; bestsellers: $2-25.
Terms: Works on consignment; 33⅓% commission. Retail price set by craftworker or joint agreement. Requires exclusive area representation. Send resume, slides/samples with SASE or call for appointment. Reports in 3 weeks. Work may be shipped or hand delivered.
Profile: "'Crafts from beginning to end' best describes our shop. We have all varieties of craft supplies and have the finished product for the person who prefers to buy their crafts. Our shop is attractively decorated in rustic woods, is quite large and is one of the largest in southern Connecticut. Items are displayed in an area of the store called 'Gallery of Crafts.' This is a shelf and wall display with an area of about 26x15'." Heaviest wholesale buying time: September-December; best selling time: August-December.

CURRENT CRAFTS, 3208 Whitney Ave., Mt. Carmel CT 06518. (203)288-9868. Contact: Don DeStefano. Estab. 1961. Represents 300 craftworkers. Heaviest wholesale buying time: spring and summer; best selling time: winter.
Acceptable Work: Considers candlemaking; glass art; jewelry; leatherworking; metalsmithing; pottery; wall hangings; and woodcrafting. Finished one-of-a-kind and handmade production-line items. Price range: $1-200; bestsellers: $5-50.
Terms: Buys outright. Shop sets retail price. Query with transparencies or photos. Reports in 30 days. Dealer pays shipping to shop and insurance for exhibited work.

THE DOUGLAS GALLERY, INC., 1117 High Ridge Rd., Stamford CT 06905. (203)322-7233. Contact: Douglas Jayne. Considers sculpture. Maximum size: 2' square. Sculpture must have pedestal. Works on consignment; 33⅓% commission. Price range: $25-2,000; bestsellers: $150-800. Retail price set by joint agreement. Requires exclusive area representation. Send slides or photos of work. SASE. Gallery pays insurance for exhibited work. 2-6 months exposure.

DOWN ON THE FARM, LTD., Banner Rd., Moodus CT 06469. (203)873-9005. Contact: Joyce Simon. Craft/gift shop and gallery. Estab. 1977. Represents 185 American craftworkers.
Acceptable Work: Considers all crafts except tole painting. Specializes in fine one-of-a-kind and handmade production-line items. Price range: $2.95-$600; bestsellers: $13.95, $80-200.
Terms: Buys outright and works on consignment; 40% commission. Craftworker sets retail price; "we reserve right to raise or lower within reasonable limitations." Requires exclusive area representation within 25 miles. Send resume and slides or call for appointment. Reports in 4 weeks. Work may be shipped or hand delivered. Dealer pays shipping and insurance.
Profile: "We are part of a larger craft center located on a working poultry farm. The center is housed in a restored chicken coop (200 ft. by 25 ft.). Gallery space is 100 ft. by 25 ft. (2500 sq. ft). We are in a country environment but close enough to major metro areas, New York and Boston. Consigned items displayed for 3 months. Display units are hand crafted and designed by our resident furniture designer (gallery/museum-style display). Besides the shop, the center houses 6 rental spaces for rental, teaching and other related facilities. We operate a glassblower's studio on the premises. We will be adding another restored coop (with approximately 20 studios) to the center in the near future. One of our greatest satisfactions has been in helping craftspeople establish themselves, and we hope to continue to do so in the future. Customers are of all ages and interests with incomes ranging from $5,000 to over $75,000." Heaviest wholesale buying time: winter-spring; best selling time: summer and pre-Christmas.

THE ELEMENTS, 14 Liberty Way, Greenwich CT 06830. (203)661-0014. Gallery Manager: Sue Fox. Gallery. Estab. 1973. Represents 300 craftworkers.
Acceptable Work: Considers basketry, batik, ceramics, clothing, glass art, jewelry, metalsmithing, pottery, wall hangings, weavings and woodcrafting. Specializes in contemporary crafts. One-of-a-kind and handmade production-line items. Price range: $15-2,000; bestsellers: $25-40.
Terms: Buys outright and works on consignment; 40% commission. Retail price set by joint agreement. Prefers exclusive area representation. Send resume and slides. SASE. Reports in 2-4 weeks. Work must be shipped or hand-delivered. Dealer pays insurance on exhibited work.
Profile: "We have 1-person, group and theme shows. In addition to the featured work, we have a representative collection of work by gallery artists on display." Heaviest wholesale buying time: fall; best selling time: Christmas and spring.

FARMINGTON VALLEY ARTS CENTER, INC., Box 220, Avon Park N., Avon CT 06001. (203)678-1867. Executive Director: Betty Friedman. Nonprofit gallery. Estab. 1974. Works on consignment; 20% commission. Craftworker sets retail price. Gallery pays insurance on exhibited work. Exhibitions change monthly.
Acceptable Work: Considers batik; clothing; glass art; jewelry; leatherworking; metalsmithing; needlecrafts; pottery; quilting; soft sculpture; weavings; wallhangings; woodcrafting; and sculpture. Fine one-of-a-kind; utilitarian and/or decorative. Price range: $10-500; bestsellers: $10-150.
Profile: "The gallery features work by outstanding artists/craftsmakers who are not normally shown in this area. In conjunction with the gallery approximately 20 artists maintain studios at the Arts Center; the majority of which function as small shops and galleries as well as work space. Classes, workshops and lectures are held at the Arts Center, often in conjunction with the special gallery exhibitions." Eight exhibitions/year plus holiday exhibit/sale November and December of quality New England crafts.

GUILFORD HANDCRAFT CENTER, Box 221. Guilford CT 06437. (203)453-5947. Director: Beth Parrott. Craft/gift shop/gallery. Estab. 1968. Represents 100 craftworkers.
Acceptable Work: Considers batik, ceramics, clothing, glass art, jewelry, leatherworking, metalsmithing, pottery, quilting, soft sculpture, wall hangings, weavings and woodcrafting. Specializes in contemporary limited production and one-of-a-kind designer pieces. Price range: $5-500. Special shows run 4-5 times/year for 6-8 weeks.
Terms: Consignment and limited wholesale; 33⅓% commission. Craftworker sets retail price. New work juried first Wednesday of month. Send slides and price list. Reports in 2 weeks. Work may be shipped or hand-delivered. Dealer pays insurance on exhibited work.
Profile: "The shop is part of a craft center which also includes a school and exhibition gallery and serves southern Connecticut. Approximately 75% of the work is on display and displays are changed weekly." Customers: collectors, upper middle class members of the community, artists, students and craftsmen. Heaviest wholesale buying time: fall and spring; best selling time: October-December.
To Break In: "Concise presentation with complete inventories appreciated. Applications and

requests for information must include SASE."

LUTA STUDIOS, Rt. 9A, Deep River CT 06417. (203)526-5812. Contact: Nancy Mazzoni. Estab. 1971. Represents 3-6 craftworkers. Considers all crafts. Finished, one-of-a-kind and production-line, handmade items; utilitarian and/or decorative. Price range: $1.50-350; bestsellers: $3-35. Buys outright. Craftworker sets retail price. Write.
Profile: "Items displayed 4-6 weeks in gallery setting with spot lighting. Items moved after several weeks for optimum attention." Heaviest wholesale buying time: fall and spring. Best selling time: Christmas and summer. "High quality, well-displayed crafts." Customers age 25-65 with $18,000-35,000 income; they buy crafts for artistic value.

THE MYSTIC RIVER GUILD, 13 Water Street, Mystic CT 06355. (203)536-6688. Contact: Patricia Camp. Craft/gift shop and gallery. Represents 15-20 craftworkers.
Acceptable Work: Considers all crafts. One-of-a-kind and handmade production-line items. Price range: $1.50-750; bestsellers: $2.50-25.
Terms: Buys outright and works on consignment; 33⅓% commission. Retail price set by joint agreement. Requires exclusive area representation. Call for appointment. Reports in 2 weeks. Work may be shipped or hand delivered. Dealer pays insurance on exhibited work.
Profile: "We are a small exclusive retail shop with high end gifts and decorative accessories (⅓ crafts, ⅓ arts, ⅓ commercial items). Our wholesale operation (P.O. Box 271, Mystic) represents several outstanding crafters, mainly in the Northeast. The retail shop doubles as a showroom. New items generally get a preferential area display for about a month. Very exceptional items get newspaper ad promotion. After initial impact has slowed, items reverse to conventional wall or showcase display. We try to give every consigned item about 6 months prior to return to the crafter unless the item contributes to general ambiance. There's no periodic price reduction policy. Local customers are affluent (25,000+ income) and there's a surprising number of young people in modest (10-18,000 income) bracket who do not hesitate to make a major commitment for really high quality items. In the fall, there are less 'lookers'—older with more purchasing power, but fewer needs."
To Break In: "We prefer not to handle 'cutesy artsy craftsy' items; buyers are becoming increasingly sophisticated about crafts and will pay for real quality; if buyers think 'Oh, I could make that myself if I only had the time', the item will be a poor seller."

MYSTIC SEAPORT MUSEUM STORE, Mystic CT 06355. (203)536-8010. President: Thomas H. Aageson. Museum gift shop. Estab. 1938. Represents 50-75 craftworkers.
Acceptable Work: Considers candlemaking; ceramics; clothing; dollmaking; jewelry; metalsmithing; needlecrafts; pottery; quilting; soft sculpture; weavings; and wall hangings. "We are searching for work that represents the 19th century, either reproductions or adaptations. We also need items that reflect a maritime theme." Price range: $1-1,500.
Terms: Works on consignment and buys outright; 40% commission. Craftworker sets retail price. Requires exclusive area representation. Reports in 2 weeks. Dealer pays shipping to shop if outright purchase, and insurance for exhibited work.
Profile: "The shop is an integral part of Mystic Seaport, a nonprofit museum. As an educational institution we represent the 19th century and the country's maritime heritage. It is the country's largest maritime museum. Our museum store selections represent this period and/or nation's maritime heritage." Best selling time: summer.

PEYTON ORIGINALS, Box 124, Brookfield Center CT 06805. (203)775-0044. Contact: Paul or Elizabeth Peyton. Craft and gift shop/manufacturer of handcrafted gifts. Estab. 1970. Considers glass art; needlecrafts; pottery; and unusual candles. Finished handmade production-line items; utilitarian and/or decorative. Nothing over $25; bestsellers: $10-20. Buys outright; shop sets retail price. Best selling season: October-December.

THE QUEST FOR HANDCRAFTS, Forty Boutiques Mall, Ridgeway Center, 2299 Summer St., Stamford CT 06905. (203)324-2260. Managers: Ruth A. and B.N. Schrauf. Craft shop. Estab. 1974. Represents 300 craftworkers who are professional in their work and shipping procedures.
Acceptable Work: Considers all crafts, except decoupage and tole painting. "Ceramics is the best seller." One-of-a-kind and handmade production-line items. Price range: $3-300; bestsellers: $3-60.
Terms: Buys outright. Shop sets retail price. Send resume and slides with SASE or call for appointment. Reports in 2 weeks; does not report in December. Work may be shipped or hand delivered.

Profile: "We sell unique, creative work of top quality almost entirely made by American craftsmen. We advertise ourselves as a year-round craft fair. New items are first displayed in the window, then rotated to positions in the shop. We arrange constantly as we are cramped for space." Customers: mostly ages 30-40, $18,000-60,000 incomes, interested in the arts. "We also have many visitors from foreign countries looking for something uniquely American to take home for themselves and others." Heaviest wholesale buying time: September-October; best selling time: June and December.
To Break In: "Craftworker must: 1) include a packing list with each shipment; 2) have consistent quality of work; 3) have proper packing; 4) fulfill orders within a reasonable time period—30-60 days."

THE SHOP—GUILFORD HANDCRAFT CENTER, Box 221, Guilford CT 06437. (203)453-5947. Shop/Gallery Director: Pamela Holeman. Craft shop. Estab. 1968. Represents 75-100 craftworkers.
Acceptable Work: Considers batik; ceramics; clothing; glass art; jewelry; leatherworking; metalsmithing; pottery; quilting; soft sculpture; wall hangings; weavings; and woodcrafting. Fine one-of-a-kind and handmade production-line items. Price range: $12-250; bestsellers: $10-60.
Terms: Works on consignment and limited wholesale; 25% commission. Craftworker sets retail price. Dealer pays insurance for exhibited work; unsold consigned pieces returned after 90 days. All work subjected to jury selection. Submit slides and/or samples first Wednesday of each month.
Profile: "This is a nonprofit school, exhibit and sales center. We show a wide range of work representing all geographic areas. Recent grant from Connecticut Commission on the Arts has facilitated expansion of marketing, promotion and publicity for The Shop." Customers are sophisticated, collection-oriented. Best selling time: Christmas and summer months.

THE SILO, Upland Road, New Milford CT 06776. (203)355-0300. Contact: Ruth Henderson. Gallery/gift shop/country kitchen store. Estab. 1972. Represents 24 craftworkers with production capabilty to handle orders and with high level of creativity and individuality in work.
Acceptable Work: Considers batik; ceramics; decoupage; glass art; metalsmithing; needlecrafts; pottery; quilting; soft sculpture; weavings; wall hangings; and woodcrafting. Finished and primitive handmade production-line items; utilitarian and/or decorative. Price range: $4-2,000; bestsellers: $10-50.
Terms: Works on consignment; buys outright; and selects work for special exhibitions. 40% commission. Retail price set by consultation. Prefers exclusive area representation. Reports in 4 weeks. Only items with prepaid receipt and return postage accepted.
Profile: "Arts and crafts selected for exhibition remain on exhibition for roughly 4 weeks; display technique is at the craftworker's discretion with approval of The Silo. The Silo has been described as bringing the best of Bloomingdale's and Bendel's to Connecticut. Customers are chiefly professionals; artists; writers; musicians; Broadway producers; fashion designers—the 'in' crowd of western Connecticut, chiefly New Yorkers who maintain second homes in the area."

THE SILVERWORKS, The Market Place, 125 Main St., Westport CT 06880. (203)226-9636. Contact: Hedy Adler. Craft/gift/silversmith shop. Estab. 1975. Represents 6-10 craftworkers.
Acceptable Work: Considers glass art, jewelry, metalsmithing, pottery, soft sculpture and woodcrafting. Specializes in contemporary fine art one-of-a-kind pieces. Price range: $10-150.
Terms: Buys outright, net 30 and works on consignment; 40% commission. Retail price set by shop or joint agreement. Requires exclusive area representation. Send slides/catalog or call for appointment. Reports in about 1 week. Work may be shipped or hand delivered. Dealer pays insurance on exhibited work, unless item is faulty.
Profile: Small shop recently relocated in a mall on a main shopping street. A workshop is located in the rear of the store. Items displayed in glass showcases or on shelves. "Westport is well-known for shoppers in the high income bracket." Heaviest wholesale buying time: spring-fall.
To Break In: "Mail the same quality product as the samples—too often it is not!"

SOCIETY OF CONNECTICUT CRAFTSMEN, Box 37, Rt. 9A, Deep River CT 06417. (203)526-5812. Contact: Nancy Mazzoni. Estab. 1935. Represents about 250 member craftworkers. Contact SCC for membership details.
Acceptable Work: Considers batik; candlemaking; ceramics; dollmaking; glass art; leatherworking; metalsmithing; mobiles; needlecrafts; pottery; sculpture; tole paintings; wall

hangings; weavings; and woodcrafting.
Terms: Price range: $1.50 and up; bestsellers: $1.50-35. 25% commission. Craftworker sets retail price. Reports on jury review in spring and fall in *SCC Newsletter*.

STRONG CRAFT GALLERY, Civic Center Shops, Hartford CT 06103. (203)522-9083. Manager: Julie Branner. Craft shop. Estab. 1975. Represents 250 craftworkers.
Terms: Send slidies or call for appointment. Requires exclusive area representation. Reports on inquiries in 2 weeks.
Profile: "This is a branch of the main shop in Maine and most of the same work is carried in both places, the character is similar, but Hartford sells much more glass—both stained glass mirrors and boxes, planters and hand-blown glass of all kinds. The Hartford customer tends to be younger and more aware of new style trends. Best selling time: Christmas."

THE SUNSHINE FACTORY, 142 New Haven Ave., Milford CT 06760. (203)878-9797. Contact: Chris or Muriel Swihura. Gallery/craft shop/plant shop/tea room. Estab. 1976. Represents 300 craftworkers.
Acceptable Work: Considers batik; candlemaking; clothing; dollmaking; glass art; jewelry; leatherworking; metalsmithing; needlecrafts; pottery; quilting; soft sculpture; tole painting; wall hangings; weaving; woodcrafting; pressed flowers; dough work; sandcasting; and stationery. Especially needs woodworking, stained glass and quilts. Price range: 50¢-$400; bestsellers: $5-15.
Terms: Works on consignment; 40% commission. Craftworker sets retail price. Requires exclusive Milford representation. Reports in 1 week. Work may be shipped or hand-delivered, subject to our approval of samples. Dealer pays return shipping.
Profile: "Craftwork is exhibited with the help of antiques and collectibles (oak pews, Vermont glass pie cases for jewelry, old sleds, old stoves and a jungle of ferns and greenery). We are in a large lovely old home with a tea room upstairs. The Tea Room is our gallery restaurant serving homemade soups, breads, desserts, and also helps us showcase our crafts and antiques. We use our fireplace all winter and have established a very friendly atmosphere. We handle a great deal of customer orders. 60% of our customers are from out of town; most are women although we see more men every day."

THENDARA STUDIO GALLERY, 590 Oxford Rd., Oxford CT 06483. (203)263-0400. Contact: Millicent McKee. Gallery/studio. Estab. 1973. Represents 3 craftworkers.
Acceptable Work: Considers batik, glass art, pottery, soft sculpture, wall hangings, weavings and woodcrafting. One-of-a-kind designer crafts only. Price range: $2 minimum; bestsellers: $2.50-300.
Terms: Works on consignment; 30% commission. Retail price set by joint agreement. Send resume, slides or call for appointment. SASE. "Bring slides or work in to be juried." Reports in 1-2 weeks. Work may be shipped or hand-delivered. Display time: 1 month.
Profile: "We are a fine arts and crafts gallery. To make sure the craftworkers are good, they must have a following to exhibit here." Best selling time: spring-winter.

THE TRESKUNOFF STUDIO, INC., 70 Main Street, Ansonia CT 06401. (203)734-1435. President: Edwin J. Jacek. Gallery. Estab. 1917. Represents 60 craftworkers.
Acceptable Work: Considers ceramics, decoupage, glass art, metalsmithing, scrimshaw and woodcrafting. One-of-a-kind and handmade production-line items. Price range: $4.95-175; bestsellers: $65-120.
Terms: Buys outright and works on consignment. Retail price set by joint agreement. Call for appointment with SASE. Reports in 1 week. Work may be shipped or hand delivered.

UPSTAIRS POTTERY, 198 West St., Cromwell CT 06416. (203)635-0808. Contact: Helen Yaglowski. Craft shop. Estab. 1977. Represents 6 local stoneware potters using no molds.
Acceptable Work: Considers pottery. Primitive and fine one-of-a-kind pieces. Price range: $3-75; bestsellers: $5-20.
Terms: Works on consignment; 40% commission. Craftworker sets retail price. Reports in 1 month. Hand-delivered work only. Dealer pays insurance for exhibited work.
Profile: "It is the only full-time pottery shop in a large area. Our customers are in the late 20's, early 30's and are getting into the natural nonplastic material area, looking for things not mass-produced." Best selling time: Christmas.

VOLTAIRE'S SHOP & GALLERY, Rt. 2, New Milford CT 06776. (203)354-4200. Contact: Mrs. P. Voltaire. Craft/gift shop and gallery. Estab. 1956. Represents 45-50 craftworkers.

Acceptable Work: Considers batik, ceramics, clothing, glass art, jewelry, leatherworking, metalsmithing, pottery, soft sculpture, wall hangings, weavings and woodcrafting. Especially needs hand wrought iron sculpture, chandeliers and candleholders. Specializes in contemporary and fine crafts. One-of-a-kind and handmade production-line items. Price range: $1-1,500; bestsellers: $10-50.
Terms: Buys outright and works on consignment; 40% commission on consignments; 50% on purchases. Retail price set by joint agreement. Requires exclusive area representation. Send slides or call for appointment. Reports in 2 weeks. Work may be shipped (never C.O.D.) or hand delivered. Dealer pays shipping for purchased work and return shipping for consignment work. Gallery covers certain risks within limits, but additional insurance coverage paid by craftsman.
Profile: "We are known as a contemporary, 'good design' establishment. Many New Yorkers of above average incomes who have second homes in the area are our customers." Best selling time: Christmas and summer.

WASHINGTON ART ASSOCIATION, Washington Depot CT 06794. (203)868-2878. Executive Secretary: Joan Talbot. Gallery. Estab. 1952. Represents about 60 craftworkers during the Christmas sale; 4-10 during the craft show.
Acceptable Work: Considers all crafts. Fine one-of-a-kind and handmade production-line items. Price range: $1.50-1,000; bestsellers: $1.50-250.
Terms: Works on consignment; 25% commission. Craftworker sets retail price. Sometimes charges $50/week per room for exhibit space; group shows have $5 entry fee.
Profile: "It is a nonprofit gallery run by volunteers. Usually crafts are invited for a 3-week exhibit. Work is selected by a committee except for open craft show at Christmas when work is taken on consignment." Wide range of customers. Best selling time: Christmas and August.

WEBB & PARSONS, 134 Elm St., New Canaan CT. (203)966-1400. Directors: Pat Parsons and Carol and Bill Webb. Gallery. Estab. 1970. Represents contemporary American artists and craftsmen. Considers all crafts, functional and nonfunctional. Price range: $1-5,000. Works on consignment; 40% commission. Send slides.

WHY NOT 1, 71 Church St., Greenwich CT 06830. (203)661-8383. Contact: Lyn Lally. Craft shop. Estab. 1978. Represents 30-35 American craftworkers.
Acceptable Work: Considers wearable craft, sterling jewelry, soft sculpture, leatherworking, metalsmithing, pottery, weaving and woodcrafting. Especially need unique functional items. One-of-a-kind pieces. Price range: $5-250.
Terms: Buys outright and works on consignment; 40% commission. Retail price set by joint agreement. Requires exclusive area representation. Reports in 2 weeks. Work may be shipped or hand delivered. Dealer pays shipping to shop and insurance on exhibited work.
Profile: "Our gallery is an elegant white with wrought iron and black accents."

Delaware

DELAWARE MUSEUM OF NATURAL HISTORY, Box 3937, Greenville DE 19807. (302)658-9111. Museum Shop Manager: Alicia Ann Chomo. Museum gift shop. Estab. 1972. Represents 3 craftworkers.
Acceptable Work: Considers glass art, jewelry, needlecrafts, scrimshaw, shell art, stationery, wall hangings and weavings. Especially needs shell jewelry and inexpensive animal carvings. Specializes in contemporary handmade production-line items. "At the present, we are only showing local people who have made shell jewelry or crafts, but this is open to change, depending on items submitted. For IRS purposes, we may only sell items which relate, in any way, to our specimens on exhibit. We deal with animals, shells and birds. Any items with this subject matter are acceptable." Price range: $1-100; bestsellers: $1-20.
Terms: Buys outright and works on consignment; 40% commission. Gallery sets retail price. Contact in any manner which is convenient. SASE. Reports in 2 weeks. Dealer pays insurance on exhibited work. Display time: usually 3 months.
Profile: Displays in glass cases and on glass shelving. "The shop features museum publications as well as items which relate directly to specimens on exhibit." Customers: school children, ages 8-14 spending 25¢-$2; senior citizens, ages 65+ on fixed incomes spending $1-5; families with 2+ children, ages 20+ (children, 1-6 years old) with lower middle incomes, spending $1-2 for children's gifts. Heaviest wholesale buying time: early April and early November; best selling time: May-June (for school groups) and especially November-December (for tour groups and Christmas shoppers).
To Break In: "Offer moderately-priced items which can be restocked quickly by our shop if the

demand so indicates. Do not push for an immediate answer concerning handling of your items. Stay within the prices indicated."

GALLERY 18, Box 593, Nassau DE 19969. (302)684-4829. Contact: W.E. Reifsnyder. Craft shop/gallery/frame shop. Estab. 1969. Represents 2-3 craftworkers.
Acceptable Work: Considers ceramics; glass art; jewelry; leatherworking; metalsmithing; wall hangings; and weavings. Fine one-of-a-kind and handmade production-line items. Price range: $10-70; bestsellers: $10-50.
Terms: Buys outright. Gallery sets retail price. Requires exclusive area representation. Reports in 2 weeks. Dealer pays insurance for exhibited work.
Profile: Customers are middle-level executives and professionals, 30-60 years old. Best selling time: spring-fall.

GRASSROOTS HANDCRAFTS, 39 E. Main St., Newark DE 19711. (302)453-9751. Contact: Marilyn Barnekov or Vonna Taylor. Craft shop. Estab. 1975. Represents 75 craftworkers. Considers batik; candlemaking; ceramics; clothing; glass art; jewelry; leatherworking; metalsmithing; pottery; quilting; wall hangings; weavings; and woodcrafting. One-of-a-kind and handmade production-line items; utilitarian and/or decorative. Bestsellers: $5-215. Takes very little consignment and prefers buying outright; 33⅓% commission. Retail price set by joint agreement. Requires exclusive area representation. Dealer pays shipping if buying work; and insurance for exhibited work.
Profile: "We are near a university but have customers of all ages from the community. We also have a summer shop in Rehoboth Beach, Delaware." Best selling time: Christmas.

WARE GALLERY, 1800 Breen Lane, Wilmington DE 19810. (302)475-4208. Contact: Dorothy Truman. Craft shop/gallery/gift shop. Estab. 1951. Represents 15-20 craftworkers. Considers batik; ceramics; dollmaking; glass art; jewelry; leatherworking; metalsmithing; needlecrafts; pottery; quilting; soft sculpture; wall hangings; weavings; and woodcrafting. Fine one-of-a-kind pieces; utilitarian and/or decorative. Price range: $5-250; bestsellers: $5-25. Works on consignment and buys outright; 33% commission. Craftworker sets retail price. Requires exclusive area representation. Hand-delivered work only.
Profile: "Shop is uncrowded and well-lighted. Work is displayed in conjunction with paintings on walls." Best selling time: fall-spring.

WARE GALLERY, GIFTS, 2208 Millers Rd., Ardentown DE 19810. (302)475-9804. Contact: Joan Ware Colgan. Gallery/gift shop. Estab. 1950. Represents about 15 craftworkers, mostly local. Considers batik; ceramics; decoupage; glass art; jewelry; leatherworking; needlecrafts; pottery; soft sculpture; wall hangings; weavings; and woodcrafting. All styles; utilitarian and/or decorative. Price range: $1-100; bestsellers: $1-20. Works on consignment and sometimes buys outright; 25% commission. Craftworker sets retail price. Hand-delivered work only. Consigned pieces kept until sold or craftworker requests return. Best selling time: Christmas.

WINTERTHUR MUSEUM BOOKSTORE & GIFT SHOP, Winterthur DE 19735. (302)656-8591. Supervisor: Bobbi Bruni. Museum gift shop and bookstore. Estab. 1951. Represents 15-20 craftworkers.
Acceptable Work: Considers candlemaking, ceramics, metalsmithing, needlecrafts, export porcelain, designer jewelry, pottery, quilting, tole painting and woodcrafting. "American colonial crafts preferred, such as pottery, tinsmiths, candlemaking, weaving, needlework and cabinetmaking on a small scale. Museum represents American decorative arts from 1640-1860. However, we will stretch into the Victorian period." Folk one-of-a-kind and handmade production-line items. Price range: $1-120; bestsellers: $10-30.
Terms: Buys outright. "We buy very little to test the items, then with experience will reorder for a short time." Shop sets retail price. Prefers exclusive area representation. Call for appointment. Reports in 1 week. Work may be shipped or hand-delivered.
Profile: Displays in glass cases and on shelves. Customers: college age and up. Heaviest wholesale buying time: summer; best selling time: fall-Christmas.

Florida

ANIMAL CRACKERS, 3400 Gulf Blvd., St. Petersburg Beach FL 33706. (813)360-2079. Contact: Kay Ehrenkonig. Gift shop. Estab. 1978. Represents 15-20 craftworkers.
Acceptable Work: Considers children's clothing, dollmaking, needlecrafts, quilting, soft sculpture and tole painting. Specializes in children's gift items (i.e. dolls, stuffed animals, pillows,

music boxes, purses, clothing); kitchen or wall decorations; and Christmas ornaments and decorations. One-of-a-kind and handmade production-line items. Price range: $1-85; bestsellers: $1-30.

Terms: Works on consignment; 40% commission. "We may buy outright after work proves to be a good seller." Retail price set by joint agreement. Send resume, slides/photos with SASE. Reports in 1 week. Work may be shipped or hand delivered. Dealer pays insurance on exhibited work.

Profile: "The shop is located in the main lobby of the Don Cesar Beach Resort Hotel. The decor follows a circus theme. The dispay cases are styled like circus wagons with shelving within. The center island display is a brass cradle. All items are displayed constantly. The customers range from children to grandparents. The summer people are budgeted while the winter people have good to excellent incomes." Heaviest wholesale buying time: September-October; best selling time: November-March.

To Break In: "I appreciate craftworkers who deliver items ready for display that are reasonable in price. Original and unique items are always the best sellers."

THE BANANA BOX AT YBOR SQUARE, 1901 N. 13th St., Tampa FL 33605. (813)247-6972. Contact: Bettie Perez. Gift and antique shop. Represents 12-15 craftworkers.
Acceptable Work: Considers ceramics; jewelry; miniatures of all kinds; metalsmithing; pottery; woodcrafting; rubbings; copper enameling; dolls; note cards; and books. "We have a special need for Spanish crafts since Ybor Square's history is Spanish. Also is a need for $20-65 marquetry; pewter animals and boxes; unusual mirrors; small furniture accents; shelves; stools; and clocks. We are inclined towards inspirational or works that have some meaning, both functional and artistic. Boxes of all types are a specialty with us—$1-10." Price range: $1.95-250; bestsellers: $1.95-50.
Terms: Buys outright. Retail price set by joint agreement. Requires exclusive area representation on some items. Submit samples and SASE. Reports in 4 weeks.
Profile: "We are in a unique historical area that is being restored. There is much interest in antiques; old art forms; collectibles; and art shows. We have a big tourist season; there's always an interest in Florida artists but some of my best sellers are from New England and California." Best selling time: fall-winter.

BOUNTY SHOP, 219 Atlantic Blvd., Atlantic Beach FL 32233. (904)246-7855. Contact: Dody Fleckenstein. Considers ceramics; sculpture; jewelry; metalsmithing; glass; leather; tie dying; and batik. Price range: $5-200. Retail price set by joint agreement. Send transparencies or photos.

THE CENTER OF MODERN ART, INC., Box 297, Micanopy FL 32667. (904)466-3459. Chairpersons, Board of Artists: Bill Hutchinson and Cynthia Edmonds. Gallery and gift shop. Estab. 1967. Represents 50-100 craftworkers.
Acceptable Work: Considers all crafts. Specializes in contemporary American arts and crafts. One-of-a-kind, designer pieces. Price range: $3-500; bestsellers $3-100.
Terms: Works on consignment; 33⅓% commission. Must have approval of the Board of Artists; send resume and 5 slides of work. Reports in 4 weeks. Craftworker sets retail price unless advice is sought. Work may be shipped or hand delivered.
Profile: "The Center of Modern Art is a non-profit educational gallery dedicated to presenting the best of contemporary arts and crafts. It is located in the small historic town of Micanopy, Florida (state's second oldest city) and in a partly restored historic building. It is accessible to an Interstate and Federal highway (I-75, US 441) and 9 miles south of Gainesville (pop. 95,000 SMSA) and the University of Florida. Items accepted for shows in the gallery are displayed by the Board of Artists in the most visually pleasing manner. We have an abundance of props, space, cases, and lighting. The shop displays crafts through the year and rearranges and rotates stock monthly. Items sold are paid to the artist monthly and all unsold items are returned at the end of the show year. Currently the center has a membership of 200 who patronize regularly. Artists from all areas know and come to the center. The University of Florida provides a great number of students, staff, and faculty who are regular visitors and workers of the Center. Patrons are art wise and economically well-off. Occassional student groups conduct tours at the Center." Open: last week of September-last week of May. Best selling time: October-December. "The main event is a specially priced and promoted Christmas Show. The center has 9 different show openings per year; sales are best on opening days."
To Break In: "The Center accepts the best in art and crafts for its seasonal shows. Application for a show is needed at least 9 months in advance. The Center shop however continually seeks craftsmen for shop exhibits. Notification of shop acceptance is immediate."

CRAFTS & THINGS, 121 Harrison St., Rockledge FL 32922. (305)636-6381. Contact: Thelma M. Murrell. Craft and gift shop. Estab. 1977. Represents 160 craftworkers.
Acceptable Work: Considers batik; ceramics; clothing; decoupage; jewelry; needlecrafts; pottery; wall hangings; weavings; woodcrafting; and any unique, quality handmade items. "Quilts and infants clothing are always in great demand. No clothing for children over 6 years-old." Fine one-of-a-kind and handmade production-line items. Price range: $1-500; bestsellers: $2-25.
Terms: Works on consignment and buys outright; 33⅓% commission. Retail price set by joint agreement. Payment made by 10th of month following sales. Dealer pays return UPS shipping.
Profile: "We specialize in quality, handmade items." Unsold consigned pieces returned after 90 days. Customers are local residents and tourists visiting Cape Canaveral. Best selling time: Christmas.

CREATIVE ART GALLERY, 324 Park Ave. N., Winter Park FL 32789. (305)647-6858. Director: Madeline Landing Pots. Gallery. Estab. 1962. Represents 10 member craftworkers.
Acceptable Work: Considers batik, ceramics, clothing, dollmaking, glass art, jewelry, metalsmithing, needlecrafts, pottery, soft sculpture, wall hangings, weavings and woodcrafting. One-of-a-kind and handmade production-line items. Price range: 50¢-3,000; bestsellers: $5-100.
Terms: Members only; acceptance is voted upon by member artists. "All work is juried for technical competence and artistic value." Works on consignment. Craftworker sets retail price. Call for appointment. Reports in 1 week.
Profile: "We are a nonprofit cooperative gallery. Items are put in a new gallery exhibit each month." Best selling time: Christmas.

THE CREATIVE CONSPIRACY, 13064 Indian Rocks Rd., Lango FL 33540. (813)596-5565. Contact: Mary Jane Robbins. Craft shop. Estab. 1976. Represents over 100 craftworkers. "I prefer to work with artists in my own area, or ones I can at least meet and talk with; that way, they feel more a part of my shop. I do have people in North Carolina and Tenneseee sending items to me in Florida, which I think is great. Most have seen the shop while on vacation."
Acceptable Work: Considers children's clothing, dollmaking, glass art, needlecrafts, pottery, quilting, soft sculpture, tole painting, wall hangings, weavings and woodcrafting. Especially needs items for men and teenagers; items that can be personalized; and unusual Christmas items. No kits. "If you have tags with your logo, please use them, but no addresses on items." One-of-a-kind pieces in stained glass and pottery, but mostly handmade production-line items. Price range: 50¢-$250; bestsellers: $5-50.
Terms: Works on consignment; 40% commission. Retail price set by joint agreement. Sometimes requires exclusive area representation. Send resume with SASE. Dealer pays insurance on exhibited work.
Profile: "We are located in an old 6-room house, complete with fireplace and kitchen. We display our items in the rooms they would go in (kitchen items in kitchen, etc.). We have a country look in many of our items, but we try to display with a decorator look our more expensive woven wallhangings and stained glass items." Customers: ages 25-60; above average incomes, well-traveled and "know quality and originality when they see it". Heaviest wholesale buying time: October-March; best selling time: November-March.

CREATIVE HANDS, 2109 E. Hwy. 580, Dunedin FL 33528. (813)733-4965. Contact: Mel Murphy. Craft/gift shop. Estab. 1976. Represents 200 craftworkers.
Acceptable Work: Considers all crafts except those made from plastics, sequence, feathers, plumes, etc. Price range: 50¢-$300; bestsellers: 99¢-$55. Buys outright and works on consignment; 50% commission. Retail price set by joint agreement. Send resume and photos with SASE. Reports in 2 weeks. Work may be shipped or hand-delivered.
Profile: "1,850 square feet of space located on a busy state road in an 8-unit shopping center. We have a very good turnover ratio. 80% of our customers are retired or semi-retired. Heaviest wholesale buying and best selling time: October-April."

A DIFFERENT DRUMMER, 194 Miracle Strip Pkwy. SE, Fort Walton Beach FL 32548. (904)243-1834. Contact: Karen Ward. Craft and gift shop. Estab. 1974. Represents 75-100 craftworkers.
Acceptable Work: Considers candlemaking; ceramics; decoupage; dollmaking; glass art; jewelry; needlecrafts; pottery; quilting; soft sculpture; tole painting; wall hangings; weavings; and woodcrafting. Primitive handmade production-line items. Price range: 69¢-$150; bestsellers: $3.50-30.

Terms: Works on consignment; 40% commission. Retail price set by joint agreement. Requires exclusive area representation. Reports in 2 weeks. "Payment is made on the 10th of the month following the month of sale; articles must remain in shop at least 60 days." Dealer pays insurance for exhibited work.
Profile: "The shop is managed by a professional artist and craftswoman. Our summer tourist season brings traffic from all over the US. From November 1-January 1 we transform our shop into 'The Wonderful World of Christmas' which attracts all income levels and ages." Best selling time: Christmas and June-Labor Day.

DISCOVERY CENTER, 231 SW 2nd Ave., Fort Lauderdale FL 33301. (305)462-4115. Art Director: Rich Yasko. Museum gallery. Estab. 1973. Represents 4 craftworkers.
Acceptable Work: Considers all crafts. Specializes in colonial dollmaking, weaving, natural basketry and silkscreen. One-of-a-kind crafts. Price range: $20-500; bestsellers: $20-50.
Terms: Works on consignment; 25% commission. Craftworker sets retail price. Call for appointment with resume and slides. Reports in 2 weeks. Dealer pays insurance on exhibited work.
Profile: "We are a children's museum of science and art. Large shows have an initial reception (approximately 250-300 attendance). Exhibits will remain hung or displayed for no longer than 2 months. Whenever there is not an exhibit on display, the area is reserved for the artists-in-residence. We have at this time 6 artists-in-residence who work in a studio at the museum facility free of charge. All materials are supplied and most equipment (that the artists feel is necessary) is provided. In addition, we invite 'visiting artists' to do public demonstrations at our facility on weekends (materials provided for these artists also)." Customers: 60% adult, 40% children. Best selling time: winter.

FIBRATIONS WEAVING STUDIO & GALLERY, 14115 S. Dixie Hwy., Suite D, Miami FL 33176. (305)233-0221. Contact: B. Clark. Craft shop/gallery/workshop/supply studio. Estab. 1973. Represents several Florida craftworkers.
Acceptable Work: Considers batik; clothing; dollmaking; quilting; wall hangings; and weaving. "We have a special need for one of a kind clothing; tapestries; wall hangings; and decorative items." Price range: $5-500; bestsellers: $10-100.
Terms: Works on consignment; 30% commission. Retail price set by joint agreement. Prefers exclusive area representation. Reports in 3-4 weeks. Dealer pays insurance for exhibited work; "we are protected against theft only."
Profile: "We have a workshop atmosphere combined with high quality displays." Customers are fellow craftsmen; fiber students; shop and gallery owners; decorators; tourists; and local neighbors. Best selling time: November-January. Shop closed in August.

FRANKLIN STREET MALL, Tampa Downtown Development Authority, 512 N. Florida Ave., Tampa FL 33602. (813)223-8518. Mall Administrator: Reba F. Cook. Maintains a registry of craftspeople who set-up at the Mall. "Anyone coming into our area can obtain a temporary permit for the duration of their visit by contacting our office."

FRIENDS OF THE MUSEUM, INC., Box 8311, Tampa FL 33674. (813)932-8719. Treasurer, Manager: Terri Garnhart. Museum gift shop. Estab. 1968. Represents 10 craftworkers.
Acceptable Work: Considers batik; candlemaking; ceramics; decoupage; jewelry; leatherworking; needlecrafts; pottery; wall hangings; weavings; and woodcrafting. Fine one-of-a-kind pieces. Price range: $1-75; bestsellers: $2-10.
Terms: Works on consignment and buys outright; 25-50% commission. Shop sets retail price. Reports in 4 weeks. Dealer pays for return shipping; return shipping insurance; and insurance for exhibited work.
Profile: "In comparison to other museum shops our lines are much more varied; something for everyone at reasonable prices. Geared for children 6-12 years old with $1-2 to spend." Best selling time: summer.

THE GREEN FLASH, Box 348, Captiva Island FL 33924. (813)472-3305. Contact: Nancy Simonson. Shell shop. Estab. 1974.
Acceptable Work: Considers sea shell craft. Handmade production-line items OK. Price range: 50¢-$25; bestsellers: 50¢-$25.
Terms: Works on consignment; 33⅓% commission. Retail price set by joint agreement. Call for appointment. Reports same day. Work may be shipped or hand-delivered. Craftworker pays insurance on exhibited work.
Profile: "We are located on the Gulf of Mexico, which is noted for shelling." Items are

displayed on shelves. Customers: young children, wealthy tourists, retired millionaires. Heaviest wholesale and best selling time: winter.

GROVE HOUSE, INC., 3496 Main Hwy., Coconut Grove, Miami FL 33133. (305)445-5633. Executive Director: Thyrza Jacocks. Craft shop/gallery. Estab. 1960. Represents 200-400 Florida craftworkers.
Acceptable Work: Considers batik; ceramics; dollmaking; glass art; metalsmithing; needlecrafts; pottery; quilting; soft sculpture; wall hangings; weavings; and woodcrafting. Price range: $5-1,500; bestsellers: $20-250.
Terms: Works on consignment; 35% commission. Craftworker sets retail price. Reports in 2 weeks. Dealer pays return shipping and insurance for exhibited work.
Profile: "We are a nonprofit cooperative." Customers are middle income with large age spread. Best selling time: November-March.

GROVE NORTH, INC., 18430 W. Dixie Highway, North Miami Beach FL 33180. (305)935-0220. Director: Beverly Swatt. Gallery. Estab. 1977. Represents 80-90 craftworkers.
Acceptable Work: Considers batik, candlemaking, ceramics, glass art, jewelry, leatherworking, metalsmithing, pottery, quilting, soft sculpture, wall hangings, weavings and woodcrafting. Specializes in high quality gift and decorative accessories. One-of-a-kind and handmade production-line items. Price range: $3.50-800; bestsellers; $50-200.
Terms: Buys outright and works on consignment; 33⅓% commission. Retail price set by joint agreement. Send resume, slides or call for appointment. Reports in 1 week. Requested work may be shipped or hand delivered.
Profile: "Our gallery is in one of the oldest homes in N.M.B.—a Florida pine 65 year old home with hardwood floors, window boxes and a hedge outside. It is quaint and we have tried to keep a homey atmosphere (a couch 50 years old, 100 year old dining room furniture). Pieces are displayed in a setting to give our customers ideas as to their decorative abilities." Customers: 30-60, well educated, interested in the arts and middle to upper income. Heaviest wholesale buying time: August-October; best selling time: October-December.

HALIFAX HISTORICAL SOCIETY, INC., Box 5051, Daytona Beach FL 32018. (904)255-5976. President: Florence D. Nordquist. Museum gift shop located at 128 Orange Ave., Daytona Beach FL 32018. Estab. 1978.
Acceptable Work: Considers candlemaking; dollmaking; needlecrafts; quilting; wall hangings; weavings; and any pioneer craft. Primitive and fine one-of-a-kind pieces. Minimum price: $2.50.
Terms: Works on consignment; 40% commission. Retail price set by joint agreement. Requires exclusive area representation. Reports in 3 weeks. Prefers UPS.
Profile: "The store follows the general motif of a country store. All items are of a type that would interest collectors. We advertise in some national magazines and papers. We are in a tourist area." Best selling time: January through August.

THE HEN'S NEST, 6098 150th Ave. N., Clearwater FL 33520. (813)531-1045. Contact: Faye Wine. Craft shop. Estab. 1978. Represents 10 craftworkers.
Acceptable Work: Considers dollmaking, needlecrafts, quilting, soft sculpture, wall hangings and weavings. Especially needs handmade dolls, patchwork pillows and handmade toys. Specializes in "decorative and colorful pillows, toys and dolls. Mostly pastels and ginghams." One-of-a-kind and handmade production-line items. "Everything must be neatly made with good fabric and stuffing." Price range: $2-200; bestsellers: $12 (pillows), $16 (dolls) to $50 (dolls and mice).
Terms: Buys outright and works on consignment; 25% commission. Retail price set by joint agreement. Send slides or call for appointment. Reports in 1 week. Work may be shipped or hand-delivered. Dealer pays insurance on exhibited work.
Profile: "My shop specializes in dolls. (I usually have 50 or more dolls at all times.) Dolls are displayed in chairs, beds and on doll stands; pillows on shelves or hanging; wall hangings on walls; and stuffed toys on the shelves." Customers: young children to grandmothers, and doll collectors. Heaviest wholesale buying time: October; best selling time: Christmas.

HISTORICAL ASSOCIATION OF SOUTHERN FLORIDA, INC., 3280 S. Miami Ave., Miami FL 33129. (305)854-3289. Business Manager: Consuelo Maingot. Museum gift shop. Estab. 1941. Represents 6 Florida craftworkers who "manufacture products dealing specifically with the history of south Florida as illustrated in our museum gallery displays."
Acceptable Work: Considers jewelry; woodcrafting; and Seminole Indian crafts. Primitive

handmade production-line items. Price range: $1-100; bestsellers: $2-10.
Terms: Works on consignment; 50% commission. Retail price set by joint agreement. Reports in 1 month. Dealer pays shipping to shop.
Profile: "Our present museum shop is small. Items are displayed in display cases; on the wall; book shelves; or whichever of these is appropriate." Customers are older members of the museum; school age tour groups; and tourists. Best selling time: December-April.

HOUSE OF FINE ART, INC., 9476 Harding Ave., Surfside FL 33154. (305)868-6870. Contact: Iris G. Klein. Gallery/gift/frame/art supplies shop. Estab. 1961. Represents 10-12 US craftworkers.
Acceptable Work: Considers bagel basketry, batik, candlemaking, ceramics, decoupage, dollmaking, glass art, pottery, scrimshaw and sculpture (metal, sand, soft and wood). Especially needs sand sculpture. Fine one-of-a-kind and handmade production-line items. Price range: $2-75; bestsellers: $2-25.
Terms: Buys outright and works on consignment; 40% commission. Retail price set by joint agreement. Sometimes requires exclusive area representation. Send resume, slides, SASE or call for appointment. Dealer pays material insurance for exhibited work only, not artist value.
Profile: Our shop has 1 wall for paintings only and the other walls have glass shelves or pegboard for crafts and sculpture. Items are never on the floor or out of eye reach. Customers: ages 25-70; average to upper incomes. Heaviest wholesale buying and best selling time: winter (November-June).

HOWARD GALLERIES, LTD., 148 Pompano Fashion Sq., Pompano Beach FL 33062. (305)781-9481. President: H.B. Solomon. Considers sculpture. Maximum size: 48x36". Minimum price: $25; bestsellers: $100-300. Buys outright or on consignment. Retail price set by joint agreement. Requires exclusive area representation. Write for interview or send photos of work. SASE. Gallery pays shipping from gallery and insurance on exhibited work. 60 days minimum exposure.

JACKSONVILLE ART MUSEUM SHOP, 4160 Boulevard Center Dr., Jacksonville FL 32207. (904)398-8336. Contact: Ruth Hall. Estab. 1968. Considers most crafts; especially interested in well-made ceramic work. Primitive and finished one-of-a-kind and handmade production-line items; utilitarian and/or decorative. Price range: $2.50-75; bestsellers: $5-15. Buys outright or on consignment; 30% commission. Craftworker sets retail price. Write. Tries to report within 10 days. Dealer pays shipping from shop and insurance for exhibited work.
Profile: Best selling time: November-December. "We are a museum shop in a teaching institution and we seek items to stimulate classroom discussion."

LIGHTHOUSE GALLERY, INC., Box 3814, Tequesta FL 33458. (301)746-3101. Administrative Director: Elizabeth Long. Gallery. Estab. 1964.
Acceptable Work: Considers batik, ceramics, glass art, jewelry, leatherworking, metal smithing, pottery, scrimshaw, soft sculpture and woodcrafting. One-of-a-kind designer pieces. Price range: $5-200.
Terms: Works on consignment; 30% commission. Craftworker sets retail price. Requires exclusive area representation. Send slides, resume with SASE. Reports in 2 weeks. Work may be shipped or hand delivered.
Profile: "We are a small cultural center with art exhibits, a School of Art, lectures, films and concerts. Exhibits change monthly. The Center is supported by membership dues, a charity ball and other fund raising events. Items would be displayed in a small gift shop for a period of approximately six weeks at a time." Customers: 70% retired professionals or business executives; 30% industrial white collar workers and small businessmen. Heaviest wholesale buying time: October-April; best selling time: November-February.

LOCH HAVEN ART CENTER SHOP, 2416 N. Mills Ave., Orlando FL 32803. (305)896-4231. Managers: Carol Bechtel and Marguerite Lineham. Museum gift shop. Estab. 1969. Represents 2 craftworkers.
Acceptable Work: Considers batik, glass art, jewelry, pottery, wall hangings and weaving. Fine one-of-a-kind pieces. Price range: $1-100; bestsellers: $1-25.
Terms: Works on consignment; 34% commission. Retail price set by joint agreement. Reports in 4 weeks. Dealer pays return shipping and insurance for exhibited work.
Profile: "We have an Artist-of-the-Month series which we use to exhibit selected artists on a monthly basis." Best selling time: Christmas.

Shops and Galleries   129

MUSEUM OF ARTS & SCIENCES, 1040 Museum Blvd., Daytona Beach FL 32014. (904)255-0285. Director: Gary Russell Libby. Gift shop. Buys crafts outright or on consignment. Price range: $1-30. "Minimum of 20% commission on all sales."

MUSEUM OF THE ARTS GIFT SHOP, 426 E. Las Olas Blvd., Ft. Lauderdale FL 33301. (305)463-5184. Buys original art and crafts outright or on consignment; 33⅓% minimum commission. Price range: 50c-$100 for such items as small booklets to African/pre-Columbian artifacts. Museum holds Annual Hortt Memorial Competition & Exhibition, with residents of Broward, Dade, Monroe and Palm Beach counties invited.

MUSEUM OF FINE ARTS SHOP, 255 Beach Drive N., St. Petersburg FL 33701. (813)896-2667. Shop Manager: Mrs. Edgar Andruss. Museum gift shop. Estab. 1965. Represents 4-5 craftworkers.
Acceptable Work: Considers ceramics; glass art; and pottery. Fine one-of-a-kind pieces. Price range: $3.50-30.
Terms: Works on consignment and buys outright; 40-50% commission. Shop sets retail price. Requires exclusive area representation.
Profile: Customers are high income, age 45-60; "we are now trying to appeal to younger group." Best selling time: fall-winter.

PENSACOLA MUSEUM OF ART, 407 S. Jefferson St., Pensacola FL 32501. (904)432-6247. Director: Brigitte Huybregts. Museum gallery/gift shop. Estab. 1954. Represents 4 craftworkers. Considers batik; ceramics; dollmaking; glass art; jewelry; metalsmithing; needlecrafts; pottery; quilting; soft sculpture; wall hangings; weaving; and woodcrafting. One-of-a-kind pieces; utilitarian and/or decorative. Price range: $5-100; bestsellers: $10-30. Works on consignment and buys outright; 30% commission. Retail price set by joint agreement. Shipping and in-transit insurance are negotiable; dealer pays insurance for exhibited work.
Profile: "We are located in a historic building—Old City Jail." Best selling time: Christmas.

THE PINK PETUNIA, 97 St. George St., St. Augustine FL 32084. (904)829-9363. Contact: Kay or G.H. Welborn. Craft and gift shop. Estab. 1968. Represents 100 craftworkers. Price range: 75c-$125; bestsellers: $3-75. Works on consignment and buys outright; 40% commission. Shop sets retail price if items are purchased outright; craftworker sets retail price for consigned items. Requires exclusive area representation. Reports as soon as possible. Dealer pays return shipping; in-transit insurance if returning purchases; and insurance for exhibited work.
Acceptable Work: Considers batik; candlemaking; decoupage; dollmaking; glass art; jewelry; needlecrafts; pottery; quilting; wall hangings; weavings; woodcrafting; macrame; woodblock prints; trapunta; enamels; and collages. All styles; utilitarian and/or decorative.
Profile: "We have just moved into larger quarters in what was once the Pan American Center complete with Hispanic garden and typical Spanish architecture. We feature exclusive and well-displayed crafts." Best selling time: spring and summer.

ROOFTOP GALLERY, Harbor House, 423 Front St., Key West FL 33040. (305)294-6863, 294-5892. Contact: Barbara Doremus. Gallery/gift shop. Estab. 1970. Represents 7-8 craftworkers.
Acceptable Work: Considers gyotaku, jewelry, wall hangings, weavings and woodcrafting. Especially needs gold jewelry. Specializes in fine and contemporary handmade production-line items. Price range: $5-250; bestsellers: $5-30.
Terms: Buys outright and works on consignment; 40% commission. Retail price set by joint agreement. Requires exclusive area representation. Send slides. Reports in 2 weeks. Dealer pays shipping to shop. Display time: 30 days, to test acceptance.
Profile: "Rooftop will carry only items well-designed, well-made and sensibly priced. We have established over a period of 7 years a reputation for integrity and fairness in pricing plus an unusually select line of merchandise. We are housed in an old brick building (with small display space) on Key West's waterfront." Customers: mostly tourists. Heaviest wholesale buying and best selling time: winter.

THE STRAWBERRY WALRUS, 1324 S. Ft. Harrison Ave., Clearwater FL 33516. (813)443-7493 or 441-9236. Owners: Kay Sloan and Jim Thornton. Crafts/antique shop. Estab. 1977. Represents 30 craftworkers.
Acceptable Work: Considers batik, candlemaking, ceramics, dollmaking, needlecrafts, pottery, quilting, soft sculpture, tole painting, wall hangings, weavings and woodcrafting. Especially needs gifts for men and boys and handmade baskets. Exhibits primitive pieces, tradi-

tional handcrafts and Appalachian-style work. One-of-a-kind and handmade production-line items OK. Price range: 99¢-$50; bestsellers: 99¢-$30.
Terms: Buys outright and works on consignment; 40% commission. Retail price set by joint agreement. Requires exclusive area representation. Call for appointment. SASE. Reports in 1 week. Work may be shipped or hand-delivered. Craftworker pays insurance on exhibited work.
Profile: "Great pains are taken to display crafts attractively and our setting (a restored turn-of-the-century house) is conducive to creating a charming atmosphere. Antique furnishings (also for sale) are arranged in vignettes and create a backdrop for our crafts."

SURPRISES IN STORE, 1025 Gulf Life Dr., Jacksonville FL 32207. (904)396-7061. Manager: Marianne Hocker. Museum gift shop. Estab. 1968.
Acceptable Work: Considers batik, dollmaking, jewelry, pottery, wall hangings and weavings. Handmade production-line items only. Price range: $4-50; bestsellers: up to $10.
Terms: Buys outright and works on consignment; 33⅓% commission. Retail price set by joint agreement. Call for appointment. Reports in 2 weeks. Work may be shipped or hand-delivered.
Profile: Customers: tourists, children and families. Heaviest wholesale buying time: fall; best selling time: Christmas.

TEMPLE MOUND MUSEUM, Box 1449, Fort Walton Beach FL 32548. Curator: Mrs. Yulee W. Lazarus. Museum gift shop. Estab. 1962. Best selling time: summer.
Acceptable Work: Considers ceramics; decoupage; jewelry; leatherworking; needlecrafts; pottery; wall hangings; and weavings in Southeastern Indian designs. Primitive one-of-a-kind and handmade production-line items. Price range: 75¢-$30; bestsellers: 75¢-$15.
Terms: Buys outright. Shop sets retail price. Requires exclusive area representation. Submit photos or description. Reports in 2 weeks. Dealer pays for shipping to shop.

TREASURED TIMBERS, 13145 Gulf Blvd., Madeira Beach FL 33708. (813)393-0807. Contact: Dan Zwally and John Godfrey. Craft/gift shop. Estab. 1977. Represents 8-10 craftworkers.
Acceptable Work: Considers candlemaking, ceramics, glass art, metalsmithing, pottery, scrimshaw and woodcrafting. Especially needs wood items with nautical flair (figure heads, ship carvings). Specializes in nautical and rustic crafts. One-of-a-kind, but mostly handmade production-line items. Price range: $5-1,500; bestsellers: $5-200.
Terms: Buys outright (on selected items) and works on consignment; 30% commission. Retail price set by joint agreement. Write with slides/photos or call for appointment. Reports in 2 weeks. Work may be shipped or hand delivered. Dealer pays insurance on exhibited work, except theft.
Profile: "We have rustic handmade items, furniture, a ship's hatch cover, tables, custom woodwork, candle light with loads of salty decoration." Heaviest wholesale buying time: September-October; best selling time: November-April.

TUTTLES SEAHORSE SHELL SHOP, 342 Periwinkle Way, Sanibel Island FL 33957. Contact: Pauline and Bob Tuttle. Gift shop. Estab. 1960. Represents 10 local craftworkers.
Acceptable Work: Considers candlemaking; ceramics; jewelry; wall hangings; and weavings as related to shell craft. Price range: 59¢-$450; bestsellers: 59¢-$50.
Terms: Buys outright. Retail price set by shop. Requires exclusive area representation. Reports daily. Hand-delivered work only.
Profile: "We carry only locally made items. Every item must have seashells or be marine life related. The island is famous for shelling beaches." Customers are tourists. Best selling time: winter.

THE TWENTY FOUR COLLECTION, Box 24, Miami FL 33153. Gallery. Estab. 1975. Represents 20 craftworkers. Considers ceramics; clothing; glass art; jewelry; needlecrafts; soft sculpture; wall hangings; weavings; and woodcrafting. Primitive and fine one-of-a-kind pieces; utilitarian and/or decorative. Price range: $20-2,500; bestsellers: $50-300. Works on consignment and buys outright; 40% commission. Retail price set by joint agreement. Requires exclusive area representation. Reports in 2 weeks. Dealer pays shipping to shop and insurance for exhibited work. Best selling time: fall.

THE WEB, INC., 4135 Aurora St., Coral Gables FL 33146. (305)446-7731. President: Donna Keller. Craft, batik and weaving supplies, and equipment shop. Estab. 1975. Represents local craftworkers only.
Acceptable Work: Considers batik; clothing; quilting; soft sculpture; wall hangings; and

weaving. Price range: $3-700; bestsellers: $3-80.
Terms: Works on consignment; 25% commission. Retail price set by joint agreement. Reports in 1 week. Hand-delivered work only. Customers are 24-45 years of age; craft oriented; and with income of $10,000-50,000. Best selling time: November-December, March-April.

Georgia
AUTUMN LEAVES, 3-B Public Sq., Dahlonega GA 30533. (404)864-7305. Contact: Jan Campbell. Craft/gift shop. Estab. 1976. Represents 25 craftworkers.
Acceptable Work: Considers tole painting; clothing; books; dollmaking; jewelry; leatherworking; metalsmithing; needlecrafts; quilting; and woodcarving. Especially needs men's items; woodcarvings; baskets; and silver jewelry. Price range: 25¢-$100; bestsellers: 40¢-$20.
Terms: Works on consignment; 40% commission. Gallery sets retail price. Requires exclusive area representation. Reports in 1 month. Work may be shipped or hand-delivered. Dealer pays return shipping and insurance for exhibited work. Displays work "as long as craftsman desires."
Profile: Work is displayed "on shelves; jewelry in cases. Customers are from the college in town; tourists of all ages; steady traffic from Atlanta." Best selling and heaviest wholesale buying time: May-October.

BANKS HALEY GALLERY—THE GALLERY SHOP, Box 571, Albany GA 31707. (912)435-0977. Contact: Shelley M. Greggs. Museum gift shop and gallery. Estab. 1978.
Acceptable Work: Considers batik, ceramics and jewelry. Specializes in fine art jewelry, and unusual ceramics and pottery. One-of-a-kind pieces only. Price range: $3-50; bestsellers: $10.
Terms: Buys outright. Shops sets retail price. Send resume and slides with SASE. Reports in 3 weeks. Work may be shipped or hand-delivered.
Profile: "The Banks Haley Gallery is a non-profit organization. It houses monthly traveling exhibits for the benefit of the community. The Gallery Shop is a small gift shop that offers unique and original pieces of fine art work. Some reproductions of classic sculpture are also sold. All items are recorded, priced and set out for display within a 10-day period. Items remain on display for 4-6 months. After 6 months, items are placed in a sale case. They remain there until sold." Customers: art-oriented. Heaviest wholesale buying time: late summer-autumn; best selling time: Christmas.

ELAINE COYNE GALLERIES, 943 S. Main, Stone Mountain GA 30083. (404)469-7907. Contact: Elaine Coyne. Craft shop. Estab. 1973. Represents 10 craftworkers.
Acceptable Work: Considers ceramics; glass art; jewelry; leatherworking; metalsmithing; pottery; and soft sculpture. Especially needs leather bags; glass blowing; and pottery. Fine handmade production-line items. Price range: $1-200; bestsellers: $10-25.
Terms: Works on consignment and buys outright; 35% commission. Gallery sets retail price. Requires exclusive area representation. Reports in 4 weeks. Work may be shipped or hand-delivered. Dealer pays insurance for exhibited work.
Profile: "We like to display a series and then take custom orders, as well as sell displayed pieces. Shop is located in a beautiful little old town at the tip of Stone Mountain." Best selling and heaviest wholesale buying time: Christmas and summer.

THE DOLL HOUSE, INC., 375 Pharr Rd. NE, Atlanta GA 30305. (404)261-0691. Manager: Melissa Stuart. Doll house and furnishings store. Estab. 1973. Represents 20 craftworkers. Price range: $1-1,500; bestsellers: $1-400. Buys outright. Shop sets retail price. Reports in 1 week. Work may be shipped or hand-delivered. Dealer pays return shipping.
Acceptable Work: Considers ceramics; needlecrafts; miniature furniture in all finishes and styles; miniature china; moldings; windows; and electrical work. One-of-a-kind handmade production-line items; decorative only. Especially needs fine 18th century English reproductions (Hepplewhite, Chippendale, Duncan Phyfe, etc.), and fine Victorian pieces in rosewood, walnut and mahogany.
Profile: "Work is displayed in glass cases, dollhouse interiors and vignettes, etc. We sell only miniatures scaled exactly 1"-1'. We are the largest miniature store in the Southeast."

GEORGIA MOUNTAIN ARTS ASSOCIATION, Box 67, Tallulah Falls GA 30573. (404)965-6561. Manager: Lassie Bradshaw. Craft shop. Estab. 1967. Represents 75 member craftworkers. (Members must live in northeast Georgia.) Price range: $1-200; bestsellers: $10-200. Works on consignment and buys outright; 25% commission. Craftworker sets retail price. Work may be shipped or hand-delivered. Dealer pays shipping and insurance. Heaviest wholesale buying time: winter; best selling time: April-December.

Acceptable Work: Considers batik; jewelry; pottery; quilting; wall hangings; weavings; and woodcrafting. Primitive and handmade production-line items; utilitarian and/or decorative.

HOMEPLACE, 1676 S. Lumpkin St., Athens GA 30606. (404)549-0829. Contact: Barbara Fuller. Craft and gift shop. Estab. 1971. Represents 10 craftworkers. Price range: $5-75; bestsellers: $10-15. Works on consignment; 33⅓% commission. Retail price set by joint agreement. Requires exclusive area representation. Reports in 1 week. Work may be shipped or hand-delivered.
Acceptable Work: Considers ceramics; needlecrafts; pottery; quilting; wall hangings; weavings; and woodcrafting. Especially needs pottery; weavings; quilts; and homemade toys. Finished, one-of-a-kind and handmade production-line items; utilitarian and/or decorative.
Profile: "We have 5 rooms in a Victorian house, many white shelves; sometimes items are in windows. Customers are above average in income, from a university community, sophisticated in taste and well traveled." Heaviest wholesale buying time: fall; best selling time: pre-Christmas.

ISLAND ART CENTER, Box 673, Demere Rd., St. Simons Island GA 31522. Associate Director: Mrs. W.C. Hendrix. Museum gift shop and community arts center. Estab. 1956.
Acceptable Work: Considers all crafts except decoupage and kits. One-of-a-kind and handmade production-line items. Price range: $1.50-50; bestsellers: $3-20.
Terms: Works on consignment; 25% for members of arts association, 30% for non-members. Craftworker sets retail price; shop advises. Send resume or call for appointment. Requested work may be shipped or hand delivered.
Profile: "We are a community arts center, are non-profit, and are listed in multiple tourist guides. Part of our charter commitment is to promote arts in the area and this means promoting the artists/craftsmen. We're primarily visual arts, but only because we don't have access to quality craftsmen. Counters and glass cases are used according to the item. We have a specially constructed compartment shelf arrangement for most craft items." Best selling time: September-May for locals; summer for tourists (who want mostly area items).

LEATHER ETC, INC., Box 111, Old St., Helen GA 30545. (404)878-2537. President/manager: Maggie Garrett. Gift shop/leather workshop. Estab. 1977. Represents 12 craftworkers.
Acceptable Work: Considers leather, handsewn or woven clothing, glass art, jewelry, leatherworking, metalsmithing, pottery, scrimshaw, wall hangings and weavings. Especially needs hats and bags. "We are interested in dealing primarily with original and unusual leather goods from the southeastern United States (mountain areas in particular), but we do not limit ourselves to that." One-of-a-kind and handmade production-line items. Price range: $1-250; bestsellers: $1-20.
Terms: Buys outright and works on consignment; 40% commission. Retail price set by joint agreement. Requires exclusive area representation. Send slides/photos or call for appointment. Reports in 2 weeks. Work may be shipped or hand delivered. Dealer pays insurance on exhibited work.
Profile: "We are primarily a seasonal, tourist-oriented business, located in an Alpine-style village in the foothills of the lush Blue Ridge Mountains of scenic northeast Georgia. Our atmosphere is rustic/contemporary (barnwood, stained glass, mirrors, carpet, track lights). Our shop is small but quality is high. Care is taken to protect fragile or easily soiled items from over-handling and mistreatment. Small items are displayed under glass. We appeal to a wide range of people but the largest percentage of our customers are from 21-38, working types from large cities, from Pennsylvania to Florida, but mostly Atlanta. They tend to be stylishly casual which, I suppose, is a phrase that describes us." Heaviest wholesale buying time: spring and summer; best selling time: summer and fall.
To Break In: "As we are a seasonal business (June-October), projected delivery time must be accurate, within one week. Terms should be specific, not implied. We find that following standard business practices makes for enduring relationships.

MARK OF THE POTTER, INC., Rt. 3, Clarkesville GA 30523. (404)947-3440. Contact: Glen or John LaRowe. Estab. 1968. Represents 30-40 craftworkers. Considers glass art; jewelry; pottery; some wall hangings; weavings; and woodcrafting. Finished, one-of-a-kind and handmade production-line items only; utilitarian and/or decorative. Price range: $2-300; bestsellers: $2-30. Buys outright. Retail price set by craftworker or joint agreement. Requires exclusive area representation. Query with transparencies or photos. Reports in 3 weeks. LaRowe pays shipping from shop to craftworker. Heaviest wholesale buying time: spring and late summer. Shop located in converted gristmill.

THE MUD DAUBER'S NEST, Box 361, 7001 Blackhawk Trail, Chatsworth GA 30705. (404)695-3797. Contact: Virginia Keese. Craft shop. Estab. 1975. Represents 75 craftworkers. Price range: $1-200; bestsellers: $1-20. Works on consignment and buys outright; 40% commission. Retail price set by joint agreement. Reports in 2 weeks. Work may be shipped or hand-delivered. Displays work 60 days minimum.
Acceptable Work: Considers all crafts. Especially needs dolls; stuffed toys; hand puppets; and items for boys of all ages. Primitive handmade production-line items; utilitarian and/or decorative.
Profile: "I take the same care of other craftsmen's work as I do my own. The items are attractively displayed." Best selling and heaviest wholesale buying time: spring, summer and fall.

STOREHOUSE, INC., 2737 Apple Valley Rd. NE, Atlanta GA 30319. (404)262-2926. Craft Buyer: Banks O. Godfrey Jr. Specialty store for contemporary home furnishings. Estab. 1969. Represents 35 craftworkers.
Acceptable Work: Considers ceramics, glass art, pottery, wall hangings, weavings and baskets. "Special need for more weaving." Price range: $2-350; bestsellers: $5.50-50.
Terms: Buys outright. Shop sets retail price. Requires exclusive area representation. Reports in 1 week. Dealer pays shipping.
Profile: "We are a chain of 15 stores of contemporary home furnishings. Each store has a major department of crafts." Best selling time: fall.

STOREHOUSE, INC., 3106 Early St. NW, Buckhead, Atlanta GA 30305. See above.

STOREHOUSE, INC., 3228 Northlake Parkway, Northlake 2, Atlanta GA 30345. See above.

STOREHOUSE, INC., 6277 Roswell Rd., Sandy Springs Plaza, Atlanta GA 30328. See above.

Hawaii

BISHOP MUSEUM, Box 6037, Honolulu HI 96818. (808)847-3511. Manager: Sandi L. Halualani. Museum gift shop. Estab. 1889. Represents 50 craftworkers whose work relates to Hawaii or its overlaying cultures.
Acceptable Work: Considers ceramics; dollmaking; jewelry; Hawaiian quilting; wall hangings; weavings; woodcrafting; basketry; and shell jewelry. Price range: $1.40-800; bestsellers: $5-250.
Terms: Works on consignment and buys outright; 40-50% commission. Retail price set by joint agreement. Reports in 3 weeks. Work may be shipped or hand-delivered.
Profile: "If the items are accepted, first orders are usually taken on consignment for 30 days. If successful, then items are bought outright."

CONTEMPORARY ARTS CENTER OF HAWAII, 605 Kapiolani Blvd., Honolulu HI 96813. (808)525-8047. Director: Laila Roster. Gallery. Estab. 1962. "Generally, our exhibitions are by artists and craftsmen who are from Hawaii, either living here, working here or born here. Some affiliation is necessary for our tax status and framework."
Acceptable Work: Considers batik, ceramics, soft sculpture, wall hangings and weavings. Price range: $100-2,000; bestsellers: $100-800.
Terms: Invitational exhibition only; planned 2 years in advance. Retail price set by joint agreement. Send resume and slides with SASE or call for appointment. Reports in 3 weeks. Work may be shipped or hand delivered.
Profile: "We are a non-profit gallery/museum existing within the newspaper building (2 major dailies in this city). Our collection is exhibited throughout the building and may be viewed by the public at all times. A large gallery in the center of the building is the exhibition space, where the show changes monthly. They are generally one-person exhibitions rather than group. Work is for sale, but we do not keep work beyond the exhibition time."

CONVERSATION PIECE, 2250 Kalakaua Ave., Honalulu HI 96815. (808)923-3383. Manager: Ms. Somusa Ratanarak. Craft gallery. Represents 100+ craftworkers.
Acceptable Work: Considers adult games, children's toys, dolls, handblown glass, jewelry, leatherworking, pillows, pottery, silverwork and woodwork. One-of-a-kind and handmade production-line items. Price range: $5-500.
Terms: Buys outright. Gallery sets retail price. Write with resume and illustrations of work; do not send samples.
Profile: "Conversation Piece carries only the highest quality crafts handmade by American and

European artisans. Uniqueness and good craftsmanship are crucial."

CROSSFIRE GALLERY, Box 604 Kealakikua HI 96750. Craft shop/gallery. Estab. 1975. Represents 10 local craftworkers.
Acceptable Work: Considers glass art, jewelry, leatherworking, scrimshaw. One-of-a-kind and handmade production-line items. Price range: $9-3,000.
Terms: Buys outright and works on consignment; 45% commission. Retail price set by joint agreement. Requires exclusive area representation. Send resume. Reports in 2 weeks. Work must be mailed or shipped.
Profile: "We believe in order to sell a piece, it must be properly displayed and we work at achieving this goal." Customers: tourists. Heaviest wholesale buying time: autumn (before November); best selling time: December-February.
To Break In: "Keep up with production! Working with craftspeople, there is always the problem of the craftsworkers not keeping up with demand."

FOLLOWING SEA, 1441 Kapiolani Blvd., Honolulu HI 96814. Contact: Michael Gibson. Represents about 250 craftworkers from 35 states.
Acceptable Work: Considers ceramics; jewelry; metalsmithing; glass art; leatherworking; batik; woodcrafting; and weaving. Price range: $1-4,500.
Terms: Buys outright and sometimes works on consignment; 35-50% commission. Craftworker sets retail price. Send transparencies or photos. Gallery pays shipping.
Profile: From early spring through fall, features one-man and group shows. Craftworkers juried year-round and selected works are offered for display and sale through 4-week show periods. Show schedule available. "We are endeavoring to develop one of the finest representations of contemporary American craftsmanship in the country, and a truly valid representation of each craft medium and each area of the country."

THE HAND & EYE, INC., 2855 Kihei Place, Honolulu HI 96816. (808)737-9996. President: Robert Karr. Craft/gift shop/gallery. Estab. 1970. Represents 155 craftworkers. "All artists must be residents of the state of Hawaii working in an art field. Exception is during schooling when residing on the mainland."
Acceptable Work: Considers all crafts, except candlemaking and clothing. Especially needs ceramics of commercial size and any items relating to Hawaii. One-of-a-kind pieces only. Price range: $2-4,500; bestsellers: $6-150.
Terms: Buys outright and works on consignment; 40% commission. Retail price set by joint agreement. Call for appointment. Reports in 2 weeks. Work may be shipped or hand delivered. Dealer pays insurance on exhibited work. Display time: show runs 4 weeks; remaining items stay 4 additional weeks.
Profile: "We are the island's largest stocked selling gallery, a promoter and developer of some of the island's finest artists, and dedicated to the encouragement and development of talented artists. Items are placed in boutique areas and current artist displays." Customers: young married adults, above average incomes, college educations, patrons of the arts. Heaviest wholesale buying time: fall; best selling time: fall-winter.

KAY'S ALOHA ART GALLERY, 101 Aupuni St., Room 201, Hilo, Hawaii 96720. (808)935-0711 or (808)935-4998. Contact: Kay Yamamoto. Gift shop/gallery. Estab. 1971. Represents 25-30 craftworkers, mainly from Big Island.
Acceptable Work: Considers batik, ceramics, glass art, wood block prints, collage, jewelry and pottery. Specializes in local craftwork (coconut, olivine). One-of-a-kind and handmade production-line items. Price range: 50¢-1,500; bestsellers: $2.50-75.
Terms: Works on consignment; 33⅓% commission. Retail price set by craftworker and sometimes by joint agreement. Call for appointment. Reports immediately. Work must be hand-delivered. "One-man shows last 3-4 weeks and the artist helps hang his own show. Craftworker should pick up other unsold artwork after 3 months. Work is hung on space-available basis."
Profile: "The gallery is in a popular hotel annex building, across from a shopping mall. It is small and does not take too many items, but it is most interesting and different. We have well-to-do professional people and art connosseurs who buy work of well-known local artists. Mainly middle income tourists who buy paintings, quality gift and souvenir items, and jewelry. Ages teens-70." Heaviest wholesale buying time; summer and Christmas; best selling time: summer, but especially August and October.

RARE DISCOVERY COLLECTABLES, 1050 Ala Moana Blvd., Honolulu HI 96814.

(808)524-7119. Contact: Mark Izbicki. Craft shop/gallery. Estab. 1974. Represents 100 craftworkers.
Acceptable Work: Considers batik; candlemaking; ceramics; dollmaking; glass art; jewelry; leatherworking; metalsmithing; pottery; soft sculpture; wall hangings; weavings; and woodcrafting. Especially needs furniture and art glass. Fine one-of-a-kind and handmade production-line items. Price range: 50¢-$6,000; bestsellers: $30-350.
Terms: Works on consignment and buys outright; 40% commission. Retail price set by joint agreement. Reports in 2 weeks. Work may be shipped or hand-delivered. Dealer pays shipping and insurance.
Profile: "There is 300 square feet devoted to each craftsman. Customers are middle-upper class; 50% are tourists from all over the world." Shows last 45 days. Heaviest wholesale buying time: February, June, August and October; best selling time: December.

U.F.O. & PLANTS, 94-875 Waipahu St., Waipahu HI 96797. (808)671-3343. Contact: Lynette L. Arakawa. Craft shop/art studio. Estab. 1976. Represents 5 craftworkers. Price range: 50¢-$500; bestsellers: $10-30. Works on consignment and buys outright; 30% commission. Craftworker sets retail price. Reports in 2 weeks. Work may be shipped or hand-delivered. Displays work 90 days.
Acceptable Work: Considers batik, ceramics; clothing; glass art; jewelry; pottery; soft sculpture; wall hangings; weavings; and woodcrafting. All styles; utilitarian and/or decorative.
Profile: "Shop has a home-grown Hawaiian atmosphere. It is a casual working studio-shop arrangement." Heaviest wholesale buying time: August-December; best selling time: spring and winter.

VESTIBULE SHOP, Box 6037, Honolulu HI 96816. (808)847-3511. Shop Manager: Sandi Halualani. Supervisor, Retail Sales: Ron Lockwood. Museum gift shop. Estab. 1898. Represents 40-50 Hawaiian and Pacific Island craftworkers.
Acceptable Work: Considers ceramics, clothing, decoupage, jewelry, quilting, tapa cloth, wall hangings, weavings and woodcrafting. Specializes in contemporary and primitive crafts. One-of-a-kind and handmade production-line items. Price range: $5-750; bestsellers: $5-75.
Terms: Buys outright and works on consignment; 50% commission. Retail price set by joint agreement. Call for appointment; no appointments taken on Monday. Reports in 2 weeks. Work must be hand-delivered. Dealer pays insurance on exhibited work. Display time: 30 days.
Profile: "Items are displayed on open racks or enclosed in glass cases. The shop is a unique blend of contemporary and ancient craft items along with an excellent collection of books on Hawaii and the Pacific." Customers: mostly tourists. Heaviest wholesale buying time: spring-fall; best selling time: summer and winter.

Idaho

BOISE GALLERY OF ART, Box 1505, Boise ID 83701. Contact: Ric Collier. Gallery/museum gift shop. Estab. 1937. Represents 35 craftworkers. Heaviest wholesale buying time: early fall; best selling time: late fall.
Acceptable Work: Considers batik; ceramics; glass art; jewelry; leatherworking; metalsmithing; needlecrafts; pottery; small textiles; and woodcrafting. Fine one-of-a-kind and handmade production-line items (not plastic). Price range: $2-100; bestsellers: $5-50.
Terms: Works on consignment; 30% commission. Craftworker sets retail price. Work may be shipped or hand-delivered. Dealer pays return shipping and insurance. Displays work 6 months.

LAKESIDE GALLERY SCHOOL OF ART, 611 Lakeside Ave., Coeur d'Alene ID 83814. (208)664-9052. Manager: Opal Brooten. Gallery/gift shop. Estab. 1967. Represents 20 craftworkers.
Acceptable Work; Considers batik; ceramics; dollmaking; jewelry; leatherworking; metalsmithing; pottery; wall hangings; and weavings. Primitive and fine one-of-a-kind pieces Bestsellers: $5-150.
Terms: Works on consignment; 30% commission. Craftworker sets retail price. Reports in 1 week. Work may be shipped or hand-delivered. Shows are 3-4 weeks; consignment work displayed 3 months maximum.
Profile: "Customers are in the middle income bracket; mostly young married couples and 45-50 years old." Shows are 3-4 weeks; consignment work 3 months maximum. Best selling time: October-December.

"TUESDAY'S CHILD" ART GALLERY, 3018 Overland Rd., Boise ID 83705. Contact: Elaine

Burtch. Gallery. Estab. 1972. Represents 75-100 craftworkers.
Acceptable Work: Considers batik, ceramics, glass art, jewelry, pottery, wall hangings, weaving and woodcrafting. Specializes in fine and contemporary one-of-a-kind crafts. "Do not send seconds, only the best of your line." Price range: $10-400; bestsellers: $10-100.
Terms: Buys outright and works on consignment; 40% commission. Artist sets retail price on consigned items; gallery on work bought outright. Requires exclusive area representation. Send slides with SASE, or call for appointment (if local). Reports in 2 weeks. Work may be shipped or hand delivered. Display time is 90 days (consigned work); until sold (bought outright).
Profile: "We are changing displays constantly to create a new look. Work is displayed on a variety of props, from church pews and glass shelves to baskets. There are plants and semi-classical music." Customers: ages 20-45, professionals ("who have moved to Boise from other cities where they have enjoyed quality galleries and shopping priviledges"), $35,000+ incomes. Best selling time: June-Christmas.

Illinois

THE ALBATROSS, 1834 W. Lawrence, Chicago IL 60640. (312)271-7445. Contact: Art Perez. Craft/gift and jewelry shop. Estab. 1975. Customers: ages 18-60. Best selling time: Christmas. Christmas.
Acceptable Work: Considers jewelry, metalsmithing and scrimshaw. Specializes in contemporary gold and silver design Indian jewelry. One-of-a-kind and handmade production-line items. Price range: $5-80; bestsellers: $10-150.
Terms: Buys outright. Gallery sets retail price. Send resume. Reports in 1 week. Work must be shipped.
To Break In: "Do not show us a good sample and then send us junk merchandise. Keep fair pricing."

AMERICAN SOCIETY OF ARTISTS, INC., 1297 Merchandise Mart Plaza, Chicago IL 60654. (312)751-2500. American Artisan Director: Judy Edborg. Membership Chairman: Helen Del Valle. Showroom. Estab. 1972. Has membership of about 500 craftworkers and artists.
Acceptable Work: Considers batik; glass art; jewelry; leatherworking; metalsmithing; pottery; quilting; soft sculpture; tole painting; wall hangings; weavings; and woodcrafting. Prefers decorative work. Price range: $10-1,000; bestsellers: $15-200.
Terms: Works on consignment. "Artist receives amount agreed upon ASA; commission is dependent on discount to buyer." Retail price set by joint agreement. Reports in 1 week. Work may be shipped or hand-delivered only from members and only after pre-notification and agreement.
Profile: "We have continually changing exhibits of work by members from across the nation. Things are on a casual basis, i.e. when an artist is able to bring or ship work. We suggest size, type, etc. of work. Those exhibiting are invited to demonstrate during 'marketweeks.'" Customers: galleries, shops and decorators. Best selling time: Christmas.

AMISH FARM MARKET, Rt. 1, Box 191, Arthur IL 61911. Manager: Jonas M. Schrock. Estab. 1966. Represents 5 local Amish craftworkers.
Acceptable Work: Considers clothing; dollmaking; needlecrafts; and woodcrafting. Handmade production-line items. Price range: 60¢-$7.95; bestsellers: $1-2.50.
Terms: Works on consignment; 20% commission. Retail price set by joint agreement. Requires exclusive area representation. Reports in 2 weeks. Hand-delivered work only. Best selling and heaviest wholesale buying time: summer.

THE ARKWRIGHT & HIS FRIENDS, 5 Long Grove Rd., Rt. 2, Box 294-C, Long Grove IL 60047. (312)634-3130. Partners: Patricia Lewis or Joan Zasadil. Craft shop. Estab. 1976. Represents 300 craftworkers.
Acceptable Work: Considers batik; ceramics; dollmaking; glass art; jewelry; leatherworking; metalsmithing; needlecrafts; pottery; quilting; soft sculpture; wall hangings; weavings; woodcrafting; and unique Christmas ornaments. Price range: $1.50-600; bestsellers: $5-100.
Terms: Works on consignment; 40% commission. Craftworker sets retail price. Requires exclusive area representation. Reports in 1 month. Work may be shipped or hand-delivered.
Profile: "We carry only handcrafts. We are located in a unique restored turn of the century village which houses a cluster of antique shops, boutiques, gift shops and restaurants. Long Grove is a major tourist attraction in the Chicagoland area." Heaviest wholesale buying time: spring and fall; best selling time: April-December.

ARTISAN SHOP & GALLERY, 1515 Sheridan Rd., Plaza del Lago, Winnetka IL 60091. (312)251-3775. President: Lila Goddard. Craft shop/gallery. Estab. 1968. Represents 350 craftworkers.
Acceptable Work: Acceptable Work: Considers batik, ceramics, clothing, dollmaking, pottery, glass art, jewelry, quilting, soft sculpture, wall hangings, weavings, and wood crafting. Especially needs wall pieces—fiber, soft sculpture, art glass, and creative adult and children's toys. Contemporary one-of-a-kind and handmade production-line pieces. Price range: $2,500 maximum; bestsellers: $300.
Terms: Buys outright and works on consignment; 40% commission. Retail price set by joint agreement. Requires exclusive area representation. Send resume and slides. Reports in 2 weeks. Work may be shipped or hand delivered. Dealer pays return shipping and insurance on exhibited work.
Profile: "Our gallery shows the finest quality American handcrafts. We show the works of over 350 artist-craftsmen working in multi-media. Our shows are bi-monthly."

ARTIST EXHIBITION & REGISTRY SERIES, 1712 2nd Ave., Rock Island IL 61201. (309)793-1213. Executive Director: Vincent Tolpo. Gallery. Estab. 1977. Considers all crafts. "Gallery show, featuring 1-3 local artists, changes monthly. Craftworker must attend opening show. Work may be offered for sale." Craftworker sets retail price. Dealer pays insurance for exhibited work.

ARTISTS IN WOOD, 1119 Tower Rd., Schaumberg IL 60195.(312)893-3144 or 882-1661. President: Claude Michaelson. Gallery/gift shop. Estab. 1977. Represents 12 craftworkers who produce original wood carved items. Price range: $5-750. Works on consignment and buys outright; 40% commission. Retail price set by joint agreement. Reports in 2 weeks. Work may be shipped or hand-delivered. Dealer pays insurance for exhibited work.
Profile: "We are a complete wood gallery featuring only domestic carvings of all types and styles. Customers are in upper and upper middle income bracket." Displays work 30 days minimum. Heaviest wholesale buying time: spring and fall.

ARTS INTERNATIONAL, LTD., 58 E. Walton St., Chicago IL 60611. (312)943-1793. Director of Artists Relations: David Oates. Considers sculpture. Maximum size: 48x36. Price range: $50 minimum; bestsellers: $50-250.
Terms: Buys outright. Retail price set by joint agreement. Requires exclusive area representation. Query with slides. SASE. Gallery pays shipping from gallery and insurance on exhibited art.

B.C. HEADACHE, 22 E. Grand Ave., Fox Lake IL 60020. (815)385-8098. Manager: Betty Ann Brendel. Craft/gift shop. Estab. 1977. Represents 23 craftworkers.
Acceptable Work: Considers candlemaking, clothing, jewelry, leatherworking, metalsmithing, macrame, pottery, wall hangings, weavings and woodcrafting. Specializes in bright-colored contemporary and novelty crafts. Handmade production-line items only. Price range: $2-169.95; bestsellers: $12-45.
Terms: Works on consignment; 40% commission. Shop sets retail price. "Prices are set to be sold at the highest amount." Requires exclusive area representation. Send photos with SASE. Work may be shipped or hand delivered. Dealer pays insurance on exhibited work.
Profile: "We are a small shop—the only craft/variety store in the area." Display time: 4-12 weeks, depending on the time of year. "Some crafts are seasonal. All crafts are either hung in the open or shelved within view from the entire store. Fox Lake attracts many tourists from all over. In the summer—boating; in the winter—snowmobiling, skiing. All during the year, there are retirees and vacationers." Heaviest wholesale buying time: fall (before Christmas shopping); best selling time: fall-spring.
To Break In: "A lot of craftworkers work very hard on their products. Some sell faster than others. Patience is the only tip I have to offer being a craftsperson myself. Sometimes it can get very discouraging. Keep up the good work."

MERRILL CHASE GALLERIES, LTD., 225 Fence Lane, Hillside IL 60162. (312)449-5100. Contact: Robert Chase. Considers sculpture. Price range: $15-65,000.
Terms: Buys outright and works on consignment. Retail price set by joint agreement. Requires exclusive area representation. Send slides or photos. SASE. Gallery pays shipping to gallery and insurance on exhibited work.

COLLECTORS' SHOWROOM, 325 N. Wells, Chicago IL 60610. (312)644-3180. President:

Ruth Friedland. Gallery. Estab. 1970. Represents 250 artists.
Acceptable Work: Considers nonfunctional pottery and stone sculpture; soft sculpture; wall hangings; weavings and wood. Fine one-of-a-kind pieces. Especially needs art forms for corporate art programs. Price range: $50-25,000.
Terms: Works on consignment; 50% commission. Retail price set by joint agreement. Reports in 4 weeks. Work may be shipped or hand-delivered. Dealer pays insurance for exhibited work.
Profile: "We are specifically designed as an art form resource for architects and designers and corporate collectors."

THE COMSTOCK LODE, 450 Duane, Glen Ellyn IL 60137. (312)858-3230. Contact: Jean Weliver. Gallery. Estab. 1974. Represents 70 craftworkers.
Acceptable Work: Considers jewelry; especially needs rings. Fine one-of-a-kind and handmade production-line items. Price range: $2-400; bestsellers: $20-150.
Terms: Works on consignment and buys outright; 25% commission. Retail price set by joint agreement. Reports in 2 weeks. Work may be shipped or hand-delivered. Dealer pays return shipping and insurance for exhibited work. Displays work 3-12 months.
Profile: "Work is locked in glass cases. Our shop has exceptional variety and quantity at reasonable prices. Customers are sophisticated; under 40; middle income; conservative." Heaviest wholesale buying time: fall; best selling time: October-June.

CONTEMPORARY ART WORKSHOP, 542 W. Grant Pl., Chicago IL 60614. (312)525-9624. Contact: Lynn Kearney. Gallery/art center. Estab. 1950. Represents 2-30 craftworkers.
Acceptable Work: Considers ceramics; glass art; metalsmithing; soft sculpture; wall hangings; weavings; and woodcrafting. Fine one-of-a-kind pieces. Price range: $15-2,000.
Terms: Works on consignment; 33⅓% commission. Retail price set by joint agreement. Reports in 4 weeks. Hand-delivered work only. Shows last 1 month.
Profile: "We are a nonprofit art center and gallery started and run by artists." Best selling time: September-May.

THE CONTEMPORARY QUILT, 2863 N. Clark St., Chicago IL 60657. (312)528-0360. Contact: "Kay." Craft and supply shop. Estab. 1972. Represents 15-20 craftworkers.
Acceptable Work: Considers clothing; dollmaking; quilting; soft sculpture; and woodcrafting. One-of-a-kind and handmade production-line items. Price range: $3-600; bestsellers: $3-300.
Terms: Works on consignment and buys outright; 20-30% commission. Retail price set by joint agreement. Call. Reports in 1 month. Work may be shipped or hand-delivered. Dealer pays return shipping and insurance on exhibited work. Displays work 3 months or more. Best selling time: Christmas.

CRAFT CLOCKS & GIFTS, Rt. 82 and North Ave., Elmhurst IL 60126. Owners: Ruth Hall Smith and Robert J. Smith. Gift shop. Price range: $1-3,200; bestsellers: $1-250. Buys outright. Shop sets retail prices. "Always send a query first to R.H. Smith, preferably accompanied by photos." Reports in 3 weeks. Work may be shipped or hand-delivered.
Acceptable Work: Considers dollmaking; metalsmithing; needlecrafts; pottery; tole painting; woodcrafting; craft clocks; dollhouses; and miniatures.
Profile: Customers are all ages and in the middle income bracket. Heaviest wholesale buying time: late summer months; bestselling time: November-January.

CRAFT CONNECTION, LTD., 2555 N. Clark, Chicago IL 60614. (312)549-0899. President: Marcia Fensin. Gallery. Estab. 1977. Represents 80-100 craftworkers.
Acceptable Work: Considers batik; ceramics; clothing; dollmaking; jewelry; pottery; quilting; soft sculpture; wall hangings; weavings; woodcrafting; stained glass; and glassware. Fine handmade production-line items. Price range: $2-380; bestsellers: $3-25.
Terms: Works on consignment and buys outright; 40% commission. Retail price set by joint agreement. Reports in 1 month. Work may be shipped or hand-delivered. Dealer pays shipping to shop and insurance for exhibited work.
Profile: "Most craftspeople's items are displayed together. Names of maker on all; tagged with price and materials and cleaning methods if necessary. Customers are 18-35; mainly single with $12,000/year income."

CRAFT PRODUCTS COMPANIES, Rt. 83 and North Ave., Elmhurst IL 60126. Manager: Vic Zirkel. See Craft Products Companies, St. Charles, Illinois. 60174.

CRAFT PRODUCTS COMPANIES, 2200 Dean St., St. Charles IL 60174. (312)584-9600. Vice

President: Ruth Smith. Craft, gift and mail order shop/museum gallery. Estab. 1940. Price range: $1-4,000; bestsellers: $3.95-800. Buys outright. Retail price set by joint agreement. Requires exclusive area representation. Reports in 3 weeks. Work may be shipped or hand-delivered by previous arrangement. Payment for return shipping is negotiable. Dealer pays insurance for exhibited work.
Acceptable Work: Considers ceramics; dollmaking; glass art; metalsmithing; needlecrafts; tole painting; woodcrafting; and scaled miniatures of all kinds. Especially needs clockmakers; miniaturists and woodcrafters. Fine handmade production-line items; utilitarian and/or decorative.
Profile: "We display representative samples at all times, then order additional quantities as needed. We are currently looking for unusual miniatures and inexpensive to moderately-priced items for the holiday season."

CREATIVE GIFT STUDIO, INC., 411 Main St., Glen Ellyn IL 60137. (312)469-2317. Contact: Dale B. Atkins. Gift shop. Estab. 1962. Price range: $1-200; bestsellers: $5-50. Works on consignment and buys outright; 30% commission. Retail price set by joint agreement. Requires exclusive area representation. Reports in 2 weeks. Work may be shipped or hand-delivered by previous agreement. Dealer pays insurance for exhibited work.
Acceptable Work: Considers candles; ceramics; glass art; jewelry; leather products; pottery; tole painting; wall hangings; weavings; and woodcrafting. All styles; utilitarian and/or decorative.
Profile: Work is displayed "on counters, shelves, walls or windows, depending on size and type of article. Customers have income of $5,000-100,000 annually."

CREATIVELY YOURS STUDIO, 929 Alpine Rd., Rockford IL 61108. Contact: Liz Hill. Craft and gift shop. Estab. 1973. Represents 150 craftworkers.
Acceptable Work: Considers candlemaking; dollmaking; glass art; jewelry; leatherworking; metalsmithing; pottery; soft sculpture; tole painting; wall hangings; weavings; and woodcrafting. Especially needs tole painting; sculpture; candles; jewelry; and toys. Fine one-of-a-kind and handmade production-line items. Price range: $1-200; bestsellers: $3.50-35.
Terms: Works on consignment; 40% commission. Retail price set by joint agreement. Requires exclusive area representation. Reports in 3 weeks. Work may be shipped or hand-delivered. Dealer pays return shipping. Displays work 3 months.
Profile: "We display an artist's work for up to 3 months, continually changing display of merchandise to focus on various crafts and seasons." Customers are women; middle and high middle income; 16-65 years old. Best selling and heaviest wholesale buying time: Christmas.

DYECO, Conover Square, Oregon IL 61061. (815)732-2411. Contact: D. Dean Dye. Series of craft/art/gift shops. Represents 8 craftworkers; "must be excellent in their field." Price range: $1-500; bestsellers: $4-50. Buys outright. Requires exclusive representation within 25 miles. Reports in 1 week. Work may be shipped or hand-delivered. Dealer pays return shipping. "We have 130,000 square feet of a former piano plant, remodeled into a mall of 31 very different shops."
Acceptable Work: Considers all crafts except quilting and tole painting. All styles; utilitarian and/or decorative.

EARTH GLASS STUDIO, INC., 7433 N. Harlem Ave., Niles IL 60648. (312)647-9470. President: Sandra Iussig Bohn. Craft shop/gallery/gift shop. Estab. 1972. Represents 10 craftworkers.
Accceptable Work: Considers glass art. Fine one-of-a-kind and handmade production-line items. Price range: $5-800; bestsellers: $10-300.
Terms: Works on consignment; 33⅓% commission. Retail price set by joint agreement. Reports in 3 weeks. Hand-delivered work only. Dealer pays insurance for exhibited work (theft and fire only). Best selling time: Christmas.

EVA'S INTERIORS, 276D Rt. 2, Long Grove IL 60047. (312)634-1373. Buyer: Eva Homor. Craft/gift shop/interior design studio. Estab. 1978. Represents 100-150 craftworkers.
Acceptable Work: Considers batik, ceramics, glass art, pottery, scrimshaw, soft sculpture, tole painting, wall hangings, weavings, woodcrafting and pillows. Especially needs one-of-a-kind handcrafted furniture and accessory pieces. Specializes in natural materials, rustic and nautical articles. One-of-a-kind and handmade production-line items. Price range: $5-500; bestsellers: $5-150.
Terms: Works on consignment; 50% commission (exceptions made on pieces over $300). Retail

price set by joint agreement. "Since we are a small community of approximately 60 shops, we have to have items exclusively in Long Grove. Do not contact me if anyone else in town has your work." Send slides with SASE. Reports in 2 weeks. Work may be shipped or hand delivered. Dealer pays insurance on exhibited work. Display time: 3 months maximum (except items over $300).
Profile: "We are located in a very old town in the country just minutes from downtown Chicago. The shop is rustic in nature with exposed wood beams and brick walls. Display areas are natural sisal or barnwood backed. Our customers come from the surrounding 6 states. Convention groups are bused here for the day. Also local homeowners (homes range in the $200,000+ price range." Best selling time: summer and Christmas.

EVERYTHING CREATIVE BY SUSIE SELLS, 330 W. State St., Sycamore IL 60178. (815)895-3331. Contact: Sue Alexander, 216 W. State St., Sycamore IL 60178. Gift shop. Estab. 1970. Represents 40 craftworkers.
Acceptable Work: Considers all crafts except clothing. Especially needs prints, cards and poetry. One-of-a-kind and handmade production-line items. Price range: $5-100; bestsellers: $10-25.
Terms: Buys outright and works on consignment; 50% commission. Retail price set by joint agreement, "but usually the artist tells us how much he wants and we must double that for our price." Send resume, slides and prices. Reports in 1 week. Work may be shipped or hand delivered.
Profile: "We are a small country town with an aggressive business district—near a big city. We have a barn-like, somewhat antique, decor. Items are displayed on the wall, on shelves, on tables or in cases. We try to sell all items in 2 months or less. Otherwise the turnover is not profitable. Customers are 18-35 years old with higher than average income. Heaviest wholesale buying time: fall-winter.

FIBERWORKS, 2364 N. Lincoln, Chicago IL 60614. (312)327-0444. Contact: Kathy Jahnke. Craft shop/gallery. Estab. 1976. Represents 10 craftworkers.
Acceptable Work: Considers batik, clothing, needlecrafts, quilting, soft sculpture, wall hangings and weavings. Especially needs functional and/or wearable weavings. One-of-a-kind and handmade production-line items. Price range: $10-600; bestsellers: $18-250.
Terms: Buys outright and works on consignment; commission based on sliding scale (25%, 33%, 40%). Retail price set by joint agreement. Send slides or call for appointent. Reports in 2 weeks. Work may be shipped or hand-delivered. Display time: 3 months.
Profile: "We are located in a 'young people' area of the city with a high density of single working people." Heaviest wholesale buying time: fall-winter; best selling time: winter (especially Christmas).

FINE ARTS CENTER OF CLINTON, 119 W. Macon St., Clinton IL 61727. (217)935-5055. Director: Vera MacGillivray. Gallery. Estab. 1960.
Acceptable Work: Considers batik; ceramics; decoupage; jewelry; metalsmithing; quilting; wall hangings; weavings; and woodcrafting. Primitive and fine one-of-a-kind pieces. Price range: $10-500; bestsellers: $10-100.
Terms: Works on consignment; 20% commission. Craftworker sets retail price. Rental gallery fee: $25. Requires exclusive area representation. Reports in 2 weeks. Work may be shipped or hand-delivered. Center pays return shipping and insurance for exhibited work. Displays work 1 month.
Profile: "Large exhibits are in the gallery; small exhibits in a large locked case." Heaviest wholesale buying time: September-May; best selling time: October-December.

THE FIRE WORKS, 7637 N. Greenview, Chicago IL 60626. (312)465-8655. Contact: James Zerwin. Concessionaire. Estab. 1972.
Acceptable Work: Considers glass art. Especially needs handblown lampwork. Specializes in contemporary bright-colored crafts. One-of-a-kind and handmade production-line items. Price range: $1-25; bestsellers: $5-13.
Terms: Buys outright. Dealer sets retail price. Call for appointment. Reports in 1 week. Work may be shipped or hand delivered. Dealer pays insurance for exhibited work.
Profile: "I have temporary displays in department and chain stores." Customers are female; 10-50 years old, with income under $10,000/year. Best selling and heaviest wholesale buying time: Christmas and Mother's Day.

FRAN'S MINIATURES, 3831 N. Lincoln, Chicago IL 60613. Contact: Fran Hasler. Craft shop. Estab. 1977. Represents 5-10 craftworkers.

Acceptable Work: Considers 1" scale miniatures only. One-of-a-kind and handmade producton-line items. Price range: 50¢-$50; bestsellers: $1-12.
Terms: Buys outright. Retail price set by joint agreement. Write with SASE. Reports in 2 weeks. Work may be shipped or hand delivered. Customers are urbanites. Heaviest wholesale buying time: fall; best selling time: Christmas.

FREEPORT ART MUSEUM, 511 S. Liberty, Freeport IL 61032. (815)235-9755. Director: Linda Prestwich. Sales exhibitions and gift shop. Estab. 1975. Considers all crafts. Price range: $10-200. Works on consignment with agreement; 10% commission. For consideration by exhibition review committees, send slides and resume. Dealer provides mailing, advertising and complete news service for each artist/craftsperson.

FROG TOOL CO., LTD., 541 N. Franklin St., Chicago IL 60610. (312)644-5999. President: Richard Watkins. Mail order store. Estab. 1969.
Acceptable Work: Considers forged or other woodworking tools, especially hand tools. Handmade production-line items only. Price range: $1-400. Buys outright. Shop sets retail price. Write. Reports in 2 weeks.
Profile: "Presently we are buying from Europe. We will buy work from anyone who can produce the quality that we require and who can furnish us with the volume that is needed. We are a mail order woodworking tool sales and retail store. Items will be inserted in our mail order catalog." Customers: male, white, ages 18-70. Best selling time: fall and winter.
To Break In: "We need serious producers who can make quantities of from 50-1000 pieces of a kind of high quality forged or cast woodworking tools. Part-time hobbyists should not apply for these jobs. Craftsmen should be able to produce the items in their own shop.

THE GALLERY, 450 Duane, Glen Ellyn IL 60137. Contact: Jean Weliver. Estab. 1979. Represents 70 craftworkers.
Acceptable Work: Considers original prints, drawings, paintings and fibre. "Glen Ellyn is a center for nature lovers so natural themes go well." No fantastic art or art nouveau. Price range: $2-400; bestsellers: $20-150.
Terms: Works on consignment and buys outright; 25% commission. Retail price set by joint agreement. Reports in 2 weeks. Work may be shipped or hand-delivered. Accepts only high quality, small pieces; keeps slide file of larger work. Dealer pays insurance for exhibited work. Displays work 3-12 months.

GALLERY YOLANDA, 148 E. Ontario, Chicago IL 60611. (312)266-7608. Director: Yolanda Kelley. Gallery. Estab. 1975. Represents 8-10 craftworkers.
Acceptable Work: Considers ceramics; metalsmithing; sculpture; soft sculpture; and wood sculpture. Finished and one-of-a-kind pieces. Especially needs fine art ceramics. Price range: $40-12,000; bestsellers: $300-8,000.
Terms: Works on consignment and buys outright; 50% commission. Retail price set by joint agreement. Reports as soon as possible. Work may be shipped or hand-delivered. Dealer pays insurance for exhibited work.
Profile: "We have window displays and shows that last 1 month usually. Our gallery is unique because it does not intimidate the browser or buyer; the artists are always welcome. It is in the manner of a European Salon where visitors and buyers feel like welcome guests in my home." Heaviest wholesale buying time: August-June; best selling time: fall-Christmas.

GLASSBLOWING SHOPPE, F204A Woodfield Mall, Schaumburg IL 60194. (312)885-8339. Contact: Pat or Jim Mains. Gift shop. Estab. 1970. Represents 30-40 craftworkers.
Acceptable Work: Considers glass art only. Specializes in spun items, from baby rattles to rocking chairs. Price range: $2-500; bestsellers: $5.95-24.95.
Terms: Buys outright. Shop sets retail price. Call for appointment. Reports in 1 week.
Profile: "We are a small retail shop located in a large shopping center. We demonstrate glass blowing at times in the store, but items are showcased. We desire new contacts continuously." Most customers buy on impulse. Best selling time: Christmas.

THE HOBBY HORSE SHOPPE, 2122 Pontoon Rd., Granite City IL 62040. (618)876-5566. Contact: Jo Ann Kalert. Craft/gift shop. Estab. 1976. Represents 15-20 craftworkers.
Acceptable Work: Considers clothing, dollmaking, jewelry, needlecrafts, pottery, quilting, tole painting, wall hangings, weavings and woodcrafting. Especially needs placemats, potholders, candles, bridal items and baby things. Specializes in calico and patchwork with some breadwork. Price range: $3.50-$40; bestsellers: $3.50-20.

Terms: Works on consignment; 30% commission. Retail price set by craftworker or by joint agreement. Send slides with SASE. Reports in 2 weeks. "Send items prepaid." Work may be shipped or hand delivered.
Profile: "I am in a small shopping center. The item is first displayed in a place where people will see it when they come in the door and moved accordingly. I will handle an item indefinitely as long as it is selling. If not, I will keep 6 months and then return to sender. I also teach tole and decorative painting and have wood items and paints to go along with this. Students are here 4 nights a week, plus on Saturdays for classes." Heaviest wholesale buying time: September-March; best selling time: September-December.

HOWARD ART GALLERIES, INC., 5106 N. Broadway, Chicago IL 60640. President: Albert Kodner; Vice President: Howard Kodner. Auction gallery. Estab. 1945.
Acceptable Work: Considers ceramics, glass art, jewelry, metalsmithing, pottery, scrimshaw, soft sculpture, tole painting, wall hangings, weavings, woodcrafting, paintings and lithos. Specializes in fine one-of-a-kind and handmade production-line items. Price range and bestsellers: minimum—$25.
Terms: Buys outright and works on consignment; 25% commission. Retail price set by joint agreement. Requires exclusive area representation. Send resume and slides or call for appointment. Reports "when we have need for various auctions, exhibitions or sales. Work may be shipped or hand delivered. Craftworker pays insurance on exhibited work unless it is very high quality art or jewelry. "Only good works of art or very unusual items."

ILLINOIS RAILWAY MUSEUM, Box 431, Union IL 60180. Contact: Book Store Manager. Estab. 1953.
Acceptable Work: Considers railroad-oriented crafts. Handmade production-line items. Price range: $30 maximum; bestsellers: $3-15.
Terms: Retail price set by joint agreement. Submit photos; description; and information. Reports in 4 weeks. Work may be shipped or hand-delivered. Dealer pays insurance for exhibited work.
Profile: "We are situated in a depot built in 1851 and located as the center of interest in an operating museum with 150 pieces of railroad equipment." Heaviest wholesale buying time: spring; best selling time: summer.

IT'S A SMALL WORLD, 555 Lincoln Ave., Winnetka IL 60093. (312)446-8399. Owner/buyer: Mary Jane Graham. Miniature gallery. Estab. 1972. Represents 400 craftworkers.
Acceptable Work: Considers miniature furniture and accessories. Scale must be 1"-1'. One-of-a-kind and handmade production-line items. Price range: $1-2,000; bestsellers: $10-200.
Terms: Buys outright and sometimes works on consignment; 40% commission. Retail price set by joint agreement. Sometimes requires exclusive area representation. Send samples or photos. Reports in 1 week. Work may be shipped or hand delivered. Dealer pays insurance on exhibited work.
Profile: "Miniatures for the collector. All kinds of high quality furniture, silver, glass, ceramic lighting, needlepoint. Have been featured by NBC and CBS TV specials, major magazines and newspapers. We're considered the Tiffany of miniature shops." Items are displayed in windows for 2 weeks or in illuminated jewelry-type locked cases. Customers: ages 28-72, interested in collecting, $40,000 incomes. Best selling time: November-December.

JEANNINE'S CERAMICS, 1412 E. Perkins Rd., Urbana IL 61801. (217)344-0640. Contact: Jeannine Baker. Ceramic shop. Estab. 1970. Represents 15 craftworkers. Price range: 50¢-$150; bestsellers: 50c-$30.
Terms: Buys outright. Reports in 1 week. Work may be shipped or hand-delivered. Best selling and heaviest wholesale buying time: fall.

JOLIET CERAMIC ARTS & CRAFTS, INC., 64 N. Desplaines St., Joliet IL 60431. (815)723-8616. Contact: Carol A. McGuire or Helen M. Petrilla. Craft and gift shop. Estab. 1966. Represents 300 Illinois and Indiana craftworkers.
Acceptable Work: Considers ceramics and pottery. Finished and handmade production-line items. Price range: 25¢-$600; bestsellers: $1-300.
Terms: Works on a special order basis. Retail price set by joint agreement. Reports in 1 week. Heaviest wholesale buying time: September-December; best selling time: fall and Christmas.

KOEHNLINE GALLERY, 7900 Nagle, Morton Grove IL 60053. (312)967-5120, ext. 396.

Contact: Bernard Krule. Estab. 1972. Primarily handles fine art photography. Considers sculpture. Maximum size: 4x6. Price range: $15-3,000. Works on consignment. Send resume and slides or photos. Gallery pays insurance on exhibited work. Audience of 300 receives mailing with each show. 2 weeks minimum exposure.

LAKEVIEW SALES/RENTAL GALLERY, 1125 W. Lake Ave., Peoria IL 61614. (309)686-7000. Procurer of Art: George Ann Danehower. Sales/rental gallery. Estab. 1964. Represents Illinois craftworkers.
Acceptable Work: Considers batik, ceramics, pottery, wall hangings and weavings. One-of-a-kind items only. Price range: $25-999; bestsellers: $125-250.
Terms: Works on consignment; 30% commission. Retail price set by joint agreement. Send resume and slides. Reports in 4 weeks. Work may be shipped or hand delivered. Dealer pays insurance on exhibited work. Six month contract to sell or rent work.
Profile: "The sales/rental gallery deals mostly in paintings and ceramics. The Museum shop will deal in very fine unusual one-of-a-kind pieces. We share space. Ceramics and pottery are displayed on glass and chrome shelves in the center of the room. Others are hung." Customers: middle income, interested in art. Heaviest wholesale buying and best selling time: fall, "so we need more art works in the fall."

This soft sculpture doll, made by Ramona Audley, causes several double-takes as customers pass through Mindscape Gallery, Evanston, Illinois. The gallery, located in the center of a university town, has 3,000 square feet and provides all display props. "One of the biggest problems is getting craftsmen to realize that a gallery is here to help them—not exploit them," says Ronald Isaacson, Director of Mindscape.

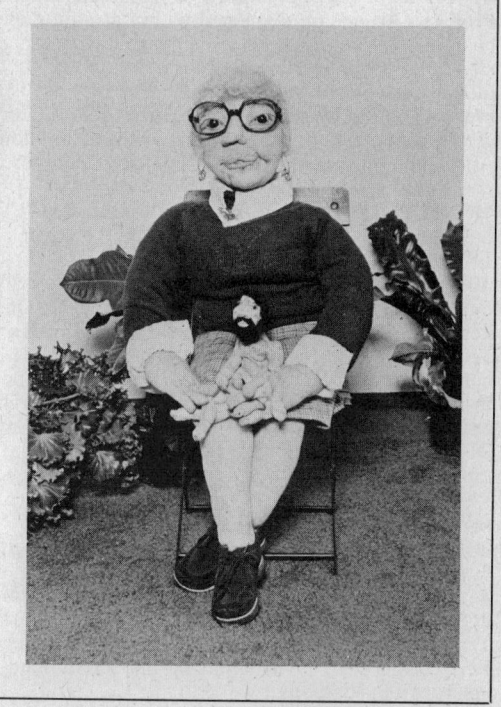

THE LOOM ROOM, 546 Crescent, Glen Ellyn IL 60137. (312)858-8057. Contact: Gary R. Babbitt. Craft/gift/supply shop/gallery. Estab. 1976. Represents 8-12 craftworkers.
Acceptable Work: Considers baby items such as stuffed animals, bibs and toys; candlemaking; ceramics; clothing; dollmaking; glass art; leatherworking; needlecrafts; pottery; quilting; scrimshaw; soft sculpture; wall hangings; functional weavings and woodcrafting. No kits. One-of-a-kind and handmade production-line items. Price range: $1.25-500; bestsellers: $4-35.
Terms: Buys outright and works on consignment; 30% commission. Retail price set by joint agreement. Requires exclusive area representation. Send resume, slides, SASE or call for appointment. Reports in 2 weeks. Work may be shipped or hand-delivered. Dealer pays insurance on exhibited work. Display time: minimum of 60 days.
Profile: "My shop is in an old house converted into several shops. I have 2 rooms on the second floor. It's a rustic, relaxed, low-key shop specializing in handwoven items. I also sell yarns, looms and equipment and give lessons. The majority of the weaving sold is my own work, but I

also sell other handcrafted items and some mass produced items (baskets, small antiques and collectibles) which compliment woven pieces. There is also a mixture of primitives and antiques, butcher block tables and burlap covered shelves for display." Heaviest wholesale buying time: late summer-early fall; best selling time: Christmas.

To Break In: "I pay promptly according to our agreement and expect only the best the craftworker has to offer. Being a craftsman myself, I understand fully how much time things take to do (costs, etc.). If the work is original, reasonably priced and quality is high, you will do very well."

MINDSCAPE GALLERY & STUDIO, INC., 1521 Sherman Ave., Evanston IL 60201. (312)864-2660. Director: Ronald Isaacson. Craft shop/gallery/rental gallery. Estab. 1974. Represents 300 craftworkers.
Acceptable Work: Considers batik; ceramics; wearables; blown and stained glass; jewelry; leatherworking; metalsmithing; pottery; woodcrafting; and commissioned architectural works. Especially needs soft sculpture; sculptural ceramics; wall tapestry; weavings; and unusual jewelry, functional and sculptural. Fine one-of-a-kind pieces. Price range: $10-3,000; bestsellers: $20-150.
Terms: Works on consignment; 40% commission. Retail price set by joint agreement. Requires exclusive area representation. Juried gallery. For application send SASE. Reports in 2-4 weeks. Work may be shipped or hand-delivered. Dealer pays insurance for exhibited work.
Profile: "Artists are displayed with a grouping of their work. The size of the display area is based on the amount of work on hand. Gallery space has 3,000 square feet. The gallery provides all display props and has a corner gallery with much window space and exposure. The premise of the gallery is to be a true reflection of what is happening in contemporary fine crafts and present it fairly for the public and artist alike." Located on the North Shore of Chicago, in the center of a major university town. Heaviest wholesale buying time: October-December and April-June; best selling time: October-December.

MOSTLY HANDMADE, INC., 508 Main St., Evanston IL 60202. (312)864-0845. Contact: Susan DePree, Mickey Nickels, Nancy Tucker or Rita Allison. Craft and gift shop. Estab. 1972. Represents 100-150 craftworkers.
Acceptable Work: Considers soft sculpture; jewelry; toys; dolls; quilted and handsewn items. Especially needs adult gifts priced at $10-30. One-of-a-kind and handmade production-line items; "We want new and unusual items." Price range: $1-400; bestsellers: $3-40.
Terms: Works on consignment and buys outright; 40% commission. Reports in 2 weeks. Prefer hand-delivered samples; out-of-town inquiries most welcome.
Profile: "Displays change constantly as new merchandise comes in daily. Customers are male and female; 25-40. $15,000 and up income; looking for the unusual, noncommercial item." Displays work 1-3 months. Heaviest wholesale buying time: September-October; best selling time: October-December.

MUELLER'S WROUGHT IRON SHOP, 22166 Nillview and Rt. 14, Barrington IL 60010. (312)382-3270 or 382-3271. Buyer: Lynn Parquette. Gift shop. Estab. 1974. Represents 3-4 craftworkers.
Acceptable Work: Considers metalsmithing; metal sculptures; and miscellaneous metal products. "We specialize in wrought metals." Price range: $5 minimum; best sellers: $15-250.
Terms: Works on consignment; commission is negotiable. Retail price set by joint agreement. Reports in 2 weeks. Work may be shipped or hand-delivered. Dealer pays shipping to shop and insurance for exhibited work.

NATURAL SELECTION, 711 W. Belmont, Chicago IL 60657. (312)477-0203. Contact: K. Ishibashi. Craft, gift and home accessories shop. Estab. 1971.
Acceptable Work: Considers batik; ceramics; jewelry; leatherworking; pottery; soft sculpture; wall hangings; weavings; woodcrafting; and paper products. Price range of bestsellers: $2-100.
Terms: Works on consignment and buys outright; 33⅓% commission. Retail price set by joint agreement. Reports in 4 weeks. Work may be shipped or hand-delivered. Payment on shipping is negotiable.
Profile: "We try to give our shop a 'natural' look: very little plastic, mainly woods, fabrics, ceramics, etc. Customers are college educated; 20-45; good incomes." Best selling and heaviest wholesale buying time: spring and fall.

NEVILLE-SARGENT GALLERY, 509 Main St.,, Evanston, Ill 60202. (312)328-9395. Contact: Jane Neville. Gallery. Estab. 1973. Represents 20 craftworkers. Customers: "more taste than

money; young." Heaviest wholesale buying time: fall; best selling time: December.
Acceptable Work: Considers batik, ceramics, glass art, mirrors, wall hangings, paperweights and especially small stained glass pieces. Specializes in fine art and contemporary crafts and posters. One-of-a-kind and handmade production-line items. Price range: $10-100; bestsellers: $10-50.
Terms: Buys outright and works on consignment; 40% commission. Retail price set by joint agreement. Requires exclusive area representation. Send slides with SASE. Reports in 4 weeks. Work may be shipped or hand delivered. Dealer pays insurance on exhibited work.

NONPAREIL, 2300 N. Clark St., Chicago IL 60614. (312)477-2933. Contact: Marjorie Freed. Craft shop. Estab. 1978. Represents 100 craftworkers.
Acceptable Work, Considers ceramics, dollmaking, glass art, jewelry, leatherworking, metalsmithing, needlecrafts, pottery, quilting, soft sculpture and woodcrafting. "We are not interested in 'stylized' work. Originality in conception and theme is very important." Specializes in fine and primitive crafts. One-of-a-kind and handmade production-line items. Price range: $5-100.
Terms: Buys outright and works on consignment; 40% commission. Retail price set by joint agreement. Requires exclusive area representation. Call for appointment. "This is essential since I am the only person to contact and am in and out. Be persistent in finding me. I must be able to see the work. Slides are not satisfactory. I report immediately but can only reply on work actually seen—not to mail inquiries." Work may be shipped or hand delivered after inspection.
Profile: "We are a very handsome shop, specializing in unique but saleable items not generally found in Chicago. Much travel is done to this end. We feel if an item does well with us it will more than compensate a craftsman for not being in neighboring stores—location is prime. Most items are always on display. If they are not selling, we ask to return them. Generally 1-2 months indicates saleability." Heaviest wholesale buying time: spring (for summer), summer and fall (for Christmas and fall); best selling time: Christmas, spring and fall.

OCTAGON SHOP, 2603 Sheridan Rd., Evanston IL 60207. (312)685-5300. Managers: Stacey Greenberger or Janet Aliapolis. Craft and gift shop. Estab. 1971. Represents 20-30 craftworkers within 100 miles.
Acceptable Work: Considers batik; ceramics; clothing; glass art; jewelry; leatherworking; metalsmithing; soft sculpture; wall hangings; and weavings. Especially needs glass paper weights and glass bowls. Fine one-of-a-kind and handmade production-line items. Price range: $1.50-185; bestsellers: $1.50-20.
Terms: Works on consignment and buys outright; 40% commission. Retail price set by joint agreement. Reports in 2 weeks. Hand-delivered work only.
Profile: Work is displayed in closed cases, on walls and on stands on the floor. "Shop does not operate for profit; it is housed in the Evanston Art Center building." Heaviest wholesale buying time: November; best selling time: November-December.

OLDE TOWN GALLERY, Main St., Mahomet IL 61853. (217)586-3211. Contact: Charlotte Williamson. Craft shop/gallery. Estab. 1977. Represents 50 craftworkers.
Acceptable Work: Considers dollmaking; drawings; jewelry; metalsmithing; needlecrafts; pottery; photographs; quilting; soft sculpture; wall hangings; and weavings. Price range: $2.50-350; bestsellers: $11-50.
Terms: Works on consignment and buys outright; 33⅓% commission. Retail price set by joint agreement. Reports in 1 month. Work may be shipped or hand-delivered. Displays work 9 months.
Profile: "Work is always out on display in its category. We are a community fine arts center; we rent space to artists who work and teach at the gallery and help keep shop as part of rent. There is usually an artist working for customers to see." Heaviest wholesale buying time: late summer-early fall; best selling time: November-December.

PEORIA ART GUILD, 1831 N. Knoxville, Peoria IL 61603. (309)685-7522. Contact: P. Atterberry. Gallery. Estab. 1878. Represents 200-250 local and regional craftworkers. Price range: $3-1,000; bestsellers: $5-150. Works on consignment; 30% commission. Retail price set by craftworker. Reports in 2 weeks. Work may be shipped or hand-delivered. Dealer pays insurance for exhibited work.
Acceptable Work: Considers ceramics; glass art; jewelry; pottery; soft sculpture; wall hangings; weavings; and woodcrafting. Fine one-of-a-kind pieces; utilitarian and/or decorative.
Profile: "We do not jury individual pieces for placement in the Guild, rather the representation

of a particular artist is decided by a committee. This allows the artist freedom of experimentation in his or her work and the ability to display a piece without the delay of waiting for jurying. We are a nonprofit, all volunteer community arts center. Our customers range from university students to professional people." Best selling time: Christmas and late fall.

PRAIRIE HOUSE, 213 S. 6th, Springfield IL 62701. (217)544-2094. Contact: Edith Myers. Considers only "superior crafts . . . no 'craftsy' types." Price range: $5-1,000. Works on consignment with one-of-a-kind items; 40% commission. Craftworker sets retail price. Requires exclusive Springfield representation. Shop pays return shipping and insurance for exhibited work.

PRESTIGE GALLERIES, INC., 3909 W. Howard St., Skokie IL 60076. (312)679-2555. Vice President: Louis Schutz.
Acceptable Work: Considers glass art; metalsmithing; and sculpture. Maximum size: 5' square. Specializes in traditional romantic (i.e. mother with child) and representational works. Price range: $10-10,000, contemporary work; $50-5,000, sculpture. Bestsellers: $500-10,000.
Terms: Buys outright or on consignment; 33⅓% commission. Retail price set by joint agreement. Requires exclusive area representation. Send slides or photos of work. 3 weeks minimum exposure.

QUILT CRAFT, 1006½ Pine St., Fox River Grove IL 60021. (312)639-4417. Contact: Marie Wierzbicki. Craft shop. Estab. 1972. Represents 10 craftworkers.
Acceptable Work: Considers quilting only. Specializes in contemporary and traditional quilts (including baby quilts), patchwork items (toys, pillows, potholders, tea cozies) and made-to-order quilted items. "Useful, colorful patchwork and quilted items are best sellers. Moderate prices and original interpretations. Cutesy things don't move. Our customers look for things that make thoughtful gifts at sensible prices. Many items are purchased for babies and small fry." One-of-a-kind and handmade production-line items. Price range: $200-600; bestsellers: $10-60.
Terms: Buys outright and works on consignment; 33% commission. Retail price set by joint agreement. Call for appointment with SASE. Reports in 2 weeks. Work may be shipped or hand delivered. Display time: 3 months (on consigned work).
Profile: "We are a quilt shop, handling supplies (not fabrics), books, kits and quilt lessons. Items are displayed on tables, chairs, walls and shelves. Since we also carry quilting supplies and instruction, many others than quilt customers are exposed to our display." Customers: ages 18-60, above average incomes. Heaviest wholesale buying time: October-November; best selling time: November-December.

RAMNAD CORPORATION-D/B/A PINK FLAMINGO, 228 E. Main St., Barrington IL 60010. (312)381-7760. President: Marian Ring. Gallery/gift shop. Estab. 1977. Represents 20 craftworkers.
Acceptable Work: Considers clothing; glass art; soft sculpture; and clothing accessories. Especially needs custom furniture and home accessories. Price range: $5-1,500; bestsellers: $15-50.
Terms: Buys outright. Gallery sets retail price. Requires exclusive area representation. Reports in 2 weeks. Work may be shipped or hand-delivered. Shipping payment is negotiable. Dealer pays insurance for exhibited work.
Profile: "Work receives a 10-day window display, if merited. We will take custom orders from customers for artists in the same medium." Heaviest wholesale buying time: August-November; best selling time: December.

THE RED OAK, Bishop Hill St., Bishop Hill IL 61419. (309)927-3539. Contact: Janet S. Arter. Gift shop. Estab. 1970. Represents 75 craftworkers.
Acceptable Work: Considers clothing; dollmaking; jewelry; leatherworking; metalsmithing; needlecrafts; quilting; tole painting; wall hangings; weavings; and woodcrafting. Especially needs quilts; woodwork; and enamelware. Primitive and fine handmade production-line items. Price range: $5-150; bestsellers: $5-25.
Terms: Works on consignment; 34% commission. Retail price set by joint agreement. Requires exclusive area representation. Reports in 1 week. Work may be shipped or hand-delivered. Dealer pays return shipping.
Profile: "Customers are greatly varied. We have a large tourist trade as we're located in a state park but we have a large area trade as well." Best selling and heaviest wholesale buying time: summer-fall.

S&A CERAMICS, 3315 N. Harlem, Chicago IL 60634. (312)736-3351. Contact: Mrs. Ann Izzo. Gift shop/ceramic studio. Estab. 1960. Represents 50 craftworkers.
Acceptable Work: Considers ceramics; decoupage; and dollmaking. Handmade production-line items. Price range: $5-500; bestsellers: $40-125.
Terms: Works on consignment and buys outright; 50% commission. Retail price set by joint agreement. Reports in 3-5 days. Hand-delivered work only. Work is displayed in large window and on shelves.

SHERI'S HOUSE OF CRAFTS, 607 S. Hamilton, Sullivan IL 61951. (217)728-4415. Contact: Sharen Schlitter. Craft shop. Estab. 1975. Represents 2 craftworkers. Heaviest wholesale buying and best selling time: fall.
Acceptable Work: Considers decoupage, dollmaking, wall hangings, weavings, macrame, brooms and magnetics. Especially needs items for bazaars. Specializes in bright-colored handmade production-line crafts. Price range: 20¢-$35; bestsellers: $1-10.
Terms: Buys outright. Retail price set by joint agreement. Requires exclusive area representation. Write with SASE. Reports in 1 week. Work may be shipped or hand delivered.

THE SIDE STREET, 434 Franklin St., Waukegan IL 60085. (312)623-5155. Contact: Arva L. Wallace. Craft gift shop. Estab. 1969. Represents over 200 craftworkers.
Acceptable Work: Considers all crafts except macrame. Price range: 50¢-$100; bestsellers: $3-25.
Terms: Works on consignment only. Retail price set by joint agreement. Requires exclusive area representation. Work may be shipped or hand-delivered. Dealer pays return shipping. Displays work 60 days minimum.
Special Needs: "Good unusual jewelry in the price range from $5-25 retail (some a little higher); $50 top limit."
Profile: "There is no limit on the type of craft. Baby things and toys are big sellers; also afghans and all knits, pillows, prints, Christmas ornaments, wood items and pottery." Best selling and heaviest wholesale buying time: October-December and June.

SPERTUS MUSEUM OF JUDAICA, MUSEUM STORE, 618 S. Michigan Ave., Chicago IL 60605. (312)922-9012. Manager: Suzanne MacDonald. Museum gallery/gift shop. Estab. 1972. Represents 30-50 Israeli artists.
Acceptable Work: Considers batik; ceramics; jewelry; pottery; wall hangings; and weavings. Fine one-of-a-kind pieces. Price range: $4.50-1,250; bestsellers: $20-200.
Terms: Works on consignment and buys outright; 50% commission. Retail price set by joint agreement. Reports in 3 weeks. Work may be shipped or hand-delivered by previous consent. Dealer pays insurance for exhibited work. Displays work 2-6 months.
Profile: "Exhibits change about every 2 months. We specialize in Israeli and Judaica items. Customers are students, museum visitors, conventioneers and tourists; 75% Jewish." Heaviest wholesale buying time: winter; best selling time: fall and spring.

SPRINGFIELD ART ASSOCIATION, 700 N. 4th St., Springfield IL 62702. (217)523-2631. Executive Director: William Bealmer. Museum gallery/rental gallery. Estab. 1933. Represents 200 craftworkers.
Acceptable Work: Considers batik; ceramics; glass art; jewelry; leatherworking; pottery; soft sculpture; wall hangings; and weavings. Especially needs ceramics and textiles. Finished and one-of-a-kind pieces. Price range: $10-300.
Terms: Works on consignment; 30% commission. Craftworker sets retail price. Reports in 3 weeks. Work may be shipped or hand-delivered. Dealer pays insurance for exhibited work. Work is featured for 2 weeks. Best selling time: September-January and April-June.

SPURGEON MERCANTILE CO., 822 W. Washington Blvd., Chicago IL 60607. Buyer: Tom Bloyd. Department store. Arts & Crafts department buys adult games; children's toys; wall hangings; and weavings for resale. Buyer sets retail price. Call or write for interview.

SUBURBAN FINE ARTS CENTER, 472 Park Ave., Highland Park IL 60035. (312)432-1888. Contact: Receptionist. Nonprofit gallery and school. Estab. 1970. Represents 1-10 Chicago area craftworkers per show. Price range: $20-1,200; best sellers: $20-250. Exhibits work; commission varies. Retail price set by joint agreement. Hand-delivered work only.
Acceptable Work: Considers batik; ceramics; quilting; soft sculpture; wall hangings; and weavings. Fine one-of-a-kind pieces; utilitarian and/or decorative.
Profile: "We have a very nice professional looking space; are located in the North Shore area

with a sophisticated audience; we are very easy to deal with and take a small percentage in relation to other galleries." Best selling time: Christmas. "Traditionally we have an exclusively crafts exhibit at Christmas time."

SUNSHINE UNLIMITED, INC., 1937 W. 95th St., Chicago IL 60643. (312)239-0107. Contact: Carol Foley, Carlie Nelson, or Liz Manz. Gift and plant shop. Estab. 1974. Represents 45 craftworkers.
Acceptable Work: Considers batik, candlemaking, ceramics, clothing, decoupage, dollmaking, glass art, needlecrafts, pottery, quilting, soft sculpture, tole painting, wall hangings, weavings and woodcrafting. Especially needs items for home and children. Specializes in contemporary and traditional handmade production-line items. "We insist on new materials being used and prefer bright cheerful colors." Price range: $1-100; bestsellers: $3-12.
Terms: Works on consignment and buys outright; 34% commission. Retail price set by joint agreement. "We accept no crafts without seeing good slides or a sample." Reports in 2 weeks. Work may be shipped or hand-delivered. Work is displayed for 90 days.
Profile: "We display on tables, shelves, racks or however we feel will display item best. Our customers range from children shopping for 'mom' to grandmothers. Also middle to upper class and appreciators of unusual items." Heaviest wholesale buying and best selling time: October 1-December 25.

TOWER GALLERY, 300 N. State St., Chicago IL 60610. (312)222-1117. Contact: Seena Swibel. Craft shop. Estab. 1970. Represents 50 craftworkers.
Acceptable Work: Considers batik; candlemaking; ceramics; glass art; jewelry; leatherworking; metalsmithing; needlecrafts; pottery; soft sculpture; wall hangings; weavings; and woodcrafting. Handmade production-line items. Price range: $2-300; bestsellers: $8-75.
Terms: Works on consignment and buys outright; 40% commission. Retail price set by joint agreement. Reports in 4 weeks. Dealer pays insurance for exhibited work.
Profile: "Shop has 3 windows; items are prominently displayed. Customers are all ages; upper middle income." Displays work 1 month. Heaviest wholesale buying time: fall; best selling time: Christmas.

THE UNIVERSITY GALLERY OF CHICAGO STATE UNIVERSITY, Department of Art, 95th and King Dr., Chicago IL 60628. (312)995-2192. Director: Robert Weitz. Gallery. Estab. 1976. Has 2 craft exhibition shows per year.
Acceptable Work: Considers batik; ceramics; jewelry; needlecrafts; pottery; quilting; soft sculpture; wall hangings; and weavings. Especially needs ceramics and fiber. Primitive and fine one-of-a-kind pieces. Price range: $75-1,800; bestsellers: $75-400.
Terms: Works on consignment via contract for exhibition purposes; 20-25% commission. Retail price set by joint agreement. Reports in 3 weeks. Work may be shipped or hand-delivered. Dealer pays return shipping and insurance for exhibited work.
Profile: "We are an urban university in a middle-class neighborhood. Our customers are students, faculty, administrators and people of our south side community. But our exhibits often attract the attention of the Chicago public at-large. Craftworker is given advertising poster/mailers for his/her exhibit and a reception. Often craftworker is asked to lecture for a fee. Work is on display for 1 month."

UPSTAIRS, 450 Duane, Glen Ellyn IL 60137. (312)858-3230. Contact: Jean Weliver. Craft shop. Estab. 1979. Represents 70 craftworkers.
Acceptable Work: Considers "serious crafts": pottery, weaving, handblown glass, and wood. Price range: $2-400; bestsellers: $20-150.
Terms: Works on consignment and buys outright; 25% commission. Retail price set by joint agreement. Reports in 2 weeks. Work may be shipped or hand-delivered. Dealer pays return shipping and insurance for exhibited work. Displays work 3-12 months. Heaviest wholesale buying time, fall; best selling time: October-June.

WEAVING WORKSHOP, 3352 N. Halsted, Chicago IL 60657. (312)929-5776. Contact: Barbara diMauro. Estab. 1970. Represents 10 craftworkers. Considers glass art; leatherwork; rugs; and tapestries. Especially needs utilitarian crafts. Finished, one-of-a-kind items OK; utilitarian and/or decorative. Price range: $5-1,000; bestsellers: $5-150. Works on consignment; 25% commission. Retail price set by joint agreement. Write. Reports in 3 weeks. Dealer pays shipping from shop and insurance for exhibited work. Heaviest wholesale buying time: fall. Customers, ages 25-40, buy crafts for unusual gifts.

Indiana

ALFORD HOUSE, 226 W. 8th St., Anderson IN 46016. (317)649-1248. Manager: June Tibbetts. Director: Joseph B. Schenk. Museum gift shop/rental gallery. Estab. 1967. Represents 60 craftworkers.
Acceptable Work: Considers candlemaking, ceramics, dollmaking, glass art, jewelry, metalsmithing, needlecrafts, pottery, quilting, tole painting and woodcrafting. One-of-a-kind and handmade production-line items. Price range: $1-50; bestsellers: $5-25.
Terms: Works on consignment; "craftworker receives full asking price, markup 30-100%". Retail price set by joint agreement. Call for appointment. Reports in 2 weeks. Work may be shipped or hand delivered. Dealer pays insurance on exhibited work.
Profile: "The shop, sales and rental gallery run to provide additional income to the Anderson Fine Arts Center. It is staffed by volunteers from Women's League. Items are tastefully displayed on shelving units and in display cases; items can also be hung." Display: continuous with occasional rotation. Customers: interests are primarily related to arts or art programs with middle and upper income levels. Heaviest wholesale buying time: fall and early spring; best selling time: Christmas, fall and late spring.

THE ALLIANCE MUSEUM SHOP, Indianapolis Museum of Art, 1200 W. 38th St., Indianapolis IN 46208. (317)923-1331. Buyer: Jeanne Scofield. Museum shop. Estab. 1975. Represents 200 craftworkers.
Acceptable Work: Considers batik; ceramics; decoupage; glass art; jewelry; metalsmithing; needlecrafts; pottery; quilting; soft sculpture; wall hangings; weavings; and woodcrafting.
Terms: Works on consignment and buys outright; 30% commission. Craftworker sets retail price on consigned work; shop sets retail price if bought outright. Reports in 1 week to 10 days. Work may be shipped or hand-delivered. Dealer pays return shipping and insurance for exhibited work. Best selling and heaviest wholesale buying time: fall.

ANDERSON FINE ARTS CENTER, Anderson IN. See Alford House.

ART CENTER MUSEUM SHOP, 120 S. St. Joseph St., South Bend IN 46601. (219)284-9102. Manager: Jennifer Buck. Museum gift shop. Estab. 1960. Represents 15-20 craftworkers; northern Indiana residents have first priority. Considers ceramics; glass art; jewelry; metalsmithing; needlecrafts; pottery; quilting; soft sculpture; weavings; wall hangings; and woodcrafting. Price range: $1-500; bestsellers: $5-50. Works on consignment (6 month contract) and buys outright; 30% commission. Craftworker sets retail price to include 30% commission. Reports in 2 weeks. Dealer pays return shipping and insurance on exhibited work.
Profile: "We are located in a new, exciting civic center designed by Philip Johnson. The shop is at the entrance to the Art Center complex and the gallery exhibition space." Best selling time: summer and Christmas.

THE BROWN COUNTY CRAFT GUILD GALLERY, Rt. 2, Box 210, Nashville IN 47448. (812)988-2124. President: Susan W. Showalter (988-7830). Rental gallery. Estab. 1978. Represents 27 Brown County area craftworkers.
Acceptable Work: Considers batik, dollmaking, glass art, hand forged ironwork, jewelry, leatherworking, metalsmithing, needlecrafts, paper cutting, pottery, quilting, seat weaving, wall hangings, weavings and woodworking. One-of-a-kind and handmade production-line items. Price range: $2-2,500; bestsellers: $4.50-45.
Terms: Must be a member of Brown County Craft Guild; live in a 35 mile radius of Nashville; and join for a minimum of 1 year. Works on consignment. Charges $40/month plus 10% commission for regular exhibiting members and $10/month plus 25% commission for associate exhibiting members. Both must work an equal amount of time in the gallery. Craftworker sets retail price. Send resume, slides and SASE. Jury procedures take place every February and August. Work must be hand-delivered.
Profile: "We are in a tourist town. The shop is owned and operated by Guild members and everyone shares the work. Members work only sold in gallery except for occasional shows by outside craftworkers." Heaviest wholesale buying and best selling time: fall. Closed in winter during the week.

COMMON PLACE, 302 Washington, Columbus IN 47201. (812)376-9915. Contact: Bill Mitchell. Gallery. Estab. 1974. Represents 100 craftworkers.
Acceptable Work: Considers batik; candlemaking; ceramics; clothing; dollmaking; glass art; jewelry; leatherworking; metalsmithing; needlecrafts; painting; pottery; quilting; wall hangings; weavings; and woodcrafting. Fine one-of-a-kind and handmade production-line items. Price range: $1-300; bestsellers: $1.50-100.

Terms: Works on consignment and (occasionally) buys outright; 30% commission. Craftworker sets retail price. Reports in 2 weeks. Work may be shipped or hand-delivered. Dealer pays shipping for exhibited work. Displays work 3 months-1 year.
Profile: "Work is displayed in glass cubes on pedestals, in jewelry cases, hanging on walls and rafters and on counters. This is a nonprofit organization. All profits from sales are returned to the community through programs of The Commons and The Columbus Service League, who are joint sponsors of the shop." Heaviest wholesale buying time: September-October; best selling time: November-December.

CONNER TRADING POST, Conner Prairie Pioneer Settlement, 30 Conner Lane, Noblesville IN 46060. (317)773-3633. Contact: Manager of the Trading Post. Museum gift shop. Estab. 1964. Represents 50-60 craftworkers.
Acceptable Work: Considers candlemaking, dollmaking, glass art, leatherworking, metalsmithing, needlecrafts, quilting, scrimshaw and woodcrafting. Especially needs child-oriented items "which parents and grandparents will buy." Specializes in Appalachian work. "We do purchase historic crafts produced with quality in mind. Our time frame is early 19th century and we especially desire pieces that represent fine craftsmanship." One-of-a-kind and handmade production-line items. Price range: 5¢-$350; bestsellers: 5¢-$85.
Terms: Buys outright and works on consignment; 33⅓% commission. Retail price set by joint agreement. Call for appointment and be prepared to bring samples; January-March not always available; weekends bad. Reports in 2 weeks. Work may be shipped or hand delivered.
Profile: "Our museum is not in a town; therefore, our visitors must be interested in Indiana-type (Appalachian, etc.) crafts to drive out here. Most of our items are on a self-serve basis and thus are handled, but there are also locked glass cases. We have a large number of discriminating adults, interior decorators who come regularly." Customers: school groups (majority 4-8th grade); scout groups; senior citizen; handicapped; small club groups; national and international conventions; local traffic (for our specialty items such as Christmas crafts, made-on-the-property crafts, and such unique items of our time period—1830's). Best selling time: June weddings and Christmas. Closed: December-March.
To Break In: "We are flexible on regular basis supply—we cannot expect true craftsmen to be machines—if we're out...we're out."

COON HOLLER, Rt. 3 Box 553, Nashville IN 47448. Manager: Midge Gaylor. Craft shop. Estab. 1978. Represents 5 craftworkers.
Acceptable Work: Considers tole painting, woodcrafting and woodcarvings. Especially needs low cost bare wood products for tole painters and woodcarvings which could retail for under $5 (ie. little animals, carved shoes, pins, necklaces). One-of-a-kind and handmade production-line items. Price range: 98¢-$150; bestsellers: $2.50-22.50.
Terms: Buys outright on some selected crafts that retail for under $5; mainly works on consignment with 20-33% commission. Shop sets retail price on outright purchases; retail price set by joint agreement on consigned items. Requires exclusive area representation. Send slides/photos with SASE. Reports in 2 weeks. Work may be shipped or hand delivered.
Profile: "We sell finished wood carvings and toleware items, and supplies for woodcarvers and tole painters. We are very emphatic about dealing honestly with customers (if a motor tool is used in the carving, we are very open about it. We *do not* want carvings done on a machine duplicator; carvings done with a motor tool are OK as long as you tell us). Items are consigned on a limited time basis arrived at by mutual agreement. The method of display rests solely with the shop personnel. Display is done in an antique style shop with crate shelves and barnboard decor. Some items are displayed in glass and wood cases. We are in a tourist area with very seasonal influx. Most customers tend to be in the average income range thus about 90% of our sales are in the under $15 range." Heaviest wholesale buying and best selling time: June-November ("we can usually project anticipated needs as early as April").

COUNTRY JOY, Rt. 3, Box 176, Possum Trot Sq., Nashville IN 47448. (812)988-6797. Contact: Joyce or George Murphy. Boutique/craft/gift shop. Estab. 1978. Represents 9+ craftworkers.
Acceptable Work: Considers all crafts. One-of-a-kind and handmade production-line items. Price range: $5.98-550; bestsellers: $5.98-15.98.
Terms: Works on consignment; 30% commission. "We prefer to handle all crafts on consignment and only consider purchasing in those instances of special merit and which we feel will sell readily." Craftworker sets retail price; shop advises. Requires exclusive area representation. Write with SASE. Reports in 2 weeks. Work may be shipped or hand delivered.
Profile: "Our community is small and there are many shops here. We have approximately 500

square feet of space and are located in a rustic-type building. It has a courtyard in the center, off of which all the shops open. The interior of the shop borders in rustic, but is compatable with all types and styles of merchandise. Our area is small, but we try to keep as many craft items on display as we can at one time so that each gets a fair representation. We display on shelves, walls, racks and furniture. We use any method of display available at the time and usually display items until they are sold, sent back or recalled (if room)." Customers: tourists, teenagers, college students (from Indiana Uviversity), senior citizens, city and country folks, artists, craftsmen, business people and factory workers. Heaviest wholesale buying time: February-September; best selling time: October. Open: March-Christmas.

F.B. FOGG, Cana St., Metamora IN 47030. (317)289-7464. Contact: Ann Johnson. Craft shop and gallery/studio. Estab. l973. Represents 25 Hoosier craftworkers; must be from within a 50 mile radius. Send resume, slides with SASE. Reports in 2 weeks.
Acceptable Work: Considers batik, ceramics, clothing, glass art, jewelry, leatherworking, metalsmithing, needlecrafts, pottery, quilting, soft sculpture, wall hangings, weavings and papier-mache. Specializes in igolochkoy (Russian needle embroidery). One-of-a-kind and handmade production-line items. Price range: $1-500; bestsellers: $1.25. Works on consignment; 40% commission. Dealer pays exhibit insurance. Craftworker sets retail price.
Profile: "We are located in the 3 lower rooms of a house built in 1873. The rooms are painted puce and mauve and have an abundance of flowering window boxes. The house is shaded by a big maple tree and is located by an old canal in a little town in the hills of southern Indiana. Much tourist enjoyment. Displays are rotated over one season (May-October 30) with antiques as background; There is a gallery room set with small tables where art surrounds the customers as they sip tea and eat crumpets. Sometimes we have 45,000 people a weekend in traffic." Heaviest wholesale buying time: May; best selling time: fall.
To Break In: "We like 3 copies of inventory—identity of pieces and prices well marked."

FLOYD COUNTY MUSEUM, 201 E. Spring St., New Albany IN 47150. (812)944-7336. Director: Alice Trottman. Gallery/museum gift shop. Estab. 1971. Represents 15 craftworkers.
Acceptable Work: Considers batik; dollmaking; glass art; jewelry; metalsmithing; pottery; soft sculpture; wall hangings; weavings; handbuilt ceramics; and original prints. Fine one-of-a-kind and handmade production-line items. Price range: $3-100; bestsellers: $3-25.
Terms: Works on consignment; 30% commission. Craftworker sets retail price. Requires exclusive New Albany representation. Send inquiry or slides. Reports in 2 weeks. Work may be shipped or hand-delivered after acceptance. Best selling time: fall-winter.

FORT OUIATENON BLOCKHOUSE TRADING POST, 909 South St., Lafayette IN 47901. (317)742-8411. Buyer: Fern Martin. Museum gift shop. Estab. 1969. Represents 5-10 18th century fur trade era craftworkers. Price range: $1-25; bestsellers: $1-12.50. Works on consignment and buys outright; 20% commission. Retail price set by joint agreement. Reports in 3 weeks. Work may be shipped or hand-delivered.
Acceptable Work: Only accepts 18th century type crafts. Considers candlemaking; clothing; dollmaking; glass art; jewelry; leatherworking; metalsmithing; needlecrafts; pottery; quilting; wall hangings; weavings; and woodcrafting.
Profile: "We are located in a reconstructed blockhouse, patterned after the structures from the French fur trade era in Indiana (18th century). The fort specializes in replica items from the fur trade era." Heaviest wholesale buying time: April-September; best selling time: September or October.

FORT WAYNE MUSEUM OF ART GIFT SHOP, 1202 W. Wayne St., Fort Wayne IN 46804. Director: James Bell. Museum gift shop. Estab. 1894.
Acceptable Work: Considers ceramics; glass art; jewelry; metalsmithing; pottery; woodcrafting; note cards; blank books; and sculpture. Price range: 49¢-$150; bestsellers: $1.50-30.
Terms: Works on consignment and buys outright; 50% commission. Retail price set by joint agreement. Reports in 2 weeks. Work may be shipped or hand-delivered. Displays work 6-12 months. Best selling and heaviest wholesale buying time: September-May.

FRIENDS OF ART BOOKSTALL, Fine Arts Museum, Bloomington IN 47405. (812)337-1333. Manager: P.M. Pizzo. Museum gift shop. Estab. 1966. Represents 4-5 craftworkers.
Acceptable Work: Considers ceramics and jewelry. Specializes in primitive and fine art crafts. Handmade production-line items only. Price range: 50¢-$50; bestsellers: $5-10.
Terms: Buys outright and works on consignment; 30% commission. Craftworker sets retail price. Call for appointment. Reports in 4 weeks. Work may be shipped or hand-delivered.

Profile: "The shop is small; we can only handle small items. Work is displayed in glass jewelry cases." Customers: ages 18-30, mostly students. Heaviest wholesale buying time: fall; best selling time: Christmas.

GOURLEY'S OLDE SHOPPE, 2242 Cragmont, Madison IN 47250. (812)273-1697. Contact: Helen Gourley. Museum gallery. Estab. 1966. Represents 20-25 area craftworkers.
Acceptable Work: Considers candlemaking; decoupage; needlecrafts; tole painting; wall hangings; weavings; and woodcrafting. Price range: 50¢-$500.
Terms: Works on consignment; 20% commission. Craftworker sets retail price. Requires exclusive area representation. Work may be hand-delivered.
Profile: "We have a living museum of antiques and crafts, displayed together. We sponsor the Historic Hoosier Hills Antique Collectors & Hand Craftsmen's Guild. We also sponsor 2 annual festivals around the Madison Court House area."

J. BOB CREATIONS, Box 223, Nashville IN 47448. Contact: Mr. and Mrs. John R. Hughes. Craft/gift shop. Estab. 1978. Represents 6 craftworkers, especially woodcrafters.
Acceptable Work: Considers glass art, jewelry, metalsmithing and woodcrafting. Specializes in primitive and fine art pieces. One-of-a-kind and handmade production-line items. Price range: $2.50-250.
Terms: Buys outright and works on consignment; 30% commission. Call for appointment and bring samples. Reports in 1 week. Work must be hand-delivered. Dealer pays for insurance on exhibited goods and sets retail price. Requires exclusive area representation.
Profile: "Our shop is located in a 25-30-year-old quaint building, which was, at one time, an art museum. We want to see people being able to afford crafts so we have a price range for everybody. We take special orders (2 weeks) and pay all the postage. Browsers are welcome. Displays are changed once a week, hoping to highlight slower items. Work is hung on board walls." Customers: mainly tourists. Heaviest wholesale buying time: early summer and early fall; best selling time: fall. Closed January-March except weekends.

MOREAU GALLERY THREE, St. Mary's College, Notre Dame IN 46556. (219)284-5717. Gallery Coordinator: Michele Fricke. Exhibit gallery. Estab. 1844.
Acceptable Work: Considers ceramics, glass art, jewelry, metalsmithing, pottery, soft sculpture, wall hangings, weavings and woodcrafting. Especially needs fiber art. Specializes in contemporary and fine designer crafts.
Terms: Exhibits only; no charge. Retail price set by joint agreement. Send resume or slides. Reports in 4 weeks. Dealer pays insurance on exhibited work.
Profile: "This is strictly an exhibition gallery. If the artist wishes, we can post a price list, but we rarely sell anything. We have 3 galleries, 2 quite large and suitable for larger pieces. The small gallery is more suitable to small precious work. All have natural and track lighting. The shows are of the 1 or 2-person variety. Normally a show runs approximately 1 month. The galleries are locked and guarded." Customers: college age students and local residents; middle-high incomes.

THE MUSEUM SHOP, 202 N. Alabama, Indianapolis IN 46204. (317)633-5007. Contact: Mrs. J.E. Burns Jr. Museum gift shop. Estab. 1970. Represents 10-12 craftworkers who make items as they were done in the 18th and 19th centuries.
Acceptable Work: Considers candlemaking; ceramics; dollmaking; jewelry; metalsmithing; needlecrafts; pottery; quilting; tole painting; and woodcrafting. Price range: 10¢-$350; bestsellers: 10¢-$15.
Terms: Works on consignment and buys outright; 34% commission. Retail price set by joint agreement. Reports in 3 weeks. Work may be shipped or hand-delivered. Dealer pays return shipping and insurance for exhibited work.
Profile: "Work is displayed with similar items and items used with, i.e. candle holders with candles. We try to display the best craftwork reflecting what people would have used and made in Indiana prior to 1910." Best selling time: Christmas and summer.

NEW HARMONY GALLERY OF CONTEMPORARY ART, Owen Block, Main St., New Harmony IN 47631. (812)682-3156. Director: John P. Begley. Gallery. Estab. 1975. Represents 40 craftworkers who live within a 200-mile radius of New Harmony or with prior connections to this area. Price range: $5-1,000; bestsellers: $15-50. Works on consignment; 30% commission. Retail price set by joint agreement. Reports in 4 weeks. Work may be shipped or hand-delivered with prior consent. Dealer pays return shipping and insurance for exhibited work.
Acceptable Work: Considers ceramics; glass art; jewelry; metalsmithing; soft sculpture; wall

Conner Trading Post, located in Noblesville, Indiana, is the museum shop for the Conner Prairie Pioneer Settlement. Customers are interested in Indiana and Appalachian crafts and the best selling times are June (for weddings) and Christmas. Being a seasonal business, the shop is closed December to March.

hangings; weavings and woodcrafting. Fine utilitarian and/or decorative pieces.
Profile: "The gallery has 1 room with constantly rotating exhibitions of individual or small groups of artists. In addition, we keep a consignment room with pieces by artists we represent constantly on display." Best selling time: summer-fall.

RAG-TIME ARTISTRY, Box 187, Nashville IN 47448. (812)988-4047 (shop); (812)988-4554 (office). Contact: Fran Rogers. Gift shop. Estab. 1978. Represents 6-8 craftworkers.
Acceptable Work: Considers dollmaking, needlecrafts, quilting, scrimshaw, weavings and woodcrafting. Especially needs kitchen items (placemats, toaster covers), dolls and toys. Handmade production-line items. Price range: $1.25-250; bestsellers: $3.50-18.
Terms: Buys outright; net 30 days. Dealer sets retail price. Requires exclusive area representation. Write with SASE. Work may be shipped or hand-delivered.
Profile: "I am striving to give to the customers an opportunity to purchase handmade items of the best quality at a reasonable price. I like to carry items for the little ones which can be of such a quality that they can be kept for years and even handed down with pride to their children. In short, I have tried to create a shop of yesterday which offers a higher type and quality of product than the everyday gift shop that sells items 'made in Japan'. Displays change from time to time—and arranged according to space available and quality of products." Best buying time: summer and fall.
To Break In: "I would want to see examples of their work. I would not buy from someone who sold to other shops in this town. Since I believe a good piece of work at a reasonable price sells itself, I do not like to work with pushy salespeople. I prefer not to have minimum orders set for more than $50, since I may want to place several smaller orders from time to time."

STATION GALLERY, 422 E. Goldsboro, Crown Point IN 46307. (219)663-8770. Gallery/frame shop. Estab. 1972. Represents 100 craftworkers. Considers batik; dollmaking; glass art; jewelry; metalsmithing; pottery; wall hangings; weavings; and woodcrafting. Fine one-of-a-kind and handmade production-line items. Price range: $5-150; bestsellers: $5-30. Works on consignment and sometimes buys outright. Craftworker sets retail price. Requires exclusive area representation. Reports in 4 weeks. Dealer pays return shipping.
Profile: "We are located in an old train station." Customers are middle to upper income professionals in mid 20's-50's. Best selling time: April-December.

TIPPECANOE COUNTY HISTORICAL ASSOCIATION, FOWLER HOUSE MUSEUM, 909 South St., Layfayette IN 47901. (317)742-8411. Buyer: Fern Martin. Museum gift shop. Estab. 1971. Represents 5-10 19th century/Victorian craftworkers. Price range: $1-25; bestsellers: $1-12.50. Works on consignment and buys outright; 20% commission. Retail price set by joint agreement. Reports in 3 weeks. Work may be shipped or hand-delivered.
Acceptable Work: Accepts 19th century Victorian work only. Considers candlemaking; accessories; dollmaking; glass art; jewelry; leatherworking; metalsmithing; needlecrafts; pottery; quilting; wall hangings; weavings; and woodcrafting.
Profile: "Representative items are on display at all times. The museum is housed in a mansion dating from the 1850s." Customers range from pre-schoolers to Senior Citizens interested in things historic; income varies." Best selling and heaviest wholesale buying time: Christmas.

THE TOY CHEST & HANDCARVED CIRCUS, West Main, Box 533, Nashville IN 47448.

(812)988-2817 (after 6 p.m.). Contact: Helen Hollis. Toy shop. Represents 5 craftworkers.
Acceptable Work: Considers dollmaking and wood toys. One-of-a-kind and handmade production-line items. Price range $5-500; bestsellers: $5-50.
Terms: Works on consignment; 40% commission. Craftworker sets retail price plus dealer adds 40% onto original price. Write, stating craft and prices, enclosing SASE. Reports in 2 weeks. Work may be shipped or hand delivered. Requires exclusive area representation.
Profile: "We carry unusual items and only want realistic-looking toys. We try to carry unique items from around the world. In back, the circus carved by Ed Hollis received TV coverage. Work is displayed on shelves, behind and in counters." Customers: mainly tourists. Heaviest wholesale buying time: March-summer; best selling time: October and summer.

TRILOGY GALLERY INC., Box 642, Nashville IN 47448. (812)988-4030. Vice President: Donn Stoffer. Gallery. Estab. 1973. Considers all quality crafts. Price range: $3-1,500; bestsellers: $15-100.
Terms: Works on consignment and buys outright; 40% commission. Craftworker sets retail price. Requires exclusive area representation. Arrange interview. Reports in 2 weeks. Dealer pays insurance for exhibited work.

VILLAGE CRAFTSMAN, Division of Cottonpatch, Inc., 605 Washington St., Columbus IN 47201. (812)376-9156. Manager: Terry Clark. Craft shop. Estab. 1972. Represents 5 craftworkers.
Acceptable Work: Considers candlemaking; clothing (leather); glass art; jewelry; leatherworking; metalsmithing; pottery; and woodcrafting. Especially needs hardwood products and pottery. Finished and one-of-a-kind pieces. Price range: $10-1,000; bestsellers: $10-100.
Terms: Works on consignment; 20-40% commission. Retail price set by joint agreement. Requires exclusive area representation. Reports in 2 weeks. Work may be shipped or hand-delivered. Dealer pays insurance for exhibited work.
Profile: Work is "either highlighted or blended with other pieces, depending on what care it needs. Jewelry is in glass; stainable items are put out of reach." Best selling and heaviest wholesale buying time: May-Christmas.

WAYNE COUNTY HISTORICAL MUSEUM, 1150 N. A St., Richmond IN 47374. Contact: Director. Museum gift shop. Estab. 1930. Represents 8 craftworkers.
Acceptable Work: Considers candlemaking, clothing, dollmaking, glass art, jewelry, metalsmithing, needlecrafts, wall hangings, weavings and woodcrafting. Especially needs blacksmithing, woodworking, weavings and various doll types. Price range: 25¢-$15; bestsellers: 25¢-$10.
Terms: Works on consignment and buys outright; 20% commission. Retail price set by joint agreement. Reports in 2 weeks. Work may be shipped or hand-delivered. Dealer pays shipping to shop and insurance for exhibited work.
Profile: "Most items are located in glass display cases in the entrance area to the museum." Heaviest wholesale buying time: early spring and midsummer; best selling time: spring-early fall.

WINTHROP GALLERY, 5228 Winthrop Ave., Indianapolis IN 46220. (317)283-1147. Contact: Herman W. Kapherr. Considers sculpture. Handles mainly 19th and 20th century American art. Buys outright. Price range: $25-3,000.

Iowa

BLUE GRASS ART AND HOBBY CENTER, Box 206C, E. Telegraph Rd., Blue Grass IA 52726. (319)381-3111. Manager: LuElla Schroder. Gift shop/china-glass studio. Estab. 1950. Represents 3 craftworkers. Price range: 50¢-$500; bestsellers: 50¢-$275. Buys outright. Gallery sets retail price. Considers ceramics; glass art; jewelry; and china-painted porcelain only. No other crafts considered.
Profile: "We carry exclusively glass, porcelain and china supplies. No one carries or teaches this full line in our area. We mail-order to all states." Best selling time: June-July and November-December.

CORNERHOUSE GALLERY & FRAME, 2753 1st Ave. SE, Cedar Rapids IA 52402. (319)365-4348. Director: Janelle V. McClain. Gallery/frame shop. Estab. 1976. Represents 50 craftworkers.
Acceptable Work: Considers batik; glass art; pottery; wall hangings; weavings; and woodcrafting. Fine one-of-a-kind and handmade production-line items. Price range: $5-500; bestsellers: $5-150.

Shops and Galleries   **155**

Terms: Works on consignment and buys outright; 40% commission. Gallery sets retail price. Requires exclusive area representation. Reports in 3 weeks. Work may be shipped or hand-delivered. Dealer pays insurance.
Profile: "Each work is displayed so as to benefit it most with sufficient space. Displays are rotated once a month with special showings of individual artists' work. We are located in a large turn-of-the-century house emphasizing a comfortable, relaxed, artistic atmosphere." Heaviest wholesale buying time: summer; best selling time: winter-spring.

DARLENE'S HOUSE OF GIFTS, 314 A. Ave. E, Box 665, Oskaloosa IA 52577. Contact: Darlene Fleck. Craft shop. Estab. 1977. Represents 75 craftworkers.
Acceptable Work: Considers all crafts connected with animals (dogs, cats, pigs, owls and horses); unique and unusual only. Handcrafted items only—no kits or plastic and no crocheted, knit or stuffed toys. Handmade production-line items only. Price range: $2-50; bestsellers: $5-20.
Terms: Buys outright and works on consignment; 34% commission. Retail price set by craftworker or joint agreement. Send resume and photos with SASE. No samples until requested. Reports in 2-3 weeks. Work must be hand-delivered.
Profile: "Shop is small (430 square feet) with a limited display area. Large items are hard to handle. Items go on display immediately as there's no storage space—30-60 day time period, unless seasonal, then pulled after holiday or season. Shop is set up like a house and presently have 20 states represented and 75 persons. We do mail order business, both retail and wholesale. We've had ads in 1977 *Christmas Ideas*, June '78 (*Better Homes and Gardens*). The area has a high percent of retirees—mostly from farm areas. We cater to the 20-45 age and lower income groups." Heaviest wholesale buying time: Christmas; best selling time: September-December.
To Break In: "SASE needed for return of photos or for a reply. Black and white photos are best, would like permission to use photos in the mail brochure."

FOURTH STREET ARTISTS GALLERY, INC., 473 W. 4th St., Dubuque IA 52001. (319)556-9363. Public Relations Director: Ruth Nash. Craft/gift shop and gallery. Estab. 1972. Represents 100 craftworkers.
Acceptable Work: Considers all crafts except decoupage and tole painting. Especially needs jewelry. "We like moderately-priced functional items of distinctive design, handmade." One-of-a-kind and handmade production-line items. Price range: 50¢-$200; bestsellers: 5¢-$30.
Terms: Works on consignment; 30% commission. "The work is juried by people with BA degrees in art and/or asthetics." Craftworker sets retail price. Send slides. Reports in 1 week. Work may be shipped or hand-delivered.
Profile: "Work is well displayed on walls, shelves or pedestals and kept until sold or reclaimed by artist (moved occasionally). We are located in a charming remodeled old house near the number one tourist attraction in Dubuque—the 4th Street cablecar. We have 3 special shows monthly, plus 3 exhibitions. Our best customers are tourists from Chicago; young, married and well-educated; people hunting for wedding presents; also visitors on weekends (relatives, old friends)." Best selling time: November-December.

GENEVA'S GIFT SHOPPE, 111 W. Bremer Ave., Waverly IA 50677. (319)352-3281. Shopkeeper: Geneva Liebau. Craft and gift shop. Estab. 1974. Represents 125 craftworkers.
Acceptable Work: Considers batik; candlemaking; ceramics; clothing; decoupage; dollmaking; glass art; jewelry; leatherworking; metalsmithing; needlecrafts; pottery; quilting; soft sculpture; tole painting; wall hangings; weavings; woodcrafting; baskets; and macrame. Price range: $1-350; bestsellers: $2-25.
Terms: Works on consignment and buys outright; 33⅓% commission. Retail price set by joint agreement. Requires exclusive area representation. Reports in 4 weeks. Work may be shipped or hand-delivered. Dealer pays fire and theft insurance for exhibited work. Displays work 3 months. Customers are mostly female. Best selling time: Christmas.

GRANNY'S ATTIC, 222 5th St., West Des Moines IA 50265. (515)255-7088. Contact: Fran Schiers. Gift shop. Estab. 1973. Represents 450 craftworkers.
Acceptable Work: Considers batik, candlemaking, ceramics, clothing, decoupage, dollmaking, glass art, jewelry, leatherworking, metalsmithing, needlecrafts, pottery, quilting, tole painting, wall hangings, weavings and woodcrafting. Especially needs painted china, children's furniture, wooden toys and handmade furniture. Fine one-of-a-kind and handmade production-line items. Price range: $1+; bestsellers: $1-15.
Terms: Buys outright and works on consignment; 50% commission. Retail price set by joint

agreement. Call in person, for appointment, or write with SASE; do not send samples. Reports in 4 weeks. Work may be shipped or hand-deliverd. "Charges 10% of selling price on consigned items removed before 90 days. After 90 days, no charge until sold."
Profile: "Jewelry is shown in glass showcase, delicate items are marked *do not handle*. Shop is a mixture of old and new." Heaviest wholesale buying time: Easter and September; best selling time: summer and Christmas.

JAN'S GALLERY, 203 5th St., West Des Moines IA 50265. (515)277-6734. President: Jan Shotwell. Gallery. Estab. 1970. Represents 30-35 craftworkers.
Acceptable Work: Considers batik; ceramics; glass art; jewelry; metalsmithing; pottery; soft sculpture; wall hangings; and weavings. Fine one-of-a-kind pieces only. Price range: $5-500; bestsellers: $5-250.
Terms: Works on consignment; 40% commission. Retail price set by joint agreement. Requires exclusive area representation. Reports in 1-2 weeks. Work may be shipped or hand-delivered. Dealer pays return shipping and insurance.
Profile: "I have 2 store front windows and 2 gallery rooms, 1 with shelving, etc. All work is displayed but I rotate windows and rearrange items every 2-3 weeks. I also have a leasing program for businesses and professional offices." Best selling time: pre-Christmas.

MADE IN IOWA SHOP, 427 Douglas, Ames IA 50010. (515)232-5331. Manager: Evelyn Baumberger. Represents Iowa craftworkers only.
Acceptable Work: Considers all fine hand-crafted original works. Primitive one-of-a-kind and handmade production-line items. Especially needs woodworking, basketry, leatherworking and weavings. Send slides or examples of works for selection committee. Price range: $1-200; bestsellers: $5-50.
Terms: Works on consignment; 30% commission. Craftworker sets retail price. Reports in 4 weeks. Work may be shipped or hand-delivered. Dealer pays insurance for exhibited work. Displays work 3-4 months.
Profile: Works are displayed in prominent area; customers are college students and people with middle incomes. Best selling time: school year and holidays.

MAIN STREET GALLERY SHOP, 232½ Main St., Ames IA 50010. (515)232-5331. Manager: Evelyn Baumberger. Represents non-Iowan craftworkers.
Acceptable Work: Considers all fine handcrafted original works. Primitive one-of-a-kind and handmade production-line items. Especially needs woodworking, basketry, leatherworking and weavings. Send slides or examples of works for selection committee. Price range: $1-200; bestsellers: $5-50.
Terms: Works on consignment; 30% commission. Craftworker sets retail price. Reports in 4 weeks. Work may be shipped or hand-delivered. Dealer pays insurance for exhibited work. Displays work 3-4 months.
Profile: The shop is adjacent to the gallery exhibition area. Works are displayed in prominent area. Customers are college students and people with middle incomes. Best selling time: school year and holidays.

THE OCTAGON ART CENTER SHOP, 232½ Main St., Ames IA 50010. (515)232-5331. Contact: Shop Manager.
Acceptable Work: Considers ceramics; jewelry; needlecrafts; glass art; leatherworking; tie dye; batik; woodcrafting; and toymaking. Price range: 50¢-$150.
Terms: Buys on consignment; 30% commission. Craftworker sets retail price. "We primarily feature local and area artists' work, but we also actively seek quality handcrafts from other parts of the country."

THE POT SHOP/ART GALLERY, Rt. 1, US Hwy. 169 S., Humboldt IA 50548. (515)332-4210. Contact: Hiram or JoAnne Shouse. Gallery/gift shop. Estab. 1977. Represents 30 craftworkers.
Acceptable Work: Considers all crafts. Price range: $1-300; bestsellers: $4-40.
Terms: Works on consignment and buys outright; 25% commission. Craftworker sets retail price. Requires exclusive area representation. Reports in 1 week after end of each month. Work may be shipped or hand-delivered. Dealer pays return shipping and insurance for exhibited work.
Profile: "We try to feature 1 craftsman at a time in special displays. We try to work with the craftsman in his 'off' season if he attends shows and fairs." Heaviest wholesale buying time: early spring and early fall.

Kansas

ACCENTS, 816 A 5th St., Clay Center KS 67432. (913)632-5995. Contact: Judy Bigler or Coni Witters. Gallery/gift shop. Estab. 1975. Represents 30 craftworkers.
Acceptable Work: Considers all crafts. Especially needs smaller items under $50. One-of-a-kind and handmade production-line items. Price range: $1.95 (tree decorations)-$195; bestsellers: $5-100.
Terms: Buys outright and works on consignment; 20-30% commission. "Some craftworkers set their own prices, others prefer that we do it." All methods of inquiry OK. Reports as soon as possible. Work may be shipped or hand delivered. "After 3 months, if the piece hasn't sold, we decide if we will keep it longer or return it."
Profile: "We have 3 rooms, and usually display similar items together. The front room has a display window with sun screen and track lighting. It is modern and natural in decor with display shelves and boxes. The middle room contains mostly yarn. The back room has an antique decor. We get a cross between the more wealthy who can afford and want good artwork and the younger craftsperson who appreciates and will buy what he can." Best selling time: October-December. Shop is advertised by newspaper and radio ads.

AGRICULTURAL HALL OF FAME, 630 N. 126th St., Bonner Springs KS 66012. (913)721-1075. Director: Harold L. Adkins. Museum gift shop. Estab. 1965.
Acceptable Work: Considers ceramics, leatherworking, pottery, quilting, painting, sculpture, woodcrafting and wood chiseling. "We have never tried anything like this—gift shop items are now mass produced. We would like to represent rural arts and crafts, although folk arts and crafts would be acceptable. We are looking for things with farm animals on them and pictures of rural living." Price range: $1-35; bestsellers: $3.
Terms: Buys outright and works on consignment; 30% minimum commission. Retail price set by craftworker or joint agreement. Bring in samples for discussion. Reports in 2 weeks. Work must be hand-delivered at present time.
Profile: "Items would be on modern display shelves but would develop suitable shelving of old wood posts. Tourists come from all over the US and several foreign countries, mostly looking for souveniers of our area." School children come in April-May, families in June-August, and senior citizens in September-November; all above average incomes. Heaviest wholesale buying time: March-April; best selling time: May-September.

THE ART BOX, 1321 Anderson, Manhattan KS 66502. (913)539-7031. President: Donna F. Rooks. Craft/gift shop. Estab. 1964. Represents 100 craftworkers.
Acceptable Work: Considers batik, candlemaking, ceramics, dollmaking, glass art, jewelry, macrame, metalsmithing, needlecrafts, pottery, scrimshaw, soft sculpture, tole painting, wall hangings, weavings, woodcrafting, stained glass, assemblages, collages and sculpture. Especially needs Christmas tree ornaments. One-of-a-kind pieces only. Price range: $1-100; bestsellers: $1-33.50.
Terms: Works on consignment; 40-60% commission on items costing less than $30, and 33⅓% to 66-2/3% commission on items costing $30 or more. Retail price set by joint agreement. "We place our shop price on after consignee states his price." Send resume, slides, SASE or call for appointment. Work accepted every Thursday. Work may be shipped or hand delivered. Display time: 3-6 months on contract basis.
Profile: "We are a nonprofit shop and have never borrowed a penny. We display on and in all types of boxes. We use telephone spools and paper mache (for tables), barn doors and counters tops. The counter came from a department store and we painted it bright yellow. We make our own price tags and consignment cards and use old sacks with our name handprinted on them. We change windows, counters, areas and furniture every week. The shop looks different constantly. We are located across the street from Kansas State University and close to Aggieville shopping area so students and visitors are good customers. Good walk-in traffic." Best selling time: fall-December and spring.

BLACKBEAR'S GREAT PLAINS STUDIO, 710 W. Douglas, Wichita KS 67203. (316)263-2793. Contact: Sandra or Patricia. Gallery/gift shop. Estab. 1955.
Acceptable Work: Considers jewelry, pottery, paintings, sculpture, beadwork and quillwork. Especially needs beadwork, quillwork and soap stone carvings. Specializes in native American pieces.
Terms: Buys outright and works on consignment; 25% commission. Requires exclusive area representation. Call for appointment at which time you should present work. Work must be hand-delivered.

CHEROKEE STRIP LIVING MUSEUM, (Affiliated National Park Museum), Box 230, Arkansas City KS 67005. (316)442-6750. Director: Herbert Marshall. Gallery/museum gift shop. Estab. 1966. Represents 12 craftworkers.
Acceptable Work: Considers ceramics; jewelry; leatherworking; pottery; wall hangings; and weavings. Primitive one-of-a-kind pieces. Price range: $2.50-500; bestsellers: $10.
Terms: Works on consignment; 20% commission. Curator sets retail price. Requires exclusive area representation. Reports in 2 weeks. Hand-delivered work only. Dealer pays insurance for exhibited work.
Profile: "Items are very well taken care of and they are not handled by the visitor. Shop is connected to a historical museum and customers are very cultural minded." Heaviest wholesale buying time: spring; best selling time: summer.

CRAFTS INCREDIBLE, INC., 7217 Mission Rd., Prairie Village KS 66208. (913)362-9430. Contact: Irene L. Marsh or Donna or Claude Adam. Craft/gift shop and gallery. Estab. 1967. Represents 225 American craftworkers.
Acceptable Work: Considers all crafts except clothing. Specializes in traditional and contemporary crafts. One-of-a-kind and handmade production-line items. Price range: 25¢-$500; bestsellers: 25¢-$25.
Terms: Buys outright and works on consignment; 40% commission. Retail price set by joint agreement. Send resume, slides, samples if possible or call for appointment. Reports in 2 weeks. Work may be shipped or hand-delivered. Dealer pays return shipping and insurance for exhibited work.
Profile: "Our displays are done in a vignette manner according to type of item (i.e. kitchen items grouped in one area, children-oriented items in another). The flavor is eclectic using old trunks and displayers—no commercial racks or shelving. Giving each item dignity is stressed. Customers are middle to upper class women, ages 25-55, suburban living." Heaviest wholesale buying time: fall and spring; best selling time: Christmas.
To Break In: " We look for craftsmen who are proud of their work and show it through care for their product in packing, inventory, correct receipts and listings as well as printed tags or biographies and a continued interest in the locations in which they place their work."

EARTH TO STONE, Box 61, Cawker City KS 67430. (913)781-4369. Contact: Barbara or Charles Stevens. Consignment gallery. Estab. 1977. Represents 10-12 craftworkers.
Acceptable Work: Considers all original work. Especially needs themes of wildlife or anything dealing with the outdoors. Price range: $1-350; bestsellers: $1-25.
Terms: Works on consignment; 33⅓% commission. Craftworker sets retail price. Reports in 4 weeks. Work may be shipped or hand-delivered.
Profile: "We have both hanging space and shelf space. Art pieces are kept on display in gallery until picked up by artist. Each artist has a 60-day consignment period, and 60 days after consignment termination to pick up pieces." Heaviest wholesale buying time: spring and fall; best selling time: summer and Christmas.

EMMETT KELLY & HISTORICAL MUSEUM GIFT SHOP, 215 S. Montgomery, Sedan KS 67361. (316)725-5179. Curator: D. Modena Lewis. Museum gift shop. Estab. 1970. Represents 1 craftworker at present time.
Acceptable Work: Considers candlemaking, ceramics, dollmaking, glass art, jewelry, leatherworking, metalsmithing, pottery and any new crafts. Especially needs and specializes in circus or animal themes—3-5" in height and in the $1-3 range; must be durable and bright and attractive in appearance. One-of-a-kind and handmade production-line items. Price range: 5¢-$10; bestsellers: 5¢-$5.
Terms: Buys outright. Retail price set by joint agreement. Requires exclusive area representation. Send resume with SASE or call for appointment. Reports in and display time: 2 weeks in summer, 4+ weeks in fall and spring. Work may be shipped or hand delivered.
Profile: "Since we are a free museum, out gift shop profits assist in maintenance and operation. All work is done at the museum in one small section." Items are displayed in glass cases inside entrance to Museum. Heaviest wholesale buying time: late fall-early spring; best selling time: summer.

FREDONIA ARTS COUNCIL, INC., Box 355, Fredonia KS 66736. Contact: Director. Interested in craftworkers exhibiting work in the Council's gallery. Works with sculptors; ceramists; weavers; and other craftworkers. Submit slides of work and resume. February 28 deadline for following September-May season.

KANSAS HERITAGE CENTER, Box 1275, Dodge City KS 67801. (316)227-2823. Director: Jane R. Robison. Museum gift shop. Estab. 1966. Represents 15 craftworkers. "We try to exhibit products produced in Kansas and surrounding areas."
Acceptable Work: Considers all crafts related to Kansas and the Old West. Especially needs wheat weaving, quilting, sun bonnets, sterling silver items and wood carvings. Handmade production-line items only. Price range: $2-5,000; bestsellers: $6-20.
Terms: Buys outright. Retail price set by joint agreement. Send slides. SASE. Reports in 3 weeks. Work may be shipped or hand-delivered. Dealer pays insurance on exhibited work.
Profile: "Our shop is small—featured areas are changed often in the summer." Customers: educators, students and citizens from Kansas; tourists. Heaviest wholesale buying time: spring; best selling time: summer.

THE MUSEUM OF NATURAL HISTORY—MUSEUM SHOP, University of Kansas, Lawrence KS 66045. (913)864-4450. Manager: Pam Sellen. Museum gift shop. Estab. 1968. Represents 3-4 craftworkers. "We especially encourage local craftspeople."
Acceptable Work: Considers ceramics, clothing, glass art, jewelry, metalsmithing, pottery, wall hangings, weavings and woodcrafting. "We are always looking for crafts depicting or related to natural history. The size of the shop restricts us from carrying large items." One-of-a-kind and handmade production-line items. Price range: $2-50; bestsellers: $2-25.
Terms: Buys outright but mostly works on consignment; 30% commission. Retail price set by joint agreement. Send resume. Reports in 2 weeks. Work may be shipped or hand-delivered.
Profile: "Displays are set up in cases, on shelves and on counter tops. We're a relatively small shop with clientele composed of primarily students, staff and faculty of the university, as well as local and out-of-state visitors. The customers are most readily enticed by reasonably-priced items which are different and practical, although decorative pieces do well, also." Heaviest wholesale buying time: late spring-early fall; best selling time: Christmas.

PATCHWORK PARLOR, 905 Main, La Crosse KS 67548. (913)222-3536. Contact: Enola Kirby. Gift shop. Estab. 1975. Represents 75 craftworkers.
Acceptable Work: Considers ceramics, clothing, dollmaking, needlecrafts, quilting, soft sculpture, tole painting, wall hangings, weavings and woodcrafting. Especially needs baby items and dolls. Specializes in bright, neatly finished and small gift-type items. Handmade production-line items only. Price range: $1-250; bestsellers: $1.50-35.
Terms: Works on consignment. "Craftworker sets wholesale price; shop adds 30% commission to make retail price. Send resume and photos. SASE. Reports in 2 weeks. Work may be shipped or hand-delivered. Dealer pays insurance on exhibited work.
Profile: "We are a small shop on the main street of a small rural town. There's a prominent featured display (on/in trunks and antiques) on a rotating basis." Customers: some tourists, mostly regular local residents; low-medium (some high) incomes. Heaviest wholesale buying time: pre-Christmas and May-June; best selling time: pre-Christmas.

PRAIRIE FLOWER CRAFTS, Pioneer St., Alden KS 67512. (316)534-2405. Contact: Sara Fair Sleeper. Craft shop. Estab. 1970. Represents 2 craftworkers. Considers all crafts. Especially needs work with sunflower designs (state flower). Price range: $1-800; bestsellers: $5-100. Works on consignment and buys outright; 30% commission. Craftworker sets retail price. Reports in 4 weeks. Hand-delivered work only.
Profile: "When an item is consigned to our shop, the artist records when, what and price of item and records same when taking it out of the shop." Best selling time: fall and before Christmas.

SECOND HAND ROSE, 507 Washburn, Topeka KS 66606. (913)232-1411. Contact: Carol Hollis. Quilt shop. Estab. 1975. Represents 20 craftworkers.
Acceptable Work: Considers batik, clothing, needlecrafts, quilting, soft sculpture, wall hangings and weavings. Especially needs soft sculpture and quilted or appliqued wall hangings and apparel. Specializes in fine art, but also has contemporary and primitive quilt-related items. One-of-a-kind items only. Price range: $25-300; bestsellers: $25-150.
Terms: Buys outright and works on consignment; 40% commission. Retail price set by joint agreement. Send resume, slides and information sheet listing size, colors, etc. Reports in 2 weeks. Work may be shipped or hand delivered. Display time: month.
Profile: "The shop is a quilt shop with antiques and supplies. I design clothing and art pieces that are related to quilting and applique. The shop has periodical monthly showings of artists in the field of quiltmaking. A wall hanging is always hung on the wall, and should have some means to hang. Quilts are either hung or displayed on quilt racks." Customers: mostly around

35 years-old with middle to high-middle incomes. Heaviest wholesale buying time: late summer-early fall; best selling time: fall-winter.

SENIOR CITIZENS HANDCRAFT SHOPPE, 73 S. 7th St., Kansas City, KS 66101. (913)321-4499. Manager: Glenn A. Snyder. Craft/gift shop. Estab. 1971. Represents 200 craftworkers, 55+ years old.
Acceptable Work: Considers: batik, candlemaking, ceramics, clothing, decoupage, dollmaking, glass art, jewelry, leatherworking, metalsmithing, needlecrafts, quilting, wall hangings, weavings and wood. Specializes in contemporary handmade production-line items. Price range: 25¢-$125; bestsellers: $1-75.
Terms: Works on consignment; 25% commission, or 15% if works 1 day/month. "Articles left at their own risk." Craftworker sets retail price. Call in person. Work may be shipped or hand delivered.
Profile: "We are mainly set up to help senior citizens needing something to do or additonal income. Most of our help is volunteer and not super salespeople." Customers: lower to middle incomes. "We also have sales or bazaars at a shopping center, and go to several towns that have festivals and fairs." Best selling time: Christmas.

SIGN OF THE ACORN, 4816 E. Douglas, Wichita KS 67208. Contact: Mary Leedom or Mary Ann Ranney. Shop/gallery. Considers ceramics; sculpture; glass; weavings; and wall hangings. Price range: $5-1,200. 40% commission. Craftworker sets retail price. Requires exclusive area representation. Gallery pays shipping on returned work to craftworker and insurance for exhibited work. Items displayed 4 weeks minimum.

STUDIO ARTS, 1218 W. 6th, Topeka KS 66606. (913)234-2242. Contact: Bern Ketchum. Gallery/supply shop/picture framing/pottery studio. Estab. 1977. Represents 1-2 craftworkers.
Acceptable Work: Considers glass art, jewelry, pottery and woodcrafting. Specializes in fine art designer arts/crafts. Price range: $10-600; bestsellers: $10-300.
Terms: Works on consignment; 30% commission. Craftworker sets retail price. Send slides. SASE. Reports in 2 weeks.
Profile: "Our display space is somewhat limited. Most of our exhibits are 1 or 2-man shows for a period of 4-6 weeks." Customers: $20,000+ incomes. Heaviest wholesale buying and best selling time: pre-Christmas.

THE TALENT TREE, 213 Delaware, Suite B-4, Leavenworth KS 66048. (913)651-7833. Contact: Joy Loftus. Craft shop. Estab. 1977. Represents 260 craftworkers.
Acceptable Work: Considers all crafts. Price range: 35¢-$500; bestsellers: $10-200.
Terms: Works on consignment. Craftworker sets retail price. Call for an appointment. Work must be hand-delivered.
Profile: Work is displayed on wall space, shelves and from ceiling hangers. Displays work 60 days. Best selling time: fall and winter.

TOPEKA PUBLIC LIBRARY GALLERY OF FINE ARTS, 1515 W. 10th, Topeka KS 66604. (913)233-2040. Director: Larry D. Peters. Gallery. Estab. 1975. Represents about 40 craftworkers in annual judged exhibition. Cash awards given for exhibition winners. Gallery is not specifically for sales.
Acceptable Work: Considers batik; ceramics; glass art; jewelry; metalsmithing; pottery; quilting; soft sculpture; wall hangings; weavings; and woodcrafting. Fine one-of-a-kind pieces. Price range: $20-1000; bestsellers: $20-60.
Terms: Items sold only after exhibition. Craftworker sets retail price. Rental gallery fee: 20%. Work may be shipped or hand-delivered. Gallery pays insurance for exhibited work. Exhibits work 1 month.
Profile: "We exhibit with some emphasis on each individual piece. All small items are under glass for protection. Customers are middle class and mostly middle aged." Shows are in April.

WHITE BUFFALO GALLERY, 1010 N. Main, Suite 1, Wichita KS 67203. (316)263-3136. Contact: Joan M. Cawley. Gallery. Estab. 1974. Represents 15-20 craftworkers.
Acceptable Work: Considers batik, ceramics, pottery, wall hangings, weavings, baskets and woodcrafting. Especially needs unusual, pleasantly-priced ceramic pieces. Style can be primitive in nature, but prefers contemporary, signed pieces (unless it is woven basket in which signing is impossible). "The gallery is primarily devoted to easel art by native Americans. If the artist is non-Indian, the work is mostly of a southwestern flavor (earthy, natural colors,

contemporary in nature, one-of-a-kind), or an original graphic (stone lithograph, etching, wood block). Baskets and pottery and unusual decorative items are offered." One-of-a-kind and handmade production-line pieces. Price range: $5-3,000; bestsellers: $5-500.
Terms: Buys outright and works on consignment. "Works by new artists are generally consigned. The gallery takes 40% commission; if purchased, the artist receives 50% of retail price. Craftworker sets retail price. Requires exclusive area representation. Send slides. Reports in 2 weeks. Work may be shipped or hand delivered.
Profile: "The shop is on three levels with an open staircase and many charming 'nooks' so that the items on display may be hung as if in a home. Also, the fixtures, if placed in a case, are all antiques so that art items are placed in a natural atmosphere. This is not the usual retail display seen in retail shops. The age—strongest buying power—is 30-45. Because of the signed posters, we do cater to many young collectors, too, and the income area represents all ranges. Most of the clients are art collectors." Heaviest wholesale buying time: early fall; best selling time: October-December.
To Break In: "We appreciate promptness in delivery when items are requested from the craftsperson; also, prices that are established that are realistic and that remain fairly stable. We like to have a price range—not all one price or all high prices. We do not wish to work with an artist whose pricing is inconsistent or who will sell at a lower price than established for the gallery. If the artist undercuts the gallery, we will no longer handle that artist's work."

Kentucky

APOLLOS ART, Main, Box 74, Gamaliel KY 42140. (502)457-2642. Contact: Mrs. Clyde England. Studio. Estab. 1975. Represents 5 craftworkers.
Acceptable Work: Considers clothing; needlecrafts; quilting; wall hangings; and weavings. Fine, one-of-a-kind and handmade production-line items.
Terms: Price range: $1-150; bestsellers: $1-8. Works on consignment; 25% commission. Retail price set by joint agreement. Reports in 2 weeks. Work may be shipped or hand-delivered. Dealer pays insurance for exhibited work.
Profile: "I change displays frequently. My shop is in my home, but I display in local business places, state parks, etc. Customers range from age 20-70; high school and college students; some retired and on fixed incomes." Heaviest wholesale buying time: Christmas and fall; best selling time: Christmas and spring.

APPALACHIAN ARTS & CRAFTS, 102 Center St., Berea KY 40403. (606)986-1239. Contact: Don or Nancy Graham. Craft/gift shop. Estab. 1971. Represents 200 craftworkers.
Acceptable Work: Considers candlemaking, ceramics, clothing, decoupage, dollmaking, glass art, jewelry, leatherworking, metalsmithing, needlecrafts, pottery, quilting, woodcrafting and natural materials. Especially needs throw rugs, placemats and patchwork items. "Products are mostly Appalachian, but we take things from outside the area if it fits with our basic theme of Appalachian crafts. Keep prices realistic." Price range: 15¢-$575; bestsellers: 15¢-$25.
Terms: Buys outright. Only takes quilts on consignment; 40% commission. Shop sets retail price; consignment retail set by joint agreement. Requires exclusive area representation. Call for appointment with SASE. Reports in 4 weeks, longer in summer. Work may be shipped or hand delivered. Dealer pays insurance on exhibited work.
Profile: "We started out as exclusively Appalachian crafts (which we still have mostly) yet we have branched into general gifts that fit our theme. Quilts are hung in full view on the walls." Customers: tourists. Heaviest wholesale buying time: spring and summer; best selling time: summer and fall.

BAKERY SQUARE GALLERY, 1324 E. Washington St., Louisville KY 40206. (502)587-7024. Contact: Lucy Marret or Kathy Scherer. Gallery. Estab. 1974. Represents 6-10 craftworkers.
Acceptable Work: Considers dollmaking, soft sculpture, wall hangings, metalsmithing, needlecraft, paper mache, appliques and woodcrafting. Specializes in contemporary work. One-of-a-kind and handmade production-line items. Price range: $12-500; bestsellers: $50-250.
Terms: Prefers to buy outright but also works on consignment; 40% commission. Retail price set by joint agreement. Sometimes requires exclusive area representation. Send slides. Reports in 2 weeks. Work may be shipped or hand delivered.
Profile: "We carry whimsical and sophisticated contemporary work and have an everchanging and unusual exhibit of fine quality prints, accessories, soft sculpture and sculpture. We're known by artists as the place in Louisville to find unusual items." Displays set by joint agreement. "The gallery is in a restored building and is the largest tour attraction in Louisville." Heaviest wholesale buying time: spring and fall; best selling time: Christmas.

BENCHMARK GALLERY, Box 422, Berea KY 40403. (606)986-9413. Manager: Daphne Osolnik. Craft and gift shop. Estab. 1972. Represents 100 American craftworkers.
Acceptable Work: Considers candlemaking; batik; ceramics; dollmaking; baskets; glass art; jewelry; leatherworking; metalsmithing; needlecrafts; pottery; enamels; quilting; wall hangings; weavings; woodcrafting; and prints. Price range: $1-1,500; bestsellers: from under $15 to as high as $50.
Terms: Buys outright and occasionally works on consignment; 33⅓% commission. Requests exclusive area representation "when possible; it is a small place." Reports in 4 weeks on consigned items. Dealer pays return shipping and insurance (break-in and fire) for exhibited work.
Profile: "An individual show can be arranged for a week or 2. Craftworker should plan to stay, demonstrate and sell. 20% commission."

CENTURY GALLERY, INC., 2001 Triplett, Owensboro KY 42301. (502)685-5374. Secretary-Treasurer: Linda C. Overby. Gallery/gift shop. Estab. 1972. Represents 8-15 craftworkers.
Acceptable Work: Considers ceramics, glass art, jewelry, metalsmithing, pottery, quilting, soft sculpture, wall hangings, weavings and woodcrafting. One-of-a-kind and handmade production-line items. Price range: $15-400; bestsellers: $20-100.
Terms: Buys outright and works on consignment. "Normally, we ask the craftworker to state what he/she wants to receive and we mark that price up 20-40%". Requires exclusive area representation. Send resume or call for appointment. Reports in 1 week. Work may be shipped or hand-delivered. Dealer pays insurance on exhibited work.
Profile: "We have a fairly large gallery which does a good business in custom framing." Has special 1-2 month advertised exhibits. "Work is displayed as it could be in the home; also in window displays." Customers: young marrieds to older well-established couples; young unmarried business people; professionals; $15,000+ incomes. Heaviest wholesale buying time: fall and spring; best selling time: Christmas.

COFFEETREES AT STEWART'S, 501 River City Mall, Louisville KY 40202. (502)584-3261, ext. 289. Contact: Rod Beck. Gallery/gift shop. Estab. 1974. Represents 200 Kentucky craftworkers.
Acceptable Work: Considers batik, candlemaking, jewelry, leatherworking, hand-forged iron, pewter work, pottery, quilting, scrimshaw, soft sculpture, wall hangings, weavings and woodcrafting. One-of-a-kind and handmade production-line items. Price range: 50¢-$3,500; bestsellers: $4.50-50.
Terms: Buys outright and works on consignment; 40% commission. Retail price set by joint agreement. Requires exclusive area representation. Send resume. Reports on inquires in 1 week. Work may be shipped or hand delivered.
Profile: "Our shop is located in a major department store in downtown Louisville. All displays are changed monthly."

COLLECTOR'S GALLERY, Civic Center Mall, Suite 301, Lexington KY 40507. (606)233-1121. Contact: C.N. Starr. Gallery and gift shop. Estab. 1972. Represents 12 craftworkers.
Acceptable Work: Considers batik, ceramics, decoupage, glass art, jewelry, leatherworking, metalsmithing, pottery, scrimshaw, soft sculpture, tole painting, wall hangings, weavings, woodcrafting and sculpture. Especially needs crafts related to horses. One-of-a-kind and handmade production-line items OK. Price range: $5-150; bestsellers $25-75.
Terms: Buys outright and works on consignment; commission negotiable. Retail price set by joint agreement. Send slides or call for appointment. Reports in 1 week. Work may be shipped or hand-delivered. Dealer pays insurance for exhibited work.

THE CROSSROADS MUSEUM OF ART, 121 E. Reynolds Rd., Lexington KY 40503. (606)273-2215. Contact: Ann Tower. Gallery. Estab. 1978. Represents 40 craftworkers.
Acceptable Work: Considers ceramics, glass art, metalsmithing, pottery, scrimshaw, soft sculpture, woodcrafting, painting and photography. Exhibits primitive and fine art designer crafts. One-of-a-kind pieces OK. Price range: $15-1,000; bestsellers: $15-50.
Terms: Buys outright and works on consignment; 20-40% commission. Craftworker sets retail price. All methods of contact OK. Work may be shipped or hand-delivered. Dealer pays insurance on exhibited work.

CLARA M. EAGLE GALLERY, Price Doyle Fine Arts Center, Murray State University, Murray KY 42071. (507)762-3784. Director: Richard Jackson. Exhibit Gallery. Estab. 1970.

Acceptable Work: Considers all crafts. One-of-a-kind and handmade production-line items.
Terms: Exhibits only; no commission. Craftworker sets retail price. Send slides. Reporting time varies. Exhibits are selected 1 year in advance. Work may be shipped or hand-delivered. Gallery pays insurance on exhibited work.
Profile: "Items are displayed as an exhibition for usually a 1 month period. There are several galleries (1 large, 100'x40'; 3 smaller spaces)."

EDGEMONT YARN SERVICE, INC., Rt. 5, Box 132, Maysville KY 41056. (606)564-3193. President: Jean Adair. Craft and supply shop. Estab. 1960. Represents 2 craftworkers. Considers jewelry; metalsmithing; and needlecrafts. Price range: 10c-$500. Works on consignment; 5% commission plus material cost. Reports the day after inquiry. "We are located in an historic town established in 1783. Our shop is in a house built in 1824." Best selling time: Christmas.

EMERGENCY WORKSHOP, Box 8, Barbourville KY 40906. (606)546-4622. Director: Rebecca Spears. Gallery/wholesaler. Estab. 1966. Represents 50 craftworkers with basic emergency needs. Shop gives cash advances to people needing emergency funds who then produce crafts and receive retail credit to repay debt. Price range: $1-150; bestsellers: $2-60. Buys outright. Reporting time varies. Work may be shipped or hand-delivered. Dealer pays return shipping and insurance for exhibited work.
Acceptable Work: Considers dollmaking; quilting; woodcrafting; pieced table clothes; dresses; skirts; and corn shuck placemats. Primitive and fine handmade production-line items.
Profile: "When a craft is brought in or made in the shop, it becomes the property of Emergency Fund. We attempt to sell it at the fair retail price and proceeds revert to the fund. Customers are families whose income is less than $300/month." Heaviest wholesale buying time: fall-winter; best selling time: spring-summer.

The woodworking of Co-owner Warren May is the main feature of The Upstairs Gallery in Berea, Kentucky. But, Warren said other craftmen's work makes the gallery special. "We feel great loyalty to their work and strive to represent them well." The gallery and gift shop has its busiest selling times in fall and spring.

THE GALLERY, 487 High St., Hazard KY 41701. (606)436-5102. Contact: Audrey C. Rogers. Craft and gift shop. Estab. 1976. Represents 30-40 Appalachian craftworkers. Price range: $2-400; bestsellers: $10-200. Works on consignment and buys outright; 40% commission. Retail price set by joint agreement. Reports in 4 weeks. Work may be hand-delivered or shipped. Dealer pays insurance for exhibited work. Best selling and heaviest wholesale buying time: summer and fall.
Acceptable Work: Considers candlemaking; ceramics; clothing; dollmaking; jewelry; leatherworking; pottery; quilting; wall hangings; weavings; and woodcrafting.

GALLERY OF MINIATURES, INC., 317 Seay St., Glasgow KY 42141. (502)651-2856. President: Mary M. Pace. Museum gallery/gift shop. Estab. 1977. Represents 40-50 craftworkers.
Acceptable Work: Considers ceramics, clothing, decoupage, dollmaking, glass art, leatherworking, metalsmithing, needlecrafts, pottery, scrimshaw, soft sculpture, tole painting, wall hangings, weavings and woodcrafting. "These items must be on a miniature scale of 1" to 1'. At the time, I do not stock dollhouses, but I am interested in doing so. I can use any items of furniture, accessories, room setting, dioramas, vignettes, etc. on the correct scale." One-of-a-kind and handmade production-line items. Price range: $1-700; bestsellers: $3-5 and $25-30.
Terms: Buys outright and works on consignment; 30% commission. Retail price set by joint agreement for consigned items; gallery sets retail price for items bought outright. Send resume or call for appointment as introduction (include SASE); if interested a slide or photo is requested (dealer pays return postage). Reports in 1 week. Work may be shipped or hand-delivered. Dealer pays insurance on exhibited work.
Profile: "Most of the items are displayed in lighted display cases or lighted miniature room settings. Our museum has 32 room settings done by well-known miniaturists in the US. I know of no other exhibit displayed like the Thorne rooms that are in the Art Institute in Chicago. We have a large collection of colonial tools and implements done on the same scale. Besides furniture, we have accessories in brass, glass, pewter and china for any style or period." Customers: "all ages, from children with dollhouses to the elderly collector. The majority of our customers are past 30 with average to above average incomes." Heaviest wholesale buying time: winter and spring; best selling time: summer and fall.

GUILD GALLERY, 811 Euclid Ave, Lexington KY 40502. (606)266-2215. Estab. 1970. Represents 200 Kentucky craftworkers.
Acceptable Work: Considers all crafts except clothing, scrimshaw and tole painting. Specializes in Appalachian folk crafts. One-of-a-kind and handmade production-line items.
Terms: Must be a member of the Kentucky Guild of Artists and Craftsmen, Inc. (juried membership by Standards Committee).
Profile: "Proceeds from the Guild Gallery are used in year 'round educational projects, ranging from exhibitions to workshops."

HEADLEY-WHITNEY MUSEUM, 4435 Old Frankfort Pike, Lexington KY 40511. (606)252-1073. Director of Sales: Becky Riffe. Museum gift shop. Estab. 1968. Represents 5-10 craftworkers.
Acceptable Work: Considers batik, ceramics, clothing, dollmaking, glass art, jewelry, needlecrafts, pottery, scrimshaw and woodcrafting. Especially needs items related to dollhouse exhibits, seashells and jewelry. "We have periodic needs for crafts related to current exhibitions." Specializes in fine art and some contemporary pieces. One-of-a-kind items only. Price range: $1-25,000; bestsellers: $1-40.
Terms: Buys outright and works on consignment; 30% commission. Retail price set by joint agreement. Send resume and slides or call for appointment. Reports in 4 weeks. Work may be shipped or hand delivered.
Profile: "The museum shop occupies 1 of several rooms. We have 2 lighted upright display cases (approximately 4'x5' shelves) and limited wall space may be available. Also some space for furnished cases." Customers: 6th grade student-senior citizens; mostly middle incomes. Heaviest wholesale buying time: spring; best selling time: summer and fall.

KENTUCKY GUILD OF ARTISTS & CRAFTSMEN, INC., Box 291, 213 Chestnut St., Berea KY 40403. (606)986-3192. Director: Garry Barker. Craft shop. Estab. 1961. Represents 200 member Kentucky craftworkers. Best wholesale buying and best selling time: December.
Acceptable Work: Considers batik, candlemaking, ceramics, dollmaking, glass art, jewelry, leatherworking, metalsmithing, needlecrafts, pottery, quilting, scrimshaw, soft sculpture, wall hangings, weavings and woodcrafting. One-of-a-kind and handmade production-line items. Price range: $1-3,000; bestsellers: $10-100.

Terms: Buys outright and works on consignment; 40% commission. Retail price set by joint agreement. Call for appointment. Committee meets in March and August for membership jurying. Work may be shipped or hand-delivered. Dealer pays insurance on exhibited work.

KENTUCKY HILLS INDUSTRIES, INC., Box 186, Pine Knot KY 42635. (606)354-2813. Manager: Smith G. Ross. Craft shop. Estab. 1946. Represents 58 craftworkers. Apply for membership in Kentucky Hills Industries. Buys outright. Retail price set by joint agreement. Reports in 1 week. Hand-delivered work only.
Acceptable Work: Considers dollmaking; needlecrafts; pottery; woodcrafting; cornshuck; basketmaking; and handweaving. Especially needs "any craft that has a tie with the past, graceful in design and indigenous to the area." Primitive handmade production-line items. Price range: $1-1,200; bestsellers: $1-25.
Profile: "For the most part we handle only items that have utility and those that harken back to the early days. We sell mostly to young homemakers." Heaviest wholesale buying time: summer; best selling time: summer and fall.

LOG HOUSE SALES ROOM, .778, Berea College, Berea KY 40404. (606)986-9341. Manager: Haley Robinson. Gift shop. Represents 100 craftworkers. Buys outright. Gallery sets retail price. Work may be shipped or hand-delivered. "We handle mostly Appalachian handmade crafts and Berea College student craft items." Best selling and heaviest wholesale buying time: fall and spring.
Acceptable Work: Considers candlemaking; ceramics; jewelry; leatherworking; metalsmithing; needlecrafts; pottery; quilting; wall hangings; weavings; and woodcrafting. Handmade production-line items; utilitarian only. Price range of bestsellers: under $10.

LOUISVILLE SCHOOL OF ART GALLERY, 100 Park Rd., Anchorage KY 40223. (502)245-8836. Associate Director: Diana Arcadipone. Gallery/supply shop. Estab. 1912. Represents 1+ craftworkers/month.
Acceptable Work: Considers batik, ceramics, glass art, jewelry, metalsmithing, pottery, quilting, soft sculpture, wall hangings, weavings and woodcrafting. Specializes in contemporary fine crafts. Price range: $20-2,000; bestsellers: $20-1,000.
Terms: Exhibits only; no commission. Craftworker sets retail price. Send resume and slides with SASE. Reports in 1 week. Work may be shipped or hand delivered. School pays insurance for exhibited work. Gallery provides news releases and mailed invitations. Display time: 1 month.
Profile: "We are a gallery (within a school) which offers local as well as nationally known artists, and also has traveling shows of contemporary fine arts and crafts. Pieces are displayed however the piece warrants protection." Best selling time: Christmas.

MAIN STREET USA ANTIQUES, (formerly The Gazehound Crafts), 263 E. Main St., Lexington KY 40507. (606)255-0931. Contact: Ken Morris. Antique/craft shop. Estab. 1977. Represents 3 craftworkers.
Acceptable Work: Considers all crafts except clothing. Especially needs scrimshaw. One-of-a-kind and handmade production-line items. Price range: $2-5; bestsellers: $4-20.
Terms: Buys outright and works on consignment; 20% commission. Craftworker sets retail price. Write letter for information. Reports in 1 week. Work may be shipped or hand-delivered. Dealer pays insurance on exhibited work. Display time: 90 days.
Profile: Shop located in downtown area. Customers: ages 20-70. Heaviest wholesale buying and best selling time: summer.

METRO ARTS CENTER, 8360 Dixie Hwy, Louisville KY 40215. (502)937-2055. Director: Melvin D. Rowe. Gallery/community art center. Estab. 1969. Represents 1-2 craftworkers.
Acceptable Work: Considers batik, glass art, jewelry, metalsmithing, pottery, quilting, soft sculpture, wall hangings, weavings and woodcrafting. One-of-a-kind and handmade production-line items. Bestsellers: $5-20.
Terms: Exhibition only; no commission. Craftworker sets retail price. Send slides. Reports in 2 weeks. Exhibitions are selected 1 year in advance. "Upon selection of an exhibitor, he/she will be sent a data sheet listing all necessary information." Gallery hosts opening reception and handles all publicity. Work may be shipped or hand delivered. Display time: 1 month.
Profile: "The Metro Arts Center is a non-profit educational facility. Walls are white-painted peg board (75 linear feet), floor space (350 square feet), black pedestals of assorted sizes and glass cases.

ONE STEP UP GIFTS, 323 Romany Rd., Lexington KY 40502. (606)269-1345. Contact: Shirley Jeter. Gift shop. Estab. 1973. Represents 150-200 craftworkers. Buys outright. Reports in 2 weeks. Work may be shipped or hand-delivered. Dealer pays insurance for exhibited work.
Acceptable Work: Considers all crafts. Fine one-of-a-kind and handmade production-line items. Price range: 50c-$660; bestsellers: $1.50-15.
Profile: "We specialize in unusual well-made and functional handcrafted gifts. We look for items not available in other shops. We accent reasonable prices and quality workmanship as well as uniqueness and practicality. Customers are 20-50; middle to upper income." Heaviest wholesale buying time: fall; best selling time: fall and winter.

OWENSBORO AREA MUSEUM, 2829 S. Griffith Ave., Owensboro KY 42301. (502)683-0296. Director: Joe Ford. Museum gift shop. Estab. 1966. Price range: 10c-$25; bestsellers: 25c-$20. Buys outright. Gallery sets retail price. Reports in 1 week. Best selling time: before Christmas.
Acceptable Work: Considers candlemaking; ceramics; jewelry; needlecrafts; pottery; quilting; wall hangings; weavings; and woodcrafting. Primitive handmade production-line items.

OWENSBORO MUSEUM OF FINE ART, 901 Frederica St., Owensboro KY 42301. (502)685-4978. Director: Mary Bryan Hood. Museum gift shop/gallery. Estab. 1977. Represents Midwestern or Southern craftworkers. Considers all crafts.
Terms: Works on consignment; 30% commission. Craftworker sets retail price. "Submit slides or photographs and a resume listing education, exhibition record and awards."
Profile: "We are only the second fine art museum to be formed in the state of Kentucky. We promote regional artists in 2 ways. First, we offer an opportunity for exhibitions in our galleries; and secondly, we offer an opportunity for sales through our Gift Shoppe."

PARAMOUNT ARTS CENTER, Box 1546, Ashland KY 41101. (606)324-3175. Director: Linda L. Ball. Craft shop/gallery/rental theater. Estab. 1973.
Acceptable Work: Considers candlemaking, ceramics, dollmaking, glass art, jewelry, leatherworking, metalsmithing, pottery, quilting, wall hangings, weavings and woodcrafting. Specializes in Appalachian work. Handmade production-line items.
Terms: Buys outright. Craftworker sets retail price. Send resume. Reports in 2 weeks. Work must be hand-delivered.
Profile: Also sponsors Arts and Crafts Festival annually during the fourth of July weekend. Usually 75 craftworkers attend.

SCHWAB'S PIPES 'N STUFF, 2335 Lexington Mall, Richmond Rd., Lexington KY 40502. (606)266-1011. Contact: Paul and Pat Schwab. Gift/tobacco shop. Estab. 1977. Represents 2 craftworkers; "We could use more."
Acceptable Work: Considers handmade pipes and male oriented gifts. Especially needs pipes, chess sets and backgammon sets. One-of-a-kind and handmade production-line items. Price range: $8-200; bestsellers: $5-35.
Terms: Works on consignment; 33⅓% commission. Retail price set by joint agreement. Requires exclusive area representation. Write or call for appointment. Reports in 1 week. Work may be shipped or hand-delivered. Dealer pays insurance on exhibited work. Display time: 60 days.
Profile: Shop is located in a busy shopping center mall. Heaviest wholesale buying time: fall; best selling time: Christmas.

J.B. SPEED ART MUSEUM SHOP, 2035 S. 3rd St., Louisville KY 40208. (502)636-3894. Shop Manager: Danielle Faversham. Museum gift shop. Estab. 1972. Represents 2-3 craftworkers. "We prefer to handle the work of local (state-wide or nearby states) craftsmen."
Acceptable Work: Considers ceramics, jewelry, pottery and soft sculpture. One-of-a-kind and handmade production-line items. Price range: $4-300; bestsellers: $4-15.
Terms: Buys outright and works on consignment; 30% commission. Retail price set by joint agreement. Prefers exclusive area representation. Call for appointment. "We usually see craftworkers and salesmen on Mondays. The buying is done largely by the shop manager and 1 or more committee members (a volunteer group of 4 women who carry on much of the behind-the-scenes work of the shop)." Reports in 3 weeks. Work may be shipped or hand-delivered.
Profile: "We have a rapidly growing (about to expand) shop in the entrance foyer of the museum. There are 3 lighted glass display cases, plus many open shelves and 2 jewelry cases (1 for gold, 1 for silver). Displays are changed radically 3 times/year; minimal changes occur almost weekly." Customers: patrons of museum and students (University of Louisville).

Heaviest wholesale buying time: late spring and fall; best selling time: pre-Christmas.

THE UNFINISHED UNIVERSE, 505 E. High St., Lexington KY 40508. (606)252-3289. Partners: Joel Evans, Patrick White and Ricka White. Craft shop/gallery/antique shop. Estab. 1973. Represents 5 craftworkers.
Acceptable Work: Considers batik; candlemaking; ceramics; clothing; pottery; quilting; wall hangings; weavings; and woodcrafting. "We specialize in custom woodworking designs. Anything from a traditional table to an indoor cat playground." Price range: $1-3,000; bestsellers: $5-60. Works on consignment and buys outright; 20% commission. Retail price set by joint agreement. Reports in 1-2 weeks. Work may be shipped or hand-delivered. Displays work a maximum of 2-3 months.
Profile: Customers are all ages and types from "college students to architects to jewel collectors, middle class families, etc."

THE UPSTAIRS GALLERY, 114 Main St., Berea KY 40403. (606)986-9293. Contact: Frankye or Warren A. May. Gallery/gift shop. Estab. 1973. Represents 28-30 craftworkers.
Acceptable Work: Considers batik; ceramics; handmade toys; pottery; weavings; woodcrafting; and handmade furniture. Finished, one-of-a-kind and handmade production-line items. Price range: $5-2,000; bestsellers: $10-200.
Terms: Works on wholesale and/or consignment; 20% commission. Craftworker sets retail price. Requires exclusive area representation. Reports in 4 weeks. Work may be hand-delivered. Dealer pays return shipping and insurance for exhibited work.
Profile: "Since our gallery features the woodworking of owner Warren May, we are set up so that we don't have to make a living off another person's work. We feel that our other craftsmen's work makes us special and we feel great loyalty to their work and strive to represent them well." Best selling time: fall and spring.

UPSTAIRS POTTERY & CRAFTS, Bakery Square, 1324 E. Washington St., Louisville KY 40206. (502)584-2406. Contact: Joann Ryan. Craft shop. Estab. 1977. Represents 40 craftworkers.
Acceptable Work: Considers batik, ceramics, metalsmithing, pottery, soft sculpture, and especially needs jewelry, woodcrafting, wall hangings, weavings and glass art. "In the last few months, I have tried stained glass and handcrafted furniture and the pieces have sold within a few days. This market could be very lucrative if I can find the craftsmen." One-of-a-kind and handmade production-line items. Price range: $2-150; bestsellers: $3-70.
Terms: Works on consignment ; 40% commission. Buys jewelry outright. Craftworker sets retail price. Requires exclusive area representation. Write with catalogue/photos/samples/or description of work. Work may be shipped or hand delivered. Dealer pays insurance on exhibited work.
Profile: "We are located in Bakery Square which is an old renovatd bakery with 3 floors and 32 specialty shops in Old Butchertown of Louisville. The shop is on the second floor with about 800 ft. of floor space. Items are on display for 6 months. I use shelves and cubes for displaying pottery, plexiglass cases for jewelry. Lighting is with flood lights. Also, we use a few antiques to display pottery." Customers: 18-50, upper middle and high incomes. Heaviest wholesale buying time: spring and fall; best selling time: summer and Christmas.
Profile: "I want very high quality and no students unless they are ready to graduate. Must be located near Louisville for pottery. Jewelry can be from all over. I want potters who are willing to supply me with unusual pieces."

VALUR BOUTIQUE LTD., Garden Springs Shopping Center, 820 Lane Allen Rd., Lexington KY 40504. (606)277-0614. Manager: Evelyn Welch. Consignment shop. Estab. 1978. Represents 200 craftworkers.
Acceptable Work: Considers all crafts except metalsmithing and scrimshaw. Price range: $1-325; bestsellers: $3-50.
Terms: Works on consignment; 25% commission. Pays at the end of each month. Retail price set by joint agreement. Write or call for appointment. Work may be shipped or hand-delivered. Dealer pays insurance on exhibited work. Display time: 1 month minimum; after 3 months, considers price change.
Profile: Shop is located in "a new shopping center backing up the oldest mall in the city." Customers: medium to high incomes. Heaviest wholesale buying and best selling time: holidays.

YEN NAN GALLERY, 3220 Nicholasville Rd., Lexington KY 40503. (606) 272-7660. Contact:

Ms. Yen Hsu and Ms. Nan Sturm. Craft/gift shop and gallery. Estab. 1977. Represents 45 craftworkers.
Acceptable Work: Considers batik, candlemaking, dollmaking, glass art, jewelry, leatherworking, metalsmithing, pottery, quilting, scrimshaw, soft sculpture, wall hangings, weavings, woodcrafting, paintings, prints and dry flowers. One-of-a-kind and handmade production-line items OK. Price range: $1-550; bestsellers: $12-80.
Terms: Buys outright and works on consignment; 40% commission. Retail price set by joint agreement. Requires exclusive area representation. Send slides or call for appointment. Reports in 4 weeks. Work may be shipped or hand-delivered. Dealer pays insurance on exhibited work.

Louisiana

ALROD ENTERPRISES, 728 Toulouse, New Orleans LA 70130. (504)522-6106. Contact: Al Willis or Rod Reeves. Craft and gift shop. Estab. 1972. Represents 150 craftworkers.
Acceptable Work: Considers clothing; dollmaking; jewelry; needlecrafts; pottery; quilting; tole painting; wall hangings; weavings; and woodcrafting. Especially needs items for boys and for babies. Price range: $1-300; bestsellers: $1.99-200.
Terms: Works on consignment and buys outright; 50% commission. Shop sets retail price. Requires exclusive area representation. Reports in 1 week. Work may be shipped or hand-delivered. Dealer pays return shipping and insurance for exhibited work.
Profile: "All merchandise is prominently displayed a long as it is in the shop. Customers are middle to upper income."

CEZAR, 301 Royal St., New Orleans LA 70130. (504)581-2100. Contact: Charles DeBlieux. Gift shop/gallery. Estab. 1962. Represents 40-50 craftworkers.
Acceptable Work: Considers batik, ceramics, glass art, jewelry, metalsmithing, pottery, wall hangings, weavings and woodcrafting. Specializes in contemporary crafts. One-of-a-kind and handmade production-line items with a few utility items (tablewares). Price range: $2-1,250; bestsellers: $5-150.
Terms: Buys outright and sometimes works on consignment; 33⅓% commission. Retail price set by shop or joint agreement. Requires exclusive area representation. Send slides and be prepared to send samples on request. Reports in 1 week. Work may be shipped or hand delivered. Dealer pays insurance on exhibited work.
Profile: "Cezar is our principal shop/gallery located on the prime corner of Royal St. Large windows make entire shop a showcase; wall covering grass cloth—perfect background for wall pieces; custom-made display cabinets and pedestals; one entire wall niched for individual piece presentation. Favored art pieces displayed until sold and receive special spots and flood lighting. There are more expensive and exclusive articles at this "Vieux Carre" location—an oasis amidst antique shops. I travel to Europe each year to shop for stock. The majority of artists/craftsmen in the US producing the quality of work I enjoy have their own retail establishments and are not interested in mine. My selections are restricted to those things I like—owner is not disagreeable, only proud." Customers: early to late middle age, home decorators, median to high incomes, and "those who afford winter holidays and exhibit that rare combination of taste and money." Heaviest wholesale buying time: September-March; best selling time: October-March, except January.

CHITIMACHA CRAFT, Rt. 2, Box 224, Jeanerette LA 70544. (318)923-7547. Contact: Faye Stouff. Craft shop. Estab. 1970. Represents 2 craftworkers.
Acceptable Work: Considers pine needle and cane reed baskets and some beadwork. Handmade production-line items; decorative only. "We have only handmade articles by members of the tribe; customers are all ages."
Terms: Price range: $2-25. Works on consignment; no commission. Retail price set by joint agreement. Reports in 1 week. Work may be shipped or hand-delivered.

THE CRAFT ALLIANCE, 1075 Dalzell, Shreveport LA 71104. (318)222-1780. Director: Roger Runge. Gallery/school/studio/art center. Estab. 1972. Represents about 10-12 Shreveport craftworkers—members of the Craft Alliance at one time.
Acceptable Work: Considers batik, jewelry, pottery, soft sculpture, wall hangings and weavings. Contemporary one-of-a-kind and handmade production-line items. Price range: $2.50-600; bestsellers: $2.50-20.
Terms: Works on consignment; 25-30% commission. Craftworker sets retail price. Call for appointment. Reports in 2 weeks. Work must be hand-delivered.
Profile: "Gallery space: usually has one-man show for 3-4 weeks with nothing else in the

gallery; direct mail invitations, artist's reception; 30% commission. Sales area: typical display on shelves, counters, etc.; all work is mixed in together; 90 day display. Since we are a nonprofit organization, the gallery shows are concerned more with exhibition of contemporary crafts, exposure, and education rather than sales." Heaviest wholesale buying and best selling time: Christmas.

HIGHLAND HOUSE, 8501 Highland Rd., Baton Rouge LA 70808. (504)769-0582. Contact: Genny Nadler. Craft shop. Estab. 1977. Represents 40 craftworkers.
Acceptable Work: Considers all crafts, except decoupage and tole painting. Specializes in fine and contemporary crafts. One-of-a-kind and handmade production-line items. Price range: 95¢-$350; bestsellers: $5-50.
Terms: Buys outright and works on consignment; 33⅓% commission. Retail price set by joint agreement. Send slides. Reports in 2 weeks Work may be shipped or hand delivered. Dealer pays insurance on exhibited work. Uses photo advertising.
Profile: "Our store is a rustic wood building, set in the outskirts of a wealthy residential area. We display on railroad ties, rough cut lumber pedestals, shelves and antique jewelry cases." Customers: mainly craftsmen and artists; middle to high incomes; mid-30's. Heaviest wholesale buying time: late summer-fall; best selling time: Christmas.

IDEA FACTORY, 838 Chartres, New Orleans LA 70116. (504)524-5195. Manager: Margaret A. Bacon. Craft shop. Estab. 1974. Represents 6+ professional craftworkers.
Acceptable Work: Considers dollmaking, soft sculpture and woodcrafting. Especially needs wooden toys and soft sculpture. One-of-a-kind and handmade production-line items. Price range: $1-200; bestsellers: $5-50.
Terms: Buys outright and works on consignment; 40% commission. Retail price set by joint agreement. Requires exclusive area representation. Send slides. Reports in 2 weeks. Work may be shipped or hand-delivered. Dealer pays insurance on exhibited work. Display time: 3 months for consigned work.
Profile: "We are craftworkers producing graphics in wood, mostly custom work—names, letters, numbers, commercial signs, logos. We will purchase any craft items showing good ideas in design and craftsmanship." Customers: tourists and local residents. Heaviest wholesale buying and best selling time: winter.

THE KATY-DID, 711 Jefferson Hwy, Suite 10, Baton Rouge LA 70806. (504)924-6974. Contact: Polly des Bordes. Gift shop. Estab. 1972. Represents 75-85 Southern craftworkers, mainly from Louisiana.
Acceptable Work: Considers baby clothing, dollmaking, glass art, jewelry, pottery, quilting, soft sculpture, wall hangings, weavings, woodcrafting, toymaking, basketry and Christmas items. "Quilts must be hand quilted with no less than 5 stitches per inch but preferably 6-9 stitches per inch, traditional or original designs." One-of-a-kind and handmade production-line items. Price range: $2-400; bestsellers: $2-200.
Terms: Buys outright but prefers working on consignment; 40% commission. Craftworker sets retail price; shop advises. Prefers exclusive area representation. Send letter with color photos and description, including size and price, or call for appointment (if local). Reports in 2 weeks. Work may be shipped or hand delivered. Dealer pays insurance on exhibited work. "Except for our quilts and more expensive woodworking, any item that has not generated positive consumer interest after 90 days is returned to the craftworker."
Profile: "Ours is a small shop (less than 500 sq. ft.) but every inch is utilized. We display a different quilt each week on a folding screen in our display window. We also use shelf units and wooden crates to display some items. Most customers are wise shoppers who come to us looking for well-made and unique items for themselves and to give as gifts"; middle to excellent incomes. Heaviest wholesale buying time: August-December; best selling time: September-Christmas.
To Break In: "It is our policy not to duplicate a craftperson's work unless the newly offered item is remarkably different. There are some items that time and trial have proven to be unmarketable in our area. It's best to check with us first before sending or making something we might not need."

LE MAGASIN, Lafayette Natural History Museum & Planetarium, 637 Girard Park Dr., Lafayette LA 70503. (318)233-6611. Director: Beverly D. Latimer. Secretary: Rose M. Must. Museum gift shop. Estab. 1977. Represents 10 craftworkers.
Acceptable Work: Considers dollmaking, jewelry, metalsmithing, needlecrafts, pottery, quilting, wall hangings, weavings and woodcrafting. Specializes in regional handmade production-line items. Price range: 10¢-$50; 25¢-$10.

Terms: Buys outright and works on consignment; 30% commission. Shop sets retail price. Send color photos or slides of work, selling prices and availability. Reports in 2-3 weeks. Work may be shipped or hand-delivered.
Profile: "We have a small store with a large display case, shelving and cabinets for storage. Large items are seldom handled." Customers: children to adults; interested in astronomy, regional crafts, jewelry and books. Heaviest wholesale buying time: fall-Christmas; best selling time: spring and fall.

LOOM ROOM, INC., 623 Royal St., New Orleans LA 70130. (504)522-7101. President: Glenna Geisert. Craft/gift shop. Estab. 1975. Represents 60 craftworkers.
Acceptable Work: Considers handwoven articles. Especially needs line of jewelry. Specializes in functional weavings. One-of-a-kind and handmade production-line items. Price range: $1.35-350; bestsellers: $5.50-50.
Terms: Buys outright, or will consider consignment. Requires exclusive area representation. Send introductory letter and slides. "If we are interested, we will ask for articles/samples to be sent." Reports in 1 week. Work may be shipped or hand-delivered. Display time: 2 months.
Profile: "Besides carrying handwoven articles, we also carry yarns and weaving supplies. Our turnover rate is 2.5 months. Customers are young adults and professional people. 75% of our business is tourist and convention business." Heaviest wholesale buying time: February and August-September; best selling time: October-December.

LOUISIANA CRAFTS COUNCIL, 139 Broadway, New Orleans LA 70118. (504)861-8267. Manager: Lynne Higbee. Craft shop/gallery/school. Estab. 1961. Represents 25-30 craftworkers. "Craftworkers must live in Louisiana to show in our shop and to teach classes, but to exhibit in our gallery, they can reside anywhere in the US."
Acceptable Work: Considers batik, ceramics, clothing, dollmaking, glass art, jewelry, leatherworking, metalsmithing, needlecrafts, pottery, quilting, scrimshaw, soft sculpture, wall hangings, weavings and woodcrafting. Specializes in contemporary crafts. One-of-a-kind and handmade production-line items. Price range: $3-400; bestsellers: $5-35.
Terms: Works on consignment; 25% commission. Craftworker sets retail price. Call or stop at shop on Tuesday-Saturday (10 am-4 pm) Work may be shipped or hand-delivered. Display time: 6 months in shop; 1 month in gallery.
Profile: "Craft items must pass a standards committee for quality. Items are displayed on shelves and walls. We are a nonprofit organization which assists craftsmen with low commissions and free publicity." Customers: middle aged; middle to high incomes. Best selling time: Christmas.

THE MAGI, 301 Royal St., New Orleans LA 70130. (504)581-2100. Contact: Charles DeBlieux. Gift shop/gallery. Estab. 1962. Represents 40-50 craftworkers.
Acceptable Work: Considers batik, ceramics, glass art, jewelry, metalsmithing, pottery, wall hangings, weavings and woodcrafting. Specializes in contemporary crafts. One-of-a-kind and handmade production-line items with a few utility items (tablewares). Price range: $2-1,250; bestsellers: $5-150.
Terms: Buys outright and sometimes works on consignment; 33⅓% commission. Retail price set by shop or joint agreement. Requires exclusive area representation. Send slides and be prepared to send samples on request. Reports in 1 week. Work may be shipped or hand delivered. Dealer pays insurance on exhibited work.
Profile: "The Magi shop is our senior establishment and is located in one of the most successful of all shopping centers in the Southeast. Large pieces cannot be accommodated. I travel to Europe each year to shop for stock. The majority of artists/craftsmen in the US producing the quality of work I enjoy have their own retail establishments and are not interested in mine. My selections are restricted to those things I like—owner is not disagreeable, only proud." Customers: early to late middle age, home decorators, median to high incomes, and "those who afford winter holidays and exhibit that rare combination of taste and money". Heaviest wholesale buying time: September-March; best selling time: October-March, except January.

MARATHON EAST ART CENTER, 610 Herndon, Shreveport LA 71101. (318)222-9400. Contact: M. Elaine Garrett. Craft/gift shop/gallery. Estab. 1977. Represents 60 member craftworkers. "We specialize in local art found in a 200-mile radius of the city."
Acceptable Work: Considers batik, ceramics, jewelry, metalsmithing, needlecrafts, pottery, tole painting, wall hangings, weavings, woodcrafting and serigraphs. One-of-a-kind items only. Price range: $6-3,000; bestsellers: $5-1,500.

Terms: Works on consignment; 15% commission. Craftworker sets retail price. Call for appointment. Reports in 1 week. Work may be shipped or hand delivered. Dealer pays insurance on exhibited work. "Work is displayed on an 8 week rotation, appropriate equipment supplied by the art center. Artists have the option of using their own equipment also."
Profile: "The art center is made up of 4 galleries, a frame shop, art supplies, classes and it distributes a monthly newsletter." Customers: banks, interior designers, office outfitters, ages 25-35, $20,000-40,000 incomes. Heaviest wholesale buying time: spring and fall; best selling time: summer-fall.

CAMILLE MAHER ANTIQUES & GIFTS, 5408 Magazine St., New Orleans LA 70015. (504)897-6849. Contact: Camile Maher. Gift and antique shop. Estab. 1974. Represents 40-50 craftworkers.
Acceptable Work: Considers ceramics; decoupage; dollmaking; jewelry; metalsmithing; needlecrafts; pottery; quilting; soft sculpture; tole painting; wall hangings; weavings; woodcrafting; paintings; prints; and soft toys. Price range: $3-350; bestsellers: $5-50.
Terms: Works on consignment and buys outright; 33⅓% commission. Gallery sets retail price. Requires exclusive area representation. Reports in 1-2 weeks with SASE. Work may be shipped or hand-delivered. Dealer pays shipping on requested material.
Profile: Shop is "in a quaint old Victorian cottage crammed with a melange of old things, handcrafted items, with a surprise here and there of something very modern, like soft sculpture. Customers tell me they like the mix of nostalgia and new." Best selling and heaviest wholesale buying time: Christmas.
To Break In: "Please send full description of item you make: materials, size, etc. Also send a picture or two with SASE for return of pictures. Send your final price and SASE for reply."

OUACHITA COUNCIL ON AGING, 3113 Breard St., Monroe LA 71201. (318)387-0535. Executive Director: Christine E. Gray. Gift shop. Estab. 1976. Represents craftworkers 60 years or older.
Acceptable Work: Considers ceramics, clothing, decoupage, dollmaking, needlecrafts, quilting, wall hangings, weavings and woodcrafting. Handmade production-line items only. Price range: $1-300; bestsellers: $13-80.
Terms: No charge or commission for exhibiting. Craftworker sets retail price. Stop at shop. Work may be shipped or hand delivered. Display time: 1 month.
Profile: "Our Calico Corner is located in Humphries Center for senior citizens. We average $1,000/month in sales." Community has about 80,000 people. Customers: many young couples. Heaviest wholesale buying time: October, December and March; best selling time: November-December.

THE PIONEER SHOPPE, 3026 College Dr. Baton Rouge LA 70808. (504)927-2912. Manager/Buyer: Caryn Schoeffler. Gift shop. Estab. 1976. Represents 10-12 craftworkers.
Acceptable Work: Considers dollmaking, needlecrafts, quilting, soft sculpture and woodcrafting. Especially needs Christmas ornaments/decorations and wooden Colonial accessory pieces. Specializes in needlework items (for children), toys and gifts. Handmade production-line items only. Price range: $1-50; bestsellers: $4.50-10.
Terms: Buys outright. Shop sets retail price. "We will not take anything that can be found in more than 3 places." Send resume and slides. Reports in 2 weeks. Work may be shipped or hand delivered.
Profile: "We are a retail furniture store and gift business handling gift lines bought from regular markets as well as from local craftspeople. We discontinue any lines sold by large, well-known stores. We cater to the unique. Quite a bit of repeat business from customers. Most items are displayed on antiques and reproduction antiques and are constantly moved to different locations so that a display does not become old." Customers: tourists, ages 25-65, middle to upper incomes, interested in antiques. Heaviest wholesale buying time: spring and fall; best selling time: Christmas.
To Break In: "I buy small quantities of each item so as not to saturate my market with unchanging merchandise. I may discontinue a popular line for a while only to carry it again after my customers are used to not seeing it in my shop."

PONCHATOULA COUNTRY MARKET, INC., 10 E. Pine St., Ponchatoula LA 70454. Manager: Hazel Watts. Recruitment Chairman: Hobby Van Der Weyden. Craft shop. Estab. 1973. Represents 35 local craftworkers, including those in Southern Louisiana and Mississippi.
Acceptable Work: Considers all crafts. Especially needs basketry, stained glass and leatherwork. One-of-a-kind and handmade production-line items. Price range: open; bestsellers: $5-10.

Terms: "Individual craftsmen rent selling space and must arrange for someone to operate it whenever the market is open." Craftworker sets retail price. Send slides. SASE. Reports in 2 weeks.
Profile: "We are located in the old railroad depot in the center of town. We are open 10 months of the year on Tuesday, Thursday and Saturday and are classified as a tourist attraction." The average *double* selling space is 8x8 shaped like a U. Best selling time: October-December and April-May.

ROUNTREE GALLERY, INC., 812 N. 2nd St., Monroe LA 71201. (318)325-0057. President: Mary Lou Rountree. Rental gallery. Estab. 1977. Represents 3 craftworkers.
Acceptable Work: Considers batik, glass art, jewelry, leatherworking, metalsmithing, pottery, quilting, soft sculpture, wall hangings and weavings. Specializes in fine art designer crafts. Price range: $4-380; bestsellers: around $100.
Terms: Buys outright and works on consignment; 33⅓% commission. Retail price set by joint agreement. Requires exclusive area representation. Send resume, slides or visit with portfolio. Reports in 3 weeks. Work may be shipped or hand delivered.
Profile: "Displays pots on sculpture stands and shelves; fabric items on the wall or in a hand-built porch swing located in the special crafts room. Labels are typed, lengthy and mounted on matboard. I usually feature an artist for about 6 weeks, often with an opening reception. The gallery is in a renovated old home in a largely residential old neighborhood." Customers: upper incomes; interested in fine art; educated. Heaviest wholesale buying time: spring and fall; best selling time: winter.

SHADETREE ANTIQUES, Drawer R, Royal at Ferdinand, St. Francisville LA 70775. (504)635-6116. Shopkeeper: Marjorie Collamer. Antique/craft/natural food shop. Estab. 1974. Represents 12 craftworkers.
Acceptable Work: Considers batik, candlemaking, ceramics, clothing, jewelry, metalsmithing, needlecrafts, pottery, quilting, wall hangings, weavings, woodcrafting, cornshuck mats and split oak baskets. One-of-a-kind and handmade production-line items. Price range: $180 maximum; bestsellers: 80¢-$16.
Terms: Buys outright. Retail price set by joint agreement. Write or call for appointment. Reports in 2 weeks. Work may be shipped or hand delivered.
Profile: "We are a small antique craft shop located in historic St. Francisville, Louisiana on a hill (above the Mississippi River). The shop is the front portion of a fine, old restored home. We have recently opened a natural food store on the premises as well. We have old showcases and cypress storage boxes used in displays. We are always open to the craftworker's ideas on display of his/her items. We meet people from all over because the riverboats make a weekly stop in St. Francisville." Heaviest wholesale buying time: fall and early spring; best selling time: fall, early spring, Christmas and early March (during the Audubon pilgrimage).

DIXON SMITH INTERIORS, 1655 Lobdell St., Baton Rouge LA 70806. Contact: Dixon Smith. Gallery/antique shop/interior designer. Estab. 1946. Represents 10 craftworkers.
Acceptable Work: Considers batik, ceramics, jewelry, pottery, quilting, wall hangings, weavings and woodcrafting. One-of-a-kind and handmade production-line items. Price range: no limit.
Terms: Buys outright and works on consignment. Dealer pays insurance on exhibited work. Requires exclusive area representation. Visit shop with actual work or call for appointment. Work may be shipped or hand-delivered.

SPORTS ART, 617 Bienville St., New Orleans LA 70130. Contact: J. Peter Eaves. Considers traditional sculpture. Specializes in wildlife, hunting and fishing themes. Price range: $20-10,000. 30% commission. Retail price set by joint agreement. Exhibited art insured. Mailings sent with each show.

2 + 2 LTD. GALLERY, 5163 General DeGaulle, New Orleans LA 70114. (504)394-5265. Director: Lou Eckert. Gallery/frame shop. Estab. 1972. Represents 20-25 craftworkers. Price range: $3-150; bestsellers: $5-25. Works on consignment; 40% commission. Craftworker sets retail price. Requires exclusive area representation. Reports in 4 weeks. Work may be shipped or hand-delivered.
Acceptable Work: Considers dollmaking; glass art; pottery; soft sculpture; wall hangings; weavings; and woodcrafting. Fine one-of-a-kind pieces only. Especially needs pottery; unusual ceramic pieces; soft sculpture; pillows; and one-of-a-kind wooden toys.
Profile: "Work is displayed artfully according to the type of item. We switch displays monthly;

some are stored and redisplayed throughout the year. Heaviest wholesale buying time: early spring and early fall; best selling time: spring and fall.

UNIVERSITY OF SOUTHERN LOUISIANA UNION CRAFT SHOP, Box 44507, University of Southern Louisiana, Lafayette LA 70504. (318)264-6372. Director: Mike Flaherty. Craft shop/gallery. Estab. 1970. Considers batik; ceramics; jewelry; leatherworking; and pottery. "Customers are students of this campus; minimal income."
Terms: Teaches programs and workshops and has gallery shows 4 times per semester. "We program usually 1 year in advance. Art Gallery programs are decided on by USL Union Art Advisory Board, comprising of Union staff, the craft shop director and certain applied and fine arts faculty." Reports in 4 weeks. Work may be shipped or hand-delivered. Dealer pays insurance. Shows last for 3 weeks.

Maine

ABACUS GALLERY, Box 3, Boothbay Harbor ME 04538. (207)633-2166. Contact: Dana Heacock or Sal Scaglione. Craft shop/gallery. Estab. 1971. Represents 150 craftworkers.
Acceptable Work: Considers batik; glass art; graphics; jewelry; leather; metalsmithing; pottery; quilting; soft sculpture; wall hangings; weavings; and woodcrafting. Fine one-of-a-kind and handmade production-line items. Price range: $1-1,500; bestsellers: $1-50.
Terms: Works on consignment and buys outright; 40% commission. Shop sets retail price. Requires exclusive area representation.

THE ACADIA CORPORATION, 85 Main St., Bar Harbor ME 04609. (207)288-5592. Merchandise Manager: Dave Woodside. Gift shop. Estab. 1947. Represents 30-50 craftworkers. "Our first preference is for Maine crafts; the second for New England crafts. Other crafts considered if not available in New England. (We do sucessfully carry several lines from as far away as California.)"
Acceptable Work: Considers ceramics, glass art, jewelry, needlecrafts, pottery, scrimshaw, woodcrafting, Christmas decorations and reproduced prints. Specializes in "rustic and/or nautical designs, suggestive of Maine and New England or using New England materials, utilitarian and decorative". Handmade production-line items. Price range: $1-295; bestsellers: $3-15.
Terms: Buys outright. Shop sets retail price. Prefers exclusive area representation. Send slides. Reports in 2 weeks. Work may be shipped or hand-delivered.
Profile: "We are a National Park concessioner, involved very heavily with Mrs. Mondales 'Native Handcraft' project to place handcrafts in national parks. Shops are small with heavy traffic. The shops are basically rustic so all displays must conform to this. One shop is located at a high-class restaurant, another in downtown Bar Harbor (summer tourist town), and the other two are at park attractions. Initially, there is a small to medium display. The size varies thereafter according to saleability and supply." Customers: tourists "interested in most crafts which portray the uniqueness of Maine in some way"; young families; well-to-do young couples to older folk. Heaviest wholesale buying time: January-May; bestsellers: June-September.
To Break In: "We strive for a minimum retail volume of $100 per item, thus, production and ability to fill reorders is highly important."

ACADIAN CRAFTS ASSOCIATION, 29 St. Catherine St., Madawaska ME 04756. (207)728-3295. Manager: Theresa Violette. Wholesale/mail order shop. Estab. 1970. Represents 40-70 St. John Valley women craftworkers. Considers clothing. Fine and handmade production-line items; utilitarian only. Price range: $18-57. Buys outright. Retail price set by joint agreement. Reports in 2 weeks. Hand-delivered work only. Dealer pays shipping to shop and in-transit insurance. Heaviest wholesale buying time: summer; best selling time: fall.

BAY STUDIO CRAFTS, 3 Belmont Ave., Belfast ME 04915. Contact: Frances Armington. Craft shop located at the corner of Main and High Sts. Estab. 1976. Represents 100 craftworkers.
Acceptable Work: Considers candlemaking; ceramics; clothing; decoupage; dollmaking; glass art; jewelry; leatherworking; metalsmithing; needlecrafts; pottery; tole painting; woodcrafting; macrame; and other. Handmade production-line items. Price range: 79¢-$100; bestsellers: $1.50-20.
Terms: Works on consignment and buys outright; 33⅓% commission. Craftworker sets retail price. Requires exclusive area representation. Reports in 4 weeks. Work may be shipped or hand-delivered with previous approval. Dealer pays shipping to shop, in-transit insurance and

insurance for exhibited work if on consignment. Heaviest wholesale buying time: spring and fall; best selling time: summer and pre-Christmas.

BOSTON BAKED BEADS, 8 Mt. Desert St., Bar Harbor ME 04609. Winter off-season address: 64 Wendell St., Cambridge MA 02138. Contact: Paul DeVore or Gail Gutradt. Craft/gift shop. Estab. 1974. Represents 50 craftworkers.
Acceptable Work: Considers batik, candlemaking, ceramics, dollmaking, glass art, jewelry, metalsmithing, needlecrafts, pottery, small quilts, wall hangings, weavings, woodcrafting, beads, cards, silkscreen, stationery, posters, mobiles and wind chimes. Especially needs sea- and nature-oriented items, handmade cards, imaginative Christmas ornaments, and items for men (besides leather). Specializes in fine and bright-colored handmade production-line items. Price range: 50¢-$75; bestsellers: $5-$10.
Terms: Buys outright. Shop sets retail price. Send resume, slides with SASE. Reports in 2 weeks. Work may be shipped or hand-delivered.
Profile: Roomy retail shop "where we highlight items to their best advantage. We emphasize delightful handmade items of high quality." Customers are primarily tourists, families, young campers, middle to upper incomes, with some elderly, city sophisticates and singles. "They're interested in nature, hiking, sailing, camping, etc. Many vacationers are doing their Christmas shopping." Heaviest wholesale buying time: May-August; best selling time: summer. "Our season runs from May 15-October 15, so we order early to give craftworkers lead time."
To Break In: "We need sure, quick delivery and communication. We can give adequate (long-range) notice for initial order, but need good delivery for re-orders because we're a summer shop with an intense, but short season."

THE COOL MOOSE, 102 Main St., Bridgton ME 04009. (207)647-2446. Contact: Peter Lowell. Craft/gift shop. Estab. 1968. Represents 4 craftworkers.
Acceptable Work: Considers jewelry, leatherworking, wall hangings, weavings and woodcrafting. One-of-a-kind and handmade production-line items: Price range: $5-60; bestsellers: $5-15.
Terms: Buys outright and works on consignment; 50% commission. Retail price set by joint agreement. Requires exclusive area representation. Call for appointment. Reports in 4 weeks. Work may be shipped or hand delivered. Dealer pays insurance on exhibited work.
Profile: "Most items are handmade on the premises as we have been working in leather, wood and metals for 11 years." Heaviest wholesale buying and best selling time: summer.

THE DANCING DEER, 10-12-D Mt. Desert St., Bar Harbor ME 04609. Winter off-season address: 64 Wendell St., Cambridge MA 02138. Contact: Paul DeVore or Gail Gutradt. Craft/gift shop. Estab. 1974. Represents 50 craftworkers.
Acceptable Work: Considers batik, candlemaking, ceramics, dollmaking, glass art, jewelry, metalsmithing, needlecrafts, pottery, small quilts, wall hangings, weavings, woodcrafting, beads, cards, silkscreen, stationery, posters, mobiles and wind chimes. Especially needs sea- and nature-oriented items, handmade cards, imaginative Christmas ornaments, and items for men (besides leather). Specializes in fine and bright-colored handmade production-line items. Price range: 50¢-$75; bestsellers: $5-$10.
Terms: Buys outright. Shop sets retail price. Send resume, slides with SASE. Reports in 2 weeks. Work may be shipped or hand-delivered.
Profile: Roomy retail shop "where we highlight items to their best advantage. We emphasize delightful handmade items of high quality." Customers are primarily tourists, families, young campers, middle to upper incomes, with some elderly, city sophisticates and singles. "They're interested in nature, hiking, sailing, camping, etc. Many vacationers are doing their Christmas shopping." Heaviest wholesale buying time: May-August; best selling time: summer. "Our season runs from May 15-October 15, so we order early to give craftworkers lead time."
To Break In: "We need sure, quick delivery and communication. We can give adequate (long-range) notice for initial order, but need good delivery for re-orders because we're a summer shop with an intense, but short season."

EASTERN MAINE CRAFTS CO-OP, Box 22, Steuben ME 04680. (207)546-2269. Secretary/Treasurer: Peter Weil. Craft shop located in Milbridge, Maine. Estab. 1973. Represents 10-12 New England craftworkers.
Acceptable Work: Considers any good designer-craftsman work from Main-based artisans. Fine one-of-a-kind and handmade production-line items. Price range: $3.50-400; bestsellers: $3.50-50.
Terms: Works on consignment; 40% commission. Craftworker sets retail price. Requires exclusive area representation. Send resume, slides, SASE or call for appointment. Reports in 2

weeks. Work must be hand-delivered. Dealer pays burglary insurance only. "We expect a consigner to keep us in store all summer. Work is displayed for the entire season."
Profile: "We are in a converted house in eastern Maine. Each person's work is displayed in a section of its own. Special exhibit items are displayed 2-3 weeks in the central location of the gallery. Customers are tourists and summer residents age 30 and up; above average income and education." Open mid June-October 1.

ESPECIALLY MAINE, US Rt. 1, Arundel ME 04046. (207)985-3749. Gift and mail order shop. Estab. 1974. Represents 30 craftworkers.
Acceptable Work: Considers candlemaking; ceramics; clothing; glass art; jewelry; leatherworking; metalsmithing; needlecrafts; and pottery. Fine handmade production-line items. Price range: 50¢-$450.
Terms: Buys outright. Gallery sets retail price. Requires exclusive area representation. Work may be shipped or hand-delivered. Dealer pays shipping and insurance for exhibited work. Best selling and heaviest wholesale buying time: fall.

WILLIAM A. FARNSWORTH LIBRARY & ART MUSEUM, Box 466, Rockland ME 04841. (207)596-6457. Shop Manager: Jan Lamont. Director: Marius B. Peladeau. Museum gift shop. Estab. 1948. Represents many craftworkers, with an emphasis on Maine craftworkers and the alumni of Haystack Mountain School. Best selling and heaviest wholesale buying time: summer.
Acceptable Work: Considers all crafts. Price range: under $50; bestsellers: under $25.
Terms: Works on consignment: 40% commission. Craftworker sets retail price. Work is "displayed in Museum Shop sales area; breakable pieces in cases or behind glass".

THE GAMEKEEPER, INC., Box 1016, Bangor ME 04401. (207)947-8806. President: Gwethalyn M. Phillips. Game and toy shop. Estab. 1977. Represents 8-10 craftworkers.
Acceptable Work: Considers games and toys in any medium. Especially needs cribbage boards ranging from $5-30. One-of-a-kind and handmade production-line items. "I have a hard time buying an item that the craftperson sells wholesale in area shows." Price range: $5-680; bestsellers: $5-20.
Terms: Buys outright. Gallery sets retail price. Call for appointment and bring samples and nonreturnable catalog/price sheet. Reports immediately with appointment, 1 week if not. Work must be hand-delivered. Dealer pays shipping to shop and insurance for exhibited work.
Profile: "We specialize in high quality games (mostly for adults) and a few toys. We mix manufactured goods with handcrafted goods." Customers: intellectual with mid-upper incomes. Heaviest wholesale buying time: late spring and October; best selling time: summer (July-August) and Christmas.

HANDCRAFTERS GALLERY, 18 Exchange St., Portland ME 04101. Contact: Peter or Gail Kahn. Craft shop. Estab. 1973. Represents 100 craftworkers. Bestsellers: $25. Buys outright. Gallery sets retail price. Requires exclusive area representation. Work may be shipped or hand-delivered.
Acceptable Work: Considers ceramics; clothing; glass art; jewelry; pottery; soft sculpture; wall hangings; and weavings.

HARPSWELL HOUSE GALLERY, 49 Winter St., Topsham ME 04086. (207)725-7694. Contact: Winthrop L. Brown. Craft/gift shop. Estab. 1960. Represents 25-40 craftworkers. Customers: college students and faculty, Naval Air Station personnel, plus summer and retired residents; above average incomes and education. Heaviest wholesale buying time: spring-fall; best selling time: summer and Christmas season.
Acceptable Work: Considers ceramics, glass art, silver and gold jewelry, metalsmithing, pottery, china, and crystal. Prefers New England crafts. No tourist items. Specializes in contemporary work. One-of-a-kind and handmade production-line items. Price range: $2.50-200; bestsellers: $5-50.
Terms: Works on consignment. Craftworker sets retail price. Requires exclusive area representation. Call for appointment.

HERITAGE METALCRAFT, INC., Rt. 202, S. Windham ME 04082. (207)892-6739. President: Wayne R. Holmquist. Craft shop. Estab. 1967. Represents craftworkers who work in forged, cast or hammered copper metal items.
Acceptable Work: Considers decorative and functional metalcraft only. 90% are handmade production-line items; 10% are one-of-a-kind. Price range: $2.50-2,000; bestsellers: $5-100.

Terms: Buys outright. Gallery sets retail price. Reports in 1 week. "Send catalog, pictures, description, pricing, packaging and normal shipping method. If production item, give time requirements for reorders and state volume available per year and on what basis." Work may be shipped or hand-delivered.
Profile: "We operate craft store, mail order and wholesale to dealers throughout US and Canada. Customers are mostly home owners." Heaviest wholesale buying time: June and December; best selling time: Christmas.

HERON POINT GALLERY, Rt. 2, Brunswick ME 04011. Director: Nell Burbank. Gallery. Estab. 1975. Represents 10-20 craftworkers.
Acceptable Work: Considers batik; ceramics; glass art; jewelry; metalsmithing; needlecrafts; pottery; wall hangings; weavings; sculpture; cards; and notes. Fine one-of-a-kind pieces. Price range: $1.25-200; bestsellers: $2.50-20. Works on consignment and buys outright; 25% commission. Retail price set by joint agreement. Work may be shipped or hand-delivered. Dealer pays shipping to shop. Displays work 4-6 weeks minimum.
Profile: Gallery is "well lighted and uncrowded. The location has a view of Quohog Bay, sculpture terrace with woods background." Displays work 4-6 weeks. Heaviest wholesale buying time: spring; best selling time: summer.

HOBBIT HOUSE, Shore Rd., Ogunquit ME 03907. (207)646-9427. Contact: Ruth or Bill Kocsis. Gift shop. Estab. 1972. Represents over 100 craftworkers.
Acceptable Work: Considers decoupage; dollmaking; glass art; jewelry; leatherworking; metalcraft; needlecrafts; pottery; quilting; wall hangings; woodcrafting; and internal carvings in Plexiglas. Especially needs blown glass; paper weights; and procelain bells. Fine one-of-a-kind pieces. Price range: $1-200; bestsellers: $1-150.
Terms: Buys outright. Gallery sets retail price. Requires exclusive area representation. Work may be shipped or hand-delivered. Dealer pays shipping.
Profile: "All items are displayed to the best advantage possible, space limitations considered. Customers are teenagers to the elderly; middle income. We have repeat sales to those who are always interested in the newest, most novel and imaginative in handcrafts." Heaviest wholesale buying time: spring and winter; best selling time: summer.

H-O-M-E, INC., Rt. 1, Orland ME 04472. (207)469-7961. Marketing Director: Arleen Morris. Cooperative craft shop. Estab. 1970. Represents 500 Maine craftworkers.
Acceptable Work: Considers all crafts. Price range: 50¢-$300; bestsellers: 50¢-$75.
Terms: Works on consignment; 30% commission. Retail price set by joint agreement. Reports immediately. Work may be shipped or hand-delivered with previous approval. Displays work 6 months.
Profile: "H-O-M-E is a private nonprofit organization. Many of its activities are of a public service nature. The cooperative craft shop is one of its activities. All activities are geared to helping people become more self sufficient. The H-O-M-E craft shops were established as an outlet for low income people to subsidize their income through the sale of crafts. There is a membership fee of $10 yearly." Heaviest wholesale buying time: prior to summer and Christmas; best selling time: summer and Christmas. Also holds annual craft fair in August.

THE ISLAND STORE, Spruce Head Island ME 04859. (207)594-7475. Contact: Erika E. Pilver. General store/gift and craft shop. Represents 24 craftworkers. Price range: 99¢-$75; bestsellers: $1.50-5. Works on consignment and buys outright; 33⅓% commission. Gallery sets retail price on crafts bought outright; craftworker sets retail price on consignment work. Reports in 1 week. Work may be shipped or hand-delivered. Dealer pays insurance for exhibited work.
Acceptable Work: Considers batik; candlemaking; decoupage; glass art; jewelry; leatherworking; metalsmithing; and needlecrafts. Fine one-of-a-kind and handmade production-line items.
Profile: "Displays are changed several times a season. Location is right on the shore in a fishing village. Customers are a few retired 'summer people' who sometimes purchase designer items and many tourists who purchase inexpensive items for gifts." Heaviest wholesale buying time: spring; best selling time: summer.

JAFFRAY & CHASE, LTD., Blue Hill ME 04614. (207)374-9957. Contact: Deenee Chase or Margie Jaffray. Craft/gift shop and boutique. Estab. 1976. Represents 10 craftworkers.
Acceptable Work: Considers all crafts. One-of-a-kind and handmade production-line items. Price range: $2-300.
Terms: Buys outright and works on consignment. Retail price set by joint agreement. Requires exclusive area representation. Call for appointment.

Profile: "We carry needlepoint originals, hand knits, wool knitting yarn, unique gifts and clothes and unusual cards and notes. Displays are moved about in the shop. Customers are well-to-do summer residents and native people; middle to upper income; mostly women but a good many men and children also." Heaviest wholesale buying time: winter and spring; best selling time: summer.

JANE-GRAY SHOPPE, Rt. 2, Box 206, Dexter ME 04930. Contact: Jane Gilbert. Gift/antique shop. Estab. 1977. Represents 10 craftworkers.
Acceptable Work: Considers clothing, decoupage, dollmaking, jewelry, needlecrafts, quilting, soft sculpture and woodcrafting. Specializes in Maine and area crafts. One-of-a-kind pieces only. Price range: $1-40; bestsellers: $1-25.
Terms: Works on consignment; 20% commission. Retail price set by joint agreement. Call for appointment. Reports in 2 weeks. Work must be hand-delivered.
Profile: "I have a 48'x32' Gambrel roof new building. We utilize a gallery second floor as well as ground floor. New gifts are kept separate from antiques. Items are treated with respect and kept as long as craftsman wants, or left to my discretion." Heaviest wholesale buying time: spring-fall; best selling time: summer.

THE LAMP POST CRAFT SHOP, 335 Penobscot Ave., Millinocket ME 04462. (207)723-4225. Contact: Ronald or Susan Legere. Craft shop. Estab. 1974. Represents 54 craftworkers.
Acceptable Work: Considers ceramics, clothings, decoupage, dollmaking, glass art, jewelry, leatherworking, pottery, quilting, tole painting and woodcrafting. One-of-a-kind pieces.
Terms: Works on consignment; 25% commission. Retail price set by joint agreement. Requires exclusive area representation. Reports in 3 weeks. Work may be shipped or hand-delivered. Dealer pays insurance. Heaviest wholesale buying time: fall and spring; best selling time: fall.

Pedestals are used to display 3-dimensional works such as these unusual items at the Maple Hill Pottery Craft Gallery, Auburn, Maine. "Whimsical and unusual crafts sell well here," says owner Nancy Lee. "An artist's work is grouped together and great effort is made to create the best environment for it."—Photo by Robert F. George.

THE LEFT BANK, Atlantic Ave, Boothbay Harbor ME 04538. (207)633-4815 or 633-5228. Contact: Richard Macdonald. Craft shop. Estab. 1977. Represents 20 craftworkers.
Acceptable Work: Considers ceramics, clothing, glass art, jewelry, leatherworking, metalsmithing, pottery, quilting, soft sculpture, wall hangings, weavings, and woodcrafting. Especially needs pottery, fiber and iron works. Specializes in fine art and contemporary items. Price range: $6-800; bestsellers: $6-300.

Terms: Works on consignment; 25% commission. Craftworker sets retail price. Send resume, slides and SASE or call for appointment. Reports in 2 weeks. Work may be shipped or hand delivered. "I will not accept less than $200 wholesale from an individual craftsperson."
Profile: "Basically, the shop is an outlet for my own fine glass production. However, as I have space left over, I invite others to display. Each craftworker gets his own wall or cube space depending upon needs. Our walls are white with 4 foot areas, divided by 18" deep verticle separators so each person can have his own focus point. The shop is earthy and the objects selected are refined. The public seems to like this and we have excellent traffic, and a well-educated and appreciative clientele. We have vacationers from all over the Eastern Seaboard and the world who can afford the resorts in Boothbay Harbor. Also, there are yachtsmen as our shop overlooks the harbor. Our paying audience is basically 25-50 year-old professionals." Open: May 15-October 15.
To Break In: "Don't send me dogs or seconds to get rid of. Send a balanced order and price range of popular items. Don't take stock away before the season ends. All things being equal, the craftworker will be well cared for, will receive excellent exposure, and saleable work in any price range will move."

THE LUBEC CRAFTS COUNCIL, INC., The Wharf Shop, Water St., Lubec ME 04652. (207)733-4701. Contact: Robert O. Voight. Estab. 1970.
Acceptable Work: Considers candlemaking; glass art; jewelry; leatherworking; metalsmithing; pottery; wall hangings; weavings; and woodcrafting. Finished, one-of-a-kind items only. Price range: $2-300; bestsellers: $5-25.
Terms: Buys outright. Retail price set by joint agreement. Write. Reports in 4 weeks. Council pays shipping from shop and insurance for exhibited artwork. Best selling time: summer.

MAINE CRAFT STORE, Blue Hill ME 04614. (207)374-5645. Contact: Rufus A. Candage. Craft shop. Estab. 1974. Represents 150 craftworkers.
Acceptable Work: Considers all crafts except tole painting. Price range: 10¢-$500; bestsellers: $2.25-50.
Terms: Works on consignment; 30% commission. Craftworker sets retail price. Reports in 4 weeks. Work may be shipped or hand-delivered. Best selling and heaviest wholesale buying time: summer.

MAPLE HILL POTTERY CRAFT GALLERY, RFD 3, Auburn ME 04210. (207)782-8768. Craft shop/gallery. Year-round location at Engine House, Court and Spring Sts., Auburn ME 04210. See below.

MAPLE HILL POTTERY CRAFT GALLERY, RFD 3, Auburn ME 04210. Summer address: Perkins Cove, Ogunquit ME 04210. (207)782-8768. Contact: Nancy Lee. Craft shop/gallery. Estab. 1974. Represents 50 craftworkers.
Acceptable Work: Considers fiber work such as weaving, clothing, wall hangings, soft sculpture and quilting; jewelry; and ceramics. Especially interested in jewelry in the $18-60 range, unique clothing and creative fiber. "Whimsical and unusual crafts sell well." Gallery has one-of-a-kind and production-line items. Price range: 75¢-$600; bestsellers: $4.50-60.
Terms: Craft shop buys outright. Gallery pieces taken on consignment; 40% commission. Craftworker sets retail price. Requires exclusive area representation. Reports in 2 weeks. Work may be shipped or hand-delivered. Dealer pays shipping to shop on purchased work and insurance for exhibited work.
Profile: "An artist's work is grouped together and great effort is made to create the best environment for it. I use pedestals for the 3-dimensional pieces, Plexiglas caps over these when the work needs to be protected. The work is hung on muslin-covered walls." Heaviest wholesale buying time: February-July; best selling time: summer.

THE MARKETPLACE, INC., 107 Exchange St., Portland ME 04111. (207)774-1376. President: Ellen M. Higgins. Craft and gift shop. Estab. 1972. Represents 75-100 northern New England craftworkers.
Acceptable Work: Considers batik; candlemaking; ceramics; clothing; dollmaking; etchings; glass art; jewelry; metalsmithing; pottery; silkscreens; soft sculpture; wall hangings; weavings; and woodcrafting. Miniatures in 1"-1' scale or anything pertaining to children is a specialty. "The emphasis is on whimsical and unusual." Fine one-of-a-kind and handmade production-line items. Price range: $1-500; bestsellers: $1-25.
Terms: Buys outright. Retail price set by joint agreement. Requires exclusive area representation. Reports in 2 weeks. Work may be shipped or hand-delivered. Dealer pays insurance for exhibited work.

Profile: "A body of work gets displayed together but we try to mix media which allows a double display. Our shop is 3,000 square feet broken up into architectural areas and full of articles of every medium chosen for excellence of design and execution." Heaviest wholesale buying time: May-December. Best selling time: summer and pre-Christmas.

MUSEUM SHOP, BOWDOIN COLLEGE MUSEUM OF ART, Walker Art Building, Brunswick ME 04011. (207)725-8731, ext. 275. Contact: Lynn C. Yanok or Mary L. Poppe. Museum gift shop. Estab. 1961. Represents several craftworkers.
Acceptable Work: Considers ceramics; decoupage; glass art; jewelry; metalsmithing; and pottery. Especially needs work "in the reproduction of objects from our permanent collection—but only with exclusive distribution rights and without large minimum order requirements." Price range: $1-50; bestsellers: $5-25.
Terms: Buys outright and occasionally accepts consignment; commission is negotiable. Retail price set by joint agreement or by museum staff. Requires exclusive area representation. Reports in 10 days. Work may be shipped or hand-delivered by advance agreement only. Dealer pays shipping to shop.
Profile: "Items generally turn over quickly enough so that no rotation or retirement period is necessary." Heaviest wholesale buying time: Christmas, and buys outright; 33⅓% commission. Craftworker sets retail price. Reports in 2 weeks. Work may be shipped or hand-delivered. Dealer pays shipping to shop.

THE PASCOS, Kennebunkport ME 04046. (207)967-4722. Contact: Henry or Priscilla Pasco. Craft shop. Estab. 1942. Represents 125 craftworkers, mostly from New England.
Acceptable Work: Considers batik, handblown glass, jewelry, metalsmithing, stoneware, metal or fabric wall hangings and woodwork. One-of-a-kind and handmade production-line items. Price range: $5-75.
Terms: Buys outright. Craftworker sets retail price. Requires exclusive area representation. Call for appointment. "If one is really interested in crafts, one must see and feel the objects and meet the craftsman. Arrive on time, neatly dressed and able to be enthusiastic and ready to take criticism, whether good or bad." Reports immediately. Work may be shipped or hand delivered.
Profile: "Henry and Priscilla are both weavers displaying their wares. Also, in this way, we know what goes into the work of other crafts. We do not show 1000 items, if we have that many at one time. All displays are changed every 2-3 weeks—no favoritism is shown. If we have bought a $5 item of good design, it may sit beside a $25 item." Open: May-December.

PINE TREE KILN, Rt. 1, West Sullivan ME 04689. (207)422-3377. Contact: Ruth Vibert. Craft shop/gallery/gift shop. Estab. 1948. Represents 15-20 craftworkers.
Acceptable Work: Considers batik; candlemaking; ceramics; glass art; jewelry; leatherworking; metalsmithing; pottery; wall hangings; weavings; and woodcrafting. Especially needs leather; woven wall hangings; and jewelry. One-of-a-kind and handmade production-line items. Price range: $1.75-350; bestsellers: $5-30.
Terms: Works on consignment and buys outright; 33⅓% commission. Craftworker sets retail price. Reports in 2 weeks. Work may be shipped or hand-delivered. Dealer pays shipping to shop.
Profile: "We display a craftsman's work all together in one place, identified as his work. We show work as long as it continues to sell. The shop is a handsome converted barn; has been going for 30 years and has an old, regular and loyal clientele. Customers are from old, well-established, wealthy summer colonies." Heaviest wholesale buying time: spring-early summer; best selling time: June-October.

PLUM DANDY, Rt. 2, Box 469A, Goose Rocks Rd., Kennebunkport ME 04046. Formerly in Wells, Maine. (207)967-4013 (shop) or 967-3463 (office). Buyer: Linda Haydock. Craft/gallery located at Dock Square, Kennebunkport ME 04046. Estab. 1974. Represents 150+ craftworkers.
Acceptable Work: Considers basketweaving, batik, beads, candlemaking, ceramics, Christmas items, clothing, fiberwork, jewelry, metalsmithing, needlecrafts, pottery, silkscreening, soft sculpture, wall hangings and weavings. No leather, macrame, patchwork or applique items, traditional crafts, or items made on sewing machine, e.g., potholders, aprons, baby bibs, etc. Especially needs stoneware pottery with no strongly visible wheel rings and dinnerware; craftsperson willing to provide pottery or wood sculpture on an open stock basis as well as take special orders; new hat designs; and flamboyant jewelry under $35 retail. Specializes in fine contemporary crafts. One-of-a-kind and handmade production-line items. Price range: 20¢-$175; bestsellers: $2.50-50.

Terms: Buys outright and occasionally on consignment; 40% commission. Retail price set by gallery or joint agreement. Requires exclusive area representation. Query with slides/photos, price list, resume and SASE; or call for appointment. Will not return reply or slides/photos without SASE. Reports in 1-2 weeks. (Inquiries made in July-August may not be answered until winter.) Work may be shipped or hand delivered. Dealer pays insurance for exhibited work; negotiates payment for shipping and in-transit insurance. Display time: maximum 6 months (consignment).
Profile: Uses shelves for pottery, niches for weavings and wall pieces and tables for dinnerware. "The window display changes once a week and the featured decorator cubes change 10-14 days." Customers: ages 12-60 with lower middle to middle incomes, interested in home decoration and gifts (locals); ages 25-50 with upper middle incomes (tourists). Heaviest wholesale buying time: Febuary-April; best selling time: July-September.

THE PUMPKIN PATCH, Box 178, Searsport ME 04974. (207)548-6047. Contact: Robert F. Sommer. Craft and antique shop. Estab. 1974. Represents 10 Maine craftworkers.
Acceptable Work: Considers candlemaking; pottery; quilting; weavings; woodcrafting; and graphics. Price range: $2-100; bestsellers: $5-30.
Terms: Buys outright. Retail price set by joint agreement. Reports in 1 week. Work may be shipped or hand-delivered.
Profile: "Displays are constantly changed, integrating handworks and antiques. Each craftsman is highlighted in his own setting with background information on the artist, object and skill. Shop is an old sea captain's house and in a quaint coastal community." Heaviest wholesale buying time: May-July; best selling time: May-October.

RICKER BLACKSMITH SHOP, Campbell Hill, Cherryfield ME 04622. (207)546-7954. Contact: George A. Brace. Blacksmith shop. Estab. 1801. Represents 1 craftworker who works in metal or wrought iron. One-of-a-kind and handmade production-line items. Price range: $5-200; bestsellers: $5-60. Exhibits work; does not buy or consign. Work may be shipped or hand-delivered.
Profile: "This is the oldest family-run blacksmith shop in the East. It has been in our family since 1801." Best selling time: summer and fall.

THE SEA CHEST, Parker Point Rd., Box 456, Blue Hill ME 04614. (207)374-2250. Contact: Mr. or Mrs. M. Bullard. Craft/gift shop. Estab. 1970. Represents 20 craftworkers.
Acceptable Work: Considers all crafts except batik. Price range: $1-450; bestsellers: $5-100.
Terms: Buys outright and works on consignment; 30% commission. Retail price set by joint agreement. Send resume and call for appointment. SASE. Reports in 2 weeks. Work must be hand-delivered.
Profile: "Being on the coast, we have a nautical theme, but our crafts are the unusual in handmade items." Heaviest wholesale buying time: spring and pre-Christmas; best selling time: summer-fall.

THE SEA CRAFTERS, Box 770, Ocean Ave., Kennebunkport ME 04046. (207)967-2059. Contact: Hilary Cobb. Gift shop; puts out gift catalog. Estab. 1966. Represents 35-45 craftworkers.
Acceptable Work: Considers ceramics; clothing; decoupage; dollmaking; glass art; jewelry; leatherworking; metalsmithing; needlecrafts; pottery; soft sculpture; and woodcrafting. Primitive and fine pieces. Price range: $1-500; bestsellers: $5-45.
Terms: Works on consignment and buys outright; 33 1/3% commission. Retail price set by joint agreement. Requires exclusive area representation. Reports in 2 weeks. Work may be shipped or hand-delivered. Dealer pays shipping and insurance for exhibited work.
Profile: "Items are generally displayed with related merchandise; period of display as agreed with craftsman, usually during tourist season of June-September. We specialize in merchandise with a nautical theme, primarily useful or decorative items for the home. We normally display over 1,750 items ranging from jewelry to large furniture, all shown in our 1785 colonial building featuring original handhewn post and beam construction." Heaviest wholesale buying time: spring-summer; best selling time: July-August.

SHERRYMIKE POTTERY/GALLERY, 19 Pleasant St., Hallowell ME 04347. (207)622-1906. Contact: Adele Nichols. Craft shop/gallery. Estab. 1960. Represents 90 craftworkers, mostly from Maine. Fine one-of-a-kind and handmade production-line items. Price range: $1.50-325; bestsellers: $8-20. Buys outright. Craftworker sets retail price. Requires exclusive area representation. Reports in 1 week. Dealer pays insurance for exhibited work. Best selling time: summer-Christmas.

Acceptable Work: Considers batik; candlemaking; dollmaking; glass art; jewelry; leatherworking; metalsmithing; pottery; soft sculpture; wall hangings; weavings; and woodcrafting. "Pottery is always big; weaving sales have increased; and jewelry is a steady."

STRONG CRAFT GALLERY, Bar Harbor Rd., Ellsworth ME 04605. (207)667-2595. Contact: Roslyn Strong. Craft gallery. Estab. 1970. Represents 250 craftworkers.
Acceptable Work: Considers cards, glass art, jewelry, leatherworking, metalsmithing, pottery, scrimshaw and woodcrafting. One-of-a-kind and handmade production-line items. Price range: $1.50-300; bestsellers: $4-75.
Special Needs: "I would like to see more wrought iron and wood pieces (prices up to $75 mostly). Inexpensive jewelry ($5-20) sells well. I find my larger more important pieces have slowed down. We sell a lot of utilitarian pottery (casseroles, mugs, pitchers, honey pots), some very simple, some very decorative and one-of-a-kind. We need small items for the casual buyer and large fine pieces for serious collectors."
Terms: Buys outright and works on consignment; 33⅓% commission. Retail price set by joint agreement ("but sometimes we have to raise a price to cover freight and packing"). Requires exclusive area representation. Send slides or samples of small items, or call for appointment. "I rely on finding new craftspeople at the major shows, but welcome slides and samples if the work has already been sold at wholesale." Reports in 2-3 weeks. Work may be shipped or hand-delivered.
Profile: "We have a wholesale business that sells to interior decorators and furniture stores across the country (as well as here in the gallery). Usually I like to show the work of 1 potter in 1 place with a sign showing his name. At other times, we display teapots or pitchers together. Flamewear and delicate porcelain usually have displays of their own. In the summer, many of our customers are tourists who have been here before and who expect to find new work that is smartly styled, of high quality and with a wide range of prices. We have shows during the summer, usually for 2-4 weeks, and we publicize." Heaviest wholesale buying time: spring; best selling time: summer.

SUNRISE, 115 Main St., Bar Harbor ME 04609. (207)288-5190. Managers: Michael and Leah Rae Donahue. Craft shop. Estab. 1970. Represents 75-100 craftworkers.
Acceptable Work: Considers clay, leather, fiber, metal, wood and glass. Specializes in fine jewelry and leather. "We have more production-line items than one-of-a-kind, but sell both." Price range: $1-500; bestsellers: $20-75.
Terms: Buys outright and sometimes works on consignment ("if production costs prohibit a wholesale price that is reasonable"); 30% commission. Retail price set by joint agreement. Requires exclusive area representation. Send slides and call for appointment. Reports in 1 week. Work may be shipped or hand-delivered. Dealer pays insurance on exhibited work. Display time: up to 3 months.
Profile: "The shop has large glass display windows in the front providing excellent natural light; spot lights are used to pick up the darker corners. The walls are white on 2 sides with the third being diagonal varnished hardwood to provide hanging space for leather bags. The floors are brightly varnished hardwood. Work is displayed by craftworker. Handbags are hung, smaller leather pieces are in glass cases. Jewelry is in glass cases with conventional trays and props. During the tourist season, we get every kind of walking tourist imaginable as we are right in the center of town on Main Street. The average buyer is of middle to upper income brackets and concerned with both design and function." Heaviest wholesale buying time: early spring; best selling time: August-September. Open June-September.

SWAMP JOHN'S, Perkins Cove, Ogunquit ME 03907. (207)646-9414. Contact: Thomas Young. Craft shop. Estab. 1970. Represents 10-12 craftworkers.
Acceptable Work: Considers jewelry and leatherworking. Fine, one-of-a-kind and handmade production-line items; utiliarian only. Price range: $15-900; bestsellers: $25-100.
Terms: Buys outright. Gallery sets retail price. Requires exclusive area representation. Work may be shipped or hand-delivered. Dealer pays shipping and insurance for exhibited work.
Profile: "Since most everything is bought outright, it is usually displayed until it sells. Everything is displayed attractively; jewelry in exotic hardwood cases and in a manner to make it appealing to the consumer. We carry exclusive works from the other shops in our area." Heaviest wholesale buying time: March-April; best selling time: summer.

TOMTEGARD, INC., SCANDINAVIAN DESIGN INTERIORS, Central St., Rockport ME 04856. Contact: Doris Nuesse or Marcia Sims. Furniture and accessory store. Estab. 1974. Represents 5 New England craftworkers.

Acceptable Work: Considers ceramics; pottery; wall hangings; weavings; woodcrafting; and furniture. Fine, one-of-a-kind and handmade production-line items only. Price range: $3-150; bestsellers: $3-90.
Terms: Buys outright and works on consignment; 33⅓% commission. Retail price set by joint agreement. Requires exclusive area representation. Reports as soon as possible. Work may be shipped or hand-delivered. Dealer pays insurance for exhibited work.
Profile: "We are a modern design shop specializing in the 'Scandinavian look' on the Maine Coast." Displays work 6-12 months. The average customer is 35-60 years old. Heaviest wholesale buying time: spring; best selling time: summer.

THE VICTORIAN STABLE, Box 185, Damariscotta ME 04543. (207)563-3810. Mrs. M.H. Plummer. Craft shop/gallery. Estab. 1969. Represents 150 Maine craftworkers.
Acceptable Work: Considers batik, decoupage, dollmaking, glass art, jewelry, leatherworking, metalsmithing, needlecrafts, paper mache, pottery, quilting, scrimshaw, soft sculpture, tole painting, wall hangings, weavings and woodcrafting. "All hanging items should have appropriate hardware." One-of-a-kind and limited production items. Price range: $5-300; bestsellers: $5-100.
Terms: Works on consignment; 25% commission. Retail price set by joint agreement. "It's helpful if the item is priced for sale including our commission." Call for appointment. Reports in 3 weeks. Dealer pays fire insurance only.
Profile: "Items are displayed in the stalls and on the main floor of an elegant stable." Upper income and repeat customers. Heaviest wholesale buying time: spring; best selling time: summer and fall.

THE WHARF SHOP, Lubec ME 04652. Contact: R.O. Voight. Craft/gift shop "with wood stoves and other energy devices". Estab. 1970. Represents 5-10 Maine craftworkers. Heaviest wholesale buying time: spring; best selling time: summer.
Acceptable Work: Considers candlemaking, ceramics, glass art, jewelry, leatherworking, metalsmithing, needlecrafts, pottery, wall hangings, weavings and woodcrafting. One-of-a-kind designer pieces only. Price range: $1-250.
Terms: Buys outright and works on consignment; 20% commission. Retail price set by joint agreement. Write with SASE. Reports in 1 week. Work may be shipped or hand delivered. Dealer pays insurance on exhibited work.

YANKEE ARTISAN, 119 Front St., Bath ME 04530. (207)443-6215. Craft shop. Estab. 1970. Represents 100 Maine craftworkers.
Acceptable Work: Considers batik; candlemaking; ceramics; clothing; dollmaking; jewelry; leatherworking; needlecrafts; pottery; quilting; soft sculpture; wall hangings; weavings; and woodcrafting. One-of-a-kind and handmade production-line items. Price range: 25¢-$150; bestsellers: 25¢-$55.
Terms: Works on consignment. Retail price set by joint agreement. Hand-delivered work only. Unsold consigned pieces returned after 6 months.
Profile: "We're located in historic district on downtown waterfront." Best selling time: July-August and December.

Maryland

APPALACHIANA, 10400 Old Georgetown Rd., Bethesda MD 20014. (301)530-6770. President: Joan A. Farrell. Vice President: Ann S. Powell. Craft shop. Estab. 1970. Represents 300 craftworkers.
Acceptable Work: Considers ceramics; candles; jewelry; metalsmithing; pottery; quilts; wall hangings; weavings; and woodcrafting. Price range: $1-400; best sellers: $1-30.
Terms: Buys outright. Retail price set by shop. Reports in 2 weeks. Work may be shipped or hand-delivered. Dealer pays insurance on exhibited work.
Profile: "Volume and diversity make our shop unique." Heaviest wholesale buying time: fall; best selling time: fall-Christmas.

ARTS/OBJECTS, 1004 Reisterstown Rd., Baltimore MD 21208. (301)484-5355. Owners: Irvin and Nita Borenstein. "Mini-department store." Estab. 1961. Represents 75-100 craftworkers.
Acceptable Work: Considers batik; ceramics; metalsmithing; glass; pottery; quilts; soft sculpture; weavings; and wall hangings. Special need for one-of-a-kind art pieces. Price range: $1-500; bestsellers: $15-100.
Terms: Buys outright. Retail price set by joint agreement; "we must make 100% mark-up." Requires exclusive area representation. Reports in 2 weeks. Work may be shipped or hand-

delivered; dealer pays insurance on exhibited work.
Profile: "We are a mini-department store. We have an art gallery, but we also show crafts mixed with commercially-made items. We do custom floral (silk, dried, paper) and use many containers. In addition, we have an interior design studio which uses many one-of-a-kind 'art pieces.'" Heaviest wholesale buying time: fall, preparing for Christmas; best selling time: Christmas season. Customers are "high income, well-educated, sophisticated. They expect the finest and most unusual."

BALTIMORE MUSEUM OF ART, Art Museum Dr., Baltimore MD 21218. (301)396-6338. Manager: Margaret Baker. Museum gallery/gift shop. Represents 10-12 craftworkers.
Acceptable Work: Considers batik; ceramics; decoupage; dollmaking; jewelry; needlecrafts; pottery; quilting; soft sculpture; wall hangings; weavings; and woodcrafting. Primitive and fine one-of-a-kind peices. "We're always looking for craftworkers who will carry out an idea based on some item from our collection. I usually spy a talent, then ask to use his talent in our direction." Price range: 25¢-$150; bestsellers: $1-25.
Terms: Works on consignment; 40% commission. Retail price set by joint agreement. Reports in 1 week. Work may be shipped or hand-delivered.
Profile: "A large percentage of our gifts are items based on the Museum's collection, exclusive to us. We stock a large selection of art books, re-inforcing our collection." Small items displayed in locked cases, larger items on wall shelves out of customers' reach. Heaviest wholesale buying time: September-October; best selling time: fall-Christmas.

BECKY'S COUNTRY NOOK, Frederick County Square, Frederick MD 21701. (301)663-1155. Owner: Becky Higginbotham. Craft shop "representing craftworkers on a wholesale and retail basis." Estab. 1975. Represents 125 craftworkers.
Acceptable Work: Considers clothing; decoupage; dollmaking; glass art; needlecrafts; pottery; quilting; soft sculpture; tole painting; wall hangings; weavings; woodcrafting; and Christmas ornaments. "Everything must be of a country or traditional nature." Handmade production-line items. Price range: 50¢-$60; bestsellers: $1.50-30.
Terms: Works on consignment and buys outright; 40% commission. Retail price set by joint agreement. Reports in 2 weeks. Work may be shipped or hand-delivered; dealer pays insurance on exhibited work.
Profile: "We handle everything of traditional/country nature, from corsages and Christmas ornaments to quilts and furniture. Items are displayed as best to give a country, homey overall look to the shop." Heaviest wholesale buying time: spring-summer; best selling time: October-December.

CALICO CAT, INC., 2137 Gwynn Oak Ave., Baltimore MD 21207. (301)944-2450. President: Bruni Obriecht. Gallery and gift shop. Estab. 1968. Represents 200 craftworkers.
Acceptable Work: Considers candles; clothing; decoupage; dollmaking; glass art; jewelry; pottery; quilting; and woodcrafting. Price range $1-350; bestsellers: $5-30.
Terms: Works on consignment and buys outright; 30% commission. Retail price set by craftworker. Reports in 3 weeks. Query first.
Profile: Crafts displayed together, apart from the gallery. Also sponsors craft demonstrations. Best selling and heaviest wholesale buying time: Christmas season.

CHESAPEAKE BAY MARITIME MUSEUM SHOP, Box 83, St. Michaels MD 21663. (301)745-2916. Manager: V. Louise Stewart. Museum gift shop. Estab. 1969. Represents 10-12 craftworkers. "We prefer work done by local craftspeople but will accept craftwork from other areas as long as the theme is correct."
Acceptable Work: Considers candlemaking, ceramics, clothing, decoupage, dollmaking, glass art, jewelry, needlecrafts, pottery and small woodcrafted items. Especially needs sailor dolls and soft sculptures in theme. "All craftwork must pertain to the Chesapeake Bay—being nautical or wildfowl in nature." Also needs "wooden models of Hoopers Strait Lighthouse located here on Museum grounds." Specializes in driftwood painting, ceramics (in nautical colors and decorations) and handcarved items (no scrimshaw). No bright flashy colors. One-of-a-kind (usually on consigned work) and mostly handmade production-line items (bought outright). Price range: 50¢-$500; bestsellers: $1-19.95.
Terms: Buys outright and works on consignment; 25% commission. Retail price set by joint agreement. Prefers exclusive area representation. Send slides/photos with SASE. Reports in 1-2 weeks. Work may be shipped or hand delivered. "We hold consigned work through the busy season (May-September 30). A check is mailed within a week of the sale of the item. Items may be removed at any time by the craftsman if he feels he has a better opportunity to sell elsewhere."

Profile: "We are located on the grounds of the Chesapeake Bay Maritime Museum. There are bus tours coming from DC and metropolitan areas for lunches and dinners (at the Crab Claw Restaurant next door) so they visit the shop. The museum has docking facilities for a large number of boats and also has tours scheduled during the peak season." Customers: school groups (early spring); senior citizens of low incomes (spring, summer and fall); young marrieds and singles (spring and summer); government and embassy workers; boaters (late summer and fall); and tourists. Heaviest wholesale buying time: late February-April (for handmade production-line items), late April-early May (for consigned and one-of-a-kind items); best selling time: July-September.
To Break In: "Be sure you can supply the quantities which you quote on time."

THE CRAFT GALLERY, LTD., White Flint, Kensington MD 20795. (301)770-6990. Contact: Marvin Wies. Craft shop/gallery. Estab. 1969. Represents 200 American craftworkers.
Acceptable Work: Considers batik; ceramics; glass art; jewelry; leatherworking; metalsmithing; pottery; soft sculpture; and woodcrafting. Fine one-of-a-kind and handmade production-line items. Price range: $1-$1,000; bestsellers: $1-50.
Terms: Buys outright. Shop sets retail price; "We will discuss retail prices with craftsperson." Dealer pays shipping to shop.
Profile: "We're in a 125-store shopping mall catering to mostly college educated, government employees and professionals. Heaviest wholesale buying time: summer; best selling time: fall-Christmas.

THE CRAFT STUDIO OF TAKOMA PARK, 7040 Carroll Ave., Takoma Park MD 20012. (301)270-3138. Contact: D. Macchiavelli. Craft shop and gallery. Estab. 1977. Represents 40-50 craftworkers. "Craft artists working in the East are easier and less expensive to deal with as far as shipping."
Acceptable Work: Considers batik, candlemaking, ceramics, clothing, jewelry, pottery, soft sculpture, wall hangings and weavings. "I am interested in enameled work, semi-production type, and also wood forms, including kitchen items. I am very interested in designer crafts in any area, whether it be quilts, contemporary or traditional—the criteria is high quality professional." Also takes handmade production-line items. Price range: 50¢-$300; bestsellers: $8-25.
Terms: Buys outright and works on consignment; 33 1/3% commission. Retail price set by joint agreement on consignment work. Send slides/brochure. Reports in 4 weeks. Requested work may be shipped or hand-delivered.
Profile: "We are located in an area outside of Washington DC which is having some re-growth and restoration of its historic architecture. Therefore, most of our area is very aware of the beauty of preserving and renewing architecture and ideals. Our atmosphere is casual and warm, to encourage conversation with our customers. Our craftwork is displayed as creatively as possible. We do not display according to artist, or subject matter. I like to have an array of work interspersed to encourage browsing. I re-display work in the shop every couple of weeks. Consignment work can stay up to one year, depending on the type of work it is, but generally changes completely every six months." Heaviest wholesale buying time: September-January (for Christmas); best selling time: October-February.
To Break In: "I am very interested in original concepts and designs of work. I stress high-quality in the work and differing techniques are very welcome. Being prompt in filling orders is a must."

THE EIGHT HANDS AT THE FARM WOMEN'S MARKET, 7155 Wisconsin Ave., Bethesda MD 20014. (301)652-9600. Vice President/Publicity: Jacqui Melpolder. Craft shop and gallery. Estab. 1966. Represents 40 craftworkers.
Acceptable Work: Considers batik; ceramics; clothing; dollmaking; glass art; jewelry; leatherworking; metalsmithing; needlecrafts; pottery; and woodcrafting. "Would like more variety in printmaking—we have batik, woodblock and lithographs now." Price range 75¢-$250; bestsellers: $5-75.
Terms: Works on consignment and buys outright; 33 1/3% commission. Reports in 4 weeks. Work may be shipped or hand-delivered.
Profile: Jewelry and metalwork are displayed in locked cases; all other items are shown on open shelves and wall displays. Heaviest wholesale buying time: June; best selling time: fall. "Our customers range from US Senators to national news personalities to small children; with most being in the middle to upper income bracket."

ELLICOTT B&O R.R. STATION MUSEUM, Main St. & Maryland Ave., Ellicott City MD 21043. Director: Sally Bright. Museum gift shop. Estab. 1976. Represents 5 craftworkers.

Acceptable Work: Considers ceramics, clothing, jewelry, leatherworking, metalsmithing and needlecrafts relating to railroad or historical (1830) theme. Especially needs small leather items, scrimshaw, soft sculpture and wooden items pertaining to railroading design. Specializes in handmade production-line items. Price range: 10¢-100; bestsellers: 10¢-$10.
Terms: Buys outright. Retail price set by joint agreement. Send slides and resume with SASE. Reports in 2 weeks. Work may be shipped or hand-delivered.
Profile: "As a small gift shop in a railroad museum we try to carry unique items centering around railroading. We have a large tourist type flow, but also an equally large number of repeat customers who are railroad enthusiasts." Heaviest wholesale buying time: prespring and prefall; best selling time: summer and Christmas.

FAVORITE THINGS, York & Monkton Rds., Hereford MD 21111. (301)472-2466. Owner: Betsy Swann. Specialty shop, emphasizing dollhouses and miniatures. Estab. 1973. Represents 10-15 craftworkers. Price range: $1.50-700; bestsellers: $1.50-100. Works on consignment and buys outright; 33% commission. Retail price set by joint agreement. Work may be shipped or hand-delivered.
Acceptable Work: Considers ceramics; dollmaking; jewelry; pottery; soft sculpture; and especially, dollhouses and miniatures. Primitive and fine handmade production-line items.
Profile: "Whimsey, variety and quality make our shop unique." Heaviest wholesale buying and best selling time: pre-Christmas. Most customers are in the upper and middle to upper income bracket.

GALLERY ON THE PARK, 1111 Sligo Creek Pkwy., Takoma Park MD 20012. (301)270-6633. Owners: Jack and Vaughn Hammond. Craft shop/gallery. Estab. 1973. Represents 40-50 craftworkers.
Acceptable Work: Considers batik; candlemaking; handcrafted ceramics; glass art; jewelry; leatherworking; metalsmithing; pottery; soft sculpture; weavings; wall hangings; and woodcrafting. "We're always looking for items with circus motif." Fine one-of-a-kind and handmade production-line items. Price range: $1-100; bestsellers: $1-50.
Terms: Works on consignment and buys outright; 33% commission. Retail price set by joint agreement. "We'll be happy to answer inquiries, but we rarely order or accept items we have not seen and approved in person. Call for an appointment; bring a representative sampling of work and/or photos; be organized; have a price list and order forms. And, don't promise what can't be delivered." Reports in 2 weeks.
Profile: "We display craft items grouped by artist's name. Minimum display time: 30 days; 60 maximum on consignment items. Our warm, relaxed atmosphere and reasonable prices make our shop unique." Heaviest wholesale buying time: fall and winter. "Our customers are mostly moderate income. Many are repeat customers, the majority having little knowledge of crafts/art, but are interested in learning."

THE GREAT CHASE, c/o The Tifanee Tree, 4949 Allan Rd., Chevy Chase MD 20016. (301)656-6228. Owners: Frances and Edward Garfinkle. Craft/gift shop located at White Flint, North Bethesda, Maryland 20795. See The Tifanee Tree, Chevy Chase, below.

HANDS OF MAN, 1709 Reisterstown Rd., Baltimore MD 21208. (301)484-2114. Contact: Edie Brown or Sue Talles. Craft shop. Estab. 1974. Represents 200 craftworkers.
Acceptable Work: Considers batik, ceramics, glass art, jewelry, leatherworking, metalsmithing, pottery, soft sculpture, wall hangings, weavings, quilting, dollmaking and woodcrafting. Price range: $2-500; bestsellers: $5-30.
Terms: Works on consignment and buys outright; 40% commission. Dealer sets retail price. Send slides or call for appointment. Reports in 2 weeks. Work may be shipped or hand-delivered. Dealer pays insurance on exhibited work.
Profile: "We represent many craftworkers, and we're in a large area with 5 other boutiques. Our traffic flow is good, and our display is also excellent, though it changes constantly." Best selling time: Christmas and June, "but there's a steady flow throughout the year." Shop located in an upper income area.

MARSON LTD., 6 Shawan Rd., Cockeysville MD 21030. (301)666-7161. Owners: A.G. Marsiglia and S. Gamson. Gallery. Estab. 1971. Currently emphasizes Oriental art.
Acceptable Work: Considers batik and prints. Fine one-of-a-kind items; decorative. Price range: $5-3,500; bestsellers: $5-125.
Terms: Buys outright. Work may be shipped or hand-delivered; dealer pays insurance on exhibited work.

Profile: "We specialize in original Oriental art and have over 1,000 shows annually, through traveling sales representatives at universities, museums and art centers. Each piece of art is individually matted and the opening covered with Mylar. It's also labelled with the artist's name, country of origin, birth date, medium, title and price." Best selling time: fall.

MARYLAND HISTORICAL SOCIETY MUSEUM SHOP, 201 W. Monument St., Baltimore MD 21201. (301)685-3750, ext. 30. Contact: Shop Manager. Museum gift shop. Estab. 1977. Prefers Maryland craftspeople.
Acceptable Work: Considers glass art, jewelry, metalsmithing, pottery, quilting and scrimshaw. Specializes in fine art with a nostalgic flavor and Maryland background. One of a kind and handmade production-line items.
Terms: Buys outright. Shop sets retail price. Contact by all means OK. Reports in 1 week. Work may be be shipped or hand-delivered.
Profile: Work is displayed behind glass and on open shelves. "Because we are a historical museum we try to have our items represent some historical type." Customers are school children, researchers and other persons interested in Maryland history. Best selling time: preChristmas.

POTTER'S GUILD OF BALTO, INC., 201 Homeland Ave., Baltimore MD 21212. (301)433-9738. President: Elaine Ozol. Gallery. Estab. 1955. Represents 50 Baltimore craftworkers. Specializes in pottery. One-of-a-kind items. Price range: $1-200; bestsellers: $4-50. "We accept members who are professional potters, willing to volunteer some time towards the maintenance and operation of the guild." Retail price set by craftworker.
Profile: "Work is done by individual professional craftworkers. We're a guild whose members exchange ideas, attend many workshops, teach and try to improve/promote the craft." Displays change monthly, "except during Christmas when it runs from November-December." Best selling time: Christmas. "Many students and educators are customers, most from middle to upper income."

THE STORE, LTD., Village of Cross Keys, Baltimore MD 21210. (301)323-2350. Owners: Betty Cooke and William O. Steinmetz. Design store. Estab. 1965. Represents approximately 10 designers and craftpeople.
Acceptable Work: "We represent all materials—fabric, metal, clay, wood, leather, glass, etc. Our items are primarily utilitarian, i.e., clothing, gourmet utensils, toys, boxes. The standards for our store are high for design, style and workmanship." Bestsellers: $50-200.
Terms: Works outright and on consignment; 33⅓% commission. Retail price set by joint agreement. Work may be shipped or hand-delivered; dealer pays insurance on exhibited work.

THE TIFANEE TREE, Montgomery Mall, Bethesda MD 20034. (202)333-4323. Contact: Frances or Edward Garfinkle. Craft shop and gallery. Estab. 1970. Represents 200-300 craftworkers.
Acceptable Work: Considers candlemaking, ceramics, dollmaking, glass art, jewelry, metalsmithing, pottery, scrimshaw, soft sculpture, wall hangings, weaving and woodcrafting. Fine one-of-a-kind and handmade production-line items. Price range: $1-$1,500; bestsellers: $10-100.
Terms: Buys outright and works on consignment; 40% commission. Retail price set by joint agreement. Send slides or call for appointment. Reports within 3 weeks. Work may be shipped or hand-delivered. Dealer pays insurance on exhibited work.
Profile: "Ours is a gallery of crafts, displayed in a setting of what we call 'organized clutter,' permeated by a feeling of fantasy and whimsy. In a very full setting, we do our best to give each artist an important display. We feature the name and area of country and generally play up the craftsperson." Display period: 4-6 weeks. "Customers are 20-50, professional people ($25,000+ incomes) with an overall sophisticated taste." Heaviest wholesale buying time: summer; best selling time: fall-Christmas.

THE TOMLINSON CRAFT COLLECTION, 711 W. 40th St., Baltimore MD 21211. (301)338-1572. Contact: Ginny Tomlinson. Craft shop/gallery. Estab. 1971. Represents 400 craftworkers.
Acceptable Work: Considers batik; candles; ceramics; clothing; glass art; jewelry; leatherworking; metalsmithing; pottery; quilting; soft sculpture; wall hangings; weavings; and woodcrafting. Fine one-of-a-kind and handmade production-line items. Price range: $15-500; bestsellers: $3-50.

Terms: Buys outright; a few large pieces accepted on consignment. Retail price set by joint agreement. Reports as soon as possible. Work may be shipped or hand-delivered by previous consent. Dealer pays return shipping and insurance for exhibited work. Heaviest wholesale buying time: April-May and November-December; best selling time: December.

THE VILLAGE LEATHER SHOP, 6417 Windsor Mill Rd., Woodlawn MD 21207. (301)944-7671. Owner: Hank Yeatman. Craft shop. Estab. 1970. Represents 2 craftworkers.
Acceptable Work: Considers jewelry and leatherworking; especially needs handmade buckles. Price range: $2-500; bestsellers: $5-125.
Terms: Works on consignment and buys outright; 10-20% commission. Retail price set by joint agreement. Reports in 2 weeks. Work may be shipped or hand-delivered; dealer pays insurance on exhibited work.
Profile: Shop is in a rustic setting. Heaviest wholesale buying time: summer and fall; best selling time: summer, fall and Christmas. Customers are "in the 25-50 range, middle to upper middle class."

WASHINGTON COUNTY MUSEUM OF FINE ARTS, Box 423, City Park, Hagerstown MD 21740. (301)739-5727. Director: H. Paul Kotun. Museum gift shop. Estab. 1931. Represents 6-10 craftworkers.
Acceptable Work: Considers ceramics, glass art, jewelry, leatherworking, metalsmithing, quilting, soft sculpture, wall hangings, weavings and woodcrafting. Primitive, fine art and contemporary crafts. One-of-a-kind and handmade production-line items. Price range: $1.50-500; bestsellers: $1.50-100.
Terms: Buys outright and works on consignment; 20% commission. Retail price set by gallery or joint agreement. Requires exclusive area representation. Send resume or call for appointment. Reports in 2 weeks. Work may be shipped or hand delivered. Dealer pays insurance on exhibited work.
Profile: Gift shop is in lobby area. Permanent display in glass cases and on counter tops. Customers: child-adult. Heaviest wholesale buying time: July-November; best selling time: November-December.

Massachusetts

ALIANZA, 140 Newbury St., Boston MA 02106. (617)262-2385. Contact: Karen Rotenberg. Craft/gift shop. Estab. 1965. Represents 60 craftworkers.
Acceptable Work: Considers ceramics, glass art, jewelry, metalsmithing, pottery, soft sculpture, wall hangings, weavings and woodcrafting. Especially needs "soft sculpture or other related craft items for our new 'Softworks' boutique." Specializes in a mixture of primitive and contemporary crafts. One-of-a-kind and especially handmade production-line items. Price range: $5-300; bestsellers: $5-50.
Terms: Buys outright. Shop sets retail price. Requires exclusive area representation. Call for appointment. Work may be shipped or hand delivered. "Always give a reasonable delivery date."
Profile: "Alianza is a unique mixture of Latin American ethnic crafts displayed on handcarved Mexican furniture, and contemporary American crafts shown on white pedestals. There is a great emphasis on color, a common element in both groupings. This fall, we expanded the range of our handcrafts with the opening of 'Softworks'—a separate boutique at Alianza featuring sculptural pillows, soft mirrors, satin flowers, etc. We are located on Newbury Street which has a high concentration of galleries and select boutiques attracting a receptive audience of all ages, generally affluent and well educated." Heaviest wholesale buying time: spring-summer; best selling time: fall, especially December.

ARTISAN'S GALLERY, South Market, Faneuil Hall Marketplace, Boston MA 02109. See Artisan's Cooperative, Chadds Ford, Pennsylvania.

ARTISAN'S COOPERATIVE, 16 Center St., Nantucket Island MA 02554. See Artisan's Cooperative, Chadds Ford, Pennsylvania.

ARTISAN'S COOPERATIVE, Straight Wharf, Nantucket Island MA 02554. Seasonal, May-October. See Artisan's Cooperative, Chadds Ford, Pennsylvania.

AYN'S SHUTTLE SHOP, Box 1207, Lake Ave., Oak Bluffs-Martha's Vineyard MA 02557. (617)693-0134. Owner: Ann Chase. Craft and gift shop. Estab. 1955. Represents 40 craftworkers.

Acceptable Work: Considers batik; ceramics; Christmas ornaments; dollmaking; glass art; jewelry; leatherworking; metalsmithing; needlecrafts; pottery; tole painting; wall hangings; weaving; and woodcrafting. "We're always looking for something new; e.g., I'd like some more pottery, dinnerware sets, unusual note paper and something for the men. It would be best in earth-tone colors, with samples on display for orders." Fine handmade production-line items. Price range: $2-150; bestsellers: $2-30.
Terms: Works on consignment; 30% commission. Retail price set by joint agreement. Reports in 2 weeks. Work may be shipped or hand-delivered; dealer pays insurance on exhibited work.
Profile: "We're the only handicraft shop in this area; we're well established and business increases every year. All items are in full view. I've found that several items of the same craft displayed together sell better than having several types mixed together." Heaviest wholesale buying time: spring-summer; best selling time: summer. Customers are primarily tourists "who want something different than what's at home. If they like it, they'll buy it regardless of income."

BOSTON ATHENAEUM GALLERY, 10½ Beacon St., Boston MA 02108. (617)227-0270.
Acceptable Work: Considers ceramics; decoupage; glass art; jewelry; mobiles; needlecrafts; pottery; sculpture; soft sculpture; wall hangings; and weavings. Price range: $25-10,000.
Terms: No commission. Retail price set by craftworker. All methods of contact OK. SASE. 1 month exposure.

BOSTON BAKED BEADS, 12-D Mt. Desert St., Bar Harbor ME 04609. Off-season, October-April address: 64 Wendell St., Cambridge MA 02138. Owners: Paul DeVore and Gail Gutradt. Craft and gift shop. Estab. 1974. Represents 50 craftworkers.
Primitive and fine handmade production-line items. Price range: 25¢-$50; bestsellers: 25¢-$20.
Terms: Buys outright. Retail price set by shop. Reports in 2 weeks. Work may be shipped or hand-delivered.
Profile: "We specialize in handcrafted beads—about 100 varieties. Customers are encouraged to create their own jewelry in the store." Heaviest wholesale buying time: February-April. "Our customers are mainly young families."

CARDS & SHARDS, 45 S. Main St., Cohasset MA 02025. (617)383-0729. Contact: Dick or Sue Straley. Gift shop. Estab. 1965. Represents 12 craftworkers.
Acceptable Work: Considers ceramics, clothing, glass art, jewelry, metalsmithing, pottery, scrimshaw, tole painting, wall hangings, weaving, and woodcrafting. No fine art crafts. One-of-a-kind and handmade production-line items. Price range: $10-150; bestsellers: $10-100.
Terms: Works on consignment; 40% commission. Craftworker sets retail price. Requires exclusive area representation. Call for appointment. Reports in one week. Work may be shipped or hand delivered.
Profile: "Displays are placed for the best viewing (about 1 month). If items aren't moving, merchandise is moved for a different appearance." Has special displays and advance promotion. Shop located in an affluent community. Best selling and heaviest wholesale buying time: May-December.

CAT'S CRADLE, 244 Commercial St., Provincetown MA 02657. Contact: Alice Foley. Craft shop. Estab. 1976. Represents 40 craftworkers.
Acceptable Work: Specializes in pottery but has some other media as well. Unique clay work of any type, especially that which relates to Provincetown clientele or seashore. No gimmickry or tourist pieces. One-of-a-kind and production-line items. Price range: up to $200; bestsellers: $10-50.
Terms: Works some on consignment and buys outright; 30% commission. Retail price set by joint agreement. Requires exclusive area representation. Shipping by UPS only. Dealer pays shipping on outright purchases by shop.
Profile: Shop is in center of town in second oldest house in Provincetown. Customers are tourists. Best selling time: summer.

THE CRAFT BASKET, 118 Water St., Williamstown MA 01267. (413)458-8247. Owner: Dorothy L. Loomis. Craft shop. Estab. 1978. Represents 80-100 craftworkers, preferably from New England.
Acceptable Work: Considers batik, candlemaking, clothing, decoupage, glass art, jewelry, small metalsmithing, needlecrafts, pottery, quilting, stuffed animals, wall hangings, weavings and woodcrafting. Especially needs crafts appealing to college students (clothing, decor,

jewelry); items for children 4-14 years-old (toys, games, clothing in the $5-20 price range); stationery; and weavings (utilitarian, apparel, household). One-of-a-kind and handmade production-line items. Price range: $1.25-300; bestsellers: $1.25-60.
Terms: Buys outright and works on consignment; 40% commission. Retail price set by joint agreement. Call for appointment; "prefer to see the actual work. Sometimes possible for me to visit the craftsperson on scouting trips." Reports in 2 weeks. Work may be shipped or hand delivered. Dealer pays insurance on exhibited work. Display time: 3 months.
Profile: "We're located in a converted home. Work is displayed on counters and cases of natural wood with generous use of color for backgrounds. Samples of all work is continuously on display. Business hours are adjusted to meet seasonal patterns. We have regular program of newspaper and radio advertising and local promotions. Regularly scheduled demonstrations by our suppliers to acquaint customers with the crafts and foster appreciation. Located in an area of educational institutions, art appreciation and tourism." Customers: educators, industrial management, personnel, college students, artists/craftsmen, tourists; sophisticated but practical. "The way-out work does not move well." Heaviest wholesale buying time: late summer-early spring; bestselling time: December and June-August.

CRAFT CENTER, 25 Sagamore Rd., Worcester MA 01605. (617)753-8183. Manager: Alyce Pazeian. Craft shop and gallery. Estab. 1945. Represents 100 craftworkers.
Acceptable Work: Considers ceramics, glass art, jewelry, metalsmithing, pottery, soft sculpture, wall hangings, weaving, and woodcrafting. Especially needs functional stoneware pottery, small wooden objects and "any gift item for men." Specializes in fine art and contemporary crafts. One-of-a-kind and handmade production-line items. Price range: $6-200; bestsellers: $8-60.
Terms: Buys outright and works on consignment; 40% commission. Craftworker sets retail price. Requires exclusive area representation. Send at least 5 good slides plus price list and delivery method or call for appointment. Reports in 2 weeks. Work may be shipped or hand-delivered. Dealer pays insurance on exhibited work.
Profile: Displays work in cases and on shelves for at least 1 month. "We're also a craft school, plus we sponsor major craft exhibitions in our gallery." Customers are middle to upper income. Heaviest wholesale buying time: April-June; best selling time: fall.

CRAFTILY YOURS, Berkshire Common, Pittsfield MA 01201. (413)499-4285. Owners: Patrick or Anne McKernan. Craft/gift shop/gallery. Estab. 1976. Represents 100-150 New England area craftworkers.
Acceptable Work: Considers batik, candlemaking, dollmaking, glass art, jewelry, leatherworking, metalsmithing, needlecrafts, pottery, quilting, scrimshaw, soft sculpture, wall hangings, weavings, woodcrafting, photography, paintings and etchings. One-of-a-kind and handmade production-line items OK. Price range: $1-200; bestsellers: $1-45.
Terms: Buys outright and works on consignment; 33⅓% commission. Retail price set by joint agreement. Requires exclusive city representation. Call for appointment. Reports immediately. Work may be shipped or hand-delivered. Dealer pays insurance on exhibited work.
Profile: "Each craftperson's work is displayed in an area of the shop where there are varied types of crafts. For example, one cubicle has a shelf containing pottery, another containing woodworking, another quilted mats and dried flowers in baskets on the floor. We try to keep each artisan's work all together, except for window display. In addition to handcrafted items, we also serve as a gallery for local artists who wish to display and/or sell their work on a consignment basis."

DANFORTH MUSEUM SHOP, 123 Union Ave., Framingham MA 01701. (617)620-0050. Chairman: Elaine Marks. Museum gift shop. Estab. 1975. Represents 100 craftworkers.
Acceptable Work: Considers ceramics; glass art; jewelry; and pottery. Primitive and fine one-of-a-kind items; utilitarian and/or decorative. Price range: $3-250; bestsellers: $8-50.
Terms: Works on consignment; 35% commission. Retail price set by craftworker. Report time varies according to season. Work may be shipped or hand-delivered.
Profile: "Located inside the museum, the shop has display cases, shelves and bins." Best selling time: winter. "Customers are middle and upper income people with art and craft interests."

DIFFERENT DRUMMER, 41 Central St., Wellesley MA 02181. (617)235-8772. Contact: Grace M. Loerch or Ruth Westlake. Gift shop. Estab. 1973. Represents 30+ craftworkers.
Acceptable Work: Considers batik, ceramics, glass art, jewelry, leatherworking, metalsmithing, pottery, wall hangings, weavings and woodcrafting. Especially needs lively decora-

tive accessories. Specializes in contemporary crafts. One-of-a-kind and handmade production-line items. Price range: $1.50-500; bestsellers: $1.50-25.
Terms: Buys outright. Shop sets retail price. Requires exclusive area representation. Send resume, slides or call for appointment. SASE. Reports in 2 weeks. Work may be shipped or hand delivered.
Profile: "Usually we keep the work of a particular artist displayed in 1 area, unless we are using an item to highlight or complement a special arrangement. A new artist is featured in a center island to introduce the work to our customers. We like to have photos of this person when possible." Customers: young to middle aged professionals, 30,000-50,000 incomes; interested in schools, politics and the arts. Heaviest wholesale buying time: late summer-early fall; best selling time: holidays (especially Christmas) and May-June.
To Break In: "Be organized, know how to price, be fair in charging for packing, and send clean ready to display merchandise."

DIVIDED HOUSE INC., 255 Elm St.—Rt. 110, Salisbury MA 01950. (617)462-8423. Contact: Mary or Larry Cuddire. Gift shop. Estab. 1972. Represents 3-5 craftworkers.
Acceptable Work: Considers dollmaking, scrimshaw and woodcrafting. Especially needs dollhouse miniatures. "Most of the crafts in our shop would pertain to the dollhouse and miniature business. These are the finer pieces that appeal to the adult collector, but not necessarily expensive." One-of-a-kind and handmade production-line items. Price range: 49¢-$140; bestsellers: 49¢-$95.
Terms: Buys outright and works on consignment; 30% commission. Retail price set by joint agreement. Call for appointment. Reports in 1 week. Work may be shipped or hand delivered.
Profile: "We are in a 300 year-old house. Decor is arranged in the rooms on the first floor. Dollhouses are made in the workshop next door." Heaviest wholesale buying time: Christmas and summer; best selling time: Christmas.
To Break In: "Have brochure for follow-up or business cards. Know what prices you need (not just going by what is seen on the retail shelf). Don't just duplicate what is already on the market. Do try new things and ideas."

DODGE HOUSE ART GALLERY, 426 Main St., Chatham MA 02633. (617)945-1231. Contact: H. Latham Kent. Gallery. Estab. 1968. Represents 25 craftworkers.
Acceptable Work: Considers ceramics; glass art; and pottery. Especially needs "small, realistic sculptures." Fine one-of-a-kind pieces. Price range: $10-500; bestsellers: $10-150.
Terms: Works on consignment; 33⅓% commission. Retail price set by joint agreement. Requires exclusive area representation. Reports in 1 week. Work may be shipped or hand-delivered; craftworker pays insurance on exhibited work.
Profile: "Items are displayed in an antique setting. The gallery is housed in a 1750 homestead. We specialize in fine quality, original artwork sensibly priced." Best selling time: June-Labor Day. "Our customers appreciate traditional artwork."

ECHOES (formerly Ali Baba), 99 Mt. Auburn St., Harvard Square, Cambridge MA 02138. (617)864-2777. Contact: Anne Brinton or Frank Cullen. Museum style gift shop. Estab. 1975. Represents 20+ craftworkers.
Acceptable Work: Open to any moderately-priced work in any media, including polymers and other less traditional substances, (except as noted below). All items must be period pieces, museum reproductions or art themes from any culture or period (African, European, Modern Art, Asian, etc.). These can be jewelry, sculptures, greeting cards, ceramics, glass art, stationery, or plastics. No animal slaughter products (leather, fur, bone, ivory, scrimshaw, shells, feathers, bone ash or human life support products in critical supply such as coral). Production-line items only. Price range $5-75; bestsellers: $10-20.
Terms: Buys outright on 30 day billing. Shop sets retail price. Requires exclusive area representation on most items. Call for appointment. Ship work UPS; include invoices. Shop pays shipping on goods purchased outright.
Profile: New and expanding shop in high volume area. Prefer hard-line goods to soft lines but are not rigid. Heavy female clientele, well educated. Fashion lead market area. Heaviest wholesale buying time: April-November; best selling time: Christmas, late spring and late summer.

ELLIOT DESIGNS JEWELRY, 8 Arnold St., Needham MA 02194. (617)449-3131. President: Herschel Queen. Jewelry studio and gallery. Estab. 1960.
Acceptable Work: Considers contemporary gold and silver jewelry only. One-of-a-kind and handmade production-line items. "We take only extremely fine finished pieces that stick to

gold and silver for their main qualities. We do not purchase any plastics or other metals. We like semi-precious and precious stones (no jasper): malachite, turquoise, tourmaline, pearl, etc. We do like some wood combinations. Our best sellers are earrings, neckpieces and rings in that order. Price range: $2-1,500; bestsellers: $18-65.
Terms: Buys outright and works on consignment. Retail price set by joint agreement. Write with resume and describe products, prices and qualities. Prepare to ship samples if we request. Reports in 2 weeks. Work may be shipped or hand delivered.
Profile: "We have 5 galleries, our studio gallery in Needham and a gallery at 4 locations listed under 'Shops for Pappagallo.' All shops are done in contemporary styling using much natural wood with a very large accessory groupings of antique cases and furniture. Customers range from students in the Boston colleges to upper and highest incomes in the Newbury St. and Chestnut Hill shops. Our customers prefer to frequent our shops because they can buy an unusually large selection of pieces—from earrings to match their clothing purchases to pill/powder vials, custom made wedding bands and other specially made and ordered pieces, commonplace to exotic." Heaviest wholesale buying time: fall; best selling time: fall and December.

ESSEX INSTITUTE MUSEUM SHOP, 132 Essex St., Salem MA 01970. (617)744-3390. Managers: Mrs. Dwain Smith and Mrs. Albert Goodhue. Museum gift shop. Estab. 1972. Represents 10 craftworkers.
Acceptable Work: Considers ceramics, metalsmithing, pottery, scrimshaw and tole painting. Especially needs museum-oriented and Salem, Massachusetts-oriented items. Also "interested in having our logo and other museum designs reproduced on pottery and toleware." Specializes in fine arts. Handmade production-line items only. Price range: $3-25; bestsellers: $10-15.
Terms: Buys outright. Retail price set by joint agreement. Send resume. Reports in 3 weeks. Work may be shipped or hand delivered. "Important items should be well-packed and insured by sender." Display time: 1 year.
Profile: "We have a small museum shop for 12 months a year plus a boutique in the carriage house 4 months a year." Customers: school age, and middle aged to senior citizens; tourists. Heaviest wholesale buying time: spring and late summer; best selling time: summer-fall.

BRIAN FAUNCE JEWELERS, 448 Main St., Hyannis, Cape Cod MA 02601. (617)775-1373. Contact: Brian Faunce. Craft shop. Estab. 1969. Represents 2 craftworkers.
Acceptable Work: Considers jewelry only. One-of-a-kind and handmade production-line items. Price range: $3-500; bestsellers: $6-20, $40-100.
Terms: Buys outright. Shop sets retail price. Send slides or call for appointment. Reports in 2 weeks. Work may be shipped or hand delivered.
Profile: "We are located in the oldest building on Main St. (fully restored under guidelines of National Historical Register) and use antique display cases and artifacts to display jewelry. Due to our policy of non-pressure selling and complete customer satisfaction, we have an abnormally high percentage of repeat customers for fine handcrafted jewelry." Heaviest wholesale buying and best selling time: summer-Christmas.

FOLKLORICA, 1504 Fareuil Hall Marketplace, Boston MA 02109. (617)367-1201, Contact: Ellen Kenwood Gross. Folk art gallery and jewelry emporium. Estab. 1973. Represents 6-10 craftworkers. Has stores in Boston and Stockbridge; Boston store open year-round, Stockbridge store open summers only.
Acceptable Work: Considers jewelry, ceramics, glass and wall hangings. Especially needs unusual jewelry, small wall hangings, ceramics and glass; with a "very primitive art decor or antique look, or an oriental feel." One-of-a-kind and handmade production-line items. Price range: $10-150; bestsellers: $10-25.
Acceptable Work: Buys outright and works on consignment; 34% commission. Retail price set by joint agreement. Requires exclusive area representation. Call for appointment. Reports in 1 week. Work may be shipped or hand-delivered. Dealer pays insurance on exhibited work.
Profile: "Our merchandise is unusual and prices are very reasonable. Work is displayed to enhance the visual beauty of each piece. Sophisticated upper middle-class clientele, 25-45 years old." Heaviest wholesale buying time: spring-fall; best selling time: summer and fall.
To Break In: "Have clean work and good delivery. Be ready to handle special orders for early delivery."

DANIEL FRISHMAN GALLERY, 933 Main St., Osterville MA 02655. Winter address: 14 Castle Heights Rd., Andover MA 01810. Contact: Daniel Frishman. Considers sculpture and pottery. Price range: $10-10,000.

Terms: 40% commission. Retail price set by joint agreement. Gallery may share shipping expenses. Requires exclusive area representation. Commission taken on any art sold locally after showing. Send transparencies or photos. Exhibited art insured. Sponsors openings. Open annually June-September.

THE GALLERIES, LTD., 464 Washington St., Wellesley MA 02181. (617)235-8296. Contact: Manager. Gallery. Estab. 1971. Represents 15 craftworkers.
Acceptable Work: Considers glass art and jewelry only. Jewelry must be silver, brass, or glass; weavings. Especially needs tapestries and large scale design items. "We are custom design consultants in crafts and therefore will only consider quality, professional work." One-of-a-kind pieces only. Price range: $30-5,000.
Terms: Works on consignment; 40% commission. "More specifically interested in working as crafts agents." Retail price set by joint agreement. Requires exclusive area representation. Send resume and slides with SASE or call for appointment. Reports in 4 weeks. Work may be shipped or hand-delivered, after approval only.
Profile: Work is displayed 30 days minimum. Shop is in a suburban location in a converted store front with large window areas. Customers are upper-middle class, affluent professionals; also designers and architects.
To Break In: "Interested only in top of the line items. We are essentially out of the small crafts business and dealing mostly in designer items. Do not come in without a specific appointment and interrupt sales activities. Be prepared to deliver contract items on schedule."

GALLERY OF WORLD ART INC., 745 Beacon St., Newton Centre MA 02159. (617)332-1800. Art Director: Susan Morrill. Considers sculpture. Maximum size: 72" square. Works on consignment; 40% commission. Retail price set by joint agreement. Requires exclusive area representation. Arrange interview to show slides on larger work, samples on small.

THE GARRET GALLERIES, 340 Huron Ave., Cambridge MA 02138. (617)864-2660. Contact: Beryl Jacobson. Gallery. Estab. 1972. Represents 50 craftworkers.
Acceptable Work: Considers glass art and jewelry only. Jewelry must be silver, brass, or glass, no beads. One-of-a-kind and handmade production-line items. Price range of jewelry: $8-150; bestsellers: $15-45.
Terms: Buys outright and works on consignment; 40% commission. Craftworker sets retail price. Send slides. Reports in 1 week. Requested work may be shipped or hand delivered. Dealer pays insurance on exhibited work.
Profile: "Handcrafted jewelry is a large part of the gallery business with original contemporary prints by professional artists making up the rest. Jewelry is displayed in glass cases both in the gallery and in the large street window. All items are displayed constantly." Customers: sophisticated urban professionals with high incomes, and some students. Best selling time: October-June.
To Break In: "Must have new items on a regular basis with a varied price structure."

THE GIFT HORSE OF STURBRIDGE, INC., Rt. 20, Box 513, Sturbridge MA 01566. (617)248-5584. Buyer: Mrs. Barbara Cowher. Gift shop. Estab. 1975. Represents 50-60 craftworkers.
Acceptable Work: Considers all crafts. One-of-a-kind and handmade production-line items. Price range: 59¢-$300; bestsellers: $2.50-30.
Terms: Buys outright and works on consignment; 30% commission. Retail price set by joint agreement. Requires exclusive area representation. Send slides with SASE or samples which can be returned. Reports as soon as possible. Work may be shipped or hand delivered.
Profile: "We attempt to put our shop together in such a way as to present all our merchandise with combinations of textures and colors to enhance each item. Sometimes we find a whole impact display is best. We often have a featured 'craftsperson of the month' accompanied by advertising to enhance this. We also put out a yearly catalog. Ours is a unique shop dealing primarily with tourists and with an ever growing repeat clientele. We like collector-type items." Heaviest wholesale buying time: spring-fall; best selling time: spring-December.
To Break In: "We require well done crafts. No craftsperson is too 'small' to be considered—none is too 'big'!"

GRANDMOTHER'S TRUNK, 75 Great Rd., Maynard MA 01754. (617)897-8089. Proprietor: Debbie Regan. Craft, gift and antique shop located on 2 Powder Mill Road. Estab. 1974. Represents 5-20 craftworkers.
Acceptable Work: Considers ceramics, clothing, dollmaking, glass art, jewelry, pottery, scrim-

shaw, soft sculpture, tole painting, wall hangings, weavings, woodcrafting, doll furniture and prints. "We're always looking for left-handed products (e.g., cards, aprons, stationery, T-shirts, mustache mugs) at reasonable prices. Also, crafts depicting horses, trains and antique cars are in demand, as are miniatures and doll furniture." One-of-a-kind and handmade production-line items. Price range: $1-100; bestsellers: $1-$20.
Terms: Buys outright and works on consignment; 33⅓% commission. Retail price set by joint agreement. Send photos and price list with SASE. Reports in 3 weeks. Work may be shipped or hand-delivered. Dealer pays insurance on exhibited work.
Profile: "Our theme: old-fashioned miscellaneous or what can be found in grandmother's trunk. Also incorporates 'left-handed complements'—a corner featuring quality products for lefties. Crafts are grouped and displayed to harmonize with the furniture and antiques we sell. Usual display time is 90 days. Being situated next to Concord and near various large corporations gives us a clientele from other regions and countries, in addition to regular, local customers." Heaviest wholesale buying and best selling time: fall.
To Break In: "Every letter should have a straightforward business-like approach listing products, materials used, dimensions and prices, and also include photos and SASE."

THE HANDCRAFTER, Whalers Wharf, 237-241 Commercial, Provinceton MA 02657. (617)487-1966. Owner: Dale Elmer. Craft and gift shop, plus summer shops rented to craftworkers. Estab. 1963. Represents 40 craftworkers. Price range: $2-350; bestsellers: $2-30. Works on consignment and buys outright; 33⅓% commission. Retail price set by joint agreement. Reports in 2 weeks. Work may be shipped or hand-delivered if a prior agreement has been made; dealer pays insurance on exhibited work.
Acceptable Work: Considers candlemaking; ceramics; glass art; jewelry; leatherworking; metalsmithing; pottery; and woodcrafting. Crafts must reflect sea themes; e.g., whales, fish, sailboats, lighthouses, seagulls. No scrimshaw.
Profile: "What makes us unusual is our location—on the beach, adjacent to the National Seashore, and in the center of a historical town (where the Mayflower Compact was made in the harbor)—and the fact that there are 40 artists and craftworkers producing and selling in our shop." Size: 10,000 square feet. Display time: 1-4 months, depending upon sales. Heaviest wholesale buying time: April 15-July 15; best selling time: May 15-September 15. "This town has a rich heritage of working artists and craftworkers, as well as galleries, ranging from average to excellent, so our customers are quite knowledgeable."

HANDSCAPES, Box 733, Dennis Port MA 02639. (617)394-6657. Contact: Diane L. Thibault. Gift shop. Estab. 1975. Represents 100 craftworkers.
Acceptable Work: Considers candlemaking; dollmaking; glass art; jewelry; leatherworking; metalsmithing; pottery; wall hangings; weavings; and woodcrafting. Especially needs seaside or nautical themes. Fine one-of-a-kind and handmade production-line items. Price range: $1.25-100; bestsellers: $2-18.
Terms: Works occasionally on consignment but mostly buys outright; 40% commission. Retail price set by joint agreement. Requires exclusive area representation. Reports in 2-3 days. Work may be shipped or hand-delivered, if a prior contract has been made. Dealer pays insurance on exhibited work.
Profile: "Although we have a gallery section, more and more gallery and shop items are being intermingled. This is to break down artificial barriers and assumptions; e.g. that price equals art. A $12 bowl can be as beautiful as a $3,500 wood sculpture, and we may have them displayed side by side." Heaviest wholesale buying time: winter; best selling time: summer. "This being a tourist area, 85% of our business is between July 1-October 1. However, we're open year-round. The bulk of our customers are middle income families who are shopping for a 'souvenir' of Cape Cod. As such, our shop has educational value since most of our customers don't come looking for quality crafts, but many end up buying them."

HANDWORKS, Box 371, Winter St., Edgartown MA 02539. (617)693-9215 or 627-9754. Contact: John or Claudia Bradford. Craft shop and mail order. Estab. 1972. Represents 75-100 craftworkers.
Acceptable Work: Considers candlemaking, jewelry, leatherworking, pottery, scrimshaw, soft sculpture and woodcrafting. Handmade production-line items only. Price range: 95¢-$150; bestsellers: $1-40.
Terms: Buys outright and works on consignment; 40% commission. Retail price set by joint agreement. Requires exclusive area representation on some items. Send slides/catalog or call for appointment. "If you will be at a craft show in the area, let us know." Usually reports in 1-2 weeks; July-August in 1-2 months; "for best response, write in March-April." Work may be

shipped or hand-delivered, if pre-arranged agreement has been made.
Profile: "We are a shop featuring both contemporary and traditional crafts along with well designed noncraft items (furniture, lamps, cards, prints). Our shop is in a high traffic tourist area (Martha's Vineyard Island). Items that are fast moving get prime exhibit space. Some items which are slower movers but very unique in design will be given prime space also. We also can sell some crafts through our mail order catalog sent out in the fall. Craftsman must be able to supply in quantity and time desired by us (will discuss with craftsman)." Customers are "tourists and island residents, mid to late 20s, middle income and up, looking for the unusual at reasonable prices." Heaviest wholesale buying time: late winter-spring; best selling time: summer.
To Break In: "We enjoy dealing with craftsmen who are experienced in dealing on a wholesale basis and can supply us within a reasonable time. Items small enough to be carried in luggage or easily packed and shipped go well with our tourist clientele."

HIGH STREET OF BOSTON, Box 161, Chestnut Hill MA 02167. Owner: William Hunter. Gift shop. Estab. 1972. Represents 50 craftworkers. Price range: up to $200; bestsellers: up to $20. Works on consignment and buys outright; 34% commission. Retail price set by shop. Requires exclusive area representation. Reports "as soon as possible." Work may be shipped or hand-delivered.
Acceptable Work: Considers batik; candlemaking; ceramics; clothing; decoupage; dollmaking; glass art; jewelry; leatherworking; metalsmithing; needlecrafts; pottery; quilting; soft sculpture; tole painting; wall hangings; weavings; woodcrafting; and paintings. All styles; utilitarian and/or decorative.
Profile: "All work is original." Heaviest wholesale buying time: spring and summer; best selling time: summer and fall. "Customers are of discriminating taste, they appreciate the sea, nature and quality."

THE IDEA, 673 Massachusetts Ave., Arlington MA 02174. (617)641-0200. Contact: Carma Forgie. Book/stationary shop. Estab. 1976. Represents 20 craftworkers.
Acceptable Work: Considers ceramics, dollmaking, jewelry, metalsmithing, needlecrafts, pottery, quilting, wall hangings, weavings, woodcrafting, baskets and silkscreen. One-of-a-kind (needlework, pottery, silkscreen) and handmade production-line items (jewelry, baskets, woodcrafting). "We like the unusual and good taste is a must." Price range: $1.50-285; bestsellers: $1.50-15.
Terms: Buys outright and works on consignment; 33⅓% commission. "We like people who can fill special orders." Craftworker sets retail price. Requires exclusive area representation. Send slides or call for appointment. Reports in 1 week. Work must be hand-delivered. Dealer pays insurance on exhibited work.
Profile: "We carry mostly stationery/office supplies and books. The shop attempts to get a complete line of these. Crafts are to add interest and be an alternate gift item when none of the books or stationery items fits the occassion. We do not have much space (on walls, shelves, or in display cases)." Customers: cosmopolitan, above average education, average incomes. Heaviest wholesale buying time: August-December; best selling time: Christmas.

IMAGE GALLERY, Main St., Stockbridge MA 01262. Director: Clemens Kalischer. Gallery. Estab. 1965.
Acceptable Work: Considers ceramics; glass; jewelry; metalsmithing; fiber sculpture; wall hangings; and wood. Fine one-of-a-kind pieces suitable for an art gallery only. Price range: $20-5,000.
Terms: Works on consignment; 35% commission. Retail price set by joint agreement. Requires exclusive area representation. Reports in 4 weeks. Work may be shipped or hand-delivered. Exhibitions last 4-6 weeks.

JOURNEYMAN, INC., 55 Boylston St., Harvard Square, Cambridge MA 02138. (617)876-0170. Contact: Frank Cullen, Donald McNeilly or Margaret Bailey. Contemporary craft shop. Estab. 1971. Represents over 100 craftworkers.
Acceptable Work: "We keep the largest selections of silver and pottery in our area thus emphasize those 2 media. We also sell blown glass; stain glass mirrors; low-line gold jewelry; and handmade lampshades. We do not use or sell *any* products that are the result of the slaughter of animals. This means leather; fur; bone; scrimshaw; ivory; shells; feathers; etc. For potters and glass blowers this means no bone ash. In stain glass or pottery hangings, no leather thongs. Also please don't use human life support products that are in critical supply (coral)." Mostly production-line, some one-of-a-kind items. Price range: $5-200; bestsellers: $10-40.

Terms: Retail price is set by joint agreement. Requires exclusive area representation. Shipping by UPS only. Journeyman pays shipping to shop if outright purchase; and pays insurance on exhibited work.
Profile: Very prominent location. Fashion lead market. Customers are mostly women; average 30 years old; upper middle income; well-educated; professionals. Many out-of-staters. Best selling time: Christmas.

LEVERETT CRAFTSMEN & ARTISTS INC., Montague Rd., Leverett MA 01054. (413)549-6871. Contact: Stephen Hamilton. Craft shop and museum gallery; also rents studio space for classes/workshops. Estab. 1966. Represents 80-90 craftworkers, most living within a 40-mile radius.
Acceptable Work: Considers batik; ceramics; dollmaking; glass art; jewelry; leatherworking; metalsmithing; needlecrafts; pottery; quilting; soft sculpture; wall hangings; weavings; and woodcrafting. All styles; utilitarian and/or decorative. Price range: 75¢-$500; bestsellers: $4.50-140.
Terms: Works on consignment; 40% commission. Retail price set by craftworker, with guidance of the salesroom manager when requested. Reports after "all work has passed our jury." Work may be shipped or hand-delivered; dealer pays insurance on exhibited work.
Profile: "Salesrooms have a gallery flavor. As a nonprofit, educational organization, salesrooms are also exhibition spaces. Special monthly exhibits are in a separate gallery." Juries held 6 times per year. Best selling time: August-December. "People who buy things are aged 30-55, professional or university, with an income of over $20,000. Art lovers, with less income, also purchase select items for themselves."

LITTLETON GALLERY, Box 202, 225 Great Rd., Littleton MA 01460. (617)486-4969. Contact: Evalyn Wood. Craft/gift shop and rental gallery. Estab. 1974. Represents 150 craftworkers.
Acceptable Work: Considers batik, candlemaking, clothing, decoupage, glass art, jewelry, leatherworking, needlecrafts, pottery, quilting, soft sculpture, scrimshaw, tole painting, wall hangings, weavings, cards, and woodcrafting. Specializes in fine one-of-a-kind and handmade production-line items. Price range: $1-45; bestsellers: $5-20.
Terms: Works on consignment and buys outright; 33⅓% commission. Retail price set by joint agreement. Requires exclusive area representation. Send slides/photos or call for appointment. "We have a jury system consisting of 3 partners and we all decide." Reports in 1 week. Work may be shipped or hand delivered.
Profile: Has featured artist showings and conducts craft classes. "Sometimes we feature specific artist/craftperson and release news articles to local papers. Items are displayed at our discretion for 3 months or longer after the show." Customers are primarily women, "young homemakers, secretaries, professional people." 18-40, $10-25,000 incomes. Heaviest wholesale buying and best selling time: fall.

LONDON VENTURERS CO., 2 Dock Sq., Rockport MA 01966. (617)546-7161. Owner: J. Manera. Gallery. Estab. 1968. Represents 12 craftworkers. Considers glass art; jewelry; wall hangings; and weavings. Fine one-of-a-kind pieces only; utilitarian and/or decorative. Price range: $1-2,000; bestsellers: $10-200.
Terms: Works on consignment and buys outright; 40% commission. Retail price set by gallery. Requires exclusive area representation. Reports in 2 weeks. Craftworker pays insurance on exhibited work.
Profile: Best selling and heaviest wholesale buying time: summer. Customers are "30-40 years old, married and in the $20,000 income bracket. They buy crafts for their artistic value."

MacIVOR REDDIE GALLERY, Art Institute of Boston, 700 Beacon St., Boston MA 02215. (617)262-1223. Gallery Committee Member: Sissy Willis. College gallery. Estab. 1912. Represents 1-6 craftworkers.
Acceptable Work: Considers ceramics; pottery; soft sculpture; wall hangings; and woodcrafting. Price range: $10-2,500; bestsellers: $10-250.
Terms: Works on consignment; 20% commission. Retail price set by craftworker. Reports in 4 weeks. Work should be hand-delivered; dealer pays insurance on exhibited work while at the Art Institute only.
Profile: Nonprofit gallery with free admission, "exhibiting work of artists involved in the fields students will one day enter: painting, sculpture, ceramics, printmaking, advertising and corporate design, illustration, photography. Shows run for a month, and are both group and individual showings." Best selling time: winter of the academic year.

MASSACHUSETTS AUDUBON SOCIETY GIFT SHOP, S. Great Rd., Lincoln MA 01773. (617)259-9500. Manager/Buyer: Mrs. George K. Lewis. Nonprofit organization craft shop. Estab. 1950.
Acceptable Work: Considers batik, ceramics, decoupage, glass art, jewelry, metalsmithing, pottery, wall hangings, and weavings. "All crafts must, in some way, be nature-oriented." Specializes in fine art and contemporary crafts. One-of-a-kind and handmade production-line items. Price range: 50¢-$750; bestsellers: $2.50-100.
Terms: Works occasionally on consignment, but mostly buys outright. Retail price set by joint agreement. Requires exclusive area representation. Call for appointment. Work may be shipped or hand delivered.
Profile: "Massachusetts Audubon is the oldest Audubon society in the country. We're located in a solar experiment building, which attracts great attention. Also, we've developed a wide reputation for exceptional crafts." Heaviest wholesale buying time: spring-fall; best selling time: April-June, September-December. 'Most customers are environmentally aware."

MUSEUM OF AFRO AMERICAN HISTORY, Dudley Station, Box 5, Boston MA 02119. (617)445-7400 or 267-4160. President: Byron Rushing. Museum gallery/gift shop located at 719 Tremont St. in the south end section of Boston. Estab. 1967. Represents African and Afro American craftworkers with an emphasis upon New England, South Carolina, Georgia, Louisiana, Haiti and Ethiopian sources.
Acceptable Work: Considers dollmaking; quilting; soft sculpture; wall hangings; weavings; basketry; and woodcrafting. Primitive and fine one-of-a-kind pieces; utilitarian. "We specialize in Afro American crafts that have some connection with the year-round history exhibit program." Price range: 50¢-$150; bestsellers: 50¢-$25.
Terms: Works on consignment and buys outright; 50% commission. Retail price set by gallery. Requires exclusive area representation. Reports in 3 weeks. Work may be shipped or hand-delivered; museum pays insurance on exhibited work.
Profile: Crafts displayed in gallery atmosphere. Showing times vary from 1-12 months. Heaviest wholesale buying time: fall; best selling time: December, February (Black history month), May and June. Customers come from all races; lower and middle income.

PADDLEWICKER, 17 Church St., Lenox MA 01240. (413)637-3179. Contact: Joni Frankel. Craft shop and gallery. Estab. 1971. Represents Berkshire area craftworkers, "although we will consider craftworkers from Massachusetts proper, New York, New Hampshire and Vermont if they have quality items." Price range: $3-100; bestsellers: $3-26. Works on consignment and buys outright; 30-40% commission. Retail price set by joint agreement. Requires exclusive area representation. Reports in 4 weeks. Work may be shipped or hand-delivered.
Acceptable Work: Considers batik cards; candlemaking; ceramics; dollmaking; glass art; jewelry; needlecrafts; pottery; quilting; soft sculpture; wall hangings; weavings; woodcrafting; paintings; and sculpture. Fine one-of-a-kind and handmade production-line items; utilitarian and/or decorative.
Profile: Crafts are displayed on shelves or behind glass, possibly in a special exhibit. Crafts are shown for a maximum of 3 months. "We concentrate on work by local artisans, emphasizing quality items at a reasonable price." Heaviest wholesale buying time: spring; best selling time: summer. Customers are "both locals and New York tourists, anywhere in the $12,000-25,000 income bracket."

PERCEPTIONS, INC., 75 Main St., Concord MA 01742. (617)369-6797. Craft shop and gallery. Estab. 1972. Represents 150 craftworkers.
Acceptable Work: Considers batik; ceramics; clothing; glass art; jewelry; leatherworking; metalsmithing; pottery; soft sculpture; wall hangings; weavings; woodcrafting; and prints. "We're always interested in seeing new designs in all categories, particularly weavings and jewelry." Fine one-of-a-kind and handmade production-line items. Price range: $1-1,200; bestsellers: $1-200.
Terms: Works on consignment and buys outright; 33⅓% commission. Retail price set by craftworker. Requires exclusive area representation. Reports in 2 weeks. Work may be shipped or hand-delivered; dealer pays insurance on exhibited work.
Profile: "Each piece is given plenty of space, rotating as possible. We're unique because there is no other contemporary craft shop in this area." Heaviest wholesale buying time: "we order at major craft fairs"; best selling time: Christmas. Customers are "liberal, affluent and relatively young."

PETERSHAM CRAFT CENTER & CRAFT SHOP, Rt. 32, Petersham MA 01366. (617)724-3415. Gallery, craft and gift shop. Estab. 1954. Represents 40 craftworkers. Price range: 50¢-$350; bestsellers: $1-25. Works on consignment and buys outright; 25% commission. Retail price set by joint agreement. Reports in 2 weeks. Work may be shipped or hand-delivered.
Acceptable Work: Original and well designed crafts. Considers ceramics; clothing; decoupage; dollmaking; jewelry; needlecrafts; pottery; quilting; wall hangings; weavings; and woodcrafting. Especially needs "interesting toys; woven placemats; clothing; and useful pottery." Primitive and fine one-of-a-kind pieces; utilitarian and/or decorative.
Profile: Crafts are displayed for 6 months, then returned if not sold. Shop is run by volunteers, who also conduct arts and crafts classes. Best selling time: summer and fall.

POOR RICHARD'S GALLERY, 56 Rocky Neck Ave., East Gloucester MA 01930. (617)283-8665. Contact: Richard or Nancy Korb.
Acceptable Work: Considers batik; glass art; metalsmithing; mobiles; pottery; and sculpture. Maximum size: 2x3. Specializes "to some degree" in New England marine themes.
Terms: Buys outright or works on consignment; 40% commission. Price range: $5-300. Craftworker sets retail price. Requires exclusive area representation. Send slides or photos of work. SASE. Gallery pays shipping from gallery and insurance on exhibited work.
Profile: "The shop is located in the heart of the Rocky Neck Art Colony." Work is exhibited from April 1-October 30.

QUAIGH DESIGNS, Chandlers Row, Pleasant St., Marblehead MA 01945. (617)631-4016. Owner: Lilias MacBean Hart. Craft shop. Estab. 1968. Represents 85 New England craftworkers.
Acceptable Work: Considers batik; candlemaking; ceramics; glass art; jewelry; leatherworking; metalsmithing; needlecrafts; pottery; wall hangings; weavings; and woodcrafting. Fine handmade production-line items. Price range: $1-250; bestsellers: $4-40.
Terms: Buys outright. Gallery sets retail price. Requires exclusive area representation. Only replies if interested. Work may be shipped or hand-delivered. Dealer pays shipping to shop.
Profile: "We're open year around. Each craftperson's work is usually displayed in one place. We always buy items which are useful, a good price, well designed and professionally presented. Our customers are local." Heaviest wholesale buying time: Christmas; best selling time: summer-fall and Christmas.

SERENITY LEATHER & CRAFTS, Box 325, West Stockbridge MA 01266. (413)232-4235. Contact: Phil or Grace Morarre. Craft shop. Estab. 1974. Represents 30 craftworkers.
Acceptable Work: Considers batik, candlemaking, ceramics, clothing, glass art, jewelry, leatherworking, needlecrafts, pottery, quilting, scrimshaw, soft sculpture, wall hangings, weavings and woodcrafting. One-of-a-kind and handmade production-line items. Price range: 60¢-$300; bestsellers: 60¢-$65.
Terms: Buys outright and works on consignment; 33⅓% commission. Retail price set by joint agreement. Call for appointment. Reports in 1 week. Work may be shipped or hand-delivered.
Profile: "We make 95% of leatherwork ourselves, on the premises. Other crafts are mostly bought outright, although many start out on consignment. If items do not sell within 6 months, they are taken out." Heaviest wholesale buying time and best selling time: summer.

SHOPS FOR PAPPAGALLO, 145 Newbury St., Boston MA 02116. See Elliot Designs Jewelry, Needham MA.

SHOPS FOR PAPPAGALLO, Faneuil Hall Marketplace, Boston MA 02109. See Elliot Designs Jewelry, Needham MA.

SHOPS FOR PAPPAGALLO, Harvard Square at Crimson Galleria, The Mall at Chestnut Hill, Newton MA 02192. See Elliot Designs Jewelry, Needham MA.

SHOPS FOR PAPPAGALLO, Nagog Village, Acton MA 01718. See Elliot Designs Jewelry, Needham MA.

THE SNEAK BOX STUDIO, Box 1055, Concord MA 01742. (617)369-8312. Contact: Charles F. Murphy. Represents 10 craftworkers.
Acceptable Work: Considers decoys and bird carvings, but may accept any medium if subject pertains to wildfowl or birds. Finished one-of-a-kind and handmade production-line items. Price range: $1-1,000; bestsellers: $20-500.

Terms: Buys outright or on consignment. Craftworker sets his price and studio then sets retail price. Requires exclusive area representation. Write or query with transparencies or color photos. Reports in 1 week.
Profile: Consigns items for 12 weeks minimum. All items displayed and many photographed and added to mail order literature. Customers are mostly collectors.

Although most of the leatherwork is produced by the owners themselves, Phil and Grace Morarre, other crafts are bought and consigned at Serenity Leather & Crafts of West Stockbridge, Massachusetts. Many new crafts start on consignment, but if they sell well, they are bought outright. Items have a 6-month display time.

THE SOCIETY OF ARTS & CRAFTS, 175 Newbury St., Boston MA 02116. (617)266-1810. Director: Cyrus D. Lipsitt. Craft shop/gallery. Estab. 1897. Represents 300-400 US craftworkers.
Acceptable Work: Considers batik, ceramics, glass art, jewelry, leatherworking, metalsmithing, needlecrafts, pottery, quilting, scrimshaw, soft sculpture, wall hangings, weavings and woodcrafting. Specializes in contemporary and traditional crafts. One-of-a-kind and handmade production-line items. Bestsellers: under $50-200.
Terms: Buys some work outright, but mainly works on consignment; 40% commission. Retail price set by joint agreement. Send slides or call for appointment. Reports in 3 weeks. Work may be shipped or hand-delivered after being approved for showing. The Society of Arts & Crafts pays insurance on exhibited work.
Profile: "We are a nonprofit craft organization operating a retail shop, a craft exhibition center, library, workshops, lectures, craftsman referral service, apprenticeship placement service. Open year-round in an historic area of Boston where most of the art galleries and convention centers are located. Pieces are displayed as a grouping of the individual artist, shown on pedestals, artists' names are with the work, work is retained for a period of 3 months at the discretion of the society. Our customers' age range is generally from the 20s up, with varied interests. They turn to us for what's being done in the crafts of excellent quality and expect to find a broad range of media. They have good to excellent incomes. Many have an 'eye to quality.' "
To Break In: "Be professional—work should arrive at the gallery with packing slip including retail prices of items, well packed to avoid breakage; allow enough time when delivering in person for the work to be checked over for quality and condition. When shipping send it by a delivery service that delivers to the shop—do not arrange for the work to have to be picked up at some terminal. Use a service like UPS and insure the work."

Shops and Galleries 199

THE SPECTRUM OF AMERICAN ARTISTS & CRAFTSMEN, INC., 369 Old King's Hwy., Brewster MA 02631. (617)385-3322. President: Addison H. Pratt Jr. Craft shop/gallery. Estab. 1966. Represents 225 craftworkers and artists.
Acceptable Work: Considers batik; candlemaking; ceramics; dollmaking; glass art; jewelry; leatherworking; metalsmithing; needlecrafts; pottery; soft sculpture; wall hangings; weavings; and woodcrafting. Fine one-of-a-kind and handmade production-line items. Price range: 75¢-$1,500.
Terms: Works on consignment and buys outright; commission varies. Retail price set by joint agreement on consigned items. Reports in 2 weeks. No work should be sent without prior agreement.
Profile: "Crafts receive prominent display in a spacious atmosphere." Heaviest wholesale buying time: "early in the year"; best selling time: summer. Customers are primarily tourists.
Sales Tip: "An appointment to show your work is absolutely necessary. Early in the year is the best time. We do not view work during the height of our season."

THE SPECTRUM OF AMERICAN ARTISTS & CRAFTSMEN, INC., 433 Main St., Hyannis MA 02601. See above.

THE SPECTRUM OF AMERICAN ARTISTS & CRAFTSMEN, INC., 26 Main St., Nantucket MA 02554. See above.

STORROWTON VILLAGE MUSEUM, 1305 Memorial Ave., West Springfield MA 01089. (413)736-0632. Director: June Cook. Museum gift shop. Estab. 1970. Represents 10-25 craftworkers.
Acceptable Work: Considers candlemaking; ceramics; clothing; dollmaking; glass art; jewelry; leatherworking; metalsmithing; needlecrafts; pottery; quilting; tole painting; and woodcrafting. All crafts must be early American orientation; "no plastic." Especially needs blown glass, tin and pottery in the $5-10 price range. Price range: 50¢-$100; bestsellers: 50¢-$30.
Terms: Works on consignment and buys outright; 35% commission. Retail price set by craftworker; however, advisory board juries all articles for price and appropriateness. For special events, charges $10/64 square feet for exhibit space. Reports in 4 weeks. Work may be shipped or hand-delivered.
Profile: Located in a colonial village shopping area. Display is "in the old-style village motif." Displays work 30 days. Heaviest wholesale buying and best selling time: summer.

SUTTER'S MILL, 233 Main St., Northampton MA 01060. (413)586-1470. Owner: John Sutter. Craft and gift shop. Estab. 1968. Represents 20 craftworkers. Considers ceramics; glass art; jewelry; pottery; and woodcrafting. Specializes in custom-designed jewelry and settings. Fine one-of-a-kind and handmade production-line items; utilitarian and/or decorative. Price range: $5-1,500. Buys work outright. Retail price set by joint agreement. Requires exclusive area representation. Reports in 2 weeks. Work may be shipped or hand-delivered; dealer pays insurance on exhibited work. Best selling time: Christmas.

TERRA-COTTA, INC., 765 Massachusetts Ave., Cambridge MA 02139. (617)864-1454. President: Martin B. Fishman. Craft/gift shop. Estab. 1968. Displays in showcases and windows.
Acceptable Work: Considers ceramics, glass art, jewelry, pottery, scrimshaw, soft sculpture and woodcrafting. Specializes in fine art and contemporary crafts. Handmade production-line items only. Price range: $11-250.
Terms: Buys outright and works on consignment. Shop pays insurance on exhibited work. Call for appointment with SASE. Reports in 4 weeks. Work may be shipped or hand delivered.

VLADA, Box 721, Stockbridge MA 01262. (413)298-3656. Contact: Vlada. Craft and gift shop. Estab. 1970. Represents 40 craftworkers.
Acceptable Work: Considers batik; weaving; candlemaking; clothing; jewelry; leatherworking; pottery; and soft sculpture ("will take other things if they appeal"). Especially needs "interesting and well-made summer dresses, tops, skirts and men's shirts." Fine one-of-a-kind and handmade production-line items. Price range: $2.50-250.
Terms: Works on consignment; 33⅓% commission. Retail price set by joint agreement. Work may be shipped or hand-delivered, if a prior agreement has been made.
Profile: "We're a small shop dealing in unusual and well-made clothes, accessories and crafts. Display time agreed upon receipt of crafts." Heaviest wholesale buying time: spring-early summer; best selling time: summer and pre-Christmas. Customers are a "wide range of tourists and local people who come to New England's summer 'cultural' area."

VORTEX STAINED GLASS STUDIOS, Main St., W. Stockbridge MA 01266. (413)232-4243. Manager: Dwight O'Niel. Owner: Raymond Dorazio. Stained glass studio/gallery. Estab. 1973. Represents 3 craftworkers.
Acceptable Work: Considers glass art only. Especially needs mouth blown glass lamps. "We love art glass lamps and don't have facilities to make them ourselves." One-of-a-kind and handmade production-line items. Price range: $5-2,000; bestsellers: $10-300.
Terms: Buys outright and works on consignment; 30% commission. Retail price set by joint agreement. Send resume and slides. Reports in 1 week. Work must be hand-delivered. Dealer pays insurance on exhibited work.
Profile: "Ours is a working studio concentrating on the finest craftsmanship possible in stained glass. We produce original windows, doors, mirrors and Tiffany-type lamps. We are also distributors of stained glass and stained glass tools and supplies. We have a display area 25'x40' in which we display our own work for the most part, and other exceptional stained glass and blown art glass pieces. We rarely sell other people's work, but when we see very original well-crafted pieces (especially of blown glass), we may take some on consignment. We keep pieces exhibited until we sell them." Customers: ages 30-50, professionals, good to excellent incomes, many artists. Best selling time: May-January.

THE WEE SPINNAKER, 11 Elm St., Cohasset MA 02025. (617)383-6395. Contact: Ann, Bobbie or Judy. Craft shop. Estab. 1977. Represents approximately 200 craftworkers.
Acceptable Work: Considers batik, selected clothing, decoupage, dollmaking, jewelry, leatherworking, needlecrafts, pottery, quilting, scrimshaw, soft sculpture, tole painting, wall hangings, weavings and woodcrafting. Especially needs unique items for children and special gifts for adults. One-of-a-kind and handmade production-line items OK; but prefers one-of-a-kind. Price range: 25¢-$100; bestsellers: $5-25.
Terms: Buys outright occasionally, but usually works on consignment; 40% commission. Retail price set by joint agreement. Requires exclusive representation on South Shore area of Boston. Send photos with SASE. Reports in 2 weeks maximum. Work may be shipped or hand-delivered after items have been reviewed and discussed.
Profile: "We are a shop of *unique* items for children and special gifts for adults. We are located in the small, original blacksmith shop in our charming seaside town. The shop is attractive from the outside and is stunning on the inside because it is filled with bright, sunny, unique items. People have gone out of their way to say exactly this! Some of our items have been hand carried to Europe, etc. Any new item is displayed well, pointed out by staff person in shop. After 30 days or so, if we are getting negative feedback, we ask that it be removed. We try to maintain contact with our consignee and come back to him with color suggestions, etc., always giving him feedback information. Our customers range from small children to grandparents, from a varied background." Heaviest wholesale buying and best selling time: June-December.

WISTARIAHURST MUSEUM, 238 Cabot St., Holyoke MA 01040. (413)536-6771. Director: Marie Quirk. Museum gallery. Shows 4 craftworkers at a time. Exhibition mainly, although items may be priced for sale.
Acceptable Work: Considers batik; ceramics; dollmaking; glass art; metalsmithing; pottery; quilting; paintings; prints; and textiles. "We're always interested in scheduling a craft exhibit of quality, well-designed pieces." Fine one-of-a-kind items. Retail price set by craftworker.
Terms: Does not charge for exhibit space, but a donation is desired. In lieu of donation, percentage fee on sales requested. Reports in 3 weeks. "For exhibition, items must be seen to ascertain the standards needed for museum display." Museum pays insurance on exhibited items.
Profile: "Items appropriate for hanging are hung in the gallery. Small items are shown in locked cases. Other large items are exhibited on standards and tables." Best selling time: summer, fall and Christmas. "The gallery is located in a Victorian mansion on an estate, and the architectural features attract much attention. Many groups schedule meetings and special programs at the museum, and many ethnic groups also participate in exhibits and programs."

WOMENCRAFTS INC., Box 190, Provincetown MA 02651. Contact: A.E. Picoff or V. Walker. Craft and gift shop. Estab. 1976. Represents 150 women craftworkers.
Acceptable Work: Considers batik; candlemaking; ceramics; clothing; decoupage; dollmaking; glass art; jewelry; leatherworking; metalsmithing; needlecrafts; pottery; quilting; soft sculpture; wall hangings; weavings; woodcrafting; and silkscreened t-shirts. Especially needs items that retail under $10. Price range: 50¢-$500; bestsellers: $1-30.
Terms: Works on consignment and buys outright; 40% commission. Retail price set by joint agreement. Requires exclusive area representation. Work may be shipped or hand-delivered; dealer pays insurance on exhibited work.

Profile: Heaviest wholesale buying time: spring and summer; best selling time: summer. Customers are primarily tourists and feminists.

WONDERFUL THINGS, INC., 232 Stockbridge Rd., Great Barrington MA 01230. (413)528-2473. President: Lucille Tanguay. Gallery/craft and gift shop. Estab. 1973. Represents 300 craftworkers, "most are from the Northeast because of the fairs we visit."
Acceptable Work: Considers batik; candlemaking; ceramics; clothing; miniatures; dollmaking; glass art; jewelry; leatherworking; metalsmithing; pottery; quilting; soft sculpture; tole painting; wall hangings; weavings; and woodcrafting. Price range 1¢-$500; bestsellers: $5-150.
Terms: Works on consignment and buys outright; 35% commission. Retail price set by joint agreement. Reports in 4 weeks maximum. Work may be shipped or hand-delivered if prior agreement has been made. Dealer pays insurance on exhibited work.
Profile: "We're a total craft center, selling everything from supplies to finished crafts. There are 3 rooms for living, 8 rooms for working and 12 rooms for selling 30,000 items—we're really like 6 shops in one 8,000-foot location." Best selling time: July-December. "We're growing at a rate of 20% yearly because we appeal to anyone with an interest in or appreciation of crafts."

WORCESTER ART MUSEUM, 55 Salisbury St., Worcester MA 01608. Contact: Barbara Siff. Gift shop buys cards, crafts and jewelry outright.

Michigan

ANN ARBOR ART ASSOCIATION, 117 W. Liberty, Ann Arbor MI 48104. (313)994-8004. Administrative Assistant: Susan Monaghan. Gift shop/gallery/studio/school. Estab. 1977. Represents 250 craftworkers, mostly from Michigan.
Acceptable Work: Considers batik, ceramics, original dollmaking, glass art, jewelry, metalsmithing, pottery, soft sculpture, wall hangings, weavings and woodcrafting. Specializes in fine art and contemporary crafts. "Must be of high quality. We don't accept artsy-craftsy or 'cute' items." One-of-a-kind and handmade production-line items. Price range: $1-900; bestsellers: $4-100.
Terms: Works on consignment; 33.4% commission (if member of AAAA), 40% commission (if nonmember of AAAA). Craftworker sets retail price. Juries the first Tuesday of each month. "Bring 6-12 items. Please come the first time prepared to spend some time discussing and preparing contracts and pricing individual pieces." Reports in 1-2 days. Work may be shipped or hand delivered. "We ask for a 3 month commitment."
Profile: "We are a sales/rental gallery shop with a large area and storefront in downtown Ann Arbor. We are located in an historic building in an area that is becoming an 'Old Town.' Craft items are strictly for sale. Most crafts are on continual displays. Jewelry and miniatures have locked cases. Since we also have an education program and studios, we have a lot of art interested people coming through." Heaviest wholesale buying time: fall; best selling time: Christmas.

THE ART GLASS ALCOVE, 142 Butler St., Saugatuck MI 49453. (616)857-3431. Owner: Andrea Eming. Gift shop. Estab. 1972. Represents 35-40 craftworkers. Price range: 75¢-$400; bestsellers: $3.50-25. Works on consignment and buys outright; 33⅓% commission. Retail price set by shop. Requires exclusive area representation. Reports in 2 weeks. Work may be shipped or hand-delivered.
Acceptable Work: Considers batik; candlemaking; ceramics; glass art; jewelry; leatherworking; metalsmithing; pottery; wall hangings; weavings; woodcrafting; prints; and cards. "I'd like to strengthen my metalsmithing area." Primitive handmade production-line items.
Profile: "Our shop is designed with virtually no poor display areas—our main shelving is pigeon-holed, so it lends itself to our creating special themes. We try to use as much of nature as possible: driftwood, rocks, crates, rope. We usually allow items to be displayed 3-4 weeks before changing them." Heaviest wholesale buying time: spring; best selling time: summer. "We're located in a resort town so we get all kinds of people, from the penniless student to the yacht owner. Primarily, though, we deal with vacationers with a set amount of money to spend."

ARTISANS GALLERY, 107 Howard, Petoskey MI 49770. (616)347-6466. Contact: Russell or Frances Secrest. Craft shop. Estab. 1970. Represents 100 craftworkers.
Acceptable Work: Considers batik; candlemaking; ceramics; glass art; jewelry; leatherworking; metalsmithing; needlecrafts; pottery; soft sculpture; wall hangings; weavings; and woodcrafting. Fine one-of-a-kind and handmade production-line items; utilitarian only. Price range: $2-1,000; bestsellers: $2.50-50.

Terms: Buys outright. Retail price set by joint agreement. Reports in 1 week. Work may be shipped or hand-delivered. Best selling time: summer. "Customers are moderately conservative."

ARTS & CRAFTS UNLIMITED, Midtown Mall, Iron Mountain MI 49801. (906)774-8031. Contact: Barb Raffin. Craft/framing shop. Estab. 1977. Represents 5 craftworkers.
Acceptable Work: Considers decoupage, glass art, jewelry, tole painting, wall hangings, weavings, woodcrafting and macrame. Specializes in modern one-of-a-kind and handmade production-line items. Price range: 2¢-$55; bestsellers: 2¢-$6.
Terms: Buys outright and works on consignment; 20% commission. Craftworker sets retail price. Write with SASE. Reports once a month. Work may be shipped or hand delivered. "Craftworkers must sign a consignment agreement, protecting their work from copy." Display time: 4 weeks, unless seasonal.
Profile: Items are displayed in the window or in the 2200 square foot shop. Classes are also offered. Customers: ages 8-70, middle class. Heaviest wholesale buying time: May-December; best selling time: June-December.

BURKID'S, 320 Main, Frankfort MI 49635. (616)352-7001. Owner: Susan Kidder. Gift shop. Estab. 1971. Represents 30-75 craftworkers.
Acceptable Work: Considers batik, candlemaking, glass art, jewelry, leatherworking, metalsmithing, pottery, quilting, scrimshaw, soft sculpture, tole painting, wall hangings, weavings and woodcrafting. No kits, prefabricated or commercial products. Especially needs unusual candles, stained glass and soft sculpture. Specializes in contemporary, bright-colored items. One-of-a-kind and handmade production-line items. Price range: 50¢-$250; bestsellers: $1-35.
Terms: Buys outright and works on consignment; 25% commission. Retail price set by joint agreement. Requires exclusive Frankfort representation. Send resume or slides. Reports in 2 weeks. Work may be shipped or hand delivered. Display time: 3 months (longer if sells well).
Profile: "We are a unique gift shop in a high traffic resort area. I like to keep each craftworker's work together with a sign telling about the artist and his work." Customers: average ages are 30-60; average to above average incomes. "In summer, we have very wealthy customers." Heaviest wholesale buying time: late spring-early summer; best selling time: May-Christmas (especially June-August).

CAPITOL ART GALLERY, Plaza Hotel, Michigan at Capitol, Lansing MI 48933. (517)372-6550 (ext. 127). Cooperative rental gallery. Estab. 1977. Represents 50 Michigan craftworkers. Best selling time: September-January 30.
Acceptable Work: Considers ceramic sculpture, glass art, metalsmithing, pottery, scrimshaw, sculpture, wall hangings, weavings, and woodcrafting. Special exhibiting collections and one-person shows.
Terms: Rental space: $3/item per each month; or $30/month for 10-20 items; or $3/month for small items grouped with $75 total retail. Craftworker sets and receives total retail price. Send slides or samples. Must be juried by a 4 artist/member panel. Reports in 2 weeks. Work may be shipped or hand delivered.

CLASSICAL GLASS, 249 E. Liberty Plaza, Ann Arbor MI. Owners: Richard and Sandra Marks. See Marks Studio/Gallery, Tecumseh, Michigan.

THE CLAY GALLERY, Stone Village Art Center, 1701 Probert Rd., Jackson MI 49203. (517)789-7913. Director: Sandra Beaman. Gallery. Estab. 1977. Represents 10 craftworkers.
Acceptable Work: Considers clay medium only: ceramics, sculpture and wall hangings. Fine one-of-a-kind and handmade production-line items. Bestsellers: $3-800.
Terms: Buys outright but mostly works on consignment; 40% commission. Retail price set by joint agreement. Reports in 4 weeks; send slides, which will then be viewed by a jury. Work may be shipped or hand-delivered.
Profile: Each craftworker has his/her own display of 25-150 items. "We're a large gallery with a ceramic library for reference and slide lectures on participating craftworkers and their work." Best selling time: Christmas, spring and fall. Customers are "aged 20-40, middle to lower income, professional people with cultural interests."

CRANBROOK ACADEMY OF ART MUSEUM BOOKSTORE, 500 Lone Pine Rd., Bloomfield Hills MI 48013. (313)645-3315. Buyer/Manager: Linda Parks. Museum bookstore. "We are strictly a bookstore and only carry art books, postcards, exhibition posters and notecards. We do stock cards and books printed by craftsmen/artists."

Shops and Galleries 203

CRANBROOK INSTITUTE OF SCIENCE, 500 Lone Pine Rd., Bloomfield Hills MI 48013. (313)645-3226. Bookshop Manager: Gloria B. Esau. Museum gift shop. Estab. 1931. Represents 1-2 craftworkers.
Acceptable Work: Considers bird or animal ceramics, Indian dollmaking, glass art, jewelry, metalsmithing, needlecrafts, pottery, soft sculpture, Eskimo sculpture, and porcupine quill baskets. Especially needs natural history note paper; any crafts pertaining to science; and authentic American Indian material. Specializes in primitive and Appalachian one-of-a-kind pieces. Price range: 25¢-$300; bestsellers: $2-10.
Terms: Buys outright and works on consignment; commission negotiable. Retail price set by joint agreement. Write for appointment; SASE. Reports in 3-4 weeks. Work may be shipped or hand-delivered. Display time: 6 weeks.
Profile: Nonprofit organization. "Very modern and accessible to traffic flow. Has planetrium." Items displayed behind glass doors. Customers: ages 8-75, interested in natural history, American Indians, rock hounding, astrology and ornithology. Heaviest wholesale buying time: July 15-November 15, sometimes spring; best selling time: autumn.

DETROIT ARTISTS MARKET, 1452 Randolph St., Detroit MI 48226. (313)962-0337. Gallery Manager: Margaret Conzelman. Gallery. Represents 175-200 craftworkers from the 60-mile radius of Detroit.
Acceptable Work: Considers batik; ceramics; jewelry; metalsmithing; soft sculpture; wall hangings; weavings; blown glass; woven pillows; placemats; skirts; stoles; scarves; and throws. Fine one-of-a-kind pieces. Price range: $2-100; bestsellers: $5-45.
Terms: Works on consignment; 25-30% commission. Work may be shipped or hand-delivered; however, work will not be shipped back, it must be claimed in person.
Profile: "Established during the Depression, the shop is nonprofit and run by a board of directors. Its sole purpose is to give local artists and craftworkers a place to exhibit and sell their work." Best selling time: November-January. "Customers are primarily young business people, in their early 20s and 30s." Work is submitted to a jury; if accepted, it is shown on a rotating basis.

HUGUETTE FISHER GALLERY INC., 752 Pine St., Muskegon MI 49440. (616)722-4773. President: Huguette Fisher. Gallery, gift shop and custom framing. Estab. 1974. Represents 20-25 craftworkers.
Acceptable Work: Considers batik; ceramics; glass art; jewelry; soft sculpture; wall hangings; weavings; and woodcrafting. "Ceramic and raku should be used as sculptures for the home and wall reliefs." Primitive and fine one-of-a-kind pieces; decorative only. Price range: $10-500; bestsellers: $10-150.
Terms: Works on consignment and buys outright; 40% commission. Retail price set by joint agreement. Reports in 4 weeks. Work may be shipped or hand-delivered; dealer pays insurance on exhibited work.
Profile: "We're the only 'fine art' gallery in Muskegon. With our displays, we work out a theme several times a year." Heaviest wholesale buying time: fall and winter; best selling time: spring, summer and Christmas. "Our customers are middle to lower income, many are professionals; in addition, we do work with offices and buildings."

FRANKENMUTH HISTORICAL MUSEUM, 613 S. Main, Frankenmuth MI 48734. (517)652-9701. Director: Carl R. Hansen. Museum gift shop. Estab. 1973. Represents 6 craftworkers.
Acceptable Work: Considers ceramics; jewelry; leatherworking; pottery; and woodcrafting. Primitive handmade production-line items; utilitarian. Price range: 75¢-$100; bestsellers: 75¢-$30.
Terms: Works on consignment; 25% commission. Retail price set by joint agreement. Reports in 1 week. Work may be shipped or hand-delivered.
Profile: Indefinite display time. Heaviest wholesale buying time: spring-fall; best selling time: summer and fall.

GALLERIA INTERNAZIONALE, LTD., 1911 Wieneke Rd., Saginaw MI 48603. (517)799-1982. President: Luciana Weiss. Gallery. Estab. 1973. Represents 100 craftworkers.
Acceptable Work: Considers jewelry; pottery; soft sculpture; wall hangings; weavings; and woodcrafting. Primitive and fine one-of-a-kind pieces.
Terms: Works on consignment and buys outright; 40% commission. Retail price set by joint agreement. Requires exclusive area representation. Reports in 4 weeks. Work may be shipped or hand-delivered. Work displayed for 3-month period.

GALLERY ONE, 306 Howard St., Petoskey MI 49770. (616)347-9842. Contact: Jack Perry. Gallery. Estab. 1968. Represents 50 craftworkers.
Acceptable Work: Considers ceramics, glass art, jewelry, pottery, soft sculpture, wall hangings, weavings and woodcrafting. Specializes in fine one-of-a-kind and handmade production-line items. Price range: $2-500; bestsellers: $2-300.
Terms: Buys outright and works on consignment; 40% commisson. Craftworker sets retail price. Requires exclusive area representation. Send resume and slides. Reports in 3 weeks. Work may be shipped or hand delivered. Dealer pays insurance on exhibited work. If items are not sold in 10-12 months, they will be returned (if on consignment).
Profile: "We have been dealing in paintings, sculpture, pottery and jewelry for the past 10 years. Items will be rotated in display areas. We're located in Petoskey's famous summer shop area where customers come from all over the country. Also in the mid-west ski center." Heaviest wholesale buying time: spring; best selling time: summer.

THE GALLERY SHOP, 230 E. Fulton, Grand Rapids MI 49503. (616)459-9272. Craft Buyer: Mrs. Carter S. Bacon. Museum gift shop. Estab. 1962. Represents 50 craftworkers.
Acceptable Work: Considers batik; candlemaking; ceramics; decoupage; dollmaking; glass art; jewelry; leatherworking; metalsmithing; needlecrafts; pottery; soft sculpture; wall hangings; weavings; and woodcrafting. Price range: $1-250; bestsellers: $10-35.
Terms: Buys outright. Requires exclusive area representation. Reports in 2 weeks. Work may be shipped or hand-delivered; Grand Rapids Art Museum pays insurance on exhibited work.
Profile: "We're a small shop, and we change arrangements frequently. We usually try to have all art types represented." Heaviest wholesale buying time: February-September; best selling time: September-December.

THE GENTLE SIDE OF LIFE, 2006 E. Michigan Ave., Lansing MI 48912. (517)482-2864. Owner: Pat Lindemann. Manager: Renee Lindemann Dart. Craft/supply shop/gallery. Represents 200 craftworkers, preferably from Lansing and surrounding areas.
Acceptable Work: Considers all crafts. One-of-a-kind and handmade production-line items. Price range: 50¢-800; bestsellers: $5-50.
Terms: Works on consignment; 25-35% average commission. "We do not buy outright, although may consider if price is right on small popular items." Shop sets retail price; "suggestions from artist welcome. We add on our commission to your cost, so keep this in mind when setting your wholesale price." Call for appointment. "We appreciate advance notice from artists with large pieces or many items." Reports immediately. Work must be hand-delivered. Dealer pays insurance on exhibited work.
Profile: "We are a community art shop with the local artist in mind. Special orders are an important part of our business. Shop has 2 rooms—1 devoted mainly to wall art (paintings, photos, etc), and the other to functional and smaller decorative pieces. Decor is in natural colors (barnwood, rustic-looking shelving). Seasonal merchandise is welcomed but must be removed promptly after season is over." Customers: those interested in gift shopping or home decorating. Best selling time: Christmas. "For 2 months after Christmas, we find our walls and shelves quite bare. We need fresh merchandise during this time to keep our shop interesting to our customers."
To Break In: "Don't expect expensive merchandise, however well made, to move as quickly as small inexpensive pieces that a customer may purchase at the spur of the moment."

GUILD OF SHAKER CRAFTS, INC., 401 W. Savidge St., Spring Lake MI 49456. (616)846-2870. Shopkeeper: Elizabeth Kammeraad. Craft/gift shop and Shaker furniture showroom. Represents 10 craftworkers.
Acceptable Work: Considers primitive crafts, candlemaking, dollmaking, glass art, jewelry, metalsmithing, needlecrafts, pottery, quilting, soft sculpture, wall hangings, weavings and woodcrafting. Especially needs Early American crafts. Specializes in primitive and Appalachian one-of-a-kind and handmade production-line items. Price range: 75¢-$1,000; bestsellers: $5-400.
Terms: Buys outright and works on consignment; 40% commission. Retail price set by joint agreement. Requires exclusive area representation. Call for appointment. Reports in 2 weeks. Work may be shipped or hand delivered.
Profile: "A group of craftsmen joined together to reproduce Shaker furniture. We make reproductions of originals designed before 1850. Items are attractively displayed in the showroom." Customers: interested in Shaker furniture. Heaviest buying time: spring and fall; best selling time: summer to pre-Christmas.

HABITAT GALLERIES, INC., 1820 N. Telegraph Rd., Dearborn MI 48128. (313)274-1220. Contact: Thomas Boone or Ferdinand Hampson. Gallery. Estab. 1971.
Acceptable Work: Considers ceramics, glass art, jewelry, metalsmithing and woodcrafting. Fine art pieces only. Price range: $3.50-7,500.
Terms: Buys outright and works on consignment; 40% commission. "A strong, firm reasonable price (retail) should be set by craft artist long before approaching us." Requires exclusive area representation. Send resume and slides with SASE. Reports in 4 weeks maximum. Dealer pays insurance on exhibited work.
Profile: "We are a high quality contemporary American fine art and craft gallery. Large (over 3,000 square feet) exhibition space. Run around 20 exhibitions a year. Represent most American glassblowers. Customers are interested in good art." Work is displayed on pedestals and wood or glass shelving. Heaviest wholesale buying time: early spring and late fall; best selling time: special exhibitions and holiday seasons.
To Break In: "Be unique and only send best work. Never undercut our prices. We will drop any artist that does this."

THE HOOT OWL, 10 W. Silver Lake Rd. N., Traverse City MI 49684. (616)947-9494. Contact: Helen Gould. Craft shop/gallery. Estab. 1967. Represents 12-15 craftworkers. Considers ceramics; dollmaking; glass art; jewelry; metalsmithing; pottery; wall hangings; weavings; and woodcrafting. Price range: $5-50; bestsellers: $8-25. Works on consignment and buys outright; 40% commission. Retail price set by joint agreement. Requires exclusive area representation. Reports in 2 weeks. Dealer pays insurance for exhibited work.
Profile: "We are located in an old lakeside inn whose interior was designed by a former student and friend of Frank Lloyd Wright. We give time and thought to display. Fragile items may be placed out of reach of children but we do not restrict customer's handling items. Customers are mostly professional, middle class; many are involved with the National Music Camp at Interlochen 5 miles away." Heaviest wholesale buying time: spring, in some cases consignment in June. "We are a summer shop."

HURON CITY MUSEUMS, 7930 Huron City Rd., Port Austin MI 48467. (577)428-4123.

Habitat Galleries, Inc., Dearborn, Michigan demands a high level of craftsmanship, professionalism and creativeness for the items they exhibit. The work of over 500 craftworkers is displayed in 3,000 square feet of exhibition space and attracts many customers who are interested in fine art and craft items. The heaviest selling times are during special exhibitions and holiday seasons.

Director: David P. Dane. Museum gift shop. Estab. 1949. Represents 10-12 craftworkers.
Acceptable Work: Considers ceramics, clothing, dollmaking, jewelry, needlecrafts, pottery, quilting, scrimshaw, wall hangings, weavings and woodcrafting. Specializes in Victorian handcrafts and household pieces. One-of-a-kind and handmade production-line items. Price range: $1-125; bestsellers: $1-25.
Terms: Works on consignment; 30% commission. Retail price set by joint agreement. Call for appointment. Reports in 3 weeks. Work may be shipped or hand-delivered.
Profile: "Items are displayed and sold in office of 19th century general store. Store itself is authentically furnished and exhibited. Huron City is a restored village founded in 1857. The major buildings were constructed in the 1880s and are now restored and furnished with their original furnishings. Most of our visitors are resorters dropping in from the highway. Heaviest wholesale buying time: March-May; best selling time: July-August."

INDIAN HILLS TRADING CO., Indian Hills Reservation, Box 546, Petoskey MI 49770. (616)347-3789. Owner: Victor S. Kishigo. Trading post. Estab. 1970. Represents craftworkers from 50 North American Indian tribes.
Acceptable Work: Considers all Indian arts, particularly pottery. Needs quill boxes; black ash baskets; beadwork; woodcarvings; and featherwork. Price range: $3-3,700; bestsellers: $10-150.
Terms: Buys outright or trades for finished Indian art. Retail price set by shop.
Profile: "Indian Hills is owned and operated by a full-blooded Ottawa Indian. We not only sell the best quality Indian art, but also raw materials and craft supplies for the Indian craftworker. Catalog available for $1 to cover shipping and handling; refundable with first purchase of $10 or more." Heaviest wholesale buying time: late winter-early spring; best selling time: summer.

IRON COUNTY MUSEUM, Box 272, Caspian MI 49915. (906)265-2617. Curator: Marcia Bernhardt. Office Manager: Audrey Ridolphi. Museum gift shop. Estab. 1968. Represents 6-7 craftworkers on the average; during the Ferrous Frolics Festival, represents 25.
Acceptable Work: Considers candlemaking; decoupage; dollmaking; jewelry; metalsmithing; pottery; quilting; wall hangings; weavings; woodcrafting; and rosemaling. Wants pioneer crafts. "We'd like to develop a low-price range line of crafts—e.g., candles, old-fashioned cards, weavings, etc." Primitive one-of-a-kind pieces.
Terms: Works on consignment; 10% commission. Retail price set by craftworker. Charges $1 plus 10% commission for exhibit space during the Ferrous Frolics. Reports in 2 weeks. Work should be hand-delivered.
Profile: Crafts are displayed in glass cases. "Our principal business is our museum on pioneer life. It's located on a 5½ acre tract and consists of 9 buildings, most of which are circa 1890." Heaviest wholesale buying and best selling time: summer. Ferrous Frolics held the third weekend in July, preceded by a week long art show featuring 1 outstanding local artist. For the Frolics, tables are set up outdoors and artists sell their own work.

KALAMAZOO NATURE CENTER, 7000 N. Westnedge, Kalamazoo MI 49007. (616)381-1574. Shop Buyer: Janet Duffield. Museum gift shop. Estab. 1960. Represents 6 craftworkers. Price range: $1-50; bestsellers: $1-15. Works on consignment; 50% commission. Retail price set by joint agreement. Reports in 2 weeks. Work may be shipped or hand-delivered; dealer pays insurance on exhibited work.
Acceptable Work: Considers candlemaking; dollmaking; leatherworking; metalsmithing; needlecrafts; pottery; quilting; tole painting; wall hangings; weavings; woodcrafting; and homespun crafts. All work must be natural history, outdoor or environmentally oriented. Primitive one-of-a-kind and handmade production-line items.
Profile: Work shown in glass cases. Displays work 6 months. Heaviest wholesale buying and best selling time: fall, Christmas and spring. "Customers are families with a strong interest in the outdoors and the environment."

LAKEWINDS GALLERY, 405 Phoenix, South Haven MI 49090. Chairman: Steve French. Cooperative gallery. Estab. 1976. Represents 10 southwest Michigan craftworkers.
Acceptable Work: Considers batik; ceramics; jewelry; needlecrafts; pottery; soft sculpture; wall hangings; weavings; paintings; and photographs. Fine one-of-a-kind pieces. Price range: $15-200; bestsellers: $15-100.
Terms: Handles crafts of cooperative members only. Retail price set by craftworker. "Each member assumes an equal share of the rent."
Profile: "Our shop is a cooperative gallery put together by and for area artists for the exhibition and sale of their work. Each member arranges his/her work in an agreeable manner amidst the

other members' work, and is responsible for maintenance and rotation of stock." Best selling time: May-September and Christmas.

LANSING ART GALLERY, 425 S. Grand Ave., Lansing MI 48933. (517)484-9649. Executive Director: Marte E. Milks. Rental gallery/gift shop. Represents 300+ Michigan and Midwest craftworkers.
Acceptable Work: Considers batik, ceramics, clothing, glass art, jewelry, metalsmithing, needlecrafts, prints, scrimshaw, soft sculpture, wall hangings, weavings and woodcrafting. One-of-a-kind items only. Price range: $1-800; bestsellers: $50-150.
Terms: Works on consignment; 35% commission. Charges $40-150/month for exhibition space rental. Craftworker sets retail price. Work is juried monthly by committee. Send resume and slides. SASE. Reports within 4 weeks. Work may be shipped or hand-delivered.
Profile: "The Lansing Art Gallery, located in the Center for the Arts building in downtown Lansing, has 4 galleries: main gallery, salon gallery, rental & sales gallery and gift shop. They total approximately 1,800 square feet of open floor space. Exhibit areas, refined wall space and exhibit display stands will accommodate most size works. Special display arrangements are always available. The galleries provide a spacious viewing area in a relaxed atmosphere. There's an annual Christmas showing called 'Market Place' (entry forms must be received by August). 1 artist to 3-artist showings are scheduled 6-12 months in advance." Customers: professionals with above average incomes. Best selling time: October-April.

LEAVES 'N' WEAVES, 211 Washington, Grand Haven MI 49417. (616)846-4880. Owner: Nancy Vander Vere. Craft/gift shop. Estab. 1973. Represents 12 craftworkers.
Acceptable Work: Considers candlemaking; glass art; needlecrafts; pottery; soft sculpture; wall hangings; weavings; woodcrafting; and macrame. Primitive and fine one-of-a-kind pieces. Price range: $5-100; bestsellers: $5-30.
Terms: Works on consignment and buys outright; 33% commission. "We handle items on consignment first; then, if it sells, we buy outright." Retail price set by craftworker. Requires exclusive area representation. "Call before coming to shop." Reports in 1 week. Work may be shipped or hand-delivered; dealer pays insurance on exhibited work.
Profile: "We have a large upstairs plant shop, and the handcrafted items are integrated there. There are also some handcrafted items on the first floor, which is a contemporary gift shop." Customers are age 20-50, professional people with "interests revolving around the outdoors and Lake Michigan."

McKENDREE COLLABORATIVE, 1443 Wealthy SE, Grand Rapids MI 49506. (616)458-0267. Contact: Mona Erickson. Craft shop. Estab. 1974. Represents 4 craftworkers.
Acceptable Work: Considers glass art; jewelry; leatherworking; and metalsmithing. Fine one-of-a-kind and handmade production-line items. Price range: $15-500; bestsellers: $15-60.
Terms: Buys outright. Retail price set by craftworker. Reports in 2 weeks. Work may be shipped or hand-delivered.
Profile: "We have 900 square feet of display area; included are 6 antique showcases. We're unique in our area in providing handcrafted goods in a broad price range." Heaviest wholesale buying time: fall; best selling time: holidays.

MARKS STUDIO/GALLERY, 302 E. Chicago, Tecumseh MI 49286. (517)423-5858. Owners: Richard and Sandra Marks. Craft shop and gallery. Estab. 1972. Represents 12 Midwestern and East Coast craftworkers.
Acceptable Work: Considers jewelry; metalsmithing; and glass art; especially blown and stained glass. Fine one-of-a-kind and handmade production-line items. Price range: $1-1,250; bestsellers: $10-200.
Terms: Works on consignment and buys outright; 33⅓% commission. Retail price set by joint agreement. Requires exclusive area representation. Reports in 3 weeks. Work may be hand-delivered; dealer pays insurance on exhibited work.
Profile: "Our gallery is a working stained glass studio." Items displayed for 60 days. Heaviest wholesale buying time: fall; best selling time: fall and spring. "Our customers are very art aware."

MICHIGAN STATE UNIVERSITY MUSEUM GIFT EMPORIUM, Museum, W. Circle Dr., Michigan State University, E. Lansing MI 48824. Contact: Peg Dickman. Museum gift shop.
Acceptable Work: Considers cornhusk dollmaking, jewelry, needlecrafts, pottery, weavings, Ukranian eggs, Christmas ornaments and tinware (cookie cutters). "Resale items *must* be museum-oriented." One-of-a-kind and handmade production-line items. Price range: $1.50-50; bestsellers: $1.50-10.

Terms: Buys outright. Requires exclusive area representation. Call for appointment.
Profile: Shop has limited space in Natural History Museum; collections include decorative arts and folk art." Customers: college students and general public. "Hundreds of elementary school children tour the facility to view exhibits." Heaviest wholesale buying time: October-November; best selling time: Christmas.

MOSER'S DRIED FLOWER BARN, Box 65, Springlake MI 49456. (616)842-0641. Owners: John and Reini Moser. Gift shop. Estab. 1975. Represents 2-3 craftworkers.
Acceptable Work: Considers pottery, wall hangings, weavings and woodcrafting. "We limit our items to those relating to dried flower arranging, though there are always exceptions. We are not interested in buying dried arrangements." Specializes in primitive and fine one-of-a-kind and handmade production-line items. Price range: $2.50-60; bestsellers: $2.50-15.
Terms: Buys outright. Shop sets retail price. Requires exclusive area representation. Send resume, slides or photos. Reports in 2 weeks. Work may be shipped or hand delivered.
Profile: "Dried arrangements and wall hangings in natural colors are arranged in a primitive antique setting." Customers: ages 20-50, mostly female in middle to upper incomes. Heaviest wholesale buying time: summer-fall; best selling time: summer-Christmas.

MURIEL ORIGINALS, 1047 Michigan Ave., Benzonia MI 49616. (616)882-7203. Owner: Murial Trapp. Interior decoration shop. Estab. 1948. Represents 4 craftworkers. Considers original jewelry and pottery. "We handle only our own pots." All styles; utilitarian and/or decorative. Price range: $1.50-250; bestsellers: $10-20. Works on consignment; 33% commission. Best selling time: summer.

MUSEUM OF ARTS & HISTORY SHOP & RENTAL GALLERY, 1115 6th St., Port Huron MI 48060. (313)982-0891. Director: Stephen R. Williams. Museum gift shop/rental gallery. Estab. 1968. Represents 5 craftworkers from the 6 counties surrounding Port Huron (St. Clair, Tuscola, Lapeer, Huron, Sanilac, Macomb).
Acceptable Work: Considers batik, ceramics, glass art, jewelry, metalsmithing, needlecrafts, pottery, quilting, wall hangings, weavings and woodcrafting. One-of-a-kind designer pieces only. Price range: $15-250; bestsellers: $15-100.
Terms: Works on consignement; 25% commission. Craftworker sets retail price. Call for appointment. Reports in 2 weeks. Work may be shipped or hand-delivered. Dealer pays insurance on exhibited work.
Profile: "The Museum of Arts & History is a general museum. Two dimensional items are displayed in the sales and rental gallery; large 3-dimensional objects in sales and rental gallery; jewelry and other small items in locked Museum shop display case." Heaviest wholesale buying time: fall; best selling time: fall and summer.

MUSEUM SHIP VALLEY CAMP, Box 1668, Sault St. Marie MI 49783. (906)632-3658. Manager: Thomas J. Manse. Museum gift shop. Estab. 1968. Represents 1 craftworker at present time.
Acceptable Work: Considers all marine-oriented crafts. One-of-a-kind and handmade production-line items. Price range: $1.95-25; bestsellers: $2.95-3.
Terms: Buys outright. Retail price set by joint agreement. Send resume and slides. Reports in 4 weeks. Work must be mailed. Items are displayed from June-October. "We are a ship's store and sell to 55,000 people a year, mainly families on summer vacations." Heaviest wholesale buying and best selling time: April-October.

120 IN THE SHADE, c/o Hobies Rest., 109 E. Allegan St., Lansing MI 48933. (517)487-4470 or 337-2639. President: Beverly Rollins. Gallery. Estab. 1974. Represents 50-100 craftworkers.
Acceptable Work: Considers batik, ceramics/pottery, dollmaking, glass art, jewelry, metalsmithing, needlecrafts, soft sculpture, wall hangings, weavings and woodcrafting. "We are open to other media." Especially needs 3-dimensional work. Specializes in fine art designer crafts. Price range: $2-2,500 ("some exceed this"); bestsellers: $5-300.
Terms: Buys outright and works on consignment; 20-40% commission. Retail price set by joint agreement. Send resume, slides and call for appointment. "I prefer to have work shown to us—a minimum of 3 pieces. We must have a resume and b&w glossy photo, preferably of artist at work, for our news releases." Reports in 1 week. Work may be shipped or hand-delivered. Dealer pays insurance on exhibited work up to $100/piece, and only on 10 items/artist at any particular time.
Profile: "Shop is 40x40' with movable walls and space placements; many plants; skylight; and 20' ceilings. When we feature an artist, we have a minimum of 20 pieces, maximum 300. We

write a feature article for the area press, hold a poster campaign and have an invitational mailing." Items displayed on walls, in 5 locked glass cases and randomly throughout shop. Best selling time: Christmas.

THE PEACEABLE KINGDOM, 111 W. Liberty, Ann Arbor MI 48104. Contact: C. Wilfong. Gift shop. Estab. 1974.
Acceptable Work: Considers batik, candlemaking, ceramics, dollmaking, jewelry, leatherworking, quilting, soft sculpture. Especially needs dollmaking and soft sculpture. Specializes in folk art and contemporary crafts. One-of-a-kind and handmade production-line items. Price range: $5-300; bestsellers: $25-150.
Terms: Buys outright and works on consignment; 30% commission. Retail price set by joint agreement. Send resume and slides. Reports in 3 weeks. Dealer pays insurance on exhibited work.
Profile: "Small low-key shop with relaxed atmosphere in 1868 building." Located in university town. Best selling time: fall-Christmas.

PRIEHS DEPARTMENT STORE, 60-66 Macomb St., Mount Clemens MI 48043. (313)463-4567. General Manager: George W. Priehs. Department store. Write with resume and samples/illustrations of work.
Resale Items: Mrs. W. Cummings, buyer of hosiery, budget lingerie, candy, books, gifts, cards and stationery. Considers adult games; carvings; sculpture; children's toys; Christmas ornaments; dinnerware; dolls; furniture; jewelry; pillows; and silverwork. Handmade production-line items only. Prices set by store depending upon item's quality, workmanship and originality.
Props: Milo D'Oriole, display manager, store planning and development, and equipment buyer. Considers buying carvings; sculpture; Christmas ornaments; handmade furniture; and pottery.

REEDCRAFT WEAVERS, 153 N. Michigan, Beulah MI 49617. (616)882-5575. Contact: Lewis Small. Estab. 1940. Represents 5 craftworkers.
Acceptable Work: Considers candlemaking; jewelry; needlecrafts; and wall hangings. Especially needs woven towels; napkins; and lunch cloths. Finished handmade production-line items only. Price range: 20¢-$26; bestsellers: $1.35-26.
Terms: Buys outright or on consignment; 50% commission. Shop sets retail price. Requires exclusive area representation. Write. Reports in 1 week.
Profile: Items shown in glass cases and hanging displays. Best selling time: summer; heaviest wholesale buying time: spring. Shop located in "barn"; daily handweaving demonstration. Customers are tourists with middle to upper incomes.

REFLECTIONS ART GALLERY, Box 521, Leland MI 49654. Proprietor: Richard Braund. Craft shop. Estab. 1970. Represents 25 craftworkers.
Acceptable Work: Considers ceramics, glass art, jewelry, metalsmithing, pottery, soft sculpture, wall hangings, weavings and woodcrafting. One-of-a-kind and handmade production-line items. Price range: $3-125; bestsellers: $10-36.
Terms: Buys outright and works on consignment; 40% commission. Retail price set by joint agreement. Requires exclusive area representation. Send resume and slides. Reports in 3 weeks. Work may be shipped or hand delivered. Dealer pays some insurance on exhibited work. Items crafted should be signed.
Profile: "We are a small rough sawn wood shop in an old fishing village, now a national historic site. Items are moved often. We use old crates and blocks of wood for redistribution. The town is an exlusive resort for high income people and above. Has a new marina alongside the old village. Customers are highly educated with high incomes from all over the US." Heaviest wholesale buying time: late spring-early summer; best selling time: middle summer.

THE SIGN OF THE COPPER LANTERN, Box 899A, Royal Oak MI 48068. (313)545-7872. Owner: Peg Smith. Craft and gift shop. Estab. 1972. Represents 50-70 Michigan craftworkers.
Acceptable Work: Considers most professional crafts, including batik; candlemaking; ceramics; glass art; jewelry; metalsmithing; pottery; wall hangings; and woodcrafting. Needs "good metal workers, especially in copper," and unusual toys. "We also encourage our craftworkers to devise kits, when it fits their discipline." Price range: $1-500; bestsellers: $5-35.
Terms: Works on consignment (33⅓% commission) and buys outright, (50%). Retail price set by joint agreement. Requires exclusive area representation. Reports in 3 weeks. Work may be shipped or hand-delivered, "but only if we have committed to purchase and agreed upon when

and where delivery is to happen." Dealer pays shipping and insurance on exhibited work.
Profile: Owns 2 stores, a seasonal summer store on Main Street in Mackinaw City, Michigan, and a year-round store on Woodward in Berkley, Michigan. "We run our stores like gift shops. The commercial lines of little-known book publishers, small classic imported toys and the Rock Shop (Michigan minerals only) are the only other things we show besides Michigan art work." Uses gallery-type spotlighting plus general window and store displays. Maximum display time: 3 months. Heaviest wholesale buying time: spring and late summer; best selling time: summer in the Mackinaw store, October-December in the Berkley store. "Our greatest customer volume is women, age 25-50. Of all our customers 70% are from southeastern Michigan, 20% from the balance of the state, and 10% are regular customers from throughout the US."

STUDIO OF NATURAL ARTS, Box 5, Wire Rd., Paradise MI 49768. (906)492-3557. Owner: Sara L. Kuehne. Gallery. Estab. 1978. Represents 75 craftworkers, preferably from Michigan's Upper Peninsula.
Acceptable Work: Considers batik, dollmaking, folk art, pottery, rosemaling, soft sculpture, sculpture, tole painting, wall hangings, weavings and woodcrafting. Especially needs stuffed toys. Specializes in fine arts and crafts. One-of-a-kind and handmade production-line items. Price range: $5 minimum; bestsellers: $5-85.
Terms: Works on consignment; 30% commission. Retail price set by craftworker. Requires exclusive area representation. Send resume and slides or call for appointment. SASE. Reports in 2 weeks. Work may be shipped or hand delivered.
Profile: "The building is constructed of rough sawn lumber to retain a natural theme. In contrast, there is track lighting. Gallery is surrounded by tall birch and poplar trees." Customers: tourists. Heaviest consignment time: spring; best selling time: May-October.

SUNFLOWER SHOP, 116 E. Main, Northville MI 48167. (313)349-1425. Owner: Marie Bonamici. Gallery/gift shop. Estab. 1970. Represents 6-8 professional craftworkers.
Acceptable Work: Considers jewelry; pottery; wall hangings; weavings; and prints. Price range: $2-495; bestsellers: $20-150.
Terms: Works on consignment and buys outright; 33⅓% commission. Retail price set by shop. Requires exclusive area representation. Reports in 3 weeks. Hand-delivered work only. Dealer pays insurance on exhibited work.
Profile: Heaviest wholesale buying time: August-September; best selling time: November-December. Customers are middle to upper income with an interest in art. "We deal with many professional people and collectors."

THE WILD WEFT, 415 N. Fifth, Ann Arbor MI 48103. (313)761-2466. Contact: Mildred Diamond or June Wendel. Gallery/weaving supply shop. Estab. 1971. Represents 5 craftworkers.
Acceptable Work: Considers batik, needlecraft, wall hangings and weavings. Specializes in handwoven one-of-a-kind crafts. Price range: $30-300; bestsellers: $35.
Terms: Works on consignment; 25% commission. Craftworker sets retail price. Send resume and slides. Reports in 2 weeks. Work may be shipped or hand delivered. Dealer pays insurance on exhibited work. Display time: 1 month.
Profile: "We are primarily a weaving supply shop. However, we have a small exhibit area. Our format is to invite a weaver to display for a month at a time. We hold classes also." Best selling time: Christmas.

WIND & SUN CREATIONS, Rt. 2, Gobles MI 49055. (616)628-2568. Contact: Peter or Connie Czuk. Craft/gift shop. Estab. 1976. Represents 15-25 craftworkers.
Acceptable Work: Considers all crafts. "Wood is our main craft. Peter works with redwood burl and other exotic woods himself so wooden items go well." One-of-a-kind and handmade production-line items. Price range: $1-2,000; bestsellers: $4-500.
Terms: Buys outright but mostly works on consignment; 20-40% commission. Retail price set by craftworker or joint agreement. Requires exclusive area representation. Send slides with SASE. Reports in 2 weeks. "We exhibit at shows and meet many artists and craftsmen there." Work may be shipped or hand delivered. "Do not send work through the mail unless we have reviewed the work beforehand." Dealer pays insurance on exhibited work. Consignment work may stay 4-6 months, depending on when submitted.
Profile: "We are located in a rural area outside of Kalamazoo, Michigan. Our shop has quite a history asociated with it. At one time, it was the 'hub' (general store, post office, school) of a productive mint plantation. Our workshop is in the same building, behind the show room. Small items are displayed in glass and oak show cases. The interior of the shop has hardwood floors

with cherry, barnwood and pine siding. People from higher income groups come out for Pete's work and they are quite interested in other craft items. Items must be high quality because the buyers look for it." Heaviest wholesale buying time: pre-Christmas; best selling time: pre-Christmas and summer.

WOODLAND WORKSHOP, Birch Point Rd., Brimley MI 49715. (906)248-3398. Contact: Olive Craig. Craft shop/gallery. Estab. 1967. Represents 35-40 Michigan craftworkers.
Acceptable Work: Considers batik, glass jewelry, leatherworking, metalsmithing, pottery, wall hangings, weavings, and especially needs woodcrafting (functional or carvings). One-of-a-kind and handmade production-line items. Price range: 15¢-$250; bestsellers: $1-100.
Terms: Works on consignment; 33⅓% commission. Craftworker sets retail price, shop may advise. Call for appointment. Reports in 1 week. Work may be shipped or hand delivered. Dealer pays insurance on exhibited work.
Profile: "We are privately owned. Items are displayed to their best advantage. Pieces are moved around so returning customers see them in different perspectives." Customers: traveling public, mainly family vacationers. "There is an increasing number of professional people because of customers telling friends about us." Heaviest wholesale buying and best selling time: May-August.
To Break In: "Must be steady production (not necessarily the same items). Items should be ready to go on display (proper hanging devices, smooth surfaces on bottoms of pots)."

Minnesota

ART CRATE, INC., 3000 White Bear Ave., Maplewood Plaza, St. Paul MN 55109. (612)770-3110. See Art Crate, New Richmond, Wisconsin.

BROOKLYN CENTER COMMUNITY CENTER, 6301 Shingle Creek Pkwy., Brooklyn Center MN 55430. (612)561-5448. Contact: Kathy Flesher.
Terms: "Artists must hang own show and assume responsibility for their work in case of stolen property. We carry no insurance." Craftworker sets retail price. Call or write. 2 weeks exposure minimum.
Profile: "Our small gallery is available without charge to local artists/craftsmen. It is a small portion of a complete community center operation. We would be interested in showing traveling shows."

THE CANDLING MILL, 400 Sibley St., St. Paul MN 55101. (612)226-9891. President: Sherry Sandey. Gift shop. Estab. 1971. Represents 10 craftworkers. Heaviest wholesale buying time: fall; best selling time: fall and summer.
Acceptable Work: Considers candlemaking and candle-related crafts. One-of-a-kind and handmade production-line items. Price range: $2.50-65; bestsellers: $1-20.
Terms: Buys outright and works on consignment. Retail price set by joint agreement. Prefers exclusive area representation. Call for appointment. Reports in 2 weeks. Dealer pays return shipping and insurance for exhibited work.

ENDION STATION, 208½ W. Superior, Duluth MN 55802. (218)727-3534. Owners: Michael and Patricia Spencer. Craft shop/gallery. Estab. 1971. Represents 20 craftworkers.
Acceptable Work: Considers batik; ceramics; glass art; jewelry; leatherworking; pottery; quilting; soft sculpture; wall hangings; weavings; and woodcrafting. Price range: $1-200; bestsellers: $1-50.
Terms: Works on consignment and buys outright; 30% commission. Retail price set by joint agreement. Reports in 2 weeks. Work may be shipped or hand-delivered. Dealer pays insurance on exhibited work.
Profile: Work is grouped by exhibitor. Heaviest wholesale buying time: September-October; best selling time: October-December. Customers are women age 12-45 with lower to upper-middle income; they buy crafts for their usefulness and for gifts.

GRASS ROOTS, 400 Sibley, Park Square Ct., St. Paul MN 55101. (612)292-0988. Owner: Laurie Gluesing-Simpson. Gift shop. Represents 75-80 craftworkers, preferably from the upper Midwest.
Acceptable Work: Considers all crafts. Specializes in traditional one-of-a-kind items. Price range: $2-375; bestsellers: $5-50.
Terms: Buys outright and works on consignment; 33⅓% commission. Retail price set by joint agreement. "Craftworker cannot do art fairs in the immediate area, unless price agreements are set." Send slides or call for appointment. SASE. Work may be shipped or hand delivered.

Dealer pays insurance on exhibited work. Display time: 3 months.
Profile: "All items are displayed if possible. Quilts are hung on racks; cloth items are hung from chains suspended from the ceiling; other items are displayed on shelves, in an old trunk (currently used for display of rugs) and window space. We are in a restored warehouse in an historic area of St. Paul. The store is open on nights of play performances." Customers: primarily women, ages 25-45, middle to upper-middle incomes. "Advertising is being done to reach educated upper income buyers." Heaviest wholesale buying time: fall; best selling time: pre-Christmas.

THE HEART OF THE ARTICHOKE, 222 E. Clark St., Albert Lea MN 56007. (507)373-4258. Craft/gift shop. Represents 150-200 craftworkers.
Acceptable Work: Considers all crafts. One-of-a-kind and handmade production-line items. Price range: 25¢-$500; bestsellers: $5-20.
Terms: Buys outright and works on consignment; 30% commission. Retail price set by joint agreement. Send resume and photos. Reports in 2 weeks.
Profile: "We try to put new items in the front room when they are first brought in. Then they go to a specific area and are kept for 6 months or more. Items are displayed from walls, ceilings, display cases and in/on pieces of antique furniture." Heaviest wholesale buying and best selling time: pre-Christmas.

THE HONEYCOMB, Rt. 2, Lewiston MN 55952. (507)523-3642. Contact: Mrs. Clifford Babcock. Estab. 1973. Represents 50 craftworkers. Best selling time: pre-Christmas season and summer. Customers are ages 30-50 with middle incomes.
Acceptable Work: Considers candlemaking; ceramics; decoupage; dollmaking; glass art; jewelry; needlecrafts; quilting; wall hangings; weavings; and woodcrafting. Finished one-of-a-kind and handmade production-line items OK. Price range: $1-50; bestsellers: $2-10.
Terms: Works on consignment. Retail price set by joint agreement. Write. Reports in 1 week. Dealer pays insurance for exhibited work.

KALICO KORNER, 101 S. Broadway, Box 94, Alden MN 56009. (501)874-3458. President: Lucy Stiehl. Treasurer: Shirley Phinney. Secretary: Lois Hemmingsen. Craft/gift shop. Estab. 1974. Represents 100-150 craftworkers.
Acceptable Work: Considers candlemaking; ceramics; children's clothing; decoupage; dollmaking; jewelry; needlecrafts; pottery; quilting; soft sculpture; tole painting; wall hangings; weavings; and woodcrafting. Especially needs moderately priced holiday items; handmade toys; and ceramics. Primitive handmade production-line items. Price range: $1.50-50; bestsellers $2.50-25.
Terms: Works on consignment. "Craftworker sets his price; we add 30%. He always gets the amount he sets. He should keep in mind ours is added so item isn't over-priced." Reports in 3 weeks. Work may be shipped or hand-delivered.
Profile: "We have an ideal location in a small town atmosphere. Crafts are displayed with antiques, with better pieces kept under glass." Open 10-4 daily, 1-4 Sundays. Best selling time: fall-winter. Customers are both tourists and residents of the surrounding rural area.

LUMBERTOWN USA, Box 387, Brainered MN 56401. President: Peg Madden. Estab. 1954. Represents 3 craftworkers practicing Midwestern crafts of the 1870s.
Acceptable Work: Considers clothing; glass art; quilting; and woodcrafting. Primitive one-of-a-kind and handmade production-line items. Price range: 25¢-$150.
Terms: Works on consignment; 40% commission. Retail price set by joint agreement. Work may be shipped or hand-delivered; craftworker pays insurance on exhibited work.
Profile: "Lumbertown USA is a genuine restoration and replica of an 1870 lumbertown." Season runs May 25-September 15. Customers are older tourists with middle incomes.

LUTHERAN BROTHERHOOD—LUTHERAN CENTER GALLERY, 701 Second Ave. S., Minneapolis MN 55402. (612)340-7261. Fine Arts Coordinator: Joan Sheldon. Gallery. Estab. 1971. Represents 1+ craftworkers/month.
Acceptable Work: Considers all crafts except clothing, decoupage and quilting. "Pottery and jewelry have a big following." One-of-a-kind items preferred, "but will show some handmade production-line items." Price range: $5-300; bestsellers: $5-150.
Terms: Exhibits only; no commission. Craftworker sets retail price. Send resume and slides. Reports in 8 weeks, "depending on how our scheduling is going for the year. We usually book a year in advance." Work may be shipped or hand-delivered. Lutheran Brotherhood pays insurance on exhibited work and return transit. Craftworker pays insurance *to* gallery. Display time: 1 month.

Profile: "Hanging items are shown on display panels; more fragile items are shown in locked display cases; some pieces are displayed in the open. The gallery was established for the enjoyment of our employees as well as the downtown business community. We try to introduce a wide variety of craftworkers and mediums to those who regularly view the works in the gallery. In many cases, ours is the only gallery that displays works affordable enough for those working in the downtown area to buy." Customers: young people beginning to collect fine art pieces. Best selling time: pre-spring (before graduations, confirmations, etc.) and October-November.

MAD MONEY BOUTIQUE, c/o Sun Bay, Moose Lake MN 55767. (218)485-4958. Owner: Sheri Sundby. Craft shop/gallery. Estab. 1973.
Acceptable Work: Considers ceramics; clothing; dollmaking; jewelry; leatherworking; metalsmithing; pottery; soft sculpture; tole painting; wall hangings; weavings; and woodcrafting. Fine one-of-a-kind and handmade production-line items OK. Price range: $2-275; bestsellers; $4-30.
Terms: Works on consignment and buys outright; 33% commission. Retail price set by joint agreement. Reports in 2 weeks. Work may be shipped or hand-delivered. Dealer pays insurance on exhibited work.
Profile: "Our purpose is to present well-designed crafts and fine arts. The reaction over the years has been continuously supportive and complimentary, and the customers always comment on the unique visual treatment of the merchandise." Heaviest wholesale buying time: spring-summer; best selling time: late spring-fall. "Customers are generally tourists or summer residence dwellers: professors, naturalists, unique individuals who appreciate fine craftsmanship. They're often repeat customers who bring their guests to share what they've found 'in the middle of nowhere.'"

MINNESOTA LANDSCAPE ARBORETUM GIFT SHOP, 3675 Arboretum Dr., Chaska MN 55318. (612)443-2460. Manager: Lenore Johnson. Gift shop. Estab. 1974. Represents 15 craftworkers.
Acceptable Work: Considers batik; ceramics; glass art; jewelry; leatherworking; metalsmithing; pottery; wall hangings; weavings; and woodcrafting. Fine one-of-a-kind and handmade production-line items. Price range: 50¢-$200; bestsellers: $1-45.
Terms: Works on consignment and buys outright; 40% commission. Retail price set by joint agreement. Reports in 1 week. Work should be hand-delivered for consideration. "Our system of ordering, payments and invoicing is sometimes a problem because it's regulated by the University of Minnesota and we must conform to their statutes."
Profile: "We handle only nature-related items and try to have pieces that can't be found in mainline gift shops or department stores." Work is hung on walls and displayed in cases. Heaviest wholesale buying and best selling time: summer/fall. "Customers are mostly people who are interested in gardening, plants, animals and nature. During the summer we get many one-time customers. Some of our best buyers are arboretum members."

NORMANDALE COLLEGE GALLERY, 9700 France Ave. S., Bloomington MN 55431. (612)831-5001. Contact: J. Jack Bean. Considers graphics, pottery, jewelry, weaving and glass enameling. Retail price set by craftworker. Prices range: $15+. Send resume and slides or photos. Gallery pays shipping.

THE PEDDLERS, 2826 Piedmont Ave., Duluth MN 55811. (218)727-6955. Contact: Shirley Plaisted or Barb Dryer. Gift shop. Estab. 1977. Represents 180 craftworkers.
Acceptable Work: Considers all crafts, except metalsmithing and scrimshaw. "We are looking for the person who does craftwork for the person 'who has everything.' We do not do well with fine art." Handmade production-line items only. Price range: $1-140; bestsellers: $4-25.
Terms: Buys outright and works on consignment. "The craftworker sets his own price, we sell the item for what we feel it would best sell for. Not everything can be sold for the same percentage locked onto it." Send resume and photos. Reports in 1 week. Work may be shipped or hand delivered. Dealer pays insurance on exhibited work.
Profile: "Our shop is done in red, white and black. We have red and white checked curtains, bags, and wrapping paper. We also do house parties. Our handmade things are displayed on antique furniture. Each item is displayed in proper setting (i.e. baby things together with childrens). We also group things together by color. We are located in a neighborhood plaza. As a result we can get to know our customers as friends." Best selling time: spring and fall.

PLAINS ART MUSEUM, Box 37, Moorhead MN 56560. (218)236-7171. Director: James O'Rourke. Assistant Director: Rolf Lund. Museum gallery. Estab. 1960. Represents 12-18

craftworkers. Heaviest wholesale buying and best selling time: fall-winter.
Acceptable Work: Considers batik, ceramics, clothing, dollmaking, glass art, jewelry, leatherworking, metalsmithing, pottery, scrimshaw, soft sculpture, wall hangings, weavings and woodcrafting. One-of-a-kind designer pieces. Price range: 10¢-$2,000; bestsellers: 50¢-$40.
Terms: Works on consignment; 60% commission. Craftworker sets retail price. Requires exclusive area representation. Send resume and slides with SASE or call for appointment. Reports in 4 weeks. Requested work may be shipped or hand-delivered.

SANDEEN'S SCANDINAVIAN GIFT & ART SHOP, 1315 White Bear Ave., St. Paul MN 55106. (612)776-7012. Contact: Gail Sandeen. Gift shop. Estab. 1956. Price range: 59¢-$385; bestsellers: $1-30. Buys outright. Shop sets retail price. Work may be shipped or hand-delivered.
Acceptable Work: Considers candlemaking; ceramics; clothing; dollmaking; glass art; jewelry; metalsmithing; needlecrafts; pottery; wall hangings; weavings; woodcrafting; rosemaling; and dalmalning. "We specialize in Scandinavian and European style crafts. We are always looking for unusual and well-made unfinished woodenware items suitable for decoration by rosemaling or dalmalning. Always open for new lines of artwork or giftware which is Scandinavian." Heaviest wholesale buying and best selling time: September-December.

3 ROOMS UP, 4316 Upton Ave. S., Minneapolis MN 55410. (612)926-1774. Partner: Patricia Burrets. Craft shop/gallery. Estab. 1971. Represents 125 local craftworkers.
Acceptable Work: Considers batik; dollmaking; glass art; jewelry; metalsmithing; pottery; soft sculpture; wall hangings; weavings; woodcrafting; graphics; embossings; prints; trapunto; and basketry. Price range: $1-150; bestsellers: $1.50-40.
Terms: Works on consignment; 34% commission. Retail price set by joint agreement. Queries are answered "immediately; works are juried every 2 weeks, after which time we report." Work may be shipped or hand-delivered. New items are displayed for a trial period of 3-6 months.
Profile: "Our shop emphasizes quality craft/artwork at moderate prices. We have 4-5 shows/year, featuring 1 or more artists working in 1 medium. We're always looking for new things, well done, to show at reasonable prices." Works often grouped together by genre or color. All framed and finished pieces are hung. Accepts consignments "at any time"; best selling time: fall-Christmas. Customers are primarily women, age 20-50, middle to upper-middle class.

TIDEPOOL GALLERY, 3907 W. 50th St., Edina MN 55424. (612)926-1351. Manager: Bayle Greenberg. Gift shop. Estab. 1973. Represents 12-15 craftworkers.
Acceptable Work: Considers batik; candlemaking; ceramics; glass art; jewelry; metalsmithing; needlecrafts; pottery; soft sculpture; wall hangings; weavings; woodcrafting; wind chimes; pictures; flower arrangements; boxes; mirrors; and sand paintings. All crafts must relate to the ocean, and preferably be made from shell, coral, driftwood or sand. Fine one-of-a-kind and handmade production-line items. Price range: $2-135; bestsellers: $5-50.
Terms: Works on consignment and buys outright; 33% commission. Retail price set by joint agreement. Reports in 1 week. Work may be shipped or hand-delivered; dealer pays insurance on exhibited work.
Profile: "We deal exclusively in seashells, coral and sea-inspired crafts. We're the only shop of this kind in the upper Midwest; we're a branch of Tidepool Gallery, Malibu, California. Depending on the item, work is shown on center aisle tables, rough-hewn shelves or on the walls. Displays are changed every 2-3 weeks. Heaviest wholesale buying time: fall-Christmas; best selling time: fall-Christmas and April-June.

UP NORTH HANDCRAFTS/LADY SLIPPER DESIGNS, 314 Houston Ave., Crookston MN 56716. (218)281-3720. Shop Manager: Lisa Schumacher. Gallery, wholesale handcraft distributor and craft/gift shop. Estab. 1973. Represents 150 rural Minnesota craftworkers.
Acceptable Work: Considers batik; ceramics; dollmaking; glass art; jewelry; leatherworking; metalsmithing; needlecrafts; pottery; quilting; soft sculpture; tole painting; wall hangings; weavings; and woodcrafting. Price range: $1-200; bestsellers: $1-25.
Terms: Buys outright; 30% commission on gallery sales. Reports in 6 weeks. Work may be shipped or hand-delivered. Insurance by arrangement.
Profile: "In the gallery, exhibits last 2-3 weeks; may be 1 artist or a group show." Heaviest buying time: spring for retail store; spring, summer and early fall for wholesaling. Best selling time: summer for retail; fall for wholesale. "Our wholesale accounts vary from large department stores to small gift shops—accounts are scattered all over the country." Retail shop

customers are primarily visitors to Itasca State Park.

WINDSOR GALLERY, 5019 France Ave. S., Minneapolis MN 55410. (612)927-6041. Owner: D.J. Long. Gallery. Estab. 1961. Represents 3 craftworkers. Best selling time: fall-winter. Customers are age 25-50, upper income.
Acceptable Work: Considers batik; soft sculpture; wall hangings; and weavings. Fine one-of-a-kind and handmade production-line items; decorative only. Price range: $10-300; bestsellers: $10-100.
Terms: Works on consignment; 33% commission. Retail price set by craftworker. Requires exclusive area representation. Reports in 2 weeks. Work may be shipped or hand-delivered; dealer pays insurance on exhibited work. Work is displayed for 3 weeks minimum.

THE WINONA COUNTY HISTORICAL SOCIETY MUSEUM SHOP, 160 Johnson St., Winona MN 55987. (507)454-2723. Director: William D. Gernes. Museum craft/gift shop. Estab. 1976. Represents 60 craftworkers. "We have some responsibility to represent current trends, but more importantly we offer the traditional crafts of the Upper Mississippi Valley and the ethnic crafts of our area immigrant groups—Germans, Poles, Swedes, Norwegians and Luxemburgers."
Acceptable Work: Considers dollmaking; leatherworking; metalsmithing; needlecrafts; pottery; quilting; wall hangings; weavings; woodcrafting; wrought iron; stationery; ethnic Christmas ornaments; and rosemaling. Primitive handmade production-line items. Price range: 35¢-$150; bestsellers: 75¢-$10.
Terms: Works on consignment; 33% commission. Retail price set by joint agreement. Requires exclusive area representation for craftworkers not from the immediate area. Reports in 3 weeks. Work may be shipped or hand-delivered. Maximum display time, 1 year.
Profile: "We're the sole retailer of quality crafts in the city and are given added stability by our association with the Winona County Historical Society. Our shop sells traditional crafts exemplifying crafts' continuing role in the upper Midwest's development." Displays employ old-fashioned store fixtures, wicker baby buggies and steamer trunks. Customers are vacationers and gift buyers, income $15,000-30,000, with an interest in history and handicrafts.

Mississippi

COTTONLANDIA FOUNDATION, Box 1635, Greenwood MS 38930. (606)453-0925. Contact: Peggy H. McCormick. Gallery/museum gift shop. Estab. 1969.
Acceptable Work: Considers batik; ceramics; glass art; jewelry; leatherworking; needlecrafts; pottery; quilting; wall hangings; and weavings. Primitive and fine one-of-a-kind pieces. Price range: $1 and up.
Terms: Buys outright. Retail price set by joint agreement. Reports in 1 week. Work may be shipped or hand-delivered.
Profile: "Pictures are hung on rods and cams; 3D work on tables and stands in gallery; shop display is informal on shelving. Shop features cotton-related items." Displays gallery work 8 weeks. Heaviest wholesale buying time: spring and fall; best selling time: summer and Christmas.

DAR GIFT SHOP, 100 Orleans St., Nutchez MS 39120. (601)445-4555. Executive Director: Carolyn Nugent. Gift shop. Estab. 1953. Represents handicapped craftworkers. Considers handmade production-line dollmaking only. Price range and bestsellers: $1-12. Buys outright and works on consignment. Retail price set by joint agreement. Work may be shipped or hand delivered. Displays are on open tables with saleswomen. Customers: tourists and elderly. Heaviest wholesale buying and best selling time: spring and summer.

SERENDIPITY, 516 Linden St., Corinth MS 38834. (601)287-5173. Contact: Mary H. Kennedy or Margaret Mathis. Craft shop. Estab. 1976. Represents 140 craftworkers.
Acceptable Work: Considers ceramics; decoupage; dollmaking; jewelry; needlecrafts; pottery; quilting; tole painting; woodcrafting; and religious books. "Special need for wood products; baby gifts; and kitchen items." Price range: $1-450; bestsellers: $5-125.
Terms: Works on consignment; 30% commission. Craftworker sets retail price. Reports in 4 weeks. Dealer pays return shipping; in-transit insurance; and insurance for exhibited work.
Profile: "The shop is in a lovely old home with appropriate items in each room." All ranges of customers. Heaviest wholesale buying time and best selling time: fall.

THE VALLEY, 1423 Washington St., Box 111, Vicksburg MS 39180. (601)636-6121. General Manager: Ray L. Bolmes. Department store. Buys and consigns baskets; carvings and sculpture; dinnerware; dolls; furniture; jewelry; pillows; pottery; silverwork; wall hangings; and weavings. Display department uses baskets; carvings; sculpture; and handmade furniture. One-of-a-kind and handmade production-lines OK. Store sets retail price. Write or call for interview.

WOODVILLE MUSEUM OF SOUTHERN DECORATIVE ARTS, Box 328, Woodville MS 39669. (601)888-6809. Contact: Ernesto Caldeira. Museum gift shop. Estab. 1976. Represents 10-50 craftworkers. Considers all crafts. Price range: 50¢-$75; bestsellers: $1-5. Works on consignment; 25-50% commission. Craftworker sets retail price. Work may be shipped or hand-delivered. Museum pays insurance for exhibited work.
Profile: "We are the only museum shop in southwestern Mississippi; are located on the court house square". Heaviest wholesale buying time: early spring; best selling time: March-April and September-December.

Missouri

AMANDA'S, Mutton Hollow, Box 59, Branson MO 65616. (417)334-4947. Contact: Amanda Cashman. Craft/gift shop. Estab. 1970. Represents 50-100 craftworkers.
Acceptable Work: Considers baskets, ceramics, chairs, decoupage, dollmaking, jewelry, woven mats, needlecrafts, pillows, quilting, rugs, tole painting, wall hangings, weavings, and woodcrafting. Especially needs "quilts that are large and well-made; handquilted only." Specializes in primitive pieces. One-of-a-kind and handmade productionline items. Price range: $1-500.
Terms: Works on consignment; 40% commission. Retail price set by joint agreement. Send resume. SASE. Reports in 2 weeks. Work may be shipped or hand delivered. "Anything mailed to me would be returned at the craftsman's expense if craft not suitable."
Profile: Shop is 3-story. "We display in a country-style in keeping with the area." Customers: tourists. Heaviest wholesale buying time: April-October; best selling time: April-September.

THE ARK, 51 N. Gore, Webster Groves MO 63119. (314)968-2200. Contact: Arline R. Korte. Craft/gift shop and gallery. Estab. 1971. Represents 100+ craftworkers. "We do not take any items that are done by our 20 board members." Best selling time: October-December.
Acceptable Work: Considers all crafts except leatherworking, metalsmithing, and scrimshaw. Specializes in fine art one-of-a-kind pieces. "Only quality items and prefer uniqueness." Price range: $1.50-395.
Terms: Works on consignment; 50% commission. Retail price set by joint agreement. Requires exclusive area representation. Call for appointment. Reports in 2 weeks. Work must be hand-delivered.

BARN GALLERY & FRAME SHOP, 1209 W. 103 St., Kansas City MO 64114. Owner: K.D. Gilbert. Gallery. Estab. 1948. Represents 15 professional craftworkers.
Acceptable Work: Considers batik, ceramics, scrimshaw, sculpture and woodcarving. Especially needs woodcarvings. One-of-a-kind items only. Bestsellers: $300-500.
Terms: Works on consignment; 34% commission. Requires exclusive area representation. Call for appointment. Dealer pays insurance on exhibited work ("up to a certain point").

BITS & PIECES INC, 230½ Nichols Rd., Kansas City MO 64112. (816)561-7686. Owner: Jacqueline Schulz. Miniatures and dollhouse shop. Estab. 1971. Represents 35 craftworkers. Considers all types of miniatures. All styles; 1 inch scale. Price range: 25¢-$3,000; bestsellers: $2-50. Buys outright. Retail price set by shop. Reports in 2 weeks. Work may be shipped or hand-delivered. Heaviest wholesale buying and best selling time: fall. "We build and furnish dollhouses and rooms on a 1 inch equals 1 foot scale."

CALIFORNIA CLOTHING, CO., Box 1221, 620 S. Main, St. Charles MO 63301. Owner: Stephanie Stupperich. Shop for handmade and recycled clothing. Estab. 1975. Represents 10 craftworkers.
Acceptable Work: Considers clothing and jewelry. "No macrame or leather." Price range: $1-50; bestsellers: $5-20.
Terms: Works on consignment; 25% commission. Retail price set by joint agreement. Reports in 2 weeks. Work may be shipped or hand-delivered.
Profile: "This shop is the only one of its kind in a tourist area of historical buildings and other attractions." Clothes must be appropriate to the season. Displays work 3 months. Best selling time: fall. Customers are "college girls, young working women and housewives, age 17-35. They're interested in flattering quality clothing rather than the bizarre."

COUNTRY CRAFT BOUTIQUE, Rt. 1, Box 455, Branson MO 65616. (417)338-2424. Contact: Jan Young or Billie Penrod. Craft/gift shop. Estab. 1976. Represents 20-25 craftworkers.
Acceptable Work: Considers dollmaking, jewelry, metalsmithing, needlecrafts, quilting, tole painting, woodcrafting and folk crafts. Especially needs quilts, woodcarvings, folk toys, jewelry and baskets. Items should have a practical use. No kits. Specializes in Ozark-type work and concentrating in tole painting and woodworking. Handmade production-line items only. Price range: 50¢-$250; bestsellers: $2-10, $50-100.
Terms: Buys outright but prefers working on consignment; 40% commission. Retail price set by joint agreement. Write or call for appointment; must have slides for screening. Reports in 2 weeks. Work may be shipped or hand-delivered. "We reserve the right to return merchandise after 30 days, if it does not receive customer interest."
Profile: "Branson is a tourist area. People come into this area for the lakes, scenery and because the area is promoted as an Ozark craft area. We are a gift shop concentrating on craft items, not the mass-produced souvenier shop. Our shop was an older house and we left the floor plan as it was. Work is displayed around antique pieces (wood boxes, barrels, baskets). We try to maintain the rustic Ozark atmosphere." Customers: young married to retired people, middle to upper middle income, tourists. Heaviest wholesale and best selling time: April-October.

CRAFT ALLIANCE GALLERY, 6640 Delmar Blvd., St. Louis MO 63130. (314)725-1151. Gallery Director: Dorothy Farley. Gallery. Estab. 1964. Represents 70 craft artists.
Acceptable Work: Considers batik; ceramics; clothing; glass art; jewelry; metalsmithing; stitchery; pottery; soft sculpture; wall hangings; enamels; weavings; and woodcrafting. "Work must represent contemporary American craft-art." Fine one-of-a-kind and handmade production-line items (limited edition). Price range: $2.50-3,000; bestsellers: $12-75.
Terms: Works on consignment; 33⅓% commission. Only work by juried member artists is shown. Work is juried twice annually. Retail price set by craftworker. Reports in 1 week. Work may be shipped or hand-delivered; dealer pays insurance on exhibited work while on premises.
Profile: Nonprofit gallery with standards and policies determined by member-artists. "Part of it is gallery-like, another part is shop-like in its displays." Best selling time: November-December. Customers are age 18-65.

CRAFT PLACE, 506 S. Main St., St. Charles MO 63301. (314)723-9398. Partner: Christine Raecke. Gallery/gift shop/studio. Estab. 1973. Represents 50-60 craftworkers.
Acceptable Work: Considers batik, glass art, jewelry, metalsmithing, mobiles, pottery, soft sculpture, wall hangings, weavings and woodcrafting. Specializes in fine contemporary crafts. One-of-a-kind and handmade production-line items. Price range: $2-400; bestsellers: $5-200.
Terms: Buys outright and works on consignment; 33⅓% commission. Craftworker sets retail price. Requires exclusive area representation. Send slides. Reports in 3 weeks. Work may be shipped or hand delivered. Dealer pays insurance on exhibited work.
Profile: Shop is in a "Victorian home located in the restored beauty of one of Missouri's oldest river-front towns. Work is displayed on burlap or old brick walls, or in stone or brick display areas. Bells and windchimes hang from a 9 foot gold leafed tree (wrought iron). Mobiles hang from 12 foot ceilings." Customers: good to excellent incomes. Heaviest wholesale buying time: spring-fall; best selling time: summer and pre-Christmas.

CUSTOM HOUSE, 701 S. Main St., St. Charles MO 63301. (314)723-6433. Owner: Duane Thornton. Craft shop. Estab. 1971. Price range: $10-2,000; bestsellers: $100-700. Works on consignment; 30% commission. Retail price set by joint agreement. Requires exclusive area representation. Send samples or photos. Reports in 1 week. Work should be hand-delivered.
Acceptable Work: Considers jewelry; quilting; woodcrafting; clocks; and custom built furniture. Primitive and fine one-of-a-kind pieces; utilitarian and/or decorative.
Profile: "Our shop features only handmade, original items and customers can also place order of their own design. Displays are constantly changing; if customer response is negative, items are removed, usually after 8 weeks." Heaviest wholesale buying time: June-October; best selling time: June-December.

DARLINE'S ANTIQUES & NEEDLECRAFT, 1106 Pine St., Rolla MO 65401. (314)364-7505. Gift shop/boutique. Represents 10-15 craftworkers.
Acceptable Work: Considers ceramics, decoupage, dollmaking, glass art, needlecrafts, quilting, tole painting, wall hangings, weavings and woodcrafting. Especially needs inexpensive home decorating items. Specializes in contemporary, bright colored items. One-of-a-kind and handmade production-line items. Price range: $2-100; bestsellers: $5-25.

Terms: Works on consignment; 40% commission. Retail price set by joint agreement. Requires exclusive area representation. Call for appointment. Reports in 1 week. Work may be shipped or hand-delivered. Dealer pays insurance on exhibited work.
Profile: "We are located on the main street of the town and directly across from Missouri School of Mines University. We are a local tourist attraction." Heaviest wholesale buying time: fall-spring; Best selling time: Christmas and summer.

EUCLID LEATHER LOFT, 9 S. Euclid, St. Louis MO 63108. (314)367-5514. Contact: Roger and Fern Steffen. Leather shop. Estab. 1972.
Acceptable Work: Considers leatherworking, metal, wood and stone buckles. Handmade production-line items OK. Price range: $5-100; bestsellers: $30-60.
Terms: Buys outright. Retail price set by joint agreement. Send resume, slides and SASE. Reports in 3 weeks.
Profile: "Our shop is a store front shop in a redeveloped urban area. Since the quality of leather items can vary so easily, we will look only at well finished items. Plain items that feature good leather work, rather than artsy/craftsy decorations, seem to sell best."

THE FARMER'S DAUGHTER, 4103 Pennsylvania, Kansas City MO 64111. (816)561-1777. Contact: Judy Christy. Gift shop. Estab. 1976. Represents 10-20 craftworkers.
Acceptable Work: Considers candlemaking, ceramics, clothing, dollmaking, glass art, jewelry, needlecrafts, pottery, quilting and woodcrafting. "I prefer functional items rather than purely decorative. Crafts with an old-fashioned feeling do well (e.g., wooden toys, rag dolls, quilt items)." Handmade production-line items. Price range: $2-425; bestsellers: $5-40.
Terms: Buys outright and occasionally takes large items on consignment; 40% commission. "Consignment items are usually removed after 90 days if no interest in them is evidenced." Retail price set by joint agreement. Call for appointment; reports in 1 week. Work may be shipped or hand-delivered. Dealer pays insurance on exhibited work.
Profile: "We are located in a restored area. The shop is in an 1850 vintage building converted to small shops, reataurants, offices. We have used lots of wood and antique fixtures for display. 'Careful clutter' makes the shop warm and inviting to browsers." Heaviest wholesale buying time: summer and fall prior to Christmas; bestselling time: pre-Christmas.

THE RALPH FOSTER MUSEUM, The School of the Ozarks, Point Lookout MO 65726. (417)334-6411. Director: Marvin E. Tong Jr. Museum gallery/gift shop. Estab. 1933. Represents 6 craftworkers; Ozarks region of Missouri, Arkansas and Oklahoma craftworkers preferred.
Acceptable Work: Considers ceramics; decoupage; dollmaking; jewelry; leatherworking; metalsmithing; needlecrafts; pottery; quilting; woodcrafting; and native Ozarks crafts. Especially needs inexpensive woodcarvings; metalwork; ceramics; jewelry; native Ozarks crafts such as baskets; split hickory chairs; ceramics; and cast iron. Price range: $3-100; bestsellers: $3-25.
Terms: Buys outright. Retail price set by joint agrement. Rental gallery fee: $30/$100. Reports in 2 weeks. Work may be shipped or hand-delivered. Displays work 30 days maximum.
Profile: "We are the only museum in the area that is a legitimate museum with no admission charge; 368,000 visitors in 1978. May through August visitors are young married couples interested in the Ozarks and its crafts. September to October visitors are older retired couples on tours of the Ozarks." Heaviest wholesale buying time: March-April; best selling time: May-October.
To Break In: "Visit buyer with selection of samples, have price list available and be able to supply on a regular basis."

GATEWAY GALLERY OF ARTS & CRAFTS, 103 Newton, Verallies MO 65084. Contact: Jan O'Haro or Dorsey Letchworth. Craft/gift shop/gallery. Estab. 1970. Represents 100 craftworkers. Best selling time: summer and Christmas.
Acceptable Work: Considers candlemaking, ceramics, decoupage, dollmaking, glass art, jewelry, leatherworking, metalsmithing, needlecrafts, pottery, quilting, tole painting, wall hangings, weavings and woodcrafting. Especially needs leatherworking. Specializes in fine art designer crafts and Appalachian work—a good cross section. One-of-a-kind and handmade production-line items. Price range: 35¢-$200; bestsellers: $1.98-20.
Terms: Works on consignment plus $1/month charge. Craftworker sets price and gallery adds 40% mark-up. Call in person with SASE. Reports immediately. Work may be shipped or hand delivered. "Old merchandise not selling must be taken from the shop and replaced with new and different items every 90 days. Dues will be payable at that time for the 90 day period. Items will be held for 60 days and if not called for, will become property of the shop to be handled as best seen fit."

THE GATHERING, 919 W. 44th St., Kansas City MO 64111. (816)931-9393. Contact: Carolyn Cameron or Willie Morgan. Gallery/supplier. Estab. 1976. Represents 60 craftworkers.
Acceptable Work: Considers ceramics, dollmaking, metal, pottery, wood, glass, and fiber (clothing, weaving, stitchery, paint on silk or fabric, batik, quilted/stuffed sculptural and wall pieces). "Special emphasis on fiber." One-of-a-kind pieces. Price range: $1.50-1,000; bestsellers: up to $100.
Terms: Works on consignment; 40% commission. "All work must be juried before acceptance. We jury on the 3rd Sunday of each month. Work sometimes must be held until that time." Query with slides; submit actual pieces if possible. SASE. Reports in 2 weeks. Work may be shipped or hand delivered. Dealer pays return shipping and insurance for exhibited work.
Profile: "We are dealing with tomorrow's market in this area of the country. Seeking to improve the understanding of the artist/craftsman and to give exposure to those persons working in those fields."

GINGHAM GOOSE, 427 N. Sappington, Glendale MO 63122. (314)965-6821. Partners: Sheran Cronin, Jan Schuster, Maureen Wagner and Barbara Monaco. Gift shop. Estab. 1977. Represents 90-120 craftworkers.
Acceptable Work: Consides candlemaking, ceramics, clothing, decoupage, dollmaking, glass art, jewelry, metalsmithing, needlecrafts, pottery, quilting, tole painting, wall hangings, weavings, woodcrafting and antiques. "Children and baby gifts are big year round. Crafts made from natural materials (barnwood, corn cob, straw) seem to do best." Handmade production-line items only. Price range: $1-50; bestsellers: $3-12.
Terms: Works on consignment; 40% commission. Retail price set by joint agreement. Write with samples or drop in. SASE. Reports in 3 weeks. Work may be shipped or hand delivered.
Profile: "We use a lot of antiques for displaying crafts." Items are on display for 90 days. Best selling time: October-December.

THE GLASS WORKBENCH, INC., 515 S. Main St., St. Charles MO 63301. (314)723-3557. President: Joanne Bishop. Craft shop. Estab. 1975. Represents 4 craftworkers. Considers stained glass art. Fine one-of-a-kind and handmade production-line items; utilitarian and/or decorative. Price range: $2.50-500; bestsellers: $2.50-65. Buys outright.
Profile: "We primarily handle our own design items. Classes, kits and craft supplies are also available for the stained glass beginner." Heaviest wholesale buying time: fall; best selling time: Christmas.

GRANDMA'S FOLLY, 401 S. Main St., St. Charles MO 63301. (314)724-5656. Owner: C. Thompson. Children's gift shop. Estab. 1974. Represents 75 craftworkers.
Acceptable Work: Considers clothing; dollmaking; needlecrafts; quilting; wall hangings; weavings; and woodcrafting—"anything to wear or play with related to children." Needs all types of clothing and toys. Fine one-of-a-kind and handmade production-line items; utilitarian and/or decorative. Price range: 50¢-$125; bestsellers: $2.50-20.
Terms: Works on consignment and buys outright; 40% commission. Retail price set by joint agreement. Requires exclusive representation within a 10 mile radius. Reports in 4 weeks. Work may be shipped or hand-delivered; dealer pays insurance on exhibited work and return shipping.
Profile: "We specialize in items for special little people." Work displayed for 30 days; "longer, if it seems necessary." Heaviest wholesale buying time: fall; best selling time: October-November. Customers are mothers, grandmothers and young women.

HOBBY SHOP, 209 E. Main, Union MO 63084. (314)583-5252. Contact: Ervin J. Aholt. Craft shop. Represents 2 craftworkers.
Acceptable Work: Considers candlemaking; decoupage; dollmaking; jewelry; leatherworking; needlecrafts; tole painting; wall hangings; weavings; and woodcrafting. Fine one-of-a-kind pieces. Price range: $1-25; bestsellers $3-10.
Terms: Works on consignment; 20% commission. Retail price set by joint agreement. Reports in 1 week. Work may be shipped or hand-delivered. Displays work 30 days maximum. Best selling and heaviest wholesale buying time: fall.

McCLENDON'S ART FACTORY, 4248 Troost, Kansas City MO 64110. (816)931-5791. Contact: Time McClendon. Gift shop/gallery. Estab. 1971. Represents 15 craftworkers.
Acceptable Work: Considers batik, candlemaking, ceramics, clothing, glass art, jewelry, leatherworking, metalsmithing, pottery, soft sculpture, wall hangings, weavings and woodcrafting. One-of-a-kind items only. Price range: $3-2,000; bestsellers: $5-100.

Terms: Works on consignment; 33⅓% commission. Retail price set by joint agreement. Send resume and slides with SASE or call for appointment. Reports in 2 weeks. Work may be shipped or hand delivered. Dealer pays insurance on exhibited work.
Profile: "The shop has white painted walls, palm trees and plants creating a comfortable but electrifying atmosphere blended in with very unique antiques. A reception is held for each artist who gives a one-man showing. Items remain as long as they sell, until the artist requests their removal, or an average of one month or longer." Customers: ages 18+ with $8,000-30,000 incomes. Heaviest wholesale buying time: fall, spring, and occasionally in the summer; best selling time: winter (especially around Christmas) and other holidays (Valentine's Day, Mother's Day, Labor Day).

MORGIE'S, 524 S. Main St., St. Charles MO 63301. (314)723-3468. Manager: Morgie Felt. Craft/gift shop. Estab. 1977. Represents 40 craftworkers.
Acceptable Work: Considers ceramics; clothing; decoupage; dollmaking; glass art; jewelry; needlecrafts; pottery; quilting; soft sculpture; tole painting; wall hangings; weavings; metalworking and woodcrafting. Price range: 99¢-$125; bestsellers: $1.99-60.
Terms: Works on consignment and buys outright; 40% commission. Retail price set by joint agreement. Requires exclusive area representation. Work may be shipped or hand-delivered. Dealer pays insurance for exhibited work.
Profile: "Items are shown in a casual grouping; some under glass. We are located in a courtyard by a gazebo overlooking the Missouri River. Customers are tourists and residents; interested in history." Best selling time: summer-Christmas.

MUSEUM OF ANTHROPOLOGY SALES DESK, UNIVERSITY OF MISSOURI-COLUMBIA, 104 Swallow Hall, University of Missouri, Columbia MO 65201. (314)882-3764. Director: Dr. Lawrence H. Feldman. Museum gift shop. Estab. 1973.
Acceptable Work: Considers ceramics; clothing; pottery; wall hangings; weavings; and woodcrafting. "We need items used around the home, among peasant cultures." One-of-a-kind and handmade production-line items; utilitarian. Price range: 50¢-$60; bestsellers: 50¢-$20.
Terms: Works on consignment and buys outright; commission varies. Gallery sets retail price. Reports in 1-2 weeks. Work may be shipped or hand-delivered. Dealer pays shipping to shop and insurance for exhibited work.
Profile: "Items are put in a locked display case. Customers are college students with poverty level income and somewhat better-off University staff and occasional tourists." Best selling time: July-August and November-December.

MUSEUM OF ART & ARCHAEOLOGY, UNIVERSITY OF MISSOURI, 1 Pickard Hall, University of Missouri, Columbia MO 65211. Museum shop manager: Florene B. Fratcher. Museum gift shop. Estab. 1976.
Acceptable Work: Considers glass art, jewelry, needlecrafts and pottery. "All items must be related to the museum collections." Specializes in reproductions of ancient glass, pottery and jewelry. Price range: $3-35.
Terms: Buys outright and works on consignment; commission varies. Shop sets retail price. SASE. Reports in 1-2 weeks. Work may be shipped or hand-delivered.
Profile: "There is 1 small room opposite the elevator on the main museum floor (second floor of the building). Displays are changed every 2 months." Customers: university students, faculty and visitors. Best selling time: November-December.

OLD COUNTRY STORE & MUSEUM, Rt. 1, Milo MO 64767. (417)876-6280. Contact: Mrs. John A. Logan. Craft museum gift shop. Estab. 1975. Represents local craftworkers.
Acceptable Work: Considers ceramics; dollmaking; metalsmithing; barn wood picture frames; dollhouses; dollhouse furniture; and miniatures. Fine one-of-a-kind and handmade production-line items. Price range: $1-300; bestsellers: $1-75.
Terms: Works on consignment and buys outright; 25% commission. Retail price set by joint agreement. Hand-delivered work only.
Profile: "My store not only sells staple groceries and picnic items, but also used books, miniature 3-D scenes, dolls, doll cradles, doll beds, dollhouses, dollhouse furniture and miniatures. Everything but the books and groceries is made right here in the community and there is no other store nearby that does that." Heaviest wholesale buying time: April; best selling time: May-October.

OLD MILL CRAFTS, Rt. 1, Box 6, Augusta MO 63332. (314)228-4496. Contact: Betty Bade. Craft and antique shop. Estab. 1976. Represents 10 craftworkers. Considers all crafts. One-of-a-kind and handmade production-line items. Price range: 10¢-$150; bestsellers: $15-50. Works on consignment; 30% commission. Craftworker sets retail price. Requires exclusive area representation. Work may be shipped or hand-delivered. "We are located in a barn that was once an old mill." Best selling time: fall.

OMEGA POTTERY SHOP, Box 13, Reeds Spring MO 65737. Pottery/Owner: Mark Oehler. Estab. 1972. Represents 3 craftworkers.
Acceptable Work: Considers pottery, wall hangings and weavings. Specializes in traditional and contemporary utilitarian crafts. One-of-a-kind and handmade production-line items. Price range: $4-200; bestsellers: $4-25.
Terms: Buys outright and works on consignment; 30% commission. "I will buy outright if I have the capital at the time." Retail price set by joint agreement. Send resume and slides. SASE. Reports in 1 week. Work may be shipped or hand delivered.
Profile: "My shop is in the Ozarks near Table Rock Lake and area attractions. Items are displayed equally with my work. My customers are people interested in objects of the hand as opposed to mass production; people with the time, money and education to seek out one-of-a-kind items. Mostly tourist traffic, but much return business from regular visitors." Best selling time: April-December.

ONE MANZ FAMILY ARTS & CRAFTS, 918 Westwood Mini Mall, Caruthersville MO 63830. (314)333-1324. Contact: Charles Manz. Arts/crafts/gift shop. Estab. 1977. Price range: 50¢-$50; bestsellers: $2-5. Buys outright. Reports in 2 weeks.
Acceptable Work: Considers batik; candlemaking; decoupage; dollmaking; jewelry; leatherworking; metalsmithing; quilting; wall hangings; weavings; woodcrafting; and especially needs tole painting.
Profile: Customers are "from 15-65; from lawyers to welfare." Best selling and heaviest wholesale buying time: Christmas.

OZARK MARKET BASKET, 1611 S. 3rd St., Ozark MO 65721. (417)485-2755. Contact: Dick or Joann Ege. Craft/gift shop. Estab. 1973. Represents 60 craftworkers.
Acceptable Work: Considers calico chickens, pillows, quilting, soft sculpture, tole painting and woodcrafting. "We use a lot of chicken related items. We sell a lot of finished wood shelves, coat racks and mirrors." Specializes in contemporary, bright colored crafts. Handmade production-line items only. Price range: 50¢-$100; bestsellers: 50¢-$15.
Terms: Buys outright. Shop sets retail price. Call for appointment. Reports in 1 week. Work may be shipped or hand delivered.
Profile: "We display with old cabinets and wooden crafts to create a bright country look. We have a shop that features decor items (wooden coat racks, floral arrangements, lots of calico, etc.). We teach tole painting classes." Customers: middle incomes; rural residents; housewives, homemakers and some tourists; early 20s to middle age. Heaviest wholesale buying time: summer-fall; best selling time: fall-Christmas.
To Break In: "Have a sample and price decided before trying to sell. Fill orders in a reasonable time and have all items as well-made as samples."

PATCHWORK, 25 N. Gore, Webster Groves MO 63119. (314)961-2983. Contact: Joan I. Scott. fabric/gift shop.
Acceptable Work: Considers needlecrafts, quilting, soft sculpture and wall hangings. Handmade production-line items only. Price range: $3.25-30.
Terms: Buys outright. Craftworker sets retail price. Work may be shipped or hand delivered.
Profile: "We have the largest selection of calico fabrics in St. Louis. Along with that, we buy soft good gift items that we find at shows (Atlanta, New York, California, Texas, etc.). We teach quilting and rugbraiding." Heaviest wholesale buying and best selling time: pre-Christmas.

PATTERSON'S CORNER, 102 E. College, Independence MO 64050. (816)252-5770. Co-owner: Barbara J. Patterson. Gift shop. Estab. 1977. Represents 20 craftworkers.
Acceptable Work: Considers ceramics, decoupage, dollmaking, glass art, jewelry, leatherworking, metalsmithing, miniatures, needlecrafts, pottery, scrimshaw, soft sculpture, tole painting, wall hangings, weavings and woodcrafting. Specializes in doll houses, furniture and accessories. One-of-a-kind and handmade production-line items. Price range: 50¢-$400; bestsellers: $2-100.
Terms: Buys outright but mostly works on consignment; 40% commission. Gallery sets retail price. Send resume, slides or call for appointment. SASE. Reports in 1-2 weeks. Work may be

shipped or hand-delivered. "Please have items and prices listed."
Profile: Displays in window, on tables, wall shelves, walls and in hanging boxes. Heaviest wholesale buying time: summer-Christmas; best selling time: fall-Christmas.

PICKWICK PLACE, 621 S. Pickwick, Springfield MO 65802. (417)869-0469. President: Rebecca Giboney. Craft/gift/antique shop. Estab. 1976. Represents 10-15 craftworkers.
Acceptable Work: Considers batik, candlemaking, ceramics, dollmaking, needlecrafts, pottery, quilting, scrimshaw, soft sculpture, wall hangings, weavings and woodcrafting. Specializes in primitive and Appalachian crafts; prefers a country look. Has some original art quilts. Price range: $1-500.
Terms: Buys outright (small items) and works on consignment (expensive items); 33⅓% commission. Craftworker sets retail price. Requires exclusive area representation. Send resume, slides or call for appointment. Reports in 2 weeks. Work may be shipped or hand delivered. Display time: 3 months (depending upon item).
Profile: "We have a small shop. We try to have the unusual and seem to be succeeding in establishing a reputation for doing just that. We constantly change our shop displays so our items are displayed differently each month" Customers: many antique buffs, return clientele, high income people and working women. Heaviest wholesale buying and best selling time: fall.

QUILT COUNTRY ENTERPRISES, INC., 616 Ward Pkwy., Kansas City MO 64112. (816)561-3311. President: Mary Alys Corcoran. Quilt shop. Estab. 1974. Represents 100 quilt craftworkers.
Acceptable Work: Considers clothing, quilting and wall hangings; all quilted. Price range: $1-3,000; bestsellers: $100-500.
Terms: Buys outright. Reports in 2 weeks. Dealer pays insurance for exhibited work.
Profile: "Quilt Country in Kansas City offers the largest selection of quilts for sale anywhere. Our calico fabric selection is also extensive and we have a complete line of supplies for the do-it-yourself person."

RAACH'S PLAZA GALLERY INC., 630 W. 50th, Kansas City MO 64112. (816)753-2047. President: F.A. Raach.
Acceptable Work: Considers batik; ceramics; glass art; jewelry; mobiles; pottery; sculpture; soft sculpture; wall hangings; weavings; and woodcrafting. Price range: $10-10,000; bestsellers: $100-500.
Terms: Works on consignment; 33⅓% commission. Gallery sets retail price. Requires exclusive area representation. Query with slides of work. SASE.

J. ROACH GALLERIES, 26 N. 9th St., Columbia MO 65201. (314)449-8717. Contact: Jay Roach. Craft shop/gallery/gift shop. Estab. 1974. Represents 90-100 craftworkers.
Acceptable Work: Considers ceramics; glass art; jewelry; metalsmithing; pottery; wall hangings; and weavings. Finished and handmade production-line items. Price range: $3.50-1,000; bestsellers: $10-400.
Terms: Buys outright. Craftworker sets retail price. Requires exclusive area representation. Work may be shipped or hand-delivered. Dealer pays insurance for exhibited work.
Profile: "There are 3 colleges here; customers are college students with some money; and housewives and working women 30-45 years old. We really like to have the arrangement with our craftspeople that whatever does not sell in a reasonable amount of time can be exchanged for credit or for other merchandise." Best selling time: December.

ST. CHARLES ARTISTS GUILD, 524 South Main St., St. Charles MO 63301. President: Chiara Moerschel. Gallery. Estab. 1966. Represents 70 craftworkers. "We are a nonprofit organization; members set values on their work; 20% is donated to the guild." Price range: $1-1,000; bestsellers: $1-100. Craftworker sets retail price. Membership fee: $18/year. Work must be hand-delivered.
Acceptable Work: Considers batik; ceramics; pottery; paintings, prints; drawings; wall hangings; and weavings.
Profile: "One section is set aside where any member can exhibit frequently. Other sections feature special shows and exhibits, usually on a monthly basis. Customers are tourists from all over US and town people interested in crafts and fine art for their home. Average customer will spend $10-25." Best selling time: summer and pre-Christmas.

ST. LOUIS ART MUSEUM—MUSEUM SHOP, Forest Park, St. Louis MO 63110. Managers: Mary Wool and Mary Gonos. Museum gift shop. Estab. 1958.

Master woodcarver Peter Engler admires a Western scene by a true backwoodsman, Ivan Denton, at Silver Dollar City, Inc., Marvel Cave Park, Missouri. Silver Dollar City is an Ozark theme park with crafts represented in several shops. Prices range from less than $100 to more than $7,000, the latter figure being for a life-size wooden Indian with the buyer's own likeness beneath a big headdress.

Acceptable Work: Considers batik, jewelry, pottery, soft sculpture, wall hangings and weavings. Especially interested in having an exclusive on a stuffed animal. "As a nonprofit organization, all purchases must relate directly to art or the art museum. We are not interested in silver jewelry as much as we are other kinds." One-of-a-kind and handmade production-line items. Price range: $2-300; bestsellers: $10-100.
Terms: Buys outright. Shop sets retail price. Write with slides or photos. Reports in 3 weeks. Work may be shipped or hand-delivered.
Profile: "At the moment, we are mainly a book store, but do sell a great deal of handmade jewelry and could handle a few exceptional items." Customers: tourists (looking for souvenirs) or local, well-to-do, sophisticated people knowledgeable in art.

TOM SAWYER DIORAMAS & AUNT POLLY'S HANDCRAFTS, 323 N. Main, Hannibal MO 63401. (314)221-3525. Manager: Fran Hafner. Museum craft shop/dioramas. Estab. 1970. Represents 70 craftworkers.
Acceptable Work: Considers ceramics, china, dollmaking, knitting, needlecrafts, quilting, rug weaving and woodcrafting. Especially needs hand painted thimbles and baby quilts. Specializes in contemporary, bright-colored items. "½ of our customers arrive on buses. We need as many small items as large. Keep in mind Tom, Becky and the river." One-of-a-kind and handmade production-line items. Price range: 20¢-$195; bestsellers: $1-135.
Terms: Works on consignment; 40% commission. "If item is quite reasonably priced, we might buy outright." Payment sent to craftworker when sold. Retail price set by joint agreement. Requires exclusive area representation. Call for appointment. Reports in 2 weeks. Work must be hand-delivered; "we accept restocking items mailed."
Profile: Shop is in the "historic area of Mark Twain's boyhood home. The front of the building is dedicated to crafts. The remainder is Art Sieving's famous dioramas. ½ of items are in cases; other wooden items are on tables; quilts, afghans and rugs have special display rack's. Visitors relive the adventures of Tom Sawyer." Customers include national and foreign visitors and tourists. Heaviest wholesale buying time: spring to pre-Christmas; best selling time: summer-fall.

MARTIN SCHWEIG GALLERY, 4657 Maryland Ave., St. Louis MO 63108. (314)361-3000. Director: Lauretta Schumacher. Gallery. Estab. 1950s.
Acceptable Work: Considers batik; ceramics; dollmaking; jewelry; pottery; soft sculpture; wall hangings; weavings; and woodcrafting. Primitive and fine one-of-a-kind pieces.
Terms: Exhibits work for 3 week periods. 33⅓% commission. Retail price set by joint agreement. Reports as soon as possible. Hand-delivered work only.
Profile: "No display cases are available; walls are used for hanging and pedestals are available. Media coverage is given." Best selling time: fall and spring.

SERMON-ANDERSON, INC., 10815 Winner Rd., Independence MO 64052. (816)252-9192. Buyer: R.T. Sermon. Gallery/gift, furniture and design shop. Represents traditional craftworkers.
Acceptable Work: Considers all crafts except dollmaking and scrimshaw. One-of-a-kind and handmade production-line items. Price range: $1-100; bestsellers: $5-100.
Terms: Buys outright and works on consignment; 20-33% commission. Gallery sets retail price. Sometimes requires exclusive area representation. Send slides or samples of work. Reports in 2-3 weeks. Work may be shipped or hand-delivered. Dealer pays insurance on exhibited work.
Profile: "We maintain 4 separate buildings ranging from a 1-room summer house for basketry, dried flowes, etc. to a 3-story 26 room building. These are rooms complete as in home or office, with furniture, furnishings, accessories and backgrounds as well. We also have a country store where smaller, inexpensive items are displayed in proper atmosphere (jewelry, glasscrafts, needlecrafts, candles, ceramics and pottery). We also have a courtyard opened seasonally." Customers: older age group, substantial incomes, young marrieds seeking items for their home. Heaviest wholesale buying time: late February-December; best selling time: fall and holidays.

SILVER DOLLAR CITY, INC., Marvel Cave Park, MO 65616. (417)338-2611. Product Manager: John Swift. Theme park with crafts in several shops. Estab. 1960. Represents 200 craftworkers with crafts representing 1880 theme. Heaviest wholesale buying time: January-May; best selling time: May-October.
Acceptable Work: Considers candlemaking, dollmaking, glass art, jewelry, leatherworking, metalsmithing, needlecrafts, pottery, wall hangings, weavings, basketry, broommaking, toys, and woodcrafting. Handmade production-line items. Price range: 15¢-$5,000.
Terms: Buys outright. Shops set retail price. Send list of samples with prices or call for appointment. Reports in 2 weeks. Work may be shipped or hand-delivered.

THE STUFFED STOCKING, 616 S. Main St., St. Charles MO 63301. (314)946-7714. Director: Beverly Jean Klug. Craft shop/gallery. Estab. 1969. Represents over 500 craftworkers. Price range: 50c-$500. Works on consignment; 40% commission. Retail price set by joint agreement. Requires exclusive area representation. "Do not send samples; send nonreturnable photo." Reports once a month. Work may be shipped or hand-delivered.
Acceptable Work: Considers batik; decoupage; dollmaking; leatherworking; metalsmithing; needlecrafts; pottery; quilting; soft sculpture; tole painting; wall hangings; infant toys and clothing; and woodcrafting. Major emphasis on quilts. Finished, one-of-a-kind and handmade production-line items; utilitarian and/or decorative.
Profile: "The Stuffed Stocking is located in the only historical district in the St. Louis area. Some 30 shops, restaurants and galleries are located on a cobblestone street with gas lights and a park along the Missouri River. Customers are upper income women in the $30,000 bracket. The shop maintains a card index and does mailings." Heaviest wholesale buying time: July-December; best selling time: summer-Christmas.

TOYMAKERS SHOP, 412 Main, Joplin MO 64801. (417)781-3160. Managers/Owners: Glen or De Kelly. Craft/miniature/toy shop. Estab. 1977. Represents 3 craftworkers.
Acceptable Work: Considers needlecrafts, wooden toys, dollmaking (china and bisque), doll houses, doll furniture and doll clothes. Includes Barbie doll sizes. One-of-a-kind and handmade production-line items. Price range: 10¢-$1,000; bestsellers: 29¢-$5.
Terms: Works on consignment; 50% commission. Retail price set by joint agreement. Send slides. SASE. Reports in 2 weeks. Work may be shipped or hand delivered.
Profile: "We display in type trays and peg boards. We also repair dolls and toys." Heaviest wholesale buying time: July-November; best selling time: December.

THE UNUSUAL SHOP, Rt. 4, Box 176, Festus MO 63028. (314)937-0410. Contact: Judy Jackson. Gift shop. Estab. 1976. Represents 6-8 craftworkers.
Acceptable Work: Considers candlemaking; clothing; dollmaking; jewelry; needlecrafts; quilt-

ing; soft sculpture; tole painting; woodcrafting; hand-painted china; and antiques. Especially needs miniatures; baby gifts; gifts useful to older people; and things of interest to men. One-of-a-kind and handmade production-line items. Price range: $1-150; bestsellers; $3-10.
Terms: Works on consignment; 40% commission. Gallery sets retail price. Reports in 2 weeks. Work may be shipped or hand-delivered; "contact us before shipping." Dealer pays return shipping and insurance for exhibited work.
Profile: "The shop has an unusual atmosphere created by antiques, original Ben Franklin stove that is used daily in winter." Displays work 3 months minimum. Best selling time: spring and fall.

VILLAGE MINIATURES, 910 Clayton Rd., Ballwin MO 63011. (314)527-4020. Partner: Shirley Franz. Collector's miniature shop. Estab. 1972. Represents 130 craftworkers.
Acceptable Work: Considers dollhouse 1"-1' miniatures. One-of-a-kind and handmade production-line items. Especially needs handcrafted furniture and unusual accessories. Price range: 25¢-$1,125; bestsellers: $1.50-50.
Terms: Works on consignment and buys outright; 40% commission. Craftworker sets retail price. Requires exclusive area representation. Reports in 2 weeks. Work may be shipped or hand-delivered. Dealer pays return shipping and insurance for exhibited work.
Profile: "We display work in miniature room settings of different periods. Items are displayed as long as they are popular. We are the only exclusively miniature shop in the greater St. Louis area and are located in a 70-year-old restored dairy barn." Heaviest wholesale buying time: August-December; best selling time: October-December.

THE WEAVERS' STORE, 110 N. 10th St., Columbia MO 65201. (314)442-5413. Contact: Barbara Overby. Gallery/weaving supplies. Estab. 1977. Represents 5 fiber artists. Price range: $1-700. Works on consignment; 30% commission. Retail price set by joint agreement. Reports in 3 weeks. Work may be shipped or hand-delivered. Dealer pays shipping to shop. Main gallery shows last 2-4 weeks.
Acceptable Work: Considers batik; clothing; needlecrafts; soft sculpture; wall hangings; and weavings. Fine one-of-a-kind and handmade production-line items; utilitarian and/or decorative.
Profile: Gallery provides publicity with shows; "we sell only fiber arts, no kit work."

THE WHEELHOUSE, 210 E. Main St., Arrow Rock MO 65320. (314)442-8696. Owners: Ed and Carolyn Collings. Craft/gift/supply shop and workshop. Estab. 1972. Represents 4 craftworkers.
Acceptable Work: Considers candlemaking, glass art, jewelry, leatherworking, metalsmithing, pottery and woodcrafting. Early American reproductions only. Handmade production-line items only. Price range: $2-100; bestsellers: $3-15.
Terms: Buys outright and works on consignment; 33⅓% commission. Retail price set by joint agreement. Requires exclusive area representation. Send resume, slides or stop by shop. Reports in 2 weeks. Work may be shipped or hand delivered. Display time: 1-3 months.
Profile: Shop is "located in the historic community of Arrow Rock adjacent to Missouri State Park and campgrounds." Customers: tourists and area residents. Heaviest wholesale buying time: spring; best selling time: summer. Open May-September.

THE WILD FLOWER, Rt. 2, Box 169½, Waynesville MO 65583. (314)336-5800. Owner: Nadine Stokes. Gift/flower shop. Estab. 1977. Represents 8-10 craftworkers.
Acceptable Work: Considers decoupage, dollmaking, glass art, needlecrafts, pottery, quilting, scrimshaw, tole painting and woodcrafting. Especially needs unique macrame pieces, basketweaving and quilts. Specializes in fine art designer crafts. Price range: $4-150; bestsellers: $6-40.
Terms: Works on consignment; 30% commission. "I might buy outright if item can be used with flower arranging." Send slides. SASE. Reports in 2 weeks. Work may be shipped or hand delivered.

WILD OATS, 14 Church St., Ferguson MO 63135. (314)521-5566. Contact: Kathy Noelker. Gift shop. Estab. 1975. Represents 75 craftworkers.
Acceptable Work: Considers batik, candlemaking, decoupage, dollmaking, glass art, needlecrafts, pottery, quilting, soft sculpture, tole painting, wall hangings, weavings and woodcrafting. Handmade production-line items only. Specializes in country antiques and handcrafted gifts. Price range: $1-150; bestsellers: $1.95-25.
Terms: Works on consignment; 40% commission. Retail price set by joint agreement. Call for

appointment. Reports in 1 week. Work may be shipped or hand delivered.
Profile: "The aroma of potpourri and candles enhance our friendly old-fashioned store setting. An effort is made to display items attractively among country antiques and old store fixtures." Customers: ages 20-50; $20,000-40,000 incomes. Heaviest wholesale buying and best selling time: Christmas."
To Break In: "Always take a sample of your work to the shop you wish to sell, rather than trying to describe your work."

WILDERNESS ROAD CLOCKWORKS, Box 194, Reeds Spring MO 65737. Owner: Pat Schlobohm. Craft/gift shop. Estab. 1976. Represents over 200 craftworkers.
Acceptable Work: Considers candlemaking, ceramics, Christmas items, clocks, clothing, decoupage, dollmaking, glass art, jewelry, miniatures, music boxes, quilting, scrimshaw, tole painting and woodcrafting. Specializes in country one-of-a-kind and handmade production-line items. Price range: 10¢-$800; bestsellers: 10¢-$100.
Terms: Buys outright. Send slides and price. Reports in 2 weeks.
Profile: "There are 7 rooms with things displayed on shelves, in cases or on furniture we make. We have glass cases for more delicate items. Most of the walls and shelves are rough wood. We have an old post office as display also." Customers: tourists, retirees and local trade. Heaviest wholesale buying time: summer; best selling time: summer-fall.
To Break In: "Promptness and dependability seem to be the biggest problems."

WORLDS FAIR, Bagnell Dam Strip, Box 468, Lake Ozark MO 65049. (314)365-2711. Contact: Joe Cole. Gift shop. Estab. 1974. Considers batik, glass art, leatherworking, quilting, scrimshaw, tole painting, wall hangings and weavings. Price range: $5-30. Buys outright and works on consignment. Retail price set by joint agreement. Call for appointment.
Profile: "We are in a high traffic area, located on the strip at Bagnell Dam. We have an upstairs to our building which contains 2,400 square feet of area. We are interested in getting craftsmen who would like to rent a booth for the season." Customers: mainly ages 15-30, tourists, semi-permanent residents. "We have a lot of people coming from the cities looking for different and unusual items." Heaviest wholesale buying time: spring and early summer. Closed: January-February.

WOVEN IMAGES, 2450 Grand Ave, Suite WV 224, Kansas City MO 64108. (816)471-7265. Contact: Mary Ellen or Cathie Joslyn. Craft shop. Estab. 1973. Represents 10-20 craftworkers.
Acceptable Work: Considers needlecrafts, wall hangings and weavings. Specializes in fine art and contemporary crafts. One-of-a-kind and handmade production-line items. Price range: $2500; bestsellers: $2-50.
Terms: Works on consignment; 30% commission. Retail price set by joint agreement. Send resume and slides with SASE. Reports in 4 weeks. Work may be shipped or hand delivered.. Dealer pays insurance on exhibited work.
Profile: Carries needlecraft supplies and consigned and commissioned fiber art. "We are in an area of a high degree of tourism within a complex which houses Western International Hotel and Hallmark Cards, Inc." Customers: upper middle income. Best selling time: Christmas and summer.

YANKEE PEDDLER COUNTRY CRAFTS, Hospital Rd., Osage Beach MO 65065. (314)348-5054. Contact: Kaye Clemens or Sandra Shupe. Craft/gift shop and gallery. Estab. 1975. Represents 4 craftworkers.
Acceptable Work: Considers tole painting. Especially needs calico items and pottery (wheel thrown). "No shoddy work, no decoupage. If we can find craftworkers with a different unusual craft, especially items out of calico and crafts that go with our primitive antiques, we will buy." Specializes in primitive one-of-a-kind items. Price range: $3-125; bestsellers: $12.50-45.
Terms: Works on consignment. Dealer sets retail price. Write with SASE. Reports in 4 weeks. Work may be shipped or hand delivered.
Profile: "We own a primitive antique and gift shop with an art studio for classes. We have our art gallery in our studio with a Christmas shop off the studio where we display Christmas crafts year 'round. We use country calico wallpaper throughout the shop with old barnwood. We are in a tourist area (seasonal: March-December) and we display our crafts with antiques." Customers: tourists, housewives and artists; ages 21-65; and interested in art, decorating homes, and buying for gifts. Heaviest wholesale buying and best selling time: spring-fall.

Montana

DOUG ALLARD'S FLATHEAD INDIAN TRADING POST, Box 464, St. Ignatius MT 59865. (406)745-2951. Contact: Doug Allard. Craft shop/gallery/gift shop/museum. Estab. 1974. Represents hundreds of Indian craftworkers.
Acceptable Work: Considers decoupage; dollmaking; jewelry; pottery; quilting; woodcrafting; and beadwork. Especially needs Indian-made beadwork using 13/0 cut beads. One-of-a-kind pieces. Price range: 5¢-$650; bestsellers: $15-63.
Terms: Buys outright. Gallery sets retail price. Reports in 3 weeks. Hand-delivered work only.
Profile: "Customers are all ages; tourists and locals." Heaviest wholesale buying time: April, May and November; best selling time: summer.

ART UNLIMITED, 429 2nd St., Whitefish MT 59937. (208)862-5155. Contact: Laurie Carlson. Art supply and gift shop. Estab. 1975. Represents 7 craftworkers.
Acceptable Work: Considers ceramics; jewelry; pottery; wall hangings; weavings; and macrame. Especially needs interesting gift ideas that are indicative of the Montana area in the $7-15 price range. Finished, one-of-a-kind and handmade production-line items. Price range: $1.50-125; bestsellers: $7 minimum.
Terms: Buys outright. Retail price set by joint agreement. Requires exclusive area representation. Work may be shipped or hand-delivered. Dealer pays insurance.
Profile: "We teach everything we sell and try to give a personal touch." Best selling and heaviest wholesale buying time: summer and Christmas.

ARTIFACTS GALLERIES LTD., Box 1989, Bozeman MT 59715. (406)586-3755. Director: Patricia B. Noteboom. Craft shop/gallery. Estab. 1977. Represents 90-100 craftworkers; "emphasis on area craftspeople, but not to the exclusion of quality crafts from other parts of the country."
Acceptable Work: Considers batik, candlemaking, ceramics, clothing, glass art, jewelry, leatherworking, metalsmithing, needlecrafts, pottery, quilting, contemporary scrimshaw, soft sculpture, wall hangings, weavings and woodcrafting. Especially needs contemporary jewelry (limited production and one-of-a-kind); and goods for gentlemen. Specializes in contemporary crafts. No primitive or folksy crafts. Price range: $5-500; bestsellers: $5-100.
Terms: Buys outright. "Occassionally, we have a 3 month trial period of consignment for market testing purposes"; 40% commission. Retail price set by joint agreement. Requires exclusive area representation. Send resume and slides with SASE. Reports in 2 weeks. Work may be shipped or hand-delivered. Dealer pays insurance on exhibited work. Display time: 3 months for consigned work; 1 month for gallery shows.
Profile: "The gallery has been designed with glass displayed in special mirrored units; jewelry in cases; ceramics on cubes, shelves, etc; wearables on wall surfaces and racks; and hangings suspended from gridwork ceiling. Shop is adjacent to a fine restaurant and open some evenings for browsing by diners." Customers: year around tourists, local clientele from college age to wealthy retired folks. Heaviest wholesale buying time: spring and fall; best selling time: summer and Christmas.

BITTERROOT POTTERY, Rt. 1, Box 74, Victor MT 59875. (406)961-3307. Contact: Peggy Steffes. Craft shop/pottery studio. Estab. 1972. Represents 2 craftworkers.
Acceptable Work: Considers pottery; wall hangings; and weavings. Fine one-of-a-kind and handmade production-line items. Price range: $1-200; bestsellers: $15-35.
Terms: Buys outright; 35% commission. Craftworker sets retail price. Reports in 1 week. Work may be hand-delivered. Best selling and heaviest wholesale buying time: August, October and November.

CASTLE GALLERY, 622 N. 29th, Billings MT 59101. (406)259-6458. Directors: Mary Reed and Tom Nelson. Gift/framing shop/gallery. Estab. 1975. Represents 10 craftworkers.
Acceptable Work: Considers batik, glass art, jewelry, pottery, soft sculpture, wall hangings and weavings. One-of-a-kind pieces only. Price range: $500 maximum; bestsellers: $10-60.
Terms: Buys outright and works on consignment; 33⅓% commission. Craftworker or shop sets retail price. Send slides or call for appointment. Reports in 2 weeks. Work may be shipped or hand delivered. Dealer pays 30% of the insurance; craftworker pays rest.
Profile: "The Castle looks like an old castle actually copied after Palmer Potters Home (who copied his home after English Castle). It was built as a private residence and now houses a gallery (one-person shows) and a sales gallery (art related gifts). We have 1- or 2-person shows in 3 rooms in our main gallery. Invitations are sent to our and the artist's list of guests to attend the show and we hold an artists reception for each show. Show length: 1 month. We do have 2

juried shows each year." Customers: ages 16-80.
To Break In: "Items should be finished (i.e. pictures ready to hang, complete with screw eyes or hanger). Prices should be visible and easily read."

CHUCK'S GALLERY, Box 286, (106 S. Main St.), Twin Bridges MT 59754. (406)684-5702. Contact: Chuck or Virginia Watts. Craft/gift shop/gallery/unisex hair-styling. Estab. 1974. Represents 50+ craftworkers.
Acceptable Work: Considers batik, candlemaking, glass art, jewelry, leatherworking, metalsmithing, pottery, scrimshaw, tole painting, wall hangings, weavings and woodcrafting. Especially needs sculpture and carvings developed from native stone and wood of wild-life and fish (either realistic or abstract). "We exhibit primitive especially, but enjoy mixing craft styles in the gallery." One-of-a-kind and handmade production-line items. Price range: $1-1,000; bestsellers: $5-150.
Terms: Buys outright and works on consignment; 30% commission. "We may try a new craftworker on a consignment basis, but switch to buying outright, if craft proves a good-mover in our area." Retail price set by joint agreement. Requires exclusive area representation. Send slides or call for appointment. Reports in 2 weeks. Work may be shipped or hand-delivered. Dealer pays insurance on exhibited work. "We give new consigned pieces a 3 month test period. We like to have 3-4 parties or openings each year with invitations, publicity, champagne, etc. and will usually feature an artist and a craftworker together at these affairs. That show will then continue 3-5 weeks."
Profile: "We display in a simply, yet rustic elegant setting making use of barnwood, local stone, rough sawed wood cubes of various sizes used in a variety of arrangements. We try to feature the newcomers. The hair-styling element creates a daily year-round flow of traffic which is very important during the non-summer months of the year." Customers: tourists; seasonal fishermen and hunters (with wives); local ranchers and their families; persons interested in the arts. Heaviest wholesale buying and best selling time: summer and pre-Christmas.
To Break In: "I want to see attention to detail, an original piece—not a copy, and I'm particularly interested in the craftworker who will utilize the material native to his area in developing his concept, design and the finished work."

COPPER KING MANSION, 219 West Granite, Butte MT 59701. (406)792-7580. Contact: Ann Cote Smith. Craft/gift shop and museum gallery. Estab. 1967. Represents 20 craftworkers.
Acceptable Work: Considers ceramics, clothing, glass art, jewelry, leatherworking, metalsmithing, needlecrafts, pottery, quilting, soft sculpture, tole painting, wall hangings, weavings and woodcrafting. Specializes in fine art crafts. One-of-a-kind and handmade production-line items. Price range: $5-500; bestsellers: $5-25.
Terms: Works on consignment; 40% commission. Craftworker sets retail price. Reports in 2 weeks. Work may be shipped or hand delivered. Dealer pays insurance on exhibited work.
Profile: "Our gallery is located in a National Historical Site and thousands of visitors tour each year." Displays are on shelves or in cases. Displayed in late spring, summer, or early fall. Heaviest wholesale buying and best selling time: summer.
To Break In: "All crafts must be prepriced before being sent. A complete inventory should be sent with the crafts."

EMPORIUM, 1400 1st Ave. N., Great Falls MT 59401. (406)727-8255. Director: Elizabeth Rak. Sales shop of community cultural center. Features handcrafted work done solely by Montana artists, currently 20 artists are represented.
Acceptable Work: Considers batik, ceramics, glass art, jewelry, metalsmithing, pottery, soft sculpture, wall hangings, weavings and woodcrafting. Specializes in fine crafts, especially pottery. One-of-a-kind and handmade production-line items. Price range: $2-400+; bestsellers: $5-150.
Terms: Buys outright and works on consignment; 30% commission. Craftworker sets retail price. Send slides or call for appointment. Reports in 3 weeks. Work may be shipped or hand-delivered. "We carry insurance only for gallery exhibitions and not in the sales shop."
Profile: The Emporium is a part of Paris Gibson Square, a community cultural center. Built as a high school in 1896, it is now on the National Register of Historic Places. The building is three stories and houses a large fine arts exhibition space with monthly exhibits; the Conservatory, a luncheon restaurant; a local genealogy society, artists in residence, class facilities and areas for groups to meet. A featured artist's work is shown for approximately 1 month in an area of the Emporium. Work of different artists, as well as the featured artist, is shown at all times." Customers: local residents and summer tourists. Heaviest wholesale buying time: early fall and pre-summer; best selling time: October-November.

THE FIBERWORKS GALLERY, Room 301-302 Level 3 Stapleton Bldg, Billings MT 59101. Contact any member. Gallery. Estab. 1978. Represents 15 craftworkers.
Acceptable Work: Considers batik, clothing, dollmaking, needlecrafts, quilting, soft sculpture, wall hangings and weavings. One-of-a-kind fiber work only. Price range: $10-500; bestsellers: $10-150.
Terms: "The works have to be predominately fiber, have to be juried in, and we have an agreement which all participants must sign giving us exclusive rights to show their work in this area. There are fees for participating, as well as commissions, depending upon the fee structure. Craftworker sets retail price. Send slides. Reports in 2 weeks. Work may be shipped or hand-delivered.
Profile: "We are a partnership of 8 local fiberists with contributing partners juried in by the partners. We keep work a maximum of 6 months, displayed appropriately and in keeping with other pieces."

HAND MADE USA, INC., 526 Coronado Center, Albuquerque NM 87110. (505)883-5861. President Don Byrne. Craft shop located at A-15 Rimrock Mall, Billings MT 59102. Estab. 1976. Represents 110 craftworkers.
Acceptable Work: Considers all crafts. Price range: $1-1,000; bestsellers: $5.95-200.
Terms: Works on consignment and operates as a high volume coop with a basic booth fee and percentage; 24% commission. Craftworker sets retail price. Shop reports each month with a copy of all sales tickets. Work may be shipped or hand-delivered. Dealer pays insurance for exhibited work.
Profile: "Each craftsman has his own display booth, arranged the way he likes his craft displayed." Best selling time: summer, fall and Christmas.

HELLROARIN' GALLERY, Box 1026, Red Lodge MT 59068. (406)446-1940. Director: Tom Egenes. Gift shop—estab. in 1945; gallery—estab. in 1977.
Acceptable Work: Considers batik, ceramics, glass art, jewelry, leatherworking, metalsmithing, needlecrafts, pottery, soft sculpture, wall hangings, weavings, woodcrafting, and especially needs ceramics and sculpture. Specializes in contemporary and fine art crafts. One-of-a-kind pieces only. Price range: $15-2,500; bestsellers: $20-100.
Terms: Buys outright, but mostly works on consignment; 33⅓% commission. Craftworker sets retail price. Requires exclusive area representation. Send resume and slides with SASE; also send for contract and additional information. Reports in 3 weeks. Work may be shipped or hand delivered. Dealer pays insurance on exhibited work.
Profile: "The gallery is on the mezzanine floor above the gift shop. The gallery has a bronze tin-type ceiling, white cypress walls with antique decor and a ceiling fan over the mezzanine. There's 1800 square feet of floor space and 80 track light fixtures. Work is on display 6-8 weeks. It is displayed on walls, sculpture cubes and easels and lighted with spots from track lighting. We do fairly well considering we've only been open for a few years. We're starting to draw more from the surrounding area (Billings, Montana and Cody, Wyoming)." Customers: middle aged, high income. Heaviest wholesale buying time: June-November; best selling time: July-August and November-December.

HOCKADAY CENTER FOR THE ARTS CRAFT SHOP, Box 83, Kalispell MT 59901. (406)755-5268. Director: John Brice. Considers all arts and craft items. Most items taken on consignment; 331/3% commission. 40% discount for items purchased outright. Also sponsors annual outdoor art festival and sale. Write for more information.

THE MAGIC MUSHROOM GALLERY, Southgate Mall, Missoula MT 59801. (406)549-9322. Buyer: Kaye Caskey. Gallery/gift shop. Estab. 1970. Represents 100 craftworkers.
Acceptable Work: Considers batik; ceramics; glass art; jewelry; pottery; quilting; soft sculpture; wall hangings; weavings; and woodcrafting. Price range: $5-500; bestsellers: $5-100.
Terms: Buys outright. Gallery sets retail price. Requires exclusive area representation. Reports in 2 weeks. Work may be shipped or hand-delivered.
Profile: "Customers are college students to housewives; mill workers to doctors. Best customers are lawyers, doctors, professional women and business people." Heaviest wholesale buying time: fall; best selling time: Christmas.

POTS 'N STUFF, Box 613, Ronan MT 59864. (406)676-2500. Contact: Donna L. Aadsen. Craft shop/gift shop. Estab. 1976. Represents 3 craftworkers. Price range: $5-100; bestsellers: $5-50. Buys outright. Gallery sets retail price. Requires exclusive area representation. Reports in 4 weeks. Work may be hand-delivered. Dealer pays insurance for exhibited work.

Acceptable Work: Considers candlemaking; ceramics; pottery; and macrame. Finished, one-of-a-kind and handmade production-line items.
Profile: "This is the only exclusive gift and macrame shop in our area. Customers are from all age groups and all social and economic groups." Heaviest wholesale buying time: summer; best selling time: Christmas.

J. K. RALSTON MUSEUM & ART CENTER GIFT SHOP, Box 50, Sidney MT 59270. (406)482-3500. Director: Linda K. Mann. Considers ceramics and sculpture. Price range: $5-200. Works on consignment; 25% commission.

REEDER'S ALLEY & CO., Reeder's Alley, Helena MT 59601. (406)442-1519. Contact: Ray Dominick. Gallery/gift shop. Estab. 1974. Represents 12 craftworkers, preferably from Montana, Western US and Midwest US.
Acceptable Work: Considers glass art, jewelry, metalsmithing, pottery, wall hangings, weavings and wood carvings. One-of-a-kind and handmade production-line items. Price range: $5-250; bestsellers: $6-50.
Terms: Buys outright and works on consignment; 35% commission. Retail price set by joint agreement. Requires exclusive area representation. Send slides or call for appointment. SASE. Reports in 3 weeks. Work may be shipped or hand-delivered. Dealer pays insurance on exhibited work. Display time: 6 months.
Profile: Shop is in "historic area selling to local persons for gifts and home decor, and to tourists in the summer months." Heaviest wholesale buying time: early fall and pre-summer; best selling time: October-December and June-August.
To Break In: "We look for quality and dependability; those who can deliver items at the proper time—the beginning of the selling seasons."

TOWN & COUNTRY GALLERY, Box 92, Dillon MT 59725. (406)683-5525. Contact: Lorene Lovell. Gift shop/gallery also selling art supplies. Estab. 1972. Represents 250 craftworkers.
Acceptable Work: Considers all crafts except ceramics, decoupage, needlecrafts, and soft sculpture. One-of-a-kind and handmade production-line items. Price range: $1-2,000; bestsellers: $5-25.
Terms: Buys outright and works on consignment: 30% commission. Retail price set by craftworker. Send resume with SASE. Reports in 2 weeks. Work may be shipped or hand-delivered. Dealer pays insurance on exhibited work.
Profile: "The shop is in an old log house and I really try to keep a good variety of items." Heaviest wholesale buying and best selling time: Christmas and tourist season.

WEST YELLOWSTONE MUSEUM, Box 411, West Yellowstone MT 59758. (406)646-7814. Director: Joel C. Janetski. Museum gallery/gift shop. Estab. 1972. Represents 4-6 craftworkers, usually from the intermountains. Heaviest wholesale buying time: spring-May; best selling time: July-August.
Acceptable Work: Considers batik, ceramics, pottery, wall hangings, weavings and woodcrafting. Specializes in primitive pieces. "We have the best luck with items related to the region (i.e. Yellowstone Park). One-of-a-kind and handmade production-line items. Price range: $1-500; bestsellers: $3-20.
Terms: Buys outright and works on consignment; 40% commission. Craftworker sets retail price. Send slides. Reports in 1-2 weeks. Work may be shipped or hand delivered.

WESTERN HERITAGE GALLERY, 4289 N. Montana Ave., Helena MT 59601. (406)442-4154. Manager: Bernadine H. Wright. Craft shop/gallery. Estab. 1976. Represents 22 craftworkers of Indian extraction. Price range: $2.50-600; bestsellers: $10-50. Works on consignment; 25% commission. Gallery sets retail price. Requires exclusive area representation. Reports in 1 week. Work may be shipped or hand-delivered. Dealer pays return shipping and insurance for exhibited work.
Acceptable Work: Considers ceramics; glass art; jewelry; metalsmithing; pottery; wall hangings; and weavings. Primitive one-of-a-kind pieces.
Profile: Shop provides advertising. Displays work 3 months. "Customers are all ages; Indians; middle class; many are collectors of Indian art." Heaviest wholesale buying time: spring/summer; best selling time: summer.

WINGS WEST GALLERY, (formerly The Art Gallery), 13 S. Willson, Bozeman MT 59715. (406)587-0092. Contact: Anita Kristensen. Gallery/gift shop. Estab. 1977. Represents 24 craftworkers whose work deals with Western wildlife or scenery typical of the Montana area.

Acceptable Work: Considers glass art; jewelry; metalsmithing; pottery; stained glass; weavings; and woodcrafting. Especially needs small, inexpensive items ($5-15 retail); impulse items. Fine one-of-a-kind pieces. Price range: $10-1,000 (no limit); bestsellers: $15-150.
Terms: Works on consignment and buys outright; 40% commission. Retail price set by joint agreement. Reports in 1 week. Work may be shipped or hand-delivered only if approved. Dealer pays insurance for exhibited work. Displays work 1 year maximum.
Profile: "Items are grouped whenever possible; the shop is tiny and I am very selective in buying; all items accepted are on display at all times. I am the only gallery in this city which imports the works of nationally recognized artists." Heaviest wholesale buying time: fall and spring.

YELLOWSTONE ART CENTER, 401 N. 27th St., Billings MT 59101. (406)259-1869. Manager: Katherine H. Haughey. Museum gift shop. Estab. 1967. Represents 10-12 craftworkers.
Acceptable Work: Considers ceramics; glass art; jewelry; pottery. Fine one-of-a-kind and handmade production-line items. Price range: $2.50-100; bestsellers: $2.50-60.
Terms: Works on consignment and buys outright; 25% commission. Craftworker sets retail price. Reports in 1 month. Work may be shipped or hand-delivered. Dealer pays shipping to shop and insurance for exhibited work.
Profile: "Pottery is displayed on shelves; jewelry in cases. Customers are college age through early 40s; middle income." Displays work 1 year. Heaviest wholesale buying time: February-November; best selling time: December.

Nebraska

OLD MARKET CRAFTSMEN'S GUILD, 511 S. 11th St., Omaha NE 68102. (402)346-8887. No collect calls. Director: Nancy Gruver. Craft shop/gallery. Estab. 1972. Represents 50 craftworkers.
Acceptable Work: Considers batik, ceramics, glass art, jewelry, pottery, soft sculpture, wall hangings, weavings and woodcrafting. Especially needs persons working in fiber and soft sculpture and woodcrafters. Specializes in contemporary American crafts of a high professional quality. One-of-a-kind and handmade production-line items. Price range: $3-500; bestsellers: $3-50.
Terms: Buys outright but works mainly on consignment; 40% commission. "We prefer to consign—money flow makes it difficult to buy outright from everyone. We do have a consignment agreement form, good record keeping and prompt payment." Craftworker sets retail price. Requires exclusive area representation. Send resume and slides or call for appointment. Reports in 2 weeks. Work may be shipped or hand delivered. Dealer pays insurance on exhibited work. 3 month period of display—can be extended if agreeable to consigner and gallery.
Profile: "We consider ourselves primarily a contemporary crafts gallery. We have work available year round for purchase, and, in addition, we do 6-8 major regional or national shows per year. Work is displayed on walls or pedestals, also built in shelving—gallery has a very contemporary look and we are sensitive to displaying work well." Customers: ages 20-65, middle class ($5-50,000 incomes) and broad general interests. "We seem to have established a good firm base of repeat customers." Heaviest wholesale buying time: pre-Christmas; best selling time: late spring-summer and Christmas.

WEST NEBRASKA ARTS CENTER, Box 62, Scottsbluff NE 69361. (308)632-2226. Executive Director: Michael Shonsey. Museum gallery. Estab. 1967. Represents 8 craftworkers per year.
Acceptable Work: Considers all crafts. Especially needs pottery, fiber, mixed media and sculpture. "Works need to be considered as a show and not individually" Specializes in fine art crafts but "also interested in true folk stuff." One-of-a-kind pieces. Price range: $5-1000; bestsellers: $10-30.
Terms: Works on consignment; 35% commission. Work is reviewed by Selection Committee. Craftworker sets retail price. Send resume and slides. Reports in 4 weeks. Work may be hand-delivered or shipped. Insurance on exhibited work is negotiated. "Items are displayed as part of a 1-3 person exhibit, displayed on walls or on pedestals. The shows generally run 1 month."
Profile: We are part of a nonprofit Arts Center located in an old library building in the extreme western part of Nebraska. There is a variety of types of shows: national, regional, local; painting, photography, crafts, etc. We are looking for balance in our shows. Customers are 30-70, have $20,000+ incomes, newly interested in the arts, usually community minded, female." Best selling time: winter. "Good sales record: approximately $5000/year sales."

Nevada

SIERRA NEVADA MUSEUM OF ART SHOP, 549 Court St., Reno NV 89501. (702)324-3333. Gallery/gift shop. Estab. 1976. Prefers local craftworkers. Price range: $1-500; bestsellers: $5-30. Works on consignment and buys outright; 33⅓% commission. Craftworker sets retail price. Work may be shipped or hand-delivered by prior consent. Dealer pays shipping to shop and insurance for exhibited work. Heaviest wholesale buying time: pre-Christmas and January; best selling time: Christmas.
Acceptable Work: Considers ceramics; clothing; glass art; jewelry; leatherworking; pottery; quilting; soft sculpture; wall hangings; weavings; and woodcrafting. Fine one-of-a-kind and handmade production-line items.

SUN CIRCLE CRAFTS GALLERY, 1223 Arizona St., Boulder City NV 89005. (702)293-4679. Contact: Phil or Eileen Vanderwal. Craft shop/gallery. Estab. 1977. Represents 40-45 craftworkers.
Acceptable Work: Considers all crafts except clothing, decoupage and tole painting. Especially needs leather (not clothes), handsewn work, dolls and unusual candles. "We exhibit a combination of fine art designer crafts and Appalachian style works. Earth tones and natural colors go best." Price range: $3-500; bestsellers: $3-45.
Terms: Buys outright and works on consignment; 40% commission. Retail price set by craftworker, though gallery may offer its suggestions. Requires exclusive area representation. Send resume and slides with SASE. Reports in 2 weeks. Work may be shipped or hand-delivered. Dealer pays insurance on exhibited work.
Profile: "We display works on wooden spools and wooden shelves and counters. Antiques are also used as displays for handsewn work. Cedar shingles and the wood interior give the gallery a warm, homey atmosphere. Customers are generally in the 25-50 age group—middle to upper class." Heaviest wholesale buying time: summer and fall before Christmas season; best selling time: "we sell steadily throughout the year, but February-March are slightly slow, and November-December are excellent."
To Break In: "Provide good slides of your work so we can really tell what it is like. We are interested in people who will stand behind the quality and craftsmanship of their work."

New Hampshire

THE ARTIFACTORY, 25 Lebanon St., Hanover NH 03755. (603)643-2277. Contact: Gordy Thomas. Craft/gift shop. Estab. 1974. Represents 45-50 American craftworkers.
Acceptable Work: Considers candlemaking, ceramics, glass art, jewelry, leatherworking, metalsmithing, pottery and woodcrafting. Especially needs boxes of all kinds (jewelry, sculptural) and jewelry for men. Specializes in contemporary crafts, but some traditional work. Exhibits one-of-a-kind, but mainly handmade production-line items. Price range: $1-250; bestsellers: $5-50.
Terms: Buys outright. Retail price set by joint agreement. Send slides or call for appointment. "We do most of our buying at shows but are usually eager to see new work at other times, too." Reports in 2 weeks. Work may be shipped or hand-delivered.
Profile: "We try to display work in a way that will direct the eye to the piece rather than to the display. Our displays are primarily wood, glass, cork and other natural materials—and rather neutral, colorwise. Jewelry and finer small pieces are in antique display cases on velvet, velour, coral, cork, wood and glass. The displays are lit with stained glass lamps and floods and the light is generally soft rather than harsh. The atmosphere in our shop is relaxed and informal and our standards of aesthetics and workmanship are high. Our shop is part of the Dartmouth College community (Hanover, New Hampshire) and most of our regular customers are local and/or associated with Dartmouth. The income level is middle to moderate and artistically our market is a little less conservative than most in this part of the country." Heaviest wholesale buying time: spring-fall; best selling time: July-December.

ARTISAN'S WORKSHOP, Main St., New London NH 03257. (603)526-4227. Manager: Muffin Bushueff. Art/craft shop. Estab. 1975. Represents 30-40 northern New England craftworkers. Heaviest wholesale buying time: spring-autumn; best selling time: summer and winter.
Acceptable Work: Considers batik; candlemaking; glass art; jewelry; leatherworking; pottery; and woodcrafting. Especially needs blown glass; pottery; batik (smaller items); serigraphs; woodcuts; and unusual, moderately-priced utilitarian pieces of wood and stone. Finished, one-of-a-kind and handmade production-line items. Price range: $2-150; bestsellers: $2-25.
Terms: Works on consignment and buys outright; 33% comission. Retail price set by joint agreement. Reports in 2 weeks. Work may be shipped or hand-delivered. Dealer pays return shipping and insurance for exhibited work.

AYOTTES' DESIGNERY, Box 287, Center Sandwich NH 03227. Contact: Robert Ayotte. Craft shop/handweaving studio. Estab. 1958. Represents 30 craftworkers; preferably from northern New England.
Acceptable Work: Considers candlemaking; glass art; jewelry; leatherworking; metalsmithing; pottery; woodcrafting; and black iron work. Fine one-of-a-kind and handmade production-line items. Price range: $1-500; bestsellers: $40 maximum.
Terms: Buys outright. Requires exclusive area representation. Reports in 1 month. Work may be shipped or hand-delivered.
Profile: "We have been in business for 20 years and have established a reputation and repeat clientele. We pride ourselves on quality craftsmanship and unique designs in our own handweaving." Heaviest wholesale buying time: spring; best selling time: July-August.

A recent pottery show at The Golden Toad, Milford, New Hampshire, featured the work of local potter, Barbara Knutson. "Changing shows and displays frequently makes everything look new and fresh as well as encouraging customers to drop in often," says Sandy Hammond, owner of the shop.

BERNIER STUDIO, Rt. 25, Wentworth NH 03282. (603)764-5720. Manager: Carol Ann Bernier. Gift shop. Estab. 1968. Represents 25 craftworkers.
Acceptable Work: Considers batik, ceramics, clothing, decoupage, dollmaking, glass art, jewelry, leatherworking, metalsmithing, pottery, quilting, wall hangings, weavings and woodcrafting. Handmade production-line items. Price range: $3-50; bestsellers: $5-15.
Terms: Buys outright. Shop sets retail price. Send resume and slides. Reports in 1 week. Work may be shipped or hand-delivered. Dealer pays shipping to shop and insurance for exhibited work.
Profile: "Our shop is in an old colonial home and a renovated barn. We have 6 rooms of gifts, books and antiques. It's very clean and carefully put together to give all our merchandise the best possible visual contact with our customers. Crafts we don't sell one year, we put out the next, but every year we rearrange the whole shop to give it a new look." Customers: out-of-state tourists. "Our customers come back every year because of our fine quality crafts." Heaviest wholesale buying time: spring; best selling time: summer. Open May-October.

GOLDEN APPLE—KEENE CRAFT CENTER, Fairbanks Plaza, Keene NH 03431. (603)357-3639. Contact: Alice White. Craft/gift shop/gallery. Estab. 1978. Represents 40 craftworkers.
Acceptable Work: Considers batik, candlemaking, decoupage, dollmaking, glass art, jewelry, needlecrafts, pottery, quilting, scrimshaw, soft sculpture, tole painting, wall hangings, weavings and woodcrafting. Especially needs New England-type country gifts. One-of-a-kind and handmade production-line items. Price range: $2-250; bestsellers: $2-25.
Terms: Buys outright and works on consignment; 30% commission. Retail price set by joint agreement. Prefers exclusive area representation. Send slides or call for appointment. Reports in 2 weeks. Work may be shipped or hand-delivered. Dealer pays insurance on exhibited work.
Profile: "We rotate our stock if possible to give all items a fair chance at selling. We pick some items for window displays if appropriate. We appeal mostly to the housewife, but are working to get younger customers (college age) and men to shop for gifts." Heaviest wholesale buying and best selling time: Christmas and July, August and October (for tourists).

THE GOLDEN TOAD, 35 Amherst St., Milford NH 03055. (603)673-4307. Contact: Sandy Hammond. Craft shop/gallery. Estab. 1972. Represents 100-150 East Coast craftworkers.
Acceptable Work: Considers batik; candlemaking; dollmaking; glass art; jewelry; leatherworking; metalsmithing; pottery; soft sculpture; wall hangings; weavings; and woodcrafting. Especially needs items men would like. Primitive handmade production-line items. Price range: $1-300; bestsellers: $10-20.
Terms: Buys outright. Requires exclusive area representation. Reports in 2 weeks. Work may be shipped or hand-delivered. Dealer pays shipping to shop.
Profile: "Customers are middle class to upper middle class; educated; with incomes of $20,000 and up." Displays work 3 months. Heaviest wholesale buying time: early fall; best selling time: Christmas and summer.

THE GUILD OF STRAWBERY BANKE, INC., 93 State St., Portsmouth NH 03801. (603)438-8004. Director of Merchandise: Carol Olson. Museum gift shop. Estab. 1965. Represents 100 craftworkers.
Acceptable Work: Considers candlemaking; ceramics; decoupage; dollmaking; glass art; needlecrafts; pottery; quilting; tole painting; and woodcrafting. Price range: $3-250; bestsellers: $5-35.
Terms: Buys outright. Retail price set by joint agreement. Reports immediately. Work may be shipped or hand-delivered. Dealer pays shipping to shop.
Profile: "We have 3 shops; if an item does not sell in one shop, it is moved to another shop. Our average customer is between 30 and 50; high middle to high income." Heaviest wholesale buying time: spring; best selling time: August-September and November.

LEAGUE OF NEW HAMPSHIRE CRAFTSMEN, 205 N. Main St., Concord NH 03301. Director: Merle D. Walker. Craft shop. Estab. 1932. Represents an unlimited number of craftworkers; must be state juried members of the League who meet residency requirements.
Acceptable Work: Considers all crafts except candlemaking and ceramics. Price range: $1-1,000; bestsellers: $10-150.
Terms: Works on consignment and buys outright; 33% commission. Craftworker sets retail price.
Profile: "We are constantly working on new methods of displaying objects to encourage appreciation in the consumer. Buyers are mostly middle years, middle incomes and have a

developed appreciation level of the crafts." Heaviest wholesale buying time: spring-summer; best selling time: August and December.

LEAGUE OF NEW HAMPSHIRE CRAFTSMEN, Wolfeboro Arts and Crafts, Rt. 28, Wolfeboro NH 03894. (603)569-3489. Craft shop. Represents New Hampshire craftworkers. Craftworkers must meet residential requirements. Considers all crafts. Price range: 10¢-$650. Works on consignment. "All crafts must be juried by standards committee through a personal appointment." Craftworker sets retail price. Work may be shipped or hand-delivered. Best selling time: summer and fall.

LEAGUE OF NEW HAMPSHIRE CRAFTSMEN, HANOVER SHOP, 13 Lebanon St., Hanover NH 03755. (603)643-5050. Manager: Jane MacKinnon. Craft/gift shop. Estab. 1933. Represents 2,000 New Hampshire craftworkers. Best selling time: fall.
Acceptable Work: Considers all crafts except candlemaking. One-of-a-kind and handmade production-line items. Price range: 15¢-$800; bestsellers: 15¢-$25.
Terms: Works on consignment and buys outright; 40% commission. Craftworker sets retail price. Reports in 2 weeks after local jurying. Work may be shipped or hand-delivered. Shop pays return shipping and insurance for exhibited work.

New Jersey

ART LEASE & SALES GALLERY, Friends of New Jersey State Museum, 205 W. State St., Trenton NJ 08625. (609)394-5310. Contact: Carol Rosenthal or Ann Gips. Museum/craft gallery. Estab. 1972. Represents 35-40 craftworkers.
Acceptable Work: Considers batik; ceramics; jewelry; metalsmithing; needlecrafts; pottery; quilting; soft sculpture; wall hangings; and weavings. Especially needs hand woven items; and jewelry. Fine one-of-a-kind pieces. Price range: $4.50-1,000; bestsellers: $35-100.
Terms: Works on consignment; 40% commission. Craftworker sets retail price. Work may be shipped or hand-delivered. Dealer pays insurance for exhibited work. Displays work 2-3 months.
Profile: "Our customers are in their early 20's to early 70's with the largest concentration in the 35-55 age group. They have interest in the fine and performing arts." Heaviest consignment time: October and November; best selling time: mid-November to January.

THE BEA HIVE, 504 Cedar Lane, Teaneck NJ 07666. (201)836-1366. Contact: Bea Westin or Naomi Koncius. Craft and gift shop. Estab. 1975. Represents 100-200 craftworkers. Price range: $5-300; bestsellers: $10-30. Buys outright. Retail price set by joint agreement. Requires exclusive area representation. Reports in 2 weeks. Work may be shipped or hand-delivered. Dealer pays insurance for exhibited work.
Acceptable Work: Considers batik; candlemaking; ceramics; glass art; jewelry; leatherworking; metalsmithing; pottery; quilting; soft sculpture; wall hangings; weavings; and woodcrafting. Especially needs personalized items in baby gifts, name plaques, and gifts for men, etc. Fine one-of-a-kind and handmade production-line items.
Profile: "We display work in 2 large windows. New merchandise is displayed in the window and inside the shop. Windows are changed once a month completely, although new things are added every few days." Heaviest wholesale buying time: September-December and April, May and June; best selling time: Christmas.

BEARPAW LEATHER SHOP, 36 Main St., Clinton NJ 08809. (201)735-7351. Contact: Jean Gries. Craft shop. Estab. 1972. Represents 40 craftworkers. Considers leatherworking. Fine one-of-a-kind and handmade production-line items. Especially needs bags and wallets; designer art pieces are always welcome. Price range: $2-750; bestsellers: $20-100. Buys outright. Reports in 2-3 weeks. Work may be shipped or hand-delivered. Dealer pays shipping to shop.
Profile: "I will keep something until I sell it. Bearpaw is full of antiques and beautiful display cases. If I could sum up the shop in one word, it would be 'comfortable.' Customers are 27-35; quality is their main interest; income of $12,000-30,000." Heaviest wholesale buying time: June-September; best selling time: October-December.

BEAUTIFUL THINGS, 1838 E. 2nd St., Scotch Plains NJ 07076. (201)522-1666. Contact: Paula Gollhardt Leighton. Craft and gift shop. Estab. 1973. Represents 75-100 craftworkers.
Acceptable Work: Considers dollmaking; glass art; jewelry; leatherworking; pottery; soft sculpture; and woodcrafting. Especially needs gift items to sell for under $20; and production pottery items like juice squeezers and ladles. Interested in any item with rainbow motif. Fine

one-of-a-kind and handmade production-line items. Price range: $2-300; bestsellers: $10-35.
Terms: Buys outright. Gallery sets retail price. Write for information. No replies unless SASE enclosed. Reports in 4 weeks. Work may be shipped or hand-delivered. Dealer pays shipping to shop.
Profile: "We feature our own jewelry; we have high quality and good taste with a total price range; we also mix crafts with some commercial items and some imported." Heaviest wholesale buying time: late summer and fall; best selling time: Christmas.

BEAUTIFUL THINGS, 452 Springfield Ave., Summit NJ 07901. See above.

BLUE ONION, 285 Closter Dock Rd., Closter NJ 07624. (201)767-3074. Contact: Lillian Lane. Gift shop. Estab. 1973. Represents 5 craftworkers.
Acceptable Work: Considers all crafts. Especially needs silver or porcelain jewelry, good sounding wind chimes, mouth-blown glass art, small weed pots, and baskets year 'round; unusual tree ornaments, paper mache figures (old-fashioned feeling, e.g., Charles Dickens), dolls, angels, animals (in ceramics, fabric, metals), small wreaths of natural materials, spices, cornhusks for Christmas; handpainted porcelain eggs and rabbits for Easter; handpainted pumpkins, figures of raffia made into ladies, men, witches, ghosts to hang on front doors for Halloween. Handmade production-line items. No contemporary or costly items. Price range: $5-50; bestsellers: $5-25.
Terms: Buys outright and works on consignment; 40% commission. Shop sets retail price. Requires exclusive area representation. Send samples. SASE. Reports in 1 week. Work may be shipped or hand-delivered.
Profile: "My shop is small with displays mostly on/in old refinished oak furniture. I combine most crafts in with regular gift items that look well together or are color coordinated. For instance, a Raggedy Ann Doll sits in an old Haywood-Wakefield antique high chair.) Most of my clients are traditional, country, French and colonial lovers. Therefore, simple silver jewelry, pottery, dolls, stained glass mirrors must fit into these categories and act as our interesting unusual accessories. Modern is not for me." Customers: mostly women, middle to upper middle incomes, suburban, some teenagers and college folks (looking for gifts for parents and friends). Heaviest wholesale buying and best selling time: fall-Christmas.
To Break In: "My shop is a small one in a small town. The folks come in and they buy for each other. I, therefore, have found in my 5 years that I must deal, not in quantity, but in ones, constantly finding new items that my customers have not seen the last time they were in. My staple items number no more than 5 or 6.

BY HAND FINE CRAFT GALLERY, 211 Kings Hwy. E, Haddonfield NJ 08033. (609)429-2550. Contact: Arlene R. Ludin. Craft gallery. Estab. 1976. Represents 175 craftworkers. Price range: $3-3,000; bestsellers: $10-250. Works on consignment and buys outright; 30-40% commission. Retail price set by joint agreement. Reports in 2 weeks. Work may be shipped or hand-delivered. Dealer pays insurance for exhibited work. Shows are 2 weeks.
Acceptable Work: Considers batik; ceramics; glass art; leatherworking; metalsmithing; pottery; soft sculpture; wall hangings; weavings; and woodcrafting. Fine one-of-a-kind and handmade production-line items.
Profile: "Items purchased are held until sold and constantly moved. Each piece is given as important a place as possible. The look of the gallery changes constantly. Customers are mostly women; interested in the arts; most are 25-40 years old; upper middle income." Heaviest wholesale buying time: April and November; best selling time: December, April and August.

CLINTON HISTORIAL MUSEUM VILLAGE, Box 5005, 56 Main St., Clinton NJ 08809. (201)735-4101. Director: Gloria Lazor. Museum gift shop. Estab. 1965. Represents 5 craftworkers. Price range: $1-200; bestsellers: $1-10. Works on consignment; 40% commission. Gallery sets retail price. Reports in 4 weeks. Hand-delivered work only. Dealer pays insurance for exhibited work. Displays work 3 months. Customers are family groups; 30-45 with an income of $15,000. Heaviest wholesale buying time: spring; best selling time: summer.
Acceptable Work: Considers candlemaking; ceramics; decoupage; dollmaking; glass art; jewelry; metalsmithing; needlecrafts; pottery; quilting; and woodcrafting. Primitive one-of-a-kind and handmade production-line items.

CRAFTSMEN TWO, 2700 S. Main Rd., Vineland NJ 08360. (609)696-1199. Contact: Judy Shapiro or Beverly Rosenthal. Craft shop. Estab. 1978. Represents 90 craftworkers.
Acceptable Work: Considers dollmaking, glass art, jewelry, leatherworking, metalsmithing, pottery, quilting, soft sculpture, wall hangings, weavings and woodcrafting. Specializes in

contemporary and traditional crafts. Handmade production-line items. Price range: $1.50-200; bestsellers: $10-50.
Terms: Buys outright and works on consignment; 33% commission. Craftworker sets retail price. Send description of work, photos or call for appointment. Reports in 3 weeks. Work may be shipped or hand-delivered. Dealer pays insurance on exhibited work.
Profile: "We use the first floor (including the kitchen and bath) of an old Victorian house for our shop. We have antique furniture as display pieces. We also have an art gallery in one of the bedrooms upstairs. We usually group items from the same craftworker together with the craftperson's name displayed. If it is a very unusual piece, the item is displayed by itself. We usually change our displays around every 3-4 weeks and take an item off the floor after a couple of months." Customers: middle incomes, "but this only puts a limit on the number of very expensive items we can carry." Heaviest wholesale buying time: Christmas.

CRAFTWORKS, INC., 12 N. Van Brunt St., Englewood NJ 07631. (201)567-3881. Contact: Raye Cooke or Lorraine Cilluffo. Craft shop/pottery studio. Estab. 1975.
Acceptable Work: Considers batik; ceramics; glass art; jewelry; pottery; soft sculpture; wall hangings; weavings; and woodcrafting. One-of-a-kind and handmade production-line items. Price range: $3-300; bestsellers: $10-25.
Terms: Works on consignment and buys outright; 30% commission. Craftworker sets retail price. Requires exclusive area representation. Reports in 3 weeks. Work may be shipped or hand-delivered. Dealer pays shipping and insurance for exhibited work.
Profile: "Work is displayed to its best advantage; like styles or shapes grouped together; functional displayed separately; displays change monthly." Heaviest wholesale buying time: fall and late winter; best selling time: spring and late fall.

DEXTERITY, LTD., 26 Church St., Montclair NJ 07042. (201)746-5370. Contact: Shirley Zafirau. Craft shop/mail order firm. Estab. 1974. Represents 250 craftworkers.
Acceptable Work: Considers all crafts. Finished, one-of-a-kind and handmade production-line items. Price range: $1.25-250.
Terms: Buys outright. "We find net 30 terms most convenient." Gallery sets retail price. Requires exclusive area representation. Reports in 3-4 weeks. Dealer pays shipping to shop.
Profile: We offer a large "selection of the best in crafts we can find; we offer service and beautifully packaged gifts; people react verbally to the visual impact of our display, shop and atmosphere. We would like advance notice of price increases and an opportunity to place orders at the old prices." Heaviest wholesale buying time: orders placed February-June for September-November delivery; best selling time: November-December and April-May.

DISCOVERY ART GALLERIES, 1191 Valley Rd., Clifton NJ 07013. Gallery. Estab. 1971. Represents 3 craftworkers.
Acceptable Work: Considers ceramics, glass art, metalsmithing, soft sculpture, wall hangings, weavings and woodcrafting. One-of-a-kind and handmade production-line items. Price range: $10-250; bestsellers: $20-60.
Terms: Works on consignment; 50% commission. Dealer pays insurance on exhibited items. Retail price set by joint agreement. Requires exclusive area representation. Send resume, slides with SASE. Reports in 3 weeks. Work may be shipped or hand delivered.
Profile: "We handle mainly contemporary art (paintings, prints, sculpture) and most of the artists are in museum collections. Work is placed on shelves or hung and is usually rotated after a month. Most active collectors here seem to be about 35-45 years old, employed in business professions—income ranges about $16,000-40,000." Heaviest buying time and best selling time: November-March and May-June.

THE DOLLHOUSE FACTORY, Box 456, 157 Main St., Lebanon NJ 08833. (201)236-6404. President: R.V. Dankanics. Dollhouse miniatures shop. Estab. 1971. Represents 30-50 craftworkers.
Acceptable Work: Considers ceramics, dollmaking metalsmithing, pottery, quilting, tole painting, wall hangings, weavings and woodcrafting. Must be dollhouse-related items. Price range: 10¢-$10,000; bestsellers: $1-100.
Terms: Buys outright and works on consignment; 33⅓% commission. Dealer pays insurance on exhibited work. Retail price set by joint agreement. Send slides/samples or call for appointment. Reports in 1 week. Work may be shipped or hand-delivered.
Profile: "We are a complete dollhouse center fully serving every facet of the dollhouse and miniature field (from machinery, tools, and supplies of the trade to the finest in finished items for the discriminating collector). Work is always on display in locked glass showcases."

Heaviest wholesale buying time: fall; best selling time: fall and winter.
To Break In: "Have samples of your work at hand. We are interested in quality items only."

DOLLHOUSE FURNITURE & ACCESSORIES SHOP, Box 83, Adelphia Rd., Rt. 524, Adelphia NJ 07710. (201)431-2942. Contact: Mrs. Mary Anne Marin. Craft/gift shop. Estab. 1968. Represents 18 craftworkers. Send resume, slides with SASE or call for appointment. Reports in 2-3 weeks. Work may be shipped or hand delivered.
Acceptable Work: Considers ceramics, clothing, dollmaking, glass art, metalsmithing, needlecrafts, pottery, scrimshaw, tole painting, wall hangings, weavings and woodcrafting. Especially needs reproduction-antique bisque and porcelain dolls—kits and/or dressed dolls preferred. One-of-a-kind and handmade production-line items. Price range: $1-2,000. Buys outright, consigns work; 50% commission. Craftworker pays insurance on exhibited work. Retail price set by joint agreement or craftworker only. Requires exclusive area representation.
country road—approximately 1/2 mile east of New Jersey State Highway, Rt. 9. We are located in historic Monmouth County." Customers: upper incomes.

DOUBLETREE GALLERY, 5 Alvin Place, Upper Montclair NJ 07043. (201)783-5022. President: Jerri Weiss. Gallery/coop. Estab. 1972. Represents coop members. Price range: $1.50-1,500; bestsellers: $4-32. Works on consignment; 33⅓% commission. Craftworker sets retail price. Reports in 2 weeks. Work may be hand-delivered. Dealer pays insurance for exhibited work. Displays work 4-6 weeks for invitational shows.
Acceptable Work: Considers batik; ceramics; clothing; dollmaking; glass art; jewelry; leatherworking; metalsmithing; pottery; quilting; soft sculpture; wall hangings; weavings; and woodcrafting. Finished, one-of-a-kind and handmade production-line items.
Profile: Shop is run by nonprofit organization. "Customers are affluent professionals; and most have some knowledge of art and/or crafts." Heaviest wholesale buying time: fall; best selling time: fall and spring.

EARTH & FIRE CERAMIC STUDIO & GALLERY, 20 Morris St., Morristown NJ 07960. (201)455-9368. Contact: Michael Feno or Sy Shames. Gallery/ceramic studio. Estab. 1969. Represents 2 craftworkers. Works on consignment. Craftworker sets retail price.
Acceptable Work: Considers ceramics and pottery. Fine one-of-a-kind and handmade production-line items. Price range: $12-600; bestsellers: $18-90.
Profile: "Our items are displayed beautifully in a very elegant, uncrowded manner. We show unusual slab constructed pottery and one-of-a-kind ceramic objects." Best selling time: spring to Christmas.

FLY BY NIGHT, 252 Riverside Square, Hackensack NJ 07601. (201)489-0484. Contact: Arcadji Vetlov. Craft shop/gallery. Estab. 1970 Represents 36 craftworkers. Heaviest wholesale buying and best selling time: summer and winter.
Acceptable Work: Considers batik, ceramics, clothing, jewelry, metalsmithing, needlecrafts, pottery, quilting, wall hangings, weavings and woodcrafting. Especially needs "new and innovative designs in wearing apparel." Specializes in fine one-of-a-kind and handmade production-line items. Price range: $1.50-1,000; bestsellers: $5-50.
Terms: Buys outright and works on consignment; 33% commission. Retail price set by joint agreement. Requires exclusive area representation. Send resume, slides or call for appointment. Reports in 1 week. Work may be shipped or hand-delivered. Dealer pays insurance on exhibited work.

FROM THE HANDS OF MAN, 398 Main St., Metuchen NJ 08804. (201)548-0003. Manager: Suanne Fancis. Gift/jewelry shop. Estab. 1975. Represents 12-24 craftworkers.
Acceptable Work: Considers glass art, jewelry, leatherworking, pottery and scrimshaw. Specializes in fine art and functional crafts. One-of-a-kind and handmade production-line items. Price range: $10-200; bestsellers: $10-80.
Terms: Buys outright and works on consignment; 30% commission. Retail price set by joint agreement. Send slides/catalogue or call for appointment. Work may be shipped or hand delivered. Dealer pays insurance on exhibited work. Display time for consignment items set by joint agreement.
Profile: "Pieces displayed individually and by style. We have recently renovated the shop with custom-built displays, spot lighting and good atmosphere on Main St. in small upper class town." Customers: ages 20-45, well-educated, cosmopolitan. Heaviest wholesale buying and best selling time: Christmas.

To Break In: "Must be reliable and friendly and have ability and desire to reproduce and deliver."

GALLERY 187, 187 Sherwood Place, Englewood NJ 07631. (201)567-6187. Contact: Diann E. Goldberg. Gallery. Estab. 1977. Represents 6 craftworkers.
Acceptable Work: Considers ceramics, glass art, jewelry, pottery, soft sculpture, wall hangings, weavings and woodcrafting. One-of-a-kind and handmade production-line items. Price range: $25-600.
Terms: Buys outright and works on consignment; 35-50% commission. Retail price set by joint agreement. Requires exclusive area representation. Send resume or call for appointment. Reports in 2 weeks. Work may be shipped or hand-delivered. Dealer pays insurance on exhibited work.
Profile: "This is primarily a fine arts gallery with professional gallery presentation of items (i.e., sculpture stands, enclosed cases, track lighting)." Customers: adults with upper-middle incomes.

All types of customers—from dollhouse hobbyists to the discriminating collectors—are found buying items in The Dollhouse Factory, Lebanon, New Jersey. This miniature and supply shop carries all types of dollhouse and miniature-related items which are always on display in glass cases.

GALLERY 2W0, 34 Washington Ave., Westwood NJ 07675. (201)666-1696. Contact: Joyce Kaplan. Craft shop/gallery. Estab. 1967. Represents 7-8 craftworkers. Heaviest wholesale buying time: fall; best selling time: fall and spring.
Acceptable Work: Considers batik; pottery; soft sculpture; wall hangings; weavings; and woodcrafting. Finished, one-of-a-kind pieces. Price range: $10-500.
Terms: Works on consignment; 40% commission. Retail price set by joint agreement. Requires exclusive area representation. Reports in 2 weeks. Work may be shipped or hand-delivered. Dealer pays insurance for exhibited work.

HAND FEATS, 40 Main St., Madison NJ 07940. (201)822-1616. Manager: Eileen Madden. Craft

shop. Estab. 1970. Price range: $2-300. Works on consignment and buys outright; 34% commission. Retail price set by joint agreement. Reports in 2 weeks. Work may be shipped or hand-delivered.
Acceptable Work: Considers candlemaking; ceramics; glass art; jewelry; leatherworking; metalsmithing; pottery; and woodcrafting.
Profile: "In our area there aren't any shops quite as diversified as ours. We deal with leather boots, shoes, jewelry and crafts, a combination that makes for a really pleasurable shopping experience." Heaviest wholesale buying time: fall; best selling time: Christmas.

HORSE FEATHERS WEST, 185 E. Ridgewood Ave., Ridgewood NJ 07450. (201)444-6633. Contact: Joyce Solney. Craft/gift shop. Estab. 1976. Represents 40-50 craftworkers.
Acceptable Work: Considers candlemaking, ceramics, glass art, jewelry, leatherworking, metalsmithing, pottery, scrimshaw, soft sculpture, wall hangings, weavings and woodcrafting. Specializes in utilitarian, especially likes whimsy porcelain or stoneware. One-of-a-kind and handmade production-line items. Price range: $4-350; bestsellers: $10-20 and $40-60 items.
Terms: Buys outright and works on consignment; 30-40% commission. Retail price set by joint agreement. Requires exclusive area representation. Send resume and slides with SASE. Reports in 3 weeks. Work may be shipped or hand-delivered. Dealer pays insurance on exhibited work.
Profile: Crafts are displayed according to craftworker (i.e., pottery is displayed together with it broken down by craftworker). Shop is woodsy, casual and large. Heaviest wholesale buying time: spring-fall; best selling time: pre-Christmas.

HOUSE OF BERNARD, 353 Millburn Ave., Millburn NJ 07041. (201)376-8088. Contact: Berry or Shirley Bernard. Estab. 1961. Represents 60 out-of-town craftworkers. Considers batik; ceramics; jewelry; metalsmithing; pottery; wall hangings; and weaving. Primitive and finished, one-of-a-kind and handmade production-line items OK. Price range: $1-thousands of dollars; bestsellers: $5-50. Buys outright. Retail price set by joint agreement. Requires exclusive area representation. Write. Reports in 2 weeks. Dealer pays shipping to shop and insurance for exhibited work. Best selling time: Christmas. Customers are ages 20-50 with $20,000 incomes and are informed about art.

INTUITION, 75A Brighton Ave., West End NJ 07740. (201)870-1699. Contact: Beverly L. Hanapole. Craft shop/gallery. Estab. 1977. Represents 50-75 craftworkers.
Acceptable Work: Considers all crafts except decoupage, needlecrafts, scrimshaw and tole painting; especially needs furniture consignments. Specializes in fine contemporary crafts. Fine one-of-a-kind and handmade production-line items only. Price range: $2-1,000; bestsellers: $5-150.
Terms: Buys outright and works on consignment; 40% commission. Dealer pays insurance on exhibited work. Retail price set by craftworker or by joint agreement. Requires exclusive area representation. Send resume with slides. Reports in 2 weeks. Work may be shipped or hand-delivered.
Profile: "All work of each craftsman is grouped in a way to best show all aspects of his/her work. Certain outright buys (things that turn over fast) are moved from place to place within the shop on a monthly basis—this also allows for the featured work of the month (consigned) to be spotlighted." Professionally-designed shop with complete mobility of display in mind. Displays are primarily glass shelving and cases and black fiber drums. "Being a suburb of New York City and also a college town, we get quite an art-oriented clientele—with most in the high middle and above incomes." Heaviest wholesale and best selling time: summer ("we are 1 block from the beach") and Christmas. "We change consigned work monthly and have mailers designed and sent to our entire mailing list so this brings our *real* devotees around on a monthly basis.
To Break In: "We like to show people who are 'together' enough to know the value of their work. We appreciate delivery on the date promised and if working on an outright buy—first order C.O.D. then net 30."

JEAN JOHNSON MINIATURES, 421 Higgins Ave., Brielle NJ 08730. (201)528-7478. Contact: Jean Johnson. Miniature shop. Estab. 1973. Represents 150 craftworkers.
Acceptable Work: Considers miniatures in ceramics; clothing; dollmaking; glass art; metalsmithing; needlecrafts; pottery; quilting; tole painting; woodcrafting; and room settings. All styles; decorative only. Especially needs Victorian, heavily-detailed miniatures. Price range: 50¢-$1,000; bestsellers: $3-125.
Terms: Works on consignment and buys outright; 20% commission. Retail price set by joint

agreement. Reports in 4 weeks. Work may be shipped or hand-delivered. Dealer pays insurance for exhibited work. "We display work in the shop and at miniature shows in 5 states." Best selling time: Christmas.

KORNBLUTH GALLERY, 7-21 Fairlawn Ave., Fair Lawn NJ 07410. (201)791-3374. Contact: Lillian Kornbluth. Gallery. Estab. 1959. Represents 20 craftworkers and 20 additional at Christmas.
Acceptable Work: Considers batik, ceramics, glass art, jewelry, leatherworking, metalsmithing, needlecrafts, pottery, soft sculpture, wall hangings, weavings and woodcrafting. Especially needs sculptural wall hangings. Specializes in fine art one-of-a-kind and handmade production-line items. Price range: $15-2,000; bestsellers: $15-200.
Terms: Works on consignment; 40% commission. Craftworker sets retail price. Prefers exclusive area representation. Send resume and slides with SASE. Reports in 2 weeks. Work may be shipped or hand-delivered.
Profile: "We amalgamate fine, expensive paintings and sculpture with fine crafts. We do 3-4 major craft shows a year with a sampling on display at other times. Each show is mounted and designed as carefully as we do our paintings and sculpture with a total view of the effect of the show as well as the display of each item to its best advantage." Best selling time: December-June.

L'ATELIER GALLERY OF ARTS AND CRAFTS, Box 413, Cape May NJ 08204. (609)884-8662. Contact: Beau Sinkler and Carol McDowell. Gallery. Estab. 1978. Represents 15 craftworkers.
Acceptable Work: Considers dollmaking, jewelry, metalsmithing, needlecrafts, pottery, soft sculpture, wall hangings, weavings, stained glass and hand-painted pillows. Especially needs hand-spun yarns and textiles (i.e. hats and other small crocheted items and unique wall hangings). Exhibits mostly nostalgic pieces with a Victorian flavor. One-of-a-kind and handmade production-line items OK. Price range: $1.25-800; bestsellers: $10-150.
Terms: Buys outright and works on consignment; 40% commission. Craftworker sets retail price. Send slides, brochures, prints, samples, SASE or call for appointment. Reports in 1 week. Work may be shipped or hand-delivered. Dealer pays insurance for exhibited work.
Profile: "We rotate our displays every few weeks and occasionally feature one particular artist or craftsperson for a 2-week period. Displays are generally simple and uncluttered; we try to maintain a spacious, airy feeling in the gallery. Since we are a seashore resort, many items reflect local surroundings: birds, water, dunes, boats, etc. However, other works sell equally well, provided they are extremely well made."

MAIN STREET CRAFT COOPERATIVE, 37b N. Main St., Glassboro, NJ 08028. Contact: David Gray or Bill Kelmer. Craft shop. 1974. Represents 8-10 craftworkers, preferably from S. Jersey. "We'd like craftspeople to become working partners in the business."
Acceptable Work: Considers batik, candlemaking, ceramics, clothing, glass art, jewelry, leatherworking, metalsmithing, pottery, scrimshaw, wall hangings, weavings and woodcrafting. Specializes in contemporary functional pieces. Handmade production-line items. Price range: $1-100; bestsellers: $4-45.
Terms: Buys outright, takes memberships, and works on consignment; 34% commission. Craftworker pays insurance on exhibited work and sets retail price. Call for appointment or visit. Reports in 2 weeks. Work may be shipped or hand delivered.
Profile: "We are in a small, old, separate building standing back from the road. The minimum time for consignment is 2 months and there is open easy-access displays except for jewelry. Since Glassboro is a university town, we have a lot of college students, professors and middle class townspeople." Heaviest wholesale buying time: fall; best selling time: Christmas.

MARY ANNE MARINACCIO DOLL HOUSE FURNITURE & ACCESSORIES, Box 83, Adelphia Rd., Rt. 524, Adelphia NJ 07710. (201)431-2942. Contact: Mary Anne Marinaccio. Craft and gift shop. Estab. 1969. Represents 6 craftworkers. Considers dollmaking and dollhouse furniture and accessories. 1"-1' scale. Handmade production-line items. Price range: 50¢-$500. Works on consignment; 30-50% commission. Retail price set by joint agreement. Reporting time varies. Work may be shipped or hand-delivered.

THE MINI GALLERY, THE NEWARK MUSEUM, Box 540, 49 Washington St., Newark NJ 07101. (201)733-6635. Exhibits coordinator: Jean West. Museum gallery. Estab. 1973. Sponsors 1- and 2-man shows of New Jersey professional craftworkers.
Acceptable Work: Considers batik, ceramics, glass art, jewelry, quilting, soft sculpture, wall

hangings, weavings and woodcrafting. One-of-a-kind and handmade production-line items. Price range: $10-1,000; bestsellers: $10-50.
Terms: Send resume and slides. Slides are reviewed once a year and a schedule is made. Work may be shipped or hand delivered. Museum pays insurance on exhibited work.

MORRIS MUSEUM SHOP, Box 125, Convent Station NJ 07961. (201)538-0454. Contact: Judith Chapin or Claire Cain. Museum gift shop. Represents 6 craftworkers. Price range: 10¢-$95; bestsellers: 10¢-$8. Works on consignment and buys outright; commission varies. Retail price set by joint agreement. Requires exclusive area representation. Reports in 2 weeks. Work may be shipped or hand-delivered. Dealer pays shipping to shop and in-transit insurance. Displays work 6-12 months.
Acceptable Work: Considers batik; ceramics; dollmaking; glass art; jewelry; pottery; needlecraft; wall hangings; weavings; and woodcrafting. Especially needs batik hangings; weavings; boxes; miniatures; and animals in pottery, ceramics or wood. All styles.
Profile: "We try to display each craft item to its best advantage; also find changing display periodically, that is, shifting location, helps items to sell. We are a family museum with exhibits for young and old in both arts and sciences. Approximate income of customers: $5,000-200,000." Heaviest wholesale buying time: fall and spring; best selling time: fall.

ONLY ORIGINALS, 759 Somerset St., Watchung NJ 07060. (201)756-7475. Contact: Dot Kenney. Craft shop/gallery. Estab. 1970. Represents 10 craftworkers.
Acceptable Work: Considers batik; ceramics; jewelry; pottery; wall hangings; weavings. Especially needs mobiles, wall hangings and sculpture. One-of-a-kind pieces. Price range: $5-200; bestsellers: $10-35.
Terms: Works on consignment: 30% commission. Retail price set by joint agreement. Requires exclusive area representation. Reports in 4 weeks. Work may be shipped or hand-delivered. Dealer pays return shipping and insurance for exhibited work.
Profile: "Work is displayed in wall displays and shelf displays. Customers are middle-aged; with above average income." Displays work 6-8 weeks. Heaviest wholesale buying time: spring; best selling time: fall.

PAST & PRESENTS, 10 Herman Street, Glen Ridge NJ 07028. (201)748-3693. Contact: Marnie de Carville. Craft/antique shop. Estab. 1978. Represents 15 craftworkers.
Acceptable Work: Considers batik, clothing, dollmaking, jewelry, metalsmithing, pottery, quilting, wall hangings, weavings and woodcrafting. One-of-a-kind and handmade production-line items. Price range: $1.25+; bestsellers: $1.25-15.
Terms: Buys outright and works on consignment; 30% commission. Shop sets retail price. Prefers exclusive area representation. Work may be shipped or hand-delivered. "Consignment items are kept for 3 months, with payments monthly."
Profile: "We display our crafts in, on and around our antiques; or give them a separate and special area, as seems appropriate. Customers find the melange of old crafts (antiques) with new crafts refreshingly different." Customers: ages 8-80, middle incomes. "We are near several schools." Heaviest wholesale buying time: spring and fall; best selling time: pre-Christmas.

PAULA'S PLACE, 1 W. Main St., Marlton NJ 08053. (609)983-6880. Contact: Paula Vallen. Craft shop. Estab. 1974. Represents 80 craftworkers. Price range: $5-250; bestsellers: $15-40. Works on consignment and buys outright; 33% commission. Retail price set by joint agreement. Requires exclusive area representation. Reports in 4 weeks. Work may be shipped or hand-delivered. Dealer pays shipping and insurance. Displays work 3-4 weeks.
Acceptable Work: Considers batik; ceramics; clothing; glass art; jewelry; leatherworking; pottery; quilting; soft sculpture; wall hangings; weavings; and woodcrafting. Especially needs wall hangings; soft sculpture; and functional pottery in large, interesting pieces. Fine one-of-a-kind and handmade production-line items.
Profile: "Work is displayed in special section with sign denoting exhibit; announcements are sent to customers and advertising done in local papers. Customers are in late 20's to mid 30's; middle class; $15,000-25,000 income." Heaviest wholesale buying time: summer; best selling time: fall.
To Break In: "Visit shop if possible, see if your craft fits in; send information, pictures and prices."

THE PEDDLERS CELLAR, 9 Main St., Chester NJ 07930. (201)879-6369. Contact: Ginny Hardy. Gift shop. Estab. 1971. Represents 150 craftworkers. Price range: 50¢-$600; bestsel-

lers: $1.50-20. Works on consignment; 40% commission. Retail price set by joint agreement. Do not send samples unless requested. If interested reports in 2 weeks. Work may be shipped or hand-delivered. Dealer pays return shipping.
Acceptable Work: Considers all crafts. Especially needs dolls, baby and children's items, wind chimes, Christmas ornaments, pottery, wood work and ceremics. Primitive handmade production-line items.
Profile: Customers are "women; married; age 19-70; and interested in doing crafts themselves". Heaviest wholesale buying time: late summer; best selling time: Christmas.

PETERS VALLEY, Star Route, Layton NJ 07851. (201)948-5202. Contact: Linda Davis. Craft shop/gallery. Estab. 1969. Represents over 100 regional craftworkers. Price range: $1-1,000; bestsellers: $15-175. Works on consignment; 33% commission. Retail price set by joint agreement. Work may be shipped or hand-delivered. Dealer pays insurance for exhibited work.
Acceptable Work: Considers batik; ceramics; clothing; glass art; jewelry; leatherworking; metalsmithing; pottery; soft sculpture; wall hangings; weavings; and woodworking. Fine one-of-a-kind and handmade production-line items.
Profile: "We are located in a national park and are part of a crafts community with craft studios open to the public. Customers are 18-55; middle to upper income; interested in crafts." Displays work 90 days. Best selling time: summer and fall.

RAGGEDY ANN ANTIQUE DOLL & TOY MUSEUM, 171 Main St., Flemington NJ 08822. (201)782-1243. Contact: Jean Bach. Museum gallery and gift shop. Estab. 1962. Represents 8 craftworkers.
Acceptable Work: Considers doll clothing, dollmaking and anything to do with antique dolls or Raggedy Ann items. One-of-a-kind and handmade production-lne items. Price range: $1.25-18; bestsellers: $2-5.
Terms: Buys outright. Retail price set by joint agreement. Requires exclusive area representation. Call for appointment or write with SASE. Reports in 1 week. Work must be hand-delivered. Dealer pays insurance on exhibited work. Display time: year.
Profile: "We are located in and old Victorian brick mansion filled with the charm of a bygone era. Each item of interest is described on a printed card near it." Heaviest wholesale buying and best selling time: summer. Open: June-January.

WILLIAM RIS GALLERIES, 9725 Second Ave., Stone Harbor NJ 08247. See William Ris Galleries, Camp Hill, Pennsylvania.

THE SANDPIPER, 536 Lake Ave., Bay Head NJ 08742. (201)892-9090. Contact: Mrs. James McGregor. Gift shop. Estab. 1965. Represents 35-40 craftworkers.
Acceptable Work: Considers clothing, decoupage, metalsmithing, needlecrafts, pottery, quilting, tole painting and woodcrafting. Handmade production-line items only. Price range: $2.50-200.
Terms: Works on consignment; 33⅓% commission. Retail price set by joint agreement. Requires exclusive area representation. Call for appointment. Work may be shipped or hand-delivered. Dealer pays insurance on exhibited work. "Consignment may be left for 1 season to be picked up after the 1st of each year."
Profile: "We are a small handcraft, gift and pantry shop. We are also a basic summer shop surrounded by a community of wealth." Best selling time: summer."

THE SUNSHINE SHOPPE, 55 W. Shore Ave., Dumont NJ 07628. (201)387-0909. Contact: Doris Gripenburg or Gail Meyers. Craft shop. Estab. 1976. Represents 50 craftworkers.
Acceptable Work: Considers candlemaking, ceramics, decoupage, glass art, jewelry, leatherworking, miniatures, needlecrafts, pillows, pottery, baby quilting, soft sculpture, tole painting, wall hangings, weavings, woodcrafting, wood toys, Christmas decorations, and especially needs patchwork items and stuffed toys and dolls. No clothes or large items. Specializes in contemporary and personalized items for childrens rooms and Appalachian work. One-of-a-kind and handmade production-line items. Price range: 59¢-$30; bestsellers: 59¢-$10.
Terms: Works on consignment; 40% commission. Retail price set by joint agreement. Send slides/photos/drawings with SASE. Reports in 2 weeks. Work may be shipped or hand-delivered. Dealer pays return shipping and insurance for exhibited work. Contacts craftworker after 2 months of no sales to lower price or take back merchandise.
Profile: "We are a very small store (but growing rapidly) and seek a variety of colorful, small items for display. Items are displayed on wall shelves, in cases or hung." Customers: ages

30-40, middle income and "looking for handcrafts rather than just a gift. They often make things themselves." Heaviest buying time: fall; best selling time: fall-Christmas and Mother's and Father's Days.
To Break In: "Please pack your items well. Also, depending on your craft, be aware that newspaper will leave print smudges on your items—use foam material, tissue or old pattern paper to wrap."

THISTLEDOWN GALLERY, 851 Rabway Ave., Westfield NJ 07090. Thistledown Gallery, Grafton, VT 05146 (in summer). Contact: Mrs. Robinson. Gallery/gift shop. Estab. 1970. Represents 156 Vermont and New England craftworkers.
Acceptable Work: Considers batik, candlemaking, ceramics, glass art, jewelry, leatherworking, metalsmithing, pottery, quilting, wall hangings, weavings and woodcrafting. "Mod does not go in this area." One-of-a-kind and handmade production-line items. Price range: $1-200.
Terms: Buys outright and works on consignment; 33⅓% commission. Retail price set by joint agreement. Call for appointment. Work may be shipped or hand-delivered.
Profile: "A rustic barn setting alongside fashionable inn with well-to-do tourist customers and average shoppers." Heaviest wholesale buying time: June and late summer; best selling time: fall.
To Break In: "Don't short on the shop wholesaler in favor of current direct sales or shows."

TOOL & TALENT—HANDCRAFTS OF DISTINCTION, 229 Raritan Ave., Highland Park NJ 08904. (201)246-0878. Contact: Roselee Borow. Craft shop/gallery/gift shop. Estab. 1973. Represents 100-150 American craftworkers.
Acceptable Work: Considers batik, ceramics, glass art, enameling and functional jewelry, leatherworking, metalsmithing, pottery, scrimshaw, soft sculpture, wall hangings, weavings and woodcrafting. Especially needs furniture and sterling silver jewelry in the $10-30 range. Specializes in one-of-a-kind jewelry. Fine one-of-a-kind and handmade production-line items. Price range: $3-$2,000; bestsellers: $10-150.
Terms: Buys outright and works on consignment; 40% commission. "Really fine pieces are consignment only." Retail price set by joint agreement. Requires exclusive area representation. Send slides with SASE or call for appointment. Reports in 2 weeks. Work may be shipped or hand-delivered. Dealer pays shipping to shop and insurance for exhibited work ("We are covered for theft if there is a break-in but no coverage on shoplifting"). New work is displayed in window for 1 month at the longest. Thereafter it is used within the gallery up to a year, if not sold. Advertises at Christmas and various gift seasons.
Profile: "We have a lovely gallery with excellent window and interior displays. ½ of the space is for jewelry; the balance is devoted to all other crafts, which are generally purchased as gifts." Customers: primarily professionals, ages 25-50, fairly well-to-do (doctors, lawyers, Rutger's University people). Heaviest wholesale buying time: early spring and summer; best selling time: winter and late spring.
To Break In: "We only buy what we see—if orders do not live up to what we have already inspected, they are returned. We are known for the high quality of the crafts we carry. Over-pricing guarantees no sales so prices must be realistic."

UNIVERSAL GALLERIES, INC., Millside Manor Arcade, Delran NJ 08075. (609)764-1601. Estab. 1978. Sponsors 24 shows annually for members only. Membership $125. $65 exhibit fee. No commission. Limited space. Write or phone for membership application.

VAN CLINE & DAVENPORT LTD., 792 Franklin Ave., New Jersey NJ 07417. (201)891-4588. President: Stephen Lord van Cline. Gallery. Estab. 1875. Sponsors 1-man shows. Considers porcelain with detail and originalilty. Works on consignment; 50% commission.

THE WALL GALLERY, 55 Summit Ave., Summit NJ 07901. (201)273-5552. President: Muriel S. Bloom. Craft shop/gallery. Estab. 1975. Represents 150 craftworkers. Price range: $10-500. Works on consignment and buys outright; 40% commission. Craftworker sets retail price. Requires exclusive area representation. Reports first of the month. Work may be shipped or hand-delivered. Payment for return shipping is negotiable. Dealer pays insurance for exhibited work. Displays work 6 months minimum.
Acceptable Work: Considers (only for wall) batiks; ceramics; weavings; embroideries; metalsmithing; rugs; glass art; woodcrafting; soft sculpture; and other wall hangings. Primitive and fine one-of-a-kind pieces; decorative only.
Profile: "Work is displayed immediately on receipt. Our stock is from all over the world." Best selling time: winter and spring.

WHALE'S TALE, 312 Washington Mall, Cape May NJ 08204. (609)884-4808. Contact: Hilary Russell. Estab. 1974. Represents 20 craftworkers. Considers batik; candlemaking; ceramics; dollmaking; glass art; jewelry; pottery; soft sculpture; wall hangings; weavings; and woodcrafting. Finished one-of-a-kind and handmade production-line items. Price range: $2-160; bestsellers: $2-20. Buys outright or on consignment; 40% commission. Retail price set by joint agreement. Requires exclusive area representation. Query with transparencies or photos. Reports in 2 weeks. Dealer pays shipping and insurance.
Profile: "Display structures are versatile and we're able to build them around the work displayed." Most crafts displayed 1 month. Heaviest wholesale buying time: spring and summer; best selling time: summer and fall. "A large number of 25-35 year olds who appreciate the work of serious craftspeople (as opposed to hobbyists) pass through shop in summer."

WHEATON VILLAGE, Glasstown Rd., Millville NJ 08332. (609)825-6800. Merchandising Manager: Ben Weston. Craft shop/museum gallery/museum gift shop. Estab. 1970. Represents 12-20 craftworkers. Price range: $1-700; bestsellers: $5-15. Buys outright. Retail price set by joint agreement. Work may be shipped or hand-delivered.
Acceptable Work: Considers candlemaking; ceramics; clothing; dollmaking; glass art; jewelry; leatherworking; metalsmithing; needlecrafts; pottery; quilting; tole painting; wall hangings; weavings; woodcrafting; and reproductions of 19th century (especially glass). Primitive one-of-a-kind and handmade production-line items.
Profile: "Shops are part of a reconstructed 19th century museum village." Heaviest wholesale buying time: spring and summer; best selling time: summer and fall.

THE YELLOW DOOR, 24 Washington Ave., Tenafly NJ 07670. Contact: Betty Turino. Estab. 1973. Represents 375-400 craftworkers. Considers batik; candlemaking; ceramics; glass art; jewelry; metalsmithing; soft sculpture; wall hangings; weavings; and woodcrafting. Finished one-of-a-kind and handmade production-line items. Price range: $8-1,500; best sellers: $8-75. Buys outright or on consignment; 40% commission. Gallery sets retail price. Requires exclusive area representation. Write. Dealer pays return shipping and insurance on exhibited work.
Profile: Items displayed 3-4 weeks. Heaviest wholesale buying time: April-May, September-November; best selling time: October-February, March-August. Customers are 30-55, urban-oriented and affluent.

New Mexico

ARTISTS' CO-OP GALLERY, 125 W. Palace Ave., Santa Fe NM 87501. (505)988-2582. Gallery/rental gallery. Estab. 1971. Represents 7 Santa Fe craftworkers. Must be member of Beiriga Co-op.
Acceptable Work: Considers batik, ceramics, clothing, glass art, needlecrafts, pottery, quilting, soft sculpture, wall hangings, weavings, woodcrafting and raku. Especially needs wall hangings (multi-media). Specializes in fine and contemporary crafts. One-of-a-kind and handmade production-line items. Price range: $3-1,000; bestsellers: $3-125.
Terms: Works on consignment; 15% commission. Requests a 1 year commitment. Space fee: $30/month—first and last months rent paid upon joining. Members must work 2-3 days a month at the gallery. Craftworker sets retail price. "Come to a meeting with samples of work (6:30 pm, first Wednesday of any month—work is juried by members)." Reports in 1 week. Work must be hand-delivered.
Profile: "We are a 13-14 member cooperative. We show both fine arts and crafts. The work is changed often in our large front room and we have a backroom where work is on continuous display. Each show lasts 3 weeks; 1 or 2 man shows are for 2 weeks. Customers: tourists (some wealthy); and good local traffic." Best selling time: summer and pre-Christmas.

BLUE DOOR GALLERY/GIFT SHOP, Drawer N, Taos NM 87571. (505)758-2233. Contact: Jay Slinde or LaVonne Moynihan. Gallery/gift shop. Estab. 1972. Represents 50 craftworkers.
Acceptable Work: Considers batik; ceramics; clothing; dollmaking; jewelry; needlecrafts; pottery; tole painting; wall hangings; and sand paintings. Especially needs weavings. Price range: $5-4,000; bestsellers; $20-200.
Terms: Works on consignment and buys outright; 33% commission. Retail price set by joint agreement. Reports in 2 weeks. Work may be shipped or hand-delivered.
Profile: "Display time is indefinite; we show work in open and locked cases, on walls and shelves; we have 5 rooms." Heaviest wholesale buying time: spring and fall; best selling time: summer-fall.

CASA DE COLORES, 602 Canyon Rd., Santa Fe NM 87501. Contact: Karen DeMott. Studio/

gallery. Estab. 1978. Represents 2 craftworkers.
Acceptable Work: Considers batik; jewelry; soft sculpture; pottery; sculpture; wall hangings; weavings; and silk screening. Fine and one-of-a-kind pieces. Price range: $10-500.
Terms: Works on consignment; 33⅓% commission. Retail price set by joint agreement. Requires exclusive area representation. Mail slides and photos and description of materials and prices. Reports in 3 weeks. Work may be shipped or hand-delivered. Dealer pays insurance for exhibited work.
Profile: Work is displayed on open shelves, closed cases and in wall displays. Customers are middle to upper income tourists. Heaviest wholesale buying time: spring; best selling time: summer.

CASE TRADING POST—WHEELWRIGHT MUSEUM, Box 5153. Santa Fe, New Mexico 87502. (505)982-4636. Manager: Noel Pitcher. Museum gift shop/gallery. Estab. 1937. Represents 50-100 native American craftworkers.
Acceptable Work: Considers all Native American crafts especially ceramics, dollmaking, jewelry, pottery and scrimshaw. Specializes in primitive, traditional and contemporary crafts. One-of-a-kind items only. Price range: $5-5,000; bestsellers: $5-2,500.
Terms: Buys outright and works on consignment; 30% commission. Retail price set by joint agreement. Send resume and slides. Reports in 4 weeks. Work may be shipped or hand delivered. Dealer pays insurance on exhibited work. "Pieces sent by mail must be insured by craftworker.
Profile: "All items are dislayed in antique cases or mounted on walls (tapestries, weavings). The shop is a replica of a 1890's Navajo Trading Post with most items in the shop for sale." Customers: many local patrons and tourists interested in native American art. Heaviest wholesale buying time: May-August; best selling times: April-October.

CLAY & FIBER GALLERY, Box 439, Taos NM 87571. (505)758-8093. Contact: Art or Mark Adair. Craft shop/gallery. Estab. 1974. Represents 60-75 craftworkers. Work is displayed "on walls, shelves and pedestals." Best selling and heaviest wholesale buying time: summer and fall.
Acceptable Work: Considers batik; ceramics; clothing; glass art; jewelry; pottery; quilting; soft sculpture; wall hangings; weavings; and woodcrafting. Fine one-of-a-kind and handmade production-line items. Price range: $3-1,500; bestsellers: $10-500.
Terms: Works on consignment and buys outright; 40% commission. Craftworker sets retail price. Requires exclusive area representation. Reports in 1 week. Work may be shipped or hand-delivered upon request from gallery. Shipping payment is negotiable. Dealer pays insurance for exhibited work.

THE CONTEMPORARY CRAFTSMAN, 112 Don Gaspar, Santa Fe NM 87501. (505)988-1001. Director: Jane Gann. Gallery. Estab. 1976. Represents 120 craftworkers.
Acceptable Work: Considers batik; ceramics; clothing; dollmaking; glass art; jewelry; leatherworking; metalsmithing; needlecrafts; pottery; quilting; soft sculpture; wall hangings; weavings; woodcrafting; furniture; baskets; and stained glass. Fine one-of-a-kind and handmade production-line items. Price range: $3-1,200; bestsellers: $3-700.
Terms: Works on consignment and buys outright; 34% commission. Retail price set by joint agreement. Reports in 4 weeks. Work may be shipped or hand-delivered by prior arrangement. Dealer pays return shipping and insurance for exhibited work.
Profile: Displays employ shelves, pedestals, glass display cases and wall space. "We make a concerted effort to educate people about the fine quality of work in New Mexico and the rest of the country." Heaviest wholesale buying time: spring-fall; best selling time: June-Christmas.

DE VARGAS ARTS & CRAFTS FAIR, Box 205, Santa Fe NM 81501 (505)988-1110. Contact: Jane Dunn. Gallery/rental gallery/art promotion shop. Estab. 1974. Represents 75-100 craftworkers. Heaviest wholesale buying time: summer-fall; best selling time: Christmas and summer.
Acceptable Work: Considers batik; candlemaking; ceramics; clothing; dollmaking; glass art; jewelry; leatherworking; metalsmithing; needlecrafts; pottery; wall hangings; weavings; and woodcrafting. Fine one-of-a-kind pieces. Price range: $5-12,000; bestsellers: $15-250.
Terms: Works on consignment and buys outright; 20-40% commission. Retail price set by joint agreement. Work may be shipped or hand-delivered. Dealer pays limited insurance for exhibited work.

DEL SOL, INC., La Fonda Hotel, Shelby and Water Streets, Santa Fe NM 87501. (505)983-

3927. Contact: Celina Garcia. Craft/gift shop. Estab. 1976. Represents 20 craftworkers. "We display work on shelves, hung on walls and in niches in the wall." Best selling time: summer.
Acceptable Work: Considers batik; candlemaking; ceramics; decoupage; dollmaking; glass art; hand blown glass; silver; brass; copper art; jewelry; leatherworking; metalsmithing; needlecrafts; pottery; quilting; wall hangings; weavings; and woodcrafting. Price range: $1-300; bestsellers: $6-150.
Terms: Works on consignment and buys outright; commission varies. Gallery sets retail price. Reports in 3 weeks. Work may be shipped or hand-delivered.

DEWEY-KOFRON GALLERY, 112 E. Palace Ave., Santa Fe NM 87501. (505)982-8478. Contact: Ray Dewey. Arts/crafts gallery. Estab. 1976. Represents 30 craftworkers whose work relates to Indian and contemporary Southwest and New Mexico folk art.
Acceptable Work: Considers jewelry; metalsmithing; pottery; wall hangings; weavings; and woodcrafting. Primitive and fine one-of-a-kind pieces. Price range: $20-15,000; bestsellers: $300-1,500.
Terms: Works on consignment and buys outright; 33% commission. Retail price set by joint agreement. Requires exclusive area representation. Reports in 2 weeks. Work may be shipped or hand-delivered. Dealer pays return shipping.
Profile: Work is displayed in enclosed cases and on wall space. "We are selective and limited in what we show and have an excellent location near Santa Fe Plaza." 80% of customers are from out of state; aged 24-55; basically collectors; have over $20,000 per year income. Heaviest wholesale buying time: December-June; best selling time: June-December.

EL GRINGO, Box 2356, Taos NM 87571. (505)758-8311. Contact: C.H. Burlingame. Craft shop/gallery/gift shop. Estab. 1972. Represents 15 craftworkers.
Acceptable Work: Considers glass art; jewelry; leatherworking; metalsmithing; pottery; woodcrafting; statuary, and ojos (God's eyes). Special need for pottery. Fine handmade production-line items. Price range: $5-100; bestsellers: $5-8.
Terms: Works on consignment and buys outright; 40% commission. Retail price set by joint agreement. Reports in 1 week. Dealer pays return shipping.
Profile: "Work is enclosed in jewelry cases, placed on pedestals or shelves. Our store is in a good location. We stay open long hours in the summer (8:30 a.m. to 10 p.m.) 7 days a week." Customers are all tourists of upper middle income. Heaviest wholesale buying time: spring-summer; best selling time: summer.

EL RINCON, Box Q, Taos NM 87501. (505)758-9188. Contact: Rowena Meyers Martinez. Museum gift shop/gallery. Estab. 1970. Represents 35 craftworkers.
Acceptable Work: Considers dollmaking; jewelry; pottery; wall hangings; weavings; woodcrafting; tin craft; and beadwork. Price range: $5-1,800; bestsellers: $20-75.
Terms: Buys outright. Gallery sets retail price. Reports in 1 week. Hand-delivered work only.
Profile: "We are a museum of Indian and Spanish Colonial cultural items. Work is displayed in showcases, on shelves and wallspace." Heaviest wholesale buying time: summer; best selling time: summer-fall.

HAND MADE USA, INC., 526 Coronado Center, Albuquerque NM 87110. (505)883-5861. President: Don Byrne. Craft shop. Estab. 1976. Represents 110 craftworkers.
Acceptable Work: Considers all crafts. Price range: $1-1,000; bestsellers: $5.95-200.
Terms: Works on consignment and operates as a high volume coop with a basic booth fee and percentage; 24% commission. Craftworker sets retail price. Shop reports each month with a copy of all sales tickets. Work may be shipped or hand-delivered. Dealer pays insurance for exhibited work.
Profile: "Each craftsman has his own display booth, arranged the way he likes his craft displayed." Best selling time: summer, fall and Christmas.

HAND MAIDEN, El Centro Mall, 102 E. Water St., Santa Fe NM 87501. (505)982-8368. Contact: Kathe Brogan. Craft/gift shop. Estab. 1971. Represents 15 Southwestern craftworkers.
Acceptable Work: Considers candlemaking; ceramics; leatherworking; pottery; and woodcrafting. Especially needs utilitarian stoneware; pottery and soft leather bags. Specializes in utilitarian items. Price range: $2-150; bestsellers: $10-40.
Terms: Buys outright. Gallery sets retail price. Reports in 2 weeks. Work may be shipped or hand-delivered. Dealer pays shipping to shop and insurance for exhibited work.
Profile: "We display work on open shelves and walls and in glass cases; customers are

tourists." Heaviest wholesale buying time: spring; best selling time: summer.

HOUSE & TABLE, 20 Sena Plaza, Santa Fe NM 87501. (505)982-5265. Contact: Robert Olds. Craft/gift shop. Estab. 1967. Represents 6 craftworkers. Heaviest wholesale buying time: spring; best selling time: summer.
Acceptable Work: Considers ceramics; clothing; metalsmithing; pottery; soft sculpture; wall hangings; weavings; woodcraftings; and furniture. Primitive one-of-a-kind and handmade production-line items. Price range: $2-150; bestsellers: $5-25.
Terms: Works on consignment and buys outright; 40% commission. Retail price set by joint agreement. Reports in 1 week. Work may be shipped or hand-delivered. Dealer pays shipping to shop after agreeing to buy and insurance for exhibited work.

HUNTRESS STAINED GLASS, 109 Washington Ave., Santa Fe NM 87501. (505)983-1866. Contact: Judy Wilson. Glass gallery/custom order studio. Estab. 1971. Represents 5-6 craftworkers.
Acceptable Work: Considers glass art. Fine one-of-a-kind and handmade production-line items. Price range: $15-1,500; bestsellers: $20-50.
Terms: Works on consignment; 33% commission. Retail price set by joint agreement. Reports in 5 weeks. Work may be shipped or hand-delivered. Dealer pays shipping to shop.
Profile: Work is "back lit; shown in hanging displays. Customers are home owners; builders; restaurant owners; municipalities; and churches." Best selling and heaviest wholesale buying time: summer.

INSTITUTE OF AMERICAN INDIAN ARTS MUSEUM, Cerrillos Rd., Santa Fe NM 87501. (505)988-6281. Museum Director: Charles Dailey. Museum gallery/gift shop/junior college. Estab. 1962. Represents 200-300 native American craftworkers, or those which make Indian-related artwork.
Acceptable Work: Considers all native American crafts. "Work must be either native American or in the nature of inspiration, derivation, etc." One-of-a-kind items only. Price range: $1-1,000; bestsellers: $6-90.
Terms: Works on consignment; 20% commission. "We purchase for the collection through Federal purchasing, from 1-man shows and from student sales." Craftworker sets retail price. Send resume and slides. Reports in 3 weeks. "Our museum committee meets for jurying of shows as necessary." Work may be shipped or hand delivered. "All artwork on federal property is protected by the federal law; one must request payment for value on broken items." Display time: 3-6 weeks.
Profile: "Item is displayed in the way the artist requests—if different than a logical or customary method. Our Arts and Crafts Junior College is maintained expressly for the purpose of training native Americans in areas of arts and crafts, museum training and creative writing." Heaviest wholesale buying and best selling time: December, May-September.

JELLYBEANS, 602 Canyon Rd., Santa Fe NM 87501. (505)988-5227. Contact: Rebecca Carter. Needlework shop. Estab. 1974. Represents 100 craftworkers.
Acceptable Work: Considers needlecrafts. Finished, one-of-a-kind and handmade production-line items. Especially likes Southwestern designs. Also interested in handmade items for the miniature enthusiast. Price range: $1-500; bestsellers: $15-40.
Terms: Buys outright. Gallery sets retail price. Requires exclusive area representation. Reports in 2 weeks. Work may be shipped or hand-delivered by previous arrangement. Dealer pays shipping to shop.
Profile: "Most of our designs are handpainted and are of the best quality materials. Customers are locals and tourists; middle to upper income." Best selling time: summer.

LA PALOMA GALLERY, Box 3037, Taos NM 87571. (505)758-2921. Contact: Jane Mohon. Craft shop/gallery. Estab. 1977. Represents 10 craftworkers.
Acceptable Work: Considers ceramics; glass art; jewelry; metalsmithing; pottery; wall hangings; weavings; woodcrafting; and mounted butterflies in glass cases. Primitive and fine one-of-a-kind pieces. Price range: $5-600; bestsellers: $10-50.
Terms: Works on consignment and buys outright; 40% commission. Retail price set by joint agreement. Requires exclusive area representation. Reports in 2 weeks. Work may be shipped or hand-delivered.
Profile: "We display work on display stands, shelves and enclosed cases and walls." Heaviest wholesale buying time: spring-summer; best selling time: summer.

LA POSADA GIFT SHOP, 330 E. Palace Ave., Santa Fe NM 87501. (505)988-1990. President: Josephine Turner. Treasurer: Verena Doak. Craft/gift shop. Estab. 1970. Represents 30 craftworkers.
Acceptable Work: Considers ceramics, clothing, cone craft, decoupage, glass art, jewelry, metalsmithing, needlecrafts, pottery and woodcrafting. One-of-a-kind and handmade production-line items. Price range: 15¢-$300; bestsellers: $2.80-30.
Terms: Buys outright and works on consignment; 33⅓% commission. Retail price set by joint agreement. Call for appointment with samples. Reports immediately. Work must be shipped or hand-delivered. "If we lose or break anything, we pay craftsperson." Display time: 1 year.
Profile: "We feature local items (Indian, Spanish American). We're in a motel near center of town and have 6 acres." Best selling time: summer-Christmas.

LAS NOVEDADES, Box 1162, E. Kit Carson Rd., Taos NM 87571. (505)758-4439. Contact: Angie Martinez. Gift shop. Estab. 1969. Represents 5 craftworkers. Heaviest wholesale buying time: May and June; best selling time: July, August and September.
Acceptable Work: Considers jewelry; leatherworking; metalsmithing; pottery. Primitive and handmade production-line items. Price range: $12-25; bestsellers: $12 maximum.
Terms: Works on consignment and buys outright; 50% commission. Craftworker sets retail price. Reports in 1 week. Work may be shipped or hand-delivered. Dealer pays insurance for exhibited work.

THE MARKET, Box 1111, Taos NM 87571. (505)758-3195. Contact: Peggy Williamson or Jo Livingston. Craft shop/gallery. Estab. 1966. Represents 100 Southwestern comtemporary craftworkers. "Only full-time professional craftsmen who can supply consistently."
Acceptable Work: Considers ceramics, glass art, jewelry, metalsmithing, pottery, wall hangings, weavings and woodcrafting. Contemporary crafts only. Specializes in fine designer crafts, especially ceramics and one-of-a-kind jewelry in silver and gold. One-of-a-kind and handmade production-line items. Price range: $2-5,000; bestsellers: $5-50.
Terms: Buys outright and works on consignment; 33⅓% commission. Retail price set by craftworker or joint agreement. Requires exclusive area representation. Send resume and slides or call for appointment. Reports in 1 week. Work may be shipped or hand delivered.
Profile: "We are located on Kit Carson Road, which is (and always has been for 30 years) a street of painting galleries and Indian art shops. We were the first gallery to feature the contemporary craftsman *exclusively*. We carry no imports, no manufactured items and display all artists continuously." Customers: young tourists and professionals. Heaviest wholesale buying and best selling time: May 15-October 15.

MAXWELL MUSEUM GIFT SHOP, University of New Mexico, Albuquerque NM 87131. (505)277-3766. Manager: Sally J. Nusbaum. Buyer: Beverly J. Barsook. Museum gift shop. Estab. 1968.
Acceptable Work: Considers authentic American Indian crafts only. One-of-a-kind and handmade production-line items. Price range: $10-1,500; bestsellers: $20-500.
Terms: Works on consignment and buys outright; 50% commission. Retail price set by joint agreement. Work may be shipped with permission and hand-delivered by prior appointment. Dealer pays return shipping and insurance for exhibited work.
Profile: "Customers are primarily college students and adults traveling." Best selling time: Chrismas and summer.

THE MELTING POINT GLASSWORKS & POTTERY, 821 Canyon Rd., Santa Fe NM 87501. (505)988-2662. Contact: Daphne Morrissey. Craft shop/gallery. Estab. 1976. Represents 10 craftworkers.
Acceptable Work: Considers ceramics; glass art; and pottery. Fine one-of-a-kind and handmade production-line items. Price range: $3-500; bestsellers: $4-75.
Terms: Works on consignment; 40% commission. Craftworker sets retail price. Reports in 4 weeks. Hand-delivered work only. Dealer pays insurance for exhibited work.
Profile: "We are fortunate to have our studios on the premises. Work is fully lighted and displayed on shelves, not overcrowded." Best selling and heaviest wholesale buying time: summer.

THE MUSEUM SHOP AT THE INTERNATIONAL FOLK ART MUSEUM, Box 2087, Santa Fe NM 87501. (505)982-3016. Buyer: Liz Buchanan. Museum gift/craft shop. Estab. 1952. Represents 10-20 American craftworkers.
Acceptable Work: Considers batik, ceramics, dollmaking; glass art; jewelry; metalsmithing;

needlecrafts; pottery; wall hangings; weavings; woodcrafting; baskets; and toys. Only folk art, Spanish Colonial and local crafts based on a folk tradition. One-of-a-kind pieces. Price range: $2-200; bestsellers: $5-30.
Terms: Works on consignment and buys outright; commission varies. Retail price set by joint agreement. Reports immediately after personal appointment. Work may be shipped or hand-delivered. Dealer pays insurance for exhibited work.
Profile: Work is displayed in "glass enclosed cases, open shelves and securely locked storage closets and bins." Customers are tourists; collectors; school groups; people doing research; and local residents. Best selling time and heaviest wholesale buying time: summer.

MUSEUM SHOP—PALACE OF THE GOVERNOR, Box 2087, Santa Fe NM 87501. (505)982-3016. Buyer: Liz Buchanan. Museum gift shop. Estab. 1964. Represents over 100 Indian and Spanish-American craftworkers.
Acceptable Work: Considers dollmaking; jewelry; needlecrafts; pottery; wall hangings; weavings; woodcrafting; and pottery figures. Primitive and one-of-a-kind pieces. Price range: 75¢-$3,500; bestsellers: $10-400.
Terms: Buys outright. Retail price set by joint agreement. Reports in 3 weeks. Work may be shipped or hand-delivered upon agreement to buy. Dealer pays insurance for exhibited work. Displays work 3-12 months.
Profile: Work is displayed in "enclosed cases, walls; we have burglar alarms and museum guards. We are located in an historic city and building. We deal with craftsmen whose backgrounds are more ancient than the city." Best selling and heaviest wholesale buying time: summer.

NEW MEXICO ART LEAGUE, 3401 Juan Tabo NE, Albuquerque NM 87111. (505)293-5034. Director: Jean Rosenburg. Gallery. Estab. 1929. Represents 14 New Mexico craftworkers. Price range: $5-1,000; bestsellers: $45-100. Works on consignment; 33% commission. Craftworker sets retail price. Reports in 2 weeks. Work may be shipped or hand-delivered. Displays work 1 month minimum. Best selling time: summer.
Acceptable Work: Considers ceramics; metalsmithing; pottery; wall hangings; weavings; and woodcrafting. Fine one-of-a-kind pieces.

1 OF A KIND, 706 Canyon Rd., Santa Fe NM 87501. (505)988-4867. President: Hilary Harts. Craft shop. Estab. 1976. Represents 17 member craftworkers.
Acceptable Work: Considers all crafts except decoupage; soft sculpture; and tole painting. Primitive and fine one-of-a-kind pieces. Price range: $2-500; bestsellers: $5-50.
Terms: 10% commission. Craftworker sets retail price. Reports in 4 weeks. Only members' work shown.
Profile: Work is displayed on "walls, in display cases and on shelves. One coop member is in charge of display. There is no middle man between craftsman and customer". Best selling time: summer.

THE OWL'S NEST, Box 1726, The Plaza North, Taos NM 87501. (505)758-4478. Owner: Dorothy Archibald. Craft shop/gallery/gift shop. Estab. 1972. Represents 18-20 craftworkers.
Acceptable Work: Considers batik; stained glass art; metalsmithing; pottery; soft sculpture; wall hangings; weavings; woodcrafting; furniture; lamps; rugs; sand painting; baskets; and handmade cards and stationery. Fine one-of-a-kind pieces. Price range: 50¢-$2,700; bestsellers: under $50.
Terms: Works on consignment and buys outright; 35% commission. Craftworker sets retail price. Requires exclusive area representation. Reports in 1 week. Hand-delivered work only (initially).
Profile: "Work is displayed on counters, open shelves, locked cases and walls." Heaviest wholesale buying time: spring; best selling time: summer.

PEDDLER'S CART GALLERY, 7602 Menaul NE, Albuquerque NM 87110. (505)298-2770. Contact: Carolyn Ouellette. Gallery. Estab. 1965. Represents 100 craftworkers.
Acceptable Work: Considers ceramics; jewelery; pottery; tole painting; wall hangings; weavings; and woodcrafting. Fine one-of-a-kind pieces. Price range: $1.50-125; bestsellers: $1.50-40.
Terms: Works on consignment and buys outright; 40% commission. Retail price set by joint agreement. Reports in 4 weeks. Work may be hand-delivered. Dealer pays shipping to shop and insurance for exhibited work.
Profile: "Customers are individualistic; represent the upper income group; aged 22-70."

Heaviest wholesale buying time: late summer; best selling time: Christmas.

PICURIS PUEBLO MUSEUM CENTER, Box 228, Penasco NM 87553. (505)587-2671. Director: John Keesing. Museum gift shop. Estab. 1969. Represents 25-50 Indian craftworkers. All craftsmen are required to sign a certificate of authenticity.
Acceptable Work: Considers clothing, dollmaking, jewelry, leatherworking, needlecrafts, scrimshaw, wall hangings, weavings, woodcrafting and any Indian craft. Must be made in the traditional manner, using only natural materials. One-of-a-kind and handmade production-line items. Price range: $1-1,000; bestsellers: $25-250.
Terms: Buys outright and works on consignment; 25% commission. Retail price set by joint agreement. Call for appointment; purchases generally made immediately. Work may be shipped or hand-delivered. Dealer pays insurance on exhibited work.
Profile: "The Picuris Pueblo Museum is primarily a show place for both historical and contemporary exhibits dealing with the Picuris Indians and the Indians of the Southwest. The shop is used to provide a market for quality Indian-made arts and crafts, with emphasis on local area Indians, but no restrictions to such. The gift shop portion of the museum is comprised of approximately 1,200 square feet, and contains 7 glass show cases, and a large amount of hanging area. There are also areas set up for free-standing floor displays. We do not set a time limit on displays for sale, although we do limit items not for sale." Customers: 30+ year olds, "a definite interest in accurate information on Pueblo Indians, and this means they are interested only in authentic merchandise." Heaviest wholesale buying and best selling time: April-October, especially July-August.

POPOVI DA INDIAN ARTS & CRAFTS, Rt. 5, Box 309, San Ildefonso Pueblo, Santa Fe NM 87501. (505)455-2456. Contact: Anita Da. Estab. 1949. Represents 100 Southwestern Indian craftworkers. Customers are tourists; they buy crafts for artistic value and gifts.
Acceptable Work: Considers beadwork; dollmaking; jewelry; leatherworking; metalsmithing; needlecrafts; pottery; sand painting; sculpture; wall hangings; weavings; and woodcrafting. One-of-a-kind primitive and finished items. Price range: $9-5,000; bestsellers: $10-200.
Terms: Buys outright or occasionally on consignment; 10-20% commission. Retail price set by joint agreement. Requires exclusive area representation. Call for interview. Dealer pays insurance for exhibited work. Heaviest wholesale buying time: April-September.

PRIMITIVES & CONTEMPORARIES, 601 Canyon Rd., Santa Fe NM 87501. (505)983-8068. Contact: Jerilou Mayans. Craft shop/gallery. Estab. 1976. Represents 25 craftworkers.
Acceptable Work: Considers batik; dollmaking; quilting; wall hangings; weavings; and woodcrafting. Primitive and fine one-of-a-kind pieces. Price range: $10-500; bestsellers: $30-150.
Terms: Works on consignment and buys outright; 40% commission. Retail price set by joint agreement. Requires exclusive area representation. Query first. Reports in 2 weeks; enclose SASE. Dealer pays return shipping and insurance for exhibited work. Displays work 3 months.
Profile: "Special items are displayed in the front window. Attention is given to floor displays using plants and furniture. Information about craftsperson is mounted next to items. Best selling time: summer-fall.

QUIVIRA SHOP, 114 Old Santa Fe Trail, Box 1941, Santa Fe NM 87501. (505)983-7852. Manager: Larry Torres. Indian arts and crafts shop. Estab. 1971. Represents 100 American Indian craftworkers. Work is displayed "in enclosed glass cases and on walls." Best selling time: March-November.
Acceptable Work: Considers only Indian dollmaking (kachinas); jewelry; pottery; wall hangings; weavings; and beadwork. Fine one-of-a-kind pieces. Price range: $10 minimum; bestsellers: $10-250.
Terms: Buys outright. Retail price set by joint agreement. Reporting time varies. Hand-delivered work only. Dealer pays return shipping and insurance for exhibited work.

RETURN, Box 53, Taos NM 87501. (505)758-3993. Contact: Charlotte Hopper. Gallery. Estab. 1976. Represents 36 craftworkers. "Southwestern mystical theme centered on northern New Mexico artists but also looking at artists from other regions with compatible new age consciousness."
Acceptable Work: Considers all crafts, "mainly interested in refined workmanship and theme compatibility." All styles. Price range: $2.50-8,725; bestsellers: $30-150.
Terms: Works on consignment; 40% commission. Retail price set by joint agreement. Reports in 2 weeks. Dealer pays return shipping; in-transit insurance; and insurance for exhibited work.
Profile: "Display environment created by the artists to emulate nature and ancient Indian civilization of Chaco Canyon. Extensive rock work, fine wood work, stained glass in decor. A

museum quality in environment and work." Customers are successful young business people to older fine arts and crafts collectors. Best selling time: summer.

TONY REYNA INDIAN SHOP, Box 1892, Taos Pueblo, Taos NM 87571. Contact: Tony or Ann Reyna. Estab: Shop #1 at Taos Indian Reservation, 1950; Shop #2 at the Kachina Lodge, 1960. Representing Southwestern Indian arts.
Acceptable Work: Considers jewelry; drums; rugs; paintings; beadwork; carvings; baskets; and pottery. Finished, one-of-a-kind handmade items OK. Price range: $10-2,000; bestsellers; $10-350.
Terms: Buys outright. Retail price set by joint agreement. Write. Reports in 2 weeks. Dealer pays insurance for exhibited work.
Profile: Best selling time: March-June. Shop is Indian-owned and operated. Tourist customers buy crafts for artistic value. No mail orders.

RUYBALID'S INDIAN SHOP & SANTA FE ARTS & CRAFTS, 113-117 E. Palace, Santa Fe NM 87501. (505)982-0525. Contact: Victor Ruybalid. Craft and gift shop. Estab. 1957. Represents 3 craftworkers.
Acceptable Work: Considers ceramics; dollmaking; glass art; jewelry; leatherworking; metalsmithing; needlecrafts; pottery; wall hangings; weavings; woodcrafting; ojos; and rugs. Primitive and fine one-of-a-kind pieces. Price range: $1-2,500; bestsellers: $35-2,500.
Terms: Buys outright. Gallery sets retail price. Reports immediately. Work may be shipped or hand-delivered for approval.
Profile: "We are one of the older dealers of Indian jewelry and are located in an historic adobe building." Best selling and heaviest wholesale buying time: summer.

SCHELU ARTISANS, 401-B San Felipe NW, Old Town, Albuquerque NM 87104. (505)765-5869. Contact: Doris Lusk. Gallery. Estab. 1973. Represents 100 craftworkers.
Acceptable Work: Considers batik; ceramics; jewelry; metalsmithing; pottery; soft sculpture; wall hangings; weavings; and woodcrafting. Especially needs wall hangings; pottery; jewelry; and decorator pieces. Price range: $2.50-600; bestsellers: $14-250.
Terms: Works on consignment and buys outright; 40% commission. Retail price set by joint agreement. Reports in 2 weeks. Work may be shipped or hand-delivered. Dealer pays insurance for exhibited work. Displays work 1 month minimum.
Profile: "We display work depending on item; on pedestals and on wall space. Displays and work are moved and rotated frequently to inspire sales. We show mostly Southwestern style of work; offer customers decorating service and custom orders." Heaviest wholesale buying time: spring and September-October; best selling time: summer and Christmas.

SHALAKO SHOP, INC., Box 970, Community Center, Los Alamos NM 87544. (505)662-2539. Contact: Edward B. Grothus. Estab. 1957. Represents 2 craftworkers. Heaviest buying and selling time: Christmas and summer. Customers buy crafts for gifts.
Acceptable Work: Considers candlemaking; ceramics; glass art; jewelry; leatherworking; metalsmithing; needlecrafts; pottery; wall hangings; weavings; woodcrafting; works in copper, brass and tile; and ecological and futuristic crafts. Primitive and finished one-of-a-kind and handmade production-line items. Price range: 50¢-$1,500; bestsellers: $50.
Terms: Buys outright. Retail price set by joint agreement. Arrange appointment. Negotiates payment for shipping and insurance.

SHOP OF THE RAINBOW MAN, INC., 107 E. Palace, Santa Fe NM 87501. (505)982-0791. Contact: Gwen Windus. Craft shop/gallery/gift shop. Estab. 1945. Represents 6 craftworkers.
Acceptable Work: Considers ceramics; dollmaking; glass art; jewelry; woodcrafting; sandpaintings; and tiles. Finished and handmade production-line items. Price range: $6.50-475; bestsellers: $100-300.
Terms: Buys outright. Retail price set by joint agreement. Reports in 1 day. Work may be shipped or hand-delivered.
Profile: "We display work in show cases, windows and hanging on walls. Our customers are all ages, interests and incomes." Heaviest wholesale buying time: spring; best selling time: summer.

STREETS OF TAOS, 200 Canyon Rd., Santa Fe NM 87501. (505)983-8268. Contact: Hilda Street. Craft shop/gallery/gift shop/trading post. Estab. 1947. Represents 16 craftworkers. Work is displayed in showcases, on walls and tables. Heaviest wholesale buying time: spring; best selling time: summer.
Acceptable Work: Considers clothing; jewelry; pottery; and woodcrafting. Primitive and fine

one-of-a-kind items. Especially needs unusual handmade shirts and Indian made jewelry. Price range: $20-2,000; bestsellers: $100-1,000.
Terms: Buys outright. Gallery sets retail price. Reports in 1 week. Work may be shipped or hand-delivered. Shipping payment is negotiable.

THE STUDIO GALLERY, 3529 Constitution NE, Albuquerque NM 87106. (505)262-0672. Contact: Tom W. Thomason. Gallery. Estab. 1962. Represents 35 craftworkers.
Acceptable Work: Considers all crafts except decoupage and tole painting. Especially needs good leather and fiber work. Specializes in fine and contemporary one-of-a-kind crafts and editions. Price range: 50¢-$3,000; bestsellers: $1.50-400.
Terms: Works on consignment; 40% commission. Craftworker sets retail price. Send resume and slides with SASE. Reports in 2 weeks. Work may be shipped or hand-delivered. Dealer pays insurance for exhibited work. Displays work 3 months minimum.
Profile: "We have a gallery-type display and usually have one-man or small group exhibits which are mentioned in the newsletter." Customers: 30-50, professionals, $20,000+ incomes. Best selling time: summer and Christmas.

SUNRISE OF SANTA FE, 111 Old Santa Fe Trail, Santa Fe NM 87501. (505)982-2993. President: Don Bush. Gallery. Estab. 1976. Represents 35 New Mexico, Arizona and Colorado jewelry craftworkers.
Acceptable Work: Considers jewelry. Fine one-of-a-kind and handmade production-line items; decorative only. Price range: $10-1,500; bestsellers: $30-150.
Terms: Works on consignment and buys outright; 40% commission. Retail price set by joint agreement. Requires exclusive area representation. Reports as soon as possible. Hand-delivered work only. Dealer pays return shipping and insurance for exhibited work.
Profile: "Work is displayed in handcrafted wood cases using natural materials (woods, cork, minerals, etc.) for background." Customers are 25-45 years old; middle to upper income; 20% of business is local; 50% tourists. Heaviest wholesale buying time: spring-summer; best selling time: spring-fall.

THE TRADING COMPANY, Box TTT, Taos NM 87571. (505)758-8819. Contact: Thelma Dodson. Trading company. Estab. 1978. Represents 10-15 craftworkers.
Acceptable Work: Considers batik; ceramics; clothing; dollmaking; glass art; jewelry; leatherworking; metalsmithing; needlecrafts; pottery; quilting; tole painting; wall hangings; weavings; woodcrafting; beading; and rugs. Primitive, finished and one-of-a-kind pieces. Price range: $3-8,000.
Terms: Arrangements with craftworkers vary. Retail price set by joint agreement. Reports in 2 weeks. Work may be shipped or hand-delivered. Dealer pays return shipping.
Profile: "We display work in enclosed showcases, on walls, shelves and tables. We'll trade anything: artifacts, antiques and crafts." Heaviest wholesale buying time: spring-summer; best selling time: spring-fall.

WHATSMENOT?, 703 Canyon Rd., Santa Fe NM 87501. (505)988-4241. Craft shop. Estab. 1976. Represents 6-7 craftworkers.
Acceptable Work: Considers batik; candlemaking; ceramics; glass art; jewelry; leatherworking; pottery; wall hangings; weavings; and woodcrafting. Primitive and fine one-of-a-kind pieces. Price range: $2-200; bestsellers: $30-50.
Terms: Works on consignment and buys outright; 30% commission. Craftworker sets retail price. Reports same day. Work may be shipped or hand-delivered. Dealer pays insurance for exhibited work.
Profile: "Work is displayed in enclosed cases, open counters, tables and wall space." Heaviest wholesale buying time: early spring; best selling time: May-September.

THE WHEELWRIGHT MUSEUM, Box 5153, Santa Fe NM 87502. (505)982-4636. Director: Susan Brown McGreevy. Museum gallery.
Acceptable Work: Considers ceramics; dollmaking; jewelry; metalsmithing; pottery; sculpture; and weavings. Maximum size: 6x8'. Historical and contemporary Indian art only. Price range: $50-1,500.
Terms: Works on consignment; 30% commission. Artist sets retail price. Query, send samples or call or write for interview. No samples returned. Museum pays shipping from gallery and insurance. Exhibition department handles installation. 1-2 months exposure.

WINONA TRADING POST, 211-213 Galisteo St., Box 324, Santa Fe NM 87501. (505)988-4811.

Contact: Pierre Bovis. Estab. 1965. Represents 100 Indian craftworkers.
Acceptable Work: Considers beadwork; jewelry; pottery; and quillwork. One-of-a-kind primitive and finished items only. Minimum price: $10.
Terms: Buys outright or on consignment; 30% commission. Retail price set by joint agreement. Requires exclusive area representation. Write. Reports in 1 week. Dealer pays shipping from shop.

New York

ADIRONDACK FOLKWARES, Box 42, Speculator NY 12164 (summer); Caroga Lake Stage, Gloversville NY 12078 (winter). (518)548-3681 (summer); (518)725-1343 (winter). Proprietor: Lyn Clark Pegg. Craft/antique/stove shop. Represents 70 Adirondack craftworkers. "With one or two exceptions, all of our participants are New York residents (both full-time and part-time).
Acceptable Work: Considers all crafts, except ceramics and glass art. Especially needs leatherwork. Specializes in functional folk crafts. Price range: $1.50-150; bestsellers: $3.50-25.
Terms: Buys outright but prefers working on consignment; 33⅓% commission. Retail price set by joint agreement. Send resume. Reports in 2 weeks. Work may be shipped or hand delivered. Dealer pays insurance on exhibited work.
Profile: "Ours is a warm, colorful and exciting selection of crafts and fine art, all displayed in the midst of and along with antiques—furniture, tools, kitchenware—and wood stoves. There is a personal feeling, as the creative energies of folk, both past and present, is sensed. Since we are located in a summer resort region, our heaviest trade is between Memorial weekend and Labor Day. During that time, all accepted items are displayed, and multiples are kept in reserve. A limited selection is presented in our fall/winter catalogue." Customers: mostly vacationers (some long-standing camp residents, others are 1-2 week resort or campground vacationers), middle to upper middle incomes, interested in purchasing a gift or momento from the region. Heaviest wholesale buying time: spring; best selling time: summer.

ADIRONDACK STORE, Box 991, Lake Placid NY 12946. Craft/gift shop and gallery. Estab. 1955. Represents 25 craftworkers.
Acceptable Work: Considers baskets, candlemaking, ceramics, furniture, jewelry, leatherworking, metalsmithing, needlecrafts, pottery, quilting, soft sculpture, weavings and woodcraftng. Especially needs items "with a woodsy theme like woodland animals and flowers." Specializes in fine bright-colored crafts. One-of-a-kind and handmade production-line items. Price range: $2-1000; bestsellers: $5-25.
Terms: Buys outright and works on consignment; 40% commission. Retail price set by joint agreement. Requires exclusive area representation. Call for appointment. Reports in 2 weeks. Work may be shipped or hand delivered. Display time for consignment items: 6 months.
Profile: "All items are displayed and changed regularly." Customers: middle age, high income, interests in outdoors and sports. Heaviest wholesale buying time: June-December; best selling time: July-August and November-December.

ALBRIGHT-KNOX ART GALLERY—THE GALLERY SHOP, 1285 Elmwood Ave., Buffalo NY 14222. (716)882-8700 (ext. 219). Manager: Leta K. Stathacos. Museum gift shop. Estab. 1975. Represents contemporary craftworkers.
Acceptable Work: Considers contemporary-designed crafts in glass art, jewelry, soft sculpture and woodcrafting. No textiles or weavings; glass must be in a specific sculptural form. Especially needs Christmas ornaments, playing cards and contemporary toys. Designer pieces and limited handmade production-line items. Price range: 75¢-$100; bestsellers: $1-10.
Terms: Buys outright and works on consignment; 50% commission. Retail price set by joint agreement. Sometimes requires exclusive area representation. Send resume and slides or call for appointment. Reports in 8 weeks maximum. Work may be shipped or hand-delivered. Dealer pays insurance for exhibited work upon receipt of items.
Profile: "We are a contemporary art museum. The shop makes every effort to display the items attractively. Information on the craft-artist is available. Customers include many students, art lovers, world travelers and tourists. The community is very supportive and we have a large segment of Canadians and especially Torontonians as regular visitors to the Museum exhibitions and shop." Best selling time: September-December.
To Break In: "I always like to 'test my market first,' so small quantities are a must to start off with. The most marketable item can be priced out of existence; common sense of business (reality) is important."

ALL BY HAND, 7810 3rd Ave., Brooklyn NY 11209. (212)745-8904. Contact: Lou Gaita. Craft shop. Estab. 1976. Represents 25 craftworkers. Reports in 2 weeks. Work may be shipped or

The Elder Craftsmen, a nonprofit shop in New York City, represents over 500 craftworkers age 60 and over. Handling work from elderly persons in more than 30 states, the co-op also serves as a model for similar shops throughout the country.

hand-delivered. Dealer pays shipping. "Do not send unsolicited samples unless they are not to be returned; always include a packing slip." Best selling time: Christmas; heaviest wholesale buying time: summer.
Acceptable Work: Considers ceramics; glass art; jewelry; leatherworking; pottery; and woodcrafting. Handmade production-line items only. Price range: $1-350; bestsellers: $10-25. Buys outright. Gallery sets retail price.

THE ANTHONY GALLERY, Box 222, Main St., Moravia NY 13118. Director: Lucy Stevens. Craft shop/gallery. Estab. 1968. Represents 75 craftworkers.
Acceptable Work: Considers candlemaking, ceramics, clothing, decoupage, doll clothes, glass art, jewelry, needlecrafts, quilting, woodcrafting and especially needs pottery, tole painting, leatherworking and silver wire jewelry. Specializes in traditional one-of-a-kind items. Price range: $1.50-60; bestsellers: $1.50-25.
Terms: Works on consignment; 20% commission. "Checks are sent to consignors as items are sold. We handle several very fast-moving items by buying outright." Craftworker sets retail price. "Price items before they reach us." If out-of-town, send slides with SASE; if local, call in person. Reports in 2 weeks. Work may be shipped or hand delivered.
Profile: "It is a nonprofit service organization, run by a gallery guild and by-laws. We have an exhibitor that we feature every month—an area artist or craftsman. Each item and display is marked. We ask that exhibitors rotate displays every 3 months so that we have fresh items. In summer, many of our customers are tourists passing through the Finger Lakes Region or campers at the Fillmore State Park. Local people buy more practical things." Heaviest wholesale buying time: June and October; best selling time: November-December.

ANYTHING GOES, 197 Main St., Hudson Falls NY 12839. (518)747-4326. Contact: Carolyn Malan. Craft shop. Estab. 1977. Represents 8 craftworkers from local LARAC organization.
Acceptable Work: Considers candlemaking, clothing, decoupage, dollmaking, glass art, jewelry, macrame, needlecrafts, pottery, quilting, tole painting, wall hangings, weavings and woodcrafting. One-of-a-kind and handmade production-line items. Price range: $1-225; bestsellers: $25-50.

Terms: Buys outright. Dealer sets retail price. Requires exclusive area representation. Call for appointment. Report immediately. Work may be shipped or hand delivered.
Profile: "Most crafts are rotated, but on constant display. I do not have production crafts, but like only originals." Customers: ages 15+, handcraft enthusiasts, good incomes. Heaviest wholesale buying and best selling time: holidays.
To Break In: "I buy from craftsmen who sell wholesale and who do not do shows. Also, no flea market people."

ARC EN CIEL STAINED GLASS, LTD., c/o Kata Gallery, 130 Green St., Soho NY 10012. (212)925-8772. Contact: Richard Cronk and Doris Goldfischer. Gallery/supply shop/school of stained glass. Estab. 1975. Considers original blown and stained glass. Works on consignment. Retail price set by joint agreement. Work may be shipped or hand-delivered. Send slides and resume. "We are located in Soho, the heart of New York's contemporary art center." Best selling time: fall-Christmas.

ART ADVENTURES, 888 Madison Ave., New York NY 10021 (212)628-2267. Contact: Sandi Berman. Craft/gift shop. Estab. 1969. Represents 20-30 craftworkers.
Acceptable Work: Considers ceramics, clothing, jewelry, soft sculpture and fashion accessories. "We seem to be selling more low-fire functional ceramics than anything else." Specializes in contemporary crafts; "always representational in design and shape. No abstracts." One-of-a-kind and handmade production-line items. Price range: $20-250; bestsellers: $20-75.
Terms: Buys outright. Shop sets retail price. Send slides or call for appointment. Reports immediately by phone if interested; if not, slides are returned in a few days. Work may be shipped or hand delivered. "We don't want to be responsible for sending items back and repacking them."
Profile: Gallery is "split level with wood walls and floors, double height display windows, natural wood display fixtures and good lighting from a beamed ceiling. Items are always on display until sold." Customers: sophisticated with money to spend, gay, 45 years-old to retired. Heaviest wholesale buying time: fall; best selling time: fall-winter.
To Break In: "Keep us informed of new additions to lines and be prompt with shipments."

ART LATITUDE, 29 E. 73rd St., New York NY 10021. (212)288-9200. Director: Ruth Raible. Gallery. Estab. 1978. Represents 50 craftworkers.
Acceptable Work: Considers all crafts except candlemaking, decoupage and scrimshaw. Specializes in fine art designer crafts. Price range: $25-2,500.
Terms: Works on consignment; 50% commission. Retail price set by joint agreement. Requires exclusive area representation. Send resume and slides. Reports in 3 weeks. Work may be shipped or hand delivered. Dealer pays insurance on exhibited work. Display time: approximately 4 weeks.
Profile: "We are an international gallery exhibiting fine art and fine crafts. We have professional hung exhibitions monthly. We sell to young and new as well as established collectors."

ARTISAN HOUSE, 80 Main St., Northport NY 11768. (516)261-3800. Contact: G. Jackier or M. Lenaerts. Craft shop/gallery. Estab. 1972. Represents 400 craftworkers. Best selling time: Christmas and summer.
Acceptable Work: Considers batik; candlemaking; clothing; glass art; jewelry; leatherworking; metalsmithing; pottery; soft sculpture; wall hangings; weavings; woodcrafting; graphics; wooden toys; handmade cards; and basketry. Price range: $1-250; bestsellers: $1-40.
Terms: Works on consignment and buys outright; 40% commission. Retail price set by joint agreement. Requires exclusive area representation. Reports in 2 weeks. Work may be shipped or hand-delivered. Dealer pays shipping to shop and insurance for exhibited work. Displays consigned work at least 3 months.

THE ARTISANS GALLERY LTD., 6 Bond St., Great Neck NY 11021. (516)829-6747. Gallery. Estab. 1978. Represents 25 craftworkers.
Acceptable Work: Considers batik, ceramics, dollmaking, glass art, jewelry, pottery, trapunto, soft sculpture, wall hangings, and woodcrafting. One-of-a-kind and handmade production-line items. Price range: $15-800; bestsellers: $35-200.
Terms: Works on consignment; 40% commission. Retail price set by joint agreement. Requires exclusive area representation. Send slides or resume or call for appointment. Reports in 1 week. Work may be shipped or hand-delivered. Dealer pays insurance on exhibited work. Work is exhibited 4-6 weeks.
Profile: "This is the first gallery opened in this area. People are delighted they don't have to

travel to NYC for fine crafts. Our shop is modern in white with natural wood cabinets. Color is derived from the crafts and art glass. I am embarking on a campaign and advertise in major newspapers. I also send invitations mentioning the exhibiting craftsperson. This is a high income area.''

ARTPARK STORE, Box 371, Lewistown NY 14094. (716)754-8250. Manager: Joan McDonough. Craft shop/gallery. Estab. 1974. Usually represents artists-in-residence.
Acceptable Work: Considers batik; clothing; dollmaking; glass art; jewelry; leatherworking; metalsmithing; pottery; soft sculpture; wall hangings; weavings; and woodcrafting. Price range: $5-500; bestsellers: $5-100.
Terms: Works on consignment; commission varies. Craftworker sets retail price. Reports in 2 weeks. Work may be shipped or hand-delivered. Dealer pays return shipping and insurance for exhibited work.
Profile: "Artist's work grouped together, will not be placed next to another working in the same medium. Length of time is flexible, payment in 30 days." Only open in summer; heaviest wholesale buying time: spring.

ARTWEAR, 409 W. Broadway, New York NY 10012. President: Robert Lee Morris. Gallery. Estab. 1977. Represents 12-15 craftworkers.
Acceptable Work: Considers jewelry. Specializes in avante garde—"a pure, clean and strong design." One-of-a-kind and handmade production-line items. Price range: $10-5,200; bestsellers: $30-200.
Terms: Works on consignment; 50% commission. Retail price set by joint agreement. Requires exclusive area representation. Send resume and slides. Reports in 1 week. Work may be shipped or hand delivered. Dealer pays insurance on exhibited work. "You *must* visit Artwear before considering submitting work."
Profile: "We are an extremely competitive gallery—only 1 out of every 50 jewelers are accepted." Customers are interested in high fashion; many collectors. Best selling time: August-December.

ARTWORKS, 208 W. State St., Olean NY 14760. (716)372-1740. Contact: Bette Hestle. Craft shop/gallery. Estab. 1973. Represents 15-20 craftworkers. Best selling and buying time: fall.
Acceptable Work: Considers batik; candlemaking; clothing; dollmaking; glass art; jewelry; leatherworking; metalsmithing; pottery; wall hangings; weavings; and woodcrafting. Fine one-of-a-kind and handmade production-line items. Price range: $1.65-200; bestsellers: $3-25. Buys outright. Retail price set by joint agreement. Work may be shipped or hand-delivered. Dealer pays return shipping and insurance for exhibited work.

BALDWIN POTTERY INC., 540 La Guardia Place, New York NY 10012. (212)475-7236. President: Judith Baldwin. Estab. 1960. Represents 12 craftworkers. Primitive or finished ceramics OK. Price range: $3-150; bestsellers: $3-50. Works on consignment. Craftworker sets retail price. Requires exclusive area representation. Write or call. Reports in 2 weeks. Negotiates payment for shipping and insurance.
Profile: Window and central display area provided. "Try not to keep old merchandise (have sales or exchange these for new items)." Customers are ages 20-40, middle-class.

BARNES GALLERIES, LTD, 1 Nassau Blvd, Garden City S. NY 11530. (516)538-4503. Director: Mr. Barnes. Gallery. Estab. 1970. Represents 3 craftworkers.
Acceptable Work: Considers batik, glass art, jewelry, metalsmithing, needlecrafts, pottery, wall hangings, weavings and woodcrafting. Specializes in primitive and fine one-of-a-kind crafts. Price range: $10-500; bestsellers: $20-200.
Terms: Works on consignment; 40% commission. Retail price set by joint agreement. Requires exclusive area representation. Reports in 3 weeks. Work may be shipped or hand delivered. Display time: 2-4 weeks.
Profile: "We are located in one of the best known towns in the US—Garden City." Customers: ages 35-55, $25,000+ incomes. Best selling time: fall.

BARBARA BARRON FIBRE CREATIONS, 1943 New York Ave., Huntington Station NY 11746. (516)549-4242. President: Barbara Barron. Craft studio. Represents 6 fiber artists only. Price range: $1.50-2,100; bestsellers: $1.50-100. Works on consignment and buys outright; 40% commission. Retail price set by joint agreement. Requires exclusive area representation. Reports in 2 weeks. Work may be shipped or hand-delivered. Dealer pays return shipping and insurance for exhibited work. Send photos or slides.

Acceptable Work: Considers batik; needlecrafts; quilting; soft sculpture; wall hangings; and weavings. Especially needs fine one-of-a-kind unusual items. Especially needs macrame; wall hangings; soft sculpture; quilting; weaving; and pillows. Price range: no limit.
Profile: Has showrooms in New York, Dallas, Chicago, Miami in designer buildings. Dealer also goes to retail shows and will take items around the country to these shows.

THE BEACH PLUM TREE, 52 Main St., E. Hampton NY 11937. (516)324-5066. Contact: Lynn Kroll. Craft/gift shop. Estab. 1972. Represents 20-25 craftworkers.
Acceptable Work: Considers batik, ceramics, glass art, pottery, wall hangings, weavings and woodcrafting. Especially needs glass art. Specializes in fine and contemporary crafts. One-of-a-kind and handmade production-line items. Price range: $5.50-275; bestsellers: $10-40.
Terms: Buys outright and works on consignment; 40% commission. Requires exclusive area representation. Send slides and call for appointment. Work may be shipped or hand-delivered. Dealer pays insurance on exhibited work.
Profile: "We are a seasonal shop for crafts, imports, home furnishings and accessories." Customers: tourists; ages 25-80; and middle to upper incomes. Heaviest wholesale buying time: March-October; best selling time: May-October. Open March-December.

BEAUTIFUL WOODS INC., 230 E. 59th St., New York NY 10022. (212)759-7246. Contact: Renee Levy. Designer showroom. Estab. 1977. Represents 2-3 craftworkers.
Acceptable Work: Considers woodcrafting. "Special need for quality wall sculptures from wood; mirrors with wood; and crafts combining wood and other elements." Fine one-of-a-kind pieces. Price range: $75-7,000; bestsellers: $400-2,500.
Terms: Works on consignment and buys outright; 25-50% commission. Requires exclusive area representation. Reports in 1 week. Dealer pays shipping and in-transit insurance.
Profile: "We sell wholesale to decorators and architects and are the only showroom in New York handling fine wood furniture for the designer trade."

BEDFORD/DOWNING GLASS, 202 E. 83rd St., New York NY 10028. (212)861-2634. Contact: Ingo Williams. Craft shop. Estab. 1972. Represents 3-4 craftworkers who work in leaded glass. Considers glass art only. Fine one-of-a-kind handmade production-line items. Price range: $15-600; bestsellers: $15-300. Works on consignment; 25% commission. Gallery sets retail price. Reports in 1 week. Work may be shipped or hand-delivered. Work is "displayed in living room style." Best selling and buying time: spring and fall.

THE BEE SKEP, Rt. 2, Bee Skep Lane, Granville NY 12832. (518)632-5313. Contact: Carol L. Liedtke. Craft and gift shop. Estab. 1975. Represents 60 craftworkers. Price range: 15¢-$155; bestsellers: $2-20. Works on consignment and buys outright; 40% commission. Gallery sets retail price. Reports in 4 weeks. Work may be shipped or hand-delivered.
Acceptable Work: Considers batik; candlemaking; ceramics; decoupage; dollmaking; glass art; jewelry; leatherworking; metalsmithing; needlecrafts; pottery; quilting; soft sculpture; tole painting; wall hangings; weavings; woodcrafting; quilling; tinsel art; fused glass; and Christmas ornaments. All styles; utilitarian and/or decorative
Profile: Work is in "glass display cases, shelves, small items in baskets. At least 1 year of displaying time. The Bee Skep is set in a wooded valley where visiting customers view a spectacular waterfall and stream." Heaviest wholesale buying time: early spring and late summer; best selling time: summer, fall and holidays.

BELLARDO LTD., 100 Christopher SE, New York NY 10014. (212)675-2668. Contact: Paul Bellardo. Gallery. Estab. 1967. Represents 50 craftworkers.
Acceptable Work: Considers ceramics; glass art; jewelry; leatherworking; metalsmithing; pottery; wall hangings; and weavings. One-of-a-kind designer pieces only. Price range: $24-3,500; bestsellers: $45-300.
Terms: Works on consignment and buys outright; 50% commission. Retail price set by joint agreement. Requires exclusive area representation. Reports in 2 weeks. Work may be shipped or hand-delivered. Dealer pays shipping and insurance for exhibited work.
Profile: Displays individuals and groups "in or out of the main windows for as long as the shop wishes to show the artist's work". Heaviest wholesale buying time: September; best selling time: November-December.

BENSON GALLERY, Bridgehampton NY 11932. (516)537-0598. Director: Elaine Benson. Estab. 1966. Represents 2-3 craftworkers. Considers all crafts. Price range: $25-10,000; bestsellers: up to $250. Works on consignment; 40% commission. Retail price set by gallery or joint agreement. Requires exclusive area representation. Query with transparencies or photos. Reports in 1-2 weeks. Dealer pays insurance for exhibited work. Items exhibited for 2-week periods during May-September.

WESLEY BERGEN, 65 W. 55th St., New York NY 10019. (212)246-6279. Contact: Wesley Bergen. Considers jewelry and metalsmithing. Price range: $10-5,000. Retail price set by joint agreement. Dealer pays insurance for exhibited work. Openings sponsored. Advanced designs only. Submit color transparencies or b&w photos.

BEYOND EXPRESSION, INC., 7 Hill St. Bedford Hills NY 10507. (914)666-9881. Proprietor: Roberta Hopkins. Craft/gift shop. Estab. 1977. Represents 30-40 craftworkers.
Acceptable Work: Considers batik, candlemaking, ceramics, dollmaking, glass art, jewelry, metalsmithing, pottery, scrimshaw, soft sculpture, wall hangings, weavings. "I'm setting up a boutique so I'll need clothing in spring." Specializes in contemporary crafts. One-of-a-kind and handmade production-line items. Price range: $2-200; bestsellers: $2-50. "Expensive items (over $100) don't sell well."
Terms: Buys outright and works on consignment; 33⅓% commission. Prefers working on consignment for boutique items. Retail price set by joint agreement. Requires exclusive area representation. Send slides or call for appointment. Reports in 2 weeks. Work may be shipped or hand delivered. Dealer pays insurance on exhibited work. Consignment items returned if not sold by 3 months.
Profile: "We're in an old Victorian house used exclusively as a shop. Each room has another type of business (i.e. crafts, jewelry, antiques, etc.). Some rooms are rented to other people, but don't have handcrafted items. I own the house and have five rooms myself. Displays are in showcases and on walls." Customers: well-to-do, teens to middle age. Heaviest wholesale buying time: fall; best selling time: Christmas, Mothers Day and graduation.

BFM GALLERY LTD., 150 E. 58 St., New York NY 10022. President: Bernice Steinbaum. Gallery. Estab. 1977. Represents 30 contemporary American craftworkers.
Acceptable Work: Considers batik, ceramics, glass art, pottery, soft sculpture, wall hangings, weavings and woodcrafting. Specializes in fine designer crafts. Price range: $50-10,000.
Terms: Works on consignment; 50% commission. Retail price set by joint agreement. Send resume and slides. SASE. Dealer pays insurance on exhibited work.
Profile: "Items are displayed in room settings to harmonize craft and context." Customers: professional interior space designers, architects and collectors.

BLUE MOUNTAIN DESIGNS, Blue Mountain Lake NY 12812. President: Edith C. Mitchell. Craft shop/gallery. Estab. 1965. Represents 100 craftworkers, preferably from Northeast US.
Acceptable Work: Considers batik, candlemaking, clothing, dollmaking, glass art, jewelry, leatherworking, metalsmithing, pottery, soft sculpture, wall hangings, weavings and woodcrafting. Specializes in contemporary one-of-a-kind and handmade production-line items. Price range: $2-500; bestsellers: up to $50.
Terms: Buys outright and works on consignment; 30% commission (with payment on the 1st of the month). Craftworker sets retail price. Call for appointment with SASE. Reports in 2 weeks. Work may be shipped or hand delivered. Dealer pays insurance on exhibited work. Display time for special exhibits: 2-3 weeks; consigned work: up to 6 months.
Profile: Customers: primarily summer tourists. "We like to share with everyone; if someone can't afford a $50 pot, we have an excellent one for $10." Heaviest wholesale buying time: spring and summer; best selling time: spring-fall.

BOSWORTH HANDCRAFTS, 132 Indian Creek Rd., Ithaca NY 14850. (607)272-6716. Managers: Edward and Helen Bosworth. Craft shop/gallery/studio. Represents approximately 30 craftworkers.
Acceptable Work: Considers batik, candlemaking, ceramics, clothing, dollmaking, glass art, jewelry, metalsmithing, needlecrafts, pottery, soft sculpture, wall hangings, weavings and woodcrafting. Especially needs contemporary designs in pewter; blown glass (decorative); porcelain; and small weavings. Specializes in fine art designer and contemporary bright-colored items. One-of-a-kind and handmade production-line items. Price range: $2-500; bestsellers: $2-45.
Term: Buys outright and works on consignment; 30% commission (consignors usually paid quarterly). Retail price set by craftworker or joint agreement. Prefers exclusive area representation. Send resume, slides (if requested) with SASE or call for appointment. Reports as soon as possible. Work may be shipped (prefers UPS) or hand-delivered. Dealer pays some insur-

ance on exhibited work (as if sold with commission). Display time: 3 month trial period for new consignors.

Profile: Shop is an "open light gallery with 4 rooms, high windows, good overhead lighting, and radiant heat in the ceiling. It has white walls with varied strong colored sections, wood shelving and handcrafted display tables. It's set in a rural area with trees, flowers, vines, patio and birds all about. Also easy parking. The atmosphere is peaceful, friendly and informal. Customers are largely from a University community (Cornell, Ithaca Colleges) with only some students since they need a car to get here. On the whole, we have a mature clientele—traveled, sophisticated, selective. Many have become friends and come for special gifts. Some bring visitors, many foreign." Heaviest wholesale buying time: late summer-fall; best selling time: late spring-early winter.

To Break In: "Attach retail price tags to all articles. Pack carefully for shipping and insure against damage. Communicate with us directly about any dissatisfaction and we will try to clear them up."

BROOKLYN MUSEUM GALLERY SHOP, 188 Eastern Pkwy, Brooklyn NY 11238. (212)638-5000. Buyer: Brigid Kernan. Museum gift shop. Estab. in 1950s.

Acceptable Work: Considers batik, ceramics, jewelry, needlecrafts, pottery, toys, wall hangings, weavings and woodcrafting. Specializes in primitive, Appalachian and ethnic items. "We carry jewelry, textiles, old one-of-a-kind pieces from the US and many other countries, toys, prints (not contemporary). We are moving into American contemporary crafts, as well." One-of-a-kind and handmade production-line items. Price range: maximum $250; bestsellers: maximum $75.

Terms: Buys outright. Shop sets retail price. Send slides/photos marked with prices. "Please indicate if slide/photos may be kept for our files. Indicate delivery time of goods and discount offered." Reports in 4 weeks. Work may be shipped or hand-delivered.

Profile: "The shop has the feeling almost of a marketplace, i.e., a wide range and quantity of items—not a stark, contemporary look. The shop is well known for its wide range of unusual pieces: ethnic objects, crafts from all over the world." Customers: $20,000 average incomes; 62% ages 16-35, 37% over 35. Heaviest wholesale buying time: February-March and summer; Best selling time: September-December and March-June.

BROOKSIDE MUSEUM, Ballston Spa NY 12020. (518)885-4000. Display Curator: Betsey Krug. Museum craft/gift shop. Estab. 1976. "We're looking for local craftsmen (Saratoga County or at least New York State) who would like to sell crafts especially of Early American flavor on consignment".

Acceptable Work: Considers candlemaking, ceramics, dollmaking, glass art, leatherworking, metalsmithing, needlecrafts, pottery, quilting, scrimshaw, wall hangings, weavings and woodcrafting. Specializes in fine art designer crafts from the colonial period (weavings, pottery, needlework, dolls and toys). Price range: 10¢-$1,500.

Terms: Buys outright and works on consignment. Retail price set by joint agreement. Send slides or call for appointment. Reports in 2 weeks. Work may be shipped or hand delivered.

Profile: "Items are displayed on open counter surface until sold. The shop is small and is at the rear of an historical museum. We are in a transitional period moving from a gift shop decor to more of a handcrafted stock. Many children of ages 5-13 come through the shop as well as well as historical society members of ages 40-80. With new stock, I hope to attract a different age group between 20-35." Heaviest wholesale buying time: spring.

CANTON GALLERY, INC., 10 Court St., Canton NY 13617. President: Patricia M. Sennett. Gallery. Estab. 1975. Represents 11 member craftworkers.

Acceptable Work: Considers batik, ceramics, jewelry, pottery, wall hangings and weavings. One-of-a-kind pieces only. Price range: $4-350; bestsellers: $4-25.

Terms: Craftworker sets retail price. "Must be an owner of stock in the corporation. Prospective members submit work to be juried by membership for admission to the company as a stockholder and exhibitor." SASE. Reports in 4 weeks. Displays every 4-5 weeks.

Profile: "We are a cooperative comprised of selected artists who buy into the corporation, do their own 'sitting' on a shift basis. We have a close relationship with local colleges and the community. Craftworkers are asked to change their own exhibit. When we have been approached directly, we have had to refuse many, because of limited wall and exhibition space although their work may have been well-received by the corporate members." Customers: college students, faculty, business people. Best selling time: holidays.

CARROLL-CONDIT GALLERIES, 210 Mamaroneck Ave., White Plains NY 10601.

(914)946-1490. Contact: Lou Iona and Maureen Hanna. Craft shop/gallery. Estab. 1970. Represents 12 craftworkers.
Acceptable Work: Considers batik, ceramics, jewelry, pottery, wall hangings, weavings and woodcrafting. Specializes in quality decorative and functional contemporary crafts. "Our bestsellers are quality functional pottery and wall hangings." One-of-a-kind and handmade production-line items. Price range: $10-150; bestsellers: $10-50.
Terms: Buys outright and works on consignment; 40% commission. Retail price set by craftworker or joint agreement. Requires exclusive area representation. Send slides or call for appointment. Reports in 2 weeks. Work may be shipped or hand delivered.
Profile: "We are primarily an art gallery with quality crafts mixed in." Customers: young married, affluent. Best selling time: November-January.

CHARLES TOWN FACTORY OUTLET COMPLEX, (formerly the Sperry Univac plant), 311 Turner St., Utica NY 13501. (315)724-4617. Craft Marketing Coordinator: Diane L. Kelly. Shopping complex. Estab. 1979.
Acceptable Work: Considers all crafts. No wholesalers, retailers or jobbers.
Terms: Rental charge: $10/day with rate decreasing for longer rentals. Yearly rental prices are available upon request. Spaces are 9x9', 9x18', 18x18' or larger. Unlimited booths available. Write for information. SASE. Reports in 1 week.
Profile: "Among factory outlet stores, restaurants and an off-track betting parlor are permanent arts and crafts booths for craftsmen who would like to open a permanent store or would like to rent a booth on a daily basis or year around. Booths are lighted, heated and indoors. The complex consists of 5 buildings, 4 floors each, interconnected by hallways and exterior courtyards surrounding a lake and wharf area. The brick structure which is sandblasted along with the wood columns and hardwood floors gives this complex the atmosphere of the old market place.

THE CHOCOLATE SOUP, 249 E. 77th St., New York NY 10021. (212)861-2210. Contact: Anna Youree. Children's shop. Estab. 1967. Represents 30 craftworkers.
Acceptable Work: Considers clothing, dollmaking, quilting and knitwear (sweaters, mittens, hats, etc.). Specializes in children's crafts that are brightly colored and old-fashioned in flavor. Handmade production-line items preferred. Price range: $10-80; bestsellers: $10-15.
Terms: Buys outright. Craftworker sets retail price. Requires exclusive area representation. Call for appointment. Reports in 1 week. Work may be shipped or hand-delivered.
Profile: "We are a special children's shop featuring handmade clothes, toys and quilts for children. We feature all of our merchandise, giving them star billing. When a customer comes in we discuss with them what is unique about each piece. Customers are of middle-upper class income, ages 20-60. Heaviest wholesale buying time: September; best selling time: Christmas.

CHRISTINA'S, 52 Fall St., Seneca Falls NY 13148. (315)568-8826. Manager: Christine Andrews. Craft shop. Estab. 1978. Represents 14 craftworkers.
Acceptable Work: Considers batik, candlemaking, ceramics, decoupage, dollmaking, glass art, jewelry, metalsmithing, pottery, scrimshaw, soft sculpture, wall hangings, weavings and woodcrafting. Exhibits contemporary fine art designer crafts. One-of-a-kind and handmade production-line items OK. Price range: $6-1,000; bestsellers: $6.50-100.
Terms: Buys outright and works on consignment; 25% commission. Retail price set by joint agreement. Requires exclusive area representation. Send resume and samples. Reports in 1 week. Work may be shipped or hand-delivered. Craftworker pays insurance for exhibited work.

CLAY CRAFTS COMMUNITY, 222 W. 79th St., New York NY 10024. (212)595-2222. Contact: Deena Kolbert. Craft shop. Estab. 1978. Represents 75 to 100 craftworkers. Works on consignment; 50% commission. Retail price set by joint agreement. Send slides. Shipping and/or hand delivery accepted.
Acceptable Work: Considers all crafts, primarily ceramics. Fine one-of-a-kind and handmade production-line items. Price range: $4-800; bestsellers: under $25 or over $100.
Profile: "Exhibits are rearranged monthly. Customers are middle class and multi-ethnic. Please do not come in without appointment." Best selling time: Christmas, summer and other holidays.

THE CLAY POT, 162 7th Ave., Brooklyn NY 11215. (212)788-6564. Contact: Riva Rosenfield. Craft shop. Estab. 1968. Represents 70 craftworkers.

Acceptable Work: Considers candlemaking; ceramics; glass art; jewelry; leatherworking; metalsmithing; pottery; raku; wall hangings; weavings; and handcrafted greeting cards. Fine one-of-a-kind and handmade production-line items. Museum quality work. Price range: 75¢-$150; bestsellers: 25¢-$75.
Terms: Buys outright. Craftworker sets retail price. Requires exclusive area representation. Reports in 4 weeks. Work may be shipped or hand-delivered. Dealer pays shipping to shop.
Profile: "We serve the 4 million population of Brooklyn with quality production items. Customers are upwardly mobile New Yorkers, aware and interested in identifying with the objects around them." Heaviest wholesale buying time: spring and fall.

CLEAR LIGHT STUDIO, 10852 Main St., Clarence NY 14031. (716)759-6480. Contact: Donna Ioviero or Bill Jobling. Craft shop/gallery. Estab. 1976.
Acceptable Work: Considers batik; candlemaking; clothing; stationery; prints; metalsmithing; pottery; and soft sculpture. Fine art one-of-a-kind designer pieces only. Price range: $4-175; bestsellers: $4-45.
Terms: Works on consignment; 25% commission. Requires exclusive area representation. Send slides and description of work. Reports in 2 weeks. Work may be shipped or hand-delivered only by prior arrangement.
Profile: "We have only 4 shows per year, usually on weekends. Customers are all ages, middle and upper class." Heaviest wholesale buying time: Christmas; best selling time: summer and Christmas.

CLOUDS, 1 Mill Hill Rd., Woodstock NY 12498. Directors: Robert Ohnigian and Robert Orsini. Craft shop/gallery. Estab. 1974. Represents 150 craftworkers.
Acceptable Work: Considers jewelry, handblown glass and fine porcelain. Fine one-of-a-kind and handmade production-line items. Price range: $5-1,000.
Terms: Works on consignment and buys outright; 40% commission. Requires exclusive area representation. Work may be shipped or hand-delivered. Dealer pays insurance for exhibited work.
Profile: Shop "is specifically American contemporary; on a gallery level more than a shop." Heaviest wholesale buying time: fall and winter; best selling time: Christmas and August.

CONSORTIUM FOR CHILDREN'S SERVICES, 123 E. Water St., Syracuse NY 13202. (315)471-8331. Shop Manager: Patricia H. Ludington. Gift shop. Estab. 1973. Represents 100-150 craftworkers.
Acceptable Work: Considers batik, ceramics, jewelry, pottery, soft sculpture, wall hangings, weavings and woodcrafting. Specializes in toys, children's items, kitchen items and metal sculpture (metal trees, etc.). One-of-a-kind and handmade production-line items. Price range: $1-200; bestsellers: $5-100.
Terms: Buys outright and works on consignment; 33⅓% commission. Retail price set by joint agreement. Call for appointment or stop at shop with sample. SASE. Reports in 2 weeks. Work may be shipped or hand delivered. Display time: 30+ days.
Profile: Nonprofit shop whose funds are used for children's services in community agencies. "We purchased and renovated the building (vintage 1834)." Customers: young marrieds to elderly; mostly middle to high incomes. Heaviest wholesale buying time: spring and fall; best selling time: fall-Christmas and April-June.

CONTEMPORARY ART GLASS GALLERY, 806 Madison Ave., New York NY 10021. (212)879-4655. Director: Douglas Heller. Gallery. Estab. 1973. Represents 20 studio glass artists. One-of-a-kind designer pieces only. Price range: $30-1,600; bestsellers: $35-400.
Terms: Works on consignment; 40% commission. Retail price set by joint agreement. Requires exclusive area representation. Reports in 3 weeks. Work may be shipped or hand-delivered. Dealer pays return shipping and insurance for exhibited work.
Profile: Items are displayed in "well lit show cases; shop has knowledgeable sales help." Customers are middle to high income group who have well-developed tastes; serious collectors. Best selling time: October-June.

CORNING GLASS CENTER, Centerway, Corning NY 14830. (607)974-8276. Director: John P. Fox, Jr. Museum gift shop. Estab. 1951. Represents 35 craftworkers.
Acceptable Work: Considers glass art only. One-of-a-kind and handmade production-line items. Price range: $20-5,000.
Terms: Buys outright. Retail price set by craftworker or joint agreement. Send slides or call for appointment. Reports in 4 weeks. Work may be shipped or hand-delivered.

Profile: "We are a collectors shop specializing in glass. We have back lighted displays." Heaviest wholesale buying time: January-April; best selling time: May-October.

THE COUNTRY GALLERY, Main St., Verona NY 13478. (315)363-2179. Director: Bette McBain. Gallery/gift shop. Estab. 1973. Represents 35-50 craftworkers "but we are expanding."
Acceptable Work: Considers batik; pottery (both stoneware and porcelain); wall hangings; weavings; silk screen; etchings; and block-prints. Also buys fine one-of-a-kind and handmade production-line items. "We are concentrating on wall work and pottery, but will consider anything that will fit well in our gallery which caters to the above average income and highly selective customers. We are always looking for good new potters." Price range: $5-1,000; bestsellers: $10-400.
Terms: Works on consignment for first order and buys outright; 35% commission. Gallery sets retail price when work is purchased outright; craftworker sets retail price on consigned items. Requires exclusive area representation. Reports in 2 weeks if SASE is included in query. Work may be shipped or hand-delivered. Dealer shares shipping costs on acceptance and pays insurance for exhibited work.
Profile: "Work is beautifully displayed; gallery provides some individual shows and advertising. Building goes back to the Civil War period." Displays work 90 days to 1 year. Heaviest wholesale buying time: spring to early December; best selling time: spring to Christmas.

THE CRAFT BARN, Box 8, Florida NY 10921. (914)651-7949. Contact: Marjorie L. Zap. Craft shop. Estab. 1958. Represents 25 United States and countless international craftworkers.
Acceptable Work: Considers candles; ceramics; clothing; glass art; jewelry; leatherworking; metalsmithing; pottery; and woodcrafting. Handmade production-line items. Price range: $1.50-200; bestsellers: $10-20.
Terms: Buys outright. Requires exclusive area representation. Reports in 1 week. Work may be shipped or hand-delivered by prior arrangement. Dealer pays return shipping.
Profile: Items are shown "in a 200-year-old barn. Direct importers of international traditional handcrafts. Gold and silver jewelry workshop with 2 full time craftspeople on staff." Customers' taste is basically traditional. Summer and Christmas shoppers will buy some higher priced one-of-a-kind crafts. Heaviest wholesale buying time: spring and late summer; best selling time: summer and Christmas. Closed mid-January to mid-March.

CRAFT DESIGNS UNLIMITED, 548 La Guardia Place, New York NY 10012. (212)477-1690. Contact: Kim Hanson. Considers most types of craft work, primarily interested in weaving, but currently exhibiting stained glass and jewelry. Price range: $10-400; bestsellers: $25-100. Buys outright or on consignment; 25-40% commission. Call for interview. Reports in 1 week. Dealer pays insurance for exhibited work. Items displayed 3 weeks minimum. Gallery also sells imported weavings and gifts.

THE CRAFTS BARN, 61 Market St., Potsdam NY 13676. (315)265-9806. Manager: Verna Duprey. Craft shop. Estab. 1970. Represents 50-75 craftworkers.
Acceptable Work: Considers batik; candlemaking; clothing; dollmaking; jewelry; leatherworking; metalsmithing; needlecrafts; pottery; quilting; wall hangings; weavings; woodcrafting; and original Indian basketry. One-of-a-kind and handmade production-line items. Especially needs items to sell to Olympic visitors to Lake Placid, New York: crafts indigenous to northern New York or related to winter sports. Price range: $1-150; bestsellers: $1-35.
Terms: Works on consignment and buys outright; 30% commission. Craftworker sets retail price. Reports in 7-10 days. Work may be shipped or hand-delivered.
Profile: "Items must meet approval of the Quality Control Board; then placed on display for a period of not less than 3 months. This is the only retail outlet for handcrafted articles in our area." Best selling time: summer and fall.

THE CRAFTSMAN'S GALLERY LTD., 16 Chase Rd., Scarsdale NY 10583. (914)725-4644. Contact: Sybil Robins. Craft Gallery. Estab. 1973.
Acceptable Work: Considers batik; ceramics; glass art; jewelry; leatherworking; metalsmithing; pottery; quilting; soft sculpture; wall hangings; weavings; and woodcrafting. Fine one-of-a-kind and handmade limited production items. Especially needs wood; blown glass; fiber, wall hangings, stained glass. Price range: $10-2,000.
Terms: Works on consignment; commission varies with price. Retail price set by joint agreement. Requires exclusive area representation. Send slides or photos, and information. SASE. Reports in approximately 6 weeks. Work may be shipped or hand-delivered. Dealer pays insurance for exhibited work.

Profile: "Pieces are displayed as unique works of art for an agreed upon length of time, usually 5 weeks. Customers are 30-60, married, well-educated with income of $20,000 plus." Do not send unrequested material.

CRAFTSMEN CORNER, INC., 192 E. Main St., Mt. Kisco NY 10549. (914)666-2231. President: Mrs. Mullane. Treasurer: Mrs. Amuso. Craft and gift shop. Estab. 1973. Represents 125-135 craftworkers over the age of 55.
Acceptable Work: Considers ceramics; dollmaking; jewelry; and knitted and crocheted items. Utilitarian and/or decorative. Price range: 50¢-$125; bestsellers: 50¢-$35.
Terms: Works on consignment; 25% commission. Retail price set by joint agreement. Reports in 4 weeks. Hand-delivered work only. Dealer pays insurance for exhibited work.
Profile: Shop has "window displays; glass counters for jewelry and small items. All open shelves on wall and tables in center of store have articles draped and displayed." Heaviest retail selling time: September until Christmas and before Easter.

CREATIONS & CRAFTS CO., 11 W. 37 St., New York NY 10018. (212)221-3299. President: A. Shah. Craft shop/store/gift shop. Estab. 1974. Represents 20 craftworkers. Heaviest buying and selling time: August-December.
Acceptable Work: Considers clothing; jewelry; leatherworking; needlecrafts; woodcrafting; beads; lapidary; and stones. Price range: 50¢-$500.
Terms: Works on consignment and buys outright; 40% commission. Retail price set by joint agreement. Reports in 4 weeks. Work may be shipped or hand-delivered. Dealer pays return shipping and insurance for exhibited work.

CREATIVE WOMEN'S COLLECTIVE, 236 W. 27th St., 12th Flr., New York NY 10001. (212)924-0665. Organization of Women Artists. Estab. 1973. Represents 8 craftworkers and artists, members only.
Acceptable Work: Considers jewelry, small wall hangings, small textile items, weavings, silk-screened cards and macrame. Fine one-of-a-kind and handmade production-line items. Price range: 35¢-$50; bestsellers: 35¢-$12.
Terms: Works on consignment. Retail price set by joint agreement. Reports in 2 weeks. Hand-delivered work only. "Since we sell work only by our members and students, persons wishing to sell through us must either join the collective or become our students."
Profile: "We sell crafts only occasionally at fairs, exhibits, conferences and open houses or fundraisers. The group specializes in producing work related to issues of the Women's Movement. We help other women's groups and others working for social change to produce graphics related to these issues." Best selling time: Christmas.

DAMRON HALL, 172 Prince St., New York NY 10012. (212)966-4345. Contact: Michael Damron Stowers. Craft shop/gallery. Estab. 1974. Represents 12-15 craftworkers.
Acceptable Work: Considers jewelry and nonfunctional ceramics and glass art. Especially needs blown glass. Specializes in nonfunctional contemporary and fine art one-of-a-kind pieces. Price range: $18-2,500; bestsellers: $25-55, $70-150.
Terms: Buys outright and works on consignment; 40% commission. "New consigned work is displayed for at least 6 weeks—usually in the gallery window. If response is good, we then buy outright and represent the artist on a continuing basis." Retail price set by craftworker or joint agreement. Send slides, call for appointment or visit gallery. "We prefer to meet the artist in person and see 1-2 examples of work (rather than slides and resume)." Reports in 1 week. Work may be shipped or hand delivered. Dealer pays insurance on exhibited work.
Profile: "The gallery is small and quiet as opposed to the usual large bright space. The size, however, is a limiting factor in the size of work we can show. Large, flat work is a problem as well as work intended to stand on the floor." Customers: young, professional and urban from New York, Montreal and Boston; $25,000+ incomes. Heaviest wholesale buying time: fall; best selling time: fall-winter.
To Break In: "We expect the artist to be of a good business head and to know what he/she wants for their work."

DESIGNS IN SILVER, ETCETERA, 230 E. Main St., Port Jefferson NY 11777. (516)928-2037. Contact: Charles Kohn. Estab. 1976. Represents 23 craftworkers.
Acceptable Work: Considers candlemaking; ceramics; glass art; jewelry; leatherworking; metalsmithing; pottery; wall hangings; weavings; and woodcrafting. All styles.
Terms: Price range: $1.75-500; bestsellers: $1.75-300. Buys outright and works on consignment; 40% commission. Retail price set by joint agreement. Requires exclusive area represen-

tation. Query with transparencies or photos. Reports as soon as inquiry is received. Dealer pays shipping from shop and insurance.
Profile: Items displayed 1 month minimum. Displays are on walls, windows, tables, pedestals and showcases. Each craft is treated independently as required. Crafts arrranged in museum-like atmosphere where everything can be viewed without distracting items surrounding them.

DFC GALLERY, DIVISION OF DESIGNERS FURNITURE CENTER INTERNATIONAL, 150 E. 58th St., New York NY 10022. (212)755-5611. Showroom Coordinator: Florence Ferber.
Acceptable Work: Considers carvings, sculpture, furniture, pottery, wall hangings, weavings and pillows. One-of-a-kind items only. Price range: $50-2,000.
Terms: Buys outright and works on consignment. Store sets retail price. Send resume with slides/photos or call for appointment.
Profile: "We are a contemporary furniture showroom selling residential and contract furniture to designers, architects, and their clients. We must have high quality crafts. They are integrated into our displays."

DOUST ART GALLERIES, 204 E. Arbordale Rd., Syracuse NY 13219. (315)488-7686. See below.

DOUST ART GALLERIES, 621 S. Warren St., Syracuse NY 13202. (315)471-0291. Contact: Paula Naselli. Museum craft/gift shop/gallery/picture framing. Estab. 1876. Represents 300 craftworkers.
Acceptable Work: Considers all crafts except needlecraft and scrimshaw. Specializes in fine art, Appalachian and contemporary crafts. One-of-a-kind and handmade production-line items. Price range: $1-100; bestsellers: $5-50.
Terms: Buys outright and works on consignment; 40% commission (payment at end of month). Retail price set by craftworker or joint agreement. Send resume, slides with SASE. Reports in 1 week. Work may be shipped or hand delivered. Dealer pays insurance on exhibited work. Display time: 60 days. Must be able to provide volume.
Profile: "We have over 2,000 people daily at 2 locations." Customers: young people with average incomes. Best selling time: October-December.

EARTHCRAFT, Syracuse Mall, 100 S. Salina St., Syracuse NY 13202. (315)471-0125. Contact: Larry Obrist. Craft shop/boutique. Estab. 1974. Represents 5 craftworkers.
Acceptable Work: Considers ceramics, clothing, brooms, jewelry, leatherworking, metalsmithing, pottery, quilting and scrimshaw. Specializes in leather goods and accessories—clothing, jewelry, pipes, papers and ceramics. One-of-a-kind and handmade production-line items. Price range: $1-300; bestsellers: $1-100.
Terms: "I try things on consignment and may buy later"; 33⅓% commission. Dealer pays insurance on exhibited work. Retail price set by joint agreement. Call for appointment. Reports in 1 week. Work may be shipped or hand delivered.
Profile: "Space is assigned to the craftworker and he may do his own display or I will display it. We are located next to the Village Square, a collection of craftworkers in the Square Mall (a downtown department store)." Customers are ages 15-50; many young professional people. Heaviest wholesale buying time: late summer and fall; best selling time: fall and Christmas.

EARTHWORKS & ARTISANS, 251 W. 85th St., New York NY 10024. (212)873-5220. Director: Claire DesBecker. Estab. 1970. Represents 10 craftworkers.
Acceptable Work: Considers candlemaking, ceramics, glass art, jewelry, pottery and woodcrafting. Especially needs Christmas tree ornaments and porcelain jewelry. Specializes in fine, one-of-a-kind and handmade production-line items. Price range: $3-300; bestsellers: $8.50-75.
Terms: Buys outright and works on consignment; 40% commission. Retail price set by joint agreement. Send resume and color slides/b&w prints with SASE. Reports in 2 weeks. Work may be shipped or hand delivered. Dealer pays insurance for exhibited work.
Profile: "Items spend one week in a window display with the name of the artist, and arrangement in the studio." Customers: $25-30,000 incomes, Jewish, New Yorkers, knowledgable in the arts and craft techniques, appreciative of exceptional quality of workmanship. Heaviest wholesale buying time: summer-early fall; best selling time: fall-spring.

EARTHWORKS POTTERY, 255 E. 74, New York NY 10021. (212)650-9337. Contact: Margaret Simonds. Craft shop/gallery. Estab. 1971. Represents 15 New York craftspeople.
Acceptable Work: Considers glass art, pottery, wall hangings and weavings. "Emphasis is on superbly crafted pottery, mostly contemporary, although we have a wide selection of a more

classic design. We are not interested in gimmicky or funky pottery, but rather in lovingly-crafted pieces." One-of-a-kind and handmade production-line items. Price range: $5-1,000; bestsellers: $5-50.
Terms: Works on consignment; 50% commission. Craftworker sets retail price. Call for appointment, then work may be hand-delivered. Dealer pays insurance on exhibited work.
Profile: "New outstanding pottery is displayed in our windows for a 2 week period, then moved to our prominent display areas in the gallery. Connected with this business is the well-known ceramics restoration studio known as the M. Simonds Studio. Customers are young adults of above-average income (we are located in one of the wealthiest areas in NYC), and a small group of very well-to-do adults (our restoring customers), who do purchase our more expensive pottery." Best selling time: winter and summer.

THE ELDER CRAFTSMEN, 850 Lexington Ave., New York NY 10021. (212)535-8030. Estab. 1955. Represents 500 age 60+ crafters.
Acceptable Work: Considers decoupage, silver, and macrame jewelry; needlecrafts; and soft sculpture. Especially needs copper enamel dishes; ashtrays; inlaid wood boxes; decorative painted wooden toys; trays; boxes; picture frames; baby toys; gifts; sweaters; and quilts. Finished, one-of-a-kind and handmade production-line items only. Price range: $4-125; bestsellers: $10-25.
Terms: Works on consignment; 35% commission. Retail price set by joint agreement. Prefers exclusive area representation. Write or send samples or photos. Reports in 3 weeks. Items displayed 3 months minimum. Best selling time: September-December and Easter. "We make crafts to order."

ELECTRUM JEWELRY, 10 Main St., East Hampton NY 11937. (516)324-3232. Contact: Susan Kalman. Fine jewelry shop. Estab. 1975. Represents 10-12 craftworkers.
Acceptable Work: Considers jewelry made with precious metals (gold and sterling), natural stones (in most cases) and a fine finishing. Especially needs men's jewelry and innovative and youthful designs in wedding bands and engagement rings. Fine, one-of-a-kind and handmade production-line items. Price range: $50-500; bestsellers: $100-250.
Terms: Buys outright and works on consignment; 50% average commission. Retail price set by joint agreement. Requires exclusive area representation. Send slides or call for appointment. Reports in 1 week. Work may be shipped or hand-delivered. Dealer pays shipping and insurance.
Profile: "Ours is a small personal touch shop where we do our own custom jewelry. We use non-commercial display methods, refined promotion and selling techniques. Period of display is usually through summer. We have a prime location in the center of East Hampton, Long Island, which is an ocean resort." Customers: ages 25-50, "mostly professionals who have their weekend and vacation homes here. Average income is high, many have very sophisticated tastes and are willing to pay for quality and fine design." Heaviest wholesale buying time: spring and fall; best selling time: summer and Christmas.

THE ELEMENTS, 766 Madison Ave., New York NY 10021. (212)744-0890. Gallery Manager: Kay Eddy. Gallery. Estab. 1977. Represents 300 craftworkers.
Acceptable Work: Considers ceramics, baskets, fiberwork, glass art, jewelry, metalsmithing, wall hangings and woodcrafting. Specializes in contemporary, fine crafts; one-of-a-kind. Price range: $15-2,000; bestsellers: $25-150.
Terms: Works on consignment; 50% commission. Craftworker sets retail price. Prefers exclusive area representation. Send resume and slides with SASE. Reports in 2-4 weeks. Solicited items may be shipped or hand-delivered. Gallery pays isurance on exhibited work.
Profile: "We have one person shows, group shows and theme shows. In addition to the featured work, we have a representative collection of work by gallery artists on display."

EVERSON MUSEUM, 401 Harrison St., Syracuse NY 13202. (315)474-6064. Public Information Manager: Marlana Timmons. Museum gallery/gift shop. Estab. 1965. Represents 3-5 US craftworkers. Heaviest wholesale buying time: winter; best selling time: winter and summer.
Acceptable Work: Considers ceramics, glass art, jewelry, pottery, scrimshaw, wall hangings, weavings and woodcrafting. Specializes in American art. One-of-a-kind and handmade production-line items. Price range: $1-100; bestsellers: $1-50.
Terms: Works on consignment; 33⅓% commission. Retail price set by Managing Committee. Send resume. Reports in 6-8 weeks for gallery displays. Work must be hand-delivered. Museum pays insurance on show exhibits. Display time: 3 months.

FIBERFORMS & POTS, Tinker Square, Woodstock NY 12498. (914)679-9042. Contact: Cici Chase. Craft shop/small gallery. Estab. 1978. Represents 25-30 craftworkers, but wants to increase to about 75. Reports in 1 week. Work may be shipped or hand delivered.
Acceptable Work: Considers ceramics, clothing, glass art, jewelry, pottery, wall hangings, weavings, woodcrafting and soft sculpture; especially needs clothing—sweaters, hats, shawls and scarves. Specializes in well-designed and executed contemporary work. One-of-a-kind and handmade production-line items. Price range: $2-1,000; best sellers: $9-115. Buys outright; 33⅓ to 40% commission. Retail price set by joint agreement. Requests exclusive Woodstock representation.
Profile: "The shop is approximately 35x18'—well-lit and with interesting angular walls and shelving units of pine and glass. We are inside an old clapboard building remodeled during the summer/spring of 1978. It contains 12 stores. My customers are local people with good jobs and incomes who are interested in the arts, the environment and the area, as well as the seasonal Woodstock resident and tourist trade (April-December)." Best selling time: summer and pre-Christmas.
To Break In: "Make sure all things are signed (either stamped or labeled)—hang tags should be on clothing as well as artist labels. I request a biography and photos of work from each artist to share with the customers. All work must be expertly finished."

FIFE & DRUM GIFT SHOPPE, Rt. 9, Box 315, Chestertown NY 12817. (518)494-3742. Contact: Ed or Helen Devlin. Gift shop. Estab. 1974 (Chestertown); 1978 (Lake George). Represents 40-50 craftworkers.
Acceptable Work: Considers candlemaking, ceramics, decoupage, dollmaking, glass art, jewelry, leatherworking, macrame, metalsmithing, needlecrafts, pine cone art, pottery, quilting, slate art, wall hangings, wood toys and woodcrafting. Especially needs lamps, clocks, wood sculpture, blown glass animals, blown art glass, scrimshaw or etchings on slate, pottery (particularly in tones of greens, blues and sand combinations) and woodworking. Specializes in Early American crafts. Handmade production-line items only. Price range: 80¢-$250; bestsellers: 80¢-145.
Terms: Buys outright and works on consignment; 65% commission. Retail price set by joint agreement. Requires exclusive area representation. Send slides or bring actual work/samples. Reports in 3 weeks. Work may be shipped or hand delivered. Dealer pays insurance on exhibited work.
Profile: "We use subdued earthy background colors and out of the ordinary displays. We give each item the optimum in level, lighting and position. The shop is usually considered a quaint colonial gift shoppe where you can find the gift most everyone would enjoy." Located in a resort area. Customers: ages 6-60, middle-upper middle incomes ($16,000-200,000). Heaviest wholesale buying time: spring-summer; best selling time: summer.

FIFE & DRUM GIFT SHOPPE, 337 Canada St., Lake George NY 12845. (518)668-5770. See above.

FOCUS CRAFTS & FURNISHINGS, INC., 4 Purchase St., Rye NY 10580. (914)967-3015. Contact: Joan Tillman. Craft shop. Estab. 1970.
Acceptable Work: Considers batik; ceramics; woodcrafts. Prefer handmade production pieces, functional.
Terms: Price range: $3-150. Buys outright. Gallery sets retail price. Work may be shipped or hand-delivered. Dealer pays shipping to shop.

FORMS AND FOLIAGE, LTD., Wolf Road Park, Albany NY 12205. (518)458-1313. President: David Sofer. Vice-president: Martin Weber. Craft shop. Estab. 1975. Represents 250 contemporary craftworkers from the northeastern US.
Acceptable Work: Considers batik, candlemaking, ceramics, glass art, jewelry, leatherworking, pottery, scrimshaw, wall hangings, weavings and woodcrafting. Especially needs sterling silver and 14-k-gold jewelry. Specializes in contemporary crafts. One-of-a-kind and handmade production-line items. Price range: $4-1,000; bestsellers: $30-50.
Terms: Buys outright and sometimes works on consignment; 34% commission. Retail price set by joint agreement. Requires exclusive area representation. Send slides with a personal cover letter; make appointment before bringing work to store. Reports in 2 weeks. Work may be shipped or hand-delivered. Dealer pays shipping to shop and insurance.
Profile: "Each artist's work is grouped together with identification of artist and state. Most customers are in their upper 20's and older with contemporary taste in home accessories, jewelry and art." Heaviest wholesale buying time: spring and fall; best selling time: summer-fall.

FORT DELAWARE—MUSEUM OF COLONIAL HISTORY, Rt. 97, Narrowsburg NY 12764. (914)252-6660. Director: Ethel M. Poley. Craft/gift shop. Estab. 1957. Represents 12+ craftworkers.
Acceptable Work: Considers batik, candlemaking, ceramics, clothing, dollmaking, needlecrafts, pottery, quilting, wall hangings, weavings and woodcrafting. Colonial type of handcrafted articles only. Specializes in primitive and Appalachian-type crafts. Price range: $1.50-25; bestsellers: $5-10.
Terms: Works on consignment; 15% commission. Craftworker sets retail price. Requires exclusive area representation. Work may be shipped or hand delivered after prior arrangements.
Profile: Items have a limited display area. "The Fort consists of a stout stockade, surrounding dwelling cabins, blockhouses, gun platform, store houses, blacksmith shed, candle shed, armory, and animal yard. Staff members provide lively lectures/demonstrations illustrating many of the day-to-day tasks performed by the first colonial inhabitants. Customers: seasonal, mostly travelers and campers. Best selling time: July-August. Open: 1 weekend in May, weekends in June and from the last Saturday in June-Labor Day.

GALERIE PAULA INSEL, 987 3rd Ave., New York NY 10022. (212)355-5740. Director: Paula Insel. Gallery. Estab. 1958.
Acceptable Work: Considers batik, ceramics, decoupage, glass art, leatherworking, metalsmithing, needlecrafts, pottery, soft sculpture, tole painting, wall hangings, weavings and woodcrafting. "In the future, we will eventually cover all the crafts." Specializes in fine and contemporary crafts. One-of-a-kind items only. Price range: $25-1,000.
Terms: Works on consignment; 40% commission. Retail price set by joint agreement. Requires exclusive area representation. Write with SASE. Work may be shipped or hand-delivered. "Work is usually exhibited 2 weeks, then placed in other locations."
Profile: "We are located in one of the busiest streets in the world. We are in the decorators market and I was the first one here."

GALERIE INTERNATIONALE, 1095 Madison Ave., New York NY 10028. (212)861-7877. Manager: E.M. Martin. Considers batik; decoupage; glass art; pottery; sculpture. Buys outright or on consignment; 33% commission. Retail price set by joint agreement. Send slides of work. SASE.

GALLERY 84 INC., 1046 Madison Ave., New York NY 10021. (212)628-4920. Director: Cecile Fine. Considers mobiles; sculpture; and wall hangings. Maximum size: 14'x54''x60''. 25% commission. Artist sets retail price. Query. Artist is requested to bring 3 works to be viewed to become member. SASE. 3 weeks maximum exposure.

GALLERY NORTH, Box 1145, Setauket NY 11733. (516)751-2676. Director: Elizabeth Goldberg. Assistant: Alexandra Randall. Gallery. Estab. 1965. Represents 50-100 craftworkers.
Acceptable Work: Considers batik; ceramics, glass art; jewelry; pottery; wall hangings; weavings; and woodcrafting. Handmade production-line items only. Price range: $5-400; bestsellers: $5-50.
Terms: Works on consignment; 33% commission. Retail price set by joint agreement. Requires exclusive area representation. Reports in 1 month. Work may be shipped or hand-delivered. Dealer pays insurance for exhibited work. Customers are from the local area with modest incomes. Best selling time: October-December.

GALLERY OF CONTEMPORARY METALSMITHING, 250 Mill St., Rochester NY 14614. (716)546-1224. Director: Deborah Norton. Gallery. Estab. 1977. Represents 25 craftworkers.
Acceptable Work: Considers jewlery and metalsmithing; all styles. "I am looking for highly sophisticated, professional, unique work. No bent wire jewelry!" One-of-a-kind and handmade production-line items. Price range: $6-3,500; bestsellers: $30-300.
Terms: Works on consignment; 40% commission. Dealer pays insurance on exhibited work. Craftworker sets retail price. Requires exclusive area representation. Send slides. Reports in 4 weeks. Shipping of work prearranged.
Profile: "Items are always displayed with the artist's name. My displays change with each show and are highly individualistic and totally non-traditional. Very few items are displayed in each case. Our shows change every 2 months. Shop is set in a loft setting (3,500 square feet)." Best selling time: Christmas season."

GALLERY PLACE, Baron Steuben Place, Corner of Market St. & Centerway, Corning NY

14830. (607)936-6564. Manager: Roz Collins. Cooperative craft shop/gallery. Estab. 1976. Represents 35-45 member craftworkers.
Acceptable Work: Considers batik, ceramics, glass art, jewelry, leatherworking, metalsmithing, pottery and sculpture. Specializes in fine contemporary one-of-a-kind items. Price range: $1-1,200; bestsellers: $15-35.
Terms: "We are a cooperative gallery—members pay $15/month rent and give 8 hours service or pay for a substitute. The gallery takes a 10% commission on sales. It is run by a board of 9 members elected by the whole membership." Craftworker sets retail price. Send resume and slides with SASE for membership consideration. Reports in 3 weeks. Work must be hand-delivered.
Profile: "The gallery is located in the Market Street Restoration Area which attracts many tourists. Craft items remain on display until sold or removed by artist. We hold a one-man show each month for a different member."

THE GALLERY SHOP AT THE JAMAICA ARTS CENTER, 161-04 Jamaica Ave., Jamaica NY 11432. (212)658-7400. Director: Vivian Warfield. Estab. 1976. Represents 50 craftworkers. Considers batik; jewelry; and ceramics. Primitive and finished one-of-a-kind and handmade production-line items. Price range: 50¢-$300; bestsellers: $2.50-30. Buys outright or on consignment; 33% commission. Craftworker sets retail price. Write. Reports in 2 weeks. Dealer pays shipping from shop and insurance for exhibited work. Work displayed in lighted cabinets, opera glass shelving and wall space. Best selling time: Christmas. Customers buy crafts for gifts.

GIFT HAUS, 5651 Main St., Williamsville NY 14221. (716)634-6888. Contact: Judith Nachbar. Gift shop. Estab. 1973. Represents 600-800 craftworkers. Best selling time: 4th quarter.
Acceptable Work: Considers all crafts; one-of-a-kind and handmade production-line items. Price range: 25¢-$500; bestsellers: 89¢-$150.
Terms: Works on consignment and buys outright; 40% commission. Gallery sets retail price. Reports in 4-6 weeks. Work may be shipped or hand-delivered by prior arrangement. Dealer pays shipping to shop and insurance. Consigns for 6 months and changes windows at least every 3 weeks.

GILLARY GALLERY, 62 Maiden Lane, Jericho NY 11753. (516)681-2015. Director: Sylvia R. Gillary.
Acceptable Work: Considers ceramics; glass art; jewelry; pottery; and sculpture. Maximum size: 48x36". Specializes in modern, contemporary, realistic, impressionistic and primitive work. Statues must have pedestals. Price range: $150-2,000, sculpture; $10-500, jewelry; bestsellers: $150-300.
Terms: Works on consignment; 40% commission. Retail price set by joint agreement. Query or call for interview. 6 weeks maximum exposure.

GLASSMASTERS GUILD, 621 Avenue of the Americas, New York NY 10011. (212)924-2868. Manager: Lili Lihn. "Glassmasters Guild is a combination stained glass supply shop and gallery of blown and lead glass work." Send slides or call for appointment. Reports in 4 weeks. Work may be shipped or hand-delivered.
Acceptable Work: Considers contemporary stained and blown glass art. One-of-a-kind and handmade production-line items. Price range: $15-6,000; bestsellers: $20-300.
Terms: Buys outright and works on consignment; 40% commission. Glassmasters Guild pays insurance on exhibited work. Retail price set by joint agreement. Send slides or call for appointment. Reports in 1 month. Work may be shipped or hand delivered.
Profile: Stained glass artworks are mounted on walls, hung in windows or in the middle of the gallery. Work is also placed in display cases. Exhibits displayed 4-5 weeks. Customers are both hobbyists and professional stained glass craftspeople; serious collectors; tourists; and people who prefer giving handcrafted gifts to manufactured items. Heaviest wholesale buying and best selling time: fall-winter.

GRAHAM GALLERY, 1014 Madison Ave. (78th St.), New York NY 10021. (212)535-5767. Contact: Robert Graham or Terry Davis. Considers sculpture. Price range: $100-100,000.
Terms: Buys outright or on consignment; 40% commission. Requires exclusive area representation. Query with slides or samples of work. SASE. 4 weeks exposure.

THE HAMMOND GALLERY & SILVER SHOP, 157 Main St., Cooperstown NY 13326. (607)547-8921. Contact: Bud or Jean Hammond. Speciality silver and gold jewelry, craft and

antique shop. Estab. 1975. Represents 40 American craftworkers.
Acceptable Work: Considers batik, candlemaking, ceramics, glass art, leatherworking, metalsmithing, pottery, woodcrafting, silkscreen, prints and especially needs wooden toys. Specializes in contemporary work. One-of-a-kind and handmade production-line items. Price range: $1-200; best sellers: $3-45.
Terms: Buys outright. Dealer pays insurance on exhibited work. Retail price set by joint agreement. Requires exclusive area representation. Call for appointment or send resume and slides. Reports in 1 week. Work may be shipped or hand delivered.
Profile: "Our shop is mainly a crafts gallery. We feature our own silver and gold jewelry. We also carry American handcrafts, artwork and antiques. We do not confine ourselves in terms of media or geographical areas, but look for the best of American craftsmen. Each craftsman's work is individually and prominently featured. Our backgrounds are set up to accent and complement the pieces. A short biographical sketch is included with each. Large tourist business. Heaviest wholesale buying time: spring-fall; best selling time: summer and pre-Christmas.
To Break In: "We prefer to deal with professionals who can supply us within a reasonable amount of time. We do, however, consider all work except jewelry."

HAND OF THE CRAFTSMAN, 58 S. Broadway, Nyack NY 10960. (914)358-6622. Contact: Janet or Sheldon Haber. Craft shop/gallery. Estab. 1971. Represents 75 full-time designer craftworkers living and working in the US.
Acceptable Work: Considers batik, candlemaking, ceramics, dollmaking, glass art, jewelry, leatherworking, metalsmithing, pottery, soft sculpture, wall hangings, weavings and woodcrafting. Especially needs designer jewelry in silver and gold; handmade belt buckles; and bells in all media. Specializes in modern and traditional designer originals (mostly functional). One-of-a-kind and handmade production-line items. Price range: $5-250; bestsellers: $5-125.
Terms: Buys outright. Retail price set by joint agreement. Requires exclusive area representation. Send resume, slides with SASE or call for appointment. Reports in 2 weeks. Work may be shipped or hand-delivered. Dealer pays insurance for exhibited work.
Profile: "As a shop with a growing reputation for fine crafts, we attempt to keep a cross section of each craftsman's work on permanent display. We are most interested in full-time designer craftsmen who can be relied upon to keep improving and producing, thereby keeping his/her display fresh and interesting. Our is an attractive, bright, cheerful, unpretentious gallery of the very best craftworks. As designer-craftsmen ourselves, we know and love fine crafts and are always willing to talk crafts with our customers." Customers: mainly professionals (doctors, teachers), knowledgeable and sensitive to fine craftwork. Heaviest wholesale buying time: late winter and late summer; best selling time: late spring, July-December.
To Break In: "We look for 'spread'—a variety of items, a choice of colors, styles, glazes. We prefer serious full-time craftsmen and we cherish originality of design and sensitivity to materials. The best craftsmen keep experimenting and adding new and different items to their catalogue."

HANDMADE, 6 N. Front St., New Paltz NY 12561. (914)255-6277. Contact: Ann Rodman. Craft/gift shop. Estab. 1974. Represents 50 craftworkers.
Acceptable Work: Considers batik, candlemaking, ceramics, glass art, jewelry, leatherworking, pottery, soft sculpture, wall hangings, weavings and woodcrafting. Handmade production-line items only. Price range: $3-100; bestsellers: $5-60.
Terms: Buys outright. Retail price set by joint agreement. Send resume and catalog. Reports in 1 week. Work may be shipped or hand delivered.
Profile: "We are in an old, renovated barn on the ground floor. It has a low ceiling, heavy beams, beautiful arched windows and white walls (some stone, some plasterboard). There's a dance studio upstairs and a clothes shop next door." Customers: "half are college age since we are in a college town; others are in their 40s, middle class and professionals." Heaviest wholesale buying time: spring-fall; best selling time: winter and summer.

HANDWORKS, 5 East St., Honeoye Falls NY 14472. (716)624-4950. Contact: Shirley Hughes. Craft shop/gallery. Estab. 1976. Represents 25-35 craftworkers.
Acceptable Work: Considers batik, glass art, jewelry, leatherworking, metalsmithing, pottery, printmaking, quilting, toys, wall hangings, weavings and woodcrafting. Especially needs blown and stained glass and batik wall hangings. One-of-a-kind and handmade production-line items. Price range: $1-200; best sellers: $2-10 and $30-45.
Terms: Buys outright and works on consignment; 30% commission. Dealer pays insurance on exhibited work. Retail price set by joint agreement. Send resume with SASE or call for

appointment. Reports in 2 weeks. Work may be shipped or hand delivered.
Profile: Work is displayed 90 days minimum; all articles displayed at all times. Shop is located in business section of a small town south of Rochester, New York. Customers are primarily young marrieds or professional people either restoring old Victorian houses or building energy efficient contemporary homes. "My shop is small and all space is used for display, therefore, I must limit the amounts of any one item to a choice of only a few colors or sizes."
To Break In: "Specify 'orders taken' or not and then deliver in a reasonable amount of time. As a potter/weaver myself I realize it's easy to overbook. I have just received a leather order from 8 months ago; as a shopkeeper, it's annoying when you have to keep putting off customers. They just take their business elsewhere."

HANOVER SQUARE GALLERY, 121 E. Water St., 2nd Floor, Syracuse NY 13202. (315)474-0476. Contact: Henry and Dolores Gernhardt. Gallery. Estab. 1976. Represents 100 contemporary artists and craftworkers.
Acceptable Work: Considers batik, candlemaking, ceramics, clothing, glass art, jewelry, leatherworking, metalsmithing, pottery, soft sculpture, wall hangings, weavings, woodcrafting, small sculpture, contemporary prints and small paintings. One-of-a-kind and handmade production-line items OK. Price range: $5-3,000; bestsellers: $25-500.
Terms: Buys outright and works on consignment; 40% commission. Retail price set by joint agreement. Requires exclusive area representation. Send resume, slides and SASE. Reports in 3 weeks. Work may be shipped or hand-delivered. Dealer pays insurance on exhibited work.
Profile: "Our gallery consists of approximately 1,000 square feet. The building dates back to 1840, contains a bird cage elevator that opens onto the Gallery and is listed in the National Register of Historic Places. The Gallery itself is contemporary in feeling with white walls, grey carpeting and work in the shop area displayed on abstracta and glass shelves. We run shows every 5-6 weeks where we feature an artist, craftsman or have a group."

HAVEN HOUSE, 4864 Ridge Rd., Lockport NY 14094. (716)434-5450. Contact: Mrs. G.H. Thompson. Gift/antique shop. Estab. 1967. Represents 25 craftworkers.
Acceptable Work: Considers candlemaking, dollmaking and Christmas ornaments. "I am interested only in items that are well done and different (not copied from one of the womens magazine patterns). I do find different things for my shop, but it takes a great deal of looking." Wants finished-looking products. Price range: $1-75.
Terms: Buys outright. Gallery sets retail price. Reports as soon as possible. Samples may be shipped or hand-delivered. Dealer pays shipping.
Profile: "Located in a cedar building (with a fireplace) which resembles an 1810 house, we have Early American antique furniture (pine, cherry) for display and sale. We also have a year round Christmas room. Items are attractively displayed using antique props; customers attention is directed to new items." Customers: middle to upper incomes. Best selling time: July-December.

HERE COMES THE SUN, Star Rt., Warrensburg NY 12885. Contact: Christine Cabhal. Craft/gift shop. Estab. 1975. Represents 30 craftworkers.
Acceptable Work: Considers dollmaking, glass art, jewelry, leatherworking, pottery, quilting, soft sculpture and woodcrafting. Especially needs Olympic items. One-of-a-kind and handmade production-line items. Price range: 75¢-200; bestsellers: $1-35 (jewelry); $65-200 (quilts).
Terms: Buys outright and works on consignment. Shop sets retail price. Enclose SASE. Reports in 2 weeks. Work may be shipped or hand delivered. Display time: 1 month maximum.
Profile: Shop located in small 1-room cabin (30x30). Customers: tourists; middle incomes; average age of 35. "Many stop to see the quilts if they're displayed outside or in our big front window." Heaviest wholesale buying time: spring; best selling time: summer and Christmas.

THE HIRED HAND, 1324 Lexington Ave., New York NY 10028. (212)722-1355. Contact: Fran Stein. Craft and calico fabric shop. Estab. 1974. Represents 150 craftworkers. Price range: $1.50-75; bestsellers: $2-50.
Acceptable Work: Considers dollmaking; needlecrafts; quilting; soft sculpture; and patchwork/applique. Especially needs dolls; applique pillows; and crib quilts. Primitive one-of-a-kind and handmade production-line items; utilitarian only.
Terms: Works on consignment and buys outright; 45% commission. Retail price set by joint agreement. Reports in 1 week. Work may be shipped or hand-delivered. Dealer pays return shipping and insurance for exhibited work.
Profile: "We specialize in softwares and we sell quilting supplies. We try to price things moderately for quick sales." Work displayed on shelves and plank walls. Best selling time: Christmas.

HOBBS PLACE, 25 Bridge St., Seneca Falls NY 13148. (315)568-6275. Contact: Howard R. Lainhart. Gallery/gift shop. Estab. 1976. Represents 4 craftworkers. Best selling time: winter and summer.
Acceptable Work: Considers ceramics; decoupage; jewelry; leatherworking; pottery; wall hangings; weavings; woodcrafting; and hologram jewelry. Price range: $10-1,000; bestsellers: $65-100.
Terms: Works on consignment and buys outright; 25-35% commission. Retail price set by joint agreement. Reports in 4 days. Work may be shipped or hand-delivered. Displays work in glass case.

HOLLY WOODWORKING, Old Forge NY 13420. (315)369-3757. Contact: Keith Hollister. Gift Shop. Estab. 1957. Represents 5 craftworkers.
Acceptable Work: Considers candlemaking, jewelry, pottery and woodcrafting. Especially needs woodcarving and woodsy items.
Terms: Buys outright and works on consignment. Retail price set by joint agreement. Write with SASE for terms.

HORSE FEATHERS, 81 S. Broadway, Nyack NY 10960. (914)425-3323. Contact: Gordon Rauer. Craft/gift shop. Estab. 1973. Represents 30 craftworkers.
Acceptable Work: Considers candlemaking, ceramics, glass art, jewelry, leatherworking, pottery, scrimshaw and woodcrafting. No "too modern" crafts. Especially needs utilitarian pieces. Price range: $2-150; bestsellers: $10-40.
Terms: Buys outright. Gallery sets retail price. Requires exclusive area representation. Call for appointment. Reports as soon as possible. Work may be shipped or hand-delivered. Dealer pays shipping to shop and in-transit insurance. "We strongly prefer UPS."
Profile: "We are an unusual blend of crafts, jewelry, antiques, Icelandic sweaters and Chinese groceries. Heaviest wholesale buying time: June-October; best selling time: Christmas.

INCORPORATED GALLERIES, 1449 2nd Ave., New York NY 10021. (212)628-1902. Contact: Bruce Wittenstein or Riis Layman. Craft shop/gallery. Estab. 1975. Represents 100-125 craftworkers.
Acceptable Work: Considers all crafts except candlemaking, clothing, decoupage, needlecrafts, scrimshaw and tole painting. Specializes in contemporary, one-of-a-kind work. Price range: $10-1,500; bestsellers: $20-25 and $125. Work must be signed.
Terms: Works on consignment; 50% commission. Retail price set by joint agreement. Send resume and slides with SASE or call for appointment. Reports in 2 weeks. Work may be shipped or hand-delivered. Gallery pays insurance on exhibited work.

INTERNATIONAL ART GALLERY, 1453 Broadway, Hewlett NY 11557. (516)374-9021. Contact: William George. Rental gallery/frame shop. Estab. 1962. Represents 4-5 craftworkers.
Acceptable Work: Considers batik, ceramics, glass art, jewelry, metalsmithing, needlecrafts, pottery, soft sculpture and woodcrafting. One-of-a-kind designer pieces only. Minimum price: $25; bestsellers: up to $700.
Terms: Works on consignment; 33⅓% commission. Fee varies according to space. Retail price set by joint agreement. Send slides and resume with SASE. Reports in 4 weeks. Hand-delivered work only.
Profile: "All items are given a separate area of gallery for best display. Time is usually 4 weeks or depends on sales. We sell my oils and my daughter's graphics and work by members of the creative artist league. We also do framing and restore old oils." Customers are of above average income. Heaviest wholesale buying time: summer-fall; best selling time: spring-fall.

S.F. ISZARD CO., 150 N. Main St., Elmira NY 14902. (607)734-7171. Assistant General Merchandise Manager: Robert Hooker. "We are a 2-unit department store."
Acceptable Work: Buys and consigns baskets; carvings and sculpture; Christmas ornaments; dinnerware; handbags and leather accessories; jewelry; pillows; pottery; and silverwork. One-of-a-kind and handmade production-lines OK. Retail price range: $5-100.
Terms: Store sets retail price. Submit resume; illustrations of work; and arrange interview.

ITHACA HOUSE GALLERY, 108 N. Plains St., Ithaca NY 14850. (607)272-1233. Contact: Sherry Hathaway. Gallery. Estab. 1969. Represents 11 craftworkers. Best selling time: Christmas and spring.
Acceptable Work: Considers batik; ceramics; prints; soft sculpture; wall hangings; and

weavings. One-of-a-kind designer pieces only; decorative. Price range: $2.50-125; bestsellers: $5-125.
Terms: Works on consignment; 30% commission. Retail price set by joint agreement. Work may be shipped or hand-delivered by previous agreement.

JEWELLRY WORKSHOP & GALLERY, 150 Spring St., New York NY 10012. (212)226-5303. Gallery/school. Estab. 1976. Represents 6-7 craftworkers.
Acceptable Work: Considers jewelry and metalsmithing. Specializes in classical jewelry. One-of-a-kind and handmade production-line items. Price range: $18-5,000; bestsellers: $18-250.
Terms: Buys outright and works on consignment; 40% commission. Retail price set by joint agreement. Send slides. Reports in 2 weeks.

JEWISH MUSEUM SHOP, 1109 5th Ave., New York NY 10028. (212)860-1866. Manager: Ceil Skydell. Museum gift shop. Represents 10-12 craftworkers.
Acceptable Work: Considers batik, ceramics, glass art, jewelry, metalsmithing, needlecrafts, pottery, soft sculpture, wall hangings, weavings and woodcrafting. Especially needs Judaica. Specializes in fine one-of-a-kind and handmade production-line items. Price range: $6-200; bestsellers: $5-100.
Terms: Buys outright. Retail price set by joint agreement. SASE. Reports in 2 weeks. Work may be shipped or hand-delivered.
Profile: Museum shop with a variety of Judaica books, lithos, ceremonial objects and jewelry. Heaviest wholesale buying and best selling time: pre-Hanukkah and Passover.

JORICE DESIGNS, INC., 1057 2nd Ave., New York NY 10022. (212)752-0129. President: Maurice Mogulescu. Craft shop/gallery. Estab. 1976. Represents 40 craftworkers.
Acceptable Work: Features art glass and ceramics; pottery; wall hangings; weavings; woodcrafting; stained glass boxes; and mirrors. One-of-a-kind designer pieces. Price range: $10-250; bestsellers: $10-65.
Terms: Works on consignment and buys outright; 50% commission. Retail price set by joint agreement. Reports in 2 weeks. Work may be shipped or hand-delivered. Dealer pays shipping and insurance for exhibited work.
Profile: "Send us 3 or 4 sample pieces with price list of typical pieces and photos of other pieces. If we like the work we will keep the samples and establish contact with the artist. If not we will return them at our expense." Best selling time: fall and Christmas; heaviest wholesale buying time: summer and fall.

J-P's GALLERY, 55 Deer Park Ave., Babylon NY 11702. (516)587-8129. Contact: J.P. Westpfahl. Craft/gift shop and gallery. Estab. 1977. Represents 30 craftworkers.
Acceptable Work: Considers all crafts. One-of-a-kind and handmade production-line items. Price range: $1.50-350; bestsellers: $1.50-25.
Terms: Buys outright and works on consignment; commission varies. Gallery sets retail price. Prefers exclusive area representation. Send slides/photos, preferably samples, or call for appointment. Reports immediately. Work may be shipped or hand-delivered. Dealer pays insurance for exhibited work.
Profile: "Either they or we put up a special showing display and we send out a customers mailing, advertised in the *NY Times* and *Newsday*. The showings last 2 weeks (the items are on consignment at this time), then we leave it up to mutual agreement as to the future of the crafts. This system works out very well." Customers: middle to upper incomes; "all our customers are repeat, and nothing has ever been returned." Heaviest wholesale buying time: Easter, Mother's Day, Father's Day, graduation, June-July weddings and October; best selling time: October-Christmas.
To Break In: "We like to have a sizeable display from the craftsperson. Ship on time and have quality work. Don't try to ship seconds; we are craftsmen ourselves and are very critical of quality."

JULIE: ARTISANS' GALLERY, 687 Madison Ave., New York NY 10021. (212)688-2345. Contact: Julie, Rick, Paul and Ellen. Craft gallery. Estab. 1973. Represents 200 craftworkers, primarily American.
Acceptable Work: Considers ceramics, clothing, dollmaking, glass art, jewelry, leatherworking, needlecrafts, pottery, quilting, soft sculpture, wall hangings, weavings and woodcrafting. Especially needs anything wearable and non-wearable of museum quality. Specializes in contemporary crafts. One-of-a-kind and some handmade production-line items. Price range: $10-4,000.

Terms: Works on consignment; fixed commission. Gallery sets retail price. "Write or phone for an appointment, or better yet, submit slides for viewing, stating price of each object. Do not send actual work." Reports in 4 weeks. Work may be shipped or hand-delivered if accepted. Dealer pays return shipping and insurance.
Profile: "Our shop is technically perfect with a view leaning towards fantasy and whimsy as well as humor. Pieces are displayed on a rotating basis, except for special exhibitions, where all pieces concerned are displayed at the same time." Best selling time: Christmas.

JUST ACCESSORIES, INC., 112 W. 34th St., Rm. 710, New York NY 10001. (212)564-5168. President: Richard N. Bloch. Gift shop. Estab. 1961. Represents 2-3 craftworkers. Fine handmade production-line items only. Price range: $15-60. Best selling time: holidays.
Terms: Buys outright. Gallery sets retail price. Reports in 1 week. Work may be shipped or hand-delivered. Dealer pays return shipping and insurance for exhibited work.

KATA GALLERY, 130 Greene St., Soho, New York City NY 10012. (212)925-8772. Contact: Frank Dituri. Gallery. Considers stained glass, blown glass and sculpture. Works on consignment; 50% commission. Work must be for sale. Work may be shipped or hand-delivered. Send slides and resume. Has group shows and 1-man shows.

KIRKLAND ART CENTER, On the Park, Clinton NY 13323. (315)853-8871. Gallery/gift shop. Estab. 1960. Price range: $1-100; bestsellers: $1-10. Best selling time: Christmas.
Acceptable Work: Considers all crafts. All styles; utilitarian or decorative.
Terms: Works on consignment and buys outright; 25% commission. Craftworker sets retail price on consigned items. Work may be shipped or hand-delivered. Dealer pays insurance for exhibited work. Bring in work, send slides and resume or send illustrated catalog. Exhibits work 3 months before returning.

THE KIVA: ARTISAN'S GALLERY, 37 Popham Rd., Scarsdale NY 10583. (914)723-1474. Contact: Sandy Bernstein, Sue Herrmann or Kiki Suslow. Craft gallery. Estab. 1977. Represents 10+ craftworkers.
Acceptable Work: Considers all high quality crafts: functional and non-functional in every medium. Specializes in contemporary, fantasy-oriented work. One-of-a-kind preferred but will consider quality production work. Price range: $5-5,000; bestsellers: $20-350.
Terms: Works on consignment; 40-50% commission. Retail price set by joint agreement. Requires exclusive area representation. "Submit good slides or photos with size and price wanted by the artist and detailed description of work." Reports in 2 weeks. Work may be shipped or hand-delivered. Dealer pays return shipping and insurance on exhibited work. Display time: 6-8 weeks.
Profile: "The Kiva deals in fantasy and functional creative crafts of high quality. The gallery is 850 sq. feet with multi-level display areas and theatrical lighting allowing great flexibility in exhibiting work. The prominent window display area faces a well traveled street. Sculpture, porcelain etc. is displayed in cases or on lucite cubes. A shelving system is available when required. The backround is neutral to show work at its best advantage. Our customers come to us expecting to find the exciting and unusual."

KNOCK ON WOOD, 1601 Trumansburg Rd., Ithaca NY 14850. President: David Hoffman. Craft shop. Estab. 1974. Represents 10 craftworkers.
Acceptable Work: Considers batik: ceramics; glass art; jewelry; leatherworking; metalsmithing; pottery; soft sculpture; wall hangings; weavings; and woodcrafting. Price range: $1-300; bestsellers: $1-65.
Terms: Works on consignment and buys outright; 33% commission. Craftworker sets retail price. Reports in 4 weeks. Work may be shipped or hand-delivered. Dealer pays return shipping and insurance for exhibited work. Best selling time: Christmas; heaviest wholesale buying time: late fall.
To Break In: "Develop a good catalog, either pictorial or with line drawings, with terms and prices set out clearly."

LYNN KOTTLER GALLERIES, 3 East 65th St., New York NY 10021. (212)734-3491. Director: Lynn Kottler. Rental gallery. Estab. 1949.
Acceptable Work: Considers batik, ceramics, decoupage, glass art, jewelry, leatherworking, metalsmithing, pottery, soft sculpture, tole painting, wall hangings, weavings, woodcrafting, drawings, sculpture and assemblage. Original contemporary work only. Minimum price: $50; bestsellers: $400-3,000.

Terms: Sponsors 2 exhibitions every 2 weeks. $225 for 3-man exhibits; $650 for 1-man exhibits; both plus 10% commission. Send resume, slides with SASE or call for appointment. Reports in 1 week. Work may be shipped or hand delivered. Retail price set by craftworker or joint agreement. Gallery pays insurance up to $5,000. Work is displayed for two weeks.
Profile: "We supply pedestals for sculpture and we hang the show. Attractive catalogues listing the artist's name and titles of works will be available free, also opening reception party. The artist's name will appear in advertisements and listings, including the *New York Times*. All reviews will be mailed to the artist." Closed: July-August.

KRUGER GALLERY, 842 Madison Ave., New York NY 10021. (212)734-6436. President: Laura Kruger. Gallery. Estab. 1975. Considers jewelry. Price range: $15-5,000; bestsellers: $75-350.
Terms: Works on consignment. Retail price set by joint agreement. Requires exclusive area representation during show.. Submit photos and arrange interview. SASE. Reports in 2 weeks. Dealer pays return shipping and insurance for exhibited work.
Profile: Gallery sponsors regular one-man shows and provides openings and promotions. Shows run a minimum of 6 weeks with the possibility of becoming part of gallery's stable of craftworkers.

LA GALERIE ROUGE, Seneca Turnpike Nichols Plaza, New Hartford NY 13413. (315)724-1756. Contact: Rick Bianco. Gallery/art supplier. Estab. 1970. Represents 7 craftworkers.
Acceptable Work: Considers candlemaking; glass art; pottery; and silkscreening. One-of-a-kind and handmade production-line items. Price range: $2-150.
Terms: Works on consignment; 30% commission. Retail price set by joint agreement. Requires exclusive area representation. Work may be hand-delivered and is displayed 30 days minimum. Best selling time: fall-Christmas.

JACK LEBOWITZ DESIGNS, 139-43 85 Dr., Jamaica NY 11435. (212)523-4123. President: Jack Lebowitz. Craft shop/gallery. Estab. 1963. Represents 10 craftworkers who work to Lebowitz's designs. Price range: $50-5,000; bestsellers: $50-2,000. Buys outright. Gallery sets retail price. Requires exclusive area representation. Work may be shipped or hand-delivered. Dealer pays insurance on exhibited work.
Acceptable Work: Considers ceramics; leatherworking; metalsmithing; pottery; soft sculpture; wall hangings; weavings; and woodcrafting. Fine one-of-a-kind designer pieces only.

THE LEE SHOP, 43 Greenwich Ave., New York NY 10014. (212)989-7215. Contact: Lee Erdberg. Craft shop. Estab. 1965. Represents 20 craftworkers. Considers leather garments, bags and accessories. Price range: $15-350. Buys outright. Craftworker sets retail price. Requires exclusive area representation. Work may be shipped or hand-delivered. Special needs: leather goods. Best selling and buying time: autumn.
Sales Tip: "It would be helpful if craftworkers considered the retail price while working, so that they produce an item that has a viable price in the store."

THE LONGHOUSE MUSEUM, Rt. 5, Oneida NY 13032. (315)363-1330. Contact: Dick C. Brewer. Museum gift shop. Estab 1960. Represents 3-10 craftworkers.
Acceptable Work: Considers candlemaking, ceramics, decoupage, dollmaking, jewelry, scrimshaw and woodcrafting. Specializes in primitive and Appalachian crafts. One-of-a-kind and handmade production-line items. Price range: 50¢-$350; bestsellers: $1-5.
Terms: Buys outright. Retail price set by joint agreement. Call for appointment with SASE. Reports in 4 weeks. Work may be shipped or hand delivered.
Profile: "We have pegboard walls and wooden display benches. It's full, but homey. I have a large outdoor area and hope to have an outdoor craft area where craft people can display and sell their own materials on some weekends." Customers: many school groups (grades 7-12). Heaviest wholesale buying time: spring; best selling time: summer.

LUMINERE CREATIONS, INC., 15 Charles St., New York NY 10014. (212)989-7858. President: Miss Shulman. Gallery/gift shop. Estab. 1969. Represents 120 craftworkers.
Acceptable Work: Considers ceramics; glass art; metalsmithing; pottery; and especially needs wall treatments in mirror and glass from $20-50. Fine one-of-a-kind and handmade production-line items. Price range: $5-1,500; bestsellers: $10-50.
Terms: Works on consignment but mostly buys outright; 40% commission. Gallery sets retail price. Requires exclusive area representation. Reports in 1-3 weeks. Work may be shipped or

hand-delivered. Deals pays return shipping and insurance for exhibited work.
Profile: "Window and shelf display on all items for 2 weeks; inside store display another 2-6 weeks in scattered positions." Best selling time: September-December; heaviest wholesale buying time: September-October. Cosmopolitan customers.

THE MAD MONK, 500 6th Ave., New York NY 10011. (212)242-6678. President: Carl Monk. Director: Larry Steiger. Craft shop. Estab. 1969. Represents 80 craftworkers.
Acceptable Work: Considers ceramics and pottery only. Most are functional. One-of-a-kind utilitarian and/or decorative. Price range: $3-5,000; bestsellers: $4-150.
Terms: Buys outright. Retail price set by joint agreement. Send resume or call for appointment. Reports in 1 week. Work may be shipped or hand-delivered. Dealer pays shipping to shop.
Profile: "We have 'Please Touch' signs. We are probably the only ceramics store in New York which buys pottery on a substantial scale." Customers: mainly young, earthy, moderate incomes. Heaviest wholesale buying and best selling time: pre-holidays.

MAIN STREET DEPARTMENT STORE, 8 Main St., Hastings on Hudson NY 10706. (914)478-3553. Secretary-Treasurer: Drew Gorman. Department store. Men's, women's, children's, gifts and crafts departments buy and commission crafts. Works with out-of-town but prefers local craftworkers. Write or call for interview; include photos/samples.
Resale Items: Considers adult games, baskets, carvings and sculpture, children's toys, Christmas ornaments, dolls, furniture, handbags and leather accessories, jewelry, pillows, pottery, silverwork, wall hangings and weavings. One-of-a-kind and handmade production-line items OK. Retail price range: $1-500; craftworker sets retail price.
Props: Considers baskets, carvings and sculpture, children's toys, Christmas ornaments, handmade furniture, pillows, pottery and wall hangings. One-of-a-kind and handmade production-line items OK.
Profile: "We have wood floors, a tin ceiling, antique cabinets and large floor space. Items are displayed on the floor, in cabinets throughout the departments and in windows. There is also a separate craft department." Customers: high incomes, high education, interested in sports, crafts and hobbies. Heaviest wholesale buying time: late summer; best selling time: back-to-school time and Christmas.

THE MAINE SCENE, 100 Johnson Terrace, Staten Island NY 10309. Contact: Joyce or Edward Collord. Craft shop/gallery/gift shop. Estab. 1967. Represents 50 craftworkers. Considers; dollmaking; glass art; jewelry; metalsmithing; needlecrafts; pottery; quilting; nautical decorations; and woodcrafting. Handmade production-line items. Price range: 50¢-$75; bestsellers: $2.50-27.
Terms: Works occasionally on consignment and buys outright; 40% commission. Retail price set by joint agreement. Reports in 1 week. Accepts mailed or shipped items with return postage included; dealer pays shipping to shop if outright purchase.

MARI GALLERIES OF WESTCHESTER, LTD., 133 E. Prospect Ave., Mamaroneck NY 10543. (914)698-0008. President: Carla Reuben. Vice-president: Claire Kaufman. Craft gallery. Estab. 1966. Represents 6-10 craftworkers/exhibition.
Acceptable Work: Considers all crafts. Especially needs clothing. Fine and primitive handmade production-line pieces; decorative only.
Terms: Works on consignment; 40% commission. Craftworker sets retail price. Requires exclusive area representation. Write or call. Reports as soon as possible. Work may be shipped or hand-delivered. Dealer pays insurance for exhibited work. Display time: 5 weeks with appropriate flyers and publicity.
Profile: "Our gallery is set in a 200-year-old barn in the center of town—very contemporary and unique." Fine art is on the main level, crafts on the upper level, fine arts/crafts and art wearables on lower level.

MARINE MUSEUM GIFT SHOP, Bluff Rd., Amagansett NY 11930. (516)267-6544. Director: Tina Saposhnik. Museum gift shop. Estab. 1976. Represents 20-30 craftworkers.
Acceptable Work: Considers all nautical or sea-oriented crafts. One-of-a-kind and handmade production-line items. Price range: 50¢-$300; bestsellers: 50¢-$12.50.
Terms: Works on consignment; 33⅓% commission. Retail price set by craftworker or joint agreement. Send cover letter, slides/photos and price list. Reports immediately. Work may be shipped or hand delivered.
Profile: "We are a museum dealing with the whaling industry and present fishing industry. We also are a center in the community for classes, poetry readings, theatre groups, and we have a

space for photograph and drawing exhibits in the summer." Heaviest wholesale buying time: spring; best selling time: summer.

MERKEL'S DEPARTMENT STORE, 74-76 Margaret St., Plattsburgh NY 12901. Buyer: Deborah McNamee. Department store. Write with illustrations of work, send samples or call for interview. Store sets retail price.
Resale Items: Buys baskets; Christmas ornaments; dinnerware; dolls; handbags and leather accessories; jewelry; pillows; pottery; wall hangings; and weavings for resale. Will consider "anything that would be interesting for the store." Considers one-of-a-kind designer and production-line crafts.
Props: Considers one-of-a-kind crafts. Buys outright.

MERRY JANE'S COUNTRY SHOPPE, 232 Frew Run Rd., Rt. 1, Frewsburg NY 14738. (716)569-2344. Proprietor: Mary Jane Nelson. Craft/gift shop. Estab. 1972. Represents 4 craftworkers.
Acceptable Work: Considers candlemaking, dollmaking, needlecrafts, tole painting, wall hangings, weavings and woodcrafting. Especially needs baskets and candles. Specializes in primitive, fine art and Appalachian items; no contemporary crafts. "Pieces must look old and mellow and must have an unusual air about them." One-of-a-kind items only. Price range: $4.50-75; bestsellers: $12-50.
Terms: Buys outright and works on consignment; 40% commission. "We've tried both ways but buying outright is easier due to our location and season." Retail price set by shop or joint agreement. Requires exclusive area representation. Send resume, slides with SASE. Reports in 2 weeks. Work may be shipped or hand delivered. Dealer pays insurance on exhibited work. Display time: 1 season.
Profile: "Our crafts are mostly done by the co-owners. We have customers who are professional people interested in early good authentic one-of-a-kind articles ages 40-70 on very good incomes. They do not ask how much; they simply say they want an article. If our customers see 2 of anything they're turned off!"

MEUNIERS, 140 Montague St., Brooklyn Heights NY 11201. (855)7835. Contact Elisabeth or Paul Meunier. Craft/gift and gourmet shop. Estab. 1958. Represents 75 craftworkers.
Acceptable Work: Considers glass art, woodcrafting and especially ceramics, pottery and jewelry. One-of-a-kind and handmade production-line items. Price range: $10-300.
Terms: Craftworker sets retail price. Requires exclusive area representation. Send resume, slides or call for appointment. Work may be shipped or hand delivered.
Profile: "There is a craft corner and a jewelry alcove. The shop is informal with no pressure. People come for good design, fine work, and the individuals." Customers: professionals and families; high rent area. Heaviest wholesale buying time: spring and summer.

THE MILL GALLERY, Ballard Mill Center for the Arts, Ballard Mill Park, Malone NY 12953. (518)483-5190. Director: Nancy McMahon. Estab. 1977. Exhibition space temporarily located at Wead Library, Elm St., Malone NY 12953 (2nd floor). (518)483-0909. Plans to move to B.M.C.A. Represents 1-20 craftworkers.
Acceptable Work: Considers blacksmithing, ceramics, dollmaking, glass art, jewelry, leatherworking, metalsmithing, needlecrafts, quilting, wall hangings, weavings, woodcrafting, and especially needs soft sculpture, jewelry and pottery. Primarily one-of-a-kind pieces. Price range: $10-1,000; bestsellers: $10-700.
Terms: Works on consignment; 25% commission. Retail price set by joint agreement. Send resume, slides with SASE or call for appointment. Reports in 2 weeks. Display time: 2-6 weeks.
Profile: "We are a fine arts and crafts gallery with changing exhibits, approximately 15/year. We are funded by state and federal funds and have a nonprofit, tax-exempt status."

MINI MUNDUS SHOP, 970 Lexington, New York NY 10021. (212)288-5855. Contact: Kathryn Falk. Craft shop/gift shop with second location at 1030 Lexington Avenue. Estab. 1975. Represents 35 craftworkers. Price range: $1-500; bestsellers: $1-100. Works on consignment and buys outright; 33% commission. Retail price set by joint agreement. Reports in 2 weeks. Work may be shipped or hand-delivered. Catalog can be obtained for $4.75; includes all items from both shops.
Acceptable Work: Miniatures in dollhouses; ceramics; dollmaking; glass art; needlecrafts; pottery; wall hangings; weavings; woodcrafting; and miniature furniture and accessories. Fine one-of-a-kind and hand-made production-line items only. 1"-1' scale.
Profile: "Work is displayed in glass cases. It is the only miniature shop in New York that carries

a complete miniature line of furnishings and building and decorating parts." Best selling time: before Christmas.

MUSEUM OF HOLOGRAPHY BOOKSTORE, 11 Mercer St., New York NY 10013. (212)925-0581. Manager: Lee Zemann. Museum gift shop. Estab. 1976. Represents 10 craftworkers.
Acceptable Work: Considers glass art, jewelry, metalsmithing and holograms (3-D laser light images). "We need people to help incorporate our existing holograms into fine jewelry and usable gift items (pendants, boxes, etc.). We need jewelers to set holographic discs; glass people to make boxes with holographic lids; and people to design interesting displays and frames. We also need craftspeople who cast small objects (with lots of detail) to use as models for holograms." Specializes in contemporary images (i.e., space, abstracts). One-of-a-kind and handmade production-line items. Price range: $6.50-500; bestsellers: $6.50-35.
Terms: Buys outright and works on consignment; 40% commission. Retail price set by joint agreement. Call for appointment. Reports in 2 weeks. Work may be shipped or hand delivered. Dealer pays insurance on exhibited work.
Profile: "Items are displayed in frames (mounted on the wall) or in display case units. Holography uses laser light to produce 3-D images. Each image needs to be lit at a specific angle in order to be viewable." Customers are interested in art and science. Best selling time: Christmas.

THE MUSICAL MUSEUM, Deansboro NY 13328. (315)841-8774. Curator: Arthur H. Sanders. Museum gallery/gift shop. Estab. 1948. Represents 2-6 craftworkers. Best selling time: summer and November; heaviest wholesale buying time: summer.
Acceptable Work: Considers all crafts with a musical motif except clothing, quilting and soft sculpture. Especially needs musical jewelry. Primitive one-of-a-kind pieces preferred; utilitarian. Price range: 10¢-$100; bestsellers: $6-10.
Terms: Works on consignment and buys outright; 40-60% commission. Retail price set by joint agreement. Reports in 1 week. Work may be shipped or hand-delivered.

Edward Hoit is one of 100-120 craftworkers who produce items for the North Country Arts & Crafts Store, Inc., Malone, New York. Local townspeople and tourists occasionally find demonstrations, such as broommaking, being held when visiting the shop. The outlet is located only 60 miles from Lake Placid, New York.

MY SISTER, 10 E. 40th St., New York NY 10022. (212)868-3330. Contact: Ina Eckhaus. Boutique. Estab. 1973. Represents 8-10 craftworkers.
Acceptable Work: Considers all accessories and jewelry; expecially needs unusual jewelry and knitted scarf and hat sets for adults and children. Interested in other unusual crochet items such as stoles, "or anything that is new and attractive." Price range: $10-200; bestsellers: $15-100.
Terms: Works on consignment; commission varies. Retail price set by joint agreement. Arrange appointment to show work. Reports in 4 weeks. Work may be shipped or hand-delivered if previously arranged. Work that is shipped is done at the expense of the artist.
Profile: Items are "shown to all customers, usually in conjunction with other accessories that will show the item off to best advantage. Best selling and heaviest wholesale buying time: fall and winter. Customers are fashion-oriented, so "be aware of what women are wearing today."

NATURAL LEATHER, 203 Bleecker St., New York NY 10012. (212)533-6530. Contact: Phil or Dick. Craft shop. Estab. 1969. Represents 20-30 craftworkers. Considers leatherworking and metalsmithing. "Much of what we sell we make or buy from people we know. I buy about two-thirds of my stock." Handmade production-line items only. Price range: $5-400; bestsellers: $5-165. Buys outright. Gallery sets retail price. Reports in 2 weeks. Customers are about half tourists, and about half from Greenwich Village and New York City.

NEW YORK EXCHANGE FOR WOMAN'S WORK, 541 Madison Ave., New York NY 10022. Manager: V. Doerfler. Craft/gift shop. Estab. 1878. Represents 500 craftworkers with financial need. Not restricted to women.
Acceptable Work: Considers ceramics, clothing, decoupage, dollmaking, glass art, leatherworking, needlecrafts, quilting, scrimshaw, soft sculpture, tole painging and woodcrafting. Prefers small items due to limited space. One-of-a-kind items only. Price range: $1-750.
Terms: Works on consignment; 30% commission. Craftworker sets retail price; shop advises. Visit shop on Wednesday morning between 10-11:30 with SASE. "No information will be mailed unless postage is furnished as we are nonprofit." Reports immediately. Work may be shipped or hand delivered. "The Exchange does not hold itself responsible for loss caused by damage, fire or theft having taken all reasonable precautions. Please note this rule before becoming a consignor."
Profile: "We will keep an item for 1 year. It is on display at least 50% of this time." Consignors have included "a gentleman, who recently went blind who supplies us with tabletop-sized sculpture; a former schoolteacher, aged 84, who helps supports herself by making baby clothes; and a destitute woman conceived a sleeveless jacket that was so successful that eventually she was able to establish herself as a dress designer in New York City."

THE NIDDY NODDY, 416 Albany Post Rd., Croton-on-Hudson NY 10520. (914)271-9724. Contact: Irene Miller. Textile craft shop. Estab. 1966. Represents 12 craftworkers. Price range: $1.50-650. Works on consignment and buys outright; 33⅓ commission. Retail price set by joint agreement. Work may be shipped or hand-delivered. Dealer pays return shipping and insurance for exhibited work. Reports "immediately."
Acceptable Work: Considers batik; clothing; dollmaking; needlecrafts; quilting; and soft sculpture.

9 ARTISANS, INC., 142 7th Ave. S., New York NY 10014. (212)691-1695. Manager: Dan Beck. Cooperative craft shop/gallery. Estab. 1976. Represents 14-18 member craftworker.
Acceptable Work: Considers batik; enamel art; glass art; jewelry; leatherworking; pottery; soft sculpture; wall hangings; and weavings. Especially needs members working in wood, wrought iron and metal. One-of-a-kind designer pieces and handmade production-line items only. Price range: $4-1,200.
Terms: Shows work of members only; does not buy or consign. Craftworker sets retail price. Reports in 2 weeks.

NORTH COUNTRY ARTS & CRAFTS STORE, INC., Elm St., Malone NY 12953. Craft shop. Contact: Beth Bailey, (518)483-7851; or Alice Wand, (513)483-7851. Represents 100-120 craftworkers.
Acceptable Work: Considers all crafts. Especially needs pottery and silver jewelry. No plastic flowers, preformed plastic parts, molded pottery/candles from commercial molds, macaroni, or items from kits. Specializes in traditional and functional crafts "with a homespun feeling". Handmade production-line items only. Price range: 50¢-$100; bestsellers: 50¢-$10.
Terms: Works on consignment; 30% commission. Craftworker sets retail price. Send work or

call in person. Reports in 1 week. Work may be shipped or hand delivered. Store has liability insurance, but not responsible for loss due to fire or theft. "There is a maximum time limit of 1 year that the item may remain in the store."
Profile: "Our shop contains local crafts ranging fom traditional knit and crocheted items to Mohawk Indian baskets. Items are displayed on tables, racks or on the wall. We are about 60 miles from Lake Placid and hope for extra good sales during the Olympic season." Customers: local townspeople and tourists (especially from Quebec). Heaviest consignment and best selling time: summer and holidays.

NORTH VIEW GALLERY, 91 Main St., Dobbs Ferry NY 10522. (914)693-3790. Director: Barbara Contorelli. Gallery. Estab. 1976. Represents 8 craftworkers.
Acceptable Work: Considers candlemaking, ceramics, glass art, jewelry, leatherworking, metalsmithing, pottery and scrimshaw. One-of-a-kind and handmade production-line items. Price range $5-200; bestsellers: $10-60.
Terms: Buys outright and works on consignment; 35% commission. Retail price set by joint agreement. Send slides or call for appointment. Reports in 2 weeks. Work may be shipped or hand delivered. Dealer pays insurance on exhibited work.
Profile: "We sell contemporary fine arts and crafts all year round, especially during Christmas, and also do custom picture framing. There is a special platform with jewelry cases sunken in, fabric wrapped shelves and a room divider with shelves. We also have a distinctive large window to display work. Our clientele is from middle, upper-middle class incomes who are fairly familiar with art. They seek unique very functional crafts and are looking for well priced items. They favor landscape and seascape paintings." Heaviest wholesale buying time: Christmas-November; best selling time: Christmas.
To Break In: "We seek craftsmen who are good businessmen and are reliable. Craftsmen must keep up with supply and demand."

OF CABBAGES & KINGS, 587 E. Boston Post Rd., Mamaroneck NY 10543. (914)698-0445. President: Rona Kurz. Gallery. Estab. 1977. Represents 90-100 craftworkers.
Acceptable Work: Considers batik, clothing, pottery, jewelry, leatherworking and soft sculpture. Especially needs glass art, metalsmithing, wall hangings, weavings, woodcrafting and ceramics. Specializes in fine art designer crafts in contemporary syles. Price range: $10-1,200; bestsellers: $15-100.
Terms: Prefers consignment, but will consider buying outright; 40% commission. Retail price set by joint agreement. Send slides or call for appointment. Reports in 2 weeks. Work may be shipped or hand-delivered. Dealer pays insurance on exhibited work.
Profile: "Our shop is very contemporary and attractive. We display items in mobile cubes and on walls of cork and burlap. Our focal point is a gazebo-like structure with a straw roof and straw backdrop which frames a series of shelves. Our customers are bright, sophisticated people with an interest in the unique and contemporary. We purchase most of our crafts in the months preceding Christmas, as well as in the late winter and early spring for wedding gifts." Bestselling time: pre-Christmas.

OXFORD GALLERY, 267 Oxford St., Rochester NY 14607. (716)271-5885. Co-directors: Edythe Shedden and Glorya Mueller. Considers sculpture; soft sculpture; and wall hangings. Specializes in contemporary and ethnic arts. Price range: $75-10,000, sculpture; bestsellers: $100-1,000. Works on consignment; 40% commission. Retail price set by craftworker. Requires exclusive area representation. Call for interview. "We have an important 'letter of agreement' and we require an insurance release." 4-6 weeks exposure.

PARAFFINALIA, 122 Washington Ave., Endicott NY 13760. (607)754-0192. Contact: Donn or Jayne Kemp. Craft shop. Estab. 1972. Represents 15 craftworkers.
Acceptable Work: Considers ceramics; dollmaking; glass art; jewelry; leatherworking; metalsmithing; pottery; wall hangings; weavings; and woodcrafting. Fine one-of-a-kind and handmade production-line items. Price range: $2-300; bestsellers: $5-60.
Terms: Works on consignment and buys outright; 33% commission. Craftworker sets retail price. Requires exclusive street representation. Work may be shipped or hand-delivered. Dealer pays shipping to shop and insurance for exhibited work if bought outright.
Profile: "Item is displayed in best environment for work agreed to by craftsman and dealer. Usually work is displayed for up to 3 months; longer if there is big turnover." Heaviest wholesale buying time: fall; best selling time: Christmas and summer.

THE PEDESTAL, 50 State St., Pittsford NY 14534. (716)381-7640. Gift shop. Estab. 1971. Represents 50 craftworkers.

Acceptable Work: Considers ceramics, glass art, jewelry (other than metals), leatherworking, metalsmithing, pottery, scrimshaw and some woodcrafting. Specializes in decorative and functional contemporary pieces. "We also carry a huge selection of music boxes." One-of-a-kind and handmade production-line items. Prices up to $250; bestsellers: $5-25.
Terms: Buys outright. Requires exclusive area representation. Call for appointment. "Appointments/advance phone calls are important as we don't like to send people away just because we are too busy to talk business." Work may be shipped or hand delivered.
Profile: "Our shop is located in a suburban area which is made up of 30 businesses dealing primarily with handcrafts. Because we try not to cross the lines of the other shops, we do not sell all types of crafts. We combine American handcrafts with imported goods at a ratio of 2:1; gourmet corner included. We prefer to purchase groupings of a new item and to make a special display of the initial delivery in order to get a response. If an item or line does not sell well after a period of 6 months to a year, we reduce the price and sell out the line." Customers: ages 20-45, professionals with relatively high incomes. Heaviest wholesale buying time: spring and fall; best selling time: summer and pre-Christmas.
To Break In: "We don't like to deal with double-pricing on the part of our craftspeople, and request that local people keep the wares priced at full retail if they attend local shows."

THE PENGUIN'S PANTRY, 143 Main St., Bellport NY 11713. (516)286-0776. Contact: Nancy Ljungqvist. Gourmet/gift shop. Estab. 1968. Represents 5-10 craftworkers.
Acceptable Work: Considers candlemaking, ceramics, metalsmithing, pottery, woodcrafting, Christmas ornaments, baskets and kitchen crafts. Especially needs wooden items (chopping blocks, salad bowls, cutting boards, cheese boards), mugs, tea pots, oriental items, and tiles. Spcializes in fine contemporary bright-colored works. One-of-a-kind and handmade production-line items. Price range: $10-150.
Terms: Buys outright and works on consignment; 33⅓% commission. Retail price set by joint agreement. Requires exclusive area representation. Call for appointment. Reports immediately. Work may be shipped or hand delivered. Dealer pays insurance on exhibited work.
Profile: Customers: young married couples, elderly, middle incomes. Heaviest wholesale buying time; fall-spring; best selling time: summer-Christmas.

PERFORMERS' OUTLET, 222 E. 85th St., New York NY 10028. (212)249-8435. President: Jerald Thomas Young. Craft and gift shop. Represents 350 craftworkers. Estab. 1969.
Acceptable Work: Considers batik; candlemaking; ceramics; decoupage; dollmaking; glass art; jewelry; needlecrafts; pottery; quilting; soft sculpture; wall hangings; weavings; and woodcrafting. Price range: $5-70; bestsellers: $10-25.
Terms: Works on consignment and buys outright; 50% commission. Retail price set by joint agreement. Write or call. Reports in 4 weeks. Work may be shipped or hand-delivered. Dealer pays shipping and insurance for exhibited work.
Profile: "We specialize in theatre people's art and craft work. Customers are middle to upper-middle class; 20-40 age range; well educated and well travelled." Best selling time: fall-Christmas; heaviest wholesale buying time: fall.

PHOENIX GALLERY, 30 W. 57th St., New York NY 10019. (212)245-5095. Director: Betty Unger. Considers mobiles and sculpture. Specializes in contemporary art. Price range: $200-5,000. Works on consignment; 25% commission. Retail price set by joint agreement. Query.

PINCHPENNY GALLERY, 564 Lexington Ave., Mt Kisco NY 10549. (914)666-6525. President: Bertram J. Lange. Estab. 1966. Represents 3 craftworkers. Considers soft sculpture and woodcrafting; especially needs New England oriented woodworkings and decoys. Price range: $50-450. Best selling time: summer and November-December; heaviest wholesale buying time: early spring. Customers are primarily managerial and professional with incomes of $10,000-500,000.
Terms: Buys outright. Retail price set by joint agreement. Requires exclusive area representation. Work may be shipped or hand-delivered.

POT-POURRI GALLERY OF AMERICAN CRAFTS, 85 N. Main St., Florida NY 10921. (914)651-7418. Contact: Louis or Dianne Mendez. Craft shop/gallery. Estab. 1968. Represents 135 craftworkers. Price range: $1-$7,500; bestsellers: $150 maximum. Works on consignment and buys outright; 40% commission. Retail price set by joint agreement. Requires exclusive area representation. Make appointment to show work. Reports as soon as possible. Work may be shipped or hand-delivered. Dealer pays return shipping and insurance for exhibited work.

Acceptable Work: Considers batik; candlemaking; ceramics; blown glass; jewelry; metalsmithing; pottery; soft sculpture; vests; wall hangings; weavings; and woodcrafting.
Profile: "Special shows have approximately 6 weeks duration, otherwise no time limitation on displays; try to group items according to type." Best selling time: summer and Christmas; heaviest wholesale buying time: early spring and fall.

POTTERY & SOUTH 4TH, 177 W. 4th St., New York NY 10014. (212)675-7478. Contact: Ellen Richman, Nancy Fern, Jerry Marshall and Alix Leff. Estab. 1975. Coop. Represents 6 craftworkers. Works on consignment; 40% commission. Retail price set by joint agreement. Work may be hand-delivered.
Acceptable Work: Considers ceramics; pottery; wall hangings; weavings; and especially soft sculpture and jewelry. Fine one-of-a-kind and handmade production-line items. Price range: $1-200; bestsellers: $5-56.
Profile: "Items will be displayed along with a name card or biographical writing. Displays are changed or rotated around shop weekly. We are a coop, so our prices are reasonable. All members of coop work in shop, so customers and artists have direct interaction. Because we are located in Greenwich Village we get a large tourist traffic along with neighborhood customers."

THE QUEENS MUSEUM, New York City Bldg., Flushing Meadow Park, Flushing NY 11368. (212)592-2405. Contact: Barbara Sperber. Museum gift shop. Estab. 1972.
Acceptable Work: Considers all crafts except clothing and tole painting. Fine one-of-a-kind pieces and handmade production-line items. Bestsellers: $100 maximum.
Terms: Works on consignment and buys outright; 40% commission. Retail price set by joint agreement. Work may be hand-delivered by pre-arrangement only. Dealer pays insurance for exhibited work. Items are exhibited for approximately 8 weeks.

RAINBOW'S END, 56 Mamaroneck Ave., White Plains NY 10601. (914)948-1057. Contact: Paul or Loretta Croese. Craft shop. Estab. 1977. Represents 100+ craftworkers. "We welcome all US craftspeople. They may be of foreign origin, but live in the US. We are tired of 'imports'—let's help our own craftspeople!"
Acceptable Work: Considers all crafts except clothing; especially needs items with rainbow themes. One-of-a-kind and designer pieces. Price range: 25¢-$425; bestsellers: $5 items and those in the $25-50 price range.
Terms: Buys outright; 50% markup. Retail price set by joint agreement. "We prefer you don't sell in the same town unless a different item than we carry. We always like to meet you in person—this is not always possible. Give us a call or notify us when you are doing a show in our area (or reasonably close). Let us know if you belong to a large crafts group. We may travel if we can make many contacts all at once. When you write, give us all information at once—wholesale prices, minimum orders, terms. Introductions get thrown away if not clear. Please call before coming as we can't do business if you come at a busy hour." Reports in 2 weeks. Work may be shipped or hand delivered.
Profile: "We use primarily stucco, wood and earthy materials in our display. Media is mixed to a certain extent (e.g. not all pottery is lumped together). With jewelry, we either put the work of 1 person alone or display in categories (e.g. gold, scrimshaw, etc.). Items are rotated or put away and taken out so as not to appear as if they aren't selling. We have a small shop—bottom floor and half mezzanine level. There are many young customers buying jewelry—ages 14-30. Lots of collectors (of unicorns, owls, pigs, etc.) come in. We try to hunt things out for those we know collect particular things. Our older customers tend to spend less." Heaviest wholesale buying time: summer and pre-Christmas.
To Break In: "It seems that customers like little explanations of the things you make—for instance, a picture of you at the potters wheel and/or an explanation of technique."

RAINTREE BOOK & ART SHOP, Fayetteville Mall, Fayetteville NY 13066. (315)637-5158. Contact: Achilles Nickles. Gallery. Estab. 1974. Represents 15 craftworkers.
Acceptable Work: Considers all crafts except clothing; leatherworking; needlecrafts; and tole painting. Fine one-of-a-kind and handmade production-line items. Price range: $3.50-395.
Terms: Works on consignment and buys outright; 40% commission. Retail price set by joint agreement. Requires exclusive area representation. Reports in 3-4 weeks. Work may be shipped or hand-delivered. Dealer pays return shipping. Buys/consigns most crafts in the summer for the fall and Christmas seasons.

ROADS GALLERIES, 400 E. 57th St., New York NY 10022. (212)486-1441. President: Louis

Horwin. Estab. 1974. Represents 100 craftworkers.
Acceptable Work: Considers batik, metalsmithing, soft sculpture, wall hangings and weavings. Finished, one-of-a-kind and handmade production-line items only; decorative. Price range: $100-1,300; bestsellers: $300-500.
Terms: Works on consignment; 40% commission. Retail price set by joint agreement. Send slides/photos or call for appointment. Reports in 4 weeks. Dealer pays shipping from gallery and insurance for work.
Profile: "We sell office decorations to corporations. We show photos or slides to the customers; if there's interest, we have the item sent to us."

ROME HISTORICAL SOCIETY FT. STANWIX MUSEUM, 113 W. Court St., Rome NY 13440. (315)336-5870. Executive Director: Joseph G. Vincent. Gallery/gift shop. Estab. 1936. Represents 4 craftworkers. Price range: 10¢-$100; bestsellers: $2-25. Works on consignment and on loans for exhibits; 25% commission. Retail price set by joint agreement. Reports in 1 day. Work may be shipped or hand-delivered. Dealer pays insurance for exhibited work. Heaviest wholesale buying time: spring; best selling time: spring-summer.
Acceptable Work: Considers clothing; decoupage; dollmaking; glass art; jewelry; leatherworking; metalsmithing; pottery; quilting; soft sculpture; tole painting; wall hangings; weavings; and woodcrafting. American Indian items welcomed.

ROSCOE CRAFT CENTER, Box 93, Roscoe NY 12776. (607)498-5500. Manager: Helen Orobello. Craft shop/gallery/gift shop. Estab. 1972. Represents 25-30 craftworkers. Price range: $1.25-500. Works on consignment and buys outright; 33% commission. Retail price set by joint agreement. Requires exclusive area representation. Reports as soon as possible. Work may be shipped or hand-delivered. Dealer pays return shipping.
Acceptable Work: Considers all crafts except candlemaking and clothing.
Profile: Displays work in gallery 3-4 weeks; in gift shop for an indefinite period of time. Heaviest wholesale buying time: spring and fall; best selling time: summer and Christmas.

SALISBURY MANOR, Old Rt. 23, Leeds NY 12451. (518)943-9299. Proprietor: Kay Stamer. Craft/gift/antique/eccentricity shop. Estab. 1975. Represents 5-10 craftworkers.
Acceptable Work: Considers all crafts except batik, candlemaking and scrimshaw. One-of-a-kind and handmade production-line items. Price range: $2.50-250; bestsellers: $5-50.
Terms: Buys outright and works on consignment; 33⅓% commission. Retail price set by joint agreement. Send slides or call for appointment. SASE. Reports in 4 weeks. Work may be shipped or hand delivered.
Profile: "We are located on a country lane in an historical manor house of stone. The front portion of the manor is the shop setting. Pieces are displayed on antiques and hung on walls in room settings." Customers: educated and high incomes. Heaviest wholesale buying time: late spring and mid-fall; best selling time: summer and Christmas.

SCARBOROUGH GALLERY OF ARTS & CRAFTS, 28 N. Greeley Ave., Chappaqua NY 10514. (914)238-8367. Director: C.A. Gowen. Gallery. Estab. 1969. Represents US craftworkers, preferably those who have exhibited in American Craft Council-sponsored shows.
Acceptable Work: Considers batik, ceramics, dollmaking, glass art, jewelry, leatherworking, pottery and toymaking. Specializes in fine functional crafts. One-of-a-kind and handmade production-line items. Price range: $5-500; bestsellers: $10-60.
Terms: Buys outright (in experienced well-selling situations) and works on consignment; 40% commission. Retail price set by joint agreement. Requires exclusive area representation. Send catalog with photos or call for appointment. Does not report unless interested; returns work immediately if return-postage included. Work may be shipped or hand delivered. Dealer pays insurance on exhibited work.
Profile: "We are an art and craft gallery with a good reputation for fine quality in Westchester, a small commuter town. We also do a good framing business. New items are displayed with preference (i.e. front of store, window)." Heaviest wholesale buying time: summer-fall; best selling time: fall-spring.

THE SHAKER MUSEUM, Shaker Museum Rd., Old Chatham NY 12136. (518)794-9100. Director: Peter Laskovski. Museum gift shop and bookstore. Estab. 1950. Represents 5 craftworkers. Price range: 75¢-$350; bestsellers: $2-25. Works on consignment and buys outright; 40% commission. Retail price set by joint agreement. Requires exclusive area representation. Reports in 2 weeks. Work may be shipped or hand-delivered. Dealer pays return shipping.

Acceptable Work: Considers candlemaking; ceramics; clothing; dollmaking; leatherworking; metalsmithing; needlecrafts; pottery; quilting; wall hangings; weavings; and woodcrafting. Emphasis on simple utilitarian items in the Shaker style. All styles; utilitarian only. Heaviest wholesale buying time: spring-summer; best selling time: summer.

THE SHOP, ADIRONDACK LAKES CENTER FOR THE ARTS, Box 101, Blue Mountain Lake NY 12812. (518)352-7715. Program Director: Patricia Struthers. Craft shop of art center. Estab. 1967. Price range: $5-400; bestsellers: $5-50. Works on consignment; 30% commission. Reports in 3 weeks. Work may be shipped or hand-delivered by prior arrangement. Best selling time: May-October.
Acceptable Work: Considers all areas; quality utilitarian and/or decorative.

THE SHOP, ALBANY INSTITUTE OF HISTORY & ART, 125 Washington Ave., Albany NY 12210. (518)465-1281. Manager: Martha T. Gibson. Museum gift shop. Estab. 1962. Represents 5-6 craftworkers.
Acceptable Work: Considers batik, ceramics, jewelry, glass art, pottery, quilting, tole painting, wall hangings and weavings. Must correspond to museum image. Specializes in fine one-of-a-kind designer crafts. Price range 5¢-$50; bestsellers: 5¢-$20.
Terms: Works on consignment; 34% commission. Retail price set by joint agreement. Call for appointment. Reports in 2 weeks. Hand-delivered work only. Dealer pays in-transit insurance. Items are prominently displayed for 2-3 weeks, then held for 3 months.
Profile: Customers are young business women 25-30 years old; museum members, 40-60 years old: middle income. Heaviest wholesale buying time: fall; best selling time: fall-Christmas.

A SHOW OF HANDS, 2310 Broadway, New York NY 10024. (212)874-9193. Managers: Lynn Bender and Valencia Saczynski. Craft shop. Estab. 1970. Represents 35 craftworkers.
Acceptable Work: Considers batik; ceramics; clothing; dollmaking; glass art; jewelry; leatherworking; needlecrafts; pottery; quilting; wall hangings; weavings; marbelized paper; applique and stitchery in clothing and hangings; and mobiles. Fine one-of-a-kind and handmade production-line items only. Price range: $1-1,000; bestsellers: $25-100.
Terms: Works on consignment; 30% commission. Craftworker sets retail price. Reports in 4 weeks.
Profile: This is a "collective made up of very talented craftsmen who all feed into the direction and goals of the shop—setting policy and being part of how their work is displayed and sold. It gives a craftsman a chance to show new work and experiment with what sells." Best selling time: holidays and spring.

SIMPLE GIFTS INC., 354 Central Ave., Albany NY 12206. (518)465-0525. Manager: Walt Chura. Craft shop. Estab. 1976. Represents 25 craftworkers.
Acceptable Work: Considers calligraphy, candlemaking, decoupage, glass art, jewelry, metalsmithing, needlecrafts, pottery, scrimshaw, silkscreen, wall hangings, weavings and woodcrafting. Especially needs woodcraft items (simple, under $50) and copies of Shaker designs. No leather, plastic or erotic items. "We do not carry flashy mod stuff. Crafts with a 'message' (religious, spiritual, inspirational) do best for us—but not cute items. Fine-crafted functional items and relatively inexpensive childrens' items are good." One-of-a-kind and handmade production-line items. Price range: 30¢-$325; bestsellers: 30¢-$15.
Terms: Occassionally buys outright but mostly works on consignment; 33⅓% commission. Retail price set by joint agreement ("although craftworker has more weight"). Requires exclusive Albany City area representation. Send photos/samples with SASE or call for appointment. Work may be shipped or hand delivered. Dealer pays insurance on exhibited work.
Profile: "We are a non-profit religious educational organization. We carry crafts as a reflection of the creative gift from God and to offer people works of beauty in a plastic age. Our image is rustic, simple, homey. Whenever possible, we use display fixtures supplied by the worker. We use wood and woodgrain fixtures a lot. Otherwise glass case or table display is common. We have Shaker pegs along 1 wall. Some wall space is used." Heaviest wholesale buying time: early spring and early fall ("the spring items tend to be less expensive"); best selling time: May-June and November-December.

SIMPLY NATURAL, Rt. 23, Hermon NY 13652. Contact: Syd Gelbwaks. Craft shop. Estab. 1978. Price range: $10-250. Works on consignment; 40% commission. Retail price set by joint agreement. Reports in 3 weeks. Work may be shipped or hand-delivered. Dealer pays return shipping and insurance for exhibited work. Likes to display work "from March through October."

Shops and Galleries **285**

Acceptable Work: Considers clothing; pottery; quilting; wall hangings; weavings; handspun yarns and garments from handspun yarns. Primitive one-of-a-kind and handmade production-line items; utiltiarian and/or decorative.

SONNENBERG GARDENS, GARDEN GIFTS, 151 Charlotte St., Canandaigua NY 14424. (716)394-4922. Manager: Catherine Gifford. Gift shop at greenhouse location. Estab. 1973. Represents 5 craftworkers. Price range: 90¢-$25; bestsellers: $1-7. Works on consignment and buys outright; 33⅓ commission. Craftworker sets retail price. Reports in 4 weeks. Work may be shipped or hand-delivered. Dealer pays return shipping and insurance for exhibited work.
Acceptable Work: Considers ceramics; glass art; jewelry; pottery; woodcrafting and items relative to plants, flowers and gardens that are not affected by temperature or humidity. All styles. Especially needs well designed, inexpensive useful containers for plants and flowers; flower holders; and wall hanging containers.
Profile: "Craft consignment shows rotate once a month and are promoted and advertised; purchased inventory is on general display." Heaviest wholesale buying time: April-July; best selling time: June-August.

SOUTHOLD HISTORICAL SOCIETY MUSEUM, Main Rd and Maple Lane, Southold, Long Island NY 11971. (516)765-5500. Director: George D. Wagoner. Museum gift shop. Estab. 1970. Represents 6-8 craftworkers.
Acceptable Work: Considers ceramics, dollmaking, glass art, pottery, scrimshaw, tole painting and woodcrafting. Specializes in graphical and historical crafts of the 17th, 18th and 19th centuries. "Everything must be antique and museum related. Handmade production-line items only. Price range: 50¢-$110; bestsellers: 50¢-$35.
Terms: Buys outright. Gallery sets retail price. Requires exclusive area representation. Send resume.
Profile: "The shop is in an area of a house-museum displaying 17th, 18th and 19th century reproductions of glass, porcelain, silver, pewter, stone, books, dolls, etc." Customers: children to senior citizens; upper incomes. Heaviest wholesale buying time: early spring and late summer; best selling time: summer and Christmas.

SPOT ARTS & CRAFTS SHOP, INC., 178 Front St., Owego NY 13827. (607)687-5705. Coordinator: Anita Zelle. Craft shop. Estab. 1973. Represents 100-150 craftworkers.
Acceptable Work: Considers all crafts. One-of-a-kind and hand-made production-line items. Price range: 50¢-$275; bestsellers: 50¢-$45.
Terms: Works on consignment; 25% commission. Craftworker sets retail price. Reports as soon as possible. Work may be shipped or hand-delivered if samples are okayed.
Profile: "This is a store front shop on the Susquehanna River in 1880's brick row buildings. No other similar shop in geographic area that sells handmade items exclusively." Best selling time: fall and Christmas; heaviest wholesale buying time: summer.

SPRING STREET ENAMELS GALLERY, 171 Spring St., New York NY 10012. (212)431-8151. Director: Joan Itzcovitz. Gallery/workshop. Estab. 1977. Represents 40-50 craftworkers.
Acceptable Work: Considers enamel art in all interpretations; handblown art glass; unusual stained glass; unusual gold and silver jewelry. Specializes in enamel artwork (cloisonne, champleve, limoges, bassetaille) in all interpretations: jewelry, sculpture, wall pieces, boxes, bowls, etc. Also works with enamel in combinations with other media. One-of-a-kind and handmade production-line items. Price range: $25-3,000; bestsellers: $50-300.
Terms: Works on consignment; 50% commission. Retail price set by joint agreement. Requires exclusive area representation. Send resume and actual art work/slides. "Actual artwork is the best representation of an artist." Reports in 3 weeks. SASE. Work may be shipped or hand delivered. Artists pays postage both ways. Gallery pays insurance on exhibited work. One-person shows: 6 weeks. "There is an on-going group show of gallery artists and there are also invitationals."
Profile: "We are a loft gallery (2,000 square feet). Fine enamel art and art glass is displayed in a beautiful and unusual setting of plants and fresh flowers. In addition to traditional wall space, white brick walls are used for wall pieces. Jewelry is displayed on sculpture stands, in unusual arrangements in glass cases and as art on the walls. The workshop is separated from the gallery by a wall of burlap. The public is invited to see the students working in the medium. The public is always receptive, impressed, and very often inspired to buy. On weekends, the workshop is used as an extension of the gallery, displaying additional art works in a tasteful setting. We are located in the heart of Soho (the art center of New York) so have a large international tourist clientele. They include UN personnel, theatre people, professionals and artists; mainly upper middle incomes."

ELLEN SRAGOW LTD., 43 5th Ave., New York NY 10003. (212)929-2734. Contact: Ellen Sragow. Gallery. Estab. 1974. Represents 2 fiber artists.
Acceptable Work: Considers wall hangings, weavings and fine arts (including painting, photography and sculpture). One-of-a-kind, designer pieces only.
Terms: Works on consignment and on commission basis; 50% commission. Retail price set by joint agreement. Call for appointment at which time you should present slides and resume. Reports in 1 week. Solicited work may be shipped or hand-delivered.
Profile: Gives presentations to architects and interior designers. Does not actively solicit commission, but will show slides when asked for fiber work.

THE STUDIO, 15 Main St., Lake Placid NY 12946. (518)523-3589. Contact: Marge Augenthaler. Estab. 1968. Represents 100-150 craftworkers.
Acceptable Work: Considers non-abstract ceramics, decoupage, dollmaking, glass art, jewelry, metalsmithing, needlecrafts, pottery, quilting, tole painting, wall hangings, and woodcrafting. Especially needs figure skating and winter sports craft themes. Finished one-of-a-kind and handmade production-line items; utilitarian and/or decorative (likes nature themes). Price range: $2-1,000; bestsellers: $2-75.
Terms: Buys outright or on consignment; 33% commission. Retail price set by joint agreement. Requires exclusive area representation. Call for interview or send transparencies or photos. Reports in 1 week. Dealer pays shipping from shop; negotiates shipping to shop and insurance.
Profile: Consigned items displayed 6 months maximum. Heaviest wholesale buying time: spring; best selling time: summer and fall. Tourist customers ages 18 with middle to upper incomes; they buy crafts for artistic value.

SUFFOLK MARINE MUSEUM GIFT SHOP, Montauk Hwy., West Sayville NY 11796. (516)567-1733. Director: Roger B. Dunkerley. Museum gift shop. Estab. 1978. Represents 10 craftworkers.
Acceptable Work: Considers glass art, jewelry, needlecrafts, scrimshaw, soft sculpture, woodcrafting, ship models, decoys and ropework. "The craft items must bear some relationship to our collection, which consists of artifacts pertaining to the maritime history of Long Island (and artifacts typical of same). Sailor crafts are encouraged." One-of-a-kind and handmade production-line items. Price range: 25¢-$100; bestsellers: 25¢-$5.
Terms: Buys outright and works on consignment; 33.4% commission. Retail price set by joint agreement. Send slides with SASE or call for appointment. Reporting time varies according to time of year. Work must be hand-delivered. Dealer pays insurance on exhibited work.
Profile: "The museum's gift shop is an extension of the museum gallery, most especially in theme. It is designed to enable local craftsmen or those working with local materials or in marine crafts to display their work in a manner profitable to both museum and craftsman. It is located in a highly visible section of the museum and is a stop for most visitors. We have a variety of show places: glass cases, counter tops, shelves and walls. Our audience is very diverse, but is weighted heavily in favor of family groups and school children." Heaviest wholesale buying time: spring; best selling time: summer and fall.

THE SUNSHINE GALLERY, 547 Warburton Ave., Hasting-on-Hudson NY 10706. (914)478-0002. Contact: Lyn Higgins. Represents 60 artisans from Westchester County and surrounding New York areas.
Acceptable Work: Considers quilts, pottery, stained glass, jewelry, candlemaking, stuffed dolls and animals, batik, weavings, basketry, porcelain figures, dried flower and weed art, pillows, baby things, copper enamel, wood carvings, old linens, glassware, plants and collectibles. Price range: $4-400; bestsellers: $4-25.
Terms: Works on consignment; 33⅓% commission. Craftworker sets retail price. Reports at the end of each 30-day period. References furnished upon request. Write or call for information.

SUZUKI GALLERY, 38 E. 57th St., New York NY 10022. Director: Katsko Suzuki. Considers sculpture. Buys outright or on consignment; 50% commission. Price range: $500-5,000, sculpture. Retail price set by joint agreement.

SYNECHIA ARTS CENTER INC., 150 North St., Middletown NY 10940 (914)343-0546. Director: Nan Ginsburg. Gallery and gift/supply/frame shop. Estab. 1972. Represents 10-50 craftworkers.
Acceptable Work: Considers all crafts. One-of-a-kind and handmade production-line items. Price range: $1-500; bestsellers: $5-40.

Terms: Exhibits only. "When sold, craftsperson receives 70% of the retail price of the article sold." Craftworker sets retail price. Send resume, slides or call for appointment. Reports in 2 weeks. Work may be shipped or hand delivered. Gallery Association of New York State pays insurance on exhibited work. Exhibit time: 1 month.
Profile: "Synechia is dedicated to the advancement of the arts. A non-profit membership organization, it is in part funded by the NY State Council on the Arts. It consists of a large gallery, framing shop, art supply center and photo darkroom facility. A low cost school of visual arts offers an opportunity for art students to learn varied disciplines of art from a faculty of professional practicing artists." Items are displayed on the wall, in cases and on counter tops. Customers: $10,000-60,000 incomes. Best selling time: holidays and summer.
To Break In: "If craftspeople would be willing to demonstrate their techniques in an afternoon workshop, this helps sell. Craftspeople should display a few examples of higher priced items along with a variety of less expensive pieces which therfore sell better."

THE THREE CROWNS, Box 144, Pittsford NY 14534. (716)586-5160. Contact: George Gordon. Craft shop. Estab. 1966. Represents 50+ craftworkers with 4-6 years technical training from an accredited college or university.
Acceptable Work: Considers batik, ceramics, glass art, jewelry, metalsmithing, pottery, hand woven textiles, woodcrafting and copper enamel. "Ceramics tends toward bright colored and/or decorative." Fine one-of-a-kind items only. Price range: $3-150; bestsellers: $7.50-25.
Terms: Buys outright and works on consignment; 33⅓% commission. Craftworker sets retail price. Requires exclusive area representation. Send resume and slides or call for appointment. Reports in 1 week. Work may be shipped or hand-delivered. Dealer pays insurance for exhibited work.
Profile: "I designed and built the building which includes an 8x8 fountain area and circular stairway to offer area. I have counters and shelves which are moved from time to time. Operation also includes handtools and solid brass hardware for woodworkers (and my own woodworking). Most items (except jewelry which is in cases) are moved every 30 days; entire shop is rearranged at least every 3 months. There is ample display space (1,200 square feet) and only pieces of highest quality and design are offered; also services such as wrapping and delivery. We serve an area from Buffalo to Syracuse plus visitors from all over the US. Most customers are middle class, except for a substantial number of doctors and their wives. Our customers are very loyal."

A TOUCH OF WHIMSY, 210 Central Park S., Suite 14B, New York NY 10019. (212)246-5320. President: Joan Rowland. Crafts gallery. Estab. 1973. Represents 150 craftworkers. Considers all crafts. Fine one-of-a-kind pieces. Price range: $10-2,500; bestsellers: $10-500.
Terms: Works on consignment; 50% commission. Retail price set by joint agreement. Reports in 1 week. Work may be shipped or hand-delivered. Dealer pays insurance for exhibited work. Make appointment.
Profile: "We have special invitational events, often for 1 day only. We specialize in social and political satire." Best selling time: winter and spring.

TWO RIVERS GALLERY/ROBERSON CENTER FOR THE ARTS & SCIENCES, 22 Front St., Binghamton NY 13905. (607)723-6921. Director: Mrs. Judith M. Carey. Craft shop/gallery/rental gallery. Represents 100 craftworkers.
Acceptable Work: Considers batik; ceramics; clothing; dollmaking; glass art; jewelry; leatherworking; quilting; soft sculpture; wall hangings; weavings; and woodcrafting. Especially needs clothing and ceramic sculpture. Fine one-of-a-kind and handmade production-line items. Price range: $2.25-400; bestsellers: $20-55.
Terms: Works on consignment; 35% commission. Craftworker sets retail price. Reports in 3 weeks. Work may be shipped or hand-delivered. Dealer pays return shipping and insurance for exhibited work during annual Christmas show only.
Profile: Museum has quality exhibit design; time period of display depends on artist, usually not more than 6 months; clientele is very sophisticated. Best selling time: Christmas and September.

THE UNCOMMON, 2079 S. Clinton Ave., Rochester NY 14618. (716)273-4981. Contact: Fran Becker. Gallery/gift shop. Estab. 1977. Represents 50-60 craftworkers. Considers ceramics; glass art; jewelry; metalsmithing; pottery; and woodcrafting. Fine one-of-a-kind and handmade production-line items; utilitarian and/or decorative (emphasis on utilitarian). Price range: $3-325; bestsellers: $5-60. Works on consignment; 40% commission. Craftworker sets retail price; gallery may advise adjustment. Requires exclusive area representation. Send slides;

work is juried. Reports in 2 weeks. Dealer pays insurance for exhibited work.
Profile: "This is a craftsman-owned shop with careful selection of crafts exhibited. The presence of School for American Craftsmen in the community has increased the awareness of crafts. Shop is located in middle to upper income area." Best selling time: Christmas and spring.

THE UNICORN CITY CORPORATION, 55 Greenwich Ave., New York NY 10014. (212)243-2017. Contact: Marty Proctor. Craft shop/gift shop. Estab. 1961. Represents 15 craftworkers. Price range: $5-1,800; bestsellers: $10-25. Works on consignment and buys outright; 50% commission. Gallery sets retail price. Requires exclusive area representation. Reports in 3 weeks. Work may be shipped. Best selling time: Christmas.
Acceptable Work: Considers batik; candlemaking; ceramics; dollmaking; glass art; jewelry; leatherworking; metalsmithing; pottery; soft sculpture; wall hangings; and weavings. Only uses unicorn designs. All styles.

VERZYL GALLERY, 377 Rt. 25A, Northport NY 11768. (516)261-8962. Director: June C. Verzyl. Considers ceramics; pottery; and sculpture. Works on consignment; 33% commission. Minimum price: $100, sculpture; bestsellers: $200-800. Craftworker sets retail prices, but gallery will not exhibit work Verzyl feels is overpriced. "No exclusive representation, but we hope an artist will not overextend in the area. We welcome artists at any time during business hours." One-man shows are given 3 weeks exposure.

VILLAGE CRAFTS & CURIOS, 17 Church St., Greenwich NY 12834. (518)692-2281. Contact: Helen A. Hoag. Craft shop/gallery. Estab. 1970. Represents 75-100 craftworkers.
Acceptable Work: Considers batik, candlemaking, clothing, dollmaking, glass art, jewelry, leatherworking, metalsmithing, needlecrafts, pottery, quilting, wall hangings, weavings, woodcrafting, and especially enameling. Especially needs good leather bags of simple design. "No cutesy items. One-of-a-kind and handmade production-line items. Price range: $1-700; bestsellers: 50¢-$10.
Terms: Buys outright and sometimes works on consignment; 30% commission. Retail price set by joint agreement. Requires exclusive area representation. Send slides. Reports in 3 weeks. Work may be shipped or hand-delivered.
Profile: "We are a small high-class craft shop in my home. We rotate displays approximately twice a month. We try to be very careful in selection of crafts—color and placement are very important to us. We take only original designs." Customers: many young adults, elderly, summer tourists and college associated people. Heaviest wholesale buying time: February and June; best selling time: summer and Christmas.

THE VILLAGE SILVERSMITH, 149 Main St., Bellport NY 11713. (516)286-1660. Contact: Dwight Trujillo. Craft shop. Estab. 1970. Represents 5-8 craftworkers. Price range: $5-700; bestsellers: $5-50. Works on consignment and buys outright; 33⅓% commission. Retail price by joint agreement. Requires exclusive area representation. Reports in 3 weeks. Work may be shipped or hand-delivered. Dealer pays return shipping and insurance for exhibited work.
Acceptable Work: Considers ceramics; glass art; jewelry; leatherworking; metalsmithing; wall hangings; weavings; and woodcrafting.
Profile: "All crafts are displayed in lighted cases and mingled with other craftsmen's work. We have wall and counter cases plus large front windows." Work is displayed 1-3 months. "We aim for the 18-40 age group when designing." Heaviest wholesale buying time: summer and winter; best selling time: spring and winter.

WARD-NASSE GALLERY, 178 & 131 Prince St., New York NY 10012. (212)925-6951 or 475-9125. Director: Harry Nasse. Price range: $3-3,000, sculpture; bestsellers: $100-300. Works on consignment; no commission. Artist sets retail price. Query. Gallery pays insurance for exhibited work. "This is an artist-run gallery and members vote in January and June to determine which artists are exhibited."

THE WEAVING PLACE LTD., 1038 New York Ave., Huntington Station NY 11746. (516)271-6434. President: Louise Orkin. Secretary/Treasurer: Cecile Kramer. Gallery/weaving shop/school. Estab. 1977. Represents 7 craftworkers.
Acceptable Work: Considers soft sculpture, wall hangings and weavings. Specializes in all types of woven wall hangings, handcrafted baskets, crochet, macrame hangings, placemats and novelty woven pieces. One-of-a-kind items only. Price range: $5-350.
Terms: Works on consignment; 33⅓% commission. Craftworker must sign consignment

agreement. Retail price set by joint agreement. Call for appointment with SASE. Reports in 2 weeks. Work may be shipped or hand delivered. Dealer pays insurance on exhibited work.
Profile: "We are located in an old house. Antiques are downstairs and The Weaving Place is upstairs. The gallery at this time would rank third (first classes; second—supplies). We are trying to generate interest in buying finished work. Weavings are hung throughout the shop and in our hall gallery." Customers: ages 18-65, upper incomes, suburban women. Best selling time: Christmas.

WEBER GALLERIES, 7863 Thompson Rd., N. Syracuse NY 13212. (315)458-7855. Contact: Jo Weber. Craft shop/gallery/school/supply shop. Estab. 1977. Represents 10-12 craftworkers.
Acceptable Work: Considers glass art, pottery, wall hangings, weavings, woodcrafting, unique clothing, jewelry, leatherworking, metalsmithing, soft sculpture and functional pottery. Specializes in fine contemporary crafts. One-of-a-kind and handmade production-line items. Price range: $2-350; bestsellers: $4-90.
Terms: Works on consignment; 35% commission. Craftworker sets retail price. Send slides with SASE or call for appointment (bringing samples). Reports in 1 week. Work may be shipped or hand delivered. "Crafts must be priced (tags or labels) and we must be provided with a dated list of all items."
Profile: "We are located in a large old 2-room school house; 1 room is for the art supply store and craft sales; the halls are for monthly shows of arts and crafts, and the second room is used for classes. There is a usual gallery array of assorted white boxes and platforms which are moved constantly to look fresh." Customers: generally professionals, students, artists. Best selling time: April-Christmas.

WESTLAKE GALLERY LTD., 210 E. Post Rd., White Plains NY 10601. (914)682-8123. Vice President: Catharine Westlake. Gallery. Estab. 1976. Represents 75 craftworkers.
Acceptable Work: Considers batik, clothing, glass art, jewelry, leatherworking, pottery, soft sculpture, wall hangings, weavings and woodcrafting. Specializes in quality contemporary collectable crafts. One-of-a-kind and handmade production-line items OK. Price range: $2-2,000; bestsellers: $20-150.
Terms: Buys outright and works on consignment; 50% markup on items bought outright, 40% commission on consignment pieces. Craftworker sets retail price ("we are also happy to advise on pricing"). Requires exclusive area representation. Send slides or call for appointment. "Items on consignment will be insured at the artist's price as opposed to retail price."
Profile: "Westlake Gallery is a fine art and craft gallery geared to the collector. We also do custom framing, restoration and appraisals. The main gallery space is 20x60'. The mezzanine is 32x32'. Our fine art and sculpture exhibits change every 6 weeks and in addition to our permanent collection of crafts, special crafts exhibitions are held several times a year. Careful consideration is given to display each item to its best advantage using pedestals, fabrics, special jewelry cases and display counters. Items on consignment are held for varying periods of time agreed upon by artist and gallery in advance. Many of our customers are collectors, quite knowledgeable in choosing quality crafts. We have many special events and exhibits which serve to educate the public in the areas of fine art and craft, thereby creating new collectors. Most buying is done during February and June for delivery throughout the year." Best selling time: Christmas and spring.
To Break In: "Be professional, deliver work when promised. Be prepared to supply technical and biographical information and publicity photos for special exhibitions. We often request information far in advance of shows so we can properly prepare publicty and invitations. Having both work and information on time benefits both gallery and craftspeople."

THE WHEELBARROW, 135 Main St., Cold Spring Harbor, Long Island NY 11724. (516)367-4604. Contact: Mrs. Mahan. Craft shop/gallery/gift shop. Estab. 1967. Represents 300 craftworkers. Considers all crafts except candlemaking. All styles. Price range: $1-300; bestsellers; $5-50. Works some on consignment and buys outright; commission negotiable. Shop sets retail price. Requires exclusive area representation. Insurance for exhibited work negotiable.
Profile: "We are in a historic area; our crafts are all American." Best selling time: Christmas.

THE WHIMSEY CRAFTSHOP & GALLERY, Lake Rd., Aurora NY 13026. (315)364-8486. Contact: Judith Erdely. Craft shop/gallery. Estab. 1971. Represents 30 craftworkers.
Acceptable Work: Considers all crafts. Especially needs quilts. One-of-a-kind designer pieces, handmade production-line items and primitive pieces. Price range: 50¢-$150; bestsellers: 50¢-$25.

Terms: Works on consignment and buys outright; 33% commission. Retail price set by joint agreement. Reports in 1 month. Work may be shipped or hand-delivered. Dealer pays insurance for exhibited work.
Profile: "We hold special shows lasting from 1 weekend to 1 month. Unless it is a show, all work is dispersed throughout shop although larger works find their way to the top or other special areas." Heaviest wholesale buying time: summer and winter; best selling time: fall and spring.

WHITE UNICORN GALLERY, 15 N. Buckhaut St., Irvington NY 10533. (914)591-7545. President: Doris Brown. Vice-President: John Brown. Craft/gift/supply shop and gallery. Estab. 1975. Represents 15-20 craftworkers.
Acceptable Work: Considers all crafts except clothing. One-of-a-kind items only. Price range: $3-400; bestsellers: $4-40.
Terms: Buys outright and works on consignment; 30% commission. Shop sets retail price. "Price is based on what craftworker wants for it." Requires exclusive area representation. Call for appointment. Reports in 1 week. Work may be shipped or hand delivered.
Profile: Located in Victorian house. Has 3 rooms (900 square feet) and a hall used for crafts ("mixed with needlepoint displays and antiques"). Also has modern building addition (1,000 square feet) used as a gallery for painting and sculpture. Customers: upper incomes; suburbanites; executives, commuters, writers, artists; college aged married couples; and wealthy retired folks. Heaviest wholesale buying and best selling time: spring and Christmas.

THE WICKER GARDEN, INC., 1318 Madison Ave., New York NY 10028. (212)348-1166. President: Pamela McGinley Scurry. Gift shop. Estab. 1977. Represents 125 craftworkers.
Acceptable Work: Considers applique, dollmaking, pillows and quilting. Especially needs unusual, bright colored pillows, toys for boys, and children's things. Fine handmade production-line items. Price range: $3-300; bestsellers: $7.50-30.
Terms: Buys outright. Shop sets retail price. Reports in 1 week. Work may be mailed or shipped. Dealer pays return shipping; in-transit insurance; and insurance for exhibited work.
Profile: "Work is displayed amidst antique Victorian wicker that is repaired to perfection and set in a bright garden atmosphere. The color is lime green and white. The shop and/or its items have been shown in 40 magazines during the past 2 years. The accessories that complement the wicker are brightly colored pillows, quilts, baby toys, silk flowers, silkscreens, handpainted picnic baskets, aprons, pillows and umbrellas. The colors are lime greens, lemon yellow, pure white, hot pinks, cornflower blue, pastels and lots of laces. Customers are 30-45 years of age, well-traveled, educated, upper-middle class and expect super quality for good price value."

WILKES GALLERY, INC., 101 Main St., Northport NY 11768. (516)261-4007. Contact: John or Jeannette Cuomo. Craft shop/gallery/gift shop. Estab. 1968. Represents 12-20 craftworkers. Price range: $2.50-100; bestsellers: $1.50-50. Works on consignment; 40% commission. Retail price set by joint agreement. Requires exclusive area representation. Work may be shipped or hand-delivered. Dealer pays insurance for exhibited work.
Acceptable Work: Considers batik; ceramics; decoupage; jewelry; leatherworking; metalsmithing; pottery; wall hangings; weavings; and woodcrafting. Especially needs work with a fishing or nautical theme. All styles.
Profile: Shop has "window displays as we are located on Main Street, with overwhelming walk by traffic; also additional items in several local newpapers announcing new crafts." Heaviest wholesale buying time: summer and November-December; best selling time: July-August.

WILL-O-THE-WICK, LTD., 1138 Lexington Ave., New York NY 10021. (212)535-1558. Contact: H. Cascante. Candle store. Estab. 1973. Represents 6 craftworkers. Considers candlemaking. Especially needs a wide range of novelty candles. Price range: $3-25; bestsellers: $5-18. Buys outright. Reports in 2 weeks. Work may be shipped or hand-delivered. Dealer pays insurance for exhibited work.
Profile: Items are placed immediately on display; no special time limit. Customers are in the middle and upper income brackets. Bestselling and heaviest wholesale buying time: fall.
To Break In: "Artists should do some research first. Find out from potential buyers what they want. Develop a line that is different, not a variation or copy of what many others are already doing."

WINDOW ON MAIN STREET, Box 575, Naples NY 14512. (716)374-5050. Manager: Judith Reifsnyder. Gallery. Estab. 1976. Represents 20 craftworkers.
Acceptable Work: Considers ceramics; glass art; jewelry; metalsmithing; pottery; wall hang-

ings; weavings; and woodcrafting. Emphasis is on one-of-a-kind designer pieces. Price range: $6-1,000; bestsellers: $6-35.
Terms: Works on consignment; 35% commission. Craftworker sets retail price. Reports in 4 weeks. Hand-delivered work only.
Profile: "We're a cooperative gallery run by artists. Membership dues are $18 per year; a member may have a show and also keep work on display for the April-December season. We are located in a tourist and culturally active area." Best selling time: July, August-October and December.

WONDROUS THINGS, INC., Rt. 129, Croton-on-Hudson NY 10520. (914)271-3044. Contact any officer. Craft shop/gift shop. Estab. 1972. Represents 100 craftworkers. Price range: $3-165; bestsellers: $3-$15. Works on consignment and buys outright; 30% commission. Craftworker sets retail price. Reports in 4 weeks. Work may be shipped or hand-delivered after contracted.
Acceptable Work: Considers all crafts except clothing. Especially needs stained glass; leather; and wrought iron. Fine one-of-a-kind and handmade production-line items.
Profile: "We feature handmade gifts; we sell supplies and we give classes in silver jewelry, pottery, stained glass and watercolor painting."

THE WORKS GALLERY EAST, INC., 28 Jobs Lane, Southampton NY 11968. (516)283-1407. Contact: John Albano or Frank Pereira. Gallery. Estab. 1976. Represents 40-50 craftworkers. Price range: $20-2,000; bestsellers: $50-300. Works on consignment and buys outright; 40% commission. Retail price set by joint agreement. Requires exclusive area representation. Reports in 2-3 weeks. Work may be shipped or hand-delivered. Dealer pays shipping to shop and insurance for exhibited work. "Customers are extremely wealthy New Yorkers, 30-50 years of age, who appreciate good work." Heaviest wholesale buying time: early spring; best selling time: summer.
Acceptable Work: Considers batik; ceramics; glass art; jewelry; leatherworking; metalsmithing; pottery; quilting; soft sculpture; wall hangings; weavings; and woodcrafting. One-of-a-kind designer pieces.

North Carolina

ACT 1, GALLERY, 111 E. Caswell St., Kinston NC 28501. (919)527-2517. Director: Pat Crawford. Gallery Manager: Susan Parrot. Associate Director: Steve Peeples. Craft shop/gallery. Estab. 1977. Represents 5-10 craftworkers.
Acceptable Work: Considers ceramics, glass art, pottery, wall hangings, and especially needs batik, jewelry, leatherworking, metalsmithing and weavings. "We still encourage pottery and ceramics sales, but these are more easily available in our area." Fine one-of-a-kind pieces. Price range: $3-500; bestsellers: $10-50.
Terms: Works on consignment; 25% commission. Craftworker sets retail price. Reports in 2 weeks. Work may be shipped or hand-delivered. Dealer pays insurance on exhibited work.
Profile: "Items are displayed on shelves within view from street. Featured items are placed in street windows." Best selling time: fall.

ALLANSTAND, 16 College St., Asheville NC 28801. (704)253-2051. Manager: Mary Hudson. Craft shop. Estab. 1930. Represents over 100 member Appalachian craftworkers.
Acceptable Work: Considers batik, ceramics, dollmaking, glass art, jewelry, leatherworking, metalsmithing, needlecrafts, pottery, quilting, soft sculpture, wall hangings, weavings, woodcrafting, print making, toys, vegetable dyed yarns and anything made with native materials. Specializes in traditional and contemporary designer and handmade production-line items. Price range: $1-700; least expensive bestsellers: $5-20; most expensive bestsellers: $300-400.
Terms: Must be a member of the Southern Highland Handicraft Guild; membership strictly judged by Standards Committee and Board of Trustees; open to craftworkers living and working in Southern Appalachian Mountain Region. Buys outright. Craftworker sets wholesale price; shop doubles for retail. Work may be shipped or hand-delivered; guild shop pays for all shipping and insurance.
Profile: "We attempt to display each craftsman's work to its very best advantage. We like getting a firm commitment—especially on delivery times!" Best selling time: Easter-Christmas.

BLUE RIDGE HEARTHSIDE CRAFTS, Box 1388, Boone NC 28607. (704)264-9078. General Manager: Joe Patelidas. Craft shop/wholesaler. Estab. 1968. Represents members only.
Acceptable Work: Considers batik, candlemaking, ceramics, clothing, dollmaking, glass art,

jewelry, leatherworking, metalsmithing, needlecrafts, pottery, quilting, soft sculpture, wall hangings, weavings and woodcrafting. Specializes in traditional and contemporary crafts. One-of-a-kind and handmade production-line items. Price range: 50¢-$1,000; bestsellers: 50¢-$250.
Terms: Buys outright. Retail price set by joint agreement. Reports in 2 weeks. Send resume. SASE. Work may be shipped or hand-delivered. Dealer pays shipping.
Profile: Customers: middle to high incomes. Best selling time: summer and fall.

THE CALICO KITTEN, Box 57, Beaufort NC 28516. Contact: Mrs. Bill Rike. Gift shop. Estab. 1977. Represents 15 craftworkers.
Acceptable Work: Considers batik, ceramics, clothing, jewelry, needlecrafts, pottery, quilting, soft sculpture, wall hangings, weavings and woodcrafting. Especially needs baby gifts, unique toys, and accessories for contemporary families (wall hangings, soft sculptures). Specializes in contemporary and Appalachian crafts. One-of-a-kind and handmade production-line items. Price range; $2-500; bestsellers: $5-60.
Terms: Buys outright and works on consignment; 35-40% commission. Sometimes takes special orders from customers. Retail price set by joint agreement. Prefers exclusive area representation. Send resume, brochure and slides. Reports in 2 weeks. Dealer pays insurance on exhibited work.
Profile: "We have contemporary decor with eye-catching natural wood shelving and walls. New items are displayed immediately (whenever possible) and there is a 2 week change of major displays." Customers: ages 25-40; upper middle incomes, local people, tourists (in summer especially). Heaviest wholesale buying time: spring and fall; best selling time: summer and fall.

JOHN C. CAMPBELL FOLK SCHOOL, Rt. 1, Brasstown NC 28902. (704)837-2775. Manager: Gladys Rogers. Craft shop. Estab. 1925. Represents 55 craftworkers. Works on consignment and buys outright; 30% commission. Retail price set by joint agreement. Reports in 2 weeks. Hand-delivered work only.
Acceptable Work: Considers candlemaking; jewelry; leatherworking; metalsmithing; pottery; soft sculpture; wall hangings; weavings; and woodcrafting. Especially needs quilting and stitchery. Price range: 50¢-$200; bestsellers: 50¢-$80.
Profile: "We are in a rural mountain setting, located within a folk school." Heaviest wholesale buying time: winter; best selling time: summer.

CAROLINA ARTS GALLERY, 3300 Womans Club Dr., Raleigh NC 27612. (919)782-2533. Director: Mary S. Proctor. Craft shop of the Raleigh Womans Club. Estab. 1950. Represents North Carolina craftworkers only. Call or write for appointment. Reports in 1 week. Work may be shipped or hand delivered.
Acceptable Work: Considers ceramics, glass art, jewelry, metalsmithing, limited needlecrafts, pottery, wall hangings, weavings and woodcrafting. One-of-a-kind and production-line items. Price range: $2.50-50; bestsellers: $2.50-25. Works on consignment: 33⅓% commission. Shop sets retail price.
Profile: "Traffic at our gallery depends on club activities and activities from rental of club facilities—we do not do any advertising; however, we are realizing an increase in business from the general public."

CAROLINA MOUNTAIN ARTS & CRAFTS, Box 573, Murphy NC 28906. (704)644-5688. Contact: Manager. Estab. 1973. Represents 550 North Carolina, Tennessee and Georgia member craftworkers. Best selling time: Easter-Thanksgiving.
Acceptable Work: Considers candlemaking; ceramics; decoupage; dollmaking; jewelry; leatherworking; metalsmithing; needlecrafts; pottery; macrame; quilting; tole painting; wall hangings; weavings; and woodcrafting. Price range: $1-200; bestsellers: $3-5.
Terms: Works on consignment; 40% commission. Craftworker sets retail price. Write or visit shop. Reports in 2-3 weeks.

CAROLISTA JEWELRY DESIGNERS, 137 E. Rosemary St., Chapel Hill NC 27514 (summer: May-September, Box 201, Nags Head NC 27959). Contact: W. G. Baum. Estab. 1962. Considers ceramics; sculpture; tapestries; woven objects; glass; tie dye; and batik. Price range: $5-3,000. Work taken on consignment first year; often bought outright afterwards. 25-40% commission. Requires exclusive area representation. Send resume.

THE CENTER SHOP, 750 Marguerite Dr., Winston-Salem NC 27106. (919)725-1904. Manager:

Sandy Whitworth. Museum gift shop. Estab. 1977. Represents 40 craftworkers.
Acceptable Work: Considers batik, candlemaking, ceramics, jewelry, leatherworking, pottery, soft sculpture, wall hangings and weavings. Exhibits contemporary work. One-of-a-kind and handmade production-line items OK. Price range: $4.50-1,100; bestsellers: $20-40.
Terms: Buys outright and works on consignment; 33⅓% commission. Craftworker sets retail price. Send resume and slides. Work may be shipped or hand-delivered. Dealer pays insurance on exhibited work.

THE COUNTRY COTTAGE, Rt. 1, Box 295A, Beulaville NC 28518. (919)298-3771. Contact: Mrs. Jean C. Sanderson. Craft/gift shop. Estab. 1974. Represents 5-6 craftworkers.
Acceptable Work: Considers ceramics, decoupage, needlecrafts, quilting, tole painting, woodcrafting or flower arrangements. Especially needs leatherworking, pottery, weavings, candles and handmade Christmas ornaments. "We exhibit traditional, decorative and useful handmade things that are not extremely expensive. Also bright colors—things for the home." One-of-a-kind and handmade production-line items. Price range: $2-300; bestsellers: $2-25.
Terms: Works on consignment until sees how they sell; 25% commission. Also special orders from sample. Dealer pays insurance on exhibited work but not on shipping. Retail price set by joint agreement. Call for appointment (if local) or write with SASE (out-of-town). Reports in 3 weeks. Work may be shipped (if insured) or hand delivered.
Profile: "We are located in a little red barn (with brick floors and checked curtains) on our farm, 3 miles from Beulaville, 30 miles from Jacksonville, Goldsboro, and Kinston. We sell brass, pewter, candles, baskets, dried and silk flowers, Armetale, children's gifts and craft supplies. Our displays are on rough wood shelving, barrels and ladders and we display to the best advantage of each item. If it needs extra protection, it goes in glass cases. We usually leave items for as long as the craftworker desires, unless no interest is shown. This is primarily a farming area. However, many customers are with local textile and poultry industries. They include middle to upper middle class incomes. They also enjoy beautiful things and appreciate handcrafts. Many bring out-of-town guests 'out to the shop on the farm.' " Heaviest wholesale buying and best selling time: fall-Christmas; slowest is summer.

GOLDSBORO ART CENTER, Herman Park Center, 901-A E. Ash St. Goldsboro NC 27530. (919)736-3335. Gallery. Estab. 1971. Represents 90 craftworkers. Price range: $1-500; bestsellers: $5-50. Works on consignment; 20% commission. Craftworker sets retail price. Reports in 1 week. Work may be shipped or hand-delivered. Dealer pays return shipping and insurance for exhibited work.
Acceptable Work: Considers batik; dollmaking; jewelry; pottery; wall hangings; and weavings. Especially needs weavings and batik. Fine one-of-a-kind and handmade production-line items; utilitarian and/or decorative.
Profile: "We sell and exhibit only original art, no reproductions of any kind; we are completely nonprofit and we have classes and monthly exhibits." Best selling time: summer and Christmas.

GRANNY'S CLOSET, Rt. 3, Box 283, Plymouth NC 27962. (919)793-5944. Contact: Juanita or Mary Lee Ambrose. Estab. 1972. Represents 10 craftworkers.
Acceptable Work: Considers needlecrafts, quilting and woodcrafting. Specializes in needlework (counted cross-stitch, crewel, needlepoint), quilts, pocketbooks and macrame. Handmade production-line items. Price range: $12-165; bestsellers: $10-25.
Terms: Works on consignment; 30% commission. Craftworker sets retail price. Stop at shop with work. Reports in 4 weeks. Work must be hand-delivered.
Profile: "We carry a large line of needlework supplies and sell quite a lot during the year, especially during the holidays for customers wanting to do thier own thing. Our items are often seen, and then customers go home and copy the item. Around Christmas, we do a great deal of business in our gift line." Customers: ages 12-80; moderate incomes; many out-of-towners. Best selling time: Christmas.

GREEN HILL ART GALLERY, INC., 712 Summit Ave., Greensboro NC 27405. (919)273-6696. Contact: Executive Director. Nonprofit, educational facility. Gallery. Estab. 1974. Exhibits only original works of North Carolina artists.
Acceptable Work: Considers all crafts, 2-D and 3-D. Group, educational, theme exhibitions; utilitarian and decorative. Price ranges: $10-900; bestsellers: $10-200.
Terms: Exhibits only; 25% commission. Craftworker sets price. Reports in 4 weeks. Work may be shipped or hand-delivered if selected to exhibit. Gallery insures all exhibits. Artists/craftsmen should submit slides and resume, slides returned within 20 days.

GUILD CRAFTS, 930 Tunnel Rd., Asheville NC 28805. (704)298-7903. Manager: Louise Bell. Craft shop. Estab. 1954. Represents over 100 member Appalachian craftworkers.
Acceptable Work: Considers batik, ceramics, dollmaking, glass art, jewelry, leatherworking, metalsmithing, needlecrafts, pottery, quilting, soft sculpture, wall hangings, weavings, woodcrafting, print making, toys, vegetable dyed yarns and anything made with native materials. Specializes in traditional and contemporary designer and handmade production-line items. Price range: $1-700; least expensive bestsellers: $5-20; most expensive bestsellers: $300-400.
Terms: Must be a member of the Southern Highland Handicraft Guild; membership strictly judged by Standards Committee and Board of Trustees; open to craftsmen living and working in Southern Appalachian Mountain Region. Buys outright. Craftworker sets his wholesale price; shop doubles for retail. Work may be shipped or hand delivered. Guild shop pays for all insurance.
Profile: "We attempt to display each craftsman's work to its very best advantage. We like getting a firm commitment—especially on delivery times!" Best selling time: Easter-Christmas.

HIGH POINT MUSEUM CRAFT SHOP, 1805 E. Lexington Ave., High Point NC 27262. Shop Manager: Linda Gill. Craft museum gift/craft shop. Estab. 1971. Represents only a few craftworkers.
Acceptable Work: Considers candlemaking, ceramics, dollmaking, jewelry, leatherworking, metalsmithing, needlecrafts, and pottery. Especially needs quilting, tole painting and weavings. One-of-a-kind and handmade production-line items. Price range: $4.50-20; bestsellers: $5-8.
Terms: Buys outright. Shop sets retail price. Requires exclusive area representation; "but not totally enforced." Send resume or call for appointment. Reports in 1 week. Work may be shipped or hand-delivered. "We would like to write special articles in the newspaper about the craftsperson and their work prior to the exhibit and handling of the items. We would also like to have the craftsperson be present at the museum with his work on a specially publicized Sunday or Saturday afternoon."
Profile: "We are a small museum gift shop run entirely by volunteers of the Museum Guild." Customers: school children (ages 8-15); college-age adults (ages 18-25); special groups (garden clubs, societies); and out-of-town visitors and families. Heaviest wholesale buying time: summer; best selling time: fall.

INDIAN MUSEUM OF THE CAROLINAS, 607 Turnpike Rd., Laurinburg NC 28352. (919)276-5880. Director: Michael R. Sellon. Museum gift shop. Estab. 1972. Represents 6-8 craftworkers; American Indian crafts only.
Acceptable Work: Considers dollmaking; jewelry, cornhusk dolls; and stone arrow points. Handmade production-line items; utilitarian and/or decorative. Price range: 50¢-$20; bestsellers: 50¢-$8.95.
Terms: Buys outright. Reports in 2 weeks. Museum sets retail price. Shipment is negotiated. Dealer pays insurance for exhibited work.
Profile: "We display exceptional works for periods of up to 1 month." Best selling time: November and May.

JUGTOWN POTTERY, Rt. 2, Seagrove NC 27341. (919)464-3266. Directors: Nancy Sweezy or Vernon Owens. Craft shop. Estab. 1921. Represents 25 craftworkers.
Acceptable Work: Considers candlemaking, dollmaking, needlecrafts, quilting, wall hangings, weavings and woodcrafting. Specializes in Appalachian folkcrafts. Handmade production-line items only. Price range: $2.50-150; bestsellers $2.50-20.
Terms: Buys outright. Dealer sets retail price. Send slides. Reports in 2-3 weeks. Work may be shipped or hand delivered (only with joint agreement).
Profile: "A display is made to the item's best advantage as we see it in a log cabin shop with Jugtown pottery. The items are mixed together on tables and a variety of shelves. Handcrafts, mostly pottery, is made here in a traditional style. We are well established in North Carolina and have visitors from all states in the US and many foreign countries." Customers: middle and upper incomes with interests in homes/gardens and academics. Heaviest wholesale buying time: late summer-early fall; best selling time: fall, summer, spring.

THE KILN ROOM, Box 145A, Rt. 1, Banner Elk NC 28604. (704)963-5865. Contact: Lee Magdanz. Craft shop and pottery studio. Estab. 1973. Represents 25-30 American craftworkers. Send resume and slides. Reports in 3 weeks. Work may be shipped or hand-delivered.
Acceptable Work: Considers batik, candlemaking, glass art, jewelry, leatherworking, metal-

smithing, pottery, scrimshaw and woodcrafting. Especially needs handwoven placemats, beads, greeting and note cards, buckles, windchimes and candles. One-of-a-kind and handmade production-line items. Price range $1-200; bestsellers: $5-20. Buys outright and works on consignment; 30% commission. Retail price set by joint agreement.
Profile:"We are a craft shop/pottery studio on a creek with a trout pond—done in an old wood barn within the Million Dollar Summer and Winter Resort Area in the Western North Carolina Mountains. We make arrangements, in a rustic setting, which show work off well for the type it is." Heaviest wholesale buying and best selling time: June-August.
Profile: "Be consistent, available and reasonable in price.

KINSTON ARTS COUNCIL, 111 E. Caswell St., Kinston NC 28501. (919)527-2517. Director: Pat Crawford. Associate Director: Steve Peeples. Gallery/arts council. Estab. 1965. Represents 5-10 craftworkers.
Acceptable Work: Considers batik; ceramics; glass art; jewelry; leatherworking; metalsmithing; needlecrafts; pottery; quilting; soft sculpture; tole painting; wall hangings; weavings and woodcrafting. Especially needs jewelry and metalsmithing. Fine one-of-a-kind pieces; utilitarian and/or decorative. Price range: $4-75; bestsellers: $4-35. Works on consignment; 20% commission.
Terms: Craftworker sets retail price. Reports in 2 weeks. Work may be shipped or hand-delivered. Dealer pays insurance for exhibited work.
Profile: "All crafts are placed on shelves which are highly visible to the street and gallery. We handle only one-of-a-kind fine art crafts and, since we operate as an arts council, there is a ready made clientele in the people who use the building." Heaviest wholesale buying time: summer-fall; best selling time: fall-winter.

LITTLE ART GALLERY, North Hills Mall, Raleigh NC 27609. (919)787-6317. Contact: Ruth Green. Craft shop/gallery. Estab. 1968. Represents 50 craftworkers.
Acceptable Work: Considers glass art; jewelry; pottery; wall hangings; and weavings. "I would like a good weaving exhibit on consignment. Most of the weavers will only sell, and I feel I have a market, if I can keep the work for 4-6 months." Price range: $6-300; bestsellers: $15-50.
Terms: Works on consignment and buys outright; 40% commission. Craftworker sets retail price. Work may be shipped or hand-delivered. Dealer pays shipping.
Profile: "A show is up for 1 month. Work is on various walls and stands; our regular contributors remain up." Heaviest wholesale buying time: August; best selling time: Christmas.

MACO CRAFTS, INC., Rt. 2, Box 1190, Franklin NC 28734. (704)524-7878. Manager: Margaret Ramsey. Represents 250 local craftworkers. Considers quilts and furniture. Finished, one-of-a-kind and handmade production-line items only. Price range: $1-385; bestsellers: $5-235. Retail price set by joint agreement. "15% commission for craftsmen that work in the shop as volunteers 8 hours a month only." Write. Reports immediately. Dealer pays shipping to shop. Best selling time: summer and fall. Customers buy crafts to use as unusual gifts.

MIDLAND CRAFTERS, INC., Box 100, Pinehurst NC 28374. (919)295-6156. Contact: Mr. or Mrs. R.F. Stearn. Gallery/gift shop. Estab. 1960. Represents 1,500 craftworkers. Considers all crafts. All styles; utilitarian and/or decorative. Price range: 15¢-$4,500; bestsellers: $2-30. Works on consignment and buys outright. Gallery sets retail price. Requires exclusive area representation. Reports in 1 week. Work may be shipped or hand-delivered. Dealer pays shipping to shop on purchased items.
Profile: "We're located in an old weaving mill. Display is our specialty with work of each crafter shown in lighted niche or grouped on counter." Heaviest wholesale buying time: late winter and early fall; best selling time: spring and late fall.

NECESSITIES, INC., 1308 Dixie Trail, Raleigh NC 27607. (919)781-5298. Contact: Becky W. Penny. Gallery/gift shop. Estab. 1975. Represents 10 craftworkers. Best selling and heaviest wholesale buying time: fall and winter.
Acceptable Work: Considers batik; clothing; dollmaking; glass art; jewelry; metalsmithing; needlecrafts; pottery; wall hangings; weavings; and woodcrafting. Price range: $5-750; bestsellers: $5-150. Works on consignment and buys outright; 25% commission. Craftworker sets retail price. Reports in 1 week. Work may be shipped or hand-delivered. Displays work 3 months maximum.

NEW MORNING GALLERY, 7 Boston Way, Asheville NC 28803. (704)274-2831. Contact: John Cram. Craft shop/gallery. Estab. 1972. Represents 200 craftworkers.
Acceptable Work: Considers ceramics; furniture; glass art; jewelry; and pottery. Fine one-of-a-kind and handmade production-line items; utilitarian and/or decorative. Price range: $4-4,000; bestsellers: $4.50-60.
Terms: Works on consignment and buys outright; 40% commission. Craftworker sets retail price. Requires exclusive area representation. Reports in 1 week. Work may be shipped or hand-delivered with prior agreement. Dealer pays shipping to shop and insurance for exhibited work. Shows are 1 month or more.
Profile: "We have an extensive display system of oak shelving and a wall oak glass case for art glass." Best selling time: summer and Christmas.

NORTH CAROLINA LEAGUE OF CREATIVE ARTS & CRAFTS, INC., 115 Brookstown Ave., Winston-Salem NC 27101. (919)723-4800. President: Betty Place. Art and craft shop. Estab. 1975. Represents 200-250 artists and craftworkers.
Acceptable Work: Considers all crafts except ceramics; patterns; and kits. Especially needs glass; leather, other than belts; weavings; and original stitchery. Price range: 75¢-$800; bestsellers: $3-30.
Terms: Works on consignment; 33⅓% commission. Retail price set by joint agreement. Work may be shipped or hand-delivered. Reports immediately. Dealer pays insurance for exhibited work. Work is displayed 3-6 months.
Profile: "We are a total way of life for an artist or craftsperson to work. Resident craftworker pays on $20-30/month rent and takes 80% of sales." Heaviest wholesale buying time: summer and early fall; best selling time: March-June and October-December.

NORTH CAROLINA MUSEUM OF ART—THE MUSEUM STORE, 107 E. Morgan St., Raleigh NC 27611. (919)733-3288. Manager: Mrs. Frances H. Myers. Museum gift shop. Estab. 1956. Represents 8 regional craftworkers.
Acceptable Work: Considers jewelry only. "Present space is very limited for display of craft items, but a future store in a new building, to be occupied sometime in 1980-1, should have space for expanded inventory." Especially needs jewelry around $25. "We show mostly silver and brass/bronze." One-of-a-kind and handmade production-line items. Price range: $5-150; bestsellers: $2-18.
Terms: Buys outright. Retail price set by joint agreement; 100% markup of wholesale price. Send slides or call for appointment. SASE. "We accept pieces for consideration and then place an order for the ones we want. Craftspeople should submit goods with an untotaled invoice so that items which we do not keep can be deleted. We will total the kept items and then make arrangements for payment." Reports in 1 week. Work may be shipped or hand-delivered. Dealer pays insurance and return shipping costs.
Profile: "We immediately display a jeweler's work. Each artist's work is identified. Periodically, we may request that new items be sent in exchange for pieces not selling. Our trade depends on attendance stimulated by museum exhibits program." Customers: area residents, museum membership, adult tours, student and school groups, tourists. Heaviest wholesale buying time: pre-Christmas and pre-holidays; best selling time: Christmas.
To Break In: "Artists may provide business cards to be distributed to interested customers."

NORTHWEST GALLERY, Highway 115 and Armory Rd., North Wilkesboro NC 28659. (919)667-2841. Director: Martha Barksdale. Craft shop/gallery. Estab. 1970.
Acceptable Work: Considers batik, candlemaking, dollmaking, glass art, jewelry, needlecrafts, pottery, quilting, wall hangings, weavings and woodcrafting. Specializes in fine art designer and Appalachian crafts. Price range: $1-75; bestsellers: $1-7.50.
Terms: Works on consignment: 20% commission. Occasionally buys outright. A check is sent by the 10th of each month to the craftworker. Retail price set by joint agreement. Send resume and slides. Reports in 1 week. Work may be shipped or hand-delivered.
Profile: "We are primarily an art gallery. The craft section stays the same year around exhibiting local and mountain crafts, mostly from North Carolina. Consignment items are listed, tagged and entered in our 'Hands of Man' book. As each item is sold, this is marked on artists sheets and in the bookkeeping book." Customers: school tours and local people. Heaviest wholesale buying time: Christmas; best selling time: Christmas and June (weddings, graduation).
To Break In: "When sending consignment items, be sure they are priced with the 20% commission taken into consideration."

PARKWAY CRAFT CENTER, Blowing Rock NC 28605. Contact: Trudy Thompson (May 1-October 31) at (704)295-7938 or Robert W. Gray, James Gentry, Carol Smith (November 1-April 30) at (704)298-7928. Craft shop. Estab. 1950. Represents over 100 Appalachian craftworkers. Must be a member of the Southern Highland Handicraft Guild; membership strictly judged by Standards Committee and Board of Trustees; open to craftsmen living and working in Southern Appalachian Mountain Region. Work may be shipped or hand delivered.
Acceptable Work: batik, ceramics, dollmaking, glass art, jewelry, leatherworking, metal, needlecrafts, pottery, quilting, soft sculpture, wall hangings, weavings, woodcrafting, print making, toys, vegetable dyed yarns and anything made with native materials. Specializes in traditional and contemporary designer and handmade production-line items. Price range: $1-700; least expensive bestsellers: $5-20; most expensive bestsellers: $300-400. Buys outright. Craftworker sets his wholesale price; shop doubles for retail. Guild shop pays for all insurance.
Profile: "We attempt to display each craftsman's work to its very best advantage. This craft center is located in the historic Cone House on the Blue Ridge Parkway. Weekly demonstrators are featured showing steps in the making of the various objects which are for sale.

PIEDMONT CRAFTSMEN, INC., 300 South Main St., Winston-Salem NC 27101. (919)725-1516. Contact: Lida Lowrey. Craft shop and gallery. Estab. 1971. Represents 200 member craftworkers.
Acceptable Work: Considers batik, ceramics, clothing, glass art, jewelry, leatherworking, metalsmithing, pottery, quilting, soft sculpture, wall hangings, weavings and woodcrafting. Specializes in fine or contemporary designer and handmade production-line items. Price range: $2-3,000; bestsellers: $20-70.
Terms: Must be member of Piedmont Craftsmen, Inc.; membership is juried each spring and those eligible must come from either North or South Carolina, Georgia, Virginia, Tennessee, Alabama, Maryland or Florida. Write for jury forms at above address. Buys outright and works on consignment; 33⅓% commission. Dealer pays insurance on exhibited items. Craftworker sets retail price.
Profile: Customers: middle class homemakers and professionals. Best selling time: Christmas.

QUALLA ARTS & CRAFTS MUTUAL, INC., Box 277, Cherokee NC 28719. (704)497-3103. Manager: Betty DuPree. Indian art and craft shop. Estab. 1946. Represents 250 Eastern Cherokee Indian craftworkers. Heaviest wholesale buying time: winter; best selling time: summer.
Acceptable Work: Considers dollmaking; pottery; wall hangings; weavings; baskets; and beadwork. Primitive and fine work OK. Price range: $1.50-350.
Terms: Shop sets retail price. "We are an Indian owned and operated coop." Reports in 10 days.

RUMPELSTILTSKIN, 4 All Souls Crescent, Asheville NC 28803. (704)274-4609. Contact: Linda or Richard Biehusen. Craft/gift shop. Estab. 1977. Represents 35 craftworkers. Call or write enclosing slides/photos. Reports in 2 weeks. Work may be shipped or hand delivered.
Acceptable Work: Considers batik, candlemaking, clothing, decoupage, glass art, leatherworking, metalsmithing, wall hangings, weavings and woodcrafting. Especially needs jewelry and pottery from North Carolina and surrounding Appalachian areas. Also needs weavings, leather belts and smoking pipes (both meerschaum and briar) from any area. Specializes in contemporary work with small amount of traditional Appalachian work in summer and early fall. Price range: 35¢-200, but flexible; bestsellers: $5-20. Buys outright and works on consignment; 40% commission. Dealer pays insurance on exhibited work. Craftworker sets retail price on consigned work.
Profile: "We try to group each craftworker's items together with a name card with the grouping. Also, the craftsman's name is written on the sales slip. We try to move items around as much as possible (even whole groupings of pottery) from month to month." Heaviest wholesale buying time: spring and fall; best selling time: Christmas, late summer and early fall.
To Break In: "Pay attention to detail and quality in work. Set prices which do not put things out of reach to those who appreciate them. We are really fairly flexible and open to new things."

STAINED GLASS ASSOCIATES, Box 1531, Raleigh NC 27602. (919)266-2493. Contact: Robert J. Wysocki. Craft shop/studio. Estab. 1958. Represents 5 craftworkers.
Acceptable Work: Considers glass art; panels for individual residences and businesses. Fine one-of-a-kind pieces; utilitarian and/or decorative. Bestsellers: $57.50-585.
Term: Retail price set by joint agreement. Requires exclusive area representation. Reports in 1

week. Dealer pays return shipping and insurance for exhibited work.
Profile: "The stained glass objects are displayed within sight of the working distance and area of stained glass windows being assembled. Hanging display is used in studio area."

STONE MOUNTAIN CRAFTS, INC., Star Rt., Box 15, Traphill NC 28685. (919)957-8055. Contact: Ruth W. Holbrook. Craft shop. Estab. 1970. Represents 30 low income craftworkers.
Acceptable Work: Considers clothing, corn shuck items, denim items, dollmaking, jewelry, leatherworking, needlecrafts, quilting, woodcrafting and knitted and crocheted Christmas tree decorations. One-of-a-kind in some pieces only. Price range: 26¢-$100; bestsellers: 26¢-$26.
Terms: Works on consignment; 25% commission. Shop sets retail price. SASE. Reports in 4 weeks. Work must be hand-delivered.
Profile: "We display items in a 150 year-old building, located in the entrance to Stone Mountain State Park." Customers: low income. Heaviest wholesale buying and best selling time: summer.

STOREHOUSE, 288 N. Hills Mall, Raleigh NC 27609. See Storehouse, Inc., 2737 Apple Valley Rd. NE, Atlanta, Georgia.

THE TRADE PATH, 604 Idol Dr., High Point NC 27262. (919)869-7014. Contact: Mike or Candy Murrow. Estab. 1975. Represents 25 craftworkers, preferably North Carolina.
Acceptable Work: Considers jewelry, leatherworking, pottery, quilting, scrimshaw, stone carvings and soft sculpture. Specializes in primitive pottery and beads and fine art gold and silver jewelry. One-of-a-kind only. Price range: $1-$700; bestsellers: $5 minimum.
Terms: Buys outright, works on consignment and barters. Also takes custom orders when customer is interested in handmade original designs. Craftworker sets wholesale price; shop sets retail price. Write with SASE. Reports in 2 weeks. Work may be shipped or hand-delivered.
Profile: "Our business has 6 display cabinets consisting of: gold and ivory jewelry display; silver jewelry; pre-Columbian pottery and woven baskets; etc. Our store is a division of a furniture store across the walk. It's a very rustic store with wooden planks and shelves, and a large window plant display. We have furs and paintings on leather and skins hanging on the walls." Customers: ages 10-50; medium incomes. Heaviest wholesale buying time: after Christmas and during gem festivals in the summer; best selling time: summer-winter.

VILLAGE CRAFTSMEN, Box 248, Howard St., Ocracoke Island NC 27960. (919)928-5541. Contact: Philip or Julia Howard. Craft shop. Estab. 1970. Represents 100 craftworkers. Price range: $1-250; bestsellers: $1-50. Buys outright. Shop sets retail price. Prefers exclusive area representation. Reports as soon as possible. "Do not send unsolicited samples unless you do not need to have them returned." Work may be shipped or hand-delivered. Dealer pays shipping to shop on merchandise ordered and in-transit insurance on same.
Acceptable Work: Considers batik; candlemaking; clothing; glass art; jewelry; leatherworking; metalsmithing; needlecrafts; pottery; quilting; wall hangings; weavings; woodcrafting; wrought iron; soap; baskets; and beads. Primitive handmade production-line items; utilitarian and/or decorative.
Profile: "We are located on a turn-of-the-century picturesque sandy lane on an island off the coast of North Carolina. Although our customers are generally tourists, we stock quality-made American crafts which we display with creativity." Heaviest wholesale buying time: spring and summer; best selling time: late spring, summer and early fall.

YANCEY COUNTY COUNTRY STORE, Box 8, Town Square, Burnsville NC 28714. (704)682-3779. Contact: Mrs. G.A. Downing. Craft and gift shop. Estab. 1967. Represents 100 mountain craftworkers.
Acceptable Work: Considers candlemaking; ceramics; clothing; decoupage; dollmaking; glass art; jewelry; leatherworking; pottery; quilting; wall hangings; weavings; and woodcrafting. Primitive and fine handmade production-line items; utilitarian and/or decorative. Price range: $1-350.
Terms: Works on consignment; 25-33⅓% commission. Retail price set by joint agreement. Work may be shipped or hand-delivered. Dealer pays insurance for exhibited work.
Profile: "Our shop is like a museum, with many old things not for sale, etc. Customers are from all states and 24 foreign countries." Best selling and heaviest wholesale buying time: summer.

North Dakota

ARACHNE, 620 Main, Fargo ND 58102. (701)232-0354. Contact; Suzanne Smemo. Craft/gift/

supply shop. Estab. 1975. Represents 10 craftworkers of Fiber Craft Guild and Goya.
Acceptable Work: Considers clothing, dollmaking, needlecrafts, soft sculpture, wall hangings and weavings. Especially needs clothing, hand spinning and knitting. One-of-a-kind and handmade production-line items. Price range: $2-350; bestsellers: $4-125.
Terms: Works on consignment; 30% commission. Retail price set by joint agreement. Requires exclusive area representation. Send resume and slides. Reports in 1 week.
Profile: "The shop is a mixture of studio, gallery, supply shop and a meeting place for craftspeople. I have limited space in the shop, but gallery space is available in the mall area in front of the store." Customers: college students, business and professional people, and summer tourists. Heaviest wholesale buying time: fall-summer; best selling time: fall-Christmas.

THE BOOKTIQUE, Straus Mall, Valley City ND 58072. (701)845-1104. Owner: Dort Hamilton. Craft consignment shop. Estab. 1978. Represents 50 craftworkers.
Acceptable Work: Considers batik, candlemaking, ceramics, decoupage, dollmaking, glass art, jewelry, leatherworking, needlecrafts, pottery, quilting, soft sculpture, tole painting, wall hangings, weavings and woodcrafting. Especially needs batik, jewelry, soft sculpture, tole painting, stained glass and scrimshaw. One-of-a-kind and handmade production-line items OK. Price range: 75¢-$50; bestsellers: $2-6.50.
Terms: Works on consignment; 30% commission. Retail price set by joint agreement. Send resume or slides or come in. Reports in 2 weeks. Work may be shipped or hand-delivered. Dealer pays insurance for exhibited work.

THE COLLAGE, 23 N. 3rd St., Grand Forks ND 58201. (701)772-7900. Contact: Barb Lander. Craft shop/gallery/gift shop. Estab. 1974. Represents 100 craftworkers. Price range: $2.50-150; bestsellers: $5-45. Works on consignment and buys outrights; 33⅓% commission. Retail price set by joint agreement. Rental gallery fee: $3, 1 time only. Reports in 1 week. Work may be shipped or hand-delivered. Dealer pays insurance. Displays work 90 days.
Acceptable Work: Considers batik; candlemaking; clothing; dollmaking; glass art; leatherworking; metalsmithing; needlecrafts; pottery; quilting; soft sculpture; tole painting; wall hangings; weavings; woodcrafting; patchwork; wooden toys; and sandcasting. Fine one-of-a-kind and handmade production-line items; utilitarian and/or decorative.
Profile: "Customers are students and faculty, air base personnel and the general public of all ages." Heaviest wholesale buying time: August-November; best selling time: September-December.

THE FAIR, 315 Central Ave., Valley City ND 58072. General Merchandise Manager: R. Munkeby. Department store. Buys crafts outright; consigns crafts for resale; and sponsors craft shows.

MINOT ART GALLERY, Box 325, Minot ND 58701. (701)838-4445. Director: Beth Kjelson. Gallery/gift shop. Estab. 1970. Represents 5 craftworkers.
Acceptable Work: Considers all crafts except ceramics. Especially needs glassware. Fine and contemporary one-of-a-kind pieces. Price range: $3.50-300; bestsellers: $2.50-200.
Terms: Works on consignment; 30% commission. Craftworker sets retail price. Send resume, slides, SASE or call for appointment. Reports in 4 weeks. Work may be shipped or hand-delivered. Dealer pays fire insurance up to $5,000 on exhibited work. Display time: 3 months maximum in shop; 1 month maximum in gallery (for one-person exhibits). Gallery arranged all newspaper features for both one-person and group exhibitions.
Profile: Exhibits in 2 first floor showrooms and hall, and 2 upper level showrooms and hall. All walls are light-colored. Displays on counters, chrome stands, boxes and tables for 3-dimensional work. Space is available for crates and boxes. Customers: college students and faculty; farmers; tourists; Air Force base personnel; and business/industry-oriented people. Best selling time: September-December.

UNIVERSITY OF NORTH DAKOTA ART GALLERIES, Box 8136, University Station, Grand Forks ND 58202. (701)777-4195. Director: Laurel J. Reuter. Gallery. Estab. 1971. Gallery is for exhibition, but work may be for sale. Work may be shipped or hand-delivered. Dealer pays shipping and insurance. Exhibitions are 3-6 weeks.
Acceptable Work: Considers batik; ceramics; clothing; glass art; jewelry; metalsmithing; quilting; soft sculpture; wall hangings; weavings; and clay. Fine one-of-a-kind pieces; decorative only.

Ohio

ANYTHING GOES: THE CRAFT GALLERY, 595 S. 3rd St., Columbus OH 43215. (614)221-0873. Contact: Rhoda Adlerstein. Craft shop/gallery. Estab. 1976. Represents 60-80 craftworkers.
Acceptable Work: Considers batik, candlemaking, ceramics, decoupage, dollmaking glass art, jewelry, leatherworking, needlecrafts, pottery, scrimshaw, soft sculpture, wall hangings, weavings and woodcrafting. Specializes in contemporary and folk art. One-of-kind and hand-made production-line items. Price range $1-300; bestsellers: $5-25.
Terms: Works on consignment: 33⅓% commission. Retail price set by joint agreement. Requires exclusive German Village representation. Send resume, slides or call for appointment. Reports in 1 week. Work may be shipped or hand delivered.
Profile: "German Village is a reconstructed area of 100-150 year old homes and shops. Quality merchandise is needed. We carry primarily handcrafted items by central Ohio craftspeople, quality handcrafted imports, and handcrafted jewelry from around the world. We're seeking to expand to include craftspeople from all over the US. Items are displayed in our Gallery Room for 1 month, then in an ongoing display in two other rooms for as long as we (and the craftperson) desire to keep it there (or until sold)." Customers: tourists, local people (20-40, middle and upper middle, professionals). Heaviest buying time: spring-summer; best selling time: November-December for local customers, July and August for tourists.

ARTISTREE, 2727 Erie Ave., Cincinnati OH 45208. (513)871-4400. Co-managers: Sharon Ramsay/Pat Crotty. Craft cooperative. Estab. 1977. Represents 25-35 craftworkers who must be able to work in shop.
Acceptable Work: Considers batik, clothing, dollmaking, jewelry, needlecrafts, pottery, quilting, soft sculpture, wall hangings, weavings, woodcrafting, work in natural dry material, rug weaving and hand braided rug hooking, copper enameling, pressed flower collages, macrame and stained glass. Especially needs leather, wood, weaving and unusual jewelry. One-of-a-kind and handmade production-line items. Price range: $2-150; bestsellers: $15-30.
Terms: Craftworker buys shares which allow him/her to exhibit 20 items; no commission. Retail price set by craftworker. Call for appointment to present work; reports in 1 week. Work must be hand-delivered.
Profile: The Artistree is located above historic Hyde Park, an exclusive area of Cincinnati, in a restored building. Work is displayed with the name of the creator, with displays rotated on a monthly basis. All displays are wooden and were constructed by a member of the cooperative.

ASHTABULA ARTS CENTER, 2928 W. 13th St., Ashtabula OH 44004. (216)964-3396. Contact: Gloria Kaull, Kathy Mahar or Caron Van Gilder. Gallery/gift shop/arts center. Estab. 1953. Represents 15-20 craftworkers. Price range: $1-5,000; bestsellers: $7-500. Works on consignment; 20-30% commission. Works through committee approval for exhibition in gallery. Retail price set by joint agreement. In exhibit gallery craftworker sets retail price. Reports in 4 weeks. Work may be shipped or hand-delivered at craftworker's expense. Dealer pays insurance for exhibited work.
Acceptable Work: Considers batik; ceramics; clothing; dollmaking; glass art; jewelry; pottery; soft sculpture; wall hangings; and weavings. All styles; utilitarian and/or decorative.
Profile: "Work is displayed in glass cases or hung on exhibit walls. There is excellent exposure as we conduct classes all year; we average 1,200 people through the center each week. Customers are 25-45; female; culturally oriented with above average income." Best selling time: pre-Christmas.

CAMPUS MARTIUS MUSEUM, 601 2nd St., Marietta OH 45750. (614)373-3750. Museum gift shop. Prefers local craftworkers but no real restrictions. Price range: 25¢-$40; bestsellers; 25¢-$5. Buys outright. Retail price set by joint agreement. Prefers exclusive area representation. Work may be shipped or hand-delivered.
Acceptable Work: Considers Ohio and West Virginia items, including candles; dolls; jewelry metalsmithing; pottery; and woodcrafts. Especially needs low price items of quality for school children. Utilitarian and/or decorative.
Profile: "Craft items for sale are displayed in glass cases, on shelves, or on a wall." Heaviest wholesale buying time: early spring; best selling time: May-October.

CEDAR POINT, INC. Merchandise Department, Sandusky OH 44870. (419)626-0830. Crafts Manager: Gene Goff. Craft shop. Estab. 1971. Represents 10-20 craftworkers per week. Considers all crafts except glass art. All styles; utilitarian and/or decorative. Price range: $1-50; bestsellers: $1-10. Craftworkers set up and sell on a percentage of their gross sales. Craft-

worker sets retail price. Reports as soon as possible between January 1-mid-August. Samples may be shipped or hand-delivered. Dealer pays return shipping for samples only and insurance for exhibited work.
Profile: "We are a Visiting Crafts Center and do not handle the items. The craftsmen set up a display and sell themselves. We get customers of all ages and incomes since we are located in an amusement park." Best selling time: mid-May through mid-September.

CINCINNATI MUSEUM OF NATURAL HISTORY COLLECTORS SHOP, 1720 Gilbert Ave., Cincinnati OH 45202. (513)621-3889. Business Manager: Sue Riggs. Museum gift shop. Estab. 1945.
Acceptable Work: Considers ceramics, leatherworking and jewelry. Specializes in work of natural materials and of ethnic origins. One-of-a-kind items only. Price range: $1-125; bestsellers: $5.
Terms: Buys outright and works on consignment; 25% commission. Retail price set by joint agreement. Call for appointment.

CONTEMPORARY STAINED GLASS & THE CREATIVE ARTS, 213215 King Ave., Columbus OH 43201. (614)299-7838. Contact: Bill McCoy. Craft shop. Estab. 1974. Represents 10-20 craftworkers. Best selling time: pre-Christmas.
Acceptable Work: Considers glass art, pottery, quilting, soft sculpture, wall hangings, weavings and woodcrafting. Especially needs blown glass, sculpture and metalworking. Specializes in contemporary to ultra-modern one-of-a-kind pieces. Price range: $1-1,500; bestsellers: $30-100.
Terms: Buys outright and works on consignment; 30% commission. Craftworker sets retail price. Send resume and slides with SASE or call for appointment. Reports in 2 weeks. Work may be shipped or hand-delivered. Items are displayed until sold or exchanged.

THE CRAFTY FOX, 3240 E. Market, Warren OH 44484. Contact: Lynne Boling. Gift shop. Estab. 1973. Represents 300 craftworkers. Price range: $1-100; bestsellers: $1-10. Works on consignment and buys outright; 25% commission. Retail price set by joint agreement. Rental gallery fee: $3/year. Requires exclusive area representation. Reports in 1-4 weeks. Work may be shipped or hand-delivered. Displays work 6 months maximum. Customers are upper middle class housewives. Heaviest wholesale buying time: summer; best selling time: September-December.
Acceptable Work: Considers all crafts. Fine handmade items; utilitarian and/or decorative.

CREATION ART & CRAFT CENTER, 717 Chillicothe St., Portsmouth OH 45662. (614)353-8838. Contact: Fred Tindall or Ann Arthur. Craft shop/gallery. Estab. 1976. Represents 12 craftworkers.
Acceptable Work: Considers batik; ceramics; decoupage; glass art; jewelry; leatherworking; pottery; tole painting; wall hangings; weavings; and woodcrafting. Especially interested in pottery. Price range: 4¢-$2,400.
Terms: Buys outright. Gallery sets retail price. Reports in 4 weeks. Work may be shipped or hand-delivered. Displays work 6-12 months.
Profile: Will consider 1-person shows or demonstrations. Customers are middle class and have incomes of approximately $15,000 per year. Best selling and heaviest wholesale buying time: winter.

CREATIVE CLUTTER BY VERGENE, 22 S. Market St., Troy OH 45373. Contact: Vergene Wetz. Gift shop. Estab. 1970. Represents 5-10 craftworkers. Price range: $1.95-100; bestsellers: $2.50-20. Works on consignment: 25-33⅓% commission. Retail price set by joint agreement. Requires exclusive area representation. Reports immediately. SASE. Pays monthly in person for work sold. Hand-delivered work only. Bring samples of work at first contact.
Acceptable Work: Considers batik; dollmaking; glass art; needlecrafts; Shaker style furniture; children's barnwood plaques; doll furniture; ceramics; floral arrangements; and door ornaments. All styles; utilitarian and/or decorative.
Profile: "Work is displayed in windows and grouped on walls. We are a home accessory shop mostly; we carry some fabric for upholstery and draperies." Best selling time: Christmas and Mother's Day.

CREATIVE TREASURES ARTISANS' COOPERATIVE, 1360 N. Fairfield Rd., Dayton OH 45432. (513)426-9651. Manager: Constance Sheldon. Member-owned, member-operated non-profit corporation. Estab. 1978. Represents 110 craftworkers.

Acceptable Work: Considers all crafts; especially needs metalsmithing, batik and weaving. One-of-a-kind and handmade production-line items. Price range: 59¢-$400; bestsellers: 59¢-$30.
Terms: "The artist purchases yearly membership units. For each unit the artist may have on display 10 items, and agrees to work 4½ hours/month in the shop. One unit equals 10 items, 4½ hours; 2 units is 25 items, 9 hours; 4 units is 55 items, 18 hours. Items may be replaced as soon as something is sold. Members are paid 100% of their selling price; payment is made monthly. All expenses: rent, utilities, insurance, etc. come from membership fee. The cooperative is governed by a board of 7 trustees elected by and from the membership. It is a democratic cooperative with a constitution and bylaws." Craftworker sets retail price. Call for appointment. Hand-deliver work. Items remain until sold or artist removes them.
Profile: "Items are not grouped by artist unless requested. Display equipment is updated to accommodate the types of items coming into the shop. Because of space, only 170 units will be available. A waiting list is maintained. Much of our business is local. Most customers are housewives in the middle to upper income bracket. Holidays are good selling times, with Christmas, Mother's Day and Easter being the leading times."

DESIGNER CRAFTSMAN SHOP, Columbus Museum of Art, 480 E. Broad St., Columbus OH 43215. Selections Chairman: Sally Burke. Museum contemporary craft shop. Estab. 1970. Represents 80-100 craftworkers.
Acceptable Work: Considers batik, ceramics, glass art, jewelry, leatherworking, metalsmithing, pottery, quilting, soft sculpture, wall hangings, weavings and woodcrafting. Specializes in contemporary fine one-of-a-kind crafts. Price range: $3.75-600; bestsellers: $3.75-65.
Terms: Buys outright and works on consignment; 40% commission. Craftworker sets retail price. Send slides. Committee meets the third Wednesday of each month to evaluate new craftspeople. Display changes every 30 days.
Profile: "Most articles are displayed on shelving or in showcases, depending upon value and fragility." Heaviest buying time: early fall; best selling time: November-December.
To Break In: "Have realistic prices, good records and submit slides or actual work for selection committee."

DOLLHOUSE WORLD, 20391 Miller Ave., Euclid OH 44119. (216)486-6664. Contact: Jean Schroeder. Dollhouse and miniature shop. Estab. 1973. Represents 15 craftworkers.
Acceptable Work: Considers dollhouses; miniature furniture and accessories; all 1"-1' scale. Fine one-of-a-kind and handmade production-line items; utilitarian and/or decorative. Price range: $1-500; bestsellers: $2-200.
Terms: Works on consignment and buys outright; 30-40% commission. Retail price set by joint agreement. Sometimes requires exclusive area representation. Reports in 2 weeks. Work may be shipped or hand-delivered. Dealer pays return shipping and insurance for exhibited work.
Special Needs: "Exquisite Oriental pieces; moderately priced Victorian pieces; English Tudor style furniture. I would also like to develop a line of bed coverings, crewel type, etc."
Profile: "We usually have more expensive furniture in locked glass cases; held for a period of 6 months-1 year; other items are on racks and shelves, open and closed. I want to use a few good craftsmen who will follow my ideas and still be creative and have ideas of their own that we can discuss. For new people I want to work on a consignment basis to start and if all goes well would buy outright on an exclusive basis." Best selling and heaviest wholesale buying time: Christmas.

DON DRUMM STUDIOS & GALLERY, 437 Crouse St., Akron OH 44311. (216)434-4452. Contact: Don or Lisa Drumm. Rental gallery. Estab. 1960. Represents 500 craftworkers.
Acceptable Work: Considers ceramics; dollmaking; glass art; jewelry; leatherworking; metalsmithing; pottery; soft sculpture; wall hangings; and weavings. Especially needs gifts in the $10-50 price range. Fine one-of-a-kind and handmade production-line items; utilitarian and/or decorative. Price range: $10-1,000; bestsellers: $25-250.
Terms: Buys outright and works on consignment for shows; 40-60% commission. Retail price set by joint agreement. Requires exclusive area representation. Reports in 2 weeks. Work may be shipped or hand-delivered; prefers UPS. Dealer pays shipping to shop (will not accept COD) and insurance for exhibited work.
Profile: "Our gallery consists of different rooms of display; items are changed and moved around featuring things in special changing displays. A large number of items are functional crafts." Best selling time: winter and Christmas sales.

ARTHUR L. FELDMAN FINE ARTS, 53 The Arcade, Cleveland OH 44114. (216)861-3580.

Contact: A.L. Feldman. Considers ceramics. Specializes in internationally known artists. Price range: $100-10,000, prints/ceramics; bestsellers: $200-500. Buys outright. Gallery sets retail price. Query. Gallery pays shipping to gallery.

FRENCH ART COLONY, 530 1st Ave., Box 472, Gallipolis OH 45631. (614)446-3834. Curator: Jan Thaler. Nonprofit museum gallery. Estab. 1964.
Acceptable Work: Considers batik, glass art, jewelry, metalsmithing, pottery, wall hangings and weavings. Fine one-of-a-kind pieces only. Price range: $5-100; bestsellers: $5-25.
Terms: "We are primarily a gallery. We do exhibit craft items 3 or 4 times a year. Artists who are invited to exhibit may price their work for sale. All sold items are then picked up at the end of the show." Displays work 30 days. Send slides and resume. Reprts in 3 weeks. Accepted work may be shipped or hand-delivered.

THE GALLERY, Box 293, Put-in-Bay OH 43456. (419)285-3611. Contact: Thomas S. Houser or Sandra Littman. Craft shop/gallery. Estab. 1969. Represents 40 craftworkers. All styles; utilitarian and/or decorative. Price range: $2-200; bestsellers: $2-35. Works on consignment and buys outright; 30% commission. Craftworker sets retail price. Shipping to shop negotiable; dealer pays return shipping, transit insurance and insurance for exhibited work.
Acceptable Work: Considers batik; candlemaking; ceramics; clothing; decoupage; dollmaking; glass art; jewelry; leatherworking; metalsmithing; needlecrafts; pottery; quilting; tole painting; wall hangings; weavings; and woodcrafting.
Profile: "We are a seasonal shop, summer only, located on South Bass Island. Customers are tourists, boaters and cottage people."

THE GALLERY ON MAIN STREET, 114½ W. Main St., Circleville OH 43113. (614)474-2078. Contact: Buyer. Craft shop/gallery/gift shop and non-profit art cooperative. Estab. 1973. Represents 130 craftworkers. Considers all crafts. "Pumpkin motif is popular because of 'Pumpkin Show' held annually in October." All styles; utilitarian and/or decorative. Price range: $1-85; bestsellers: $2-25. Works on consignment; 25% commission. Retail price set by joint agreement; requires exclusive area representation. 3 months minimum exposure. Best selling time: Christmas.

GOLDEN HOBBY SHOP, 906 E. Broad St., Columbus OH 43205. (614)222-8329. Director: Carol Seitz. Operated by the Columbus Recreation and Parks Department. Craft shop. Estab. 1971. Represents 1,500 Franklin County craftworkers over 60 years of age. Price range: 10c-$220. Works on consignment; 10% commission. Retail price set by joint agreement. Reports immediately. Work may be shipped or hand-delivered. Dealer pays insurance for exhibited work. Displays work 1 year. Best selling time: Easter and August through December.
Acceptable Work: Considers all crafts except soft sculpture. Primitive and fine one-of-a-kind pieces; utilitarian and/or decorative.

THE GOLDEN KITE, 58 N. Main St., Centerville OH. (513)435-7326. Contact: Amy Kayes. Gift shop. Estab. 1977. Represents 45 craftworkers.
Acceptable Work: Considers batik, candlemaking, ceramics, clothing, decoupage, dollmaking, glass art, jewelry, leatherworking, metalsmithing, needlecrafts, pottery, quilting, scrimshaw, tole painting, wall hangings, weavings and woodcrafting. Especially needs tole painting, metalsmithing, pottery and leatherworking. One-of-a-kind and handmade production-line items OK. Price range: $2.50-325; bestsellers: $2.50-45.
Terms: Craftworker buys a year membership, either half or full share, and works 8 hours/month in the shop. No commission is taken. Craftworker sets retail price. Send resume. SASE. Reports in 1 week. Work must be hand-delivered. Dealer pays insurance on exhibited work.

THE HAMLET, 3687 Ira Rd., Bath OH 44210. (216)666-2583. Contact: Joyce Vyhnalek. Craft shop/gift shop. Estab. 1970. Represents 220 craftworkers. Price range: 35c-$150; bestsellers: 35c-$40. Works on consignment; 30% commission. Craftworker sets retail price. Requires exclusive area representation. Work may be shipped or hand-delivered. Dealer pays insurance for exhibited work.
Acceptable Work: Considers batik; ceramics; clothing; decoupage; dollmaking; glass art; jewelry; leatherworking; metalsmithing; needlecrafts; pottery; quilting; soft sculpture; tole painting; and woodcrafting. All styles; utilitarian and/or decorative.
Profile: "We are located in a building that is over 120 years old and set among tall pines out in the country. We get a large percentage of tourists. Most of our customers are upper middle

class and professional types." Best selling time: September-December.

THE HOLDEN ARBORETUM, 9500 Sperry Rd., Mentor OH 44060. (216)946-4400. Contact: Tree House Manager. Museum gift shop. Estab. 1977. Represents 5 craftworkers. Price range: $1-200; bestsellers: $5-50. Works on consignment; commission is negotiable. Retail price set by joint agreement. Reports in 3 weeks. Work may be shipped or hand-delivered. Displays work 1-3 months.
Acceptable Work: Considers batik; glass art; jewelry; pottery; quilting; wall hangings; weavings; and woodcrafting. Especially needs crafts dealing with birds, wildflowers or wildlife. All styles; utilitarian and/or decorative.
Profile: "The Holden Arboretum is a 2,700 acre museum of woody plants. The gift shop is surrounded by a beautiful expanse of land. It is a comfortable building with fireplaces and picture windows. Customers enjoy the out-of-doors." Best selling time: holidays.

HUFF'S HANG-UPS, 5569 Fulton Rd., Canton OH 44718. (216)499-0730. Contact: Barb or Donna Huff. Craft shop. Estab. 1976. Represents 10 craftworkers.
Acceptable Work: Considers ceramics, scrimshaw, soft sculpture, wall hangings, weavings and woodcrafting. Especially needs macrame and pottery. Handmade production-line items. Price range: $3-100; bestsellers: $10-50.
Terms: Buys outright. Retail price set by joint agreement. Send slides with SASE. Reports in 1 week. Work must be hand-delivered.
Profile: Shelves are handcrafted. Sells macrame and weaving supplies as well as crafts. Customers are 30-50 years old with average to above average incomes. Heaviest wholesale buying time: fall; best selling time: fall-Christmas.

THE LADY BUG SHOP, 235-A Main St., Milford OH 45150. Contact: Nancy Applegate. Gift shop. Estab. 1976. Represents 60 craftworkers.
Acceptable Work: Considers clothing, dollmaking, needlecrafts, quilting, soft sculpture, wall hangings, weavings and woodcrafting. Specializes in country-style or quilt-related items—calicos, crayon colors, natural materials. Handmade production-line items. Price range: 60¢-$375; bestsellers: $1.75-35.
Terms: Buys outright. Retail price set by joint agreement. Call or write for appointment. Reports in 3 weeks.
Profile: We are located in a 100-year-old house on Main Street and handle children's gifts and clothing, kitchen gifts and unique Christmas items.

THE LITTLE GALLERY & THINGS ORIGINAL, Springfield Art Center, 107 Cliff Park Rd., Springfield OH 45501. (513)325-4673. Manager: Gesa Eimer. Museum gift shop located in a park. Estab. 1971. Represents 100 craftworkers.
Acceptable Work: Considers batik, ceramics, clothing, glass art, jewelry, metalsmithing, needlecrafts, pottery, quilting, soft sculpture, wall hangings, and woodcrafting. Especially needs dolls, toys and weavings. Specializes in one-of-a-kind and handmade production-line designer crafts. Price range: $1.50-250; bestsellers: $5-50.
Terms: Works on consignment; 25% commission. Craftworker sets retail price. Call for appointment. Reports in 2 weeks. Work may be shipped or hand-delivered.

THE MASSILLON MUSEUM, 212 Lincoln Way E., Massillon OH 44646. (216)833-4061. Director: Mary M. Merwin. "We are not a gallery to promote sales, but have exhibitions to promote the artists and craftsmen who wish exposure. They must be professional." Considers batik; ceramics; glass art; jewelry; metalsmithing; mobiles; pottery; sculpture; soft sculpture; wall hangings; and weavings. Maximum size: 4x9'. Price range: $10-50, crafts. 20% commission on sold work. Artist sets retail price. Send slides. SASE. Gallery pays insurance on exhibited work. "We endeavor to exhibit the work of Ohio artists and craftsmen who meet the standards."

THE MILFORD POTTERY, 235-B Main St., Milford OH 45150. (513)831-1463. Contact: Catherine A. Gatch. Craft shop. Estab. 1976. Represents 8-10 craftworkers. "Prefer Cincinnati area craftsmen, but will accept others." Considers pottery. All styles; utilitarian and/or decorative. Price range: $1-200; bestsellers: $1-30. Works on consignment and buys outright; 30-40% commission. Retail price set by joint agreement. Reports in 1-2 weeks. Work may be shipped or hand-delivered.
Profile: "We normally display items mixed with other craftsmen's work. However, in the case of a major showing of someone's work, we will set up a separate display of 1 person's work."

Best selling and heaviest wholesale buying time: summer and Christmas.

MILLER GALLERY, 2722 Erie Ave., Cincinnati OH 45208. (513)871-4420. Contact: Barbara, Norman or Laura Miller. Gallery. Estab. 1962. Represents 20 craftworkers. Price range: $3-1,000; bestsellers: $10-70. Works on consignment and buys outright; 40% commission. Craftworker sets retail price. Requires exclusive area representation. Reports in 2 weeks. Work may be shipped or hand-delivered. Dealer pays insurance for exhibited work.
Acceptable Work: Considers ceramics; glass art; jewelry; pottery; soft sculpture; wall hangings; weavings. Especially needs hand blown art glass; unique fiber works; art jewelry; fine glazed porcelain; and fine glazed stoneware. Fine one-of-a-kind handmade items; utilitarian and/or decorative.
Profile: "New items get prime space the first month; regular space the next 3 months, then are rotated between storage and display. Customers are in the upper socio-economic level; educated; income from $15,000-200,000." Heaviest wholesale buying time: pre-Christmas; best selling time: Christmas.

THE PATCHWORK FACTORY, INC., 671 Sawburg Ave., Alliance OH 44601. (216)823-6708. Contact: Betty Malone. Craft and gift shop. Estab. 1972. Represents 150-200 craftworkers.
Acceptable Work: Considers candlemaking; ceramics; clothing; decoupage; dollmaking; glass art; jewelry; leatherworking; needlecrafts; pottery; quilting; soft sculpture; tole painting; wall hangings; weavings; and woodcrafting. Especially needs patchwork; wood items; and stained glass. Fine one-of-a-kind and handmade production-line items; utilitarian and/or decorative. Price range: 75¢-$780; bestsellers: $3-300.
Terms: Works on consignment; 33⅓% commission. Retail price set by joint agreement. Work may be hand-delivered. We do not insure work. If item is damaged we pay for repairs or buy the item if damage is due to our negligence.
Profile: "We have some displays of a mixture of all types of crafts together; but mostly show the same types of work grouped together." Best selling and heaviest wholesale buying time: early fall to holidays.

PEOPLES & CULTURES SHOP-IN-THE-FLATS, 1330 Old River Rd., Cleveland OH 44113. (216)621-3749. Manager: Amparo Hernandez. Estab. 1972. Represents 150 craftworkers from the Greater Cleveland area.
Acceptable Work: Considers batik; ceramics; decoupage; dollmaking; jewelry; leatherworking; metalsmithing; quilting; needlecrafts; pottery; soft sculpture; wall hangings; weavings; and woodcrafting related to cultural heritage. Especially needs clothing with ethnic stitchery; new culturally-related crafts; toys; games; pillows; instruments; and cooking utensils. Primitive or finished, one-of-a-kind or handmade production-line items. Price range: 90¢-$500; bestsellers: $1-2.50 Christmas ornaments.
Terms: Works on consignment; 30% commission. Retail price set by joint agreement. Make appointment to show work to selection jury. Reports in 2 weeks.
Profile: New crafts exhibited in feature display. Best selling time: Christmas and spring. "Customers are all ages, colors, creeds, incomes—those interested in diverse cultures of Cleveland."

PERA'S SUMMER RESORT, Amusement Park, Lake Rd., Geneva on the Lake OH 44043. (216)466-8659. Contact: Martha Pera Woodward. Summer resort has locations for rent for craftworkers Memorial Day-Labor Day. Submit resume or actual work; call for interview. Reports in 2 weeks.

POTPOURRI INC., 585 Dover Center, Bay Village OH 44140. (216)871-6500. Manager: Dorli Rosenzopf. Estab. 1968. Represents 50 craftworkers. Considers candlemaking; ceramics; glass art; jewelry; pottery; and tole painting. Especially needs woodcrafting and metal sculpture. Prefers "early American style, nothing super modern—it doesn't sell here." Finished handmade production-line items OK; utilitarian and/or decorative. Price range: $2-250; bestsellers: $5-25. Works on consignment; 40% commission. Retail price set by joint agreement. Requires exclusive area representation. Query with transparencies or photos. Reports in 3 weeks.
Profile: Items displayed 3 months minimum. Heaviest wholesale buying time: Christmas. Customers are middle-aged housewives with middle and upper incomes; they buy crafts for gifts.

QUAINT CORNERS, 109 N. Lake St., Madison OH 44057. (216)428-1812. Contact: Doris

McIntosh. Craft/gift/antique shop. Estab. 1960. Represents 25-35 craftworkers. Heaviest wholesale and best selling time: pre-Christmas.
Acceptable Work: Considers candlemaking dollmaking, jewelry, needlecrafts, pottery, quilting, scrimshaw, tole painting, wall hangings and weavings. Especially needs dolls. Handmade production-line items only. Price range: $1-100.
Terms: Buys outright and works on consignment. Retail price set by joint agreement. Requires exclusive area representation. Send resume. Reports in 2 weeks.

SCANDESIGIN, INC., 2917 Mayfield Rd., Cleveland Heights OH 44118. (216)321-3463. Contact: William Singelis. Furniture store. Estab. 1970. Considers batik, ceramics, glass art, jewelry, pottery, wall hangings and weavings..
Terms: Works on consignment; 40% commission. Craftworker sets retail price. Send slides or call for appointment. Dealer pays insurance on exhibited work.
Profile: Store of contemporary and Scandinavian furniture. "If we have a show, work is exhibited in the gallery for approximately 4 weeks with an opening reception for artist; otherwise, we place pieces in gallery and around shop. Heaviest buying and best selling time: Christmas and June.

SEVENTEENTH COLONY HOUSE, Box 186, 3991 Main St., Hilliard OH 43026. (614)889-1204. Contact: G. Theodore. Gift shop. Estab. 1969. Represents 4-6 craftworkers.
Acceptable Work: Considers glass art; jewelry; metalsmithing; pottery; and woodcrafting. Especially needs pewter; glass paper weights; lamps; figurines and jewelry; bronze figurines; and wood. Price range: $10-1,000; bestsellers: $25-300.
Terms: Works on consignment and buys outright; 40% commission. Retail price set by joint agreement. Requires exclusive area representation. Reports in 4 weeks. Work may be shipped or hand-delivered. Dealer pays shipping to shop. Displays work 2 weeks maximum.
Profile: Customers are 25-55; couples with both people working; income of $30,000 and up. Heaviest wholesale buying time: fall; best selling time: fall and winter.

SHAKER LAKES REGIONAL NATURE CENTER, 2600 S. Park Blvd., Shaker Heights OH 44120. (216)321-5935. Manager: Mrs. John Drollinger, Jr. Gift shop. Estab. 1970.
Acceptable Work: Considers only nature-related goods (jewelry of natural materials, etc). Handmade production-line items OK. Price range: $1-36; bestsellers: $2-6.
Terms: Buys outright. Shop sets retail price. Does not require exclusive area representation. Send brochure or other descriptive material. Reports in 2 weeks.

THE SPIRIT TREE, 16740 S. Park Blvd., Shaker Hts. OH 44120. (216)921-1201. Shop Manager: Mrs. J.P. Van Sweringen. Museum gift shop. Estab. 1969. Represents 12 craftworkers.
Acceptable Work: Considers needlecrafts, pottery, wall hangings, weavings and wooden miniatures. "We are interested only in Shaker-type items or associated crafts." Price range: 50¢-$40; bestsellers: 50¢-$20.
Terms: Buys outright and occassionally works on consignment; commission varies. Retail price set by joint agreement. Send resume. Reports in 2 weeks. Work may be shipped or hand-delivered.
Profile: "We are a small attractive gift shop in a Shaker museum with continuous displays in cases or shelves. We try to limit items to things wooden and simple. There's not a lot of traffic through the shop and customers don't seem to buy expensive items." Heaviest wholesale buying time: spring (for miniature show in August) and summer (for Christmas); best selling time: fall.

STORY BOOK CRAFTS, 6021 Dayton Rd., Springfield OH 45502. (513)864-7781. Contact: Elmo or Betty Spriggs. Craft shop/gallery/gift shop/glassblowing studio. Estab. 1955. Represents 332 "Master Craftsmen." Price range: $1.50-5,000; bestsellers: $8.50-425. Works on consignment and buys outright; 33⅓% commission. Retail price set by joint agreement. Requires exclusive area representation. Reports as soon as possible. Work may be shipped or hand-delivered. Dealer pays shipping and insurance for exhibited work. Displays work 30 days.
Acceptable Work: Considers batik; candlemaking; ceramics; glass art; jewelry; leatherworking; metalsmithing; pottery; soft sculpture; wall hangings; weavings; woodcrafting; bronze sculptures; copper and silver enamels; crystalline porcelains; lithophanes; and grandfather clocks. Limited one-of-a-kind items; utilitarian and/or decorative. "We are now getting into bronze sculpture, wildlife, figures, fantasy, etc." Price range: $85-5,000.
Profile: "We have excellent spot lighting and backgrounds to best suit the art objects; lighted all

glass cases for protection of items such as jewelry. Our customers range from 20-late 60's; interested in fine art; many are collectors; income ranges from $15,000 to many who are in the millionaire bracket. Many commission special work."

SYNERGY, 314 W. 4th St., Cincinnati OH 45506. (513)323-6470. Contact: G. Steinberg. Gallery of wearables. Estab. 1977. Represents 5 craftworkers. Price range: $1-1,500; bestsellers: $15-50. Works on consignment and buys outright; 30% commission. Gallery sets retail price. Requires exclusive area representation. Reports in 3 weeks. Work may be shipped. Dealer pays insurance for exhibited work. Displays work 1 month.
Acceptable Work: Considers clothing; jewelry; and personal accessories. All styles; utilitarian and/or decorative.
Profile: "We publicize individual shows to a mailing list of 5,000. Customers are looking for unique and beautiful items; are in late 20's through 60's." Heaviest wholesale buying time: fall; best selling time: fall and winter.
To Break In: "Would like to see a complete presentation of slides, photos, etc., with prices, colors, sizes and fabrics; also description of unusual craft processes in use and list of shows craftperson has participated in."

The Little Gallery & Things Original, Springfield, Ohio, is located in a park and carries the work of 100 craftworkers. This museum gift shop, specializing in one-of-a-kind and handmade designer crafts, has a special need for dolls, toys and weavings.

THOUGHT FORM & FANTASY, 2909 Mayfield Rd., Cleveland Heights OH 44118. (216)371-1527. Proprietress: Kris Kollar. Craft/gift shop, gallery and studio. Estab. 1977. Represents 50 craftworkers.
Acceptable Work: Considers all crafts except decoupage and tole painting. Especially needs "things of interest to men—both for gifts and to entice the men who come in to buy for themselves". One-of-a-kind and handmade production-line items. Price range: $1.50-750.; bestsellers: $5-95.
Terms: Buys outright and sometimes works on consignment; 65% commission. Retail price set by joint agreement. Send slides with SASE or call for appointment. Reports in 2 weeks. Work may be shipped or hand delivered. Dealer pays insurance on exhibited work.
Profile: "The shop is an interesting combination of antiques, cards, plants and artwork. I have a good reputation for quality at reasonable prices." Customers: late teens-retirement, respect for art, good to excellent incomes. Heaviest wholesale buying and best selling time: Christmas and summer wedding season.

TOMAR, 2757 Observatory Ave., Cincinnati OH 45208. (513)871-2044. Contact: Thomas R. Bryant. Estab. 1956. Represents 12 craftworkers.
Acceptable Work: Considers ceramics, decoupage, glass art, jewelry, pottery, wall hangings, weavings and woodcrafting. Especially needs hand turned bowls, trays, vases of rare or exceptionally decorative grainings or markings in exotic woods. Contemporary one-of-a-kind

and handmade production-line items OK. Price range: $10-400; bestsellers: $10-25.
Terms: Buys outright. Retail price set by joint agreement. Requires exclusive representation. Send slides. Reports in 1 week. Work may be shipped or hand-delivered.
Profile: "Our shop is rather eclectic in that we sell very unique, old and antique decorative accessories and art as well as very contemporary items. We carry also crystal, dinnerware and interesting textiles from many countries."

THE TREEHOUSE, THE HOLDEN ARBORETUM, 9500 Sperry Rd., Mentor OH 44060. (216)946-4400. Manager: Sandy Bole. Museum gift shop. Estab. 1977. Represents 8-10 craftworkers.
Acceptable Work: Considers glass art, jewelry, pottery, wall hangings, weavings and woodcrafting. Specializes in nature-related items, especially trees and birds. One-of-a-kind and handmade production-line items. Price range: $5-200; bestsellers: $5-25.
Terms: Works on consignment; 30% commission. Craftworker sets retail price. Send resume or call for appointment. Reports in 2 weeks. Work may be shipped or hand-delivered. Dealer pays insurance on exhibited work. Display time: 3 months minimum.
Profile: Shop is small with books and educational materials, bird feeding supplies, plants and gifts (oriented to country living). "Items are displayed in a country setting in a shop overlooking a pond and crabapple collection. We use wooden shelves and baskets for display. We usually acccept only a small number of items due to the size of the shop and limited storage facilities." Customers: school groups to senior citizens; bird watchers, hikers, cross-country skiers; interested in the outdoors, nature and the environment. Heaviest wholesale buying time: late winter and fall; best selling time: spring and Christmas.

ROSS WIDEN GALLERY, 5120 Mayfield Rd., Lyndhurst OH 44124. (216)461-3430. Contact: Mrs. Widen. Gallery. Estab. 1947. Represents 10-12 craftworkers. Price range: $5-1,500; bestsellers: $100 maximum. Works on consignment; 33⅓% commission. Retail price set by joint agreement. Requires exclusive area representation. Reports in 2 weeks. Work may be shipped or hand-delivered. Dealer pays insurance for exhibited work.
Acceptable Work: Considers batik; ceramics; glass art, jewelry; pottery; soft sculpture; wall hangings; weavings; and woodcrafting. All styles; utilitarian and/or decorative.
Profile: "We don't usually exhibit local persons very often as they are seen in other local galleries. Our customers are middle-aged; intelligent; and are in upper income brackets." Best selling time: fall and winter.

WORTHINGTON HISTORICAL SOCIETY GIFT SHOP, 1188 Circle on Green, Worthington OH 43085. (614)885-7441. Contact: Gloria Newman. Gift shop. Represents 5 craftworkers.
Acceptable Work: Considers candlemaking, ceramics, dollmaking, jewelry, metalsmithing, needlecrafts, pottery, quilting, soft sculpture, tole painting, wall hangings, weavings and woodcrafting. Specializes in primitive and Appalachian crafts. One-of-a-kind and handmade production-line items. Price range: $1-35; bestsellers: $1.50-25.
Terms: Buys outright in small quantities. Retail price set by joint agreement. Send resume and slides. Reports in 3 weeks. Work may be shipped or hand-delivered.
Profile: "Our shop is located in the basement of a restored historical home. It has brick walls and glass enclosed display cabinets. We may hang the item, or place it on old trunks, old chairs, in glass cabinets or in an old hutch. The shop is small now, but we plan to expand soon." Customers: local people interested in restored historical homes and museums and tourists; average to excellent incomes. Heaviest wholesale buying time: fall to pre-Christmas.

Oklahoma

ADA GIFTS & CRAFTS, 715 E. Main, Ada OK 74820. (405)332-5540. Contact: Jimmie Nell Blum. Craft and gift shop. Estab. 1976. Represents 20-30 craftworkers. Price range: $1.50-45; bestsellers: $2-15. Works on consignment and buys outright; 40% commission. Retail price set by joint agreement. Reports in 2 weeks. Work may be shipped or hand-delivered. Dealer pays return shipping.
Acceptable Work: Considers batik; candlemaking; ceramics; decoupage; glass art; jewelry; pottery; wall hangings; weavings; and woodcrafting. Primitive and fine one-of-a-kind pieces; utilitarian and/or decorative. Especially needs pillow making and new designs for planters and plant hangers.
Profile: "We are located in an old residence with a relaxed atmosphere and an emphasis on people and service. Customers are university students; women aged 18-50; and Indians with an interest in jewelry and weavings." Best selling time: winter.

ALEX'S IMPORTS, 1000 Falcon Rd., Altus OK 73521. (405)482-9634. Manager: R. Alexander. Craft/gift shop. Estab. 1976. Represents local craftworkers.
Acceptable Work: Considers ceramics, clothing, decoupage, dollmaking, glass art, jewelry, leatherworking, metalsmithiing, pottery, wall hangings, weavings and woodcrafting. One-of-a-kind and handmade production-line items.
Terms: Works on consignment; 40% commission. Retail price set by joint agreement. Visit shop with work. Work must be hand-delivered. Display time: 30 days.
Profile: "I have an import business and sell craftwork done by people around Altus. I bought out BG and Angie's Imports and have to change and add more items."

THE APPLE BASKET, 1019 8th, Woodward OK 73801. (405)256-6813. Contact: Frankie Herzer. Gift shop. Estab. 1972. Represents 100 craftworkers.
Acceptable Work: Considers batik; candlemaking; ceramics; decoupage; dollmaking; glass art; jewelry; leatherworking; metalsmithing; needlecrafts; pottery; quilting; soft sculpture; tole painting; wall hangings; weavings; and woodcrafting. Especially needs slogan plaques and Western and country-styled crafts. Primitive and fine one-of-a-kind pieces. Price range: $1-150; bestsellers: $5-50.
Terms: Works on consignment; 40% commission. Retail price set by joint agreement. Requires exclusive area representation. Reports in 1 week. Work may be shipped or hand-delivered.
Profile: "Customers are 25-50 years old; art oriented; high income." Displays work 3-12 months. Best selling time: 2nd and 4th quarters.

THE ART SHOPPE & GALLERY, 1010 C Ave., Lawton OK 73501. (405)355-6907. Manager: Debbie Stevens. Gallery. Estab. 1975. Represents 15 craftsmen/artists.
craftsmen/artists.
Acceptable Work: Considers batik, glass art, metalsmithing, pottery, scrimshaw, soft sculpture, stoneware, wall hangings, weavings and woodcrafting. Especially needs wire sculpture, stoneware and bronze crafting. No African art. Specializes in Western and Southwestern fine art. One-of-a-kind pieces. Price range: $5-3,000; bestsellers: $5-300.
Terms: Works on consignment; 30% commission. Craftworker sets retail price. Requires exclusive Lawton representation. Send resume, slides or photos. Reports in 2 weeks. Work may be shipped or hand-delivered. Special shows last 2-3 weeks; regular gallery showings last 6 weeks; new craftworkers' works are kept 60 days to test public response.
Profile: "The gallery is an open room. Permanent displays are on and along the walls. Movable wooden panels and burlap-covered display boxes are used in the middle of the room for special shows. In another part of the building, we carry art supplies and custom-framing. Fort Sill, a large military base is adjacent to Lawton, so a lot of our customers are military officers and retired military. Average to above-average incomes." Heaviest wholesale buying; time: late summer-early fall; best selling time: fall.

BYRDS FLORAL, 307 7th St., Perry OK 73077. (405)336-4326. Contact: Charlotte Byrd. Floral/gift shop. Estab. 1972. Represents 1 craftworker at present. Heaviest wholesale buying time: spring; best selling time: summer.
Acceptable Work: Considers candlemaking, ceramics, glass art, jewelry and pottery. Especially needs candles, hand-blown glass and baby ceramics. Specializes in fine, contemporary and bright-colored items. One-of-a-kind and handmade production-line items. Price range: $1-275; bestsellers: $1-10.
Terms: Buys outright and works on consignment; 25% commission. Retail price set by joint agreement. Send literature. "No telephone calls please. We order most of our crafts from catalogs or information left by salespeople." Work may be shipped or hand-delivered. Dealer pays insurance on exhibited work.

CARAVAN GALLERY, LTD., 6029 S. Sheridan, Tulsa OK 74145. (918)494-7717 or (918)258-5563. Contact: Mrs. Wilma Mitchell. Considers traditional and abstract sculpture and jewelry. "We request a broad representation of work—6 to 20 pieces, depending on the medium. Lately, we've been handling more contemporary, exclusively American artists. Our clientele tends to be young businessmen and middle-aged persons of upper-middle class income." Price range: $5-2,000; bestsellers: $200-500. 40% commission. Exclusive representation in the Tulsa area required, plus commission on art sold 60 days after show. Send photos or brochures of work. Sponsors openings. Exhibited art insured.

CHICKASAW COUNCIL HOUSE MUSEUM, Rt. 1, Box 14, Tishomingo OK 73460. (405)371-3351. Contact: Beverly J. Wyatt. Museum gift shop. Estab. 1971. Represents 20

Chickasaw Indian craftworkers. Price range: 75¢-$50; bestsellers: $1-22.50. Works on consignment; 30% commission. Retail price set by joint agreement. Reports in 1 week. Work may be shipped or hand-delivered. Dealer splits cost of shipping. Heaviest wholesale buying time: spring-summer; best selling time: summer.
Acceptable Work: Considers ceramics; jewelry; leatherworking; metalsmithing; pottery; wall hangings; and weavings. All styles; utilitarian and/or decorative.

THE GAZEBO, LTD., 4972 S. 79th East Ave., Tulsa OK 74145. (918)664-7094. President: Norma Caylor. Gift shop. Estab. 1967. Represents 25-35 craftworkers. Price range: 50¢-$325 bestsellers: $3-150. Buys outright. Gallery sets retail price. Requires exclusive area representation. Reports in 2 weeks. Work may be shipped or hand-delivered. Dealer pays insurance for exhibited work. Displays work 3 months maximum.
Acceptable Work: Considers ceramics; dollmaking; glass art; jewelry; metalsmithing; needlecrafts; pottery; wall hangings; weavings; miniatures; rocks and minerals; and woodcrafting. Especially needs anything new in the miniature field. Finished, one-of-a-kind and handmade production-line items; decorative.
Profile: "My shop is interested mostly in miniatures, dollhouses, 1''-1' scale; any and every kind of miniature." Displays work 3 months maximum. Heaviest wholesale buying time: August; best selling time: Christmas.

GILCREASE MUSEUM GIFT SHOP, 1400 N. 25 W Ave. Tulsa OK 74127. (918)581-5313. Manager: Shirley Massongill. Gift shop. Estab. 1964. Represents 70 craftworkers. Price range: 10¢-$600; bestsellers: 10¢-$100. Buys outright. Keystone sets retail price. Work may be shipped or hand-delivered. Dealer pays shipping and insurance.
Acceptable Work: Considers jewelry; metalsmithing; needlecrafts; pottery; woodcrafting; and beadwork. Fine one-of-a-kind and handmade production-line items; utilitarian and/or decorative.
Profile: "We handle mostly reproductions from the Museum collection and top quality Indian crafts. Customers are interested in the arts; 25-60 years old; middle to high income." Heaviest wholesale buying time: spring and fall; best selling time: April-December.

GINGER JAR CERAMICS, 117 E. Illinois St., Vinita OK 74301. (918)256-2124. Manager: Judy McMullin. Craft/gift shop. Estab. 1971. Represents 2-5 craftworkers.
Acceptable Work: Considers candlemaking, ceramics, decoupage, dollmaking, jewelry, needlecrafts, quilting, tole painting, wall hangings and weavings. Especially needs doll body and dress patterns; porcelein dolls; and incising and air spraying ceramics pieces. Specializes in free-hand sketch and painted designs on ceramics. "Indians, horses and cowboys are popular items here. Some items with town and state on it sell for $3-5 for souvenirs in the summer months." One-of-a-kind and handmade production-line items. Price range: $1-35; bestsellers: $1.50-25.
Terms: Works on consignment; 30% commission. Retail price set by joint agreement. Requires exclusive area representation. Call for appointment. Reports in 4 weeks. Work may be shipped or hand-delivered. "Craftworkers must keep a personal record of their items such as number of pieces and price of each one."
Profile: "The gift shop is a large showroom at the front of the building." Customers: low to middle incomes; some tourists with upper incomes in summer. Heaviest wholesale buying time: Christmas and Easter; best selling time: summer and Christmas.

GRASS HUT ODDITIES, 4800 N. McArthur, Oklahoma City OK 73122. (405)789-8160. Contact: Lavita Tarver. Gift/head shop. Estab 1975.
Acceptable Work: Considers candlemaking, ceramics, clothing, decoupage, jewelry, leatherworking, metalsmithing, soft sculpture, wall hangings, weavings and woodcrafting. Espcially needs good belts and headbands. Specializes in contemporary and bright-colored items. One-of-a-kind and handmade production-line items. Price range: $10.95-225; bestsellers: $29.95-125.
Terms: Buys outright and works on consignment; 60% commission. Retail price set by joint agreement. Sometimes requires exclusive area representation. Call for appointment. Reports in 1 week. Work may be shipped or hand-delivered. Display time: 3-6 weeks.
Profile: Shop has 2,300 square feet and sells "tapes, LPs, cigar cases and leather goods in a contemporary art decor." Customers: ages 18-40 with upper incomes. Heaviest wholesale buying time: spring-summer and Christmas; best selling time: summer and Christmas.

GREEN COUNTRY ART CENTER, 1825 E. 15th, Tulsa OK 74104. (918)932-4259. Director:

R.L. Schellstede. Gallery. Estab. 1967. Considers paintings and sculpture. Fine one-of-a-kind pieces; decorative only. Especially needs woodcarvings and metal sculptures. Price range: $10-several thousands; bestsellers: $25-500. Buys outright. Retail price set by joint agreement. Requires exclusive area representation. Reports in 1-2 weeks. Work may be shipped or hand-delivered.
Profile: "A special showing might be only a few days, special opening and advertising. Ordinary consignment to be in gallery 4-6 weeks. Customers are young married couples who buy gifts and work for decorating apartments; collectors who are usually older businessmen." Heaviest wholesale buying time: early summer; best selling time: late summer-fall.

HOUSE OF GIFTS & CRAFTS, 9 S. Main, Miami OK 74354. Contact: Darlene Beck. Craft/gift shop. Estab. 1971. Represents 13-15 craftworkers.
Acceptable Work: Considers decoupage, dollmaking, glass art and tole painting. Specializes in fine contemporary crafts. One-of-a-kind and handmade production-line items. Price range: $2-400; bestsellers: $15-25.
Terms: Works on consignment; 30% commission. Retail price set by joint agreement. Requires exclusive area representation. Send resume. SASE. Reports in 3 weeks. Work may be shipped or hand-delivered.
Profile: "The items are displayed both on walls and in various area of the shop. We try to keep only 1 or 2 displayers of similar-type items. We report how items are doing within 1 month. We are in an active craft area and have a lot of craftworkers. Most of our customers know what they want and are very selective." Heaviest wholesale buying and best selling time: September-December.

KNOB ALLEY, 516 S. Knoblock, Stillwater OK 74074. (405)377-3111. Contact: Alvin K. Fischer. Gift shop. Estab. 1972. Represents 10 craftworkers.
Acceptable Work: Considers glass art, quilting, soft sculpture, wall hangings, woodcrafting, and especially needs batik, ceramics, needlecrafts and weavings. Specializes in fine, contemporary and traditional crafts. One-of-a-kind and handmade production-line items. Price range: $1-1,000; bestsellers: $10-100.
Terms: Works on consignment; 30% commission. "Will consider purchasing with 100% markup." Craftworker sets retail price; shop advises. Send resume and photos/slides. Reports in 2 weeks. Work may be shipped or hand delivered. Dealer pays insurance on exhibited work.
Profile: "We are located in a restored house with five gallery showrooms. Works are shown on bronze Mylar walls and linen fabric covered walls. High percentage of customers are college-educated with good to excellent incomes. Crafts are exhibited in gallery showrooms with vignette settings of examples of how pieces can be used." Heaviest wholesale buying and best selling time: pre-Christmas and Mother's Day.

LEA'S HALLMARK SHOP, 201 W. 6th St., Okmulgee OK 74447. Contact: W.D. Barnes. Gift shop. Estab. 1976. Represents 1 craftworker.
Acceptable Work: Considers needlecrafts; wall hangings; and weavings. Handmade production-line items. Price range: $1-15; bestsellers: $3-10.
Terms: Works on consignment; 25-35% commission. Reports in 2 weeks. Work may be shipped or hand-delivered. Dealer pays insurance for exhibited work.
Profile: "Approximate income of customers: $10,000-12,000; young married to elderly." Displays work 30 days. Heaviest wholesale buying time: July and September; best selling time: November-December.

THE MABEE-GERRER MUSEUM, 1900 W. MacArthur Dr., Shawnee OK 74801. (405)273-9870. Director: Robert G. Dodson. Estab. 1918. Price range: $5-150. Works on consignment; 40% commission. Retail price set by joint agreement. Requires exclusive area representation. Reports in 4 weeks. Work may be shipped or hand-delivered. Dealer pays insurance.
Acceptable Work: Considers batik; candlemaking; ceramics; glass art; jewelry; leatherworking; metalsmithing; pottery; soft sculpture; wall hangings; weavings; and woodcrafting. Primitive and fine one-of-a-kind pieces; utilitarian and/or decorative.
Profile: "We have a combination of over 400 oil paintings; 300 prints and 6,000 artifacts from all civilizations of ancient history and some primitive cultures of today. Customers are middle class of typical age range with emphasis on youth."

NANCY'S CORNER, 275 Williams Center Forum, Tulsa OK 74172. Contact: Nancy Patton. Craft shop/gift shop. Estab. 1973. Represents 10-20 craftworkers. Price range: $5-750; bestsel-

lers: $5-125. Works on consignment or buys outright; 30% commission. Retail price set by joint agreement. Requires exclusive Tulsa area representation. Work may be shipped or hand-delivered by prior consent. Dealer pays shipping to shop and insurance for exhibited work only if ordered.
Acceptable Work: Considers silver jewelry; needlecrafts; pottery; quilting; baskets; soft sculpture; wall hangings; weavings; and woodcarving. Fine one-of-a-kind and handmade production-line items; utilitarian and/or decorative.
Profile: "Our store is furnished with Shaker reproductions and primitive antique pieces, a good background for handmade things. The college educated young married people seem to be our steadiest customers." Heaviest wholesale buying time: summer; best selling time: Christmas.

NORTHFORK INDIAN SHOP, Box 882, Eufaula OK 74432. (918)689-5442. Contact: Howard D. Dixon. Indian craft shop. Estab. 1977. Represents 10 Indian craftworkers.
Acceptable Work: Considers jewelry, leatherworking, pottery, wall hangings, weavings and woodcrafting. Especially needs beadwork, rugs and wall hangings. Specializes in Indian crafts. Price range: $10-600; bestsellers: $10-100.
Terms: Buys outright. Shop sets retail price. Send resume or call for appointment. Reports in 4 weeks. Work may be shipped or hand-delivered.
Profile: Shop is "approximately 2,000 square feet of carpeted space with a large stone fireplace across 1 end of the room. The outside of the building is unpainted and built using an 1850 design. We have lighted glass showcases for all jewelry." Customers: average age is 50 with above-average incomes. Heaviest wholesale buying time: mid-winter (for summer) and summer (for Christmas); best selling time: summer.

OKLAHOMA INDIAN ARTS & CRAFTS CO-OPERATIVE, Box 966, Anadarko OK 73005. Manager: Netti Standing. Estab. 1955. Represents 60 craftworkers. Best selling and heaviest wholesale buying time: summer.
Acceptable Work: Considers Indian art; beadwork; metalwork; featherwork; sewing; and dollmaking. Finished handmade production-line items. Price range: 85¢-$800; bestsellers: 85¢-$40.
Terms: Buys outright. Gallery sets retail price. Requires exclusive area representation. Reports in 4 weeks. Work may be hand-delivered. Dealer pays shipping to shop and in-transit insurance.

THE PERSIMMON SEED, 1436 S. Carson, Tulsa OK 74119. (918)587-7973. Contact: Inez Running-rabbit. Gallery. Estab. 1962. Represents 4 craftworkers. Price range: $40-1,000; bestsellers: $40-100. Works on consignment; 40% commission. Gallery sets retail price. Rental gallery fee: 25%. Reports in 2 weeks. Work may be hand-delivered.
Acceptable Work: Considers dollmaking; jewelry; leatherworking; metalsmithing; needlecrafts; pottery; and quilting. Primitive and fine one-of-a-kind pieces; utilitarian and/or decorative.
Profile: Customers are educated in the arts. Heaviest wholesale buying time: spring and fall; best selling time: fall.

BEN M. PICKARD GALLERY, 541 NW 39 St., Oklahoma City OK 73118. (405)524-3514. Contact: Ben M. Pickard. Gallery. Estab. 1967.
Acceptable Work: Considers ceramics, fiberwork, metalsmithing, works on paper (prints, drawings), pottery, sculpture (wood, metal, glass—primitive, contemporary), wall hangings, weavings, woodcrafting, and especially needs glass art. Specializes in contemporary one-of-a-kind crafts. Price range: $50-2,000.
Terms: Works on consignment; 50% commission. Retail price set by joint agreement. Requires exclusive area representation. Send resume and slides. Reports in 4 weeks. Work may be shipped or hand delivered. Dealer pays insurance on exhibited work.
Profile: "Items revolve. The gallery likes to have 2-3 excellent works plus complete slides of artists' available work on hand. It takes 15 months to establish a market." Customers: private collectors and professionals (architects, designers) and businesses in the Southwest area; middle to upper incomes, college education, ages 25-50. Heaviest wholesale buying and best selling time: January-August.

SHAWNEE ARTS & INTERIORS, 429 W. Midland, Shawnee OK 74801. (405)273-5335. Contact: Maxine Jones. Craft and gift shop. Estab. 1975. Represents 3 craftworkers. Works on consignment and buys outright; 20% commission. Retail price is set by shops in area. Reports in 1 week. Hand delivered work only.

Acceptable Work: Considers batik; ceramics; decoupage; dollmaking; glass art; jewelry; pottery; metal sculpture; soft sculpture; tole painting; wall hangings; weavings; macrame; and handcrafted stoneware. "We are going into more soft goods, such as tote bags; aprons; and decorative items for kitchen and bathrooms."
Profile: "We teach 10 classes in our shop every week. I have free workshops for churches, schools, etc. I've taught art for 6 years in public school and have a masters degree in North American Indian art. The area is approaching a renaissance in appreciating and creating art." Best selling time: October-January.

STEPHENS COUNTY HISTORICAL MUSEUM, Box 1294, Fuqua Park, Duncan OK 73533. (405)252-0717. Director: Charlotte L. Jenkins. Museum gift shop. Estab. 1977. Represents 3-4 craftworkers. Price range: 10c-$10; bestsellers: 10c-$3. Buys at wholesale price; 10% commission. Retail price set by joint agreement. Reports in 4 weeks. Work may be shipped or hand-delivered.
Acceptable Work: Considers decoupage; dollmaking; glass art; jewelry; metalsmithing; needlecrafts; pottery; quilting; tole painting; and woodcrafting. Especially needs "souvenir type gifts depicting Southwestern themes: oil field or Indian artifacts. Would like to develop a line of ashtrays (ceramic or inexpensive metal) with museum logo." Finished crafts; utilitarian and/or decorative.
Profile: "Work is displayed in glass cases that can be locked. Some have mirrors and fluorescent lights." Heaviest wholesale buying time: spring; best selling time: summer and pre-Christmas.

TALBOT FLOWER & GIFT, 149 E. Main, Wilburton OK 74578. (918)465-2263. Contact: Jerri Stanford. Flower/gift shop. Estab. 1965. Represents 5 craftworkers.
Acceptable Work: Considers all crafts. One-of-a-kind items only. Price range: $5-75; bestsellers: $5-25.
Terms: Works on consignment; commission negotiable. Retail price set by joint agreement. Requires exclusive area representation. Send slides or call for appointment. Reports in 2 weeks. Work may be shipped or hand-delivered.
Profile: "We handle Hallmark items, do all-occasion flower needs and have gift items (jewelry boxes, porcelain items, handcrafted items). When we get a new item, we display it in well-lighted shelves or on round display tables. Our town is small so we are able to chat with our customers, draw their attention to our new items and briefly describe the artist and his work." Customers: junior high students to senior citizens; medium incomes. Heaviest wholesale buying and best selling time: Mother's Day, Valentine's Day and Christmas.

TALENTS & CO. ART GALLERY, 2118 W. Willow, Enid OK 73701. (405)234-5511. Contact: Cynthia Gordhamer or Jean Fleming. Gallery. Estab. 1975. Represents 65 craftworkers.
Acceptable Work: Considers batik, ceramics, jewelry, metalsmithing, pottery, soft sculpture, wall hangings, weavings and woodcrafting. One-of-a-kind items only. Price range: $2-300; bestsellers: $5-75.
Terms: Buys outright but mostly works on consignment; 40% commission. Retail price set by joint agreement. Send resume or call for appointment. Reports in 1 week. Work may be shipped or hand-delivered. Dealer pays insurance on exhibited work. Display time: minimum of 90 days.
Profile: "We are located in an exclusive shopping center (recently moved from a downtown location) dealing in quality art. Our gallery is decorated casually and many of our customers come to relax and rest." Customers: ages 25+; interested in oil, wheat and cattle; upper-middle to high incomes. Heaviest wholesale buying and best selling time: fall.
To Break In: "We prefer to know personally the artists whose work we display."

TUCKER TOWER MUSEUM, Box 1649, Lake Murray, Ardmore OK 73401. (405)223-2109. Curator: G.T. Lofton. Museum gift shop. Estab. 1952. Represents 6-10 Indian craftworkers.
Acceptable Work: Considers ceramics, jewelry, pottery and rugs. Specializes in primitive, contemporary and bright-colored work. One-of-a-kind and handmade production-line items. Price range: $10-200; bestsellers: $5-25.
Terms: Buys outright and works on consignment; 50% commission. Retail price set by joint agreement. Send resume with SASE. Reports in 3 weeks. Work may be shipped or hand delivered.
Profile: "The museum is owned and operated by the Tourism Department, State of Oklahoma, and displays minerals, fossils, western and Indian artifacts and handcrafted Indian items. Work is displayed in closed cases with no time limit unless craftworker specifies." Customers:

tourists and Indian art collectors. Best selling time: summer-fall.

26 EAST ART CENTER, INC., 26 E. 18th St., Tulsa OK 74119. (918)582-3382. President: Nelson P. Kifer. Craft shop/gallery. Estab. 1972. Represents 60-80 craftworkers. Price range: $5-2,000; bestsellers: $4-600. Works on consignment; 40% commission. Craftworker sets retail price. Reports in 1 week. Work may be shipped or hand-delivered. Dealer pays return shipping. "We direct our merchandise to the 35-50 year olds." Best selling time: fall and spring.
Acceptable Work: Considers batik; ceramics; glass art; jewelry; pottery; and soft sculpture. Finished and one-of-a-kind pieces; utilitarian and/or decorative.

WEWOKA TRADING POST, 524 S. Wewoka, Wewoka OK 74884. (405)257-5580. Contact: Idabel Bishop. Estab. 1974. Represents 25 local craftworkers. Considers dollmaking; jewelry; Seminole patchwork; wall hangings; and weavings. Especially needs Seminole beadwork and sculpture. Finished one-of-a-kind items only; utilitarian and/or decorative. Price range: 25c-$250. Buys outright or on consignment; 25% commission. Retail price set by gallery or joint agreement. Write.

Oregon

THE ART MERCHANT, Box 443, Sisters OR 97759. (503)549-4571. Contact: Vallerie Robinson. Gallery/gift shop/rental gallery. Estab. 1976. Represents 50 craftworkers.
Acceptable Work: Considers batik; dollmaking; jewelry; metalsmithing; pottery; soft sculpture; wall hangings; weavings; and woodcrafting. Price range: $2-11,500; bestsellers: $10-500.
Terms: Buys outright. Retail price set by joint agreement. Requires exclusive area representation. Reports in 4 weeks. Work may be shipped or hand-delivered. Dealer pays return shipping and insurance.
Profile: "Artist must be approved by panel; after acceptance work is shown continuously." Displays work 1-3 months. Best selling time: summer.

BURGETT'S MYRTLEWOOD SHOPS, Box 1067, Bandon OR 97411. (503)347-2248. Contact: Jim or Joan Burgett. Craft and gift shop. Estab. 1936. Represents 40 craftworkers. Price range: 50c-$2,600; bestsellers: $5.95-22. Buys outright. Retail price set by joint agreement. Requires exclusive area representation. Reports immediately. Work may be shipped or hand-delivered. Dealer pays insurance for exhibited work.
Acceptable Work: Considers candlemaking; jewelry; tole painting; and woodcrafting. Especially needs $5-10 items in hardwoods. All styles; utilitarian and/or decorative.
Profile: "We are located in a scenic area on the Oregon coast; customers are tourists from western US and Canada." Best selling time: summer.

CASA DEL SOL, 82 N. Main St., Ashland OR 97520. (503)482-5443. Contact: John Connors. Craft shop/gallery. Estab. 1971. Represents 10 craftworkers. Price range: $3-5,000; bestsellers: $3-30. Works on consignment; 34% commission. Retail price set by joint agreement. Requires exclusive area representation. Reports in 2 weeks. Hand-delivered work only. Displays work 1 month in shows. "Customers are in their 20's on up; well-educated and of moderate to good income." Heaviest wholesale buying time: spring; best selling time: summer.
Acceptable Work: Considers batik; candlemaking; ceramics; dollmaking; glass art; pottery; soft sculpture; and woodcrafting. Fine one-of-a-kind and handmade production-line items; utilitarian and/or decorative.

COLUMBIA ART GALLERY, 514 State, Hood River OR 97051. Director: Deb Martz. Gallery/gift shop. Estab. 1973. Represents 8-10 craftworkers. Price range: 75¢-$2,000; bestsellers: $1-500. Works on consignment; 25% commission. Retail price set by joint agreement. Reports in 1 month. Work may be shipped or hand-delivered. Dealer pays return shipping and insurance for exhibited work. Displays work 6 weeks.
Acceptable Work: Considers batik; ceramics; handmade clothing; glass art; jewelry; leatherworking; metalsmithing; pottery; quilting; soft sculpture; wall hangings; weavings; and woodcrafting. Especially needs silver work small sculptural things; batik; window screens; and blown glass goblets. Fine pieces only; utilitarian and/or decorative.
Profile: "We are located in an old mansion on the Columbia River bank and have a highly sophisticated clientele." Best selling and heaviest wholesale buying time: Christmas and spring.

CONTEMPORARY CRAFTS ASSOCIATION, 3934 SW Corbett Ave., Portland OR 97201. (503)223-2654. Contact: Marlene Gabel. Craft shop/gallery. Estab. 1938. Represents 800 craftworkers.

Acceptable Work: Considers batik; ceramics; glass art; jewelry; leatherworking; metalsmithing; needlecrafts; pottery; quilting; soft sculpture; wall hangings; weavings; and woodcrafting. Fine one-of-a-kind contemporary pieces. Price range: $3-5,000.
Terms: Works on consignment; 25% commission. Craftworker sets retail price. Reports in 2 weeks. Work may be shipped or hand-delivered with prior agreement. Dealer pays insurance for exhibited work.
Profile: "If our space allows, most pieces are exhibited in our consignment and sales gallery (shelves, stands, wall space)." Best selling time: Christmas.

COOS ART MUSEUM, 515 Market Ave., Coos Bay OR 97420. (503)267-3901. Director: Maggie Karl. Museum gallery/museum gift shop/rental gallery. Estab. 1965. Represents over 100 craftworkers. Price range: 25¢-$200; bestsellers: $10 minimum. Works on consignment; 25-30% commission. Craftworker sets retail price. Requires exclusive area representation. Reports immediately. Hand-delivered work only. Dealer pays insurance for exhibited work. Best selling time: Christmas.
Acceptable Work: Considers all crafts except clothing; decoupage; and tole painting. Especially needs jewelry. Primitive and fine one-of-a-kind pieces; utilitarian and/or decorative.

FAVELL MUSEUM OF WESTERN ART & INDIAN ARTIFACTS, Box 165, Klamath Falls OR 97601. (503)882-9996. Contact: Gene Favell. Considers glass art; jewelry; metalsmithing; pottery; sculpture; and woodcrafting. Specializes in Western and Indian art. Sculpture must have pedestals. Price range: $5-200, Indian crafts. Buys outright or on consignment; 35% commission. Retail price set by joint agreement or craftworker. Sometimes requires exclusive area representation. Query with samples or call for interview. SASE. 1 month minimum exposure.

GALES CREEK ENTERPRISES OF OREGON LIMITED, Star Rt., Box 1318, Glenwood OR 97120. (503)357-3574. Manager: Paul V. Class. Streetcar shop. Estab. 1959. "We have an operating shop moving in the direction of the American Village Institute program concentrating on village industry. Our commercial customers are mostly museums, restaurants, and cities who want quality exhibits and have the funding needed for this type of work. Each streetcar, body or complete tram is set on horses; stripped of all paint inside and out; rusted metal is removed and body prepared for new materials. Craftworkers then insert stained glass or inlay, carpenters' joinery, etc. Final painting is done by museum staff." Write for more information. "American Village Institute products are adult student made as a result of seminar program. Send for free newspaper and details."

HORNER MUSEUM GIFT AREA, Oregon State University, Gill Coliseum, Corvallis OR 97331. Field Representative: Karen S. Piepmeier. Museum gift shop. Estab. 1976.
Acceptable Work: Considers only crafts that reflect the exhibits in the museum. Exhibits in the museum deal with history, natural history, and anthropology. Fine pieces only. Price range: 25¢-$25; bestsellers: 25¢-$10.
Terms: Works on consignment; 50% commission. Gallery sets retail price. Reports as soon as possible. Work may be hand-delivered. Displays work 1 year.
Profile: "When an item is accepted in the gift area, it is priced and displayed on a shelf or in a case with its price. Customers are primarily museum visitors." Heaviest wholesale buying time: summer; best selling time: fall, winter and spring.

KATS, 777 NW 9th St., Corvallis OR 97330. (503)752-9021. Contact: Janice. Boutique. Estab. 1975. Represents 6-10 craftworkers.
Acceptable Work: Considers ceramics, clothing, jewelry, needlecrafts, soft sculpture and weavings. Specializes in contemporary crafts. One-of-a-kind and handmade production-line items. Price range: $2.50-600; bestsellers: $5-30.
Terms: Buys outright and works on consignment; 30% commission. Retail price set by joint agreement. Send slides or call in person. Reports in 2 weeks. Work may be shipped or hand delivered.
Profile: Customers: mainly women; ages 17-37; middle incomes. Heaviest wholesale buying time: pre-Christmas; best selling time: Christmas.

MAUDE I. KERNS ART CENTER, 1910 E. 15th Ave., Eugene OR 97403. (503)345-1571. Contact: Director. Craft shop, gallery and rental gallery. Estab. 1955. Represents 145 craftworkers in the craft shop, 100 in rental sales.
Acceptable Work: Considers batik; candlemaking; dollmaking; toys; glass art; jewelry;

leatherworking; metalsmithing; pottery; quilting; soft sculpture; wall hangings; weavings; and woodworking. Fine one-of-a-kind and handmade production-line items. "All work must be of original design and made from natural materials—no assembled work accepted." Price range: $1.50-150; bestsellers; $1.50-35.
Terms: Works on consignment; 30% commission. Retail price set by craftworker. All work is juried before acceptance. Reports in 4 weeks. Work may be shipped or hand-delivered; dealer pays insurance on exhibited work.
Profile: "We represent quality crafts which are selected by a jury once a month. Consignment periods are 6 months, after which time items are reevaluated." Best selling time: May, September and December.

LAWRENCE GALLERY, Box 187, Sheridan OR 97396. (503)843-3633. Contact: Gary Lawrence. Fine arts and crafts gallery. Estab. 1977. Represents 150 craftworkers.
Acceptable Work: Considers batik, ceramics, glass art, jewelry, pottery, sculpture, soft sculpture, wall hangings, weavings and woodcrafting. Fine one-of-a-kind pieces, except for pottery, which can be handmade production-line items. Price range: $2.50-5,000; bestsellers; $5-500.
Terms: Works on consignment; 35-40% commission. Craftworker sets retail price. "We have jury composed of 5 artists who view all work. Once an artist is accepted, all of his work is generally allowed, unless it's of noticeably low quality. The jury strives for high quality. Out-of-area artists who want to be juried should send slides and a resume." Reports in 3 weeks. "We pay the artist often within 1 week, 4 weeks at most." Work should be hand-delivered; "must contact us before shipping."
Profile: Gallery has 3,000 square feet of display space and track lighting. Shows last 3-5 weeks. "Because of our large gallery, we prefer to keep pieces 3 months and exhibit them even when they're not in a specific show." Customers: mostly middle-aged; upper-middle to upper incomes; beginning buyers and collectors." Best selling time: summer and Christmas.

MOSSY CREEK POTTERY & GALLERY, Box 368, Gleneden Beach OR 97388. Owner: Bob Richardson. Craft shop and gallery. Estab. 1973. Represents Oregon craftworkers.
Acceptable Work: One-of-a-kind and production-line items. Price range: $3-300.
Terms: Works on consignment; 30% commission. Retail price set by joint agreement. Requires exclusive area representation. Reports in 4 weeks or less. Work should be hand-delivered, if a prior agreement has been made.
Profile: "We handle limited amounts of crafts during our season on a full-time basis. Some or all of each artist's work is always on display, with displays changing constantly as sales occur." Best selling time: summer. "Our customers are very knowledgeable, and are looking for the best. Most are tourists visiting the Oregon coast."

MUSEUM SHOP, PORTLAND ART MUSEUM, 1219 SW Park, Portland OR 97205. (503)226-2811, ext. 56. Museum gift shop. Estab. 1969. Represents 5 craftworkers.
Acceptable Work: Considers ceramics, dollmaking, needlecrafts, pottery and soft sculpture. "Objects must pertain to the permanent collection of our museum or a traveling show." One-of-a-kind and handmade production-line items. Price range: 75¢-$600; bestsellers: $1-25.
Terms: Buys outright and works on consignment: 50% commission. Retail price set by joint agreement. Send resume or call for appointment. Reports in 4 weeks. Work may be shipped or hand delivered. Dealer pays insurance on exhibited work.
Profile: "We are an art museum gift shop dealing mainly with reproductions of the old masters. There is some representations of ethnic art. We are staffed entirely by volunteers." Customers: medium to excellent incomes. Heaviest wholesale buying and best selling time: fall.

OREGON ELECTRIC RAILWAY HISTORICAL SOCIETY, Star Rt., Box 1318, Glenwood OR 97120. (503)357-3574. Contact: Paul Class. Museum gift shop. Museum estab. in 1957; shop estab. in 1978.
Acceptable Work: Considers decoupage, glass art, metalsmithing and woodcrafting. Must be related to the trolley era. One-of-a-kind and handmade production-line items. Price range: $1-25.
Terms: Buys outright and works on consignment; 50% commission. Retail price set by joint agreement. Send slides with SASE. Reports in 4 weeks. Work must be hand delivered.
Profile: "We are a new gift shop designed within the museum to increase sales. 1 sample of each item is placed in a show case or on the display rack. Families coming for a day in the park pass through the museum/depot and gift shop." Heaviest wholesale buying time: March-May; best selling time: June-September.

OREGON HISTORICAL SOCIETY, 1230 SW Park Ave., Portland OR 97205. (503)222-1741. Bookshop Manager: Sue Bright. Museum gift shop. Estab. 1900. Represents 4-5 Northwest coast craftworkers.
Acceptable Work: Considers clothing, needlecrafts, scrimshaw, soapstone sculpture, wall hangings, weavings and woodcrafting. Especially needs clothing, scrimshaw and soapstone sculpture of regional design and character for under $20. Specializes in primitive pieces. One-of-a-kind and handmade production-line items. Price range: $1-35; bestsellers: $1-20.
Terms: Buys outright and occasionally works on consignment; 50% commission. Retail price set by joint agreement. Send slides or call for appointment. Reports in 1 week. Work may be shipped or hand delivered.
Profile: Shop is "in the Oregon Historical Center, a 50,000 square foot museum/library complex in downtown Portland. Items are displayed behind glass counters or in glass cases." Customers are interested in Northwest and Oregon history. Best selling time: summer and December.

THE OREGON SCHOOL OF ARTS & CRAFTS GIFT GALLERY & CRAFT SUPPLY STORE, 8245 SW Barnes Rd., Box 5784, Portland OR 97225. (503)228-4741. Sales Manager: Gloria Baer-White. Craft/book/supply shop. Estab. 1974. Represents Northwest craftworkers.
Acceptable Work: Considers all crafts. "All work must be original in design and ready for installation."
Terms: Works on consignment; 30% commission. Retail price set by joint agreement. Write or phone for appointment.
Profile: "The Oregon School of Arts and Crafts has recently moved to a brand new $1,600,000 craft center. The Hoffman exhibition gallery, augmented by monthly fliers and an aggressive public relations department, stimulates a large and diverse clientele."

THE RED COCK CRAFTSMEN'S OUTLET, 1423 NW Hwy. 101, Lincoln City OR 97367. (503)994-2518. Contact: Laurel Soeby. Craft and gift shop. Estab. 1972. Represents 30 craftworkers, mainly from Oregon and the Northwest.
Acceptable Work: Considers batik, candlemaking, jewelry, needlecrafts, pottery, scrimshaw, wall hangings, weavings, woodcrafting, prints, photography, and fiber arts. "I'd like new and unusual things, particularly in jewelry and glass. I'd like to also get more children's things and some metalwork." Specializes in contemporary and primitive crafts. One-of-a-kind and handmade production-line items. Price range: $1-150; bestsellers: $5-20.
Terms; Buys outright, but mainly works on consignment; 30% commission. Craftworker sets retail price. Requires exclusive area representation. Call for appointment. Reports in 3 weeks, longer in the summer. Work may be shipped or hand-delivered, if a prior agreement has been made.
Profile: "Works are displayed so they can be touched, in settings similar to how they might be displayed in the home (with the exception of small items such as jewelry). Displays are revamped constantly. Customers are age 20-50, $10,000-50,000 annual income; they generally tend to be a young thinking, upwardly mobile group interested in all kinds of arts and crafts." Heaviest wholesale buying time: spring-summer; best selling time: summer-fall.

RIVER GALLERY, Rt. 1, Box 193, Nehalem OR 97131. (503)368-5711. Owner: Carey Tate. Gallery. Estab. 1974. Represents 25 craftworkers.
Acceptable Work: Considers batik; ceramics; glass art; jewelry; metalsmithing; pottery; soft sculpture; wall hangings; weavings; woodcrafting; and sculpture. "We are seeking weavers, potters and metal sculptors." Primitive and fine one-of-a-kind pieces. Price range: $5-500; bestsellers: $5-300.
Terms: Works on consignment; 34% commission. Retail price set by gallery. Requires exclusive area representation. Reports in 1 week. Work may be shipped or hand-delivered.
Profile: "The gallery is located in a 1900 building in the rustic atmosphere of the Oregon coast. Items are given prime showing for 1 month, then up to 3 months in available space." Heaviest wholesale buying time: spring and summer; best selling time: summer and Christmas. Customers are upper income bracket, tourists and vacationing property owners.

SUNBOW GALLERY, 206 SW Stark St., Portland OR 97204. (503)221-0258. Co-owners: Janice Butler, Tonie Tollen, Sandie Clark and Lynda Toney. Craft shop and gallery. Estab. 1976. Represents 100 craftworkers.
Acceptable Work: Considers batik; clothing; glass art; jewelry; leatherworking; pottery; soft sculpture; wall hangings; weavings; woodcrafting; toys; and handbound books. Fine one-of-a-kind and handmade production-line items.

Terms: Price range: $1-1,000; bestsellers: 50¢-$90. Works on consignment; 33⅓% commission. Retail price set by joint agreement. Fee charged for exhibit gallery space; craftworker pays flyer expenses for show. Reports in 3 weeks. Slides of work may be mailed; hand-delivered work only.
Profile: Work is displayed for 90 days. Monthly shows feature a certain artist or group. "Our customers are downtown business and working people and gallery followers."

THE WHIFFLETREE, 189 Liberty NE, Salem OR 97301. (503)399-9281. Contact: Sandi Conrad. Plant and gift shop. Estab. 1975. Represents 5-6 craftworkers.
Acceptable Work: Considers candlemaking, glass art, pottery, scrimshaw, soft sculpture and woodcrafting. Specializes in contemporary utilitarian crafts. "Items must be appropriate for the shop—pottery is primarily to plant pots. We also like leaded glass with flowers, stone art and rock planters—not paintings. Basically anything unusual that would make a good gift item." One-of-a-kind and handmade production-line items. Price range: $2.99-145; bestsellers: $10-30.
Terms: Buys outright and works on consignment; 35% commission. Shop sets retail price on pieces bought outright; craftworker on consigned work. Requires exclusive area representation. Call for appointment with SASE. Reports in 1 week. Work may be shipped or hand delivered.
Profile: "Plants are about 50% of our business with unusual gift items—things to please the senses (incense, organic soaps, window hangings, pottery). Pieces are displayed to their best advantage and to give the customer ideas on how to use an item." Customers: 15-50, upper-middle class. Heaviest wholesale buying and best selling time: Christmas (October-November).
To Break In: "Expensive one-of-a-kind items do *not* sell well here. Unusual decorative items that the average person can relate to sell well. Pieces need to be somewhat functional."

WHITE BIRD GALLERY, Box 502, Cannon Beach OR 97110. (503)436-2681. Contact: Evelyn Georges. Fine art and crafts gallery. Estab. 1971. Represents 50 craftworkers. Considers batik; ceramics; clothing; glass art; jewelry; pottery; quilting; soft sculpture; wall hangings; weavings; and woodcrafting. "We have a special need for large platters." Fine one-of-a-kind and some handmade production-line items; utilitarian and/or decorative. Price range: $5-500; bestsellers: $25-150. Works on consignment and buys outright; 33⅓% commission. Retail price set by joint agreement. Requires exclusive area representation. Reports in 3-4 weeks. Shipping is negotiable; dealer pays insurance for exhibited work.
Profile: "After 7 years in the same location we feel we have earned our excellent reputation for quality crafts. We are a beach town so we draw many tourists as well as our own following." Best selling time: summer.

WOOLY LLAMA, 543 SW 6th, Corvallis OR 95330. (503)753-6561. Contact: Charlotte Attig. Craft/gift shop and gallery. Estab. 1975. Represents 11 craftworkers.
Acceptable Work: Considers clothing, jewelry, needlecrafts, pottery, scrimshaw, soft sculpture, wall hangings, weavings and baskets (natural, pine needle, coiled). Specializes in primitive and contemporary crafts. One-of-a-kind and handmade production-line items. Price range: $5-200; bestsellers: $5-175.
Terms: Works on consignment; 30% commission. Craftworker or shop sets retail price. Send slides or call for appointment. Reports in 1 week. Work may be shipped or hand delivered.
Profile: "We are a weaving shop with a gallery. Items are moved often and usually in glass cabinets. They are advertised in the town paper and store newsletter." Best selling time: December-January.
To Break In: "Keep prices low enough so that they will sell. Do quality unusual work."

Pennsylvania

ARTESANS GALLERY, Box 411 AA, Oakdale PA. (412)923-1177. Contact: Kathleen Zimbicki. Craft shop. Estab. 1976. Represents 45 craftworkers. Price range: $2-200. Works on consignment and buys outright; 30% commission. Retail price set by joint agreement. Best selling time: Christmas.
Acceptable Work: Considers batik; glass art; jewelry; leatherworking; metalsmithing; pottery tole painting; wall hangings; weavings; and woodcrafting.

ARTISAN'S COOPERATIVE/COOPERATIVE CRAFT MARKETING CENTER, Box 216, Chadds Ford PA 19317. Executive Director: Deirdre Bonifaz. Marketing outlet center. Estab. 1973 in support of rural artisans. Represents 50 low income, rural groups and individuals,

primarily from Appalachia, deep South, New England and as far west as Minnesota.
Acceptable Work: Considers batik, candlemaking, ceramics, glass art, leatherworking, metalsmithing, pottery, quilting, soft sculpture, wall hangings, handwoven clothing, woodcrafting, folk toys, broomcraft, basketry, patchwork, applique, stained glass, silkscreen, and hand-forged iron work. Specializes in traditional crafts. Price range: $3-1,500; bestsellers: $3.75-475.
Terms: Buys outright. Shop sets retail price. Requires exclusive area representation. Send slides or "any information relating to techniques employed, current price list, etc." Requested work may be shipped or hand delivered.
Profile: Shop has "high quality authentic crafts throughout; vivid colors in displays and a feeling of fantasy. Displays are changed frequently as new items are acquired and as seasons change. However, products from organization members are constantly on display. Technical assistance is provided to member groups/individuals enabling them to cope with a growing market and assist in developing self-sustaining businesses." Customers are in middle to high income bracket, professionals, all ages. "Member groups are grassroots community organizations independently striving to serve their members, mostly women, who live in rural, isolated areas of US (Appalachia, deep South, New England). There are individual members as well. We purchase a percentage of crafts from nonmembers who complement, but do not compete with, work from members." Heaviest wholesale buying time: August-December; best selling time: Christmas (Nantucket, Massachusetts shop: May-Sept, especially July-September).
To Break In: "Craftspeople must be able to demonstrate ability to meet production deadlines and maintain a consistently high level of quality in their work. Craftspeople must be interested in deriving a livelihood from their craft."

ARTISAN'S COOPERATIVE, Suburban Square, Ardmore PA. See above.

ARTISAN'S COOPERATIVE, New Market, Philadelphia PA. See above.

ARTISAN'S GALLERY, Chadds Ford PA. See Artisan's Cooperative, Chadds Ford PA.

BARE WALL GALLERY, 712 Green St., Harrisburg PA 17102. (717)236-8504. Contact: Ronn Fink. Gift/needlepoint shop. Estab. 1972. Represents 25 craftworkers, preferably a member of a guild or coop.
Acceptable Work: Considers batik, candlemaking, ceramics, jewelry, metalsmithing, needlecrafts, pottery, scrimshaw, stationery products, wall hangings, weavings, woodcrafting and wooden toys. No crochet or knit items. Especially needs notecards and silkscreen. One-of-a-kind and handmade production-line items; utilitarian items only. Price range: $5-150; bestsellers; $10-40.
Terms: Buys outright. Craftworker sets retail price. Requires exclusive Harrisburg representation. Send slides or call for appointment. SASE. Reports in 1 week except December 1-January 15. Work may be shipped or hand delivered. Dealer pays shipping to shop.
Profile: "There are 5 rooms in a 1906 townhouse, one block from the state capitol building. Displays usually in a window or on a table to oneself with a card indicating maker and hometown. A glossy of the artist is displayed with work if provided and preferred. We have a TV ad when slides are suitable and an occasional print media ad devoted to the artist. We try to develop a personality for the artist so that the public will ask for his things again." Customers: middle to upper incomes; ages 23-60; many state workers in decision-making positions; growing gay segment with large disposible incomes. Heaviest wholesale buying time: June, March and September; best selling time: December and June (for brides)."
To Break In: "Craftsmen striving to be professional need help in developing their lines and in setting up merchandising practice. The most frequent problems craftsmen seem to have are limited selection of items, fluctuating prices and little respect for order dates. We do not welcome any craftsmen who charge packing fees, handling charges, etc. The retail price should be true, reflecting the actual cost of production from studio to retail shelf."

BEATRICIA & THE KID, 107 S. Main St., New Hope PA 18938. (215)862-9103. Director: Beatricia. Craft shop and gallery. Estab. 1978. Represents 100 craftworkers.
Acceptable Work: Considers batik, ceramics, glass art, jewelry, leatherworking, pottery, quilting, soft sculpture, wall hangings and weavings. Specializes in fine one-of-a-kind and handmade production-line items. Price range: $5-1,500; bestsellers: $20-250.
Terms: Works on consignment; 45% commission. Retail price set by joint agreement. Requires exclusive area representation. Send resume and slides with SASE or call for appointment. Reports in 2 weeks. Work may be shipped or hand delivered. Dealer pays insurance on exhibited work.

Profile: "We have high quality crafts—two dimensional art work and photography. The building was built to house the work. Things are kept together." Display time: 6 weeks (1-man show), longer on a regular basis. Best selling time: spring, summer and fall.
To Break In: "Be professional and do artwork on a high creative level."

BIRD IN THE HAND, INC., 427 Broad St., Sewickley PA 15143. (412)741-8286. Contact: Katharine N. Amsler. Estab. 1969. Represents 50 craftworkers. Considers ceramics; glass art; jewelry; leatherworking; pottery; wall hangings; weavings; and woodcrafting. Finished, one-of-a-kind items OK; utilitarian and/or decorative. Price range: $5-1,000. Buys outright or on consignment; 40% commission. Retail price set by joint agreement. Requires exclusive area representation. Write or query with transparencies or photos. Reports in 2 weeks. Dealer pays shipping from shop and insurance for exhibited work.
Profile: Gallery has 2 floors, each with separate shows. One-man show on lower level runs about 1 month; upper level displays work on walls, boxes and cases for 6 months maximum. Heaviest wholesale buying time: Christmas season. Customers buy crafts for artistic value and usefulness.

THE BLUE SKY GALLERY, 3861 Old William Penn Hwy., Murrysville PA 15668. (412)325-2713. Director: Mimsie Stuhldreher. Gallery. Estab. 1972. Represents 100 craftworkers.
Acceptable Work: Considers candlemaking; glass art; functional and decorative ceramics; metalsmithing; fibers; and woodcrafting. Price range: $3-400; bestsellers: $3-50.
Terms: Works on consignment and buys outright; 40% commission. Retail price set by joint agreement. Requires exclusive area representation. Reports in 3 weeks. Work may be shipped or hand-delivered by previous arrangement. Dealer pays shipping and insurance. Shows are 4 weeks; consignment work is shown for 3 months.
Profile; "Crafts are displayed in the old kitchen, for the most part. Framed and matted items in another room. The shows are held in the inn parlor. We are housed in a handsome, red brick, 160 year old building. Customers are young to middle aged with middle income." Heaviest wholesale buying time: late summer and early fall; best selling time: November and December.

CANDLEWIC COMPANY, 35 Beulah Rd., New Britain PA 18901. (215)348-9285. Vice President: Elizabeth Binder. Craft shop/wholesale candle supplier. Estab. 1964. Represents 6 craftworkers who manufacture candleholders.
Acceptable Work: Considers candlemaking; glass art; woodcrafting; and "any item for candles." One-of-a-kind and handmade production-line items. Price range: $1.25-75; bestsellers: $5.50-15.
Terms: Works on consignment; buys outright; 50% commission. Shop sets retail price. Reports in 1 week.
Profile: "All candle items purchased in bulk, 1 dozen-2 dozen per item. We also manufacture candles at shop." Tourist area. Best selling time: September-December.

CENTER OF THE HISTORY OF AMERICAN NEEDLEWORK, Box 8162, Pittsburgh PA 15217. (412)422-8749. Director: R. Maines. Study center. Estab. 1974. Represents 1-10 needle and textile arts craftworkers who are Center members.
Acceptable Work: Considers batik; clothing; dollmaking; jewelry; needlecrafts; quilting; soft sculpture; wall hangings; and weavings. Price range: 50¢-$400; bestsellers: $5-15.
Terms: Displays work; 25% commission. Craftworker sets retail price. Reports in 2 weeks. Work may be shipped or hand-delivered. Dealer pays insurance for exhibited work. Displays work 6 weeks.
Profile: "We are entirely non-exclusive with regard to form and style; we do not as yet have an exhibit fee, nor do we charge admission; our goal is to further interest and research in the needle and textile arts." Sells craft items November-December only. "We also do an occasional individual sales show; artisans who wish to be considered for this purpose should send slides during August for consideration in September, for the coming calendar year."

CHMIELEWSKI GALLERY, 1131 Hamilton St., Allentown PA 18101. (215)439-0900. Contact: Linda Chmielewski. Gallery. Estab. 1976. Represents 10-15 craftworkers.
Acceptable Work: Considers batik, ceramics, pottery, soft sculpture, glass art, metalsmithing, wall hangings and weavings. Especially needs flat ceramic wall pieces and fiber wall hangings. Specializes in primitive, fine art, contemporary, bright colored, inlaid work and salt glaze one-of-a-kind pieces. Price range: $2-250; bestsellers: $8-35.

Terms: Works on consignment; 40% commission. "We ask craftsperson what their desired price is and then if we feel it necessary, we advise." Requires exclusive area representation. Send resume and slides with SASE or call for appointment. Reports in 2 weeks. Work may be shipped or hand-delivered. Craftworker and dealer pay insurance on exhibited work.
Profile: "We are a fine arts gallery that handles mostly graphics. Our crafts are very selective in that we look for fine workmanship and items that show new areas of work in crafts. We handle some painting. Our work is mainly contemporary with some traditional watercolorists exhibiting. We represent around 150 artists, both on consignment and gallery owned. The gallery does do consulting in homes and offices as well as having a custom framing service. We like to give items 1-2 months initial exposure depending on the time of the year. If the items do sell, we continue our working relationship to represent the craftsman. If no response, the work returns to the artist. Articles are displayed on pedestals, tables and ceramic display boxes. Average client is middle-aged, middle to upper income and a professional. Many are interested in beginning to collect art for value and interest as well as decoration. Some of our customers are art investors." Heaviest wholesale buying time: fall and spring; best selling time: fall and early winter.
To Break In: "We welcome craftsmen who know what they have to offer and we are confident with their work. An artist who is a good presenter with fine crafted items and an understanding of the business end of selling art is one step ahead in our gallery."

THE CLAY PLACE GALLERY, 5600 Walnut St., Pittsburgh PA 15232. (412)441-3799. Director: Elvira L. Peake. Gallery/craft and supply shop. Estab. 1973.
Acceptable Work: Considers pottery and sculpture clay works and occasionally glass and enamels. Price range: $4-250; bestsellers: $4-150.
Terms: Works on consignment; 33% commission. Buys outright; 50% commission. Craftworker sets retail price. Requires exclusive area representation during show. Query with slides and photos. SASE. Reports in 4 weeks. Dealer pays insurance for exhibited work.
Profile: "We hold 11 one-person shows and 1 group show each year. We sponsor the openings and provide promotion. Craftworker installs exhibit."

THE COLLECTION, 5424 Walnut St., Pittsburgh PA 15232. (412)682-6668. Jewelry shop. Estab. 1977. Represents 10-12 craftworkers.
Acceptable Work: Considers wedding bands and engagement rings. Fine, one-of-a-kind and handmade production-line items. Price range: $32-2,500; bestsellers: $32-300.
Terms: Works on consignment and buys outright; 50% commission. Craftworker sets retail price. Requires exclusive area representation. Reports in 2 weeks. Work may be shipped or hand-delivered. Dealer pays shipping and insurance.
Profile: "Each goldsmith has his own tray or trays with nameplate; velvet and cork and felt display materials and recessed lighting in cases."

CRAFT STORE, 39 Maplewood Mall, Philadelphia PA 19144. (215)842-3620. Partners: Rose Malley, Dori Flood, Margaret Waltner. Craft shop. Estab. 1971. Represents 100 craftworkers. Price range: $4-150; bestsellers: $7.50-20. Works on consignment and buys outright; 33⅓% commission. Retail price set by joint agreement. Reports in 4 weeks. Hand-delivered work only. Work is displayed on a 30-day trial basis.
Acceptable Work: Considers batik; ceramics; clothing; glass art; jewelry; leatherworking; metalsmithing; pottery; soft sculpture; wall hangings; weavings; woodcrafting; and puppets. Fine one-of-a-kind and handmade production-line items; utilitarian and/or decorative.
Profile: "All 5 partners are craftspeople. We feel we do craftspeople a service by displaying and selling their wares in an interesting environment. The partners do not receive a salary. Customers are 20-30 years old; professionals and homemakers." Heaviest wholesale buying time: fall; best selling time: Christmas and June.

CREATIVE HANDS, Peddlers Village, Lahaska PA 18931. (215)794-7012. Partners: Friedl Allen and Florence Kummer. Gift/craft shop. Estab. 1963. Represents 25 craftworkers.
Acceptable Work: Considers batik, candlemaking, ceramics, decoupage, glass art, jewelry, metalsmithing, pottery, quilting, wall hangings, weavings and woodcrafting. Specializes in fine contemporary items. Price range: $4-80; bestsellers: $3-30.
Terms: Buys outright and works on consignment; 30% commission. Retail price set by joint agreement. Requires exclusive Peddlers Village representation. Prefers call for appointment with samples, but may send slides. Reports in 2 weeks. Work may be shipped or hand-delivered. Dealer pays shipping. Display time: 2 months.
Profile: "We coordinate in color and best location. We find most of our craftwork at the craft

fairs in Baltimore, Rhinebeck, Boston, Fredericksburg and local Bucks County." Heaviest wholesale buying time: spring and fall; best selling time: May-January.

DANDELION 2, 1700 Locust St., Philadelphia PA 19103. (215)546-7655. Contact: Beth Fluke. Craft and jewelry shop. Estab. 1969. Represents 60 craftworkers.
Acceptable work: Considers batik; candlemaking; ceramics; glass art; jewelry; pottery; and soft sculpture. Price range: $5-100; bestsellers: $10-50.
Terms: Buys outright. Retail price set by joint agreement. Reports in 2 weeks. Work may be shipped or hand-delivered by prior arrangement.
Profile: Customers are 20-40 years old; center city professionals and students. Heaviest wholesale buying time: spring-summer; best selling time: Christmas.

DEEPWOOD CRAFTS GALLERY, 137 E. Pitt St., Bedford PA 15522. (814)623-9175. Contact: Penny Henry. Craft shop/gallery. Estab. 1971. Represents 50-75 craftworkers.
Acceptable Work: Considers wall hangings; pottery; jewelry; toys; and Christmas tree ornaments. Utilitarian and/or decorative. Price range: $1.50-300; bestsellers: $10 and up.
Special Needs: Especially needs Christmas tree ornaments and items for young men and boys. "Hope to have a year-round Christmas tree corner—fiber, metal, clay and other media. Also looking for unusual candles."
Terms: Buys outright and may consider consignment. Gallery sets retail price. Requires exclusive area representation. Work may be shipped. Dealer pays shipping to shop and insurance for exhibited work.
Profile: "Each item is treated as something special. I use a lot of driftwood, barn boards, etc. I move things after a period of time so it doesn't look 'old hat.' Customers are young marrieds and tourists." Heaviest wholesale buying time: summer; best selling time: fall.
Sales Tip: "I like 30 day terms. It's a big help for a buyer. Also, cards or tags with some personal information is always of interest and helps sell. I do appreciate a small *first* order sometimes until I know how well a piece is going to move."

HELEN DRUTT GALLERY, 1625 Spruce St., Philadelphia PA 19103. (215)735-1625. Director: Helen Drutt. Gallery. Estab. 1974. Represents 35 craftworkers.
Acceptable Work: Considers ceramics; clothing; glass art; and jewelry. Fine one-of-a-kind pieces.
Terms: Works on consignment; 40% commission. Retail price set by joint agreement. Requires exclusive area representation. Reports in 3 months. Dealer pays return shipping and insurance for exhibited work.
Profile: "The gallery is committed to an exhibition schedule of 8 shows per year in addition to representing the work of the artists continually. It makes an effort to educate the community and to make critical definitions in the field."

ELDER CRAFTSMEN OF PHILADELPHIA, 1628 Walnut St., Philadelphia PA 19103. (215)545-7888. Director: Evelyn Samuel. Nonprofit craft shop. Estab. 1960. Represents 500 craftworkers age 60 or older. Price range: $1-400.
Acceptable Work: Considers ceramics; clothing; decoupage; needlecrafts; pottery; quilting; and woodcrafting. One-of-a-kind handmade items.
Terms: Works on consignment; 25% commission. Retail price set by joint agreement. Crafts may be shipped or hand-delivered. Work is displayed in windows and inside displays. Best selling time: Christmas.

THE EMPORIUM, Rt. 7, Box 381, Johnstown PA 15905. (814)288-2843. Contact: Jack or Pat Roseman. Craft shop/bookstore. Estab. 1974. Represents 50+ craftworkers.
Acceptable Work: Considers batik, candlemaking, ceramics (not molded), clothing, glass art, jewelry, leatherworking, metalsmithing, pottery, quilting, scrimshaw, soft sculpture, wall hangings, weavings, woodcraftings and handmade furniture. Fine, one-of-a-kind and handmade production-line items. Specializes in contemporary designs with a traditional feeling. Price range: $4-300; bestsellers: $20-50.
Special Needs: Especially needs men's gifts; fantasy subjects (dragons, unicorns, wizards), frogs and horses in any medium; oil lamps; canister sets; wine sets; bracelets; leather hats; and chess sets. "We usually avoid flashy modern items."
Terms: Buys outright. Retail price set by joint agreement. Requires exclusive area representation. Send slides. Reports in 2 weeks. Work may be shipped or hand delivered.
Profile: "We are located in a 100-year-old remodeled church in a scenic suburb. Shop has rustic wood interior; original wood ceilings 20' high with balconies; walls are wormy chestnut and

cedar shingles. We utilize natural materials: dry weeds, stones, rough wood, etc." Customers: college students (ages 18-40); young blue collar workers ($15,000-20,000 incomes); nurses; professionals (attorneys, architects, doctors); families. Heaviest wholesale buying time: spring and summer; best selling time: Christmas and July-August.
To Break In: "Be realistic about delivery dates. If there's a change, notify me. Prepricing saves us a lot of time. Use liquor boxes with partitions for pottery and ship only by UPS. Keep us posted on current items, even if we don't purchase anything for a while. Jars with large corks sell better than lidded jars."

EVERHART MUSEUM SALES SHOP, Nay Aug Park, Scranton PA 18510. Contact: Mrs. W.R. Julius Jr. Museum gift shop. Estab. 1968. Represents 20-25 craftworkers. Buys outright. Gallery sets retail price. Reports in 3-4 weeks. Work may be shipped or hand-delivered. Dealer pays shipping to shop. Best selling time: April-December.
Acceptable Work: Considers ceramics; dollmaking; glass art; jewelry; pottery; and woodcrafting. All styles; utilitarian and/or decorative. Price range: $2.50-50; bestsellers: $2.50-25.

EVERYDAY PEOPLE, 6th and Reed Ave., Monessen PA 15062. (412)684-3450. Directors: Joyce Mosely/Gerogene Sacchini. Craft shop/school. Estab. 1974. Represents 50 low income, elderly and handicapped craftworkers. Works on consignment; 20% commission. Craftworker sets retail price. Work may be hand-delivered. Stop by shop for interview.
Acceptable Work: Considers candlemaking; ceramics; clothing; dollmaking; jewelry; needlecrafts; pottery; quilting; wall hangings; and weavings. Primitive and one-of-a-kind pieces; utilitarian and/or decorative. Price range: 50¢-$35; bestsellers: $1-5.
Profile: "There is a rotating arrangement; prices are reduced 10% after 2 months; another 10% after another 2 months; returned after 6 months. Our purpose is to supplement the income of elderly and low income as well as handicapped people. Customers are middle income school students and housewives." Best selling time: Christmas and late summer.

The Artisan's Cooperative/Cooperative Craft Marketing Center in Chadds Ford, Pennsylvania represents both group members and individual craftworkers. The work of a nonmember is displayed when it complements the work of members. The atmosphere created is one of fantasy emphasizing traditional crafts in vivid colors.

FONTANA GALLERY, 307 Iona Ave., Narberth PA 19072. Director: Joy Kushner. Considers mobiles and sculpture. Maximum size: 50" square. Works on consignment; 40% commission. Retail price set by joint agreement. Requires exclusive area representation. Send slides or photos of work. SASE.

FORT PITT MUSEUM GIFT SHOP, Point State Park, Pittsburgh PA 15222. Manager: Nancy Bonati. Museum gift shop. Estab. 1976. Represents 12 craftworkers.
Acceptable Work: Considers candlemaking, ceramics, dollmaking, jewelry, leatherworking, metalsmithing, needlecrafts, pottery, quilting, scrimshaw, tole painting, wall hangings, weavings and woodcrafting. "We carry merchandise that is colonial in nature. We also carry prints and note cards. One-of-a-kind and handmade production-line items. Price range: $1-400.
Terms: Works on consignment; usually 40% commission. Retail price set by joint agreement. Send resume and slides. SASE. Reports in 1 week. Work may be shipped or hand-delivered. Dealer pays insurance on exhibited work.
Profile: "We are a small gift shop inside the Fort Pitt Museum. The display theme carries out the mood of the period; we use many barrels, hooks, shelves and enclosed cases for the more expensive items." Customers: ages 20; interested in the Revolutionary period. Best selling time: April-November.

THE FRAME FACTORY, 266 S. Main St., Doylestown PA 18901. (215)345-9225. Contact: Carolyn Sadowski. Gallery. Estab. 1975. Represents 5 craftworkers.
Acceptable Work: Considers batik, wall hangings and weavings. Framable items only. Price range: $20-300; bestsellers: $40-80.
Terms: Buys outright and works on consignment; 25% commission. Retail price set by joint agreement. Requires exclusive area representation. Call for appointment. Reports in 1 week. Work must be hand-delivered. Craftworker sets retail price.
Profile: Displays on wall or easel. "We are a do-it-yourself and custom frame shop with gallery. Friendly, bright cheery atmosphere." Customers: ages 16-70; mainly Caucasian; middle to upper incomes. Best selling time: Christmas.

FRIENDS OF THE FREE LIBRARY GIFT SHOP, Logan Square, Philadelphia PA 19103. (215)567-4562. Contact: Manager. Gift shop. Estab. 1975. Represents local craftworkers.
Acceptable Work: Considers ceramics; glass art; jewelry; soft sculpture; and woodcrafting. Fine, one-of-a-kind and handmade production-line items; utilitarian and/or decorative. Price range: 50c-$75; bestsellers: $2-10.
Terms: Works on consignment; negotiable commission. Retail price set by joint agreement. Reports in 1 week. Work may be shipped or hand-delivered. Dealer pays insurance for exhibited work. Work displayed under glass is shown for 2 months; work on walls displayed 1 month.
Profile: "We are located in the Free Library of Philadelphia and support the library through our sales. Customers are library employees, city employees and library users." Heaviest wholesale buying time: late summer-fall; best selling time: winter holidays.

GALLERY 500, 500 Germantown Pike, Lafayette Hill PA 19444. (215)825-3222. Contact: Rita Greenfield. Craft shop/gallery. Estab. 1968. Represents 50 craftworkers. Customers are between 20 and 45; middle socio-economic level.
Acceptable Work: Considers batik; ceramics; glass art; jewelry; leatherworking; pottery; soft sculpture; wall hangings; weavings; and woodcrafting. Fine, one-of-a-kind and handmade production-line items; utilitarian and/or decorative. Price range: $6-1,000; bestsellers: $10-200.
Terms: Works on consignment and buys outright; 40% commission. Retail price set by joint agreement. Requires exclusive area representation. Reports in 4 weeks. Work may be shipped or hand-delivered. Dealer pays shipping and insurance. Displays work about 1 month.

GOLDEN DOOR GALLERY, Parry Barn, 52 S. Main St., New Hope PA 18938. (215)862-5529. Director: Mary Gardner. Considers sculpture. Specializes in representational art, "although we do carry a few abstracts." Works on consignment; 40% commission. Price range: $30-5,000. Retail price set by joint agreement. Usually requires exclusive area representation. Send photos of work. SASE. Gallery pays insurance on exhibited work. Displays work 2-6 months.

THE GOLDSMITH SHOP, 5600 Walnut St., Pittsburgh PA 15232. Contact: Ronald F. McNeish. Considers jewelry; metalsmithing; and handmade pipes. Price range: $10-20,000. Buys outright. Retail price set by joint agreement. Requires exclusive area representation.

Prefers to see samples. Items displayed 2 weeks minimum. Openings sponsored.

GOUNDIE HOUSE MUSEUM SHOP, 501 Main St., Bethlehem PA 18018. Manager: Vivian M. Paul. Museum gift shop. Estab. 1967. Represents craftworkers who work in craft or materials relating to the period from 1741-1850.
Acceptable Work: Considers candlemaking; dollmaking; glass art; leatherworking; metalsmithing; needlecrafts; pottery; hand quilting; tole painting; woodcrafting; paper craft; and miniatures. All styles; utilitarian and/or decorative. Price range: 30c-$980; bestsellers: $1-25.
Terms: Works on consignment and buys outright; 50% commission. Craftworker is required to set his price; retail price is determined from that. Reports in 1-2 weeks. Work may be hand-delivered. Dealer pays insurance for exhibited work.
Profile: "The shop is located in an 1810 restored Federal home; 2 rooms are museum rooms. Because of the structure, there are no contemporary display units used, but all items are shown in antique and suitable furnishings." Best selling and heaviest wholesale buying time: Christmas.

THE HAHN GALLERY INC., 8439 Germantown Ave., Philadelphia PA 19118. (215)247-8439. Directors: Maurice and Roslyn Hahn. Gallery. Estab. 1974. Represents 15-25 craftworkers. Price range: $10-1,000; bestsellers: $5-50. Works on consignment and buys outright; 40% commission. Retail price set by joint agreement. Requires exclusive area representation. Reports in 1 month. Work may be shipped or hand-delivered. Dealer pays shipping and insurance.
Acceptable Work: Considers ceramics; glass art; paperweights; metalsmithing; pottery; soft sculpture; wall hangings; weavings; and woodcrafting. Fine, one-of-a-kind and handmade production-line items; utilitarian and/or decorative.
Profile: "We tend to maintain continuous small displays of each craftperson's work; occasionally we feature some with larger displays and works in windows. We are a complete art gallery which represents artists. We have 3 week changing shows, group shows and we give our artists publicity and exposure as artists." Heaviest wholesale buying time: summer; best selling time: Christmas.

HANDWORKS, 848 Walnut St., Allentown PA 18102. (215)820-5431. Proprietress: Irma Rosenzweig. Estab. 1974. Represents 100 craftworkers.
Acceptable Work: Considers batik, candlemaking, ceramics, dollmaking, glass art, jewelry, leatherworking, metalsmithing, needlecrafts, pottery, woodcrafting and especially needs metal sculpture. One-of-a-kind and handmade production-line items. Price range: 35¢-$100; bestsellers: $1.50-50.
Terms: Buys outright (out of town) and works on consignment (in town). Retail price set by joint agreement. Requires exclusive downtown area representation. Send resume. Reports in 2 weeks. Work may be shipped or hand delivered. Dealer pays insurance on exhibited work.
Profile: "I have a shop 1 block off the Hamilton Mall in downtown Allentown. Business is not what it used to be since a large suburban mall opened. Plans to build a convention center across from me will help the shops downtown. I display on shelves, peg board and tables and give each item very special care. I have had no problems with breakage or shop-lifting. I will display an item for 2 months." Customers: middle income, middle age, recognize the quality of handcrafted things. "I treat my customers with great care so they keep coming back."
To Break In: "Do not promise delivery unless absolutely sure order can be filled. Again this year, I have had many disappointments even though I ordered in August. Do not change price before shipment is made and expect to be paid the higher price."

HERITAGE HOUSE, 314 E. 8th Ave., Homestead PA 15120. (412)464-1300. Manager: Cheryl Panfil or Carol Wagner. Gift shop. Estab. 1975. Represents 200 craftworkers. Price range: $1-100; bestsellers: $1-35. Works on consignment. Retail price set by joint agreement. Reports in 4 weeks. Work may be shipped or hand-delivered. Dealer pays return shipping and insurance for exhibited work. Crafts are displayed for 90 days.
Acceptable Work: Considers clothing; decoupage; dollmaking; jewelry; leatherworking; needlecrafts; quilting; tole painting; wall hangings; weavings; and woodcrafting. Especially needs leather, metal and wood crafts and items made as men's gifts. Primitive handmade production-line items; utilitarian and/or decorative.
Profile: "New items are prominently featured and often listed as new items in the store in general advertising. Customers are all ages with low to moderate income." Heaviest wholesale buying time: late summer and early fall; best selling time: Christmas.

HERRON STAINED GLASS STUDIOS, 85 S. Watson Ave., Washington PA 15301. (412)225-3079. Contact: Charlotte Herron. Stained glass studio with retail crafts, gifts and supplies. Estab. 1970. Represents 10 American craftworkers.
Acceptable Work: Considers batik, glass art, metalsmithing, pottery, tole painting and woodcrafting. No imports, kits or copies. Price range: $1.50-500+ (maximum price is for commissioned windows); bestsellers: $1.50, $35-125.
Terms: Buys outright, but may work on consignment; 30% commission. Craftworker sets retail price. Requires exclusive area representation. Send resume, slides and SASE. Reports in 1 week. Samples sent will be returned if postage included. Work may be shipped or hand delivered.
Profile: "We are principally a stained glass studio with a retail shop/gallery of gifts and supplies. The quaint retail shop displays items that relate to antiques and artistic settings. Displays are changed constantly as merchandise is sold. We are well acquainted with our merchandise and advertise to customers about new items that they might be interested in." Customers: ages 30+, collectors of fine arts, well-educated, $15,000+ incomes, professionals (doctors, lawyers, etc.). Heaviest wholesale buying time: June-December.

THE HOLE IN THE WALL GALLERY, 3099 Leechburg Rd., Lower Burrell PA 15068. (412)335-8888. Contact: Ron or Sidney Raymond. Gallery/gift shop. Estab. 1971. Represents 25-35 craftworkers. Price range: $4-400; bestsellers: $5-20. Buys outright. Reports in 2 weeks. Work may be shipped or hand-delivered. Dealer pays insurance for exhibited work. Customers are female; 15-45 years old. Best selling and heaviest wholesale buying time: Christmas, May and June.
Acceptable Work: Considers batik; candlemaking; ceramics; glass art; jewelry; leatherworking; metalsmithing; needlecrafts; pottery; quilting; soft sculpture; wall hangings; weavings; and woodcrafting. Fine, one-of-a-kind and handmade production-line items; utilitarian and/or decorative.

I & WE, 5320 Germantown Ave., Philadelphia PA 19144. (215)438-5757. Contact: Stan Levin. Gift shop. Estab. 1973. Represents 22-30 craftworkers.
Acceptable Work: Considers batik; candlemaking; ceramics; decoupage; glass art; jewelry; leatherworking; pottery; and soft sculpture. Handmade production-line items and primitive pieces. Maximum price: $35; bestsellers: $10-15.
Terms: Works on consignment and buys outright; 30% commission. Retail price set by joint agreement. Reports immediately. Work may be shipped or hand-delivered. Dealer pays return shipping and insurance for exhibited work. Heaviest wholesale buying time: June; best selling time: November-April.

INTERNATIONAL ART GALLERY, 212 Valley Brook Rd., McMurray PA 15317. (412)833-3788. Contact: Margaret Woolf. Craft shop/gallery. Estab. 1960. Represents 50-75 craftworkers. Price range: $5-200; bestsellers: $10-40. Works on consignment and buys outright; 33⅓% commission. Retail price set by joint agreement. Requires exclusive area representation within a 10-mile radius. Reports in 4-8 weeks. Work may be shipped or hand-delivered. Dealer pays shipping to shop and insurance for exhibited work.
Acceptable Work: Considers ceramics; glass art; jewelry; metalsmithing; pottery; quilting; tole painting; wall hangings; and weavings. Especially needs enameling (small utilitarian pieces) and metal sculpture (wall and standing pieces). Fine, one-of-a-kind and handmade production-line items; utilitarian and/or decorative.
Profile: "We have craftsmen from Maine to California. Customers are young and middle aged; middle to high income." Heaviest wholesale buying time: summer; best selling time: November-December.

RICHARD KAGAN STUDIO & GALLERY, 326 South St., Philadelphia PA 19147. (215)925-2370. Contact: Richard Kagan. Gallery. Estab. 1973. Represents 15 woodworkers. Finished, one-of-a-kind and handmade limited production wood items. Price range: $75-10,000; bestsellers: $500-2,500. Works on consignment and buys outright; 30-40% commission. Craftworker sets retail price. Requires exclusive area representation. Reports in 2 weeks. Work may be shipped or hand-delivered. Dealer pays return shipping and insurance for exhibited work. Work is displayed 6-12 months.
Profile: "We exhibit wood furniture and objects exclusively. Woodwork represented is of museum quality and status. Customers are 25-60 years old; income is $10,000-100,000." Displays work 6-12 months. Best selling time: spring and fall.

KIPP GALLERY, Indiana University of Pennsylvania, Indiana PA 15701. (412)357-2530. Chairperson: Ned O. Wert. Museum gallery. Estab. 1970. Represents 12-20 craftworkers.
Acceptable Work: Considers batik, ceramics, clothing, glass art, jewelry, metalsmithing, pottery, quilting, sculpture, soft sculpture, weavings and woodcrafting. One-of-a-kind pieces only. Price range: $12,000 maximum.
Terms: Exhibits only. Work may be offered for sale; no commission. Craftworker sets retail price. Send resume and slides. Reports in 3 weeks. Work must be hand-delivered. Dealer pays insurance up to $20,000 per show.
Profile: "We are a professional non-sales gallery well publicized in Pennsylvania and we appeal to craftworkers who are seeking shows (group and one-man). A professional staff reviews applicants and schedules a complete gallery program 1 year in advance. We are funded by Student Coop and NEA to promote the arts to a 5 county area as well as the university community of 18,000."

LANGMAN GALLERY, 218 Old York Rd., Jenkintown PA 19046. Director: Richard Langman. Gallery. Estab. 1972. Represents 10-30 craftworkers. Price range: $25-5,000.
Acceptable Work: Considers batik; ceramics; clothing; glass art; jewelry; metalsmithing; quilting; soft sculpture; wall hangings; weavings; and woodcrafting. Fine, one-of-a-kind museum quality pieces only.
Terms: Works on consignment; 40% commission. Retail price set by joint agreement. Requires exclusive area representation. Reports in 2 weeks. Dealer pays return shipping and insurance for exhibited work.
Profile: Our craft/art show is one of the largest privately sponsored national exhibits in the country. All inquiries should include color slides or photos with prices and SASE." Displays work 6 weeks. Heaviest wholesale buying time: fall and winter; best selling time: November-December.

LEBANON COUNTY HISTORICAL SOCIETY MUSEUM STORE, 924 Cumberland St., Lebanon PA 17042. (717)272-1473. Manager: Patricia L. Attwood. Museum gift shop. Estab. 1976. Represents 15-25 Pennsylvania folk art craftworkers. Price range: $3-100; bestsellers: $3-50. Buys outright. Gallery sets retail price. Rental gallery fee: $1 per adult. Reports in 2 weeks. Work may be shipped or hand-delivered. Dealer pays shipping to shop.
Acceptable Work: Considers candlemaking; dollmaking; glass art; jewelry; metalsmithing; needlecrafts; pottery; quilting; tole painting; wall hangings; weavings; and woodcrafting. Primitive and fine one-of-a-kind pieces; utilitarian and/or decorative.
Profile: "We display work in showcases, wall hangings and in antique corner cupboards, etc. Customers are 20-60 years old with $10,000 and up income." Best selling time: fall and Christmas.

MAIN LINE CENTER OF THE ARTS, Old Buck Rd. and Lancaster Ave., Haverford PA 19041. (215)525-0272. Administrative Director: Eleanor Daitzman. Art center. Estab. 1937. Represents 25-40 craftworkers. Price range: $5-250; bestsellers: $5-150. Works on consignment. Craftworker sets retail price. All inquiries should be made by late spring for show in October. Work may be shipped or hand-delivered.
Acceptable Work: Considers all crafts. All styles; utilitarian and/or decorative.
Profile: "We have 3 new galleries with attractive cloth covered walls, excellent professional lighting and large jewelry case." Best selling time: fall.

MAPLESHADE POTTERY, Box 7, Rt. 4, Indiana PA 15701. (412)463-3005. Partner: W. Stump. Craft shop. Estab. 1976. Represents 10-20 craftworkers. Price range: 25c-$500; bestsellers: $10-20. Works on consignment and buys outright; 40% commission. Craftworker sets retail price. Reports in 4 weeks. Work may be shipped or hand-delivered. Dealer pays insurance for exhibited work. Heaviest wholesale buying time: fall and late spring; best selling time: Christmas and summer.
Acceptable Work: Considers batik; candlemaking; glass art; jewelry; leatherworking; metalsmithing; pottery; wall hangings; weavings; and woodcrafting. Especially needs leather, wood and glass. All styles; utilitarian and/or decorative.

MEADOWCROFT VILLAGE, Rt. 2, Avella PA 15312. (412)587-3412. Crafts Coordinator: Linda Jones. Restoration village and outdoor museum. Estab. 1968. Represents 8-10 craftworkers.
Acceptable Work: Considers candlemaking, ironwork, quilting, tinwork, tole painting and woodcrafting. Especially needs traditional late 18th to early 19th century crafts and reproduc-

tion items. Specializes in traditional and early American crafts, especially reproductions of interior decoration items (stencilwork, quilts, coverlets, glass), pottery, lighting devices and bandboxes. Handmade production-line items. Price range: $5-150; best sellers: $5-20.
Terms: Buys outright and works on consignment; 50% commission. Shop sets retail price. Send slides. Reports in 2 weeks. Work may be shipped and hand-delivered. Dealer pays insurance on exhibited work.
Profile: "We have a craft shop display during the season and some off-site shows and fairs." Has an annual attendance of 30,000 people, mostly school children, adults with families, and senior citizens. Heaviest wholesale buying time: March-May; best selling time: May-October.

MERCER MUSEUM SHOP, Pine St., Doylestown PA 18901. (215)345-0210. Manager: Margaret M. Lawrence. Museum gift shop. Estab. 1971. Represents 10-15 craftworkers whose work relates to the museum's 18th and 19th century theme: "The Tools of the Nation Maker": implements and crafts employed by the men and women who built our nation, particularly in eastern Pennsylvania.
Acceptable Work: Considers candlemaking, dollmaking, jewelry, metalsmithing, needlecrafts, pottery, quilting, tole painting, ceramics, glass art, leatherworking, scrimshaw, weavings and woodcrafting. Especially need Early American Pennsylvanian pieces. One-of-a-kind and handmade production-line items. Price range: $2-350; bestsellers: $3-35.
Terms: Buys outright and works on consignment; 40-50% commission. Shop sets retail price. Prefers exclusive area representation. Send slides or call for appointment. Reports in 2 weeks. Requested work may be shipped or hand delivered.
Profile: Carries souvenirs, books and gifts related to museum collections. Volunteer sales force. "We are a small, cozy shop with a traditional display." Display time: up to 6 months, longer for special pieces such as museum reproductions. Customers: "tourists and local suburbanites interested in history and tradition. High income, generally, but value demanded. Also school children in groups." Heaviest wholesale buying time: February and October; best selling time: May-September and Pre-Christmas.

MIRYAM'S FARM, Tohickon Hill Rd., Pipersville PA 18947. (215)766-8956. Contact: Miryam Rene Ralph. Craft/gift shop/gallery/farm. Estab. 1972. Represents 10-20 craftworkers.
Acceptable Work: Considers all crafts except glass art and tole painting. One-of-a-kind and handmade production-line items. Price range: $1-200; bestsellers: $5-75.
Terms: Buys outright and works on consignment. Retail price set by joint agreement. Phone, write, or stop at farm. Work may be shipped or hand delivered. Display time: 1-6 months.
Profile: "At Miryam's, the Medieval Guilds are reborn through teaching, practice, demonstration and experimentation in a variety of crafts. There are weekend workshops, a monthly art exhibition, and on the second Sunday of each month, musical recitals or the world of theatre and dance add to the activities. Farm animals create an environment where rural farm life and arts and crafts go hand in hand."

MOSTELLER'S INC., 19-27 N. Church St., West Chester PA 19380. (215)696-0582. General Merchandise Manager: James L. Mosteller. Department store. Write with resume and illustrations of work to arrange interview.
Resale Items: Home furnishings department will consider buying or consigning adult games; baskets; carvings and sculpture; Christmas ornaments; dinnerware; dolls; handbags and leather accessories; jewelry; pillows; silverwork; and wall hangings. One-of-a-kind designer, and production-lines OK. Retail price range: $1-100; set by joint agreement. "Need gift type items especially at Christmas."
Props: Anthony D'Orazio, display manager. Considers buying or leasing baskets; carvings and sculpture; children's toys; Christmas ornaments; handmade furniture; pillows; pottery; and wall hangings. One-of-a-kind designer and production-line crafts OK.
Shows: Advertising and Sales Promotion department sponsors 1 show annually. "Hope to start smaller shows throughout the year." Write for prospectus.

MUSEUM SHOP, PHILADELPHIA MUSEUM OF ART, Box 7646, Philadelphia PA 19101. (215)763-8100. Contact: Kathleen O'Neill. Museum gift shop. Estab. 1928. Represents 20-25 craftworkers.
Acceptable Work: Considers ceramics, glass art, jewelry, metalsmithing, pillows, pottery, soft sculpture and woodcrafting. Especially needs good glass and inexpensive items for children. Specializes in contemporary crafts, reproductions of pottery and jewelry antiques and handmade production-line jewelry (sterling silver, macrame). Price range: $2.50-200; bestsellers: $7.50-40.

Terms: Buys outright. Shop sets retail price. Prefers exclusive area representation. Send introductory letter, resume, price list and slides with SASE. Reports in 2 weeks. Work may be shipped or hand-delivered. Dealer pays shipping to shop.
Profile: "The shop is newly renovated and very contemporary in design. We have a very large shop (3300 square feet) with locked and well lit display cases made of wood and glass. Approximately 1/3 of our shop is used for crafts. We feature an artist with a grouping of pieces and a sign with the name and place of the studio." Customers: tourists, Philadelphia area groups, and interested in the arts. Heaviest wholesale buying time: June-July; best selling time: September-Christmas.

OLD BEDFORD VILLAGE, Box 1976, Bedford PA 15522. (814)623-1156. Manager: Marian Miller. Craft shop. Estab. 1976. Represents 45 craftworkers. "In the craft shop, preference is given to Bedford County craftspeople, then to Pennsylvania craftspeople, then to craftspeople from other areas."
Acceptable Work: Considers batik; candlemaking; clothing; dollmaking; jewelry; leatherworking; metalsmithing; pottery; quilting; wall hangings; weavings; and woodcrafting. Primitive and fine handmade production-line items; decorative only. Price range: $1-400; bestsellers: $1-12.
Terms: Buys outright. Retail price set by joint agreement. Reporting time varies. Work may be shipped or hand-delivered. Dealer pays shipping to shop.
Profile: "Old Bedford Village is a park comprised of log buildings moved from various locations to the Old Bedford Village site. The Village represents the historical period from 1750-1850. The houses are furnished in period pieces; in several of the buildings craftsmen demonstrate how crafts were done in this period. The craft shop is open 7 days a week April-October. The Village is closed through the winter with the exception of the Christmas celebration the week before Christmas. Items are displayed on shelf space and in 2 glass cases. There are also items displayed on the wall. Stock is rotated periodically. Our shop offers only juried handcrafted items." Best selling and heaviest wholesale buying time: summer tourist season.

OLD MILL VILLAGE, Rt. 848, Box 434, New Milford PA 18834. (717)465-3800. Property Head: Edyth Williams. Museum village gift shop. Estab. 1962. Represents 20 craftworkers.
Acceptable Work: Considers candlemaking, chair caning, ceramics, dollmaking, glass art, leatherworking, needlecrafts, pottery, quilting, rugmaking, wall hangings, weavings, and especially glass blowing and tin work. Specializes in educational history of past crafts. One-of-a-kind and handmade production-line items. Price range: $1-500; bestsellers: $2.75-10.
Terms: Works on consignment; 30% commission (only 10% if on work hour agreement). Craftworker sets retail price. Requires exclusive area representation. Send resume. Work may be shipped or hand-delivered.
Profile: Group of gift shops. Customers: tourists from US. Heaviest wholesale buying time: spring-summer; best selling time: summer-fall. Open weekends from Memorial Day- October 1.

THE OPEN DOOR ART SHOP, 319 Market St., Lewisburg PA 17837. Contact: Irene Mahon. Craft shop/gallery. Estab. 1970. Represents 150 craftworkers. Price range: 25¢-$365; bestsellers: $3-30. Buys outright. Craftworker sets retail price. Requires exclusive area representation. Reporting time varies. Work may be shipped or hand-delivered with consent. Dealer pays shipping and insurance for exhibited work. Work is displayed for 1 month.
Acceptable Work: Considers batik; ceramics; clothing; dollmaking; glass art; jewelry; leatherworking; metalsmithing; needlecrafts; pottery; quilting; wall hangings; weavings; woodcrafting; limited edition prints; books of poetry; papercraft; and soft toys. Especially needs silver jewelry. Fine, one-of-a-kind and handmade production-line items; utilitarian and/or decorative.
Profile: "Customers are all ages; middle income." Heaviest wholesale buying time: summer; best selling time: winter and spring.

OVERLY-RAKER VILLAGE, Rt. 1, McConnellsburg PA 17233. (717)485-4705. Contact: Helen Overly. Estab. 1972. Represents 20-25 craftworkers. Considers candlemaking; dollmaking; glass art; jewelry; leatherworking; metalsmithing; pottery; quilting; and woodcrafting. Finished, one-of-a-kind and handmade production-line items only; utilitarian and/or decorative. Price range: $5-100; bestsellers; $15-40. Buys outright. Retail price set by joint agreement. Write. Reports in 2 weeks.
Profile: "We have a full time visual display person who will display a line in a professional setting. Window treatments usually change bi-weekly; in-store displays rotate weekly. Cus-

tomers are upper middle to upper class; very design conscious and extremely quality oriented." Heaviest wholesale buying time: pre-Christmas; best selling time: Christmas.

THE PEDDLER'S SHOP, 379A W. Lancaster Ave., Wayne PA 19087. (215)688-5781. Contact: Ruth Bailey. Gift shop. Estab. 1970. Represents 250 US craftworkers.
Acceptable Work: Considers candlemaking, clothing, dollmaking, glass art, jewelry, leatherworking, metalsmithing, needlecrafts, pottery, scrimshaw and woodcrafting. Handmade production-line items only. Price range: $1-250; bestsellers: $5-20.
Terms: Buys outright. Does not buy on pro forma. Deals only on standard terms: 1-2% in 10 days, net 30; or net 30. Shop sets retail price. Normally requires exclusive area representation. Call for appointment. Reports immediately. Work may be shipped or hand delivered.
Profile: "Items are prominently displayed, usually grouped with compatible items." Customers: ages 15-50; middle to upper incomes. Heaviest wholesale buying time: early spring-early fall; best selling time: summer and Christmas.
To Break In: "Must meet delivery schedules. Prices should hold while order is being processed or we should be notified. C.O.D.s not appreciated since our credit rating is excellent."

WILLIAM PENN MUSEUM SHOP, Box 1026, Harrisburg PA 17120. (717)787-2678. Manager: Miss O'Brien. Museum gift shop. Estab. 1972. Represents 25-30 Pennsylvania craftworkers.
Acceptable Work: Considers candlemaking; ceramics; clothing; dollmaking; glass art; jewelry; metalsmithing; needlecrafts; pottery; quilting; tole painting; wall hangings; weavings; woodcrafting; papercrafts; and quilling. Especially needs tinware. Price range: 50¢-$100; bestsellers: 50¢-$5.
Terms: Works on consignment and buys outright; 30% commission. Retail price set by joint agreement. Requires exclusive area representation. Reports in 4 weeks. Work may be shipped or hand-delivered. Dealer pays shipping.
Profile: "Display locations are changed every 3-4 weeks. We relate items to Pennsylvania history and the exhibits in our museum. Customers: 75% are children between 7 and 12 with up to $5 to spend; 25% are adults that spend from $1-10." Work displayed 3 months. Heaviest wholesale buying time: December-February; best selling time: March-July.

THE PHILADELPHIA ART ALLIANCE, 251 S. 18th St., Philadelphia PA 19103. (215)545-4302. Considers all crafts. Price range: $10-1,500. Works on consignment; 30% commission. Craftworker sets retail price. Query or write for interview. Gallery pays insurance on exhibited work. Work is exhibited for 6 weeks.

THE PUMPKIN PATCH, R.R. 1, Taylorsville Rd., Washington Crossing PA 18977. (215)493-5411. Contact: Al and Dana K. Dudek. Craft shop. Estab. 1977. Represents 100-150 craftworkers.
Acceptable Work: Considers batik, candlemaking, ceramics, dollmaking, jewelry, metalsmithing, needlecrafts, pottery, quilting, soft sculpture, tole painting, wall hangings, weavings and woodcrafting. Especially needs "items with a Colonial era flavor and items appealing to men and boys." One-of-a-kind and handmade production-line items. Price range: 50¢-$200; bestsellers: $1-25.
Terms: Buys outright and works on consignment; 33⅓% commission. Retail price set by joint agreement. Send slides or call for appointment. "In lieu of slides or photographs, brochures or other literature would be accepted." SASE. Reports in 2 weeks. Work may be shipped or hand-delivered. Dealer pays insurance on exhibited work.
Profile: "Our shop is a former tenant farmer's house, dating to 1753, that we have restored, using display pieces to compliment the architecture. It is located near the historic site where Washington crossed the Delaware in 1776. Stock is frequently rearranged, so that each craftperson's items receive equal exposure. It is displayed around a large, open fireplace, off handhewn beamed ceilings and on antique furniture." Customers: moderate to high incomes. Heaviest wholesale buying time: summer; best selling time: Easter and Christmas.

THE PYRAMID SHOP, The University Museum, University of Pennsylvania, Philadelphia PA 19104. (215)243-4022. Manager/Buyer: Nancy Flood. Museum gift shop. Estab. 1972. Represents 2 craftworkers.
Acceptable Work: Considers ceramics, clothing, dollmaking, glass art, jewelry, leatherworking, metalsmithing, needlecrafts, pottery, scrimshaw, toys, wall hangings, weavings and woodcrafting. Items must be archaelogical museum-related (pottery, masks, jewelry, figurines, etc.). "Items needed are for children and items they might buy as gifts for adults."

Specializes in primitive and bright-colored pieces. One-of-a-kind but mostly handmade production-line items. Price range: 5¢-$6; bestsellers: 5¢-$2.50.
Terms: Buys outright. Retail price set by joint agreement. Send slides, samples or call for appointment. Reports in 2 weeks. Work may be shipped or hand delivered.
Profile: "We are an archaelogical museum (North American Indians, Middle and South America, Egypt, China, Near East, Africa, Asiatic and Mediterranean world). Our shop is located in the museum and is primarily for children. Merchandise must, therefore, be inexpensive. The purpose of the shop is to provide reasonably-priced goods which will remind children of their visit. Many of our things are on self-serve display shelves and in bins. More breakable items are placed behind the counter, as are smaller and more expensive items. The store is very small." Customers: children on school trips; some adults: parents; university students; tourists. Heaviest wholesale buying time: fall and spring; best selling time: pre-Christmas and middle to late spring.

THE QUILTERY, Benfield Rd., Rt. 4, Boyertown PA 19512. Contact: Marjorie P. Cannon. Mail order shop. Estab. 1971. Represents 25 craftworkers. Price range: $75-750; bestsellers: $250. Buys outright. Price set by joint agreement. Reports in 1 week. Work may be shipped. Dealer pays shipping and insurance.
Acceptable Work: Considers quilting. All styles; utilitarian and/or decorative. "I provide all quilt fabrics according to customers' specifications. Do not like to have any 'foreign' fabrics introduced by the quilters."
Profile: "Work receives national exposure in publications such as *House and Garden, Early American* and *Yankee*. Customers are interested in the finest quality, handmade, traditional home furnishings. Nearly all are women, all ages. Money is no object to them." Best selling and heaviest buying time: all months except December.

WILLIAM RIS GALLERIES, 2208 Market St., Camp Hill PA 17011. (717)737-8818. Director: Barbara Schreckengaust. Craft shop/gallery. Estab. 1966. Represents 125 professionally trained craftworkers.
Acceptable Work: Considers batik, ceramics, glass art, jewelry, pottery, sculpture, wall hangings, weavings, woodcrafting, paintings, graphics, collage, and enameled plates and plaques with birds, animals, and flowers. Specializes in fine and contemporary crafts. One-of-a-kind and handmade production-line items. Price range: $5-800; bestsellers: $5-250.
Terms: Buys outright and works occasionally on consignment; 40% commission. "All show exhibitions are consignment at 60% to artist and 40% to gallery." Retail price set by gallery or joint agreement. Requires exclusive area representation. Send resume and slides or call for appointment. Reports in 2 weeks. Work may be shipped or hand delivered. Dealer pays shipping.
Profile: "Exhibitions of art work and craftwork are held monthly at the gallery in Camp Hill, Pennsylvania. Exhibitions of art work are held in the summer months in Stone Harbor, New Jersey. Gallery in Hershey has two shows yearly. Exhibits are on display about 4 weeks." Customers: late 20's to 60 with middle and upper incomes. Heaviest wholesale buying time: spring and fall; best sellers: spring, summer and fall through December 31.
To Break In: "Make appointments, do not just drop in. Keep delivery dates."

WILLIAM RIS GALLERIES, 939 W. Governor Rd., Briar Barn, Hershey PA 17033. See above.

SCHUYLKILL COUNTY COUNCIL FOR THE ARTS, 1440 Mahantongo St., Pottsville PA 17901. (717)622-2788. Director: David S. Marshall. Museum gallery and gift shop. Estab. 1975. Represents 1 craftworker at present, but is expanding; prefers Pennsylvania craftworkers.
Acceptable Work: Considers batik, candlemaking, ceramics, clothing, glass art, jewelry, pottery, soft sculpture, wall hangings, weavings and woodcrafting. Specializes in quality contemporary pieces. One-of-a-kind and handmade production-line items. Price range: $4-500.
Terms: Works on consignment; 22% commission. Retail price set by joint agreement. Send resume and slides. Reports in 2 weeks. Work may be shipped or hand delivered.
Profile: "The gallery and gift shop are housed in the Schuylkill County Council for the Arts, a non-profit corporation. The gift shop will serve as as revenue-generating operation; the small gallery will serve as an educational facility for county residents. Display period—one month. Displays will be held in a bookshop and in small gallery space for crafts of exceptional merit." Heaviest wholesale buying time: fall; best selling time: winter.

SCUBCO, Box 182, 94 N. Branch St., Sellersville PA 19860. (215)257-2526. Contact: Mrs.

Elizabeth W. Wismer. Craft shop. Estab. 1967. Represents 2 handicapped craftworkers. Considers weavings, rugs, placemats, handbags, and pillows. Specializes in bright colored handloomed crafts. Works on consignment. Craftworker sets retail price. Call for appointment with SASE. "We are an early American rug shop with hand operated looms—also a show room for displaying items." Customers: some young adults but mostly mature persons. Best selling time: summer and fall-Christmas.

BETTY SEIDEL SHOPS, Cherryville Inn, Cherryville PA 18035. (215)767-2403. Contact: Betty Seidel. Museum gift shop. Estab. 1937. Represents 40 craftworkers. Price range: $2-500; bestsellers: $20-500. Buys outright. Craftworker sets retail price. Requires exclusive area representation. Work may be shipped or hand-delivered. Dealer pays shipping to shop.
Acceptable Work: Considers ceramics; clothing; decoupage; dollmaking; glass art; jewelry; needlecrafts; soft sculpture; decorated eggs; and porcelain bread dough. Fine one-of-a-kind pieces; utilitarian and/or decorative.
Special Needs: Especially needs elegant boxes (Victorian style); mirrors; memorabilia boxes; elegant lamps; wall hangings; decoupage; dolls; and soft sculptured pillows.
Profile: "We are famous for our ultra displays. Each and every piece of merchandise is put in a very special setting so that it is shown off to the best advantage. Customers are business and professional types; retired upper class." Best selling time: Easter-spring and July-December.

CHARLES E. SHOOP, 5539 Walnut St., Pittsburgh PA 15232. (412)621-9766. Contact: Charles E. Shoop or Charles Wojton. Gift shop. Estab. 1960. Represents 35-40 craftworkers. Price range: $1-2,000; bestsellers: $10-50. Buys outright. Craftworker sets retail price. Requires exclusive area representation. Reports in 2 weeks. Work may be shipped or hand-delivered. Dealer pays shipping to shop and insurance for exhibited work. Displays work until sold. "Customers are all ages, interests and incomes; we are in an area surrounded by colleges and private schools." Heaviest wholesale buying time: spring and fall; best selling time: fall.
Acceptable Work: Considers ceramics; dollmaking; glass art; jewelry; metalsmithing; pottery; soft sculpture; tole painting; and woodcrafting. Fine, one-of-a-kind and handmade production-line items; utilitarian and/or decorative.

C. LESLIE SMITH SILVERSMITH SHOP, 921 Hamilton Mall, Allentown PA 18101. (215)432-4504. Contact: C. Leslie Smith. Craft shop/gift shop. Estab. 1952. Represents 10-12 craftworkers. Price range: $1.50-1,000; bestsellers: $10-50. Buys outright. Craftworker sets retail price. Requires exclusive area representation. Reports in 2 weeks. Work may be shipped or hand-delivered. Dealer pays insurance for exhibited work. Heaviest wholesale buying time: fall; best selling time: Christmas.
Acceptable Work: Considers candlemaking; ceramics; glass art; jewelry; leatherworking; metalsmithing; pottery; wall hangings; weavings; and woodcrafting. Fine, one-of-a-kind and handmade production-line items; utilitarian and/or decorative.

THE STORE, 719 Allegheny River Blvd., Verona PA 15147. (412)828-6121. Director: Elizabeth Raphael. Craft shop/gallery. Estab. 1972. Represents 400 craftworkers. Price range: $1-3,000; bestsellers: $5-40. Buys outright. Gallery sets retail price. Reports in 1 week. Work may be shipped or hand-delivered. Dealer pays shipping. Call or write. If you write, send slides or photos.
Acceptable Work: Considers batik; ceramics; clothing; dollmaking; glass art; jewelry; leatherworking; metalsmithing; needlecrafts; pottery; quilting; soft sculpture; wall hangings; weavings; and woodcrafting. "Only American designer handcrafts." Finished, one-of-a-kind and handmade production-line items; utilitarian and/or decorative.
Profile: "I believe we have the largest inventory of designer handcrafts in the country. We use our front room as a gallery (to introduce all new work every other month) but always have a full selection of crafts in the larger space that is the 'regular' store." Heaviest wholesale buying time: June and January; best selling time: November-December.

THE SUN SHOP, 491 Lancaster Ave., Frazer PA 19355. (215)647-0374. Contact: Bob Frantz. Craft and plant shop. Estab. 1972. Represents 20 craftworkers.
Acceptable Work: Considers ceramics, glass art, jewelry, pottery and woodcrafting. Especially needs planters. Specializes in contemporary functional pottery. Handmade production-line items only. Price range: $4-75; bestsellers: $10-25.
Terms: Buys outright. Retail price set by joint agreement. Send slides, brochure or call for appointment. Reports in 3 weeks. Work may be shipped or hand delivered. Dealer pays insurance; negotiates shipping cost.

Profile: "We are a full service plant shop with a greenhouse and 2 rooms where plants and crafts share space equally." Display period: 1 year. "Most crafts are displayed together but segregated by the craftsperson." Customers: suburban families, age 25-40, $20-30,000 incomes. Heaviest wholesale buying time: winter and summer; best selling time: spring and Christmas.
To Break In: "Keep packing and shipping fees at a minimum to help keep retail prices reasonable."

TEASEL CRAFTS, 63 E. State St., Doylestown PA 18901. (215)345-9288. Contact: Carol Cress or Pat Gompper. Craft shop. Estab. 1975. Represents 75-100 craftworkers.
Acceptable Work: Considers batik; candlemaking; ceramics; dollmaking; glass art; jewelry; leatherworking; needlecrafts; pottery; quilting; soft sculpture; tole painting; woodcrafting; macrame; and baby clothing. Price range: 50¢-$75; bestsellers: $2-40.
Terms: Works on consignment; 33⅓% commission. Retail price set by joint agreement. Reports in 2 weeks. Work may be shipped or hand-delivered. Dealer pays insurance for exhibited work.
Profile: "Items are shown to best advantage and displays are rearranged often. We are a good mix of local, non-professional craftspeople and professionals." Work displayed 3 months minimum. Heaviest wholesale buying time: June-December; best selling time: pre-Christmas.

THE WALNUT STREET THEATRE GALLERY, 825 Walnut St., Philadelphia PA 19107. (215)574-3562. Coordinator: Dorothy Smallwood. Estab. 1972. Work displayed in 2 theatre lobbies; work may be offered for sale; 20% commission. Craftworker sets retail price. "Submit slides or photos plus educational information. Committee reviews work of craftworkers during the year." Dealer pays insurance for exhibited work.
Profile: "The Gallery includes craftworkers in most of our shows. We have approximately 6 shows annually running for 6 weeks with an average of 15 artists in each. We promote the show by press releases; opening reception; and special interviews on radio, TV, etc."

WELL FANCY THIS, 1218 Chestnut St., Philadelphia PA 19107. (215)922-6415. Contact: Florence Shakalum. Gallery. Estab. 1976.
Acceptable Work: Considers all craft items "that would be suitable for a cocktail table, beside a lamp. I'm interested in primarily decorative ceramics, small wood carvings or anything to blend with my own craft—driftwood art/wall hangings. No items like stringwork, knitting or crocheting." One-of-a-kind items only. Price range: $10-200; bestsellers: $25.
Terms: Works on consignment; 50% commission. Craftworker sets retail price. Requires exclusive area representation. Send resume and slides. Reports in 1 week. Work may be shipped or hand-delivered. Display time: 60 days.
Profile: "We are a small showroom/gallery with round tables and circular cloths. There is a stacked step arrangement (boxes covered with velvet). No shelving is available for masses of the same item." Customers: ages 20-40, interested in conversation pieces. "Most of the people like interpretive items. For instance, in my driftwood, everyone sees something different in the shapes." Heaviest wholesale buying and best selling time: Christmas.

WINFIELD HOUSE, Rt. 15, Winfield PA 17889. (717)524-7006. Manager: Tripat Singh. Craft shop. Estab. 1972. Represents 75 craftworkers. Price range: $1-350; bestsellers: $1-10. Works on consignment and buys outright; 33% commission. Craftworker sets retail price. Requires exclusive area representation. Reports in 1 week. Work may be shipped or hand-delivered. Dealer pays shipping and insurance. Best selling and heaviest wholesale buying time: fall.
Acceptable Work: Considers batik; candlemaking; ceramics; clothing; glass art; jewelry; leatherworking; metalsmithing; pottery; tole painting; wall hangings; weavings; and woodcrafting. All styles; utilitarian and/or decorative.

WOODMERE MUSEUM SHOP, 9201 Germantown Ave., Philadelphia PA 19118. (215)247-0476. Contact: Gladys Geiger. Museum gift shop. Estab. 1977. Represents 25-30 craftworkers. Price range: $3-500; bestsellers: $3-150. Works on consignment; 20% commission. Craftworker sets retail price. Reports in 3 weeks. Work may be shipped or hand-delivered with consent. Dealer pays insurance for exhibited work. Displays work for 2 months.
Acceptable Work: Considers batik; ceramics; clothing; dollmaking; jewelry; needlecrafts; pottery; soft sculpture; wall hangings; weavings; woodcrafting; and small antiques. Finished and one-of-a-kind pieces; utilitarian and/or decorative.
Profile: "All items must first be approved by the Museum Shop committee. Correspondence and photos are acceptable. Work for consideration by committee must be hand-delivered." Heaviest wholesale buying time: early fall; best selling time: November-December.

THE WORKS CRAFT GALLERY, 319 South St., Philadelphia PA 19147. (215)922-7775. Contact: Ruth or Rick Snyderman. Estab. 1965. Represents 230 craftworkers. Consider batik; ceramics; glass art; jewelry; metalsmithing; pottery; quilting; soft sculpture; wall hangings; weavings; and woodcrafting. One-of-a-kind and handmade production-line items only; utilitarian and/or decorative. Price range: $3.50-1,800; bestsellers: $5-40. Buys outright or on consignment; 40% commission. Craftworker sets retail price. Requires exclusive center city representation. Send transparencies or photos and arrange interview. Reports in 2 weeks. Gallery pays shipping and insurance for exhibited work.
Profile: Craftworker's item(s) displayed as a unit and marked with name and medium. Items rotated weekly in gallery. Heaviest wholesale buying time: October-December.

Rhode Island

ANYART CONTEMPORARY ARTS CENTER, 5 Steeple St., Providence RI 02903. (401)861-0830. Director: Elaine Kaufman. "We are a nonprofit gallery and do not sell anything. The artist deals with the public directly. We exist as an alternative space to museums and profit-making galleries. We are supported by grants, memberships and donations." Estab. 1975. Customers are fine arts and theatre-oriented people, plus some writers.
Acceptable Work: Considers batik, ceramics, glass art, jewelry, leatherworking, metalsmithing, pottery, wall hangings, weavings, woodcrafting, bookbinding and sculpture. Fine one-of-a-kind items only.
Terms: Send resume and slides with SASE. Exhibition committee meets the second Monday of each month. Artist hangs own show, unless help requested.

COOPER & FRENCH, LTD., 130 Thames St., Newport RI 02840. (401)849-6512. Director: Marve H. Cooper. Estab. 1974. Represents over 50 craftworkers. Considers ceramics; glass art; jewelry; metalsmithing; pottery; quilting; soft sculpture; wall hangings; weavings; and woodcrafting. Finished handmade decorative work that appeals to the serious collector. Price range: $25-1,500. Buys outright or on consignment for exhibitions. 40% commission. Craftworker sets retail price. Query with transparencies or photos, or arrange interview. Reports in 1 week. Dealer pays shipping to shop and insurance on exhibited work. Heaviest wholesale buying time: spring and fall; best selling time: summer and Christmas. Best exhibiting time: spring and summer.

FAYERWEATHER CRAFT CENTER, Box 206, W. Kingston RI 02892. (401)789-9072. Director: Eleanor H. Sickler. Craft and gift shop. Estab. 1966. Represents 40 craftworkers. Price range: $1-100; bestsellers: $1-20. Works on consignment; 33⅓% commission. Retail price set by joint agreement. Work may be shipped or hand-delivered. Dealer pays insurance on exhibited work, but we are not responsible for shoplifting.
Acceptable Work: Considers batik; candlemaking; ceramics; clothing; decoupage; jewelry; leatherworking; metalsmithing; needlecrafts; quilting; tole painting; wall hangings; weavings; and woodcrafting. All styles; utilitarian only.
Profile: A nonprofit organization offering classes, workshops and demonstrations. Located on Route 138 at the intersection of Route 108 and Kingston. Season runs May 1-December 23. Located in a historic home built in 1820. Work is displayed on tables. Best selling time: summer and Christmas. Most customers are connected with the University of Rhode Island, which adjoins Kingston.

LENORE GRAY GALLERY, INC., 15 Meeting St., Providence RI 02903. Director: Lenore Gray. Considers sculpture; soft sculpture; wall hangings; and weavings. Specializes in contemporary art. Sculpture must have stand. Works on consignment; negotiates commission. Retail price set by joint agreement. Requires exclusive area representation. Send slides. SASE. Gallery pays insurance on exhibited work.

SLATER MILL MUSEUM SHOP, Slater Mill Historic Site, Roosevelt Ave., Pawtucket RI 02862. (401)725-8638. Shop Manager: Letitia Carter. Museum gift shop. Estab. 1967. Represents 20-25 craftworkers from the Rhode Island Association of Craftsmen. Price range: $1-40; bestsellers: $1.50-30. Works on consignment; 25-30% commission. Retail price set by joint agreement. Hand-delivered work only.
Acceptable Work: Considers ceramics; clothing; dollmaking; glass art; jewelry; leatherworking; needlecrafts; pottery; quilting; wall hangings; weavings; and woodcrafting. All styles; utilitarian and/or decorative.
Profile: Exclusively handles work of the Rhode Island Association of Craftsmen. "Consignment items are inventoried and displayed, with a check written to the artist for a sale.

Craftsmen are encouraged not to leave items on display past 1 year." Best selling time: late spring, summer and Christmas. Many customers are tourists.

THE SPECTRUM OF AMERICAN ARTISTS & CRAFTSMEN, INC., Bannister's Wharf, Newport RI 02840. See The Spectrum of American Artists and Craftsmen, Inc., Brewster, Massachusetts.

WELCOME ROOD STUDIO, S. Killingly Rd., Foster RI 02825. (401)397-3045. Contact: Elizabeth Zimmerman. Estab. 1970. Represents 6 local craftworkers. Considers primarily stoneware pottery; also glass art, metalsmithing, quilting, soft sculpture, wall hangings, weavings and woodcrafting. Finished, one-of-a-kind and production-line items only; utilitarian and/or decorative. Price range: $3.50-100; bestsellers: $3.50-25. Works on consignment; 25% commission. Retail price set by joint agreement. Arrange interview. Reports in 4 weeks.
Profile: Crafts remain in shop until sold. All items, except wall hangings, are rearranged monthly. Best selling time: fall-Christmas. "It is primarily a salesroom for the stoneware pottery produced on the premises. Other work is an addition to this, but does not receive the same volume turnover." Customers are primarily young married couples; they buy crafts for usefulness.

ZERO WAMPUM, 63 Tower Hill Rd., Wakefield RI 02879. (401)789-7172. Contact: Amy Klingensmith. Gift shop. Estab. 1971. Represents 10 craftworkers. Price range: up to $100; bestsellers: $5-30. Buys outright. Retail price set by joint agreement. Reports in 2 weeks. Work may be shipped or hand-delivered; Heaviest wholesale buying time: spring and fall; best selling time: summer and winter.
Acceptable Work: Considers candlemaking; jewelry; pottery; soft sculpture; weavings; house-oriented goods or personal items; unique collectables; cards; handwoven rugs; house accessories; Christmas ornaments; and some jewelry (silver or 14 K gold).

South Carolina

ALLENS' CREATIONS INC. FRAME & ART GALLERY, Box 452 University Square Mini Mall, Clemson SC 29631. (803)654-3594. Contact: Doris Allen. Gallery and frame/gift shop. Estab. 1976. Represents 5-10 craftworkers.
Acceptable Work: Considers glass art, jewelry, pottery, scrimshaw, woodcrafting and flaw-free needlecrafts (made from quality materials). No cardboard or pressure sensitive tapes. One-of-a-kind and a few handmade production-line items. Price range: $2-50; bestsellers: $5-10.
Terms: Buys outright but mostly works on consignment; 33⅓% commission. Retail price set by craftworker or joint agreement. Send resume or call for appointment. Reports in 1 week. Work may be shipped or hand delivered. Dealer pays insurance on exhibited work. Display time: 90 days.
Profile: "We specialize in museum mounting of artwork, needlework framing, laminating shrink wrapping and local and student arts and crafts. Breakable items are put in glass cases. Others are in modernly decorated open spaces." Customers: early 20s, $15-40,000 incomes, and interested in limited edition collections. Heaviest wholesale buying and best selling time: Thanksgiving-Christmas.

ANDERSON COUNTY ARTS COUNCIL, 405 N. Main St., Anderson SC 29621. (803)224-8811. Executive Director: Sue A. Parks. Gallery/gift shop. Estab. 1976. Represents 20-25 craftworkers.
Acceptable Work: Considers batik; candlemaking; clothing; dollmaking; glass art; jewelry; leatherworking; metalsmithing; needlecrafts; pottery; quilting; soft sculpture; wall hangings; weavings and woodcrafting. Price range: 15¢-$300; bestsellers: $1-20.
Terms: Works on consignment. 33⅓% commission, nonmembers; 20%, members. Retail price set by craftworker. Requires a one-time $5 entry fee. Reports in 4 weeks on sales; inquiries in 1 week. Work may be shipped or hand-delivered; dealer pays insurance on exhibited work.
Profile: "When received, items are inventoried and then displayed in cases or on the walls. There's no time limit on displays." Best selling time: Christmas. Customers are generally members of the Arts Council, middle to upper income bracket.

THE ARTS COUNCIL OF SPARTANBURG COUNTY, INC., 385 S. Spring St., Spartanburg SC 29301. (803)583-2776. Assistant Director: Ava J. Hughes. Local arts center with exhibition areas.
Acceptable Work: Considers batik, glass art, jewelry, leatherworking, metalsmithing, needlecrafts, pottery, quilting, scrimshaw, soft sculpture, wall hangings, weavings and woodcrafting.

One-of-a-kind designer pieces only. Price range: $3-5,000; bestsellers: $3-100.
Terms: "We exhibit works of artists for a commissiion of 33⅓% on all sales." Craftworker sets retail price. Send resume and slides with SASE. Reports in 4 weeks maximum. Center pays insurance on exhibited work. Work is displayed a maximum of 4 weeks.
Profile: "We are a local arts center serving an area of over 100,000 people. Local school groups, scouts, senior citizens and other special interest groups visit and tour our facilities. We are the 'umbrella' organization of 49 arts-related groups in this area."

THE BOHEMIAN, 2736 Devine St., Columbia SC 29205. (803)256-0629. Contact: Karen R. Murphy. Boutique with adjoining gallery. Estab. 1976. Represents 9-10 craftworkers; "but we are growing."
Acceptable Work: Considers batik, clothing, jewelry, pottery, woodcrafting, clay and wood sculpture and other sculptural objects. Specializes in "creative, contemporary styles. We try to have an earthy, but finely-styled appeal." One-of-a-kind and handmade production-line items. Price range: $3-700; bestsellers: $8-90.
Special Needs: Especially needs unusual functional and/or sculptural woodwork and stoneware or porcelain pottery that is functional or sculptural.
Terms: Prefers to buy outright, but may work on consignment only on very expensive items; 33⅓% commission. Retail price set by joint agreement. Requires exclusive area representation. Send slides and price list with SASE. Reports in 3 weeks. Accepted work may be shipped or hand-delivered. Shop has insurance covering consigned pieces.
Profile: "The Bohemian's shop interior is a series of arched sections, one side of the store being a creative shop for women's clothing and accessories. The main gallery for art objects is a sunken area in the middle of the shop, combining white stucco and natural woods for display. The main goal of our shop is to offer our area a creative alternative for buying and for just visiting. Being located in one of the older, restored sections of town (and one of the most affluent), and also near the state university, we get a wide range of customers." Heaviest wholesale buying time: fall and early spring; best selling time: Christmas and spring.

THE BUTTERFLY, 1902 Ebenezer Rd., Rock Hill SC 29730. (803)366-7914. Owners: Gladys Leonard and Linda Perkins. Gift shop. Estab. 1975. Represents 300 craftworkers.
Acceptable Work: Considers batik; candlemaking; ceramics; Christmas decorations; dollmaking; glass art; jewelry; leatherworking; metalsmithing; needlecrafts; pottery; quilting; soft sculpture; tole painting; wall hangings; weavings; and woodcrafting. Needs quilts and "always looking for original new types of crafts." Price range: 79¢-$600.
Terms: Works on consignment and buys outright; 35% commission. Retail price set by joint agreement. Requires exclusive area representation. Send pictures, description and price list. Reports in 4 weeks. Work may be shipped or hand-delivered.
Profile: Located in 19th century house with 8 rooms of crafts. Work displayed on antiques and handcrafted furniture throughout the house. Heaviest wholesale buying time: late summer; best selling time: fall-winter. "Customers are from the upper socio-economic strata, college students and young marrieds."

COUNTRY SHOP, Old Corner Rd., Rt. 3, Marion SC 29571. (803)423-6663. Contact: Dorothy G. Martin. Craft shop. Estab. 1976. Represents 8 craftworkers.
Acceptable Work: Considers dollmaking, needlecrafts, pottery, quilting, tole painting, wall hangings, weavings, woodcrafting and handmade furniture. Handmade production-line items only.
Terms: Buys outright, but sometimes works on consignment. Dealer sets price on outright sales; craftworkers sets price on consignment if within reason. Call in person. Reports immediately. Work must be hand-delivered.
Profile: "The shop is small and I work alone with some help from my family. They all make handcrafts. My best customers are young married couples but I have a good all-round business."

EXHIBITORS GALLERY, 205 E. Bay St., Charleston SC 29401. Contact: Penny Ross or Bert Glassman. Gallery. Estab. 1976. Represents 40 craftworkers.
Acceptable Work: Considers batik, glass art, jewelry and pottery. One-of-a-kind and handmade production-line items. Price range: $5-2000.
Terms: Works on consignment; 40% commission. Craftworker sets retail price. Requires exclusive area representation. Send resume and slides. Reports in 1 week. Work may be shipped or hand delivered.
Profile: "We are a contemporary art gallery with one-person shows each month, preview rights

and a large mailing list. Carrying local and East Coast artists. Pottery and sculpture is exhibited at all times. Change all exhibits every 6 weeks." Heaviest wholesale buying and best selling time: pre-Christmas.

FINE ARTS CENTER OF KERSHAW COUNTY, INC., Box 845, Camden SC 29020. (803)432-0473. Executive Director: Lise Swensson. Arts center/gallery. Estab. 1975.
Acceptable Work: Considers batik, needlecrafts, pottery, quilting, wall hangings and weavings. Primitive and fine one-of-a-kind pieces. Price range: $10-100.
Terms: Works on consignment; 20% commission. Craftworker sets retail price. Reporting time varies. Work may be hand-delivered. Displays work 1 month.
Profile: "Crafts are displayed on walls, pedestals and in showcases. Customers are middle to upper-class adults; middle-aged to elderly." Best selling time: late fall.

THE GALLERY, 385 S. Spring St., Spartanburg SC 29301. (803)582-7616. Gallery. Estab. 1969.
Acceptable Work: Considers all crafts. Primitive and fine one-of-a-kind pieces. Price range: $2-1,000; bestsellers: $10-300.
Terms: Works on consignment; 33% commission. Retail price set by joint agreement. Reports in 1-4 weeks. Work may be shipped or hand-delivered. Dealer pays insurance for exhibited work (up to $500). Initial contact should be made with slides or photos that can be returned to the craftsperson.
Profile: "The Gallery schedules 9 changing exhibits per year. Crafts are displayed in one area of the gallery at all times on lighted shelves, some with locking glass covers, except during the middle of November to the middle of December at which time we schedule our 'Annual Crafts Show' and craftwork fills the entire gallery." Heaviest wholesale buying time: fall; best selling time: Christmas.

HARBOUR TOWN CRAFTS, Harbor House 7, Box 3065, Hilton Head Island SC 29928. (803)671-3643. Contact: Mrs. C. Alden Baker. Craft shop. Estab. 1971. Represents 250-300 craftworkers.
Acceptable Work: Considers dollmaking; jewelry; metalsmithing; pottery; wall hangings; weavings; and woodcrafting. "We're located in a plush resort, so we strive to have unusual, top grade crafts." Fine one-of-a-kind and handmade production-line items. Price range: $1.50-500; bestsellers: $8.50-90.
Terms: Buys outright. Retail price set by joint agreement. Requires exclusive area representation. Send slides of work for consideration. Dealer pays insurance on exhibited work.

HOUSE OF GLASS, 642 Harden St., Columbia SC 29205. (803)799-0638, no collect calls. Contact: Ms. Craig Hunter. Gift and home/office accessories shop. Estab. 1973. Represents 10-15 craftworkers with signed work and others making handmade production-line items. Would like to locate craftworkers in Southeast for reasons of customer identification and ease of shipment, but will work with others.
Acceptable Work: Considers baskets; needlecrafts; handscreened stationery, notes and greeting cards; weavings for table tops (mats and napkins); utilitarian and art glass (crystal, lucite and mirror); and small beveled and/or stained glass pieces with possibility of job development (on commission basis) with architectural contacts. Especially needs craftworkers working in blown glass and crystal; construction items in glass and mirror (wind chimes, mobiles, window hangings, boxes, ornaments, candleholders, wall sconces); copper-wheel engraving; and detailed acid etching. "At Christmas, we add very special handmade ornaments in all media. We also look for extraordinary toys, such as puppets, puzzles, old-fashioned toys, unique animals and dolls. We specialize in mostly fine designer clear glass and crystal in clear glass with only a few art nouveau pieces in color. We seem to lean toward Scandinavian design, but have a recent interest in Victorian and art noveau revival." Price range: $1-350; bestsellers: $3-125.
Terms: Buys outright (depending upon expense and ability to move in quantity) and works on consignment; 35% commission. "Craftspersons should present invoices in a professional manner and be prepared to offer terms common to the trade (i.e., 1/10, net 30)." Retail price set by joint agreement. Prefers exclusive area representation. Willing to cosponsor opening events with artist in attendance and would help set up interviews and appearances with media (artist's travel expenses at his own expense). Send resume with SASE, slides/photos, price list, conditions for custom work and samples of small nonreturnable work. Reports in 2 weeks, except Christmas. Work may be shipped UPS or hand-delivered after acceptance in writing following review of slides/photos. Do not ship on initial inquiry unless small, inexpensive nonreturnable items.

Profile: "Most of our display is against matte black walls with wall-hung glass shelves lit by track spots with table and wooden cube islands free-floating as appropriate for the merchandise. We are located in a revitalized neighborhood near the University of South Carolina and state office buildings. We know most of our customers by name and have a friendly, low-pressure approach with the emphasis on repeat business—very loyal customers." Customers are discriminating; predominately 20-45 year-old well-educated professionals who are active in the arts; middle to high incomes. Heaviest wholesale buying and best selling time: fall, Valentine's Day, Christmas, graduation and wedding season (early spring-summer).
To Break In: "Our customers are very interested in how items are made, particularly in the case of highly technical crafts, such as glass blowing. Explanations that our salespeople can understand and share with the customer would create more interest. Well-prepared written and pictorial information that could be included in the display would help very much to educate us and the customer. Tags giving background of the artist and the item would interest both the buyer and the potential recipient in the case of gifts. Although the craftworker may think of his works as 'works of art,' as certainly they are, he must be realistic and keep his prices competitive with similar manufactured goods unless items are so distinctive that there is just no comparable quality at the price."

OLD SLAVE MART MUSEUM & GALLERY, 6 Chalmers St., Charleston SC 29401. (803)722-0079. Director: Louise A. Graves. Museum of black heritage. Estab. 1937. Represents 100-200 black craftworkers.
Acceptable Work: Considers batik; candlemaking; ceramics; decoupage; dollmaking; glass art; jewelry; leatherworking; metalsmithing; needlecrafts; pottery; quilting; soft sculpture; tole painting; wall hangings; weavings; and woodcrafting. Primitive and finished, one-of-a-kind and handmade production-line items. Price range: 25¢-$75; bestsellers: $2-10.
Terms: Buys outright or on consignment; 25% commission. Retail price set by joint agreement. Query with transparencies or photos, or arrange interview. Reports in 2-3 weeks. Dealer pays shipping from shop and insurance for exhibited work. Items displayed approximately 6 weeks.
Profile: Items arranged in glass cases in relation to other crafts and art. Heaviest wholesale buying time; fall and spring; best selling time: spring-summer. Only shop in Charleston featuring work of black artists/craftworkers. Over 35,000 visitors annually. Customers buy for artistic value and gifts.

PHOEBUS, Box 5725, Richmond VA 23220. Contact: Joe or Suny Monk. Jewelry store/craft gallery located at 500-A Plantation Center, Rt. 278, Hilton Head Island, South Carolina. Estab. 1977. Represents 35 craftworkers.
Acceptable Work: Considers batik, ceramics, glass art, jewelry, pottery, soft sculpture, wall hangings, weavings, woodcrafting and "might like to see one-of-a-kind vests of highest quality." Interested in fine art designer crafts—mostly functional, but exceptionally well-executed; "only the best in production pieces. We try to handle the finest crafts avialable—to select only a few craftspeople to represent in each medium. We sell quite a bit of jewelry—handcrafted in the $20-80 range. We also are always looking for unusual items—humorous or funky or strange. We try to keep an expensive ($400-1,000) conversation piece in the shop. We have done particularly well with articulated sculptures." Price range: $5-500; bestsellers: $5-75.
Terms: Buys outright, but sometimes works on consignment with new craftworkers "if necessary"; 40% commission. Gallery sets retail price "in line with retail prices charged by craftsperson." Requires exclusive area representation. Send resume and slides with SASE. Reports in 3 weeks. "All items received from craftspersons are displayed (with the exception of duplicate items). An item in stock over 6 months may be put away temporarily then reinstalled in 2 months."
Profile: "Our customers are tourists to Hilton Head Island. They are upper middle to upper income professional people. They tend to be 30-45 years old but also we have retired persons who are vacationing. They are interested in athletics and come from all over the East Coast area." Heaviest wholesale buying time: spring; best selling time: summer.
To Break In: "Quality in technique plus original designs or form is our most important criteria. Craftspeople must be able to fill reorders on same or similar items. Shipping and *good* packing are paramount to our receiving pieces in salable condition."

SKULL CREEK CRAFT SHOP, Box 1562, Hilton Head SC 29928. (803)785-6480. Manager: Sue Hill. Craft shop. Estab. 1976. Represents 50 craftworkers.
Acceptable Work: Considers batik, candlemaking, dollmaking, glasswork, jewelry, pottery, quilting, scrimshaw, wall hangings, weavings and woodcrafting. "The items must be of high

quality, reflecting the individual's own sense of design." Price range: $1.25-300.
Terms: Buys outright. Retail price set by joint agreement. Prefers exclusive area representation. Visit shop. "We like to meet as many of the craftsmen as possible." Reports in 1 week. Work may be shipped or hand-delivered.
Profile: "The shop is located next to the restaurant in one of the plantations on the island. "We like to have a good variety of American-made handcrafted items. The emphasis is on Southeastern crafts, but any American-made works will be considered." Customers: ages 21-70. Heaviest wholesale buying and best selling time: spring and summer.

THE TURTLE, 135 Meeting St., Charleston SC 29401. Manager: Emily Parker Marshall. Art gallery/gift shop. Estab. 1970. "Prefer that craftsmen be regional to the crafts which are represented in the Southeast section of our country, but will consider the individual by what product he represents. Mainly interested in the high quality of the craft without too much expense to the customer."
Acceptable Work: Considers batik, ceramics, glass art, jewelry, pottery, scrimshaw and woodcrafting. Specializes in high quality, well-designed, simple styles; some contemporary, mostly conservative in nature. One-of-a-kind and handmade production-line items. Price range: $1-100; bestsellers: $2-35.
Terms: Buys outright and works on consignment dependent on craft and time of year; 30% commission. "We do not keep an item taken on consignment for more than 4 months. Since we are nonprofit, we cannot pay for advertising." Retail price set by joint agreement. Requires exclusive Charleston metropolitan representation. Send slides with SASE or call for appointment. Reports in 4 weeks. Work may be shipped or hand-delivered.
Profile: "We are a small shop located directly inside the only art gallery in Charleston. We get a great deal of business from those searching out the unique gift—totally art-oriented, creative products." Heaviest wholesale buying time: end of winter; best selling time: spring.

South Dakota

AGRICULTURAL HERITAGE MUSEUM, South Dakota State University, Brookings SD 57007. (605)688-6226. Director: John C. Awald. Museum gift shop. Estab. 1967.
Acceptable Work: Considers candlemaking; ceramics; clothing; dollmaking; metalsmithing; pottery; quilting; wall hangings; weavings; and woodcrafting. Primitive one-of-a-kind and handmade production-line items. Price range: give aways—$100; bestsellers: $1-10.
Terms: Buys outright. Gallery sets retail price. Reports in 2 weeks.
Profile: "Ours is a theme museum. We emphasize the development of agriculture in the state of South Dakota from a humanistic approach. The materials we sell are directly related towards our role as educators in this area." Heaviest wholesale buying time: spring and fall; best selling time: Christmas.

CIVIC FINE ARTS ASSOCIATION MUSEUM SHOP, 235 W. 10th St., Sioux Falls SD 57102. (605)336-1167. Director: Raymond Shermoe. Womens' Art Guild museum gift shop/rental gallery. Estab. 1961. Represents 50 craftworkers.
Acceptable Work: Considers batik, ceramics, glass art, jewelry, metalsmithing, pottery, tole painting, wall hangings, weavings and woodcrafting. Specializes in contemporary work. One-of-a-kind and handmade production-line items. Price range: $2-85; bestsellers: $1.50-20. Display time: approximately 6 months.
Terms: Works on consignment; 20% commission. Craftworker sets retail price. Requires exclusive area representation. Send resume and slides with SASE. Reports in 2-3 weeks. Work may be shipped or hand-delivered. Dealer pays insurance on exhibited work.
Profile: "Work is handled with care, displayed as best as possible." Customers: ages 15-80; $12,000-100,000 incomes; interested in fine arts. Heaviest wholesale buying time: spring and winter; best selling time: winter (November-December).

DACOTAH PRAIRIE MUSEUM, Box 395, Aberdeen SD 57401. (605)229-1608. Shop Manager: Sheila Enderson. Museum gift shop. Estab. 1969. Represents 25 local craftworkers.
Acceptable Work: Considers candlemaking, ceramics, decoupage, dollmaking, pottery, quilting and woodcrafting. "We need pieces that are related to our collections." Handmade production-line items. Price range; $1-20; bestsellers: $2-5
Terms: Buys outright and works on consignment; 40% commission. Retail price set by joint agreement. SASE. Reports in 2 weeks.
Profile: "We have a tourist trade only." Heaviest wholesale buying time: Christmas; best selling time: summer and Christmas.

DEADWOOD GULCH ART GALLERY, 665 Historic Main St., Deadwood SD 57732. (605)578-3636. Gallery/gift shop. Estab. 1967. Represents 3-4 craftworkers. Considers ceramics; pottery; wall hangings; weavings; and woodcrafting. Finished utilitarian pieces only. Works on consignment; 30-40% commission. Retail price set by joint agreement. Requires exclusive area representation. Work may be hand-delivered. Heaviest wholesale buying time: spring; best selling time: summer.

FRIENDS OF THE MIDDLE BORDER MUSEUM, Box 1071, 1311 S. Duff St., Mitchell SD 57301. (605)996-2122. Director: William W. Anderson. Museum gift shop. Estab. 1952. Represents 15-20 craftworkers.
Acceptable Work: Considers dollmaking; glass art; jewelry; leatherworking; metalsmithing; needlecrafts; pottery; quilting; soft sculpture; tole painting; wall hangings; weavings; and woodcrafting. Primitive one-of-a-kind and handmade production-line items. decorative. Price range: $1-125; bestsellers: $2-25.
Terms: Works on consignment and buys outright; 20% commission. Retail price set by joint agreement. Reports in 1 week. Work may be shipped or hand-delivered. Dealer pays return shipping and insurance.
Profile: "Most items are marked and put on display behind glass if necessary or in the open, but always in view. We have heavy traffic 5 months of the year (May-September). We are open by appointment other times of the year." Heaviest wholesale buying time: April and May; best selling time: summer.

THE GARRET, 119 W. 3rd St., Mitchell SD 57301. (605)996-4111. Gallery/gift shop. Estab. 1971. Represents 60-70 South Dakota, North Dakota, Minnesota, Iowa and Nebraska craftworkers.
Acceptable Work: Considers batik; glass art; jewelry; metalsmithing; needlecrafts; pottery; wall hangings; weavings; woodcrafting; rosemaling; Indian beadwork; assemblages; and signed lithographs. Fine one-of-a-kind pieces. Price range: $1-2,000; bestsellers: $5-150.
Terms: Works on consignment and buys outright; 25% commission. Retail price set by joint agreement. Reports in 1 week. Work may be shipped or hand-delivered. Dealer pays insurance for exhibited work.
Profile: "Work is displayed in a small but comfortable sales room. Some items are suspended, some placed in shelving, some hung on walls." Heaviest wholesale buying time: spring and fall; best selling time: summer and Christmas.

HATTIE'S STAINED GLASS & GIFTS, 4200 S. Minnesota Ave., Sioux Falls SD 57105. (605)339-1111. Contact: Gary Hartenhoff. Craft/gift shop. Estab. 1977. Represents 80 craftworkers.
Acceptable Work: Considers candlemaking, glass art, leatherworking, metalsmithing, pottery, quilting, scrimshaw, soft sculpture, tole painting, wall hangings, weavings and woodcrafting. Specializes in primitive pieces. Price range: $2-1,000; bestsellers: $5-50.
Terms: Buys outright and sometimes works on consignment; 40-60% commission. Craftworker sets retail price; shop advises. Prefers exclusive area representation. Send slides. SASE. Reports in 2 weeks. Work may be shipped or hand-delivered. Dealer pays insurance on exhibited work.
Profile: "Our shop is located in the New Northlander Center situated in one of the nicer areas of Sioux Falls. The Northlander Center is a $1,500,000 restaurant (one of the finest supper clubs in this area) with 2 shop areas. Hattie's is one of the retail shops. 90% of our merchandise is handcrafted, making us the most unique shop in this area. We have approximately 1,000 square feet on the 1st floor with a balcony of 500 square feet. The shop front and interior is a San Franciscan Victorian style." Customers: restaurant patrons. Heaviest wholesale buying time: February-April (for tourists) and September-October (for Christmas); best selling time: May-August (for tourists) and November-December (for Christmas).
To Break In: "We expect the same delivery time in all seasons—not fast delivery in slow months and unbearable delays in fast months. Consistency in delivery is very important. If we are not exclusive, we insist that our retail price not be cut by competitors or craftsperson selling directly to the public."

W.H. OVER MUSEUM, The University of South Dakota, Vermillion SD 57069. (605)677-5228. Director: June Sampson. Museum gallery, friends of the museum gift shop. Estab. 1968. Represents approximately 40 craftworkers.
Acceptable Work: Considers beadwork, candlemaking, ceramics, featherwork, jewelry, leatherworking, needlecrafts, painting (hide and parfleche), pipe carvings, pottery, quillwork,

quilting, ribbonwork and other native American crafts. "We try to keep the items in the gift shop and the people who demonstrate in the gallery closely connected to our purpose of interpreting the cultures of this area. Therefore, we emphasize native American crafts, especially the crafts of the Sioux, and crafts of the pioneer cultures that settled this area (e.g., Scandinavian, German)." One-of-a-kind and handmade production-line items. Price range: $1-400; bestsellers: $5-25.
Terms: Buys outright and on consignment; 25% commission. Shop sets retail price. Call for appointment. Reports in 4 weeks. Work may be shipped or hand-delivered.
Profile: "The museum is a natural history museum on the campus of the University of South Dakota. In addition to habitat groups, the prehistoric and historic cultures of the state are represented in permanent exhibits (Hall of Man and Pioneer Hall). The changing gallery allows items that are normally in storage to be displayed as well as traveling exhibitions to be featured. The Friends of the Museum Gift Shop features many craft items of a regional theme. Items are displayed in cases or on shelves in the gift shop." Customers: community people, University students, school children and out-of-state tourists. Heaviest wholesale buying time: early spring-summer; best selling time: summer (for tourists) and Christmas.
To Break In: "A tag printed up describing yourself and you craft helps let buyers know that they are purchasing a unique item made by an artisan."

THE PIERRE NATIONAL BANK, 420 S. Pierre St., Box 998, Pierre SD 57501. (605)224-7391. Marketing Officer: Jim Larson. Bank. Estab. 1889. Represents 1 craftworker. Only displays work.
Acceptable Work: Considers ceramics; decoupage; glass art; jewelry; and soft sculpture. Price range open.
Terms: Craftworker sets retail price. Requires exclusive area representation. Reports in 2 weeks. Work may be shipped or hand-delivered. Displays work 2 weeks. "We have easels and some floor space available. We will do our best to display work to the best advantage or follow specific directions."

PRAIRIE PEOPLES HANDICRAFT MARKET, INC., Armour SD 57313. (605)928-3937. Chairman of the Board: Judy Winter. Gift shop. Estab. 1971. Represents 150 craftworkers.
Acceptable Work: Considers batik; candlemaking; ceramics; clothing; decoupage; jewelry; leatherworking; needlecrafts; pottery; quilting; wall hangings; weavings; and woodcrafting. Primitive handmade production-line items only. Price range: 25¢-$125; bestsellers: 25¢-$25.
Terms: Works on consignment: 35% commission. Craftworker sets retail price. Reports in 4 weeks. Work may be shipped or hand-delivered. Craftworker determines length of display time.
Profile: "We are in a rural area, but most of our customers are middle class; middle to low income." Best selling time: summer and Christmas.

RED CLOUD COOP ARTS & CRAFTS, Box 161, Pine Ridge SD 57770. (605)867-5167. Contact: Zona Fills the Pipe. Museum/crafts center. Estab. 1969. Represents 20 local Sioux craftworkers.
Profile: Considers beadwork, wooden Indian dollmaking, beaded vest leatherworking, crochet ponchos, quillwork, wall hanigings and weavings. Specializes in traditional Oglala Sioux artifacts. Handmade production-line items. Price range: $8-250; bestsellers: up to $100 (quilts).
Terms: Exhibits and demonstrates; no commission. Board of Directors sets retail price. Requires exclusive area representation. Visit shop and ask for information.
Profile: "We are a self-help program for the local people of the reservation. We have a 14x16 room, below the Billy Mills Hall in Pine Ridge, with showcases, art exhibits and tables (for beading, sewing, etc.). Many art items are on walls." Customers: low incomes. Heaviest wholesale buying time: winter; best selling time: summer.

ROSSER'S ARTS & CRAFTS CENTER, 617 Spencer Ave., Gregory SD 57533. (605)835-8864. Contact: Carol Rosser. Craft shop. Estab. 1974. Represents 12 craftworkers.
Acceptable Work: Considers decoupage; dollmaking; jewelry; leatherworking; needlecrafts; pottery; wall hangings; and weavings. Handmade production-line items only. Price range: $1-75.
Terms: Works on consignment; 20% commission. Retail price set by joint agreement. Requires exclusive area representation. Reports "immediately." Work may be shipped or hand-delivered.
Profile: "We take great care in displaying items; usually use a protective covering of clear

plastic. We arrange for eye appeal. Customers are moneyed ranch people and students interested in crafts." Heaviest wholesale buying time: spring and fall; best selling time: all months except January, February and July.

SOUTH DAKOTA MEMORIAL ART CENTER SHOP, Medary Ave. at Harvey Dunn St., Brookings SD 57007. (605)688-5423. Contact: Rex Gulbranson. Museum gift shop. Estab. 1970. Represents 15 craftworkers.
Acceptable Work: Considers metalsmithing, pottery, quilting, soft sculpture, wall hangings and weavings. Especially needs jewelry, ceramics and woodcrafting. Specializes in contemporary work. Fine one-of-a-kind and handmade production-line items. Price range: $2.50-25; bestsellers: $6-12.50.
Terms: Works on consignment and buys outright; 30% commission. Retail price set by joint agreement. Send resume and slides. Reports in 3 weeks. Work may be shipped or hand-delivered. Dealer pays shipping and insurance.
Profile: "The shop is located in the South Dakota Memorial Art Center on the campus of South Dakota State University. The center offers a series of changing monthly temporary exhibitions." Shop is located in a long corridor adjacent to the temporary exhibitions galleries, and because of this has a great deal of exposure. Heaviest wholesale buying time: fall; best selling time: summer and winter.

WESTERN WOODCARVINGS, Box 747, Custer SD 57730. (605)673-4404. Contact: Dale Schaffer. Museum gallery/gift shop. Estab. 1972. Represents 30 Western-style craftworkers.
Acceptable Work: Considers woodcrafting. Fine one-of-a-kind and handmade production-line items; decorative only. Price range: 5¢-$1,500; bestsellers: $10-100.
Terms: Buys outright. Shop sets retail price. Requires exclusive area representation. Reports in 2 weeks. Dealer pays return shipping.
Profile: "We have a large collection of animated woodcarvings." Customers are almost exclusively tourists. Best selling time: summer.

Tennessee

ARROWCRAFT SHOP & GALLERY, Box 567, Gatlinburg TN 37738. (615)436-4604. Contact: Faye Cook, shop; or Bette Raymond, gallery. Craft shop/gallery. Estab. 1926. Represents 30-40 craftworkers. Shop has traditional and contemporary production items; gallery has one-of-a-kind innovative pieces.
Acceptable Work: Considers batik; ceramics; glass art; jewelry; metalsmithing; pottery; quilting; soft sculpture; wall hangings; weavings; and woodcrafting. "Seeks excellence in craftmenship and design." Fine one-of-a-kind and handmade production-line items. Price range: $2-50 in shop; $50-600 in gallery.
Terms: Gallery works on consignment and shop buys outright; 40% commission. Gallery price set by joint agreement. Reports in 3 weeks. Work may be shipped or hand-delivered. Shop pays insurance for exhibited work.
Profile: "The shop has its roots deep in the heritage of east Tennessee and the Appalachians. Hand weaving is its specialty with work done by some 70 local weavers under direction of Arrowcraft weaving designer." Heaviest wholesale buying time: late spring-early fall; best selling time: summer-fall. The gallery has constantly changing exhibits and sales.

BOUTZ FAMILY GLASSBLOWERS, Box 74, Lookout Mountain TN 37350. (615)266-5019. Contact: Donavon Boutz. Craft shop. Estab. 1968. Represents 20 craftworkers. Price range: $2.50-500; bestsellers: $2.50-25. Buys outright. Gallery sets retail price. Requires exclusive area representation. Reports in 2-4 weeks. Work may be shipped or hand-delivered. Dealer pays shipping to shop and insurance for exhibited work.
Acceptable Work: Considers ceramics; glass art; jewelry; pottery; and woodcrafting. All styles; utilitarian and/or decorative.
Profile: "Our shop has a very wide selection in an attractive setting with good customer traffic." Heaviest wholesale buying time: spring-summer; best selling time: summer and Christmas.

COMMUNITY CRAFT COOPERATIVE, Rt. 1, Clinton TN 37716. (615)494-9854. Coordinator: Doris Nicholson. Craft Center Developer: Sharon Fields. Craft shop. Estab. 1972. Represents 100 craftworkers. "Must live in the general area because volunteer work is required. We strive to have 50% low-income members."
Acceptable Work: Considers clothing, dollmaking, glass art, jewelry, leatherworking, metalsmithing, needlecrafts, pottery, quilting, wall hangings, weavings, woodcrafting, cornshuck-

A craft and antique shop is one of 32 structures at the Museum of Appalachia, Norris, Tennessee. The museum is open during daylight hours year-round. The buildings have a lived-in look and feeling to portray actual conditions in the past. The museum specializes in Appalachian crafts; therefore "items should have a natural appearance," says Manager John Rice Irwin.

ery and natural materials. Especially needs broommaking and basketry. Specializes in Appalachian and traditional crafts. One-of-a-kind and handmade production-line items. Price range: 25¢-$250. Bestsellers: $1-10.
Terms: Works on consignment; 30% commission. Craftworker sets retail price; shop advises. Call for appointment or come to shop. Reports in 4 weeks, maximum. Work may be shipped or hand delivered. Display time: 1 year; "then, if crafts are not picked up, they become property of the store."
Profile: "The building was an old grocery store we have fixed up and converted to a craft shop. It is a cooperative which especially encourages low-income craftspeople, both in improving their crafts and in marketing them." Displays on shelves, walls, tables, some special display racks. Customers: tourists and local people. Best selling time: pre-Christmas and summer.

THE COMPLEX, 711 W. 17th St., Knoxville TN 37916. (615)523-5573. President: David Chappell. Craft shop. Estab. 1973. Represents 30 craftworkers.
Acceptable Work: Considers ceramics, glass art, jewelry, metalsmithing, pottery, wall hangings and weavings. Specializes in fine and contemporary crafts. One-of-a-kind and handmade production-line items. Price range: $10-250; bestsellers: $15-50.
Terms: Buys outright. Retail price set by joint agreement. Requires exclusive area representation. Call for appointment. Reports in 2 weeks.
Profile: "The shop is a multi-level, interior-decorated in rough cut wood. Merchandise is displayed on rough wood pedestals and crates, and is separated by artist. We deal with name craftsmen and promising craftsmen on a national scale (18 states), giving us a broad variety of approaches and styles." Customers: ages 18-65; students to corporate presidents. Heaviest wholesale buying time: fall and spring; best selling time: Christmas.

CORNERSTONE CRAFTS, Box 1074. Pigeon Forge TN 37863. Contact: Marian or Karen Biggs. Gift shop. Estab. 1977. Represents 20 craftworkers.
Acceptable Work: Considers candlemaking, ceramics, dollmaking, jewelry, leatherworking, metalsmithing, pottery and woodcrafting. "We consider anything unusual; things that would reflect the mountain atmosphere." One-of-a-kind and handmade production-line items. Price range: $2-150; bestsellers: $2.95-30.
Terms: Buys outright and occasionally works on consignment (only those things which have doubt as to their salability). Retail price set by joint agreement. Requires exclusive area representation. Send photos with SASE. Reports in 2 weeks. Work may be shipped or hand delivered. Dealer pays insurance on exhibited.
Profile: "Our shop is located in an area called Old Forge Village. The main attraction is 'The Old Mill' which is a national historic place. Also located across the street from our shop is the Pigeon Forge Pottery which has been there about 40 years. There are many shops here but so many have the same merchandise. We look for the unusual and try to find things that cannot be found in other shops. We keep it uncluttered so that all items can be easily seen." Customers:

middle to high incomes, mostly tourists. Heaviest wholesale buying time: spring-summer; best selling time: summer (April-October).

THE CRAFT CRANNY, 2216 Bandywood Dr., Nashville TN 37215. (615)298-4691. Contact: Nancy Saturn. Craft shop. Estab. 1970. Represents 100 craftworkers. Price range: $2-250; bestsellers: $2-50. Buys outright. Craftworker sets retail price. Requires exclusive area representation. Slides of work may be sent. Dealer pays shipping to shop and insurance for exhibited work.
Acceptable Work: Considers all crafts except needlecrafts, decoupage and tole painting. All styles; utilitarian and/or decorative.
Profile: "All work is shown until it is sold. Displays are moved around weekly seeking fresh background to enhance each piece." Customers are 20-45 years old with average to upper incomes. Heaviest wholesale buying time: fall; best selling time: Christmas and June. "Shop puts on an annual Crafts Fair (in June) at which 100 craftspeople are invited to exhibit."

EAST TENNESSEE CRAFTS INC., Village Green Craft Shop, Box 653. Norris TN 37828. Craft Clerk Secretary: Jean Hunt. Craft shop. Estab. 1976. Represents 100 Tennessee craftworkers. Price range: 50¢-$175; bestsellers: $2.50 minimum. Works on consignment and buys outright; 25% commission. Craftworker sets retail price. Requires exclusive area representation. Work may be shipped or hand-delivered. Dealer pays return shipping.
Acceptable Work: Considers clothing; dollmaking; glass art; jewelry; leatherworking; needlecrafts; pottery; quilting; wall hangings; weavings; woodcrafting; nature hangings; macrame; barnboard picture frames; and wood clocks and lamps. Primitive one-of-a-kind and handmade production-line items; utilitarian and/or decorative.
Profile: "Everything in our shop has been handcrafted by a Tennessee craftsperson. We blend traditional and contemporary crafts, feeling that one complements the other. Our customers are tourists in the summer; all ages, interest and incomes; and locals from surrounding towns who are repeat customers." Best selling time: May 30-September 10.

GALLERY III, 122 Stadium Dr., Hendersonville TN 37075. (615)824-7675. Contact: Pat Beaver. Craft shop/gallery. Estab. 1968. Represents 50 craftworkers. Price range: $2-150; bestsellers: $10-40. Buys outright. Retail price set by joint agreement. Reports in 3 weeks. Work may be shipped or hand-delivered. Dealer pays shipping to shop.
Acceptable Work: Considers glass art; jewelry; metalsmithing; pottery; quilting; wall hangings; weavings; and woodcrafting. All styles; utilitarian and/or decorative.
Profile: "Our customers know that they are buying the best when they buy from us and we stand behind everything and expect our craftsmen to do the same. Customers are upper middle income, educated, aged 25-45." Heaviest wholesale buying time: fall; best selling time: fall and winter.

GEPPETTO'S, 716 Parkway, Tipton Terrace Mall, Gatlinburg TN 37738. (615)436-6665. Contact: John or Pamela Perlingero. Toys/games/children's accessories shop. Estab. 1977. Represents 10 craftworkers. Heaviest wholesale buying and best selling time: June-October.
Acceptable Work: Considers clothing, dollmaking, needlecrafts, quilting, soft sculpture, wall hangings, weavings and woodcrafting. Especially needs handcrafted dolls and wall hangings for childrens' rooms. Must pertain to children. One-of-a-kind and handmade production-line items. Price range: $1-150; bestsellers: $1-30.
Terms: Buys outright. Retail price set by joint agreement. Requires exclusive area representation. Send resume, slides, SASE or call for appointment. Reports in 2 weeks. Work may be shipped or hand delivered. Dealer pays insurance on exhibited work.

GLASS BLOWERS OF GATLINBURG, Box 723, Gatlinburg TN 37738. (615)436-9179. Contact: Bob Myrick. Craft shop. Represents 3 craftworkers.
Acceptable Work: Considers candlemaking and glass art. Handmade production-line items only. Price range: 59¢-$300; bestsellers: $1-30.
Terms: Shop sets retail price. Send resume with SASE. Reports in 4 weeks. Work may be shipped or hand delivered.
Profile: "We demonstrate the art of blowing glass, candlemaking and engraving fine crystal. Work is displayed in cases, on glass or mirrors and under spotlights." Customers: ages 20-50, middle incomes. Heaviest wholesale buying time: winter; best selling time: summer.

HUNTER MUSEUM OF ART, 10 Bluff View, Chattanooga TN 37403. (615)267-0968. Museum Shop Buyers: Mrs. R. C. Thatcher, Jr. and Eleanor Cunningham. Coordinator of Exhibits:

Bradley Burns. Museum gallery/gift shop. Estab. 1951. "Since it is a regional gallery, craftworkers must live within a 50-mile radius."
Acceptable Work: Considers batik, ceramics, glass art, jewelry, metalsmithing, needlecrafts, pottery, quilting, soft sculpture, wall hangings, weavings and woodcrafting. Specializes in fine one-of-a-kind pieces. Price range: $5-500; bestsellers: $30-100.
Terms: Gallery works on consignment; 30% commission. Gift shop buys outright. Retail price set by joint agreement. Send resume and slides. Reporting time varies. Work may be shipped or hand delivered. Dealer pays insurance on exhibited work.
Profile: "We are a museum of American art primarily." Customers: all ages, culturally-oriented, middle to upper incomes. Best selling time: Christmas.

THE LEATHERCRAFTER, Rt. 11, Waldens Ct. Rd., Sevierville TN 37863. (615)453-2069 Contact: Kathy Williams. Craft shop. Estab. 1975. Represents 2 craftworkers.
Acceptable Work: Considers leatherworking and belt buckles only. Especially needs handmade belt buckles and bags. Handmade production-line items only. Price range: $5-100; bestsellers: $10-40.
Terms: Buys outright. Shop sets retail price. Send slides with SASE or call for appointment. Reports in 1 week. Work may be shipped or hand delivered.
Profile: "Our products are displayed on wood chip walls. It is a leathery, but neat and clean-looking store." Customers: vacationers. Heaviest wholesale buying time: June-July; best selling time: June-November, especially October.

LITTLE BIT OF HEAVEN, (formerly Christian Book Center), 734 Parkway, Gatlinburg TN 37738. (615)436-5433. Manager: Daniel Saffelder. Book/gift shop. Estab. 1977. Represents Christian craftworkers.
Acceptable Work: Considers all crafts. Christian items only. Price range: $5-40; bestsellers; $8.
Terms: Buys outright and works on consignment; 40-50% commission. Retail price set by joint agreement. Send resume, slides with SASE or call for appointment.
Profile: "We are a reatil store in a summer tourist area. Consigns only through October 31. Customers are all ages and those who love Jesus." Heaviest wholesale buying and best selling time: summer.

LIVERY STABLE, 455 Parkway, Gatlinburg TN 37738. (615)436-9831. Contact: M. Spiegel. Craft shop. Estab. 1968. Represents 3 craftworkers.
Acceptable Work: Considers leatherworking, pottery, woodcrafting and any mountain crafts. Especially needs "all types of small and large leather goods (wallets, coin pouches, carrying bags, belt bags, belts, purses, handbags). Handmade production-line items only. Price range: $5-55; bestsellers: $5-40.
Terms: Net 30/60. Owner sets retail price. Send resume, slides/photos//catalog/samples with SASE. Reports in 1 week. Work may be shipped or hand delivered.
Profile: "We are growing yearly because of the blessings of God on our effort to support the work of Jesus Christ here in our community and fine work. Work is displayed in mid-1800 decor with antiques and stable atmosphere. Wood and antiques are used as displays along with old display cases." Customers: tourists from the Great Smoky Mountains National Park (8-12 million/year). Heaviest wholesale buying time: May-November; best selling time: summer.

MUSEUM OF APPALACHIA, Box 359, Norris TN 37828. (615)494-7680. Manager: John Rice Irwin. Museum gift shop. Estab. 1968. Represents 20 craftworkers.
Acceptable Work: Considers candlemaking, ceramics, dollmaking, leatherworking, pottery, and woodcrafting. "Items should have a natural appearance." Specializes in Appalachian crafts. One-of-a-kind and handmade production-line items. Price range: $1-20; bestsellers: $2-5.
Terms: Buys outright and works on consignment; 30-40% commission. Retail price set by joint agreement. Call for appointment. Reports in 1 week. Work may be shipped or hand delivered.
Profile: Museum consists of many buildings (with a lived-in look and feeling), one of them a craft and antique shop. Heaviest wholesale buying time: February-March; best selling time: summer and autumn.

OATES GALLERY, 97 N. Tillman, Memphis TN 38111. (901)323-5659. Director: Rena Dewey. Considers sculpture. Buys outright and works on consignment. Retail price set by joint agreement. Requires exclusive area representation. Send photos; if gallery is interested, will arrange interview. SASE. Gallery pays insurance on exhibited work and may pay shipping and in-transit insurance.

Profile: Work is displayed 2-4 weeks. Some work may be displayed that is not for sale during an exhibition.

THE PLUM NELLY SHOP, 1201 Hixson Pike, Chattanooga TN 37405. (615)266-0585. Contact: Celia Marks. Estab. 1971. Represents 300 out-of-town craftworkers. Considers candlemaking; ceramics; metalsmithing; pottery; and woodcrafting. "We use the Southern Highland Handicrafts Guild standards in judging crafts to be bought for our shop; however, we don't limit ourselves to the crafts accepted for membership in that organization." Finished, one-of-a-kind and handmade production-line items only; utilitarian and/or decorative. Price range: $1-200; bestsellers: $3-35. Buys outright. Retail price set by joint agreement. Requires exclusive Chattanooga representation. "We usually spot new work at craft fairs and shows, but frequently craftsmen know us by reputation and write to set up an appointment to show their work." Reports in 2 weeks. Dealer pays shipping from shop and insurance on exhibited work. "Send work by UPS; it is then automatically insured while in-transit."
Profile: "We buy with considerable discrimination and time period between purchase and sale is not of great concern to us." Heaviest wholesale buying time: spring and summer; best selling time: Christmas. Customers are young career women and male executives in their 30's.
To Break In: "I am an ex-food editor and author of 2 cookbooks and therefore am extremely practical in my approach to functional items. Those items to be used in the kitchen come in for special scrutiny (i.e., handles large enough to grasp while holding a cloth pot holder, smooth bottoms, dishwasher-safe, etc.)."

QUILTER'S HAVEN, Box 151, Bell Buckle TN 37020. (615)275-2292. Contact: Mildred W. Locke. Quilter's supply shop. Estab. 1975. Represents 10 craftworkers. Price range: $1-500. Buys outright. Reports in 3 weeks. Work may be shipped or hand-delivered.
Acceptable Work: Considers quilting; utilitarian and/or decorative. Especially needs traditional quilts (grandmother's flower garden, Dresden plate, double wedding ring) approximate size 90x108; preferably all cotton with fabrics washed before being made.
Profile: "My shop is in a 100-year-old house on a farm. I ship quilts all over the United States."

RIDGEWAY GALLERY, 132 Ridgeway Center, Oak Ridge TN 37830. (615)483-6690. Manager: Mirjam Koehler.
Acceptable Work: Considers ceramics; sculpture; tapestries; rugs; glass; jewelry; and metalsmithing. Price range: $2-1,000.
Terms: Buys outright (50% discount) or on consignment (33⅓ commission). Craftworker sets retail price. Send transparencies or photos. Gallery pays half shipping costs and insurance for exhibited work. Items displayed 6 months minimum. Sponsors openings.

SERENDIPITY GALLERIES, 120 East Vine, Murfreesboro TN 37130. Director: Mrs. Louis Rowland. Gallery. Estab. 1967. Represents 30-35 craftworkers. Price range: $3-500; bestsellers: $2.50-25. Works on consignment and buys outright. Retail price set by joint agreement. Reports in 4 weeks. Work on consignment may be shipped or hand-delivered by prior arrangement. Dealer pays insurance for exhibited consignment work.
Acceptable Work: Considers woodcrafting, weaving, pottery and most other crafts. One-of-a-kind pieces; utilitarian only. Especially needs contemporary pottery: cups, mugs and casseroles.
Profile: "We are the only shop in a city of 20,000; customers have middle income to upper middle; professional people; some have art background." Displays work 4-8 weeks. Heaviest wholesale buying time: mid-spring; best selling time: fall-winter.

STOREHOUSE, INC., 4105 Hillsboro Rd., Nashville TN 37215. See Storehouse, Inc., 2737 Apple Valley Rd. NE, Atlanta, Georgia.

STUDENTS' MUSEUM, Box 6108, Knoxville TN 37914. (615)637-1121. Director: Edna Clark. Museum gift shop. Estab. 1976. Represents student craftworkers.
Acceptable Work: Considers batik, dollmaking, pottery and quilting. Specializes in contemporary crafts done by local students. One-of-a-kind and handmade production-line items. Price range; 10¢-$5; bestsellers: $1-3.
Terms: Buys outright and works on consignment; 50% commission. Shop sets retail price. Send resume. "Don't come without an appointment. Try to come Tuesday afternoons when the Sales Shop Buyers are here." Reports in 2 weeks. Work may be shipped or hand delivered.
Profile: "The museum is a non-profit educational institute with science, natural history, drama,

arts and crafts." Customers: student of all ages. Heaviest wholesale buying and best selling time: spring.

STUDIO S GALLERY, 1426 Avon Rd., Murfreesboro TN 37130. (615)896-0789. Contact: Lewis D. Snyder. Craft gallery. Estab. 1970. Sponsors 1 and 2-man shows. Considers needlecrafts; pottery; wall hangings; weavings; and woodcrafting. Fine one-of-a-kind and handmade production-line items; utilitarian and/or decorative. Retail price set by joint agreement. 30% commission on gallery shows. Hand-delivered work only.
Profile: "We operate a production shop and gallery." Customers are college to middle age; middle income and up. Best selling time: summer-fall.

TULLAHOMA FINE ARTS CENTER, 401 S. Jackson St., Tullahoma TN 37388. (615)455-1234. President: Lucy F. Hollis. Gallery. Estab. 1969. Considers batik, jewelry, needlecrafts, pottery, wall hangings and weavings. Specializes in fine one-of-a-kind crafts. Price range: $2.50-$250; bestsellers: $5-100. Retail price set by craftworker or joint agreement. Send resume or slides. Heaviest wholesale buying time: post-holidays; best selling time: holidays and May.

VILLAGE CRAFTS, 5204 Kineston Pike, Knoxville TN 37919. (615)584-2562. Contact: Alex Woodcox. Craft shop. Estab. 1975. Represents 30-40 Tennessee craftworkers.
Acceptable Work: Considers batik; ceramics; leaded and stained glass; jewelry; metalsmithing; pottery; wall hangings; weavings; and woodcrafting. Primitive and fine one-of-a-kind pieces. Price range: 98¢-$300; bestsellers: $3-30.
Terms: Works on consignment and buys outright; 30% commission. Craftworker sets retail price. Work may be hand-delivered. Dealer pays shipping to shop if work is purchased.
Profile: "Customers are 20-70, intellectual and from students to people with upper bracket incomes." Displays work 60 days. Best selling and heaviest wholesale buying time: pre-Christmas.

WHIFF 'N POUFF, 18 The Village, Gatlinburg TN 37738. (615)436-7458. Contact: Barbara Blaker. Gift shop/boutique. Estab. 1970. Represents 12-15 craftworkers.
Acceptable Work: Considers clothing, decoupage, jewelry, leatherworking and needlecraft accessories. Especially needs handmade tops, purses, jewelry and accessories. "I would prefer handcrafts that appear to originate in this area."Specializes in decoupage: repousse; handcarved and handpainted wooden purses; hand decorated, embroidered and appliqued blouses; and raffia dolls. Price range: $11.50-85.
Terms: Buys outright. Shop sets retail price. Sometimes requires exclusive area representation. Write or call for appointment and describe crafts. Reports in 1 week. Work may be shipped or hand delivered.
Profile: "In a charming Bavarian-type village right in the middle of Gatlinburg, Tennessee, are 18 boutique shops. We have three. Whiff 'n Pouff is about 20 feet square with 2 stories decorated with French provincial furniture, marble fireplace and shag carpeting. Items are given key positions until proven either successful or not. If not, I reduce them to my cost and don't reorder." Customers: middle class, teen to senior citizens. Heaviest wholesale buying time: spring-summer; best selling time: June-October.

Texas
AMARILLO ART CENTER SALES GALLERY, Box 447, Amarillo TX 79178. (806)372-8356. Manager: Jackie Wilson. Museum gift shop/gallery. Estab. 1972. Represents 50 craftworkers.
Acceptable Work: Considers batik, glass art, jewelry, leatherworking, metalsmithing, needlecrafts, pottery, quilting, soft sculpture, tole painting, wall hangings, weavings and woodcrafting. One-of-a-kind and handmade production-line items. Price range: 50¢-$1,500; bestsellers: $6-60.
Terms: Buys outright and works on consignment; 30% commission. Retail price set by joint agreement. Send resume and slides. Reports in 2 weeks. Work may be shipped (paid by craftworker) or hand-delivered. Dealer pays insurance on exhibited work. "An artist gallery show (20 or more pieces) is hung for 4 weeks. Individual items are accepted for 60-90 day periods."
Profile: "We're a nonprofit institution, operating under the auspices of Amarillo Art Center. Our gallery space for individual shows totals about 80 linear feet. The shop has about 80 linear feet of hanging space and 1,200 square feet of floor space. Items are checked in and inspected for damage or flaws." Customers: mostly females, ages 30-60 with 30,000+ incomes. Heaviest wholesale buying and best selling time: Christmas.

THE ART CENTER, Box 5396, 1300 College Dr., Waco TX 76708. (817)752-4371. Director: Paul Rogers Harris. Museum gift shop/gallery. Estab. 1972. Represents 10 craftworkers.
Acceptable Work: Considers batik, candlemaking, ceramics, glass art, jewelry, leatherworking, metalsmithing, pottery, quilting, soft sculpture, wall hangings, weavings and woodcrafting. One-of-a-kind and handmade production-line items. Price range: $1-50; bestsellers: $1-20.
Terms: Buys outright and works on consignment; 40% commission. Retail price set by joint agreement. Requires exclusive city representation. Reports in 3 weeks. Dealer pays insurance for exhibited work. Display time: 10-12 months.
Profile: "We have staggered shelving, special lighting on glass shelves and a glass case for jewelry. Items are attractively displayed and regularly rotated for maximum exposure. The unique selection of craft items sets our shop apart from other retail stores in the area." Customers: upper incomes ($15,00-50,000); ages 30-45. Heaviest wholesale buying time: late summer-early fall; best selling time: holidays.

BEAUMONT ART MUSEUM SALES GALLERY, 1111 9th St., Beaumont TX 77702. (713)832-3432. Assistant to the Director: Georgia Baier. Museum gift shop. Estab. 1972.
Acceptable Work: Considers all crafts. Especially needs jewelry, boxes, pottery, baskets and wall hangings. Price range: $25-100; bestsellers: $25-35.
Terms: Buys outright and occasionally on consignment; commission negotiable. Shop sets retail price. Requires exclusive area representation. Reports in 2 weeks. Work may be shipped or hand-delivered. Museum pays insurance on exhibited work.
Profile: Customers: young women and some tourists. Heaviest wholesale buying time: late summer and Christmas.

BELLFORT FRAME & ART CENTER, 7732 E. Bellfort, Houston TX 77061. (713)649-5855. Gallery/frame shop. Estab. 1968. Represents 3 craftworkers. Price range: $20-500. Works on consignment and buys outright; 30% commission. Retail price set by joint agreement. Reports in 1 week. Work may be shipped or hand-delivered. Dealer pays return shipping.
Acceptable Work: Considers needlecrafts; pottery; tole painting; wall hangings; weavings; and woodcrafting. Primitive and fine one-of-a-kind pieces; utilitarian and/or decorative.

BIG THICKET MUSEUM, Box 198, Saratogo TX 77585. (713)274-2971. Director: Nick G. Rodes. Museum gift shop. Estab. 1970. Represents craftworkers whose work deals with pioneer or rustic crafts. Price range: $1-100; bestsellers: $1-50. Works on consignment and buys outright; 30-50% commission. Gallery sets retail price. Reports in 2 weeks. Work may be shipped or hand-delivered.
Acceptable Work: Considers all crafts except soft sculpture. All styles; utilitarian and/or decorative.
Profile: "We are the only museum within a 40-mile radius. We are limited to Big Thicket natural or cultural history items. Local people shop us heavily at Christmas." Best selling and heaviest wholesale buying time: spring-summer.

BLACK'S ART GLASS STUDIO, 3225 N. Flores, San Antonio TX 78212. (512)736-5201. Contact: G. Vernon Black. Glass studio. Estab. 1942. Represents 7 craftworkers. Considers glass art. Supplies for hobbyists.

CERAMIC HUT, 140 W. 3rd, Colorado City TX 79512. (915)728-3942. Contact: Johnnie Hammond. Estab. 1971. Represents 2 craftworkers. Considers ceramics; decoupage; tole painting; wall hangings; and weavings. Especially needs vases, 9-10" high. Finished handmade production-line items only; utilitarian and/or decorative. Price range: $75-250; bestsellers: $30-250. Buys outright. Shop sets retail price. Requires exclusive area representation. Write first. Reports in 3 weeks.
Profile: Displays items 2 weeks. Heaviest wholesale buying season: November-December. Only shop in a 40-mile area. Customers ages 25-65; income of age 25 about $500 per month. They buy crafts for originality.

CHAPARRAL, 2505 River Oaks Blvd., Houston TX 77019. (713)522-2501. President: Dawsie Crain. Embroidery center. Estab. 1962. Represents 10 craftworkers. Price range: 25c-$1,000; bestsellers: $7.50-50. Works on consignment and buys outright: 40% commission. Retail price set by joint agreement on consigned items. Reports in 1 week. Work may be hand-delivered or shipped.
Acceptable Work: Considers clothing; needlecrafts; quilting; and soft sculpture. One-of-a-kind and handmade production-line items; utilitarian and/or decorative.

CONTEMPORARY GALLERY, 2425 Cedar Springs, Dallas TX 75201. (214)747-0141. Contact: R.H. Kahn. Gallery. Estab. 1964. Represents 10 craftworkers. Price range: $10-5,000. Works on consignment and buys outright; 40% commission. Retail price set by joint agreement. Requires exclusive area representation. Reports in 2 weeks. Work may be shipped or hand-delivered. Dealer pays insurance for exhibited work.
Acceptable Work: Considers ceramics; glass art; jewelry; pottery; soft sculpture; wall hangings; weavings; and woodcrafting. One-of-a-kind designer pieces; utilitarian and/or decorative.
Profile: "One-man exhibits are for 6 weeks; general display has no time limitation."

CRAFT INDUSTRIES, 78 Woodlake Sq., Houston TX 77063. (713)789-8170. Contact: Linda Lee. Craft shop/gallery. Estab. 1969. Represents 50 North American craftworkers, preferably Texan.
Acceptable Work: Considers batik, ceramics, handblown glass, metalsmithing, needlecrafts, pottery, quilting, soft sculpture, wall hangings, weavings and woodcrafting. Especially needs functional stoneware pottery. Specializes in "functional work with a small gallery area devoted to sculpture and wall hangings." One-of-a-kind and handmade production-line items. Price range: $3-6,000; bestsellers: $3-450.
Terms: Works on consignment; 40-50% commission. Retail price set by joint agreement. Requires exclusive area representation within a 3-mile radius. Send resume and slides with SASE. Reports in 4 weeks. Work may be shipped or hand-delivered. Display time: 3 months minimum.
Profile: "Our shop is within a complex which houses a total system of education for the public including classes, supplies, and workshops in clay and weaving as well as finished crafts. We find that by illustrating the process within the shop, we sell more than simply by being a gallery situation. The shop is 2,500 square feet, while the studio is 600 square feet. The gallery area provides exhibits on pedestals and risers; another room in the shop exhibits on shelves and pedestals." Customers: ages 20+ (especially women ages 28-40); middle to upper middle incomes. Heaviest wholesale buying and selling time: September-December.
To Break In: "Have a businesslike attitude. Know your product and prices. Stability of supply is important."

DALLAS MUSEUM OF FINE ARTS MUSEUM SHOP, Dallas Museum of Fine Arts, Fair Park, Dallas TX 75226. (214)421-4188. Manager: Susan H. Brown. Museum gift shop. Estab. 1965. Represents 50 craftworkers.
Acceptable Work: Considers some batik (doesn't sell well), ceramics, jewelry, small wall hangings and weavings, and hand-made marbled paper. Specializes in contemporary blown glass, pottery (all hand-delivered, therefore all from Texas and Louisiana), some weavings, jewelry and other varied media: wood, papier mache. Price range: $3-1,250; bestsellers: $3-35.
Terms: Works on consignment; 33⅓% commission. Craftworker sets retail price. Send resume and slides. Reports in 1-4 weeks. Work (with the exception of pottery) may be shipped or hand-delivered. Dealer pays insurance on exhibited work.
Profile: "Small items in enclosed, lighted, locked cases; wall hangings on upright display units and walls; large pottery on low shelves, ceiling lights are moved occasionally to expose them to different traffic. Our craft shop exists to serve the museum's visitors and members (they receive a 10% discount on purchases). We also stock a large selection of books on art, design, technique, etc. and imports from various countries. We have a small shop and cannot have very many pieces from a lot of craftsmen." Best selling time: December.

THE DOOR KNOB, INC., 3022 Sandage, Ft. Worth TX 76109. President: Betty Mellina. Gift shop. Estab. 1970. Represents 8-10 craftworkers.
Acceptable Work: Considers ceramics, dollmaking, jewelry, glass art, metalsmithing (tin items) needlecrafts, quilting, soft sculpture tole painting and woodcrafting. Especially needs dolls, baby items and woodcarvings (particularly birds, animals and folk art). "I prefer traditional designs—Appalachian work. I like unique items—not too contemporary." Handmade production-line items. Price range: $2.95-50; bestsellers: $5-15 and $25-35.
Terms: Buys outright. Retail price set by dealer. Send samples or slides and resume. Reports in 4 weeks. "If I'm slow in answering, it doesn't mean I'm not interested—just swamped." Work may be shipped or hand-delivered.
Profile: "I try to give handcrafted items priority display area. My shop has a country look and I handle antiques, so more traditional items do well—but I am also near Texas Christian University so bright, unusual items go well. My shop is quite small and I have very little storage area, therefore, I cannot buy in quantities." Heaviest wholesale buying time: early fall and early spring; best selling time: fall, Christmas and spring.

THE DUNLAP CO., 200 Greenleaf Ave., Ft. Worth TX 76107. (817)336-4985. Merchandise Manager, Home Furnishings: Pat Stewart Benson. Department store. Write with illustrations of work and resume.
Resale Items: Home furnishings department will consider baskets, carvings, sculpture, Christmas ornament, dinnerware, furniture, pillows, pottery, silverwork, wall hangings and weaving for resale. "For most items we need production work that can supply between 5 and 20 stores." Retail price range: $3-300; set by store "based on cost and item."
Props: Home furnishings department will consider buying baskets, carvings and sculpture, Christmas ornaments, handmade furniture, pillows, pottery and wall hangings. One-of-a-kind or handmade production-lines OK.

EL PASO MUSEUM OF ART GIFT SHOP, 1211 Montana, El Paso TX 79902. (915)543-3800. Contact: Susan Neessen or Joan Goetting. Museum gift shop. Estab. 1961. Represents 15-20 craftworkers. Price range: 10¢-$400; bestsellers: $5-25. Works on consignment and buys outright; 15% commission. Craftworker sets retail price. Reports immediately. Work may be shipped or hand-delivered.
Acceptable Work: Considers ceramics; jewelry; metalsmithing; needlecrafts; pottery; wall hangings; weavings; woodcrafting; and stained glass. All styles; utilitarian and/or decorative.
Special Needs: "There does not appear to be local craftsmen in the field of glass; we would like to know sources for fine paper, stationery, Shaker boxes or other crafts that are indigenous to definite areas of the nation." Also Christmas ornaments, Christmas marketable gifts. Any item with a Southwestern flavor.
To Break In: "Make written inquiry first addressed to the gift shop chairman. We prefer a full price range indication on items; we would be pleased to received slides which can be returned if desired. Definitely do not send items which have not been ordered by purchase order." Best selling time: fall.

GEORGE FILLEY DEPARTMENT STORE, 214 S. Main St., Victoria TX 77901. Contact: George Filley. Department store. Antique department buys baskets; carvings and sculpture; dinnerware; dolls; furniture; jewelry; pottery; silverwork; wall hangings; and weavings for resale. Display department considers handmade furniture and pottery for use as props. Store sets retail price. Send samples.

FORT WORTH MUSEUM OF SCIENCE & HISTORY—GIFT SHOP, 1501 Montgomery St., Fort Worth TX 76107. (817)732-1631. Gift shop supervisor: Mrs. Ollie Stewart. Museum gift shop. Estab. 1960. Represents 6 craftworkers.
Acceptable Work: Considers dollmaking, jewelry, leatherworking, metalsmithing, pottery, scrimshaw, soft sculpture, wall hangings, weavings and woodcrafting. Specializes in "primitive, ethnic, geographical and teaching artifacts for the youngsters. Tourists look for things based mostly on natural materials (i.e., mineral specimens, seashells of speciman quality, ethno-geographical handcrafts). We carry no souvenirs as such, no novelties, and everything must relate to science and/or history." One-of-a kind and handmade production-line items. Price range: 50¢-$600; bestsellers: $3.50-5.
Terms: Buys outright and occasionally works on consignment; 33⅓% commission. Shop sets retail price. Call for appointment. Reports in 4 weeks. Work may be shipped or hand-delivered. Display time: up to 3 months.
Profile: Shop located "at the front entrance of the museum on a corner of halls connecting the main rotunda and a major hall to exhibits. Items are displayed in either open display cases or, in the event of expensive items, in glass jewelry counters or locked glass cases. We are as much a children's center and school as we are a museum. There is an excellent planetarium, science clubs and classes, as well as crafts for pre-school through adult levels." Heaviest wholesale buying time: pre-Christmas; best selling time: pre-Christmas and summer.

GREEN-FIELD GALLERIES, 1131 E. Yandell Dr., El Paso TX 79902. (915)533-5690. Managing Director: Edgar Schnadig. Gallery. Estab. 1962. Represents 10-20 craftworkers.
Acceptable Work: Considers batik, ceramics, glass art, leatherworking, pottery, soft sculpture, wall hangings, weavings and woodcrafting. One-of-a-kind items only. Price range: $2.95-300; bestsellers: $6-45.
Terms: Buys outright and works on commission; 40% commission. Gallery sets price on items bought outright; craftworker sets price on consigned pieces. May request exclusive area representation. Reports in 2 weeks.

HAND MADE USA, INC., 526 Coronado Center, Albuquerque NM 87110. (505)883-5861.

President Don Byrne. Craft shop located at Odessa, Texas. Estab. 1976. Represents 110 craftworkers.
Acceptable Work: Considers all crafts. Price range: $1-1,000; bestsellers: $5.95-200.
Terms: Works on consignment and operates as a high volume coop with a basic booth fee and percentage; 24% commission. Craftworker sets retail price. Shop reports each month with a copy of all sales tickets. Work may be shipped or hand-delivered. Dealer pays insurance for exhibited work.
Profile: "Each craftsman has his own display booth, arranged the way he likes his craft displayed." Best selling time: summer, fall and Christmas.

HEMPWILL-WELLS CO., 13th & J Sts., Lubbock TX 79408. (806)763-3411 or 795-4333. Display Director: Mrs. Vern Wiggins. Department store. Display department buys Christmas ornaments; handmade furniture; and wall hangings for use as props. Particularly interested in spring on formulating plans for Christmas windows and interiors. Handmade production-lines only. "Only large items are appropriate for our large display areas." Write with illustrations of work.

HELEN JOHNSON GALLERY, Box 1159, San Antonio TX 78294. (512)224-7865. Contact: Helen Johnson. Gallery. Estab. 1971. Represents 25 craftworkers. Price range: 35c-$2,000; bestsellers: 35c-$300. Works on consignment and buys outright; 60% commission to the artist, 40% to the artist. Retail price set by joint agreement. Requires exclusive area representation. Reports in 4 weeks or longer. Work may be shipped or hand-delivered with prior approval.
Acceptable Work: Considers ceramics; jewelry; metalsmithing; pottery; and woodcrafting. Especially needs pottery that sells for a reasonable price. Fine one-of-a-kind and handmade production-line items; utilitarian and/or decorative.
Profile: "We are next to the convention center; our customers are all age groups, all income brackets and from all over the world." Heaviest wholesale buying time: spring and early fall; best selling time: March-November.

McCALL'S AT OLD CITY PARK, 1717 Geno St., Dallas TX 75215. (214)421-0901. Contact: Mary Jane Hinnant. Museum gift shop. Estab. 1975. Represents 80 craftworkers whose work can "be identified with the north Texas history of 1840-1910."
Acceptable Work: Considers candlemaking, ceramics, clothing, decoupage, dollmaking, jewelry, leatherworking, needlecrafts, pottery, quilting, wall hangings, weavings and woodcrafting. "Only items representative of the north Texas area from 1840-1910." One-of-a-kind and handmade production-line items OK. Price range: 5¢-500; bestsellers: $3-25.
Special Needs: Especially needs toys and gifts for men. "Only the highest quality of workmanship is considered."
Terms: Buys outright. Shop sets retail price. "Write and describe item made. I will answer letter and either reject or ask for sample." Reports in 1 week. Work may be shipped or hand-delivered.
Profile: Country store located in a cultural/living history museum located in an urban area with a heavy tourist traffic. "All agest visit our store. We strive for high quality workmanship and prices are reasonable. I purchase year-round, but our heaviest selling time is October through December."

THE MAIL TRAIN, 5134 Cedar, Bellaire TX 77401. (713)668-0805. Contact: Barbetta T. Wood. Needle art shop with some crafts related to needlework and mail order. Heaviest wholesale buying time: spring and fall.
Acceptable Work: Considers dollmaking, needlecrafts and quilting. Handmade production line designer crafts only. Price range: $1-75; bestsellers: $5-40.
Terms: Buys outright and works on consignment; 33⅓% commission. Shop sets retail price. Work may be shipped or hand-delivered if requested.
Profile: "A complete needlework shop with all items needed for needlework plus custom made dolls and miniatures. We offer class instruction in all areas as well as individual instruction. Display depends on the item. Some pieces get front window display for 1 or more weeks, while others are displayed in shop cabinets behind glass and others are hung on walls or are draped for display." Heaviest wholesale buying time and best selling time: fall and winter.
To Break In: "We prefer to supply the materials needed for these crafts/needle people."

THE MUSEUM SHOP, West Texas Museum Association, Box 4499, 4th St., and Indiana Ave., Lubbock TX 79409. (806)742-2436. Supervisor: Sue Putteet. Museum gift shop. Estab. 1971. Represents 100-125 craftworkers. Price range: 20c-$500; bestsellers: $15-250. Works on con-

signment and buys outright; 40% commission. Requires exclusive area representation. Reporting time varies. Work may be shipped or hand-delivered with prior permission. Dealer pays insurance for exhibited work.
Acceptable Work: Considers batik; ceramics; clothing; decoupage; dollmaking; glass art; jewelry; leatherworking; metalsmithing; needlecrafts; pottery; soft sculpture; wall hangings; weavings; woodcrafting; basketry; and fabrics.
Profile: "Work is displayed in locked cases; some things on shelves. We want work to relate to museum exhibits and/or collection." Heaviest wholesale buying time: spring and fall; best selling time: winter.

NARANJO'S AMERICAN INDIAN ARTS, 10001 Westheimer, #20A, Houston TX 77042. (713)783-0833. Contact: Al or Stella Naranjo. Craft shop/art gallery/metalsmithing school. Estab. 1975. Represents 200 American Indian craftworkers. Price range: $1-5,500; bestsellers: $5-200. Works on consignment and buys outright; 33⅓% commission. Retail price set by joint agreement. Reports in 1 week. Work may be shipped or hand-delivered. Dealer pays return shipping and insurance.
Acceptable Work: Considers clothing; jewelry; leatherworking; metalsmithing; needlecrafts; pottery; wall hangings; weavings; and woodcrafting. Primitive and fine one-of-a-kind pieces; utilitarian and/or decorative. Especially needs Indian baskets, beadwork, contemporary jewelry and weavings.
Profile: "We are the only Indian Art Gallery in Houston. Customers are teenagers to elderly people with middle to high income; single and young marrieds; professional people; and some art collectors." Heaviest wholesale buying time: September-November; best selling time: October-December.

THE PARLOUR, 2124 The Strand, Galveston TX 77550. (713)762-4006. Contact: Judith Copeland. Estab. 1975. Represents 200 craftworkers. Considers candlemaking; dollmaking; glass art; jewelry; leatherworking; metalsmithing; needlecrafts; pottery; quilting; wall hangings; weavings; and woodcrafting. Finished, one-of-a-kind and handmade production-line items OK; utilitarian and/or decorative. Price range: $1.50-200; bestsellers: $5-30. Buys outright or on consignment; 33⅓% commission. Retail price set by joint agreement. Requires exclusive area representation. Write. Reports in 2 weeks. Dealer pays shipping from shop and insurance for exhibited work.
Profile: Items displayed 3 months maximum; marked down after 45 days. Best selling time: summer-Christmas. Customers are tourists, local residents and medical students; they buy crafts for gifts. "This area is restored Victorian on the order of a small New Orleans."

SANDIE'S SHOWCASE, 2511 State Line, Texarkana TX 75501. (214)792-3071. Contact: Sandie Walker. Gallery/gift shop. Estab. 1971. Represents 8 craftworkers. Price range: $2.50-500; bestsellers: $15-150. Buys outright. Retail price set by joint agreement. Requires exclusive area representation. Reports in 4 weeks. Work may be shipped or hand-delivered with permission. Dealer pays return shipping.
Acceptable Work: Considers batik; ceramics; jewelry; needlecrafts; pottery; quilting; soft sculpture; wall hangings; weavings; and woodcrafting.
Profile: "We carry a wide range, primitive to finer pieces, of unusual items and have a wide appeal in price range, age groups and tastes. Personalized service is our biggest asset."

SHOP OF THE SOUTHWEST, 170 S. West Missouri, Midland TX 79701. Contact: Shop Chairman. Museum gift shop. Estab. 1971. Represents 10 craftworkers.
Acceptable Work: Considers jewelry, pottery, scrimshaw and quilting. Specializes in work from the Southeast and Central America. One-of-a-kind and handmade production-line items OK. Price range: $5-650; bestsellers: $30-50.
Terms: Buys outright. Shop sets retail price. Requires exclusive Midland representation. Send slides with SASE. "If we don't get back to you, we're not interested. Do *not* send work unless it is ordered by shop. We will not return unordered merchandise."

THE SKETCH BOX, 1011, W. 5th Ave., Corsicana TX 75110. (214)874-8845. Contact: Frances Look. Considers batik; glass art; jewelry; mobiles; pottery; sculpture; tole paintings; weavings; and woodcrafting. Maximum size: 5x4. Specializes in Southwestern landscapes, and Indian and Western art. Works on consignment: 30% commission. Price range: $10-95, tole paintings. Retail price set by joint agreement. Requires exclusive area representation. Query with slides or photos. SASE. Work is displayed 3-6 weeks.

SOL DEL RIO, 1020 Townsend, San Antonio TX 78209. (512)828-5555. Director: Dorothy Katz. Gallery. Estab. 1970. Represents 15 craftworkers. Heaviest wholesale buying time: fall; best selling time: fall and spring.
Acceptable Work: Considers batik; ceramics; glass art; jewelry; pottery; quilting; soft sculpture; wall hangings and weavings. "We are a contemporary gallery, but do exhibit primitive pieces and fine designer crafts." Price range: $2-1,000; bestsellers: $2-200.
Terms: Works on consignment and buys outright; 40% commission. Retail price set by joint agreement. Requires exclusive area representation. Send resume and slides with SASE. Reports in 1 week. Work may be shipped or hand-delivered. Dealer pays insurance for exhibited work.

SOPHIENBURG MUSEUM SHOP, 401 W. Coll, New Braunfels TX 78130. (512)629-1572. Contact: Linda P. Dietert. Museum gift shop. Estab. 1977. Represents 10 craftworkers. Price range: 25¢-$35. Consignment; 33⅓% commission. Retail price set by joint agreement. Work may be shipped or hand-delivered. Dealer pays return shipping and insurance for exhibited work. Displays work 90 days. Best selling time: June-December.
December.
Acceptable Work: Considers dollmaking; jewelry; metalsmithing; quilting; and woodcrafting. Primitive one-of-a-kind and handmade production-line items; utilitarian and/or decorative.

SPORTSMAN'S GALLERY, 5015 Westheimer, Houston TX 77056. Contact: Mike Mahoney. Considers Western sculpture. Openings sometimes sponsored. Exhibited art insured. 8 weeks exposure.

STOREHOUSE, INC., 2102 Highland Mall, Upper Level, Austin TX 78752. See Storehouse, Inc., Apple Valley Road, Atlanta, Georgia.

STOREHOUSE, INC., 8415 Preston Center Plaza, Dallas TX 75225. See Storehouse, Inc., Apple Valley Road, Atlanta, Georgia.

STOREHOUSE, INC., 13601 Preston Rd., Carillon Plaza, Dallas TX 75240. See Storehouse, Inc., Apple Valley Road, Atlanta, Georgia.

STOREHOUSE, INC., Champion Forrest Plaza, 5470 FM1960 West, Houston TX 77069. See Storehouse, Inc., Apple Valley Road, Atlanta, Georgia.

STOREHOUSE, INC., 173 Greenspoint Mall, Houston TX 77060. See Storehouse, Inc., Apple Valley Road, Atlanta, Georgia.

STOREHOUSE, INC., 268 Sharpstown Center, Houston TX 77032. See Storehouse, Inc., Apple Valley Road, Atlanta, Georgia.

STOREHOUSE, INC., 1721 S. Post Oak Rd., Houston TX 77027. See Storehouse, Inc., Apple Valley Road, Atlanta, Georgia.

STOREHOUSE, INC., 463 Town & Country Village, Houston TX 77024. See Storehouse, Inc., Apple Valley Road, Atlanta, Georgia.

STOREHOUSE, INC., 6547 San Pedro Ave., San Antonio TX 78216. See Apple Valley Road, Atlanta, Georgia.

THE SYNDICATE, 1066 Valley View Center, Dallas TX 75240. (214)233-6694. Contact: Steven Dean. Gift shop/rental gallery. Estab. 1976. Represents 60-90 craftworkers. Considers all types art and crafts. Price range: 50¢-$2,500; bestsellers: $3-60. Works on consignment, buys outright and rents space plus commission; 25% commission. Retail price set by joint agreement. Requires exclusive representation in mall where store is located. Reports monthly with checks. All work is juried. Dealer pays insurance for exhibited work.
Profile: "We're located in major shopping malls rather than free standing or open center stores. We have the look of an exclusive boutique but with reasonable pricing. Welfare and success of craftworker first consideration; we have very strong reputation for fairness to craftworker." Customer averages 18-49 years; middle and lower middle class; good mix of apartment and single family home dweller; and median income of $15,750. Best selling time: winter.

THE URSULINE GALLERY AT THE SOUTHWEST CRAFT CENTER, 300 Augusta, San Antonio TX 78209. (512)224-1848. Director: Luann Cohen. Gallery. Estab. 1975. Represents 75 craftworkers. Price range: 75¢-$4,000; bestsellers: $5-100. Works on consignment; 60% commission. Retail price set by joint agreement. Reports in 1 week. Work may be shipped or hand-delivered. Dealer pays insurance for exhibited work. Displays work 6 months. Best selling time: Christmas, spring and summer.
Acceptable Work: Considers batik; candlemaking; ceramics; clothing; dollmaking; glass art; jewelry; leatherworking; metalsmithing; needlecrafts; pottery; woodcrafting; quilting; soft sculpture; wall hangings; weavings; oils; watercolors; prints; and other fine art. Especially needs glass and wood. Fine one-of-a-kind and handmade production-line items; utilitarian and/or decorative.

WATKINS, INC., Box 89, Quanah TX 79252. (817)663-2261. General Manager: Douglas Jeffrey. Department store. Fabric department buys and consigns Christmas ornaments; dinnerware; pillows; wall hangings; and weaving for resale. Handmade production-lines only. Retail price range: $2-30; set by store. Write with resume and samples.

WITTE MUSEUM SHOP, 3801 Broadway, San Antonio TX 78209. (512)826-0647. Manager: Erich Menger. Museum gift shop. Estab. 1968. Represents 20 craftworkers. Price range: $1-1,200; bestsellers: $1-40. Works on consignment and buys outright; 30-40% commission. Retail price set by joint agreement. Reports in 2 weeks. Work may be shipped or hand-delivered. Heaviest wholesale buying time: fall and spring; best selling time: Christmas and summer.
Acceptable Work: Considers candlemaking; ceramics; clothing; dollmaking; glass art; jewelry; pottery; wall hangings; weavings; and woodcrafting. Especially needs anything with armadillos on it. All styles; utilitarian and/or decorative.

ZJAY GALLERY, 283 Cicero, San Antonio TX 78218. Contact: Pat Pickett. Gallery/gift shop. Estab. 1975. Represents 15 craftworkers. Price range: $5-425; bestsellers: $15-225. Works on consignment and buys outright; 33⅓% commission. Gallery sets retail price as well as craftworker. Reports in 4 weeks. Work may be shipped or hand-delivered. Dealer pays return shipping and insurance for exhibited work.
Acceptable Work: Considers glass art; jewelry; pottery; soft sculpture. Especially needs jewelry made in silver with smooth elegant lines with and without stones; and earth tone pottery. Fine handmade production-line items; utilitarian and/or decorative.
Profile: "We specialize in items created by black Americans. Customers are young adults." Displays work 3 months. Heaviest wholesale buying time: early spring; best selling time: summer.

Utah

BRIGHAM CITY MUSEUM & GALLERY, Box 583, Brigham City UT 84302. (801)723-6769. Director: Frederick M. Huchel. Museum and gallery. Estab. 1970. Represents 5 craftworkers.
Acceptable Work: Considers ceramics; clothing; dollmaking; glass art; jewelry; leatherworking; needlecrafts; pottery; quilting; and woodcrafting. Price range: $5-300; bestsellers: $5-20.
Terms: Works on consignment; 20% commission. Craftworker sets retail price. Requires exclusive area representation. Reports in 2 weeks. Hand-delivered work only. Displays work 3½ weeks.
Profile: "We have a greater variety of displays than most, including a historical museum, an art gallery, and a wildlife/natural resources museum. We serve all the citizens of our local and extended community area and we are a major stopping place for tourists through this area." Heaviest wholesale buying time: spring and fall; best selling time: summer.

CHILDRENS EDUCATIONAL TOYS, 3363 S. 700 W, Salt Lake City UT 84119. (801)266-3020. Vice President/Buyer, educational toy department: John Gustafson. Department store. Works with out-of-town craftworkers only. Send photos.
Resale Items: Considers children's toys, dolls, furniture and wall hangings. Handmade production-line items only. Retail price range: $5-1,500; set by store.
Props: Considers children's toys and wall hangings. One-of-a-kind and handmade production-line items OK.

THE GALLERY SHOP, Salt Lake Art Center, 20 South West Temple, Salt Lake City UT 84101. (801)328-2762. Contact: Manager. Collector's gallery. Estab. 1974. Represents 75 Western craftworkers.

Acceptable Work: Considers ceramics; clothing; glass art; jewelry; metalsmithing; needlecrafts; pottery; quilting; soft sculpture; wall hangings; weavings; and woodcrafting. Primitive and fine one-of-a-kind pieces. All consigned work is juried into gallery. Price range: $3.25-200; bestsellers: $5-50.
Terms: Works on consignment and buys outright; 35% commission. Craftworker sets retail price. Work may be shipped or hand-delivered. "A piece is usually displayed 3-6 months, depending on the time it was brought in. If a grouoping is brought in, we try to display it in a prominent spot where it will receive the most attention. The group is then featured for a month and then rotated to another position." Dealer pays return shipping and insurance for exhibited work.
Profile: "Items are displayed 3-6 weeks and rotated monthly. We appreciate strong support from our Art Center members, the general public and a good tourist trade. Heaviest wholesale buying time fall; best selling time Christmas.

JOANNE'S ANTIQUE AND GIFT SHOPPE, 457 S. University Ave., Provo UT 84601. Contact: JoAnne Tappa. Gift/antique shop. Estab. 1974.
Acceptable Work: Considers antique decoupage, baby items, dollmaking, kitchen items, needlecrafts, pillows, quilting, scrimshaw, soft sculpture, tole painting and woodcrafting. Especially needs Christmas items (ornaments, wreaths, dolls and other Christmas-related items). Specializes in a country-antique theme (mostly patchwork and calico items). One-of-a-kind and handmade production-line items. Price range: $350 maximum (for quilts).
Terms: Buys outright and works on consignment (all quilts); 30% commission. Craftworker sets retail price. Requires exclusive area representation. Send resume and clear precise photos of work. SASE. Reports in 2 weeks. Work may be shipped or hand-delivered. Display time for consigned items: 6 months.
Profile: "We feature oak and pine country-style antiques in a beautiful old restored 2-story home on a busy main Provo street. We mix handmade items that blend with antiques. Crafts are displayed among such antique pieces as amoires, kitchen cabinets, oak tables and chairs, oak and iron beds, etc." Customers: middle-age residents, some college students and some ski tourists; middle incomes. Best selling time: Christmas.

KIMBALL ART CENTER, Box 1478, Park City UT 84060. (801)649-8882. Secretary/Treasurer: Marilyn Modling. Museum gift shop/gallery/school. Estab. 1976. Represents 75 craftworkers.
Acceptable Work: Considers all crafts except scrimshaw and tole painting. One-of-a-kind designer pieces only. Price range: $600 maximum; bestsellers: $10-150.
Terms: Works on consignment; 75% commission. Craftworker sets retail price. Send resume, slides, actual work or call for appointment. SASE. "All work must go through a jury committee." Reports in 3 weeks. Work may be shipped (returned COD collect) or hand-delivered. Dealer pays insurance on exhibited work.
Profile: Displays are free standing, on walls and on pedestals; reviewed after 6 months. Customers: tourists, convention groups, adults and children. Best selling time: winter ski season (November-May).

LAUGHING GYPSY, 2546 Washington Blvd., Ogden UT 84401. (801)399-3703. Manager: Nancy Jo Larson. Craft and gift shop. Estab. 1975.
Acceptable Work: Considers glass art, jewelry, leatherworking, scrimshaw, wall hangings, weavings and woodcrafting. Handmade production-line items only. Price range: $2-50; bestsellers: $2-32.
Terms: Works on consignment (net 30 days); 20-50% commission. Dealer sets retail price. Send resume or call for appointment. Reports in 4 weeks. Work may shipped or hand-delivered. Dealer pays insurance on exhibited work.
Profile: "We are a small store priding itself in carrying unique items. Business is located above a restaurant and below a teenage disco. By day customers are professional women ages 21-30 and men ages 30-50; by night customers are teenagers who like to disco dance."

TAYLOR-LONDON'S OLD CURIOUSITY SHOP, c/o 2460 E. 7600 S., Salt Lake City UT 84121. Contact: John Taylor, Carolyn Berlin or Robert Holt. Gallery/antiques/framing. Estab. 1977. Represents 8-12 craftworkers.
Acceptable Work: Considers ceramics; glass art; needlecrafts; pottery; soft sculpture; and woodcrafting. Especially needs needlepoint. Primitive and fine one-of-a-kind pieces. Price range: $10-15,000; bestsellers: $15-500.
Terms: Works on consignment; 40% commission. Retail price set by joint agreement. Reports

in 2 weeks. Work may be shipped or hand-delivered. Dealer pays return shipping and insurance for exhibited work.
Profile: "Items are displayed with proper lighting and in or out of display cabinets, depending on the item and size. Customers are 30 and have an income range of $25,000+." Heaviest wholesale buying time: fall and spring; best selling time: Christmas and fall.

Vermont

BECKERHOFF IN STOWE, LTD., Box 62, Stowe VT 05672. (802)253-7668. Contact: Helen Beckerhoff. Jewelry shop. Estab. 1977. Represents 10 craftworkers.
Acceptable Work: Considers jewelry. Fine one-of-a-kind and handmade production-line items. Price range: $3.50-1,500; bestsellers: $5-500.
Terms: Buys outright. Retail price set by joint agreement. Reports in 1 week. Work may be shipped or hand-delivered. Dealer pays return shipping and insurance.
Profile: "Purchased work is displayed with other jewelry; exhibits are advertised and displayed separately. Customers are 15-60, sports oriented and have incomes of $10,000 and up." Displays work 2-6 weeks. Heaviest wholesale buying time: spring; best selling time: summer and fall.

BUSYFINGERS GIFT SHOP, Rt. 2, Box 167, Orleans VT 05860. (802)754-2084. Contact: Judith Soucier. Gift shop. Estab. 1975. Represents 3-6 craftworkers.
Acceptable Work: Considers ceramics, dollmaking, jewelry, needlecrafts, quilting, wall hangings, weavings and woodcrafting. One-of-a-kind items only. Price range: $2-60; bestsellers: $2-30.
Terms: Works on consignment; 20% commission. Retail price set by joint agreement. Call for appointment with SASE. Reports in 2 weeks. Work may be shipped or hand delivered. Dealer pays insurance on exhibited work.
Profile: Displays mainly on walls. Customers: tourists. Heaviest wholesale buying time: spring-summer; best selling time: May-September.

THE CALEDONIA COBBLER, 61 Eastern Ave., St. Johnsbury VT 05819. (802)748-2312. Contact: Cynthia or Richard Corey. Craft shop. Estab. 1973. Represents 50-60 craftworkers.
Acceptable Work: Considers batik, candlemaking, glass art, jewelry, leatherworking, metalsmithing, scrimshaw and woodcrafting. Especially needs 14K gold jewelry of unusual hammered designs or stonework; leather gift items; cloisonne and fine enamel work. Specializes in contemporary crafts. One-of-a-kind and handmade production-line items. "We carry lots of reorderable items (e.g., jewelry), but sell many pieces just because they are fairly unique. Our customers are sometimes conservative so we don't sell too massive pieces of jewelry." Price range: $1-600; bestsellers: $5-100.
Terms: Buys outright and works on consignment; 33⅓% commission. Retail price set by joint agreement. Requires exclusive area representation. Call for appointment or send returnable samples. Reports in 3 weeks. Work may be shipped or hand delivered. Dealer pays insurance on exhibited work.
Profile: "We have a small store right now, but are presently negotiating for larger quarters. We're rustic in appearance and low-key in approach. We do feature a focus on certain items and run advertisements periodically to inform the public about the qualities of these gifts. This amounts to an informal show for a few weeks at a time." Customers: mostly local young professionals; some ski vacationers and summer tourists with upper incomes. Heaviest wholesale buying time: Christmas; best selling time: Christmas and July-early August.
To Break In: "I am not too prompt with bookkeeping, so to avoid mixups I keep separate accounts for all consignment people. This way I can settle up at the convenience of the craftsperson (i.e., monthly, quarterly)."

A CANDLE IN THE NIGHT, 181 Main St., Brattleboro VT 05301. (802)257-0471. Manager: Larry Simons. Craft shop. Estab. 1973. Imports and crafts. Specializes in clothing, jewelry, rugs, tiles, boxes, brass and hammocks including the works of 5-10 craftworkers. Most crafts bought outright, larger items taken primarily on consignment at 33% commission. Exclusive area representation required and all items subject to individual approval.
Acceptable Work: Considers batik; clothing; fabric; jewelry; weavings; and woodcrafting.
Profile: "All small items are exhibited in antique showcases. There are large display windows facing the street and inside a small attractive mall. Well stocked store of ever-changing goods—not a gallery. Heaviest wholesale buying in spring and fall for summer and Christmas seasons.

THE CARRIAGE BARN, Rt. 3, Enosburg Falls VT 05450. (802)933-2263. Contact: Gwen Kinney. Craft shop. Estab. 1976. Represents 50 craftworkers, preferably from Vermont.
Acceptable Work: Considers batik, candlemaking, clothing, dollmaking, glass art, jewelry, leatherworking, metalsmithing, needlecrafts, pottery, quilting, tole painting, wall hangings, weavings and woodcrafting. One-of-a-kind and handmade production-line items. Price range; $1-200; bestsellers: $3-30.
Terms: Buys outright and works on consignment; 30% commission. Craftworker sets retail price. Call for appointment. SASE. Reports in 3 weeks. Work may be shipped or hand-delivered. Dealer pays insurance on exhibited work.
Profile: "The Carriage Barn is a craft shop situated in a renovated 100-year-old horse carriage barn of an operating dairy farm located in rural Vermont. We display our goods on antique tables and cupboards with other shelving made of rough wood." Customers: moderate to upper incomes; tourists; and craftsmen/artists. Heaviest wholesale buying time: spring and fall; best selling time: summer and Christmas.
To Break In: "Two things I feel are important in anyone I deal with are dependability and straight forward honesty."

COLD HOLLOW CIDER PRESS, Rt. 100, Waterbury Center VT 05677. (802)244-8560. Contact: Francine or Eric Chittenden. Gift/craft shop/cider mill in rustic renovated old barn. Estab. 1974. Represents 40 craftworkers.
Acceptable Work: Considers batik, candlemaking, ceramics, clothing, glass art, jewelry, leatherworking, metalsmithing, needlecrafts, pottery and quilting; especially needs woodcrafting. Prefers Vermont crafts. One-of-a-kind and handmade production-line items. Price range: $2-100; bestsellers: $2-20.
Terms: Buys outright and works on consignment; 25% commision. Retail price set by joint agreement. Call for appointment. Reports in 1 week. Work may be shipped or hand-delivered. Dealer pays insurance on exhibited work.
Profile: "We are constantly arranging our displays and they must be seen to be appreciated." Customers are mostly tourists with a relatively high income; also local persons. Heaviest wholesale buying and best selling time: summer and fall.
To Break In: "Be consistent in availability and costs as well as pride in finished piece."

COLONIAL VERMONT, INC., Rt. 7, Shelburne VT 05482. (802)985-2742. Contact: R. Gazley. Estab. 1965. Represents several craftsmen. Considers furniture, woodcrafting and pottery. Finished, one-of-a-kind utilitarian items preferable. All prices. Buys on consignment; 40% commission. Retail price set by joint agreement. Requires exclusive area representation. Write. Reports in 2 weeks. Dealer pays insurance for exhibited work.

CORNWALL CRAFTS, Rt. 2, Middlebury VT 05753. (802)462-2438. Contact: Nancy Means Wright. Craft and furniture shop. Estab. 1958. Represents 40-50 Vermont craftworkers. Price range: $1-700; bestsellers: $1-50. Works on consignment and buys outright; 30-40% commission. Showroom sets retail price. Requires exclusive area representation. Reports in 1 week. Work may be shipped or hand-delivered with prior permission. Dealer pays insurance for exhibited work.
Acceptable Work: Considers batik; candlemaking; ceramics; decoupage; glass art; leatherworking; metalsmithing; some needlecrafts; pottery; some quilting; soft sculpture; wall hangings; weavings; and woodcrafting. Fine one-of-a-kind and handmade production-line items.
Profile: "We are located in an old barn. We have quality handcrafted furniture and crafts, low-keyed atmosphere and are family-run. We have moderate prices and price down, not up. We give very personal service." Heaviest wholesale buying time: June-October; best selling time: July-December.

COTTAGE CRAFTS OF VERMONT, Box 214, Weston VT 05161. (802)824-3930. Contact: Clancy or Hank Parker. Craft shop. Estab. 1975. Represents 200 craftworkers.
Acceptable Work: Considers batik; ceramics; dollmaking; glass art; jewelry; leatherworking; metalsmithing; pottery; quilting; soft sculpture; wall hangings; and weavings. Especially needs medium-priced leather goods; glass (not stained glass pieces); jewelry (bone, for example) and items that can be personalized by the craftworker for the customer. Price range: $1-400; bestsellers: $10-75.
Terms: Buys outright. Gallery sets retail price. Requires exclusive area representation. Reports in 2 weeks. Work may be shipped or hand-delivered. Dealer pays return shipping and insurance for exhibited work.

Profile: "We are one of the few craft shops offering good quality crafts nationwide via mail order catalogs; we also feature Indian crafts. Work is displayed by general category. Shop customers range from blue collar workers on vacation to extremely high income families. Our mail order customer is above average in taste and income, usually a collector who spends $30-200 by mail." Displays work from Memorial Day through Columbus Day. Heaviest wholesale buying time: February-April and July-August; best selling time: July-August and October-November.

COTTONBROOK GALLERY, Rt. 1, Mountain Rd., Stowe VT 05672. (802)253-8121. Contact: Vera Beckerhoff. Craft shop/gallery. Estab. 1973. Represents 50 craftworkers. Price range: $3-150; bestsellers: $5-50. Works on consignment and buys outright; 40% commission. Requires exclusive area representation. Work may be shipped or hand-delivered. Dealer pays shipping to shop and insurance for exhibited work if wholesale.
Acceptable Work: Considers jewelry; metalsmithing; quilting; and wall hangings. Especially needs hand-printed cards. Handmade production-line items.
Profile: "We move items around and try to display a full selection. We are located in a barn; run by a professional craftsperson and our customers are interested in crafts and moving towards a greater appreciation in art." Best selling and heaviest wholesale buying time: summer-fall.

THE CRAFT SELLER, 71 Main St., Poultney VT 05764. (802)287-9713. Contact: Vicki Swenor. Craft shop. Estab. 1976. Represents 75 craftworkers.
Acceptable Work: Considers unusual clothing, decoupage, dollmaking, jewelry, leatherworking, needlecrafts, pottery, quilting, soft sculpture, wall hangings, weavings, woodcrafting, slate products (especially clocks), macrame and calico appliques (featuring wall hangings and special order pictures of homes and favorite landscapes). "I'm very interested in handling weavings of all types—especially moderately priced wall hangings—and pillows to add to our large collection." Specializes in "calicos and appliques with a nice mixture of pottery and wood." One-of-a-kind and handmade production-line items. Price range: $1-200; bestsellers: $1-50.
Terms: Buys outright under certain circumstances but prefers to handle crafts on consignment (especially at first); 33% commission; $3 fee for consignors to discourage those who aren't interested in selling on a regular basis. Craftworker sets retail price. "We appreciate having our consignors come into the store so they can get the feel of what we're trying to present to the public, and at what price ranges we sell our items. We do not set any prices but would encourage reasonably-priced, well-made, creative efforts." Send photos and SASE. Reports as soon as possible. Work may be shipped, but prefers hand-delivered. Dealer pays insurance on exhibited work.
Profile: "Our craft business has recently been combined with our fabric business (specializing in calicos) to complement our craft items. A newly opened 2nd floor with plaster walls and exposed beams sets off the enormous variety of crafts, fabrics, antiques, and collectibles. Year round business is supported by customers (with moderate income) from our small college town population. Summer and fall foliage season brings tourists to our area—most with a good income. We have a strong return business and tourists always expect to find something new and different." Heaviest wholesale buying time: pre-summer-November; best selling time: summer, October, Christmas.

DAKIN FARM, Ferrisburg VT 05456. (802)877-2936. Contact: Sam Cutting. Craft and gift shop. Estab. 1955. Represents 20 craftworkers. Price range: 50¢-$50; bestsellers: $1-10. Buys outright. Gallery sets retail price. Reports in 10 days. Work may be shipped or hand-delivered. Dealer pays return shipping. Heaviest wholesale buying time: spring and fall foliage; best selling time: summer and Christmas.
Acceptable Work: Considers candlemaking; ceramics; clothing; and woodcrafting. Primitive handmade production-line items; utilitarian Vermont products only.

DECORATIVE THINGS, DBA THINGS, INC., 100 Dorset St., S. Burlington VT 05401. (802)862-1715. President: Madonna Wright. Gift shop. Estab. 1969. Represents 10 craftworkers. Considers ceramics, glass art, jewelry, leatherworking and metalsmithing. Especially needs clothing. Handmade production-line items only. Price range: $3-100; bestsellers: $10. Buys outright. Dealer sets retail price. Call for appointment. Work may be shipped or hand-delivered. Customers are mainly female, 19-45. Heaviest wholesale buying time: summer; best selling time: winter.

EBENEZER ALLEN COUNTRY STORE & GIFT SHOP, Burlington Square Mall, Burlington

VT 05401. (802)863-4215. Gift shop. Contact: Jon Luck. Estab. 1971. Represents 40-50 craftworkers.
Acceptable Work: Considers candlemaking, ceramics, dollmaking, glass art, jewelry, leatherworking, metalsmithing, pottery, quilting, scrimshaw and woodcrafting. Finished one-of-a-kind and handmade production-line items. Price range: $5-350; bestsellers: $5-150.
Terms: Buys outright. Shop sets retail price. Requires exclusive area representation. Send resume, slides/photos or call for appointment. Reports in 2 weeks. Work may be shipped or hand delivered. Dealer pays shipping to shop and insurance for exhibited work.
Profile: "Our store is located in a mall situation, consisting of 1,900 square feet. Crafts and manufactured items are combined. One part of the shop is like a country store with old fashioned candies, antiques, etc, while the other section is more formal. If the item sells well in our shop, we continue to carry it. Our customers range from 15-75. There are three colleges in this community, including a medical school and medical center. Average income is $15,000 up." Heaviest wholesale buying time: June and October; best selling time: summer and Christmas.
To Break In: "Must be able to supply crafts in amply supply in a reasonable length of time."

THE ENCHANTED DOLL HOUSE, Manchester Center VT 05255. (802)362-1327. President: Barbara Haviland. Vice President: Jack Guidera. Craft/toy shop. Estab. 1963. Represents "a large number" of craftsmen.
Acceptable Work: Considers dollmaking; soft sculpture; miniatures; and dollhouses. Especially needs toys and collector's items (dolls, dollhouses, miniatures and stuffed animals). Prefers hand-made items. Price range: $1.25-2,000; bestsellers: $65.
Terms: Buys outright. Shop sets retail price. Requires exclusive area representation. Reports immediately. Work may be shipped or hand-delivered. Dealer pays shipping.
Profile: "We are housed in an 1850 farmhouse; we have 12 rooms of toys, dolls, crafts, dollhouses and books." Best selling time: summer and fall.

ETHAN ALLEN GIFT SHOPPE, Rt. 1, Pownal VT 05261. (413)458-3497. Contact: Charles Gray. Craft shop. Estab. 1958. Represents 5 craftworkers. Considers clothing, leatherworking, wall hangings, weavings and woodcrafting. Handmade production-line items only. Price range: $2-20; bestsellers: $1-15. Works on consignment; negotiable commission. Shop sets retail price. Requires exclusive area representation. Send resume, slides with SASE or call for appointment. Reports in 3 weeks. Work may be shipped or hand-delivered. Displays work 30-60 days. Customers: tourists, ages 15-60, middle to upper incomes. Heaviest wholesale buying time: spring; best selling time: summer and fall.

THE FAIRBANKS MUSEUM & PLANETARIUM, Main and Prospect Sts., St. Johnsbury VT 05819. (802)748-2372. Director: William G. Brown. Estab. 1889. Represents 10 craftworkers.
Acceptable Work: Considers all crafts. One-of-a-kind and handmade production-line items. Price range: up to several hundred dollars.
Terms: Buys outright and works on consignment, and loans for exhibition. Retail price set by joint agreement. Write brief letter. Reports in 2 weeks. Shop pays insurance on exhibited work.
Profile: "The Fairbanks Museum and Planetarium is northern New England's center for exhibits and public programs on science and the humanities. The museum's main building was built in 1990-91 and is listed on the National Register of historic places. The museum shop and special exhibition gallery are located in the main building in very attractive space. There's about 50,000 visitors per year, their interests and background vary." Heaviest wholesale buying time: spring; best selling time: summer and fall.

FARMER HODGE'S ROADSIDE STAND & COUNTRY CHRISTMAS SHOP, Rt. 5, Fairlee VT 05045. (802)333-4483. Contact: Beverly Hodge. Craft/gift shop. Estab. 1953. Represents 15 craftworkers.
Acceptable Work: Considers candlemaking, ceramics, clothing, dollmaking, glass art, leatherworking, metalsmithing, needlecrafts, pottery, quilting, tole painting, wall hangings, weavings and woodcrafting. Especially needs stained glass ornaments. Specializes in bright-colored items. Price range: $1-75; best sellers: $25-75.
Terms: Works on consignment; 30% commission. Craftworker sets retail price. Send resume. Reports in 1 week. Work may be shipped or hand delivered. Display time: open.
Profile: "We have a large roadside gift shop and a 7-room Christmas shop to display items in." Customers: ages 21-75; average incomes. Best selling time: fall.
To Break In: "Have your name on the item so the customer may know who made the item and where it was made."

THE FEDERAL ESTABLISHMENT, 58 N. Main St., Albans VT 05478. (802)524-2735. Contact: Roger King-Hall. Estab. 1974. Represents 20 craftworkers. Considers batik; candlemaking; glass art; jewelry; leatherworking; metalsmithing; pottery; quilting; soft sculpture; wall hangings; weavings; and woodcrafting. Finished handmade production-line items; utilitarian and/or purely decorative. Price range: $1-50; bestsellers: $1-18. Buys outright; 34% commission. Retail price set by joint agreement. Write. Reports in 1 month.

FRIENDS & COMPANY, Box 150, Windsor VT 05089. (802)674-6830. Manager: Gina Wenz. Craft shop. Estab. 1974. Represents 50 craftworkers.
Acceptable Work: Considers batik, candlemaking, clothing, dollmaking, glass art, jewelry, leatherworking, metalsmithing, needlecrafts, pottery, quilting, scrimshaw, soft sculpture and woodcrafting. Handmade production-line items only. Price range: $2-150; bestsellers: $5-25.
Terms: Buys outright. Occassionally works on consignment; 25% commission. Retail price set by joint agreement. Send slides and mailing to introduce work and self. Reports in 1 week. Work may be shipped or hand-delivered. Display time: 3 months (for trial period).
Profile: "We are in an old bank building with original vault for jewelry display. Items are featured when new to the shop." Heaviest wholesale buying time: late spring-summer and October-Christmas; best selling time: summer and Christmas.
To Break In: "No hobbyists, and please be prepared for reorders. Don't price yourself right back into a 9-to-5."

F.H. GILLINGHAM & SONS, 16 Elm Street, Woodstock VT 05091. (802)457-2100. President: Mrs. Billings. Department store. Write for appointment.
Resale Items: Considers batik, ceramics, clothing, glass art, jewelry, leatherworking, metalsmithing, pottery, wall hangings, weavings, woodcrafting (especially reproductions), marble and soapstone. Specializes in fine art and contemporary crafts. One-of-a-kind and handmade production-line items OK. Price range: $10-4,500; retail price set by joint agreement.
Profile: "We were founded in 1886 and are now in our fourth generation management. Craftworkers must be on time with deliveries and prices must hold for six months." Heaviest wholesale buying time: April; best selling time: June-December.

THE GOLDEN PHEASANT, Box 99, Chester VT 05143. (802)875-2552. Proprietor: Ruth Vanderhoof. Gift shop. Estab. 1975. Represents 15-20 craftworkers. "I try to use the craftspeople in the area, but I have crafts from New Hampshire, Maine and Massachusetts."
Acceptable Work: Considers ceramics, clothing, dollmaking, glass art, jewelry, pottery, quilting, slate painting and woodcrafting. Handmade production-line times only. Price range: $1.35-200; bestsellers: $1.50 (candles) to $27 (crib quilts).
Terms: Buys outright and works on consignment; 33⅓% commission. Craftworker sets retail price on consigned items. Requires exclusive Chester representation. Send resume or call for appointment. SASE. Reports in 3 weeks. Work may be shipped or hand delivered. Dealer pays insurance on exhibited work.
Profile: "My shop is small, but I am particular about the display of all my merchandise. I rearrange monthly and seldom have like merchandise displayed together. I have several antique pieces used for display. The shop is L-shaped and is attached to the Chester Inn. One section is wall-papered; another paneled in roughboard." Customers: local residents; tourists. Heaviest wholesale buying and best selling time: September-October.

GOOD STUFF GIFTS, Box F, Main St., Stowe VT 05672. (802)253-4526. Contact: Amy E. Good. Craft shop. Estab. 1977. Represents 30 craftworkers, "preferably from Vermont or New England, but will consider others if work is unusual and of excellent quality".
Acceptable Work: Considers batik, candlemaking, ceramics, dollmaking, glass art, jewelry, leatherworking, pottery, quilting, soft sculpture and woodcrafting. Fine one-of-a-kind and handmade production-line items. Especially needs small inexpensive stuffed animals and small ceramic vases. Specializes in bright-colored, contemporary and useful items. Price range: $1-40; bestsellers: $1-10.
Terms: Buys outright and works on consignment; 30% commission. Gallery sets retail price. Prefers exclusive area representation. Send slides/photos or call in person. Reports in 2 weeks. Work may be shipped or hand-delivered. Dealer pays shipping to shop and insurance. Display time: 1 year.
Profile: "Most things are displayed on large natural wood tables; some things are hung on the barn board walls. I change displays periodically as I run low on or receive more items. I usually keep all of one artist's work together. I handle mostly crafts that no one else in the area carries and a large selection of inexpensive, useful items." Customers range from winter skiers to

tourists of all ages with middle to upper middle incomes who want gift items. Heaviest wholesale buying time: late spring; best selling time: summer-fall.

GREEN MOUNTAIN STAINED GLASS, Box 831, Manchester Center VT 95255. (802)362-3612. Contact: Harlan Levey. Craft/gift shop. Estab. 1977. Represents 3 craftworkers.
Acceptable Work: Considers ceramics, glass art, pottery, soft sculpture and woodcrafting. Specializes in finished fine craft pieces. One-of-a-kind and handmade production-line items. Price range: $3-500; bestsellers; $10-30.
Terms: Buys outright. Retail price set by joint agreement. Send resume. Reports in 2 weeks. Work may be shipped or hand delivered.
Profile: "We are a small store (expanding) in a good tourist area, specializing in a limited number of crafts. The owners are both working stained glass craftspeople. Each item is displayed in a setting consisting of one of our stained glass lamps, a piece of oak furniture, possibly a picture on the wall and lots of plants." Customers: ages 30-50; upper middle incomes; professionals. Heaviest wholesale buying time: spring; best selling time: summer and fall.

GREEN MOUNTAIN SUGAR HOUSE, Rt. 1, Ludlow VT 05149. Contact: Ann Harlow Rose or David S. Harlow. Gift shop. Estab. 1967. Represents 20-25 Vermont or New England craftworkers. Price range: $1-75. Works on consignment and buys outright. Gallery sets retail price. Requires exclusive area representation. Reports in 2 weeks. Work may be shipped or hand-delivered. Dealer pays return shipping and insurance for exhibited work.
Acceptable Work: Considers candlemaking; ceramics; glass art; jewelry; leatherworking; wall hangings; weavings; and woodcrafting. All styles.
Profile: "Our customers are 95% tourists and skiers." Best selling and heaviest wholesale buying time: summer-fall.

GREENMONT GUILD HALL, West Rd., Bennington VT 05201. (802)442-3397. Contact: Dorothy G. Ertell. Craft shop/gallery. Estab. 1973. Represents 7-10 craftworkers.
Acceptable Work: Considers ceramics, clothing, glass art, metalsmithing, wall hangings, weavings and woodcrafting. Specializes in fine art designer crafts. One-of-a-kind and handmade production-line items OK. Price range: $3-150; bestsellers: $3-35.
Terms: Works on consignment; 33⅓% commission. Retail price set by joint agreement. Send slides or photos, and call for appointment. Reports in 2 weeks. Work may be shipped or hand-delivered.
Profile: "Our shop has handled weaving supplies and equipment for 5 years in conjunction with the weaving studio. The gallery, a separate room, handles our own weaving as well as crafts from other artists." Work is hung on the wall, displayed on shelving units or hung from the ceiling. Best selling time: summer-Christmas.

HAWKINS HOUSE, Rt. 7, Shaftsbury VT 05262. (802)447-0488. Contact: Ron Spivak. Craft shop/gallery. Estab. 1977. Represents 200 craftworkers, primarily from New England. ' 'We do; however, carry work of special merit from other areas."
Acceptable Work: Considers batik, candlemaking, ceramics, clothing, glass art, jewelry, leatherworking, metalsmithing, pottery, quilting, scrimshaw, soft sculpture, wall hangings, weavings and woodcrafting. ' 'We have a showroom for Vermont cabinetmakers. We take orders for work on exhibit plus custom design for clients." Especially needs furniture and furnishings (lamps, quilts). "We have an excellent handwoven clothing line and would like to expand into skirts, blouses. We now have woolens, capes, ponchos, vests, jackets. We are always looking for new quality pottery work, especially those with textured, decorated and painted surfaces." Specializes in contemporary work of quality. "We occasionally handle works of humor in good taste." One-of-a-kind and handmade production-line items. Price range: $2-2,000; bestsellers: $5-95.
Terms: Most production work is bought outright but special exhibits and special pieces may be on consignment. On works retailing under $150, 40% commission; on works retailing over $150, 33% commission. Craftworker sets retail price unless guidance is requested. Send slides or call for appointment; prefers to see actual work. Reports immediately when review in person. Work may be shipped or hand-delivered. Dealer pays insurance on exhibited work.
Profile: "We are Southern Vermont's largest outlet for professional crafts. Located in an historic setting within a 3,000 square foot barn that has been completely renovated into a modern bi-level shop and gallery. The two levels are flooded with light with ceilings of 14 and 20 foot heights. Production work is exhibited on the upper level. A balcony overlooks the double

height lower level where we display our furniture and furnishing showroom, wall hangings, quilts, and special works. We also have resident craftspeople and working crafts studios on the premises—weaver's, jeweler's and artist's. Additional studio space is available and we seek other craftspeople." Customers: 25-40, summer residents and tourists, and middle to upper income professionals (doctors, lawyers, pharmacists). Heaviest wholesale buying time: April-June, reorders during summer. "Our season is busiest starting in July, grows through the summer, is very heavy during the fall foliage and Christmas months. January-May are slowest."

To Break In: "Several important factors in good business: 1) deliver work on time; 2) acknowledge orders and reorders; 3) advise if order will be late and by how much; 4) advise in advance of price rises on production work and if possible, allow shop cut-off date for purchasing at old prices."

HOGBACK MOUNTAIN GIFT SHOP, INC., Rt. 9, Marlboro VT 05344. Museum craft/gift shop. Estab. 1938. Represents only a few craftworkers. Works on consignment. Requires exclusive area representation. Write for information. Work may be shipped or hand-delivered. Best buying and selling time: summer.

JAMAICA TRADING CO., Rt. 30, Jamaica VT 05343. (802)874-4106. Contact: Sally Gardner. Gift shop. Estab. 1976. Represents 6-10 area craftworkers.
Acceptable Work: Considers candlemaking, ceramics, jewelry, pottery and soft sculpture. Specializes in Appalachian-type work and bright-colored items. Handmade production-line items. Price range: $2-50; bestsellers: $2-20.
Terms: Buys outright and works on consignment; 33⅓% commission. Retail price set by joint agreement. Send resume. SASE. Reports in 1 week. Work may be shipped or hand-delivered.
Profile: "We are a tourist business. Half the store is antiques while the other half has a little of everything." Customers: summer tourists with children, spending part of foliage season; older visitors of higher income; and especially skiers ages 20-35 from New York and Connecticut. Heaviest wholesale buying time: mid-May for July 1 delivery and mid-October for January 1 delivery; best selling time: summer and October.
To Break In: "We've cut back on craftworkers because too many cannot deliver on time and when their items sell well, they can't fill reorders promptly."

THE JAY COUNTRY STORE, Jay Village, Rt. 242, Jay VT 05859. (802)988-4040. Proprietors: Richard and Ronnie Vander Veer. Craft shop and country store. Estab. 1975. Represents 45 craftworkers. "We prefer Vermont craftspersons with New England as a second choice, but would consider anything interesting."
Acceptable Work: Considers candlemaking, clothing, dollmaking, glass art, jewelry, needlecrafts, pottery, quilting, tole painting, wall hangings, weavings, woodcrafting, potpourri, applique, and especially needs basketry, metalwork, leatherwork and soft sculpture. Specializes in contemporary bright-colored items. One-of-a-kind and handmade production-line items. Price range: $1.50-300; bestsellers: $5-55.
Terms: Buys outright and works on consignment; 30% commission. Retail price set by joint agreement. Requires exclusive area representation. Send catalogue with SASE or call for appointment. Reports immediately. Work may be shipped or hand delivered.
Profile: "We are a country store in a resort ski area with a little bit of everything in the way of groceries, wine, cheese and general items. We have a large craft area and exhibits are casual. We try to group a person's work to emphasizes it, and it's there constantly until it sells. We use boxes, trunks and barrels for display." Customers are mainly Canadians. Heaviest wholesale buying time: September-February; best selling time: December-March and July-August.

KENNEDY BROTHERS WOODENWARE, 11 Main St. Vergennes VT 05491. (802)877-2975. Buyer: Chris Duclos. Gift shop. Estab. 1937. Represents 15 New England craftworkers.
Acceptable Work: Considers ceramics, decoupage, glass art, jewelry, leatherworking, metalsmithing, pottery, tole painting and woodcrafting. Specializes in New England traditional crafts. Handmade production-line items only. Price range: $1-1,500; bestsellers: $1.75-20.
Terms: Buys outright. Retail price set by joint agreement. Call for appointment. Reports in 2 weeks. Work may be shipped or hand delivered.
Profile: "We're the largest gift shop in Vermont, specializing in our own woodenware. Customers can watch the woodenware being made. Items are displayed with other New England crafts in our converted factory space." Customers: adults in middle to upper income; 75% travelers, 25% from Vermont. Heaviest wholesale buying time: March-June and September-October; best selling time: July-October and December.

LANGDON BRIDGE CRAFTS, 94 State St., Montpelier VT 05602. (802)229-0714. President: Cynthia Rumley. Gift shop. Estab. 1975. Represents 75 craftworkers, preferably from Vermont, but also from New England.
Acceptable Work: Considers batik, candlemaking, ceramics, decoupage, dollmaking, glass art, jewelry, leatherworking, metalsmithing, needlecrafts, pottery, quilting, wall hangings, weavings, woodcrafting, macrame and silkscreen. Specializes in contemporary Vermont crafts. Production-line items only. Price range: $2-185; bestsellers: $2-15.
Terms: Buys outright and works on consignment; 33% commission. Retail price set by joint agreement. Requires exclusive area representation. Call for appointment. Reports in 1 week. Work may be shipped or hand delivered. Dealer pays insurance on exhibited work. "Present your product with a positive attitude and have a price range in mind."
Profile: "The shop is within a hotel arcade. It has 1 large, modern, carpeted decor room with good window display area." Customers: local (all ages and incomes) and older women tourists. Heaviest wholesale buying time: summer and fall; best selling time: fall and Christmas.

THE LOOKING GLASS, INC., 41 Central St., Woodstock VT 05091. (802)457-3345. Vice President/Buyer: Linda Steele. Children's wear shop. Estab. 1975. Represents 5 craftworkers.
Acceptable Work: Considers batik, clothing, jewelry, leatherworking, quilting and toys. Children's items only. Especially needs "well-designed children's clothing. Items must be unique, yet have utilitarian value for practical-minded mothers. We deal in sizes infant to 14-year olds." One-of-a-kind and especially handmade production-line items. Price range: $5-75; bestsellers: $5-30. "Successful items for us must have utilitarian value. Soft sculpture pillows don't sell, but we sell dozens of handcrafted appliqued recycled denim jumpers and 3-piece dress-panty-bonnet sets."
Terms: Buys outright and works on consignment; 30% commission. Prefers to start on consignment and progress to buying outright. Retail price set by joint agreement. Requires exclusive area representation within a 30-mile radius. Send slides, samples or visit shop. SASE. Reports in 2 weeks. Work may be shipped or hand delivered.
Profile: "We are a quality children's wear shop located in a small, wealthy tourist area. We specialize in handcrafted children's wear (approximately 20% of our volume). Our volume with our largest craftsperson supplier approaches $4,000/year at wholesale. Handcrafted items are used in windows as focus centers and are displayed on walls." Customers: upper income parents and grandparents. Heaviest wholesale buying time: May-August (for tourists), July-Christmas (for Christmas) and January (for spring); best selling time: September 15-October 30 foliage season, July 4-September 15 summer season, Thanksgiving-December 25 holiday season, February 15-March 30 spring season.
To Break In: "We operate with 1-2 salespeople. If you visit and we have a customer, please let us sell. We have refused to deal with craftspeople because they showed ignorance of business needs. Also, while we do not attempt to mold craftspeople with our ideas, we often work with craftspeople to make their good ideas more marketable."

THE MILLER'S THUMB, Greensboro VT 05841. (802)533-2960. Contact: Gertrude W. Corwin. Craft shop/gift shop. Estab. 1966. Represents 60 Vermont craftworkers. Price range: 50¢-$250; bestsellers: $1-50. Works on consignment and buys outright; 33% commission. Retail price set by joint agreement. Reporting time varies. Work may be shipped or hand-delivered with prior permission. Dealer pays shipping to shop and insurance for exhibited work.
Acceptable Work: Considers all crafts except dollmaking; soft sculpture; and tole painting. Especially needs leather crafts and handweaving. Quality stressed. Fine one-of-a-kind and handmade production-line items.
Profile: "Our building is a remodeled grist mill with stream running underneath; we have an uncommercial atmosphere and give personal attention. Customers have interests from farming to high-level business and professional people." Heaviest wholesale buying time: spring. Shop open late June-September.

NORTON HOUSE MUSEUM, Wilmington VT 05363. (802)464-5102. Contact: Sue Wurzberger. Museum gift/candle/fabric shop. Estab. 1967. Represents 150+ craftworkers.
Acceptable Work: Considers candlemaking, ceramics, clothing, dollmaking, glass art, jewelry, leatherworking, metalsmithing, needlecrafts, pottery, quilting, scrimshaw, soft sculpture, tole painting, wall hangings, weavings and woodcrafting. Specializes in Colonial and 19th century handcrafts. "We prefer historical items but will not exclude others." Handmade production-line items only. Price range: $1-30; bestsellers: $1-8.
Terms: Buys outright. Craftworker sets retail price. Send resume with SASE. Reports in 4

weeks. Work may be shipped or hand delivered..
Profile: "The Norton House Museum is run and operated by the Second Battery Vermont Light Artillery, a nonprofit corporation commanded by James Dassatti. Each year, Norton House sponsors the Wilmington Americana Week Craft show, exhibiting many modern and old fashion crafts." Customers: young to middle age, middle class, interest in Early American home crafts. Best selling time: spring and fall.

OLD MILL CRAFT SHOP, Box 35, Jericho VT 05465. (802)899-4982. Manager: Willadine O. Cochran. Craft shop. Estab. 1974. Represents 80 craftworkers, preferably from Vermont.
Acceptable Work: Considers all crafts. Finished articles only. One-of-a-kind and handmade production-line items. Price range: 24¢-$225; bestsellers: 24¢-$15.
Terms: Works on consignment; 30% commission. Craftworker sets retail price. Call in person. Reports in immediately. Work may be shipped or hand delivered.
Profile: "The shop is for selling local craft items. We have no working craftpersons. We are a non-profit business. All workers at the shop are volunteers and all profits go to the restoration of the mill. Items are put on the floor within a few days (if brought on Saturday, item goes on the floor that day). Depending on the kind of item, we may keep it from 3 months to a year before it is marked down or returned to the craftsperson." Heaviest wholesale buying time: summer and Christmas; best selling time: summer, fall and Christmas.

ORANGE OX, Box 1207, Manchester Center VT 05255. Proprietors: Don and Vicky French. Craft shop. Estab. 1976. Represents 5 craftworkers.
Acceptable Work: Considers needlecrafts, ironwork, copper lanterns and reproduction colonial chandeliers. Especially needs handmade ironwork (i.e., pokers, shovels, other fireplace accessories). Specializes in colonial one-of-a-kind reproductions. Price range: $6-200; bestsellers: $6-12.
Term: Buys outright. Retail price set by joint agreement. Requires exclusive area representation. Write for information. Reports in 2 weeks. Work may be shipped or hand delivered.
Profile: We have a small area displaying Iron Fireplace Tools, lanterns and chandeliers, plus some paintings on wood and brass items. We also make and sell homemade fudge." Items displayed on walls and ceiling. Customers: ages 20-70, mainly 25-45. Heaviest wholesale buying time: spring and summer; best selling time: summer and fall.

THE OWL'S NEST GIFT SHOP, 74 Broad St., Lyndonville VT 05851. (802)626-5170. Contact: Joan A. Hallett. Craft/gift shop. Estab. 1978. Represents 20-50 Vermont craftworkers.
Acceptable Work: Considers all crafts. Especially needs "good pottery designs and candles (hand dipped and of unusual designs)." Prefers one-of-a-kind items. Price range: 59¢-$150; bestsellers: $5-15.
Terms: Buys outright and works on consignment. "Craftworkers are asked to set their price and I will mark it up 30%." Requires exclusive area representation. Send slides or call for appointment. Reports in 4 weeks. Work may be shipped or hand-delivered. Dealer pays insurance on exhibited work. "Craftworkers are welcome to take any of their crafts out of my shop if they have a buyer before I sell them."
Profile: "Shop is all done in barnboards and kept as rustic as possible. Cow watering bowls, barn beams and pegs are used for displaying gifts." Customers: locals and ski tourists in winter; tourists in summer and fall. "This is a great foliage viewing area. Also, as this is a college town, we get many students and their families."

PIPPIN APPLE JEWELRY, Box 115, White River Jct. VT 05001. (802)295-5136. President: Pat Pippin. Craft/jewelry shop. Estab. 1976. Represents 10 craftworkers.
Acceptable Work: Considers jewelry, metalsmithing, scrimshaw, soft sculpture, tole painting, wall hangings and weavings. Specializes in silverwork. Handmade production-line items only. Price range: $1-150; bestsellers: $5-30.
Terms: Buys outright and works on consignment; 70% commission. Retail price set by joint agreement. Requires exclusive area representation. Send resume and photos before shipping work. Reports in 2 weeks.
Profile: "Our shop is small and cozy. Wall space has paintings and clocks on it and another has a rainbow painted on it. I prefer the use of antique showcases and an informal shop to that of commercialized display racks. Displays and placements of jewelry are always changing to give prime location to many things. Our shop is in a tourist area but it is not set up as commercially touristy." Heaviest wholesale buying and best selling time: May-October.
To Break In: "No extravagant and high-priced pieces as spur of the moment buying warrants reasonable price and design to appeal to the majority of buyers for volume sales. Space is a premium."

THE POMFRET SHOP, Central St., Woodstock VT 05091. (802)457-3397.Contact: Mr. or Mrs. D. Cleveland. Estab. 1972. Represents 40 craftworkers. Considers ceramics; glass art; metalsmithing; needlecrafts; pottery; quilting; wall hangings; weavings; and woodcrafting. Especially needs garden sculpture; plant containers; fountains; bird baths; houses; feeders; and Christmas decorations. Primitive and finished, one-of-a-kind and handmade production-line items OK. Price range: $5-350; bestsellers: $5-20. Buys outright or on consignment; 33% commission. retail price set by joint agreement. Requires exclusive area representation. Query with color transparencies or b&w prints. Reports in 2 weeks. Dealer pays shipping to shop.
Profile: "We have just recently moved to larger quarters on the mainstreet in Woodstock which consequently has generated more traffic. An adjoining enclosed garden enables us to display garden sculptures and plant containers to their best advantage. All crafts are displayed with maker's name. Best selling times are winter and spring. We are looking for unique one-of-a-kind handicrafts."

POMPANOOSUC MILLS, 50 Burlington Sq. Mall, Burlington VT 05401. (802)862-8208. Manager: Dick Matheson. Showroom. Estab. 1973. Represents 10-15 craftworkers. "Some preference given to Vermont craftsmen, but if it's the right item, we'll take it from anywhere."
Acceptable Work: Considers batik, candlemaking, ceramics, metalsmithing, needlecrafts, quilting, scrimshaw, soft sculpture, wall hangings, weavings and woodcrafting. Specializes in natural materials usually suitable for contemporary settings. Some one-of-a-kind pieces, but mostly handmade production-line items. Price range: $4-150; bestsellers: $7-40.
Terms: Buys outright and works on consignment; 33⅓% commission. Retail price set by joint agreement. Prefers exclusive area representation. Call for appointment if local, SASE if not local. Reports in 1 week. Work may be shipped or hand delivered. Dealer pays insurance on exhibited work.
Profile: "We are a showroom/direct outlet for handcrafted butcherblock and contemporary furniture. We carry unique, handcrafted items and some imported handcrafted items which complement our furniture. These are often purchased as gifts and impulse additions to the customer's own home. Generally, there is a low turnover of craftworkers we buy from. Things we like which also sell, we'll reorder again and again. As much as possible, we integrate the item into a homelike setting (i.e., a wall hanging over a couch; a clock not in a jumble of other clocks; art or prints might be grouped; handpainted scene candles, cutting boards, or similar small items would usually be displayed primarily on a table or shelf unit in a group). Although we are very selective about what we think is suitable for our store, we are informal, friendly and delighted to have a chance to consider new things. Motto: It never hurts to look." Customers: ages 20-40, 2-income families, tourists. Best selling time: summer and Christmas.

QUAIGH DESIGN CENTRE, INC., Box 114, Wilmington VT 05363. (802)464-2780. Contact: Lilias MacBean Hart. Craft shop. Estab. 1968. Represents 85 New England craftworkers. Price range: $1-250; bestsellers: $4-40. Buys outright. Gallery sets retail price. Requires exclusive area representation. Only replies if interested. Work may be shipped or hand-delivered. Dealer pays shipping to shop.
Acceptable Work: Considers batik; candlemaking; ceramics; glass art; jewelry; leatherworking; metalsmithing; needlecrafts; pottery; wall hangings; weavings; and woodcrafting. Fine handmade production-line items.
Profile: "Each craftperson's work is usually displayed in one place. We always buy items which are useful, a good price, well designed and professionally presented. Our customers range from the local resort worker to the odd millionaire." Heaviest wholesale buying time: spring-summer; best selling time: summer-fall and Christmas.

QUIMBY COUNTRY, Averill VT 05901. (802)822-5533. Manager: June W. LaRou. Gift shop. Estab. 1894.
Acceptable Work: Considers decoupage, jewelry, needlecrafts, pottery, tole painting, and woodcrafting. Handmade production-line items only. Price range: $3-15.
Terms: Buys outright. Shop sets retail price. Send slides or catalog with pictures. Work must be mailed or shipped.
Profile: "We have a small shop located in the office of the resort. We are in the midst of a mountain area of lakes and forests in northern Vermont, bordering Canada and New Hampshire." Activities include fishing, horseback riding, swimming, water skiing, tennis, hiking, sailing, golf, square dancing and cookouts. Customers: summer tourists. "Many purchase gifts as Christmas presents." Heaviest wholesale buying time: May-June; best selling time: July-August.

THE RED CUPBOARD, Rt. 4, West Woodstock VT 05091. (802)457-3722. Contact: Donald E. Amero. Gift shop. Estab. 1957. Represents 20 craftworkers. Considers candlemaking, ceramics, clothing, decoupage, dollmaking, glass art, jewelry, leatherworking, pottery and woodcrafting. Handmade production-line items only. Price range: $4-30; bestsellers: $4-10. Buys outright. Shop sets retail price. Send slides. Reports in 2 weeks. Work may be shipped or hand delivered. Heaviest wholesale buying time: spring; best selling time: summer.

THE RED STORE & ASHERY, 2 Summer St., Montpelier VT 05602. (802)223-3531. Contact: Helene Lang. Craft/gift shop. Estab. 1976. Represents 15 craftworkers.
Acceptable Work: Considers candlemaking, ceramics, decoupage, dollmaking, needlecrafts, pottery, quilting, tole painting and woodcrafting. "We desire crafts in keeping with our 1869 country store motif." Specializes in primitive, Appalachian and brightly-colored crafts. "Cozy home-spun-type items, nothing very sophisticated—more the folksy-type of item. Must be well-made." One-of-a-kind and handmade production-line items. Price range: $1.50-200; bestsellers: $1.50-15. "Please keep price modest: $1, $5, $10."
Terms: Buys outright and works on consignment; 75% commission. Retail price set by joint agreement. Prefers exclusive area representation. Send resume, slides with SASE or call for appointment. Reports in 1 week. Work may be shipped or hand delivered. Dealer pays insurance on exhibited work. Display time: full season (July 4 to mid-October).
Profile: "We are an 1869 old-fashioned country store which sells books, gifts, crafts and penny candy. Items are put in shelf and counter displays usually arranged with appropriate books." Customers: urbanites from Montreal, ruralites from Vermont, elderly, antique seekers, retirees, vacationers, children. Heaviest wholesale buying time: spring, summer and autumn; best selling time: summer and autumn.

SAMARA, Box 1115, Stowe VT 05672. (802)253-8318. Contact: Lynn W. Miles. Craft shop. Estab. 1972. Represents 100 US craftworkers.
Acceptable Work: Considers batik, candlemaking, dollmaking, glass art, jewelry, leatherworking, metalsmithing, pottery, quilting, scrimshaw, soft sculpture, wall hangings, weavings and woodcrafting. Specializes in contemporary crafts with many bright-colored and some fine art crafts. One-of-a-kind and handmade production-line items. Price range: 25¢-$200; bestsellers: $1-50.
Terms: Buys outright and sometimes works on consignment; 33⅓% commission. Craftworker sets retail price. Send slides with SASE. Reports monthly. Work may be shipped or hand-delivered. Dealer pays insurance for exhibited work.
Profile: "Every item in the shop is handcrafted by primarily local craftsmen with special attention given to display. Custom work is available in most media. We have many tourists from urban centers such as Boston, New York and Montreal—mostly skiers in winter, all ages, all incomes." Heaviest wholesale buying time: pre-summer and pre-Christmas; best selling time: July-August and December.

SANTA'S LAND, Rt. 5, Putney VT 05346. (802)387-5550. Buyer: Tina Brewer. Christmas village. Gift shop. Estab. 1970. Represents 2+ craftworkers.
Acceptable Work: Considers candlemaking, ceramics, dollmaking, glass art, jewelry, needlecrafts, quilting, wall hangings, weavings and Christmas arrangements. Especially needs Christmas ornaments. One-of-a-kind pieces OK; handmade production-line items in glass only. Price range: $1-125; bestsellers: $1-10.
Terms: Buys outright and works on consignment. Shop sets retail price. Requires exclusive area representation. Send resume. Reports in 3 weeks. Work may be shipped or hand-delivered. Dealer pays insurance on exhibited work.
Profile: "We are a Christmas village with a series of shops and craftpersons in residence." Activities include petting zoo, enchanted animal forest, Alpine railroad, mistletoe mill, Christmas tree shop, Santa's post office, park, antique German carousel, Austrian Haflinger horses and Santa's home. "There are 2 additional Christmas shops: Rutland, Vermont, and Wells, Maine. If items do not move well in 1 month, we change the displays." Customers: young families and grandparents. Heaviest wholesale buying time: June-December; best selling time: summer-fall."

L. J. SERKIN CO., 51 Elliot St., Brattleboro VT 05301. (802)257-7044. Proprietors: John or Lucy Serkin. Craft shop. Estab. 1972. Represents 80 craftworkers.
Acceptable Work: Considers batik, ceramics, glass jewelry, leatherworking, metalsmithing, pottery, and functional handweaving. Must have good finishing. Handmade utilitarian production-line items. Price range: $3-150; bestsellers: $10-50.

Terms: Buys outright. Craftworker sets retail price. "Please have pricing worked out; 50% wholesale for us to be interested." Requires exclusive area representation. Send slides or call for appointment. Reports in 2 weeks. Work may be shipped or hand-delivered. Dealer pays shipping.
Profile: "Most work is displayed by craftsman (i.e. each person's work is displayed as a whole)." Customers: early 20's to late 70's; middle class and up." Heaviest wholesale buying time: May and November; best selling time: summer and December.

THE SHOP AT THE INN, 74 West the Ferry Rd., Shoreham VT 05770. (802)897-5081. President: Cleo. Country store. Estab. 1975. Represents 5 craftworkers. "I would like to have as many Vermont crafts as possible, but would accept some from other Northeastern states."
Acceptable Work: Considers batik, candlemaking, ceramics, clothing, glass art, jewelry, leatherworking, needlecrafts, pottery, quilting, wall hangings, weavings and woodcrafting. Handmade production-line items. Price range: $3.50-175; bestsellers: $3.50-12.
Terms: Works on consignment; 30% commission. Craftworker sets retail price. Requires exclusive area representation. Call for appointment. Work may be shipped or hand delivered.
Profile: "We are a country store in a small village on the road to Ticonderoga Ferry. Many tourists come by for we have a reputation for interesting gifts at a good price. Most items are displayed in a gift area on old furniture or hung on white brick walls trimmed in cedar." Heaviest wholesale buying time: spring and fall; best selling time: summer-Christmas.

THE SILK PURSE & THE SOW'S EAR, Box 169, Bethel VT 05032. (802)234-5368. Contact: Donna Nelson. Craft shop studio. Estab. 1976. Represents 125 craftworkers. "Although we carry mostly New England crafts and a few imports, we are open to other regions of the US."
Acceptable Work: Considers candlemaking, clothing, dollmaking, glass art, jewelry, leatherworking, metalsmithing, needlecrafts, pottery, quilting, wall hangings, weavings and woodcrafting. No kits. Especially needs candles; boxes made out of leather, wood and glass; and lampshades. One-of-a-kind and handmade production-line items. Price range: 35¢-$400; bestsellers: $5-100.
Terms: Buys outright and works on consignment; 33⅓% commission. Craftworker sets retail price. Requires exclusive area representation within a 10-mile radius. Call for appointment. Reports in 1 week. Work may be shipped or hand delivered. "We pay for crafts that are stolen or damaged, but prefer that the craftworker insures own pieces in case of fire or a larger loss."
Profile: "We are a 4-part business: retail shop, furniture restoration, caning and custom woodworking. We have 3 seasons—summer, fall and Christmas—and suggest that items stay on display all 3 seasons. We discourage items being pulled out for craft fairs and just before Christmas. We are located near a second home resort and near major routes." Customers: tourists (in summer and fall seasons); locals (throughout the year); above average incomes. Heaviest wholesale buying time: pre-Christmas; best selling time: Christmas and fall foliage.
To Break In: "We advise that a reasonable retail price be established and that the craftworker sell at that price everywhere (fairs, other retail outlets, etc.). Keep acurate records. Have crafts ready to display and stock the store regularly; do not have a half empty display."

THE SKIN TRADE, Box 533, Waitsfield VT 04573. (802)496-3265. Contact: Terry A. Redlich. Craft and retail clothing store. Estab. 1976. Represents 10-15 craftworkers, preferably from New England "unless too exceptional to pass up. I deal only with leatherworkers, jewelers, weavers and knitters."
Acceptable Work: Considers jewelry, leatherworking, furs and handknit and handwoven clothing. Shop carries mostly clothing and accessories. Especially needs handstitched sheepskin jackets, vests and ear muffs, silver hair combs and reasonably priced jean-style pants. Specializes in contemporary work "but am open-minded". One-of-a-kind and handmade production-line items. Price range: $7-400; bestsellers: $15-60.
Terms: Buys outright and works on consignment (on expensive items); 30% commission. "I'm not heavily into consignment, but when I do bring an item in, it can usually remain for as long as the craftworker desires." Retail price set by joint agreement. Requires exclusive area representation. Call in person. Reports immediately. Work may be shipped or hand delivered.
Profile: "The shop is retail with 90% of the leather work done by me. We have mostly tourists as I'm located in a popular ski resort. Summers also attract many people. There's also many people with second homes located here." Heaviest wholesale buying time: summer, fall and Christmas; best selling time: summer, fall and winter.
To Break In: "Be pleasant, be on time and work must be consistent."

THE SOFT TOUCH, LTD., 161 Main St., Burlington VT 05401. (802)862-8506. President: E.

Michael Goldblatt. Craft shop/gallery/gift shop. Estab. 1976. Represents 10-15 craftworkers. Price range: $1-1,500; bestsellers: $1-50. Works on consignment and buys outright; 25% commission. Craftworker sets retail price. Reports in 4 weeks. Work may be shipped or hand-delivered. Dealer pays insurance for exhibited work.
Acceptable Work: Considers candlemaking; ceramics; clothing; glass art; jewelry; leatherworking; metalsmithing; pottery; quilting; soft sculpture; wall hangings; weavings; and woodcrafting. Primitive and fine one-of-a-kind pieces. Especially needs quilts for waterbeds; blown glass; and unusual stone or wood carvings.
Profile: "Art should be framed, or matted at the very least. Work is wall displayed, lighted; an attempt is made to draw attention to each piece or a special showing is given to a specific artist. Free area advertising to displaying exhibitor." Best selling and heaviest wholesale buying time: fall-winter.

STONE SOLDIER POTTERY, Jacksonville VT 05342. (802)368-7077. Contact: Connie Burnell. Craft shop. Estab. 1968. Represents 35-40 craftworkers. Price range: $2-500; bestsellers: $2.50-100. Buys outright. Craftworker sets retail price. Requires exclusive area representation. Reports in 2 weeks. Work may be shipped or hand-delivered. Dealer pays shipping to shop and insurance.
Acceptable Work: Considers glass art; jewelry; leatherworking; metalsmithing; pottery; soft sculpture; wall hangings; weavings; woodcrafting; and blown and stained glass. Fine one-of-a-kind and handmade production-line items. Especially needs stained glass; candles; and jewelry.
Profile: "We make pottery on the premises; our customers are young and middle aged, mostly college-educated with an appreciation for crafts." Heaviest wholesale buying time: spring and fall; best selling time: summer-fall and Christmas.

SUNSHINE SNOWY DAY, Box 1305, Stowe VT 05672. (802)244-7546. Contact: John Wetmore. Craft shop. Estab. 1970. Represents 24 craftworkers, "prefer New England craftworkers but not strictly limited." Considers candlemaking; ceramics; clothing; glass art; jewelry; leatherworking; metalsmithing; pottery; soft sculpture; wall hangings; weavings; and woodcrafting. All styles. Price range: $1.50-250; bestsellers: $8.75-40. Buys outright. Retail price set by joint agreement. Reports in 2 weeks. Dealer pays shipping to shop and all insurance. Best selling time: fall.

THREE BAGS FULL—TOYS, 33 Central St., Woodstock VT 05091. (802)457-3940. Contact: Joan R. Cronshey. Toy store. Estab. 1977. Represents 5 craftworkers, preferably from New England.
Acceptable Work: Considers dollmaking, soft sculpture, toys and woodcrafting. "I would like to have crafts which are aimed at the toy buying consumers and have a certain amount of whimsical appeal." Specializes in bright-colored one-of-a-kind and handmade production-line items. Price range: $12-18; bestsellers: $5-10.
Terms: Works on consignment; 30% commission. Retail price set by joint agreement. Requires exclusive area representation. Reports in 1 week. Work may be shipped or hand delivered. Dealer pays insurance on exhibited work.
Profile: "It is a small store which handles mostly unusual toys, crafts, puzzles and books. The colors are bright, hopefully a place to please the child in all of us. The displays are rearranged seasonally, highlighting various items. New and unusual toys or crafts head straight for the window display area." Customers: late twenties to early thirties; tourists; $30,000-35,000 average incomes. Heaviest wholesale buying time: early summer and fall-Christmas; best selling time: late summer-early fall.
To Break In: "I realize that crafts are time consuming to make and therefore, deserve a high price; however simple craft items (e.g., toothfairy pillows) don't sell well as it is felt that they are not unusual enough. I'm looking for uniquely designed toys at a fair price."

THE TOY CHEST, Box 248, Shelburne VT 05482. (802)985-3888. Contact: Sam Levin. Gift/toy shop. Estab. 1968. Represents 5 craftworkers.
Acceptable Work: Considers dollmaking, jewelry, needlecrafts and woodcrafting. Especially needs wood toys, wood carvings, Christmas decorations and dolls. Handmade production-line items only. Price range: 25¢-100; bestsellers: $10-45.
Terms: Buys outright. Retail price set by joint agreement. Requires exclusive area representation. Call for appointment. Reports in 1 week. Work may be shipped or hand delivered.
Profile: "Primarily handles wood toys from around the world." Customers: 75% tourists; 25% locals; mostly parents and grandparents. Heaviest wholesale buying time: spring-fall; best

selling time: summer-fall. Open June-December.

THE TOY STORE, INC., Box 311, Waitsfield VT 05673. (802)496-3270. President: Dorothy B. Raphael. Toy store. Estab. 1977. Represents 4-5 craftworkers. Considers soft, wood and bisque toys.
Terms: Buys outright. Craftworker sets retail price. Requires exclusive area representation. Call for appointment. SASE. Reports in 2 weeks. Work may be shipped or hand delivered.
Profile: "I have a small toy store with quality toys not in competition with discount stores. I would like to have unique toys and be the sales representative in this area." Customers: mostly grandparents and young mothers. Heaviest wholesale buying and best selling time: Christmas.

TRANQUIL THINGS, Box 338, 43 Main St., Derby Line VT 05830 (802)873-3454. Contact: Pat Wright. Craft/gift shop. Estab. 1973. Represents foreign import firms and craftworkers and 15-20 American craftsmen.
Acceptable Work: Considers batik, clothing, glass art, jewelry, leatherworking, metalsmithing, needlecrafts, pottery, scrimshaw, soft sculpture, wall hangings, weavings and woodcrafting. Plans later to include dollmaking. Specializes in primitive and contemporary items. One-of-a-kind and handmade production-line items. "We sell commercial factory-produced gift items as well as handcrafted ones. The chief criteria in choice are the quality and unusualness of the item at a reasonable price." Price range: $1-260; bestsellers: $3-10.
Terms: Buys outright and sometimes on consignment; 30% commission. Retail price set by shop or joint agreement. Prefers exclusive area representation. Send slides with SASE or call for appointment. Reports in 1 week. Craftworker pays insurance on expensive items; dealer on inexpensive items. "We do not order what we cannot pay for, however much we may admire it, and so we do always pay promptly."
Profile: "Our shop is presently 3 rooms in a 100+ year-old house. We display all things constantly and as appropriately as we can under these somewhat crowded conditions. Our business comes from 4 main sources: 1) local people, many of whom do not have a great deal of money to spend (I feel it important to have quality merchandise at modest prices for them); 2) travelers who see reference to us in guides (they are generally from the city and have more money to spend); 3) Canadians, since we are on the border (they, in many cases, have money to spend but import duties and currency exchange are problems); 4) people who like what we sell and will come many miles to see what we have (we are steadily building up such a clientele)." Heaviest wholesale buying time: spring and fall; best selling time: summer and Christmas.
To Break In: "I prefer to personally select the items to be sold. I am very unhappy when craftspeople show me superior items and then send inferior ones. I also like to receive merchandise when it is promised, or at least be advised if a delay is inevitable."

TRILLIUM FINE CRAFTS, The 1820 House, Box 504, Main St., Norwich VT 05055. (802)649-1695. Contact: Barbara S. Woodard or Marcia Hall. Craft shop. Estab. 1978. Represents 50 craftworkers.
Acceptable Work: Considers ceramics, clothing (limited), glass art, jewelry (including pins), leatherworking, needlecrafts, pottery, contemporary quilting, soft sculpture, mobiles, small wall hangings, small weavings and handmade notecards. Specializes in fine, functional, contemporary and bright-colored crafts. One-of-a-kind and handmade production-line items. Price range: $1-300; bestsellers: $1-50 (handscreened notecards).
Terms: Buys outright. Retail price set by joint agreement. Requires exclusive area representation. Send resume and slides if out-of-town; call for appointment (if local). "Please contact us if possible before coming in. Much can be discussed over the phone." Reports in 1 week.
Profile: "Each craftperson's work is given its own display or grouping. The shop has quilted walls, providing some specialized display area." Customers: mainly ages 20-50; local professionals; tourists; "many craft-oriented people and customers with an appreciation of handcrafted wares." Heaviest wholesale buying time: spring-summer (for summer and Chrismas traffic); best selling time: summer-fall and pre-holidays.
Tips: "Know the prices you want for your work. I always want to know something about you and your work; any resume material, descriptions or information is appreciated—verbal or written."

UNICORN, 15 Central St., Woodstock VT 05091. (802)457-2480. Contact: Andrea Vassallo or Jeffrey Kahn. Craft/gift shop. Estab. 1977. Represents over 6 craftworkers.
Acceptable Work: Considers clothing, glass art, jewelry, quilting, wall hangings, weavings and woodcrafting. Specializes in functional items but carries whimsical items as well, especially

unicorns. One-of-a-kind and handmade production-line items. Price range: $3-150; bestsellers: $5-30.
Terms: Buys outright (preferably) and works on consignment; 40% commission. Retail price set by joint agreement. Prefers to see samples, but slides OK. Reports in 1 week. Work may be shipped or hand delivered. Dealer pays insurance on exhibited work. Display time: 2 months.
Profile: "We deal in imported and domestic made crafts of all kinds with a heavy concentration in baskets, jewelry, clothing and toys. Most items would be shown from all directions with a fair amount of handling for those things that are not easily damaged. We rely on a tourist trade of all ages. There is also a constant local clientele. Most customers are in the middle to upper income bracket." Heaviest wholesale buying time: spring and late summer; best selling time: July-March.

VERMONT CRAFTS MARKET, INC., Main St., Box 17, Putney VT 05346. (802)387-5981. Contact: Kenneth Brown or Barbara Martocci. Mail order shop. Estab. 1975. Represents 250-300 US craftworkers.
Acceptable Work: Considers all crafts. Finished and handmade production-line items. Price range: $7.50-700; bestsellers: $16.95-300.
Terms: Buys outright. Shop sets retail price. Send slides with prices and availability. "Generally, we prefer to order samples for catalog consideration after we have seen slides, photos or a letter. Work is kept 6-8 weeks for consideration." Work may be shipped or hand delivered. Dealer pays shipping if work was solicited. Run in catalog usually 6 months.
Profile: "We are a mail order catalog distributed throughout the US. There's photography with copy describing size, color dimensions and at times methods used in production." Customers: middle to upper middle class, middle aged. Heaviest wholesale buying time: August-November, January-April; best selling time: September-November.
To Break In: "Volume production capability a must. Products used by us must be able to be reproduced very closely to the original. Keep wholesale cost as absolutely low as can be and still make a decent profit. High catalog production costs can often make our high mark-up result in unrealistic retail prices."

VERMONT HISTORICAL SOCIETY, Pavilion Office Bldg., Montpelier VT 05602. (802)828-2291. Assistant Treasurer: Virginia McManis. Museum gift shop. Estab. 1838. Represents 30-35 Vermont craftworkers.
Acceptable Work: Considers candlemaking, ceramics, dollmaking, glass art, jewelry, leatherworking, metalsmithing, pottery, soft sculpture and woodcrafting. Especially needs inexpensive leather and ceramics items. Handmade production-line items only. Price range: 75¢-$10; bestsellers: 75¢-$3.
Terms: Buys outright and works on consignment; 30% commission. Gallery sets retail price. "Either stop in with samples of your work or call to talk to us. Have your wholesale price set in advance." Reports in 2 weeks. Work may be shipped or hand-delivered. Dealer pays insurance on exhibited work. Display time: 3 months.
Profile: "It's a small museum shop located at the Vermont Museum. Along with the crafts, we sell Vermont-made maple products; jams and jellies; and over 400 Vermont-related books. We try to keep inexpensive items in stock. Our customers are school age, mainly elementary school groups and tourists of all ages and backgrounds." Heaviest wholesale buying time: spring-summer; best selling time: spring-fall and Christmas.

VERMONT STATE CRAFT CENTER AT WINDSOR HOUSE, Box 110, Main St., Windsor VT 05089. (802)674-6729. Contact: Denis Kenny. Craft shop/gallery/gift shop/educational center. Estab. 1975. Represents 250 Vermont craftworkers.
Acceptable Work: Considers all crafts made in Vermont. No kits or imports. One-of-a-kind and handmade production-line items. Price range: 30¢-$500; bestsellers: $1-20.
Terms: Buys outright and works on consignment; 30% commission. Retail price set by joint agreement. Must be juried. Call for appointment with SASE. Work may be shipped or hand-delivered. Customers: tourists and local people, and especially young to middle aged. Heaviest wholesale buying time: spring-summer; best selling time: summer-fall foliage time.

WAY AHEAD BOUTIQUE, Box 788, Manchester Center VT 05255. (802)362-3886. Owner: Patt Nichols. Gift shop. Estab. 1977. Represents 30 craftworkers.
Acceptable Work: Considers batik, candlemaking, ceramics, clothing, jewelry, pottery, scrimshaw, wall hangings and weavings. Specializes in contemporary one-of-a-kind and handmade production-line items. Price range: $3-80; bestsellers: $5-25.
Terms: Works on consignment; 33% commission. Retail price set by joint agreement. Requires

exclusive area representation. Send slides. SASE. Reports in 3 weeks. Work may be shipped or hand delivered. Dealer pays insurance on exhibited work.
Profile: "We are a retail business specializing in imported clothing (from India, Guatemala and Mexico) and smoking paraphernalia. All crafts must be in perfect selling condition and will be returned at the end of 3 months in the same condition. (May be left longer; this is the decision of the craftworker and the shopkeeper.) It is preferred that the craftworker supply display upon presentation of his/her goods." Customers: ages 15-40; fashion-minded with incomes from $50 to $250 weekly. Heaviest wholesale buying time: summer and winter; best selling time: Christmas and summer.

WESTON BOWL MILL, Main St., Weston VT 05161. (802)824-6219. President: Sam Lloyd. Manufacturer/retailer/wholesaler. Estab. 1946. Represents 12 craftworkers.
Acceptable Work: Woodcrafting only. Handmade production-line items. Price range: $1-100; bestsellers: $1-25.
Terms: Buys outright. Retail price set by joint agreement. SASE. Work must be hand-delivered.
Profile: "60% of our stock is made on the premises; 40% is made elsewhere; and 95% are wooden items." Customers: 100,000 visitors per year, mostly tourists and skiiers. Heaviest wholesale buying time: spring-fall; best selling time: late summer-fall.

Virginia

ACADIA GIFTS, 411 King St., Alexandria VA 22314. (703)549-8090. Contact: Betty I, Johnson. Gift shop. Estab. 1977. Heaviest wholesale buying time: winter and spring; best selling time: summer and Christmas.
Acceptable Work: Considers ceramics, decoupage, glass art, scrimshaw, soft sculpture, wall hangings, weavings and woodcrafting. Handmade production-lines only. Price range: $3-100; bestsellers: $10-25.
Terms: Buys outright. Retail price set by joint agreement. Requires exclusive area represenation. Send resume. Reports as soon as possible. Work may shipped or hand-delivered.

ALEXANDRIA BICENTENNIAL MUSEUM SHOP, 201 S. Washington, Alexandria VA 22314. (703)548-1812. Director: Ms. Dene Garbow. Museum gift shop. Estab. 1974. Represents 4-6 craftworkers.
Acceptable Work: Considers ceramics; decoupage; dollmaking; glass art; jewelry; needlecrafts; pottery; quilting; and woodcrafting. One-of-a-kind and handmade production-line items. Price range: $1-50; bestsellers: $1-30.
Terms: Works on consignment and buys outright; 40-50% commission. Retail price set by joint agreement. Reports in 3 weeks. Work may be shipped or hand-delivered. Dealer pays insurance for exhibited work.
Profile: "A new item is put on display in a prominent place; often a sign is made explaining the new item. We only want American crafts—reproductions of colonial crafts." Best selling and heaviest wholesale buying time: Christmas.

ANDERSON GALLERY, Virginia Commonwealth University, 907½ W. Franklin St., Richmond VA 23220. Director: Harriet Dubowski. University gallery. Estab. 1970. Represents 2-3 craftworkers.
Acceptable Work: Considers ceramics; glass art; jewelry; metalsmithing; pottery; soft sculpture; wall hangings; weavings; and woodcrafting. Fine one-of-a-kind pieces.
Terms: Takes work for exhibit only, with sales as a service with 25% commission. Craftworker sets retail price. Reports in 4-8 weeks. Work may be shipped or hand-delivered. Gallery pays insurance for exhibited work.
Profile: "Exhibits change monthly; crafts are displayed in a manner appropriate to the work. Customers are from the University and surrounding Richmond communities." Best selling and heaviest wholesale buying time: Christmas.

BAYLY MUSEUM SHOP, UNIVERSITY OF VIRGINIA, Rugby Rd., Charlottesville VA 22903. Manager: Janice F. Bowen. Museum gift shop. Estab. 1977. Represents 10 craftworkers.
Acceptable Work: Considers batik; ceramics; glass art; jewelry; metalsmithing; needlecrafts; pottery, soft sculpture; and woodcrafting. Price range: under $1-1,000; bestsellers: $1-100.
Terms: Works on consignment; 25% commission. Craftworker sets retail price. Work may be shipped or hand-delivered. Museum pays insurance for exhibited work.
Profile: "Size is a handicap; items need to be relatively small. Customers are students, faculty

wives and the general public." Best selling and heaviest wholesale buying time: Christmas.

BROOKNEAL DEPARTMENT STORE, 101 Main St., Brookneal VA 24528. Vice President: Katharine R. Holt. Department store.
Acceptable Work: Gift department buys (and sometimes consigns) dinnerware; handbags and leather accessories; jewelry; silverwork; wall hangings; and weavings. Handmade production-lines only. Display department uses carvings, sculpture and wall hangings. Handmade production-lines only. Retail price range: $3-50; set by store. Write with illustrations of work.

THE CAVE HOUSE, 279 E. Main., Abingdon VA 24210. (703)628-7721. Manager: Tina Blanton. Craft shop operated by Holston Mountain Arts & Crafts Co-op. Estab. 1971. Represents 200 craftworkers who live within a 40 mile radius of the shop.
Acceptable Work: Considers batik; ceramics; dollmaking; glass art; jewelry; leatherworking; metalsmithing; needlecrafts; pottery; quilting; tole painting; wall hangings; weavings; woodcrafting; baskets; crocheting; knitting. Especially needs baskets, brooms and quilts. Primitive, and fine handmade production-line items. Price range: 75¢-$400; bestsellers: $2-15.
Terms: Works on consignment; 40% commission. Craftworker sets retail price. Work may be shipped or hand-delivered. Shop pays insurance for exhibited work.
Profile: "We are located in a big, old house in historical district of Abingdon. Many wealthy people come to Abingdon to see a play, take part in the Virginia Highlands Festival or to visit the Martha Washington Inn." Displays work 6 months. Best selling time: Christmas and summer.

CRAFTERS' GALLERY, Rt. 2, Box 215, Charlottesville VA 22901. (804)295-7006. Contact: Bob Leiby or Don Nelson. Craft shop/gallery. Estab. 1974. Represents 100 craftworkers.
Acceptable Work: Considers batik; ceramics; glass art; jewelry; leatherworking; metalsmithing; pottery; quilting; soft sculpture; wall hangings; weaving; and woodcrafting. One-of-a-kind and handmade production-line items; utilitarian only. Price range: $1-1,600; bestsellers: $20-70.
Terms: Works on consignment and buys outright; 40% commission. Craftworker sets retail price. Requires exclusive area representation. Reports in 2 weeks. Work may be shipped or hand-delivered, if requested. Shipping costs are shared; dealer pays insurance for exhibited work.
Profile: "We are noted for fine display; our building is an old barn with several rooms. Customers are professional, moneyed and sophisticated." Best selling time: November-December, May and summer.

THE DANVILLE MUSEUM OF FINE ARTS & HISTORY SHOP, 975 Main St., Danville VA 24541. (804)793-5644. Manager: Martha Corr. Museum gift shop. Estab. 1975. Represents approximately 50 craftworkers.
Acceptable Work: Considers most unusual work of highly executed quality. Especially needs handwork of all kinds—unusual (knit, crochet, needlepoint, etc.), stuffed animals and dolls, and handmade jewelry. Specializes in fine art, one-of-a-kind designer crafts—Victorian items, Civil War items, Jefferson Davis items. Handmade production-line items OK. Price range: 50¢-$250; bestsellers: 50¢-$50.
Terms: Buys some work outright, but mostly works on consignment; 30% commission. Retail price set by joint agreement. Call for appointment or send resume with SASE. Reports in 2 weeks. Work may be shipped or hand-delivered. "Items accepted are kept in the shop for 4 months. If there is no sale for them at the end of the 4 month period the items may be picked up or exchanged for newer and different items."
Profile: "We are located in the Maj. W.T. Sutherlin Mansion which housed Jefferson Davis in 1865 and served as the last capitol of the Confederacy. The shop is in a growing stage and will expand its location in the near future. Customers are drawn from the guests and visitors to the museum and galleries as well as from the local citizens. Collectors of Civil War memorabilia, history buffs, artists and writers all visit this shop. People looking for gifts of all kinds, i.e. baby gifts, birthday gifts, wedding gifts, etc. are customers. Incomes range from good to the very wealthy." Heaviest wholesale buying and bestselling time: fall for Christmas.

DAWNTREADER, 11 Elliewood Ave., Charlottesville VA 22903. (804)977-3200. Contact: Wilhem F. Golluh. Craft shop. Estab. 1976. Represents 6 craftworkers. Price range: 25c-$250; bestsellers: 25c-$20. Buys outright; 33⅓% commission. Retail price set by joint agreement. Requires exclusive area representation. Reports in 2 weeks. Hand-delivered work OK. Dealer pays return shipping and insurance for exhibited work.

Acceptable Work: Considers jewelry and metalsmithing. Fine one-of-a-kind and handmade production-line items; decorative only. Especially needs sterling inlay pendants (small).
Profile: "Work is put in center display for a few weeks, and if it does not sell, it is moved to a side display. Customers are college students and middle-aged housewives." Heaviest wholesale buying time: September-December; best selling time: October-December.

DEPARTMENT OF TOURISM, CITY OF PETERSBURG, Petersburg VA 23803. (804)733-7690. Director of Tourism: John Elliott. City government. Estab. 1850. Would like to represent 10 craftworkers. Considers all crafts; deals mainly with 19th century period. All styles; utilitarian and/or decorative. Price range: $1-400; bestsellers: $1-15. Works mostly on consignment and buys some outright; commission is negotiable. Director sets retail price. Requires exclusive area representation. Reports in 2 weeks. Work may be shipped or hand-delivered. Heaviest wholesale buying time: spring; best selling time: spring-fall.

EVANS FARM COUNTRY STORE, 1696 Chain Bridge Rd., McLean VA 22101. Buyer: Caroline Van Wagoner. Craft gift and antiques shop. Estab. 1962. Represents 25 craftworkers.
Acceptable Work: Considers ceramics; clothing; decoupage; glass art; jewelry; needlecrafts; wall hangings; weavings; and woodcrafting. Especially needs weaving and rug braiding. Handmade production-line items. Price range: $2.50-500; bestsellers: $2.50-60.
Terms: Works on consignment and buys outright; 40% commission. Retail price set by joint agreement. Reports in 2 weeks. Work may be hand-delivered. Displays work 3 months. Heaviest wholesale buying time: spring and fall; best selling time: summer and Christmas.

FERRUM CRAFT SHOP, Rt. 1, Box 242, Ferrum VA 24088. (703)365-7256. Director: Lois Scott. Craft shop. Estab. 1969. Considers all crafts. Price range: $1-650. Works on consignment; 25% commission. Craftworker sets retail price.
Profile: "The shop is a project of Franklin County Community Action. Its original purpose was to help supplement low income people by selling their crafts. We now accept crafts from anyone, anywhere. This gives us an excellent variety of crafts. There is a craft and price for everyone."

FIRST IMPRESSIONS, 13809 Lee Hwy., Centreville VA 22020. (703)631-9019. Contact: Harriet Hollway. Estab. 1972. Represents 300 craftworkers (mostly local).
Acceptable Work: Considers all crafts; especially needs traditional styles. Fine one-of-a-kind and handmade production-line items. Price range: 75¢-$50; bestsellers: $1.50-22.
Terms: Works on consignment; 33% commission. Retail price set by joint agreement. Write. Reports in 2 weeks. Dealer pays "break-in" insurance for exhibited work.
Profile: Items displayed among antiques. Best selling time: fall and spring; heaviest consignment time: late summer and fall.

FREDERICKSBURG GALLERY OF ART, 813 Sophia St., Fredericksburg VA 22401. (703)373-5646. Director: Marcia Chaves. Gallery. Estab. 1962. Represents 20 craftworkers.
Acceptable Work: Considers batik; glass art; jewelry; metalsmithing; pottery; weavings; and woodcrafting. Fine one-of-a-kind items. Price range: $1.50-200; bestsellers: $2-30.
Terms: Works on consignment; 33⅓% commission. Craftworker sets retail price. Reports in 3 weeks. Work may be shipped or hand-delivered. Dealer pays return shipping and insurance for exhibited work.
Profile: "Items are handled with great care and display is changed often. We are in an old historic building and are on the historic tour guide of Fredericksburg." Best selling and heaviest wholesale buying time: fall.

GALLERY 3, 213 1st St. SE, Roanoke VA 24011. (703)343-9698. President: Andy Williams. Gallery. Estab. 1969. Represents 30 craftworkers.
Acceptable Work: Considers batik, ceramics, jewelry, pottery, quilting, soft sculpture, wall hangings and weavings. One-of-a-kind and handmade production line designer crafts only. Price range: $10-300; bestsellers: $10-30.
Terms: Buys outright; 50% markup. "We expect to retail at the same price that the artist would sell at a craft show directly." Requires exclusive area representation. Send slides. Reports in 2 weeks. Work may be shipped or hand-delivered after reviewed by gallery.
Profile: Located in Roanoke's farmers market, just blocks from downtown. Area is being redeveloped. "We redo gallery every 1-2 weeks using Formica cubes, Plexiglas stands and antique furniture to display." Customers are young professionals, commercial accounts with office buildings—many large accounts with banks. Heaviest wholesale buying time: spring and

summer for fall; best selling time: pre-Christmas.

GREEN SPRING FARM GALLERY, 4601 Green Spring Rd., Alexandria VA 22312. (703)941-6066. Director: Irv Brobeck. County arts council. Estab. 1964. Represents craftworkers from Fairfax County and surrounding area.
Acceptable Work: Considers batik; ceramics; glass art; jewelry; needlecrafts; pottery; wall hangings; weavings; and woodcrafting. Finished, one-of-a-kind and handmade production-line items. Price range: $2-150; bestsellers: $2-50.
Terms: Works on consignment; 25% commission. Craftworker sets retail price. Reports immediately. Work may be hand-delivered.
Profile: "Shop is located in an historic house (circa 1764) restored and open to the public. Customers are all ages and middle income." Displays work 1 month. Best selling time: spring-summer and winter holidays.

GUILD GALLERY, 501 State St., Bristol VA 24201. Manager: Evelyn Gordon. Craft Shop. Estab. 1969. Represents 100+ craftworkers who are members of the Southern Highland Handicraft Guild. "Membership depends upon approval of an applicant's work by our Standards committee and Board of Trustes, and is open to eligible craftsmen living and working in the Southern Appalachian Mountain Region."
Acceptable Work: Considers batik, ceramics, dollmaking, glass art, jewelry, leatherworking, metalsmithing, needlecrafts, pottery, quilting, soft sculpture, wall hangings, weavings and woodcrafting. Items should be of native materials; both traditional and contemporary designer crafts. Price range: $1 (folk toys)-700 (small furniture); bestsellers: $5-20.
Terms: Buys outright. "Craftsman sets his wholesale price; shop doubles for retail." Requires exclusive area representation. Work may be shipped or hand-delivered. Dealer pays insurance on exhibited work.

HAND WORK SHOP, INC., 7 N. 6th St., Richmond VA 23219. (804)649-0674. Executive Director: Ruth T. Summers. Craft shop/gallery. Estab. 1963. Represents 150-200 craftworkers.
Acceptable Work: Considers batik; candlemaking; ceramics; jewelry; leatherworking; metalsmithing; pottery; quilting; wall hangings; weavings; woodcrafting; blown glass; and forged iron. Fine one-of-a-kind and handmade production-line items. Price range: 75¢-$600; bestsellers: $5-45.
Terms: Works on consignment and buys outright; 33⅓% commission. Retail price set by joint agreement. Requires exclusive area representation. Reports in 2 weeks. Work may be shipped or hand-delivered. Dealer provides insurance while work is on consignment. Displays work 3 months.
Profile: "We are a tax exempt nonprofit organization dedicated to the appreciation of fine designer craft work. We sponsor gallery shows plus a large retail craft fair annually in November. Customers have an income of $15,000-30,000; are in the 25-55 year range." Displays work 3 months. Heaviest wholesale buying time: January-February; best selling time: September-December.

HOUSE OF ALEXANDER, Coliseum Mall, Hampton VA 23666. (804)826-2086. Manager: Richard Mandell. Gallery. Estab. 1970.
Acceptable Work: Considers batik, ceramics, glass art, jewelry, metalsmithing, needlecrafts, pottery, quilting, scrimshaw, wall hangings, weaving and woodcrafting. One-of-a-kind and handmade production-line items. Price range: $5.50-600; bestsellers: $20-75.
Terms: Works on consignment; 50% commission. Retail price set by joint agreement. Call for appointment or send slides. Reports in 1 week. Work may be shipped or hand-delivered. Dealer pays insurance on exhibited work.
Profile: "6,400 square-foot art gallery with frame shop with emphasis toward limited editions, sculpture, stoneware, handcrafted silver jewelry and local crafts. The mall attracts a complete spectrum of customers." Heaviest wholesale buying and best selling time: Christmas.

THE KNOTTY PINE, 113 King St., Alexandria VA 22314. (703)836-7475. Contact: Lorraine Eggenberger. Handcrafted furniture and gifts. Estab. 1975. Represents 20 craftworkers. Price range: $8-50; bestsellers: $8-30. Works on consignment. Gallery sets retail price. Requires exclusive area representation. Reporting time varies. Work may be shipped or hand-delivered. Dealer pays shipping and insurance for exhibited work.
Acceptable Work: Considers ceramics; leatherworking; pottery; quilting; wall hangings; weavings; and woodcrafting. Primitive one-of-a-kind and handmade production-line items; utilitarian and/or decorative.

Profile: "Our customers are 25-35 years old; married couples." Displays work 3 months. Heaviest wholesale buying time: fall; best selling time: Christmas and summer.

OLDE ENGLAND FRAMING, c/o Gallery 3, 213 1st St. SE, Roanoke VA 24011. (703)343-9698. President: Andy Williams. Gallery. Estab. 1969. Represents 30 craftworkers.
Acceptable Work: Considers batik, ceramics, jewelry, pottery, quilting, soft sculpture, wall hangings and weavings. One-of-a-kind and handmade production line designer crafts only. Price range: $10-300; bestsellers: $10-30.
Terms: Buys outright; 50% markup. "We expect to retail at the same price that the artist would sell at a craft show directly." Requires exclusive area representation. Send slides. Reports in 2 weeks. Work may be shipped or hand-delivered after reviewed by gallery.
Profile: Located in suburban Roanoke's Tanglewood Mall. "We redo gallery every 1-2 weeks using Formica cubes, Plexiglas stands and antique furniture to display." Customers are young professionals, commercial accounts with office buildings—many large accounts with banks. Heaviest wholesale buying time: spring and summer for fall; best selling time: pre-Christmas.

THE PEANUT PATCH, Box 183, Main St., Courtland VA 23837. (804)653-2028. Contact: Judy S. Riddick or Gaynelle E. Riddick. Craft shop. Estab. 1973. Represents 200 craftworkers. Price range: 50¢-$330; bestsellers: $2.50-15. Works on consignment and buys outrght; 40-50% commission. Retail price set by joint agreement. Reports in 2 weeks. Work may be shipped or hand-delivered if previously arranged. Dealer pays shipping to shop if bought outright.
Acceptable Work: Considers ceramics; clothing; decoupage; dollmaking; glass art; jewelry; metalsmithing; needlecrafts; pottery; quilting; tole painting; and woodcrafting. Fine one-of-a-kind and handmade production-line items; utilitarian and/or decorative.
Special Needs: "We always hunt for peanut and pig items, since this is pig and peanut country. We like fine quilts and nice patchwork items."
Profile: "We display our crafts to fit in with the decor of the shop. Customers are adults; middle and upper income; many tourists." Displays work 6 months or longer. Heaviest wholesale buying time: fall; best selling time: fall-winter.

THE STONEWALL JACKSON HOUSE, 8 E. Washington St., Lexington VA 24450. (703)463-2552. Associate Director: Barbara J. Crawford. Museum gift shop. Estab. 1979. "In 1954, the house was turned into a memorial, but underwent complete restoration recently and was completed in the fall of '79.
Acceptable Work: Considers candlemaking, ceramics, dollmaking, leatherworking, metalsmithing, needlecrafts and pottery. "We are interested in items that relate to Stonewall Jackson, life in the mid-1850s, the Civil War or traditional crafts of Virginia." Handmade production-line items only. Price range: 25¢-$75; bestsellers: $1-10.
Terms: Buys outright and works on consignment; 33⅓% commission. Retail price set by joint agreement. Send resume and slides. Reports in 1 week. Work may be shipped or hand delivered. Dealer pays insurance on exhibited work.
Profile: "Most of the visitors to the Jackson House are interested in the Civil War hero, Virginia, or the historic town of Lexington which is the home of Washington and Lee University and Virginia Military Institute. The Jackson House is an historic site which charges an admission to visitors for an interpretative tour. The gift shop serves as the receiving room for visitors to the house before they start their tour. Almost all items are in display cases. The exhibits will be changed about once a month." Heaviest wholesale buying time: spring; best selling time: April-September.
To Break In: "Develop an item that is unique to Jackson and the house where he lived as a professor at Virginia Military Institute before the Civil War."

STRASBURG MUSEUM, Strasburg VA 22657. (703)465-3175. Manager: Bobbi Walker. Estab. 1972. Represents 8-10 craftworkers. Price range: $1-30. Buys outright. Gallery sets retail price. Reports in 4 weeks. Work may be hand-delivered. Dealer pays insurance for exhibited work.
Acceptable Work: Considers ceramics; clothing; dollmaking; leatherworking; needlecrafts; pottery; quilting; and woodcrafting. Primitive and fine one-of-a-kind pieces; utilitarian and/or decorative. Especially needs items in the low price range; items that might appeal to school children as souvenirs.
Profile: "We have local crafts and artwork on sale; we also give pottery classes and take special orders." Displays work 5 months. Heaviest wholesale buying time: April-August; best selling time: summer.

UNIQUE SHOP, 213 King St., Alexandria VA 22314. (703)836-6686. Contact: Ethel Beun.

Craft/gift shop. Estab. 1969. Represents 50 craftworkers.
Acceptable Work: Considers ceramics; decoupage; glass art; jewelry; metalsmithing; needlecrafts; pottery; quilting; soft sculpture; tole painting; wall hangings; weavings; and woodcrafting. Primitive and fine handmade production-line items. Price range: $1-75; bestsellers: $2-15.
Terms: Works on consignment and buys outright; 33⅓% commission. Craftworker sets retail price. Work may be shipped or hand-delivered. Dealer pays return shipping and insurance for exhibited work. Heaviest wholesale buying time: late summer; best selling time: Christmas.

VIRGINIA HANDCRAFTS, INC., 2008 Langhorne Rd., Lynchburg VA 24501. (804)846-7029. Manager: Jan Spinelli. Craft shop/gallery. Estab. 1965. Represents 200 craftworkers.
Acceptable Work: Considers batik; candlemaking; glass art; jewelry; leatherworking; metalsmithing; soft sculpture; wall hangings; weavings; pottery; and woodcrafting. Fine one-of-a-kind and handmade production-line items. Price range: $1-750; bestsellers: $15-300.
Terms: Works on consignment and buys outright; 40% commission. Gallery sets retail price. Requires exclusive area representation. Reports in 2 weeks. Work may be shipped or hand-delivered. Dealer pays shipping and insurance for exhibited work.
Profile: "We work hard on effective display; try to change as frequently as possible. Our customers are all ages and income brackets, but we do have Lynchburg's most affluent citizens making up a large percentage of our clientele." Heaviest wholesale buying time; August-September; best selling time: October-December.

VIRGINIA MUSEUM-COUNCIL SALES SHOP, Boulevard & Grove Ave., Richmond VA 23221. (804)257-0886. Contact: Crafts Coordinator. Museum craft shop. Estab. 1962. Represents 150-200 Virginia craftworkers. Considers all crafts.
Terms: Open to Virginia residents, those born in the state or having minimum 3-year residency. Must have recently shows in Virginia Museum Biennial juried show or have been included in a nationally recognized invitational. Buys outright and works on consignment; 30% commission. Write for more information.
Profile: Shop is run by the Womens Council of Virginia Museum. Customers: many tourists, but includes all ages, incomes, interests. Best selling time: Christmas and May-June.

VIRGINIA POLYTECHNIC INSTITUTE & STATE UNIVERSITY ART GALLERY, Department of Art, Virginia Polytechnic Institute and State University, Blacksburg VA 24061. (703)951-5547. Contact: Dean Carter. University art gallery. Considers all crafts; utilitarian and/or decorative. Bestsellers: $5-200. Retail price set by joint agreement. Reports in 4 weeks. Work may be shipped or hand-delivered.
Profile: "Small items are shown in closed glass cases. When unlocked, area is always supervised. Customers are students, faculty and townspeople." Displays work 1 month. Best selling time: Christmas.

WILLIAMSBURG ART GALLERY, 170 2nd St., Williamsburg VA 23185. (804)826-2086. Manager: Richard Mandell. See House of Alexander above.

WOODCHOP, 35 Main St., Warrenton VA 22186. Contact: Roy Anderson. Department store. Buys various crafts for resale. Handmade production-lines and one-of-a-kind designer pieces OK. Retail price set by joint agreement. Write with resume and illustrations or samples of work.

YARN BAZAAR, 714 King St., Alexandria VA 22314. (703)548-0408. Contact: Pat Baehler or Sylvia Dudycha. A yarn, needlework, weaving and spinning supply shop. Estab. 1958.
Acceptable Work: Considers all kinds of needlecrafts, weavings and handspuns. Fine one-of-a-kind pieces. Price range: $2-200; bestsellers: $2-20.
Terms: Works on consignment and buys outright; 30% commission. Retail price set by joint agreement. Requires exclusive area representation. Work may be shipped or hand-delivered.
Profile: "We have recently moved into a large open area store. Knitting yarns, needlepoint, crewel, kits, etc. are displayed as you enter with weaving and spinning supplies located in the back room—busy classroom upstairs." Heaviest wholesale buying time: summer; best selling time: fall.

J.M. YEATTS GALLERY, 364 Walnut Ave SW, Roanoke VA 24016. (703)344-6338. Contact: Lyn or Jim Yeatts. Gallery. Estab. 1971. Represents 25 craftworkers.
Acceptable Work: Considers batik, dollmaking, glass art, jewelry, metalsmithing, pottery,

some quilting, scrimshaw, soft sculpture, wall hangings and weaving. "Always on the look out for fine art statements in crafts, the unique expressive image." Specializes in fine art designer crafts. One-of-a-kind only. Price range: $8-300; bestsellers: $30-50.
Terms: Works on consignment; 33⅓% commission. Retail price set by joint agreement. Requires exclusive area representation. Send resume and slides with SASE. Reports in 1 week. Work may be shipped or hand-delivered. Unsold items will be returned C.O.D.
Profile: Located in 60-year-old house with high ceilings. Gallery is around a central fireplace core. Customers are ages 30-50 with 25,000+ incomes. Many loyal collectors. Best selling time: September-March.
To Break In: "Please don't undercut your dealer at fairs in area or juggle your prices so that the client begins to shop prices instead of craft."

Washington

ALPHA DOUBLE PLUS, Box 98457, Des Moines WA 98457. (206)246-1570. Contact: Morton Silverbow. Estab. 1973. Represents 40 gay craftworkers. Considers batik; ceramics; glass art; jewelry; metalsmithing; needlecrafts; pottery; soft sculpture; wall hangings; weavings; and woodcrafting. Especially needs figurative works. All styles; utilitarian and/or decorative. Price range: $5-175; bestsellers: $5-35. Buys outright or on consignment; 50% commission. Gallery sets retail price. Query with transparencies or photos. Reports in 3 weeks. Dealer pays shipping from shop and insurance. Heaviest wholesale buying time: spring and fall. Affluent customers.

BONNEVILLE GALLERY, 3102 Harborview Dr., Box 32, Gig Harbor WA 98335. (206)858-9890. President: M.V. Bonneville. Craft shop/gallery. Estab. 1969. Represents 50 craftworkers. Price range: $3.50-1,000. Works on consignment and buys outright; 35% commission. Retail price set by joint agreement. Work may be shipped or hand-delivered. Dealer pays return shipping and insurance for exhibited work. Heaviest wholesale buying time: spring and fall; best selling time: summer and fall.
Acceptable Work: Considers batik; ceramics; clothing; jewelry; soft sculpture; wall hangings; and weavings.

CANNON SHOP, Fort Lewis Military Museum, Fort Lewis WA 98433. (206)967-4523. Manager: Betty Vertrees. Museum gift shop. Estab. 1973. Considers jewelry; metalsmithing; and pottery. Primitive handmade production-line items; utilitarian and/or decorative. Price range: 15c-$20. Works on consignment and buys outright. Retail price set by gift shop manager. Dealer pays insurance for exhibited work.
Profile: "Largest military museum west of Rockies and only military museum in Pacific Northwest. Customers are retired military (some on active duty) and many civilians." Best selling time: May-September.

GAIL CHASE GALLERY, 22 103rd NE, Bellevue WA 98004. (206)454-1250. Contact: Gail Chase. Craft shop/gallery. Estab. 1969. Represents 85 craftworkers.
Acceptable Work: Considers batik, ceramics, clothing, metalsmithing, soft sculpture, wall hangings, weavings, and especially needs textiles, glass, jewelry, and pottery. Specializes in primitive and fine one-of-a-kind pieces. Price range: $3.50-150; bestsellers: $3.50-25.
Terms: Buys outright and works on consignment; 40% commission. Retail price set by joint agreement. Requires exclusive area representation. Send slides and price list with SASE or call for appointment. Reports in 2 weeks. Work may be shipped or hand-delivered. Dealer pays return shipping and insurance for exhibited work.
Profile: "It is a prestigious gallery to belong to and has an excellent reputation. An item is kept in the gallery 4-6 months, occasionally longer. The gallery encourages slow moving items to be replaced. Customers are age 30-55, with incomes of $20,000-40,000." Heaviest wholesale buying time: fall; best selling time: winter. " I sell ⅓ of all crafts in the last 6 weeks of the year. Over ½ of all sales are gifts."

COMMUNITY ART GALLERY, 408½ N. Pearl St., Ellensburg WA 98926. (509)925-2670. Director: Eveleth Green. Non-profit exhibit and sales gallery. Estab 1968.
Acceptable Work: Considers batik, ceramics, clothing, dollmaking, glass art, jewelry, leatherworking, metalsmithing, needlecrafts, pottery, quilting, scrimshaw, soft sculpture, wall hangings, weavings, woodcrafting and handblown glass. One-of-a-kind designer pieces OK. Price range: $1-1,500.
Terms: Works on consignment; 20-30% commission. Craftworker sets retail price. Send resume or slides. Work may be shipped or hand-delivered. Dealer pays insurance on exhibited work.

Profile: "We have 2 rooms that are always sales rooms. There are 6 exhibit rooms, plus an additional room when needed. We set up exhibits in 6-7 rooms each month for a period of 3½ weeks. These shows are varied and have dimension through wall pieces and 3 dimensional pieces. We usually feature a painter and 2-4 craftsmen. During November and December we have an annual Christmas sale during which everything must be for sale. We change our sales rooms every 2-3 months and add work as sold."

THE COUNTRY CRAFTSMEN, Rt. 1, Box 529, Long Beach WA 98631. (206)642-2644. Contact: Bonny Lowry. Estab. 1975. Represents 50 craftworkers. Considers all media with a country-type look. Finished, one-of-a-kind and production-line, handmade items OK; utilitarian and/or decorative. Price range: 10c-$200; bestsellers: 15c-$15. Works on consignment; 33⅓% commission. Craftworker sets retail price. Write or submit work in person. Reports in 2 weeks. Dealer pays shipping from shop and insurance for exhibited work.
Profile: Craftworkers are notified each month as to whether they have made sales. Best selling time: summer; heaviest wholesale buying time: February and August. Shop, located in retirement and family tourist area, looks like a cottage. "We are strictly country-casual in a countrified setting." Customers ages 30 with average incomes.

CREATIVE CRAFTS, 370 Capital Mall, Olympia WA 98502. (206)754-8151. Manager: Robert Martin. Rental gallery. Estab. 1977. Represents 70 craftworkers. Price range: $1-1,600; bestsellers: $5-50. Handles crafts on rental and commission basis. Craftworker sets retail price. Reports in 4 weeks. Work may be shipped or hand-delivered.
Acceptable Work: Considers batik; candlemaking; dollmaking and soft goods; glass art; jewelry; leatherworking; metalsmithing; needlecrafts; pottery; quilting; tole painting; wall hangings; weavings; and woodcrafting. Fine handmade production-line items; utilitarian and/or decorative.
Profile: "Each craftsman has his own display designed and built by him, according to the theme of the store and with certain guidelines." Best selling time: Christmas.

CREATIVE CRAFTS, 2103 S. Sea Tac Mall, Federal Way WA 98003. (206)839-1530. See above.

CREATIVE CRAFTS, Vancouver Mall, Vancouver WA 98662. (206)256-7761. See above.

FIFTH AVENUE GALLERY, 1312 5th Ave., Seattle WA 98101. (206)624-3233. Contact: Carl Brecht. Craft shop/gallery/gift shop/vacuum mounting press/restoration and conservation of oil paintings and antique prints. Represents 24-30 craftworkers. Considers batik; decoupage; quilting; wall hangings; weavings; and woodcrafting. All styles; purely decorative. Price range: $25-18,000; bestsellers: $50-1,200. Works on consignment and buys outright. Gallery sets retail price. Requires exclusive area representation. Reports in 2 weeks. Dealer pays return shipping; shipping insurance; and insurance for exhibited work. Best selling time: May and December.

GALLERY NIMBA, 8041-32 NW, Seattle WA 98117. (206)783-4296. Director: Mrs. Lehmann. Gallery. Estab. 1969. Buys outright. Shop sets retail price.
Acceptable Work: Considers batik, jewelry, metalsmithing, wall hangings, weavings and woodcrafting and antiques from Africa. Specializes in ceremonial primitive African art. Price range: $25-30,000; bestsellers: $1-300.

THE LEGACY, LTD., 71 Marion Viaduct, Seattle WA 98104. (206)624-6350. Contact: Mardonna McKillop. Considers metalsmithing; pottery; sculpture; and woodcrafting. Maximum size: 3x6'. Specializes in Indian and Eskimo art based on traditional themes and produced by native artists. Price range: $60-1,200, sculpture; $200-3,000, woodcarvings. Bestsellers: $20-300. Buys outright or on consignment; 30-40% commission. Retail price set by joint agreemet. Requires exclusive area representation. Send slides of work. SASE. Dealer pays shipping from shop and insurance for exhibited work. Items displayed 3-6 weeks.

MIZPAH ART GALLERY, 1128 96th St. E., Spanaway WA 98387. (206)847-6842. Contact: Beverly Shipton. Gallery. Estab. 1974. Represents 3 craftworkers. Price range: $2.50-300; bestsellers: $10-200. Works on consignment; 40% commission. Craftworker sets retail price. Reports in 4 weeks. Work may be shipped. Dealer pays return shipping.
Acceptable Work: Considers glass art; metalsmithing; and pottery. Fine one-of-a-kind pieces; utilitarian and/or decorative.
Profile: "Our gallery is run with Christian principles and love, integrity being the most

important commodity. I have a beautiful relationship with my artists and craftspeople and I want it to remain so." Displays work 3 months. Best selling time: Christmas and summer.

MUSEUM OF NATIVE AMERICAN CULTURES, Box 3044 Terminal Annex, Spokane WA 99220. (509)326-4550. Assistant Director: Jim DeWalt. Museum gallery/gift shop. Estab. 1975.
Acceptable Work: Considers jewelry, needlecrafts, pottery, soapstone and scrimshaw. Especially needs soapstone carvings. Specializes in native American crafts (beadwork, weavings, pottery, basketry). One-of-a-kind and handmade production-line items. Price range: $5-500; bestsellers: $5-35.
Terms: Buys outright and works on consignment; 40% commission. Shop sets retail price. "Keep in mind items consigned to the gallery must be allowed a margin of mark-up." Send resume or call for appointment. Reports in 1-2 weeks. Work may be shipped or hand-delivered. Dealer pays insurance on exhibited work. Display time: 30 days minimum for consignment work.
Profile: "We are a gallery/shop located in a major museum (which is near the center of the city)." Heaviest wholesale buying time: spring-summer; best selling time: summer.

THE MUSHROOM GALLERY, 714 Sprague Ave. W., Spokane WA 99201. (509)747-6427. Contact: Joy Arsenault. Craft shop/gallery/gift shop. Estab. 1975. Represents 75-100 craftworkers. Price range: $20-500; bestsellers: $5-300. Works on consignment and buys outright; 40% commission. Retail price set by joint agreement. Reports in 2 weeks. Work may be shipped or hand-delivered. Dealer pays insurance for exhibited work.
Acceptable Work: Considers batik; ceramics; dollmaking; glass art; jewelry; soft sculpture; wall hangings; and weavings. Fine one-of-a-kind and handmade production-line items; utilitarian only.
Profile: Work is "displayed in groupings with antiques or simple sculpture stands, combined with other crafts. The gallery and gifts are rearranged every 3 months. Customers are local people interested in the arts, sports and civic affairs; moderate to high income." Best selling time: pre-Christmas and summer.

NORTHWEST CRAFT CENTER, Seattle Center, Seattle WA 98109. (206)624-7563. Manager: Ruth Nomura. Craft shop/gallery. Estab. 1963. Represents 200 Northwest resident craftworkers. Price range: $2-500; bestsellers: $5-50. Works on consignment; 40% commission. Craftworker sets retail price. Reports in 4 weeks. Work may be shipped or hand-delivered. Best selling time: summer and Christmas.
Acceptable Work: Considers batik; ceramics; jewelry; metalsmithing; and pottery.

PACIFIC CENTER OF THE ARTS & CRAFTS, Box 448, Grayland WA 98547. (206)267-1351. Contact: Ed or Sovia Pratt. Craft shop/gallery/gift shop. Estab. 1970. Represents 200 craftworkers. Price range: 50c-$1,500; bestsellers: under $10-under 300. Works on consignment; 33⅓% commission. When an artist is demonstrating, shop takes only 25% commission. Retail price set by joint agreement. Requires exclusive area representation. Reports in 1 week. Work may be shipped or hand-delivered.
Acceptable Work: Considers candlemaking; ceramics; decoupage; dollmaking; glass art; jewelry; metalsmithing; needlecrafts; pottery; tole painting; wall hangings; weavings; and woodcrafting. Fine one-of-a-kind and handmade production-line items; utilitarian and/or decorative.
Profile: "We have a large variety of handcrafts and art, paintings and art supplies all under one management in an unusual setting: an old school house." Heaviest wholesale buying time: spring-early fall; best selling time: February-October.

PATTY'S PLACE, 515 5th Ave. S., Edmonds WA 98020. (206)774-6446. Contact: Patty Price. Quilt, gift and craft shop. Estab. 1972. Represents 50 craftworkers. Price range: 50c-$375; bestsellers: $5-125. Works on consignment and buys outright; 35% commission; 20% on quilts. Retail price set by joint agreement. Work may mailed in only by mutual agreement. Dealer pays return shipping.
Acceptable Work: Considers quilts; patchwork items; needlecrafts; soft sculpture; pottery; small paintings; wall hangings; weavings; and woodcrafting. Fine one-of-a-kind and handmade production-line items; utilitarian and/or decorative.
Profile: "We try to group items so they complement each other. We are located in an old house built in 1894 and have carefully selected items in all price ranges. Customers are mostly married women, ages 20-80. Heaviest wholesale buying time: fall; best selling time: fall-winter.

POTTERY NORTHWEST, 226 1st Ave. N., Seattle WA 98109. (206)285-4421. Director: Sid

Morton. Gallery/studio workshop. Estab. 1966. Represents 55 craftworkers. Considers ceramics and pottery. Fine one-of-a-kind and handmade production-line items; utilitarian and/or decorative. Price range: $10-100; bestsellers: $10-40. Retail price set by joint agreement. Reports in 4 weeks. Dealer pays insurance for exhibited work.
Profile: "We are 1 of the few galleries that handles only ceramics." Customers are 20-50 years and of middle to high middle income. Best selling time: October-January and June, July and August.

SKYLIGHT GALLERY, 115 N. Laurel, Port Angeles WA 98362. (206)457-0009. Proprietor: Kay Myers. Gallery. Estab. 1971. Represents 100 craftworkers. Price range: $1-500; bestsellers: $3.50-50. Works on consignment; 40% commission. Retail price set by joint agreement. Requires exclusive area representation. Reports in 1 week. Work may be shipped or hand-delivered. Displays work 6 months maximum.
Acceptable Work: Considers batik; ceramics; dollmaking; glass art; jewelry; metalsmithing; pottery; soft sculpture; wall hangings; and weavings. Especially needs wood, metal and leather. Designer pieces; utilitarian and/or decorative.
Profile: "Customers are all ages; teenagers to senior citizens. Most are interested in pottery and jewelry." Best selling time: Christmas and summer.

VALLEY ART CENTER, INC., 842 6th St., Clarkston WA 99403. (509)758-8331. Contact: Pat Rosenberger. Gallery/gift shop. Estab. 1967. Represents 100 craftworkers. Price range: $5-75; bestsellers: $5-25. Works on consignment; 25% commission. Craftworker sets retail price. Requires exclusive area representation. Reports in 2 weeks. Work may be shipped or hand-delivered. Dealer pays insurance for exhibited work. Displays work 3 months.
Acceptable Work: Considers batik; ceramics; decoupage; dollmaking; glass art; metalsmithing; needlecrafts; pottery; quilting; tole painting; wall hangings; weavings; and woodcrafting. Fine one-of-a-kind pieces; utilitarian and/or decorative.
Profile: "Displays are rotated weekly so that by the end of the 3 months, the items have received the widest possible exposure." Best selling time: early summer and Christmas.

THE WEED LADY & OTHER WONDROUS WARES & GINGHAM GALLERY, 832 102nd NE, Bellevue WA 98004. (206)455-3056. Manager: Charmel Huffman. Craft shop/gallery/gift shop. Represents 20 craftworkers. Price range: $1-500; bestsellers: $1.50-50. Works on consignment and buys outright; 30% commission. Retail price set by joint agreement. Requires exclusive area representation. Work may be shipped or hand-delivered.
Acceptable Work: Considers batik; decoupage; dollmaking; stained glass art; ceramic jewelry; needlecrafts; pottery; quilting; wall hangings; weavings; soft sculpture; woodcrafting; ornaments; pressed flower pictures; and clothespin dolls. One-of-a-kind and handmade production-line items; utilitarian and/or decorative.
Profile: "We are the only shop with such a variety of special services: preserving and drying floral materials; offering classes, etc." Best selling and heaviest wholesale buying time: prior to all holidays.

THE WEED LADY & OTHER WONDROUS WARES & GINGHAM GALLERY, 408 Main St., Edmonds WA 98020. (206)775-3800. See above.

THE WOOD SHOP, 402 Occidental Ave. S., Seattle WA 98104. (206)624-1763. Contact: Marcia or Will Norwood. Craft/gift/toy shop. Estab. 1972. Represents 75 craftworkers.
Acceptable Work: Considers batik, ceramics, dollmaking, jewelry, pottery, soft sculpture and woodcrafting. Especially needs toys. Handmade production-line items. Price range: $1-75: bestsellers: $5-75.
Terms: Buys outright and works on consignment: 33⅓% commission. Retail price set by joint agreement. Call for appointment. Reports immediately.
Profile: "We are primarily a toy and gift store with a heavy concentration of toys. Crafts are very important, particularly practical items. We make wooden toys and dulcimers in the store." Customers: young adults to middle age with upper middle incomes. Heaviest wholesale buying time: fall and summer.

YAKIMA VALLEY MUSEUM SHOP, 2105 Tieton Dr., Yakima WA 98902. (509)248-0748. Chairman: Mary Picatti. Museum gift shop. Estab. 1976. Represents 3-6 craftworkers.
Acceptable Work: Considers basketry (Indian and Eskimo), decoupage, dollmaking, Indian pottery, quilting and scrimshaw. "A museum shop can carry items which relate to its museum collection and no other—according to the IRS. Our collection includes wagons, historical

artifacts, Southwest and Northwest Indian artifacts, and Eskimo artifacts. This limits the craft selection.''
Terms: Works on consignment; 25% commission. Retail price set by joint agreement. Write or call for information. Reports as soon as possible.

Washington D.C.

BENCSIK GALLERY, 5029 Connecticut Ave. NW, Washington DC 20008. Director: R. Kornemann. Gallery. Estab. 1960. Represents 5 craftworkers.
Acceptable Work: Considers batik; ceramics; decoupage; glass art; jewelry; metalsmithing; needlecrafts; pottery; quilting; soft sculpture; tole painting; wall hangings; weavings; and woodcrafting. Price range: $5-10,000; bestsellers: $20-100.
Terms: Works on consignment; 50% commission. Retail price set by joint agreement. Requires exclusive area representation. Reports in 4 weeks. Minimum 1 month display.
Profile: Very well-educated, cultured, sophisticated customers of high income. Many diplomats, congressmen, and socialites. Good age mix.
To Break In: "We accept any media, any artist—complete unknowns. We're willing to work hard to back and establish the reputations of a few really fine artists and craftsmen. We *must* have biographies; clippings; show notices; slides; or actual samples submitted to us by mail first. *Must* include SASE or package for anything to be returned. Will consider allowing craftspeople to work and demonstrate in our gallery; good exposure.''

THE CORCORAN SHOP, The Corcoran Gallery of Art, 17th St., and New York Ave. NW, Washington DC 20006. (202)638-3211. Adminstrator: Ellen Wright. Represents 1-2 craftworkers.
Acceptable Work: Considers jewelry; soft sculpture; and hand-printed notecards. "Our gift items are contemporary and well-designed; we have a total absence of folk crafts or ethnic art.'' Fine one-of-a-kind and handmade production-line items; decorative only. Price range: 80¢-$125; bestsellers: 80¢-$20.
Terms: Buys outright. Retail price set by joint agreement. Work may be shipped or hand-delivered. Dealer pays return shipping and insurance for exhibited work.
Profile: "Customers are age 30 or older and interested in art; middle-class or above.'' Best selling time: Christmas.

CRAFTSMEN OF CHELSEA COURT, 1311 Connecticut Ave. NW, Washington DC 20036. Director: Jon Boswell. Craft shop. Estab. 1970. Represents 750 craftworkers.
Acceptable Work: Considers ceramics; glass art; jewelry; metalsmithing; soft sculpture; wall hangings; and woodcrafting. Especially needs well designed and executed silver and gold jewelry; art glass; and unusual ceramics. Fine one-of-a-kind and handmade production-line items. Price range: $10-2,500; bestsellers: under $35-150.
Terms: Buys outright; 40% commission. Gallery sets retail price. Requires exclusive area representation. Reports in 2 weeks. Work may be shipped or hand-delivered. Dealer pays shipping to shop.
Profile: "Customers are 25-55; medium to upper income. We are in an area near art galleries and theaters and cater to residents of the metropolitan area.'' Heaviest wholesale buying time: April-September; best selling time: November-December, spring and early summer.

EARTHWORKS INC., 1724 20th St. NW, Washington DC 20009. (202)332-4323. Manager: Jon Gettman. Head shop. Estab. 1971. Represents 50+ craftworkers.
Acceptable Work: Considers candlemaking, ceramics, glass art, jewelry, leatherworking, metalsmithing, pottery, scrimshaw, woodcrafting and smoking accessories. "We carry only items which are useful as accessories in the use of soft drugs (i.e. marijuana or cocaine). This includes pipes, waterpipes, stash boxes, tooting straws, silver spoons and the like.'' One-of-a-kind and handmade production-line items; utilitarian only. Price range: $2-350; bestsellers: $10-100.
Terms: Buys outright. Retail price set by joint agreement. Send slides. Reports in 1 week. Work may be shipped or hand-delivered. Dealer pays shipping to shop and insurance for exhibited work.
Profile: "Customers average age is 22-35; average income is $15,000-35,000; government workers and professional people.'' Heaviest wholesale buying time: September-November; best selling time: November-December.

GALLERY K, 2032 P St. NW, Washington DC 20036. (202)765-9283. Contact: Komei Wachi.

Gallery. Estab. 1976. Represents only craftworkers working in primative and folk crafts.
Acceptable Work: Considers ceramics, needlecrafts, quilting, soft sculpture, wall hangings and weavings. One-of-a-kind pieces only. Price range: $100-1,500; bestsellers: $300-500.
Terms: Works on consignment; 40% commission. Retail price set by joint agreement. Send resume and slides. Shows last for a specified period of time (i.e., 4 weeks). Dealer pays insurance on exhibited work.
Profile: Customers are collectors of contemporary arts and some crafts collectors. Best selling time: fall.

GALLERY 10 LTD., 1519 Connecticut Ave. NW, Washington DC 20036. (202)232-3326. Considers contemporary fine art in all media. Maximum size: 6x9'. Work must be ready to install. Price range: $50-1,000. 40% commission. Retail price set by joint agreement. Query. Send slides or photos if in Eastern region. 4 week exposure.

INDIAN CRAFT SHOP, Interior Bldg, 1801 C St. NW, Washington DC 20240. (202)737-4381. Manager: C. Gilmore. Craft shop. Estab. 1937. Represents American Indian craftworkers only.
Acceptable Work: Considers dollmaking, jewelry, pottery, baskets, wall hangings, weavings and woodcrafting. American Indian crafts only. No antiques. Specializes in traditional crafts. One-of-a-kind handmade items. Price range: $2-3,000.
Terms: Buys outright. Retail price set by joint agreement. Call for appointment. SASE. Reports as soon as possible. Work may be shipped or hand-delivered.
Profile: "We are a small shop in a government building." Customers: foreign visitors, federal employees, tourists visiting capital and collectors. Best selling time: October-December.

LAMBDA RISING, 2012 S St. NW, Washington DC 20009. (202)462-6969. Manager: Nancy Stockwell. Gay book and gift shop.
Acceptable Work: Considers all fine art. "We will only accept work which reflects a gay (male or lesbian) theme or has been completed by a gay artist." Minimum price: $5; bestseller range: $5-80.
Terms: Works on consignment; 25% commission. Artist sets retail price. Query with samples. SASE. Shop pays insurance on exhibited work. Work held until sold.

THE MIDNIGHT SUN, 1700 Pennsylvania Ave. NW, Washington DC 20006. (202)393-4769. President: A. Kranish. Gift shop and gallery. Estab. 1965. Represents 100-150 craftworkers. Best selling time: Christmas and heaviest wholesale buying time: spring-summer.
Acceptable Work: Considers art glass; jewelry; and functional pottery. One-of-a-kind and handmade production-line items; utilitarian only. Price range: $2.50-150; bestsellers: $2.50-35.
Terms: Buys outright. Gallery sets retail price. Reporting time varies. Work may be shipped or hand-delivered.

PRESERVATION SHOPS, National Trust for Historic Preservation, 740-748 Jackson Place NW, Washington DC 20006. (202)638-5200 ext. 208. Director, Preservation Shops: Shelley Hodupp. Museum gift shop. Represents 15 craftworkers, but "wants to expand."
Acceptable Work: Considers ceramics, glass art, jewelry, metalsmithing, pottery, soft sculpture and woodcrafting. One-of-a-kind and handmade production-line items. Price range: $5-100; bestsellers: $5-50.
Terms: Buys outright. "We are not able to pay in advance or COD. We will process invoices for immediate payment." Shop sets retail price. Send slides or call for appointment. Reports in 4 weeks. Work may be shipped or hand-delivered.
Profile: "The National Trust operates small shops in 8 historic house museums on the East coast, and a book shop in Washington. We are interested in expanding our crafts in each of the shops. All of the purchasing is done through Washington headquarters. Crafts are displayed in groupings along with other relevant items and books. We have a lot of tourists and are building our shops to be places in the communities to come for crafts and regular shopping." Heaviest wholesale buying time: summer and winter; best selling time: fall and spring.

SERAPH, 1132-29th St. NW, Washington DC 20007. (202)337-5077. President: Patricia Ridgeway. Vice President: Marian A. Smith. Craft shop/gallery. Estab. 1978. Represents 50-60 craftworkers.
Acceptable Work: Considers clothing, dollmaking, studio glass, jewelry, leatherworking, metalsmithing, needlecrafts, quilting, fiber art, weavings and woodcrafting. Especially in-

terested in original folk art. One-of-a-kind (especially glass art) and handmade production-line items.
Terms: Buys outright and works on consignment; 40% commission. Dealer sets retail price. Requires exclusive area representation. Send slides, then call for appointment. Reports in 2 weeks. Dealer pays insurance on exhibited work.
Profile: "We are an American craft gallery attempting to carry original and beautiful crafts." Customers: educated, $20,000 incomes, some teenagers. Heaviest wholesale buying time: late winter and early summer.

SMITH-MASON GALLERY MUSEUM, 1207 Rhode Island Ave. NW, Washington DC 20005. (202)462-6323. Director: Helen S. Mason. Works on consignment; 40% commission. Artist sets retail price. Query with samples or send slides or photos of work. SASE. Gallery pays insurance on exhibited work. 6 weeks maximum exposure.
Acceptable Work: Considers batik; ceramics; glass art; jewelry; metalsmithing; pottery; and sculpture. Specializes in contemporary art. Price range: $50-5,000, paintings/sculpture/prints: $50-1,000, prints.

SMITHSONIAN MUSEUM SHOPS, Room 222, Museum of Natural History, Washington DC. Buyer: Gretchen Eggleston. Craft shop and museum gift shop. Represents 50 American craftworkers.
Acceptable Work: Considers batik, candlemaking, ceramics, dollmaking, glass art, needlecrafts, pottery, soft sculpture, wall hangings, weavings and woodcrafting. One-of-a-kind and handmade production-line items OK. Price range: $3-5,000; bestsellers: $3-25.
Terms: Buys outright and works on consignment; 40% commission. Retail price set by joint agreement. Send resume and slides. Reports in 3 weeks. Work may be shipped or hand-delivered. Dealer pays insurance on exhibited work.

A.D. SMULL GALLERY, 1606 20th St., NW Washington DC 20009. (202)232-8282. Director: A.D. Smull. Gallery. Estab. 1976. Considers fibers; soft sculpture; fantasy clothing; painted fabrics; weaving; porcelain; stoneware; raku; small humorous ceramic sculpture; and off loom sculpture. Price range: $5-500; bestsellers: $25-300. Works on consignment and buys outright sometimes; 50% commission. Retail price set by joint agreement. Requires exclusive area representation during show. Contact dealer with query, slides and photos; and arrange interview. SASE. Reports in 2 weeks. Dealer pays return shipping; in-transit insurance; and insurance for exhibited work. Work must be offered for sale. Work usually displayed 4-6 weeks.

THE TIFANEE TREE, 3112 M St. NW, Washington DC 20007. (202)333-4323. Owners: Frances and Edward Garfinkle. Craft/gift shop. Estab. 1970. Represents 300 craftworkers.
Acceptable Work: Considers candlemaking, ceramics, dollmaking, glass art, jewelry, metalsmithing, pottery, scrimshaw, soft sculpture, wall hangings, weaving and woodcrafting. Fine one-of-a-kind and handmade production-line items. Price range: $1-$1,500; bestsellers: $10-100.
Terms: Buys outright and works on consignment; 40% commission. Retail price set by craftworker or joint agreement. Send slides or call for appointment. Reports within 4 weeks. Work may be shipped or hand-delivered. Dealer pays insurance on exhibited work.
Profile: "Ours is a gallery of crafts, displayed in a setting of what we call 'original clutter,' permeated by a feeling of fantasy and whimsy. In a very full setting, we do our best to give each artist an important display. We feature the name and area of country and generally play up the craftsperson." Display period: 4-6 weeks. "Customers are 20-50, professional people ($25,000 income) with an overall sophisticated taste." Heaviest wholesale buying time: summer; best selling time: fall-Christmas.

West Virginia

THE ALLEY RAT, 13 Heritage Village, 11th St. at 2nd Ave., Huntington WV 25701. (304)529-2621. Contact: Kay or Bas Bringham. Craft/gift shop. Estab. 1970. Represents 30 craftworkers. Considers ceramics, decoupage, dollmaking, glass art, metalsmithing, soft sculpture, tole painting, wall hangings, weavings, woodcrafting, and especially needs pottery and candlemaking. One-of-a-kind and handmade production-line items. Price range: 50¢-$150; bestsellers: $1-10. Buys outright and works on consignment. "Don't promise delivery if you aren't sure of being able to." Requires exclusive area representation. Reports in 1 week. Work may be shipped or hand delivered. Dealer pays return shipping to craftsman and insurance on exhibited work. Located in a mall. Changes displays on slow items. Customers: mainly ages 19-35.

THE APPLE BARREL, 78 Holland Ave., Morgantown WV 26505. (304)292-5180. Contact: Donna Crum. Gift shop. Estab. 1975. Represents 75 craftworkers.
Acceptable Work: Considers candlemaking, dollmaking, glass art, jewelry, leatherworking, pottery, quilting, scrimshaw, soft sculpture, tole painting, wall hangings, weavings and woodcrafting. One-of-a-kind and handmade production-line items. Price range: $2-200; bestsellers: $2-20.
Terms: Buys outright and works on consignment; 30% commission. Retail price set by joint agreement. Send resume, photos, and wholesale price list. Reports in 3 weeks. Work may be shipped or hand-delivered. Dealer pays insurance on exhibited work.
Profile: Shop has country store image. "We are also a dealer for primitive furniture reproductions. We will consider a special showing with a demonstration, if the craftworker is available." Customers: female, ages 22-54, $20,000 incomes. Heaviest wholesale buying time: fall; bestsellers: Christmas.
To Break In: "We would like special tags and/or cards to accompany crafts."

ARABIA'S ART GALLERY, Walton Star Route, Box 1A, Spencer WV 25276. (304)927-2200. Contact: Philip V. Arabia. Gallery. Estab. 1969. Represents 30 craftworkers.
Acceptable Work: Considers batik, candlemaking, ceramics, dollmaking, glass art, jewelry, metalsmithing, needlecrafts, pottery, quilting, wall hangings, weavings and woodcrafting. One-of-a-kind and handmade production-line items. Price range: $5-100; bestsellers: $5-35.
Terms: Buys outright. Gallery sets retail price. Bring in samples. Reports in 2 weeks. Work may be shipped or hand-delivered. Dealer pays insurance on exhibited work.
Profile: "Signs are made to give artists credit. Often the artists' exposure is increased by our bringing items out of the area to New York or Pennsylvania for art auctions. We sell art and craft supplies and hold classes for children and adults and hold art auctions as fund raisers. Gallery's aim—to bring art to the community and the community to art. Our customers are as varied as the local population. We have bank presidents and farmers, MD's and back-to-the-land enthusiasts." Heaviest wholesale buying time: summer-spring; best selling time: fall-preChristmas.

THE ART PALETTE, 1231 Ohio Ave., Box 274, Dunbar WV 25064. (304)768-3814. Contact: Lillie Dawson. Craft shop/gallery/art supplies shop. Estab. 1976. Represents 12 craftworkers. Price range: $2-125; bestsellers: $2-15. Works on consignment and buys outright; 20% commission. Craftworker sets retail price. Reports in 2 weeks. Work may be shipped or hand-delivered. Dealer pays insurance for exhibited work.
Acceptable Work: Considers batik; glass art; jewelry; leatherworking; metalsmithing; pottery; quilting; soft sculpture; tole painting; wall hangings; weavings; and woodcrafting. Primitive and fine craft pieces; utilitarian and/or decorative.
Profile: "We take local artist's work to hang, who might not otherwise have somewhere to hang their work. Our customers are all ages: school children to adults; basically artistically inclined; middle income to higher. Make an appointment before coming to the shop." Heaviest wholesale buying time: pre-Christmas; best selling time: fall.

CABIN CREEK QUILTS, Box 383, Cabin Creek WV 25035. (304)595-3928. Director: Alice H. Nida. Craft and quilt shop. Estab. 1970. Represents 100 West Virginia, low income craftworkers. Considers clothing; needlecrafts; quilting; and wall hangings. Fine, one-of-a-kind and handmade production-line items; utilitarian only. Price range: $2.50-600; bestsellers: $2.50-300. Works on consignment; members only. 20% commission. Reports in 3 weeks. Work may be shipped or hand-delivered. Coop pays shipping and insurance.
Profile: "Work is rotated about once a month. Customers are all ages; interested in handmade items and the arts; and have higher income." Best selling and heaviest wholesale buying time: summer and fall.

CABIN CREEK QUILTS, 200 Broad St., Charleston WV 25301. (304)342-0326. See above.

COLLECTOR'S CORNER, HUNTINGTON GALLERIES, McCoy Rd., Park Hills, Huntington WV 25701. (304)529-2701. Manager: Betsy Broh or Carole McCullah. Museum gift shop. Estab. 1972. Represents 50 craftworkers. Price range: $2-300; bestsellers: $5-50. Works on consignment and buys outright; 33% commission. Retail price set by joint agreement. Reports in 1 month. Work may be shipped or hand-delivered. Dealer pays insurance for exhibited work. Heaviest wholesale buying time: fall; best selling time: Christmas.
Acceptable Work: Considers ceramics; glass art; jewelry; leatherworking; needlecrafts; pottery; wall hangings; weavings; and woodcrafting. Fine one-of-a-kind pieces.

FAITH WORKSHOP, 1418 McCorkle Ave., SW, Charleston WV 25303. (304)744-4677. Contact: David Raines. Craft shop/workshop/retailer. Estab. 1977. Price range: 39¢-$500. Works on consignment; 30% commission. Craftworker sets wholesale price. Work may be shipped or hand-delivered. Dealer pays insurance for exhibited work. Best selling time: Christmas.
Acceptable Work: Considers batik; candlemaking; ceramics; clothing; decoupage; dollmaking; leatherworking; needlecraft; pottery; quilting; woodcrafting; and leaded glass.

GREENBRIER VALLEY ARTISANS' GUILD, 102 S. Jefferson St., Lewisburg WV 24901. (304)645-6910. Chairperson: Jeff Shriver. Craft shop. Represents 30 West Virginian craftspersons, members of Greenbrier Valley Artisans' Guild. Send slides. Reports in 4 weeks. Work may be shipped or hand-delivered.
Acceptable Work: Considers batik, candlemaking, clothing, glass art, jewelry, leatherworking, metalsmithing, pottery, quilting, soft sculpture, wall hangings, weavings and woodcrafting. Utilitarian and/or decorative and fine designers crafts. Price range: $1-1,000; bestsellers: $1-20. Works on consignment; 20% commission. Craftworkers pays insurance on exhibited work. Craftworker sets retail price.
Profile:" 'The Greenbrier Valley Artisans' Guild is a cooperative (juried membership; $12 annual fee) interested in promoting fine quality art and crafts in West Virginia. The shop is a cooperative effort giving the artist or craftsperson an opportunity both to make decisions concerning the operation of the store and to market his or her items." Best selling time: summer-Christmas.

MAN CLOTHING & JEWELRY CO., 209 Main St., Man WV 25635. Department store. Ladies, furniture and jewelry departments buy baskets; carvings; sculpture; Christmas ornaments; dinnerware; furniture; handbags and leather accessories; jewelry; pillows; silverwork; wall hangings; and weavings for resale. Retail price set by joint agreement.

MOUNTAIN CRAFT SHOP, American Ridge Rd., Rt. 1, New Martinsville WV 26155. (304)455-3570. Contact: Dick Schnacke. Craft shop. Estab. 1965. Represents 60 craftworkers from West Virginia. Price range: 60¢-$39; bestsellers: $1.50-6.75. Buys outright. Retail price set by joint agreement. Reports in 1 week. Work may be shipped or hand-delivered.
Acceptable Work: Considers dollmaking; folk toys; games; puzzles; and doll furniture. Primitive and handmade production-line items; utilitarian only.
Profile: "We handle solely folk toys, dolls, games, etc. Our items appeal to all ages, interests and income levels." Best selling time: summer-fall.

PARKERSBURG ART CENTER, Box 131, Parkersburg WV 26101. (304)485-3859. Director: P. Joseph Mullins. Museum gift shop and gallery. Represents 10 craftworkers.
Acceptable Work: Considers all crafts. Specializes in Appalachian and contemporary work. One-of-a-kind and handmade production-line items. Price: 25¢-$100; bestsellers: $5-35.
Terms: Buys outright and works on consignment; 30% commission. Retail price set by joint agreement. Send slides or call for appointment. Reports in 2 weeks. Work may be shipped or hand delivered. Dealer pays insurance on exhibited work.
Profile: Several small galleries and exhibitions of traveling shows. Small items are under glass and a salesperson is on duty while the shop is open. Customers: upper middle class. Heaviest wholesale buying time: September-November; best selling time: November-December.
To Break In: "Must be good work and have dependable production."

PRICKETTS FORT MEMORIAL FOUNDATION, INC., Pricketts Fort State Park, Rt. 3, Fairmont WV 26554. (304)363-3030. Curator: Kimberlee Burdette. Gift shop. Estab. 1975. Buys outright. Retail price set by joint agreement. Requires some exclusive area representation. Reports in 3 weeks. Work may be shipped or hand-delivered. Dealer pays shipping to shop.
Acceptable Work: Considers dollmaking; leatherworking; metalsmithing; pottery; quilting; basket making; and woodcrafting. High quality 18th and 19th century reproductions only. Primitive and finished pieces.
Profile: "This is not a souvenir shop. We want only approved 18th and 19th century repros." Heaviest wholesale buying time: spring and fall; best selling time: summer and winter.

SENIOR CITIZEN ARTS & CRAFTS COOP, Pineville WV 24874. (304)732-7440. Manager: Shirley Bullington. Craft shop. Estab. 1973. Represents 200 craftworkers.
Acceptable Work: Considers ceramics, clothing, decoupage, dollmaking, glass art, jewelry,

leatherworking, needlecrafts, quilting, wall hangings, weavings and woodcrafting. Specializes in Appalachian work. Price range: $1-250; bestsellers: $5-15.
Terms: Works on consignment; 10% commission. Craftworker sets retail price. Write or call for information.
Profile: "The coop is a chartered, nonprofit organization." Best selling time: Christmas.

THE SERENDIPITY ARTS AND CRAFTS SHOP, E. German St., Shepherdstown WV 25443. Contact: Helen Myers Seeley. Craft shop. Estab. 1971. Represents 12 craftworkers. Price range: $1-100; bestsellers: $4-25. Works on consignment and buys outright; 20-40% commission. Retail price set by joint agreement. Reports in 4 weeks. Work may be hand-delivered. Dealer pays insurance for exhibited work.
Acceptable Work: Considers soft sculpture; pewter; jewelry; needlecrafts; wallhangings; weavings; macrame; stained glass; quilts; wood furniture; wood toys; and assemblage. Primitive and fine one-of-a-kind pieces. Boutique room features works of outstanding American craft artists. Year-round Christmas room offers hand-made decorations.
Profile: "I get college students, art majors, scout leaders, tourists, county extension homemakers and just good out and out crafters." Heaviest wholesale buying time: Christmas; best selling time: Christmas, Easter, and tourist season (spring-late fall).

THE SHOP, Dept. of Culture and History, Cultural Center, Capitol Complex, Charleston WV 25305. (304)348-0220. Marketing Coordinator: Rebecca Stelling Winkles. Craft shop. Estab. 1976. Represents 100 West Virginia craftworkers. Price range: 50¢-$1,500; bestsellers: 50¢-$60. Buys outright. Retail price set by joint agreement. Reports in 2 weeks. Work may be shipped or hand-delivered. Dealer pays shipping and insurance.
Acceptable Work: Considers batik; candlemaking; ceramics; clothing; dollmaking; glass art; jewelry; leatherworking; metalsmithing; needlecrafts; pottery; quilting; soft sculpture; toys; wall hangings; weavings; and woodcrafting. Fine one-of-a-kind and handmade production-line items.

STUFF & THINGS, Box C, New Martinsville WV 26155. (304)455-3241. Contact: Ruth Anne Cochran. Gift shop. Estab. 1977. Represents 50-60 craftworkers.
Acceptable Work: Considers ceramics, clothing, decoupage, dollmaking, glass art, jewelry, leatherworking, metalsmithing, needlecrafts, pottery, quilting, scrimshaw, tole painting, wall hangings, weavings and woodcrafting. Especially needs handmade baskets and flower pots and Easter items in spring. No large items. Specializes in Appalachian work. Handmade production-line items only. Price range: 50¢-$100 maximum; bestsellers: $5-10.
Terms: Works on consignment; 25% commission. Craftworker sets retail price. Send resume with SASE. Reports in 1 week. Work may be shipped or hand delivered.
Profile: "We are a small shop on a main highway looking for unusual and different crafts, not bizarre items. All items are displayed. Merchandise is taken in the month after opening in April. We keep it until November unless it is Christmas-oriented. We display Christmas items from November 15-Christmas." Customers: mostly women ages 20-60. Heaviest wholesale buying time: spring and fall; best selling time: fall and Christmas. Open: April 1-December 24.

SUNRISE SHOPS, 755 Myrtle Rd., Charleston WV 25314. (304)344-8035. Manager: Alma M. McMillan. Museum gallery and gift shop. Estab. 1974. Represents 10 craftworkers. Price range: $2-500; bestsellers: $2-15. Works on consignment and buys outright; 33% commission. Craftworker sets retail price. Requires exclusive area representation. Reports in 4 weeks. Work may be shipped or hand-delivered. Dealer pays return shipping and insurance for exhibited work.
Acceptable Work: Considers batik; ceramics; glass art; jewelry; metalsmithing; pottery; wall hangings; small sculptures; and weavings. Especially needs jewelry, glass and original design Christmas ornaments. Primitive and fine one-of-a-kind pieces.
Profile: "A copy of items received with identifying number used in inventory along with an agreement of sales and display terms is sent to the craftsman. We emphasize crafts from out of state. Customers are children as well as adults; all walks of life are represented." Heaviest wholesale buying time: July-August; best selling time: October-December and May-June.

YESTERYEAR TOY COMPANY, INC., Box 3283, Charleston WV 25332. President: Marcy A. Marble. Craft and gift shop/manufacturer of handmade painted wooden toys. Estab. 1971. Price range: $3-500. Contract manufacturing or one-of-a-kind custom made in addition to own line of toys.
Acceptable Work: Considers all crafts; primarily wooden toys.

Wisconsin

THE ART BARN, Rt. 1, Country Lane, Waupaca WI 54981. (715)258-2082. Gallery. Estab. 1967. Represents 125 craftworkers. Price range: 35¢-$200; bestsellers: $10-90. Works on consignment; 30% commission. Retail price set by joint agreement. Requires exclusive area representation. Reports in 2 weeks. Work may be shipped or hand-delivered.
Acceptable Work: Considers all crafts. All styles; utilitarian and/or decorative.
Profile: Open Memorial Day to Christmas. "Work is displayed in a rustic setting, artists and crafters often grouped or grouped when possible—a 'real barn' atmosphere." Displays work 7 months. Heaviest wholesale buying time: spring; best selling time: summer.

ART CENTER, Prospect Mall, 2233 N. Prospect Ave., Milwaukee WI 53202. (414)271-9600. Contact: Peter J. Kondos. Considers all crafts. Maximum size: standard framing. Buys outright and on consignment. Specializes in traditional art. Minimum price: $5. Retail price set by gallery. Requires exclusive area representation. Query first with slides and/or photos. SASE.

ART CRATE, INC., 334 S. Knowles Ave., New Richmond WI 54071. (715)246-6861. Contact: Bette Buell. Gallery. Estab. 1972. Represents 230 craftworkers. Price range: $3-600; bestsellers: $50-75. Works on consignment and buys jewelry outright; 40% commission. Craftworker sets retail price. Reports in 2 weeks. Work may be shipped or hand-delivered. Dealer pays insurance for exhibited work.
Acceptable Work: Considers batik; candlemaking; ceramics; glass art; jewelry; leatherworking; metalsmithing; pottery; wall hangings; and weavings. Fine one-of-a-kind pieces; utilitarian and/or decorative.
Profile: "Work is displayed until written request is sent to have artist remove it. Jewelry is displayed as long as it is a current and desirable design." Heaviest wholesale buying time: fall; best selling time: Christmas and summer.
To Break In: "We only work with individual craftsmen, not through agents. A preference is for full-time artists and craftsmen for good quality work and salable items."

ART INDEPENDENT GALLERY, 706 Main St., Lake Geneva WI 53147. (414)248-3612. Contact: Richard or Mary Jane Herr. Craft shop/gallery. Estab. 1968. Represents 270 craftworkers. Price range: $3-3,000; bestsellers: $300 maximum. Works on consignment; 40% commission. Retail price set by joint agreement. Reports in 2 weeks. Work may be shipped or hand-delivered.
Acceptable Work: Considers batik; ceramics; clothing; glass art; jewelry; leatherworking; metalsmithing; needlecrafts; sculpture; wall hangings; weavings; and woodcrafting. Fine one-of-a-kind pieces; utilitarian and/or decorative.

ARTSPACE, LTD., 790 N. Jefferson St., Milwaukee WI 53202. (414)276-8989. Contact: Suzanne Berland. Craft shop/gallery. Estab. 1975. Represents 75 craftworkers. Price range: $2.50-500; bestsellers: $5-200. Works on consignment and buys outright; 40% commission. Craftworker sets retail price. Requires exclusive area representation. Reports in 2 weeks. Work may be shipped or hand-delivered if prearranged. Dealer pays insurance for exhibited work.
Acceptable Work: Considers batik; ceramics; dollmaking; glass art; needlecrafts; pottery; quilting; soft sculpture; wall hangings; weavings; and woodcrafting. Especially needs functional ceramics and well-designed, functional flameware. Fine, one-of-a-kind and handmade production-line items; utilitarian and/or decorative.
Profile: "Displays are reviewed every week; changed at regular intervals." Heaviest wholesale buying time: summer; best selling time: October-December.

ARTWORKS, INC., 1520 Main St., Marinette WI 54143. (715)732-0379. Director: Joyce Murphy. Gallery. Estab. 1973. Represents 50 member craftworkers. Price range: 75¢-$350; bestsellers: 75¢-$25. Works on consignment; 20% commission. Craftworker sets retail price. Reports in 1 week.
Acceptable Work: Considers batik; candlemaking; ceramics; clothing; dollmaking; glass art; jewelry; needlecrafts; pottery; quilting; wall hangings; weavings; and woodcrafting. One-of-a-kind pieces; utilitarian and/or decorative.

THE BERGSTROM MUSEUM SHOP, Bergstrom Art Center, 165 N. Park Ave., Neenah WI 54956. (414)722-3348. Contact: Manager. Craft shop/gallery/rental gallery. Estab. 1959. Represents 75 artists and craftworkers. Price range: $2-800; bestsellers: $7.50-150. Works on consignment and buys outright; 25% commission. Craftworker sets retail price. Reports in 2

weeks. Work may be shipped or hand-delivered. Dealer pays insurance for exhibited work.
Acceptable Work: Considers batik; ceramics; glass art; jewelry; metalsmithing; pottery; soft sculpture; wall hangings; weavings; and woodcrafting. Especially needs glass inventory and high quality Christmas items. Fine one-of-a-kind pieces; utilitarian and/or decorative.
Profile: "Since the Bergstrom has one of the foremost collections of paperweights (and Germanic glass), we stress glass items; also Wisconsin artists." Displays work 6 months. Heaviest wholesale buying time: prior to December holidays and summer.

CABIN CRAFT SHOPPES, On the Bay, Ephraim WI 54211. (414)854-2916. Contact: June or Marty Matoushek. Craft and gift shop. Estab. 1933. Price range: $2.50-1,000; bestsellers: $2.50-50. Buys outright. Gallery sets retail price. Requires exclusive area representation. Work may be shipped or hand-delivered. Dealer pays shipping to shop and insurance for exhibited work.
Acceptable Work: Considers ceramics; clothing; jewelry; leatherworking; metalsmithing; pottery; wall hangings; weavings; and woodcrafting. Fine, one-of-a-kind and handmade production-line items; utilitarian and/or decorative.
Profile: "We intermingle craftwork with production/manufactured merchandise." Heaviest wholesale buying time: spring; best selling time: summer-fall.

CENTRAL MADISON COUNCIL, Box 71, Madison WI 53701. (608)255-5793. Coordinator: Janice Durand. "Madison will have available in the spring of 1979 a new downtown mall complete with special areas designed for the display and sale of handmade crafts. The Central Madison Council (a downtown business organization) will be responsible for sponsoring and programming craft sales in the area. Persons interested in arranging special outdoor craft show and sales should write for more information."

THE CHANGING SCENE, 418 E. Silver Spring Dr., Milwaukee WI 53217. (414)964-8877. President: Betty Burns. Craft/gift shop and gallery. Estab. 1968. Represents 200 craftworkers.
Acceptable Work: Considers all crafts except scrimshaw. One-of-a-kind and handmade production-line items. Price range: $2-300; bestsellers: $3.50-10.
Terms: Buys outright and works on consignment; 40% commission on better items. Retail price set by joint agreement. Prefers exclusive area representation. Send resume and slides/samples. Reports in 3 or less weeks. Work may be shipped or hand delivered. Dealer pays all shipping and insurance for exhibited work.
Profile: "We are a well established business on a busy suburban street. Presently, we are considering adding another store in a top financial area downtown. We rotate items (grouped by artist or craftsperson). If not much interest is shown, we return goods in 3 months (for consignment); otherwise, we rotate or mark down. Our crafts show imagination and creativity." Customers: young people (many high schools in area), above average incomes and tourists. Heaviest wholesale buying time: August-December; best selling time: Thanksgiving-Christmas.

COMMUNITY CRAFTS & ARTS CO-OP, INC., 118 N. Carroll St., Madison WI 53703. Manager: Sharon Friedland. Craft shop. Estab. 1971. Represents 30 member craftworkers.
Acceptable Work: Considers batik, candlemaking, ceramics, glass art, jewelry, leatherworking, metalsmithing, needlecrafts, pottery, quilting, soft sculpture, tole painting, wall hangings, weavings and woodcrafting. Fine one-of-a-kind pieces. "We tend towards earthy, natural styles of work." Price range: $1-100; bestsellers: $3-20.
Terms: Works on consignment; 25% commission. Craftworker "must be member of coop and work in store 8 hours per month (12 hours, 20% commission; 16 hours, 15% commission). Membership fee is $10 and work is juried by the Quality Control Committee. All profits returned to member exhibitors." Craftworker sets retail price. Stop by shop or call for information. Reports in 2 weeks. Hand-delivered work only. Dealer pays insurance on exhibited work. Displays time: 6 months.
Profile: "All members serve on functional committees—a small but responsible amount of work without overburdening any member when each does his share. Group art exhibits, exchange of craft and art ideas and fellowship are all part of the co-op." Best selling and heaviest wholesale buying time: Christmas.

COUNTRY CRAFTS, Rt. 2, Plymouth WI 53073. (414)893-8095. Partner: Rebecca Summers. Gift shop/tea room. Estab. 1973. Represents 300 craftworkers. Price range: 50¢-$500; bestsellers: 50¢-$75. Works on consignment and buys outright; 25% commission. Retail price set by joint agreement. Requires exclusive area representation. Reports in 1 week. Work may be

shipped or hand-delivered. Dealer pays return shipping.
Acceptable Work: Considers all crafts except clothing. Primitive and fine one-of-a-kind pieces; utilitarian and/or decorative. Especially needs hand-blown glass.
Profile: "Some artists' work is displayed as a group; others are arranged with other works to enhance interest and use of item. We are located in a large barn in the country. Customers are all ages; 50% are women over 50; average to upper income bracket." Heaviest wholesale buying time: January-May; best selling time: May 1-October 24.

CREATIVE ARTS STUDIO, 104 Main St., Weyauwega WI 54983. (414)867-3557. Artist in residence: Barbara Danthine Radtke. Craft shop/studio. Estab. 1969. Represents 10 craftworkers. Price range: $1-500. Works on consignment and buys outright; 20% commission. Retail price set by joint agreement. Requires exclusive area representation. Reports in 2 weeks. Work may be shipped or hand-delivered. Dealer pays insurance for exhibited work.
Acceptable Work: Considers batik; candlemaking; ceramics; dollmaking; glass art; jewelry; leatherworking; pottery; wall hangings; and weavings. Fine, one-of-a-kind and handmade production-line items; utilitarian and/or decorative.
Profile: "We have 4 display rooms along with 2 large display windows; our displays change constantly. We have our studio with the shop so visitors can see what we are making and we have lots of tour groups visit us." Best selling and heaviest wholesale buying time: spring-fall.

ELVEHJEM MUSEUM OF ART, Museum Shop, 800 University Ave., Madison WI 53706 (608)263-2246. Manager: Kathy Parks. Museum gift shop. Estab. 1970. Represents 20 craftworkers. Considers batik; ceramics; and jewelry. All styles; utilitarian and/or decorative. Price range: $5-75; bestsellers: $5-15. Buys outright. Retail price set by joint agreement. Reports in 2 weeks. Work may be hand-delivered. Dealer pays shipping and insurance for exhibited work.
Profile: "We are located on the University of Wisconsin campus and near the center of downtown. Customers are primarily UW students and staff." Best selling and heaviest wholesale buying time: fall.

FIRST NATIONAL BANK, Box 30, Monroe WI 53566. President: Evan Davis. Bank. Estab. 1856. Represents 4 craftworkers. Considers decoupage; wall hangings; and weavings. Primitive and fine pieces; utilitarian and/or decorative. Price range: $10-500; bestsellers: $10-100. Displays work only. No commission. Craftworker sets retail price. Reports in 2 weeks. Work may be hand-delivered. "Schedule an interview at the displayer's best time so as not to disrupt the daily routine." Best selling time: spring and summer. Displays work 30-90 days.

A. GOLDMANN'S & SONS, 930 W. Mitchell St., Milwaukee WI 53204. (414)645-9100. General Manager: Carl M. Brown. Department store. Art and needlework and housewares departments buy adult games; baskets; carvings; pillows; pottery; sculpture; wall hangings; and weavings for resale. Handmade production-line items only. Store sets retail price. "We could sell crafts up to $30 retail." Local craftworkers should call for interview or write with illustrations of their work.

THE HAYLOFT, 760 S. Lakeshore Dr., Lake Geneva WI 53147. (414)248-8952. Manager: Laura Braden. Craft, gift and antique shop. Estab. 1976. Represents 80 craftworkers. Price range: $1-800; bestsellers: $2-75. Works on consignment and buys outright; 33⅓% commission. Retail price set by joint agreement. Reports in 4 weeks. Work may be shipped or hand-delivered. Dealer pays insurance for exhibited work.
Acceptable Work: Considers batik; ceramics; dollmaking; jewelry; leatherworking; metalsmithing; needlecrafts; pottery; quilting; soft sculpture; tole painting; wall hangings; weavings; and woodcrafting. Especially needs glass blowing. Fine one-of-a-kind pieces; utilitarian and/or decorative.
Profile: "All consignors have been pleased with the way their work is displayed. If they are not, we take suggestions and are happy to make changes. The building is an old stable and carriage house. It was built in 1900. Each horse stall is set up as an individual room with antiques. Crafts are displayed in the carriage room. Most customers have a high income." Best selling time: summer.

JOHN MICHAEL KOHLER ARTS CENTER, 608 New York Ave., Sheboygan WI 53081. (414)458-6144. Director: Ruth Kohler. Museum gift shop and gallery. Estab. 1967. Represents 60-85 craftworkers.
Acceptable Work: Considers ceramics, glass art, jewelry, metalsmithing, pottery, soft sculpture, wall hangings, weavings and wood. Especially needs glass; pillows and other fiber work;

jewelry; and ceramics and functional pottery. Fine, one-of-a-kind and handmade production-line items. Price range: $3-500; bestsellers: $5-100. Works on consignment and buys outright; 33⅓% commission. Retail price set by joint agreement. Requires exclusive area representation. Reports in 4 weeks. Work may be shipped or hand-delivered. Dealer pays shipping and insurance.
Profile: "Each work is displayed as an individual art object in an elegant gallery." Heaviest wholesale buying time: February and June-October; best selling time: October-December.

PETER J. KONDOS ART GALLERIES, 700 N. Water, Milwaukee WI 53202. (414)271-8000. Contact: Peter Kondos. Considers sculpture. Maximum height: 6'. Art must be offered for sale. Buys outright or on consignment; negotiates commission. Price range: $5-2,000; bestsellers: $5-250. Gallery sets retail price. Requires exclusive area representation. Displays work 2 weeks-1 month. Query with slides or photos of work. SASE.

THE LOOMS, Far End, Shake Rag St., Mineral Point WI 53566. (608)987-2277. Contact: Ken Colwell. Craft shop/textile museum. Estab. 1970. Represents 2-3 craftworkers. Considers wall hangings and weavings. Primitive and fine one-of-a-kind pieces; utilitarian and/or decorative. Price range: 50¢-$250; bestsellers: $2.50-100. Works on consignment; 20% commission. Buys locally only; no mailing or shipping. Craftworker sets retail price. Reports in 1-2 weeks.

MADISON ART CENTER GALLERY SHOP, 720 E. Gorham St., Madison WI 53703. (608)257-0158. Contact: Shop manager. Write with slides or photos. Photos must be fully insured and representative of artist's work. Biographical information also helpful. Works on 25% commission. All art media acceptable for 6-month consignment.

MARATHON COUNTY HISTORICAL SOCIETY, 403 McIndoe St., Wausau WI 54401. (715)848-6143. Director: Edward T. Schoenberger. Museum gallery. Estab. 1952. Considers batik; ceramics; jewelry; metalsmithing; soft sculpture; wall hangings; and weavings. Primitive and fine pieces. Exhibitions only. Craftworker sets retail price. Reports in 2 weeks. Work may be shipped or hand-delivered. Museum pays insurance.
Profile: "All possible care is given to items on display; small items are displayed in cases that are locked. The gallery of the museum is located in the home of a former lumber baron of Wausau."

MATHIS GALLERY, 328 Main St., Racine WI 53403. (414)637-1111. Contact: Emile Mathis. Gallery. Estab. 1972. Represents craftworkers whose work relates to ethnic origins. Price range: $20-100. Works on consignment and buys outright; 40% commission. Retail price set by joint agreement. Rental gallery fee: cost of installation and opening, if any, plus percentage of sales. Reports in 4 weeks. Work may be shipped or hand-delivered. Dealer pays insurance for exhibited work.
Acceptable Work: Considers glass art; quilting; wall hangings; and weavings. Primitive and fine one-of-a-kind pieces; utilitarian and/or decorative.
Profile: "Customers are 25 and up; interested in house decorating; with incomes of $30,000 and up." Displays work 4-8 weeks. Heaviest wholesale buying time: spring and late summer; best selling time: late spring and pre-Christmas.

MILWAUKEE ART CENTER WISCONSIN GALLERY, 750 N. Lincoln Memorial Dr., Milwaukee WI 53202. (414)271-9508. Curator: Jane Brite. Considers experimental art and sculpture. Maximum size: 4x4'. 30% commission. Artist sets price. Prices from $50-1,000. Open to Wisconsin artists. Call for appointments. 3,000 members notified of spring and fall collections and special openings.

MINI GALLERY, Racine Art Association of Wustum Museum of Fine Arts, Racine WI 53404. (414)636-9177. Contact: Director. Gift shop/rental gallery. Estab. 1971. Represents 8-15 craftworkers. Size of flat work limited to 3x4'; 3D work to 12x24x12". Price range: $5-$100; bestsellers: $5-35. Works on consignment; 30% commission. Craftworker sets retail price. Reports in 2 weeks. Work may be shipped or hand-delivered. Dealer pays insurance. Best selling time: pre-Christmas.
Acceptabe Work: Considers ceramics; glass art; jewelry; needlecrafts; pottery; soft sculpture; wall hangings; weavings; and woodcrafting. All styles; utilitarian and/or decorative.

NEW VISIONS GALLERY, INC., 1000 N. Oak Ave., Marshfield WI 54449. (715)387-5562. Director: Roger C. Pearce. Gallery. Estab. 1975. Represents 1-6 craftworkers. Considers all

crafts except candlemaking; decoupage; and tole painting. Price range: $5-800; bestsellers: under $35. Works on consignment; 20% commission. Retail price set by joint agreement. Work may be shipped or hand-delivered. Dealer pays insurance for exhibited work. Returns made by dealer when possible.
Profile: "The item is unpacked, checked for damage, a report is made. It is stored until displayed, either in a case or out, dependent on the size. Some pieces require additional security such as either wiring down or tape on the bottom to deter movement. We are located in the main entrance of the fifth largest clinic in the United States." Displays work 4-6 weeks.

THE PIK PLACE, 710 Beech St., West Bend WI 53095. (414)338-2444. Contact: Bette Fehring. Craft shop. Estab. 1976. Represents 100 craftworkers. Price range: $1.25-45; bestsellers: $2.25-10. Works on consignment; 30% commission. Retail price set by joint agreement. Requires exclusive area representation. Reports in 4 weeks. Work may be shipped or hand-delivered with prior approval. Dealer pays insurance for exhibited work.
Acceptable Work: Considers ceramics; decoupage; glass art; tole painting; wall hangings; weavings; macrame; patchwork; and rosemaling. Utilitarian and/or decorative. Especially needs some new ideas from a different part of the country.
Profile: "We have an old house and display items as they would appear in a home. We get customers from grade school to middle age on up. I would judge most of our customers to be in the $10,000-15,000 income bracket." Displays work 4-6 weeks. Best selling time: September-December.

RONBACH SHOP, Box 312, Boulder Junction WI 54512. (715)385-2205. Contact: Ellen Christgau. Gift shop. Estab. 1975. Represents 35 craftworkers. Price range: 50c-$60; bestsellers: $2-30. Buys outright. Requires exclusive area representation. Reports in 2 weeks. Work may be shipped or hand-delivered. Dealer pays return shipping and insurance for submitted work.
Acceptable Work: Considers glass art; jewelry; leatherworking; metalsmithing; tole painting; woodcrafting; Christmas ornaments. Especially needs original, moderately-priced, shippable articles made of natural materials. Primitive and handmade production-line items; utilitarian and/or decorative.
Profile: "All items are very visible. We use a background of barnwood walls and display units. We cannot handle very large items. We feature crafts made of natural materials. Our customers are tourists; the majority are women." Heaviest wholesale buying time: January-May; best selling time: May 15-October 15.

THE STATE HISTORICAL SOCIETY OF WISCONSIN—MUSEUM STORE, 816 State St., Madison WI 53706. (608)262-3271. Contact: Beth E. Witz. Museum gift shop. Estab. 1955. Represents 5-6 craftworkers. Price range: $1.25-50; bestsellers: 50c-$35. Works on consignment and buys outright; commission varies. Retail price set by joint agreement. Reports in 3 weeks. Work may be shipped or hand-delivered. Dealer pays shipping and insurance for exhibited work.
Acceptable Work: Considers candlemaking; ceramics; glass art; jewelry; metalsmithing; needlecrafts; pottery; woodcrafting; and plant portraits. Fine, one-of-a-kind and handmade production-line items; utilitarian and/or decorative.
Profile: "Our display area is limited; we try to remain as historical and within Wisconsin or at least mid-West in scope as possible. Displays work 60 days. Heaviest wholesale buying time: spring and Christmas; best selling time: spring.

THUMB FUN AMUSEMENT PARK, Box 128, Hwy. 42, Fish Creek WI 54272. (414)868-3418. President: D. B. Butchart. "We are presently developing a craft area in our park where craftworkers will perform their craft during operating hours and sell their products. Space is available on lease and percentage. 1890's theme." Write for more information.

TWELMEYER GALLERIES, 6415 W. North Ave., Wauwatosa WI 53213. (414)771-4114. Director: Linda A. Twelmeyer. Gallery. Estab. 1976. Represents 1 craftworker "but would like to increase." Price range: $10-1,000; bestsellers: $10-200. Works on consignment; 40% commission. Retail price set by joint agreement. Reports in 1 week. Work may be shipped or hand-delivered. Dealer pays return shipping (if work was solicited).
Acceptable Work: Considers glass art; quilting; and woodcrafting. Especially needs fine blown glass in all price ranges. Needs paper weights, vases and bibelot. Primitive and fine one-of-a-kind pieces.
Profile: "Work is shown in display cases (glassed) or on table tops (depending on fragility) or on

wall. We usually show work at least 1 month in main gallery, then rotate on/off prime area display. Our customers range from young single and married adults just starting to collect on a low budget, to established wealthy and serious collectors."

WEE LITTLES SHOPPE, W64 N713 Washington Ave., Cedarburg WI 53012. (414)377-6170. Contact: Doris Casey. Miniatures and dolls. Estab. 1972. Represents 30 craftworkers. All styles; decorative only. Price range: 10c-$900; bestsellers: 50c-$200. Works on consignment and buys outright; 30% commission. Shop sets retail price. Requires exclusive area representation. Reports up to 4 weeks. Dealer pays insurance for exhibited work.
Acceptable Work: Considers all crafts in miniature. "Special need for handcrafted miniature furniture scaled 1"-1', especially Victorian and other period furniture. Dollhouse dolls; and clothing for dollhouse dolls are in demand."
Profile: "This is a hobby for all ages but we cater to the adult collector in the middle to upper income bracket."

THE WHIFFERDILL, Rt. 1, Trempealeau WI 54661. (608)534-6271. Contact: Jeanette Sasgen. Craft and gift shop. Estab. 1975. Represents 50-75 craftworkers. Price range: $1.50-600; bestsellers; $5-150. Works on consignment; 25% commission. Craftworker sets retail price. Requires exclusive area representation. Reports in 1 week. Work may be shipped or hand-delivered. Dealer pays insurance for exhibited work.
Acceptable Work: Considers batik; candlemaking; ceramics; decoupage; dollmaking; glass art; jewelry; leatherworking; metalsmithing; pottery; tole painting; wall hangings; weavings; and woodcrafting. Primitive and fine one-of-a-kind pieces; utilitarian and/or decorative.
Profile: "We are in a rural location near a well-known supper club and at the entrance to a state park. Our customers are generally more affluent; 30-50 years old, who appreciate handcrafted items. Displays work 4-6 months. Best selling time: April-December.

Wyoming

THE BLUE DUCK, 119 Ivinson, Laramie WY 82070. Contact: Bill or Joleen Arthur. Gallery. Estab. 1977. Represents 65 craftworkers. Heaviest wholesale buying time: fall; best selling time: summer and fall tourist seasons.
Acceptable Work: Considers batik; dollmaking; glass art; jewelry; pottery; quilting; soft sculpture; wall hangings; weavings; and woodcrafting. Especially needs soft art and wall hangings. Specializes in contemporary one-of-a-kind pieces, but also carries handmade production-line items. Price range: $2.50-250; bestsellers: $3-50.
Terms: Buys outright and works on consignment; 40% commission. Reports in 2 weeks. Work may be shipped or hand-delivered. Dealer pays return shipping and insurance for exhibited work.

THE CEDAR CHEST, 1401 W. Spruce, Rawlins WY 82301. (307)324-7737. Contact: Della M. Vivian. Estab. 1976. Represents 6 craftworkers.
Acceptable Work: Considers batik; ceramics; dollmaking; jewelry; pottery; soft sculpture; and woodcrafting. Fine one-of-a-kind and handmade production-line items. Price range: $5-300; bestsellers: $5-50.
Terms: Works on consignment and buys outright; 25% commission. Retail price set by joint agreement. Requires exclusive area representation. Reports in 4 weeks. Work may be hand-delivered. Dealer pays insurance for exhibited work.
Profile: "Pictures are displayed on easels and gallery wall; batiks on wall dowels or over furniture as merchandising drape; dolls, etc. on ladder." Best selling and heaviest wholesale buying time: summer and Christmas season.

THE COYOTE DEN, Box 2767, Jackson WY 83001. (307)733-3622. Contact: Jean Fulton. Handcrafted gift shop. Estab. 1977. Represents 72 top-quality craftworkers.
Acceptable Work: Considers all crafts. Especially needs leatherworking, metalsmithing, wildlife and Western pen and ink drawings or paintings, scrimshaw, woodcrafting and any unique, handcrafted, one-of-a-kind craft. Specializes in contemporary crafts. Price range: $2 (very few)-$450; bestsellers: $10-60.
Terms: Buys occasionally, but mostly works on consignment; 40-50% commission. Retail price set by joint agreement. Has exclusive area representation on 95% of merchandise, but not required. "Need to see crafts either in person or send slides or sample with SASE." Reports in 2 weeks. Work may be shipped or hand-delivered. "In the summer, we request that we can keep the item for the full season. In the winter season, we request to keep it for at least a 45-day period to give us every opportunity to sell the item. Dealer pays insurance on exhibited work.

Profile: "Statistics say Jackson Hole has 3½ million tourists come through during the summer months. Then, as a skiing area, it is excellent from the time the snow falls. Also, from October 1 is hunting season and the hunters are good customers." Heaviest wholesale buying time: January-June; best selling time: primary time is June-August, secondary time is September-December.
To Break In: "I like to know any and all information about my craftspeople's products so I can tell my customers the history behind the product and information about the craftsperson too. This is a good selling point."

GRAND TETON LODGE CO., Box 250, Moran WY 83013. (307)543-2811. Merchandise Manager: David M. Ware. Craft shop/gallery/gift shop. Estab. 1955. Represents 50 craftworkers.
Acceptable Work: Considers candlemaking; ceramics; jewelry; leatherworking; metalsmithing; pottery; soft sculpture; wall hangings; weavings; and woodcrafting. Fine handmade production-line items. Price range: $3-200; bestsellers: $5-15.
Terms: Buys outright. Requires exclusive area representation. Reports in 4 weeks. Work may be shipped or hand-delivered. Dealer pays shipping to shop. Heaviest wholesale buying time: late winter and spring; best selling time: summer.

HAPPY PEASANT GALLERY, Box 1116, Jackson Hole WY 83001. (307)733-3792. Contact: Keith Fay. Gallery/gift shop. Estab. 1964. Represents 12 craftworkers.
Acceptable Work: Considers glass art; jewelry; pottery; wall hangings; weavings; and woodcrafting. Primitive and fine one-of-a-kind pieces. Price range: $5-500; bestsellers: $5-25.
Terms: Gallery sets retail price. Requires exclusive area representation. Reports in 2 weeks. Work may be shipped or hand-delivered. Dealer pays return shipping and insurance for exhibited work. "Customers have medium to better than average income." Best selling time: summer.

LIBERTY GIFTS, 1005 Dewar Dr., Rock Springs WY 82901. (307)382-9829. Contact: Miss Bruna. Gift shop. Estab. 1970. Represents 100 craftworkers.
Acceptable Work: Considers all crafts. One-of-a-kind items; decorative only. Price range: $5-1,000.
Terms: Works on consignment; 20% commission. Craftworker sets retail price. Requires exclusive area representation. SASE. Reports in 4 weeks. Work may be shipped or hand-delivered. Display time: 3 months.
Profile: Shop is "located on a well-traveled street. Individual service and consideration is given to each item." Customers: $25,000+ incomes. Heaviest consignment and best selling time: spring and Christmas.

PINK CORRAL GIFT SHOP, 49 W. Broadway, Box 962, Jackson WY 83001. (307)733-4667. Contact: Rollie W. Pettit. Craft shop/gallery/gift shop. Estab. 1971. Represents 12-15 craftworkers.
Acceptable Work: Considers candlemaking; ceramics; glass art; jewelry; pottery; and woodcrafting. Fine one-of-a-kind and handmade production-line items; utilitarian only. Price range: $50-1,000; bestsellers: $50-400.
Terms: Buys outright. Retail price set by joint agreement. Requires exclusive area representation. Reports immediately. Work may be shipped or hand-delivered. Dealer pays insurance for exhibited work. Heaviest wholesale buying time: March; best selling time: June-August.

A TOUCH OF GLASS, STAINED GLASS STUDIO, Art Museum Bldg., 104 Rancho Rd., Casper WY 82601. (307)234-4758. Contact: Barbara Harris. Craft shop/ gallery. Estab. 1974. Represents 2 craftworkers.
Acceptable Work: Considers glass art and wall hangings. Fine one-of-a-kind and handmade production-line items. Price range: $25-5,000.
Terms: Works on consignment; 33% commission. Gallery sets retail price. Work may be hand-delivered. Heaviest wholesale buying time: summer-fall; best selling time: winter. "Some ready-made items on hand for resale."

Canada

ARETHUSA CRAFTS, Tyne Valley, Prince Edward Island, Canada. (902)831-2102; summer only. President: Diane Farquharson. Craft shop. Estab. 1963. Represents 40 member craftworkers.
Accepable Work: Considers batik, clothing, decoupage, dollmaking, jewelry, leatherworking,

needlecrafts, quilting, wall hangings, weavings and woodcrafting. Especially needs quilts. Specializes in contemporary craft articles and bright-colored souvenirs. Handmade production-line items. Price range: $1-150; bestsellers: $5-100. "Smaller articles for take-home gifts sell best."
Terms: Works on consignment; 20% commission. Craftworker sets retail price. Send resume and photos. Reports in 2 weeks. Work must be hand-delivered. Dealer pays insurance on exhibited work. Display time: 2 months.
Profile: Shop located in an old remodeled school. Best selling time: summer and Christmas.

ART GALLERY OF ONTARIO, GALLERY SHOP, 317 Dundas St. W., Toronto, Ontario, Canada M5T 1G4. (416)361-0414. Manager: Mrs. F.B. Moore. Gallery/gift shop. Represents 20 Canadian craftworkers.
Acceptable Work: Considers all crafts. One-of-a-kind and handmade production-line items.
Terms: Works on consignment. Retail price set by joint agreement. Prefers exclusive area representation. Call for appointment. Reports immediately. "Members of the gallery enjoy 10% discount on most items."
Profile: "We sell and display handmade books and stationery. We are surrounded by an art community, but enjoy patronage from all walks of life." Heaviest wholesale buying and best selling time: fall.

ART SALES & RENTAL SOCIETY, Box 3142, S. Postal Station, Halifax, Nova Scotia, Canada B3J 3G6. President: Irma M. Teichert. Museum gift shop/rental gallery. Estab. 1976. Represents 12-15 Canadian craftworkers mostly from Nova Scotia. Considers batik; ceramics; decoupage; jewelry; metalsmithing; pottery; wall hangings; weaving; woodcrafting; toys; and dried flower arrangements. "Special need for small handwoven items and fine stoneware or porcelain pieces." Fine one-of-a-kind pieces mostly but some handmade production-line items; decorative only. Price range: $1.50-300; bestsellers: $1.50-30 small crafts; $45-85 hangings. Works mostly on consignment, buys outright occasionally; 25% commission. Craftworker sets retail price. Prefers exclusive area representation. Reports in 2 weeks. Hand delivered work only. Dealer pays insurance. Customers are knowledgeable clientele plus tourists. Best selling time: late spring-early fall.

THE ARTISANS' MARKET PLACE, 345 King St., Midland, Ontario, Canada L4R 3M7. (705)526-2757. Contact: Julia Cameron. Craft shop. Estab. 1976. Represents 75-100 Ontario craftworkers.
Acceptable Work: Considers ceramics, clothing, dollmaking, dried flowers and weeds, glass art, jewelry, leatherworking, metalsmithing, needlecrafts, pottery, quilting, soft sculpture, small stoneware sculpture, tole painting, wall hangings, weavings and woodcrafting. Especially needs leatherwork, batik, original quality quilting, soft sculpture and original jewelry. One-of-a-kind and handmade production-line items. Price range: $2-100; bestsellers: $5-30.
Terms: Buys outright and works on consignment; 34% commission. Retail price set by joint agreement. Call for appointment or stop at shop with samples. Reports in 1 week maximum. Work may be shipped or hand delivered. Dealer pays insurance on exhibited work. Display time: 90 days.
Profile: "Shop is located on the main shopping street with ample front window display. The town is a summer tourist area on Georgian Bay with about 11,000 people. New merchandise gets feature space in the shop or in frequently changing windows. If interest wanes, articles are given less obvious display." Customers: 50% tourists and summer residents (cross country skiing and skidooing in winter). 50% local residents; medium-low to high incomes; young marrieds. Heaviest wholesale buying time: spring and fall; best selling time: July-August and December.
To Break In: "We cannot compete with big city prices—Toronto is 85 miles away. Personal tags or item identification is important on handcrafted goods."

ARTISAN'S STUDIO, 400 Front St., Nanaimo, British Columbia, Canada. President: Lois Kemp. Craft shop. Estab. 1975. Represents 15-18 craftworkers from Nanaimo and surrounding area. Considers batik; clothing; dollmaking; jewelry; needlecrafts; pottery; quilting; wall hangings; weavings; woodcrafting; baskets; and macrame. Fine one-of-a-kind and handmade production-line pottery; utilitarian and/or decorative. Price range: $1-200; bestsellers: $5-70. Members: 10% commission plus membership and 2-3 days work in shop/month. Craftworker sets retail price. Customers of all ages. Best selling time: Christmas and summer.

ATIKOKAN CENTENNIAL MUSEUM, Box 1330, Atikokan, Ontario, Canada P0T 1C0.

(807)597-6585. Curator: Diane Labelle-Davey. Museum gallery. Estab. 1965. Represents 1 craftworker at a time.
Acceptable Work: Considers all crafts. No kits. One-of-a-kind and handmade production-line items. Price range: 50¢-$40; bestsellers: $2-15.
Terms: Works on consignment. Craftworker sets retail price. Call for appointment. Reports immediately. Work must be hand-delivered. Dealer pays insurance on exhibited work.
Profile: "The Atikokan Centennial Museum is both an art gallery and a museum. As many of our visitors are interested in purchasing local crafts, we provide an outlet for local craftworkers. The items are displayed in a locked case for approximately 4 weeks. As items are sold, new ones are added to the display." Exhibits largely during Christmas; best selling time: late fall.

THE BANFF CENTRE, Box 1020, Banff, Alberta, Canada T0L 0C0. (408)762-3391, ext. 375. Curator: Barry Morrison. Gallery. Estab. 1977. Considers batik; ceramics; pottery; sculpture; soft sculpture; and weaving. Craftworker sets retail price. Invitational exhibitions throughout year.

BARRONCRAFT CO., Rt. 2, Head of Chezzetcook, Nova Scotia, Canada B0J 1N0 (902)827-3567. Craft/gift shop. Estab. 1977. Represents 30-40 craftworkers.
Acceptable Work: Considers candlemaking, clothing, dollmaking, glass art, jewelry, leatherworking, needlecrafts, pottery, quilting, wall hangings, weavings and woodcrafting. No gawdy or kit-made crafts. "We try to stay with fairly conservative pieces." One-of-a-kind and handmade production-line items. Price range: $1-500; bestsellers: $2-10.
Terms: Buys outright and works on consignment; 30-40% commission. Retail price set by joint agreement. Call for appointment. Reports in 1 week. Work may be shipped or hand delivered. Dealer pays insurance on exhibited work.
Profile: "A main part of our business is in custom-made pine furniture, made on the premises. The display area is a loft of the woodworking shop. Items are displayed on plain wooden shelves using runners. We try to rotate and change dispays quite often so as to give a new appearance to regular customers. In summer, our main shop business is with tourists. In other seasons, we depend more on local traffic." Heaviest wholesale buying time: early spring and early fall; best selling time: summer and late fall.

BLUE HERON GIFT SHOP, Box 429. Baddeck, Nova Scotia, Canada B0E 1B0. (902)295-3424. Contact: E. L. MacEachern. Gift shop. Estab. 1976. Represents 20 craftworkers.
Acceptable Work: Considers candlemaking, ceramics, dollmaking, glass art, jewelry, leatherworking, pottery, quilting and woodcrafting. One-of-a-kind and handmade production-line items. Price range: $1-165; bestsellers: $5-50.
Terms: Buys outright and works on consignment; 30% commission. Craftworker sets retail price. Requires exclusive area representation. Call for appointment. Reports in 1 week. Work may be shipped or hand delivered.
Profile: "Open year 'round selling local, Canadian and imported gifts. Located in tourist area of Cape Breton Island at the beginning and the end of the famous Cabot Trail." Heaviest wholesale buying time: spring-summer; best selling time: summer and Christmas.

CABLE COOKHOUSE, Sayward, British Columbia, Canada V0P 1R0. (604)282-3444, 282-5545. Contact: Mr. or Mrs. Glen Duncan. Craft shop. Estab. 1966. Represents 9 craftworkers.
Acceptable Work: Considers ceramics; jewelry; leatherworking; pottery; wall hangings; weavings; woodcrafting; woodcarving; soapstone carving; ivory; scrimshaw; carved horn bone; and dolls that children can play with. Fine one-of-a-kind and handmade production-line items. Price range: $2-250; bestsellers: $2-45.
Terms: Works on consignment and buys outright; 40% commission. "If new craftworker, start on consignment to see how well articles sell." Retail price set by joint agreement. Requires exclusive area representation.
Profile: "Shop is open only 6 months of the year. Most crafts depict Vancouver Island, especially wood and bone articles. We find most handmade articles only interest well travelled and above average income persons. Pottery sells to all incomes but young marrieds in particular." Customers are both local and tourists of all ages.

THE CALGARY CABIN—ALBERTA CRAFTS, 264 Palliser Square E., 115-9 Ave. SE, Calgary, Alberta, Canada T2G 0P5. (403)262-3837. Manager: Doris H. Ramsay. Craft shop. Estab. 1958. Represents 250 Alberta member craftworkers.

Acceptable Work: Considers batik, candlemaking, ceramics, dollmaking, glass art, jewelry, leatherworking, metalsmithing, pottery, scrimshaw, soft sculpture, wall hangings, weavings, woodcrafting and Indian crafts. One-of-a-kind and handmade production-line items. Bestsellers: $5-15.
Terms: Must be member of Old Cabin Crafts Society (nonprofit organization). Buys outright (Indian crafts only) and works on consignment; 46% commission on articles wholesaling up to $10, 40% commission on articles wholesaling up to $30; 30% on articles wholesaling over $30. Retail price set by joint agreement. Requires exclusive area representation. Call for appointment. Reports in 1 week. Work may be shipped or hand delivered. Dealer is responsible for breakage or theft only. Display time: minimum of 3 months.
Profile: "Originated in 'Calgary's First House' (log shack at Calgary Zoo). Now located in beautiful Palliser Square." Heaviest wholesale buying time: May-June and September-October; best selling time: July-August and November-December.

CAMPBELL RIVER & DISTRICT MUSEUM, 1235 Island Hwy., Campbell River, British Columbia, Canada V9W 2C7. (604)287-3103. Curator/Administrator: Jay S. Stewart. Museum gift shop. Estab. 1964. Represents 25-30 Kwakiutl, West Coast, and Salish craftworkers.
Acceptable Work: Considers jewelry; silver and gold metalsmithing; woodcrafting (masks, plaques, poles, and rattles); Salish, West Coast and Kwakiutl basketry. "Traditional and contemporary art of the northwest coast Indians." One-of-a-kind and handmade production-line items. Price range: $5-1,000; bestsellers: $40-150.
Terms: Buys outright. Retail price set by joint agreement. Accepts work by prior arrangement. Most customers during the summer are tourists; at Christmas local people shop at the museum. Best selling time: summer and Christmas.

CANADIAN CRAFTS GIFT SHOP, Hwy. 27, Wyebridge, Ontario, Canada. Proprietor: Karlese MacArthur. Craft shop. Estab. 1970. Represents 25-30 craftworkers.
Acceptable Work: Considers dolls, glass art, jewelry, leatherwork, soft sculpture, weavings, original sketches and woodenware. Has need now of good leather work (purses, belts)--batiked and plain leather goods preferred. Good quality crafts and representative Canadian gifts, no souvenirs, (crochet poodles). No kits or prepatterned work. One-of-a-kind and handmade production-line items readily considered. Price range: $1.50-150; bestsellers: $1.50-75.
Terms: Buys outright but prefers working on consignment. Craftworker receives 2/3 of selling price. Retail price set by joint agreement. Prefers exclusive area representation. "If a piece is damaged, we pay for it."
Profile: "We are a small country store with good summer and Christmas trade. Closed January and February. The shop is rustic with barnboard and wood heat. Usually things are displayed until sold. Everything is treated with care. In very few cases things have to be returned to the consignor due to lack of interest. The display is very decorative, uncluttered and neat." Customers are tourists, urbanite (mainly Toronto) ages 20 and up. Upper middle class clientele for the most part. Heaviest wholesale buying time is April through the end of October.
To Break In: "Quality of craft is important. Craft tags or business cards attached to items appreciated as this helps build the craftworkers reputation. Person to person contact in business dealings preferred."

THE CANDLERIGGS CRAFT SHOP, Site 38, Box 7, Rt. 1, Tantallon, Halifax Co., Nova Scotia, Canada B0J 3J0. (902)823-2722. Contact: Jean or Stephen Cochrane. Craft/gift shop. Estab. 1975. Represents 150 craftworkers.
Acceptable Work: Considers all crafts except scrimshaw and soft sculpture. Especially needs Christmas items. Specializes in fine art designer crafts. One-of-a-kind and handmade production-line items. Price range: $1-800; bestsellers: $5-75.
Terms: Buys outright. Maritime artwork purchased on consignment; 40% commission. Craftworker sets retail price; shop advises. Requires exclusive area representation. Send resume, slides or samples. Reports in 2 weeks. Dealer pays insurance on exhibited work.
Profile: "The Candleriggs is considerably large with approximately 1,200 square feet of floor space, plus walls and pulleys suspended from the ceiling for quilt display. Display units consist of pine counters and bins, pine hutches and pine shelved floor units, all open for easy access. Jewelry collector items and other expensive products are housed in antique glass and wood cases. These are enhanced with old tables, chairs and pine chests which, in turn, are complemented with antique fixtures such as a spinning wheel, an old stove, bricks, barrels, crocks and even large pieces of drift wood. We handle only what can be displayed well without overcrowding." Customers: good to excellent incomes. Heaviest wholesale buying time: early spring, and fall-November; best selling time: spring-Christmas.

To Break In: "We are interested only in serious reliable craftsmen who take pride in their work. If the product speaks for itself, we ask only that the individual have a level sense of business especially in these days of uncontrolled inflation."

CHAPMAN GALLERIES LTD., 12 Sutton Close, Red Deer, Alberta, Canada T4N 3S8. (403)346-7170. Manager: L. Joan Chapman. Gallery. Considers batik; jewelry; pottery; wall hangings; and weaving. Fine designer crafts only. Price range: $2.50-5,600; bestsellers: $15-40. Works on consignment; 50% commission. Retail price set by joint agreement. Hand-delivered work; or mailing or shipping only by prior arrangement. Shipping costs by joint agreement; dealer pays insurance for exhibited work. "Gallery is in an old 2-story house and is the only fine art gallery in Red Deer." Best selling time: pre-Christmas.

THE CHRISTMAS ELVES, 211 Main St., Yarmouth, Nova Scotia, Canada B5A 1C6. (902)742-8796. Proprietor: Carmen-Jane Fairley. Craft/gift/Christmas shop. Estab. 1977. Represents 50 craftworkers.
Acceptable Work: Considers Christmas and all handcrafted articles. One-of-a-kind and handmade production-line items. Price range: $1.29-450; bestsellers: $2-15.
Terms: Buys outright and works on consignment; 33⅓% commission. Retail price set by joint agreement. Requires exclusive area representation. Write explaining craft and media, then send slides. Reports in 4 weeks. Work may be shipped or hand delivered. Shop pays insurance on exhibited work. Displays from the beginning to the end of a season. "If merchandise doesn't move in a period of days, the location is rotated until it starts moving."
Profile: "Beyond our doors, one finds the magic of Christmas. Hundreds of mini lights entwined in holly and greens are only one of the Christmas features. Displays are decorated with velvet bows and greens and shelves are outlined with 4" bell lights and holly garlands. Unusual displays featuring baskets, wooden boxes, trunks, antique highboys and any other interesting containers are all lighted from within with miniature lights and 11 point stars. There are several decorated trees complete with simulated gifts under all." Heaviest wholesale buying time: May-December 1; best selling time: May-December 31.
To Break In: "Do not wholesale to friends. In other words, do not sell to a friend at the same price you sell to me and then expect me to retail at a mark-up. If you cannot produce consistant quality handcrafts, establish the fact that you are a hobbyist only and cannot and/or will not be able to fill large orders."

THE CLAMSHELL, Vancouver Aquarium, Box 3232, Vancouver, British Columbia, Canada V6B 3X8. (604)685-3365. Merchandise Manager: Joan Ballou. Museum craft/gift shop. Estab. 1960. Represents 50-75 craftworkers.
Acceptable Work: Considers batik, candlemaking, ceramics, decoupage, glass art, jewelry, pottery, scrimshaw, soft sculpture, wall hangings, weavings and woodcrafting. Especially needs marine-oriented crafts and crafts of native peoples. One-of-a-kind and handmade production-line items. Price range: $1-1,000; bestsellers: $2-75.
Terms: Purchases outright. Shop sets retail price. Call for appointment. Reports in 1 week. Dealer pays insurance on exhibited work.
Profile: "Our store is in a beautiful foyer of the aquarium. The walls are 'windows.' We display crafts on cedar showcases in 1 section of the store." Customers: conservative, above average incomes. Heaviest wholesale buying time: fall (gift-oriented items for local residents) and spring (heavy summer traffic); best selling time: fall-summer.
To Break In: "Because we are a Canadian shop, we do always have to contend with the duty imposed upon receipt. However, I am always interested in obtaining unique nature-oriented crafts."

CLOTH & CLAY, INC., 8 Notre Dame Rd. S., St. Agatha, Ontario, Canada N0B 2L0. (519)886-7400. Contact: Nancy Martin. Craft shop/gallery. Estab. 1973. Represents 20-25 craftworkers usually from a 50-mile radius. Considers batik; clothing; dollmaking; glass art; jewelry; leatherworking; needlecrafts; pottery; quilting; soft sculpture; wall hangings; weavings; and woodcrafting. "Try to establish a Waterloo County heritage because of the strong Mennonite background here." Fine one-of-a-kind pieces; utilitarian and/or decorative. Price range: $2-1,500; bestsellers: $4-50. Works on consignment; 40% commission. Retail price set by joint agreement. Prefers exclusive area representation. Hand delivered work only.
Profile: "We are in a unique building 144 years old with a country atmosphere. There is no craft gallery near this area. The 5 owners are all practicing craftspeople who are helping to make known other craftspeople." Reports on sales the end of each month. Customers are mostly middle age, middle income. Best selling time: fall and spring.

398 Craftworker's Market '80

COLLAGE BOUTIQUE, 1162 Cedar Ave., Trail, British Columbia, Canada V1R 4B7. (604)364-2614. Craft shop/boutique. Co-managers: Phyllis Matteucci and Janet Crema. Gift shop. Estab. 1971. Represents 50-100 craftworkers.
Acceptable Work: Considers batik, candlemaking, cards, clothing, dollmaking, stained glass art, jewelry, leatherworking, metalsmithing, pottery (hand-thrown stoneware), quilting, wall hangings, weavings and woodcrafting (especially toys). Specializes in contemporary handmade production-line items. Price range: $5-$100; bestsellers $5-28.
Terms: Buys outright and works on consignment; 33⅓% commission. Retail price set by joint agreement. Requires exclusive area representation. Work may be shipped or hand delivered.
Profile: "We are one of the few local shops who touch anything homemade. We have a boutique atmosphere with cedar walls and cedar shelving sections for displaying items on." Customers are of all ages and all interests.

COOPERATIVE ARTISANALE DE CHETICAMP LTEE., Box 98, Cheticamp, Nova Scotia, Canada B0E 1H0. (902)224-2170. (902)224-2271 (in winter). Secretary/Treasurer: Luce Marie Boudrean. Craft shop/museum. Estab. 1963. Represents 400 craftworkers.
Acceptable Work: Considers doilies, hand hooked rugs, quilts, wall hangings, weavings and woodcrafting. Fine handmade production-line items.
Terms: Buys outright and works on consignment; 20% commission. Shop sets retail price. Send slides or folders. Hand-delivered work only. Dealer pays insurance on exhibited work. Customers are mostly middle aged and low income. Heaviest wholesale buying time: winter; best selling time: summer.

THE COTTAGE STUDIO LTD., Big Bras D'or, Cape Breton, Nova Scotia, Canada B0C 1B0. (902)674-2776. Manager: Roberta Clark. Craft/gift shop. Estab. 1972. Represents 30-40 craftworkers.
Acceptable Work: Considers candlemaking, ceramics, clothing, dollmaking, glass art, jewelry, leatherwoking, needlecrafts, pottery, quilting, soft sculpture, tole painting, wall hangings, weavings and woodcrafting. Especially needs woodcrafting. "I like old antique looks, lots of driftwood, barnboard and woven articles." Specializes in primitive and contemporary crafts. One-of-a-kind and handmade production-line items. Price range: $1.50-175; bestsellers: $20-85.
Terms: Buys outright and sometimes works on consignment (large expensive pieces); commission negotiable. Shop sets retail price. Requires exclusive area representation. Send resume. Reports in 3 weeks. Work may be shipped or hand-delivered.
Profile: "We are a small shop but very popular with locals and tourists." Customers: 18-30-year old teachers and nurses; elderly with excellent incomes; tourists. Heaviest wholesale buying time: March-December; best selling time: April-Christmas.

THE CRAFT GALLERY OF THE ONTARIO CRAFTS COUNCIL, 346 Dundas St. W., Toronto, Ontario, Canada M5T 1G5. (416)366-3551. Administrative Director: Joan Hyland. Gallery. Estab. 1976. Considers all professional crafts. Price range: $10-1,000. Works on consignment; 33⅓ commission. Retail price set by joint agreement. Work exhibited for up to 1 month.
Profile: "We provide regular solo shows and group exhibitions. The Council provides an opening (less cost of refreshments), standard promotion and 300 invitations."

THE CROFT, 902-9th Ave. SW, Calgary, Alberta, Canada T2P 1L8. (403)265-1621. Contact: Audrey Mabee or Betty Anne Graves. Craft shop. Estab. 1974. Represents 85-100 Canadian craftworkers, preferably with some formal training.
Acceptable Work: Considers apple people, batik, cards, woven clothing, dollmaking, glass art, jewelry, pottery, soft sculplture, wall hangings, weavings and woodcrafting. Especially needs creative weavings, pottery and toys. Specializes in primitive and fine crafts. One-of-a-kind and handmade production-line items. Price range: $1.50-600; bestsellers: $3.50-9 (mugs and sets of mini pots and bells).
Terms: Works mostly on consignment; 35% commission. Pays at the end of the month. Retail price set by joint agreement. Call or write for appointment. Reports in 1-2 weeks. Work may be shipped or hand delivered. Dealer pays insurance on exhibited work.
Profile: "A small out-of-the-way tumble-down-looking building. Inside is decorated in barnwood with lots of healthy green plants. People are encouraged to browse and enjoy themselves. Many craftsmen come for ideas. We have several antiques which fit in well with the shop and what we sell. We are very popular as a wedding gift and going-away gift place because we are surrounded by large offices." Customers: theatre goers, office people, univer-

sity art staff and students, architects, interior designers, other craftspeople; ages 18-45. Heaviest wholesale buying time: September-October; best selling time: Christmas (November-December).
To Break In: "Don't take a course and bring us all the things you made. Most of these pieces are not as professional-looking as you think. Craftpersons should have a good idea of the price they want but be flexible."

THE CROFT HOUSE GIFT SHOP, Box 2003, Charlottetown, Prince Edward Island, Canada C1A 7N7 (902)892-8651. Manager: Mary Stuart Sage. Gift shop. Estab. 1973. Represents 45-50 Canadian craftworkers, mainly from Prince Edward Island.
Acceptable Work: Considers batik, candlemaking, ceramics, clothing, decoupage, dollmaking, jewelry, pottery, quilting, scrimshaw, wall hangings, weavings and woodcrafting. Especially needs wooden crafts. Handmade production-line items. Price range: $2-1,200; bestsellers: under $5, $15-20.
Terms: Buys outright and works on consignment; 33⅓% commission. Retail price set by joint agreement; occassionally by shop. Prefers exclusive area representation. Call for appointment. Reports in 2 weeks. Work may be shipped or hand delivered. Dealer pays insurance on exhibited work. Consigned items kept only 1 tourist season.
Profile: "We are located in the largest hotel on Prince Edward Island (on the front terrace-about 400 square feet). We sell mohair and woolen garments, blankets, film and many souvenirs Small crafts are displayed on the first shelves inside the front door and on glass shelves in the middle large windows (there's a set of 3 windows)." Customers: senior citizen bus tours, conventions, family vacationers, local professional and business people. Heaviest wholesale buying time: May-June; best selling time: June-September.
To Break In: "'Made in PEI' is almost a must on all Island crafts. Don't flood the market. Use your name or initials on as many crafts as possible. Use cards or tape on weavings to give washing instructions and your name."

CROSS CANADA CRAFTS, 416 Main St., Yarmouth, Nova Scotia, Canada B5A 1G4. (902)742-7222. Manager: Susan Townson. Craft shop. Estab. 1977. Represents 40 Canadian craftworkers.
Acceptable Work: Considers all crafts except batik, ceramics and soft sculpture. Especially needs marine-oriented crafts. One-of-a-kind and handmade production-line items. Price range: 10¢-$500; bestsellers: $3-20.
Terms: Buys outright and works on consignment; 40% commission. Pays net 30. Craftworker sets retail price. Send resume and photos. Reports in 2 weeks. Work may be shipped or hand delivered. Dealer pays insurance on exhibited work.
Profile: "Our shop has pine walls with barnboard shelves. Lobster traps and antique showcases are used for displaying items. Our Indian pottery has a birch stand. We give a guided tour to our customers who are interested in the background of each craft. Therefore, each person's work is displayed in a specific area to its best advantage, with an odd piece or two placed in a different area to add interest." Customers: American tourists interested in Canadian-made crafts, especially from Nova Scotia. Heaviest wholesale buying and best selling time: summer and pre-Christmas.

JOHN M. CUELENAERE LIBRARY, 125-12 St. E., Prince Albert, Saskatchewan Canada S6V 1B7. (306)763-8496. Head Librarian: Eleanor Acorn. Library. Estab. 1973. Considers all crafts that can be hung. Work is fastened to gallery wall and displayed for 4 weeks. Will put buyer in touch with seller. Work may be shipped or hand-delivered. Library pays insurance for exhibited work.

EARTH MUSE, Box 1775, Jasper, Alberta, Canada T0E 1E0. (403)852-4773. Contact: Jean Nixon. Craft shop. Estab. 1975. Represents 20 craftworkers, preferably Canadian but have no restrictions. Considers batik; candlemaking; ceramics; decoupage; glass art; jewelry; leatherworking; metalsmithing; needlecrafts; pottery; quilting; soft sculpture; wall hangings; weavings; woodcrafting; and unique knit products. All styles; utilitarian and/or decorative. Price range: 4¢-$400; bestsellers: 4¢-$100. Buys outright. Retail price set by joint agreement. Requires exclusive area representation. Dealer pays return shipping and insurance for exhibited work. Best selling time: summer.

FANSHAWE PIONEER VILLAGE, Box 6278, Station D, London, Ontario, Canada. Contact: K. Gaukel. General store gift shop in pioneer village. Estab. 1954. Represents 12-20 craftworkers, preferably local.

Acceptable Work: Considers candlemaking; clothing; dollmaking; jewelry; leatherworking; needlecrafts; pottery; quilting; woodcrafting; and any pioneer type crafts, especially toys. Primitive one-of-a-kind and handmade production-line items. Price range: 25¢-$20; bestsellers: 25¢-$5.
Terms: Works on consignment; 20% commission. Retail price set by joint agreement. Hand-delivered work only.
Profile: "This is a general store in a pioneer village setting unique in the London area. Only pioneer-type crafts are sold. Many school groups who want small souvenirs visit the shop. We also have many middle income customers from out of the country who want Canadian pioneer crafts." Best selling time: summer.

FORT EDMONTON PARK, 10th Flr., CN Towers, c/o City Parks and Recreation, Edmonton, Alberta, Canada T5J 0K1. (403)436-5565. Director: Ken Kobylka. Museum gallery/gift shop. Estab. 1972. Represents 65 university students with historical and/or crafts background.
Acceptable Work: Considers candlemaking; leatherworking; needlecrafts; quilting; wall hangings; weavings; woodcrafting; basket weaving; and nature crafts. Handmade production-line items. Price range: $2-30; bestsellers: $3-5.
Terms: Buys outright. Shops sets retail price. Reports in 3 weeks. Dealer pays shipping to shop. "Shop sells items in line with time period of Park." Customers are mostly tourists. Best selling time: summer.

FRAEMAR ENTERPRISES LTD, 25 Main St., Box 426, Parrsboro, Nova Scotia, Canada B0M 1S0. (902)254-2762. President: Fraser Mackay. Craft/gift/supply shop. Estab. 1972. Represents 2 craftworkers.
Acceptable Work: Considers ceramics, jewelry, needlecrafts, wall hangings and weavings. One-of-a-kind crafts only. Price range: $1.95-10; bestsellers: $1.95-5, $5-10.
Terms: Buys outright. Shop sets retail price. Send work or call for appointment. Reports in 2 weeks. Work must be hand-delivered. Dealer pays insurance on exhibited work. Display time: 30-60 days.
Profile: Customers: teens to seniors, middle incomes. Heaviest wholesale buying time: winter; best selling time: summer.

GALLERY GIFT SHOP, Confederation Centre of the Arts, Box 848, Charlottetown, Prince Edward Island, Canada C1A 7L9. (902)892-2464, ext. 149. Buyer: Antoinette Sutherland. Manager: David L. Roop. Gift/craft shop/gallery. Estab. 1964. Represents 200-500 Canadian craftworkers.
Acceptable Work: Considers batik, candlemaking, ceramics, clothing, decoupage, dollmaking, glass art, jewelry, leatherworking, metalsmithing, pottery, quilting, wall hangings, weavings and woodcrafting. Specialises in fine one-of-a-kind and handmade production-line items. Price range: 25¢-$500; bestsellers: $10-25.
Terms: Buys outright and occassionally works on consignment; 25 or 33⅓% commission.. Retail price set by joint agreement. Sometimes requires exclusive area representation. Contact personally. Reports immediately. Work may be shipped or hand delivered.
Profile: "Limited display area available. We sell no souvenirs, strictly work of noted Canadian craftsmsmen" Heaviest wholesale buying time: spring; best selling time: summer.
To Break In: "Be selective where you put handcrafts. If in chain stores, drug stores, department stores, unless exclusive, items may lose their special charm and become commercial and run-of-the-mill."

GALLERY HOUSE SOL, 45 Charles St., Georgetown, Ontario, Canada L7G 2Z4. (416)877-6460. Contact: John and Gisela Sommer. Craft shop/gallery. Estab. 1962. Represents 10 Canadian craftworkers.
Acceptable Work: Considers batik; ceramics; glass art; jewelry; needlecrafts; pottery; wall hangings; and weaving. Fine one-of-a-kind pieces. Price range: $20-800; bestsellers: $20-50.
Terms: Works on consignment and buys outright; 33⅓% commission. Craftworker sets retail price. Charges fee for exhibit space; exhibitors share expense of invitations and postage. Reports in 3 weeks. Hand delivered work only. Dealer pays return shipping and insurance for exhibited work.
Profile: "The gallery is set up as a private home. Art and craft works are changed every 3 weeks and arranged to mutual advantage. It is the house of an older couple with great interest and knowledge in fine arts and crafts. We ask our visitors to enjoy with us the best we can find." Customers are mostly younger to middle-aged. Best selling time: late fall and late spring.

THE GALLERY SHOP, 1040 Moss St., Victoria, British Columbia, Canada V8V 4P1. (604)384-7018. Managing Director: Mrs. Matheson. Gift shop. Estab. 1974. Represents 150 craftworkers.
Acceptable Work: Considers batik, ceramics, decoupage, dollmaking, glass art, jewelry, leatherworking, metalsmithing, pottery, wall hangings, weavings and woodcrafting. Specializes in fine designer porcelain, glass and pottery. One-of-a-kind and handmade production-line items. Price range: $2-300; bestsellers: $2-30.
Terms: Buys outright and accepts work on consignment; 40% commission. First order is on consignment; subsequent orders are net 30. Retail price set by joint agreement. Send slides or call for appointment. SASE. Reports in 1-3 weeks. Work may be shipped or hand delivered. Dealer pays insurance on exhibited work. Display time: 3 months.
Profile: "We are in the premises of the Art Gallery of Greater Victoria, where we attempt to compliment gallery exhibitions. Shop is located in an old mansion (forms 1 wing of the modern gallery) in elegant surroundings. We also sell antique Chinese and Japanese items." Customers: gallery members, visitors to gallery, tourists, collectors. Heaviest wholesale buying time: spring and fall; best selling time: summer and Christmas.

GIBSON HOUSE MUSEUM, 5172 Yonge St., Willowdale, Willo, Ontario, Canada M2M 5P6. (807)225-0146. Contact: Mrs. I. C. Cairns. Gallery/museum gift shop. Estab. 1971. Represents 10 craftworkers. Considers candlemaking; ceramics; decoupage; jewelry; needlecrafts; pottery; quilting; tole painting; wall hangings; and weavings. Works on consignment and buys outright; 40% commission. Retail price set by joint agreement. Charges 20% or more of sales for exhibit space. Requires exclusive area representation. Reports in 4 weeks. Best selling time: fall.

GLOOSCAPS TRADING POST, Truro S.S. 1, Box 23, Truro, Nova Scotia, Canada B2N 5H2. (902)893-9268 or 895-5455. Co-owners: Bazil and Edith Peters. Craft shop. Estab. 1952. Represents 150+ craftworkers.
Acceptable Work: Considers dollmaking, jewelry, leatherworking, metalsmithing, pottery, wall hangings, weavings and woodcrafting. Especially needs North American Indian crafts. Specializes in Eskimo, Indian, Nova Scotia and Canadian one-of-a-kind and handmade production-line items. Price range: $2-500; bestsellers: $5-60.
Terms: Works on consignment; 50% commission. Retail price set by joint agreement. Requires exclusive area representation on some items. Reports as soon as possible. Work may be shipped or hand delivered.
Profile: "We are a very compact shop with many items. We have a large back-up stock in our warehouse." Heaviest wholesale buying time: April-June; best selling time: June-December. Open May-December.

HECTOR NATIONAL EXHIBITION CENTRE, Box 1210, Pictou, Nova Scotia, Canada B0K 1H0. (902)485-4563. Curator: Gary Selig. Exhibition Center. Estab. 1973. Prefers Nova Scotia craftworkers.
Acceptable Work: Considers all crafts. Especially needs craft pieces accompanied by demonstrations and/or informative literature/graphics. One-of-a-kind and handmade production-line items.
Terms: "We are not permitted to sell displayed pieces, but display for education only." Call for appointment. Reports in 3 weeks. Work may be shipped or hand delivered. Display time: 4-6 weeks.
Profile: "Items are treated as a museum artifact giving consideration to physical security and conservation problems as well as to the display which is designed to best interpret the craft items. The main gallery (1500 square feet floor space; 120 running feet wall space—suitable for hanging; 10 foot ceiling) has suspended climate control and wall to wall carpeting. There is also a foyer gallery (200 square feet of floor in front of 12 running feet of wall). Customers: general visiting public and school groups.

HERITAGE GALLERIES LTD., 905 Heritage Dr. SW, Calgary, Alberta, Canada T2V 2W8. Considers sculpture; no abstracts. Buys outright or on consignment; 33⅓% commission. Craftworker sets retail price. Write for interview.

HILLS INDIAN CRAFTS, 34 Nicol St., Nanaimo, British Columbia, Canada V9R 4S8. 753-3811. Manager: Don McPherson. Craft shop. Estab. 1970. Represents 200 craftworkers. "I try to deal with Indians, but have about equal representation of non-Indian crafts."
Acceptable Work: Considers candlemaking, ceramics, clothing, dollmaking, jewelry,

leatherworking, metalsmithing, pottery, scrimshaw and woodcrafting. Specializes in primitive, fine and bright-colored crafts. One-of-a-kind and handmade production-line items. Price range: 20¢-$2,600; bestsellers: 40¢-$120.
Terms: Buys outright. Call for appointment with SASE. Reports in 2 weeks. Work may be shipped or hand delivered.
Profile: "We are an Indian crafts store displaying Indian crafts downstairs (e.g., Cowichan sweaters, argilite carvings of the Hidas, wood carvings) and imports upstairs (e.g., Icelandic, Scotch and Irish clothing)." Heaviest wholesale buying time: summer-fall; best selling time: summer and Christmas.

HOTEL GIFT SHOP, Holiday Inn, 99 Wyse Rd., Dartmouth, Nova Scotia, Canada B3A 1L9. (902)469-1450. Contact: Sudershen Singh. Gift shop. Estab. 1975. Represents 6 craftworkers, preferably from Canada.
Acceptable Work: Considers ceramics, dollmaking, jewelry, pottery and woodcrafting. Handmade production-line items. Price range: $2.95-30; bestsellers: $2.95-15.
Terms: Buys outright and works on consignment; 40-60% commission. Retail price set by joint agreement. Send resume or call for appointment. Reports in 2-3 weeks. Work may be shipped or hand delivered. Dealer pays insurance on exhibited work.
Profile: "The shop is located in the main lobby of the Holiday Inn. We have lots of window display space and regular shelves." Customers: tourists. Heaviest wholesale buying time: spring; best selling time: summer.

HOUSE OF CRAFTS, 584 Main St., Yarmouth, Nova Scotia, Canada B5A 1J4. (902)742-7205. Proprietor: H. William MacConnell. Craft/gift shop/gallery. Estab. 1974. Represents 100 craftworkers.
Acceptable Work: Considers all crafts, except batik and ceramics. Handmade production-line items only. Price range: $1.95-300.
Terms: Buys outright and works on consignment; 33⅓% commission. Retail price set by joint agreement. Requires exclusive area representation. Send resume and forward sample of work. Reports in 1 week. Work may be shipped or hand delivered. Display time: up to 2 years.
Profile: "The craft shop is located on the main floor while the gallery is on the mezzanine. Both are housed in an 1888 library with natural wood floors, original shutters and stained glass windows." Heaviest wholesale buying time: late winter-early spring; best selling time: summer and Christmas.

E.D.R. HUNT STAINED GLASS SUPPLY LTD, Bay 15, 2280 39th Ave. NE, Calgary-Alberta, Canada T2E 6P7. (403)276-4007. President: Robert Hunt. Stained glass shop/studio/supplier.
Acceptable Work: Considers glass art and silver jewelry. One-of-a-kind and handmade production-line items. Price range: $5-1,000; bestsellers: $35-250.
Terms: Buys outright and works on consignment; 30% commission. Retail price set by joint agreement. Call for appointment. Reports in 1 week. Work may be shipped or hand-delivered. Dealer pays insurance on exhibited work. Display time: 2 months.
Profile: Shop has 1,000 square feet; wholesale warehouse has 2,000 square feet. Customers: ages 25-50; cultural groups. Heaviest wholesale buying time: spring and fall.
To Break In: "Don't price too high; be reasonable and realistic. Have some quality-printed tags. Pray hard just to get your business going."

HURONIA HANDCRAFTED GIFTS, Rt. 3, Stayner, Ontario, Canada L0M 1S0. (705)429-2108. Contact: Jean Hanagan. Gift shop. Estab. 1958. Represents 40 Canada craftworkers.
Acceptable Work: Considers candlemaking, ceramics, clothing, decoupage, dollmaking, glass art, jewelry, leatherworking, metalsmithing, needlecrafts, pottery, wall hangings, weavings and woodcrafting. Specializes in primitive, fine and Indian work. One-of-a-kind and handmade production-line items. Price range: 50¢-$500; bestsellers: $3-200.
Terms: Buys outright. Shop sets retail price. Requires exclusive area representation. Send information on work and background. Reports in 3 weeks. Work may be shipped or hand-delivered.
Profile: "We are located in an 1843 pioneer log cabin with additions. The log section creates an excellent atmosphere for display. The quantity of merchandise necessitates the use of walls, wall shelving and islands. We display outdoors in the summer and have displays and sales by craftworkers occasionally." Heaviest wholesale buying time: spring; best selling time: summer-early winter.

ISLAND CRAFTS, 335 George St., Sydney, Nova Scotia, Canada B1P 1J7. (902)539-6474. Manager: Barbara MacLeod. Wholesale and retail craft/gift shop. Estab. 1973. Represents 200 local craftworkers.
Acceptable Work: Considers candlemaking, ceramics, clothing, decoupage, dollmaking, Cheticamp hooking, jewelry, needlecrafts, pottery, quilting, soft sculpture, wall hangings, weavings and woodcrafting. One-of-a-kind and handmade production-line items. Price range: 98¢-$400; bestsellers: $3.98-$64.
Terms: Buys outright. Wholesale price set by joint agreement; retail price set by shop. Call for appointment; bring samples. Work may be shipped or hand delivered. Dealer pays insurance on exhibited work.
Profile: "We are a wholesale outlet across Canada as well as locally so provide year 'round employment for our producers. We also have a retail shop. We produce fashion garments and hold fashion shows." Customers: school children to senior citizens. Heaviest wholesale buying and best selling time: spring, fall and Christmas.

ISLANDVIEW HANDCRAFT SHOP, Rt. 1, Hunts Point, Queens County, Nova Scotia, Canada B0T 1G0. (902)683-2442. Contact: Phyllis Smith. Craft/gift/supply shop. Estab. 1972. Represents 8 craftworkers.
Acceptable Work: Considers ceramics, clothing, jewelry, knitting, needlecrafts, pillows, pottery, quilting, wall hangings, weavings and woodcrafting. Especially needs sweaters. Specializes in contemporary handmade production-line items. Price range: $1-225; bestsellers: up to $65 (Icelandic sweaters).
Terms: Buys outright and works on consignment; 33⅓% commission. Retail price set by joint agreement. Requires exclusive Nova Scotia representation. Call for appointment. Reports immediately. Work may be shipped or hand delivered. Dealer pays insurance on exhibited work.
Profile: Customers: middle-upper incomes. Heaviest wholesale buying time: winter; best selling time: summer-Christmas.

KATHY'S CRAFT SHOP, Fairview Rt. 2, Cornwall P.O., Prince Edward Island, Canada C1A 1H0. (902)675-3061. Manager: Kathy MacDougall. Craft/gift shop/studio. Estab. 1975. Represents 15 craftworkers.
Acceptable Work: Considers candlemaking, ceramics, clothing, dollmaking, jewelry, leatherworking, boat models, needlecrafts, quilting, wooden sandles with leather straps, wall hangings, weavings and woodcrafting. Specializes in contemporary crafts. Price range: $1.25-300; bestsellers: $1.75-10.
Terms: Buys outright and works on consignment; 30% commission. Retail price set by joint agreement. Write or stop at shop. Reports in 4 weeks maximum. Work may be shipped or hand delivered. Dealer pays insurance on exhibited work.
Profile: "We are a small shop in a campground setting. There are 2 show windows in front. Items are displayed on shelves and tables." Heaviest wholesale buying time: spring; best selling time: summer.
To Break In: "The articles I usually purchase have a low price range—from $1-30—because being on a campground, I find that people are usually on a budget and they tend to buy smaller articles. However, I enjoy seeing any craft and will consider any artile which is brought to my attention."

LA HAVE RIVER TRADING CO., La Have, Lunenburg County, Nova Scotia, Canada B0R 1C0. (902)688-2416. Manager: Gloria Barrett. Craft shop. Estab. 1977. Represents 20-25 Nova Scotia craftworkers, preferably local (from Lunenburg area).
Acceptable Work: Considers batik, candlemaking, ceramics, clothing, dollmaking, glass art, jewelry, leatherworking, metalsmithing, needlecrafts, pottery, quilting, wall hangings and woodcrafting. "We have a mixture of styles; we have contemporary items, but we encourage the survival of indigenous crafts." One-of-a-kind items only. Price range: 5¢-$400; bestsellers: 5¢-$40.
Terms: Generally works on consignment, but outright buying increasing; 30% average commission. Retail price set by shop or joint agreement. Requires exclusive area representation, with some exceptions. Call for appointment. Work may be shipped or hand delivered. Dealer pays insurance on exhibited work.
Profile: "The La Have River Trading Company is in a sense the revival of a retail outlet which has existed in the present building, in one form or another, for about 130 years. This reinforces our efforts to represent indigenous craftworkers. We display most items for easy viewing—we do not store a large volume of any item. Local character is reflected in the choice of display

cases, signboards, racks, shelving, etc. Displays are frequently rearranged and crafts are generously mixed." Customers: tourists from Canada, US, Europe and Asia with above average incomes; local people. Heaviest wholesale buying time: fall-winter; best selling time: spring-summer.

To Break In: "We are not a large volume shop in our present form. We prefer to work directly with craftworkers rather than with their 'agents.' Craftworkers who wish to grow with us (and learn with us) seem to be in the majority."

LAURENTIAN UNIVERSITY MUSEUM & ARTS CENTRE, Department of Cultural Affairs, Laurentian University, Sudbury, Ontario, Canada P3E 2C6. (705)675-1151, ext. 400. Director: Pamela Krueger. Museum gallery/gift shop. Estab. 1967.
Acceptable Work: Considers batik; ceramics; dollmaking; glass art; jewelry; leatherworking; metalsmithing; needlecrafts; pottery; quilting; soft sculpture; wall hangings; weavings; and woodcrafting. Fine and primitive one-of-a-kind pieces. Price range: $1-1,000.
Terms: Works on consignment; 25% commission. Retail price set by joint agreement. Reports in 2 weeks. Dealer pays return shipping and insurance for exhibited work. The newly organized shop is connected to the art gallery. Best selling time: summer and Christmas.

LE BLANC HANDCRAFT, St. Joseph On Moine, Inverness, Nova Scotia, Canada B0E 3A0. (902)224-2991. Contact: Jeannette Le Blanc. Craft shop. Estab. 1948. Represents 75 craftworkers.
Acceptable Work: Considers candlemaking, ceramics, clothing, decoupage, dollmaking, hooking (coasters, floor mats), jewelry, needlecrafts, quilting, wall hangings and weavings. Specializes in fine handmade production-line items. Price range: $1.35-395.
Terms: Buys outright and works on consignment; 20% commission. Craftworker sets retail price. Requires exclusive area representation. Call or write for appointment in December or January. Reports in 2 weeks. Work may be shipped or hand delivered. Dealer pays insurance on exhibited work. Display time: 4 months.
Profile: "My shop is 30x25 handling mostly handmade things. We hang items on walls and display on tables and shelves." Heaviest wholesale buying time: winter; best selling time: summer-fall.

LIM'S ART GALLERY, 2033 33rd Ave. SW, Calgary, Alberta, Canada T2T 1Z5. (403)246-2090. Contact: Ben Lim. Gallery/frame shop. Estab. 1975. Represents 6 craftworkers.
Acceptable Work: Considers batik, ceramics, jewelry, pottery, wall hangings and weavings. Specializes in contemporary one-of-a-kind crafts.
Terms: Buys outright and works on consignment; 40% commission. Gallery sets retail price. Call for appointment. Reports in 1 week. Work must be hand-delivered. Dealer pays insurance on exhibited work.
Profile: Items are displayed in the front window for 3 months. Customers: 35+, middle class. Heaviest wholesale buying and best sellling time: August-December.

LOCK 21 ANTIQUES & HANDCRAFTS, Box 353, Merrickville, Ontario, Canada K0G 1N0. 269-3333. Contact: Virginia Martyn. Craft/gift shop. Estab. 1973. Represents 30 craftworkers.
Acceptable Work: Considers ceramics, clothing, jewelry, metalsmithing, needlecrafts, pottery, quilting, wall hangings, weavings and woodcrafting. Especially needs braided rugs. Specializes in crafts suitable for country homes. One-of-a-kind and handmade production-line items. Price range: $2-175; bestsellers: $6-12.
Terms: Works on consignment; 25% commission. Retail price set by joint agreement. Requires exclusive area representation. Bring samples. Reports every month. Work may be shipped or hand delivered. Dealer pays insurance on exhibited work.
Profile: "We are the only shop selling items other than books, hardwares and food in a small picturesque village (40 miles from Ottawa). The shop is in a newly renovated heritage building on most prominent corner of the village. Items are given prominent display place at the front of the shop for the first month. Later, if space is needed, they are moved to other spots." Customers: mainly ages 20-40, people form Ottawa, $15,000-35,000 incomes. Heaviest wholesale buying and best selling time: summer and Christmas.

THE LOON'S NEST, Station Mall, Sault Ste. Marie, Ontario, Canada. (705)254-3700. Contact: Helen Gillespie. Craft shop. Estab. 1972. Represents 150 Canadian craftworkers. All styles; utilitarian and/or decorative. Price range: 25¢-$850; bestsellers: $6-50. Works on consignment and buys outright; 33% commission. Retail price set by joint agreement. Requires exclusive area representation. Reports in 2 weeks. "We provide a critique of the craft when requested."

Dealer pays shipping to shop and insurance for exhibited work.
Acceptable Work: Considers batik; candlemaking; clothing; glass art; jewelry; leatherworking; needlecrafts; pottery; quilting; soft sculpture; wall hangings; weavings; woodcrafting; unusual dolls; and crafts with Northern or outdoor theme. Customers are art and craft oriented professionals with income of $15,000 and up; 20-40 years of age. Best selling time: August and December.

LYNWOOD LTD., Box 178, Baddeck, Nova Scotia, Canada B0E 1B0. (902)295-2950. Contact: Mr. or Mrs. Haines. Gallery/gift/craft shop. Estab. 1974. Represents 35-40 Canadian craftworkers, preferably from eastern Canada.
Acceptable Work: Considers candlemaking, clothing, dollmaking, glass art, jewelry, metalsmithing, pottery and woodcrafting. No primitives. One-of-a-kind and handmade production line items. Price range; $1-300; bestsellers: $1-55.
Terms: Buys outright. Retail price set by joint agreement. Call for appointment. Reports in 1 week. Work may be shipped or hand delivered.
Profile: "Shop located in an old home. Items are displayed in 6 separate rooms on antique furniture." Customers: ages 16-60; well-to-do. Heaviest wholesale buying time; spring. Open from mid-May to the end of December.

MABOU VILLAGE GALLERY, 150 Tangmere Ct., Halifax, Nova Scotia, Canada B3M 1J9. (902)443-3215. Contact: Suzanne MacDonald. Estab. 1971. Art gallery. Represents 5-10 craftworkers.
Acceptable Work: Considers batik, ceramics, decoupage, jewelry, pottery, quilting, weaving and woodcrafting. Especially needs Nova Scotia-designed quilts, functional ceramics, maritime decoupage, one-of-a-kind pottery and wood art. May buy handmade production-line items such as placemats. Price range: $4-1,000; bestsellers: $4-200.
Terms: Mainly works on consignment; 33⅓% commission. Retail price set by joint agreement. Send resume. Reports in 2 weeks. Dealer pays insurance on exhibited work.
Profile: "Shop is in a small attractive wood building on a large lot on the main street of the village. The village, called 'Mabou' is located on the West Coast Ceilidh Trail which leads to the Cabot Trail in Cape Breton Island, Nova Scotia. The shop is mainly an art gallery. Pieces which blend in with artwork will be similarly displayed. A separate shelving and counter area is reserved for smaller items." Customers: "mostly those who get off the main highway and travel secondary coastal roads—those explorers of modern times." Heaviest wholesale buying time: spring. Open during the summer only.

MALTWOOD ART MUSEUM & GALLERY, University of Victoria, Box 1700, Victoria, British Columbia, Canada V8W 2Y2. (604)477-6911 (6169 local). Director/Curator: Martin Segger. Museum gallery. Estab. 1978. Considers ceramics, glass art, jewelry, metalsmithing, pottery, quilting, wall hangings and weavings. Specializes in regional, contemporary and historic crafts. One-of-a-kind and handmade production-line items. Exhibits only. Contacted by invitation only. Work may be shipped or hand delivered. Museum pays insurance on exhibited work. Customers: students, general public.

MATSQUI-SUMAS-ABBOTSFORD MUSEUM, 33660 S. Fraser Way, Abbotsford, British Columbia, Canada V2S 2B9. (604)853-0313. Curator: O. Diane Kelly. Museum gallery/gift shop. Estab. 1969. Represents 10 local craftworkers.
Acceptable Work: Considers candlemaking; jewelry; metalsmithing; needlecrafts; pottery; wall hangings; and weavings. Price range: 50¢-$50; bestsellers: 50¢-$5.
Terms: Works on consignment, buys outright and accepts donated crafts; 25% commission. Craftworker sets retail price. Reports in 4 weeks. Hand-delivered work only.
Profile: "The single most unique feature of our shop is the quality and nature of the work we carry by local craftworkers. The money we make from these projects goes to support a nonprofit organization. Our customers form a very general cross-section of the public at large, therefore our shop does not specialize in 1 particular craft or art style." Best selling time: summer.

MICMAC INDIAN VILLAGE, Box 51, Cornwall, Prince Edward Island, Canada C0A 1H0. (902)675-3800. President: Eric Inman. Craft shop. Estab. 1960. Represents Canadian Indian craftworkers.
Acceptable Work: Considers jewelry, leatherworking (moccasins), pottery, wall hangings, weavings, woodcrafting, basket work, birchbark work and quill boxes. Specializes in Indian handcrafts. Handmade production-line items only. Price range: 50¢-$450; bestsellers: 50¢-$20.

Terms: Buys outright and works on consignment; 30-50% commission. Retail price set by shop or joint agreement. Requires exclusive area representation. Send resume. Reports in 4 weeks. Work may be shipped or hand delivered. Dealer pays insurance on exhibited work.
Profile: "Our shop consists of a gift shop as well as an outdoor museum depicting the Micmac way of life in days gone by. In our gift shop, we try to offer as many Indian crafts as possible from all across, Canada. All items are displayed in the showcase or on the counter or on a wall display depending on the article to display. We have an A frame building that shows all the beams on the inside. Our counter displays are of pine boards." Customers: mainly tourists. Heaviest wholesale buying time: mid winter-early spring; best selling time: July-August.
To Break In: "We like to deal with craftworkers who are able to supply any time during our peak season when we might find a need for quick replacements."

THE MONTREAL MILITARY & MARITIME MUSEUM, Box 1024, Station A, Montreal, Quebec, Canada H3C 2W9. (514)861-6738. Manager: B. D. Bolton. Museum gift shop. Estab. 1955. Represents 3 craftworkers.
Acceptable Work: Considers candlemaking; ceramics; decoupage; dollmaking; glass art; jewelry; leatherworking; metalsmithing; pottery; quilting; and woodcraftings. "Prefer historic Canadian; military; and maritime themes." Primitive handmade production-line items. Price range: $1-500; bestsellers: $1-25.
Terms: Works on consignment and buys outright; commission varies. Retail price set by joint agreement. Dealer pays return shipping. Best selling time: May-October.

MUSEUM OF NORTHERN BRITISH COLUMBIA, MUSEUM ART GALLERY, Box 669, Prince Rupert, British Columbia, Canada V8J 3S1. (604)624-3207. Contact: Curator or Art Gallery Committee. Museum gallery. Estab. 1971. Preference given to local residents. Considers work in all media, including school classes and 'not for sale.' "The Museum Art Gallery exists primarily for display, and sales are a minor part of its life. Museum art gallery allows local exhibitors to sell; 10% commission paid to the gallery to cover costs of future displays." Retail price set by craftworker. Reporting time varies. City of Prince Rupert pays insurance for exhibited work.
Profile: "Gallery is part of museum complex but run by volunteer committee. It is covered by the security and insurance arrangements of the Museum of Northern British Columbia. About 90,000 visitors, primarily tourists, pass through the gallery annually."

NATIONAL POSTAL MUSEUM, 180 Wellington St., Ottawa, Ontario, Canada K1A 0C6. (613)998-8570. Manager: J.E. Kraemer. Pioneer post office sales counters. Considers craft items related to the post office service.
Terms: Buys outright after committee approval, and occasionally commissions work. Manager recommends retail price. Reports in 6 weeks. Museum pays for return shipping; shipping insurance; and insurance for exhibited work.

THE NEW BRUNSWICK MUSEUM SHOP, 277 Douglas Ave., St. John, New Brunswick, Canada. (506)693-1196. Sales Manager/Buyer: Vivian Hachey. Museum gift shop. Estab. 1978. Represents 10-20 craftworkers.
Acceptable Work: Considers candlemaking, dollmaking, jewelry, leatherworking, metalsmithing, pottery, soft sculpture and woodcrafting. One-of-a-kind crafts only. Price range: $1-250.
Terms: Buys outright and works on consignment; 40% commission. Retail price set by joint agreement. Send samples. Reports in 4 weeks. Work may be shipped or hand delivered. Dealer pays insurance on exhibited work.
Profile: "We will display any item as long as possible as long as there seems to be an interest in the craft by the public." Customers: ages 6-80, $12,000-75,000 incomes. Heaviest wholesale buying time: early spring. Best selling time: summer. "In the summer, we do a very successful job, it slows down for the fall, picks up at Christmas and slows down until April or May."

NORTHLAND STORE INC., Box 608, Dryden, Ontario, Canada. (807)937-5493. Manager: Bruce Perry. General store. Represents 40-60 craftworkers.
Acceptable Work: Considers beadwork, candlemaking, ceramics, clothing, decoupage, dollmaking, furniture, glass art, jewelry, leatherworking, metalsmithing, needlecrafts, pottery, quilting, wall hangings, weavings and woodcrafting. Prefers natural materials. No kits, molds or agents. One-of-a-kind and handmade production-line items. Price range: 50¢-$300; bestsellers: up to $50.
Terms: Buys outright and works on consignment; 30% commission. "Initial orders are usually

on consignment." Craftworker sets retail price unless shops feels price is unreasonable. Prefers exclusive area representation. Send resume, slides, call for appointment or visit shop. SASE. "Send or bring work along with an invoice, however small; indicative of your work (pictures or samples acceptable). You will receive a copy of our working agreement to sign and our order by return mail if we are interested in your work. We will return your samples. Articles sent from the US as samples should be small and inexpensive since we will most likely have to pay 20% duty to even see them (this is added onto the retail price.)" Reports in 1 week. Work may be shipped (insured by craftworker) or hand-delivered. Dealer pays insurance on exhibited work. Display time: 1 year.
Profile: "The store is 1 of our 2 log buildings on a main tourist area of northwestern Ontario. Items are displayed in a rustic setting in the store on shelves, walls or floor among our antique furnishings. About half of our sales are to tourists desiring to bring home something definitely handmade in a country style. We hope to open a cafe and install gas pumps this summer." Customers: tourists, highway traffic, fisherman, hunters, canoeists and campers.

THE OLD BRONTE POST OFFICE GALLERY, 86 Bronte Rd., Oakville, Ontario, Canada L6L 3B8. (416)827-7214. Craft shop/gallery. Estab. 1975. Represents 40 Canadian craftworkers.
Acceptable Work: Considers batik; ceramics; glass art; jewelry; pottery; wall hangings; weavings; woodcrafting; and sculpture—all of original design. Fine one-of-a-kind pieces. Price range: $2-200.
Terms: Works on consignment; 33⅓% commission. Retail price set by joint agreement. "For one-man shows we take ⅓ cost of sold item; and artist pays for invitations and stamps." Reports in 1 week. Dealer pays limited return shipping and limited exhibition insurance.
Profile: "We have a pleasant, relaxed atmosphere and a wide variety of shows and work." Customers are young marrieds with 2 incomes looking for furnishings and collectibles; and shoppers of wedding and shower gifts. Pottery sells well. Best selling time: fall and at one-man shows.

OLEARY LIBRARY & MUSEUM ASSOCIATION, Oleary, Prince Edward Island, Canada C0B 1V0. President: L. G. Dewar. Museum gallery/gift shop. Estab. 1973. Considers clothing and woodcrafting. Primitive pieces only. Shop sets retail price. Best selling time: summer.

ORCHARD CRAFTS, Box 367, Kentville, Nova Scotia, Canada B4N 3X1. (902)678-1262 or 678-3687. Manager: Barbara J. Jebson. Craft/gift shop. Estab. 1976. Represents 175 craftworkers.
Acceptable Work: Considers all crafts except ceramics, decoupage and quilting. Especially needs silkscreen. Specializes in fine and bright-colored items. One-of-a-kind and handmade production-line items. Price range: $1-500; bestsellers: $1-30.
Terms: Buys outright and works on consignment (if unsure seller or if expensive); 33⅓% commission. Retail price set by craftworker on consignment, sometimes by joint agreement. Prefers exclusive area representation. Call for appointment with photos. Reports as soon as possible.
Profile: "Shop is in a small home with the bottom floor made into a 2-room shop. I had spruce shelves made to display my crafts and use burlap in greens, golds and browns for draping. Whenever possible. I try to keep each craftsman's things together with a card with his name and address." Customers: tourists and college-oriented (Acadia University is only 6 miles away). Heaviest wholesale buying time: spring and fall; best selling time: Christmas.

OTHER DELIGHTS, 491 Bloor St. W., Toronto, Ontario, Canada. (416)961-5226. Manager: Gwen Brooks. Craft and gift shop. Estab. 1974. Represents 50 craftworkers.
Acceptable Work: Considers batik; candlemaking; dollmaking; ceramics; glass art; jewelry; leatherworking; needlecrafts; pottery; quilting; wall hangings; weavings; and woodcrafting. Fine one-of-a-kind and handmade production-line items. Price range: $3.50-35; bestsellers: $4-15.
Terms: Works on consignment; 40% commission. Retail price set by joint agreement. Reports in 1 week. Hand-delivered work only. Dealer pays insurance for exhibited work. Items are displayed in the window as well as on the floor for periods up to 1 year. Customers are mostly students, ages 18-25. Heaviest wholesale buying and best selling time: Christmas.

PLACE DES ARTS, 166 King Edward, Coquitlam, British Columbia, Canada V3K 4T2. (604)526-2891. Director: Leonore Peyton. Gallery/art center. Estab. 1972. Represents 10 craftworkers.

Acceptable Work: Considers batik; ceramics; glass art; jewelry; leatherworking; needlecrafts; pottery; quilting; wall hangings; weavings; and woodcrafting. Fine one-of-a-kind pieces. Price range: $3-500; bestsellers: up to $350.
Terms: Works on consignment; 15% commission. Retail price set by joint agreement. $15/exhibit space for 2 weeks in gallery. Requires exclusive area representation. Reports in 8 weeks. Dealer pays insurance for exhibited work.
Profile: "The nonprofit gallery is part of a teaching center for 600 students." Customers are middle income. Best selling time: September-July.

PRAIRIE TEXTURES, 108 10th St. NW, Calgary, Alberta, Canada T2N 1V3. (403)283-1213. Contact: Catherine Anderson or Patti-Jean Spink. Gallery. Estab. 1977.
Acceptable Work: Considers clothing, dollmaking, needlecrafts, quilting, soft sculpture, wall hangings and weavings. Especially needs embroideries and needlework with emphasis on contemporary design. Specializes in fine one-of-a-kind items. Price range: $30-500; bestsellers: $30-250.
Terms: Works on consignment; 20% commisison. Retail price set by joint agreement. Send slides or call for appointment. Reports in 1 week. Work may be shipped or hand delivered.
Profile: "We display items of specific themes during specific show periods. Therefore we accept pieces only if they are of the theme of the show. Show themes are coordinated in connection with our local art school's program. Therefore we exhibit a lot of local students' work. Interested artists may obtain a list of yearly shows and deadlines for submission." Customers: ages 30-40; middle income; professionals. Best selling time: November-December and June-September.

RUBAIYAT CRAFTS GALLERY, 120-8th Ave. SW, Calgary, Alberta, Canada T2P 1B3. (403)261-5767 or 269-2671. President: David Haight. Craft shop/gallery. Estab. 1973. Represents 75-100 craftworkers, preferably with at least 5 years of professional studio work.
Acceptable Work: Considers ceramics, glass art, jewelry, metalsmithing, wall hangings, weavings, woodcrafting, and especially off-hand blown glass and pottery. Specializes in fine art or collectible works. One-of-a-kind and handmade production-line items. Price range: $1-1,400; bestsellers: $35-200.
Terms: Buys outright. Craftworker sets retail price; shop advises. Requires exclusive area representation. Send resume and slides. Reports in 3 weeks. Work may be shipped or hand delivered. Dealer pays insurance on exhibited work.
Profile: "We have excellent display merchandising, track lighting, antique jewelry and display cases." Customers: mainly professionals or semi-professionals with $20,000 incomes. Heaviest wholesale buying time: fall approaching Christmas and May-June; best selling time: Christmas and summer (especially July-August).

SCHOOL ON THE HILL, North River Bridge, Cape Breton, Nova Scotia, Canada B0E 2J0. (902)929-2024. Manager: Jane Grose. Craft shop. Estab. 1976. Represents 35 Nova Scotia craftworkers.
Acceptable Work: Considers all crafts. Specializes in primitive crafts. One-of-a-kind and handmade production-line items. Price range: $2-350; bestsellers: $2-15.
Terms: Buys outright. Retail price set by joint agreement. Some consignment. Send resume or call for appointment. Reports in 2 weeks. Work may be shipped or hand delivered.
Profile: "The shop is an old school house with old school desks to display goods on." Customers: tourists. Heaviest wholesale buying time: June 1-June 15.

SHAW-RIMMINGTON GALLERY, 20 Birch Ave., Toronto, Ontario, Canada M4V 1C8. (416)923-3484. Director: Marie Shaw-Rimmington. Gallery. Estab. 1966. Represents 5 craftworkers.
Acceptable Work: Considers contemporary dollmaking; glass art; jewelry; soft sculpture; wall hangings; and weavings. Fine one-of-a-kind pieces; decorative only.
Terms: Works on consignment; 40% commission. Retail price set by joint agreement. Requires exclusive area representation. Customers middle income and middle age.

SHETANI GALLERY, 589 Markham St., Toronto, Ontario, Canada M6G 2L5. (416)534-4734. Director: Rhoda Lipton. Craft shop/gallery. Estab. 1976. Represents 20 craftworkers. All styles; utilitarian and/or decorative. Price range: $5-500; bestsellers: $15-50. Works on consignment and buys outright; 34% commission. Retail price set by joint agreement. "Craftspeople share cost of one-man show opening." Dealer pays return shipping on ordered items and insurance for exhibited work.
Acceptable Work: Considers ceramics; dollmaking; glass art; jewelry; leatherworking; metal-

smithing; pottery; and woodcrafting. "These are crafts that have been shown to date; this may change."
Profile: "We handle Canadian crafts." Customers are mostly upwardly mobile, well-educated women with broad interests; ages 25-45. Best selling time: Christmas and summer tourist season.

THE SHOP DOWNSTAIRS, Robert McLaughlin Gallery, Civic Centre, Oshawa, Ontario, Canada. 576-3000. Convenor: Ronni Zolumoff. Gallery gift shop. Represents 35 craftworkers. "We deal primarily with crafts of the Durham region. We do go outside the region for something very special and unique."
Acceptable Work: Considers apple dolls, batik, burlap flowers, candlemaking, ceramics, decoupage, dollmaking, jewelry, needlecrafts, pottery, quilting, silkscreening, tole painting, wall hangings and weavings. Especially needs local Indian or Eskimo crafts. Specializes in contemporary crafts; scented candles; pottery tableware; and patchwork aprons and oven mitts. One-of-a-kind and handmade production-line items: Price range: 15¢-$150; bestsellers: $3.50-32.50.
Terms: Buys outright (from gift shows) but mostly works on consignment; 30% commission (over $10), 40% commission (under $10). Retail price set by joint agreement. Call for appointment. Reports immediately. Work may be shipped or hand delivered. Dealer pays insurance on exhibited work. Display time: 3 months (consigned work). "Special items are taken in for Art Mart, Christmas or seasonal. These items will be returned earlier, if not sold, by a prearranged contract."
Profile: " We are a small boutique having textured walls with natural burlap and cork display areas. Pine showcase with mirror backs. We color-coordinate displays with woven placemats, pottery, flowers and calico." Customers: shop volunteers, gallery members, tourists, children; reasonably good incomes. Heaviest wholesale buying time: summer ("an ideal time to attend craft shows and gift shows and restock shelves for fall openings and our annual Art Mart"); best selling time: fall. "We have a large Art Mart at the end of October. The gallery is taken over by craftspeople of all types. Most customers come to do their Christmas shopping then." Closed: July-August.

SONRISE DESIGN, Box 148 Pugwash, Nova Scotia, Canada B0K 1L0. (902)243-2563. Proprietor: Peter D. Finley. Craft/gift shop/studio. Represents 4 craftworkers.
Acceptable Work: Considers candlemaking, ceramics, clothing, dollmaking, glass art, jewelry, leatherworking, metalsmithing, needlecrafts, pottery, quilting and woodcrafting. Especially needs nautical (primarily) and rural crafts. Handmade production-line items only. Price range: $1-200; bestsellers: $5-20.
Terms: Buys outright. Shop sets retail price. Send resume. "Promote your craft by description to include with my display." Reports in 2 weeks. Work may be shipped or hand delivered.
Profile: "I display in units (this section for this worker, etc.) unless items carried by a worker isn't enough for a display." Customers: 60% tourist, middle aged to elderly. Heaviest wholesale buying and best selling time: summer.

STEEPLE ARTWORKS, 1110 Gladstone Rd. NW, Calgary, Alberta, Canada T2N 3E7. (403)283-9500. Managers: Carol Snyder and Joyce O'Brien. Craft shop/rental studio. Estab. 1977. Represents 75-90 Alberta craftworkers.
Acceptable Work: Considers basketry, batik, candlemaking, clothing, dollmaking, glass art, jewelry, macrame, needlecrafts, pottery, quilting, soapstone, soft sculpture, tole painting, wall hangings, weavings and woodcrafting. Specializes in traditional and contemporary crafts. One-of-a-kind and handmade production-line items. Price range: 1,200 maximum; bestsellers: $2-30.
Terms: Studio people display and sell their own work; 30% commission. Craftworker must work one-two days/month. Retail price set by joint agreement. Call for appointment. Reports in 1 week. Work must be hand-delivered. Dealer pays insurance on exhibited work.
Profile: "The gallery is run on a cooperative basis. Classes are given by the studio people. There is room available for others to rent workshops. New items are featured as they come in. No time limit on the length of display." Best selling time: July (for tourist season) and pre-Christmas.

STUDIO WEFAN, Box 344, Annapolis Royal, Nova Scotia, Canada B0S 1A0. (902)532-5763. Contact: Daurene Lewis. Craft shop. Estab. 1975. Represents 25 craftworkers.
Acceptable Work: Considers batik, candlemaking, glass art, jewelry, leatherworking, metalsmithing, pottery, quilting, wall hangings, weavings and woodcrafting. One-of-a-kind and

handmade production-line items. Price range: 25¢-$450; bestsellers: 25¢-$125.
Terms: Buys outright and works on consignment; 40% commission. Retail price set by joint agreement. Requires exclusive area representation. Call for appointment. Work may be shipped or hand delivered. Dealer pays insurance on exhibited work. "If work is glass or another breakable craft, I do not accept full responsibility."
Profile: "The shop is primarily my weaving studio which also retails a large range of other crafts. Most jewelry and well finished metals are displayed in cases for security reasons. Shop cases are barnboard hutches made from 200 year-old boards. The studio is located in a town of less than 700 people so items should not be too assembly line-ish. I do not carry more than about 3 of any given style." Customers: mainly professionals. Heaviest wholesale buying time: winter and late summer; best selling time: summer and Christmas.

SUNBURY SHORES ARTS & NATURE CENTRE, Box 100, St. Andrews, New Brunswick, Canada E0G 2X0. (506)529-3386. Director: Henrik Kreiberg. Gallery. Estab. 1964. Represents 2 craftworkers; "emphasis on Canadian and maritime craftworkers but not restrictive."
Acceptable Work: Considers batik, ceramics, decoupage, glass art, jewelry, leatherworking, metalsmithing, pottery, needlecrafts, quilting, wall hangings and weaving. One-of-a-kind items only. Price range: 50¢-$500, but flexible.
Terms: Exhibits work only; 30% commission. Will act as occasional sales agent. Retail price set by joint agreement. Send resume and slides. Reports in 2 weeks. Work may be shipped or hand delivered. Dealer pays return shipping and insurance for exhibited work.
Profile: "We primarily exhibit and do not stand in the way of craftworkers who wish to sell some of the pieces in the show. Profit to us is incidental. The gallery has neutral backgrounds; controlled lighting; burglar and fire alarms; and a 2-3 week exhibit period in display window or gallery. St. Andrews is a summer seaside resort with tourists from Europe and North America of all ages and incomes."
To Break In: "Workshops and instructional sessions are strong assets."

3'S COMPANY GALLERY, LTD., 524A 4th Ave. SE, Medicine Hat, Alberta Canada T1A 2N6. (403)526-5881. Contact Joyce Carlson or Wendy McLaren. Gallery. Estab. 1973. Represents 6-10 craftworkers.
Acceptable Work: Considers ceramics; glass art; metalsmithing; pottery; soft sculpture; wall hangings; and weavings. Fine one-of-a-kind and handmade production-line items. Price range: $5-1,000; bestsellers: $5-250.
Terms: Works on consignment and buys outright. Retail price set by joint agreement. Prefers exclusive area representation. All shipping and shipping insurance costs are by joint agreement; dealer pays insurance for exhibited work. Best selling time: fall and winter.

THE TOY FACTORY, Murray River, Prince Edward Island, Canada C0A 1W0. (902)962-2417. President: Al Shumate. Craft/gift shop/toy factory. Estab. 1978. Represents 5 craftworkers.
Acceptable Work: Considers candlemaking, ceramics, clothing, dollmaking, glass art, jewelry, leatherworking, metalsmithing, needlecrafts, pottery, quilting, wall hangings, weavings and woodcrafting. Specializes in Canadian crafts. "Because of our size, we prefer small items that won't take up much space and yet give us variety." One-of-a-kind and handmade production-line items. Price range: $2-50; bestsellers: $2-20.
Terms: Buys outright and works on consignment; 40% commission. Retail price set by joint agreement. Call for appointment or call in person. Reports in 2 weeks. Work may be shipped or hand delivered.
Profile: "We have a very small area and of course feature the wooden toys we manufacture. The interior is barn siding with old to antique tables and sideboards used for display. We are in a small village of about 500 with 2 general stores. Since there is a craft cooperative in the village, we attempt to have different items. We allow our customers to wander through our factory to watch us make the toys. We are very safety conscious and will not handle any item that may be dangerous." Customers: many young parents and grandparents with children; tourists; middle to high-middle incomes. Heaviest wholesale buying time: spring; best selling time: summer.
To Break In: "Be realistic in pricing your wares and make sure the article is finished properly, signed or tagged, and special care instructions given. We like to tell our customers a little thumb-nail sketch about the people who made the crafts we sell."

WINDMILL CRAFT COOP ASSOCIATION, Old Woodstock School House, Highway 2, West Devon, Prince Edward Island, Canada C0B 1H0. (902)859-3275. President: Edward MacAusland. Craft shop. Estab. 1970. Represents 20 craftworkers.
Acceptable Work: Considers dollmaking, needlecrafts, pottery, quilting, wall hangings,

weavings and woodcrafting. Handmade production-line items only. Price range: $1-125; best-sellers: $1-125.
Terms: Retail price set by joint agreement. Dealer pays insurance on exhibited work. "We are only open during the summer months: from July to September 15."

WINDSONG HOUSE LTD., 105-3521 8th St. E. Saskatoon, Saskachewan, Canada S7H 0W5. (306)373-3366. Contact: Marg. Smith-Windsor. Craft/gift shop. Estab. 1977. Represents 50 Canadian craftworkers.
Acceptable Work: Considers batik, candlemaking, decoupage, dollmaking, jewelry, needlecrafts, pottery, quilting, wall hangings, weavings and wood products. One-of-a-kind and a few handmade production-line items. Price range: $5-1,500; bestsellers: $20-100.
Terms: Buys outright but mostly works on consignment; 40% commisison. Retail price set by joint agreement. Send slides or call for appointment. SASE. Reports in 3 weeks. Work may be shipped (prepaid) or hand-delivered. Dealer pays insurance on exhibited work. Display time: 3 months.
Profile: "We are a family business, all avid craftspeople. We try to specialize in those crafts of which we are familiar in order to offer specialized service and advice to our customers. The craftworker and dealer together sign a contract where method of display and special care (i.e., sun avoidance) can be stipulated."
To Break In: "Our most successful craftspeople are those who price reasonably, their products are well finished and who fill orders reliably and promptly."

WOOD ISLANDS HANDCRAFT COOP, Murray River, Prince Edward Island, Canada. (902)962-3043. Treasurer: Marie MacLeod. Craft shop. Estab. 1972. Represents 2 craftworkers
Acceptable Work: Considers batik, candlemaking, ceramics, clothing, dollmaking, jewelry, knitting, leatherworking, needlecrafts, pottery, quilting, wall hangings, weavings and woodcrafting. Especially needs pottery, knitting, batik and needlepoint. Handmade production-line items. Price range: $1-175; bestsellers: $2-25.
Terms: Works on consignment; 33⅓% commission for nonmembers, 25% commission for members. Pays at the end of July, September and December. Craftworker sets retail price. Requires exclusive area representation. SASE. Work must be hand-delivered.
Profile: "We display and sell other people's crafts as we do our own crafts." Heaviest wholesale buying and best selling time: summer.

WOOD 'N' WOOL GIFT SHOP, Box 1, Site 37, Rt. 1, Tantallon, Halifax Co., Nova Scotia, Canada B0J 3J0. (902)823-2187. Contact: Shirley Chadwick. Craft shop. Estab. 1974. Represents 50 Nova Scotia craftworkers.
Acceptable Work: Considers candlemaking, ceramics, dollmaking, mat hooking, jewelry, leatherworking, needlecrafts, pottery, quilting, wall hangings, weavings and woodcrafting. Especially needs knit wool socks, and wool and Aran sweaters. Handmade production-line items. Price range: $1.98-175; bestsellers: $5-65.
Terms: Works on consignment; 40% commission. Retail price set by joint agreement. Call for appointment. SASE. Reports in 1 week. Work may be shipped or hand delivered.
Profile: "We are a small business run by my husband and I. The shop is at Indian Harbour on the way to Peggy's Cove. Crafts are put on shelves or hung in view of the customers." Customers: tourists on limited budgets; people looking for gifts. Heaviest consignment time: March-April; best selling time: summer. Open May-October 15.

YE WISE OWL SHOPPE LTD., 237 City Centre, Kitimat, British Columbia, Canada. (604)632-5544. President: Joanne Monaghan. Craft shop/gift shop. Estab. 1973. Represents 6-12 craftworkers. Best selling time: summer (for tourist season) and winter.
Acceptable Work: Considers batik, candlemaking, ceramics, clothing, decoupage, dollmaking, glass art, jewelry, leatherworking, metalsmithing, needlecrafts, pottery, quilting, scrimshaw, wall hangings, weavings and woodcrafting. "We have items from almost every country in the world; we try to have something for everyone." Price range: $2-$1,700; bestsellers: $5-25.
Terms: Buys outright, but mainly works on consignment; 30% commission. Retail price set by joint agreement. Requires exclusive area representation. Send resume and slides with SASE. Reports in 2 weeks. Work may be shipped or hand delivered.

Puerto Rico

CENTRO ARTES POPULARES, Instituto de Cultura Puertorriquena, Norzagaray St. 98, San Juan, Puerto Rico 00902. (809)724-6250. Director: Anibal Rodriguez Vera. Craft shop. Estab. 1958. Represents 300 craftworkers.

Acceptable Work: Considers ceramics, clothing, dollmaking, jewelry, leatherworking, needlecrafts, pottery, wall hangings, weavings, woodcrafting, coconut, hiquera and bejuco. Specializes in bright-colored crafts, some rustic. Handmade production-line items only. Price range: 53¢-$900.

Terms: Buys outright. Retail price set by joint agreement. Call for appointment. Reports in 1 week. Work must be hand-delivered. "When craftworkers come for the first time, we give them a membership card of the Institute of Puerto Rican Culture if the work they have done meets our requirements. After they have this card, they have no problem when bringing other works to us."

Profile: "Our shop belongs to the government; it is located in the Institute of Puerto Rican Culture. Because of this, the store is not a modern one. Mostly its appearance is like that of a museum. When the craftworker brings the work, we store it in our warehouse; then we set the price, mark it immediately and we display it for sale. For this purpose we have wooden end tables arranged one above the other. Soon we are going to begin remodeling, but it's going to preserve its appearance." Customers: mainly tourists "interested in taking with them a genuine souvenir from Puerto Rico." Heaviest wholesale buying time: pre-Christmas; best selling time: Christmas.

MUSEO DE LA FUNDACION ARQUEOLOGICA DE PUERTO RICO, Box S-3787, San Juan, Puerto Rico 00904. (809)723-3590. Director: Haydee Venegas. Museum gift shop. Estab. 1973 Represents 8 craftworkers.

Acceptable Work: Considers ceramics, clothing, jewelry, leatherworking, needlecrafts, pottery, sculpture, wall hangings, weavings and graphic arts. "All crafts or reproductions must be inspired on pre-Columbian motifs from Central and South America, especially from Puerto Rico." One-of-a-kind and handmade production-line items. Price range: 75¢-$75; bestsellers; 75¢-$15.

Terms: Works on consignment; 25-50% commission. Craftworker sets retail price. "We require exclusive area representation if the piece is a museum reproduction." Call for appointment. Reports in 1 week. Work may be shipped or hand delivered. Dealer pays insurance on exhibited work. Work is displayed immediately and constantly while in stock.

Profile: Customers: mostly school children, tourists and professionals. Heaviest wholesale buying time: November-December; best selling time: November-February.

Virgin Islands

RAINBOW TREE, INC, 58 Company St., Christiansted, St. Croix, US Virgin Islands 00820. (809)773-7909. President: Karen J. Syence. Craft shop/gallery. Estab. 1978. Represents over 160 craftworkers.

Acceptable Work: Considers batik, candlemaking, ceramics, clothing, dollmaking, glass art, jewelry, leatherworking, needlecrafts, pottery, scrimshaw, soft sculpture, wall hangings, weavings, wind chimes, greeting cards and clothing accessories. Especially needs 100% cotton wearables (men's and women's) including bikinis, and items especially for men, boys and children. Specializes in contemporary fine art crafts, "particularly those of a tropical and/or rainbow motif." One-of-a-kind and some handmade production-line items. Price range: $1-400; bestsellers: $10-40.

Terms: Buys outright and sometimes works on consignment; 40% commission. Retail price set by joint agreement. Requires exclusive area representation. Send resume and slides/photos (preferably nonreturnable); describe work shown on slides and include wholesale prices, terms (preferably net 30) and availability. Reports in 3 weeks. Work may be shipped or hand-delivered. Dealer pays insurance on exhibited work. Consignment items are held 6 months and returned at craftworker's or our own request. The shop and merchandise are professionally advertised/publicized in a wide range of media."

Profile: "The shop is in a restored 200+ year-old Danish carriage house in the heart of historic Christiansted (tourist area). We sell on several levels of the building. Displays are changed at least one a week, including the window showcase. All personnel are conversant with particular artist methods pieces." Customers: tourists primarily from mid-Atlantic, ages 20-50, good incomes, looking for different but not heavy/bulky items for transport; locals mainly ages 15-60 (especially 20-40), looking for unique personal items and gifts especially suited for tropical climate, $10,000-100,000/year incomes. Heaviest wholesale buying time: July-September; best selling time: December-April, "with less volume and less expensive merchandise the remainder of the year."

To Break In: "We need things which stand up under high humidity and heat. Be businesslike and be clear on your prices. Avoid prohibitively high minimums. Ship what and when agreed and pack well."

Shows and Fairs

If you're not already exhibiting your crafts at shows and fairs, you're missing out on one of the most valuable markets available. Not only can you sell your work, but exhibiting in shows allows you a means of gaining wide exposure for you and your work.

One of the nicest features of shows and fairs is they benefit both the beginner and the veteran craftworker. In a *Craftworker's Market* survey, 500 professional craftworkers said shows are the beginner's best chance of breaking into the field—to gain sales, exposure, a knowledge of public response to your work, and recognition through awards. (Shows that present awards are noted by an asterisk before the listing.) The same professionals believe shows provide them with these same benefits.

Almost all shows permit participants to sell their work—and often encourage sales. And, the buyers attracted by shows are no means restricted to the day-to-day consumer, but frequently gallery and shop owners attend shows looking for new work. One Atlanta shop owner was recently overheard explaining to a craftworker that she buys nothing from craftpersons who visit her shop. All her merchandise is ordered from craftworkers showing at fairs.

In addition to making sales at the show itself, craftpersons and artist who make their cards available, frequently continue to receive orders from individuals after the show.

Exhibiting actually provides you a means of meeting your customer face to face, and witnessing his/her reaction to your work. This feedback can help you develop better-selling lines.

Alabama

ART-ON-THE-LAKE SHOW, Box 192, Guntersville AL 35976. (205)582-3833. Chairman Invitation/Registration: Mrs. James McCain. Sponsor: Twentieth Century Club. Purpose: to support the club's charity projects. Estab. 1961. Annual show held in April on the lawn and in the hallways and classrooms of Carlisle Park School. Average paid attendance: 1,500. Entries accepted until show date. Entry fee: $7.50 per artist; no restrictions on size of display area within reason. Work may be offered for sale; no commission. "Public seems to show more interest in traditional work than in the abstract." Craftworker or representative must attend show; demonstrations encouraged. Considers all crafts, "but chairman reserves right to reject unsuitable artwork." Awards 3 ribbons in craft category.
Promotion: Announcements of show appear in art and craft magazines; newspapers; and on local radio stations. "Photos suitable for newspaper articles and information concerning the entrant are desirable; however, we cannot guarantee they will be used."

*****ART ON THE ROCKS**, Box 973, Gadsden AL 35902. Sponsor: Gadsden Art Association. Annual outdoor show held the first Sunday in May. All work must be original not made from kits. Entries accepted until 1 week before show. No entry fee. Awards $25 1st and $15 2nd prize. Work may be offered for sale; 15% commission. Craftworker must attend show.
Acceptable Work: Considers batik; candlemaking; dollmaking; glass art; jewelry; leatherworking; metalsmithing; needlecrafts; pottery; soft sculpture; tole painting; weavings; wall hangings; and woodcrafting. Work must be framed or matted when applicable.

*****THE CAROLINA CRAFTSMEN'S CHRISTMAS CLASSIC—MONTGOMERY**, 3603 Old Battleground Rd., Greensboro NC 27410. (919)288-1933. Executive Director: Clyde Gilmore. Estab. 1977. Annual indoor show held 2 days in November at Montgomery, Alabama. Considers all crafts. No kits or molds. Presents purchase awards and plaques.
Terms: Entry deadline and entry fee varies. Prejudging by slides, photos or newspaper articles. Entry fee due after prejudging. Work may be offered for sale; no commission. Craftworker must attend show; demonstrations OK. Sponsor provides chairs, curtained booth space and 24-hour security.

---

* Those listings preceded by an asterisk present awards for prize-winning crafts.

CHALAKA ARTS AND CRAFTS FESTIVAL, Box 1245 Sylacauga AL 35150. Chairman: Shirley Cardwell. Sponsor: Sylacauga Parks & Recreation Department. Estab. 1968. Annual outdoor show held 2 days in June. Average attendance 1200-1500. Entries accepted until 1 week before show. Entry fee: $15/entry. Prejudging; entry fee refunded for refused work. Work may be offered for sale. Craftworker must attend show. Considers all original crafts, no kits. Presents $1,500 in cash prizes and ribbons.

FESTIVAL IN THE PARK, 1010 Forest Ave., Montgomery AL 36106. (205)265-8593. Festival Chairman: Jeanne Hackman. Festival Coordinator: Edith Upchurch. Sponsor: Montgomery Parks and Recreation, and the Festivals in the Park Committee. Purpose: "nonprofit, to encourage community participation." Estab. 1973. Annual outdoor show held 1 day in September at Oak Park. Average attendance: 20,000. Entries accepted until 4 weeks before show. Entry fee: $15 per 12x10 display area. Work may be offered for sale; no commission. Cash prizes for best exhibits. Craftworker must attend show; demonstrations OK. Registration limit: 250. Sponsor provides electricity for demonstrations. Considers all handmade crafts. Show promoted through TV; radio spots; newspapers throughout the state; and TV and radio talk shows.

INDIAN CRAFTS FESTIVAL & PIONEER FAIR, c/o DeSoto Caverns, Rt. 1, Box 50-A, Childersburg AL 35044. (205)378-7272. Sponsor: Desoto Caverns. Estab. 1975. Annual outdoor show held 2 days in April. Average attendance: 10,000. Entries accepted until 4 weeks before show. Entry fee: $12 per 12' square display area. Prejudging by 2 slides or photos; entry fee refunded for refused work. Work may be offered for sale; no commission. Craftworker must attend show; demonstrations encouraged. Registration limit: 100 craftworkers. Sponsor provides electricity for demonstration and 24-hour security. Considers all crafts.
Promotion: Show promoted by radio, TV, magazines, newspapers, signs and posters throughout the Southeast. "Any promotional material is appreciated, but must be supplied 2 months prior to show dates," said Caryl Lynn Mathis, festival coordinator.

*KENTUCK ARTS & CRAFTS FESTIVAL, Box 127, Northport AL 35476. Executive Director: Georgine Clarke. Sponsor: Kentuck of Northport, Inc. Purpose: to promote quality art and crafts. Estab. 1973. Annual outdoor show held 2 days in October. Average attendance: 15,000. Entries accepted until early summer; some categories remain open until 1 month before show. Entry fee: $30/15x15 display area. Prejudging by slides; entry fee refunded for refused work. Work may be offered for sale; no commission. Craftworkers must attend show; demonstrations OK. Registration limit: 150-200. Sponsor provides electricity for demonstrations and 24-hour security. Show is advertised by TV; radio; newspaper; billboards; posters; magazines; and bumper stickers. Submit slides for TV spots; b&w shots for newspaper; and resume for articles. Presents cash awards of $400 and purchase awards of $400.

MUCKLE'S RIDGE FESTIVAL, Box 542, Marion AL 36756. Contact: Chairperson. Sponsor: Club 15. Estab. 1973. Annual outdoor show held the first Saturday in May. Average attendance: 3,000. Considers all crafts and hobbies.
Terms: Entries accepted until 1 week before show. Entry fee: $15/10x7' display area. Work may be offered for sale; no commission. Craftworker needn't attend show; demonstrations OK. Sponsor provides electricity for demonstrations, "but only if specified on entry form."
Sales Tip: "Mother's Day is the day after, or the weekend after, the festival, therefore items suitable for gifts might increase sales."
Profile: Show takes place "around an historic court house square. The Muckle's Ridge Festival provides the opportunity for the public to join together in remembering our heritage."

NORTHWEST ALABAMA ARTS & CRAFTS FESTIVAL, Rt. 4, Box 419, Killen AL 35645. (205)757-2115 or (202)757-4487. Director: William R. Dean. Sponsor: Brooks High School History club. Estab. 1973. Annual indoor show (with some outside space) held 3 days in April. Average attendance: 15,000-18,000.
Acceptable Work: Considers all crafts. No nails may be placed in walls or floors; no frames may obstruct the view of other craftworkers.
Terms: Entries accepted until show date. Entry fee: $20 per display area with 12' lateral front footage. Work may be offered for sale; no commission. Craftworker must attend show; demonstrations encouraged. Sponsor provides electricity for demonstrations and 24-hour security protection.
Profile: "This is the largest show in northwest Alabama; craftsmen and artists come from 24 states."

Sales Tip: "Have an attractive display, be talkative with visitors, offer to demonstrate how your craft is done."

*OPELIKA ARTS FESTIVAL, Box 2095, Opelika AL 36801. (205)749-0965. Chairman: Kathy Penton. Sponsor: Opelika Arts Association. Estab. 1968. Annual outdoor show held the third Saturday in April. Average attendance: 5,000.
Acceptable Work: Considers decoupage; dollmaking; glass art; jewelry; leatherworking; macrame; needlecrafts; pottery; sculpture; tole painting; and woodcrafting. "Bring own tables; S hooks; plastic sheet in case of rain; and chairs."
Terms: Entries accepted until 3 weeks before show. Entry fee: $10/artist. Display area: 6-10 linear feet. Work may be offered for sale; no commission. Craftworker must attend show; demonstrations OK. Registration limit: 150. Sponsor provides display panels and fencing.
Awards: Presents $1,000 in cash; $300 for 1st place; $200 for 2nd place; and $100 for 3rd place, all presented with ribbons; and 8 merit awards of $50 each in painting, crafts and sculpture.

*OUTDOOR ARTS & CRAFTS FAIR, c/o The Fine Arts Museum of the South, Box 8404, Mobile AL 36608. (205)476-2512. Juried Show Chairman: Mrs. Ramsey McKinney. Sponsor: The Fine Arts Museum of the South and The Art Patrons League. Estab. 1964. Annual outdoor show held 2 days during the last full weekend of September. Average attendance: 25,000-30,000.
Acceptable Work: Considers batik, ceramics, dollmaking, glass art, jewelry, leatherworking, macrame, metalsmithing, mobiles, needlecrafts, pottery, scrimshaw, sculpture, soft sculpture, weaving and woodcrafting. No picture frames, art supplies, crocheting, knitting, millinery, clothing, commercially manufactured items, kits, molds, string art, quilling, coin jewelry, fork-spoon jewelry, novelty rock or shell crafts, driftwood, sand art, bottle sagging, candles, decoupage, decorated eggs, carpentry, or velvet, china or tole painting.
Terms: Entries accepted until 3 months before show; applications available in March. Entry fee: $30/12x6' display area. Minimum 4 pieces/category. "Exhibition is permitted only in the category(s) in which work has been accepted." Prejudging by 3 slides (2¼x2¼ or 35mm) of work in each category and 1 slide or photo of display; $5 nonreturnable prejudging fee. Entry fee refunded for refused work. Work may be offered for sale; no commission. Craftworker must attend show; demonstrations OK. Registration limit: 200 artists and craftworkers. Sponsor provides electricity (if possible), fencing, 24-hour security (Boy Scouts Troops patrol grounds), coffee and donuts (on Saturday and Sunday). "Artists should come prepared for wind and rain. Art Patrons League collects 20% of total retail sales from artists to comply with city tax rules. Slides returned when tax paid at conclusion of fair."
Awards: Presents 10 best of show awards at $100 each; $1,000 in purchase awards; and 10 merit award ribbons.
Profile: "The Outdoor Arts & Crafts Fair is family-oriented with a wide range of public appeal. The artist/craftsman should keep this in mind and offer for sale a variety of creative original work within each category, plus establish a range of prices." The 1978 fair totalled $98,000 in sales.

RIVERFRONT MARKET DAY, Box 565, Selma AL 36701. (205)872-8265. Coordinator: Sam H. O'Hara. Sponsor: Selma and Dallas County Historical Preservation Society. Estab. 1971. Annual outdoor show held 2 days in October. Average attendance: 20,000-30,000. Considers all crafts.
Terms: Entries accepted until 1 week before show. Entry fee: $20/uncovered or $30/covered display area. Work may be offered for sale; no commission. Craftworkers must attend show. Registration limit: 250. Sponsor provides electrical outlets.

SEPTEMBERFEST, (formerly Fallfest), DeSoto Caverns, Rt. 1, Box 50-A, Childersburg AL 35044. (205)378-7252. Festival Coordinator: Caryl Lynn Mathis. Estab. 1975. Annual outdoor show held 2 days in fall. Average attendance: 10,000. Considers all crafts.
Terms: Entries accepted until 4 weeks before show. Entry fee: $12/12x12' display area. Prejudging by slides and photos. Entry fee refunded for refused work. Work may be offered for sale; no commission. Craftworker must attend show; demonstrations encouraged. Registration limit: 100. Sponsor provides electricity for demonstrations and 24-hour security.
Promotion: Show is advertised by radio; TV; magazines; newspapers; and signs and posters throughout the Southeast. Submit promotional material 2 months before show.

Alaska
HOONAH ARTS FAIR, Box 157, Hoonah AK 99829. (907)945-3212. President: Bob Hutton.

Sponsor: Hoonah Arts & Crafts. Purpose: "to raise money for Hoonah Arts & Crafts." Estab. 1969. Annual indoor show held 1 day in December. Average attendance: 400. Entries accepted until 1 week before show. No entry fee. 10x10 display area. Work may be offered for sale; 10% commission. Craftworker needn't attend; demonstrations permitted. Sponsor provides chairs, electricity for demonstrations and table.
Acceptable Work: Considers batik; candlemaking; ceramics; dollmaking; glass art; jewelry; leatherworking; macrame; metalsmithing; mobiles; needlecrafts; pottery; sculpture; soft sculpture; tole painting; weaving; woodcrafting; and other crafts that are "100% handmade."

TANANA VALLEY FAIR MOSQUITO MARKET, Box 188, Fairbanks AK 99707. (907)452-3750. Director: Beth Ziegler. Purpose: "to use the space available on the fairgrounds and to supply a market for people otherwise unable to have one." Indoor show held 2 days in May, June and July. Average attendance: 500. Entries accepted until show date. Entry fee: $10/8x8 display area. Work may be offered for sale; no commission. Craftworker must attend show; demonstrations OK. Sponsor provides electricity for demonstrations; table; and 24-hour security protection. Show is promoted by radio, posters and local newspapers. Considers all crafts. To improve sales "be an active seller. Converse with the customers."

TANANA VALLEY STATE FAIR CRAFT MARKET, Box 188, Fairbanks AK 99707. (907)452-3750. Commercial space: Carl Romick. Sponsor: Tanana Valley State Fair Association. Purpose: "to give craftsmen a place to sell their products at a time and place when a good audience is available." Estab. 1971. Annual outdoor show (with some tent space) held 5 days in August. Average attendance: 80,000. Reservations accepted until show. Space rental: $45/10x15 outside display area; $50/8x8 tent space. Work may be offered for sale; no commission. Craftworker must attend; demonstrations required whenever possible. Sponsor provides limited electricity for demonstrations and 24-hour security. Considers "all crafts which have been made by the person marketing them." Show promoted by radio, newsletters, newspapers, and some magazine advertising.
Sales Tip: "Fairbanks is very craft-minded, and most items which show quality workmanship sell. Cleanliness and attractiveness of display probably do most to increase sales."

WINTERWORKS, c/o Solstia, Inc., Box 80908, Fairbanks AK 99701. (907)456-6908. Crafts Chairperson: Deborah Sather. Estab: 1975. Annual indoor show held 2 days in December. Considers all crafts by residents of Alaska.
Terms: Write for information on registration (usually held 1 week before show). Entry fee: $25/booth. Prejudging; entry fee refunded for refused work. Registration limit: 50.

Arizona

*****ARCOSANTI FESTIVAL**, 6433 Doubletree Rd., Scottsdale AZ 85253. (602)948-6145. Director: Bruce Joseph. Sponsor: Cosanti Foundation. Estab. 1975. Annual outdoor show held 2 days in fall at Arcosanti, Arizona. Average attendance: 10,000. Presents 3 cash awards.
Terms: Entries accepted until 3 weeks before show. Entry fee: $50/5x10 display area. Prejudging by slides or photos; entry fee refunded for refused work. Work may be offered for sale; 10% commission. Craftworker must attend show; demonstrations OK. Sponsor provides electricity for demonstrations and 24-hour security protection. Exhibit area has tents and some materials for use by exhibitors.
Promotion: Show is advertised by local and national media; PSA; paid advertising posters, and handbills. "Photographs of the artist working may be helpful."
Purpose: "This is a major arts festival held at Paolo Soleri's experimental town, Arcosanti. A conference is also held at the site during the festival. It is intended to bring the arts to the entire region, encourage contemporary visual and performing arts and help establish Arcosanti as a cultural center."

*****"ARIZONA CRAFTS"**, Tucson Museum of Art, 235 W. Alameda, Tucson AZ 85701. (602)624-2333. Curator of Collections: Gerrit C. Cone. Sponsors: Tucson Museum of Art, Tucson Festival Society, Tucson Commission of the Arts & Culture, Arizona Commission on the Arts & Humanities. Estab. 1950. Biennial (odd years) indoor show held 6 weeks in March/April at the Tucson Museum of Art. Average attendance: 7,000.
Acceptable Work: Considers all crafts. No kits. "All entries must be ready for installation with instructions."
Terms: Arizona resident craftworkers/artists only. Entries accepted in January. Entry fee:

$3/item; 3 items maximum; sets are counted as 1 item. Display area: 2,000 square feet. Prejudging by actual works. Entry fee not refunded for refused work. Work must be offered for sale; 25% commission. Craftworker needn't be present at show; demonstrations OK. Sponsor provides chairs, display panels, electricity for demonstrations, insurance on exhibited work and work shipped to artist, shipping costs to artists from show, table and 24-hour security. Tucson Museum of Art handles sales and taxes.
Awards: Presents $500 in cash prizes, $3,000 in purchase prizes, and group exhibition awards in each category. "5-10 artists are selected for the group show."
Promotion: Show is advertised by state, regional and national press and arts publications; radio and television interviews; and public service announcements. "An artist's biography is provided in each prospectus and must be updated with each competition entry."

*FESTIVAL ARTS & CRAFTS FAIR, 8 W. Paseo Redondo, Tucson AZ 85705. (602)622-6911. Coordinator: Jarvis Harriman. Sponsor: Tucson Festival Society, Inc. "The show is one event of the month-long Tucson Festival, whose purpose is to promote and celebrate the cultural heritage of the Southwest." Average attendance: 50,000. Entries accepted through January. Entry fee: $65/artist. Display area: 8x8. Prejudging by slides, photos or work itself; entry fee refunded for refused work. Work may be offered for sale; no commission. Craftworker must attend show; demonstrations OK. Registration limit: 140. "We provide, if requested, an open framework booth. We supply electricity to all booths. Armed guards are on duty from show closing to reopening." Show is promoted by newspaper, radio, TV, and brochures. Categories: pottery; jewelry; fabric arts; painting; prints and photos; woodcraft; and sculpture.
Acceptable Work: Considers batik; candlemaking; ceramics; dollmaking; glass art; jewelry; leatherworking; macrame; metalsmithing; mobiles; needlecrafts; pottery; sculpture; soft sculpture; tole painting; weavings; and woodcrafting.
Awards: "Best of Show" and honors for attractive presentation.

HARVEST ARTS & CRAFTS FAIR, 1204 W. Silverlake Rd., Tucson AZ 85713. Recreational Program Supervisor: Carolyn L. Lenz. Sponsor: Pima County Parks & Recreation. Purpose: "This is primarily a selling show and not an exhibition show." Estab. 1972. Annual outdoor show held 1 day in October. Attendance: 750-1,000. Entries accepted until show date. Entry fee: $4/artist. Display area: 8x8. Work may be offered for sale; no commission. Craftworker must attend show; demonstrations OK. Sponsor provides electricity for demonstrations. Show is advertised by posters; newspapers; radio, and TV. Considers all crafts made by the exhibitor only.

INDIAN ARTISTS & CRAFTSMEN OF NORTH AMERICA, 22 E. Monte Vista, Phoenix AZ 85004. Contact: Arts & Crafts Chairman. Sponsor: Heard Museum Guild. Annual show. November closing date. No entry fee. Considers sculpture, crafts and jewelry. Art must relate to North American Indian heritage. Write for specifics. Ship items prepaid to museum or hand deliver.

*NAVAJO NATION FAIR, Box 738, Window Rock AZ 86515. (602)871-4417. Director: Johnny Descheny. Sponsor: Navajo Nation and Schlitz Beer. Annual indoor/outdoor show held in September. Average attendance: 100,000. Considers all crafts.
Terms: Entries accepted until 4 weeks before show. No entry fee. Work may be offered for sale; 20% commission. Craftworker needn't attend show; demonstrations OK. Registration limit: 50 (average). Sponsor provides chairs, display panels, electricity for demonstrations, fencing, table and 24-hour security. Navajo tribe handles sales; Financial Services Department handles taxes.
Awards: Presents $25 in cash prizes; unlimited purchase prizes; ribbons; plaques; and trophys.

*SCOTTSDALE ARTS FESTIVAL, Scottsdale Center for the Arts, 7383 Scottsdale Mall, Scottsdale AZ 85251. (602)994-2301. Visual Arts Manager: John Armstrong. Purpose: "Total celebration of the arts. To give craftspeople a quality festival to display/sell through." Estab. 1969. Annual outdoor show held 2 days the last weekend of March. Average attendance: 60,000. Entries accepted until 4 weeks before show. Entry fee: $10/artist, and $100 booth rental fee after acceptance in show. Maximum 10 entries/craftworker. Prejudged by slides; no $10 fees refunded for refused work (booth rental due after prejudging). Work may be offered for sale; no commission. Craftworker must attend show. Registration limit: approximately 50. Sponsor provides chairs; display panels; and 24-hour security. Considers all crafts. Amount of cash awards varies depending upon the income from entry fees. Also grants some booth rental fee waivers. $59,000 in sales in 1979.

*TUCSON FESTIVAL ARTS & CRAFTS FAIR, 8 W. Paseo Redondo, Tucson AZ 85705. (602)622-6911. Executive Director: Jarvis Harriman. Sponsor: Tucson Festival Society, Inc. Estab. 1951. Annual outdoor show held 3 days in April. Average attendance: 50,000. Considers all professional crafts; "no 'home crafts.'"
Terms: Entries accepted until about 8 weeks before show. Entry fee: $65/8x8x8 display area. Prejudging by slides and/or photos; entry fee refunded for refused work. Work must be offered for sale; no commission. Craftworker must attend show; demonstrations OK. Registration limit: 100+. Sponsor provides electricity for demonstrations and security after fair is closed.
Awards: Best of Show pieces will be selected by a juror of regional reputation. Prizes are awarded for attractive booth decoration."

TWO FLAGS FESTIVAL OUTDOOR SHOW, Box 256, Douglas AZ 85607. (602)364-5974. Contact: Chairman. Estab. 1971. Annual outdoor show held 2 days in May. Entries accepted until 2 weeks before show. "No booth fee charge." Work may be offered for sale; 20% commission. Craftworker must attend show; demonstrations OK. Sponsor provides limited electricity. Registration limit: 40-65. Considers all handicrafts. "Would like a resume and photo from each craftsman for publicity purposes."
Sales Tip: "We would rather see a number of inexpensive items offered to sell. Higher prices do not go over well. Average customer is retired and on Social Security; plus, being a border city, we have a numerous amount of the lower income Mexican families."

*WINSLOW I-40 EXPO, Box 641, Winslow AZ 86047. (602)289-4288. President: Mabel Nagel. Sponsor: Winslow Art Association, Inc. Annual indoor show held 2 weeks in August. Average attendance: 3,000.
Terms: Entries accepted until 4 days before show. Entry fee: $4/item. Prejudging. No entry fees refunded for refused work. Work may be offered for sale; 20% commission. Craftworker needn't attend show; demonstrations OK. Sponsor provides insurance on exhibited work, insurance on work shipped to artist, and 24-hour security. Treasurer handles sales and taxes.

WINTER ARTS & CRAFTS FAIR, 1204 W. Silverlake Rd., Tucson AZ 85713. Recreation Program Supervisor: Carolyn Lenz. Sponsor: Pima County Parks & Recreation. Purpose: "to give the artist the opportunity to sell his work. This is a selling show, not an exhibit show." Estab. 1972. Annual outdoor show held 1 day in March. Attendance: 750-1,000. Entries accepted until show date. Entry fee: $4/artist. Display area: 8x8. Work must be offered for sale; no commission. Craftworker must attend show; demonstrations OK. Sponsor provides electricity for demonstrations. Show is advertised by radio; posters; newspapers; and TV. Considers all crafts made by the exhibitor. "Artist must provide all of his own presentation equipment, supplies and materials. Work ranging up to $100 sells best."

Arkansas

*ARKANSAS ARTS, CRAFTS & DESIGN FAIR, Brady Station Box 5638, Little Rock AR 72215. (501)374-7111. Coordinator: Brenda Fox Wilson. Sponsor: Little Rock Montessori Society. Estab. 1973. Annual indoor show held the 2nd weekend in November. Average attendance: 12,000. Considers all crafts.
Terms: Entries accepted until approximately 7 months before show. Entry fee: $12/artist; $60-100/8x8 minimum display area. Maximum 3 items/category; 9 total/craftworker. Prejudging by 35mm slides. No entry fees refunded for refused work. Work may be offered for sale; no commission. Craftworker must attend show; demonstrations OK. Registration limit: 200. Sponsor provides display panels, electricity for demonstrations, table and 24-hour security.
Awards: Presents $3,000 in cash prizes and $750 in purchase awards. "An out-of-state juror always selects the awards."

ARKANSAS RIVER VALLEY ARTS & CRAFTS FAIR & SALE, Box 1122, Russellville AR 72801. (501)968-5418. Corresponding Secretary: Rita Johnston. Estab. 1970. Annual indoor show held 3 days in October or November. Average attendance: 50,000. Considers all handmade or hand decorated crafts.
Terms: Entries accepted until filled (usually in June); space granted in order of application. Entry fee: $20/6x8 or 12x4 display area. Work must be offered for sale; no commission. Craftworker must attend show; demonstrations encouraged. Registration limit: 171. Sponsor

provides chairs, electricity for demonstrations and 24-hour security. Exhibitor handles sales and taxes.

BELLA VISTA ARTS & CRAFTS FESTIVAL, Bella Vista AR 72712. (501)855-3061. Festival Director: Pam Collins. Sponsor: Village Art Club. Estab. 1968. Annual outdoor show (with 3 large tents) held 3 days in October at Blowing Springs, Arkansas. Average attendance: 150,000. Considers all crafts made by exhibitor. 1978 sales grossed $77,200.
Terms: Entries accepted until 5 months before show for tent spaces. Entry fee: $15/6x10 display area inside tent, or $15/12x12 display area outside tent. Prejudging by b&w photos. Entry fee refunded for refused work. Work must be offered for sale; 10% commission. Craftworker must attend show; demonstrations OK. Sponsor provides electricity for demonstrations, fencing in tents and 24-hour security.
Promotion: Show is advertised in newspapers, magazines, radio and TV. "Send b&w photo of yourself doing your craft, and a story about yourself and your craft to the above address."

*****DELTA ART EXHIBITION**, MacArthur Park, Box 2137, Little Rock AR 72203. (501)372-4000. Director: Townsend Wolfe. Sponsor: The Arkansas Arts Center. Estab. 1958. Annual indoor show held 4 weeks in the fall. Average attendance: 13,000. 1978 sales totaled $1,600.
Acceptable Work: Considers sculpture and soft sculpture. Maximum weight: 500 lbs. Categories include paintings and sculpture.
Terms: Entries accepted until 3 weeks before show. Entry fee: $5/entry. Display area: 300 running feet. Maximum 2 entries/artist. Prejudging by slides. No entry fees refunded for refused work. Work may be offered for sale; 10% commission. Craftworker needn't attend show; no demonstrations. Registration limit: 60-80. Sponsor provides insurance on exhibited work, shipping costs to artist from show and 24-hour security. Exhibitions Department handles sales; no taxes.
Awards: Presents a $1,000 Grand Award, an additional $3,000 for purchase awards, and honorable mentions.

FUN FESTIVAL, Box 1500, Hot Springs AR 71901. (501)321-1700. Director of Special Events: Ike Isenhower. Sponsor: Hot Springs Chamber of Commerce. Purpose: "to promote Hot Springs." Estab. 1971. Annual outdoor show (with large tents provided with electricity) held 10 days in June. Average attendance: 50,000. Entries accepted until show. Entry fee: $100/artist. Display area: 12x6. Prejudging by slide or photo. Work may be offered for sale; no commission. Craftworker must attend show; demonstrations required. Registration limit: 40. Sponsor provides chairs; electricity for demonstrations; fencing; tables; and a "security guard from closing time till opening time." Show is advertised by "radio, TV, nationwide advertising, 100,000 books mailed throughout the year, and about 100,000 flyers." Considers all crafts.

GRAND PRAIRIE FESTIVAL OF ARTS, Box 65, Stuttgart AR 72160. Annual show usually held in September. Categories include art, crafts, hobbies, music, prose and poetry. Write for specifics.

HOSPITALITY HOUSE ARTS & CRAFTS FAIR, Box 488, Magnolia AR 71753. (501)234-5540. Director: Mildred J. Holmes. Estab. 1974. Annual indoor show with covered breezeways and porches held 2 days in October. Attendance: "in excess of 2,000." Considers all crafts.
Terms: Entries accepted until filled. No entry fee. Display area: 6x6 or 8x8 inside; varies outside. Work must be offered for sale; no commission. Craftworker must attend show; demonstrations OK. Inside registration limit: 45. Sponsor provides chairs, electricity for demonstrations, table and 24-hour security.
Promotion: Show is advertised in *Southern Living* magazine, *Decorating Arts & Crafts*, in newspapers in a 4-state area, by radio and TV and posters.
Sales Tip: "The buying public in this area seems to be more interested in purchasing a large amount of small inexpensive articles rather than a few large expensive items. Most of our exhibitors return each year—this indicates satisfaction with their sales."

HOT SPRING COUNTY ART & CRAFT SHOW & SALE, Extension Office Courthouse, Malvern AR 72104. (501)332-2661. Extension Agent: Mary Ellen Williams. Sponsor: Hot Spring County Extension Council. Estab. 1971. Annual indoor/outdoor show held 3 days in spring. Average attendance: 8,000.
Acceptable Work: Considers all crafts. No machine-made products. "Wooden items are always a good seller. We could use a good candlemaker."

Terms: Entries accepted until show. "The inside spots are sold first. Some people set up outside at half price with their campers. Entry fee: $10/10x6 display area. Work may be offered for sale; no commission. Craftworkers must attend show; demonstrations OK. Sponsor provides chairs, electricity for demonstrations and 24-hour security.
Promotion: Show is advertised by TV, radio, newspapers, flyers (to all counties and newspapers in home towns of craftsmen), and posters (in stores and cafes). Craftworker provides his own display signs including the name of craft, booth, etc.
Profile: "Our show takes place during the race meet at Oaklawn in Hot Springs, 23 miles away."

HOT SPRINGS ARTS & CRAFTS SHOW, c/o Extension Homemaker's Council, Courthouse, Hot Springs AR 71901. Publicity Chairman: Mrs. Billee Staples. Economist, Advisor: Susan Neeper. Estab. 1968. Annual indoor/outdoor shop held 2½ days during the first weekend in October. Average attendance:: 50,000. "This has been increasing every year. Traffic count for 1978 indicated shoppers from 23 states and Canada."
Acceptable Work: Considers all crafts. "The entry must be handcrafted and entered by the person who made it. Entry must not spill over outside of booths. No nails or other fasteners can be driven into the walls of the buildings. Exhibits should not be hung above the side of the partition."
Terms: Entries accepted until 4 weeks before show. Entry fee: $15/8x8 display area; $30/16x8 display area; or $15/camper space. Prejudging by sample, photo and full written descriptions. Entry fee due after prejudging. Work must be offered for sale; no commission. Craftworker must attend show; demonstrations OK. Registration limit: 250. Sponsor provide electricity for demonstrations, fencing, booths, and 24-hour security.
Promotion: Show is advertised by newspaper, radio, TV, word-of-mouth, craft magazines and *Southern Living Magazine*. Craftworker should provide identification signs (white signs with black print, size 6"x22").

***MAGNOLIA SIDEWALK ARTS FESTIVAL**, Box 854. Magnolia AR 71753. (501)234-5601. Chairman: Mrs. R.W. Ezelle. Sponsor: Sorosis Club Magnolia, Columbia Chamber of Commerce, Magnolia Arts Council, Arkansas State Arts and Humanities. Estab. 1950. Annual outdoor show held 1 day in May at Downtown Square. Average attendance: several hundred. Considers all crafts.
Terms: Entries accepted until show date. Entry fee: $6/10 items (adult); $3/10 items (children). Work may be offered for sale; no commission. Craftworker must attend show; demonstrations OK. Sponsor provides display panels, electricity for demonstrations and coverings in the case of rain. Craftworker handles sales and taxes.
Awards: Presents cash awards and ribbons for 1st, 2nd and 3rd places in each category.
Promotion: Show is advertised by newspapers, its reputation and letters to past participating artists. "Craftworker may furnish resume to give to the daily newspapers."

NEWTON COUNTY ARTS & CRAFTS SHOW, Box 58, Jasper AR 72641. (501)446-5692. Secretary: Ina Henderson. Semiannual indoor show held 3 days in April and 3 days in October. Entries accepted until 1 week before show. Entry fee: $10/6x8 display area. Work may be offered for sale; no commission. Craftworkers must attend show; demonstrations OK. Sponsor provides electricity for demonstrations and 24-hour security. Considers all crafts.

OKTOBERFEST, Box 1500, Hot Springs AR 71901. (501)321-1700. Director of Special Events: Ike Isenhower. Sponsor: Hot Springs Chamber of Commerce. Estab. 1975. Annual indoor show held 4 days in October. Average attendance: 27,000. Entries accepted until show date. Entry fee: $75/display area. Prejudging by slides or photos; entry fee refunded for refused work. Work must be offered for sale; no commission. Craftworker must attend show; demonstrations OK. Registration limit: 40. Sponsor provides chairs; tables; and "guard on duty on off hours." Show is advertised on radio, TV, by nationwide advertising, 100,000 books mailed throughout the year, and about 100,000 flyers. Considers all crafts.
Sales Tip: "The better types of crafts sell here. For instance, the person who does ceramics for the Fun Festival (see above) will generally bring their porcelain to this show."

OLD FASHIONED DAY ARTS & CRAFTS FAIR, 915 E. Sevier, Benton AR 72015. (501)776-0255; 776-0449. Director: Mrs. Willard Red. Sponsor: Saline County Council on Aging. Estab. 1974. Annual indoor/outdoor show held 1 day in October. Average attendance: 7,500. Considers all crafts.
Terms: Entries accepted until show date. Entry fee: $10-20/10x10 display area. Entry fee

refunded for refused work. Work may be offered for sale; no commission but donation will be accepted. Craftworker or representative must attend show; demonstrations OK. Registration limit: 135. Sponsor provides chairs and table for inside booths and electricity for demonstrations. Exhibitor handles sales and taxes.
Sales Tip: "Have exhibit clean and attractively displayed. All types of craftwork sell well."
Profile: "Our purpose is to raise local funds which can be matched by the government on a 3:1 basis to establish a Senior Adult Center for Saline County. There's food, country music, square dancing, beard growing contests, old-fashion dress revue, a horseshoe pitching tournament, and an auction of items donated by local merchants and individuals. Hayrides, games and contests are provided for children."

OUACHITA COUNTY ARTS & CRAFTS FAIR, Box 576, Camden AR 71701. (501)836-6858. CEA Staff Chairman: Mrs. Gladys Lindsey. Sponsor: Ouachita County Extension Homemaker's Council and the City of Camden. Estab. 1969. Annual indoor show held 2 days in November. Average attendance: 2,000. Considers "all handmade arts and crafts." Show is advertised by newspaper, radio, TV, posters and direct mail. 1978 sales totaled $1,296.55.
Terms: Entries accepted until 1 week before show. Entry fee: $5/5x10 display area. Work must be offered for sale; 10% commission. Craftworker must attend show; demonstrations encouraged. Registration limit: 75. Sponsor provides display panels and electricity for demonstrations.

OZARKS ARTS & CRAFTS FAIR, Rt. 1, Hindsville AR 72738. Executive Director: Blanche H. Elliott. Purpose: "to bring recognition to Ozark artists and craftsmen who work with their hands in preserving the cultural heritage of the Ozark regions." Estab. 1954. Annual indoor show (with some 60x180' tents) held 3 days in October at War Eagle, Arkansas. Average attendance: 100,000. Considers all crafts native to the Ozarks; no plastics or supplies of any kind. Presents award plaques for 10 most attractively displayed booths.
Terms: Entries accepted until show date. Entry fee: $10/6x8 display area; $20/12x8 display area. Prejudging by slides, photos and actual samples; entry fee due after prejudging. SASE. Work may be offered for sale; 10% commission. Craftworker must attend show; no demonstrations. Registration limit: 300 craftpersons who are Ozark residents of the 4-state Ozark region (Arkansas, Missouri, Kansas, Oklahoma). Sponsor provides tables and 24-hour security.

OZARK FOOTHILLS CRAFT GUILD SPRING SHOW & SALE, Box 140, Mountain View AR 72560. (501)269-3896. Director: James H. Sanders III. Sponsor: Ozark Foothills Craft Guild. Estab. 1962. Annual indoor/outdoor show (with roofed but sideless booths) held 3 days the 3rd weekend of April. Average attendance: 10,000-15,000.
Acceptable Work: Considers all crafts, except anything made out of synthetic materials or plastic (including vinyl, styrofoam, plywood). Maximum size: 11x8. "Eyes of fabric dolls or animal toys should be embroidered or sewn. No button eyes. If presenting fiber items, fiber content should be listed on the application form."
Terms: Entries accepted until 2 weeks before show. "There are exceptions made if that given area is not well covered (in terms of techniques or media)." Entry fee: $10/6x10 display area for Guild member; $15/6x10 display area for non-member. Exhibitors limited to sell from only 2 craft categories. Prejudging by "slides, and upon acceptance—once booth is set up—standards committee reviews all work relative to slides sent for prejudging. Work must maintain same standards as in slides." Entry fee not refunded for refused work. Work may be offered for sale; 10% commission. Craftworker must attend show; demonstrations encouraged. Registration limit: 100-125. Sponsor provides coverings, display panels, fencing around grounds, tables and 24-hour protection.
Promotion: Show is advertised by "TV (3 stations, 30 second spots for a week prior); radio (most stations throughout state); public service announcements; news releases in every news publication in the 5-state area; several nationally-distributed magazines (under travel and fairs); 30,000 brochures; and craft publications. Photos and material for publicity purposes (small autobiographical/aesthetic statement by craftworker for use in news releases) are requested on the application form."
Sales Tip: "Correct attitude toward the customers is most critical. A self-sufficient craftsperson with a good display, good atitude and good prices is always a best seller. Demonstrations assist sales and overall 19th century atmosphere. Items under $10 retail sell fastest, but good sales in all media. Total exhibitor sales average: $30,000."

OZARK FRONTIER TRAIL FESTIVAL & CRAFT SHOW, Box 140, Mountain View AR

72560. (501)269-3896. Director: James Sanders. Sponsor: Ozark Foothills Craft Guild. "This is a chance to expose the public at large to the finest examples of crafts produced in the Ozarks region. All income (net) is used to promote the objectives of the Guild (a nonprofit organization)." Estab. 1962. Annual indoor show (tent and 2 buildings—outside only on request) held for 3 days the 2nd full weekend in October at Heber Spings, Arkansas. Average attendance: 15,000.
Acceptable Work: Considers all crafts except anything made out of synthetic materials or plastic (including vinyl, styrofoam, plywood). Maximum size: 10x6. "Eyes of fabric dolls or animal toys should be embroidered or sewn, no buttons. If presenting fiber items, fiber content should be listed on the application form."
Terms: Entries accepted until 2 weeks before show. "Exceptions are made to time restriction if the craft area in question is needed." Entry fee: $10/Guild member; $20/nonmember. Display area: 6x10. Prejudging by "slides, and upon acceptance — once booth is set up — standards committee reviews all work relative to slides sent for prejudging. Work must maintain same standards as in slides." No entry fees refunded for refused work. Work may be offered for sale; 10% commission. Craftworker must attend show; demonstrations encouraged. Registration limit: 100-125. Sponsor provides some coverings; electricity for a fee; display panels; tables; and 24-hour protection.
Sales Tip: "Correct attitude toward the customers is most critical. A self-sufficient craftsperson with a good display, good atitude and good prices is always a bestseller. Demonstrations assist sales and overall 19th century atmosphere. Items under $10 retail sell fastest, but good sales in all media. Total exhibitor sales average: $50,000."
Promotion: Show is advertised by "TV (3 stations, 30 second spots for a week prior); radio (most stations throughout state); public service announcements; news releases in every news publication in the 5-state area; several nationally-distributed magazines (under travel and fairs); 30,000 brochures; and craft publications. Photos and material for publicity purposes (small autobiographical/aesthetic statement by craftworker for use in news releases) are requested on the application form."

PIONEER CRAFT FESTIVAL, Box 426, Rison AR 71665. (501)325-6536. Chairman: Mrs. James L. Moore Jr. Sponsor: Cleveland County Historical Society. Purpose: "to endow our museum and Pioneer Village Restoration Fund." Estab. 1971. Annual indoor show held 2 days the 3rd weekend in March. Average attendance: 10,000.
Acceptable Work: Considers all crafts "handmade from natural materials (no plastics, etc.). Purse kits are the only kits allowed."
Terms: Entries accepted until 4 weeks before show ("waiting list exhibitors will be called if there is a last-minute cancellation"). Entry fee: $5/5x6 single booth; $10/5x12 double booth; $15/8x15 triple booth. Prejudging of new exhibitors by photos or slides. Work may be offered for sale; 10% commission. Craftworker must attend show; demonstrations OK. Registration limit: 90-100. Sponsor provides electricity for exhibitors; tables; 24-hour security; and "3 locked steel buildings."
Sales Tip: "The pioneer crafts are selling best today—baskets, dolls, wood, anything unusual and different. Ceramics and macrame seem to be on the decline. Lapidary is also declining in our area. Handpainted china items sell well."
Promotion: Show is advertised by the Arkansas State Parks & Tourism Department in national papers, the *Ozark Mountaineer*, by posters in local cities, and in the calendar of events in national publications.

*****PRINTS, DRAWINGS & CRAFTS EXHIBITION**, MacArthur Park, Box 2137, Little Rock AR 72203. (501)372-4000. Director: Townsend Wolfe. Sponsor: The Arkansas Arts Center. Estab. 1968. Annual indoor juried show held for 4 weeks in the spring. Average attendance: 12,000. 1977 exhibitor sales totaled approximately $200.
Terms: Entries accepted until 3 weeks before show. Entry fee: $5 handling fee/exhibitor. Display area: approximately 300 running feet. Maximum 2 entries/entry. Work may be offered for sale; 10% commission. Craftworker needn't attend show; no demonstrations. Registration limit: 100. Sponsor provides insurance on exhibited work; shipping costs to craftworker from show; and 24-hour security.
Acceptable Work: Considers batik; candlemaking; ceramics; dollmaking; glass art; jewelry; lapidary; leatherworking; macrame; metalsmithing; mobiles; needlecrafts; pottery; soft sculpture; weaving; and woodcrafting. Categories include prints (in all media); photography (in

---

* Those listings preceded by an asterisk present awards for prize-winning crafts.

color and/or monochrome); drawings and crafts (metal, clay, textile, glass, wood, plastics and combined media).
Awards: Presents $200 awards in crafts, textiles, jewelry, ceramics, prints, drawings and photography categories. In addition, up to $2,000 in purchase awards is given.

SALINE COUNTY CRAFT FAIR, 511 Marion Ave, Benton AR 72015. (501)778-4436. Chairpersons: Beverly Bowers (address given), Eva Lee Howard (phone given). Sponsor: Saline County Fair Board. Estab. 1973. Annual indoor/outdoor show held 2 days in spring or early summer. Average attendance: 6,000. Considers all handmade crafts.
Terms: Entries accepted until show date. Entry fee: $15/8x10 display area. Work may be offered for sale; no commission. Craftworker or representative must attend show; demonstrations OK. Sponsor provides 24-hour security.

*****SUGGIN FOLKLIFE ART SHOW**, c/o Mildred Gregory, 324 Walnut St., Newport AR 72112. (501)523-6250. Sponsor: Suggin Folklife Society. Estab. 1972. Annual indoor show held 2 weeks in the spring. Average attendance: 500. Considers small sculpture.
Terms: Entries accepted until show date. Entry fee: $1-5/item being displayed. Maximum 2 entries/category; 6 total. Work may be offered for sale; no commission. Artist needn't attend show; no demonstrations. Show is advertised by newspaper and radio.
Awards: Presents purchase prizes of $50 and up; and 1st, 2nd and 3rd honorable mention ribbons. "Pick out best work and enter. Study works of the winners for future reference."

*****TOYS DESIGNED BY ARTISTS EXHIBITION**, MacArthur Park, Box 2137, Little Rock AR 72203. Director: Townsend Wolfe. Sponsor: The Arkansas Arts Center. Estab. 1973. Annual indoor juried show held 4-8 weeks in the December. Average attendance: 15,000-25,000.
Terms: Entries accepted until 3 weeks before show. Handling fee: $5/entry. Maximum 3 entries/artist. Work may be offered for sale; 10% commission. Craftworker needn't attend show; no demonstrations. Registration limit: about 60. Sponsor provides display panels; insurance on exhibited work; shipping costs to artists from show; and 24-hour security.
Acceptable Work: Considers all crafts. "Entries must be original and completed one year prior to the show. Entries are the artists' conception of a toy—not necessarily a functional toy for children to play with. Directions or diagrams on use of the toy must accompany entry where necessary."
Awards: Presents $1,000 in purchase awards. "The purchase award is the price of the object less 10%. All purchase awards become the property of the AAC for its permanent collection."
Sales: "Sales are handled by the Exhibitions Department of The Arkansas Arts Center. The AAC is a nonprofit organization and no sales taxes are charged. Sales from the 1978 show amounted to about $800."
Profile: "This unique exhibition, open to all artists in the United States, gives the artists a chance to bring together creative and original ideas, and the materials used to give form to those ideas. Childlike innovation and imagination is joined with a sophisticated treatment of color, shape, texture and line to create toys."

California

*****ALAMEDA COUNTY FAIR**, Box 579, Pleasanton CA 94566. (415)846-2881. Manager: Lee R. Hall. Assistant Manager: Peter Bailey. Estab. 1907. Annual outdoor art show (in shaded area) held 15 days in the summer. Average attendance: 400,000. Considers sculpture up to 52x52". Awards $55-100 for 1st-3rd places.
Terms: Entries accepted until 3 weeks before show. Entry fee: $2/item being displayed in competition; prejudging of actual work; no entry fees refunded for refused work. Work may be offered for sale; 10% commission. Craftworker needn't attend; demonstrations OK. Registration limit: 100. Sponsor provides electricity for demonstrations and 24-hour security.

*****AMATEUR STAINED GLASS COMPETITION**, 1906 Broadway, Alameda CA 94501. (415)522-6157. Contact: Clarine Souza. Sponsor: The Glass Factory. Estab. 1975. Annual indoor show held one month in October at Alameda. Average attendance: over 4,000.
Terms: Entries accepted until 1 week before show. Entry fee: $7.50/entry, set, pair or unit. Displayed in 3 rooms at restaurant and glass studio. Work may be offered for sale; 20% commission. Books may be exhibited. Craftworker needn't attend show; no demonstrations. Sponsor handles sales and sales tax; provides chairs, tables and 24-hour security protection.
Acceptable Work: Considers stained glass art only. No kits. "Items useful in home or business do best (i.e. lamps, windows). All entries must be properly framed so they can be hung for display. Craftworker must provide stands for free forms and lamps; lamps must be completely wired, ready to light."

Awards: Presents merchandise orders for glass and equipment, $1,000 in awards and participation awards for all entrants.

ART IN THE PARK TRADE FAIR, c/o Mary Jo Vieira, 5843 N. Utah, Merced CA 95340. (209)723-9819 or 722-7769. (Or write c/o Shirley Row, 5142 N. Utah, Merced CA 95340). Sponsor: Merced River School Parents Club. Annual outdoor show held 1 day in May at Henderson Park, Snelling, California. Average attendance: 6,000. Considers all crafts. No flea market items or antiques. Entries accepted until spaces filled. Entry fee: $10. Registration limit: 100.

***THE ARTS GUILD WINTER FESTIVAL,** 20 Laurel Ave., Belevedere CA 94920. (415)435-5750. Coordinator: Martha Hannon. Sponsor: The Arts Guild (nonprofit artist's cooperative). Purpose: "to raise money to run our artists/craftsmen cooperative so all Bay Area (San Francisco) will have a place to exhibit and sell and rent their art. We are nonprofit— but funds go for maintenance, prizes, and annual scholarships for high school artists." Estab. 1976. Annual indoor show held the month of December in 3 large rooms in the The Arts Guild Gallery. Attendance: 400-500.
Acceptable Work: Considers "all Christmas gift items—toys, ornaments, pottery, paintings, sculpture, handmade clothing, fiberworks, furniture, baked Christmas foods, weaving and jewelry. All entries must be original—no copies, prints, etc." All work must be ready for presentation. Maximum size: 20x22.
Terms: Entries accepted the last 2 days of November. Entry fee: $2/artist. Maximum 20 small pieces; 5 large pieces/artist. Prejudging by The Arts Guild members (artists and craftworkers); no entry fees refunded for refused work. Work may be offered for sale; 30% commission. Craftworker needn't attend show; no demonstrations. Sponsor provides chairs; display panels; insurance on exhibited work; tables; and 24-hour security.
Promotion: "Extensive publicity is conducted through the use of newspapers; TV; radio; flyers; and invitations."
Awards: Presents cash prizes; ribbons; and merit awards. "Enter only top original work. Jurors are expert in their media."
Sales Tip: Viewing public buys "top quality items for gift-giving at reasonable prices. Most artists/craftsmen lower their prices for this Christmas show to help The Arts Guild." Coordinator handles sales and sales tax. $1,200 profit was made in recent show.

ARTS 'N CRAFTS BY THE SEA, Box 404, Hermosa Beach CA 90254. (213)376-0951. Executive Manager: Charles A. Pinney. Sponsor: Hermosa Beach Chamber of Commerce. Estab. 1969. Annual outdoor show held 3 days during Labor Day weekend. Average attendance: 100,000.
Acceptable Work: Considers all crafts. No "manufactured or machine-crafted items—except such manufactured items needed to complement craft (i.e., gnarled wood clocks, buckles for tooled leather belts, or stamped leather belts for handcrafted belt buckles). Desire 50% or better to be handcrafted."
Terms: Entries accepted until 2 weeks before show. Entry fee: $50 plus 10% gross sales/10x10 display area, depending upon location. Prejudging "by 3 photos, slides or submissions of actual samples of item (if small)." Entry fee refunded for refused work. Work may be offered for sale. Craftworker must attend show; demonstrations encouraged. Registration limit: 250. Sponsor provides electricity for demonstrations and water.
Sales Tip: "Demonstrate; have a friendly, positive attitude; exhibit quality products and craftsmanship; provide uniqueness or unusual crafts; and price fairly. Recommend conspicuous display of artist's name and mailing address for follow-up work on order."
Promotion: Show is advertised by advanced mailings of applications; newspapers; *Holiday Magazine*; *West Arts Magazine*; and flyers distributed at other shows. Promotional materials may be provided at the craftworker's discretion.

***BEVERLY HILLS "AFFAIRE IN THE GARDENS" ART SHOW,** 450 N. Crescent Dr., Beverly Hills CA 90210. (213)550-4864. Recreation Manager: Michelle Merrill. Sponsor: Beverly Hills Recreation and Parks Department. Estab. 1976. Semiannual outdoor show held 2 days in April and 2 days in October. Average attendance: 15,000.
Acceptable Work: Considers all crafts, except clothing. No kits or machine-made crafts. Categories include oil/acrylic; photography; sculpture; watercolor; jewelry; drawing; prints; graphics; ceramics; and others.
Terms: Entries accepted until 4 weeks before show. Entry fee: $50/9x12 display area, 7' height limitation. Prejudging by pamphlets, slides, photos and previous awards. Entry fee due after

prejudging. Work may be offered for sale; no commission. Craftworker needn't attend show; demonstrations encouraged. Registration limit: 200. Exhibitor handles sales.
Awards: Presents ribbons for Best of Show, 1st, 2nd, 3rd and honorable mentions. "An artist who is able to demonstrate his/her talent (displays, portfolio, awards) is at an advantage when being judged."
Promotion: Show is advertised by papers, magazines, TV, radio, flyers, posters and banners. "Each artist is requested to submit 1-4 b&w 8x10 or 5x7 glossy prints and a brief resume. These will be used for promotion in the various media. They prefer action shots of the artist at work or artistically photographed pieces of the work. These can be sent in with the application."

Good old-fashioned fun best describes the Old Fashioned Day Arts and Crafts Fair. Sponsored by the Saline County Council on Aging, the fair provides music, dancing, beard-growing contests, an old-fashioned dress revue, a horseshoe pitching tournament, and an auction of items donated by local merchants and individuals.

BUY ARTS FOR CHRISTMAS SHOW, 3425 7th St., Riverside CA 92501. (714)684-7111. Curator of Exhibits: Katrin Wiese. Sponsor: Riverside Art Center. Estab. 1970. Indoor show held 4 weeks in November/December at Riverside. Average attendance: 10,000.
Terms: Entries accepted 2 days only, 1 week before show. Entry fee: $4/nonmember; $3.50/senior citizen and student; and $3/Riverside Art Center member. Display area: 36'x36'. Prejudging by curator. Entry fee refunded for refused work. Work must be offered for sale; 33⅓% commission. Craftworker needn't attend show; no demonstrations. Registration limit: 45. Sponsor provides display panels and 24-hour security protection.
Acceptable Work: Considers batik, ceramics, dollmaking, glass art, jewelry, lapidary, metalsmithing, mobiles, pottery, sculpture, soft sculpture and weavings. No kits or bazaar items. Maximum size: 24"x30". Framed works must have screw eyes and wire. Portfolio pieces must be matted, with some form of protection covering each piece. "Artists needing cases to protect small and/or fragile pieces or jewelry should provide their own. Reasonable, gift-type items do best (weaving, batik pillows, handcrafted lamps, ceramics and jewelry). Ceiling price: $70."

CALICO ART FESTIVAL, 8813 Excelsior Ave., Hanford CA 93230. (209)584-5884. Show Chairman/Coordinator: Willie Camara. Sponsor: Kings River Parent-Teachers Club. Estab. 1975. Annual outdoor show held 1 day in October. Average attendance: 2,000. "We will accept

any good craft, also fine arts. We are striving for a top show—with our craftspeople going away with a profit. We want people who do top work and don't mind day outdoor shows. Some of our locations are sunny—artists are responsible for their own set ups and umbrellas if needed."
Promotion: "We really promote this show and our theme is always Calico Art Festival. We are a well-known group in our area. We put ads in local papers and we get much free publicity since we are a nonprofit school organization—on radio and local TV stations. Lots of posters! If we get local extra newspaper coverage, we enjoy featuring an artist or 2; and therefore would need to have some good, interesting glossy b&w photos that could be used in a newspaper article."
Profile: "Our show is held out in the country—away from the bustle of town—pleasant and relaxing day. Many people from throughout the area are doing their Christmas shopping at this show. Also we try to make our artists and craftspeople at home with a free meal plus coffee at set-up time. We make our profit largely from the barbeque and bingo games."

CALIFORNIA CRAFTS, Crocker Art Museum, 216 O St., Sacramento CA 95814. (916)446-4677. Sponsor: Creative Arts League of Sacramento. Biennial crafts exhibition.

THE CALIFORNIA CRAFTSMAN, 559 Pacific St., Monterey CA 93940. Director: June Braucht. Sponsor: Monterey Peninsula Museum of Art. Purpose: "it's our way of having a high quality crafts exhibition for the area." Estab. 1976. Biennial indoor show held the month of October during even-numbered years. Average attendance: 2,500.
Acceptable Work: Considers ceramics; glass art; jewelry; leatherworking; macrame; metalsmithing; pottery; textile arts; and woodcrafting. Works "must be easily manageable by 2 people.
Terms: Entry fee: $5/craftworker. Maximum 3 entries/craftworker. Prejudging by slides in August; no entry fees refunded. Work may be offered for sale; 20% commission. Craftworker needn't attend show; no demonstrations. Sponsor provides insurance on exhibited work; handles all sales; and the exhibition is installed by the museum.
Awards: Awards "to be determined by the entry fees received. Judging will be done for creativity and craftsmanship."
Promotion: Show is advertised in *Craft Horizons, Artweek, Westart*, and by direct mail. "If work is accepted he (the craftworker) should provide an 8x10 glossy photograph for possible use in the catalog."

CALIFORNIA 3-DIMENSIONAL REGIONAL EXHIBIT & COMPETITION, 482 S. 2nd St., San Jose CA 95113. (408)294-4545. Business Director: Dr. Delmar Kolb. Exhibit Director: Kathleen Barrett. Sponsor: San Jose Art League. Purpose: "a recognition of the validity of the artist's creativity and acquired skills." Estab. 1970. Annual indoor show held 1 month late November-early December. Average attendance: 500/month. Presents cash awards totaling $1,000.
Acceptable Work: Considers ceramics; glass art; jewelry; macrame; metalsmithing; mobiles; pottery; sculpture; soft sculpture; weaving; and woodcrafting.
Terms: Entries accepted until 2-3 weeks before show. Entry fee: $3/item. Display area: 1,200 square feet. Prejudging by actual work; entry fee not refunded. Work may be offered for sale; 25% commission. Craftworker needn't attend show; no demonstrations. Sponsor provides display panels and 24-hour security.
Promotion: Show is advertised by *Artweek, Westart*, major California newspapers; *Ceramics Monthly*; and mailings.

CAPITAL WOODCARVERS ASSOCIATION SHOW, 7836 Vista Ridge, Citurs Heights CA 95610. (916)723-1183. Vice President: Jack Harris. Purpose: "to promote woodcarvers club and art of woodcraft." Estab. 1972. Annual indoor show held the second weekend in November. Attendance: 8,000-10,000. Entries accepted until show date. Entry fee: $5/artist, display only; $20 for sales. Display area: 4x8. Maximum 1 entry/category. Work may be offered for sale; 10% commission. Craftworker must attend show; demonstrations OK. Registration limit: 60. Chairs and tables can be rented if sponsor is given 2 weeks notice. Categories: woodcrafting; painted work; carving in the round; decorative carving; whittling; and ornamental and special. Presents ribbon awards and ribbons to all participants and class winners.
Promotion: Show is advertised on local TV; in 2 daily newspapers; and in regional shopping news publication. Craftworker should supply b&w photos, "plus business cards are optional."

CELEBRATION OF THE ARTS, 20600 Roscoe Blvd., Canoga Park CA 91306. (213)341-6434. Contact: Chairman. Sponsor: St. John's in the Valley United Methodist Church. Estab. 1970. Annual indoor/outdoor show held 2 days in May. Average attendance: 2,000. Entries accepted until 1 week before show. Entry fee: $10/10x12 display area. Awards $75 best of show and 1st, 2nd and 3rd place ribbons. Work may be offered for sale; 10% commission. Craftworker must attend show; demonstrations encouraged. Registration limit: 120. Considers all crafts. Needlework must be framed.

CHRISTMAS ART & CRAFT SALE, 234 5th St., Davis CA 95616. (916)756-4100. Director: Marian Hamilton. Sponsor: Davis Art Center. Purpose: "fundraiser for art center." Estab. 1965. Annual indoor show held 3 weeks in December. Average attendance: 2,500. Entries accepted until 4 weeks before show. No entry fee. Prejudging by slides or actual work. Work must be offered for sale; 30% commission. Craftworker needn't attend show; no demonstrations. Registration limit: 100. Sponsor provides setup and sales personnel. Show is advertised by newspapers; radio; and flyers. Considers all crafts except decoupage. "All work must be ready for display." 1978 show sales totaled $17,500.

DOWN TOWN FULTON SHOW, Art Enterprise, Box 231, Rackerby CA 95972. Contact: M.P. Schiedeck. Sponsor: Down Town Association of Fresno. Estab. 1972. Biennial outdoor show held 4 days in May and 5 days in September at Fresno, California. Considers all crafts.
Terms: Entries accepted until show date. Entry fee: $25/artist. Prejudging by slides/photos. Entry fee refunded for refused work. Work must be offered for sale; 10% commission. Craftworker must attend show; demonstrations OK. Registration limit: 100. Sponsor provides electricity for demonstrations.

DOWN TOWN NOVATO CENTER, Art Enterprise, Box 231, Rackerby CA 95972. Contact: M.P. Schiedeck. Sponsor: Merchandising Association. Estab. 1973. Outdoor show (with some overhangs) held 4 days in spring, summer and fall at Novato, California. Considers all crafts except textiles.
Terms: Entries accepted until show date. Entry fee: $25/artist. Prejudging by slides/photos; entry fee refunded for refused work. Work must be offered for sale; 10% commission. Craftworker must attend show; demonstrations OK.

***FESTIVAL OF ARTS & CRAFTS**, 11740 E. Telegraph Rd., Santa Fe Springs CA 90670. (213)864-7511. Assistant Supervisor of Recreation: Jamie Herbon. Sponsor: City of Santa Fe Springs Parks & Recreation Department. Purpose is "to give local artists and residents an opportunity to view, buy and sell artwork." Estab. 1959. Annual indoor/outdoor show held 2 days in July. Average attendance: 800. Presents best of show plaque.
Acceptable Work: In crafts division considers batik; ceramics; glass art; jewelry; lapidary; leatherworking; macrame; metalsmithing; needlecrafts; pottery; weaving; and woodcrafting. In general crafts division considers candlemaking; decoupage; dollmaking; and tole painting. In arts division considers sculpture. "Entries may not exceed weight that can be lifted by one man. Entries that are wet, unfinished, damaged, poorly framed, or not matted are unacceptable. Entries not in one piece, requiring special handling, lighting or installation are subject to committee approval." Maximum size: 5x5.
Terms: Entries accepted until first week in July for juried art; beginning of June through the first week in July for art and craft sales application. No entry fee. Display area: for sales approximately 6x6. Maximum 3 juried entries/category; only 1 category may be entered. Prejudging ("arts and crafts amateurs and professionals are judged the morning before the show opens"). Work may be offered for sale; no commission. Juried craftworkers needn't attend show. Sponsor provides chairs; table; and 24-hour security.
Promotion: Show is advertised by press releases; brochures to local schools, arts and crafts suppliers and display shops; signs and posters; and announcements on the radio and in magazines.
Sales Tip: "Have some lower-priced items." Ceramics, jewelry, novelties and paintings sell well.

FESTIVAL OF THE ARTS, Sacramento Regional Arts Council, 562A Downtown Plaza, Sacramento CA 95814. Chairman: Albert Hellenthal. Annual open-air mall show held 2 days the last weekend in September. Entry fee: $15/5x10 display area. No commission. Craftworker or representative must be present at exhibit at all times. Considers original work only. No size limit.

***FIBER SHOW**, 20 Laurel Ave., Belevedere CA 94920. (415)383-5750. Chairman: Giselle Kappus. Sponsor: Mill Valley Arts Guild. Purpose: "to give the artist a chance and place to exhibit his original work (also to sell and/or rent), but no high pressure salesmanship. The Arts

Guild is nonprofit." Estab. 1976. Annual indoor show held 3 weeks in June. Attendance: 500-700.
Terms: Entries accepted until 1 week before show. Entry fee: $6/artist. Maximum 3 entries/artist. Prejudging of original work by 3-person jury (artists-teachers); no entry fees refunded for refused work. Work may be offered for sale; 30% commission. Craftworker needn't attend show; no demonstrations. Sponsor provides coverings; display panels; insurance on exhibited work; tables; and 24-hour security.
Promotion: Show is advertised by newspaper releases; mailed and hand-delivered invitations and flyers; posters; and paid ads. Categories include weavings; clothing; and fiber. Considers all crafts except tole painting; candlemaking; decoupage; dollmaking; and glass art. Presents $200 in cash prizes; $200 in purchase prizes; and merit award ribbons.

FIESTA DE LAS ARTES, Box 404, Hermosa Beach CA 90254. (213)376-0951. Executive Manager: Charles A. Pinney. Sponsor: Hermosa Beach Chamber of Commerce. Estab. 1969. Annual outdoor show held 3 days during Memorial Day weekend. Average attendance: 50,000.
Acceptable Work: "Craft applicants must be artisans creating quality, original work in any medium. Fiesta de las Artes is not open to manufacturers and no manufactured items may be sold. No copies of commercially produced artwork or imported items will be accepted."
Terms: Entries accepted until 1 week before show. Entry fee: $50 plus 10% gross sales. Display area: 10x10. Prejudging by 3 photos, slides, or submission of actual sample (if small). Entry fee refunded for refused work. Work may be offered for sale. Craftworker or representative must attend show; demonstrations encouraged. Registration limit: 350. Sponsor provides electricity for demonstrations. Artisan must have California Resale Card.
Sales Tip: "Demonstrate; have a friendly, positive attitude; exhibit quality products and craftsmanship; provide uniqueness or unusual crafts; and price fairly." Recommend conspicuous display of artist's name and mailing address for follow-up work on order."
Promotion: Show is advertised by advanced mailings of applications; newspapers; *Peninsula News*; *You Magazine*; radio broadcast from the show; street banner campaign; and flyers distributed at other shows. Promotional materials may be provided at the craftworker's discretion.

FIRST SUNDAY IN THE PARK, Box 99, Ventura CA 93001. (805)648-7881. Contact Recreation Supervisor. Sponsor: City of San Buenaventura Park & Recreation Department. Estab. 1973. Outdoor show held in a park setting 1 Sunday during the months of February, March, April, May, June, August, September, November and December. Attendance: 2,500-5,000. Considers all crafts.
Terms: Entries due the Wednesday before the Sunday of the show. Entry fee: $15/10'x10' display area. "New entries must be prejudged before registration for the show is accepted. Review may be done by appointment at the recreation office or by special arrangements through photos." Work may be offered for sale; no commission. No registration limit. Exhibitor brochures available by writing sponsor.
Promotion: Show is advertised in local and adjoining county newspapers, radio, TV, posters and *West Arts Magazine*.

GIFT FESTIVAL, Box 848, Lodi CA 95240. (209)369-2771. Secretary/Manager: Graeme A. Stewart. Sponsor: Lodi Grape Festival & National Wine Show. Purpose: "to create interim use of the festival grounds, and provide the public with a fun and unique shopping atmosphere." Estab. 1977. Annual indoor show held 3 days in early December. Average attendance: 5,000. Contracts for booth space are on a first come, first serve basis. Entry fee: "average of $50 per 100 square feet." Work may be offered for sale; no commission. Craftworker must attend show; demonstrations encouraged. Registration limit: 80. Sponsor provides electricity for demonstrations; wooden booths; some table spaces; and 24-hour security. Show is advertised by radio and newspaper. Considers all handcrafted items. Awards $100 for Christmas tree decorating contest; and prizes to best decorated booth and exhibitor. "The public is looking for Christmas gifts that are unique and reasonably-priced. Sales can be improved by well-displayed merchandise."

***GOLDEN WEST CERAMIC SHOW**, 3433 Alma, Palo Alto CA 94306. (415)494-0666. President: Dixie Davison. Estab. 1971. Annual indoor show held 3 days in September at San Mateo, California. Average attendance: 5,000. Presents ribbons and trophies. Show is advertised by TV, radio and newspaper.
Acceptable Work: Considers ceramics, pottery and sculpture. "This is an all ceramic show. Everything must be made of clay."

Terms: Entries accepted until show date. Entry fee: $1. Entries prejudged only if too many applicants apply. Work may be offered for sale. Craftworker must attend show; demonstrations OK. Registration limit: 125. Sponsor provides chairs, coverings, electricity for demonstrations, table and 24-hour security protection.

HALF MOON BAY ART & PUMPKIN FESTIVAL, Box 274, Half Moon Bay CA 94019. (415)762-5202. Arts Chairman: Mary Bettencourt. Purpose is "to raise funds to beautify and improve this small coastal 'turn of the century' town. Proceeds purchased 16 old-fashioned street lights, Victorian benches, street trees and flowers." Estab. 1971. Annual outdoor show held 2 days in October. Average attendance: 150,000. Entries accepted until beginning of September. Entry fee: $75/10x10 display area. Prejudging by slides or photos sent with application (these will be returned). Entries also reviewed during the show. "Previous entrants with quality merchandise get preferential placement." Entry fee refunded for refused work. Work may be offered for sale; no commission. Craftworker must attend show; demonstrations OK. Limited to 200 booths per festival. Sponsor provides limited electricity for demonstrations. Considers all crafts. Presents ribbons, and prize for best pumpkin decorated in spirit of craft.
Promotion: Terry Limslew, Publicity office: (415)346-4446. Show is "heavily promoted by posters, radio, TV, newspaper publicity. Can sometimes use photos."

*****INK & CLAY**, c/o Art Department, California State Polytechnic University, 3801 Temple Ave., Pomona CA 91768. (714)598-4567. Chairman: Yoram Makow. Estab. 1972. Annual indoor show held the month of January. Average attendance: 100/day. Entries accepted until 3 weeks before show. Entry fee: $4/item being displayed. Total display area: 1,500 square feet. Prejudging. No entry fees refunded for refused work. Work may be offered for sale; 20% commission. Craftworker needn't attend show; no demonstrations. Sponsor provides insurance on exhibited work and on work shipped to artist; and 24-hour security. Categories: printmaking; ceramics. Considers ceramics weighing 300 lbs. or less. Awards $1,000 in purchase prizes.

JOHNNY APPLESEED DAY, Box 658, Paradise CA 95969. (916)877-9356. Contact: Executive Vice President. Sponsor: Chamber of Commerce. Renewed in 1977. Annual show held the first Saturday in October (commercial craftworkers, indoor; artists and hobbyist craftworkers, outdoors). Average attendance: 12,000. Entries accepted until 2 weeks before show. Entry fee: $20/8x8 display area for hobbyist craftworkers, $35/8x8 display area for commercial craftworkers. Work may be offered for sale; no commission. Artists charged a $5 hanging fee plus commission on sales. Demonstrations OK. Categories: artists (hangings only); craft items (non-commercial); and craft items (commercial). "Commercial or noncommercial determined by retail license held with State of California." Considers all crafts. Show is advertised by magazine; newspapers; radio; TV; posters; etc.

LAKE TAHOE ART & CRAFT FAIR, Box 7112, South Lake Tahoe CA 95731. Director: Wayne Denney. Sponsor: Artist Co-op. Purpose: "to promote artists." Estab. 1976. Annual outdoor show held each Friday-Sunday during tourist season (May-September). Show is advertised by radio; newspaper; posters; 30' road banner; and highway marque.
Terms: Entries accepted until show. Entry fee: $25/10x10 display area. Prejudging by slides and photos; entry fee refunded for refused work. Work may be offered for sale; 15% commission. Craftworker must attend show; demonstrations OK. Registration limit: 60. Sponsor provides coverings; electricity for demonstrations; and fencing.

THE LIVELY ARTS FESTIVAL, 303 W. Commonwealth Ave., Fullerton CA 92632. (714)525-7171, ext. 251. Coordinator: Pat Trotter. Committe Chair: Susie Pettijohn. Sponsor: Fullerton Community Services Department. "The Lively Arts Festival is planned to be an exciting celebration bringing together 'all' age groups and art forms. In doing so, we hope to provide the community with a rich resource showcase and an enriching experience both for the performer and the observer." Estab. 1974. Annual outdoor show held 2 days in the fall. Average attendance: 12,000. Entries accepted until show date. Entry fee: $20/artist. Display area: 10x10. Prejudging by slides or photos ("to make sure they are handcrafted"); entry fee due after prejudging. Work may be offered for sale; no commission. Craftworker needn't attend show; demonstrations OK. Registration limit: 100. Sponsor provides electricity for demonstrations and 24-hour security. Considers all crafts.
Promotion: Show is advertised in local, county and statewide newspapers; in *Westart Magazine*; by flyers and posters; and large mailings.

MAMA'S ART-A-FAIRE, Los Arboles Artisans Coop, Box 3051, Mission San Jose CA 94538. Manager: Mollie Howard. Purpose: "to promote this shopping center and to make money to cover expenses of show." Estab. 1972. Annual outdoor show (with overhang about 18' wide) held 2 days in May. Average attendance: 1,000. Entry fee: $15 plus 10% commission. Prejudging by slides or photos; entry fee refunded for refused work. Craftworker must attend show "unless by arrangement with us"; demonstrations OK. Registration limit: 30. Show is advertised by flyers; mailings to past customers; and ¼-page ads in 2 local papers. Considers all crafts. "Display to be in theme of show—no card tables with something thrown on. Like old wood—anything that looks professional." Total exhibitor sales average "$1,000-1,500 per day."
Sales Tip: "Well-presented items sell much better. By getting involved with the people the craftworker will make the most sales—not just sitting with arms folded or reading a book. Selling is an art—those who work at it, sell the most."

MENDOCINO ART CENTER SUMMER ART FAIR, Box 36, Mendocino CA 95460. (707)937-5818. Executive Director: Robert Avery Jr. Estab. 1960. Annual outdoor show held 2 days in August. Average attendance: 5,000.
Acceptable Work: Considers batik, ceramics, decoupage, dollmaking, glass art, jewelry, leatherworking, metalsmithing, mobiles, needlecrafts, pottery, scrimshaw, sculpture, soft sculpture, tole painting, weaving and woodcrafting. "All entries must be made by the artist." No commercial products, kits, assembled commercial components, imports or machine-made crafts. Exhibitor must provide own display equipment.
Terms: Must be member at Art Center. Membership fee: $12. Entries accepted until 4 weeks before show. Display area: 8x8 maximum. Prejudging by slides/photos. Entry fee due after prejudging. Work must be offered for sale; 15% commission, 10% for art-in-action. Craftworker must attend show; demonstrations OK. Registration limit: 100. Sponsor provides electricity for demonstrations and fencing.
Sales Tip: Bestsellers include "original handcrafted items of high quality in the $5-75 range." Total gross sales (1978): approximately $60,000.

MONTEREY COUNTY FAIR, Art Enterprise, Box 231, Rackerby CA 95972. Contact: M.P. Schiedeck. Estab. 1973. Annual outdoor show held 6 days in September at Monterey, California. Average attendance: 145,000. Considers all crafts.
Terms: Entries accepted until 1 week before show. Entry fee: $65/exhibitor. Display area: 10x10. Prejudging by slides or photos; entry fee refunded for refused work. Work may be offered for sale; 10% commission. Craftworker must attend show; demonstrations OK. Registraton limit: 60. Sponsor provides electricity for demonstrations.

MOTHER LODE ART SHOW, Box 905, Placerville CA 95667. Sponsor: Placerville Arts Association. Estab. 1966. Annual indoor show held 2 weeks in August. Average attendance: 500. Recent show sales totalled $1,500.
Acceptable Work: Considers batik; ceramics; macrame; pottery; sculpture; and weaving.
Terms: Entries accepted on entry days 1 week before show. Entry fee: $4/item. Prejudging by actual work; entry fee not refunded for refused work. Work may be offered for sale; 10% commission. Craftworker needn't attend show; no demonstrations. The artist is responsible only for bringing and picking up his work. The Arts Association hangs and staffs the show.
Awards: Presents cash awards of $60, $30, $20; purchase awards of $1,200; and ribbons for best of show, 1st, 2nd, 3rd, and honorable mention in each category.

MOUNTAIN AIRE, Box 4698, Modesto CA 95352. (209)521-6310. Sponsor: Rock 'N Chair Productions. Estab. 1974. Annual outdoor show held in conjunction with Music Festival 2 days in June. Average attendance: 10,000/day. Craft booths usually sold out by mid-April. Prejudging; entry fee refunded for refused work. Work may be offered for sale; no commission. Demonstrations OK. Considers all handmade crafts. "Wares directed toward ages 15-35 sell best."

OCTOBERFEST ART CRAFT & ANTIQUE SHOW & SALE, Box 207, Clovis Chamber of Commerce, Clovis CA 93613. (209)299-7273. Secretary: Nancy Russell. Purpose: "to promote the city of Clovis." Estab. 1972. Annual outdoor show held 1 day in October. Average attendance: 1,500. Entries accepted until 2 weeks before show. Entry fee: $12.50/10x10 display area; $17.50/10x15 display area; $22.50/10x20 display area. Work may be offered for sale; no commission. Craftworker must attend show; demonstrations OK. Registration limit: 80. Considers all crafts.

OJAI CRAFTS FESTIVAL, Box 331, Ojai CA 93023. (805)646-0117. Director: Rick Hallmark. Sponsor: Ojai Valley Art Center. Purpose: "fund-raising for on-going programs at the center." Estab. 1974. Annual indoor/outdoor show held 2 days in the fall. Average attendance: 25,000. Entries accepted until 6 weeks before show. Entry fee: $15/6x10 display area. Prejudging by slides; $5 retained for refused work. Work may be offered for sale; 10% commission. Craftworker must attend show; demonstrations OK. Registration limit: 60. Sponsor provides electricity for demonstrations. Considers all crafts. Exhibitor paid last day of show.
Sales Tip: "Items suitable for Christmas gifts sell best. The art center has a central sales booth. Handles tax, Masterchange, Visa." 1978 exhibition sales total approximately $25,000.
Promotion: Show is advertised by radio; TV; newspaper; direct mail; and posters. "Send 5 photos of work, along with a brief paragraph on background. Also send address of major paper in artist's community."

PACIFIC ARTS & CRAFTS, 1879 Shell Beach Rd., Pismo Beach CA 93449. (805)773-1188. Contact: Bob or Phyllis Newton. Estab. 1974. Annual outdoor show held every Saturday and Sunday, weather permitting. Average attendance: 2,000-6,000 weekly; holidays: 10,000. Considers candlemaking, ceramics, decoupage, doll making, glass art, macrame, needlecrafts, pottery, sculpture, tole painting, weaving and woodcrafting. No kits or machine-made crafts. "All crafts entered must be original work and marked with their prices." Exhibitors must supply their own display equipment.
Terms: Entries accepted until 1 week before show. Entry fee: $10/10x12 display area. Work must be offered for sale; 10% commission. Registration limit: 20-30. Sponsor provides electricity for demonstrations. Resale permit is necessary.

PACIFIC STATES CRAFTS FAIR, Box 31298, San Francisco CA 94131. (415)567-4999. Director: Marcia Chamberlain. Sponsor: American Craft Enterprises, Inc. Estab. 1976. Annual indoor show held 4 days (1 trade, 3 public) in August at San Francisco's Ft. Mason Center. Average attendance: 20,000. 1978 exhibitor sales totalled "almost a million dollars."
Acceptable Work: Considers batik; candlemaking; ceramics; dollmaking; glass art; jewelry; handmade musical instruments; leatherworking; macrame; metalsmithing; mobiles; needlecrafts; pottery; sculpture; soft sculpture; weavings; and woodcrafting. "Kits designed to produce an object, even though inspired and produced by a craftperson, should not be submitted. Categories not generally acceptable are the following: painting; photography; graphics; dried flowers; seed and pod decorations; cut bottles; and embellished objects such as painted boxes, weathered boards, stones, shells, buttons and decorated furniture. We ask that craftspeople make their display as creative as their work."
Terms: Professionals from the 13-states of the Pacific Region only. Entries accepted until approximately 5 months before show date. Entry fee determined by size of display area. Prejudging by 5 color slides "to be reviewed by a selection committee." Entry fee due after prejudging. Work may be offered for sale; no commission. Craftworker must attend show; demonstrations OK. Sponsor provides coverings; electricity for demonstrations; 24 hour security ("however ACE will not be liable for loss or damage").
Promotion: Show is advertised in craft publications; trade papers/publications; newspapers and multimedia.

PEACH TREE MALL, 3608 Cinnabar Ave., Carson City NV 89701. (702)883-0968. Director: Bea Griffin. Sponsor: Creative Artists Group. Estab. 1973. Annual indoor show held 4 days in January at Marysville, California. Entries accepted until show date. Entry fee: $25/display area. Work may be offered for sale; 10% commission. Craftworker must attend show; demonstrations OK. Registration limit: 100. Sponsor provides electricity for demonstrations and 24-hour security. Considers all crafts excepts jewelry. Show is advertised by newspaper and radio. "Send me pictures."

POLK STREET FAIR, c/o Terry Pimsleur & Co., 2149 Union St., San Francisco CA 94123. (415)346-4446. Contact: Terry Pimsleur. Sponsor: Polk Street Merchants Association. Annual outdoor show held 2 days in June/July. Considers all crafts.
Terms: Entries accepted until 2 months before show. Entry fee: $100/artist for both days. Display area: 10x8'. Prejudging by slides or photos; include SASE. Work may be offered for sale; no commission. Craftworker must attend show; demonstrations OK. Sponsor provides limited electricity (if notified in advance).

PROFESSIONAL ARTS, CRAFTS & INDOOR PLANTS SHOW, 10992 Ashton Ave., Los Angeles CA 90024. (213)479-7055. Producer/Director: Glen Beckman. Sponsor: Industry

Productions of California, Inc. "This show is held for American artists and craftspeople that wish to make wholesale sales and contacts with buyers for department stores, gift shops, plant shops, boutiques, etc." Estab. 1976. Semiannual indoor show held 1 week in January and 1 week in July at the Sports Arena in Los Angeles. Average attendance: 10,000. Entries accepted until 2 weeks before show. Entry fee: $250/10x10 display area. Work may be offered for sale; no commission. Craftworker must attend show; demonstrations OK. Registration limit: 200. Sponsor provides 24-hour security. Considers all crafts. Presents awards for the best exhibit and best direct mail promotion.
Sales Tip: "The show is for wholesale buyers only, and the exhibitor should have a good supply of business cards, catalog sheets and price lists. As of the January 1979 show, we have over 70 exhibitors that have qualified for the "$5,000 and Up Club" (established for exhibitors who write $5,000 and up in wholesale orders during and/or 30 days following any single event)."
Promotion: Show is advertised with "over 50,000 special invitations mailed to wholesale buyers. We provide any reasonable quantity of wholesale invitations (at no cost) to the exhibitor for mailing to his/her own wholesale customer and/or prospect list."

RIVERSIDE DOWNTOWN SATURDAY MARKET, 3900 Main St., 4th Flr., Riverside CA 92522. (714)787-7584. Manager: Stephen Schultz. Estab. 1976. Show held Friday and Saturday of every week. Entry fee: $15/craftworker. Work may be offered for sale; no commission. Craftworker must attend show; demonstrations OK. Considers all crafts. Send for brochure.

*****SAN FRANCISCO ANNUAL ARTS FESTIVAL,** 165 Grove St., San Francisco CA 94102. (415)558-3465. Director: Elio Benvenuto. Sponsor: City of San Francisco. Estab. 1932. Annual indoor/outdoor show held 5 days in September/October. Average attendance: 200,000. Presents $1,000 in purchase prizes and certificates of merit.
Acceptable Work: Considers batik; ceramics; glass art; jewelry; soft sculpture; metalsmithing; weaving; and woodcrafting.
Terms: Entries accepted until about 6 weeks before show. Entry fee: $80/8x8 display area. Prejudging by actual work. Work may be offered for sale; no commission. Craftworker must attend show; demonstrations OK. Registration limit: approximately 100 artists/craftworkers from the 9 Bay area counties only.

SAN JOSE CHRISTMAS GIFT SHOW & SALE, 1225 Vienna Dr. 322, Sunnyvale CA 94086. (408)734-3238. Producer: Ron Roupe. Estab. 1976. Annual indoor show held 5 days during Thanksgiving weekend at Santa Clara County Fairgrounds. Average attendance: 30,000. Considers all crafts.
Terms: Entries accepted until 2 weeks before show. Entry fee: $100-400/3x8 to 10x10 display areas. Prejudging by photos. Work may be offered for sale; no commission. Registration limit: 200. Craftworker handles sales and taxes.
Promotion: Show is advertised by TV, radio, newspapers and flyers.
Sales Tips: "Demonstrations are most successful for improving sales." Total gross: $200,000.

*****SAN MATEO COUNTY FAIR CRAFTS EXHIBITION,** Box 1027, San Mateo CA 94403. (415)345-3541. Contact: Lois Kelley. Sponsor: San Mateo County Fair Arts Committee, Inc. Annual indoor show held 13 days in July/August. Entries accepted until 2 weeks before show. Entry fee: $5/item. Prejudging; no entry fees refunded for refused work. Work may be offered for sale; no commission. Sponsor provides display panels and equipment. Presents $11,000 in cash scholarships, cash and merchandise or services.
Acceptable Work: Considers original batik; ceramics; glass art; jewelry; metalsmithing; pottery; soft sculpture; weavings; and woodcrafting.

SANTA CRUZ COUNTY FAIR, Box 231, Rackerby CA 95972. Contact: M.P. Schiedeck. Sponsor: Art Enterprise. Estab. 1973. Annual outdoor show held 4 days in September at Watsonville, California. Average attendance: 125,000. Entries accepted until show date. Entry fee: $35/artist. Display area: 10x10 or 10x12. Prejudging by slides or photos; entry fee refunded for refused work. Work may be offered for sale; 10% commission. Craftworker must attend show; demonstrations OK. Sponsor provides electricity for demonstrations. Considers all crafts.

*****SANTA MONICA ART SHOW,** c/o Cultural Arts Committee, 606 Broadway, Santa Monica CA 90401. (213)393-9825. Staff Coordinator: Nell Tupper. Sponsor: Cultural Arts Committee

---

Those listings preceded by an asterisk present awards for prize-winning crafts.

of Santa Monica Chamber of Commerce. Estab. 1967. Semiannual outdoor show held 2 days in spring and fall. Average attendance: several thousand.
Acceptable Work: Considers all crafts except clothing and jewelry. No kits, machine or mass-produced items. "All work must be original and must be made by the person entering."
Terms: Entries accepted until 3 weeks before show or until all spaces filled. Entry fee: $40/artist. Display area: 128-130 square feet. "Shapes vary because of other things on the mall (trees, bandstands)." Prejudging by slides, photos and samples of work. Entry fee refunded for refused work; $3 charge. Work may be offered for sale; no commission. Craftworker must attend show; demonstrations OK. Registration limit: 250 craftworkers and artists. Sponsor provides electricity for demonstrations.
Awards: Presents cash and ribbons in each of 7 categories; plus a $100 cash Sweepstakes Award for best of show.
Profile: "We are an open mall with customer access from about 10 directions. Awards are given the first morning of the show."

SANTA'S CHRISTMAS GIFT SHOW, 1225 Vienna Dr. .322, Sunnyvale CA 94086. (408)734-3238. Producer: Ron Roupe. Purpose: "to give the small business person an opportunity to sell, make money, and increase his business and business contacts." Estab. 1976. Annual indoor show held 5 days in November (Thanksgiving week) at the Santa Clara County Fairgrounds in San Jose. Average attendance: 25,000. Entries accepted up until 2 weeks before show. Entry fee: $300/10x10 display area; $400 for corners. Prejudging by photos; entry fee refunded for refused work. Work may be offered for sale; no commission. Craftworker must attend show; demonstrations welcomed. Registration limit: 150-200. Sponsor provides electricity; drapery backdrops; and 24-hour protection. Considers all crafts.
Sales Tip: "Be interested in the public—customer attention (talking and answering questions) is very important. Everything for Christmas presents sells well."
Promotion: Show is advertised by TV; radio; newspaper flyers; and word of mouth. Craftworkers should supply "whatever they feel would help them—brochures, cards, mailing lists, etc."

SAWDUST FINE ARTS AND CRAFTS FESTIVAL, Box 1234, Laguna Beach CA 92652. (714)494-3030. Secretary: Tracey Moscaritolo. Purpose: to exhibit and sell fine arts and crafts of Laguna Beach area artisans and artists. Estab. 1966. Annual outdoor show held 6 weeks, July-August. Average attendance: 250,000. Entries accepted from residents of Laguna or South Laguna only. Entry fee: $150/6 weeks of show. Work may be offered for sale; no commission. Craftworker or representative must attend show; demonstrations encouraged. Registration limit: 160. Sponsor provides electricity for demonstration; fencing; and 24-hour security. Show is advertised by a publicity and advertising budget—TV; radio; brochures; and magazines. "Each participant is asked to complete a publicity questionnaire." Considers all crafts and fine arts.

SILVERADO COUNTRY FAIR, Box 183, Silverado Canyon CA 92676. (714)649-2996. Country Fair Chairor: Leslie Wieland. Sponsor: Inter Canyon League. Estab. 1970. Annual outdoor show held 2 days the weekend before Thanksgiving. Average attendance: 10,000. Considers most handmade crafts. Best country-western theme booth gets ribbon and refund of entry fee.
Terms: Entries accepted until 2 weeks before show. Entry fee: $20/10x10 display area. Prejudging by photos; entry fee refunded for refused work. Work may be offered for sale; no commission. Craftworker or representative must attend show; demonstrations OK. Registration limit: 100. Sponsor provides fencing and 24-hour security.
Sales Tip: "This show is very good for Christmas gift buying. Artists selling gift-priced items do very well."
Profile: A country-type parade opens up the Fair. Entertainment continues in a country-western style with contests such as log-sawing, baking and beard-growing. Music all weekend.

SONOMA COUNTY FAIR, c/o Art Enterprise, Box 231, Rackerby CA 95972. Contact: M.P. Schiedeck. Estab. 1974. Annual outdoor show held 2 weeks in July at Santa Rosa, California. Average attendance: 700,000. "Show is held during Sonoma County Fair time, which insures a maximum crowd." Considers all crafts.
Terms: Entries accepted until filled. Entry fee: $150/exhibitor. Display area: 10x10. Work must be offered for sale; 10% commission. Craftworker must attend show; demonstrations OK. Sponsor provides electricity for demonstrations.

SONORA CHRISTMAS FAIR, Box 1135, Twain Harte CA 95383. Contact: Richard Burleigh. Sponsor: Fire on the Mountain Glass Shop. Estab. 1975. Annual indoor show held 3 days during Thanksgiving weekend at Sonora, California. Attendance: 10,000. Entries accepted until mid-October. Write for entry fee. Display area: 8x10. Prejudging; entry fee refunded for refused work. Work must be offered for sale; no commission. Craftworker must attend show; demonstrations OK. Registration limit: 65-70. Sponsor provides chairs and electricity for demonstrations. Considers all crafts.

*****SOUTH LAKE FESTIVAL OF THE ARTS**, 492 South Lake Ave., Pasadena CA 91101. (213)577-2630. Director: Ray Leier. Sponsor: South Lake Business Association. Purpose: "to create a place where artists may present their work to the buying public, as well as a fundraiser for the South Lake Association." Estab. 1974. Semiannual outdoor show held 3 days in the fall and spring. Attendance: 2,000-6,000. Entries accepted until 2 weeks before show; "some entries may be accepted if particular media is not filled." Entry fee: $45/artist. Display area: 4x12 "unless otherwise requested." Prejudging by "photos of work to be exhibited, plus description of display booth (no card tables allowed)"; entry fee refunded for refused work. Work may be offered for sale; no commission. Craftworker must attend show; demonstration OK. Registration limit: 150.
Acceptable Work: Considers batik; candlemaking; ceramics; dollmaking; glass art; jewelry; leatherworking; macrame; metalsmithing; mobiles; needlecrafts; pottery; sculpture; soft sculpture; weaving; woodcrafting; and "most fine crafts. Artists must provide a professional presentation of their work."

*****SOUTHERN CALIFORNIA EXPOSITION**, Del Mar Fairgrounds, Del Mar CA 92014. (714)755-1161. Exhibit/Supervisor: Lolly Stuckenschneider. Sponsor: 22nd District Agricultural Association. Estab. 1880. Annual indoor show held 2 weeks in June/July. Average attendance: 650,000. Considers all crafts.
Terms: Open only to residents of Southern California in the following counties: San Diego, Imperial, Orange, Riverside, Los Angeles, San Bernardino, Ventura and Santa Barbara. Entries accepted during 3 days approximately 4 weeks before show. Entry fee: $4/item. Maximum 3 items/category. Entry fee not refunded for refused work. Work may be offered for sale; 25% commission. Craftworker needn't attend show; demonstrations OK. Sponsor provides necessary display unit and 24-hour security.
Awards: Presents various cash awards and ribbons. "Entries that are different and unusual, not too abstract, appeal most to the judges."

SOUTHERN CALIFORNIA POWWOW, Box 112, Baldwin Park CA 91706. (213)338-5492 or 337-5300. Directors: Jill Tilander and Cecilia Fischer. Sponsor: F&T Associates. Purpose: "to spread the gem and mineral hobby mainly. But realizing that 'variety is the spice of life,' we are open to all crafts and hobbies that a person might do on a small scale, in a small shop at home. The 'little' person can't afford booths at large shows, so we hope this can be an outlet for him to spread his hobby a little." Estab. 1977. Annual show with 184 covered spaces and 115 uncovered spaces held outdoors 3 days in October at the Los Angeles County Fairgrounds in Pomona, California. Average attendance: 3,000. Entries accepted until show date. Entry fee: $50-65, covered; $65, covered corners/12x25 display area. Work may be offered for sale; no commission. "Booth must be attended during hours open to public; demonstrations highly encouraged." Sponsor provides electricity for demonstrations; and offers tables, chairs, and coverings for rent. Considers all crafts.
Promotion: Show is advertised in *Gem & Minerals, Lapidary Journal* and *Rock and Gem*; by radio; in local newspapers; information sent to over 200 gem and mineral clubs in the West; and by ads in *Desert* magazine, *Westart*, *The Goodfellow Review of Crafts*, and *Sunshine Artists, U.S.A.* "We would appreciate any copy on special things that would draw the public."

*****SOUTHLAND ART SHOW**, Box 115, Twenty-nine Palms CA 92277. (714)367-9633. President: Lee Lukes Pickering. Sponsor: Twenty-nine Palms Artists Guild. Estab. 1963. Annual indoor show held 3 weeks during November. Average attendance: 500. Entries accepted until 3 days before show. Entry fee: $2/item being displayed. Maximum 1 entry/category; 3 entries total. Prejudging of work presented at show. Work may be offered for sale; 33⅓% commission. "Works are handled on consignment with our staff handling all sales." Craftworker needn't attend show; demonstrations OK. Sponsor provides chairs; display panels; and electricity for demonstrations. Show is advertised by radio; newspapers; direct mail; and annual exhibit brochure. Awards ribbons.
Acceptable Work: Considers batik; ceramics; decoupage; macrame; mobiles; pottery; sculp-

ture; and soft sculpture. Maximum size: 20 inches in any direction. "Works must be wired and framed, or mounted when applicable."

*SUTTER STREET ART FESTIVAL, 7107 Carriage Dr., Citrus Heights CA 95610. Director: Joanne Burkett. Sponsor: Sutter Street Merchants Association. "Our profits are used for further restoration and upkeep of the historic area, and we like to promote the arts since there are many art and crafts shops here." Estab. "in the 1960s." Annual outdoor show (with some covered spaces) held 2 days in June at Folsom, California. Average attendance: 20,000. Entries accepted until 1 week before show. Entry fee: $20/artist. Display area: state needs. Prejudging by slides or photos and description of work; entry fee refunded for refused work. Work may be offered for sale; no commission. "We can handle tax for those with no resale number." Craftworker must attend show; demonstrations OK. Registration limit: 200. Sponsor provides electricity for demonstrations; and security during show hours. Show is advertised by TV; radio; newspapers; and magazines. Considers all crafts. "Exhibitors must provide own props and display supplies."
Awards: Presents $200 in cash awards and ribbons. "Our preference is for winners fitting the theme of our town. It is a gold rush mother lode setting, and we like good realism."

TEHACHAPI MOUNTAIN FESTIVAL ART FAIRE, Box 165, Tehachapi CA 93561. (805)822-5158. Sponsor: Tehachapi Valley Arts Association. Purpose: "promotion of the arts and joint venture with Tehachapi Mountain Festival which is held annually, and brings many visitors to the town." Estab. "approximately 1967." Annual outdoor show (with trees and parachutes for shade) held 2 days in August at the Tehachapi city park. Entries accepted until 3 weeks before show. Entry fee: $15/10x10 (or larger) display area. Prejudging by slides or photos; entry fee refunded for refused work. Work may be offered for sale; 10% commission for nonmembers. Craftworker must attend show; demonstrations permitted. Sponsor provides coverings; and electricity for demonstrations. Show is promoted by "publicity in local and regional newspapers (Kern County); *LA Times; Westart* magazine; local radio and TV; and posters.
Acceptable Work: Considers all crafts. "We encourage individuals and originality. We try to avoid duplications of too similar a craft at show." If hooks are needed, craftworker must provide.
Sales Tip: "Public buying mood is quite flexible, but tends to go for original and good works from less than a dollar to $100-200 price range."

THANKSGIVING FOLK-CRAFT FESTIVAL, c/o Steve Powers & Co., 5726 Gaines St. #3, San Diego CA 92110. (714)299-2638. Director: Steve Powers. Estab. 1977. Annual indoor show held 3 days after Thanksgiving, at the Scottish Rite Center in Mission Valley, San Diego, California. Average attendance: 10,000.
Acceptable Work: Considers all crafts. Especially needs unusual items in the $5-25 range.
Terms; Entries accepted until full, usually in September. Entry fee: $135/10x8 display area. Prejudging by 6 slides of actual work, plus 1 of display to be used at festival. Entry fee refunded for refused work. No commission charged. Craftworker must attend show. Registration limit: 110. Sponsor provides electricity and security.
Promotion: Show is advertised mostly by radio. "I purchase large amounts of advertising in the greater metropolitan area of San Diego. I rely mainly on a radio saturation plan and large display ads in the San Diego Union Newspaper and use a discount coupon program effectively. Press releases and promotions help draw a responsive and affluent crowd.
Profile: "We try to provide the high quality independent craftsperson an ideal marketplace for the public to purchase original gifts for the holiday season. A combined atmosphere of visual and performing arts is very condusive for sales. Music is performed continuously on stage and is non-amplified."

TOWN AND COUNTRY VILLAGE—KIWANIS ART FIESTA, 7841 Clearview Dr., Citrus Hts. CA 95610. (916)725-5802 or 482-1880. Contact: Mary Morse. Sponsor: Sacramento Suburban Kiwanis Club. Estab. 1968. Annual outdoor show held 2 days in June at Sacramento, California.
Acceptable Work: Considers batik, ceramics, glass art, jewelry, metalsmithing, scrimshaw, sculpture, soft sculpture and weavings. No kits, machine-made crafts; all work must be original.
Terms: Entries accepted until show date. Entry fee: $15/8x6 display area. Prejudging by slides or photos. Entry fee refunded for refused work. Work may be offered for sale; no commission. Craftworker must attend show; demonstrations OK. Registration limit: 350.

Awards: Presents 3 cash awards ($100, $50, $25); $200 in purchase awards (by the Kiwanis); honorable mention ribbons; and prizes for the best demonstration.

TRUCKEE OUTDOOR ARTS & CRAFTS FAIR, Box 1239, Truckee CA 95734. (916)587-2700. President: Ken Lipsitz. Sponsor: Truckee Art Guild. Estab. 1972. Annual outdoor fair held 4 days the third week of August. Average attendance: 4,000-5,000. Considers all crafts. No machine-made crafts. Show is advertised by radio, newspapers and posters.
Terms: Entries accepted until 2 weeks before show, if craft category is still open. Entry fee: $55/craftworker. Display area: 10x10. Prejudging by slides/photos. Work may be offered for sale; no commission. Craftworker must attend show; demonstrations OK. Registration limit: 150. Sponsor provides portable tables (rental fee), and booth security.

UNION STREET SPRING FESTIVAL & CRAFTS FAIR, Union Street Association, 2149 Union St., San Francisco CA 94123. (415)567-3055 or 346-4446. Coordinator: Terry Pimsleur. Purpose: "to raise funds for the association to promote and improve historic Cow Hollow area of San Francisco." Estab. 1976. Annual outdoor show held 2 days in June on 5 blocks of Union Street. Attendance: 40,000-50,000/day. Entries accepted until 4 weeks before show. Entry fee: $100/10x8 display area. Prejudging by slides or photos; entry fee refunded for refused work. Work may be offered for sale; no commission. Craftworker must attend show; demonstrations OK. Registration limit: 200-250 (merchants on Union Street have preference as to space). Sponsor provides some electricity for demonstrations; and special patrol for security ("but not responsible for loss"). Considers all crafts. "Tables must be draped and must not protrude into street beyond 10 feet from curb."
Promotion: Show is advertised in newspapers; radio; TV; posters; and radio remote broadcast. "Can sometimes use pictures."

UNIVERSITY OF SOUTHERN CALIFORNIA CRAFT CENTER, YWCA University Park, Los Angeles CA 90007. (213)741-6208. Contact: Jo Ann Fried. Estab. 1970. Semiannual show held 3 days in May and December. Entry fee: $40. Work may be offered for sale; no commission. Craftworker must attend show; demonstrations OK. Registration limit: 100. Considers all crafts.
Sales Tip: "Gold jewelry; ceramics; stained glass; and fabric arts do well. There is more likelihood of selling moderatedly priced fine works as people have come to appreciate handcrafted items. Bestsellers are $25-100."

VALLEY CRAFT GUILD CHRISTMAS SHOW, 7798 Ironwood Dr., Dublin CA 94566. (415)828-2607. Director: Donna Franks. Estab. 1971. Annual indoor show held 2 days in November. Average attendance: 2,000. Entries accepted until August. Entry fee: $15/4x5 display area; $25/8x5 display area. Maximum 1 entry/category per artist. Prejudging of actual work; entry fee refunded for refused work. Work may be offered for sale; no commission. Craftworker must attend show; demonstrations OK. Registration limit: 41. Sponsor provides chairs and electricity for demonstrations. Show is advertised by newspapers; flyers; posters; and mailers. Considers all crafts. Items in the $2-10 range tend to sell best.

*A VERY SPECIAL ART SHOW, 2409 J St., Sacramento CA 95816. Coordinator: Amy Nishamura. Sponsor: California and Sacramento Association for the Retarded. Estab. 1974. Annual indoor show held 2 weeks in October. Average attendance: 20,000.
Acceptable Work: Considers all original crafts. Must be made by artist showing work. "We prefer items to be framed. However, we will not disqualify."
Terms: Accepts mentally retarded craftworkers only. Work accepted until 1 week before show. Entry fee: 50fl per item. Display area: 8,000 square feet. Maximum 2 items per category. Work must be offered for sale; no commission. Craftworker needn't attend show; demonstrations OK. Registration limit: 400 craftworkers. Sponsor provides display panels, electricity for demonstrations, insurance on exhibited work and 24-hour security. Volunteers for show handle sales on opening night; contributing centers handle taxes.
Awards: Presents ribbons for 1st, 2nd, 3rd places, and honorable mentions. "Through this show, we hope to help the child learn to express himself/herself through their art projects; to learn to use tools; and to do neat work."
Tips: "The majority of our art work is sold on opening night. There is great demand for the art work from our show."

*WESTWOOD CLAY NATIONAL, 14400 E. Lomitas Ave., City of Industry CA 91744. (213)330-0631. Director: Lukman Glasgow. Sponsors annual contemporary ceramic shows.

Prejudging by slides. Work may be offered for sale; 20% commission. Purchase and merit awards. Write for prospectus.

WORLD SHOWS, Box 339, Stanton CA 90680. (714)995-7509. Partners: Don, Virginia or Gale. Estab. 1977. Annual shows held 40 days in November-December at various Sears' stores throughout California. Considers all crafts.
Terms: Entries accepted until show date. Entry fee: $96 for insurance. Display area: 4x6' to 10x12'. Prejudging by phone or mail. Entry fee due after prejudging; fee refunded for refused work. Craftworker must offer work for sale; 30% commission. Craftworker must attend show; demonstrations OK. Registration limit: 1-5 per store (57 stores). Sponsor provides electricity for demonstrations.
Profile: "These are concessions in high-traffic areas of Sears' stores. Show is promoted by Sears advertising. Craftworker must provide an appropriate sign and a good-looking display."

Colorado

*****ARTISTS ALPINE HOLIDAY,** Box 149, Ouray CO 81427. (303)325-4766. Secretary: Ramona Radcliff. Sponsor: Ouray County Arts Association. Purpose: "to provide and promote culture in a remote and culturally-deprived area." Estab. 1961. Annual indoor show held 1 week in August. Average attendance: 3,000. Entries accepted until 2 days before show. Entry fee: $4/item being displayed. Maximum 3 entries per category. Work must be offered for sale; 15% commission. Craftworker needn't attend show; a few demonstrations permitted if requested. Sponsor provides display panels. Show is advertised by newspapers; local TV; and radio. Considers photography and sculpture. Awards $105 in each medium; $500 in purchase prizes; and ribbons.

CARBONDALE MOUNTAIN FAIR, Box 174, Carbondale CO 81623. (303)963-1680. Director: Gwen Ackerman Hansen. Estab. 1972. Annual outdoor show held 2 days in July. Average attendance: 7,000. Considers all crafts. 1978 exhibitor sale totalled approximately $42,000.
Terms: Entries accepted until 6 weeks before show. Entry fee: $15/10x10' display area. Prejudging by slides. Entry fee refunded for refused work. Work may be offered for sale; 10% commission. Craftworker must attend show; demonstrations OK. Registration limit: approximately 100. Sponsor provides limited electricity for demonstration.

CHERRY CREEK FESTIVAL OF THE ARTS, 1400 Josephine, Denver CO 80206. (303)322-1688. Contact: Chairman. Sponsor: Cherry Creek Merchants' Association and Assistance League of Denver. Estab. 1975. Annual outdoor show (with some tents) held 2 weekends in June. Considers all crafts.
Terms: Entries accepted until 2 weeks before show. Entry fee: $50/8x8 display area. Prejudging by slides and photos for new participants. Entry fee refunded for refused work. 20% commission. Craftworker must attend show; demonstrations OK if confined within space allotted.

Richard Peck, a brass worker from Waterbury, Connecticut, demonstrates his craft at the Berlin Crafts Expo held three days at Berlin, Connecticut. This weekend event is sponsored by American Craft Expositions, Inc.

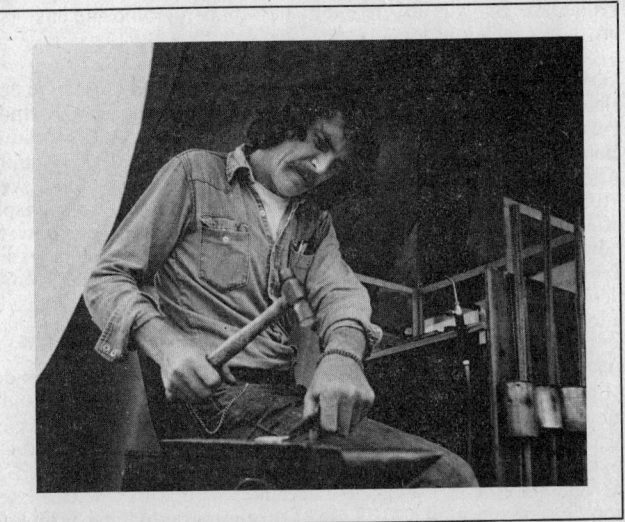

Registration limit: 138. Sponsor provides pegboard.
Promotion: Show is advertised by newspaper, radio, TV, art and craft publications and posters.

COLORADO RENAISSANCE FESTIVAL, 1078 1/2 S. Gaylord, Denver, CO 80209. (303)777-3835. Director: Rae Ann McMurtry. Sponsor: Pastimes Alive. Purpose: "a celebration of Renaissance life and spirit creating a living history involving visual and performing arts." Estab. 1975. Annual outdoor show held 8 days (4 weekends) in June, south of Denver. Average attendance: 25,000. Entries accepted until 2 weeks before show. Entry fee: $80 before February 15; $100 February 16-May 15; $150 late fee. Display area: 15x20. Period booth, costume and banner are required. Prejudging by slides. SASE. Entry fee due after prejudging. Work may be offered for sale; no commission. Craftworker must attend show; demonstrations encouraged. "If demonstrations or presentations can fit into our educational or entertainment guidelines, fees may be partially or totally excused." Registration limit: 150. Sponsor provides night security and campground area for participants. Show is advertised by local TV; radio; magazines; newspapers; and club newsletters. Considers all crafts that directly relate to the Renaissance period in theme or process.

*** CRESTED BUTTE FESTIVAL OF THE ARTS**, Crested Butte Society, Box 324, Crested Butte CO 81224. Contact: Coordinator. Estab. 1971. Annual outdoor show held 2 days during the first weekend of August.
Acceptable Work: Considers all crafts. Must be handmade by artist showing the work. No commercial traders (e.g., Indian jewelry, old quilts). "It's best to have displays viewable from at least 2 sides."
Terms: Entries accepted until 2 weeks before show. Entry fee: $30/10x10' display area; 1 displayer/booth. Prejudging by slides or photos. Entry fee due after prejudging. Work may be offered for sale; no commission. Prefers craftworker to attend show; demonstrations encouraged. Registration limit: 100. Sponsor provides electricity for demonstrations and booths (if needed; not enough for all entrants). Town of Crested Butte handles sales and taxes.
Awards: Presents ribbons and "a token gift representative of our town and festival." May possibly present purchase awards.
Profile: "We provide beautiful mountain vistas and a friendly relaxed atmosphere."

EL DIEZ Y SEIS DE SEPTIEMBRE, 408 E. Simpson St., Lafayette CO 80026. (303)665-3310. Contact: Dan Cordova or Cece Garcia. Estab. 1973. Annual outdoor show held 1-2 days "September 16 or thereabouts." Average attendance: 500. Considers all crafts except those that are highly flammable.
Terms: Entries accepted until 3 weeks before show. Entry fee: $10/10x10 display area. Prejudging; "our only requirement is that they be oriented towards an ethnic group—Indian, Mexican, etc." Entry fee due after prejudging. Work may be offered for sale; no commission. Craftworker or representative must attend show; demonstration OK. Sponsor provides electricity for demonstrations and 24-hour security.
Promotion: Show is advertised by newspapers, radio and posters. "Send photos or samples for preshow display at local businesses."

LOVELAND'S ANNUAL ARTS & CRAFTS FESTIVAL, c/o Joyce C. Musslewhite, #4 Enchanted Way, Rt.4, 480A Pole Hill, Loveland CO 80537. Sponsor: Loveland Art League. Purpose: "to make people aware of what the artists are producing and to give the artists a chance to display and sell their products." Estab. 1965. Annual outdoor show held 1 day in August. Attendance: 3,000-4,000. Entries accepted until 2 weeks before show. Entry fee: $10/artist for pre-registration; $15/artist for walk-in entries. Display area: 10x12. Work may be offered for sale; no commission. Craftworker must attend show; demonstrations OK. Registration limit: 200. Considers all original crafts and original works of art.
Promotion: Show is advertised by radio; newspapers; and TV. "When sending in the registration fee, the craftworker might include a brochure on himself and products. We use the information in our news releases."

OWN YOUR OWN ART SHOW, University of Southern Colorado Art Department, Pueblo CO 81001. (303)549-2552. Art Professors: Ed Sadbel and Bob Wands. Sponsor: USC Art Department and Pueblo Junior League. "Own Your Own Art Show is organized to stimulate sales by artists from Colorado, New Mexico, Wyoming, Montana, Idaho, Utah, Nevada and Arizona." Estab. 1961. Annual indoor show held 2 weeks in November. Attendance: 5,000-10,000.
Acceptable Work: Categories: ceramics; sculptures; textiles; jewelry; watercolors; oils and acrylics; mixed media (2-D or 3-D); photographs; and prints. Considers ceramics; jewelry;

metalsmithing; pottery; sculpture; soft sculpture; weaving; and woodcrafting.
Terms: Entries accepted until 1 week before show. Entry fee: $7/artist. Prejudging. No entry fees refunded for refused work. Work may be offered for sale; 25% commission "for USC art scholarships." Craftworker needn't attend show; no demonstrations. Registration limit: 300-500. Sponsor provides insurance on exhibited work (although limited); 24-hour security; and "the Pueblo Junior League handles all sales and sends check to artist within 2 weeks after show."
Promotion: Show is advertised in national magazines; Colorado newspapers; and TV.

ROCKY MOUNTAIN CRAFT FAIR, National Crafts Ltd., Gapland MD 21736. (301)432-8438. Director: Noel Clark. Estab. 1977. Annual indoor show held 3 days (2 days retail, 1 wholesale) in August at the Merchandise Mart in Denver, Colorado. Average attendance: 10,000. Considers all crafts. No kits or machine-made crafts. Show is advertised by newspaper and magazine ads, radio, posters and flyers. Average sales (1978): $1,100/booth.
Terms: Entries accepted until 4 weeks before show. Entry fee: $3/application. Display area: 10x10. Prejudging by 5 35mm color slides. Entry fee not refunded for refused work. Work must be offered for sale; no commission. Craftworker must attend show; demonstrations OK. Registration limit: 150. Sponsor provides 24-hour security, and an air-conditioned, fully carpeted exhibit hall.

SNOWMASS ARTS & CRAFTS FAIR, Box 5566, Snowmass Village CO 81615. (303)923-2000. Recreation Director: Laurie Rothstein. Sponsor: Snowmass Resort Association. Estab. 1969. Annual outdoor shows held 1 day in June, 2 days in July and 1-2 days in August. Average attendance: 80 craftworkers. Considers most handmade crafts.
Terms: Entries accepted until 1 week before show. Entry fee: $25-30/8x10 display area. Payment must be made at least 1 week in advance. Work must be juried and accepted at least 1 week in advance. Prejudging by slides, photos or personal review. Entry fee due after prejudging. Work may be offered for sale; no commission. Craftworker must attend show; demonstrations OK. Sponsor provides electricity for demonstrations.

*****THREADS UNLIMITED**, 809 15th St., Golden CO 80401. (303)279-3922. Executive Director: Marian Metsopoulos. Sponsor: Foothills Art Center. Estab. 1974. Annual indoor show held the month of June. Average attendance: 1,000.
Acceptable Work: Considers macrame, needlecrafts, soft sculpture, weaving, and other "work where fiber is the predominant material." Maximum size: 8x8.
Terms: "The competition is open to artists living in Colorado, Kansas, Wyoming, Nebraska, Oklahoma, New Mexico, Arizona and Utah." Entries accepted until 3 weeks before show. Entry fee: $4/artist. Maximum 2 entries/craftworker. Prejudging by actual work. No entry fees refunded for refused work. Work may be offered for sale; 30% commission. Craftworker needn't attend show; no demonstrations. Registration limit: 75 pieces. Sponsor provides $50 deductible theft insurance on exhibited work; 24-hour security; hangs show; and handles all sales and collects and pays sales tax.
Awards: Cash awards are to be determined. Judges look for "expert craftsmanship, finishing, and above all, excellent design and use of color."
Promotion: Show is advertised in newspapers; magazines; radio; and TV. Requests resumes to give buyers of work. "Buyers want to know about the artist."

WORLD SHOWS, Box 339, Stanton CA 90680. (714)995-7509. Partners: Don, Virginia or Gale. Estab. 1977. Annual shows held 40 days in November-December at various Sears' stores throughout Colorado. Considers all crafts.
Terms: Entries accepted until show date. Entry fee: $96 for insurance. Display area: 4x6' to 10x12'. Prejudging by phone or mail. Entry fee due after prejudging; fee refunded for refused work. Craftworker must offer work for sale; 30% commission. Craftworker must attend show; demonstrations OK. Registration limit: 1-5 per store (57 stores). Sponsor provides electricity for demonstrations.
Profile: "These are concessions in high traffic areas of Sears' stores. Show is promoted by Sears' advertising. Craftworker must provide an appropriate sign and a good-looking display."

Connecticut

ARTS & CRAFTS FAIR, c/o Mrs. Elayne Perry, 11 Robin Lane, Milford CT 06460. (203)878-8101. Contact: Mrs. Elayne Perry. Sponsor: Wepawang Chapter of Hadassah. Purpose: "to raise money for the Hadassah medical organization which goes to hospitals and medical centers in Israel who continually do research and training." Estab. 1972. Annual outdoor show held 1 Sunday in the spring at the Milford Green. Entries acccepted until show date. Entry fee: $15/display area. Work may be offered for sale; no commission. Craftworker must attend show; demonstrations OK. Sponsor provides electricity for demonstration. Show is advertised by radio and the local media. Craftworkers are urged to supply promotional materials about themselves and their work. Considers all crafts.

ARTS & CRAFTS FESTIVAL, Box 764, Middletown CT 06457. Sponsor: Junior Woman's Club of Middletown. Purpose: "to raise money for community projects. We profit from artists' fees and canteen setup at site." Estab. 1968. Annual outdoor show held 1 day in the spring. Entries accepted until 2 months before show. Entry fee: $15/craftworker. Display area: 12'x unlimited depth. Prejudging by slides, photos, descriptions—"whatever accompanies applications." Entry fee refunded for refused work. Work may be offered for sale; no commission. Craftworker must attend show; "demonstrations left up to the discretion of our committee." Registration limit: 100. Sponsor provides chairs; limited electricity for demonstrations; fencing; coffee; lunch; and table. Considers all crafts.
Promotion: Show is advertised by local newspapers; TV; radio; posters; and in craft magazines. "When sending in application, include photos, description, or any material available."

BERLIN CRAFT EXPO, Box 370, Farmington CT 06032. (203)224-8388. Directors: Denise Barile and Rudy Kowalczyk. Sponsor: American Craft Expositions, Inc. Estab. 1976. Annual indoor/outdoor show held 3 days in August at fair grounds in Berlin, Connecticut. Average attendance: 25,000.
Acceptable Work: Considers batik, candlemaking, ceramics, dollmaking, glass art, jewelry, leatherworking, macrame, metalsmithing, pottery, scrimshaw, sculpture, soft sculpture, weaving, woodcrafting and other "high quality craft media." No kits, manufactured or assembled items, dealers or agents.
Terms: Entries accepted until 60 days before show. Popular media close earlier. Entry fee: $75 and higher, depending upon size of area. Prejudging by 6 slides. Entry fee refunded for refused work. Work must be offered for sale; no commission. Craftworker must attend show; demonstrations encouraged. Registration limit: 250. Sponsor provides table and chairs (rental fee) and 24-hour security. Rental chairs and tables available.

BLACK EXPO & BAZAAR, 140 Goffe St., New Haven CT 06511. (203)777-3661. Contact: Director. Sponsor: Black Coalition of Greater New Haven, Inc. Estab. 1972. Annual indoor show held 4 days in October. Average attendance: 25,000. Considers all crafts.
Terms: Entries accepted until 2 weeks before show. Entry fee: $250/8x10 display area; $60/4x5 display area. Work may be offered for sale; no commission. Craftworker must attend show; demonstrations OK. Registration limit: 154. An 8x10 display area includes electricity; table; 3-side fencing; and 24-hour security. 4x5 display area includes electricity and 24-hour security.
Profile: "Black Expo & Bazaar is a showcase and appraisal of the cultural and socio-economic standing of the Afro-American communities, providing an overview of 'Grass Roots' vitality."
Sales Tip: Bestsellers include jewelry; ceramics; macrame; needlecrafts; pastel portraits; novelty items (e.g., item buttons with photos of individuals, etc.); and woodcrafts.

*****BRISTOL MUM FESTIVAL ART SHOW**, Chamber of Commerce, c/o Bristol Art League, Bristol CT 06010. Contact: Co-chairman. Annual indoor show held 10 days in September. Attendance: 1,500-2,000.
Acceptable Work: Considers framed batik and sculpture. "Entries must have been completed within the past 2 years. Artists must be over 18 years of age. No uncrating. Entries must not have been in the art show previously." Categories: oil; watercolor; mixed media; graphic; sculpture.
Terms: Entries accepted until 8-10 days before show (work must be delivered 3-4 days before show). Entry fee: $5/item being displayed. Maximum 2 entries/category. Prejudging. No entry fees refunded for refused work. Work may be offered for sale; 20% commission. Craftworker needn't attend show; demonstrations OK. Registration limit: 200. Sponsor provides display panels; electricity for demonstrations; 24-hour security; and Bristol Art League handles sales.
Awards: Awards $25-200 in cash; and honorable mention. "A judge from the area is chosen each year by the Committee. The judge views the entries 2 or 3 days before the show opens in person. The opening night of the show is awards night, and prizes are presented then."
Profile: "Held in conjunction with 2-week long festival promoted by the city of Bristol, the Chrysanthemum city of the world."

CHRISTMAS ARTS FESTIVAL, Silvermine Guild of Artists, 1037 Silvermine Rd., New Canaan CT 06840. (203)966-5617. Gallery Director: Virginia Mann. "This exhibition includes all artist members of Silvermine Guild. It is not open to any craftsperson who is not a member of the Guild. Membership is through jurying—work is submitted to be juried by the artist members of the Board of Trustees of the Silvermine Guild of Artists." Estab. 1935. Annual indoor show held from Thanksgiving until Christmas. Average attendance: 2,000. Show is advertised by publicity releases and ads that appear in local media and in the *New York Times*.

CHRISTMAS STOCKING CRAFT SHOW, Sterling House Community Center, 2283 Main St., Stratford CT 06497. (203)378-2606. Executive Director: Mary R. Hardy. Estab. 1971. Annual indoor show held 2 days in late November. Average attendance: 3,600. Considers all crafts.
Terms: Application with photos or slides for prejudging due 6 weeks before show. Entry fee: $18/6x6 plus $3 for each additional running foot of space requested up to 12. Maximum 1 category/craftworker. Work may be offered for sale; no commission. Craftworker must attend show; no demonstrations. Registration limit: 40. Sponsor provides chairs, electricity and overnight security.
Promotion: Show is advertised by news stories, radio announcements, flyers, posters and the promotion committee. Some information is requested by Committee for newspaper purposes.

CRAFT FAIR, 87 William St., Portland CT 06480. (203)342-0771. Chairman: Sari Rosenbaum. Sponsor: Middletown Chapter of Hadassah. Estab. 1971. Annual outdoor show held 1 day in September at Middletown, Connecticut. Average attendance: 10,000. Entries accepted until show date or until filled. Entry fee: $20/10x16 display area. Maximum 1 booth per craftworker. Work may be offered for sale; no commission. Craftworker or representative must attend show. Registration limit: 184. Considers all crafts.

FARMINGTON CRAFTS EXPO, Box 370, Farmington CT 06032. (202)224-8388. Directors: Denise Barile and Rudy Kowalczyk. Sponsor: American Crafts Expositions, Inc. Estab. 1972. Annual outdoor show (with tents) held 3 days in June at polo grounds. Average attendance: 20,000.
Terms: Entries accepted until 60 days before show, popular media's close earlier. Entry fee: $75 and up, depending upon size of area. Display area: 8x10 (tents) to 14x14 (outside). High quality work only. No dealers, agents, manufactured items or kits. Prejudging by 6 slides. Entry fee refunded for refused work. Work must be offered for sale; no commission. Craftworker must attend show; large demonstrations wanted. Registration limit: 200. Sponsor provides electricity for demonstrations and 24-hour security. Rental chairs and tables available.

*FESTIVAL OF ARTS, Box 486, Fairfield CT 06430. Contact: Chairman. Sponsor: Fairfield Jaycees and Jaycee Women. "This show is held for the purpose of supporting the ongoing projects of the Fairfield Jaycees, and a selected local charity or organization chosen annually by the Jaycee Women." Estab. 1969. Annual outdoor show held 1 day in September. Average attendance: 5,000. Presents cash for best in show; and 1st, 2nd and 3rd place ribbons.
Acceptable Work: Considers batik; ceramics; dollmaking; glass art; jewelry; lapidary; leatherworking; macrame; metalsmithing; pottery; sculpture; scrimshaw; nail art; bread dough; and dried flower arranging.
Terms: Entries accepted until show date as space is available. Entry fee to be announced. Prejudging by slides or photos. "Only the highest quality handmade items are accepted." Entry fee refunded for refused work. Work may be offered for sale; no commission. Craftworker needn't attend show; demonstrations OK. Registration limit: "crafts limited to 2 per category and may not exceed 40 participants." Sponsor provides a limited number of display panels.
Promotion: Show is advertised by publicity in directories; newspapers in New York, New Jersey and all of New England; radio announcements; posters; and banners used locally. "Often we will contact individuals for publicity materials as we see fit."

*GOLDENBELLS FESTIVAL ART & CRAFT MARKET, 161 Wayland St., Hamden CT 06518. (203)288-0436. Chairman: Dorothy Pomarico. Sponsor: town of Hamden. Estab. 1973. Annual indoor show held 2 days in the spring. Average attendance: 2,000. Presents cash awards ("amount determined yearly by town business contributions"); and gift certificates.
Terms: Entries accepted until 2 weeks before show. Entry fee: $12/6x10 display area. Work may be offered for sale; no commission. Craftworker must attend show; demonstrations encouraged. Registration limit: 60 craftworkers; 20-40 artists. Sponsor provides chairs, electricity for demonstrations, table and 24-hour security.
Acceptable Work: Considers batik; candlemaking; ceramics; dollmaking; glass art; jewelry;

lapidary; leatherworking; macrame; metalsmithing; mobiles; needlecrafts; pottery; sculpture; soft sculpture; tole painting; weaving; and woodcrafting. "If you're proud of your work bring it. If you're just hoping someone will take it off your hands because you can't stand it, leave it home."
Promotion: Show is advertised by radio ads and interviews; posters; handbills; TV interviews and notices; newspaper and magazine ads; billboards; and feature stories on the festival. "Personal publicity info regarding self and product will be used for newspaper articles which run every week for 2 months prior to show."
Profile: "It is a festival to welcome spring by the townspeople. The market is just 1 of several events that occur during the 2-week festival. Hamden is a very art-oriented town with a wide variety of tastes."

*GREAT DANBURY STATE ARTS & CRAFTS FAIR, 130 White St., Danbury CT 06810. (203)748-3535. Show Director: Jack Stetson. Estab. 1975. Annual indoor/outdoor show held 3 days in July. Average attendance: 25,000.
Acceptable Work: Considers all crafts. No agents, imports, kits, embellishments or strung beads.
Terms: Entries accepted until approximately 2 months before show. Entry fee: $80 for indoor space; $75 for tent space; $60 for outdoor space. Prejudging by 5 slides. SASE. Work may be offered for sale; demonstrations OK. Sponsor provides limited electricity (fee), free parking and 24-hour security.
Awards: Presents $1,500 in cash and ribbon awards to more than 300 exhibitors.
Profile: Show is housed in several permanent buildings, tents and outdoors. Events include camping on the grounds, entertainment, arts and crafts demonstrations, refreshments and music.

*GREATER HARTFORD CIVIC & ARTS FESTIVAL, 250 Constitution Plaza, Hartford CT 06103. (203)278-3378. Director: Evelyn R. Warner. Sponsor: Greater Hartford Arts Council, Downtown Council, and Greater Hartford Chamber of Commerce. Estab. 1971. Annual outdoor show (partial covering) held 9 days in June. Average attendance: 100,000. Presents cash and purchase awards and ribbons.
Acceptable Work: Eligible media include materials such as clay, fiber, glass, metal and wood.
Terms: Entries accepted until 5 weeks before show. Prejudging by actual work. Work may be offered for sale; 15% donation. Craftworker needn't attend show. Sponsor provides insurance on exhibited work.

*GREATER VERNON JAYCEES CRAFTS FAIR, Box 778, Rockville CT 06066. Co-Chairmen: Tom and Mike Sheridan. Sponsor: Greater Vernon Jaycees. Estab. 1974. Annual indoor show held 2 days in November at Vernon, Connecticut. Average attendance: 6,000. Awards ribbons.
Acceptable Work: Considers all crafts. No kits or crafts manufactured for sale by non-craftsperson. Show categories: wood carvings, woodworking, candle crafts, glass crafts, batik, leather crafts, jewelry, paintings, macrame, pottery and sculpture. "Crafters must provide their own set-ups (which should not hinder or bother any other crafter/artist). The crowd usually gathers around craftworkers who are demonstrating their skills. Sales go where the crowd goes."
Terms: Entries accepted until 5 months before show. Entry fee: $30/5x10' booth. Prejudging by 2 photos and description of craft. Entry fee refunded for refused work. Work may be offered for sale; no commission. Craftworker must attend show; demonstrations OK. Registration limit: 90-100. Sponsor provides electricity for demonstrations, 24-hour security and morning coffee and donuts.
Promotion: Show is advertised by newspapers, radio, fliers and word of mouth. "Advertising is done in more than 7 newspapers, covering more than a 200 square mile area. The show is publicized on local radio. About 5000 fliers will be passed out in local business establishments before the show. Prejudging committee goes to various shows around Connecticut and tells of our show." Proceeds help sponsor special olympics, scholarships and youth sports.

GUILFORD HANDCRAFTS EXPOSITION, Guilford Handcraft Center, Box 221, Guilford CT 06437. (203)453-5947. Exposition Chairman: Jill Coykendall. Director: Beth Parrott. "The purpose of the Exposition is to support the Guilford Handcraft Center, a nonprofit school, gallery and shop dedicated to furthering interest and participation in crafts, and exposing the

---

* *Those listings preceded by an asterisk present awards for prize-winning crafts.*

general public to crafts as an art form." Estab. 1956. Annual outdoor show (under tents on the Guilford Green) held 3 days in July. Average attendance: 50,000. Presents cash awards for best display.
Acceptable Work: Considers batik; ceramics; dolls; glass art; jewelry; leatherworking; metalsmithing; pottery; soft sculpture; fiberwork; and woodcrafting. No crafts "taken basically from nature—each piece must clearly show the impact of the artist on his materials."
Terms: "Applications available in December and due in February." Entry fee $125/10x12. Prejudging by 5 slides due with application and $10 jurying fee. Work may be offered for sale. Craftworker must attend show; demonstrations encouraged. Registration limit: 100. Sponsor provides chairs; coverings; electricity for demonstrations; table; and 24-hour security.
Promotion: Show is advertised by newspaper and radio publicity. "A brochure is distributed and available to exhibitors, as well as display posters. Newspaper releases will be made available to individual craftsmen for use in their local papers."

HARTFORD CHRISTMAS CRAFT EXPO I AND II, Box 370, Farmington CT 06032. (203)224-8388. Directors: Denise Barile and Rudy Kowalczyk. Sponsor: American Craft Expositions, Inc. Estab. 1973. Two triannual indoor shows held two weekends, 3 days each in December at Hartford, Connecticut. Average attendance: 38,000 total.
Acceptable Work: Considers batik, candlemaking, ceramics, dollmaking, glass art, jewelry, leatherworking, macrame, metalsmithing, pottery, scrimshaw, sculpture, soft sculpture, weaving, woodcrafting and "other high quality craft media." No kits, manufactured or assembled items, dealers or agents. Two shows for 2 weekends.
Terms: Entries accepted until 60 days before show. Popular media close earlier. Entry fee: $135 and up, depending upon size. Display area: 10x10 to 10x20. Prejudging by 6 slides. Entry fee refunded for refused work. Work must be offered for sale; no commission. Craftworker must attend show; demonstrations encouraged. Registration limit: 250. Sponsor provides electricity for demonstrations and 24-hour security. Rental chairs and tables available.

*****THE HUDSON VALLEY ART ASSOCIATION, INC.**, c/o Rayma Spaulding, 15 Minivale Rd., Stamford CT 06907. Annual show held first Sunday in May at White Plains, Connecticut. Entries accepted 8 days before show. Membership includes exhibition fee for 1 exhibit. Fee for nonmembers is $10. Maximum 1 entry/artist. Considers sculpture not previously exhibited in County Center. Only works done in realistic manner. Work may be offered for sale; 10% commission.
Awards: Presents Hudson Valley Art Association Gold Medal of Honor for oil, watercolor, sculpture and graphics; over $2,400 in cash awards; and honorable mention in all classes.

INTERNATIONAL GUEST EXHIBITION OF PAINTING, SCULPTURE & GRAPHICS, 1814 Newfield Ave., Stamford CT 06903. Associate Director: Darrel Couturier. Sponsor: Couturier Galerie. Estab. 1962. Annual indoor show held 4-6 weeks in the spring. Attendance: 1,000-1,500. Categories: paintings; sculpture; and graphics. Considers mobiles and sculpture.
Terms: Entries accepted until 6 months before show. No entry fee. Maximum 2-5 entries/category. Prejudging by slides or color photos. Work may be offered for sale; 40% commission. Craftworker needn't attend show; no demonstrations. Registration limit: 10-12. "Normal gallery situation."
Promotion: Show is advertised by invitations; newspaper ads; and radio. "Biography and photo of artist with a work is helpful for publicity when the work is accepted. Photos must be glossy b&w 5x7 or 8x10."

MARLBOROUGH CREATIVE ARTS FESTIVAL, Box 42, Marlborough CT 06447. (203)267-9666. President: Brenda Berger. Sponsor: Marlborough Community Arts, Inc. Estab. 1974. Annual outdoor show held 2 days in September; large tent and covered pavilion available. Average attendance: 10,000. Considers all crafts.
Terms: Entries accepted until 4 weeks before show. Entry fee: $15/craftworker. Prejudging by photos. Entry fee due after prejudging. Work may be offered for sale; no commission. Craftworker needn't attend show; demonstrations OK. Registration limit: 60. Sponsor provides coverings (tent); display panels; pegboard; electricity for demonstrations; table; and chicken wire art screens. "If craftsmen wish to use pegboard booth backings, they must supply their own S-hooks."

MEET THE ARTISTS—CHAPEL SQUARE MALL, 41 Green St., Milford CT 06460. (203)874-5672. Director: Denise Curt. Estab. 1963. Triannual indoor show held 3 days in March, May/June and November at New Haven, Connecticut. Average attendance: 4,000.

Acceptable Work: Considers photography, sculpture and batik. No kits, manufactured items, dealers, imports or work other than that of craftworker. "No burlap covered racks, but cotton or similar, non-flammable fabrics are permissable." Bestsellers: $5-400.
Terms: Entries accepted until 1 week before show. Entry fee: $35/artist per show. Display area: 5x10 walk around (unless 1 side requested only). Prejudging by slides, photos or brochure. SASE. Entry fee refunded for refused work. Work may be offered for sale; no commission. Craftworker must attend show; demonstrations OK. Registration limit: 5. Sponsor provides electricity for demonstrations and 24-hour security. "Security is there but we are not responsible."
Promotion: Show is advertised by TV, radio, newspapers, magazines, preshow mall posters, mailers, photo stories, Commission on the Arts Calendar and Chamber of Commerce State Visitors Events. Submit 5x7 b&w glossy photos, brochure and resume for promotion (include work, goals, etc.).
Sales Tip: "Craftworker should be available to converse. Be pleasant, clean and neat, informative and agreeable. No haggling/bargaining allowed—prices are *firm*."

MEET THE ARTISTS—MILFORD GREEN, 41 Green St., Milford CT 06460. (203)874-5672. Director: Denise Curt. Estab. 1963. Annual indoor show held 2 days during Memorial Day Weekend at Milford, Connecticut. Average attendance: 4,000.
Acceptable Work: Considers all crafts except ceramics and decoupage. No kits, manufactured items, dealers, imports or work other than that of craftworker. Bestsellers: $5-400.
Terms: Entries accepted until 1 week before show. Entry fee: $20/artist. Display area: 5x10 walk around (unless 1 side requested only). Prejudging by slides, photos or brochure. SASE. Entry fee refunded for refused work. Work may be offered for sale; no commission. Craftworker must attend show; demonstrations OK. Registration limit: 5. Sponsor provides electricity for demonstrations and 24-hour security.
Promotion: Show is advertised by TV, radio, newspapers, magazines, preshow mall posters, mailers, photo stories, Commission on the Arts Calendar and Chamber of Commerce State Visitors Events. Submit 5x7 b&w glossy photos, brochure and resume for promotion (include work, goals, etc.).
Sales Tip: "Craftworker should be available to converse. Be pleasant, clean and neat, informative and agreeable. No haggling/bargaining allowed—prices are *firm*."

MEET THE ARTISTS—OLDE MYSTIC VILLAGE, 41 Green St., Milford CT 06460. (203)874-5672. Director: Denise Curt. Estab. 1963. Biannual outdoor show held 2 days in August and 3 days in September at Mystic, Connecticut. Average attendance: 4,000.
Acceptable Work: Considers sculpture. No leather, decoupage, candles or jewelry. No kits, manufactured items, dealers, imports or work other than that of craftworker. Bestsellers: $5-400.
Terms: Entries accepted until 2 weeks before show. Entry fee: $30/artist (August), $80/artist (September). Display area: 5x10 walk around (unless 1 side requested only). Prejudging by slides, photos or brochure. SASE. Entry fee refunded for refused work. Work may be offered for sale; no commission. Craftworker must attend show; demonstrations OK. Registration limit: 5.
Promotion: Show is advertised by TV, radio, newspapers, magazines, preshow mall posters, mailers, photo stories, Commission on the Arts Calendar and Chamber of Commerce State Visitors Events. Submit 5x7 b&w glossy photos, brochure and resume for promotion (include work, goals, etc.).
Sales Tip: "Craftworker should be available to converse. Be pleasant, clean and neat, informative and agreeable. No haggling/bargaining allowed—prices are *firm*."

MEET THE ARTISTS—MERIDEN SQUARE MALL, 41 Green St., Milford CT 06460. (203)874-5672. Director: Denise Curt. Estab. 1963. Annual indoor show held 3 days in October at Meriden, Connecticut. Average attendance: 4,000.
Acceptable Work: Considers painting, photography, fine arts, sculpture and limited quality crafts. No kits, manufactured items, dealers, imports or work other than that of craftworker. Bestsellers: $5-400.
Terms: Entries accepted until 1 week before show. Entry fee: $35/artist. Display area: 5x10 walk around (unless 1 side requested only). Prejudging by slides, photos or brochure. SASE. Entry fee refunded for refused work. Work may be offered for sale; no commission. Craftworker must attend show; demonstrations OK. Registration limit: 5. Sponsor provides electricity for demonstrations.
Promotion: Show is advertised by TV, radio, newspapers, magazines, preshow mall posters,

mailers, photo stories, Commission on the Arts Calendar and Chamber of Commerce State Visitors Events. Submit 5x7 b&w glossy photos, brochure and resume for promotion (include work, goals, etc.).
Sales Tip: "Craftworker should be available to converse. Be pleasant, clean and neat, informative and agreeable. No haggling/bargaining allowed—prices are *firm*."

*MILFORD OYSTER FESTIVAL, 5 N. Broad St., Box 452, Milford CT 06460. (203)878-0681. Coordinator: Barbara Hernandez. Sponsor: Milford Oyster Festival, Inc. Estab. 1975. Annual outdoor show held 1 day in August. Average attendance: 55,000.
Acceptable Work: Considers all crafts, except decoupage. No kits, mass-produced and white elephant items, printed material, pot boilers or imports.
Terms: Entries accepted until 4 weeks before show. Entry fee: $15/artist. Prejudging by slides. Entry fee refunded for refused work. Work must be offered for sale; no commisssion. Craftworker must attend show; demonstrations OK. Registration limit: 200. Sponsor provides 15x15 display area, electricity for demonstrations and fencing. Exhibitor handles sales and sales taxes.
Awards: Presents 1st, 2nd and 3rd place ribbons in each category.

*NCAA JURIED SHOW, c/o NCCC, Park Place, Winsted CT 06098. (203)379-8543. Contact: Elaine Reeve. Sponsor: Northwestern Connecticut Art Association. Estab. 1971. Annual indoor show held 2 weeks in June-July. Average attendance: 500. Entries accepted until 1 week before show. Entry fee: $6-7/entry. Maximum 2 entries per craftworker. Prejudging; no entry fees refunded for refused work. Work may be offered for sale; no commission. Open to craftworkers living in the New York City area or New England. Registration limit: approximately 125 works. Presents $700 in cash prizes and $500 in purchase awards.

*NEW ENGLAND PAINTING & SCULPTURE EXHIBITION, 1037 Silvermine Rd., New Canaan CT 06840. (203)966-5617. Gallery Director: Dee Robinson. Sponsor: Silvermine Guild of Artists. Annual indoor/outdoor show held 1 month in June. Attendance: 5,000-6,000. Entries accepted until 1 month before show. Entry fee: $10/artist. Maximum 2 entries/artist. Work may be offered for sale; 33⅓% commission. Craftworker needn't attend show; no demonstrations. Sponsor provides display panels. Considers soft and other sculpture. Presents cash awards.

*OCEAN BEACH PARK ARTS & CRAFTS SHOW, 21 Shermor Pl., New London CT 06320. (203)447-3031. Director: Evelyn Kaplan. Sponsor: City of New London. Estab. 1976. Annual outdoor show held 2 days in August. Average attendance: 16,000. Considers all crafts. Bestsellers: under $50.
Terms: Entries accepted until show date. Entry fee: $15/10 linear feet of display area; depth varies. Work may be offered for sale; no commission. Craftworker needn't attend show, but at own risk. Demonstrations OK. Registration limit: 450. Sponsor provides 2 tents, plus sun shelters for some, some electricity for demonstrations and some fencing. Write for information. SASE.
Promotion: Show is advertised by local newspapers, radio and possibly TV. "We will send invitations to the craftperson's mailing lists if we are provided with them early."
Awards: Presents $500 in purchase awards; ribbons; and possibly cash awards.

OLD AVON VILLAGE ARTS & CRAFTS SHOW, Sarah L. Freedman Chapter AMC Cancer Center & Hospital, 11 Robin Rd., Apt. B-3, West Hartford CT 06119. (203)233-7192. Coordinator: Marjorie Block. May also contact Rachel Weinstein at 53 Arnold Way, West Hartford CT 06119; (203)236-5112. Annual outdoor show held 2 days in September at Avon, Connecticut. Average attendance: 3,000.
Acceptable Work: Considers all crafts. No kits, imports or flea market items. Bestsellers: seascapes or portraits.
Terms: Entries accepted until 3 weeks before show. Entry fee: $25. Display area: 8x10. Work may be offered for sale; no commission. Craftworker must attend show; demonstrations OK. Registration limit: 90. Sponsor provides electricity for demonstrations.
Promotion: Show is advertised by newspapers (especially local), television, radio and perodicals. "Any biographical material and former awards will be helpful for promotional purposes." All proceeds go for cancer research.

*ON THE GREEN, Box 304, Glastonbury CT 06033. Vice President: Don Melanson. Sponsor: Glastonbury Art Guild. Estab. 1970. Annual outdoor show held 2 days in September. Average attendance: 15,000. Entries accepted until 4 weeks before show. Entry fee: $25/member;

$35/nonmember. Display area: 10x10. Work may be offered for sale; no commission. Craftworker must attend show; demonstrations OK. Registration limit: 100. Sponsor provides fencing. Categories: judged oils, watercolors, mixed media and sculpture graphics; non-juried in the same media; and crafts. Considers all crafts. Presents 3 $50 1st prizes.

ST. JOSEPH COLLEGE ARTS & CRAFTS FAIR, 1678 Asylum Ave., W. Hartford CT 06117. (203)232-4571. Contact: Alumnae Office, St. Joseph College. Sponsor: St. Joseph College. Purpose: to raise money for scholarship fund. Estab. 1967. Annual indoor show held 2 days in March. Average attendance: 2,000. Entries accepted until 2 months before show. Entry fee: $20/display area. Prejudging by slides and/or photos; entry fee refunded for refused work. Craftworker must attend show; demonstrations OK. Registration limit: 50-60. Sponsor provides chairs and tables. Considers all crafts.

*****SLATER MEMORIAL MUSEUM**, 108 Crescent St., Norwich CT 06360. (203)887-2505, ext. 218. Museum Director: Joseph P. Gualtieri. Annual show held in April. Entry fee: $4/item; Friends of the Museum may submit 1 piece free. Maximum 2 entries per craftworker. Work may be offered for sale; 20% commission. Entries must be hand-delivered. Considers sculpture. Maximum 200 pounds. Open to Connecticut residents only. Presents cash awards of $250, $100, $75 and $50.

SPRING CRAFTS FAIR, Mattatuck Community College Art Club, 640 Chase Pky., Waterbury CT 06708. (203)757-9661 (ext. 274). Associate Professor of Art: Dr. Elizabeth Michalowski. Estab. 1972. Annual outdoor show (indoors in case of rain) held 1 day in spring, usually the first Sunday in May. Average attendance: 1,500-2,500. Acceptable Work: Considers all crafts. No kits, mass-produced or machine-made items, and no crafts made from patterns. "We may have a best or most popular display, but no decision has been reached yet."
Terms: Entries accepted until 1 week before show. Entry fee: $5-10/artist. Display area: usually 15x15. Work may be offered for sale; no commission. Prefers craftworker to attend show; encourages demonstrations. Sponsor provides chairs, electricity for demonstrations (depending on demand) and tables. Exhibitor handles sales and taxes.
Promotion: Show is advertised by a mailing to previous participants, newsletter, display advertisements, listings in area art calendars, posters, and TV and radio spots. "Publicity usually begins 2 months ahead. We could use interesting information or photos about the artist and his work which we can offer to newspapers."
Sales Tip: "This is primarily an industrial town, so we find artists with sensible prices do well. Artists who are friendly and willing to explain do well."
Profile: "Our interest in this fair is as a cultural activity and learning opportunity for our students and the community. It is always part of a 2-week Spring Arts Festival with many other activities scheduled (film, dance, demonstrations, music, class visits)."

SPRING MARKET, Connecticut Craft Professionals, Inc., Box 5463, Hamden CT 06518. Directors: Eva Orsini and Bill Richards. Purpose: to provide a wholesale and retail outlet for professional craftworkers. Estab. 1977. Annual indoor show held 1 day wholesale, 2 days retail in March at New Haven, Connecticut. Average attendance: 10,000. Entries accepted until announced deadline. Booth fee: $90/8x10 display area plus $5 application fee. Prejudging by slides; booth fee refunded for refused work. Work must be offered for sale; no commission. Craftworker must attend show; demonstrations OK. Registration limit: 150. Sponsor provides electricity and 24-hour security. Show is advertised by mailing lists; newspapers; TV; and radio. Submit b&w glossies for publicity. 1978 show sales totalled over $60,000. Considers all crafts except kits; imports; agents; embellishments; and assemblages.

SUMMER CRAFT SHOW & BAZAAR, First Church of Christ, Town St., East Haddam CT 06423. Chairman: Karl P. Stofko. Estab. 1968. Annual outdoor show held 1 day in July. Attendance: 800-1,000. Entries accepted until show date. Entry fee: $3/artist. Display area: approximately 10'. Work may be offered for sale; 10% commission. Craftworker must attend show; demonstrations OK. Registration limit: 25-30. Sponsor provides chairs. Considers all crafts.

WEST HARTFORD SPRING ARTS & CRAFTS FAIR, c/o Sheila Accortt, 21 Michael Rd., Simsbury CT 06070. (203)658-1762. Sponsor: Connecticut River Valley Region Women's American O.R.T. Purpose: fundraiser for Women's American O.R.T., "which supports a network of 700 vocational schools in 23 countries throughout the world." Estab. 1974. Annual outdoor show held 1 day in May. Average attendance: 8,000. Entries accepted until show date.

Entry fee: $15/display area measuring 2 parking stalls. Maximum 8 craftworkers/craft category. Work may be offered for sale; no commission. Craftworker must attend show; demonstrations OK (no electricity available). Registration limit: 150. Considers all crafts.
Promotion: Show is advertised by newspapers; TV; radio; and posters. Exhibitors should provide b&w photos.

WESTPORT CREATIVE ARTS FESTIVAL, 44 Imperial Ave., Westport CT 06880. (203)227-4240. Sponsor: Westport Young Woman's League. Estab. 1976. Annual indoor invitational show held 2 days in November. Average attendance: 3,600. Considers all crafts.
Terms: Entries accepted until show is full. Entry fee: $15/8x10 display area. Prejudging by slides, photos and other shows; entry fee due after invitation is issued. Work must be offered for sale; 15% commission. Craftworker must attend show; no demonstrations. Registration limit: 66-70. Sponsor provides chairs; tables on first come basis; 24-hour security protection; program; handling of Master Charge; unloading assistance; Saturday dinner and booth-sitting.
Promotion: Show is advertised by newspaper articles; paid advertising; regional publications; postcards; posters; radio spots; and directional signs and banners. Craftworker should provide as much information as possible for press releases, including glossies.

WESTPORT HANDCRAFTS FAIR, 10 Lyons Plain Rd., Westport CT 06880. Co-chairman: Bobbie Schneider. Sponsor: Westport-Weston Cooperative Nursery School. Estab. 1966. Annual outdoor/indoor (in case of rain) show held Memorial Day Weekend. Entries accepted until 3 months before show. Entry fee: $15/10x10 display area. Prejudging; "good cross section of items may be delivered by craftsman (at his expense) to place of jurying, or approximately 7 slides of photos are acceptable." Entry fee due after prejudging. Work may be offered for sale; 15% commission. Craftworker must attend show; demonstrations encouraged. Registration limit: 90-100. Sponsor provides electricity for demonstrations.
Acceptable Work: Considers batik; candlemaking; ceramics; decoupage; dollmaking; glass art; jewelry; lapidary; leatherworking; macrame; metalsmithing; needlecrafts; pottery; soft sculpture; weaving; and woodcrafting. Work must be that of attending craftworker.
Promotion: "Good write-ups with photos appear ¼ in all area papers, Connecticut magazines, *Yankee Magazine*; *New York Times*; *Connecticut Weekly*; and local papers of craftsmen." Also promoted by radio. Exhibitor should supply 5x7 or 8x10 b&w glossies.

*****YAAF EXHIBITION OF FINE ART,** Box 362, Fairfield CT 06430. Contact: Jack Farkas or Paul Strauss. Sponsor: Young Artist Association of Fairfield. Annual show. Entry fee: $7.50. Work may be offered for sale; 25% commission. Sponsor provides display equipment, but sculptures must be equipped with stands. Considers fine sculpture. Presents cash and purchase awards.

Delaware

BRANDYWINE ARTS FESTIVAL, 1307 Orange St., Wilmington DE 19801. (302)651-8364. Contact: George Sargisson. Estab. 1966. Annual outdoor show held 2 days in September. Average attendance: 12,000-15,000. Considers all crafts.
Terms: Entries accepted until 4 weeks before show. Entry fee: $40/10x10' display area. Work offered for sale; 20% commission. Craftworker or representative must attend show; demonstrations recommended. Show is advertised by brochures; billboards; posters; and flyers. Submit promotional material.
Profile: "Our purpose is to stimulate interest in the arts; to develop appreciation of the performing arts; to create the opportunity for the public to discover the countless hours of enjoyment and pleasure derived from the arts; to provide cultural expression for people of all tastes; and to present a show window for the working artists emphasizing the natural beauties of the historic Brandywine area; and to encourage all artists to share their talents with thousands of people who will be afforded an opportunity to view and purchase the art displayed."

CAPE HENLOPEN CRAFT FAIR & FOLK LIFE FESTIVAL, 119 W. 3rd St., Lewes DE 19958. (302)645-7640. Contact: Chairman. Sponsor: Lewes Historical Society. Purpose: "to raise money for Lewes Historical Society educational programs." Estab. 1972. Annual outdoor show held 2nd Saturday in July. Average attendance: 1,000. Entries accepted until 1 week before show. Entry fee: $10/artist. Prejudging by slides, photos or samples (if feasible); entry fee refunded for refused work. Work may be offered for sale; no commission. Craftworker must attend show; demonstrations required. Registration limit: 60. Sponsor provides electricity for demonstrations.

Acceptable Work: Considers batik; candlemaking; ceramics; decoupage; dollmaking; jewelry; leatherworking; metalsmithing; needlecrafts; pottery; sculpture; soft sculpture; tole painting; weaving; and woodcrafting. "Special interest in marine and historical crafts; furniture-making, for example."

Sales Tip: "Public buys items that are good quality solid craftsmanship. Not interested in items that are gaudy or that the customers might easily make themselves—such as shell animals or bead jewelry."

Promotion: Show is advertised by posters; radio; newspapers; and flyers. "Glossy photos help in promotion articles."

*CONTEMPORARY CRAFT EXHIBITION, 2301 Kentmere Pkwy., Wilmington DE 19806. (302)571-9594. Sponsor: Delaware Art Museum. Estab. 1956. Annual indoor show held 6 weeks beginning in November. Average attendance: 7,000. Limited to craftspersons from Delaware and the Northeast states (New England, New York, Pennsylvania, New Jersey, Maryland and Washington DC). Show is advertised in local papers and *Craft Horizons*.

Acceptable Work: Considers contemporary batik, ceramics, glass art, jewelry, leatherworking, lapidary, metalsmithing, needlecrafts, pottery, sculpture, soft sculpture, weaving and woodcrafting. "Work received must be conceived, designed and executed by the exhibitor."

Terms: Entries accepted until 5 weeks before show. Entry fee: $5/craftworkers. Maximum 3 entries/artist. Prejudging by slides; no entry fees refunded for refused work. Work must be offered for sale; 20% commission. Craftworker needn't attend show; no demonstrations. Registration limit: 150. Sponsor provides insurance on exhibited work; display panels; and 24-hour security.

Awards: "Selection of objects for Museum purchase will be made by the Accessions Committee of the Delaware Art Museum. These objects become a part of the Permanent Collection of the Museum. Three other cash prizes will be awarded by the judge as 'Juror's Choices.' In addition, the juror will select one craftsperson to have an exhibit at the Museum.

Sales: The 1978 show contained both functional and nonfunctional pieces of all price ranges. Sales totaled about $3,000.

CRAFTSMEN'S FAIR AT DELAWARE ART MUSEUM, 2301 Kentmere Pkwy., Wilmington DE 19806. (302)571-9594. Contact: Susan Brooks. Estab. 1972. Annual outdoor show held 1 day in June. Average attendance: 4,000. Open only to persons 18 and older in the Delaware area, including nearby Pennsylvania, New Jersey and Maryland.

Acceptable Work: Considers batik, ceramics, dollmaking, glass art, jewelry, lapidary, leatherworking, metalsmithing, mobiles, needlecrafts, pottery, scrimshaw, sculpture, soft sculpture, weaving and woodcrafting. Must be designed and executed by the exhibiting craftworker. "Embellished items must be made by the craftsperson, thus painted boxes, barnboards, decoupage, molded greenware or products of 'craft kits' are not admitted.

Terms: Entries accepted until filled. Entry fee: $15/artist. Display area: 9x9. Work must be offered for sale; no commission. Craftworker must attend show; demonstrations encouraged. Registration limit: 70. Sponsor provides electricity for demonstrations.

WILMINGTON CRAFT FAIR, 2301 Kentmere Pky., Wilmington DE 19806. (302)571-9594. Contact: Education Department. Sponsor: Delaware Art Museum. Estab. 1972. Annual outdoor show held 1 day in June. Average attendance: 4,000.

Acceptable Work: Considers batik, ceramics, blown glass; jewelry, lapidary, leatherworking, macrame, metalsmithing, needlecrafts, pottery, sculpture, soft sculpture, weaving and woodcrafting. No kits or belts. "Embellished items must be made by the craftsperson, thus painted boxes, barnboards, decoupage, molded greenware or products of craft kits are not admitted." Bestsellers: medium-priced utilitarian crafts.

Terms: Must be 18 years or older and reside in the Delaware area (including nearby Pennsylvania, New Jersey and Maryland). Entries accepted until spaces filled. Entry fee: $15/artist. Display area: 9x9. All entries are screened. Work must be offered for sale; no commision. Craftworker or representative must attend show; demonstrations OK. Registration limit: approximately 70. Sponsor provides electricity for demonstrations. "Crafts artists must furnish their own tables and chairs (a beach umbrella also suggested)."

Florida

ALTAMONTE MALL, 2918 Martel Dr., Dayton OH 45420. (513)254-2900. Director: Clarence Freeland. Annual indoor show held in Altamonte, Florida, 2 weeks in January. Closing date for entry: 1 week before show. Entry fee: $75. Prejudging. Work may be offered for sale; no commission. Craftworkers must attend show; demonstrations OK. Sponsor provides 10x10 display area. Considers all crafts.

Shows and Fairs 449

*THE ART FESTIVAL IN THE VILLAGE, Box 35, Lake Buena Vista FL 32830. Contact: Chairman. Sponsor: Walt Disney World Shopping Village. Purpose: "to provide a showcase for original art and crafts; to make the public aware of current and coming trends in creative works; and build good will for our village." Estab. 1975. Annual outdoor show held 3 days in November at Walt Disney World Village. Average attendance: 90,000. Entries accepted until August. Entry fee: approximately $75/12x10 display area. Prejudging by 3 35mm slides of work, and 1 slide of booth or display; entry fee refunded for refused work. Work should be offered for sale; no commission. Craftworker must attend show; demonstrations OK by arrangement. Registration limit: 50-60. Sponsor provides electricity for demonstrations; 24-hour security; coffee and donuts; assistance in setting up; display sitters for lunch and breaks; discount on accommodations; complimentary admission to Walt Disney World theme park; and free T-shirt. Show is advertised by radio; magazines; newspapers; TV; postcards; calendar of events; and in-flight magazines. Categories: oils and acrylics; watercolors; graphics; photography; sculpture; ceramics; mixed media; and creative crafts.
Acceptable Work: Considers batik; ceramics; glass art; jewelry; leatherworking; macrame; mobiles; pottery; sculpture; soft sculpture; weaving; and woodcrafting. No bread sculpture; mass-produced buckles and leather; or clothing.
Awards: Presents $10,000 in cash; $5,000-7,000 in purchase awards; and 51 ribbons. To win awards "maximize the potential of the media (professionally); push the media to perfection and beyond accepted limits."
Sales: "Several artists, photographers, ceramicists sold out. Some reported $9,000 in sales. Others showed low to medium sales."

*ARTS & CRAFTS FESTIVAL, St. Augustine Arts & Crafts Council, Box 547, St. Augustine FL 32084. (904)829-8175. Director: Frederick White. Estab. 1964. Annual outdoor show held 2 days during Palm Sunday weekend. Average attendance: 100,000. Entries accepted until 6 weeks before show. Entry fee: $50/12x12 display area. Prejudging by 3 slides of work and 1 slide of display; entry fee refunded for refused work. Jury fee $5. Work may be offered for sale; no commission. Craftworker must attend show; demonstrations OK. Registration limit: 144. Sponsor provides electricity for demonstrations; insurance on exhibited work; and 24-hour security. Categories: painting; glass; textiles; leather; sculpture; graphics; ceramics; mixed media; metalwork; and photography. Considers all crafts. Presents $7,200 in cash; plus purchase prizes; and ribbons.
Promotion: Show is advertised by TV; radio; and newspapers. "Exhibitors should supply biography and b&w photographs for publicity."

*ARTS POTPOURRI IN THE PARK, 344 S. Beach St., Daytona Beach FL 32074. (904)252-4769. Chairman: Ruth Bon Fleur. Sponsor: YWCA. Purpose: "to help the YWCA in our community services." Estab. 1974. Semiannual outdoor show held 2 days in April and in November. Attendance: 10,000-15,000. Entries accepted until show date. Entry fee: $15/10x20 display area. Work may be offered for sale; no commission. Craftworker must attend show; demonstrations OK. Registration limit: 200. Sponsor provides limited electricity for demonstrations. Show is advertised by local newspapers; magazine listings; radio; and TV. Considers all crafts. Awards 1st, 2nd and 3rd place ribbons.

BOCA RATON MALL ARTS & CRAFTS SHOW, 615 South 'H' St., Lake Worth FL 33460. (305)968-9029. Contact: Jim Readey. Sponsor J.J. Readey Promotions. Semiannual indoor show held 3 days in May and October at Boca Raton, Florida.
Acceptable Work: Considers all original crafts except jewelry and leather. "A drop cloth is a must. Height of racks: 6'6" maximum."
Terms: Entries accepted until 1 week before show or until spaces are filled. Entry fee: $25/12x6' display area. No refunds after closing date, unless show is cancelled. No confirmations sent—use cancelled check as confirmation. Work may be offered for sale; no commission. Craftworker must attend show; demonstrations OK. "All artists must exhibit complete hours of the show. Anyone leaving a show before closing will be refused entrance into further shows. Supply your own racks and tables. Tables must be covered to floor on all sides. Work left up overnight is at your own risk."
Promotion: "We would appreciate glossy b&w photos for publicity releases."
Profile: Located in enclosed and air conditioned mall. Anchor stores are Britts and Jeffersons.

*BOYNTON BEACH ANNUAL FESTIVAL OF THE ARTS, 128 E. Ocean Ave., Boynton Beach FL 33435. (305)732-2636. Recreation Supervisor: Laura Mudryk. Sponsor: recreation department; chamber of commerce; and the community school. Purpose: "to offer a cultural event for the surrounding areas and the citizens." Estab. 1974. Annual outdoor show held 2 days in March. Attendance: 15,000-20,000. Entries accepted until 2 weeks before show. Entry fee: $20 for professionals, $15 for amateurs. Display area: 8x12. Maximum 3 entries/category for judging, unlimited for nonjuried areas. Prejudging by 3 slides and photos. Work may be offered for sale; no commission. Craftworker must attend show; demonstrations OK. Registration limit: 200. Sponsor provides electricity for demonstrations. Categories: paintings; watercolors; sculpture; graphics; jewelry; ceramics; and mixed media. Considers batik; ceramics; jewelry; leatherworking; macrame; pottery; sculpture; weaving; and woodcrafting. Presents $1,000 in cash; and 1st, 2nd and 3rd place ribbons.

BREVARD MALL FESTIVAL OF ARTS & CRAFTS, 615 S. "H" St., Lake Worth FL 33460. (305)582-6133. Director: J.J. Readey. Annual indoor show held 3 days in February. Average attendance: 3,000. Entries accepted until 1 week before show. Entry fee: $30/12x10 display area. Prejudging by 3 slides or color photos; entry fee refunded for refused work. Work may be offered for sale; no commission. Craftworker or representative must attend show; demonstrations OK. Registration limit: 40. Sponsor provides electricity for demonstrations "if requested in advance." Considers all crafts. "Prefers batiks and needlework framed."
Promotion: Show is advertised by newspapers and radio. Exhibitor should supply 8x10 b&w glossy photos and resume for newspaper releases.

***CITRUS COUNTY FESTIVAL OF THE ARTS**, Citrus County Art League, Box 131, Lecanto FL 32661. Sponsor: Art League and Chamber of Commerce. Purpose: fundraiser. Estab. 1970. Annual outdoor show held 1 day in November at Inverness, Florida. Entries accepted up until show. Entry fee: $12/pre-registration; $15/10x10 display area. Work may be offered for sale; no commission. Craftworker needn't attend show; demonstrations OK. Show is advertised by local papers and *Sunshine Artist*. Presents cash awards for 1st, 2nd, and 3rd; ribbons for honorable mentions.

COASTLAND CENTER INVITATIONAL WINTER FESTIVAL OF ART, 615 South "H" St., Lake Worth FL 33460. (305)582-6133. Director: Jim Readey. Sponsor: Coastland Center and J.J. Readey. Estab. 1978. Annual indoor show held 3 days in February at Naples, Florida. Attendance: 30,000. Entries accepted until 1 week before show. Entry fee: $60-40/12x8 display area. Prejudging by 5 slides that are representative of work; entry fee refunded for refused work. Work may be offered for sale; no commission. Craftworker or representative must attend show; demonstrations OK. Registration limit: 50. Sponsor provides 24-hour security and electricity for demonstrations if requested in advance. Considers framed batiks; and stone metal and wood sculpture. "Most work must be framed. Portfolio may be used."
Promotion: Show is advertised by newspapers, radio and TV. Send "8x10 b&w glossy for newspaper release—also resume."

***CORAL GABLES MIRACLE MILE SIDEWALK ART SHOW**, Coral Gables Chamber of Commerce, 50 Aragon Ave., Coral Gables FL 33134. (305)446-1657. Executive Director: Tom E. Chegin. Sponsor: Chamber of Commerce and Miami Palette Club. Purpose: "to bring both culture and potential business to Coral Gables shopping area." Estab. 1964. Annual outdoor show held 3 days during the last weekend of January. Average attendance: 10,000. Entries accepted until show date; "checks accepted only until a week before the show, after that time, only money orders or certified checks will be accepted." Entry fee: $50/artist. Display area is "approximately 25' wide; artists may use no more than 50% of the sidewalk width, or approximately 7'. Description of media is required on the application." Work may be offered for sale; no commission. Artist must attend show; demonstrations OK. Considers sculpture. Presents $750 in cash; $500 in purchase prizes; and honorable mention ribbons.
Promotion: "The show is promoted year-round in artists' publications and is widely promoted locally by newspaper, TV and radio coverage—through public service, advertising and news releases during October-January."

CRAFTPRODUCERS MARKETPLACE, North Hill, Readsboro VT 05350. Directors: Charley Dooley and Riki Moss. Sponsor: Craftproducers Incorporated. Annual indoor/outdoor show held in mid-March at Sarasota, Florida. Considers all crafts. Average attendance: 6,000.
Terms: Entries accepted January-December. Entry fee: $80/8x10' display area. Prejudging by 5 slides. Work must be offered for sale; no commission. Craftworker must attend show; demonstrations OK (if arranged prior to show). Registration limit: 100. Sponsors provide chairs, electricity for demonstrations ($10 fee), tables and 24-hour security.

Shows and Fairs **451**

*DELAND OUTDOOR ART FESTIVAL, Box 781, Deland FL 32720. (305)734-1562. Co-chairman: Joyce N. Campbell. Purpose: "we love arts locally, and we want to share with others." Estab. 1965. Annual outdoor show held 2 days in March. Entries accepted until show date. Entry fee: $12/artist. Display area: 12' parking space. Work may be offered for sale; no commission. Craftworker must attend show; demonstrations OK. Categories: oils; acrylics and mixed media; watercolor; sculpture; graphics and photography; and creative crafts. Considers all original crafts. Presents $1,745 in cash awards; merit awards; best display award; and ribbons and cash prizes.
Sales Tip: You "should have name cards and literature. Many ask about the work on Saturday and come back Sunday to buy. Have attractive display racks and stands."

*FALL FOR ART, Box 1483, Sanford FL 32771. Sponsor: Sanford-Seminole Art Association. Estab. 1959. Annual outdoor show held 2 days in September. Average attendance: 10,000. Entries accepted until 2 weeks before show. Entry fee: $20/8x14 display area. Prejudging by 3 slides and/or pictures. Entry fee refunded to those refused. Work may be offered for sale; no commission. Craftworker must attend show; demonstrations OK. Categories: oils and acrylics; watercolor and pastels; graphics and photography; sculpture; and creative crafts. Presents $1,400 in cash, and ribbons and purchase awards.
Acceptable Work: Considers batik; ceramics; jewelry; lapidary; leatherworking; macrame; metalsmithing; mobiles; needlecrafts; pottery; sculpture; soft sculpture; weaving; and woodcrafting. "No sewing as in clothes, quilts or doll clothes; junk jewelry; decoupage; or commercial furniture. All work must be framed or hung (as in wall hangings and batiks). May have other works in portfolio."
Sales Tip: "To improve sales, provide a friendly personality, be willing to talk to people without 'pressure tactics,' and have a good attitude with show people (sometimes your best buyers and traders)." Artist pays own sales tax.
Promotion: Show is advertised by newspaper; radio; TV; art magazines; posters; flyers; bumper stickers; and T-shirts.

FESTIVAL OF ART, 615 South 'H' St., Lake Worth FL 33460. (305)968-9029. Contact: Jim Readey. Sponsor J.J. Readey Promotions. Semiannual indoor show held 4 days in March and October at Orange Park Mall, Jacksonville, Florida.
Acceptable Work: Considers sculpture, china painting and woodcarving. No pottery, jewelry, lapidary, leather handicraft, wax or knitting. "A drop cloth is a must. Height of racks: 6'6" maximum."
Terms: Entries accepted until 1 week before show or until spaces are filled. Entry fee: $40/12x6' display area; 6 spaces available down side corridors at $25 each. No refunds after closing date, unless show is cancelled. No confirmations sent—use cancelled check as confirmation. Work may be offered for sale; no commission. Craftworker must attend show; demonstrations OK. "All artists must exhibit complete hours of the show. Anyone leaving a show before closing will be refused entrance into further shows. Supply your own racks and tables. Tables must be covered to floor on all sides. Work left up overnight is at your own risk."
Promotion: "We would appreciate glossy b&w photos for publicity releases."

*FESTIVAL OF THE ARTS, City of Miami Beach, Bin O, Miami Beach FL 33139. (305)673-7733. Chairperson: Pearl Kipnis. Sponsor: Fine Arts Board. Purpose: "to increase interest in the creative and performing arts." Estab. 1971. Annual outdoor show held 2 days in February. Average attendance: 200,000. Entries accepted until 2 months before show. Entry fee: $50/10x10 display area. Prejudging by 3 slides from each category entered. Work may be offered for sale; no commission. Craftworker must attend show; demonstrations OK if approved by Fine Arts Board of Directors. Categories: painting, graphics and drawings, sculpture, crafts and photography. Considers all crafts.
Awards: Presents $500 1st prize; $150 2nd prize; $1,000 purchase prize; and $100 best display award. Awards total $4,350.

*FIESTA IN THE PARK, Southeast Bank Building, Suite 605, Orlando FL 32801. Program Director: Ann E. Smith. Sponsor: City of Orlando, Florida Senior Programs and Downtown Development Board. Estab. 1972. Annual outdoor show held 2 days during the first weekend in November. Average attendance: 250,000. Considers all handmade crafts.
Terms: Entries accepted until show date or until spaces filled. Entry fee: $15/10 feet display area; $5 for students and senior citizens. Work may be offered for sale; 10% commission. Craftworker must attend show; demonstrations OK (based on needed electricity). Registration limit: 425. Sponsor provides limited electricity for demonstrations and 24 hour security. Taxes

must be paid to the committee, if exhibitor does not have sales tax number; number must be on file prior to show.
Awards: Presents $50, $25 and $10 for each category as well as best in show; and ribbons for 1st, 2nd, 3rd, honorable mention, and best booth decoration. "Judging is done by an independent group, not the Fiesta Committee."
Promotion: Show is advertised by newspapers, TV, radio and magazines. "If you have an unusual craft or particular item that would interest people and draw them in to see it, please tell us about it."
Profile: "The display area is a mile and a quarter sidewalk around a lake." Bestsellers: easy to carry items.

FLORIDA FOLK FESTIVAL, Box 265, White Springs FL 32096. (904)397-2192. Assistant Director: Jim McDuffee. Program Coordinator: Barbara Beauchamp. Sponsor: Stephen Foster Center. Estab. 1953. Annual outdoor show held 4 days in May. Average attendance: 30,000.
Acceptable Work: Priority given to Florida craftsmen. Considers candlemaking; dollmaking; jewelry; lapidary; leatherworking; metalsmithing; needlecrafts; pottery; tole painting; weaving; woodcrafting; quilting; spinning; natural dyeing; and other folk crafts.
Terms: Entries accepted until 4 weeks before show. No entry fee. Display area: 6x12 or 12x12. Prejudging. Work must be offered for sale; 15% commission. Craftworker must attend show; demonstrations OK. Registration limit: 25-50. Sponsor provides coverings and 24-hour security.
Promotion: Show is advertised by news releases to all TV; radio; and newspapers in Florida and southern Georgia. Exhibitor should supply "background information on themselves as well as 8x10 b&w glossy photo showing their involvement in their craftwork."

FLORIDA FOREST FESTIVAL ARTS & CRAFTS SHOW & SALE, Box 892, Perry FL 32347. (904)584-5366. Chairman: Nadine O. Loughridge. Sponsor: Perry-Taylor County Chamber of Commerce. Purpose: "to add interest to Festival; promote local artists; and give the county's rural population a chance to see and buy arts and crafts." Estab. 1971. Annual outdoor show (with 30 canopies for rent) held 1 day in October. Average attendance: 31,000. Entries accepted until 1 week before show. Entry fee: $3/9x9 display area. Work must be offered for sale; 10% commission. Craftworker must attend show; demonstrations OK. Registration limit: 55. Sponsor provides electricity for demonstrations, and carries liability insurance. Considers all crafts. "B&w photos showing artist with work are appreciated." 1977 exhibitor sales totalled $3,708.70.

FOURTH OF JULY CELEBRATION & OPEN AIR CRAFTS FAIR, Box 265, White Springs, FL 32096. (904)397-2192. Program Director: Barbara Beauchamp. Sponsor: Stephen Foster Center. Purpose: "to showcase the folk artist in Florida and their works." Estab. 1976. Annual outdoor show held on July 4. Entries accepted until 3 weeks before show. Display area: 6x12 or 12x12. Prejudging by slides or photos. Work may be offered for sale; 15% commission. Craftworker must attend show; demonstrations OK. Registration limit: 25-100. Sponsor provides coverings and 24-hour security.
Acceptable Work: Considers candlemaking; dollmaking; jewelry; lapidary; leatherworking; metalsmithing; needlecrafts; pottery; soft sculpture; tole painting; weaving; woodcrafting; quilting; quilling; spinning; natural dyeing; pine needle crafts; palmetto; dried natural flowers of Florida; cabinetmaking; and whip braiding.
Promotion: Show is advertised by "news releases to all newspapers, TV and radio stations in south Georgia and Florida. Exhibitors should supply biographical information on themselves and glossy 5x7 b&w photo of themselves showing their involvement in craft."

GAINESVILLE MALL ARTS & CRAFTS SHOW, 615 South 'H' St., Lake Worth FL 33460. (305)968-9029. Contact: Jim Readey. Sponsor J.J. Readey Promotions. Semiannual indoor show held 3 days in January and July at Gainsville, Florida.
Acceptable Work: Considers shell craft, china painting, drawing sculpture, wood carvings and crafts. No jewelry. No plants except Bonsai. "A drop cloth is a must. Height of racks: 6'6" maximum."
Terms: Entries accepted until 1 week before show or until spaces are filled. Entry fee: $25/12x6' display area. No refunds after closing date, unless show is cancelled. No confirmations sent—use cancelled check as confirmation. Prejudging by slides or photos if have not previously shown with J.J. Readey. Work may be offered for sale; no commission. Craftworker must attend show; demonstrations OK. "All artists must exhibit complete hours of the show. Anyone leaving a show before closing will be refused entrance into further shows. Supply your

own racks and tables. Tables must be covered to floor on all sides. Work left up overnight is at your own risk."
Promotion: "We would appreciate glossy b&w photos for publicity releases."
Profile: Located in enclosed and air conditioned mall. Anchor stores are Sears, Maas Bros.; mall includes 40 other stores.

*GASPARILLA SIDEWALK ART FESTIVAL, Box 10591, Tampa FL 33679. Estab. 1970. Annual outdoor show held 1st weekend in March. Entries accepted until 3 months before show. Entry fee: $30/artist. Display area: 8x12. Prejudging by 3 slides of work; refunds $25 of entry fee for refused work. Work may be offered for sale; no commission. Craftworker must attend show; demonstrations OK. Registration limit: 300. Sponsor provides electricity for demonstrations. Presents $10,000 in cash prizes with a $2,500 best of show award.
Acceptable Work: Considers ceramics; jewelry; pottery; sculpture; and weaving. "Crocheting; knitting; millinery; picture frames; velvet paintings; manufactured or kit jewelry; ceramics cast from commercial molds; art supplies; commercial displays; decoupage; candles or wearing apparel are not eligible to be exhibited."

*GREAT GULFCOAST FESTIVAL, Rt. 7, Box 403T, Pensacola FL 32506. Contact: Art Chairman. Sponsor: Pensacola Arts Council. Estab. 1972. Annual outdoor show held 2 days in November. Average attendance: 80,000.
Acceptable Work: Considers sculpture (dimensional forms in wood, metal, plastic and clay); pottery (stoneware, raku and porcelain); fiber (batik, macrame and weaving); and crafts (jewelry, stained glass, leather, etc.). "No decorated eggs; crocheting; knitting; shellcraft; millinery; velvet painting; art supplies; picture frames; coin jewelry; manufactured belts or handbags; or mass-produced jewelry."
Terms: Entries accepted until 4 weeks before show. Entry fee: $35/artist. Prejudging by 3 2x2 slides/category entered; entry fee refunded for refused work. Work may be offered for sale; no commission. Craftworker must attend show; demonstrations encouraged. Sponsor provides security for Friday and Saturday nights. Each artist handles his own sales and collects sales tax. "The tax collector will be present on the final day of the show."
Awards: Presents $4,000 in cash; $1,000, best of show; $150 1st prize, $100 2nd prize, and $50 3rd prize in each category. "Work in portfolios will not be judged."
Promotion: Show is advertised by national magazines; TV; radio; billboards; newspapers; and through local businesses.
Profile: "The Great Gulfcoast Festival is an all volunteer effort to bring top quality arts and crafts to the people of Pensacola and surrounding towns. There are performing arts (ballet, symphony, drama); young people's art show and puppet shows; popular entertainment (bands, clowns, mimes); and historical demonstrations (weaving, soapmaking)—all free to the public."

GROUP SHOWING OF AMERICAN ARTISTS, 9476 Harding Ave., Surfside FL 33154. (305)864-8725. Contact: Iris G. Klein. Sponsor: House of Fine Art, Inc. Purpose: "to promote local and out of state American craftsmen." Estab. 1962. Annual indoor show held for 1 year. Display area: 4x8. Maximum 5-7 pieces per craftworker. Prejudging by slides; photos; and other shows. Entry fee refunded for refused work. Work may be offered for sale; 40% commission. Craftworker needn't attend show; no demonstrations. Registration limit: 6-8 at a time. Sponsor provides coverings; display panels; and electricity. Show is advertised by invitations. Submit b&w photo and resume. Considers batik; candlemaking; ceramics; decoupage; dollmaking; pottery; sculpture; and soft sculpture.

HALIFAX ART FESTIVAL, Box 504, Ormond Beach FL 32074, (904)672-1723. Co-Chairmen: Jane Clair and Kay Acquaro. Sponsor: Guild of the Daytona Beach Museum of Arts and Sciences. Estab. 1962. Annual outdoor show (some under covering) held 2 days in November. Average attendance: 40,000.
Acceptable Work: Considers batik, ceramics (no greenware), glass art, jewelry, lapidary, leatherworking, macrame, metalsmithing, pottery, scrimshaw, sculpture, soft sculpture, weavings, and woodcrafting. Work must be original.
Terms: Entries accepted until 8 weeks before show. Entry fee: $25/artist. Display area: 10x10 under covering; 12x12 outdoors. Prejudging by slides; $5 fee. Entry fee refunded for refused work. Work may be offered for sale; no commission. Craftworker must attend show; demonstrations OK. Registration limit: 175. Sponsor provides insurance on exhibited work, 24-hour security, hostessing and adjacent parking near exhibit area.

Those listings preceded by an asterisk present awards for prize-winning crafts.

Awards: Presents $5,500, cash awards; $500, purchase prizes. Framing is required for judging.

*KEY BISCAYNE ART FESTIVAL, 150 W. McIntyre, Key Biscayne FL 33149. (305)361-5418. Director: Frank DeLaurier. Sponsor: Key Biscayne Community School PTA. Purpose: "to provide the community with exposure to various artists and craftsmen and their work." Estab. 1964. Annual outdoor show held 3 days in January. Average attendance: 5,000. Entries accepted until show date. Entry fee: $75/12x12 display area due by December 1. Prejudging by slides and photos. Work may be offered for sale; no commission. Craftworker must attend show; demonstrations OK. Considers all crafts. Presents $1,000 in cash awards.

LEE SIDEWALK ARTS & CRAFTS SHOW, Box 711, Fort Myers FL 33902. (813)334-1171. Contact Special Services Department. Sponsor: Lee County Bank. Purpose: "to provide an outlet for talented craftsmen who are in the area." Estab. 1974. Annual outdoor show held 1 day in January. Average attendance: 25,000. Entries accepted until 8 weeks before show. Entry fee: $15/10x10 display area. Work must be offered for sale; no commission. Craftworker must attend show; demonstrations encouraged. Registration limit: 280. Sponsor provides electricity for demonstrations. Show is advertised by newspapers; poster; radio; and TV. Considers all crafts. "The exhibitor handles all sales and sales tax. The sponsor collects the sales tax at the end of the day, and sends it to the State Department of Revenue. 1978 sales tax totalled $920."

MERRITT SQUARE FESTIVAL OF ARTS & CRAFTS, 615 S. "H" St., Lake Worth FL 33400. (305)582-6133. Director: J.J. Readey. Estab. 1970. Annual indoor show held 3 days in January at Merritt Island, Florida. Average attendance: 8,000. Entries accepted until 1 week before show (usually full about 3 weeks before show). Entry fee: $45/12x7 display area. Prejudging by 3 slides or color photos. Work may be offered for sale; no commission. Craftworker or representative must attend show; demonstrations OK. Registration limit: 95. Sponsor provides electricity for demonstrations if requested in advance, and 24-hour security. Supply 8x10 b&w glossy photo for newspaper release.
Acceptable Work: Considers framed batik: decoupage; dollmaking; glass art; metalsmithing; mobiles; needlecrafts; pottery; sculpture; tole painting; woodcrafting; egg craft; and shell craft.

*MOUNT DORA ART FESTIVAL, Box 231, Mount Dora FL 32757. Chairman: Harlow C. Middleton. Estab. 1975. Annual outdoor show held 2 days in February. Attendance: 25,000-50,000. Considers all crafts.
Terms: Entries accepted until 5 weeks before show. Entry fee: $5 prejudging fee plus $15 if accepted. Display area: 8x14. Prejudging by slides; no prejudging fees refunded for refused work. Work may be offered for sale; no commission. Craftworker must attend show; demonstrations OK. Registration limit: 250. Sponsor provides electricity for demonstrations.
Awards: Presents $4,300 in cash awards, and $800 best of show purchase award. Categories: painting; graphics; photography; sculpture; watercolors; and crafts.
Promotion: Show is advertised "in local papers; trade magazines; TV and radio; by visiting other shows and handing out brochures; and sending brochures to all Florida colleges and universities."

OLDE TYME CRAFTS AND ARTS, 615 South 'H' St., Lake Worth FL 33460. (305)968-9029. Contact: Jim Readey. Sponsor J.J. Readey Promotions. Annual indoor show held 4 days in June/July at Orange Park Mall, Jacksonville, Florida.
Acceptable Work: Considers caning, knitting, rug hooking, weaving, handicraft, embroidery, lace making, wood carving, old-fashioned stained glass and other old-fashioned items made by hand. No basketweaving. "A drop cloth is a must. Height of racks; 6'6" maximum."
Terms: Entries accepted until 1 week before show or until spaces are filled. Entry fee: $60/12x8' display area; 6 spaces available down side corridors at $25 each. No refunds after closing date, unless show is cancelled. No confirmations sent—use cancelled check as confirmation. Prejudging by 3 slides if have not previously shown with J.J. Readey. Work may be offered for sale; no commission. Craftworker must attend show; demonstrations OK. "All artists must exhibit complete hours of the show. Anyone leaving a show before closing will be refused entrance into further shows. Supply your own racks and tables. Tables must be covered to floor on all sides."
Promotion: "We would appreciate glossy b&w photos for publicity releases."
Profile: Located in enclosed and air conditioned mall. "We suggest dressing appropriate to your craft."

ORANGE PARK MALL FESTIVAL OF ART, 615 S. "H" St., Lake Worth FL 33460.

(305)582-6133. Director: J.J. Readey. Estab. 1976. Semiannual indoor show held 4 days in the spring and fall at Jacksonville, Florida. Average attendance: 12,000/show. Entries accepted until show date. Entry fee: $40/12x7 display area. Prejudging by 3 slides or color photos; entry fee refunded for refused work. Work may be offered for sale; no commission. Craftworker or representative must attend show; demonstrations OK. Sponsor provides electricity for demonstrations if requested in advance. Considers framed batik; and stone, wood and metal sculpture.

Keith Riggeo and partner Jim La Chance, designers and builders of The Rocking Safari, enjoy their product at the Farmington Craft Expo held in Farmington, Connecticut. Sponsored by American Crafts Expositions, Inc., this three-day weekend event encourages demonstrations.

ORANGE PARK MALL WINTER CRAFT SHOW, 615 S. "H" St., Lake Worth, FL 33460. (305)582-6133. Director: J.J. Readey. Estab. 1976. Annual indoor show held 4 days in January at Jacksonville, Florida. Attendance: 20,000-25,000. Entries accepted until 1 week before show (usually fills 5 weeks in advance). Entry fee: $60/12x7 display area. Prejudging by 3 slides or color photos; entry fee refunded for refused work. Work may be offered for sale; no commission. Craftworker or representative must attend show; demonstrations OK. Registration limit: 70. Sponsor provides electricity for demonstrations if requested in advance and 24-hour security. Supply 8x10 b&w photo and resume for newspaper release. Considers all crafts except clothing and lapidary. "Like most hangings to be framed."

*****OSCEOLA ART FESTIVAL**, Box 519, Kissimmee FL 32741. Publicity Director: Kissimme/ St. Cloud Jaycees. Estab. 1965. Annual outdoor show last weekend in September. Average attendance: 15,000. Entries accepted until September 1. Entry fee: $20/artist. Display area: 12'. Work may be offered for sale; no commission. Craftworker must attend show; no demonstrations. Categories: acrylic; creative crafts; graphics; mixed media; oil; sculpture; and watercolor.
Acceptable Work: Considers all crafts. "Objects produced from commercial molds or kits will be ineligible for judging. The review committee reserves the right to remove any exhibit or work of art."
Awards: Presents $2,800 in cash awards; $3,500 in purchase prizes; and 1st, 2nd and 3rd place ribbons.

*****OUTDOOR CRAFTS FESTIVAL**, Ringling Museum's Annual Crafts Festival, Box 1838. Sarasota FL 33578. (813)355-5101. Contact: Members Council Secretary. Sponsor: Members Council, Ringling Museums. Estab. 1972. Annual outdoor show held 2 days in November. Average attendance: 13,000. Entries accepted until 10 weeks before show. "Must be Florida craftworker." Entry fee: $5 application fee plus $25/accepted craftworker. Display area: 10x12. Prejudging by "3 35mm slides of 3 different objects created within the past year in each category entered"; application fee not refunded. Work may be offered for sale; no commission. Craftworker must attend show; demonstrations OK. Registration limit: approximately 60. Sponsor provides electricity for demonstrations and 24-hour security.
Acceptable Work: Considers ceramics; enameling; glass; jewelry; leather; metal; mixed media; sculpture; textiles; and wood. "Decision of acceptance by 3-person jury. Only highly professional work accepted."
Awards: Presents best in show, $500; 4 merit awards, $200 each; 2 honorable mentions, $100 each; best presentation, $50; and purchase awards.

PARK SHORE PLAZA FESTIVAL OF ARTS & CRAFTS, 615 S. "H" St., Lake Worth FL 33460. (305)582-6133. Director. J.J. Readey. Estab. 1974. Annual outdoor show (with some spaces covered with an overhang from building) held 3 days in January at Naples, Florida. Average attendance: 8,000. Entries accepted until 1 week before show; "however it usually fills up about 6 weeks in advance, and jewelry fills about 3 months before show." Entry fee: $40/12x4 display area. Work may be offered for sale; no commission. Craftworker or representative must attend show; demonstrations OK. Registration limit: 100. Submit 8x10 b&w photo and resume for newspaper release. Considers all crafts. "In this mall inexpensive items are the fast movers."

*****PATRIOTS ART FESTIVAL**, Box 1205, Largo FL 33540. (813)581-7455. Chairman/ Executive Director: Ramon G. Florez. Sponsor: Patriotic Krewe of Largo, Inc. Estab. 1977. Annual outdoor show held 3 days in February. Average attendance: 25,000.
Terms: Entries accepted until 4 weeks before show. Entry fee: $20/8x12 display area. Work may be offered for sale; no commission. Craftworker must attend show; demonstrations OK. Registration limit: 300. Sponsor provides electricity for demonstrations and 24-hour security.
Acceptable Work: Considers all crafts except decoupage, dollmaking, lapidary and tole painting. No kits or molds. Categories: oil painting, watercolor, pottery, photography, crafts and sculpture. Exhibitor must display a card showing name, hometown and category.
Awards: Presents $600, best of show award; $100, $75, $25, honorable mentions and purchase awards; and 1st, 2nd and honorable mention ribbons.

THE PROMENADES SHOPPING CENTER FESTIVAL OF ARTS & CRAFTS, 615 South 'H' St., Lake Worth FL 33460. (305)968-9029. Contact: Jim Readey. Sponsor J.J. Readey Promotions. Annual outdoor show held 3 days in March at Port Charlotte, Florida.
Acceptable Work: Considers all original crafts. No plants except to show off macrame and

pottery. Height of racks: 6'6" maximum. "Be prepared for wind, rain, sun and cold; most spaces have no covering. A drop cloth is a must."
Terms: Entries accepted until 1 week before show or until spaces are filled. Entry fee: $25/12x6' display area. No refunds after closing date, unless show is cancelled. No confirmations sent—use cancelled check as confirmation. Work may be offered for sale; no commission. Craftworker must attend show; demonstrations OK. "All artists must exhibit complete hours of the show. Anyone leaving a show before closing will be refused entrance into further shows. Supply your own racks and tables. Tables must be covered to floor on all sides. Work left up overnight is at your own risk. No electricity available."
Promotion: "We would appreciate glossy b&w photos for publicity releases."

*SANIBEL SHELL FAIR, Box 90, Sanibel FL 33957. (813)472-2155. Chairman: Ann Joffe. Sponsor: Sanibel Community Association and Sanibel Shell Club. "Sanibel has long been known for its shelling beaches. This fair emphasizes knowledge and classification of, and appreciation for shells." Estab. 1937. Annual indoor/outdoor show held 5 days (1 day judging, 4 days open to public) in March. Entries accepted until noon on the Saturday preceding the show; exhibits due Wednesday noon preceding show. Display area: 2x20. Maximum 1 entry/category. Work may be offered for sale; no commission. Craftworker needn't attend show; no demonstrations. Sponsor provides table and 24-hour security. Categories: self-collected division; student division; scientific division; anomalies division; commercial (professional) division; and artistic division. Shell crafts only. Presents ribbons and trophies.

SARASOTA SPRING FESTIVAL OF CRAFT, Box 92, Readsboro VT 05350. (802)423-7692. Co-Directors: Charles Dooley and Riki Moss. Sponsor: Craftproducers Incorporated. Estab. 1979. Annual indoor show held 3 days in March at Sarasota, Florida.
Acceptable Work: Considers all crafts except kits, shells, embellished found objects, painted rocks and coin crafting.
Terms: Entries accepted 3 weeks before show; Entry fee: $80/10x8' display area. Prejudging by 5 slides. Entry fee due after prejudging. Work must be offered for sale. Craftworker must attend show; demonstrations OK. Registration limit: 60-70. Sponsor provides 24-hour security.

*SEAS NATIONAL, Municipal Auditorium, Panama City FL 32401. (904)763-4696. Auditorium Manager: Cecil Koon. Purpose: "to create the finest exhibit in the country, affording all artists an oportunity to compete at their own level. Hopefully we will bring the finest art to Panama City." Estab. 1964. Annual indoor show held 1 month May-June. Entries accepted until 2 weeks before show. Entry fee: $12/entry; 3 items to entry. Maximum 2 pieces per artist per category; 6 total. Work may be offered for sale; 20% commission. Craftworker needn't attend show; no demonstrations. Show is advertised by radio; TV; and magazines. Submit social security number for bond purchases. Presents cash awards. Considers mobiles; pottery; sculpture; and woodcrafting.

*7 LIVELY ARTS FESTIVAL, INCORPORATED, ART SHOW, c/o Hollywood Recreation Division, 2030 Polk St., Hollywood FL 33020. (305)921-3404. Performing Arts Coordinator: Elizabeth Wentworth. Estab. 1969. Annual outdoor show held 2 days in March. Attendance: 50,000. Considers all crafts. Presents $1500 in awards.
Terms: Entries accepted until 2 weeks before show. Entry fee: $35/12x12' display area. Prejudging by slides; entry fee refunded for refused work. If not accepted in the fine arts and crafts category, will be considered for the non-juried crafts section at $25 fee. Work may be offered for sale; no commission. Craftworker must attend show; demonstrations OK. Sponsor provides electricity for demonstrations.
Promotion: Show is advertised by radio; banners, posters, local newspapers; and *Sunshine Artists U.S.A.*

*SOCIETY OF THE ARTS' ANNUAL FESTIVAL OF THE ARTS "ARTI GRAS", Box 831, North Miami FL 33161. (305)891-7466. Chairman: Pat Bourquin. Estab. 1968. Annual outdoor show held 2 days in the spring (performing arts events are held 4 days). Attendance: 50,000-75,000. Entries accepted until 2 weeks before show. Entry fee: $30-35/12x6 display area. Work must be offered for sale; no commission. Craftworker must attend show; demonstrations OK. Registration limit: about 40. Sponsor provides electricity for demonstrations; fencing; and 24-hour security. Professional public relations firm handles promotion. Categories: paintings (oils, acrylics, watercolor); photography; sculpture and metalworking; fabrics and fibers; graphics and creative crafts. Presents $4,000 in cash and ribbons for best in category; award of merits; and purchase awards. Gift items sell best.

Acceptable Work: Considers batik; candlemaking; ceramics; jewelry; lapidary; macrame; metalsmithing; mobiles; pottery; sculpture; soft sculpture; weaving; tole painting; and woodcrafting.

SOUTH FLORIDA FAIRS & EXPOSITIONS, INC., Box 15915, West Palm Beach FL 33406. (305)793-0333. "The South Florida Fair began as an agricultural fair. It has grown to include many facets of educational, entertaining, cultural and exciting events, displays and activities." Estab. 1912. Annual indoor/outdoor show (with some tents) held 10 days in the winter. Average attendance: ½ million. Work may be offered for sale. Considers ceramics; pottery; crochet; decoupage; repousse; dollmaking; embroidery; knitting; macrame; needlework; china painting; quilting; rugs; weaving; jewelry; leatherworking; and woodworking. Florida craftworkers only. Write for brochure.

*****SPRING ARTS FESTIVAL**, Box 1530, 3000 NW 83rd St., Gainesville FL 32602. (904)372-1976 or 377-5161. Director: Karen Beach. Sponsor: Santa Fe Community College, Chamber of Commerce and City of Gainesville. Purpose: "to expose the north central Florida area residents to fine arts and crafts. This also gives area artists a chance to display their art and craftwork to a large audience." Estab. 1970. Annual outdoor show held 2 days during the first weekend in April. Average attendance: 60,000. Entries accepted until 2 months before show. Entry fee: $30/10x15 display area plus $5 application fee. Prejudging by slides; entry fee, but not application fee, refunded for refused work. Work may be offered for sale; no commission. Craftworker must attend show; demonstrations OK. Show is advertised by newspaper; radio; and magazines. Registration limit: 225. Categories: painting (oil, acrylic, mixed-media); painting (watercolor); sculpture; pottery; jewelry; fiber arts; leatherwork; graphics; photography; and open crafts.
Acceptable Work: Considers batik; ceramics; glass; jewelry; stained glass; leatherworking; macrame; metalsmithing; pottery; sculpture; soft sculpture; weaving; and woodcrafting. "No pattern or mass-produced macrame or cloth items; crocheting or knitting; novelty items; antiques; string beads; clothing; feather or shell crafts; fork, spoon or coin jewelry; or embellished items. Artwork must be in good taste and appropriate for family viewing."
Awards: Presents $6,000 in cash and $3,000 in purchase prizes. "Display work so that judges have easy access to it. Make display as attractive as possible."

*****SPRING ARTS POTPOURRI IN THE PARK**, 344 S. Beach St., Daytona Beach FL 32014. (904)252-4769. Chairman: Carol Ann Moritz. Sponsor: YWCA. Purpose: fundraiser. Estab. 1975. Semiannual outdoor show held 2 days in April and November. Average attendance: 10,000. Entries accepted until show. Entry fee: $15/10x20 display area. Work may be offered for sale; no commission. Craftworker must attend show; demonstrations OK. Sponsor provides some electricity for demonstrations. Show is advertised by magazines; newspapers; radio; flyers; posters; and TV. Considers all crafts. Presents 1st, 2nd, 3rd, honorable mention and merit ribbons.

SUWANNEE RIVER CRAFTS SHOW-SALE, Box 265, White Springs FL 32096. (904)397-2192. Director: James McDuffee. Sponsor: Stephen Foster Center (a rural folk arts center). Purpose: "to promote crafts learned by craftsmen in the Suwannee Valley area of Florida, using Florida materials (foliage) and the old-time crafts such as quilting, spinning, weaving, needlework, pine needle crafts, palmetto crafts, wood carving, wooden toys, etc." Estab. 1975. Annual indoor show held 1 month in the late spring. Average attendance: about 13,000. Entries accepted until 1 week before show. No entry fee. Prejudging by slides, photos or actual work. Work may be offered for sale; 15% commission. Craftworker needn't attend show; demonstrations OK. Registration limit: 25-50. Sponsor provides coverings; electricity for demonstrations; and 24-hour security. "People who attend most of our special events are looking for the unique folk craft that they normally do not find in shops."
Acceptable Work: Considers candlemaking; dollmaking; jewelry; lapidary; leatherworking; metalsmithing; needlecrafts; pottery; weaving; woodcrafting; quilting; spinning; and natural dyeing.
Promotion: Show is advertised "by news releases (usually 4 before show) to southern Georgia and all Florida radio, TV and daily and weekly newspapers." Submit 8x10 b&w glossy photo showing involvement with craft.

*****TARPON SPRINGS ARTS & CRAFTS SHOW**, 112 S. Pinellas Ave., Tarpon Springs FL 33589. (813)937-6109. Director: John Tarapani. Sponsor: Tarpon Springs Chamber of Commerce. Estab. 1974. Annual outdoor show held 2 days in the spring. Average attendance:

25,000-30,000. Entries accepted until March 1. Entry fee: $30/15x10 display area. Prejudging ($5 nonreturnable fee) by slides, photos or personal demonstrations; entry fee refunded for refused work. Work may be offered for sale; no commission. Craftworker must attend show; demonstrations OK. Show is advertised by artist publications, radio, television, newspapers and billboards. Categories: watercolor; oils and mixed media; sculpture; graphics; crafts; and photography. Presents $6,000 in cash, and $4,000 in purchase awards.
Acceptable Work: Considers candlemaking; dollmaking; glass art; jewelry; macrame; metalsmithing; mobiles; pottery; sculpture; woodcrafting; and soft sculpture. "No tile, beads or shell work; velvet painting; knitting; crocheting; or plants."

TITUSVILLE ART LEAGUE ANNUAL SHOW, Box 6133, Titusville FL 32780. Contact: Chairman. Estab. 1964. Annual indoor show held 1 week in the spring. Entries accepted until show date. Entry fee: $3/entry. Display area: 4x6. Prejudging: no entry fees refunded for refused work. Work may be offered for sale; no commission. Demonstrations on approval. Sponsor provides display panels. Craftworker provides display stand for unusual-size work.

TOMATO—SNOOK FESTIVAL, 615 South 'H' St., Lake Worth FL 33460. (305)968-9029. Contact: Jim Readey. Sponsor J.J. Readey Promotions. Annual outdoor show held 2 days in March at Bonita Springs, Florida.
Acceptable Work: Considers all arts, crafts and hobbies. "Be prepared for wind, rain, sun and cold; most spaces have no covering. A drop cloth is a must."
Terms: Entries accepted until 1 week before show or until spaces are filled. Entry fee: $25/12x12' display area. No refunds after closing date, unless show is cancelled. No confirmations sent—use cancelled check as confirmation. Work may be offered for sale; no commission. Craftworker must attend show; demonstrations OK. "All artists must exhibit complete hours of the show. Anyone leaving a show before closing will be refused entrance into further shows. Supply your own racks and tables. Tables must be covered to floor on all sides. Work left up overnight is at your own risk. No electricity available."
Promotion: "We would appreciate glossy b&w photos for publicity releases."
Profile: Festival also includes a music festival, a fishing contest and a street dance.

*****VERO BEACH ART CLUB WINTER ART SHOW,** 3136 Atlantic Blvd., Vero Beach FL 32960. Purpose: "to give the artist and craftsman an opportunity to show and sell his work; and to support our Vero Art Club Gallery—a nonprofit gallery." Estab. 1950. Annual outdoor show held 2 days in January. Entries accepted until 2 weeks before show or until filled. Work may be offered for sale; no commission. Craftworker must attend show; demonstrations OK. Registration limit: 200. Categories: oil; acrylic and mixed media; watercolor; photography; drawings; pastels; graphics; sculpture; and creative crafts. Presents $1,500 in cash; purchase prizes; and 1st, 2nd and 3rd ribbons.
Acceptable Work: Considers batik; candlemaking; glass art; leatherworking; macrame; metalsmithing; pottery; sculpture; tole painting; weaving; woodcrafting; and jewelry by invitation. No velvet paintings; crocheting; fork spoon jewelry; decorated eggs; knitting; novelty shell crafts; clothing; coin jewelry; or mass-produced jewelry.
Promotion: Show is advertised by special newspaper supplement listing all artists and space numbers; TV; and radio. "B&w glossy photos might be used by our local newspaper."

*****WINTER PARK MALL CRAFT SHOW,** 400 N. Orlando Ave., Winter Park FL 32789. (305)644-4476. Marketing Director: Sonja Unger Marchejano. Estab. 1970. Annual indoor show held 3 days in May. Average attendance: 15,000.
Acceptable Work: Considers batik, candlemaking, ceramics, lapidary, scrimshaw, glass art, leatherworking, macrame, metalsmithing, pottery, sculpture and woodcrafting. No crocheting, knitting, novelty shellcraft, millinery, clothing, picture frames, decoupage or string art.
Terms: Entries accepted until show date. Entry fee: $20/6x12 display area. Prejudging by slides or photos; entry fee refunded for refused work. Work may be offered for sale; no commission. Craftworker must attend show; demonstrations encouraged.
Awards: Presents $575 in cash prizes and honorable mention ribbons.
Promotion: Show is advertised by newspaper ads, radio and news releases to the media. "Anytime we have promotional information about unusual or extremely talented artists this is usually picked up by the press."

*****WINTER PARK SIDEWALK ART FESTIVAL,** Box 597, Winter Park FL 32790. Chairman: James G. Shepp. Purpose: "to provide the community with the best possible arts and crafts available today." Estab. 1959. Annual outdoor show held 3 days in March. Average attendance: 300,000.

Acceptable Work: Considers batik; ceramics; glass art; jewelry; leatherworking; metalsmithing; sculpture; soft sculpture; weaving; and woodcrafting.
Terms: Deadlines for entries on application. Entry fee: $35/craftworker plus $5 jury fee. Display area: 9x12. Prejudging by 4 slides per category (one of display); entry fee refunded for refused work. Work may be offered for sale; no commission. Craftworker must attend show; demonstrations OK. Registration limit: 90. Sponsor provides electricity for demonstrations.
Awards: Presents cash awards totaling over $10,000; best of show purchase award of $1,000; and ribbons.
Promotion: Show is advertised by local radio spots and national articles such as in *Southern Living*.

*YBOR SQUARE CHRISTMAS CRAFTS CARNIVAL, Box 2350, Tampa FL 33601. (813)247-5411. Manager: Byron B. Crowder. Sponsor: Ybor Square/Trend Publications, Inc. Estab. 1975. Annual indoor/outdoor show held 2 days in December. Entries accepted until 1 week before show. Entry fee: $20/10x10 outside display area; $30/10x10 inside display area. Prejudging by slides or photos of work; entry fee refunded for refused work. Work may be offered for sale; no commission. Craftworker must attend show; demonstrations OK. Registration limit: 80-100. Sponsor provides electricity for demonstrations; tables for rent; and 24-hour security. Show is advertised by newspapers; radio; TV; and art and crafts magazines.
Acceptable Work: Considers batik; candlemaking; ceramics; dollmaking; glass art; jewelry; lapidary; leatherworking; macrame; metalsmithing; mobiles; pottery; sculpture; tole painting; soft sculpture; weaving; and woodcrafting. "No crocheting; knitting; millinery; picture frames; manufactured or kit jewelry; ceramics cast from commercial molds; commercial displays; or wearing apparel.
Awards: Presents $200, 1st place, 4 $50 2nd places; 4 $25 3rd places; and ribbons for above winners and honorable mentions. "Our shows are judged by an outside juror."

*YBOR SQUARE FALL ARTS & CRAFTS FIESTA, Box 2350, Tampa FL 33601. (813)247-5411. Manager: Byron B. Crowder. Sponsor: Ybor Square/Trend Publications, Inc. Estab. 1975. Annual indoor/outdoor show held 2 days in October. Entries accepted until 1 week before show. Entry fee: $20/10x10 outside display area; $30/10x10 inside area. Prejudging by slides or photos; entry fee refunded for refused work. Work may be offered for sale; no commission. Craftworker must attend show; demonstrations OK. Registration limit: 80-100. Sponsor provides electricity for demonstrations; tables for rental; and 24-hour security. Show is advertised by newspapers; radio; TV; and art and crafts magazines.
Acceptable Work: Considers batik; candlemaking; ceramics; dollmaking; glass art; jewelry; lapidary; leatherworking; macrame; metalsmithing; mobiles; pottery; sculpture; tole painting; soft sculpture; weaving; and woodcrafting. "All works must be original and done by exhibitor. Crocheting; knitting; millinery; picture frames; manufactured or kit jewelry; ceramics cast from commercial molds; art supplies; commercial displays; or wearing apparel not accepted.
Awards: Presents $300, best of show; 10 awards of merit at $100 each; 10 honorable mentions at $25 each; and ribbons. "Our shows are judged by an outside juror."
Profile: "Ybor Square is the second tourist attraction in Tampa, a restored cigar factory in the old Latin quarter of the city. When Trend Publications purchased and restored Ybor Square, the atmosphere was naturally appealing to artists and craftsmen, and many of our permanent tenants themselves (antique dealers, craftsmen, specialty store owners) are heavily involved in shows throughout Florida."

*YBOR SQUARE SPRING ARTS & CRAFTS FIESTA, Box 2350, Tampa FL 33601. (813)247-5411. Manager: Byron B. Crowder. Sponsor: Ybor Square/Trend Publications, Inc. Estab. 1975. Annual indoor/outdoor show held 2 days in April. Entries accepted until 1 week before show. Entry fee: $20/10x10 outside display area; $30/10x10 inside area. Prejudging by slides or photos; entry fee refunded for refused work. Work may be offered for sale; no commission. Craftworker must attend show; demonstrations OK. Registration limit: 80-100. Sponsor provides electricity for demonstrations; tables for rent; and 24-hour security. Show is advertised by newspapers; radio; TV; and art and crafts magazines.
Acceptable Work: Considers batik; candlemaking; ceramics; dollmaking; glass art; jewelry; lapidary; leatherworking; macrame; metalsmithing; mobiles; pottery; soft sculpture; tole painting; weaving; sculpture; and woodcrafting. No crocheting; knitting; millinery; manufactured or kit jewelry; ceramics from molds; commercial displays; or wearable apparel.
Awards: Presents $300, best of show; 10 $100 awards of merit; 10 $25 honorable mentions; and ribbons. "Our shows are judged by an outside juror."

*YBOR SQUARE SUMMER CRAFTS CARNIVAL, Box 2350, Tampa FL 33601. (813)247-5411. Manager: Byron B. Crowder. Sponsor: Ybor Square/Trend Publications, Inc. Estab. 1975. Annual indoor/outdoor show held 2 days in July. Entries accepted until 1 week before show. Entry fee: $20/10x10 display area outside; $30/10x10 display area inside. Prejudging by slides or photos; entry fee refunded for refused work. Work may be offered for sale; no commission. Craftworker must attend show; demonstrations OK. Registration limit: 80-100. Sponsor provides electricity for demonstrations; tables for rent; and 24-hour security. Show is advertised by radio; TV; newspapers; and art and crafts magazines. Presents $200, 1st place; 4 $50 2nd places; 4 $25 3rd places; and ribbons for 1st, 2nd, 3rd and honorable mentions.
Acceptable Work: Considers batik; candlemaking; ceramics not made from commercial molds; dollmaking; glass art; jewelry; lapidary; leatherworking; macrame; metalsmithing; mobiles; pottery; sculpture; soft sculpture; tole painting; weaving; and woodcrafting. No comercial displays; wearables; knitting; millinery; or crocheting.

Georgia

*ALBANY ARTS FESTIVAL, Box 571, Albany GA 31707. Contact: Registration Chairman. Sponsor: Southwest Georgia Art Association. Estab. 1967. Annual indoor/outdoor show (booths available) held 2 days in April. Average attendance: 10,000. Presents $900 in cash awards; and $1,300 in purchase prizes.
Acceptable Work: Considers all crafts completed no earlier than 4 years prior to the show. "All work must be suitably mounted, framed, or matted."
Terms: Entries accepted until 4 weeks before show. Entry fee: $25/display area. Prejudging by 3 slides or photos; entry fee refunded for refused work. Work must be offered for sale; no commission. Craftworker or representative must attend show; demonstrations OK. Sponsor provides display panels; electricity for demonstrations; and 24-hour security.
Promotion: "Our show is promoted extensively in southwest Georgia, north Florida, and southeast Alabama in newspapers and on radio and TV. Artists are encouraged to include photos and information when applications are submitted."

*ARTS FESTIVAL OF ATLANTA, Suite 610, 33 North Ave., Atlanta GA 30308. (404)885-1125. Director: Pat Gann. Purpose: "to bring the artists and the public into contact, and make the arts, the creative free expression of man, an integral part of the community." Estab. 1954. Annual indoor/outdoor show held 9 days in May. Average attendance: 500,000. Entries accepted until 3 months before show. Entry fee: $100; $5 prejudging fee. Display area: 10x10. Prejudging by slides; entry fee (not prejudging fee) refunded for refused work. No commission. Craftworker must attend show; demonstrations OK. Registration limit: 150 each of the 4 days. Sponsor provides electricity for demonstrations and 24-hour security. Show is advertised by radio; TV; and the print media. Considers all crafts except candlemaking: decoupage: painted rocks; plastic, paper or feather flowers; shellcraft; T-shirts; and beads. Presents $5,000 in cash, and $1,000 in purchase prizes.

THE BERRY PATCH ARTS & CRAFT FESTIVAL, Berry Academy, Mt. Berry GA 30149. (404)234-9446, ext. 265. Director: Phil Johns. Estab. 1972. Annual outdoor show held 2 days in April. Average attendance: 5,000-8,000.
Acceptable Work: Considers all crafts including musical instruments; bobbin lace; and baskets.
Terms: Entries accepted until 6 weeks before show. Entry fee: $20/12x12 display area. Entries prejudged by photo or slide; entry fee refunded for refused work. Work may be offered for sale; no commission. Craftworker must attend show; demonstrations OK. Registration limit: 100. Sponsor provides electricity for demonstrations; 24-hour security; and attempts to meet individual needs.
Sales Tips: "Our public buys for the most part things that serve a purpose or can be used around the house. Many gifts are purchased also."
Promotion: Show is advertised by TV and radio spots in multi-state area; national and regional magazine ads and articles; newspapers in Georgia, Alabama, North Carolina, South Carolina, Florida, Tennessee and other states; and posters sent upon request to all entries. Submit photos and printed articles.

*COUNTRY ROADS, Church St., Vienna GA 31092. (912)268-4776. Director: Cathy Jones. Sponsor: Junior Woman's Club. Purpose: "to foster the development of arts and crafts." Estab. 1972. Annual indoor show held 2 days in March. Average attendance: 2,000. Entries accepted until 2 weeks before show. Entry fee: $20/8x12 display area. Maximum 2 entries/category. Prejudging by slides, photos and brochures; checks are not cashed for rejected work. Work may be offered for sale; no commission. Craftworker must attend show; demonstrations

OK. Registration limit: 20. Sponsor provides electricity for demonstrations and 24-hour security.
Acceptable Work: Considers batik; candlemaking; dollmaking; glass art; jewelry; leatherworking; macrame; metalsmithing; mobiles; needlecrafts; pottery; sculpture; soft sculpture; tole painting; weaving; and woodcrafting.
Promotion: Show is advertised by radio; TV; and newspapers—no paid advertising. "We run 13 features in our local newspaper to prepare the consumer. Each feature runs about ¼ to ½ a page. We like photos, biographical sketches, awards list and a description of technique from craftworker."

DECATUR CIVIC CHORUS ANNUAL ARTS & CRAFTS FAIR, Box 1361, Decatur GA 30031. (404)634-1382. Director: Mary Anne Sharp. Sponsor: Decatur Civic Chorus. Estab. 1972. Annual indoor show held 3 days in the fall. Average attendance: 45,000.
Acceptable Work: Considers all crafts. Maximum size: 8x10. "All display tables must be draped uniformly. The chorus has free draping for those craftsmen lacking their own. An action display attracts the most attention."
Terms: Entries accepted until 2 weeks before show. Entry fee charged. Work may be offered for sale; no commission. Craftworker must attend show. Sponsor provides coverings; display panels; electricity for demonstrations; and tables for rent.
Profile: "The Decatur Civic Chorus is a nonprofit organization. This fair enables us to travel; buy music; and covers operational expenses of our free public concerts."

*FIREHOUSE ARTS & CRAFTS FESTIVAL, Box 375, Dalton GA 30720. (404)278-0168. Sponsor: Creative Arts Guild, Inc. Estab. 1963. Annual indoor/outdoor show held 2 days in September. Entries accepted until 2 weeks before show. Entry fee: $15/artist. Display area: 10x15. Maximum 4 entries per craftworker indoors. No prejudging, but prefer new exhibitor send pictures or slides of work. Work must be offered for sale; 10% commission. Craftworker must attend show if entered for outdoor spaces; demonstrations OK. Registration limit: 100 for outdoor spaces. Categories: painting; drawing; graphics; sculpture; pottery; ceramic sculpture; handwork; creative photography; and crafts. Presents cash awards of $1,000; corporate purchase vary (1978-$12,000). 1978 show sales totaled $23,000.
Acceptable Work: Considers batik; candlemaking; ceramics; jewelry; lapidary; leatherworking; macrame; metalsmithing; pottery; sculpture; soft sculpture; weaving; and woodcrafting.
Promotion: Show is advertised by newspaper and radio public service announcements; and interview shows. Craftworker provides b&w glossy photos; background information; and resume.

*GEORGIA JUBILEE, 195 Holt Ave., Macon GA 31201. (912)743-1380. Chairman: Ken Pipkin. Estab. 1974. Annual indoor/outdoor show held 2 days (preview party Friday night) in May. Average attendance: 7,000-8,000. Entries accepted until 4 weeks before show. Entry fee: $30/juried entry; $20/crafts. Prejudging by 3 slides; entry fee refunded for refused work. Work may be offered for sale; no commission. Craftworker must attend show; demonstrations OK. Sponsor provides limited electricity for demonstrations and some security. Show is advertised by radio; TV; newspapers; and magazines. Presents cash awards of $1,150 and ribbons. Considers all crafts.

*GEORGIA MOUNTAIN FAIR, Box 444, Hiawassee GA 30546. (404)896-2256. President: Robert L. Anderson. Sponsor: Towns County Lions Club. Estab. 1950. Annual indoor/outdoor show (with tents and exhibit buildings) held 12 days in August. Average attendance: 150,000. Entries accepted until show is filled. Work may be offered for sale; 10% commission. Craftworker must attend show and "all exhibitors must have an educational exhibit, demonstrating what they sell." Registration limit: 100. Sponsor provides chairs; coverings; display panels; electricity for demonstrations; insurance on exhibited work; table; and 24-hour security.
Acceptable Work: Considers candlemaking; ceramics; decoupage; basket making; dollmaking; glass art; jewelry; leatherworking; macrame; metalsmithing; needlecrafts; pottery; sculpture; soft sculpture; tole painting; weaving; and woodworking.

GOLDEN ISLES ARTS FESTIVAL, c/o Glynn Art Association, Box 673, St. Simons Island GA 31522. (912)638-8770. Associate Director: Mrs. W.C. Hendrix. Show Chairman: Mrs. Denis Palmerin. Estab. 1969. Annual outdoor show held 2 days the second full week of October. Average attendance: 30,000. Considers all original work.

---

* Those listings preceded by an asterisk present awards for prize-winning crafts.

Terms: Entries accepted until 6 weeks before show. Entry fee: $35/display area. Prejudging by slides; entry fee refunded for refused work. Work may be offered for sale; no commission. Craftworker or agent must attend show; demonstrations encouraged. Registration limit: 175 ("we usually have 400-500 applications"). Sponsor provides display panels, security Saturday night and some electricity.
Promotion: Show is advertised by TV, billboards, radio, newspapers and periodicals. "Unusual craftsmen should submit glossies with promo material for possible 'feature' usage."

HATCHER SQUARE ARTS & CRAFTS SHOW, 615 South 'H' St., Lake Worth FL 33460. (305)968-9029. Contact: Jim Readey. Sponsor J.J. Readey Promotions. Semiannual outdoor show held 4 days in March and September at Milledgeville, Georgia.
Acceptable Work: Considers all original crafts. "A drop cloth is a must. Height of racks: 6'6" maximum."
Terms: Entries accepted until 1 week before show or until spaces are filled. Entry fee: $35/12x6' display area. No refunds after closing date, unless show is cancelled. No confirmations sent—use cancelled check as confirmation. Work may be offered for sale; no commission. Craftworker must attend show; demonstrations OK. "All artists must exhibit complete hours of the show. Anyone leaving a show before closing will be refused entrance into further shows. Supply your own racks and tables. Tables must be covered to floor on all sides. Work left up overnight is at your own risk."
Promotion: "We would appreciate glossy b&w photos for publicity releases."
Profile: Located in enclosed and air conditioned mall. "We suggest dressing appropriate to your craft."

MILLION PINES ARTS & CRAFTS FESTIVAL, Box 238, Soperton GA 30457. (912)529-4524. Sponsor: City of Soperton. Estab. 1973. Annual outdoor show held 2 days in November. Average attendance: 10,000. Entries accepted until Oct. 1. Entry fee: $25/12x12 display area. Entries prejudged by slides or photos. Entry fee refunded for refused work. Work may be offered for sale; no commission. Craftworker must attend show; demonstrations OK. Registration limit: 125. Sponsor provides electricity for demonstrations and 24-hour security. Categories: artists and craftsmen. All crafts considered. Show is advertised by newspapers; magazines; TV; and radio. Submit b&w photo and brief paragraph on exhibition.

NEW SALEM MOUNTAIN FESTIVAL, Rt. 2, Rising Fawn GA 30783. (404)675-4444. Director: Charles Counts. Sponsor: New Salem Community Improvement Club. Estab. 1974. Annual outdoor show held 2 days in October on top of Lookout Mountain. Entry fee: $20/approximately 18x20 display area. Entries prejudged by slides, photos or personal examination. Work may be offered for sale; no commission. Craftworker must attend show; demonstrations OK. Registration limit: 50. Sponsor provides electricity for demonstrations and 24-hour security. Show is advertised by TV; radio; newspapers; mailing; and brochures. Submit 8x10 glossy b&w self-photo and biographical material.
Acceptable Work: Considers batik; candlemaking; ceramics; decoupage; dollmaking; glass art; jewelry; leatherworking; macrame; metalsmithing; needlecrafts; pottery; sculpture; weaving; woodcrafting; and basketry.

OAK GROVE COUNTRY FAIR, Box 439, Pine Mountain GA 31822. (404)663-2425 or 663-4577. Chairman: Larry Thompson. Business Manager: Carolyn Thompson. Sponsor: Oak Grove Congregational Christian Church. Estab. 1972. Annual outdoor show held 2 days in August at Oak Grove Community, 5 miles north of Pine Mountain, Georgia. Average attendance: 10,000. Entries accepted until 2 weeks before show. Entry fee: $20/15x15 display area. Work may be offered for sale; no commission. Craftworker must attend show; demonstrations OK. Registration limit: 250. Sponsor provides electricity for demonstrations and 24-hour security. Show is advertised by radio; TV; direct mail; and handbills. Submit photos for promotion. Considers all crafts.

OKEFENOKEE FESTIVAL ARTS & CRAFT SHOW, Box 335, Folkston GA 31537. (912)496-7129. Chairman: Donna A. Nance. Sponsor: Charlton County Chamber of Commerce. Estab. 1969. Annual outdoor show held 2 days in October. Average attendance: 3,000-5,000. Entries accepted up until show date. Entry fee: $10/display area. Work may be offered for sale; no commission. Craftworker must attend show; demonstrations OK. Sponsor provides electricity for demonstrations. Show is advertised by TV; radio; magazines; newspapers; and mailing brochures. Considers all crafts.

*POWERS' CROSSROADS COUNTRY FAIR & ART FESTIVAL, Box 899, Newnan GA 30264. (404)253-2011. Director: Harriet Alexander. Sponsor: Coweta Festivals, Inc. Estab. 1971. Annual outdoor show held 3 days in September. Average attendance: 25,000-30,000. Entries accepted until 19 weeks before show. Entry fee: $65/16' display area; $40/10'. Prejudging by slides; entry fee refunded for refused work. Work may be offered for sale; no commission. Craftworker must attend show; demonstrations OK. Registration limit: 280. Sponsor provides 24-hour security. Show is advertised by TV; newspapers; magazines; and radio. Submit b&w glossy and publicity information. Considers all crafts. Presents $2,800 in cash and purchase prizes.

PRATER'S MILL COUNTRY FAIR, 216 Riderwood Dr., Dalton GA 30720. President: Judy Alderman. Vice President: Jane Harrell. Estab. 1971. Semiannual outdoor show held 2 days in May and October. Average attendance: 20,000 per show. Considers all crafts except poured ceramics. No kits or plastic. Everything must be "handmade of natural materials."
Terms: Entries accepted until 4 weeks before show. Entry fee: $20/15x15 display area. Prejudging by slides or photos. Entry fee due after prejudging. Work must be offered for sale; no commission. Craftworker must attend show; demonstrations OK. Registraton limit: 140. Sponsor provides electricity for demonstrations and 24-hour security. Fair representatives collect sales taxes from craftworkers without tax numbers.
Promotion: Show is advertised by all media, brochures, personal appearances, posters, and motels and restaurants. Submit b&w glossy photo, copies of press releases, previously published articles, background information, training information, other shows attended, and interesting public relations material for promotional purposes.
Sales Tips: "Have an attractive booth, talk to customers, don't look bored and don't read a book!"

WEST GEORGIA COMMONS MALL ARTS & CRAFTS SHOW, 615 South 'H' St., Lake Worth FL 33460. (305)968-9029. Contact: Jim Readey. Sponsor J.J. Readey Promotions. Indoor show held 4 days in April, June and November at La Grange, Georgia.
Acceptable Work: Considers all original crafts. No apparel. "A drop cloth is a must. Height of racks: 6'6" maximum."
Terms: Entries accepted until 1 week before show or until spaces are filled. Entry fee: $35/12x5' display area. No refunds after closing date, unless show is cancelled. No confirmations sent—use cancelled check as confirmation. Work may be offered for sale; no commission. Craftworker must attend show; demonstrations OK. "All artists must exhibit complete hours of the show. Anyone leaving a show before closing will be refused entrance into further shows. Supply your own racks and tables. Tables must be covered to floor on all sides. Work left up overnight is at your own risk."
Promotion: "We would appreciate glossy b&w photos for publicity releases."
Profile: Located in enclosed and air conditioned mall. Anchor stores are Pennys, Belk-Gallant, David Brother's Cafeteria; mall also includes 50 other stores. "We suggest dressing appropriate to your craft."

YELLOW DAISY FESTIVAL, Stone Mountain Park, Box 778, Stone Mountain GA 30086. (404)469-9831. Director, Special Events: Kathi Hayes. Estab. 1969. Annual outdoor show held 3 days in September. Average attendance: 100,000. Entries accepted until 2 weeks before show. Entry fee: $50/craftworker. Display area: 10x10 enclosed horse stall. Prejudging by 3 slides or photos and short resume; entry fee refunded for refused work. Work may be offered for sale; demonstrations OK. Registration limit: 200. Sponsor provides electricity for demonstrations and 24-hour security. Show is advertised by radio; TV; and city-wide promotions. Considers all crafts.

Idaho

*ART ON THE GREEN—ARTISANS IN ACTION, Box 901, Coeur d'Alene ID 83814. Council President: George Ives, (208)667-7888. Council Treasurer: Opal Brooten, (208)664-9052. Sponsor: Citizens Council for the Arts. Estab. 1968. Annual outdoor show (with booths) held 3 days in August. Show runs concurrently with Art on the Green—Juried Show. Average attendance: 5,000. Considers all crafts.
Terms: Booth demonstrators accepted until 6 weeks before show. Entry fee: $15/8x8x10 booth. Maximum 2 craftworkers per booth. Prejudging by slides or hand-delivered samples. Craftworker must attend show; demonstrations required. Exhibitor handles sales and taxes.

*ART ON THE GREEN—JURIED SHOW, Box 901, Coeur d'Alene ID 83814. Council Presi-

dent: George Ives, (208)667-7888. Council Treasurer: Opal Brooten, (208)664-9052. Sponsor: Citizens Council for the Arts. Estab. 1968. Annual outdoor show (with booths) held 3 days in August. Show runs concurrently with Art on the Green—Artisans in Action. Average attendance: 5,000.
Acceptable Work: Considers all crafts except decoupage, lapidary and tole painting. Maximum weight: 150 pounds; maximum length: 52". No fragile items such as unfired ceramics, and no commercially produced molds and kits. Entries not equipped for exhibiting will be disqualified.
Terms: Entries accepted until 1 week before show. Entry fee: $3/item. Maximum 2 entries. Entry fee not refunded for refused work. Work must be for sale; 20% commission.
Awards: Presents $2,400 in cash prizes and $200 in purchase awards. Judging panel consists of 3 professional artists or art teachers.

ARTS CRAFTS SHOW, Box 333, Eagle ID 83616. (208)939-6426. President: Doug Fitzgerald. Sponsor: Spectra Productions. Estab. 1972. Annual indoor show held 4 days in December at Boise, Idaho. Average attendance: 44,000. Considers all crafts.
Terms: Entries accepted until 3 week before show. Entry fee: $180/10x10 booth. Work may be offered for sale; no commission. Craftworker or representative must attend show; demonstrations OK. Registration limit: 160. Sponsor provides display panels; electricity for demonstrations; and 24-hour security.

CHRISTMAS SHOW, Box 333, Eagle ID 83616. (208)939-6426. President: Doug Fitzgerald. Sponsor: Spectra Productions. Estab. 1972. Annual indoor show held 4 days in December at Boise, Idaho. Average attendance: 35,000. Considers all crafts.
Terms: Entries accepted until 3 week before show. Entry fee: $135/10x10 booth. Work may be offered for sale; no commission. Craftworker or representative must attend show; demonstrations OK. Registration limit: 160. Sponsor provides display panels; electricity for demonstrations; and 24-hour security.

SUMMER IN THE CITY, Box 1454, Boise ID 83701. (208)336-0492. Contact: Coordinator. Sponsor: Downtown Boise Association. Estab. 1977. Annual outdoor show held 2 days in mid-July. Average attendance: 2,000. Show is advertised by radio, TV, newspapers, posters and flyers.
Acceptable Work: Considers selected crafts by invitation and confirmation by sponsor.
Terms: Entries accepted and confirmed until 2 weeks before show date. Display area: 10x10' or 10x20'. Work may be offered for sale; no commission. Craftworker must attend show; demonstrations encouraged. Sponsor provides electricity for demonstrations. Exhibitor handles sales and taxes.
Sales Tip: "Sales are improved with demonstrations. Public tends to buy quality medium-priced works. Public is very discerning in choices of media."

*SUN VALLEY CENTER'S INVITATIONAL ARTS & CRAFTS FESTIVAL, Box 656, Sun Valley ID 83353. (208)622-9491. Chairman: Mary Rolland. Sponsor: Sun Valley Center for Arts & Humanities. Estab. 1969. Annual outdoor show held 3 days during the first weekend in August. Average attendance: 10,000. Show is advertised by radio, posters and local and state newspapers. Total sales (1978): $42,500.
Acceptable Work: Considers all crafts except candlemaking, decoupage and dollmaking. No kits or machine-made crafts. "All work must be presented so that it may be hung. Wire is necessary."
Terms: Entries accepted until 1 week before show. Entry fee: $20/artist. Prejudging by slides/photos prior to closing date for entries; include SASE. Entry fee due after prejudging. Work must be offered for sale; 20% commission. Craftworker must attend show; demonstrations OK. Registration limit: 125. Sponsor provides chairs, display panels, electricity for demonstrations, table and 24-hour security. Center staff handles all sales.
Awards: Presents $100 for best overall exhibit, and merchant awards in each category (worth $25 each). "Overall presentation must be outstanding, educational and well put together."

Illinois

ADULT TOYS, Mindscape Gallery & Studio, 1521 Sherman Ave., Evanston IL 60201. (312)864-2660. Exhibition Coordinator: Deborah Farber-Isaacson. Estab. 1976. Annual indoor show held 1 month in October/November at the gallery. Average attendance: 5,000.
Acceptable Work: Considers batik, ceramics, dollmaking, glass art, jewelry, leatherworking, metalsmithing, mobiles, pottery, scrimshaw, sculpture, soft sculpture, weaving, woodcrafting and multi-media works of most types, also synthetics (e.g., polyester resin models). No kits or

"cute" items. "All pieces must be completely finished and ready for display and/or sale. No size restrictions. No price restrictions.
Terms: Entries accepted until 4 months before show. Entry fee: $5/craftworker. Maximum 25 pieces/craftworker. Prejudging by slides; no entry fees refunded for refused work. Work must be offered for sale; 40% commission. Craftworker needn't attend show; no demonstrations. Registration limit: 24. "Show is held in gallery, which provides all displays, electricity cases, illuminators, pedestals, etc."
Promotion: "Show is advertised by PR contacts and paid advertising to all metropolitan Chicago area news media, including the electronic media. We also have PR contacts with art-related publications. To be included in our publicity submit 6-12 b&w glossies (8x10 or 5x7), a personal statement (including techiniques, aims, etc.), and resume."
Sales Tip: "We suggest you include a broad range of factors: size, color, price range. However, personal style (not necessarily format) must be consistent. Gallery handles sales and taxes."

*ALBANY PARK ARTS & CRAFTS FAIR, Albany Park Chamber of Commerce, 3440 W. Lawrence, Chicago IL 60625. (312)463-5420. Chairman: Dave Cheesman. Estab. 1976. Annual outdoor show held 2 days in June.
Acceptable Work: Considers all crafts. "Jewelry; lapidary; batik; pottery; and leather. Craftspeople must submit photos or prove their work is original and not kits."
Terms: Entries accepted until 3 weeks before show. "Entries will be accepted past deadline but late entries may not be printed in free programs." Entry fee: $12/8' display area. Work may be offered for sale; no commission. Craftworker must attend show; demonstrations OK.
Promotion: Show is advertised by Albany Park Chamber of Commerce through newspaper; radio; and TV community news.
Awards: Presents gold, silver, and bronze medals with ribbons and printed award certificates.

AMERICAN ARTISTS & ARTISANS, American Society of Artists, Inc., 1297 Merchandise Mart Plaza, Chicago IL 60654. (312)751-2500. Estab. 1978. Annual outdoor show held 2 days in September in Naperville, Illinois. Considers all crafts except decoupage, dollmaking, lapidary and needlecrafts.
Terms: Entries accepted until 6 weeks before show. Entry fee: approximately $18/nonmember. Display area: 5x10. Prejudging by 5 slides or photos. Entry fee refunded for refused work. Work may be offered for sale; no commission. Craftworker must attend show; demonstrations encouraged. Sponsor provides electricity for demonstration; badges; bumper stickers; programs; and exhibit cards.
Promotion: Show is advertised by ads, posters and flyers. Submit b&w glossy photos of self with work for publicity.

*ANDERSONVILLE FESTIVAL ART FAIR, Andersonville Chamber of Commerce, 5344 N. Clark St., Chicago IL 60640. Estab. 1965. Annual outdoor show held 2 days in June. Average attendance: 10,000-15,000. Considers all crafts. Presents medal; ribbon; and certificate awards.
Terms: Entries accepted until 4 weeks before show. Entry fee: $15/8' display area. Prejudging by photos or slides; entry fee refunded for refused work. Work must be offered for sale; no commission. Craftworker must attend show; demonstrations OK.

ART IN THE BARN, Good Shepherd Hospital Field Office, 456 West Hwy. 22, Barrington IL 60010. (312)381-9600. Art Coordinator: Carolyn A. Husemoller. Sponsor: Auxiliary of Good Shepherd Hospital. Estab. 1974. Annual indoor show held 2 days in September or October. Average attendance: 2,000.
Acceptable Work: Considers all crafts. No kits or machine-made items. "Everything must be handmade and be current work. Craftsworkers must provide everything they will need for their displays, and the displays must blend in with the country atmosphere."
Terms: Entries accepted until 10 weeks before show. Entry fee: $15/display area in the upper barn (60 square feet); $10/display area in the lower barn (90 square feet). Prejudging by 4 slides; $4 jury fee. Entry fee due after prejudging. Work may be offered for sale; 15% commission. Craftworker needn't attend show; demonstrations OK. Registration limit: 60. Sponsor provides display panels in the upper barn, electricity for some demonstrations and 24-hour security. Financial secretary/treasurer of the Hospital Auxiliary handles sales and taxes.
Promotion: Show is advertised by brochures. "Quality brochures are made up by the hospital printing services and mailed to everyone in the geographic area. The public relations is handled professionally by the hospital's public relations person.
Profile: "We are bringing added revenue for the building of the Good Shepherd Hospital. The

show is held in an old rustic barn with no heat. The lower barn has 1 side exposed, overlooking a golf course." Artist's gross sales: $17,000.

ARTISTS & ARTISANS AT WORK, American Society of Artists, 1297 Merchandise Mart Plaza, Chicago IL 60654. (312)751-2500. Contact: Director. Estab. 1978. Annual outdoor show held 2 days in May at Downers Grove, Illinois.
Acceptable Work: Considers batik; candlemaking; ceramics; glass art; jewelry; leatherworking; macrame; metalsmithing; mobiles; pottery; sculpture; soft sculpture; tole painting; weaving; and woodcrafting.
Terms: Entries accepted until 6 weeks before show or until spaces filled. Entry fee: $18/nonmember. Display area: 5x10. Prejudging by slides or photos; entry fee refunded for refused work. Work may be offered for sale; no commission. Craftworker must attend show; demonstrations encouraged. Sponsor provides electricity for demonstrations.
Promotion: Show is advertised by posters; bumper stickers; flyers; paid advertising; and publicity. "Submit b&w glossy photos of self with work."

ARTS & CRAFTS IN ACTION, American Society of Artists, 1297 Merchandise Mart Plaza, Chicago IL 60654. (312)751-2500. Estab. 1978. Annual indoor show held 2 days in September at Hoffman Estates, Illinois. Entries accepted until 6 weeks before show. Entry fee: $18/nonmembers. Display area: 5x10. Prejudging by 5 slides and photos. Entry fee refunded for refused work. Work may be offered for sale; no commission. Craftworker must attend show; demonstrations encouraged. Sponsor provides electricity for demonstrations; badges; programs; exhibit cards; bumper stickers; posters; and flyers. Show is advertised by ads; bumper stickers; publicity; posters; and flyers. Submit b&w glossy photos of self with work for publicity. Considers all crafts except decoupage; dollmaking; lapidary; and needlecrafts.

AUTUMN FEST OF ARTS & CRAFTS, American Society of Artists, Inc., 1297 Merchandise Mart Plaza, Chicago IL 60654. (312)751-2500. Estab. 1978. Annual indoor show held 2 days in November at Des Plaines, Illinois.
Acceptable Work: Considers all crafts but decoupage; dollmaking; lapidary; and needlecrafts.
Terms: Entries accepted until 6 weeks before show. Entry fee: approximately $22/nonmember. Display area: 5x10. Prejudging by 5 slides or photos; entry fee refunded for refused work. Work may be offered for sale; no commission. Craftworker must attend show; demonstrations encouraged. Sponsor provides electricity for demonstrations; badges; programs; and exhibit cards.
Promotion: Show is advertised by newspapers; radio; TV; posters; and flyers. Submit b&w glossy photos of self with work for publicity.

*****BARRINGTON ART FAIR**, 1410 Lake Shore Dr. S., Barrington IL 60010. (314)381-7069. Chairman: Mrs. Richard J. Haayan. Sponsor: Barrington Woman's Club. Estab. 1958. Annual indoor/outdoor show held 1 day in August. Average attendance: 2,000-3,000. Considers all original crafts.
Terms: Entries accepted until show date; deadline for program listing is 2 weeks prior to show date. Entry fee: $2/item for exhibitor, $4/item for nonexhibitor; $12/indoor display area (5x10), $10/outdoor display area. Work may be offered for sale; no commission. Craftworker must attend show or rent exhibit sitters, available at $2/hour; demonstrations OK.
Awards: Presents $500 award for Best of Show; $125 for 1st prize, $100 for 2nd prize and $75 for 3rd prize in each category; $100 special category prize for jewelry; and $300 purchase award for best Barrington scene. "All juried items must be suitable for hanging."

BELVIDERE MALL FALL FESTIVAL OF CRAFTS, Rt. 4, 146 Park Dr., F.R.V.G., Barrington IL 60010. (312)639-5665. Show Director: Irene "Rae" Partridge. Sponsor: Merchants Association. Estab. 1964. Annual indoor show held 2 days in October at Waukegan, Illinois.
Acceptable Work: Considers all crafts. No kits, commercial molds, imports, galleries or reproductions.
Terms: Entries accepted until 1 week before show or until all spaces filled. Entry fee: $30/display area (with 10' frontage). Prejudging by 5 slides/photos, resume and SASE. Entry fee refunded for refused work. Work may be offered for sale; no commission. Craftworker must attend show; demonstrations OK. Sponsor provides electricity for demonstrations and 24-hour security. Exhibitor handles sales and taxes.
Promotion: Show is advertised by newspaper ads and articles, posters, radio, TV and mall posters. "Please send nonreturnable b&w glossy photo with resume and name and address of local paper for blanket coverage."

Sales Tip: "Craftworkers should present themselves in a professional manner; be neat in appearance; and have well constructed exhibit materials. Sales are helped when craftworkers show interest in their own work and talk with the public."

BELVIDERE MALL STARVING "AMERICAN" ARTS & CRAFTS FAIR, Rt. 4, 146 Park Dr., F.R.V.G., Barrington IL 60010. (312)639-5665. Show Director: Irene "Rae" Partridge. Sponsor: Merchants Association. Estab. 1964. Annual indoor show held 2 days in February at Waukegan, Illinois.
Acceptable Work: Considers all crafts. No kits, commercial molds, imports, galleries or reproductions.
Terms: Entries accepted until 1 week before show or until all spaces filled. Entry fee: $30/display area (with 10' frontage). Prejudging by 5 slides/photos, resume and SASE. Entry fee refunded for refused work. Work may be offered for sale; no commission. Craftworker must attend show; demonstrations OK. Sponsor provides electricity for demonstrations and 24-hour security. Exhibitor handles sales and taxes.
Promotion: Show is advertised by newspaper ads and articles, posters, radio, TV and mall posters. "Please send nonreturnable b&w glossy photo with resume and name and address of local paper for blanket coverage."
Sales Tip: "Craftworkers should present themselves in a professional manner; be neat in appearance; and have well constructed exhibit materials. Sales are helped when craftworkers show interest in their own work and talk with the public."

BLOOMINGDALE WOMEN'S CLUB FESTIVAL OF FINE ARTS, Bloomingdale State Bank, 114 E. Lake St., Bloomingdale IL 60108. Contact: Ann Yonan at 153 Greenway, Bloomingdale IL 60108, (312)893-1469; or Ann Hatt at 221 Millcreek, Bloomingdale IL 60108, (312)893-6542. Estab. 1972. Annual indoor/outdoor show held 1 day in September. Presents cash awards.
Acceptable Work: Categories are: oil/acrylics, watercolors, metals, fiber, clay/ceramics, wood, and mixed media, photography, pen-ink, charcoal, etc. "Work must be of original design and execution."
Terms: Entries accepted until about 1 week before show date. Entry fee: $12/artist. Prejudging by 5 color slides or photographs of work. Only work applied for may be exhibited. Work may be offered for sale; no commission. Registration limit: 110 artists/craftworkers.

CHILLICOTHE ART & CRAFT SHOW, Box 61, Rome IL 61562. (309)274-3001. Coordinator: Judy Kelley. Estab. 1977. Annual outdoor show held 1 day in September at Chillicothe, Illinois. Average attendance: 5,000.
Acceptable Work: Considers candlemaking; jewelry; leatherworking; macrame; pottery; sculpture; weaving; and woodcrafting.
Terms: Entries accepted until 2 weeks before show. Entry fee: $15/craftworker. Display area: 6x12. Prejudging by slides and photos. SASE. Entry fee due after prejudging. Work may be offered for sale; no commission. Craftworker must attend show; demonstrations OK. Registration limit: 50. Sponsor provides electricity for demonstrations.
Promotion: Show is advertised by radio; newspapers; and posters. Submit b&w glossies for publicity.

COUNTRY FAIR & AUCTION, 101 S. Church Rd., Bensenville IL 60106. (312)766-3632. Arts and Crafts Chairperson: Guyla Hunt. Sponsor: Bensenville Community Church. Estab. 1977. Annual indoor/outdoor show held 1 day in October. Average attendance: 400-500. Entries accepted up until show date. Entry fee: $11/8x10 display area. Work may be offered for sale; no commission. Craftworker must attend show; demonstrations OK. Registration limit: 75. Sponsor provides electricity for demonstrations. Show is advertised by radio, newspapers and posters. Considers all crafts.

COUNTRY FAIR MALL ART & CRAFT SHOW, Box 61, Rome IL 61562. (309)274-3001. Coordinator: Judy Kelley. Estab. 1979. Semiannual indoor show held 3 days in May and September at Champaign, Illinois. Average attendance: 5,000.
Acceptable Work: Considers candlemaking, pottery, jewelry, woodcrafting, metalsmithing, sculpture and tole painting.
Terms: Entries accepted until 3 weeks before show. Entry fee: $35/artist. Display area: 6x12. Prejudging by slides or photos. Entry fee refunded for refused work. Work may be offered for sale; no commission. Craftworker must attend show; demonstrations OK. Registration limit: 50. Sponsor provides electricity for demonstrations.

COUNTRYSIDE MALL ARTS & SELECTED CRAFTS FAIR, Rt. 4, 146 Park Dr., F.R.V.G., Barrington IL 60010. (312)639-5665. Show Director: Irene "Rae" Partridge. Sponsor: Merchants Association. Estab. 1973. Annual indoor show held 2 days in May at Palatine, Illinois.
Acceptable Work: Considers all crafts. No kits, commercial molds, imports, galleries or reproductions.
Terms: Entries accepted until 1 week before show or until all spaces filled. Entry fee: $30/display area (with 10' frontage). Prejudging by 5 slides/photos, resume and SASE. Entry fee refunded for refused work. Work may be offered for sale; no commission. Craftworker must attend show; demonstrations OK. Sponsor provides electricity for demonstrations and 24-hour security. Exhibitor handles sales and taxes.
Promotion: Show is advertised by newspaper ads and articles, posters, radio, TV and mall posters. "Please send nonreturnable b&w glossy photo with resume and name and address of local paper for blanket coverage."
Sales Tip: "Craftworkers should present themselves in a professional manner; be neat in appearance; and have well constructed exhibit materials. Sales are helped when craftworkers show interest in their own work and talk with the public."

COUNTRYSIDE MALL FALL FESTIVAL OF SELECTED CRAFTS, Rt. 4, 146 Park Dr., F.R.V.G., Barrington IL 60010. (312)639-5665. Show Director: Irene "Rae" Partridge. Sponsor: Merchants Association. Estab. 1973. Annual indoor show held 2 days in September at Palatine, Illinois.
Acceptable Work: Considers all crafts. No kits, commercial molds, imports, galleries or reproductions.
Terms: Entries accepted until 1 week before show or until all spaces filled. Entry fee: $30/display area (with 10' frontage). Prejudging by 5 slides/photos, resume and SASE. Entry fee refunded for refused work. Work may be offered for sale; no commission. Craftworker must attend show; demonstrations OK. Sponsor provides electricity for demonstrations and 24-hour security. Exhibitor handles sales and taxes.
Promotion: Show is advertised by newspaper ads and articles, posters, radio, TV and mall posters. "Please send nonreturnable b&w glossy photo with resume and name and address of local paper for blanket coverage."
Sales Tip: "Craftworkers should present themselves in a professional manner; be neat in appearance; and have well constructed exhibit materials. Sales are helped when craftworkers show interest in their own work and talk with the public."

COUNTRYSIDE MALL STARVING "AMERICAN" ARTS & CRAFTS, Rt. 4, 146 Park Dr., F.R.V.G., Barrington IL 60010. (312)639-5665. Show Director: Irene "Rae" Partridge. Sponsor: Merchants Association. Estab. 1973. Annual indoor show held 2 days in January at Palatine, Illinois.
Acceptable Work: Considers all crafts. No kits, commercial molds, imports, galleries or reproductions.
Terms: Entries accepted until 1 week before show or until all spaces filled. Entry fee: $30/display area (with 10' frontage). Prejudging by 5 slides/photos, resume and SASE. Entry fee refunded for refused work. Work may be offered for sale; no commission. Craftworker must attend show; demonstrations OK. Sponsor provides electricity for demonstrations and 24-hour security. Exhibitor handles sales and taxes.
Promotion: Show is advertised by newspaper ads and articles, posters, radio, TV and mall posters. "Please send nonreturnable b&w glossy photo with resume and name and address of local paper for blanket coverage."
Sales Tip: "Craftworkers should present themselves in a professional manner; be neat in appearance; and have well constructed exhibit materials. Sales are helped when craftworkers show interest in their own work and talk with the public."

***CRAFT GALLERY**, 18W118 73rd Place, Westmont IL 60559. (312)964-9062. Contact: Art Plus Associates. Sponsor: Orland Square Mall. Estab. 1977. Annual indoor show held 4 days in March at Orland Park, Illinois. Average attendance: 60,000-80,000. Considers all original crafts. Presents cash awards of $1,000 and ribbons.
Terms: Entries accepted until 6 weeks before show. Entry fee: $70/6x12 display area. Prejudging by 5 slides or photos and SASE; entry fee refunded for refused work. Work may be offered for sale; no commission. Craftworker must attend show; demonstrations encouraged. Registration limit: 150. Sponsor provides chairs; coverings; display panels; electricity for demonstrations; and 24-hour security.
Promotion: Show is advertised by area newspapers and radio. "Provide 8x10 b&w glossies of

you involved with your work along with a brief resume on your background to be considered for promotional purposes."

CRAFT SHOP CRAFTS FAIR, Craft Shop, Box 174, Southern Illinois University, Edwardsville IL 62026. (618)692-2178. Estab. 1975. Semiannual show held 3 days outdoors in May and 3 days indoors in December. Average attendance: 15,000. Considers all crafts.
Terms: Entry fee: $35 for all 3 days. Display area: 60 square feet. Prejudging by minimum of 5 slides; photos; or examples of work. Work may be offered for sale; no commission. Craftworker must attend show; demonstrations OK. Registration limit: 40, May; 40, December. Sponsor provides electricity for demonstrations; and overnight storage.

CRITTERS & COHORTS, 1521 Sherman Ave., Evanston IL 60201. (312)864-2660. Show Coordinator: Deborah Isaacson. Sponsor: Mindscape Gallery and Studio. Estab. 1977. Annual indoor show (in gallery) held 1 month in fall/winter. Average attendance: 3,000.
Acceptable Work: Considers batik; ceramics; glass art; leatherworking; metalsmithing; pottery; sculpture; soft sculpture; weaving; and woodcrafting. Especially needs anything creative and one of a kind with animal or related animal themes.
Terms: Entries due June 1. Entry fee: $5/artist. Prejudging by maximum of 5 slides indicating size, media, whole/retail price with 'front,' 'top' put on slide. Sample of work may be requested by jury. "Jury reserves right to refuse work if not up to quality of description and slides." Entry fee not refunded for refused work. Work may be offered for sale; 40% commission. Craftworker needn't attend show; no demonstrations. Registration limit: 24. Sponsor provides display panels; electricity; insurance on exhibited work; 24-hour security; all props; and display services.
Promotion: Show is advertised by advance publicity; newspapers; trade magazines; mailing lists. Submit b&w glossy for articles; statement of purpose and media description; and brief biography. "Only artists submitting proper materials will receive publicity coverage."

CROSS COUNTY MALL ART & CRAFT SHOW, Mattoon IL 61562. (309)274-3001. Coordinator: Judy Kelley. Estab. 1976. Annual indoor show held 3 days in March/October.
Acceptable Work: Considers candlemaking; leatherworking; macrame; pottery; sculpture; tole painting; and woodcrafting.
Terms: Entries accepted until 2 weeks before show. Entry fee: $35/artist. Display area: 6x12. Prejudging by slides and photos. SASE. Entry fee refunded for refused work. Work may be offered for sale; no commission. Craftworker must attend show; demonstrations OK. Registration limit: 50. Sponsor provides electricity for demonstrations.

A DAY IN THE COUNTRY, Pecatonica Junior Woman's Club, Pecatonica IL 61063. (815)239-2443. Co-chairperson: Kathy Carroll. Estab. 1971. Annual indoor show held 1 day in October. Average attendance: 7,000. Considers all crafts.
Terms: Entries accepted until 2 weeks before show. Entry fee: $15/10x10 display area. Prejudging by slides or photos. Entry fee refunded for refused work. Work may be offered for sale; no commission. Craftworker needn't attend show; demonstrations OK. Registration limit: 110. Sponsor provides electricity for demonstrations and 24-hour security.

DEERFIELD COMMONS ARTS & SELECTED CRAFTS FAIR, Rt. 4, 146 Park Dr., F.R.V.G., Barrington IL 60010. (312)639-5665. Show Director: Irene "Rae" Partridge. Sponsor: Merchants Association. Estab. 1971. Annual indoor show held 1 day in September at Deerfield, Illinois.
Acceptable Work: Considers all crafts. No kits, commercial molds, imports, galleries or reproductions.
Terms: Entries accepted until 1 week before show or until all spaces filled. Entry fee: $18/display area (with 10' frontage). Prejudging by 5 slides/photos, resume and SASE. Entry fee refunded for refused work. Work may be offered for sale; no commission. Craftworker must attend show; demonstrations OK. Exhibitor handles sales and taxes.
Promotion: Show is advertised by newspaper ads and articles, posters, radio, TV and mall posters. "Please send nonreturnable b&w glossy photo with resume and name and address of local paper for blanket coverage."
Sales Tip: "Craftworkers should present themselves in a professional manner; be neat in appearance; and have well constructed exhibit materials. Sales are helped when craftworkers show interest in their own work and talk with the public."

DEERFIELD COMMONS SPRING FESTIVAL OF SELECTED CRAFTS, Rt. 4, 146 Park Dr.,

F.R.V.G., Barrington IL 60010. (312)639-5665. Show Director: Irene "Rae" Partridge. Sponsor: Merchants Association. Estab. 1971. Annual indoor show held 1 day in June at Deerfield, Illinois.
Acceptable Work: Considers all crafts. No kits, commercial molds, imports, galleries or reproductions.
Terms: Entries accepted until 1 week before show or until all spaces filled. Entry fee: $18/display area (with 10' frontage). Prejudging by 5 slides/photos, resume and SASE. Entry fee refunded for refused work. Work may be offered for sale; no commission. Craftworker must attend show; demonstrations OK. Sponsor provides electricity for demonstrations and 24-hour security. Exhibitor handles sales and taxes.
Promotion: Show is advertised by newspaper ads and articles, posters, radio, TV and mall posters. "Please send nonreturnable b&w glossy photo with resume and name and address of local paper for blanket coverage."
Sales Tip: "Craftworkers should present themselves in a professional manner; be neat in appearance; and have well constructed exhibit materials. Sales are helped when craftworkers show interest in their own work and talk with the public."

"DISCOVER RAVINIA DAY," Highland Park Chamber of Commerce. 1811 St. Johns Ave., Highland Park IL 60035. (312)432-0284. Executive Director: Virginia Collins. Estab. 1975. Annual outdoor show held 1 day in September. Average attendance: 3,000. Entries accepted until 2 weeks before show. Entry fee: $15/artist. Display area varies. Work may be offered for sale; no commission. Suggest craftworker attends show; demonstrations OK. Registration limit: 100. Show is advertised in local and Chicago newspapers; radio; TV; and posters. Considers all crafts.

EDENS PLAZA ARTS & CRAFT FAIR, 9476 Harding Ave., Surfside FL 33154. Contact: Iris G. Klein. Sponsor: Edens Plaza Merchants Association. Estab. 1956. Annual outdoor show held 2 days in June at Wilmette, Illinois. Average attendance: 10,000-15,000. Considers all crafts.
Terms: Entry fee: $20/8x8' display area. Maximum 2 entries per craftworker. Prejudging by slides or photos (send resume and SASE). Crafts may be offered for sale; no commission. Craftworker must attend show; demonstrations OK.
Promotion: Submit b&w glossies and resume for newspaper publicity.

ELMHURST FESTIVAL CRAFTS FAIR, c/o Elmhurst Chamber of Commerce, 111 S. York St., Elmhurst IL 60126. (312)834-6060. Sponsor: Elmhurst Festival Committee. Estab. 1976. Annual outdoor show held 2 days during the year. "No established time of year; depends on other activities in the city and availability of facilities. Considers all crafts.
Terms: Entries accepted until 1 week before show. Entry fee: $15/8x10' display area. Work may be offered for sale; no commission. Craftworker must attend show; demonstrations encouraged.

*****EPSILON OMEGA ARTS & CRAFT SHOW**, 18526 Oak Ave., Lansing IL 60438. (312)895-1962. Co-chairperson: Jane Goins. Sponsor: Epsilon Omega Sorority. Estab. 1973. Annual outdoor show held 1 day in September at Wicker Park, Highland, Illinois. Average attendance: 25,000. Considers all crafts.
Terms: Entries accepted until 2 weeks before show. Entry fee: $10/8x10 display area. Work may be offered for sale; no commission. Craftworker or representative must attend show; demonstrations OK. Registration limit: 200. Sponsor provides fencing.
Awards: Presents $100, 1st; $50, 2nd; and $25, 3rd prizes in craft division. Also presents 6 ribbons.

ETHNIC/FOLK FEST OF ARTS & CRAFTS, American Society of Artists, Inc., 1297 Merchandise Mart Plaza, Chicago IL 60654. (312)751-2500. Estab. 1978. Annual outdoor show held 2 days in June at Naperville, Illinois. Considers all crafts.
Terms: Entries accepted until 6 weeks before show or until filled. Entry fee: $18/nonmembers. Display area: 5x10. Prejudging by 3 slides or photos; entry fee refunded for refused work. Work may be offered for sale; no commission. Craftworker must attend show; demonstrations encouraged. Sponsor provides electricity for demonstrations; badges; programs; and exhibit cards.
Promotion: Show is advertised by ads; bumper stickers; posters; flyers; and general publicity. Submit b&w glossy photos.

FALL FESTIVAL OF ARTS, American Society of Artists, Inc., 1297 Merchandise Mart Plaza, Chicago IL 60654. (312)751-2500. Estab. 1973. Annual indoor show held 2 days in November at Crystal Lake, Illinois.
Terms: Entries accepted until 6 weeks before show or until filled. Entry fee: $25/5x10 display area for nonmembers. Prejudging by slides and photos. Entry fee refunded for refused work. Work may be offered for sale; no commission. Craftworker must attend show; demonstrations encouraged. Sponsor provides electricity for demonstrations; badges; programs; and exhibit cards.
Promotion: Show is advertised by posters; ads; bumper stickers; flyers; and general publicity. Submit b&w photos if available (of self and work is best) plus additional information on artist and work.

***FELICIAN COLLEGE ARTS & CRAFTS FAIR**, 9476 E. Bay Harbor Dr., Bay Harbor Island FL 33154. (305)864-8725. Art Director: Iris G. Klein. Sponsor: Felician College. Estab. 1972. Annual outdoor show held 1 day in July at Chicago, Illinois. Average attendance: 4,000-5,000. Entries accepted until 4 weeks before show. Entry fee: $15/10' display area. Prejudging by slides and/or photos; entry fee due after prejudging. Work may be offered for sale; no commission. Craftworker must attend show; demonstrations OK. Sponsor provides fencing and assistance in carrying display boards. Considers all crafts. Presents $500 in purchase prizes and ribbons.
Promotion: Show is advertised by newspapers; flyers; radio (spots); and display ads. "Send b&w glossy prints and resume."

FESTIVAL, Art Department, Eastern Illinois University, Charleston IL 61920. (217)581-3410. Director, Art Fair: Bill Heyduck. Sponsor: School of Fine Arts. "This is a 3 day fine arts festival containing music, theater and art in the open air. It is a place for artists to be seen and heard as well as sell. All fees are used to support and advertise the festival." Estab. 1977. Annual outdoor show held 2 days in April. Entries accepted until 2 weeks before show. Entry fee: $10/artist; $25/group display. Display area: 8x10. Work may be offered for sale; no commission. Craftworker must attend show; demonstrations OK. Registration limit: 100. Sponsor provides chairs and table. Show is advertised by radio; TV; and newspapers. Categories: painting; drawing; prints; sculpture; and crafts. Considers all crafts except decoupage; lapidary; and tole painting.

***57th STREET ART FAIR**, c/o Susan, 5555 S. Everett, Chicago IL 60637. Secretary: Win Poole. Estab. 1947. Annual outdoor show held 2 days in June. Considers all crafts. Presents 3 cash awards of $100.
Terms: Entries accepted until about 2 months before show. Entry fee: $16/craftworker plus $2 screening fee. Prejudging by slides. Entry fee (not screening fee) refunded for refused work. Work must be offered for sale; no commission. Craftworker must attend show; no demonstrations. Registration limit: 305. Sponsor provides fencing.
Promotion: Show is advertised by radio; TV; posters; and editorial comments in newspapers and magazines. Categories: painting and drawing; sculpture; prints; and crafts.

FOUNTAIN SQUARE PLAZA STARVING "AMERICAN" ARTS & CRAFTS FAIR, Rt. 4, 146 Park Dr., F.R.V.G., Barrington IL 60010. (312)639-5665. Show Director: Irene "Rae" Partridge. Sponsor: Greater Downtown Elgin Commission. Estab. 1979. Annual outdoor show held 1 day in the summer at Elgin, Illinois.
Acceptable Work: Considers all crafts. No kits, commercial molds, imports, galleries or reproductions.
Terms: Entries accepted until 1 week before show or until all spaces filled. Entry fee: $18/10' frontage display area. Prejudging by 5 slides/photos, resume and SASE. Entry fee refunded for refused work. Work may be offered for sale; no commission. Craftworker must attend show; demonstrations OK.
Promotion: Show is advertised by newspaper ads and articles, posters, radio, TV and mall posters. "Please send nonreturnable b&w glossy photo with resume and name and address of local paper for blanket coverage."
Sales Tip: "Craftworkers should present themselves in a professional manner; be neat in appearance; and have well constructed exhibit materials. Sales are helped when craftworkers show interest in their own work and talk with the public."

---

* Those listings preceded by an asterisk present awards for prize-winning crafts.

Steve Huber, one of the 100 exhibitors at the annual Guilford Handcraft Exposition, Guilford, Connecticut, demonstrates his craft of hand spinning. Demonstrations are encouraged by promoters of the show to interest the 50,000 people attending. The expo is held on the Guilford Green, under tents, for three days each July. Crafts considered include batik, ceramics, dollmaking, glass art, leatherworking, macrame, metalsmithing, pottery, soft sculpture, weaving and woodcrafting.

FOX RIVER GROVE LIONS ARTS & CRAFTS, 9612 Witchie Dr. W., Fox River Grove IL 60021. (312)639-3327. Chairman: Frank A. Tuman. Estab. 1977. Annual outdoor show held 1 day in August. Show is advertised by newspaper; radio; and TV. Considers all crafts.
Terms: Entries accepted until 1 week before show. Entry fee: $10/10x10 display area. Work may be offered for sale; no commission. Craftworker must attend show; demonstrations OK. Registration limit: 110.

FRANCIS PARK ART & CRAFT SHOW & ETHNIC FOOD FAIR, Rome IL 61562. (309)274-3001. Coordinator: Judy Kelley. Estab. 1977. Annual outdoor show held 1 day in July at Kewanee, Illinois. Average attendance: 20,000. Show is advertised by newspaper within a 50 mile radius.
Acceptable Work: Considers candlemaking; jewelry; leatherworking; macrame; pottery; sculpture; tole painting; and woodcrafting.
Terms: Entries accepted until 2 weeks before show. Entry fee: $20/artist. Display area: 6x12. Prejudging by slides and photos. SASE. Entry fee refunded for refused work. Work may be offered for sale; no commission. Craftworker must attend show; demonstrations OK. Registration limit: 100. Sponsor provides electricity for demonstrations.

*****GLENVIEW ART FAIR**, 2122 Dewes St., Glenview IL 60025. Sponsor: Glenview Art League. Annual invitational outdoor show. Average attendance: 10,000. Submit 5 slides for jurying by July 1. Display area: 10'. Considers sculpture. Presents $900 in cash and $600 in purchase awards. No commission.

GOLD COAST ART FAIR, 26 E. Huron St., Chicago IL 60611. Sponsors: Gold Coast Association and *Near North News*. Estab. 1958. Annual outdoor show held 3 days in July or August. Average attendance: 600,000. Entry fee: $25/display area. Work may be offered for sale; no commission. Craftworker must attend show; demonstrations OK. Sponsor pays insurance for exhibited work. Considers sculpture.

GOLF MILL OUTDOOR CRAFT FAIR, Promotion Management Asst., 18127 William St., Lancing IL 60438. (312)895-3710. Coordinator: Sylvia Krugowski. Sponsor: Golf Mill Merchant Association. Estab. 1977. Annual outdoor show held in May. Entries accepted up until show. Entry fee: $24/craftworker. Display area: 8x8. Prejudging by slides or photos; entry fee refunded for refused work. Work may be offered for sale; no commission. Craftworker must attend show; demonstrations OK. Sponsor provides electricity for demonstrations. Show is advertised by all crafts publications, *Sunshine Artists*, newspaper releases; and shopping center paid advertising. Submit advance notices to your customers in area. Considers all crafts except Indian jewelry and ceramics from commercial molds.

HILLSIDE SELECTED CRAFTS FESTIVAL, Rt. 4, 146 Park Dr., F.R.V.G., Barrington IL 60010. (312)639-5665. Show Director: Irene "Rae" Partridge. Sponsor: Merchants Association. Estab. 1966. Annual indoor show held 2 days in April at Hillside, Illinois.
Acceptable Work: Considers all crafts. No kits, commercial molds, imports, galleries or reproductions.
Terms: Entries accepted until 1 week before show or until all spaces filled. Entry fee: $30/display area (with 10' frontage). Prejudging by 5 slides/photos, resume and SASE. Entry fee refunded for refused work. Work may be offered for sale; no commission. Craftworker must attend show; demonstrations OK. Registration limit: 125-140. Sponsor provides electricity for demonstrations and 24-hour security. Exhibitor handles sales and taxes.
Promotion: Show is advertised by newspaper ads and articles, posters, radio, TV and mall posters. "Please send nonreturnable b&w glossy photo with resume and name and address of local paper for blanket coverage."
Sales Tip: "Craftworkers should present themselves in a professional manner; be neat in appearance; and have well constructed exhibit materials. Sales are helped when craftworkers show interest in their own work and talk with the public."

HILLSIDE SHOPPING CENTER STARVING "AMERICAN" ARTS & CRAFTS FAIR, Rt. 4, 146 Park Dr., F.R.V.G., Barrington IL 60010. (312)639-5665. Show Director: Irene "Rae" Partridge. Sponsor: Merchants Association. Estab. 1966. Semiannual outdoor show held 2 days in February and October at Hillside, Illinois.
Acceptable Work: Considers all crafts. No kits, commercial molds, imports, galleries or reproductions.
Terms: Entries accepted until 1 week before show or until all spaces filled. Entry fee:

$30/display area (with 10' frontage). Prejudging by 5 slides/photos, resume and SASE. Entry fee refunded for refused work. Work may be offered for sale; no commission. Craftworker must attend show; demonstrations OK. Sponsor provides electricity for demonstrations and 24-hour security. Exhibitor handles sales and taxes.
Promotion: Show is advertised by newspaper ads and articles, posters, radio, TV and mall posters. "Please send nonreturnable b&w glossy photo with resume and name and address of local paper for blanket coverage."
Sales Tip: "Craftworkers should present themselves in a professional manner; be neat in appearance; and have well constructed exhibit materials. Sales are helped when craftworkers show interest in their own work and talk with the public."

HOLIDAY FESTIVAL OF ARTS & CRAFTS, American Society of Artists, Inc., 1297 Merchandise Mart Plaza, Chicago IL 60654. (312)751-2500. Estab. 1975. Annual indoor show held 2 days in November.
Acceptable Work: Considers batik; jewelry; macrame; metalsmithing; pottery; sculpture; soft sculpture; weaving and woodcrafting.
Terms: Entries accepted until 6 weeks before show or until all spaces filled. Entry fee: $25/nonmembers. Display area: 5x10. Prejudging by slides and photos. Entry fee refunded for refused work. Work may be offered for sale; no commission. Craftworker must attend show; demonstrations encouraged. Sponsor provides limited amount of electricity for demonstrations; badges; programs; and exhibit cards.
Promotion: Show is advertised by posters; flyers; newspapers, radio, TV and bumper stickers. Submit b&w photos if available (of self and work is best) plus any additional information on artist and work.

HOUBY FESTIVAL ARTS & CRAFT FAIR, 2130 S. 61st Ct., Cicero IL 60650. (312)863-2104. Executive Director: Norm Scaman. Sponsor: Cermak Road Business Association. Estab. 1969. Annual outdoor show held 2 days in October at Berwyn, Illinois. Average attendance: 15,000. Considers all crafts.
Terms: Entries accepted until 2 weeks before show. Entry fee: $15/6x10 display area. Work may be offered for sale; no commission. Craftworker or representative must attend show; demonstrations OK. Registration limit: 200.

ICE HOUSE ARTS FESTIVAL, American Society of Artists, Inc., 700 N. Michigan Ave., Chicago IL 60611. (312)751-2500. Estab. 1977. Annual indoor show held 2 days in November at Barrington, Illinois.
Acceptable Work: Considers batik wall hangings; macrame wall hangings; sculpture; soft sculpture; and woven wall hangings.
Terms: Entries accepted until 6 weeks before show or until spaces filled. Entry fee: $25. Display area: 5x10. Prejudging by slides and photos. Entry fee refunded for refused work. Work may be offered for sale; no commission. Craftworker must attend show; demonstrations encouraged. Sponsor provides limited amount of electricity for demonstrations; badges; programs; and exhibit cards.
Promotion: Show is advertised by posters; flyers; and general publicity. Submit b&w photos for publicity if available (of self and work is best) plus any additional information.

JANESVILLE MALL ART & CRAFT SHOW, Box 61, Rome IL 61562. (309)274-3001. Coordinator: Judy Kelley. Estab. 1974. Indoor show held 3 days in March, August and November. Average attendance: 15,000-20,000.
Acceptable Work: Considers jewelry; leatherworking; macrame; metalsmithing; pottery; sculpture; tole painting; weaving; and woodcrafting.
Terms: Entry fee: $40/artist (March, August); $50/artist (November). Display area: 6x12. Prejudging by slides and photos; entry fee refunded for refused work. Work may be offered for sale; no commission. Craftworker must attend show; demonstrations OK. Registration limit: 65. Sponsor provides electricity for demonstrations and 24-hour security protection.

KISHWAUKEE VALLEY ART LEAGUE SPRING ART & CRAFT FAIR, 103 E. Sunset, DeKalb IL 60115. (815)756-5218. Chairman: Virginia Lary. Kishwaukee Valley Art League. Estab. 1971. Annual outdoor show held 2 days in June at Sycamore, Illinois.
Acceptable Work: Considers all crafts. No commercially produced items, greenware, kits, molds or jewelry (which is not handmade by exhibitor). "Space must be kept neat and attractive."
Terms: Entries accepted until 1 week before show. Entry fee: $15/10x12' display area. Work

may be offered for sale; no commission. Craftworker must attend show; demonstrations OK. Registration limit: 100.

LINCOLN SQUARE ART FAIR, Lincoln Square Chamber of Commerce, 4800 N. Western Ave., Chicago IL 60625. (312)275-2800. Chairman: Dave Cheesman. Estab. 1971. Annual outdoor mall, plaza and sidewalk show held 2 days in June. Average attendance: 15,000. Considers all crafts.
Terms: Entries accepted until 4 weeks before show. Entry fee $20/8' display area. Work may be offered for sale; no commission. Craftworker must attend show; demonstrations appreciated. Submit slides or photos.
Awards: Presents gold, silver and bronze medals with ribbons, printed award certificates and cash prizes.

*LOCKPORT OLD CANAL DAYS FOLK ART & CRAFT SHOW, Box 12, Lockport IL 60441. (815)838-7316. Chairman, Folk Art Show: Wilma Stasch. Estab. 1973. Annual outdoor show held 2 days in June. Considers all crafts. Presents cash awards of $150.
Terms: Entries accepted until 4 weeks before show. Entry fee: $20/4x8' display area. Prejudging. Work may be offered for sale; no commission. Craftworker must attend show; demonstrations encouraged. Registration limit: 200.
Promotion: Show is advertised by sending notices around the country to possible contact points like craft centers and folk art museums.
Profile: "This show is designed to encourage the folk artists and craftsmen, those people who produce original work but have had little formal training. It is designed to encourage the folk art tradition in Lockport and northern Illinois where it was strong in the past but has deteriorated due to industrialization."

LOGAN RAILSPLITTING FESTIVAL, Box 352, Lincoln IL 62656. (217)732-6840. President: Dean A. Tibbs. Sponsor: Logan Railsplitting Association. Estab. 1970. Annual outdoor show held 2 days in September. Average attendance: 2,500-3,000. Considers all handmade crafts. Entries accepted until show date. Entry fee: $20/10x10' booth. Craftworker needn't attend show; demonstrations encouraged.

MACHA MARKET—CHICAGO CRAFT-HOBBY INDUSTRY SHOW, 1100 Brandywine Blvd., Box 2188, Zanesville OH 43701. (614)452-4541. Executive Director: Walter E. Offinger Jr. Sponsor: Mid-America Craft-Hobby Association, Inc. Estab. 1977. Annual indoor show held 3 days in July at Chicago. Average attendance: 6,600. Considers all crafts.
Terms: Entries accepted until 1 month before show. Entry fee: $4.75-5.25/square foot. Display area: minimum 10x10. Work may be offered for sale; no commission. Craftworker or representative must attend show. Registration limit: 400. Sponsor provides 2 chairs; 2 tables; 24-hour security; 8' high back wall drape and 3' sides with drape; waste basket; ashtrays; booth sign; 600 pounds drayage/100 square feet of exhibit space; and 1 full-page ad in directory.
Promotion: Show is advertised by direct mail to 10,000 buyers; advertising in all trade publications; and news releases to all trade publications.
Profile: Purpose: "to bring the buyers, distributors, representatives, manufacturers, teacher consultants and others involved in the industry together for a better industry. This is a show for the trade only, not a public show."

THE MALL AT CHERRY VALE ART & CRAFT SHOW, Box 61, Rome IL 61562. (309)274-3001. Coordinator: Judy Kelley. Estab. 1978. Semiannual indoor show held 4 days in March and October at Rockford, Illinois. Average attendance: 20,000-30,000.
Acceptable Work: Considers pottery, leatherworking, macrame, metal sculpture, jewelry, tole painting and woodcrafting.
Terms: Entries accepted until 3 weeks before show. Entry fee: $60/artist. Display area: 6x12. Prejudging by 3 slides, 1 of display. Entry fee refunded for refused work. Work may be offered for sale; no commission. Craftworker must attend show; demonstrations OK. Registration limit: 100. Sponsor provides electricity for demonstrations.
Promotion: Show is advertised by TV, radio and newspapers.

*MARIGOLD FESTIVAL'S "ART IN THE PARK", 309 Court St., Pekin IL 61554. (309)347-4694. Chairman: Denny Birkery. Sponsor: Pekin Chamber of Commerce. Estab. 1976. Annual outdoor show held 2 days in September. Average attendance: 10,000. Entries accepted until 2 weeks before show. Entry fee: $25/8x10 display area. Prejudging by photos or slides; entry fee refunded for refused work. Work may be offered for sale; no commission.

Craftworker must attend show; demonstrations OK. Sponsor provides 50 pegboard units. Show is advertised by radio; TV; and newspaper. Presents purchase awards of $1,000; award equals price of each winning piece. Considers all crafts but ceramics; dollmaking; needlecrafts; and soft sculpture.

MID-SUMMER FESTIVAL OF ARTS & CRAFTS, American Society of Artists, Inc., 1297 Merchandise Mart Plaza, Chicago IL 60654. (312)751-2500. Director, American Artisan Division: Judy Edborg. Estab. 1978. Annual outdoor show held 2 days in July at Carol Stream, Illinois. Considers all crafts but decoupage; dollmaking; lapidary; and needlecrafts.
Term: Entries accepted until 6 weeks before show or until spaces filled. Entry fee: $18/nonmember. Display area: 5x10. Prejudging by 5 slides or photos; entry fee refunded for refused work. Work may be offered for sale; no commission. Craftworker must attend show; demonstrations encouraged. Sponsor provides electricity for demonstrations; badges; programs; and exhibit cards.
Promotion: Show is advertised by posters; flyers; bumper stickers; and general publicity. Submit b&w glossy photos of self and work for publicity.

***MIDWEST CRAFT FESTIVAL**, 620 Lincoln Ave., Winnetka IL 60093. (312)446-2870. Director: Helen Roberson. Sponsor: North Shore Art League. Estab. 1972. Annual indoor show held 2 days in April at Northbrook, Illinois. Average attendance: 100,000.
Acceptable Work: Considers batik; ceramics; glass art; jewelry; leatherworking; macrame; metalsmithing; needlecrafts; pottery; soft sculpture (fibers); weaving; and woodcrafting.
Terms: Entries accepted until 3 months before show. $10 prejudging fee. Prejudging by 5 slides; 4 slides of single pieces and 1 may be detailed shot. No entry fees refunded for refused work. Work must be offered for sale; 15% commission. Craftworker must attend show; no demonstrations. Registration limit: 90-110. Sponsor provides chairs; coverings; display panels; and table.
Awards: Presents cash awards of $1,800; purchase awards of $500; and ribbons.

MT. PROSPECT PLAZA FALL ART & CRAFT FAIR, 1058 Mt. Prospect Plaza, Mt. Prospect IL 60056. (312)255-0644. Executive Director: Adele Jeschke. Sponsor: Mt. Prospect Plaza Merchants Association Inc. Estab. 1962. Annual outdoor show held 2 days in September. Considers pottery; ceramics; woodcraft; leather; and blown glass.
Terms: Entry fee: $15. Prejudging by photos or slides "if did not show with us previously." Work may be offered for sale; no commission. Craftworker must attend show; demonstrations OK.

MT. PROSPECT PLAZA SUMMER ART & CRAFT FAIR, 1058 Mt. Prospect Plaza, Mt. Prospect IL 60056. (312)255-0644. Executive Director: Adele Jeschke. Sponsor: Mt. Prospect Plaza Merchants Association Inc. Estab. 1962. Annual outdoor show held 2 days in June. Considers pottery; ceramics; woodcraft; leather; and blown glass.
Terms: Entry fee: $15. Prejudging by photos or slides "if did not show with us previously." Work may be offered for sale; no commission. Craftworker must attend show; demonstrations OK.

***NATIONAL INVITATIONAL FIBERS & FABRIC & CERAMIC EXHIBITION**, Springfield Art Association, 700 N. 4th St., Springfield IL 62702. (217)523-2631. Executive Director: William Bealmer. Estab. 1974. Annual indoor show held 6 weeks, March-April. Presents merit awards.
Acceptable Work: Considers batik; macrame; pottery; soft sculpture; and weaving. "All fibers and fabrics must be ready for hanging." Categories: fiber and fabric-weaving; non-loom weaving; batik; and combination.
Terms: Entries accepted until June of previous year. Prejudging by 3 slides submitted with entry. Work may be offered for sale; 30% commission. Craftworker needn't attend show; no demonstrations. Registration limit: 30-40.

NORTHGATE STARVING "AMERICAN" ARTS & CRAFTS FAIR, Rt. 4, 146 Park Dr., F.R.V.G., Barrington IL 60010. (312)639-5665. Show Director: Irene "Rae" Partridge. Sponsor: Merchants Association. Estab. late 1960s. Annual outdoor show held 1 day at Aurora, Illinois.
Acceptable Work: Considers all crafts. No kits, commercial molds, imports, galleries or reproductions.
Terms: Entries accepted until 1 week before show or until all spaces filled. Entry fee: $18.

Display area has 10' frontage. Prejudging by 5 slides/photos, resume and SASE. Entry fee refunded for refused work. Work may be offered for sale; no commission. Craftworker must attend show; demonstrations OK.
Promotion: Show is advertised by newspaper ads and articles, posters, radio, TV and mall posters. "Please send nonreturnable b&w glossy photo with resume and name and address of local paper for blanket coverage."
Sales Tip: "Craftworkers should present themselves in a professional manner; be neat in appearance; and have well constructed exhibit materials. Sales are helped when craftworkers show interest in their own work and talk with the public."

NORTHPOINT ARTS & SELECTED CRAFTS FESTIVAL, Rt. 4, 146 Park Dr., F.R.V.G., Barrington IL 60010. (312)639-5665. Show Director: Irene "Rae" Partridge. Sponsor: Merchants Association. Estab. 1971. Semiannual outdoor show (with canopy full length of stores) held 1 day in July and 1 day in September at Arlington Heights, Illinois.
Acceptable Work: Considers all crafts. No kits, commercial molds, imports, galleries or reproductions.
Terms: Entries accepted until 1 week before show or until all spaces filled. Entry fee: $18/display area (with 10' frontage). Prejudging by 5 slides/photos, resume and SASE. Entry fee refunded for refused work. Work may be offered for sale; no commission. Craftworker must attend show; demonstrations OK. Sponsor provides electricity for demonstrations and 24-hour security. Exhibitor handles sales and taxes.
Promotion: Show is advertised by newspaper ads and articles, posters, radio, TV and mall posters. "Please send nonreturnable b&w glossy photo with resume and name and address of local paper for blanket coverage."
Sales Tip: "Craftworkers should present themselves in a professional manner; be neat in appearance; and have well constructed exhibit materials. Sales are helped when craftworkers show interest in their own work and talk with the public."

NORTHWOODS CRAFT SHOW, Northwoods Merchants' Association, 4501 War Memorial Drive, Peoria IL 61613. (309)688-0445, weekdays 9-5 only. Promotion Director: Jackie Wade. Secretary: Becky Stutzman. Estab. 1975. Annual indoor show held 3 days in October. Average attendance: 35,000-40,000. Considers all crafts.
Terms: Entries accepted until 4 weeks before show. Entry fee: $50/single space. Prejudging by slides and photos; entry fee refunded for refused work. Work may be offered for sale; no commission. Craftworker must attend show and demonstration craft. Registration limit: 100. Sponsor provides limited electricity for demonstrations and 24-hour security.

NORTHWOODS MALL ART & CRAFT SHOW, c/o Judy Kelley, Box 61, Rome IL 61562. (309)274-3001. Sponsor: Northwoods Mall Merchants Association. Estab. 1979. Semiannual indoor show held 3 days in February and October at Peoria, Illinois.
Acceptable Work: Considers batik, stained glass, jewelry, macrame, metalsmithing, pottery, scrimshaw, sculpture, tole painting, weaving and woodcrafting. No commercial molds, crochet, pom-poms, magnets, needlecrafts, decoupage or polydomes. Batik must be framed.
Terms: Entries accepted until 3 weeks before show. Entry fee: $45/12x6 display area (February); $50/12x6 display area (October). Prejudging by slides and/or photos; entry fee refunded for refused work. Work must be offered for sale; no commission. Craftworker must attend show; demonstrations OK. Registration limit: 85-90. Sponsor provides electricity for demonstrations and 24-hour security.

OAK PARK VILLAGE MALL ART & CRAFT FESTIVAL, American Society of Artists, Inc., 1297 Merchandise Mart Plaza, Chicago IL 60654. (312)751-2500. Estab. 1976. Annual outdoor show held 2 days in July at Oak Park, Illinois.
Acceptable Works: Considers all crafts but decoupage; dollmaking; lapidary; leatherworking; and needlecrafts.
Terms: Entries accepted until 6 weeks before show or until filled. Entry fee: approximately $22/nonmember. Display area: 6x12. Prejudging by slides and photos; entry fee refunded for refused work. Work may be offered for sale; no commission. Craftworker must attend show; demonstrations encouraged. Sponsor provides electricity for demonstrations.
Promotion: Show is advertised by posters; flyers; radio; TV; newspapers; bumper stickers; and magazines. Submit b&w nonreturnable glossy photos plus any additional information on self and work.

*****OAKBROOK INVITATIONAL CRAFTS EXHIBITION**, Oakbrook Center Associates, 100

Oakbrook Center, Oak Brook IL 60521. Assistant Coordinator, Public Relations: Joan Quackenbush. Estab. 1968. Annual outdoor show held 2 days in July. Average attendance: 100,000.
Acceptable Work: Considers batik; ceramics; glass art; jewelry; macrame; metalsmithing; soft sculpture; weaving; woodcrafting; and enameling. Categories: fiber; clay; metal; enamel; glass; and wood.
Terms; Entries due the second week in February. Entry fee: $15. Size of display area determined by size of artist's display. Prejudging by 35mm slides; request slide entry form. Entry fee due after prejudging. Work may be offered for sale; no commission. Craftworker must attend show; no demonstrations. Registration limit: 100. Sponsor provides chairs; display panels; table; and 24-hour security.
Awards: Presents 6 cash awards of $100 each for excellence and 6 ribbons for honorable mention.
Sales Tip: "Work sold ranges from small purchases of $5-100 to works for corporate offices in the area which may range from $200-2,000. Many artists receive commissions from individual collectors, decorators and architects from this exhibition."

OLD TOWN ART FAIR, 1818 N. Wells St., Chicago IL 60614. (312)787-6545. General Chairman: Jeanne Kuhn. Sponsor: Old Town Triangle Association. Estab. 1950. Annual outdoor show held 2 days in June at Chicago. Average attendance: 30,000.
Acceptable Work: Considers batik; ceramics; glass art; jewelry; metalsmithing; pottery; sculpture; and weaving.
Terms: Entries accepted until 3 months before show. Entry fee: $5 nonrefundable application fee plus donation of 1 piece of work. Display area: 20x15'. Prejudging by slides. Work may be offered for sale; no commission. Craftworker must attend show; no demonstrations. Registration limit: 240.
Promotion: Show is advertised by posters; newspapers, TV features; and artists' magazines. "We use some of the auction donations for publicity purposes so new artists benefit from quality work donated. Artists are contacted for specific stories or features to be done."

*****OLNEY FALL FESTIVAL OF ARTS & CRAFTS**, Box 291, Olney IL 62450. (618)392-3481. Chairman: Dr. Baird Smith. Sponsor: Olney Arts Council. Estab. 1975. Annual outdoor show (covering available in case of rain) held the 3rd Saturday in September. Average attendance: 3,000-5,000. Considers all crafts.
Terms: Entries accepted until 2 weeks before show. Entry fee: $10/20x15' display area; up to 3 items accepted from each craftworker or general public for Arts Council booth. Work may be offered for sale; no commission for booth crafts; 10% for Arts Council booth. Craftworker must attend show; demonstrations encouraged. Registration limit: 100. Sponsor provides chairs, table and electricity for demonstrations.
Promotion: Show is advertised by newspaper; TV; and radio. Submit b&w photos of self or work for newspaper.
Awards: Presents $50 Best of Show awards; 2 purchase awards of $100 each; and 1st, 2nd, and 3rd place ribbons and Best of Show.

*****PLAZA ART FAIR**, Highland Area Arts Council, Freeport Art Museum, 511 S. Liberty, Freeport IL 61032. (815)235-9755. Director: Linda Prestwich. Estab. 1970. Annual outdoor show (with covering for bad weather) held 1 day in September. Average attendance: 5,000. Considers all crafts. Presents cash prizes for 1st, 2nd and 3rd places.
Terms: Entries accepted until 2 weeks before show. Entry fee: $10/15x15 display area. Prejudging by slides, photo or in person. Entry fee due after prejudging. Work may be offered for sale; no commission. Craftworker needn't attend show; demonstrations OK. Sponsor provides electricity for demonstrations.
Promotions: Show is advertised by all news media and mass mailings. Submit resume for publicity.

RANDHURST AUTUMN ART FESTIVAL, 9476 Harding Ave., Surfside FL 33154. Director: Iris Klein. Sponsor: Randhurst Corp. Estab. 1962. Annual indoor show held 3 days in October at Mt. Prospect, Illinois. Average attendance: 20,000-25,000. Considers batik and metal sculpture.
Terms: Entries accepted until September. Entry fee: $30/4x16 display area. Maximum 1 entry per craftworker. Prejudging; entry fee refunded for refused work. Work may be offered for sale; no commission. Craftworker must attend show; portrait sketching demonstrations OK. Registration limit: 140.

SANDBURG MALL ART & CRAFT SHOW, Box 61, Rome IL 61562. (309)274-3001. Coordinator: Judy Kelley. Sponsor: Sandburg Mall Merchants Association. Estab. 1976. Semiannual indoor show held 3 days in February; 3 days in November at Galesburg, Illinois. Average attendance: 10,000.
Acceptable Work: Considers candlemaking, jewelry, batik, scrimshaw, macrame, leatherworking, metalsmithing, pottery, sculpture, tole painting, weaving and woodcrafting. No plastic flowers, crochet, needlecrafts or decoupage. Batiks must be framed.
Terms: Entries accepted until 2 weeks before show. Entry fee: $40/12x6 display area (February); $45 (November). Prejudging by slides or photos and SASE; entry fee refunded for refused work. Work must be offered for sale; no commission. Craftworker must attend show; demonstrations OK. Registration limit: 85. Sponsor provides electricity for demonstrations and 24-hour security.
Promotion: Show is advertised by radio, newspapers, posters and marque. Submit b&w glossies for publicity.

*SKOKIE ART GUILD ART FAIR, 7908 Babb Ave., Skokie IL 60077 or Skokie Art Guild, c/o Aurelia Huzur, 1907 Central St., Evanston IL 60201. President: Aurelia Huzur. Estab. 1961. Annual outdoor show held 2 days in the fall. Average attendance: 300-500/day. Considers all original crafts.
Terms: Entries accepted until 2 weeks before show. Entry fee: $20/6x10 display area. Prejudging by slides or photos; entry fee refunded for refused work. Work may be offered for sale; no commission. Craftworker or representative must attend show; demonstrations OK.
Awards: Presents cash awards in each category, ribbons and 1 $50 merchandise (framing) certificate.
Promotion: Show is advertised by newspaper advertising, radio announcements and outdoor signs. "If the artist has something unusual to offer he/she should provide promotional materials. It will enable us to publicize this as something of interest. In the past, one craft publicized was paper quilling, and another was glass blowing done on the premise."
Sales: "In the last few years price has presented a problem. Public wants lots for the money put out."

*SPRING ARTS & CRAFTS FAIR, 2130 S. 61st Ct., Cicero IL 60650. (312)863-2104. Executive Director: Norm Scaman. Sponsor: Cermak Road Business Association. Estab. 1973. Annual outdoor show held 2 days in Spring. Average attendance: 2,000. Presents ribbon awards. Considers all crafts.
Terms: Entries accepted until 1 week before show. Entry fee: $10/6x10 display area. Work may be offered for sale; no commission. Craftworker or representative must attend show; demonstrations OK.

SPRING ARTS FESTIVAL, American Society of Artists, Inc., 1297 Merchandise Mart Plaza, Chicago IL 60654. (312)751-2500. Estab. 1977. Annual indoor show held 2 days in April at Crystal Lake, Illinois. Entries accepted until 6 weeks before show. Entry fee: $20/nonmembers. Display area: 5x10. Prejudging by slides and photos; entry fee refunded for refused work. Work may be offered for sale; no commission. Craftworker must attend show; demonstrations encouraged. Sponsor provides programs; badges; and exhibit cards. Show is advertised by flyers; bumper stickers; newspapers; radio; TV; magazines; posters; and general publicity. Submit, if possible, b&w glossy photo of self and work for publicity. Considers framed batik; woven wall hangings; sculpture; soft sculpture; and wood carvings.

SPRING FEST OF ARTS & CRAFTS, American Society of Artists, Inc., 1297 Merchandise Mart Plaza, Chicago IL 60654. (312)751-2500. Estab. 1978. Annual indoor show held 2 days in May at Des Plaines, Illinois.
Acceptable Work: Considers all crafts but decoupage; dollmaking; lapidary; and needlecrafts.
Terms: Entries accepted until 6 weeks before show. Entry fee: approximately $22/nonmember. Display area: 5x10. Prejudging by 5 slides or photos; entry fee refunded for refused work. Work may be offered for sale; no commission. Craftworker must attend show; demonstrations encouraged. Sponsor provides electricity for demonstrations; badges; programs; and exhibit cards.
Promotion: Show is advertised by newspapers; radio; TV; posters; and flyers. Submit b&w glossy photos of self with work for publicity.

*STARVING ARTISTS ARTS & CRAFTS FAIR, Oakton Community College, 7900 Nagle, Morton Grove IL 60201. (312)967-5120. Director: Jay Wollin. Estab. 1970. Annual outdoor

show held 2 days during Memorial Day weekend. Average attendance: 18,000. Entries accepted until 6 weeks before show. Entry fee: $25/display area with 10' minimum frontage. Prejudging by 3 slides. Work may be sold for under $35; no commission. Craftworker or representative must attend show; electricity and equipment provided for demonstrations. Registration limit: 125-150. College has liability insurance and provides security guards. Committee of non-college jurors awards 5-6 purchase prizes to use as door prizes.
Acceptable Work: Considers batik; candlemaking; ceramics; decoupage; glass art; jewelry; leatherworking; metalsmithing; pottery; soft sculpture; weavings; wall hangings; and woodcrafting.

TOY SHOW, Olde Town Gallery, Main St., Mahomet IL 61853. (217)586-3211. Owner-Manager: Charlotte Williamson. Estab. 1977. Annual indoor show held 1 day in December. Average attendance: 500. Entries accepted until 1 week before show. Display area: 8'. Work may be offered for sale; 33⅓% commission. Craftworker needn't attend show; demonstrations OK. Sponsor provides chairs; electricity for demonstrations; and table. Show is advertised by newspaper and mailing lists. Categories: antique and new handcrafts. Considers dollmaking; needlecrafts; soft sculpture; and woodcrafting.

*****VILLAGE ART FAIR**, Box 483, Oak Park IL 60302. President: Mr. Robert Kerr. Purpose: to promote interest and education in art. Estab. 1954. Annual outdoor show held first Sunday in September after Labor Day. Average Attendance: 15,000. Entries accepted until 11 weeks before show. Entry fee: $20/6x12 display area. Prejudging by 6 slides; entry fee refunded for refused work. Work may be offered for sale; no commission. Craftworker must attend show; demonstrations OK. Show is advertised by all available media. Presents cash awards of $50, $100, $150, and $100 to best new artist; purchase awards totaling $1,000; and 1st, 2nd and 3rd place ribbons. Considers batik; glass art; jewelry; macrame; metalsmithing; pottery; sculpture; soft sculpture; and weaving.

VILLAGE MALL ART & CRAFT SHOW, Box 61, Rome IL 61562. (309)274-3001. Coordinator: Judy Kelley. Estab. 1975. Semiannual indoor show held 3 days in May and 3 days in October at Danville, Illinois. Average attendance: 10,000.
Acceptable Work: Considers candlemaking; ceramics; jewelry; leatherworking; macrame; metalsmithing; pottery; sculpture; tole painting; and woodcrafting.
Terms: Entries accepted until 2 weeks before show. Entry fee: $35/craftworker. Display area: 6x12. Prejudging by slides or photos; entry fee refunded for refused work. Work may be offered for sale; no commission. Craftworker must attend show; demonstrations OK. Registration limit: 50. Sponsor provides electricity for demonstrations.
Promotion: Show is advertised by newspapers; and radio. Submit 8x10 glossies for publicity.

WATER TOWER ART & CRAFT FESTIVAL, American Society of Artists, Inc., 1297 Merchandise Mart Plaza, Chicago IL 60654. (312)751-2500. Estab. 1972. Annual outdoor show held 3 days in June.
Acceptable Work: Considers batik, candlemaking, glass art, jewelry, lapidary, leatherworking, macrame, metalsmithing, mobiles, pottery, scrimshaw, sculpture, soft sculpture, tole painting weaving, woodcrafting and unusual craft forms. "Original work only please."
Terms: Entries accepted until 6 weeks before show. Entry fee: approximately $25/nonmember. Display area: 5x10 (but may vary according to width of sidewalk, etc.). Prejudging by 4 slides of work and 1 of display set-up; entry fee refunded for refused work. Work may be offered for sale; no commission. Craftworker must attend show; demonstrations encouraged. Registration limit: 300 (but also limits number of exhibitors in each medium).
Promotion: Show is advertised by radio; TV; newspaper publicity; flyers; posters; newspaper ads; and magazines. Submit glossy b&w photos and additional information on self as an artist. Photos should be of craftsperson and his/her work.

*****WONDERFUL WORLD OF CRAFTS**, 18W118 73rd Pl., Westmont IL 60559 (312)964-9062. Contact: Art Plus Associates. Sponsor: Fox Valley Center. Estab. 1976. Annual indoor show held 4 days in October at Aurora, Illinois. Average attendance: 60,000-80,000. Considers all crafts. Presents cash awards of $1,000 and ribbons.
Terms: Entries accepted until 8 weeks before show. Entry fee: $70/6x12 display area. Prejudging by 5 slides or photos and SASE; entry fee refunded for refused work. Work may be offered for sale; no commission. Craftworker must attend show; demonstrations OK. Registration limit: 150. Sponsor provides chairs; coverings; display panels; electricity for demonstrations; and 24-hour security.

482 Craftworker's Market '80

YOUR ADVENTURE IN ART, American Society of Artists, 129 N. Merchandise Mart Plaza, Chicago IL 60654. (312)751-2500. Estab. 1978. Annual outdoor show held 2 days in October at Oak Park, Illinois. Entries accepted until 6 weeks before show. Entry fee: $22/nonmembers. Display area: 5x10. Prejudging by 5 slides or photos; entry fee refunded for refused work. Work may be offered for sale; no commission. Craftworker must attend show; demonstrations encouraged. Sponsor provides electricity for demonstrations; badges; programs; bumper stickers and exhibit cards. Show is advertised by newspapers; posters; flyers; and general publicity—radio, TV, magazines. Submit b&w photos of self and work. Considers all crafts but ceramics; decoupage; dollmaking; lapidary; and needlecrafts.

Indiana

AN AMERICAN CELEBRATION, Box 35, La Porte IN 46350. (219)324-8425. Chairman: James L. Jessup. Sponsor: La Porte Jaycees. Purpose "to add to our 4th of July celebration by bringing visitors to our community." Estab. 1973. Annual outdoor show held the Saturday before July 4. Average attendance: 1,500. Considers all crafts.
Terms: Entries accepted until 1 month before show. Entry fee: $10/14x10' display area. Work may be offered for sale; no commission. Craftworker must attend show.

ARTS & CRAFTS IN THE PARK, 211 Oakey Ave., Lawrenceburg IN 47025. (812)537-0676. Chairman: Margaret Huebner. Sponsor: Community Activities, Inc. Estab. 1970. Annual outdoor show (in shaded park) held the first Sunday after Labor Day weekend. Average attendance: 8,000.
Acceptable Work: Considers batik; candlemaking; ceramics; decoupage; dollmaking; glass art; jewelry; lapidary; leatherworking; metalsmithing; needlecrafts; pottery; sculpture; soft sculpture; tole painting; weaving; and woodcrafting.
Terms: Entries accepted until show date. Entry fee: $8/10x10 display area. Work may be offered for sale; no commission. Craftworker must attend show; demonstrations OK. Registration limit: approximately 125. Sponsor provides electricity for demonstrations.
Promotion: Show is advertised by radio; TV; newspaper; direct mail; and *National Calendar of Indoor-Outdoor Fairs*. Promotion is done quite extensively for this show at nearby Cincinnati, Ohio. "If the craftworker has an unusual craft, a b&w glossy and a brief paragraph on his background will be considered for use in newspapers."

BLOOMINGTON'S FOURTH STREET FESTIVAL OF THE ARTS & CRAFTS, Box 514, Ellettsville IN 47429. Contact: Fourth Street Festival. Estab. 1976. Annual outdoor show held 2 days in September at Bloomington, Indiana. Considers all original crafts. Entries accepted until approximately 3 months before show. Entry fee: $25. Prejudging by slides.

***CHATAUQUA OF THE ARTS**, 1119 W. Main St., Madison IN 47250. Chairman: Dixie McDonough. Sponsor: Madison Chautauqua of the Arts. "This is the only art and craft show held in this area. It is held to increase an interest in the arts and crafts." Estab. 1970. Annual outdoor show held the last weekend in September. Average attendance: 10,000-20,000.
Acceptable Work: Considers all crafts except candlemaking and ceramics. No kits; machine leather; or crafts made from molds. "Traditional items seem to sell the best."
Terms: Entries accepted until 2 weeks before show. Entry fee: $20/craftworker. Prejudging by 5 slides (4 of individual pieces and 1 of the display); entry fee refunded for refused work. Work may be offered for sale; no commission. Craftworker must attend show; demonstrations recommended. Registration limit: 50. Sponsor provides electricity for demonstrations.
Awards: Presents $850 in cash; $150 in purchase prizes plus ribbons for 1st, 2nd and 3rd places. Also gives an award for the best booth display. "Awards will be given on only finished pieces and on pieces completed within a year of the show date."
Promotion: Show is advertised by the local chamber of commerce; state tourism department; and by AAA motor magazines and clubs. "A biographic sketch listing the shows and awards the craftsperson has been in, and a b&w photo of the craftsperson which can be used in the newspaper would be helpful."

CHESTERTON ART & CRAFT FAIR, Box 783, Chesterton IN 46304. (219)926-4711. General Chairpersons: Mary and John Smith. Sponsor: Association of Artists & Craftsmen of Porter County. Estab. 1958. Annual outdoor show held 2 days during the first weekend in August. Average attendance: 10,000-11,000. Show is advertised by newspapers, radio, magazines and posters.

---

* Those listings preceded by an asterisk present awards for prize-winning crafts.

Acceptable Work: Considers batik, candlemaking, ceramics, glass art, jewelry, lapidary, leatherworking, macrame, metalsmithing, mobiles, pottery, scrimshaw, sculpture, soft sculpture, weavings and woodcrafting. "Work should be hung or otherwise properly displayed. All work must be original."
Terms: Entry fee: $35/artist. Display area: 7½x7½. Prejudging by color slides. Jury fee: $2, due after prejudging. Work may be offered for sale; no commission. Craftworker or representative must attend show; demonstrations OK (but must be arranged in advance). Sponsor provides display panel framework. Exhibitor handles sales and taxes.

CHRISTMAS GIFT & HOBBY SHOW, Box 20189, Indianapolis IN 46220. (317)255-4151. Exhibit Sales Director: Thelma B. Schoenberger. Estab. 1950. Annual indoor show held 9 days in November. Average attendance: 100,000. Considers all crafts.
Terms: Entries accepted until spaces are filled. "Show is always full 2 months prior to opening." Entry fee: $160/10x10 display area. Prejudging. Work may be offered for sale; no commission. Craftworker must attend show; demonstrations encouraged. Sponsor provides 300 watts electricity for demonstrations, 24-hour security, draped backdrop, and dividers.

*****CRAFT FAIR AT RIVERFRONT**, 16½ SE 2nd St., Evansville IN 47708. (812)422-2111. Executive Director: Jane Moore. Sponsor: Evansville Arts & Education Council. Estab. 1975. Annual outdoor show held 2 days in early May. Average attendance: 10,000. Entries accepted until 6 weeks before show. Entry fee: $20/15x20 display area. "Slides are juried by a committee of artists. Entrant must mail 3 slides or photos representing their work and entry form. Each slide must be labeled clearly with artist's name and medium and must have indication of which side is up." Entry fee partially refunded for refused work. Work must be offered for sale; 10% commission. Craftworker must attend show; demonstrations encouraged. Registration limit: 75. Sponsor provides electricity for demonstrations and 24-hour security.
Acceptable Work: Considers ceramics; jewelry; metalsmithing; mobiles; pottery; sculpture; weaving; soft sculpture; and woodcrafting. "Work is selected for showing on basis of creativity and professional art form. No articles following step-by-step instructions, or under direct supervision will be considered."
Awards: Presents 1 $200, 1 $100, and 4 $50 cash awards; and ribbons. "Awards are based on excellence. Award pieces will be exhibited together. They may be sold, but must remain through the fair before being moved."
Promotion: Show is advertised by national crafts magazines; direct mail to 1,000 artists; 1,000 notices; and local media coverage. Artists will be contacted individually for promotional materials, if needed. "Promotional materials are usually collected locally."
Profile: "Crafts Fair at Riverfront emphasizes quality crafts and gives local professional craftspersons an opportunity to sell. The demonstrations which are scheduled throughout both days serve as a means of educating viewers as to the process of creating various crafts. This is a show for the serious craftsperson and quality is heavily emphasized."
Sales Tip: "Pottery, weaving and jewelry were the most popular items, but were also the most plentiful. We need to have greater variety of media and want to encourage glassblowers, woodworkers, sculptors and furniture makers."

*****DAVIESS MARTIN COUNTY ART FESTIVAL**, Box 245, Loogootee IN 47553. (812)295-3421. Public Information Director: Dean A. Dorrell. Park Superintendent: David L. Watson. Sponsor: West Boggs Park. Estab. 1975. Annual show held 2 days in August in 12x12' tents. Average attendance: 6,000. Considers all original crafts. Presents awards first day of festival.
Terms: Entries accepted until show date. Entry fee: $10/artist. Work may be offered for sale; no commission. Craftworker must attend show. "We recommend that craftsmen demonstrate their talents as it helps promote sales." First 30 entries are given a 12x12 tent; table; and 2 chairs.

*****DRAWING & SMALL SCULPTURE SHOW**, Art Gallery, Ball State University, Muncie IN 47306. (317)285-5242. Director: William E. Story. Estab. 1955. Annual indoor show held about 7 weeks in May/June. Presents $3,000 in cash and purchase awards.
Acceptable Work: Considers ceramics, metalsmithing, sculpture, soft sculpture and woodcrafting. No kits, prints or machine-made crafts.
Terms: Entries accepted until approximately 1 month before show. Entry fee: $10/artist. Maximum 2 pieces/craftworker. Prejudging of sculpture by slides; no entry fees refunded for refused work. Work may be offered for sale; no commission. Craftworker needn't attend show; no demonstrations. Sponsor provides gallery and display equipment.

484 Craftworker's Market '80

*EAGLE CREEK ARTS & FOLK MUSIC FESTIVAL, 5901 DeLong Rd., Indianapolis IN 46254. (317)293-4827. Arts Fair Coordinator: Bill Taylor. Sponsor: Indianapolis Department of Parks. Estab. 1974. Annual outdoor show held the last Saturday and Sunday in July. Average attendance: 12,000-14,000. Presents 3 cash awards of $50 for outstanding exhibit.
Acceptable Work: Considers batik; candlemaking; ceramics; jewelry; lapidary; leatherworking; macrame; metalsmithing; mobiles; pottery; sculpture; weaving; and woodcrafting.
Terms: Entries accepted until 4 weeks before show. Entry fee: $15/10x10 display area. Prejudging by slides and/or photos; entry fee refunded for refused work. Work may be offered for sale; no commission. Craftworker must attend show; demonstrations OK. Registration limit: 75. Sponsor provides electricity for demonstrations and 24-hour security.
Promotion: Show is advertised by local and state media as well as national publications.
Profile: "We try to present to the public a grouping of top quality professional arts/crafts on exhibit and folk musicians in concert."

*FAIR ON THE SQUARE, Columbus Arts League, 302 Washington St., Columbus IN 47201. (812)372-8565. Director: Susan Weil. "Fair on the Square is a spring celebration for our local artists. It is a well-established show which the community looks forward to attending." Estab. 1964. Annual outdoor show held on Mother's Day in the Columbus library square. Average attendance: 800-1,000, depending upon weather. Entries accepted until show. Entry fee: $10/8x10 square feet in open area or 10 linear feet on fence. Work may be offered for sale; no commission. Craftworker must attend show; demonstrations OK. Registration limit: 150. Sponsor provides electricity for demonstrations and fencing. Considers all crafts. Presents $600 in cash and ribbons. "Pottery sells well if small and reasonably priced."
Promotion: "Arts division of the Guild sends newsletter to artists who have exhibited before. The show is also listed in the activity columns of the surrounding big city newspapers." Show is also advertised by local newspapers; posters; and TV.

FEAST OF THE HUNTERS' MOON, 909 South St., Lafayette IN 47901. (317)742-8411. Feast Secretary: Fern Martin. Assistance Director: Carol Waddell. Sponsor: Tippecanoe County Historical Association. Estab. 1968. Annual outdoor show held 2 days in the fall at Fort Ouiatenon Historical Park at Lafayette. "Rustic brush shelters (with covered plastic tops) are constructed prior to the Feast for all booths." Average attendance: 45,000.
Acceptable Work: Considers candlemaking; dollmaking; glass art; jewelry; leatherworking; metalsmithing; needlcrafts; pottery; sculpture; weaving; and woodcrafting. "All items must be made from natural materials (i.e., wood, stone, clay, etc.) which would have been available in the 18th century." No contemporary crafts.
Terms: Entries accepted until approximately 10 weeks prior to show. Entry fee $20/6x8 booth. Prejudging: "slides and written descriptions are submitted with application for juried selection for accepting the craftsman. He/she may bring any number of pieces of the accepted-type work." Entry fee refunded for refused work. Work may be offered for sale; no commission. Craftworker must attend show; demonstrations encouraged. Registration limit: 15. Sponsor provides chairs; brush shelter booth; and table.
Promotion: Show is advertised in local media and metropolitan Chicago, Indianapolis and St. Louis by radio; TV; and newspapers. "Also listed in tour and festival promotion publications throughout the Midwest. We occasionally request b&w glossies for newspaper releases."
Profile: "The Feast is primarily an educational festival, recreating life as it would have been lived at an 18th century French trading post. Our emphasis is on 18th century re-creation and demonstrations under primitive conditions of the traditional crafts. All participants are required to dress in 18th century costume. Colonial crafts are featured, and crafts are only a portion of the overall picture at the Feast of the Hunters' Moon. It is also a fundraising event for the Tippecanoe County Historical Association to continue archaeological exploration of the original site of Ft. Ouiatenon."

FESTIVAL ARTS & CRAFTS SHOW, 1707 Kensington Blvd., Fort Wayne IN 46805. (219)422-6949. Chairman: Betty L. Newton. Sponsor: Three Rivers Festival. Estab. 1972. Annual outdoor show held 2 days in July. Average attendance: 50,000. Considers all original crafts. Show is advertised by brochures, newspapers, TV and radio.
Terms: Entries accepted until 4 weeks before show. Entry fee: $15/10x10 display area. Prejudging by 5 slides or photos; entry fee refunded for refused work. Work must be offered for sale; no commission. Craftworker must attend show; demonstrations OK (no electricity). Registration limit: 100.

*FIESTA, 101 S. 9th St., Lafayette IN 47901. (317)742-1128. Director: Sharon A. Theobald.

Sponsors: Lafayette Art League and Lafayette Art Association. Estab. 1974. Annual outdoor show held the Saturday before Labor Day.
Acceptable Work: Considers batik; ceramics; jewelry; leatherworking; metalsmithing; pottery; soft sculpture; weavings; wall hangings; and woodcrafting.
Terms: Entries accepted until 4 weeks before show. Entry fee: $20/10x10 display area. Prejudging; entry fee refunded for refused work. Work may be offered for sale; no commission. Craftworker must attend show; demonstrations encouraged. Registration limit: 60-100. Presents cash prizes.

FOLK ARTS & MUSIC FESTIVAL, Huntington North High School, 450 McGahn, Huntington IN 46750. (219)356-4218. Chairman: Jean Gernand. Sponsor: Huntington Community School Corp. Estab. 1976. Annual indoor/outdoor show held 1-2 days in the fall. Attendance: 2,000-3,000; "more than quadrupled in its second year."
Acceptable Work: Considers all crafts. Bestsellers: stained glass; leathercrafts; and jewelry.
Terms: Entries accepted until show date. Entry fee: $5/5x12' display area or 10% of sales. Work may be offered for sale. Craftworker must attend show; demonstrations encouraged. Sponsor provides chairs; electricity for demonstrations; and table. Show is advertised by newspapers; radio; TV; posters and flyers.
Profile: "Our main purpose is to increase awareness and appreciation of all types of art, with special attention to folk arts, crafts and music."

GRABILL COUNTRY FAIR, c/o Freeman Byler, Grabill IN 46741. (219)627-3691. Sponsor: Grabill Chamber of Commerce. "Started as a farmers' country market and grew." Estab. 1972. Annual outdoor show held 3 days in September. Average attendance: 50,000.
Acceptable Work: Considers all crafts that "fit the conservative, religious atmosphere of the community."
Terms: Entries accepted until show date. Entry fee: $27.50/open display area. Work must be offered for sale. Craftworker must attend show; demonstrations encouraged. Registration limit: 80. Sponsor provides electricity for demonstrations and 24-hour security.

*****HISTORIC HOOSIER HILLS GUILD FESTIVAL**, 2242 Cragmont, Madison IN 47250. (812)273-1697. Director of Guild: Helen Gourley. Estab. 1967. Semiannual outdoor show held 4 days during Memorial Day weekend and 3 days in September. Average attendance: 20,000.
Acceptable Work: Considers all crafts, especially old-time crafts. No kits. "Cheaply made and cheaply priced crafts will be rejected by the Committee. We have a type of show which attracts only serious antique dealers and craftsmen—people who purchase only the better arts and crafts." Bestsellers: functional or wearable items.
Terms: Entries accepted until 1 week before show. Entry fee: $7/day for parking lot area. Work must be offered for sale; no commission. Craftworker must attend show; demonstrations OK. Registration limit: 50-75 (spring); 50-55 (fall).
Awards: Presents $20, $15 and $10 in cash awards. Originality, beauty and old-time crafts help in winning awards.
Promotion: Show is advertised by radio, newspapers, magazines and brochures. Craftworker should provide signs with the name of the shop or artist.

JEFFERSONVILLE ARTS & CRAFTS FESTIVAL, 907 Poppy Place, Jeffersonville IN 47130. (812)283-7842. Show Director: Robert Mode. Sponsor: Jump Committee. "We hold the show as a part of the celebration of the steamboat on the bank of the Ohio River across from Louisville, Kentucky." Annual outdoor show held 2 days the second weekend in September. Average attendance: 85,000. Entries accepted until show date. Entry fee: $10/10x10 display area. Work may be offered for sale; no commission. Craftworker must attend show; demonstrations OK. Registration limit: 150. Sponsor provides electricity for demonstrations. Show is advertised by radio; TV; newspapers; and state department of tourism. Considers all crafts.

KAMM'S BREWERY ARTS & CRAFTS FESTIVAL, Box 806, Michawaka IN 46544. (219)259-7861. Public Relations Director: Gwen Finger. Sponsor: 100 Center Development Company. Estab. 1971. Annual outdoor show held 2 days in July. Average attendance: 40,000. Considers all crafts.
Terms: Entries accepted until 3 weeks before show. Entry fee: $25/10x10' display area. Prejudging. Entry fee refunded for refused work. Work may be offered for sale; no commission. Craftworker must attend show; demonstrations encouraged. Registration limit: 150.

KOUTS ANNUAL ARTS & CRAFTS SHOW, Kouts Chamber of Commerce, Kouts IN 46347.

(219)766-3766. President: Willard Paarlberg. Estab. 1976. Annual outdoor show held 1 day in July. Average attendance: 1,000. Considers all crafts.
Terms: Entries accepted until show date. Entry fee: $10. Display area: 10x10. Work may be offered for sale; no commission. Craftworker must attend show; demonstrations OK.

LA PORTE JAYCEES ART SHOW, 3666 W. Schultz Rd., La Porte IN 46350. Contact: Jim Jessup. Sponsor: La Porte Jaycees. Annual show held in July. Considers jewelry; pottery; sculpture; and other crafts.
Terms: Entry fee: $10/craftworker (non-refundable). Write for application blank. Enter early, as spaces are limited. Prejudging as to variety. Work may be offered for sale; no commission. Craftworker must attend show; demonstrations encouraged.
Promotion: Show publicized extensively along with the annual Jaycees July 4 week-long celebration through area radio, TV and newspapers.

Pewter sculpture is a popular craft at the Hartford Christmas Craft Expo I, sponsored by American Craft Expositions, Inc. All crafts are considered and all work must be offered for sale. This show, held annually in December at Hartford, Connecticut, attracts a crowd of 25,000 and usually has 200 exhibitors.

LOWELL'S ANNUAL ARTS & CRAFTS FESTIVAL, 333 Woodland Ct., Lowell IN 46356. (219)696-7036. Director: B.E. Wheeler. Sponsor: Friends of the Library. Estab. 1972. Annual outdoor show held 2 days in the summer. Considers all crafts.
Terms: Entries accepted until 3 weeks before show. Entry fee: $20/10x8 display area. "We reserve the right to ask an artist to leave if his work should prove to be other than stated on application (an example would be if kits are presented as original work)." Work may be offered for sale; no commission. Craftworker must attend show; demonstrations encouraged. Sponsor provides electricity for demonstrations and help with setup if needed.
Awards: Presents over $500 in cash prizes; award for best demonstration; and ribbons. "Limit exhibit to 1 or 2 types of art."
Promotion: "Show is advertised in 5 trade publications; state calendar; 240 newspapers in Indiana, plus major papers out of state; 3 radio stations; and at least 1 Chicago-based TV station. Business cards are essential to have at the Festival for future business as many people

scout the fairs for future purchases. If the artist/craftsman also teaches his art, he could promote his classes through literature at the show."

*MADISON CHAUTAUQUA OF THE ARTS, Green Hills Pottery, 1119 W. Main St., Madison IN 47250. Contact: Dixie McDonough. Annual outdoor show held the last weekend in September. Considers all crafts. Presents cash prizes.
Terms: Entry fee: $20/craftworker. Prejudging by 5 slides (4 slides of individual work and 1 slide of display); "send SASE for return of slides or slides will not be returned." Craftworker must attend show. Work may be offered for sale; no commission.

*MID-STATES CRAFT EXHIBITION, 411 SE Riverside Dr., Evansville IN 47713. (812)425-2406. Contact: Craft Committee. Sponsor: Evansville Museum of Arts and Science. Estab. 1961. Annual indoor show held 4 weeks in the late winter. Average attendance: 10,000.
Acceptable Work: Considers batik; candlemaking; ceramics; dollmaking; glass art; jewelry; lapidary; leatherworking; macrame; metalsmithing; mobiles; needlecrafts; pottery; soft sculpture; tole painting only if artist makes tray, etc. also; weaving; and woodcrafting. "Craftworkers must live within 200 miles of Evansville or anywhere else in Indiana. All work must be original, made in the last 3 years, and not previously exhibited in a Mid-States Craft Exhibition. Some machine use is acceptable—potters' wheels, electric buffers and grinders for example."
Terms: Entries accepted 6 weeks before show. Handling fee: $5 for 1-3 items (limit 3); "sets may count as 1 entry." Prejudging by actual work; no refunds for refused work. Work may be offered for sale; 20% commission. Craftworker needn't attend show; no demonstrations. Sponsor provides 24-hour security, and museum staff handles display of all exhibits. Categories: ceramics; textiles; metalwork; and miscellaneous (wood, enamels, glass and other handcrafted materials). "Most sales are for home use or decoration. Under $50 items sell best."
Awards: Presents $500, $400, $275 and $100 purchase awards; and $100, $50, and 6 $75 merit awards. "Excellence of craftsmanship is most important to jurors. Creativity counts more with some jurors, while others appreciate a fine rendition of a traditional shape bowl or jar. Inflated prices do not influence jurors. They do not know what the prices are until after the judging."
Promotion: Show is advertised by direct mail brochures; press releases to news media; catalogs; and museum bulletin. "Award winners are asked to provide biographical data—this is displayed alongside work and given to news media."

NEW CARLISLE HISTORICAL DAYS, c/o Clark Hensell, Box O, New Carlisle IN 46552. (219)654-8311. Chairman: Mrs. Derm Meyer. Sponsor: Hill and Dale Men's Service Club, Inc. Estab. 1973. Annual outdoor show held 3 days in summer. Average attendance: 25,000. Entries accepted until 4 weeks before show. Entry fee: $20/12x12 display area. Work may be offered for sale; no commission. Craftworker must attend show; demonstrations OK. Show is advertised by newspapers; TV; radio; and billboards. Categories: flea market, and arts and crafts. Considers all crafts.

NILES ART GUILD ART FAIR, 7007 Fargo Ave., Niles IN 60648. Fair Chairman: Marilyn A. Brown. Purpose: "to promote local art." Estab. 1963. Annual indoor show held 2 days in April at Oak Mill Mall, Niles. Entries accepted until 2 weeks before show. Entry fee: $15, nonmember; or $10, member/10 linear feet of display space. Work may be offered for sale; no commission. Craftworker must attend show; demonstrations OK. Registration limit: 75-100. Sponsor provides 24-hour security. Show is advertised by newspapers; art magazines; and TV. Submit photos and name and address of local paper. Categories: oils and acrylics; watercolors; mixed media; sculpture; and crafts. Awards 1st, 2nd and 3rd place cash awards in each category but crafts.
Acceptable Work: Considers candlemaking; ceramics; jewelry; macrame; metalsmithing; pottery; sculpture; and woodcrafting.

OUTDOOR FINE ARTS GALLERY & ALL CRAFTS FAIR, Porter County Arts Commission, 15 Franklin St., Valparaiso IN 46383. (219)464-4080. Coordinator: Marjory Crawford. Estab. 1971. Annual outdoor show held 2 days in the summer at Lakewood Park, Valparaiso. Attendance: 5,000-10,000. Considers all crafts.
Terms: Entries accepted until 3 weeks before show. Entry fee: $20/craftworker. Prejudging by slides or photos; entry fee refunded for refused work. Work may be offered for sale; no commission. Craftworker needn't attend show (but is responsible for sales); demonstrations OK. Registration limit: 130-140. Sponsor provides electricity for demonstrations.
Promotion: Show is advertised by radio, posters and other news media within a 50-mile radius. "Good b&w photos for newspaper coverage would be helpful for publicity purposes."

*PLETCHER VILLAGE ART FESTIVAL, 1600 W. Market, Nappanee IN 46550. (219)773-4188. Contact: Richard Pletcher. Estab. 1963. Annual outdoor show held 4 days in August. Average attendance: 60,000. Considers all crafts. Awards $2,025 in cash and $1,000 in purchase prizes.
Terms: Entries accepted until about 3 months before show. Entry fee: $25/artist (this money will go toward the 15% sales commission). Display area: 12x15. Prejudging by slides or photos; entry fee refunded for refused work. Work may be offered for sale; 15% commission. Craftworker must attend show; demonstrations OK. Registration limit: 156. Sponsor provides electricity for demonstrations; fencing; and 24-hour security.

TALBOT STREET ART FAIR, 2823 W. 52nd St., Indianapolis IN 46208. (317)297-1632. Chairman: Joe Lehman. Sponsor: Indiana Artist-Craftsmen, Inc. Estab. 1955. Annual outdoor show held 2 days in June. Attendance: 20,000-30,000. Presents ribbon for best display.
Acceptable Work: Considers all crafts except decoupage. "Must be designed and made by the craftsman selling and exhibiting it."
Terms: Entries accepted until about 2 months before show. Entry fee charged. Prejudging by slides and photos of representative work. "Committee reserves the right to remove pieces if they're not up to the standard of the samples sent." Entry fee refunded for refused work. Work may be offered for sale; no commission. Craftworker must attend show; demonstrations encouraged. Registration limit: 200.
Promotion: Show is advertised by newspapers; radio; and TV. Submit biographical sketch and photos.

*TIPPECANOE REGIONAL PAINTING, PRINT & SCULPTURE BIENNIAL EXHIBITION: ARTFORMS, 101 S. 9th St., Lafayette IN 47901. Director: Sharon A. Theobald. Sponsor: Lafayette Art Association. Estab. 1909. Biennial show held odd-numbered years in May. Average attendance: 3,000-5,000. Considers sculpture by Indiana artists. Presents cash and purchase prizes totalling $1,000. Entry fee: $10. Maximum 2 works/exhibitor. Works may be offered for sale; 25% commission. Sponsor provides insurance on exhibited work.

*WABASH VALLEY EXHIBITION, 25 S. 7th St., Terre Haute IN 47807. (812)238-1676. Contact: Director. Sponsor: Sheldon Swope Art Gallery. Estab. 1943. Annual indoor show held 1 month in the early spring. Average attendance: 3,000. Entries accepted until early February. Entry fee: $5/first entry; $4/second, and $3/third entries. Maximum 3 entries per craftworker. Prejudging; no entry fees refunded for refused work. Work may be offered for sale; 20% commission. Open to craftworkers living within 160-mile radius of Terre Haute. Sponsor provides display equipment. Presents $6,000 in prizes.
Acceptable Work: Considers all media. Maximum size: 60" in any direction. Work must be framed or suitable for hanging.

WALKWAY FESTIVAL, 16 SE 2nd St., Evansville IN 47708. (812)422-2111. Executive Director: Jane E. Moore. Sponsor: Evansville Arts and Education Council. Estab. 1969. Annual outdoor show held 1 day in the spring. Average attendance: 50,000.
Acceptable Work: Considers all crafts. "There is presently an effort at upgrading the quality of work exhibited and sold."
Terms: Entries accepted until 6 weeks before show. Entry fee: $20/artist. Display area: 10-15 square feet. "Entry to show is by invitation; those interested may submit detailed descriptions of their work in advance of deadline." Work may be offered for sale; commission to be determined. Craftworker must attend show; demonstrations encouraged. Registration limit: 150. Sponsor provides electricity for demonstrations; security during 10 hours of festival; and liability insurance.
Profile: "The Walkway Festival is a 1-day event of the Ohio River Arts Festival, encompassing 16 days of arts-related activities. The Walkway Festival gives artists and craftspeople an opportunity to display and sell, while providing the community at large a fun-filled day in which to become acquainted with various arts and crafts. Our community responds marvelously to this event. The viewing and buying public range in age from children to senior citizens with all socio-economic levels represented."

WEST BOGGS ART FESTIVAL, Box 245, Loogootee IN 47553. (812)295-3421. Park Superintendent: David L. Watson. Sponsor: Boggs Park. Purpose: "to bring more people into this area; and to offer them the benefits of artists which has never been done in this area before." Estab. 1975. Annual outdoor show (with some tents) held 2 days in the summer. Average attendance: 10,000. Entries accepted until show date. Entry fee: $10, with $5 refunded upon arrival. Display area: "12x12 tents for the first few participants, after that they will have to furnish their own accommodations." Work may be offered for sale; no commission. Craftworker must attend show; demonstrations OK. Sponsor provides chairs; electricity for demonstrations; and table. Show is advertised by radio; TV; and newspaper. Considers all crafts. Work priced from $2-5 sells best.

*WICKER PARK ART FAIR, 5448 Hohman Ave., Hammond IN 46320. (219)931-0018. Program Chairman: Sandy Starrett. Sponsor: Northern Indiana Arts Association. Estab. 1970. Annual outdoor show held 2 days in May at Highland, Indiana. Average attendance: 7,000. Entries accepted until 4 weeks before show. Entry fee: $20/crafterworker. Display area: 12x12. Prejudging by 3 slides of media entered; or 6 slides (3 slides of 2 works) of sculpture pieces. $15 refunded for refused work. Work may be offered for sale; no commission. Craftworker must attend show; demonstrations OK. Registration limit: 100. Sponsor provides fencing and 24-hour security. Show is advertised by newspapers; radio; TV; and local merchants. Considers batik; jewelry; lapidary; leatherworking; metalsmithing; pottery; sculpture; soft sculpture; weaving and woodcrafting. Presents $50 1st, $30 2nd and $20 3rd prizes; and 1st, 2nd, and 3rd place ribbons.

Iowa

ART IN THE PARK, c/o Norma Thomsen, 1104 N. 17th, Clarinda IA 51632. (712)542-4744. Sponsor: Clarinda Fine Arts Council. Purpose: "to provide a market for area artists particularly, as well as for anyone from further away who wants to enter; and to educate the public on the quality and quantity of art available in our area." Estab. 1973. Annual outdoor show held 1 day usually the second or third Saturday in May. Entries accepted until show date. Entry fee: $3/artist. Work may be offered for sale; no commission. Craftworker must attend show; demonstrations OK. "Could easily accommodate up to 100 craftworkers." Sponsor provides chairs; display panels; electricity for demonstrations; and table if requested at least 1 week before show. Considers all crafts. "This show is usually close to Mother's Day, so appropriate gift items sell especially well."
Promotion: "Show is advertised by radio; articles and pictures in local and statewide papers; posters; and direct mail. "If artists' names and explanations of work are received several weeks before the show, they will be included in newspaper and radio releases."

ART IN THE PARK, Box 132, Clinton IA 52732. (315)242-9635. President: Allan Rathje. Sponsor: Clinton Art Association. Estab. 1970. Annual outdoor show held 2 days the weekend after Mother's Day. Average attendance: 4,000. Entries accepted until 1 week before show. Entry fee: $15/artist. Prejudging by slides or photos; entry fee refunded for refused work. Work may be offered for sale; no commission. Craftworker or representative must attend show; demonstrations OK. Show is advertised by newspapers; radio; posters; and magazine ads.
Acceptable Work: Considers batik; candlemaking; glass art; jewelry; paintings; leatherworking; macrame; metalsmithing; pottery; sculpture; weaving; and woodcrafting.

ART IN THE PARK, 920 Third Ave. S., Fort Dodge IA 50501. (515)573-2316. Vice President: Cheryl Parker. Sponsor: Fort Dodge Area Fine Arts Council. Annual outdoor show held the third Sunday in August. Held indoors if raining. Average attendance: 5,000-6,000.
Acceptable Work: Considers batik, candlemaking, dollmaking, glass art, jewelry, lapidary, leatherworking, macrame, metalsmithing, mobiles, pottery, painting, drawing, printmaking, scrimshaw, sculpture, soft sculpture, weavings and woodcrafting. No kits, molds or bread sculpture. "All work must be original. We discourage refrigerator-type art (e.g., fuzzy magnets)."
Terms: Entries accepted until 1 week before show. Entry fee: $5/15' wide display area. "We have strict rules for qualification." Work may be offered for sale; no commission. Craftworker must attend show; demonstrations OK. Sponsor provides electricity for demonstrations, fencing (if needed) and 24-hour security. "The State Department of Revenue sends men around to the booths to issue 1-day permits when necessary."
Promotion: Show is advertised by local and regional newspapers; radio and TV; state-wide newspapers and magazines; and nationwide magazines and newsletters. "Business cards and signs are helpful for promotional purposes."
Sales Tip: "The public likes good pottery, moderately priced jewelry, stained glass and cloth sculpture. Keep the range of prices moderate—with higher priced things kept at a minimum, but there for comparison."

*ARTS & CRAFTS SHOW, Lake City Commerce, 101 E. Main St., Lake City IA 51449. Secretary: Neola M. Mack.

Acceptable Work: Considers batik; ceramics; decoupage; dollmaking; glass art; jewelry; leatherworking; macrame; metalsmithing; needlecrafts; pottery; sculpture; tole painting; weaving; woodcrafting.
Terms: Entries accepted up until show date. Maximum 1 piece/category; total of 3. Work may be offered for sale; no commission. Craftworker must attend show; demonstrations OK.
Awards: Cash award of $15 1st prize; $9 2nd prize for adults; and $5 and $3 for youth.

BELLE OF THE BEND, Artists in Action, 204 W. 2nd St., Muscatine IA 57761. Fair Coordinator: Cheryl Weaver. Estab. 1974. Annual 1 day outdoor show held in late summer. Average attendance: 5,000-10,000.
Acceptable Work: "We would consider most original crafts with a few limitations." Categories: fine art and craft.
Terms: Entries accepted until 4 weeks before show. Entry fee: $15/10x10' display area; only 1 artist/booth permitted. Entries prejudged by slides of work. Entry fee refunded for refused work. Work must be offered for sale; no commission. Craftworker must attend show; demonstrations OK. Registration limit: 65. Sponsor provides electricity for demonstrations.
Promotion: Show is advertised by radio; TV; newspaper; Iowa Arts Council Calendar; craft magazines; posters; and newsletter. Craftworker should provide a brief resume and photos with entry fee.
Sales Tip: "All work must display a price tag and booth must display a sign that all work is for sale. Most purchases are in the low-medium price range; cash that a person would carry rather than investment range work."

*****CARROLL SIDEWALK ART SHOW**, 223 West 5th St., Carroll IA 51401. (712)792-4383. Executive Vice President: M.J. Mike Arts. Sponsor: Carroll Chamber of Commerce. Estab. 1969. Annual 1 day indoor/outdoor show (with covered canopy) held in late April.
Acceptable Work: Considers batik; decoupage; macrame; metalsmithing; mobiles; pottery; sculpture; soft sculpture; tole painting; and woodcrafting. Categories: oils; acrylics; fabric art; watercolors; pottery; 3-dimensional; sketches and drawings; prints; woodcuts and photography.
Terms: Entries accepted up until show date. Work may be offered for sale; no commission. Craftworker must attend show; demonstrations OK.
Awards: Presents $50 in cash to best of show; $50 purchase; and 1st, 2nd and best of show ribbons. Only 1 item per category will be judged.

*****COUNCIL BLUFFS OLD-TIME COUNTRY MUSIC CONTEST & PIONEER EXPOSITION**, 106 Navajo, Council Bluffs IA 51501. (712)366-1136. Director: Bob Everhart. Sponsor: Westfair. Estab. 1976. Annual indoor/outdoor show (some buildings have roofs with no sidewalls) held 3 days during Labor Day Weekend. Average attendance: 15,000-25,000.
Acceptable Work: Considers all crafts. No kits, egg or milk cartons and vinegar bottles.
Terms: Entries accepted until 4 weeks before show. Entry fee: $15/8x8 to 10x10 display space. Work may be offered for sale; no commission. Craftworker must attend show; demonstrations encouraged. Registration limit: 125. Sponsor provides display panels, electricity for demonstrations and 24-hour security. "Because of the size of this celebration, we need to make it quite clear that we do not provide tables or chairs. All craftsmen should be prepared to fill out a state sales tax application while on the grounds, if they do not already have an Iowa State sales tax permit."
Awards: Presents over $500 in cash prize for crafts ($7,000 total for show); and trophies to the top 3 winners. "The artisan must be present to win. We give extra points to working artisans; endeavors in the vein of settling pioneers also receive extra points. The display of the work is also a consideration. We feel that an artisan should be just as able to display their fine works as make it."
Promotion: Show is advertised on a national and international basis. "We have received publicity in a tremendous number of national publications. We have had in the past and expect in the future continued national network TV coverage."
Sales Tips: "This audience buys a lot of merchandise at our celebration; some in anticipation of the Christmas season, others because of the desireability of the item. Artisans should remember they are dealing with 'pioneer lovers'. We have a high repeat-craftsmen entries."

CRESCO ART & CRAFT FAIR, Box 403, Cresco IA 52136. Chairman: Ed Clark. Sponsor: Cresco Chamber of Commerce. Estab. 1960. Annual outdoor show held 1 day in August. Average attendance: 3,000. Considers all crafts. No kits or machine-made items. Show is advertised by posters and newspapers.

Terms: Entries accepted until show date. Entry fee: $4/artist. Display area: 12x8. Work may be offered for sale; no commission. Craftworker must attend show; demonstrations OK. Sponsor provides fencing. Exhibitor handles sales and taxes.

*FESTIVAL OF ART IN THE PARK, 603 S. Grand, Spencer IA 51301. (712)262-5680. Chairman: J.K. Hall. Sponsor: Chamber of Commerce. Estab. 1970. Annual outdoor show held 1 day in June.
Acceptable Work: Considers batik, ceramics, metalsmithing, pottery, mobiles, sculpture and weaving. "Only creative art whose function is secondary to its creative merit."
Terms: Entries accepted until show. Entry fee: $5/craftworker. Prejudging by slides or photos; entry fee refunded for refused work. Work may be offered for sale; no commission. Craftworker must attaend show; demonstrations OK. Electricity availability limited. Contact in advance of show.
Awards: Presents $500 in cash, $2500 in purchase awards, and ribbons. "Insure that your work resembles no one else's."
Promotion: Show is advertised by newspaper, radio, direct mail and posters. "Craftworker may send biography for promotional consideration."
Sales: 1978 sales totaled approximately $3,500.

FLIGHT BREAKFAST MAY FEST, 212 Davenport St., Audubon IA 50025. (712)563-3305. Director: John W. Sutcliffe. Sponsor: Audubon County Historical Society. Estab. 1975. Annual indoor/outdoor show held 1 day in May. Average attendance: 2,000.
Acceptable Work: Considers all original and handmade items. "We particularly want the unusual and original. Nothing made from kits or machines—unless they are antique items for sale."
Terms: Entries accepted until filled. Entry fee: $3/display area. Work may be offered for sale; no commission. Craftworker must attend show; demonstrations OK. Registration limit: about 30. Sponsor provides electricity for demonstrations and 24-hour security.
Sales Tip: "Demonstrate to attract interest. Have a neat and attractive display. Small gift type items sell the best. For exhibitors with no Iowa tax permit, tax sheets will be distributed."

MIDWEST OLD SETTLERS & THRESHERS ASSOCIATION, INC., Rt. 1, Mt. Pleasant IA 52641. (319)385-8937. Administrator: Jerry W. Shafer. Estab. 1950. Annual indoor/outdoor show held for 5 days late in August and continuing into early September. Average attendance: 250,000.
Acceptable Work: Considers batik; candlemaking; ceramics; decoupage; dollmaking; glass art; jewelry; lapidary; leatherworking; macrame; metalsmithing; needlecrafts; pottery; sculpture; soft sculpture; tole painting; weaving and woodcrafting. Exhibitor is limited to one type of craft.
Terms: All entries must be approved by craft chairman by June-July. Display area: average 8x15. Work may be offered for sale; 10% commission. Craftworker must attend show; demonstrations required. Registration limit: 75. Sponsor provides electricity for demonstrations.
Profile: "We are an annual reunion for educational purposes relating a bit of our agricultural past for today. Show has authentic crafts (must be actual craft of 1880-1920 time period) and hobby crafts (but *very* limited space for these); home or personal hobby."

MISSISSIPPI VALLEY FALL ARTS & CRAFTS FAIR, 1203 W. Locust St., Davenport IA 52804. (319)324-7643. Promotion Director: Sidney Froehlich. Sponsor: Mississippi Valley Promotions. Estab. 1976. Annual indoor/outdoor show held 3 days in September. Average attendance: 6,000-8,000. Considers all crafts made by exhibitor.
Terms: Entries accepted until 1 week before show. Entry fee: $35/10x8 indoor display space; $30/outdoor display space. Work must be offered for sale; no commission. Craftworker must attend show; demonstrations encouraged. Registration limit: 150. Sponsor provides chairs, electricity for demonstrations and fencing.

MISSISSIPPI VALLEY SUMMER ARTS & CRAFTS FAIR, 1203 W. Locust St., Davenport IA 52804. (319)324-7643. Promotion Director: Sidney Froehlich. Sponsor: Mississippi Valley Promotions. Estab. 1976. Annual indoor/outdoor show held 2 days in June. Average attendance: 6,000-8,000. Considers all crafts made by exhibitor.
Terms: Entries accepted until 1 week before show. Entry fee: $25/10x8 indoor display space; $20/outdoor display space. Work must be offered for sale; no commission. Craftworker must attend show; demonstrations OK. Registration limit: 150. Sponsor provides chairs, electricity for demonstrations, fencing, and 30"x8' table ($1 rental fee).

MISSISSIPPI VALLEY WINTER ARTS & CRAFTS FAIR, 1203 W. Locust St., Davenport IA 52804. (319)324-7643. Promotion Director: Sidney Froehlich. Sponsor: Mississippi Valley Promotions. Estab. 1976. Annual indoor show held 2 days in December. Average attendance: 6,000-8,000. Considers all crafts made by exhibitor.
Terms: Entries accepted until 1 week before show. Entry fee: $40/10x8 display space. Work must be offered for sale; no commission. Craftworker must attend show; demonstrations OK. Registration limit: 65. Sponsor provides chairs, electricity for demonstrations and 30"x8' table ($1 rental fee).

***NATIONAL ROSEMALING EXHIBITION**, 502 W. Water St., Decorah IA 52101. (319)382-3856. Contact: Betty Seegmiller. Sponsor: Norwegian-American Museum. Estab. 1967. Annual indoor show held 3 days in July. Average attendance: 15,000.
Terms: Entries accepted until 1 week before show. Entry fee: $2/entry. Maximum 2 entries per craftworker. Prejudging; entry fee refunded for refused work. Work may be offered for sale; 20% commission. Sponsor furnishes display equipment and pays insurance and shipping to artist.
Acceptable Work: Considers rosemaling on wood. "Works must measure at least 8" in one direction and contain enough decoration to reveal artist's technical skill and design ability. It is not necessary for the artist to make the article; only the painting must be original."
Awards: Presents $125-150 in cash prizes and ribbons; and Medal of Honor.

NEVADA ART FAIR, 610 J Ave., Nevada IA 50201. Manager: Janette Antisdel. Sponsor: Nevada Chamber of Commerce. Annual outdoor show held 1 day in August.
Acceptable Work: Considers all crafts. "We discourage commercial displays."
Terms: Entries accepted until 1 week before show. Entry fee: $5/10x10 display space. Work may be offered for sale; no commission. Craftworker must attend show; demonstrations OK. Registration limit: 100. Sponsor provides fencing. Exhibitor handles sales and taxes.

***THE OCTAGON ART CENTER'S CLAY & FIBER SHOW**, The Octagon Art Center, 232½ Main St., Ames IA 50010. (515)232-5331. Director: Martha Benson. Biennial indoor juried exhibit on display 4-6 weeks January-March of even-numbered years. Average attendance: 2,000-3,000.
Acceptable Work: Categories: ceramics and fiber. Considers ceramics; macrame; soft sculpture; and weaving.
Terms: Entries due early in January. Entry fee: $10/artist. Maximum 3 pieces/craftworker. Prejudging by actual work; no entry fee refunded for refused work. Work may be offered for sale; 25% commission. Craftworker needn't attend show; no demonstrations.
Awards: Presents $200, best-in-show; $100, ceramic award; and $100, fiber. Competition is open to all craftworkers over 18 years of age living within 500 miles of Ames.
Promotion: Show is advertised by radio; newspaper; flyer; posters and craft publications (*Ceramics Monthly*, *Craft Horizons*).

OPERATION T-BONE FALL FESTIVAL, 212 Davenport St., Audubon IA 50025. (712)563-3305. Director: John W. Sutcliffe. Sponsor: Audubon County Historical Society. Estab. 1972. Annual indoor/outdoor show held 1 day in September. Average attendance: 2,000.
Acceptable Work: Considers all original and handmade items. "We particularly want the unusual and original. Nothing made from kits or machines—unless they are antique items for sale."
Terms: Entries accepted until filled. Entry fee: $3/display area. Work may be offered for sale; no commission. Craftworker must attend show; demonstrations OK. Registration limit: about 30. Sponsor provides electricity for demonstrations and 24-hour security.
Sales Tip: "Demonstrate to attract interest. Have a neat and atractive display. Small gift type items sell the best. For exhibitors with no Iowa tax permit, tax sheets will be distributed."

***OTTUMWA HEIGHTS FAMILY ART FESTIVAL**, Ottumwa Heights College, Ottumwa IA 51501. (515)682-4551. President: Sister Bernadine Pieper. Sponsor: Ottumwa Heights Art Board. Estab. 1973. Annual outdoor show held the first Sunday in August. Average attendance: 3,000-5,000. $1,000 purchase award plus ribbon awards. 1977 exhibit sales totalled $10,000-12,000.
Acceptable Work: Considers batik; ceramics; decoupage; glass art; jewelry; leatherworking; macrame; metalsmithing; mobiles; pottery; sculpture; soft sculpture; tole painting; weaving

---

* Those listings preceded by an asterisk present awards for prize-winning crafts.

and woodcrafting. Work must all be artists' orginal creation. No kit work considered.
Terms: Entries accepted until 2 weeks before show. Entry fee: $15/artist. Display area: 15 linear feet. Work may be offered for sale; no commission. Craftworker must be present; demonstrations OK. Sponsor provides chairs; display panels; limited electricity for demonstrations; fencing; and table. "Displays must be set up in the morning and dismantled after 5 p.m., eliminating need for security but 'booth sitters' available."

PAPER/FIBER, Iowa City/Johnson County Arts Council, 114½ E. College, Iowa City IA 52240. (319)337-7447. President: Marcia Wegman. Estab. 1978. Annual indoor show held 3 weeks in spring. Average attendance: 4,000.
Acceptable Work: Considers batik, soft sculpture, weavings and "all works on or of paper; on or of fiber; or combinations of paper and fiber." All work must be ready for hanging. Sculpture cannot exceed 100 lbs.; maximum height: 35'.
Terms: Open only to craftworkers in Iowa, Illinois, Minnesota, Missouri, Nebraska, South Dakota and Wisconsin. Slides for prejudging due 6 weeks before show. Entry fee: $10/craftworker. No entry fees refunded for refused work. Work may be offered for sale; no commission. Craftworker needn't attend show; no demonstrations. Registration limit: 75-100. Sponsor provides insurance on exhibited work and 24-hour security.
Awards: Presents $875 in cash and $750-1,250 in purchase prizes. "Submitted slides should be highest quality color reproductions. Details of whole pieces helpful. Work should be original with the concept of paper/fiber combinations kept in mind."

*PIONEER EXPOSITION OF ARTS & CRAFTS, 106 Navajo, Council Bluffs IA 51501. (712)366-1136. Director: Bob Everhart. Estab. 1976. Annual indoor/outdoor show held 3 days during Labor Day weekend at Westfair, Iowa. Average attendance: 15,000-25,000, paid.
Acceptable Work: Considers all original crafts. "We don't want any plastic 'put together' kinds of crafts. We are interested in the 'real' thing, and, more specifically, authentic pioneer arts and crafts."
Terms: Entries accepted until 3 weeks before show. Entry fee: $15, plus gate admission for each person. Display area: 10x10 or 8x8. Work may be offered for sale; no commission. Craftworker must attend show. "Demonstrations are highly recommended. The reason we do not take a commission is because we favor the working craftsperson." Registration limit: 120. Sponsor provides some display panels, electricity for demonstrations when requested and 24-hour security.
Awards: Presents $500 in cash prizes for arts and crafts divisions, certificates of participation, and trophies to the top 3 "Mid-America" ranking. "Part of the judging is done on how well the artist and/or craftsman displays his/her wares. The more pioneerish, the better. The best thing is to be there all 3 days demonstrating your craft or art. We have had some bad experiences in the past of an artisan coming solely for the judging, and leaving immediately after—must be here to win."
Promotion: "Show is advertised by every means available to us—local newspaper, radio and TV. Listings are placed in all national magazines and articles in craft magazines directly associated with our kind of show. We were written about in the *National Geographic* magazine as a major Midwest tourist attraction."
Sales Tip: "This is a rather large crowd already buying for Christmas. Items in the under $25 range do best."

PRE-CHRISTMAS POTTERY SHOW, 513 Nebraska St., Sioux City IA 51101. Sponsor: Sioux City Art Center. Estab. 1965. Annual indoor show held 2 days in December. Average attendance: 1,500. Considers ceramics; glass art; and pottery.
Terms: Entries accepted until 2 weeks before show. Prejudging. Work may be offered for sale; 30% commission. Craftworker needn't attend show; demonstrations OK. Registration limit: 50. Sponsor provides insurance on exhibited work; insurance on work shipped to artist; shipping costs to artists from show; table; and 24-hour security protection.

*SNAKE ALLEY ART FAIR, Box 5, Burlington IA 52601. Chairmen: Tom and Ellen Francis. Sponsor: Art Guild Burlington, Inc. Estab. 1967. Show is an annual 1 day outdoor event held in June during Steamboat Days. Average attendance: 8,000-10,000.
Acceptable Work: Considers batik, glass art, jewelry, leatherworking, macrame, metalsmithing, pottery, sculpture, soft sculpture, weavings and woodcrafting.
Terms: Entries accepted up until show date. Entry fee: $15/5x10 display area. Prejudging; entry fee refunded for refused work. Work may be offered for sale; no commission. Craftworker must attend show; demonstrations OK. Sponsor provides fencing.

Promotion: Show is advertised by Guild mailing; area newspapers; radio; Chamber of Commerce brochure; and *Des Moines Register*.
Profile: "There are physical problems with the Snake Alley Site. It is an inclined grade/switchback type. Leveling devices are needed. Also a need to provide own shade."

VALLEY JUNCTION CRAFTS FAIR, Box 301, West Des Moines IA 50265. (515)279-9040. Contact: Morey Knutsen. Sponsor: Valley Junction Merchants Association. Estab. 1978. Annual outdoor show held 1 day in May. Average attendance: 2,000-3,000. Considers all crafts.
Terms: Entries accepted until show. Entry fee: $25/craftworker. Prejudging by slides and/or photos; entry fee refunded for refused work. Work may be offered for sale; no commission. Craftworker must attend show; demonstrations OK. Registration limit: 100. Sponsor provides electricity for demonstrations.

Kansas

ART IN THE PARK, Box 198, Independence KS 67301. (316)331-0108. Chairman: Ray Rothgeb. Sponsor: Independence Arts Council. Purpose: "to provide an outlet for local and area craftsmen and artists and to make available to the community art and crafts for viewing and/or purchase." Estab. 1975. Annual indoor/outdoor (covered pavilion) show held 2 days in May. Average attendance: 4,000. Entries accepted until 2 weeks before show. Entry fee: $10-15/8x10 display area. Work may be offered for sale; no commission. Craftworker needn't attend show; demonstrations OK. Registration limit: 80. Sponsor provides electricity for demonstrations if requested in advance. Considers all original crafts.
Promotion: Show is advertised by area TV; radio and newspapers; national listings; State Arts Council newsletters; and mailing to area artists. Supply material regarding awards, qualifications, etc. to chairman 4-6 weeks in advance with request for demonstration or special showing for possible use as a press release.

ARTS & CRAFTS FAIR, Courthouse, Box 100, Cottonwood Falls KS 66845. (316)273-6491. County Extension Home Economist: Connie Moss. Sponsor: Home Economics Advisory Council. Estab. 1976. Annual indoor show held 1 day in July. Average attendance: 300. Entries accepted until 2 days before show. Entry fee: $2/folding table, not card table. Work may be offered for sale; no commission. Demonstrations OK. Sponsor provides chairs and table. Show is advertised by newspaper; posters; magazines; flyers; and newsletters. Considers all crafts.

BOURBON COUNTY ARTS & CRAFTS & ANTIQUE SHOW, c/o Bourbon County Arts Council, Box 491, Fort Scott KS 66701. Cochairmen: Malinda Reagan or Penny Berry. Estab. 1972. Annual outdoor show held 1 day in late May or early June. Average attendance: 50-60. Considers all crafts and antiques. No factory manufactured items.
Profile: Entries accepted until show date. Entry fee: $10/8' table. Work may be offered for sale; no commission. Craftworker must attend show; demonstrations OK. Registration limit: 200. Sponsor provides electricity for demonstrations and printed programs naming exhibitors, their art/craft and their city.
Profile: Show takes place "on downtown sidewalks and in an old fort area. Canopies are used in shadeless grassy areas."

CHRISTMAS ARTS & CRAFTS, c/o June DeWeese, Rt. 4, Abilene KS 67410. (913)263-3474. Estab. 1976. Annual indoor show held 2 days in December. Entries accepted until filled. Entry fee: $25/8x6 display area. Prejudging by slides and photos. Entry fee refunded for refused work. Work may be offered for sale; demonstrations OK. Registration limit: 100. Sponsor provides chairs; electricity for demonstrations; table; and 24-hour security protection. Accepts all fine arts and creative crafts.
Promotion: Show is advertised on 3 TV networks; 7 radio stations; and 176 papers.

CHRISTMAS ARTS & CRAFTS, c/o June DeWeese, Rt. 4, Abilene KS 67410. (913)263-3474. Estab. 1976. Annual indoor show held 2 days in November at Topeka, Kansas. Entries accepted until filled. Entry fee: $30/8x6 display area. Entries prejudged by slides or photos; entry fee refunded for refused work. Work may be offered for sale; no commission. Craftworker must attend show; demonstrations OK. Registration limit: 200. Sponsor provides chairs; electricity for demonstrations; table; and 24-hour security. Show is advertised by 3 TV networks; 7 radio stations; and 176 papers. Considers all fine arts and creative crafts.

***HAYS ARTS & CRAFTS FAIR,** Box 896, Hays KS 67601. (913)625-7522. Executive Director:

Carol Heil. Sponsor: HAC Art Sales. Estab. 1970. Annual indoor show held 2 days the first weekend in November. Average attendance: 8,000-10,000. Considers all crafts, but limits jewelry. Presents $25, 1st prize; $15, 2nd; and $10, 3rd.
Terms: Entries accepted until 2 weeks before show. No entry fee. Display area: 10x10. Prejudging by slides or previous entries. Work must be offered for sale; 20% commission. Craftworker must attend show; demonstrations OK. Registration limit: 50 spaces. Sponsor provides chairs, electricity for demonstrations, 24-hour security and tables for a fee.
Promotion: Show is advertised by TV, radio, newspapers, flyers and posters.
Sales Tip: "The public is generally more receptive to the craft items as opposed to fine arts. Things that will help sales are an attractive display, quality work and reasonable prices." 1978 show sales totaled $12,500.

*JUNCTION CITY ART IN THE PARK, Box 403, Junction City KS 66441. (913)238-8698. Director: Dianne Schwartz. Sponsor: Junction City Arts Council. "Art in the Park affords our community with exposure to both the visual and the performing arts in a casual and festive atmosphere. It also makes a market available to local and out-of-town artists." Estab. 1973. Annual outdoor show held 1 day in September. Average attendance: 3,000. Entries accepted until 4 weeks before show. Entry fee: $10/8x8 display area. Work may be offered for sale; no commission. Craftworker must attend show; demonstration OK. Sponsor provides display panels and electricity for demonstrations. Show is advertised by wide mailing in state/out-of-state; radio; TV; and newspaper media. Presents cash awards of $100, $75, and $50. Considers all original crafts.

*MISSION CHAMBER OF COMMERCE ART FESTIVAL, 5800 Foxridge Dr., Suite 101, Mission KS 66202. (913)262-2141. Executive Secretary: Betty J. Maloney. Estab. 1969. Annual outdoor show (on sidewalk with roof overhang) held 3 days in early September. Considers all crafts.
Terms: Entries accepted until 1 week before show. Entry fee: $20/6' banquet table or 6x8 panel. Work must be offered for sale; no commission. Craftworker must attend show; no demonstrations. Registration limit: 35. Sponsor provides display panels or table.
Awards: Presents $75 Best of Show Award; 1st, 2nd and 3rd place ribbons; and additional cash awards totaling $50.
Promotion: Show is advertised by radio and newspapers. Provide b&w glossy prints for newspaper stories.
Sales Tip: Silver jewelry, wooden sculpture, pressed flowers, macrame, stained glass and pottery sell well.

NEW BEGINNINGS FESTIVAL ARTS & CRAFTS, Box 816, Coffeyville KS 67337. (316)251-4244 or (316)251-9348. Chairman Arts and Crafts Committee: Shirley Miller. Sponsor: Chamber of Commerce. Estab. 1974. Annual outdoor show (with permanent concrete canopies) held 2 days in April. Average attendance: 2,000-5,000. Entries accepted until 2 weeks before show. Entry fee: $10/8x10 (without canopy); $15/8x20. Prejudging by slides. Work must be offered for sale; no commission. Craftworker must attend show; demonstrations OK. Registration limit: 150. Sponsor provides display panels; electricity for demonstrations; and 24-hour security. Show is advertised by news releases; radio; TV; interviews; and ads.
Acceptable Work: Considers batik; glass art; jewelry; lapidary; leatherworking; metalsmithing; mobiles; painting; pottery; sculpture; weaving; and woodcrafting.

*NORTHWEST KANSAS AREA ART SHOW & SALE, c/o Mrs. Duane Aase, 606 S. Broadway, Oberlin KS 67749. Sponsor: Sappa Valley Arts Club. Estab. 1970. Annual indoor show held 4 days in late September. Average attendance: 2,000. Considers batik.
Terms: Entries accepted until show. Entry fee: $1/entry. Maximum 3 entries per craftworker. Awards cash prizes to first 3 winners in 6 divisions and ribbons. Work may be offered for sale; 10% commission. Demonstrations encouraged. Address shipped items to Decatur County Extension Office, Court House, Oberlin, Kansas 67749. No returns shipped; must be picked up.

*OLATHE ART FAIR & CRAFTS SHOW, Box 189, Olathe KS 66061. (913)764-1050. Assistant Manager: David Palmer. Sponsor: Olathe Area Chamber of Commerce. Estab. 1970. Annual outdoor show (with partial cover on 1 side of the street) held 2 days in mid-June. Average attendance: 5,000. Considers all crafts.
Terms: Entries accepted until 1 week before show; "if there are cancellations we fill them in up until show time." Entry fee: $10/table space; $15/side of art frame. Work may be offered for

sale; no commission. Craftworker or representative must attend show; demonstrations OK. Sponsor provides metal art frames and some electricity for demonstrations.
Awards: Presents ribbons and best of show plaques.
Promotion: Show is advertised by posters, newspapers, public information spots on radio and mailings. "Craftworker may submit pictures, write-ups, etc., which may be used in the advertising. Photos can be returned, if requested."

OTTAWA ARTS & CRAFTS EXPOSITION, Box 411, Ottawa KS 66067. (913)242-6770. Secretary: Libby Schmanke. Sponsor: Ottawa Community Arts Council. Estab: 1978. Annual outdoor show held the third weekend in May at the Ottawa City Park.
Acceptable Work: Considers batik, candlemaking, ceramics (not using molds), glass art, jewelry, lapidary, leatherworking, macrame, metalsmithing, mobiles, handthrown or built pottery, scrimshaw, sculpture, weaving, woodcrafting and other handmade crafts.
Terms: Entries accepted until 2 weeks before show. Entry fee: $10/8x8' display area. "Artists may not share display areas." Prejudging by slides or photos; entry fee refunded for refused work. Craftworkers may offer work for sale; no commission. Craftworker must attend show; demonstrations OK. Sponsor provides chairs, 5x8' display panels, electricity for demonstrations and 30"x8' table. "Artist may bring own display, but they must stay within designated area. We do ask the exhibitors to provide their own hooks for any wall hangings."
Profile: "We planned having the expo on the same weekend the Ottawa Carnegie Library holds the annual Skunk Run Book Sale in the same park. The book sale has been in existence for several years and draws its own numbers. In addition to this, we make every effort to utilize radio, TV, newspapers and posters for publicity purposes. As another crowd attraction we had a hot air balloon last year. We encourage artists to make available any educational materials he might have in his particular media."
Sales Tip: "The artist may improve his sales by framing or matting his items which require such; demonstrations of his art and craft; displaying an attitude which gives the public the indication that he is enjoying participating in the exposition."

*WALNUT VALLEY NATIONAL FLAT-PICKING CHAMPIONSHIP & FOLK ARTS & CRAFTS FESTIVAL, Box 245, Winfield KS 67156. (316)221-3250. Co-directors: Troy and Phyllis Boucher. Sponsor: Walnut Valley Association, Inc. Estab. 1972. Annual indoor/outdoor (covered veranda and pavilion) show held 3 days in September. Average attendance: 10,000. Considers all crafts including musical instruments and folk art. Presents cash awards of $60, $50 and $40.
Terms: Entries accepted until 2 weeks before show. Entry fee: $25/8x8' outside space; $40/8x8' inside space. Entries prejudged by slides or photos; entry fee refunded for refused work. Work may be offered for sale; no commission. Craftworker must attend show; demonstrations OK. Registration limit: 120 (75 inside, 45 outside). Sponsor provides chairs upon prior request; electricity for demonstrations; table; and 24-hour security.

*WICHITA ART MUSEUM ART & BOOK FAIR, 619 Stackman Dr., Wichita KS 67203. (316)268-4621. Contact: Secretary, Volunteer Service Division. Estab. 1959. Annual indoor/outdoor show (some under tents) held 2 days during Mother's Day weekend. Average attendance: 50,000.
Acceptable Work: Considers batik, candlemaking, ceramics, dollmaking, glass art, jewelry, lapidary, leatherworking, metalsmithing, mobiles, needlecrafts, pottery, scrimshaw, sculpture, soft sculpture, weaving and woodcrafting. No kits, molds or machine-made items. "We try to discourage 'handicraft' items (e.g., crocheted doilies, knitted pot holders). We stress original art, designs and molds."
Terms: Entries accepted until 4 weeks before show. Entry fee: $30/10x10' indoor display area. Prejudging by 3 nonreturnable slides (must be marked with full name of artist, medium, and which end is up). Entry fee refunded for refused work. Work may be offered for sale; no commission. Craftworker must attend show; demonstrations OK. Registration limit: 300. Sponsor provides 24-hour security; articles left at craftworker's discretion.
Awards: Presents 12 $150 awards; and Judges Choice ribbons. "There is no consistency from year to year as to what the judges like as they view the fair and then discuss and decide on what 12 pieces are outstanding."
Promotion: Show is advertised by radio, TV, public service announcements, newspaper articles, and several interviews on all local talk shows. "All booths must have the name of artist displayed large enough to be easily visible."

Kentucky

*ARTS & CRAFTS FESTIVAL, Land Between the Lakes, Golden Pond KY 42231. (502)924-5602. Conservationist: Ann W. Wright. Sponsor: Murray Art Guild and TVA's Land Between the Lakes. Estab. 1969. Annual outdoor show held the 3rd weekend in June. Average attendance: 25,000. Entries accepted until 2 weeks before show. Entry fee: $8 general exhibit fee plus additional fee for juried section. Maximum 2 entries/category; unrestricted in general show and sell portion of show. Work may be offered for sale; no commission. Craftworker must attend show; demonstrations encouraged. Registration limit: 250. Sponsor provides limited electricity for demonstrations. Considers all original handmade crafts except ceramics; decoupage; and lapidary. Juried entries are eligible for cash awards. "The majority of the show's visitors are tourists, and small and less expensive items sell more rapidly."
Promotion: Show is advertised by radio; TV; news releases; posters; flyers; magazine listing; and special mailing. Submit a description of work and resume.

SUE BENNETT FOLK FESTIVAL, Sue Bennett College, London KY 40741. (606)864-9714. Chairman: Madge Chesnut. Annual indoor show held 3 days in late March or early April. Average attendance: 2,000. Considers all crafts except greenware, kits and liquid embroidery.
Terms: Entries accepted until 4 weeks before show ("if unusual craft, or one we don't have any of, sometimes can be accepted later"). No entry fee. Display area: "space for long table, about 6-7 feet." Prejudging by slides or small sample. Work may be offered for sale; no commission. Craftworker must attend show; demonstrations OK. Registration limit: about 50. Sponsor provides chairs; electricity for demonstrations; table; and 24-hour security.
Sales Tip: "Adults will buy almost anything if well-made, good design and color. We have many school children who come and a lot of them bring several dollars for inexpensive items (50¢-$4)."
Promotion: Show is advertised by letters of invitation to area clubs; radio; newspapers; some TV; and posters. Submit "good b&w photographs for newspaper releases; also some interesting things about themselves and their work."

CAPITAL EXPO ARTS & CRAFTS INVITATIONAL, Capital Expo, Inc., Box 490, FRankfort KY 40602. (502)223-5329. Art & Crafts Coordinator: Alberta R. Ernst. Annual outdoor (but protected) show held 3 days the first week of June at the Capital Plaza, Frankfort, Kentucky. Estab. 1974.
Acceptable Work: Open to residents of Kentucky only. Considers all crafts.
Terms: Entry fee: $10-20. Prejudging by slides; entry fee refunded for refused work. Entries accepted until the end of April. Work may be offered for sale; no commission. Write for prospectus.

*CAPITAL EXPO FINE ART & CRAFTS SHOW, Box 496, Frankfort KY 40602. (502)223-5329. Arts and Crafts Coordinator: Alberta R. Ernst. Sponsor: Paul Sawyier Art Club. Estab. 1979. Annual indoor show held 3 days in June.
Acceptable Work: Considers all crafts except decoupage and plastic flowers. No kits, molds or reproductions. Price range: $50-1,000.
Terms: Kentucky residents only. Entries accepted until 4 weeks before show. Entry fee: $5/entry; 2 entries maximum. Prejudging by slides. Work may be offered for sale; no commission. Craftworker must attend show; demonstrations OK.
Profile: Takes place at Paul Sawyier Library Gallery (a public library). Displayed in "a modern gallery in the newly renovated historical building. Library patrons visit during regular hours. A preview party, reception and awards presentation by invitation is held the first day.

THE CAROLINA CRAFTSMENS' CHRISTMAS CLASSIC—LOUISVILLE, 3603 Old Battleground Rd., Greensboro NC 27410. (919)288-1933. Executor Director: Clyde Gilmore. Estab. 1977. Annual indoor show held 2 days in December at Louisville, Kentucky.
Acceptable Work: Considers all crafts, except ceramics. No kits or molds. Categories: fine arts and selected crafts.
Terms: Entry fee and size of display area variable. Prejudging by photos/slides and newspaper articles. Entry fee due after prejudging. Work may be offered for sale; no commission. Craftworker must attend show; demonstrations OK. Sponsor provides chairs, curtained booth space and 24-hour security.
Awards: Presents variable purchase awards and plaques.
Promotion: Show is advertised by posters, flyers, TV, radio and newspapers.

8-STATE ANNUAL, J.B. Speed Art Museum, Box 8345, Louisville KY 40208. (502)636-2893.

Director: A.F. Page. Estab. 1973. Annual indoor show held the month of September. Average attendance: 6,000. Entries accepted until 5 weeks before show. No entry fee. Maximum 2 entries per artist. Prejudging. Work may be offered for sale; no commission. Craftworkers from Kentucky, Indiana, Illinois, Ohio, Virginia, West Virginia, Tennessee and Missouri only.

*GREENUP OLD FASHIONED DAYS ARTS & CRAFTS SHOW, 203 Harrison St., Greenup KY 41144. Art Show Chairman: Dorothy K. Griffith. Sponsor: Greenup Woman's Club and Greenup Merchants Association. Annual outdoor show held first Saturday in October.
Terms: Entries accepted until show date. No entry fee. "Sales encouraged. Exhibitors responsible for own display and setup materials." Considers all crafts. Presents 12 "best" ribbons in crafts; and $25 cash award and rosette to 5 grand prize winners in each category. Four special rosettes for People's choice, Mayor's Choice, President's choice and Chairman's choice. Local craftworkers only.

*KENTUCKY GUILD OF ARTISTS & CRAFTSMEN'S FAIR, Box 291, 213 Chestnut St., Berea KY 40403. (606)986-3192 or 986-4704. Estab. 1966. Annual outdoor show held 4 days in May. Prejudging. Work may be offered for sale. Craftworker must attend show; demonstrations OK. Registration limit: 100 Kentucky Guild members. Presents Visitors' Choice Award. Considers all crafts.

KINGDOM COME SWAPPIN' MEETIN', College Rd., Cumberland KY 40823. (606)589-2145. Coordinator: Harold Patterson. Sponsor: Southeast Community College. Purpose: "to help perpetuate folkways and methods of the Appalachian area." Estab. 1964. Annual indoor show held the second Saturday in October. Average attendence: 1,500. Entries accepted until 1 week before the show. Entry fee: $5/5x8 display area. Work may be offered for sale; no commission. Craftworker must attend show; demonstrations OK. Sponsors provide chairs; coverings; and tables. Show is promoted by newspaper; radio; TV; handbills; and posters. "Primarily interested in mountain crafts. Public is primarily interested in buying crafts which are indigenous to Appalachia."

WHITE HALL STATE SHRINE'S ANNUAL LABOR DAY SHOOT, Box 517, Richmond KY 40475. (606)623-9178. Contact: Vicki Smith. Sponsor: 9th Kentucky Calvary. "Our show is for those wanting to display and sell their crafts to people from various areas around the state." Estab. 1972. Annual outdoor show held 4 days during Labor Day weekend. Attendance: 3,000-5,000. Considers all crafts.
Terms: Entries accepted throughout the event. Entry fee: $6/day. Display area: 20x20. Work may be offered for sale; no commission. Craftworker or representative must attend show; demonstrations OK. Sponsor provides 24-hour security and camping area.
Promotion: Show is advertised by TV shows; radio spots; and newspaper ads.
Profile: "Every year teams from the eastern part of the state come dressed in Civil War uniforms to compete for medals and prizes. With this we have live entertainment provided; along with an arts and crafts fair. The house, White Hall, is also open for tours. We do have a big turnout for this weekend. The area of types of people attending is very broad."

Louisiana

BOGALUSA CHAMBER OF COMMERCE ARTS, CRAFTS & ANTIQUE MART, 608 Willis Ave., Bogalusa LA 70427. (504)735-5731. Executive Director: John Moak. Purpose: fundraiser. Estab. 1975. Semiannual outdoor show (in automobile dealer's lot) held 2 days in May and October. Entries accepted until show date. Entry fee: $15/10x10 display area. Work may be offered for sale; no commission. Craftworker needn't attend show; demonstrations encouraged. Registration limit: 120. Sponsor provides chairs and table at nominal charge, coverings; electricity for demonstrations; and 24-hour security. Considers all crafts and antiques.
Promotion: Show is advertised by newspaper; radio; TV; and is usually held along with some other event that is usually tied in with the Mart. "For example, an antique auto show or free open-air concert. A photo of the artist at work stands a good chance of ending up on the front page of the *Bogalusa Daily News*."

LOUISIANA FUR & WILDLIFE FESTIVAL, c/o Carolyn Gibbs, Rt.1, Box 251, Bell City LA 70630. (318)598-2535. "The craft show is held in conjunction with the annual Louisiana Fur & Wildlife Festival. There are many different activities—art show, skinning, trap setting, retriever dog, trap shooting, etc." Estab. 1975. Annual indoor show held 2 days in January. Average attendance: 5,000. Entries accepted until 1 week before show or until filled. Entry fee:

$15/10x10 display area (more if space is needed and is available). Work may be offered for sale; no commission. Prefers craftworker attend show; demonstrations OK. Sponsor provides chairs; electricity for demonstrations; and 24-hour security. Show is advertised by national periodicals; local newspapers; radio; and TV. Considers all crafts.

LOUISIANA NATIVE CRAFTS FESTIVAL, 637 Girard Park Dr., Lafayette LA 70503. (318)233-6611. Director: Beverly D. Latimer. Sponsor: Lafayette Natural History Museum Association. Estab. 1972. Annual outdoor show (tents and canopies are used) held 2 days in fall. Average attendance: 10,000.
Acceptable Work: Considers jewelry, leatherworking, metalsmithing, pottery, weaving and woodcrafting. Criteria for entry: "the craft must have been practiced in this region prior to 1900; the product should be of Louisiana materials; or the craft must have been pertinent to the livelihood of the individual or the area."
Terms: Entries accepted until 1 week before show. Entry fee: $25/artist. Prejudging by slides, photos or actual crafts. Entry fee due after prejudging. Work may be offered for sale; no commission. Craftworker must attend show; demonstrations required. Sponsor provides chairs, coverings, electricity for demonstrations, table and 24-hour security. Exhibitor handles sales and taxes; taxes collected by the sales office (Lafayette Parish Sales Tax) during the festival.
Promotion: Show is advertised by radio, TV, posters and magazines. "We are part of Festivals Acadien (Bayou Food Festival, Cajun Music Festival, etc.). The Lafayette Parish Visitor's and Convention Bureau publicizes event in a 5-state area."

MELROSE ARTS & CRAFTS SHOW, Box 2654, Natchitoches LA 71457. (318)352-6472. Chairman: Kathy Kintzley. Sponsor: Association for the Preservation of Historic Natchitoches. Estab. 1974. Annual outdoor show held 2 days in April at Melrose, Louisiana. Average attendance: 8,000. Considers all "original and creative crafts."
Terms: Entries accepted until about 3 weeks before show. Entry fee: $10/artist; $17.50/exhibiting group. Display area: 10x20. Work must be offered for sale; 20% commission. Craftworker or representative must attend show; demonstrations OK. Sponsor provides electricity for demonstrations, fencing and 24-hour security.
Sales Tip: Moderately priced work (up to $50) sells best. 1978 sales totaled $14,000.

NEW ORLEANS JAZZ & HERITAGE FESTIVAL CRAFTS FAIR, Box 2530, New Orleans LA 70176. (504)522-4786. Crafts Coordinator: Vitrice McMurry. Sponsor: New Orleans Jazz & Heritage Foundation. Estab. 1969. Annual outdoor show (on a grassy racetrack field under many small tents) held 3 days during 3 weekends of April. Average attendance: 150,000.
Acceptable Work: Considers batik; candlemaking; ceramics; dollmaking; glass art; jewelry; lapidary; leatherworking; macrame; metalsmithing; mobiles; needlecrafts; pottery; sculpture; soft sculpture; weaving; and woodcrafting.
Terms: Entries accepted until 2 months before show. Entry fee: $100/10x10 display area. Prejudging by 3 35mm slides; entry fee refunded for refused work. Work may be offered for sale; no commission. Craftworker must attend show; demonstrations OK. Registration limit: 120. Sponsor provides coverings; electricity for demonstrations ($25 extra); table; and 24-hour security.
Promotion: Show is advertised by newspapers; TV; and radio. "Provide as much bio as possible for our publicity articles."
Sales Tip: "Quality work of all prices sell here. As usual, pottery and jewelry sell best with toys and woodwork doing next best."

NEW ORLEANS MUSEUM OF ART, NEW ORLEANS TRIENNIAL, Box 19123, City Park, New Orleans LA 70179. Contact: William A. Fagaly. Triennial show.
Acceptable Work: Considers sculpture; ceramics; fiber; and conceptual works. Open to craftworkers living and working in Kentucky, Tennessee, West Virginia, Virginia, North and South Carolina, Georgia, Florida, Alabama, Mississippi, Arkansas, Louisiana and Texas.
Terms: No entry fee. Write for entry deadlines and show dates. Maximum 3 entries per craftworker. Prejudging of 2-dimensional work by 1 2x2 slide of each item; of 3-dimensional works by 3 2x2 slides of each work, or 3 8x10 b&w photos of each work; and only paper documentation, typewritten proposals and/or 8x10 b&w photos of each work for conceptual pieces. Museum reserves the right to retain any or all slides for archives of regional contemporary artists. Juror recommends artists for one person exhibitions the next year. Work may be offered for sale; 10% purchase discount is required for purchases by museum members.

*OKTOBERFEST, 301 Lafitte St., Mandeville LA 70448. (504)626-9381. Coordinator: Jude Mogyordy. Estab. 1977. Annual outdoor show held 2 days in October. Average attendance: 5,000-10,000. Considers all original crafts.
Terms: Entries accepted until 4 weeks before show. Entry fee: to be determined (under $50). Display area: 15x15. Prejudging by slides or photos; entry fee refunded for refused work. Work may be offered for sale; no commission. Craftworker must attend show; demonstrations encouraged. Registration limit: 50. Sponsor provides electricity for demonstrations and 24-hour security.
Awards: St. Tammany Art Association awards $100, $50 and $25 cash awards. "Neatness and simplicity of exhibit help exhibitors win awards."
Promotion: Show is advertised by radio, TV, brochures, posters, newspapers and other publicity. "Photos and slides (from craftspeople) are sometimes considered for promotional purposes (i.e., papers, brochure, posters)."
Sales Tip: "People buy everything from hand-painted original clothing to pottery, weaving, fine arts, woodcrafted toys, carvings, furniture, etc. A display offering variety, individual design, and most of all, enthusiastic craftspersons, along with moderately affordable prices, will let the pieces sell themselves. Total sales are requested at the end of the last day of the festival."

RED RIVER REVEL, A CELEBRATION OF THE ARTS, 700 Clyde Fant Pkwy., Shreveport LA 71106. (318)221-1776. Sponsor: Junior League of Shreveport, Inc., Louisiana Bank and Trust Co., and the City of Shreveport. Estab. 1976. Annual outdoor show (with individual booths) held 1 week (artists can opt for 1/2 week) in September. Average attendance: 300,000. Considers all original crafts.
Terms: Entries accepted until 3 months before show. Entry fee: $40 per week; $20 per 1/2 week; and $5 prejudging fee. Display area: 8x10. Prejudging by 3 35mm slides. Entry fee refunded for refused work; $5 prejudging fee applied to booth rental on accepted work. Work may be offered for sale; 20% commission. Craftworker must attend show; demonstrations OK. Registration limit: about 50. Sponsor provides booth; electricity for demonstrations; 24-hour security; lighting; relief volunteers; and credit cards through central sales.
Sales Tip: "Highest sale in 1978 was a $500 painting; lowest sales items were $2 framed shells. 1978 artisans' sales average per artist was $792.10."
Promotion: "Festival received front page newspaper coverage week of show. TV did even the weather reports from the Revel. Radios did remotes from festival. After confirmation of acceptance is received, artists will be requested to supply glossies and biographies if possible."

*SHREVEPORT ART GUILD NATIONAL, 2911 Centenary Blvd., Shreveport LA 71104. (318)869-5169. Chairman: Carolyn Nelson. Estab. 1921. Annual indoor show held 1 month in fall. Average attendance: 2,000. Entries accepted until July 30. Prejudging by slides; no entry fees refunded for refused work. Work may be offered for sale; 10% commission. Craftworker needn't attend show; no demonstrations. Registration limit: 70. Show is advertised by local and state newspapers; local TV; and radio. Presents cash awards of $3,000 and purchase awards of $1,200. Considers ceramics and sculpture.

*SUMMER ARTS FESTIVAL, c/o Art & Humanities Council, Box 3893, Baton Rouge LA 70821. (504)344-8558. Community Relations Director: Everett Powers. "Crafts part of festival is only about 1/2 of the event—also performing arts and visual arts." Estab. 1974. Annual indoor/outdoor show held 3 days in the summer (Arts & crafts exhibits Saturday and Sunday only.) Average attendance: 100,000. Considers all crafts.
Terms: Non-prejudged entries accepted until 2 weeks before show; prejudged entries accepted until 6 weeks before show. Entry fee: $50, prejudged; $25, non-prejudged; $25, gallery display. Booth area: 8x10. Work may be offered for sale; no commission. Craftworker must attend show unless exhibiting in gallery display only; demonstrations encouraged. Sponsor provides electricty for demonstrations and accident insurance. Presents purchase awards. 1977 exhibitor sales totalled $75,000.
Promotion: Show is advertised by TV; radio; posters; and newspapers. "If entrant wants publicity, pictures and bio are encouraged—b&w only."

Maine

*ARTHRITIS ART COMMITTEE, 37 Mill St., Brunswick ME 04011. 1-2 shows sponsored annually by the Maine Chapter, Arthritis Foundation. Entries accepted until 15 days before show. Entry fee: $10, first work; $6, each additional work. Maximum 5 entries per artist. Work may be offered for sale; 25% commission. Considers framable crafts. Awards 5 $10 first prizes, ribbons and certificates.

This porcelain plate, designed by James Chalkey, won the Delaware Crafts Council Prize at the Contemporary Crafts Exchange held at the Delaware Art Museum in Wilmington. The scene below shows a scene of textiles, ceramics and wood on display at the show.

*BRIDGTON ART SHOW, Box 236, Bridgton ME 04009. (207)647-3472. Secretary: Sandra Libby. Sponsor: Bridgton Chamber of Commerce. Estab. 1971. Annual indoor show held Columbus Day weekend. Average attendance: 2,000-3,000. Entries accepted until 1 week before show. Entry fee: $20/2 entries. Entries prejudged by actual work. Work may be offered for sale; 20% commission. Craftworker needn't attend show; no demonstrations. Sponsor provides display panels; electricity; insurance on exhibited work; and 24-hour security. Considers all crafts.
Awards: Presents $1,000, 1st; $500, 2nd; $350, honorable mention; and $250, popular prize,

chosen by show's viewers. Show sales average $1,500.
Promotion: Show is advertised by posters and media advertising. "Printed materials relative to artist always welcome. They are displayed and offered for distribution to viewers."

CARIBOU FALL ARTS & CRAFTS FESTIVAL, Box 357, 111 High St., Caribou ME 04736. (207)492-5231. Coordinators: Ann Chung and Bill Johnson. Sponsor: Caribou Chamber of Commerce. Estab. 1974. Annual indoor show held 2 days in October at Caribou Armory. Average attendance: 7,000-8,000. Considers all crafts.
Terms: Entries accepted up until show date. Entry fee: $8/day/8' display area; $11/2 days/8' display area. Work may be offered for sale; no commission. Craftworker must attend show; demonstrations OK. Registration limit: 85. Sponsor provides display panel at $5/rack.
Promotion: Show is advertised by radio, TV, newspaper, listings in arts and crafts magazines, pamphlets and posters.

CARIBOU SIDEWALK ARTS & CRAFTS FESTIVAL, Box 357, 111 High St., Caribou ME 04736. (207)492-5231. Coordinators: Ann Chung and Bill Johnson. Sponsor: Caribou Chamber of Commerce. Estab. 1973. Annual outdoor show held 1 day in July. Average attendance: 3,000-5,000. Considers all crafts.
Terms: Entries accepted up until show date. Entry fee: $5/8 foot display area. Work may be offered for sale; no commission. Craftworker must attend show; demonstrations OK. Registration limit: 100. Sponsor provides display panel at $5/rack. Show is advertised by radio; TV; newspaper; listings in arts and craft magazines; pamphlets; and posters.

THE CHRISTMAS CRAFT FAIR, Kennebee Valley YMCA, Augusta ME 04330. Chairman: Marty Thornton. Purpose: "to give the town a quality crafts fair and to provide exhibitors a place to sell." Estab. 1973. Annual indoor show held 2 days in December. Entries accepted until 4 weeks before show. Entry fee: $30/8x8 display area. Prejudging by slides or past shows; entry fee refunded for refused work. Work may be offered for sale; no commission. Craftworker must attend show; demonstrations OK. Registration limit: 70. Sponsor provides chairs; electricity for demonstrations; table, if reserved at registration time; and 24-hour security. Show is advertised by newspapers; radio; posters; and trade papers. 1977 show sales totalled $24,000. Considers all crafts except ceramics and decoupage.

FRANCO-AMERICAN FESTIVAL, 145 Birch St., Lewiston ME 04240. (207)784-2926. Coordinator: Constance Cote. Estab. 1977. Annual outdoor festival held 1 week during the last week in July. Average attendance: 135,000.
Acceptable Work: Considers all crafts. No mass-produced or manufactured goods.
Terms: Entries accepted until 4 weeks before show. Entry fee: $8/10x10 display area per day (subject to change). Work may be offered for sale; no commission. Craftworker or representative must attend show; demonstrations encouraged. Sponsor provides electricity for demonstrations and fencing. Exhibitor handles sales and taxes.
Promotion: Show is advertised by radio (AM, FM), TV, newspapers and brochures throughout New England and Canada.
Sales Tip: "We have noticed that the better looking exhibits, and things with activities such as demonstrations tend to attract more people."

H.O.M.E. FAIR, Box 408, Orland ME 04472. Chairperson: Arleen Morris. Sponsor: Homeworkers Organized for More Employment. Estab. 1970. Annual outdoor show held 1st weekend in August. Average attendance: 2,000. Considers all crafts.
Terms: Entry fee: $5/H.O.M.E. member; $15/nonmember. Size of display area as needed. Work may be offered for sale; no commission. Craftworker needn't attend show; demonstrations OK. Registration limit: 80-100. Sponsor provides 24-hour security.
Promotion: Show is advertised by radio; TV; newspapers; statewide and national publications, and posters. "Greater emphasis will be placed on road signs to attract impulse tourist buying." Submit slides for TV promotion and glossies for newspaper press releases.

*****KITTERY ART ASSOCIATION SIDEWALK SALE**, 317 State Rd., Eliot ME 03903. Chairman: Carol Moreland. Purpose: to promote the arts. Annual outdoor show held 1 day in August.
Acceptable Work: Considers all crafts. Number paintings are not acceptable.
Terms: Entries accepted until 2 months before show; late entries accepted if room is available.

Those listings preceded by an asterisk present awards for prize-winning crafts.

Entry fee: $5/15x4 display area. Maximum 1 piece per artist for awards judging. Work may be offered for sale; no commission. Craftworker or representative must attend show; demonstrations OK. Registration limit: 60. Sponsor provides fencing.
Promotion: Show is advertised by newspapers; magazines; radio; TV; posters; and craftworker's organizations. Submit photo and promotional information.
Awards: Presents cash and ribbon awards.

ROTARY CRAFTS FESTIVAL, Rotary Club, Box 1755, Portland ME 04104. (207)773-7157. Estab. 1975. Annual outdoor show held 1 day in July. Average attendance: 20,000. Considers all crafts.
Terms: Entries accepted until 4 weeks before show. Entry fee: $20/10' wide display area. Work may be offered for sale; no commission. Craftworker must attend show; demonstration OK. Registration limit: 220+. Sponsor provides table, 24-hour security and liability insurance.

SEACOAST CRAFTS FAIR, Box 25, York ME 03909. (207)363-2397. Director: Rachel B. Grieg. Estab. 1967. Annual indoor show held 4 days in August. Average attendance: 3,000. Entries accepted until June 1. Entry fee: $25/8'x30'' table space (table $5 extra). Prejudging by slides; photos; or actual work. Entry fee due after prejudging. Work may be offered for sale; no commission. Craftworker must attend show; demonstrations OK. Registration limit: 50-60. Sponsor provides chairs; coverings; electricity for demonstrations; and insurance on exhibited work. Show is advertised by TV; radio; newspapers; and posters. Considers all crafts made by New England craftworkers.

Maryland

*ACADEMY OF THE ARTS, South and Harrison Sts. (Box 605), Easton MD 21601. Contact: Curator. Annual show. Entries accepted until 1 week before show. No entry fee. Artists born in Maryland, residents of the state and Maryland students may participate. Work may be offered for sale; 20% sales commission. Awards $1,000 in prizes.
Acceptable Work: Considers multimedia; collage; ceramics; and metal and wood sculpture. Sculpture may not be impermanent material. Work must have been completed in last 2 years. No title may be changed after submission of entry card. Size limit: 62x62'', 2-dimensional; 14' in total dimension; 150 lbs. Material must be shipped in crates so it can be returned.

ANNAPOLIS ARTS FESTIVAL, Box 228, Annapolis MD 21404. (301)267-7922. Executive Secretary: Kathy Greentree. Sponsor: Annapolis Fine Arts Foundation. Estab. 1962. Annual out-door show held 3 days in June. Average attendance: 25,000.
Acceptable Work: Considers batik; candlemaking; folk art; jewelry; leatherworking; macrame; metalsmithing; mobiles; pottery; sculpture; stained glass; weaving; miscellanous craft work and woodcrafting.
Terms: Entries accepted until 3 months before show. Entry fee: "no fixed amount set at this time. Contact executive secretary to confirm. Full payment of fee due 1 month prior to show." Display area: 8x10 in tent, 6x12 for fence art. Prejudging by slides only. Entry fee due after prejudging. Work may be offered for sale; no commission. Craftworker must attend show; demonstrations OK. Registration limit: 54 craftworkers; 60 fence artists. Sponsor provides tent; electricity for demonstrations; and 24-hour security.
Promotion: Show is advertised by radio; TV; newspapers; brochures; placemats; calendars; magazines; and books.

AUTUMN CRAFT FESTIVAL, c/o Sugarloaf Mountain Works, Inc., Box 319, Poolesville MD 20837. (301)279-7551. Director: Ms. Deann Verdier. See Sugarloaf Mountain Works Festival.

BALTIMORE CRAFT EXPO, Box 370, Farmington CT 06032. (203)224-8388. Directors: Denise Barile and Rudy Kowalczyk. Sponsor: American Craft Expositions, Inc. Estab. 1979. Annual indoor show held 3 days in November at the Convention Center in Baltimore, Maryland. Average attendance: 26,000. Considers all "high quality craft media. No dealers, agents, manufactured items or kits."
Terms: Entries accepted until 60 days before show. Popular media close earlier. Entry fee: $100 and up, depending upon size of display area. Display area: 10x10-10x20. Prejudging by 6 slides; entry fee refunded for refused work. Work must be offered for sale; no commission. Craftworker must attend show; demonstrations encouraged. Registration limit: 250. Sponsor provides 24-hour security protection. Rental chairs and tables available.

COLUMBIA MALL PROFESSIONAL ARTS FESTIVAL, Rt. 1, Box 153J, Auburn NH 03032.

(603)483-2742. President: Jinx Harris. Estab. 1972. Semiannual indoor show held 4 days in January and August at Columbia, Maryland. Average attendance: 25,000. Entries accepted until 1 week before show or until filled. Entry fee: $40/8x4 display area. Prejudging by slides or photos. "This is a limited craft show—careful selection of craft work." Work may be offered for sale; no commission. Craftworker must attend show; demonstrations OK. Registration limit: 150. Sponsor provides electricity for demonstrations and 24-hour security. Show is advertised by radio; TV; marquee; and post cards. Considers all crafts except ceramics; decoupage; lapidary; needlecrafts; and strung bead jewelry.

*COURTHOUSE ARTS FESTIVAL, 301 Washington Ave., Towson MD 21204. (301)494-3871. Recreation Program Coordinator: Martha F. Dearman. Sponsor: Baltimore County Department of Recreation and Parks. Purpose: "to give artists of all types a place to exhibit, compete for awards and sell their works of art in a pleasant, cultural atmosphere. And, to give people the opportunity to experience an enjoyable day with friends and to purchase original creative art works." Estab. 1951. Annual outdoor show held 1 day in early June. Average attendance: 15,000-20,000. Entries accepted until 3 weeks before show. Entry fee: $10-15 feet wide display area. Work may be offered for sale; no commission. Craftworker must attend show; demonstration OK. Sponsor provides electricity for demonstrations. Categories: art; crafts; sculpture; photography; youth; and performing arts. All categories divided into professional and amateur. Considers all crafts. Presents 3 place ribbons plus $50, 1st prize; $25, 2nd prize; and $15, 3rd prize in the professional and amateur class.
Promotion: Show is advertised by radio; TV; all newspapers; listing in events calendars and monthly magazines; posters; letters of invitation; sponsorships of awards categories; and exhibits of artists and craftworkers and photographs in commercial and government headquarters. "Craftworker should supply resume; photo of artist at work and/or photos of works. Local artists may be requested to make personal appearance on radio or TV."

*CUMBERLAND VALLEY EXHIBITION, Box 423, Hagerstown MD 21740. (301)739-5727. Director: H. Paul Kotun. Sponsor: Washington County Museum of Fine Arts. Estab. 1932. Annual indoor show held during June. Average attendance: 5,200. Entries accepted until 2-3 weeks before show. Entry fee: $10/craftworker. Maximum 2 entries per craftworker. Work may be offered for sale; 20% commission. Open to residents of the Cumberland Valley region. Considers all art. Maximum size: 2-dimensional, 72x72". Two-dimensional work must be framed.
Awards: Presents $800 in cash prizes and $600 in purchase awards, 2-dimensional art; $200 in cash prizes and $100 in purchase awards, 3-dimensional art.

*FELL'S POINT FUN FESTIVAL, 804 S. Broadway, Baltimore MD 21231. (301)675-6756. Festival Chairman: Mary T. Geeson. Sponsor: Society for the Preservation of Federal Hill and Fell's Point. Estab. 1967. Annual outdoor show held 2 days in the fall. Average attendance: 170,000. Entries accepted until 2 weeks before show. Entry fee: $20/10 ft. display area. "There is also a large flea market at $25/20'." Work may be offered for sale; no commission. Craftworker or representative must attend show; demonstrations OK. Registration limit: 200. Sponsor provides electricity for 20 exhibitors. Categories: art; arts and crafts; photography; flea market; and neighborhood collectibles. Considers all crafts except sculpture. Presents ribbons and certificates of award in all categories.
Sales Tips: "Traditional works sell best. In craft, work quality and originality are a must. This show usually is very trendy and, since it is the last outdoor one of the season, followers of these shows come and purchase hoping that the artist has lowered prices."
Promotion: Show is advertised by newspapers; TV; interviews; listing in *Maryland Happenings*; radio; and tourist information brochure.

FESTIVAL OF FROSTBURG, Box 104, Frostburg MD 21532. (301)689-3855. Chairman: Kay Parnes. Sponsor: Frostburg State College and Frostburg Community Organization. Estab. 1974. Annual outdoor show held 1 day in September. Average attendance: 3,000-4,000. Considers all crafts. No kits, imports or machine-made crafts.
Terms: Entries accepted until 2 weeks before show. Entry fee: $5/artist. Display area: 10x12. Work may be offered for sale; no commission. Craftworker must attend show; demonstrations encouraged. Exhibitor handles sales and taxes.
Promotion: Show is advertised by local radio, television and newspapers. Artists are encouraged to provide promotional materials.

FREDERICK CRAFT FAIR, National Crafts Ltd., Gapland MD 21736. (301)432-8438. Direc-

tor: Noel Clark. Estab. 1975. Annual indoor/outdoor show held 1 day wholesale and 3 days retail at Frederick, Maryland in June. Average attendance: 30,000. Considers all crafts. Average sales/booth: $2,100.
Terms: Entries accepted until March 10. Booth fee: $85-125/display area; $3 non-refundable application fee. Entries prejudged by 5-10 35mm color slides. Work must be offered for sale; no commission. Craftworker must attend show; demonstrations OK. Registration limit: 500 booths. Sponsor provides 24-hour security.
Promotion: Show is advertised by newspapers, most trade magazines, radio, TV, posters, brochures and mailings to wholesale buyers.

GERMAN AMERICAN DAY, 1215 Hillside Rd., Pasadena MD 21122. (301)437-2068. General Chairman: Kurt P. Kuenzel Sr. Sponsor: German-American Citizen Union of Maryland. Purpose: "to keep the German ethnic groups together and show the American public what we can do. Also to create interest in our heritage." Estab. 1900. Annual outdoor show (stands will have small cover or roof) held last weekend in June. Average attendance: 140,000. Entries accepted until 4 weeks before show. Display area: 8x8 or multiples by 8' front; accepts 3 craftworkers/8' table. Work may be offered for sale; 15% commission. Craftworker must attend show; demonstration OK. Sponsor provides chairs; covering; electricity for demonstrations; fencing; table; and 24-hour security. Show is advertised by radio; TV; newspapers; flyers and state of Maryland.
Acceptable Work: Considers candlemaking; ceramics; leatherworking; needlecrafts; sculpture; soft sculpture; weaving; and woodcrafting.

JONATHAN HAGER FRONTIER CRAFT DAY, Court House Annex, Washington County Tourism, Hagerstown MD 21740. (301)791-3130. Director: Betty Jane Bupp. Estab. 1972. Annual outdoor show held 1 day in August. Average attendance: 2,500-3,000. Entries accepted 6 months in advance. Work may be offered for sale; no commission. Craftworker must attend show; demonstrations OK. Registration limit: 25-30. Sponsor provides picnic size table.
Acceptable Work: Considers candlemaking; dollmaking; leatherworking; needlecrafts; pottery; weaving; and woodcrafting. Must be colonial or pioneer type.
Sales Tip: "Since this show is pioneer and colonial in concept we advise all participants to keep in mind that items for sale and merchandising of them is in the same way—loose and simple."
Promotion: Show is advertised by more than 250 newspapers; radio; TV; news releases; interviews; special features; and tourist publications. Submit b&w photo of action demonstrations, exhibits or specific details; if artist is unique, a detailed history of art and background; and for special interviews and programs some visuals will be required.

JEWISH COMMUNITY CENTER'S CRAFT SALE, 5700 Park Heights Ave., Baltimore MD 21215. (301)542-4900. Director of Fine Arts: Freda Friedman. Estab. 1973. Annual indoor show held 2 days in October. Average attendance: 4,000. Entries accepted until 3 weeks before show. Entry fee: $50/12x6 display area. Prejudging for new craftworkers by photos, slides; entry fee refunded for refused work. Work may be offered for sale; no commission. Craftworker must attend show; demonstrations OK. Sponsor provides chairs; display panels; electricity for demonstrations; table; and 24-hour security. Show is advertised by 12,000 mailed announcements; large banners; billboards; and advertisements. Considers all crafts except decoupage and dollmaking.

MARYLAND CRAFT FESTIVAL, Sugarloaf Mountain Works, Inc., Box 319, Poolesville MD 20837. (301)279-7551. Director: Ms. Deann Verdier. See Sugarloaf Mountain Works Craft Festival.

MARYLAND OKTOBERFEST INC., 1215 Hillside Rd., Pasadena MD 21122. (301)437-2068. General Chairman: Kurt P. Kuenzel Sr. Purpose: "to keep the German ethnic groups together and show the American public what we can do. Also to create interest in our hertiage." Estab. 1969. Annual indoor show held 3 days in October. Average attendance: 15,000. Entries accepted until 4 weeks before show. Display area: 8x8 or multiples by 8' front; accepts 3 craftworkers/8' table. Work may be offered for sale; 15% commission. Craftworker must attend show; demonstrations OK. Sponsor provides chairs; coverings; electricity for demonstrations; table; and 24-hour security.
Acceptable Work: Considers candlemaking; ceramics; leatherworking; needlecrafts; sculpture; soft sculpture; weaving; and woodcrafting.
Promotion: Show is advertised by radio; TV; newspapers; and flyers. Photos can be used for advance promotion.

MILLION DOLLAR MILE ART SHOW, Box 174, Havre de Grace MD 21078. (301)939-2329. Chairman: Marge Thompson. Sponsor: Soroptimist International Club. Estab. 1963. Annual outdoor show held 2 days in August. Average attendance: 20,000-25,000. Presents cash and ribbon awards.
Acceptable Work: Considers batik, candlemaking, ceramics, glass art, jewlery, leatherworking, macrame, metalsmithing, needlecrafts, pottery, scrimshaw, sculpture, weaving and woodcrafting.
Terms: Entries accepted until 2 weeks before show. Entry fee: $35/12 foot display area. Work may be offered for sale; no commission. Craftworker must attend show; demonstrations OK. Registration limit: 200. Sponsor provides fencing, insurance on exhibited work and 24-hour security.
Promotion: Show is advertised by TV, radio, art magazines, tourist listings and newspapers in Maryland, Delaware, Pennsylvania, New Jersey and Washington, DC. Craftworker should submit anything that can be used for newspaper publicity.

NATIONAL CRAFT FAIR, National Crafts Ltd., Gapland MD 21736. (301)432-8438. Director: Noel Clark. Estab. 1976. Annual indoor/outdoor show held in October 1 day wholesale and 3 days retail in Gaithersburg, Maryland. Average attendance: 15,000. Considers all crafts. Average sales/booth: $1,700.
Terms: Entries accepted until July 10, 1979. Entry fee: $75-125, plus $3 nonreturnable application fee. Entries are prejudged by 5 35mm color slides. Work must be offered for sale; no commission. Craftworker must attend show; demonstrations OK. Registration limit: 350 booths. Sponsor provides 24-hour security.
Promotion: Show is advertised by newspapers, magazines, radio, posters, brochures, TV and mailings.

PARK ARTS FESTIVAL, Box 1294, Hagerstown MD 21740. (301)791-4235. President: Mrs. Cynthia L. Staggers. Sponsor: Washington County Arts Council, Inc. Estab. 1968. Annual outdoor show is held 2 days in June. Average attendance: 10,000-15,000. Entries accepted until 3 weeks before show. Entry fee: $20/artist. Display area: space provided as necessary. Entries prejudged by slides; color photos; and personal observation whenever possible. Entry fee refunded for refused work. Work may be offered for sale; no commission. Craftworker must attend show; demonstrations OK. Registration limit: 50. Sponsor provides electricity for demonstrations; fencing; table; and 24-hour security protection. Show is advertised by newspapers; radio; TV; and brochures. Considers all crafts.

REVOLUTIONARY WAR DAYS, Tri-County Council for Southern Maryland, Box 301, Waldorf MD 20601. (301)645-2693. Tourism Planner: Clara L. Wooddy. Estab. 1967. Annual outdoor show (with tents and pavilions) held 2 days in May at Smallwood State Park, Rison, Maryland. Average attendance: 12,000.
Acceptable Work: Considers batik; candlemaking, decoupage; dollmaking; glass art; jewelry; lapidary; leatherworking; metalsmithing; needlecrafts; pottery; tole painting; weaving; woodcrafting; and any other traditional 18th century craft. "Craftsmen must demonstrate some facet of work and dress in costume. Craftsmen must provide all display material, i.e, pegboard, shelving."
Terms: Entries accepted until 4 weeks before show. Display area: 8x10' encasements. Prejudging by minimum of 3 35mm slides and resume. Work may be offered for sale; no commission. Craftworker must attend show; demonstrations required. Registration limit: 100. Sponsor provides chairs; electricity for demonstrations; fencing; table; 24-hour security; breakfast reception; and group hotel rates.
Promotion: Show is advertised by paid advertising (print only); public service announcements; press releases; feature stories; and Maryland Center for Public Broadcasting. If available craftworker should provide 35mm slides and b&w 8x10 glossies of craftworker at work.
Sales Tip: "Over the years we have established a reputation for producing a craft show which features traditional, hand-made crafts. Buyers come prepared to make major purchases. However, it is wise to have a selection of items for the modest buyers, i.e., under $10."

SPRING ARTS & CRAFTS FAIR, Sugarloaf Mountain Works, Inc., Box 319, Poolesville MD 20837. (301)279-7551. Director: Ms. Deann Verdier. See Sugarloaf Mountain Works Festival.

SPRING CRAFT FESTIVAL, Sugarloaf Mountain Works, Inc., Box 319, Poolesville MD 20837. (301)279-7551. Director: Ms. Deann Verdier. See Sugarloaf Mountain Works Festival.

SUGARLOAF MOUNTAIN WORKS CRAFT FESTIVAL, Box 319, Poolesville MD 20837. (301)279-7551. Director: Ms. Deann Verdier. Sponsor: Sugarloaf Mountain Works, Inc. Sponsors 5 annual indoor shows: Spring Arts & Crafts Fair, estab. 1976, held 3 days in April; Spring Crafts Festival, estab. 1978, held 3 days Memorial Day weekend; Maryland Craft Festival, estab. 1977, held 3 days in October; Autumn Craft Festival, estab. 1976, held 3 days in November; and Winter Crafts Festival, estab. 1978, held 3 days the first weekend in December. Average attendance for each show: 18,000.
Acceptable Work: Considers batik, candlemaking, dollmaking ("only the very best"), glass art, leatherworking, macrame, metalsmithing, mobiles, pottery, scrimshaw, sculpture, weaving and woodcrafting. "Applications will not normally be accepted in the following categories: crochet, knitting, ceramics cast from commercial molds, decoupage, embellished items, strung beads, dried flower arrangements, beaded flowers, dough art or decorated eggs. All work must be original and completely finished."
Terms: Entries accepted until filled. Entry fee: $100/8x10 or 10x10 display area. Prejudging by 4 35mm color slides representing the work to be shown. Jury slides may be left on file for future applications and possible use as promotional pictures. Work must be offered for sale; no commission. Craftworker must attend show; demonstrations encouraged. Registration limit: 250. Sponsor provides chairs at $2 each, electricity lights at $5 each, tables at $3 each and 24-hour security. "A temporary sales tax permit is issued free at the show. The 5% tax must be collected and remitted by the exhibitor. Maryland is *very* strict in enforcing the payment of this tax."
Promotion: "Baltimore and Washington love Sugarloaf shows, and last year this show was covered by all 3 TV stations. Our full-time staff will see to it that the people of Baltimore and Washington are made aware of all these popular shows."
Sales Tip: "The public in this area sees many craft shows and has come to count on the Sugarloaf Festivals for the finest in quality arts and crafts at competitive prices. To improve sales you must have a professional product, a professsional display and a professional attitude—smile, smile, smile."

WINTER CRAFTS FESTIVAL, c/o Sugarloaf Mountain Works, Inc., Box 319, Poolesville MD 20837. Director: Ms. Deann Verdier. See Sugarloaf Mountain Works Festival.

WINTER MARKET OF AMERICAN CRAFTS, Box 10, New Paltz NY 12561. (914)255-0039. Sponsor: American Craft Enterprises, Inc. Estab. 1977. Annual indoor show held 5 days (2 trade days; 2 public days) in February at Baltimore, Maryland. Average attendance: 25,000.
Acceptable Work: Considers all crafts, including handmade musical instruments. No tole painting and decoupage.
Terms: Entries accepted up until October 1 of previous year. Entry fee: approximately $175/exhibition space. Request application packet before sending material. Entries prejudged by 5 2x2 color slides; $5 nonrefundable prejudging fee. Entry fee due after prejudging. Work must be offered for sale; no commission. Craftworker must attend show; no demonstration. Registration limit: 425. Sponsor provides 24-hour security; not responsible for damage, theft, or loss of an individual's work. 1979 exhibitor sales totalled approximately $1,700,000.
Promotion: Show is advertised by multimedia press releases and advertising in local and major publications.

YE NEWE WOODLAWN CRAFTS FESTIVAL, 2131 Woodlawn Dr., Baltimore MD 21207. (301)944-7488 or 944-4942. Chairman: Phyllis Abel. Sponsor: Woodlawn Recreation & Parks Council. Estab. 1968. Annual indoor/outdoor show held 2 days during Fathers' Day Weekend. Average attendance: 5,000+. "We are adding continuous entertainment which should increase attendance and keep the crowd longer." Considers original crafts. "Many of our craftsmen have been with us for 10 years. They come from Pennsylvania, Delaware, Virginia, etc."
Terms: Write for entry deadline. Entry fee: $20/craftworker. Work may be offered for sale; no commission. Craftworker must attend show; "demonstrations are a *must*. Those exhibiting and selling only are not acceptable." Sponsor provides chairs, electricity for demonstrations, table and 24-hour security.

Massachusetts

*****ALL ARTS FESTIVAL**, Quinebaug Valley Cultural Center, Box 503, Southbridge MA 01550. (617)764-3341. General Chairman: Christine O'Brien. Sponsor: Quinebaug Valley Council for the Arts and Humanities. Estab. 1978. Annual indoor/outdoor show (juried show is indoors) held 3 days in May. Considers all crafts. No dealers.

Terms: Entries accepted until 2 weeks before show for reserved registration; entries accepted up until show, space permitting. Entry fee: $10/QVCAH member; $12/nonmember. Display area: 10'. Prejudging for juried show. Work may be offered for sale; no commission. Craftworker or representative must attend show; demonstrations encouraged. Sponsor provides fencing on reserved basis only.
Awards: Presents cash awards and ribbons.
Promotion: Show is advertised by all media. Submit resumes and any promotional information with application.

AUBURN MALL ARTS 'N CRAFTS EXPO, c/o Mall Marketing Services, Inc., 7 Goodwin Place, Boston MA 02114. President: Paul J. McDermott. Estab. 1974. Semiannual indoor show held 1 week in May and 1 week in October at Auburn, Massachusetts. Average attendance: 60,000. Considers all original crafts.
Terms: Entries accepted until 4 weeks before show or when registration limit reached. Entry fee: $60/10x10 display area. Prejuding by slides or photos; entry fee refunded for refused work. Work may be offered for sale; no commission. Craftworker must attend show; demonstrations OK. Registration limit: 50.

THE BERKSHIRE CRAFTS FAIR, Stockbridge MA 01262. Director: Paul J. Gibbons. Estab. 1973. Annual indoor show held 3 days in August at Great Barrington, Massachusetts. Average attendance: 3,000-5,000/day. Entries accepted until 4 months before show. Entry fee: $60/8x10 display area. Prejudging by 5 2x2 slides; $3 application fee. No entry fees refunded for refused work. Work may be offered for sale; no commission. Craftworker or representative must attend show; demonstrations OK. Registration limit: 95. Sponsor provides chairs; display panels; electricity for demonstrations; insurance on exhibited work; table; and 24-hour security. Show is advertised in all media. Considers all crafts including paper making, but decoupage; shell or button jewelry; silkscreening; lapidary and tole painting. 1978 show sales totalled $100,000.

BETSY ROSS ARTS & CRAFTS SHOW, Box 2204, Peabody MA 01960. (617)535-4810. President: Hal Bornstein. Treasurer: Bernice Bornstein. Sponsor: Yankee Doodle Drummer Shows Inc. Estab. 1977. Annual indoor show held 2 days in March at Woburn, Massachusetts. Average attendance: 12-40,000. Considers all crafts. No machine-made crafts or imports.
Terms: Entries accepted until show date. Entry fee: $65/12x12 display area. Prejudging by slides/photos or personal viewing. Entry fee due after prejudging. Work must be offered for sale; no commission. Craftworker must attend show; demonstrations OK. Registration limit: 300. Sponsor provides chairs, display panels, electricity for demonstrations, tables, 24-hour security, shelves, pegboard and back walls."

BOSTON CHRISTMAS CRAFT EXPO, Box 370, Farmington CT 06032. (203)224-8388. Directors: Denise Barile and Rudy Kowalczyk. Sponsor: American Craft Expositions, Inc. Estab. 1978. Annual indoor show held Thanksgiving weekend at Boston, Massachusetts. Average attendance: 28,000.
Acceptable Work: Considers batik, candlemaking, dollmaking, glass art, jewelery, leatherworking, macrame, metalsmithing, pottery, scrimshaw, sculpture, soft sculpture, weavings, woodcrafting and "other high quality craft media. No kit, manufactured or assembled items. No dealers or agents."
Terms: Entries accepted until 60 days before show, popular medias close early. Entry fee: $135 and up, depending upon size of display area. Display area: 10x10-10x20. Prejudging by 6 slides; entry fee refunded for refused work. Work must be offered for sale; no commission. Craftworker must attend show; demonstrations encouraged. Registration limit: 250. Sponsor provides 24-hour security. Rental chairs and tables available.

BOSTON SPRING CRAFTS EXPO, Box 370, Farmington CT 06032. (203)224-8388. Directors: Denise Barile and Rudy Kowalczyk. Sponsor: American Crafts Expositions, Inc. Estab. 1979. Annual indoor show held 3 days in May at Commonwealth Pier Exhibition Hall at Boston, Massachusetts. Average attendance: 25,000.
Acceptable Work: Considers batik, candlemaking, ceramics, dollmaking, glass art, jewelery, leatherworking, macrame, metalsmithing, pottery, scrimshaw, sculpture, soft sculpture, weaving, woodcrafting and "other high quality craft media. No kits, manufactured items, dealers or agents."
Terms: Entries accepted until 60 days before show. Popular medias close earlier. Entry fee:

$100 and up, depending up display area size. Display area: 10x10, 10x15 or 10x20. Prejudging by 6 slides; entry fees refunded for refused work. Work must be offered for sale; no commission. Craftworker must attend show; demonstrations encouraged. Registration limit: 250. Sponsor provides 24-hour security. Rental chairs and tables available.

BURLINGTON MALL CHILDREN'S HOUR SHOW, Rt. 1, Box 153J, Auburn NH 03032. (603)483-2742. President: Jinx Harris. Estab. 1976. Annual indoor show held 4 days in August at Burlington, Massachusetts. Average attendance: 75,000.
Acceptable Work: Considers all child-oriented crafts except ceramics; decoupage under $5; lapidary; and strung bead jewelry.
Terms: Entries accepted until 1 week before show or until filled. Entry fee: $40/8x4 display area. Prejudging by slides or photos. Work may be offered for sale; no commission. Craftworker must attend show; demonstrations OK. Registration limit: 75-80. Sponsor provides electricity for demonstrations and 24-hour security.
Promotion: Show is promoted by radio, TV and newspaper.

BURLINGTON MALL PROFESSIONAL CRAFT & SCULPTURE SHOW, Rt. 1, Box 153J, Auburn NH 03032. (603)483-2742. President: Jinx E. Harris. Estab. 1974. Annual indoor show held 4 days in January at Burlington, Massachusetts. Average attendance: 65,000.
Acceptable Work: Considers all crafts except ceramics; decoupage; lapidary; needlecrafts; strung bead jewelry or 3-D tole.
Terms: Entries accepted until 1 week before show. Entry fee: $40/8x4 display area. Prejudging by slides or photos. Work may be offered for sale; no commission, Craftworker must attend show; demonstrations OK. Registration limit: 120. Sponsor provides electricity for demonstrations and 24-hour security.
Promotion: Show is advertised by radio, TV and newspaper.

*****CHATHAM FESTIVAL OF THE ARTS**, Box 368, Chatham MA 02633. Sponsor: Creative Arts Center. Estab. 1971. Annual show held outdoors 3 days in August. Average attendance: 10,000. Entries juried in April. Entry fee: $45/100 square feet. Registration fee: $5. Prejudging by slides; if local, by samples. Entry fee refunded for refused work. Registation fee not refunded. Work may be offered for sale; no commission. Craftworker must attend show; demonstrations OK. Registration limit: 100. Sponsor provides 24-hour security; catering service; and volunteers as aides. Show is advertised by newspaper; flyers; radio; and TV. Presents 6 cash awards of $50.

THE CHRISTMAS FAIR AT PROJECT ARTS CENTER, Project, Inc., 141 Huron Ave., Cambridge MA 02138. (617)491-0187. Executive Director: Sandy Schafer. Estab. 1969. Annual crafts show and sale held indoors 4 weeks in December. Average attendance: 1,000. Entries accepted until show date. No entry fee. Prejudging by slides; photos; or actual work. Work may be offered for sale; 30% commission. Craftworker needn't attend show; demonstration OK. Show is advertised by mailing lists; public relations lists; and paid advertising. Considers all crafts but decoupage; needlecrafts; and tole painting. 1977 show sales totalled $7,000.

CONTEMPORARY CRAFTS SHOWCASE WITH ART AT THE WORCESTER CENTER, Box 3845, Indialantic FL 32903. (212)884-7952. President: Michael Picow. Sponsor: Prema Productions. Estab. 1977. Annual indoor show held 5 days in May at Worcester, Massachusetts. Average attendance: 15,000.
Acceptable Work: Considers all crafts except decoupage, dollmaking, mobiles and lapidary. No commercial casts or kits, machine-made items, coin jewelry or paintings on stones. "All displays must be neat and professional looking."
Terms: Entries accepted until 4 weeks before show. Entry fee: $65/8x10 display area, $90/8x15 display area, and $115/8x20 display area. Prejudging by 35mm slides—3 of actual work and 1 of display. Entry fee refunded for refused work. Work may be offered for sale; no commission. Craftworker must attend show; demonstrations OK. Registration limit: 80. Sponsor provides electricity for demonstrations and 24-hour security.
Promotion: Show is advertised by local newspapers, radio and posters. "8x10 b&w glossy photos would be helpful" for promotional purposes.

*****CRAFT ADVENTURE**, 1305 Memorial Ave., West Springfield MA 01089. (413)732-2361. Director: Helen H. Bardwell. Sponsor: Eastern States Exposition. Estab. early 1950s. Annual indoor show held 1 day in September; "all winning entries displayed for the duration of the 12-day fair." Average attendance: 1,000.

Acceptable Work: Considers macrame, needlecrafts, rugs, needlepoint, crewel and weavings.
Terms: Entries accepted until 3 weeks before show. Maximum 2 pieces/craftworker. Craftworker needn't attend show. Sponsor provides insurance on exhibited work and 24-hour security.
Promotion: Show is advertised by brochures; TV; press; local ads; and posters.
Awards: Presents $10 1st prize and ribbon; $7 2nd prize and ribbon; $5 third prize and ribbon; and honorable mention ribbon. Also presents The Judges Choice Trophy; Best of Show Exposition Rosette; and special awards given by craft designers and supplier.

CRAFT CENTER FAIR, 25 Sagamore Rd., Worcester MA 01605. (617)753-8183. Contact: John Russell. Sponsor: Craft Center. Estab. 1969. Annual indoor/outdoor show with tents held 2 days in May. Attendance: 6,000-8,000. Considers all crafts except decoupage and tole painting.
Terms: Entries accepted until 3 months before show. Prejudging fee: $5. Display area: 6x8, indoor; 8x10, outdoor. Prejuding by slides; no prejudging fees refunded for refused work. Work must be offered for sale; no commission. Craftworker must attend show; demonstrations OK. Registration limit: 145. Sponsor provides electricity for demonstrations, fencing, 24-hour security, camping space and food.

CRAFT FAIR, 36 Hammond St., Acton MA 01720. (617)263-7243. Show Director: William N. Clark. Estab. 1977. Annual indoor show held 2 days in November at Andover, Massachusetts. Considers all crafts.
Terms: Entries accepted up until show date. Entry fee: $50-100/display area. Prejudging by slides and photos. Work may be offered for sale; no commission. Craftworker or representative must attend show; demonstrations OK. Registration limit: 75. Sponsor provides electricity for demonstrations at $10 extra; table; and 24-hour security.
Promotion: Show is advertised by newspaper; radio; and news releases. Submit b&w glossy; if accepted for general advertising, a negative and short biography will be requested.

CRAFT FAIR, 36 Hammond St., Acton MA 01720. (617)263-7243. Show Director: William N. Clark. Estab. 1977. Annual indoor show held 2 days in November at Boxborough, Massachusetts. Considers all crafts.
Terms: Entries accepted up until show date. Entry fee: $50-100/display area. Prejudging by slides and photos. Work may be offered for sale; no commission. Craftworker or representative must attend show; demonstrations OK. Registration limit: 130. Sponsor provides electricity for demonstrations at $10 extra; table; and 24-hour security.
Promotion: Show is advertised by newspaper and news releases. Submit b&w glossy; if accepted for general advertising, a negative and short biography will be requested.

DEDHAM MALL ARTS 'N CRAFTS EXPO, c/o Mall Marketing Services, Inc., 7 Goodwin Place, Boston MA 02114. (617)523-3366. President: Paul J. McDermott. Estab. 1979. Semiannual indoor show held 1 week in May and 1 week in December. Considers all original crafts.
Terms: Entries accepted until 4 weeks before show or when registration limit reached. Entry fee: $60/10x10 display area. Prejudging by slides and/or photos; entry fee refunded for refused work. Work may be offered for sale; no commission. Craftworker must attend show; demonstrations OK. Registration limit: 50.

EASTFIELD MALL ARTS FESTIVAL, Rt. 1, Box 153J, Auburn NH 03032. (603)483-2742. President: Jinx Harris. Estab. 1968. Annual indoor show held 4 days in September at Springfield, Massachusetts. Average attendance: 40,000.
Acceptable Work: Considers all crafts except ceramics; decoupage under $5; lapidary; and strung bead jewelry.
Terms: Entries accepted until 1 week before show or until filled. Entry fee: $40/8x4' display area. Prejudging by slides or photos if not in a previous show. Work may be offered for sale; no commission. Craftworker must attend show; demonstrations OK. Registration limit: 30. Sponsor provides electricity for demonstrations and 24-hour security.

FALL ARTS & CRAFTS MARKET, 361 Washington St., Brookline MA 02146. (617)734-0100. President: Susan Radonsky. Secretary: Judy Jackson Long. Sponsor: Brookline Art Society. Estab. 1950. Annual outdoor show held 1 day in September at Chestnut Hill, Massachusetts. Average attendance: 1,000-2,000. Entries accepted until 2 weeks before show. Entry fee: $20/10x6 display area. Work may be offered for sale; no commission. Craftworker must attend show; demonstrations encouraged. Registration limit: 60. Sponsor provides security. Show is advertised by newspapers; flyers; posters; radio; and *Boston* magazine. Considers all crafts.

LONDONDERRY FAIRE, Rt. 1, Box 153J, Auburn NH 03032. (603)483-2742. President: Jinx Harris. Estab. 1974. Annual indoor show held 3 days in November at Boston, Massachusetts. Average attendance: 75,000.
Acceptable Work: Considers all crafts except ceramics; decoupage under $5; lapidary; and strung bead jewelry.
Terms: Entries accepted until 1 week before show or until filled. Entry fee: $125/10x10 display area. Prejudging by slides or photos if not in a previous show. Work may be offered for sale; no commission. Craftworker must attend show; demonstrations OK. Registration limit: 176. Sponsor provides electricity for demonstrations and 24-hour security.
Promotion: Show is advertised by radio; TV; and newspapers.

MARTHA'S VINEYARD CRAFTSMEN FAIR, c/o Ayn Chase, Box 1207, Wesley House Hotel, Oak Bluffs MA 02557. (617)693-0134. Manager: Ayn Chase. Purpose: "The show is designed mainly for Martha's Vineyard Island craftsmen. It is kept small and 1 or more crafts is represented by each craftsman. Many crafts are displayed and sold." Estab. 1968. Annual indoor show held 3 days in July. Average attendance: 5,000 and up. Entry fee: $16.50/3x5 display area; $26.50/3x10 display area. SASE with inquiry. Work may be offered for sale; no commission. Craftworker must attend show; demonstrations OK. Registration limit: 12-15. Sponsor provides chairs; display panels; electricity for demonstrations; insurance on exhibited work; table; and 24-hour security. Show is advertised by newspapers; radio; Cape Cod advertising; posters; and flyers. Considers all crafts. 1977 show sales totalled $8,000.

*****MATTOON ARTS FESTIVAL**, Box 3274, Springfield MA 01105. (413)737-0645. Co-Chairman: Lydia Campanini. Sponsor: Mattoon Street Historic Preservation Association. Estab. 1972. Annual outdoor show held 2 days in September. Average attendance: 15,000. Entries accepted until June 15. Entry fee: $25/10x10 display area. Prejudging by slides; entry fee refunded for refused work. Work should be offered for sale; no commission. Craftworker must attend show; demonstrations OK. Registration limit: 100. Sponsor provides fencing if needed; insurance on exhibited work; and security protection. Show is advertised by local and regional media. Submit promotional materials at request of Committee. Categories: fine arts and crafts. Considers all crafts.

MOUNT HOLYOKE COLLEGE PEDDLER'S FAIR, c/o Show Chairman, South Hadley MA 01075. Sponsor: Mount Holyoke Sophomore Class. Estab. 1970. Annual indoor show held 1 day in December. Average attendance: 1,500. Considers all crafts.
Terms: Entry applications sent to craftworkers by May; deadline, early September. Entry fee: $20/3x8 table, larger upon request. Prejudging by application, slides and/or past participation. SASE. Entry fee due after prejudging. Work may be offered for sale; no commission. Craftworker or representative must attend show; demonstrations encouraged. Registration limit: 80. Sponsor provides chairs, electricity for demonstrations, table, security during show, student help and snack bar.
Promotion: Show is advertised by posters, college news, local newspapers and radio. Show participants given news release to submit to their area media. "Any promotional work done by artist on his own is greatly appreciated."

NATICK MALL CHILDREN'S HOUR SHOW, Rt. 1, Box 153J, Auburn NH 03032. (603)483-2742. President: Jinx Harris. Estab. 1977. Annual indoor show held 4 days in April at Natick, Massachusetts. Average attendance: 50,000.
Acceptable Work: Considers all child-oriented crafts but ceramics; decoupage under $5; lapidary; and strung bead jewelry.
Terms: Entries accepted until 1 week before show or until filled. Entry fee: $40/8x4 display area. Prejudging by slides or photos if not in a previous show. Work may be offered for sale; no commission. Craftworker must attend show; demonstrations OK. Registration limit: 50. Sponsor provides electricity for demonstrations and 24-hour security.
Promotion: Show is advertised by radio; TV; and newspapers.

NATICK MALL CRAFT & SCULPTURE SHOW, Rt. 1, Box 153J, Auburn NH 03032. (603)483-2742. President: Jinx Harris. Estab. 1975. Annual indoor show held 4 days in July at Natick, Massachusetts. Average attendance: 60,000.

Acceptable Work: Considers all crafts except ceramics; decoupage under $5; lapidary; and strung bead jewelry.
Terms: Entries accepted until 1 week before show or until filled. Entry fee: $40/8x4 display area. Prejudging by slides or photos if not in a previous show. Work may be offered for sale; no commission. Craftworker must attend show; demonstrations OK. Registration limit: 100. Sponsor provides electricity for demonstrations and 24-hour security.
Promotion: Show is advertised by radio, TV and newspapers.

NEW ENGLAND BUYERS' MARKET PLACE, 205 N. Main St., Concord NH 03301. (603)224-3375. Purpose: "to provide professional craftpersons in the New England area an event of high quality in which to participate and sell their work. This show will be a wholesale only show." Estab. 1977. Annual indoor show held 3 days in April at Boston. Average attendance: 500-1,000. Entries accepted until October. Entry fee: approximately $100/10x10 display area. Prejudging by 5 slides, application form and $5 prejudging fee; entry fee due after prejudging. Work may be offered for sale; no commission. Craftworker must attend show; no demonstrations. Registration limit: 275-300. Show is advertised by craft publications; press releases; and direct mail campaign to 5,000 buyers across the country. Considers all crafts produced by craftworkers from Maine, Massachusetts, Vermont and New Hampshire. 1977 exhibit sales exceeded $500,000.

*NEW ENGLAND ARTIST FESTIVAL & SHOWCASE, Arts Extension Service/Division of Continuing Education, University of Massachusetts, Amherst MA 01003. (413)545-2813. Director: Bob Lynch. Estab. 1976. Annual outdoor show (some booths under tents) held 3 days in May at Northampton. Average attendance: 15,000.
Acceptable Work: Considers all crafts. No kits, machine-made work or imports. "Pieces submitted to the Visual Arts and Crafts Gallery at the festival must be prepared for display (e.g., flatwork framed or mounted)."
Terms: Entries accepted until 4 months before show. Entry fee: $35-55/display area; $3/processing fee. Display area: 10'x10'. Entries juried by slides. Entry fee due after jurying. Work must be offered for sale; no commission. Craftworker must attend show; demonstrations OK. Registration limit: 200. Sponsor provides coverings, electricity for demonstrations, insurance on exhibited work and 24-hour security. Exhibitors handle sales and sales taxes.
Awards: $1,500 total in gallery prizes and booth design awards. "Booth design awards are given with consideration to ease and attractiveness for marketing success and visual appeal." Judges choose 10-15 awards "of equal value to be given to pieces in the gallery, those demonstrating technical and aesthetic proficiency and originality."
Promotion: "All media are utilized. The NEAFAS is produced with the cooperation of the Valley Advocate Newspaper with distribution in the Amherst-Greenfield area; Springfield; and Hartford and New Haven, Connecticut. Radio, printed material and TV are strongly utilized throughout Western Massachusetts, in Southern New Hampshire and Vermont, and in Connecticut and Rhode Island. Artists may have whatever printed promo materials they'd like in their booths. Photos for press releases and printed material for our files is always helpful.
Sales Tip: "With 200-275 exhibitors, an attractive booth design can definitely increase sales by making an exhibit stand out from the rest. The viewing public buys the usual assortment of crafts, with last year's survey showing glass and leather in the lead. Large expensive items (e.g., furniture) do less business. The 1978 show figures indicated an average sale of $500/exhibitor, for a total of $91,000 (182 exhibitors)."

NEW ENGLAND CRAFT EXPO, Box 370, Farmington CT 06032. (203)224-8388. Directors: Denise Barile and Rudy Kowalczyk. Sponsor: American Craft Expositions, Inc. Estab. 1977. Annual indoor/outdoor show held 3 days in July at Topsfield, Massachusetts. Average attendance: 24,000.
Acceptable Work: Considers batik, candlemaking, dollmaking, glass art, jewelry, leatherworking, macrame, metalsmithing, pottery, scrimshaw, sculpture, soft sculpture, weavings, woodcrafting and "other high quality craft media. No kit, manufactured or assembled items. No dealers or agents."
Terms: Entries accepted until 60 days before show, popular medias close earlier. Entry fee: $75 and up, depending upon size of display area. Display area: 10x10-10x20. Prejudging by 6 slides; entry fee refunded for refused work. Work must be offered for sale; no commission. Craftworker must attend show; demonstrations encouraged. Registration limit: 250. Sponsor pro-

---

* Those listings preceded by an asterisk present awards for prize-winning crafts.

vides 24-hour security. Rental chairs and tables available.

NORTHSHORE PLAZA ARTS FESTIVAL, Rt. 1, Box 153J, Auburn NH 03032. (603)483-2742. President: Jinx Harris. Estab. 1977. Annual indoor show held 4 days in May at Peabody, Massachusetts. Average attendance: 60,000.
Acceptable Work: Considers all crafts except ceramics; decoupage under $5; lapidary; strung bead jewelry; and 3-D tole.
Terms: Entries accepted until 1 week before show or until filled. Entry fee: $40/8x4 display area. Prejudging by slides or photos if not in a previous show. Work may be offered for sale; no commission. Craftworker must attend show; demonstrations OK. Registration limit: 40. Sponsor provides electricity for demonstrations and 24-hour security.
Promotion: Show is advertised by radio, TV and newspapers.

OLD DEERFIELD CRAFT FAIR, c/o Memorial Hall Museum, Deerfield MA 01342. (413)773-8929. Contact: Tim Neumann. Estab. 1976. Semiannual outdoor show held 2 days in July and 2 days in October. Average attendance: 10,000. Entries accepted up until show date. Entry fee: $30/10x10 display area. Prejudging by 3 slides or photos; entry fee refunded for refused work. Work may be offered for sale; no commission. Craftworker must attend show; demonstrations OK. Registration limit: 80. Show is advertised by radio and newspapers. Considers all crafts.

*PEMBROKE ARTS FESTIVAL, 48 Congress St., Pembroke MA 02359. Contact: Ann Wilcox. Entry fee: $3/entry. Considers sculpture. Open to New England artists only. Work may be offered for sale; 30% commission. Presents $150, $100 and $50 cash prizes; $100 in purchase prizes; and a $50 popular prize.

WORCESTER CENTER ARTS 'N CRAFTS EXPO, c/o Mall Marketing Services, Inc., 7 Goodwin Place, Boston MA 02114. (617)523-3366. President: Paul J. McDermott. Estab. 1974. Semiannual indoor show held 1 week in February/March and 1 week in November. Considers all crafts.
Terms: Entries accepted until 4 weeks before show or when registration limit reached. Entry fee: $60/10x10 display area. Prejudging by slides and/or photos; entry fee refunded for refused work. Work may be offered for sale; no commission. Craftworker must attend show; demonstrations OK. Registration limit: 60.

WORCESTER CRAFT CENTER FAIR, 25 Sagamore Rd., Worcester MA 01605. (617)753-8153. Coordinator: Jack Russell. Estab. 1970. Annual indoor/outdoor show (with 2 large tents, open booths and a building) held 2 days the end of May. Average attendance: 6,000. Considers all crafts.
Terms: Entries accepted until approximately 3 months before show. Entry fee: $65, indoors; $55, tent space; $30, outside. Display area: 6x8. Prejudging by 5 slides accompanied by $5 nonrefundable applications fee. Work must be offered for sale; no commission. Craftworker or representative must attend show; demonstrations OK. Registration limit: 125. Sponsor provides electricity for demonstrations and 24-hour security.
Promotion: Show is advertised by newspapers, radio, flyers, posters and TV. "A request is made to the craftsmen to provide interesting data for publicity."

Michigan

ALGONAC ART FAIR, Box 422, Algonac MI 48001. (313)794-5296, after 6. Artist Chairman: Vonnie Breck. Sponsor: Algonac Sponsors of the Arts. Purpose: "to stimulate the cultural climate of our community and give good artists of the surrounding areas an outlet for their art." Estab. 1973. Annual outdoor show (with parachutes for cover, color, and attention) held 2 days Labor Day weekend. Average attendance: 5,000. Entries accepted until 2 weeks before show. Entry fee: $15/10x10 display area. Prejudging by slides; photos; recommendation by known artist; and/or personal knowledge by committee. Entry fee due after prejudging. Work may be offered for sale; no commission. Craftworker must attend show; demonstrations encouraged. Registration limit: 175. Sponsor provides electricity for demonstrations; fencing; and 24-hour security. Show is advertised by posters; flyers; newspaper; radio; and postcards. Categories: marine art; wood; weaving; oils; acrylics; watercolors; pen and ink; photography; jewelry; glass; sculpture; pottery; metal art; leather; musical instruments; and Indian art. Considers all crafts but candlemaking; decoupage; dollmaking; and lapidary.

ALL CRAFTS FAIR, 535 Quaker St., South Haven MI 49090. (616)637-1450. Executive Vice

President: A.W. Roberts. Sponsor: Greater South Haven Area Chamber of Commerce. Estab. 1977. Annual outdoor show (indoor alternate for rain) held the Sunday of Labor Day weekend. Average attendance: 5,000. Entries accepted until 1 week before show. Entry fee: $10/10x10 display area. Work may be offered for sale; no commission. Craftworker must attend show; demonstrations OK. Show is advertised by handouts; radio; newspaper; and TV. Considers all crafts.

*ALPENA ART SHOW, 1100 Wayne Rd., Alpena MI 49707. (517)356-0924. Contact: Carol Nadeau. Sponsor: Alpena Chamber of Commerce. Estab. 1977. Annual outdoor show held 2 days in July. "Artists may set up outside or in Pavillion." Average attendance: 5,000.
Acceptable Work: Considers batik, glass art, jewelry, lapidary, metalsmithing, pottery, scrimshaw, sculpture, weaving and woodcrafting. No commercial settings or fittings in jewelry or lapidary. Categories include sculpture, jewelry, mixed media, fiber, pottery, prints, photography and paintings.
Terms: Entries accepted until 4 weeks before show. Entry fee: $10/adult, $5/junior entry, $25/group. Display area: 15x15. Prejudging by 3 slides or photos. Entry fee refunded for refused work. Work may be offered for sale; no commission. Craftworker or representative must attend show; demonstrations OK. Registration limit: 100. Sponsor provides electricity for demonstrations. Artist provides own extension cords, props, etc.
Awards: Presents $10 1st prize in each category; ribbons for 1st, 2nd and 3rd in each category; and plaque for Best of Show.

THE ANN ARBOR STREET ART FAIR, Box 1352, Ann Arbor MI 48106. Purpose: "The Fair was organized to bring a showing of high quality arts and crafts to the community." Estab. 1959. Annual outdoor show held 4 days in July. Mailing list for application closed February 1; other deadlines listed in material sent to applicants. Entry fee: $4/jury fee; $40/artist. Display area: 10x10 for 2 artists. Prejudging by 5 slides in up to 3 media. No admission fees refunded. Work may be offered for sale; 3% commission. Craftworker must attend show; demonstrations by invitation.
Acceptable Work: Considers batik; ceramics; glass art; jewelry; metalsmithing; pottery; sculpture; soft sculpture; weaving; and woodcrafting.

ART GO ROUND, Box 142, Lapeer MI 48446. Sponsor: Lapeer Fine Arts Council. Estab. 1970. Annual outdoor show held 2 days in June. Average attendance: 5,000. Considers all crafts. "Everything must be handcrafted by exhibiting artist." Bestsellers: inexpensive smaller pieces. Entries accepted until show date. Entry fee: $10/artist. Display area: 6x8. Work may be offered for sale; 10% commission. Sponsor provides electricity for demonstrations and 24-hour security. Treasurer of Fine Arts Council handles sales and taxes. Send 8x10 glossy photos for promotional purposes.

"ART IN THE PARK", The Page Building, Lake Odessa MI 48849. (616)374-7455. Contact: Co-Chairperson. Sponsor: Lake Odessa Arts Commission. Estab. 1975. Annual outdoor show held the first Saturday in July (regardless of weather). Average attendance: 3,000-5,000.
Acceptable Work: Considers all crafts. No kits. Bestsellers: woodwork, jewelry and toys.
Terms: Entries accepted until show date; prefers early registration. Entry fee: $5/artist ("fee may increase"). Work must be offered for sale or order; no commission. Demonstrations encouraged. "The craftworker (unless unusual circumstances prohibit his being there) must attend and show his own work. If the work is on consignment, the artist's permission to display must be hand-written to the co-chairperson." Sponsor provides assistance in setting up. Exhibitor handles sales and taxes.
Promotion: Show is advertised by TV, radio, posters, newspapers, community bulletins and art calendars. "If the artist can provide brief summaries of his craft, his background (i.e., what led him to his work) and/or his art calendar for the year, these could be used in a promotional manner."

ART ON THE ROCKS, Box 805, Marquette MI 49855. President: Mary Frey. Sponsor: Lake Superior Art Association. Estab. 1959. Annual outdoor show held 2 days in July. Average attendance: 2,000.
Acceptable Work: Considers batik, glass art, jewelry, lapidary, leatherworking, macrame, metalsmithing, needlecrafts, pottery, sculpture, soft sculpture, weaving and woodcrafting. No copies, kits, decorated manufactured items, plants, food and crafts made from commercially-made products (jewelry mountings, greenware).

Deborah Farber-Isaacson, Exhibition Coordinator for Adult Toys, suggests that a craftworker display a broad range of sizes, colors and price ranges for best sales. This fiber doll is only one of the items displayed for adult enjoyment. The exhibition, sponsored by Mindscape Gallery and Studio, is held in Evanston, Illinois.

Terms: Entries accepted until 4 weeks before show. Entry fee: $15/12x12 display area. Prejudging by 35mm slides. Entry fee refunded for refused work. Work may be offered for sale; no commission. Craftworker must attend show; demonstrations OK.

ARTS & CRAFTS FAIR, 210 W. Hosmer, St. Charles MI 48655. Chairperson: Rebecca Wetmore. Sponsor: Wednesday Study Club. Annual indoor show held 3 days in April. Average attendance: 200-400.
Acceptable Work: Considers ceramics, glass art, jewelry, leatherworking, macrame, metalsmithing, needlecrafts, sculpture and woodcrafting.
Terms: Local craftworkers only. Entries accepted until show date. No entry fee. Work cannot be offered for sale. Craftworker needn't attend show; demonstrations OK. Registration limit: 75-100. Sponsor provides chairs, display panels, electricity for demonstrations and table.

***ARTS & CRAFTS OUTDOOR EXHIBIT**, 520 Oak St., Dundee MI 48131. Corresponding Secretary: Mrs. Roger LaVoy. Sponsor: Dundee Arts & Crafts Club. Estab. 1962. Annual outdoor show held 1 day in July. Average attendance: 2,000. Presents ribbons.
Acceptable Work: Considers all crafts. Work must be made by artist and shown in his name.
Terms: Entries accepted until 1 week before show. Entry fee: $10/4x8' display area. Work may be offered for sale; no commission. Craftworker must attend show; demonstrations OK.

ARTS & CRAFTS SHOW, Box 405, Munising MI 49862. (906)387-2138. Manager: Margarette E. La Mothe. Sponsor: Alger Chamber of Commerce. Estab. 1975. Annual outdoor show (indoor if inclement weather) held 2 days in late July. Average attendence: 1,000-2,000. Considers all handmade crafts. No kits.
Terms: Entries accepted until 1 week before show. Entry fee charged. Work must be offered for sale; no commission. Craftworker must attend show; demonstrations OK. Sponsor provides electricity for demonstrations.

*ARTS FETE, 1209 Turner, Lansing MI 48906. (517)372-6064. Manager: Dick Titus. President of Historical Society: Geneva K. Wiskemann. Sponsor: Historical Society of Greater Lansing (Box 12095, Lansing MI 48901). Estab. 1976. Annual outdoor show held 2 days in August. Average attendance: 5,000.
Acceptable Work: Considers all crafts. "All work must be original creations—no kits, machine-made crafts or Indian jewelry which is not authenticated. The artist is responsible for hanging items."
Terms: Entries accepted until 2 weeks before show. Entry fee: $45/display area. Prejudging by 35mm color slides. Entry fee refunded for refused work. Work must be offered for sale; 10% commission. "The fee may be increased and the percentage discontinued." Sponsor provides 24-hour security, emergency care, discounts on food services, assistance with housing, liability insurance, recreation program for children, tours and assistance in unloading.
Awards: Presents ribbons. "Competition is excellent so bring your best. Judges are volunteer professionals from outstanding studios, colleges, universities and successful galleries."
Promotion: Show is advertised by statewide media—radio, TV, newspaper, special interest periodicals and local calendars of events. "Good quality color slides suitable for TV airing assist in promoting the kind of work available at show. Details of work experience, special awards earned and unique character of work assists in preparation of releases."
Sales Tip: "Attractive, uncluttered, securely mounted displays and a cheerful attitude makes for a happy event and best sales. In 1978, fine art, sculpted copper, ceramics, wood carvings and violins brought top prices."
Profile: The show takes place in "Dodge Park on the lawn of the Turner Dodge House, a National Register location. There are food services, free tours of the historic house and a concert."

BLOOM 'N CRAFTS, 28500 Alden, Madison Heights MI 48071. (313)545-5585. Office Manager: Marcia Smith. Sponsor: Madison Heights Community Education. Estab. 1977. Annual indoor show held 1 day in October. Average attendance: about 1,000-1,500. Considers all handmade crafts. Show is advertised by posters, newspaper publicity, radio and TV.
Terms: Entries accepted until 3 weeks before show. Entry fee: $15 for 1 table, plus another $10 for each additional table. Display area: 6'. Prejudging by slides, photos or appointment. Entry fee due after prejudging. Work must be offered for sale; no commission. Craftworker or representative must attend show; demonstrations OK. Sponsor provides tables and chairs.

BROOKLYN ARTISTS ROSE FESTIVAL, FINE ARTS & CRAFTS SHOW & SALE, 6250 N. Lake Rd., Clark Lake MI 49234. (517)529-9144. Secretary: Grace E. McCourtie. Estab. 1973. Annual outdoor show held 1 day in June at Brooklyn, Michigan. Average attendance: 5,000. Entries accepted until 3 weeks before show; $5 late entry fee. Entry fee: $10/artist. Display area: 15x15. Prejudging by slides or photos; entry fee refunded for refused work. Work may be offered for sale; no commission. Craftworker must attend show; demonstrations OK. Registration limit: 50. Show is advertised by TV; radio; and newspapers.
Acceptable Work: Considers batik; candlemaking; ceramics; glass art; jewelry; lapidary; leatherworking; macrame; metalsmithing; pottery; sculpture; soft sculpture; weaving; and woodcrafting.

*CADILLAC FESTIVAL OF THE ARTS, Box 841, Cadillac MI 49601. (616)775-0031. Contact: Arts Coordinator. Sponsor: Cadillac Area Artists Association and Cadillac Area Council for the Arts. Estab. 1969. Annual outdoor show held 1 day in July. Average attendance: 10,000.
Acceptable Work: Considers batik, candlemaking, ceramics, glass art, jewelry, leatherworking, macrame, metalsmithing, mobiles, pottery, scrimshaw, sculpture, soft sculpture, weaving and woodcrafting. No kits, tole painting, country painting, decoupage, dried flowers, Indian jewelry, strung beads not made by artist, mass-produced buckles and hobbycraft.
Terms: Entries accepted until 10 weeks before show. Entry fee: $8/12x12' display area. Prejudging by 3-5 slides; include SASE. Entry fee refunded for refused work. Work must be offered for sale; no commission. Craftworker must attend show; demonstrations OK. Registration limit: 100. Sponsor provides electricity for demonstrations, free coffee and donuts.
Promotion: Show is advertised by radio, TV, posters, street banner, restaurant and motel signs, newspaper ads, and notices mailed with bank statements in Cadillac area banks. "Ten days before the show, area newspapers print a photo and caption of artist and work—one each day until the fair."
Awards: Presents $25 in cash awards for best of clay. Other awards possible.
Profile: Fair has "strolling minstrels, music, dance and other presentations occuring throughout the day. Area service organizations sponsor chicken barbeque, taco stands, ice cream social, beer and other fast foods."

Shows and Fairs 517

CHARLEVOIX WATERFRONT ART FAIR, Box 126, Charlevoix MI 49720. (616)547-4204. Director: Suzi Reis. Charlevoix Chamber of Commerce. Estab. 1958. Annual outdoor show held 1 day in August. Average attendance: 10,000. Sales totalled $70,000 for 1978.
Acceptable Work: Considers all crafts. No kits, machine-made crafts, prefabricated jewelry, candles, artifical flowers, molds, melted bottles or barnwood paintings.
Terms: Entries accepted until about 3 month before show. Entry fee: $20/10' display area. Prejudging by slides. Entry fee refunded for refused work. Work must be offered for sale; no commission. Craftworker must attend show; demonstrations OK. Registration limit: 150. Sponsor provides electricity for demonstrations and 24-hour security. Chamber of Commerce handles sales and taxes.
Promotion: Show is advertised by reputation, TV, radio, posters and newspapers. Send resume or brochure for promotional purposes.

CHRISTMAS CRAFT AND HOBBY SHOW, Grand Haven Community Center, 421 Columbus St., Grand Haven MI 49417. (616)842-2550. Director: Jo Ennenga. Estab. 1973. Annual indoor show held 2 days the first weekend in December. Average attendance: 2,500. Considers all crafts.
Terms: Entries accepted until 3 weeks before show. Entry fee: $1/foot. Display area: single, 6'; double, 12'. Work may be offered for sale; no commission. Registration limit: 48. Craftworker must attend show; demonstrations OK. Sponsor provides chairs, electricity for demonstrations, table and 24-hour security. Exhibitors handle own sales and taxes.
Promotion: Show is advertised by radio, newspaper, posters and direct mail. "We do this as a service to the community. The local people look forward to this as a means of gift shopping prior to Christmas."

COAST GUARD FESTIVAL CRAFTS FAIR, 1 Washington St., Grand Haven MI 49417. (616)842-4910. Contact: Director. Estab. 1972. Annual outdoor show held 2 days in August. Average attendance: 100,000. Considers all crafts.
Terms: Entries accepted until the end of June. Display area: 15x15. Prejudging by slides and photos. Work may be offered for sale; no commission. Craftworker must attend show. Registration limit: 110.

*COPPER COUNTRY GALLERY, 401 Dodge St., Houghton MI 49931. (906)482-8316. Chairperson: Mary Ann Predebon. Estab. 1977. Annual indoor show held 5 days in the spring at Hancock, Michigan (first day is devoted to set-up and opening). Average atteedance: 4,000. Show is advertised by newspapers, 3 local radio stations and posters.
Acceptable Work: Considers batik, glass art, jewelry, lapidary, leatherworking, macrame, metalsmithing, mobiles, needlecrafts, pottery, scrimshaw, sculpture, soft sculpture, weaving and woodcrafting. "No hobby crafts such as doll clothes, painted rocks, painted wood, plastercraft or poured ceramics. Two-dimensional work must be framed (except for weaving). Display will be handled by committee."
Terms: Entries accepted until 2 weeks before show. Entry fee: $20/craftworker. Display area: 10x10. Maximum 5 works/craftworker. Prejudging by slides; entry fee refunded for refused work. Work may be offered for sale; no commission. Craftworker needn't attend show; no demonstrations. Registration limit: 35. Sponsor provides chairs, display panels, insurance on exhibited work, table and 24-hour security.
Awards: Presents $100 Best of Show, $75 1st, $50 2nd and $25 3rd place prizes in both 2 and 3-dimensional categories. "The 5 pieces entered should reflect the more serious efforts of the artist showing craftsmanship, maturity of artist and mastery of media used (non-production-type work)."
Sales Tip: "Weavings are very popular. Functional works sell best of crafts (a conservative community). Works sell better if artist is on location occasionally. Opening reception will be held on first day for all participating artists and invited local patrons and professional people. Central sales desk will be provided and manned by arts council members. Sales tax will be charged and individual artist must file either on his own number or temporary permit."

CRAFT CARNIVAL V, Holy Innocents Academy, 23601 Ann Arbor Trail, Dearborn Heights, MI 48127. Mail to: 8319 Faust St., Detroit MI 48228. Director: Frances M. Palmatier. Estab. 1976. Annual indoor show held the Saturday after Thanksgiving. Average attendance: 4,000.
Acceptable Work: Considers handmade items, no kits. No flea market vendors and antique dealers.
Terms: Entries accepted until 11 weeks before show (¾ are invitational). Entry fee: $20/display area in main gym (with table & electricity); $15/display area in lower gym and annex (without

table). Electricity available on all levels—restricted to wall space only. Prejudging by personal interview or photos. Entry fee due after prejudging. Work must be offered for sale; no commission. Craftworker must attend show; demonstrations welcomed (if reservation is made with request). Registration limit: 105. Type of art and craft is limited to offer best variety. Sponsor provides chairs, electricity for demonstrations, table, and coffee and donuts during set-up time.
Promotion: Show is advertised by newspapers, radio, TV, magazines, community calendars, flyers and post card invitations. "Artists should be available for newspaper coverage and TV demonstrations if called on for morning shows. Also, the artist will be provided with printed advertising and all are asked to distribute them at shows prior to the Craft Carnival."
Sales Tips: "Over the past 4 shows, crafts to expensive metal sculpture was sold. Most were Christmas shopping with this show the only one in the area on this date year after year."

CURWOOD FESTIVAL ARTS & CRAFTS MARKET, 709 Lincoln Ave., Owasso MI 48867. Chairman: Thelma Reef. Sponsor: Shiawassee Arts Council. Estab. 1978. Annual outdoor show held 2 days in June on the lawn of Curwood Castle. Average attendance: 10,000.

*****DANISH FESTIVAL ARTS & CRAFTS SHOW**, Danish Festival, Inc., 302 S. Lafayette St., Greenville MI 48838. (616)754-6369. Managing Director: Mrs. Bart Fries. Estab. 1969. Annual outdoor show held 2 days in August. Average attendance: 50,000/day. Entries accepted until 3 weeks before show. Entry fee: $15/1 day; $25/2 days. Display area: 10x10. Prejudging by description of articles to be displayed; photos helpful but not necessary. Entry fee refunded for refused work. Work may be offered for sale; no commission. Craftworker must attend show; demonstrations encouraged. Registration limit: 130. Sponsor provides 24-hour security. Categories: artists/craftworker section and handcrafters section. Considers all crafts. Presents plaques and ribbons.
Promotion: Show is advertised by listings in numerous art magazines; and extensive coverage in state-wide radio, TV, and newspapers. "We also print a beautiful brochure which is sent to approximately 20,000 potential visitors." Uses some photos of work for publicity.
Sales Tip: If craftworker doesn't have sales tax license may use Show's for $1 which is collected with the application and entry fee.

DOWNTOWN BAY CITY SIDEWALK DAYS, 409 Bay City Bank Bldg., Bay City MI 48706. (517)893-3573. Administrative Assistant: Linda Lockard. Sponsor: Downtown Bay City, Inc. Estab. 1963. Annual outdoor show held 3 days in July. Average attendance: 150,000. Entries accepted until 1 week before show. Entry fee: $5/day. Display area: approximately 6x9. Work may be offered for sale; no commission. Craftworker must attend show; no demonstrations. Registration limit: 30-40. Show is advertised by newspapers; radio; and TV. Considers all crafts.

*****DUNDEE ARTS AND CRAFTS CLUB OUTDOOR EXHIBIT**, 520 Oak St., Dundee MI 48131. Secretary: Mrs. Roger LaVoy. Estab. 1962. Annual outdoor show held 1 day in July. Average attendance: 2,000. Entries accepted until 1 week before show. Entry fee: $10/4x8 display area. Work may be offered for sale; no commission. Craftworker must attend show; demonstrations OK. Show is advertised by all media. Presents ribbons. Considers all crafts.

EMERSON ARTS & CRAFTS FAIR, 3505 Marais, Royal Oak MI 48073. Contact: Janet Espeseth at (313)435-5308, or Gloria Kremer at 435-9653. Sponsor: Emerson Elementary School PTA. Estab. 1976. Annual indoor show held 1 day in November. Average attendance: 1,500-2,000. Considers all original crafts. Show is advertised by newspaper, radio, TV, posters, flyers and school newsletters.
Terms: Entries accepted until approximately 2 months before show. Entry fee: $10-20/10x5 or 10x4 display area. Invitations are sent to craftspeople known to Fair Committee. Others should send slides/photos or present work in person. Entry fee refunded for refused work. Work must be offered for sale; no commission. Craftworker must attend show (unless good reason for not attending, then may send representative); demonstrations OK. Registration limit: 60-70. Sponsor provides chairs, electricity for demonstrations and tables for a fee.
Sales Tip: Offer items under $5 as well as more expensive items. Have business cards with name, address and phone number for future sales. Have Visa and/or Mastercharge. Christmas items are big sellers at this time of the year, as well as different types of gift items.

FALL ART SHOW, c/o Left Bank Gallery, 503 East St., Flint MI 48503. (313)239-2921. Contact: Chairman. Estab. 1973. Annual outdoor show held 2 days in September or October. Average attendance: 3,000.

Acceptable Work: Considers batik, glass art, jewelry, lapidary, macrame, metalsmithing, mobiles, needlecrafts, pottery, sculpture, soft sculpture, weavings and woodcrafting. No kits, mass produced items or clothing.
Terms: Entries accepted until 4 weeks before show. Entry fee: $20/8x12' display area. Prejudging by 3 or more slides. Work must be offered for sale; no commission. Cratworker must attend show; demonstrations OK. Registration limit: 85 artists and craftworkers.

FESTIVAL OF THE FORKS, Albion MI 49224. (517)629-5533. Contact and Sponsor: Chamber of Commerce. Estab. 1966. Annual outdoor show held 1 day, generally the first week of October. Average attendance: 10,000-12,000. Considers all crafts. No commercial products (e.g., Avon, Stanley). Entry fee: $5/display area. Work must be offered for sale; no commission on crafts. Craftworker must attend show; demonstrations OK. Show promoted through various news media.

FLANNEL FESTIVAL, c/o Sue Wolfe, 15290 Tisdel Ave., Cedar Springs MI 49319. (616)696-2246. Sponsor: Cedar Springs Red Flannel Civic Events Council. Estab. 1977. Annual outdoor show (with indoor site in case of rain) held 1st Saturday in October. Average attendance: 20,000.
Acceptable Work: Considers all crafts; "anything of pornographic nature or matter that would be a disgrace to our show will not be accepted." Include a variety in prices and work to appeal to different ages and types of people."
Terms: Entries accepted until 2 weeks before show. Entry fee: $10/10x10 ddisplay area. No prejudging. Work may be offered for sale; no commission. Craftworker must attend show; demonstrations OK. Registration limit: 65. Sponsor provides electricity for demonstrations. "Craftsmen handle their sales and we handle sales taxes."

FOLK ARTS FAIR, 515 Stevens, Flint MI 48502. (313)767-0720. Activities Director: Bella Kritz. Sponsor: International Institute. Estab. 1932. Annual indoor show held 3 days during the first weekend of November. Average attendance: 3,000-4,000.
Acceptable Work: Considers all crafts. "The Folk Arts Fair is an international fair. Items displayed must be of an international nature."
Terms: Entries accepted until 4 weeks before show. Entry fee: $75/8 foot tables. Entries prejudged. Entry fee due after prejudging. Work may be offered for sale; 20% commission. Craftworker needn't be present at show; demonstrations OK. Registration limit: 7-10. Sponsor provides chairs, display panels, electricity for demonstrations and table. Exhibitor handles sales and taxes.

FOUNDERS WEEKEND, Box 67, Delton MI 49046. (616)623-2704. Chairman: William Kirg. Sponsor: Delton Area Chamber of Commerce. Estab. 1974. Annual outdoor show held 1 day in August. Average attendance: 5,000-6,000. Considers all crafts. "We are a rural community and things sell very well."
Terms: Write for entry deadlines. Entry fee: $3/10x10 display area. Work may be offered for sale; no commission. Craftworker must attend show; demonstrations OK. Sponsor provides electricity for demonstrations and assistance in setup.

FRANKFORT WATERFRONT ART FAIR, c/o Susan Kidder, Box 1148, Frankfort MI 49635. (616)352-7001. Chairman: Susan Kidder. Sponsor: Frankfort Chamber of Commerce. Estab. 1977. Annual outdoor show held the third Saturday in August. Average attendance: 5,000.
Acceptable Work: Considers all crafts. No kits, molds, patterns, prefabricated forms, mass-produced buckles or lapidary findings. "All work must be original in concept and execution."
Terms: Entries accepted until 3 weeks before show. Entry fee: $15/artist. Entries prejudged by slides, photos or in person. Work must be offered for sale; no commission. Craftworker must attend show; demonstrations encouraged. Registration limit: 150.

FRANKENMUTH BAVARIAN FESTIVAL, 635 S. Main St., Frankenmuth MI 48734. (517)652-6106. Contact: G. Zimmer, c/o Arts & Crafts Committee, Box 66, Frankenmuth MI 48734. Sponsor: Frankenmuth Civic Events Council. Estab. 1959. Annual outdoor show held the second week in June. Average attendance: 250,000-300,000. Closing date for entry; March 1. Entry fee:$100/12x10 display area. Maximum 1 display area per craftworker. Prejudging by slides or photos; entry fee refunded for refused work. Work may be offered for sale; no commission. Demonstration OK. Registration limit: 50. Considers all crafts.
To Break In: "Demonstration is the key to selection. We like prices that are fair for work done. List basic price list on application. Apply before March; you'll be contacted in April."

HOLIDAY GIFT SHOW, Ann Arbor Art Association, 117 W. Liberty, Ann Arbor MI 48104. (313)994-8004. Special Events Chairman: I. B. Remsen. Estab. 1976. Annual indoor show held the month of December. Entries accepted until 2 months before show. Entry fee: $50/artist. Display area: "mixed gallery." Prejudging by slides; entry fee refunded for refused work. Work may be offered for sale; 20% commission. Craftworker needn't attend show but "craftworker can volunteer time for sale to promote own work and commission rate is reduced by 5% for pieces sold by craftworker during that time." No demonstrations. Registration limit: 12-15. Sponsor provides 24-hour security. Considers all crafts but candlemaking; decoupage; dollmaking; needlecrafts; and tole painting.
Promotion: Show is advertised by newspapers; radio; and all public service forms of promotion. Artist is provided with mailing cards and flyers. Submit resume and b&w glossy of work for press releases.

HOLLY HOLIDAY ART & CRAFT SHOW, 111 College St., Holly MI 48442. (313)634-7341. Director: Daniel Rolls. Sponsor: Holly Community Education Council and NOC Historical Society. Estab. 1978. Annual indoor show held 1 day in November. Average attendance: 1,000. Considers all crafts. Handmade items only. Show is advertised by newspapers, radio announcements, posters, and art and craft publications.
Terms: Entries accepted until 3 weeks before show. Entry fee: $10/10x10 display area. Work must be offered for sale; no commission; demonstratons OK. Registration limit: 60. Sponsor provides table (for a rental fee) and chair.

*****INTERNATIONAL FESTIVAL**, 515 Stevens, Flint MI 48502 (313)767-0720. Activities Director: Bella Kritz. International Institute. Estab. 1950. Annual outdoor show held 2 1/2 days during the last weekend in June. Average attendance: 10,000.
Acceptable Work: Considers all crafts. "Since this is an international festival, all participants must have an international theme."
Terms: Entries accepted until 4 weeks before show. Entry fee: $200/commerical booth; $75/nonprofit booth. Entries prejudged. Work may be offered for sale; no commission. Craftworkers are encouraged to attend the festival; demonstrations OK ("and are helpful in sales"). Registration limit: $7-10. Exhibitor handles sales and taxes.
Promotion: Show is advertised by radio, newspapers, TV and flyers.

INVITATIONAL ANN ARBOR SPRING ART FAIR, 1725 Weldon, Ann Arbor MI 48103. Show Director: Audree Levy. Estab. 1978. Annual indoor show held 3 days in March. Entries accepted until 3 months before show. Entry fee: $110/10x12 display area. Prejudging by 3 slides; resume; and SASE. Entry fee due after prejudging. Work may be offered for sale; no commission. Craftworker must attend show; some demonstrations. Registration limit: 100. Sponsor provides 24 hour security. Show is advertised by TV; radio; and newspapers. Submit b&w photo and resume. Considers all crafts but decoupage; dollmaking; needlecrafts; and tole painting.

INVITATIONAL ANN ARBOR WINTER ART FAIR, 1725 Weldon, Ann Arbor MI 48103. Show Director: Audree Levy. Estab. 1974. Annual indoor show held 3 days in November. Average attendance: 40,000. Entries accepted until 4 months before show. Entry fee: $110/10x12 display area. Prejudging by 3 slides and resume. SASE. Entry fee due after prejudging. Work may be offered for sale; no commission. Craftworker must attend show; some demonstrations. Registration limit: 100. Sponsor provides 24 hour security. Show is advertised by TV; radio; and newspapers. Submit b&w photo and resume. Categories: fine arts and crafts. Considers all crafts but decoupage; dollmaking; needlecrafts; and tole painting.

ISLAND ART FAIR, 120 S. Bridge, Box 144, Grand Ledge MI 48837. (517)627-4867. Chairman: Lynda Trinklein. Sponsor: Ledge Craft Lane. Estab. 1974. Annual outdoor show held the last Saturday in July. Average attendance: 10,000. Considers all original and handmade crafts.
Terms: Entries accepted until filled. Entry fee: $10/10x10 display area. Work must be offered for sale; no commission. Craftworker or representative must attend show; demonstrations OK. Registration limit: 100; 20 invitational. Sponsor provides assistance in setting up, display sitters during lunch and breaks, and portable bathrooms.
Profile: Entertainment and strolling musicians are part of show.

KALKASKA ARTS & CRAFTS FESTIVAL, Box 377, Kalkaska MI 49646. Chairman: Mrs. Dale Lantzer. Sponsor: Kalkaska County Chamber of Commerce. Estab. 1971. Annual indoor show held the first Saturday in October. Average attendance: 1,000. Considers all crafts.

Terms: Entries accepted until 2 weeks before show. No entry fee. Display area: 4x8. Work may be offered for sale; 10% commission. Craftworker or representative must attend show; demonstrations encouraged. Sponsor provides chairs, electricity for demonstrations and 4x7 table.
Sales Tip: Novel crafts—children's toys, dolls, wooden trains, items crafters use (plaques, frames, dried materials, etc.) sell well.

KAZOO SCHOOL MAYFAIRE, 714 S. Westnedge, Kalamazoo MI 49007. (616)345-3239. Co-Chairperson: Vernon Kays. Sponsor: Kazoo School Inc. Estab. 1975. Annual outdoor show held 1 day, usually the third weekend in May. Considers all crafts. Work must be made by exhibitor.
Terms: Entry fee: $12/artist. Display area: approximately 10x12. Work may be offered for sale; no commission. Craftworker must attend show; demonstrations OK.

*****KEATINGTON ART FESTIVAL**, 2365 Joslyn Ct., Lake Orion MI 48035. (313)391-0623. Co-Chairmen: William Kirshman and Carroll Sheeran-Kirshman. Estab. 1978. Annual outdoor show held 2 days in August at Keatington's Antique Village. Show is advertised by newspapers, posters, flyers and magazines.
Acceptable Work: Considers glass art, batik, jewelry, pottery, sculpture and woodcrafting. No ceramics unless original designed by artist.
Terms: Entries accepted until about 3 months before show. Entry fee: $15/10x10 display area. Prejudging by slides or photos accompanied by SASE; entry fee refunded for refused work. Work may be offered for sale; no commission. Craftworker must attend show; demonstrations OK. Registration limit: 140. Sponsor provides electricity for demonstrations, overnight camping, restaurant and 24-hour security.
Awards: Presents cash and merchandise prizes and ribbons for 1st, 2nd and Best of Show awards. Honorable mentions are announced in each category.

LAFAYETTE PARK ART FAIR, 1327 Joliet Pl., Detroit MI 48207. Co-chairperson: Judy Harris. Estab. 1966. Annual outdoor show held 2 days in September. Average attendance: 10,000. Considers all crafts. No mass-produced leatherworking and nothing pre-made (e.g., commercial chains or beads). Michigan craftworkers only. Entries accepted until 4 months before show. Entry fee: $35/8x8 display area. Prejudging by slides. Entry fee due with slides. Work must be offered for sale; no commission. Craftworker must attend show; demonstrations OK. Registration limit: 100.

LIVONIA ARTS & CRAFTS FESTIVAL, 33001 5 Mile Rd., c/o LOVE, Livonia MI 48154. (313)421-2000, ext. 353. Festival Chairman: Marie Tuthill. Sponsor: Livonia Arts Commission. Estab. 1977. Annual show.
Acceptable Work: Considers ceramics; decoupage; glass art; jewelry; leatherworking; needlecrafts; weavings; macrame; and pottery.
Terms: Entry fee: $7 plus $2/electricity, if needed. Work may be offered for sale; no commission. Craftworker must attend show; demonstrations OK. Registration limit: 200.
Profile: Show includes food and free entertainment. Also free art works giveaway.

LUDINGTON ARTS & CRAFTS FAIR, 1499 Betty Ave., C8, Ludington MI 49431. (616)843-3522. Director: Mildred Pirtle. Sponsor: West Shore Art League. Annual outdoor show held 2 days in July. Average attendance: 5,000. Prejudging; entry fee refunded for refused work. Work may be offered for sale; no commission. Craftworker must attend show; demonstrations welcome. Registration limit: 200.
Acceptable Work: Fine art and well developed crafts. Considers batik; dollmaking; glass art; limited jewelry; limited leatherwork; metalsmithing; pottery; soft sculpture; weavings; wall hangings; and woodcrafting. Juried."If we have seen a work before and know the quality, it needn't be prejudged again."

*****MANISTEE WORLD OF ARTS & CRAFTS**, Box 412, Manistee MI 49660. Applications Secretary: Beth McCarthy. Sponsor: The Manistee World of Arts and Crafts. Estab. 1971. Annual outdoor show held 2 days during the weekend of July 4. "A covered assigned site is available in case of rain." Average attendance: 25,000.
Acceptable Work: Considers all crafts, "as long as it's original and shown by the artist." No kits, patterns, machine-made items (including belt buckles), copies, molds, greenware, clothing or assemblages (e.g., beads, nature crafts).
Terms: Entries accepted until 4 weeks before show. Entry fee: $12/15x15 average display area; no sharing space. Prejudging by 4 slides. Entry fee refunded for refused work. Work may be

offered for sale; no commission. Craftworker must attend show; demonstrations OK. Sponsor provides rain site, electricity for demonstrations if requested, 24-hour security, coffee, and youth to help set up the first morning. "Exhibitors must have individual sales licenses on hand; the committee does not have any record. Tax people do on-site checks for licenses."
Awards: Presents $100 each in cash prizes for Best of Show for Arts and Best of Show for Crafts; $50 each for 2nd Place in Arts and 2nd Place in Crafts; $25 each for 3rd Place in Arts and 3rd Place in Crafts. Also presents ribbons "to honor achievement in any of the creative arts". "Our patrons pledge to purchase work; individuals and industries have followed through in good faith. To win awards, be creative! Have a good visual set-up, a good attitude, and be honest and open."
Promotion: Show is advertised by periodicals, radio, TV, newspapers, 500 pamphlets (distributed locally), and applications and posters to galleries and colleges in the Midwest.
Profile: "We, after 7 years of jurying, have raised the awareness here in Northern Michigan to a point where our public is very selective. They do not want the ordinary and look for the exceptional in form *and* color. We do not jury for quality, but the people do. We have fabulous food from rolls at 6 a.m. to dinners each night and are located in a beautiful shaded park."

MIDLAND ART FAIR, The Midland Art Council of the Midland Center for the Arts, 1801 W. St. Andrews St., Midland MI 48640. (517)631-3250. Estab. 1957. Annual outdoor show held 2 days the first weekend of June. Average attendance: 10,000. Show is advertised through local and statewide PR and advertising firms. Presents 3 cash prizes of $100 each.
Acceptable Work: Considers batik, ceramics, dollmaking, glass art, jewelry, lapidary, leatherworking, macrame, metalsmithing, mobiles, needlecrafts, pottery, scrimshaw, sculpture, soft sculpture, weaving and woodcrafting. Original work only.
Terms: Submit slides for prejudging about 2 months before show. Entry fee: $25/craftworker. Display area: 8x8. Prejudging by 3 slides; entry fee due after prejudging. Work must be offered for sale; no commission. Craftworker or representative must attend show; demonstrations OK. Registration limit: 200. Sponsor provides electricity for demonstrations.

*MIDWEST ARTS & CRAFTS SHOW, 1309 Woodward, Kingsford MI 49801. (906)774-4173. Chairperson: Beth Wedin. Sponsor: Dickinson County Council for the Arts. Estab. 1967. Annual indoor/outdoor show held 2 days in late June. Average attendance: 4,000. Presents $235 in cash and ribbons. 1978 show sales totaled $12,000+.
show sales totaled $12,000+.
Acceptable Work: Considers original batik, candlemaking, dollmaking, glass art, jewelry and other original crafts.
Terms: Entries accepted until 2 weeks before show. Entry fee: $10/4x8 display area. Work may be offered for sale; no commission. Prefers craftworker attends show; demonstrations OK.
Promotion: Show is advertised by newspapers; radio; TV; and arts and craft brochures. The publicity committee contacts artists for information and photos.

*MILAN ART FAIR, Milan Arts and Crafts Club, Milan MI 48160. Purpose: "to bring good quality art and crafts to the community of Milan and surrounding area." Estab. 1969. Annual outdoor show (indoors if raining) held 1st Saturday in June. Average attendance: 1,500. Entries accepted until 2 weeks before show. Entry fee: $8/4x8 table or A-frame display area. "Admittance to the Fair is screened on the basis of originality." Work may be offered for sale; no commission. Craftworker must attend show; demonstrations encouraged. Registration limit: 75. Sponsor provides display panels if requested; and electricity for demonstrations. Presents ribbon awards for best of show; 1st, 2nd, and 3rd prizes in each category; and honorable mention. Categories: fine arts (2 dimensional) and crafts (3 dimensional). Considers all crafts. Hooks for hangings must be provided by craftworker and name must be displayed on exhibit.
Promotion: Show is advertised by local paper; Ann Arbor, Michigan, radio and newspaper coverage and ads; some ads in Detroit area papers; and posters in Michigan and Toledo, Ohio, area. Provide background and any publicity information. No guarantee return on photos.

MILHAM PARK ART FAIR, 227 Connecticut Dr., Kalamazoo MI 49002. (616)342-1029. Resident Agent: Polly Triestram. Sponsor: Kalamazoo Valley Art Association. Annual outdoor show held 1 day in August. Average attendance: 36,000. Considers all original crafts exhibited by the craftworker only. Show is advertised by TV, radio, newspapers and store fliers.
Terms: Entries accepted until 4 weeks before show. Entry fee: $5/15 feet display area. Work

---

* Those listings preceded by an asterisk present awards for prize-winning crafts.

may be offered for sale; no commission. Registration limit: 400.

THE PALMER PARK FINE ARTS FESTIVAL, 742 W. McNichols, Detroit MI 48203. (313)341-2383. Chairperson: Gwen E. Prais. Sponsor: Palmer Park Citizens Action Council. Estab. 1976. Annual outdoor show held 2 days during the 1st weekend in August. Average attendance: 15,000. Considers all handmade crafts. No kits.
Terms: Entries accepted until approximately 3 months before show. Entry fee: $35/12x10 display area. Prejudging by 3 slides/photos. Entry fee refunded for refused work. Work must be offered for sale; no commission. Craftworker preferred to attend show; demonstrations OK (if notified in advance). Registration limit: 100. Sponsor provides fencing and 24-hour security.
Promotion: Show is advertised by radio, newspapers, TV, local banners, and cultural calendars of events in local area. "We will contact those artists from whom we wish materials."
Sales Tip: "Some artists sold almost completely out last year. Many said that their sales rivaled those of Ann Arbor!"

PORTSIDE CRAFT FAIR, 704 Prospect St., East Jordan MI 49727. (616)536-2967. Chairman: Mrs. Pat Pepin. Sponsor: Portside Art and Historical Society, Inc. Estab. 1977. Annual outdoor show held 1 day in the summer. Considers all crafts.
Terms: Entries accepted until show date. Entry fee: $5/display area. Work may be offered for sale; no commission. Craftworker must attend show; demonstrations OK. Free coffee and donuts provided while setting up displays.

REED CITY DERBY DAYS, Chamber of Commerce, Reed City MI 49677. Chairman: Mrs. Jay J. Williams. Estab. 1976. Annual outdoor show with shelter area held 2 days in July. Considers all crafts. Show is advertised by newspaper and radio.
Terms: Entries accepted until show date (also during show, if possible). Entry fee: $5/8x8 display area. Work may be offered for sale; no commission. Craftworker must attend show; demonstrations OK. Sponsor provides chairs, electricity for demonstrations, fencing and table.
Profile: "Reed City Derby Days is actually a 4-day celebration the first part of July. The name comes from the soap box derby race held one of those 4 days. At the parks where the arts and crafts show is held, there is also a small carnival, beer tent, baseball, softball, tennis tournaments, chicken roasts and other events going on."

*****REGIONAL**, Hackley Art Museum, 296 W. Webster, Muskegon MI 49440. (616)722-6954. Assistant to the Director: Ann Archambault. Purpose: "to have an annual exhibition of the best artwork being done in western Michigan." Estab. 1927. Annual indoor show held 1 month in February. Average attendance: 3,000. Entries accepted until 2 weeks before show. Entry fee: $1.50/item being displayed. Display area: 4,000 square feet. Maximum 2 pieces per craftworker. "This is a museum exhibition with emphasis on artistic quality. Final exhibition is a juried show." Work may be offered for sale but emphasis not on sales; no commission. Craftworker needn't attend show; no demonstrations. Sponsor provides insurance on exhibited work and 24-hour security. Show is advertised by newspaper and brochures. Presents cash awards totalling $855. Considers all crafts but candlemaking; decoupage; dollmaking; lapidary; leatherworking; tole painting; and woodcrafting.

ROYAL OAK OUTDOOR AIR FAIR, Recreation and Public Service Department, Royal Oak MI 48068. (313)546-0900. Superintendent of Recreation: Susan Wedley. Purpose: "to provide a quality show for Royal Oak residents where they may purchase or browse through exhibits of various art media." Estab. 1971. Annual outdoor show held the third or fourth weekend in July. Average attendance: 5,000.
Acceptable Work: Considers ceramics, leaded glass, jewelry, leatherworking, metalsmithing, pottery, sculpture, weavings and woodcrafting.
Terms: Entry fee: $25/craftworker. Display area: 15x15. Prejudging by slides; entry fee refunded for refused work. Work may be offered for sale; no commission. Craftworker must attend show; demonstrations OK. Registration limit: 95.
Promotion: Show is advertised by posters; flyers; radio; and newspaper. "We will send news releases to craftworker's local newspaper if they will provide us with information."

SAGINAW WEST SIDE ART FESTIVAL, 2011 Carman Drive, Saginaw MI 48602. (517)792-1931. Chairman: Ruth B. Frieling. Sponsor: West Saginaw Civic Association. Estab. 1965. Annual outdoor show held 2 days in May or June. Average attendance: 5,000. Presents $50, $30 and $20 in cash awards.

Acceptable Work: Considers batik, ceramics, dollmaking, glass art, jewelry, lapidary, leatherworking, macrame, metalsmithing, mobiles, needlecrafts, scrimshaw, sculpure, soft sculpture, weaving and woodcrafting. No kits, commercial patterns, mass-produced components, decoupage, or assemblages of seeds, pods or driftwood.
Terms: Entries accepted until 10 weeks before show. Entry fee: $18/10x6 display area. Prejudging by slides. $15 of entry fee refunded for refused work. Work must be offered for sale; no commission. Craftworker must attend show; demonstrations OK. Registration limit: 85. Sponsor provides electricity for demonstrations and 24-hour security.

ST. CLAIR ART FAIR, Box 222, St. Clair MI 48079. (313)329-2803. Chairman: Gayle Rowland. Sponsor: St. Clair Art Association. Estab. 1971. Annual outdoor (in covered mall) show held 3 days in late June. Average attendance: 5,000-6,000. Entries accepted until mid-March. Entry fee: $20/8x8 or 8x10 display area. Prejudging. Work must be offered for sale; 10% commission. Craftworker must attend show; demonstrations OK. Registration limit: 65.
Acceptable Work: Considers batik, ceramics, glass art, jewelry, some leatherworking, metalsmithing, pottery, soft sculpture, weavings, wall hangings, painting, sculpture and some woodcrafting.

ST. JOSEPH ART ASSOCIATION'S OUTDOOR ART FAIR, Lake Bluff Park, St. Joseph MI 49085. Registration Chairman: Mrs. Del Sabin (2987 E. Windsor Dr., St. Joseph MI 49085). Estab. 1962. Annual outdoor show held the 2nd Sunday in July. Average attendance: 45,000-50,000.
Acceptable Work: Considers batik, ceramics, glass art, jewerly, leatherworking, metalsmithing, pottery, sculpture, weaving and woodcrafting. No molds, mass-produced items, bread dough, cone wreaths or weeds, paper flowers, knitting or clothing. Boxes and litter must be nonvisible to public.
Terms: Entries accepted until 8 weeks before show. Entry fee: $30/artist. Display area: 20x20. Prejudging by slides. Entry fee refunded for refused work. Work must be offered for sale; no commission. Craftworker must attend show; demonstrations OK. Registration limit: 150. Sale taxes collected by Michigan authorities.
Promotion: Show is advertised by Michigan area radio and TV; art and craft magazines; area community newspapers (*Michigan Motor News*); posters; and numerous brochures. "Craftworker provides own brochures and cards if he has them."

SAUGATUCK DOUGLAS ART FAIR, Box 176, Saugatuck MI 49453. President: Jane Van Dis. Estab. 1967. Annual outdoor show held 1 day during 2 weekends in July. Average attendance: 2,000. Considers all original crafts. No kits or machine-made crafts.
Terms: Entries accepted until show date. Entry fee: $10 for one day, $15 for both days. Display area: 10x6'. Work must be offered for sale; no commission. Craftworker must attend show; demonstrations OK.

*****SAULT SUMMER ARTS FESTIVAL**, Box 857, Sault Ste., Marie MI 49783. President: R.P. Aldrich. Sponsor: Sault Area Arts Council assisted by Chamber of Commerce and Sault Area Community Schools. Estab. 1975. Annual outdoor show held 2 days in August at the Sault area couthouse. Average attendance: 2,500. Considers most original crafts.
Terms: Entries accepted until about 2 months before show. Entry fee: $8/8x8 display area. Only 2 display areas/craftworker. Prejudging by slides; entry fee refunded for refused work. Work must be offered for sale; no commission. Craftworker must attend show; demonstrations OK. Registration limit: 100 craftworkers.
Awards: Presents $100 best of show award, ribbons in specific categories at judge's discretion and Best of Craft award. "Awards are usually more oriented to work which has a utilitarian concept—particularly in crafts. Workmanship and skill in the usage of materials is stressed. Since graphics and two-dimensional art is also part of this exhibit, competition for Best of Show is tough."
Sales Tip: "Utilitarian work sells well. This community is a tourist area and one of the high unemployment areas; however, people save and scrimp each year to get their special item from the show. Moderately priced ($5-100) pieces have the best chance of sale; however, pieces of quality above that amount do sell, but volume of this type of sale is less."

SHOLEM ALEICHEM INSTITUTE ART SHOW & SALE, 28555 Middlebelt Rd., Farmington Hills MI 48018. (313)626-9565. Contact: Sylvia Segall. Estab. 1963. Annual indoor show held 3 days in February at West Bloomfield, Michigan. Average attendance: 3,000. 1978 sales totaled $40,000+.

Acceptable Work: Considers batik, ceramics, glass art, jewelry, macrame, pottery, sculpture, weaving and woodcrafting. No bread sculpture, clothing or kit crafts. Only 6 framed works/artist.
Terms: Entries accepted until 4 weeks before show. No entry fee. Prejudging by slides and photos. Work must be offered for sale; 30% commission. Craftworker needn't attend show; no demonstrations. Sponsor provides display panels and table.
Promotion: Show is advertised by newspapers, radio, TV and mailings. Submit biography and photo of self.

*SOMERSET INVITATIONAL, 2801 Somerset Mall, Troy MI 48084. (313)643-6360. Director: Peg DuBois. Estab. 1970. Annual indoor show held 3 days in May. Entries accepted December-February. Entry fee: $55/display unit furnished by Mall. Prejudging by slides and resume; entry fee due after prejudging. Work must be offered for sale; no commission. Craftworker must attend show; no demonstrations. Registration limit: 40. Sponsor provides chairs; display panels; electricity; and 24-hour security. Show is advertised by radio; all local newspapers; and house newspapers. Announcement cards furnished for craftworker's clientele. Presents 5 $100 cash awards.
Acceptable Work: Considers batik; ceramics; jewelry; macrame; pottery; sculpture; soft sculpture; weaving; and woodcrafting.
Sales Tip: "This is a fine art show, not a craft show. Sales are realized in fine jewelry; ceramics; furniture; glass; fiber; and sculpture."

STURGIS NEWCOMERS' CLUB ARTS & CRAFTS FAIR, Sturges-Young Auditorium, Sturgis MI 49091. Chairperson: Judy Bennett. Estab. 1975. Annual indoor show held 1 day in November. Average attendance: 800. Considers all original crafts. Show is advertised by radio; TV; newspapers; and posters.
Terms: Entries accepted until filled. Entry fee: $15/3x8 display area. Work may be offered for sale; no commission. Craftworker must attend show; demonstrations OK. Registration limit: 58. Sponsor provides chairs; some electricity for demonstrations; and table.
Sales Tip: Weaving, woodcrafting and needcrafts sell especially well.

*TAWAS BAY WATERFRONT ART FAIR, 1115 Bay Dr., Tawas City MI 48763. (517)362-3198. Art Director: Paula Peterson. Sponsor: Tawas Bay Arts Council. Estab. 1960. Annual indoor/outdoor show held the first weekend in August. Average attendance: 5,000. Applications and photos due for prejudging July 1. Entry fee refunded for refused work. Work may be offered for sale; no commission. Craftworker must attend show; demonstrations OK. Registration limit: 225. Presents ribbons and cash prizes.
Acceptable Work: Considers batik; candlemaking; ceramics; glass art; jewelry; leatherworking; metalsmithing; pottery; weavings; and woodcrafting. No prefab jewelry; artificial flowers; candles from molds; knitting; crocheting; decals on wood; paper tole; ecology boxes; or dough art.

TIVOLI FAIR, 146 Walnut, Northville MI 48167. (313)348-1456. Chairman: Patricia Meyers. Sponsor: Northville Historical Society. Estab. 1972. Annual indoor show held 2 days in November. Average attendance: 3,000. Considers all handmade crafts.
Terms: Entries accepted until filled. Entry fee: $30/10x7 display area. Prejudging by slides or photos (to be sent with SASE); entry fee refunded for refused work. Work must be offered for sale; no commission. Craftworker or representative must attend show; demonstrations OK. Registration limit: 100. Sponsor provides chairs, display sitters for lunch and breaks, free coffee, overnight protection and electricity for demonstrations.

TRAVERSE BAY OUTDOOR ART FAIR, Northwestern Michigan College, 1701 E. Front St., Traverse City MI 49684. (616)946-7990. Contact: Sandy Beyer at 6839 Deepwater Point Rd., Williamsburg MI 49690. Sponsor: Northwestern Michigan Artists and Craftsmen. Estab. 1957. Annual outdoor show held the last Saturday in July. Average attendance: 10,000.
Acceptable Work: Considers all crafts. "Items under $50 sell the fastest. Also small items such as jewelry, wood products, and wooden toys."
Terms: Entries accepted until May 1. Entry fee: $15/1 artist in 12x15' booth; $20/2 artists in 12x15' booth. Prejudging by slides; entry fee refunded for refused work. Work may be offered for sale; no commission. Craftworker must attend show; demonstrations encouraged. Registration limit: 150. If craftworker doesn't have sales tax license allowed to use Fair's.
Promotion: Show is advertised by radio; TV; newspapers; magazines; and posters. "If glossies are sent with registration we might use this and background information for promotion. If we

find an exceptional work, we like to show it on a TV show promoting our fair."
Profile: "When this show began (15 years ago), we were very small. This year, we will have sent out nearly 1,000 applications. It is an event held on the campus of the college, under huge pines. It is well attended since this time of year is the very height of our tourist season."

UNIVERSITY ARTISTS & CRAFTSMEN GUILD CHRISTMAS ART FAIR, UM Artists and Craftsmen Guild, 2nd Flr., Michigan Union, Ann Arbor MI 48109. Director: Celeste Melis. Estab. 1972. Annual indoor show held 2 days in December. Average attendance: 8,000.
Acceptable Work: Considers all crafts, except decoupage, lapidary and tole painting. No kits, machine assemblages, reproductions or commercial items.
Terms: Only Guild members or UM students may apply; 3 year waiting list of 700 names. Entry fee: $30/8x8 display area. Prejudging according to Guild rules. Entry fee due after prejudging; also refunded for refused work. Work may be offered for sale; no commission. Craftworker must attend show; demonstrations encouraged. Registration limit: 150. Sponsor provides electricity for demonstrations and 24-hour security. Exhibitor handles sales and taxes; I.R.S. may collect tax during show.
Profile: "We hope to educate the public in quality craftsmanship; to provide a good market for craftspeople, and to provide a festival to celebrate the making of objects. People are looking for Christmas presents so gift items and lower-priced items sell well at this Christmas fair."
Promotion: Show is advertised by newspapers, radio, public service announcements, posters, press releases and mailings. Submit b&w photos for publicity.
Sales Tip: "Don't display too much quantity. Use professional approach, business cards and literature. We aim for a public which is aware of good quality craftsmanship." Sales total for last show: $51,000; average of $402/person.

UNIVERSITY ARTISTS & CRAFTSMEN GUILD FALL ART FAIR, UM Artists and Craftsmen Guild, 2nd Flr., Michigan Union, Ann Arbor MI 48109. Director: Celeste Melis. Estab. 1971. Annual outdoor show held 2 days in September. Average attendance: 4,000-6,000.
Acceptable Work: Considers all crafts, except decoupage, lapidary and tole painting. Guild rules identify limitations of crafts. No kits, commercial reproductions, machine-made crafts and assemblages of manufactured items.
Terms: Only Guild members may apply; 3 year waiting list of 700 names. Entry fee: $20/10x10 display area. Prejudging according to Guild rules. Entry fee due after prejudging and refunded for refused work. Work may be offered for sale; no commission. Craftworker must attend show; demonstrations encouraged. Registration limit: 85. Exhibitors handle sales and taxes; I.R.S. comes around to collect taxes.
Profile: "We hope to educate the public in quality craftsmanship; to provide a good market for craftspeople, and to provide a festival to celebrate the making of objects. This crowd is of a transient nature. The fair accompanies a football weekend. Sophisticated out-of-town buyers mixed with local buyers.
Promotion: Show is advertised by newspapers, radio, public service announcements, posters, press releases and mailings. Submit b&w photos for publicity.
Sales Tips: Don't display too much quantity. Use professional approach, business cards and literature. Our public is aware of good quality craftsmanship and expects you to be present to sell your work." Average sales/exhibitor: $200.

UNIVERSITY ARTISTS & CRAFTSMEN GUILD SPRING ARTS FESTIVAL, UM Artists and Craftsmen Guild, 2nd Flr., Michigan Union, Ann Arbor MI 48104. Director: Celeste Melis. Purpose: "to educate the public in quality craftsmanship; to provide a good market for craftspeople, and to provide a festival to celebrate the making of objects." Estab. 1978. Annual outdoor show held 2 days in May at the University of Michigan Dearborn Campus, Dearborn MI. Average attendance: 4,000. Only Guild members may apply; 3 year waiting list of 700 names. Entry fee: $60/8x8 or 6x10 display area. Prejudging. Work may be offered for sale; no commission. Craftworker must attend show; demonstrations encouraged (especially folk arts). Registration limit: 100. Sponsor provides some electricity for demonstrations; and 24-hour security. Show is advertised by newspapers; radio; public service announcements; press releases; and mailings. Submit b&w photos for promotion. Considers all crafts within Guild rules.
Sales Tip: "Don't display too much quantity. Use professional approach, business cards and literature. We aim for a public which is aware of good quality craftsmanship."

UNIVERSITY ARTISTS & CRAFTSMEN GUILD SUMMER ARTS FESTIVAL, UM Artists and Craftsmen Guild, 2nd Flr., Michigan Union, Ann Arbor MI 48109. Director: Celeste Melis.

Estab. 1970. Annual outdoor show held 4 days in July. Average attendance: 300,000.
Acceptable Work: Considers all crafts. Guild rules identify craft standards. No kits, reproductions, machine-made crafts or assemblages of commercial parts. Exhibitor handles sales and taxes; I.R.S. comes around to collect taxes.
Terms: Only Guild members or UM students may apply; 3 year waiting list of 700 names. Entry fee: $60/8x8 or 6x10 display area. Prejudging according to Guild rules. Work may be offered for sale; no commission. Craftworker must attend show; demonstrations encouraged. Registration limit: 550. Sponsor provides 24-hour security.
Profile: "Many dealers and gallery owners come to this show and there is a lot of competition."
Promotion: Show is advertised by newspapers, radio, public service announcements, posters, press releases and mailings. Submit b&w photos.
Sales Tip: "Don't display too much quantity. Use professional approach, business cards and literature. You must be present with your work. The public is interested in your philosophies of craftsmanship and quality artwork." Estimated gross: over $1 million; average of $1,500/artist.

UP IN CENTRAL PARK ART FAIR, 1 Washington St., Grand Haven MI 49417. (616)842-4910. Contact: Manager. Sponsor: Chamber of Commerce. Purpose: "to promote the arts in this area and to offer a very desirable summer activity for visitors and area residents." Estab. 1955. Annual outdoor show held 2 days in July. Average attendance: 11,000. Display area: 15x15. Prejudging by slide; photo; or sample of work. Work may be offered for sale; no commission. Craftworker must attend show. Registration limit: 110. Considers all crafts.

WARREN FESTIVAL OF ARTS, 29500 Van Dyke, Warren MI 48093. (313)573-9500. Secretary: Jan Pierce. Sponsor: Warren Cultural Commission. Estab. 1977. Annual show held 2 days at the GM Technical Center. Entry fee: $25. Prejudging by slides. Work may be offered for sale. Considers all crafts.

*****WATERFRONT ART FAIR**, c/o Pam Wilburn, Lake Bluff Estates, Gladstone MI 49837. Sponsor: Bay Area Art Association. Estab. 1971. Annual outdoor show held the first Saturday in August at Escanaba, Michigan. Average attendance: 1,200-1,500. Considers all crafts. No kits or commercial patterns. Presents cash awards, and purchase awards totalling about $300-350.
Terms: Entries accepted up until 2 weeks before show. Entry fee: $10/display area. Prejudging by description of work. First time entries submit 3 slides or photos. Work may be offered for sale; no commission. Craftworker or representative must attend show; demonstrations encouraged. Sponsor provides fencing.
Promotion: Show is advertised by TV, radio, posters, and newspapers of Central Upper Peninsula's major towns. If desired, submit b&w photos of works or self.

ZEELAND ARTS FESTIVAL, 320 E. Main St., Zeeland Community Education, Zeeland MI 49464. (616)772-6236. Coordinator: Terri Winters. Estab. 1975. Annual outdoor show (indoors if raining) held 2 days in June. Average attendance: 4,000. Entries accepted until show. Entry fee: $5/artist. Unlimited display area. Work may be offered for sale; no commission. Craftworker needn't attend show; demonstrations OK. Sponsor provides some chairs, tables and display panels; electricity for demonstrations; and 24-hour security. Show is advertised by posters; radio; newspapers; and flyers. Considers all crafts.

Minnesota

ARTS & CRAFTS FESTIVAL, Hutchinson Area Chamber of Commerce, 218 Main N., Hutchinson MN 55350. (612)879-6025. Executive Vice President: Clarice A. Coston. Estab. 1974. Annual outdoor show (indoors if inclement weather) held 2 days in the fall. Average attendance: 1,000. Entries accepted until 1 week before show. Entry fee: $20/display area. Work may be offered for sale; no commission. Craftworker needn't attend show; demonstrations OK. Sponsor provides electricity for demonstrations and tables for $3 rental fee. Considers all crafts.

ARTS & CRAFTS ON THE VILLAGE GREEN, Box 133, Bayport MN 55003. (612)439-1434. Chairman: Patricia Francois. Sponosr: Bayport Jaycee Women. Estab. 1976. Annual outdoor show held 1 day in June. Average attendance: 2,000. Considers all crafts.
Terms: Entries accepted until the day before show. Entry fee: $15/display area. Work must be offered for sale; 20% commission on consigned items. Craftworker needn't attend show; demonstrations OK. Registration limit: 125. Sponsor provides limited electricity for demonstration.

Promotion: Show is advertised by magazines, newspaper, TV, radio, flyers and posters.

DULUTH FOLK FESTIVAL, 506 W. Michigan St., Duluth MN 55802. (218)722-8563. Arts & Crafts Coordinator: Bonnie Cusick. Sponsor: Duluth Folk Festival Committee. Estab. 1926. Annual outdoor show held 1 day in August. Average attendance: 12,000.
Acceptable Work: Considers all original crafts. "Since this is an ethnic festival, representative ethnic art is preferred. All items must be handcrafted and presented by creator. No commercial advertising is allowed."
Terms: Entries accepted until full. No entry fee. Display area: 8-10' frontage. Work may be offered for sale; 15% commission. Craftworker must attend show; demonstrations OK. Sponsor provides chairs and electricity for demonstration.
Promotion: Show is advertised by newspapers, radio, TV, posters, newsletters and brochures.
Sales Tip: "The work sells well. Because of the nature of the festival, medium-priced work has the best chance of selling. However, artists often display more expensive work as promotion. Artist handles own tax."

EAST GRAND FORKS ARTS & CRAFTS, 316 Demers Ave., East Grand Forks MN 56721. (218)773-1271. Chairperson: Barbara Patterson. Sponsor: Chamber of Commerce. Estab. 1973. Annual indoor show held 2 days in October. Average attendance: 5,000. Considers all crafts.
Terms: Entries accepted until 3 weeks before show. Entry fee: $15/8x10 display area. Work may be offered for sale; no commission. Craftworker must attend show; demonstrations OK. Registration limit: 126. Sponsor provides chairs, display panels, electricity for demonstrations, table and 24-hour security.

FAIR IN THE FIELDS, 903 Johnson Ave., White Bear Lake MN 55110. (612)426-5218. President, White Bear Arts Council: Harvey Ellerd. Sponsor: White Bear Arts Council and Lakewood Community College. Estab. 1970. Annual outdoor show held the Saturday after July 4th. "In case of inclement weather, the college buildings can be used for display space." Average attendance: 5,000+.
Acceptable Work: Considers batik, ceramics, glass art, jewelry, macrame, metalsmithing, mobiles, needlecrafts, pottery, sculpture, soft sculpture, weaving and woodcrafting. "The primary criteria are original design and no mass-produced items. The sponsors are willing to consider any craft work that meet these criteria, but past experience is that some things (e.g., candles) never make it through the jurying. Usually, craftworkers with moderately-priced work (under $25) do well."
Terms: Entry is by invitation only, but reviewed and revised annually to encourage additional artists. Entries accepted until 2 weeks before show. Entry fee: $10/artist. Display area: approximately 10x10. Prejudging by samples or slides/photos. Entry fee refunded for refused work. Work may be offered for sale; no commission. Craftworker needn't attend show; demonstrations encouraged. Sponsor provides security during show hours, food service, first aid room and entertainment (madrigal and folk singers, dance groups, traveling medicine show, Shakespeare Theatre group). Exhibitor handles sales and taxes.
Promotion: Show is advertised by TV, radio, daily and weekly newspapers in the Minneapolis-St. Paul area, posters, flyers, and the Chamber of Commerce lists of events.
Profile: "We are scheduled usually to coincide with White Bear Lake's Manitou Days festival. For the past several years, the exhibit has been held in the nature area adjacent to Lakewood Community College. The buying public in the area seem to be well-educated/informed about art, and though inexpensive work usually sells faster, there is a market for the $100-500 range."

FALL ARTS FAIR, Northfield Arts Guild, Box 21, Northfield MN 55057. Contact: Arts Fair Chairperson. "The Fall Arts Fair is a celebration for support and exposure of local artists." Estab. 1961. Annual outdoor show held 1 day in September. Attendance: 6,000-8,000. Entries accepted until 3 weeks before show. Entry fee: $15/artist. Prejudging by photos; entry fee due with application. Work may be offered for sale; no commission. Craftworker must attend show; demonstrations OK. Sponsor provides display panels. Show is advertised in local papers; radio; some mention in Twin City papers; and mention in various art/craft publications.
Acceptable Work: Considers batik; ceramics; glass art; jewelry; lapidary; leatherworking; macrame; metalsmithing; pottery; sculpture; soft sculpture; weaving; and woodcrafting. "This is primarily a fine arts fair, though."

KAFFE KLATTER KRAFTS & ART FAIR, Box 385, Willmar MN 56201. Contact: Chairman.

Sponsors: Willmar Jaycee Women and the Kandiyohi County Arts Association. Estab. 1978. Annual indoor show held 1 day the end of June. Considers all crafts.
Terms: Entries accepted until show. Entry fee: $5-10/8x10 display area. Work must be offered for sale; no commission. Craftworker must attend show; demonstration OK. Registration limit: 54. Sponsor provides chairs, electricity for demonstrations and table.
Promotion: Show is advertised by radio, newspapers and local TV. "Craftworker may submit a short article for a newspaper feature article."

*MIDTOWN PROFESSIONAL ART & CRAFT FAIR, 708 W. 22nd St., Minneapolis MN 55405. (612)871-1323. Coordinator: Cindy Bebo. Sponsor: South Lyndale Avenue Merchants Association and Down East Craftsman. Estab. 1977. Annual outdoor show held 3 days during the end of May.
Acceptable Work: Considers all crafts, except dollmaking. "We are hoping to accept mostly professional artists. We prefer all or most items to sell for $5 and up." No kits or machine-made crafts.
Terms: Entries accepted until 3 weeks before show. Entry fee: $15/5x6 display area; $25/5x12; $40/5x18. Prejudging by photos and description. Entry fee refunded for refused work. Work must be offered for sale; no commission. Craftworker must attend show; demonstrations OK. Exhibitor handles sales and taxes.
Awards: Presents opportunity (to those chosen) to exhibit in Down East Craftsman's Gallery; ribbons for best display and most unique items; and discounts to all exhibitors at some of the area establishments.
Promotion: Show is advertised by flyers, radio, TV and newspapers. "Flyers are sent to the artists to distribute."
Sales Tip: "Be willing to talk to the people. Don't bury your head in a book and ignore them."

MINNEAPOLIS AQUATENNIAL NICOLLET MALL ART FAIR & MARKETPLACE, 15 S. Fifth St., Minneapolis MN 55402. (612)332-7412. Executive Vice President: Kenneth Walstad. Sponsor: Minneapolis Aquatennial Association. Estab. 1967. Annual outdoor show held 2 days for the Art Fair and 2 days for the Marketplace in July, beginning the week following the third Friday of each July. Average attendance: 75,000 daily. Acceptable Work: Considers all crafts. No antiques, sewing, kits, plaster or bread dough imitations of clay works, plastic flowers glued to wooden plaques, molds, or nonoriginal jewelry works. "We prefer working artisans to be in appropriate costume."
Terms: Entries accepted until 4 weeks before show; fills quickly. Entry fee: $15/artist per day. Display area: 10x5. Prejudging by photos. Entry fee refunded for refused work. Work may be offered for sale; no commission. Craftworker must attend show; demonstrations OK. Registration limit: 250. Sponsor provides blanket liability, but no insurance of works. Exhibitor handles sales and taxes.
Promotion: Show is advertised by the Association's travel brochure, TV and radio public service annoucements, and mailings to association members, travel agencies, travel writers and convention bureaus.

*MINNESOTA CRAFTS FESTIVAL, 811 Holly Ave., St. Paul MN 55104. Chairperson, Minnesota Crafts Festival: Irene Crowder. Estab. 1972. Annual outdoor show held 2 days in June. Considers all crafts. Presents $300 as top award and 3 $200 merit awards.
Terms: Entries accepted until 3 weeks before show. Entry fee: $35/artist (Council members); $15 membership fee. Display area: 12x12. Prejudging by 4 slides. Entry fee due after prejudging. Work may be offered for sale; no commission. Craftworker must attend show; demonstrations OK. Registration limit: 100. Sponsor provides fencing and 24-hour security.

*MINNESOTA STATE FAIR, State Fairgrounds, State Fairgrounds, St. Paul MN 55108. (612)645-2781. Contact: Entry Dept. Estab. 1911. Annual indoor show held 12 days beginning in August. Average attendance: 200,000.
Acceptable Work: Considers ceramics, glass art, jewelry, pottery, sculpture, weaving and woodcrafting. No excessively fragile or huge sculpture; and no plaster ceramics, pottery, tiles and mosaic. "All plaster sculpture must have a permanent base." Jewelry should be provided with a box, with the artist's name and address. Fastenings should be secure and well constructed wth type of materials used stated on the entry blank. Textiles should be accompanied by a label for identification."
Terms: Entries accepted until 3 weeks before show. Maximum of 3 pieces/artist. Craftworker must be from Minnesota. Prejudging by jury. Work may be offered for sale; no commission. Craftworker needn't be present; no demonstrations. Sponsor provides insurance on exhibited

work and 24-hour security. Exhibitor handles own work. "Craftworkers may list their item for sale on their entry card, but not on the piece. Customers interested in work may obtain phone numbers from the front desk."
Awards: Presents $3,000 in cash prizes; and ribbons for 1st, 2nd and 3rd places.

NORTH ST. PAUL JAYCEE WOMEN'S ARTS AND CRAFTS FAIR, 5206 Summit St., St. Paul MN 55110. (612)429-0398. President: Mary Burns. Estab. 1976. Annual indoor show held 2 days in the fall. Considers all crafts.
Terms: Entries accepted until show. Entry fee: $10/day. Display area: 10'. Work must be offered for sale; no commission. Craftworker must attend show; demonstrations OK. Registration limit: 36. Sponsor provides electricity for demonstration on first come, first served basis.

*__NORTH SHORE ART FAIR__, Box 57, Lutsen MN 55612. (218)663-7330. Chairman: Joan H. Maw. Sponsor: North Shore Arts Association. Purpose: "to educate the public and promote artists from our area." Estab. 1968. Annual indoor/outdoor show held the second weekend in July. Average attendance: 2,000. Entries accepted until show date. Entry fee: $1/item plus $20 outside booth space. Maximum 3 pieces per category per craftworker entering the judged show. Work may be offered for sale; 25% commission. Craftworker needn't attend show; demonstrations OK. Show is advertised by brochures; newspapers; TV; and radio. Considers work "in 12 media classes (children's art also accepted at no charge). Presents cash for best of show, and ribbons in all categories.

NORTH STAR ARTS & CRAFTS FESTIVAL, Rt. 4, Park Rapids MN 56470. (218)732-5421. Coordinator: Lucy Kyro. Purpose: "to give the artist and craftpeople a chance to be seen and known and sell items." Estab. 1972. Annual indoor show held 3 days in August. Entries accepted until filled. Entry fee: $25/8' space; $37/12' space; and $50/16' space. Prejudging by photos or sample of work; entry fee due after prejudging. Work may be offered for sale; no commission. Craftworker must attend show; demonstrations OK. Registration limit: 100. Sponsor provides chairs; display panels; electricity for demonstrations; table; and 24-hour security. Show is advertised by TV; radio; newspapers; and flyers. Considers all crafts made by the exhibitor.
Sales Tip: "The biggest factors in good sales are fine workmanship; good sales personality (don't sit in booths reading books); and be interested in the viewing public—talk to people."

*__RED RIVER ANNUAL__, Box 37, Moorhead MN 56560. (218)236-7171. Director: James O'Rourke. Sponsor: Friends of the Plains Art Museum. Estab. 1959. Annual indoor show held 7 weeks in the fall. Average attendance: 2,500. Entries accepted until 4 weeks before show. No entry fee. Maximum 1 entry/artist. Prejudging. Work may be offered for sale; 40% commission. Craftworker must attend show; no demonstrations. Sponsor provides 24-hour security; gallery talks; concerts; awards dinner; and luncheon with juror. Considers batik; ceramics; glass art; macrame; mobiles; pottery; sculpture; weaving; and soft sculpture.

SEPTEMBER FEST, Box 134, Owattonna MN 55060. (507)451-9990; (507)451-4540 (ext. 36). Contact: Chairperson. Sponsor: Owattonna Arts Center. Estab. 1976. Annual outdoor show held 1 day in September. Considers all crafts, except candlemaking, decoupage and tole painting. No kits or machine-made items.
Terms: Entry fee: $10/10x10 display area. Prejudging by slides/photos. Entry fee due after prejudging and refunded for refused work. Work must be offered for sale; no commission. Craftworker must attend show; demonstrations OK. Registration limit: 250. Exhibitor handles sales and taxes.
Promotion: Show is advertised by radio, TV posters and Arts Center Newsletter. Craftworker should provide his/her local newspaper's name and address.

SIDEWALK ARTS & CRAFTS FAIR, 310 NE 1st St., Little Falls MN 56345. (612)632-5155. Manager: Glen Kraywinkle. Sponsor: Chamber of Commerce. Estab. 1973. Annual outdoor show held the 1st Saturday after Labor Day. Entry fee: $2.50. Work may be offered for sale; no commission. Craftworker must attend show; demonstrations OK. Show is advertised by news releases. Considers all original crafts.

UPTOWN ART FAIR, 7201 Shannon Dr., Edina MN 55435. Administrative Director: E.A. Nieland. Sponsor: Uptown Commerical Club. Purpose: "to attract people to the area and promote broader public interest in original arts and crafts, as well as give the public an opportunity to meet artists." Estab. 1964. Annual outdoor show (on sidewalks and grassy mall)

held 3 days the second weekend in August at Minneapolis, Minnesota. Attendance: 125,000-150,000. Entries accepted until mid-May. Entry fee: $25/artist. Prejudging by photos or slides to be submitted with application by new exhibitors; entry fee refunded for refused work. Work may be offered for sale; no commission. Craftworker must attend show; demonstrations OK. Registration limit: 550-575. Considers all crafts except dollmaking; needlecrafts; soft sculpture; or handcrafts (stitchery, crochet, clothing, pillows, etc.). Must have Minnesota state sales tax permit.
Sales Tip: Work sells best when presented on "well-designed display fixtures; and prices are clearly marked. Framed art recommended as it sells better than unframed work. Also, be sure to bring a generous supply of work (we don't want artists to 'sell out' in 1 or 2 days)."

VICTORIAN CRAFT FESTIVAL, 265 S. Exchange St., St. Paul MN 55102. (612)222-5717. Contact: Edna Reasoner. Sponsor: Minnesota Historical Society. Estab. 1971. Annual outdoor show held 12 Sundays during the summer (June-August). Average attendance: 1,000-2,000.
Acceptable Work: Considers all Victorian period crafts. Categories include wood crafts; paper crafts; lacemaking; egg decorating; painting; metalwork and jewelry; spinning, weaving and rugs; needle and fabric arts; furniture repair and refinishing; glass and ceramics; and dolls and miniatures.
Terms: No entry fee. Work may be offered for sale; no commission. Craftworker must attend show; demonstrations OK.
Profile: "We have a whole summer devoted to Victorian crafts. Our hope is that visitors will have a good opportunity to concentrate on a specific Victorian craft area and learn from craftworkers. The 12 Sunday series starts with an old-fashioned Ice Cream Social. Each following Sunday will feature demonstrations of particular (or related group of) Victorian crafts."

WEAVERS GUILD FIBER FAIR, 2402 University Ave., St. Paul, Minneapolis MN 55114. (612)644-3594. Contact: Fiber Fair Committee. Sponsor: Weavers Guild of Minnesota, Inc. Purpose: fund-raiser. Estab. 1974. Annual indoor show held 3 days in November. Average attendance: 1,600. Entries received 2 days before show. Entry fee: $15/membership in Weavers Guild of Minnesota plus $3/Fiber Fair fee. Prejudging by actual work at time submitted; fees not refunded for refused work. Work may be offered for sale; 15% commission. Craftworker must attend show; demonstrations OK. "All participating craftsmen are asked to help during the show as salesmen, demonstrators, displayers, check-out, jury, etc." Sponsor provides chairs; display panels; insurance on exhibited work; and 24-hour security. Show is advertised by newspaper; radio; flyers; and posters.
Acceptable Work: Considers crafts as they relate to fiber arts including weaving; hand-spun wool; dollmaking; macrame; mobiles; needlecrafts; soft sculpture; tatting; lace; natural dyestuff; dyed handspun wool; crochet; and knitting. Bestsellers: scarves; shawls; mittens; small hangings; toys; some afghans; and throw pillows.

Mississippi

*****ART IN THE PARK**, Box 790, Meridian MS 39301. (601)693-1306. Executive Vice President: W.J. Johnson, Jr. Sponsor: Lively Arts Festival. Estab. 1977. Annual outdoor show (indoors if rain) held 1 day in April. Average attendance: 3,500. Entries accepted until 2 weeks before show. Entry fee: $25/artist for competition. Display area: 10x10. Work may be offered for sale; no commission. Craftworker must attend show; demonstrations OK. Registration limit: 100 spaces. Show is advertised by trade publications and through other publicity of the Lively Arts Festival. Presents $950 in cash, and $750 in purchase prizes.
Acceptable Work: Considers batik; candlemaking; decoupage; dollmaking; glass art; jewelry; leatherworking; macrame; metalsmithing; mobiles; needlecrafts; pottery; sculpture; soft sculpture; tole painting; weaving; and woodcrafting.

BARTER DAY, Chamber of Commerce, Drawer S, Morton MS 39117. (601)732-6135. Director: Gilbert W. Renfrow. Purpose: "gives the people in central Mississippi an opportunity to view and purchase arts and crafts that cannot be bought otherwise." Estab. 1969. Annual outdoor show held the third weekend in June. Attendance: 5,000-10,000. Entries accepted until show date. No entry fee. Display area: "varies, but usually 10x15." Work may be offered for sale; no commission. Craftworker needn't attend show; demonstrations OK. Sponsor provides coverings and electricity for demonstrations. Considers all crafts. Novel and practical items sell best. Craftworker handles sales.
Promotion: Show is advertised by radio; newspapers; posters; and leaflets. "If an artist has a unique exhibit or demonstration, he should send information 4 weeks prior to the show."

*BATESVILLE ANNUAL ART MART, Box 528, Batesville MS 38606. (601)563-3126. Secretary: Mary M. Evans. Purpose: "to promote appreciation of art, and provide an outlet for special crafts." Estab. 1966. Annual outdoor show (in pecan grove under shady trees) held 1 day in June. Average attendance: 3,000. Entries accepted until show date. Entry fee: $5/display area. Work may be offered for sale; no commission. Craftworker must attend show; demonstrations OK. Sponsor provides electricity for demonstrations. Categories: paintings, watercolor and mixed media; graphics and drawings; sculpture; crafts; and pottery. Considers all crafts. "Each year we provide purchase prizes of different amounts."

*CALICO FAIR, c/o Art Association of Columbus, Box 2251, East End Station, Columbus MS 39701. Contact: Chairman. "This annual event enables the Art Association to make money to have workshops and field trips. We also have given some scholarships; and are saving towards a building." Estab. 1968. Annual outdoor show (with a pavilion with tables) held 1 day in the fall. Average attendance: 3,000-6,000. Entries accepted until 2 weeks before show. Entry fee: $10/artist, with an additional $5 fee for admission into the awards portion of the show. Prejudging by slides or photos; entry fee refunded for refused work. Work may be offered for sale; no commission. Craftworker must attend show; demonstrations OK. Sponsor provides limited covering; electricity for demonstrations; fencing; and some tables. Considers all crafts.
Awards: Presents purchase prizes in all categories; honorable mention, 1st and 2nd place ribbons; and cash awards of merit and $200 best in show award. Purchase prizes are awarded by business and individuals. "Most judges do look at the total look (display) in picking individual prize winners. They also seem to pick someone who has a lot of items on hand—not just a few."
Sales Tip: "Crafts are good sellers. In this area people start their Christmas buying at this time—Christmas decorations, stocking stuffers—this type of thing is good."
Promotion: Show is advertised in magazines; newspapers; and TV. "Materials for promotional purposes would be helpful. If anyone would like to have advance publicity we will do what we can. Pictures should be b&w glossy and include name on the back. Resumes are also helpful. Photos will not be returned by mail, but will be held and may be picked up at the Calico Fair."

THE CANTON FLEA MARKET ARTS & CRAFTS SHOW, Box 202, Canton MS 39046. (601)859-1606. Secretary: Ginny Ray. Sponsor: Madison County Chamber of Commerce. Purpose: "to promote Canton and Madison County." Estab. 1964. Semiannual outdoor show held the second Thursday in May and October. Average attendance: 20,000. "New applications are cut off about 6 weeks before the show because the invitations go out then to persons selected by jurying." Entry fee: $17.50. Display area: 12x12. Prejudging; "invitation recipients are selected by the information on their application and the photos that they send in." Entry fee due after prejudging. Work must be offered for sale; no commission. Show is advertised by newspaper articles and craft magazines. Considers all crafts "except unfinished crafts (left for the buyer to finish) and exhibits with dried components."
Profile: "The main exhibit is located on the grounds of the Courthouse Square. Other exhibits are located on the grounds of the Old Jail Museum (i.e., additional arts and crafts, antiques, etc.). A live potted plant show and sale will be held on the grounds of the Grace Episcopal Church."

THE GREAT RIVER ROADS CRAFT FAIR, Box 1785, Natchez MS 39120. (601)442-6221. Chairman: Ted Williams. Sponsor: Jaycees. Purpose: "to promote an appreciation for the well made, hand produced article; to provide a professional atmosphere for the sale of contemporary and heritage crafts. To develop for our community a craft event which attracts tourists and to provide educational opportunities for individuals interested in artistic expressions in the craft field." Estab. 1973. Annual indoor show held 3 days on the second weekend in October. Average attendance: 5,000. Entries accepted until 3 months before show. Entry fee: $60. Display area: 10x10. Prejudging by 2-5 slides. Work may be offered for sale; no commission. Craftworker must attend show; demonstrations OK. Registration limit: 65. Sponsor provides electricity for demonstrations and booths; tables; chairs; 24-hour security; free coffee; catered supper; and free parking areas. Considers all crafts.
Promotion: Show is advertised by statewide public service announcements; newspaper ads throughout wide radius; sponsors appearance on area TV; distribution of thousands of flyers; posters; placemats in local restaurants; post cards to club members of stamping store mailing; telephone company's newsletter; notice in all craft publications which run craft columns; and radio. Submit b&w glossies of you and your work for publicity.

---

* Those listings preceded by an asterisk present awards for prize-winning crafts.

With the help of her friendly ferret, Bonnie Lee completes work on one of her unusual macrame wall hangings. She is among the 200 artists and craftspeople who display and sell their work at the Sugarloaf Mountain Works' Winter Crafts Festival in Gaithersburg, Maryland.—Photo by Tom Clark.

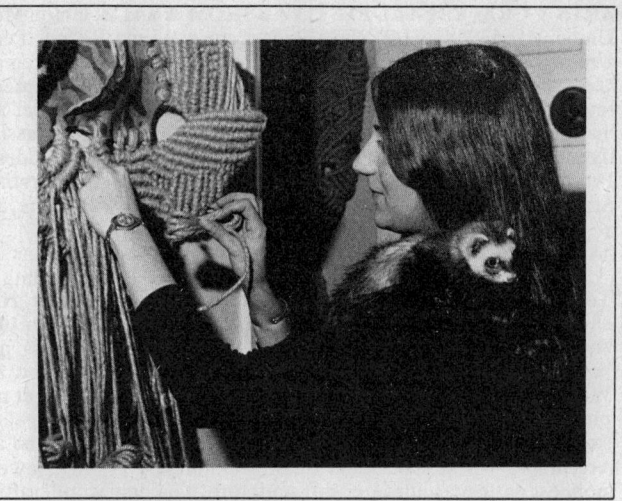

*MERIDIAN MUSEUM OF ART BI-STATE SHOW, Box 5773, Meridian MS 39301. (601)693-1501. Director: William M. Watkins, III. Sponsor: Meridian Art Association, Inc. and the Museum. Purpose: "to promote the best in visual arts throughout the states of Mississippi and Alabama, and to offer the viewing public the opportunity to take part in this promotion." Estab. 1974. Annual indoor show held the month of February. Average attendance: 800. Entries accepted until 1 week before show. Entry fee: $7 for 2 works. Maximum 2 works/artist. Prejudging by actual work. No entry fees refunded for refused work. Work may be offered for sale; 20% commission. Craftworker needn't attend show; no demonstrations. Sponsor provides insurance on exhibited work and 24-hour security. Show is advertised by newspaper; TV; direct mail; radio; and billboards. Considers all crafts; work must be ready for presentation. Maximum size: 50" in either direction, or 30 pounds. "Outrageous prices are discouraged." Museum staff handles sales.
Awards: Presents $1,200 in cash prizes. This includes $500 best in show award; 4 $100 juror awards; and 6 $50 awards of merit. "Enter dynamic show pieces and not pieces that would sell to the general public."

Missouri

ANTIQUE SHOW & COLLECTORS FLEA MARKET, Community Bldg., Hwy. 62 W. Campbell MO 63933. Contact: Nevah Clubb, 524 W. Martin, Campbell MO 63933. (314)246-2936 or 246-2258. Estab. 1977. Indoor show held the first Sunday each month. Entry fee: $6.50/8' table. Work may be offered for sale; no commission. Craftworker must attend show; demonstrations OK. Considers candlemaking; ceramics; decoupage; dollmaking; glass art; jewelry; needlecrafts; pottery; and quilting.

ARROW ROCK CRAFT FESTIVAL, Arrow Rock MO 65320. (816)837-3740. Corresponding Secretary: Buena Stolberg. Sponsor: Historic Arrow Rock Council. Estab. 1970. Annual indoor/outdoor show held 2 days during the second weekend of October. Average attendance: 3,000-6,000. Recent show totalled $3,500 in sales (10 selling craftworkers).
Acceptable Work: Considers blacksmithing, candlemaking, dollmaking, leatherworking, metalsmithing, needlecrafts, pottery, quilting, ropemaking, soapmaking, weaving and woodcrafting. No modern crafts or use of modern tools (torches, electricity, plastics). "Exhibitors dress in 19th century costumes. Modern furnishings (tables, etc.) must be covered with muslin or similar materials. Accessories must be typical of the 19th century."
Terms: Entries accepted 3½ months before show. No entry fee. Prejudging for historic authenticity by slides, photos and/or description of work. Work may be offered for sale; 10% commission. Craftworker must attend show; demonstraitons required. Registration limit: 25-30. Sponsor provides coffee and set-up assistance.
Profile: "The purpose of the craft festival is to demonstrate various crafts of the 19th century. These include household and other crafts of daily life. The festival is held in a historic village where the Santa Fe Trail began. Small and low priced items sell greater volume, but high priced quality items frequently sell out as well."

ARTS & CRAFTS FALL FESTIVAL SHOW & SALE, Union Merchants Association, Box 168, Union MO 63084. (314)583-8979. Secretary: Linda Ballou. Purpose: "to attract shoppers to Union; and for public enjoyment and availability of craft items to citizens and visitors in the area." Estab. 1975. Annual outdoor show held 1 day in September. Average attendance: "a few thousand." Entries accepted until show date. Entry fee: $2/1 parking space, or approximately 18' of space. Work may be offered for sale; no commission. Craftworker or representative must attend show; demonstrations OK. Sponsor provides fencing. Considers all crafts.
Promotion: Show is advertised by newspaper and radio advertising in the Union, Washington, St. Clair, Pacific, and Beaufort areas. Supply cards with name, address and phone number.

*AUGUST COMPETITION—EXHIBITION, 6640 Delmar St., St. Louis MO 63130. (314)725-1151. Sponsor: Craft Alliance Gallery (with funding from Missouri Arts Council). To provide a showcase for gallery member artists/craftsmen. High quality is the essence of this show. Only those living in Missouri and a 200 mile radius in Illinois are eligible. Estab. 1976. Annual indoor show held 3 weeks in August. Entries must be hand-delivered about 3-4 weeks before show. Entry fee: $10. Maximum 3 works/craftworker. All works will be juried in July. Work must be offered for sale; 40% commission. Craftworker needn't attend show. "Sponsor provides insurance on exhibited work; 24-hour security; gallery space; and staff to handle sales." Presents "at least a $150 1st prize, plus others to be announced."
Acceptable Work: Considers batik; ceramics; glass art; jewelry; macrame; metalsmithing; mobiles; pottery; sculpture; soft sculpture; weaving; woodcrafting; and any combination of the above.
Sales Tip: "Most sales are of functional work. It's difficult to anticipate what may appeal on an artistic level. We do not consider this a sales-oriented show, however; even though some definitely are consummated."
Promotion: Show is advertised by mail; newspapers; TV; radio: and magazines. "Give some educational and professional backround (space will be provided on entry forms)."

BENNETT SPRING HILLBILLY DAYS, c/o Lebanon Chamber of Commerce, Inc., Lebanon MO 65536. Estab. 1973. Annual outdoor show held 3 days in the summer. Entries accepted until about 2 weeks before show. Entry fee: $25/8' display area; $20/15' area outside main tent; $20/15' display area outside main tent plus additional footage at $1.50/foot. "Work not handcrafted will be refunded." Work may be offered for sale; no commission. Craftworker must attend show; demonstrations "strongly encouraged." Sponsor provides 24-hour security, but "the Bennett Spring Hillbilly Days committee and the Lebanon Chamber of Commerce will not be responsible for any loss, theft or damage." Considers all Ozarkian handcrafts.

BISSELL CRAFT FAIR, 1723 Mason Rd., St. Louis MO 63131. (314)822-8475. Recreation Supervisor: Michelle Burack. St. Louis County Department of Parks and Recreation. Estab. 1970. Annual outdoor show held 2 days in June at General Daniel Bissell House, North St. Louis County, Missouri. Average attendance: 5,000.
Acceptable Work: Considers all crafts. No kits or machine-made crafts. "Every craftsperson can display his work in any manner he desires as long as he stays within the booth space. Some special arrangements can be made for large spacial demonstrations."
Terms: Prejudging in February; craftworkers selected in March. "Vacancies are filled by a waiting list or by referral." Display area: 8x10. Prejudging by photos and actual work. No entry fee. Work may be offered for sale; no commission. Prefers craftworker attends show; demonstrations encouraged. Registration limit: 55. Sponsor provides electricity for demonstrations and fencing (booths are separated by hay bales and split wooden rails).
Promotion: Show is advertised by "news releases in all St. Louis County Journals and by St. Louis city papers."

BUSHWACKER ARTS & CRAFTS FESTIVAL, c/o Paula McIntosh, 330 N. Webster, Nevada MO 64772. (417)667-7744. Sponsor: Eta Theta chapter of Beta Sigma Phi. Purpose: "to raise funds for charitable purposes in the community. Our income is the fee charged for display area only." Estab. 1972. Annual outdoor show held 1 day in June. Entries accepted until show date. Entry fee: $7.50/6x9 display area. "All work is expected to be for sale unless craftsman specifies otherwise"; no commission. Craftworker must attend show; demonstrations OK. Registration limit: about 50. "Electricity for demonstrations can be arranged if asked for in advance." Show is advertised by direct mail, radio and newspapers. Considers all crafts.

CASS COUNTY LOG CABIN FESTIVAL, 400 E. Mechanic, Harrisonville MO 64701.

(816)884-5352. Secretary-Treasurer: Irene Webster. Sponsor: Chamber of Commerce and Cass County Historical Society, Inc. Purpose: "to promote demonstrations and crafts based on pioneer life. A log cabin built in 1835 is the focal point for the festival activities." Annual indoor/outdoor show (with some tents) held 3 days during the first weekend in October. Average attendance: 6,000. Entries accepted until 1 week before show. Entry fee: $20/5x7 display area inside tent, or 7x10 area outside tent. Work may be offered for sale. Craftworker must attend show; demonstrations OK. Registration limit: 60. Sponsor provides electricity for demonstrations: fencing; and 24-hour security. Show is advertised by magazines; direct mail; posters and pamphlets; and billboards. Submit descriptions of work for promotion. Considers all crafts; handmade crafts preferred. Bestsellers: work priced under $10. 1978 exhibitor sales totalled about $24,700.

CHRISTMAS CRAFT BAZAAR, Box 901, Cape Girardeau MO 63701. (314)334-9233. Director: Janet Chamberlain. Sponsor: Southeast Missouri Council on the Arts. Estab. 1972. Semiannual indoor show held 2 days in November and 2 days in late March or early April. Average attendance: 2,500-8,000.
Acceptable Work: Considers all crafts. No kits, machine-made crafts, or crafts made by non-attending craftworker. No groups.
Terms: Entries accepted until spaces are filled. Entry fee: 15/4x8 table. Entries prejudged. Work may be offered for sale; no commission. Craftworker must attend show; demonstrations encouraged. Registration limit: 160. Sponsor provides chairs and table.
Promotion: Show is advertised by 45 local papers, and public service announcements in 25 radio spots, and on 3 TV channels. Craftworker should provide b&w glossy prints for promotional purposes, if possible.
Sales Tip: "The November Bazaar is held around Christmas time to give the public an opportunity to buy early gifts. Items of this nature sell big. I wouldn't advise bringing too many items with large costs."

DUCKS UNLIMITED NATIONAL WILDLIFE ART SHOW, 1900 Erie, Suite 100, North Kansas City MO 64116. (816)842-2171. Director: David Wells. Estab. 1972. Annual indoor benefit show held 3 days in March. Average attendance: 12,000. Closing date for entry: mid-November. Entry fee: 1 original donated work. Maximum 15 entries per artist. Prejudging: donation refunded for refused work. Work may be offered for sale; no commission. Craftworker must attend show; demonstrations OK. Registration limit: 130. Considers wood and decoy carving. Emphasis placed on realism.

FALL NATIONAL CRAFT FEST, Silver Dollar City, Inc., Marvel Cave Park, MO 65616. (417)338-8212. Special Events Coordinator: Marty Munday. Estab. 1962. Annual indoor/outdoor show (with special constructed portable buildings) held 17 days beginning in September. Average attendance: 180,000. Show is advertised by TV, radio and newspapers.
Acceptable Work: Considers marquetry, dollmaking, glass art, jewelry, lapidary, crystal etching, macrame, metalsmithing, quilling, needlecrafts, scrimshaw, sculpture, soft sculpture, tole painting, weaving and woodcrafting. "All crafts must be fitting with the 1800s theme of Silver Dollar City."
Terms: Show is invitation only; entries accepted when needed. No entry fee. Prejudging by samples or slides/photos. Work may be offered for sale; 20% commission. Craftworker must attend show. "Demonstrations required 80% of the time. (Demonstration can be a blend of talking about your craft and actually making an item.) No power tools are allowed. Any modern materials which would not have existed in the late 1800s must be disguised (Elmer's Glue can be put in a mason jar.)" Sponsor provides chairs, coverings, display panels, electricity for demonstrations, counters, tables and 24-hour security.
Profile: "With our very large attendance, we feature a varied buying public. We also have only 1 craftsman in each craft. No duplication in show."

FOLK MUSIC & CRAFTS FESTIVAL, Box 339, 320 S. Curry St., West Plains MO 65775. (417)256-5948. Chairman: Olivia LaFevers. Sponsor: West Plains Council on the Arts. Estab. 1975. Annual indoor/outdoor show held 1 day in September. Average attendance: 1,000-1,500, paid. Considers all crafts.
Terms: Entries accepted until show date. No entry fee. Display area: 10x10. Work may be offered for sale; no commission. Craftworker must attend show. "This crafts show is set up as a learning experience, and all craftsmen are required to demonstrate." Sponsor provides electricity for demonstrations and some display panels.
Promotion: "Show is advertised by newspapers, TV guides, horse traders and radio stations.

Artists with promotion material may supply us, and we will use if possible."

INVITATIONAL CRAFT FAIR, 1111 E. Brookside Dr., Springfield MO 65807. (417)866-2716. Curator of Education: Jim Weaver. Sponsor: Springfield Art Museum. Estab. 1974. Annual outdoor show held 2 days in the fall. Average attendance: 6,000-8,000.
Acceptable Work: Considers batik; fine glass art; jewelry; leatherworking; metalsmithing; pottery; sculpture; soft sculpture; weaving; and woodcrafting. "No handicrafts—'fine art' quality crafts only." Bestsellers: work priced under $30.
Terms: Entries accepted until 2 weeks before show. Entry fee: $15/15x15 display area. Prejudging by 6 slides or photos; entry fee due after prejudging. Work may be offered for sale; no commission. Craftworker must attend show; demonstrations welcomed. Registration limit: 40-50. Sponsor provides electricity for demonstrations.
Promotion: Show is advertised by newspaper ads; TV public service time; posters; and news releases to radio, TV and newspapers. "A resume and b&w photo of the artist and his/her work would be helpful."

LAKE OF OZARKS ARTS & CRAFTS SHOW & SALE, 224 Oklahoma St., Rt. 2, Camdenton MO 65020. (314)346-5962. Director: Christene Burner. Estab. 1971. Annual indoor/outdoor show held 3 days in September. Average attendance: 20,000. Considers all original crafts.
Terms: Entries accepted until show date ("but usually sold out in August"). Entry fee: $15/8x10 display area. Work may be offered for sale; no commission. Craftworker or representative must attend show; demonstrations OK. Sponsor provides electricity for demonstrations and 24-hour security.

"MADE IN THE OZARKS" ARTS & CRAFTS SHOW, Eagle Rock Community Association, Eagle Rock MO 65641. Chairman, Craft Show: Mary Ann Jakeman. Estab. 1971. Annual indoor/outdoor show held 3 days during the second weekend of October. Average attendance: 2,500-3,500. Sales (1978): $10,000.
Acceptable Work: Considers all crafts. No antiques, plastic kits, food or commercially manufactured items.
Terms: Entries accepted until show date; spaces usually filled 2-3 weeks before show date. Entry fee: $10/6x6 display area. Work must be offered for sale; 10% commission. Craftworker or representative must attend show; demonstrations OK. Registration limit: 100; although some craftworkers reserve more than 1 space. Sponsor provides electricity for demonstrations (with small charge) and table for about 20 spaces. "We collect and remit sales taxes to the state of Missouri, except for those exhibitors who have their own sales tax number. They are responsible for reporting their sales.
Promotion: Show is advertised by news releases to radio, TV, newspapers and crafts magazines; posters and flyers are distributed.

MELANGE, 44 W. County Center, St. Louis MO 63131. (314)966-5950. Contact: Promotion Director. Sponsor: West County Center Merchants' Association. Estab. 1977. Annual Semiannual indoor show held 2 days in March and October.
Acceptable Work: Considers batik, dollmaking, jewelry, leatherworking, metalsmithing, pottery, sculpture, scrimshaw, soft sculpture, weavings and woodcrafting. No kits or machine-made products."An 8 foot table must be covered to the floor. All boxes must be stored under the table. Additional tables will be provided for $10 additional fee."
Terms: Entries accepted until 3 weeks before show. Entry fee: $50/10x10 display area. Prejudging by slides or photos of work and display. Entry fee due after prejudging. Work must be offered for sale; no commission. Craftworker must attend show; demonstrations OK. Registration limit: 40-50. Sponsor provides chairs, electricity for demonstrations, table and 24-hour security.

MISSOURI STATE FAIR, Craft Department or Commercial Exhibits Department, Box 111, Sedalia MO 65301. (816)826-0570. Superintendent of Craft Department: Marcedee Short (home phone: 826-3260). Concessions Manager: Arlene Rouchka. Sponsor: Missouri State Fair. Estab. 1901. Annual indoor/outdoor show held 10 days in August. Average attendance: 300,000.
Acceptable Work: Considers all crafts. "Work must be original, executed within the last 3 years." No work previously shown at Fair.
Terms: Open only to residents of Missouri who are over 16 years of age, except Junior Class. Entries accepted until 2 weeks before show. Display area: 8x10 or 10x10 (inside); 10x12 or 10x20 (outside). Maximum of 1 item/category. Work may be offered for sale; no commission.

Craftworker must attend to man booth in the Commercial area; demonstrations OK (with approval in advance of Superintendent). Sponsor provides commercial boothspace which is 3-sided with electricity. Exhibitor handles sales and taxes; taxes collected by Missouri Division of Revenue.
Awards: Presents 1st, 2nd and 3rd place cash awards. "The judges select on standards of artistic quality and the decision of the judges will be final."
Sales Tip: "Sales can be improved when work is easy to carry, of good quality and reasonably priced."

NATIVE ARTS & CRAFTS FESTIVAL, Box 327, Ozark MO 65721. (417)485-2752. Fair Coordinator: Marge Nowack. Sponsor: Utopia Federated Club. Estab. 1972. Annual indoor/outdoor show held 3 days during the first weekend in October at the Community Hall. Average attendance: 6,000-10,000.
Acceptable Work: Considers all crafts. "They have to be homemade. Nothing that is manufactured and bought."
Terms: Entries accepted until 1 week before show. Entry fee: $15/8x10 indoor and $5 outdoor display area. Work must be offered for sale; no commission. Craftworker or representative must attend show; demonstrations encouraged. Sponsor provides electricity for demonstrations. Exhibitor handles sales and taxes.
Promotion: Show is advertised by lists of events in craft magazines; KTTS and KWTO radio; all the newspapers in surrounding areas; 500 posters (sent to existing fairs in the area, motels, gas stations and restaurants); and signs on highways.
Sales Tip: "Demonstrate! When someone sees you making something, this creates much interest and usually makes better sales than the craftworker who just sits and tries to sell. You should talk with people; you'll make new friends and through your congeniality, you also make sales."

OZARK ART FEST, Box 283, Houston MO 65483. (417)967-3904. President: Jan Scheets. Ozark Art Fest Committee. Estab. 1977. Annual indoor show held 2 days during the first weekend in October. Average attendance: 5,000. Show is advertised by radio, TV, newspapers, flyers and magazines (including the Ozark Mountaineer).
Acceptable Work: Considers all crafts. "Needlework should be framed. Provide own hooks for pegboards."
Terms: Entries accepted until 1 week before show. Entry fee: $10/6x8 display area. Maximum 2 entries/category. Work may be offered for sale; no commission. Craftworker needn't attend show; demonstrations permitted. Registration limit: 50-60. Sponsor provides display panels ($4 fee), electricity for demonstrations (if requested), table ($2 fee), and 24-hour security. Exhibitor handles sales and taxes.
Awards: Presents 5 Best of Show cash prizes totaling $100; ribbon for Best of Show and for 1st, 2nd, 3rd, 4th and 5th places in each category. "Pieces need to be finished completely to be judged (i.e., paintings framed, tole pieces finished on back, ceramic pieces finished on bottom). Displays should be attractive and neat."

*****OZARK CRAFT FESTIVAL**, Battlefield Mall, Springfield MO 65804. (417)883-8444. Marketing Director: Betsy Valbracht. Sponsor: Merchant Association. Annual show held 3 days in the summer. Entry fee: $25/10x9 display area. Prejudging by slides or photos of work. "Mall will spend $1,500 to advertise work."

RENAISSANCE FESTIVAL, Kansas City Art Institute, 4415 Warwick Blvd., Kansas City MO 64111. (816)561-4852. Assistant to President, Development: Susan Hubbard. Estab. 1977. Annual outdoor show held 5 weekends (10 days) in September/October. Average attendance: 40,000. Entry fee. Prejudging by photos and slides. Work may be offered for sale; no commission. Craftworker must attend show; demonstrations OK. Considers baskets; candlemaking; carvings and sculpture; ceramics; calligraphy; children's toys; dolls; glass art; leather accessories; jewelry; lapidary; metalsmithing; mobiles; needlecrafts; pillows; pottery; wall hangings; and weavings. Craftworkers must be clothed in Renaissance period dress.

JOSEPH RUBIDOUX ARTS & CRAFTS FAIR, c/o Karen Organ, 1710 S. 40th St., Joseph MO 64507. (816)232-1323. Sponsor: St. Joseph Historical Society. Purpose: "money goes to restoration of Rubidoux Row." Estab. 1970. Annual indoor show held 3 days the first full weekend in October. Attendance: 20,000-25,000. Entries accepted until 3 weeks before show. Entry fee: $15/10x6 display area. Work may be offered for sale; no commission. Craftworker must attend show; demonstrations OK. Registration limit: 100. Sponsor provides electricity for demonstrations and 24-hour security. Show is advertised by newspaper; craft magazines; and brochures. Considers all crafts.

SANTA-CALI-GON DAYS, Box 147, Independence MO 64051. (816)252-2880. Public Relations Director: Elizabeth Hill McClure. Sponsor: Chamber of Commerce. Purpose: "to provide the community with a means of entertainment for the holiday weekend; to provide a source of fund-raising for local organization; and to promote the city to tourists." Estab. 1974. Annual outdoor show (with 4 big tents) held 4 days during Labor Day weekend. Average attendance: 250,000. Entries accepted until show date. Entry fee: $40/8x8 display area. Work may be offered for sale; no commission. Craftworker must attend show; demonstrations OK. Registration limit: 165-170. Sponsor provides some electricity for demonstrations and 24-hour security in the form of a roving policeman. Considers all crafts.
Promotion: "If work is of an unusual nature, a b&w photo and description might be included with registration." Advertising handled by Chamber of Commerce.

SPRING NATIONAL CRAFTS FESTIVAL, Silver Dollar City, Inc., Marvel Cave Park, MO 65616. (417)338-8212. Special Events Coordinator: Marty Munday. Estab. 1977. Annual indoor/outdoor show (with special constructed portable buildings) held 12 days in May. Average attendance: 95,000. Show is advertised by TV, radio and newspapers.
Acceptable Work: Considers marquetry, dollmaking, glass art, jewelry, lapidary, crystal etching, macrame, metalsmithing, quilling, needlecrafts, scrimshaw, sculpture, soft sculpture, tole painting, weaving and woodcrafting. "All crafts must be fitting with the 1800s theme of Silver Dollar City."
Terms: Show is invitation only; entries accepted when needed. No entry fee. Prejudging by samples or slides/photos. Work may be offered for sale; 15% commission. Craftworker must attend show. "Demonstrations required 80% of the time. (Demonstration can be a blend of talking about your craft and actually making an item.) No power tools are allowed. Any modern materials which would not have existed in the late 1800s must be disguised (Elmer's Glue can be put in a mason jar.)" Sponsor provides chairs, coverings, display panels, electricity for demonstrations, counters, tables and 24-hour security.
Profile: "With our very large attendance, we feature a varied buying public. We also have only 1 craftsman in each craft. No duplication in show."

SOUTH COUNTY CRAFTS SHOW & SALE, 85 S. County Centerway, St. Louis MO 63129. (314)892-5203. Assistant Promotion Director: Beverly Weber. Sponsor: South County Merchants Association. Estab. 1977. Annual indoor show held 2 days in September. Considers all crafts except jewelry.
Terms: Craftworker must have at least a $2,000 inventory. Entries accepted until 1 week before show. Entry fee: $50/10x12 display area, plus an additional $10/table. Prejudging by slides or photos; entry fee due after prejudging. Work must be offered for sale; no commission. Craftworker must attend show; demonstrations encouraged. Sponsor provides electricity for demonstrations, chairs and table.
Promotion: Show is advertised by 30-second commercial radio spots with an established jingle.
Sales Tip: "Household items, floral displays and handmade dolls sell well. Table covers should be neat, attractive and to the floor."

***TILLES PARK ARTS & CRAFTS FAIR**, 1723 Mason Rd., St. Louis MO 63131. (314)822-8475. Recreation Supervisor: Michelle Burack. Sponsor: St. Louis County Department of Parks & Recreation. Estab. 1966. Semiannual show held 2 days in September and 2 days in May at Tilles County Park. Average attendance: 25,000 per each 2 day show.
Acceptable Work: Considers all handmade crafts. "Items priced under $25 generally sell better."
Terms: Entries selected through jury process by photograph or slides. Entry fee: $12.50/70 square feet; $7.50 for students. Work may be offered for sale; no commission. Craftworker must attend show; demonstrations OK. Sponsor provides fencing.
Awards: Presents $75 for 1st Prize, $50 for 2nd Prize; and ribbons for 1st-3rd place winners and honorable mentions.
Promotion: Show is advertised by news releases in local papers throughout the city and county.

WHITE RIVER VALLEY ARTS & CRAFTS FAIR, Box 777, Forsyth MO 65653. (417)546-2741. Chairman: Jan Oliphant. Sponsor: Forsyth Chamber of Commerce. Estab. 1973. Annual indoor/outdoor show with coverings (veranda and pavillion with roof) held 3 days in August. Average attendance: 1,000. Presents ribbons.

Acceptable Work: Considers all crafts except decoupage and mobiles. No crafts made from synthetic materials (foam rubber, plastics, plaster of Paris) or commercial ceramic molds (except fine china painting).
Terms: Entries accepted until 6 weeks before show. Entry fee: $25/8x8' display area. Prejudging by slides or photos. Entry fee refunded for refused work. Work may be offered for sale; no commission. Craftworker must attend show; demonstrations OK. Registration limit: 85. Sponsor provides electricity for demonstrations and 24-hour security.

Montana

CHRISTMAS FAIR & BAZAAR, Box 585, Red Lodge MT 59068. (406)446-1370. Director: Bruce Branick. Sponsor: Carbon County Arts Guild. Estab. 1974. Annual indoor show held 2 days in December at Red Lodge. Average attendance: 500.
Acceptable Work: Considers all crafts. "We do not want anything that might be too large, any large space consuming item; we have to use common sense here. Wouldn't want automobiles or hay rakes."
Terms: Entries accepted until show date. Display area: 2,500 square feet. Maximum 6-10 entries (depending on size) per craftworker. Work may be offered for sale; 15% commission. Craftworker must attend show; demonstrations OK. Registration limit: 15. Sponsor provides chairs, display panels, electricity for demonstrations, table and 24-hour security. Arts Guild members handle sales.
Promotion: Show is advertised by "the Carbon County Arts Guild with notices to radio and newspapers in this area: Carbon County *News*, Billings *Gazette*, Clark's Fork *Bonanza*; KRBN, KOYN, KGLH radio stations; and channels 2 and 8 TV."
Sales Tips: "In this county, people buy almost anything if the price is small ($5-10). We sold around $1,200 gross at our last 2 day show."

*****ELECTRUM FESTIVAL OF THE ARTS**, Box 1231, Helena MT 59601. President: Julie Kuchenbrod. Sponsor: Helena Arts Council. Purpose: "to provide a quality show for the Northwest area." Estab. 1970. Annual indoor show held 2 days in the fall. Average attendance: 5,000-10,000. Entries accepted until 1 week before show. Entry fee: $4/item being displayed, plus $30/8x4 display area. Maximum 2 entries per craftworker per category. Work may be offered for sale; 20% commission. Craftworker needn't attend show. Considers all crafts. Presents cash awards and ribbons. Helena Arts Council handles juried show sales; "Montana has no sales tax."

FLATHEAD VALLEY ART FESTIVAL, 2nd Ave. & 3rd St., Box 83, Kalispell MT 59901. (406)755-5268. Director: John R. Brice. Sponsor: Hockaday Center for the Arts and The Flathead Valley Art Association. Purpose: "to encourage interested persons to develop arts and crafts; to interest the town and others in functions at the Hockaday Center; and to bring artisans together to share ideas." Annual outdoor show held 3 days in August. Write for entry deadline. Entry fee: $35/12x12 display area. Work may be offered for sale; no commission. Craftworker must attend show; demonstrations OK. Registration limit: 100. Sponsor provides electricity for demonstrations. Considers all crafts.
Sales Tip: "Kalispell is somewhat of a tourist town. Anything goes. Local people lean toward western themes."
Promotion: Show is advertised by radio; TV; and newspapers. Exhibitor should list type of craftwork done so list may be compiled for media.

*****J.K. RALSTON MUSEUM & ART CENTER JURIED EXHIBIT**, Box 50, Sidney MT 59270. (406)482-3500. Director: Linda K. Mann. Sponsor: Mon-Dak Historical & Arts Society. Estab. 1975. Annual indoor show held the month of October. Average attendance: 200. Entries accepted until 1 week before show. Entry fee: $3/craftworker. Maximum 2 entries per craftworker. Prejudging; entry fee refunded for refused work. Work may be offered for sale; 25% commission. No demonstrations. Work must have been done within 2 years prior to show. Sponsor provides display equipment. Crafts should be shipped prepaid; will be returned COD. Considers ceramics; metal; and soft sculpture. Maximum size: 6x4' depth; ½x1' or 5 lbs. Presents cash awards and ribbons for best of show; honorable mention; and most popular work.

Nebraska

COUNTRYSIDE VILLAGE ART FAIR, 8725 Countryside Plaza, Omaha NE 68114. (402)391-2200. Contact: Jim Chase. Sponsor: Countryside Village Merchants Association. Estab. 1970. Annual outdoor show held the first weekend in June. Average attendance: 20,000.

Entries accepted until 6 weeks before show. Entry fee: $30/8x14 display area. Prejudging; entry fee due after prejudging. Work may be offered for sale; no commission. Craftworker must attend show; demonstrations OK. Registration limit: 140.
Acceptable Work: Considers batik; oil; watercolor; acrylic; fiber; pottery; wood; metal; clay and stone sculpture; and silver/gold jewelry.

OMAHA SUMMER ARTS FESTIVAL (ARTS FESTIVAL ON THE MALL), 3860 Harney #3, Omaha NE 68131. (402)345-5401. Director: Vic Gutman. Sponsor: Summer Arts Festival, Inc. Purpose: a community event, a showcase for the arts in Omaha. Estab. 1975. Annual outdoor show held 3 days in June. Average attendance: 100,000. Entries accepted until 4 weeks before show. Entry fee: $40/craftworker. Display area: 10x10. Prejudging by 3 slides per medium; entry fee refunded for refused work. Work may be offered for sale; no commission. Craftworker must attend show; demonstrations encouraged. Registration limit: 200. Sponsor provides 24-hour security; rental of display items; free coffee and donuts; relief help; lounge; convenient parking; and reduction in hotel costs. Show is advertised by all media and 24-page supplement in newspaper. Inform your own customers of show. Considers all crafts.

Nevada

*****GOLD HILL ART FESTIVAL**, Box 510, Virginia City NV 89440. (702)847-0737. Director: Diane Gordon. Sponsor: Gold Hill Pottery and Art Gallery. Purpose: "to provide a setting for a successful festival for individual craftsmen; and to educate the public in terms of fine craftsmanship." Estab. 1974. Annual outdoor show held 3 days during Memorial Day weekend at Gold Hill, Nevada. Average attendance: 10,000-20,000. Entries accepted until March 30; prejudging done by April 15; notification of craftperson by April 30. Entry fee: $25/exhibitor. Display area: 6x12 (larger areas available for increased fee). Jury of 9 craftworkers prejudge work by slides and photos. Entry fee due after acceptance. Work may be offered for sale; no commission. Craftworker must attend show; demonstrations encouraged. Registration limit: 40. Sponsor provides 24-hour security. Show is advertised by radio; TV; local newspapers; posters; handbills; and banners. Considers batik; ceramics; candlemaking; jewelry; lapidary; leatherworking; macrame; metalsmithing; pottery; sculpture; soft sculpture; weaving; and woodcrafting. No hobby crafts. Presents $100 minimum in purchase prizes.

THE GREAT AMERICAN CRAFT SHOWS, Box 42862, Las Vegas NV 89104. Contact: Tom Greeley. Estab. 1977. Annual indoor show held 2 days in August at the Las Vegas Convention Center. Average attendance: 45,000-60,000. Considers all crafts. Heavy advertising.
Terms: Entries accepted until 3 weeks before show. Entry fee: $45/day ($90 total). Display area: 8'x10' (more if needed). Prejudging by photos/slides; include SASE. Entry fee refunded for refused work. Work may be offered for sale; no commission. Registration limit: 400. Craftworker must attend show; demonstrations OK. Sponsor pays for insurance during show.

*****MARYSVILLE MALL ART & CRAFT SHOW**, 3608 Cinnabar Ave., Carson City NV 89701. (702)883-0968. Director: Bea Griffin. Sponsor: Creative Artists Group. Estab. 1962. Annual indoor show held 4 days in January at Peach Tree Mall, Marysville, California. Average attendance: 50,000. Awards cash prizes.
Terms: Entries accepted until show date. Entry fee: $25/10x10' display area. Work may be offered for sale; 10% commission. Craftworker must attend show; demonstrations OK. Sponsor pays insurance on exhibited work.
Acceptable Work: Considers batik; candlemaking; ceramics; decoupage; dollmaking; glass art; leatherworking; metalsmithing; needlecrafts; pottery; soft sculpture; tole painting; weavings; wall hangings; woodcrafting; and all sculpture.

WORLD SHOWS, Box 339, Stanton CA 90680. (714)995-7509. Partners: Don, Virginia or Gale. Estab. 1977. Annual shows held 40 days in November-December at various Sears' stores throughout Nevada. Considers all crafts.
Terms: Entries accepted until show date. Entry fee: $96 for insurance. Display area: 4x6' to 10x12'. Prejudging by phone or mail. Entry fee due after prejudging; fee refunded for refused work. Craftworker must offer work for sale; 30% commission. Craftworker must attend show; demonstrations OK. Registration limit: 1-5 per store (57 stores). Sponsor provides electricity for demonstrations.
Profile: "These are concessions in high traffic areas of Sears' stores. Show is promoted by Sears' advertising. Craftworker must provide an appropriate sign and a good-looking display."

New Hampshire

CANAAN CRAFTSMEN'S CHRISTMAS FAIR, Canaan Elementary Gym, School St., Canaan NH 03741. Annual indoor show held 1 day the Saturday following Thanksgiving. Considers all crafts.
Terms: Open only to members of the League of New Hampshire Craftsmen. Entry fee: $1.50. Registration limit: 30 local craftworkers.

CANAAN'S MUSIC AND CRAFTS FESTIVAL, Box 172, Canaan, New Hampshire 03741. Contact: Eloise Fahrner. Estab. 1974. Annual show held 2 days during Memorial Day Weekend. Considers all crafts. Open registration with limitations in certain catagories. Entry fee: $4/day/craftworker. "The show is to benefit Canaan's Meetinghouse Restoration Fund."

CRAFTSMEN'S FAIR, 205 N. Main St., Concord NH 03301. (603)224-3375. Director: Merle D. Walker. Sponsor: League of New Hampshire Craftsmen. Annual outdoor show held 6 days in August. Average attendance: 30,000. Considers all crafts. "Participants must meet residency requirements."

*GRANITE STATE CERAMIC SHOW, 31 St. Laurent St., Nashua NH 03060. Chairman: Howard Takanaka. Sponsor: Granite State Ceramic Association. Estab. 1972. Annual indoor show held 3 days in August at Gunstock Recreation Area, Gilford, New Hampshire. Average attendance: 2,500. Considers only ceramics with no props of any kind. Presents ribbons.
Terms: Entries accepted 1 day only in the first week of August. Entry fee: $1/item. Prejudging. Work may be offered for sale; no commission. Demonstrations OK. Sponsor provides electricity for demonstrations, studio sign, 2 tables, 4' backdrop frame and 24-hour security.
Promotion: Show is advertised by radio, posters, newspaper advertisements and ceramics magazines.

LOON MOUNTAIN ARTS & CRAFTS SHOW, c/o Loon Mountain Recreation Corp., Lincoln NH 03251. (603)745-8111. Marketing Assistant: Rita M. Rand. Purpose: "to lend proper atmosphere to a well-designed, well-cared-for area which tries to offer something for everyone, and to promote arts and crafts of quality." Estab. 1967. Semiannual indoor/outdoor show held 3 days in August and in October. Average attendance: 2,000/day. Entries accepted until 1 week before show. Entry fee: "to be determined." Display area: 8x10 inside; or larger space outside if desired. Work may be offered for sale; no commission. Craftworker must attend show; demonstrations "preferred, if possible." Registration limit: about 35. Sponsor provides 24-hour security; tables; and chairs for a fee. Show is advertised by radio; newspapers; and flyers. Considers batik; candlemaking; ceramics; decoupage; jewelry; lapidary; leatherworking; macrame; metalsmithing; pottery; tole painting; weaving; and woodcrafting.

MALL OF NEW HAMPSHIRE PROFESSIONAL CRAFT & SCULPTURE SHOW, Rt. 1, Box 153J, Auburn NH 03032. (603)483-2742. President: Jinx Harris. Estab. 1978. Annual indoor show held 5 days in January at Manchester, New Hampshire. Average attendance: 70,000. Entries accepted until 1 week before show. Entry fee: $40/8x4 display area. Prejudging by slides and photos. Work may be offered for sale; no commission. Craftworker must attend show; demonstrations OK. Sponsor provides electricity for demonstrations and 24-hour security. Show is advertised by radio; TV; and newspapers. Considers all crafts except ceramics; lapidary; and strung bead jewelry.

NEW HAMPSHIRE ARTS FESTIVAL, Rt. 1, Box 153J, Auburn NH 03032. (603)483-2742. President: Jinx Harris. Estab. 1978. Annual indoor show held 5 days in April at Manchester, New Hampshire. Average attendance: 50,000. Entries accepted until 1 week before show or until filled. Entry fee: $40/8x4 display area. Prejudging by slides or photos if not in a previous show. Work may be offered for sale; no commission. Craftworker must attend show; demonstrations OK. Registration limit: 40. Sponsor provides electricity for demonstrations and 24-hour security. Show is advertised by radio; TV; and newspapers. Considers all crafts except ceramics; lapidary; strung bead jewelry; decoupage; and 3-D tole.

OLD HOME DAY, 21 A Nashua Rd., Pelham NH 03076. (603)635-7596. Chairman: Michael Coleman. Sponsor: First Congregational Church. Purpose: "to raise money for church and community." Estab. 1906. Annual outdoor show held 1 day in September. Average attendance: 8,000. Entries accepted until show is filled. Entry fee: $25/table. Work may be offered for sale; no commission. Craftworker needn't attend show; demonstrations OK. Registration limit: 25. Sponsor provides electricity for demonstrations and table. Considers all crafts; "we try to keep duplication to a minimum." Bestsellers: "items $10 and under seem to move very well." 1978 total exhibitor sales estimated at $25,000.

REGIONAL CRAFTSMEN'S FAIR, The Common, Rts. 4 and 118, Canaan NH 03741. Coordinator: Eloise Fahrner. Estab. 1970. Annual outdoor show (bring own canopies and set-up) held 3 days the last weekend in July. Entries accepted until 4 weeks before show, if show is not filled.
Terms: Entry fee: $1.50 each day per craftworker. Work may be offered for sale; no commission. Craftworker must attend show; demonstrations encouraged. Registration limit: 90. Considers all crafts. "Encourage the craftsmen to have items $4 and under—but not everything should be priced that low."

THEATRE BY THE SEA STREET FAIR, 91 Market St., Portsmouth NH 03801. (603)431-5846. Publicist: Sandi Bianco. Sponsor: Board of Trustees of Theatre by the Sea. "The Street Fair is one of the Theatre's major fund-raising activities as a nonprofit arts organization." Annual outdoor show held 1 day in the summer. Average attendance: 10,000.
Terms: Entries accepted until 1 week before show. Entry fee: $20/10' frontage. Work should be offered for sale; no commission. Craftworker or representative must attend show; demonstrations encouraged. Registration limit: 150. Sponsor provides electricity for demonstrations. Protection from sun recommended. Considers all crafts.
Promotion: Show is advertised by multiple press releases; arts magazines; TV; radio; public service announcements; and posters. "B&w studio photos can be used; feature articles can be adapted; name of participant's home town newspaper will be used for exclusive release."
Sales Tip: "Because many fair attendees are summer tourists, smaller transportable items are recommended. Moderately-priced items seem to move faster."

THE YULETIDE FAIR, 148 Concord St., Manchester NH 03104. (603)623-0313. Executive Director: Angelo Randazzo. Sponsor: Manchester Institute of Arts & Sciences. Annual indoor show held 3 days in late November or early December. Average attendance: 2,000.
Terms: Write for information on entry deadline. No entry fee. Prejudging by slides and in-person viewing. Work must be offered for sale; 30% commission. Craftworker needn't attend show but must deliver and pick up work. Registration limit: 50-60. Gallery provides complete display; insurance; handles sales; and 24-hour security. Considers all crafts. Bestsellers: "small items, suitable for Christmas gifts. Most under $30."
Promotion: Show is advertised by newspapers; radio announcements; invitations to members; and news releases. Submit business cards, pamphlets or explanatory material on the craft."

New Jersey

THE ART CENTRE OF NEW JERSEY, Annual Regional Exhibition and Sale, 16 Washington St., East Orange NJ 07017. Annual indoor show held in the spring. Maximum 2 entries per artist. Open to residents of New Jersey, New York, Connecticut and Pennsylvania. Charges 25% commission.
Acceptable Work: Considers sculpture. Size limit: sculptures, 24x24, 50 lbs. Work must be recent and original. Work sent by express or mail not accepted.
Awards: Including both cash and purchase prizes, they total about $2,000.

*****CAPE MAY COUNTY ART LEAGUE BOARDWALK ART SHOW**, 1050 Washington St., Cape May NJ 08204. Contact: Helen Dilday. Entry fee to be announced. Display area: 10'. No sales commission. Considers handcrafts. Presents awards.

CHERRY HILL MALL ARTS FESTIVAL, Rt. 1, Box 153J, Auburn NH 03032. (603)483-2742. President: Jinx Harris. Estab. 1970. Annual indoor show held 4 days in July at Cherry Hill, New Jersey. Average attendance: 65,000.
Acceptable Work: Considers all crafts except ceramics; lapidary; decoupage; strung bead jewelry; and 3-D tole.
Terms: Entries accepted until 1 week before show or until filled. Entry fee: $40/8x4 display area. Prejudging by slides or photos if not in a previous show. Work may be offered for sale; no commission. Craftworker must attend show; demonstrations OK. Registration limit: 50. Sponsor provides electricity for demonstrations and 24-hour security.
Promotion: Show is advertised by radio, TV and newspaper.

---

* Those listings preceded by an asterisk present awards for prize-winning crafts.

CHERRY HILL MALL CRAFT & SCULPTURE SHOW, Rt. 1, Box 153J, Auburn NH 03032. (603)483-2742. President: Jinx Harris. Estab. 1972. Annual indoor show held 4 days in March at Cherry Hill, New Jersey. Average attendance: 100,000.
Acceptable Work: Considers all crafts except ceramics; lapidary; decoupage; strung bead jewelry; 3-D tole; and crocheted items.
Terms: Entries accepted until 1 week before show or until filled. Entry fee: $40/8x4 display area. Prejudging by slides or photos if not in a previous show. Work may be offered for sale; no commission. Craftworker must attend show; demonstrations OK. Registration limit: 120. Sponsor provides electricity for demonstrations and 24-hour security.
Promotion: Show is advertised by radio; TV and newspaper.

CHERRY HILL MALL PROFESSIONAL CRAFT & SCULPTURE SHOW, Rt. 1, Box 153J, Auburn NH 03032. (603)483-2742. President: Jinx Harris. Estab. 1972. Annual indoor show held 4 days in October at Cherry Hill, New Jersey. Average attendance: 80,000.
Acceptable Work: Considers all crafts except ceramics; decoupage; lapidary; strung bead jewelry; and 3-D tole.
Terms: Entries accepted until 1 week before show or until filled. Entry fee: $40/8x4 display area. Prejudging by slides or photos if not in a previous show. Work may be offered for sale; no commission. Craftworker must attend show; demonstrations OK. Registration limit: 120. Sponsor provides electricity for demonstrations and 24-hour security.
Promotion: Show is advertised by radio, TV and newspaper.

CRAFT DAY IN THE PARK, Box 5005, Clinton NJ 08809. (201)735-4101. Director: Gloria Lazor. Sponsor: Clinton Historical Museum Village. Estab. 1975. Annual outdoor show held 1 day in mid-July. Average attendance: 1,000. Entries accepted until 1 week before show. Work may be offered for sale; no commission. Craftworker must attend show; demonstrations OK. Registration limit: 40. Sponsor provides electricity for demonstrations.
Acceptable Work: Considers batik; candlemaking; ceramics; decoupage, dollmaking; glass art; jewelry; lapidary; leatherworking; macrame; metalsmithing; needlecrafts; pottery; tole painting; weaving; and woodcrafting.
Promotion: Show is advertised by newspaper features; radio announcements; posters; listing in calendars of events in tri-state area; membership mailing; and newsletter.
Profile: "Our purpose is to relate colonial crafts to the total museum experience. We are an 18th and 19th century museum which displays, through our exhibits, life in these 2 periods."

This woodcarver is hard at work at the Ye Newe Woodlawn Crafts Festival in Baltimore, Maryland. "Many of our craftsmen have been with us for ten years," says Mrs. Phyllis Abel, chairman of the festival. Demonstrations are a *must* and new activities of interest to both children and adults, are planned to draw large crowds.

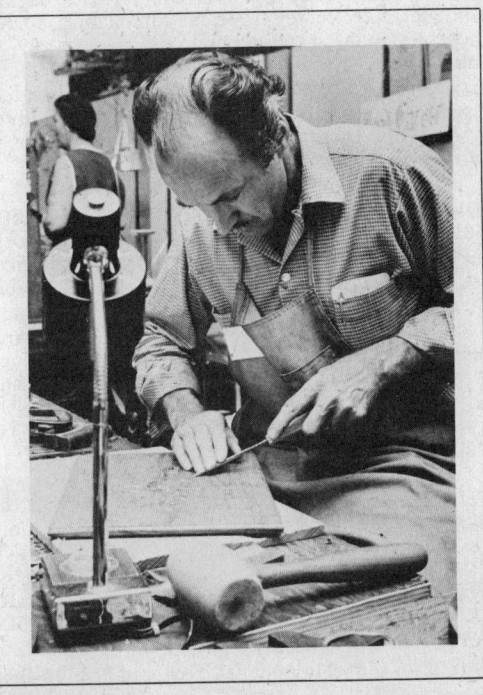

CRAFTS, 409 Wesley Ave., Ocean City NJ 08226. (609)399-7628. Chairman: Shirley A. Waldron. Sponsor: Ocean City Arts Center. Estab. 1972. The show is an annual 2 day event held in September at the Ocean City Boardwalk Music Pier. "Each craftsman is given the option of exhibiting his work within closed quarters or outdoors in a connecting pavilion." Average attendance: 3,000-4,000. Entries accepted until mid-August. Entry fee: $25/8x10 table; 2 craftsmen may share a table for $40; more than 1 table may be reserved for $10 extra. Prejudging by slides or photos; entry fee refunded for refused work. Work may be offered for sale. Craftworker must attend show; demonstrations OK. Registration limit: 60. Sponsor provides chairs; electricity for demonstrations; table; and 24-hour security protection. Show is advertised by radio; TV; direct mail; and news stories.
Acceptable Work: Considers batik; glass art; jewelry; leatherworking; macrame; metalsmithing; mobiles; pottery; soft sculpture; weaving; and woodcrafting.
Sales Tips: "The artist should do well in his sales if his work is displayed attractively. However, the craftsman demonstrating his skill does do better."

CREATIVE CRAFTS, 756 E. Broad St., Westfield NJ 07090. Co-chairwomen: Liz Shapiro, Lee Schoenfeld. Sponsor: Sisterhood—Temple Emanu-El. Estab. 1966. Annual indoor show held 5 days early in November. Average attendance: 3,500. Entries are juried up to 6 weeks prior to show.
Acceptable Work: Considers batik; ceramics; decoupage; glass art; jewelry; leatherworking; macrame; metalsmithing; mobiles; pottery; sculpture; soft sculpture; weaving; and woodcrafting.
Terms: Entry fee: $7.50. "On site" screening preferred but prejudging is done occasionally by slides or photos. Entry fee due after prejudging. Work may be offered for sale; 25% commission. Registration limit: 150. Sponsor provides display panels; theft insurance on exhibited work; insurance on work shipped to artist; shipping costs to artists from show; 24-hour security protection.
Promotion: Show is advertised by magazine; newspaper, radio; publicity and ads. Artist should provide glossy b&w photos and biographies.

CUMBERLAND COUNTY FAIR, 104 West Ave., Bridgeton NJ 08302. (609)451-2998. General Manager: Robert P. Wheaton. Sponsor: Cumberland County Cooperative Fair Association. Purpose: "we have promoted an agricultural fair since 1823—and believe a fair should encompass all areas of interest, something for everybody, to be a well-rounded fair." Estab. 1968. Annual outdoor show (with some tents) held 6 days in July at Cumberland County Fairgrounds, Millville, New Jersey. Average attendance: 80,000. Entries accepted until 2 weeks before show. Entry fee: $100/10x10 display area or 10% of sales. Work may be offered for sale; no commission. Craftworker must attend show; demonstrations OK. Sponsor provides electricity for demonstrations and 24-hour security. Considers all crafts.
Promotion: Fair is advertised by a professional advertising and public relations agency through newspapers; radio; TV; billboards; posters; and brochures. Submit photos or background information.

***DEPTFORD MALL PATRIOTS ART BRIGADE**, 131 Paradise Dr., Berlin NJ 08009. (609)767-3228. Director: Barbara Reeder and Dory Mann. Estab. 1968. Indoor show held 4 days in April and September. Average attendance: 10,000. Entries accepted until 2 weeks before show. Entry fee: $40/12x4 display area. Work may be offered for sale; no commission. Demonstrations OK. Registration limit: 100.
Acceptable Work: Considers batik; candlemaking; dollmaking; glass art; metalsmithing; needlecrafts; pottery; soft sculpture; tole painting; weavings; wall hangings; woodcrafting; ceramics; jewelry; leather by invitation only; and handmade miniature toys. No poured ceramics.
Awards: Presents ribbons. Judging by a panel of 3 college professors, professional artists and craftworkers.

ECHELON MALL ARTS FESTIVAL, Rt. 1, Box 153J, Auburn NH 03032. (603)483-2742. President: Jinx Harris. Estab. 1968. Annual indoor show held 4 days in October at Echelon, New Jersey. Average attendance: 100,000. Entries accepted until 1 week before show or until filled. Entry fee: $40/8x4 display area. Prejudging by slides or photos if not in a previous show. Work may be offered for sale; no commission. Craftworker must attend show; demonstrations OK. Registration limit: 30. Sponsor provides electricity for demonstrations and 24-hour security. Show is advertised by radio; TV; and newspaper. Considers all crafts except ceramics; decoupage; lapidary; strung bead jewelry; 3-D tole; and crocheted items.

ECHELON MALL CHILDREN'S HOUR SHOW, Rt. 1, Box 153J, Auburn NH 03032. (603)483-2742. President: Jinx Harris. Estab. 1977. Annual indoor show held 4 days in September at Echelon, New Jersey. Average attendance: 100,000. Considers all child-oriented crafts except ceramics.
Terms: Entries accepted until 1 week before show or until filled. Entry fee: $40/8x4 display area. Prejudging by slides or photos if not in a previous show. Work may be offered for sale; no commission. Craftworker must attend show; demonstrations OK. Registration limit: 60. Sponsor provides electricity for demonstrations and 24-hour security.

*INDIAN SUMMER ART SHOW, 205 N. Montpelier Ave., Atlantic City NJ 08401. (609)345-5491. Director: Florence Miller. Sponsor: Atlantic City Art Center and City of Atlantic City. Estab. 1962. Annual outdoor show held 2 days in September. Average attendance: "thousands—it is the weekend of the Miss America crowning." Presents $3,000 in cash as well as purchase prizes and ribbons. Show is advertised by newspapers, bulletins, periodicals and flyers.
Acceptable Work: Considers all crafts; limited leatherworking and jewelry (only silver and goldsmiths). Categories: fine arts and crafts.
Terms: Entries accepted until show date. Entry fee: $25/15' display area along boardwalk rail. Work may be offered for sale; no commission. Craftworker must attend show; demonstrations OK if arranged prior to show. "Displays are completely up to the exhibiting artists. They must provide backdrops—windbreakers and protection—in case of inclement weather."

INTERNATIONAL FOLK FESTIVAL, 841 Georges Rd., Brunswick NJ 08902. (201)745-2788. Executive Administrator: Jacqueline E. Rubel. Sponsor: Middlesex County Cultural & Heritage Commission. Estab. 1974. Annual indoor show held 1 day in June at Middlesex County College, Edison, New Jersey. Average attendance: 15,000.
Terms: Entries accepted until 4 weeks before show. No entry fee. Prejudging by slides; photos; or portfolio. Work may not be offered for sale. Craftworker must attend show; demonstrations encouraged. Sponsor provides chairs; electricity for demonstrations; insurance on exhibited work; table; and 24-hour security.
Promotion: Show is advertised by radio; printed media; and TV. Submit photos and resume for promotion. Considers batik; ceramics; decoupage; dollmaking; glass art; jewelry; quilting; leatherworking; macrame; metalsmithing; needlecrafts; pottery; soft sculpture; tole painting; weaving; and woodcrafting.

MOORESTOWN MALL ARTS FESTIVAL, Rt. 1, Box 153J, Auburn NH 03032. (603)483-2742. President: Jinx Harris. Estab. 1964. Annual indoor show held 4 days in November at Moorestown, New Jersey. Average attendance: 60,000.
Acceptable Work: Considers all crafts except ceramics; decoupage under $5; lapidary; and strung bead jewelry.
Terms: Entries accepted until 1 week before show or until filled. Entry fee: $40/8x4 display area. Prejudging by slides or photos if not in a previous show. Work may be offered for sale; no commission. Craftworker must attend show; demonstrations OK. Registration limit: 150. Sponsor provides electricity for demonstrations and 24-hour security.
Promotion: Show is advertised by radio, TV and newspapers.

MOORESTOWN MALL CHILDREN'S HOUR SHOW, Rt. 1, Box 153J, Auburn NH 03032. (603)483-2742. President: Jinx Harris. Estab. 1976. Annual indoor show held 4 days in June at Moorestown, New Jersey. Average attendance: 45,000.
Acceptable Work: Considers all child-oriented crafts except ceramics; decoupage under $5; lapidary; and strung bead jewelry.
Terms: Entries accepted until 1 week before show or until filled. Entry fee: $40/8x4 display area. Prejudging by slides or photos if not in a previous show. Work may be offered for sale; no commission. Craftworker must attend show; demonstrations OK. Registration limit: 100. Sponsor provides electricity for demonstrations and 24-hour security.
Promotion: Show is advertised by radio; TV; and newspapers.

MOORESTOWN MALL CRAFT & SCULPTURE SHOW, Rt. 1, Box 153J, Auburn NH 03032. (603)483-2742. President: Jinx Harris. Estab. 1975. Annual indoor show held 4 days in August at Moorestown, New Jersey. Average attendance: 60,000.
Acceptable Work: Considers all crafts except ceramics; decoupage under $5; lapidary; and strung bead jewelry.
Terms: Entries accepted until 1 week before show or until filled. Entry fee: $40/8x4 display

area. Prejudging by slides or photos if not in a previous show. Work may be offered for sale; no commission. Craftworker must attend show; demonstrations OK. Registration limit: 110. Sponsor provides electricity for demonstrations and 24-hour security. Show is advertised by radio; TV; and newspapers.

MORRISTOWN CRAFTMARKET, Box 2305-R, Morristown NJ 07960. Technical Director: Michael F. Feno. Sponsor: New Jersey Designer-Craftsmen/Kiwanis Club of Randolph Township. Estab. 1977. Annual indoor show held 2 days in October. Attendance: 15,000 in 1978.
Acceptable Work: Considers batik; candlemaking; ceramics; dollmaking; glass art; jewelry; leatherworking; macrame; metalsmithing; pottery; soft sculpture; weaving; and woodcrafting
Terms: Entries accepted until 6 months before show. Entry fee: $5/craftworker; $75 booth fee. Display area: 10x10'. Prejudging by 5 slides; no entry fees refunded for refused work. Work may be offered for sale; no commission. Craftworker must attend show; demonstrations OK. Registration limit: 135. Sponsor provides electricity for demonstrations and 24-hour security.
Promotion: Show is advertised by a paid publicist. The 1978 show sales for craftworkers totalled $175,000.

*****NATIONAL EXHIBITION**, Peters Valley Craftsmen, Layton NJ 07851. (201)948-5202. Contact: Susanne Turino. Purpose: "to exhibit exceptional pieces of raku ceramics for the enjoyment and education of the public." Annual indoor show held 6 weeks in spring at the Peters Valley Craftsmen Gallery. Average attendance: 1,200. Entries accepted until approximately 2 months before show. Entry fee: $4/item being displayed. Maximum 3 entries/craftworker. Prejudging by slides; no entry fees refunded for refused work. Work may be offered for sale; approximately 33⅓% commission. Craftworker needn't attend show; no demonstrations. Registration limit: about 20. Sponsor provides display panels; electricity for demonstrations; insurance on exhibited work; and handles sales. Show is advertised by press releases and magazines. Submit 8x10 b&w glossies for publicity. Considers wood fired ceramics. Presents purchase prizes.

NEW JERSEY FOLK FESTIVAL, American Studies Department, Hickman Hall, Douglass College, New Brunswick NJ 08903. (201)932-9174. Associate Professor of American Studies: Angus Gillespie. Sponsor: The American Studies Department of Douglass College and Rutgers University. Estab. 1975. Annual outdoor show held the last Saturday in April. Average attendance: 5,000.
Acceptable Work: Considers all crafts. No kits. "In general, our festival attempts to encourage and promote the traditional rather than the experimental crafts. No exhibits larger than 10'x8'."
Terms: Entries accepted until 3 weeks before show. Entry fee: $15/artist. Display area: 10x8. Prejudging by 4 35mm slides. Entry fee due after prejudging. Work may be offered for sale; no commission. Craftworker must attend show; demonstrations encouraged. Registration limit: 40-70. Sponsor provides display panels.
Sales Tip: "Because the festival is located on a college campus, work which would appeal to young adults would stand a larger chance of selling."

PATRIOTS ART BRIGADE, 37 Sunset Dr., Berlin NJ 08009. (609)767-3228 or 767-1874. Directors: Barbara Reeder and Dory Mann. "I feel there is much talent in our own back yard, and it is a wonderful proving ground for the experienced and inexperienced artist or craftsman." Estab. 1969. Semiannual indoor show held 4 days (Thursday-Sunday) in April and in September at Deptford, New Jersey. Average attendance: 100,000. Entries accepted until 3 weeks before show. Entry fee: $40/12' space. Prejudging by slides, personal interview, or photos; entry fee refunded for refused work. Work may be offered for sale; no commission. Craftworker must attend show; demonstrations OK. Registration limit: 60-100. Battery operated lights only. Sponsor provides 24-hour security and insurance on accidents. Considers all crafts (but ceramics; jewelry; and leatherworking by invitation only). "Work must be of professional quality."
Sales Tip: "An artist or craftsman should have 2 types of work with him—low cost items and higher priced things. We've had decorators for department stores give exclusive contracts to craftsmen which can be a permanent job for them. A Hilton Hotel manager passing through took fancy to a woodcarver and ordered several birds carved to be made into lamps for the hotel. Your best work is the surest way to sales."
Promotion: Show is advertised in local papers; *Philadelphia Enquirer* weekend magazine; *Courrier Post;* radio; and posters. "Sometimes we can get a photographer from the newspaper to take pictures of the show and interview prize winners. Sometimes we feature a really unusual craft in our preshow publicity."

QUAKER BRIDGE MALL ARTS FESTIVAL, Rt. 1, Box 153J, Auburn NH 03032. (703)483-2742. President: Jinx Harris. Estab. 1976. Annual indoor show held 4 days in June at Princeton, New Jersey. Average attendance: 60,000.
Acceptable Work: Considers all crafts except ceramics; decoupage under $5; lapidary; and strung bead jewelry.
Terms: Entries accepted until 1 week before show or until filled. Entry fee: $40/8x4 display area. Prejudging by slides or photos if not in a previous show. Work may be offered for sale; no commission. Craftworker must attend show; demonstrations OK. Registration limit: 50. Sponsor provides electricity for demonstrations and 24-hour security. Show is advertised by radio; TV; and newspapers.

QUAKER BRIDGE MALL CHILDREN'S HOUR SHOW, Rt. 1, Box 153J, Auburn NH 03032. (603)483-2742. President: Jinx Harris. Estab. 1977. Annual indoor show held 4 days in January at Princeton, New Jersey. Average attendance: 25,000.
Acceptable Work: Considers batik; candlemaking; decoupage; dollmaking; glass art; jewelry; leatherworking; animal macrame; metalsmithing; mobiles; pottery; sculpture; and soft sculpture. "This show is for child-oriented items only."
Terms: Entries accepted until 1 week before show. Entry fee: $40/8x4 display area. Prejudging by slides or photos. Work may be offered for sale; no commission. Craftworker must attend show; demonstrations OK. Registration limit: 75. Sponsor provides electricity for demonstrations and 24-hour security.
Promotion: Show is advertised by radio, TV and newspapers.

*****SUMMER MALL ART SHOW**, Shore Mall Management Office, Black Horse Pike and Tilton Rd., Pleasantville NJ 08232. (609)646-2157. Director: Florence Miller. Sponsor: Shore Mall. Estab. 1966. Annual indoor show held 3 days in August. Average attendance: hundreds. Considers all crafts. Presents $1,500 in cash awards, $200 in purchase prizes, and ribbons. Entries accepted at start of show. Entry fee: $15/10' display area. Work may be offered for sale; no commission. Craftworker must attend show; demonstrations OK. Sponsor provides 24-hour security. Show is advertised by newspapers, craft bulletins and radio.

SUPER CRAFTS SUNDAY, Box 1688, Westhampton Beach NY 11978. (516)325-1331. Promoters: Barbara Hope or Don Gaiti. Sponsor: Creative Faires, Ltd. Estab. 1978. Annual indoor show held 1 day in November at East Rutherford, New Jersey. Average attendance: 12,000.
Acceptable Work: Considers all original crafts except tole painting and decoupage. "No kits, machine-made crafts, or any craft that lacks in workmanship, style or imagination."
Terms: Entries accepted until 4 weeks before show. Entry fee: $55 (or $65 for a corner). Display area: 10x15. Prejudging by 5 slides of work and 1 slide of display; entry fee refunded for refused work. Work may be offered for sale; no commission. Craftworker must attend show; demonstrations OK. Registration limit: 175 booths. Sponsor provides electricity for demonstrations, overhead lighting and 24-hour security.
Sales Tip: "A unique, attractive or functional piece of craftwork has appeal to the public. The display of a fine craft always enhances the work's appearance, if presented properly."

*****WEST HUDSON COMMUNITY ARTS FESTIVAL**, 66 Dukes St., Kearny NJ 07032. (201)998-1067. Chairman: Phyllis Adams. Sponsor: The Halfpenny Playhouse. Purpose: to "display the artistry of New Jersey but not to the exclusion of artists in other states. To promote the goodwill of the town of Kearny and the county of Hudson to both the general public and the artistic community. To assist in improving the quality of life in the community and the encouragement of budding talent by including juniors and non-professionals who receive the same cash awards as the professionals. We deliberately inter-mix pros, non-pros, and juniors to provide the artists and public with a variety of quality and artists." Estab. 1969. Annual outdoor show held 1 day in June. Average attendance: 15,000. Entries accepted up until show date. Entry fee: $5/10' on snow or anchor-fencing; $3/senior citizen over 63; and no fee/juniors. Work may be offered for sale; no commission. Craftworker or representative must attend show; demonstrations encouraged. Sponsor provides fencing.
Awards: Presents cash awards of at least $3,000 and ribbons to best in show, 1st, 2nd, 3rd and honorable mentions in all categories. "Only honorable mentions do not receive cash awards." Average show sales totalled $50,000. Considers all crafts.
Promotion: Show is advertised by "major feature stories with pictures starting 2 weeks prior to event in all major papers including *New York Times*, *New York News* and New Jersey dailies and weeklies. Listed on all community bulletin boards of all New York and New Jersey AM and

FM radios. Heavy poster coverage of nearby affluent areas in northern New Jersey. Listed in newsletters of multiple state and private arts agencies. Listed in all events calendars of all New York and New Jersey newspapers. Ads in selected arts magazines. The minimum the artist should have available is a calling card. We find many sales are made within 3 months after events. Suggest, where financially feasible, that artists provide public with a free flyer or brochure with samples of his work included in photographs and information on his training; awards; and showing."

Sales Tip: "Our public comes from Pennsylvania, New Jersey, New York, and Connecticut. They are looking for bargains not normally available at the larger New York outdoor events. Our entrants come from as far away as Florida and Wyoming because of the heavy selling traffic. Decorative items such as flowers, rag dolls, jewelry, wall hangings and glass items are heavy sellers. Public likes to buy, where possible, those items created on the spot."

WILLOWBROOK MALL ART SHOW, Rt. 1, Box 153J, Auburn NH 03032. (603)483-2742. President: Jinx Harris. Estab. 1969. Annual indoor show held 4 days in February at Wayne, New Jersey. Average attendance: 100,000.
Terms: Entries accepted until 1 week before show or until filled. Entry fee: $40/8x4 display area. Prejudging by slides or photos if not in a previous show. Work may be offered for sale; no commission. Craftworker must attend show; demonstrations OK. Registration limit: 30. Sponsor provides electricity for demonstrations and 24-hour security.
Promotion: Show is advertised by radio, TV and newspapers.

WILLOWBROOK MALL CHILDREN'S HOUR SHOW, Rt. 1, Box 153J, Auburn NH 03032. (603)483-2742. President: Jinx Harris. Estab. 1977. Annual indoor show held 4 days in May at Wayne, New Jersey. Average attendance: 150,000.
Acceptable Work: Considers all child-oriented crafts except ceramics; decoupage under $5; lapidary; and strung bead jewelry.
Terms: Entries accepted until 1 week before show or until filled. Entry fee: $40/8x4 display area. Prejudging by slides or photos if not in a previous show. Work may be offered for sale; no commission. Craftworker must attend show; demonstrations OK. Registration limit: 125. Sponsor provides electricity for demonstrations and 24-hour security.

WILLOWBROOK MALL FIBER FAIR, Rt. 1, Box 153J, Auburn NH 03032. (603)483-2742. President: Jinx Harris. Estab. 1978. Annual indoor show held 4 days in June at Wayne, New Jersey. Average attendance: 150,000.
Acceptable Work: Considers batik; dollmaking; macrame; mobiles; needlecrafts; soft sculpture; weaving; and all crafts of fiber or combined with fibers.
Terms: Entries accepted until 1 week before show or until filled. Entry fee: $35/8x4 display area. Prejudging by slides or photos if not in a previous show. Work may be offered for sale; no commission. Craftworker must attend show; demonstrations OK. Registration limit: 100. Sponsor provides electricity for demonstrations and 24-hour security.
Promotion: Show is advertised by radio, TV and newspaper.

WILLOWBROOK MALL WOODEN WAY SHOW, Rt. 1, Box 153J, Auburn NH 03032. (603)483-2742. President: Jinx Harris. Estab. 1978. Annual indoor show held 4 days in April at Wayne, New Jersey. Average attendance: 150,000. Considers wood crafts only.
Terms: Entries accepted until 1 week before show or until filled. Entry fee: $40/8x4 display area. Prejudging by slides or photos if not in a previous show. Work may be offered for sale; no commission. Craftworker must attend show; demonstrations OK. Registration limit: 100. Sponsor provides electricity for demonstrations and 24-hour security protection.

WOODBRIDGE CENTER CRAFT & SCULPTURE SHOW, Rt. 1, Box 153J, Auburn NH 03032. (603)483-2742. President; Jinx Harris. Estab. 1975. Annual indoor show held 4 days in January, June and September at Woodbridge, New Jersey. Average attendance: 85,000.
Acceptable Work: Considers all crafts except ceramics; lapidary; decoupage under $5; and strung bead jewelry.
Terms: Entries accepted until 1 week before show or until filled. Entry fee: $40/8x4 display area. Prejudging by slides or photos if not in a previous show. Work may be offered for sale; no commission. Craftworker must attend show; demonstrations OK. Registration limit: 200. Sponsor provides electricity for demonstrations and 24-hour security.
Promotion: Show is advertised by radio, TV and newspapers.

New Mexico

ARTS & CRAFTS FAIR OF THE SOUTHWEST, Box 122, Roswell NM 88201. Contact: Exhibitors' Chairman. Sponsor: Roswell Jaycees. Estab. 1973. Annual indoor show held first weekend in May. Average attendance: 4,000. Entries accepted until March 1. Entry fee: $40/booth with 8x8' pegboard; $20/additional craftworker. Prejudging; entry fee refunded for refused work. Work must be offered for sale; no commission. Open to craftworkers ages 18. Craftworker must attend show; demonstrations encouraged. Registration limit; 100 booths.
Acceptable Work: Considers batik; candlemaking; ceramics; dollmaking; glass art; jewelry; leatherworking; metalsmithing; needlecrafts; pottery; soft sculpture; tole painting; weavings; wall hangings; woodcrafting; and mosaics. Only safety catches on jewelry are accepted as manufactured.

*****C.R.A.F.T.**, Box 737, Tucumcari NM 88401. Booth Chairman: Danny Young. Estab. 1973. Annual indoor show held 2 days during the first weekend of June. Average attendance: 2,000. Presents purchase prizes.
Acceptable Work: Considers all crafts. "The articles must be original and entirely the work of the artist. Exception: jewelry findings, frames and supports."
Terms: Entries accepted until 2 weeks before show or until spaces filled. Entry fee: approximately $25/6x8 display area. Work must be offered for sale; no commission. Craftworker must attend show; demonstrations OK. Registration limit: 70. Sponsor provides chairs, pegboard display panels, eletricity for demonstrations, table and night watchman.
Promotion: Show is advertised by newspapers, craft magazines, radio and posters. "We run pictures of artists and their wares in local newspapers."

DE VARGAS SUMMER ARTS & CRAFTS SHOW, Box 205, Santa Fe NM 87501. (505)988-1110. President: Jane Dunn. Sponsor: Southwest Arts, Inc. Purpose: fundraiser. Estab. 1975. Annual indoor show held 3 days in July. Entries accepted until 3 weeks before show. Entry fee: $50/craftworker; $50/8x4 display area. Prejudging, first year only, by slides and photos; entry fee refunded for refused work. Work may be offered for sale; no commission. Craftworker must attend show; demonstrations OK. Registration limit: 80-100. Sponsor provides electricity for demonstrations and 24-hour security. Show is advertised by radio; newspaper; posters; and direct mail. Considers all crafts.

*****NEW MEXICO ARTS & CRAFTS FAIR**, Box 30044, Albuquerque NM 87190. (505)265-3171. Manager: Ann Anthony. Estab. 1962. Annual outdoor show held the last Friday, Saturday and Sunday in June. Average attendance: 100,000. Closing date for entry: February. Entry fee: $60/booth plus $7.50 jury fee. Samples due for prejudging in February; no prejudging fees refunded for refused work. Work must be offered for sale; no commission. Open to New Mexico residents, ages 18. Craftworker must attend show and use booths. Sponsor provides lighting. Considers all arts and crafts. Presents 20 awards of $50 each.

*****NEW MEXICO CRAFTS BIENNIAL**, Box 2087, Santa Fe NM 87501. (505)827-2544. Curator: Judith Cohen. Sponsor: Museum of International Folk Art, a division of the Museum of New Mexico. Estab. 1953. Biennial indoor show suspended until 1981.

PEANUT VALLEY FESTIVAL, Campus Union, Eastern New Mexico University, Portales NM 88130. (505)562-2631. Director of Student Activities: Bill Martin. Estab. 1974. Annual indoor show held 3 days in October. Average attendance: 4,000. Entries accepted until 1 week before show. Entry fee: $15/display area. Work may be offered for sale; no commission. Craftworker must attend show; demonstrations OK. Sponsor provides display panels and electricty for demonstrations. Show is advertised by newspaper; radio; and *New Mexico Magazine*. Considers all crafts.

PLAZA ARTS & CRAFTS SHOW, Girls' Club, 301 Hillside, Santa Fe NM 87501. (505)982-2042. Director of Girls' Club: Helen Brown. Sponsor: Santa Fe Girls' Club Auxiliary. Purpose: fundraiser. Estab. 1972. Annual outdoor show held 1st Saturday in August at the Santa Fe Plaza. Average attendance: 2,000. Entries accepted until 2 weeks before show. Entry fee: $30/craftworker. Display area: 10x10. Prejudging preferred by photos; accepts slides. Entry fee refunded for refused work. Work may be offered for sale; no commission. Craftworker must attend show; demonstrations OK if space permits. Registration limit: 200. Sponsor provides trash bags; parking areas; and relief people. Show is advertised by newspapers; magazines; TV; and radio. Considers all crafts.

SANTA FE FESTIVAL OF THE ARTS, 435 Paseo de Peralta, Santa Fe NM 87501. (505)988-3924. Executive Director: Sara Sheldon. Sponsor: Santa Fe Festival Foundation. "Goals are to promote Santa Fe as a national art center and to bring national exposure to artists and craftsmen who show here." Estab. 1977. Annual indoor show held 10 days late September-early October. Average attendance: 10,000. Entries limited to craftspeople residing in New Mexico. Entries due 6 weeks before show. Judging is of actual craftwork. Entry fee: $5/craftsperson, not refundable. Accepted entries should be for sale; 20% commission to Foundation. Write for entry form at above address. Show is advertised by national magazine ads; national newspaper press releases; direct mail; TV; and radio. Submit photos and resumes for catalog.
Acceptable Work: Considers batik; ceramics; glass art; jewelry; leatherworking; macrame; metalsmithing; needlecrafts; pottery; soft sculpture; weaving; and woodcrafting. "This is a tri-cultural show with Indian, Hispanic, and other crafts. Everything is displayed as fine arts—on pedestal, in a case, or on a wall. Display up to discretion of committee."

SOUTHWEST CRAFTS BIENNIAL, Box 2087, Santa Fe NM 87501. (505)827-2544. Curator: Judith Cohen. Sponsor: Museum of International Folk Art, a division of the Museum of New Mexico. Estab. 1953. Biennial indoor show suspended until 1981.

*****SWAIA INDIAN MARKET**, Box 1964, Santa Fe NM 87501. (505)983-5220. Executive Secretary: Sally M. Kandarian. Sponsor: Southwestern Association on Indian Affairs. Purpose: "to promote quality Indian handmade arts and crafts and to provide a setting where craftworker and buyer can confront each other to the benefit of both." Estab. 1922. Annual outdoor invitational show held 2 days in August. Average attendance: 30,000. Entries accepted until 1 month before show. Entry fee: $50/6x8 display area. Maximum 3 pieces per category per artist for awards. Prejudging by slides; entry fee due after prejudging. Work may be offered for sale; no commission. Craftworker must attend show; demonstrations OK. Registration limit: 326. Sponsor provides coverings and display panels. Show is advertised by mailings and all media. Presents cash awards and ribbons. Considers all handcrafted Southwestern Indian arts.

*****TAOS FESTIVAL OF THE ARTS**, Drawer I, Taos NM 87571. (505)758-3873. Manager: Betty Armantrout. Sponsor: Taos County Chamber of Commerce. Estab. 1975. Annual indoor/outdoor show held 1 week in October. Average attendance: 2,000. Entries accepted until 4 weeks before show. Entry fee: $45/8x10 display area. Prejudging by slides; $5 of entry fee not refunded for refused work. Work may be offered for sale; no commission. Craftworker must attend show; demonstrations encouraged. Registration limit: 40. Sponsor provides 12-hour security protection. Show is advertised by national magazines; newspapers; TV; and radio. Presents 8 cash awards of $50. Considers all crafts except decoupage; mobiles; and tole painting.

New York

ADVENTURES IN CRAFTS DECOUPAGE SALE & EXHIBIT, 218 81st St., New York NY 10028. (212)628-8081. Contact: Dee Davis. Sponsor: Multiple Sclerosis. Estab. 1975. Annual indoor show held 2 weeks in March.
Terms: Entries accepted up until show. Entry fee: $5/artist. Display area: 400 square feet. Maximum 12 pieces per craftworker. Prejudging ("usually I have seen the craftsman's work at my studio"); entry fee due after prejudging. Work may be offered for sale; 2-25% commission which goes to the multiple sclerosis fund. Craftworker must serve a 2-hour shift as a salesperson; demonstrations OK. Registration limit: 35. Sponsor provides tables and 24-hour security. Considers quality decoupage.
Sales Tip: Offer variety—boxes; purses; plates; lamps; pictures; and plaques. 1977 show sales totalled $1,200.
Promotion: Show is advertised by posters; and press releases to newspapers and radio. Invitations sent by Adventures in Crafts and participants receive invitations to send.

*****ALLENTOWN OUTDOOR ART FESTIVAL**, Box 1566, Ellicott Station, Buffalo NY 14205. Contact: Chairman of Entries. Sponsor: Allentown Village Society. Estab. 1958. Annual outdoor show held 2 days during the second weekend in June. Average attendance: 300,000-400,000. Considers all crafts except decoupage and needlecrafts.
Terms: Entries accepted until 10 weeks before show. "Applications are usually mailed late January to early February. Names and addresses are accepted year 'round for mailing list." Non-refundable application fee: $5. Entry fee: $30 (subject to change). Display area: 15' street frontage. Prejudging by slides. Entry fee refunded for refused work. Work may be offered for

sale; no commission. Craftworker must attend show; demonstrations limited (no power supplied; must be kept within space). Registration limit: about 150 in crafts (470 total).
Awards: Presents cash awards and ribbons for 1st, 2nd, 3rd and honorable mention.
Promotion: Show is advertised by newspapers, radio, TV, trade magazines and posters.

*AMERICAN CRAFTS FESTIVAL, Box 20, Hasbrouck Hts. NJ 07604. Director: Brenda Brigham. Sponsor: American Concern for Artistry and Craftsmanship. Estab. 1977. Annual outdoor show held the first 2 weekends (4 days) in July at Lincoln Center for the Performing Arts, New York City. Average attendance: 95,000-100,000.
Acceptable Work: Considers basketry, batik, broommaking, candlemaking, ceramics, dollmaking, glass art, jewelry, lapidary, leatherworking, macrame, metalsmithing, needlecrafts, pottery, rag rugs, scrimshaw, soft sculpture, weaving, woodcrafting. No kits, imports, manufactured products (or embellished from commercially manufactured products), or items made primarily of pressed or dried flowers, cut bottles or shells. "The booth display must be attractive, neat and complimentary to the quality crafts exhibited."
Terms: Entries accepted until the end of April. Entry fee: $60/10x7 display area per weekend. Prejudging by 5 color slides of items representative of work to be displayed. Entry fee refunded for unselected work. Work must be offered for sale; 5% commission. Craftworker or representative must attend show; demonstrations OK. Registration limit: 125/weekend. Sponsor provides electricity for demonstrations and 24-hour security. Exhibitor handles sales and taxes.
Awards: Presents 2 $50 cash prizes for Best Display, and 2 $50 prizes for Fine Craftsmanship; 5 certificates of honorable mention for display and 5 certificates of honorable mention for fine craftsmanship. "It is expected that displays will be consistent with the craftperson's concern for good marketing technique and the cultural environment in which the festival is held. Craftsmanship must be of the highest quality combined with innovative and unique design."
Promotion: Show is advertised by radio, TV, newspaper publications, magazine articles, posters and banners. "Promotional materials may be requested from participants."
Sales Tip: "The display plays an extremely important part in the salability of a creation of art. A display enhances the craft and at the same time creates an interest for the prospective buyer."

*ART IN THE PARK, Box 641, Elmira NY 14902. Chairman: Cameron Macdonell. Sponsor: Southern Tier Arts Association Inc. Estab. 1974. Annual outdoor show held 2 days during the third weekend in May. Show occurs during the Mark Twain Festival. Average attendance: 10,000.
Acceptable Work: Considers batik, candlemaking, ceramics, glass art, jewelry, leatherworking, macrame, metalsmithing, mobiles, needlecrafts, pottery, sculpture, soft sculpture, weaving and woodcrafting. No patterns, kits or greenware.
Terms: Entries accepted until 3 weeks before show. Entry fee: $10/8x10 display area. Prejudging by slides and photos. $5 prejudging fee balance refunded for refused work. Work may be offered for sale; no commission. Craftworker must attend show; demonstrations OK. Registration limit: 150. Sponsor provides electricity for demonstrations.
Awards: Presents cash and purchase awards. Bestsellers: functional art and jewelry.

*ASID INTERNATIONAL EXPOSITION OF DESIGNER SOURCES, 730 5th Ave., New York NY 10019. (212)586-7111. Coordinator: Ed Gips. Sponsor: American Society of Interior Designers. Estab. 1971. Annual indoor show held 4 days in July. Average attendance: 2,000.
Terms: Entries accepted until 2 weeks before show. Charges entry fee for 8x10' display area. Prejudging; no entry fees refunded. Considers all crafts. Presents ribbons.

*AUTUMN ART FESTIVAL, 19 Bernard Ave., Norwood NY 13668. (315)353-9909. Chairperson: Jane Peacock. Sponsor: Village of Norwood. Estab. 1972. Annual show held in outdoor arena with open sides 2 days in September. Average attendance: 5,000. Entries accepted until 1 week before show. Entry fee: $5/artist. Work may be offered for sale; no commission. Craftworker must attend show; demonstrations OK. Sponsor provides easels and fencing. Show is advertised by newspapers; radio; TV; and many publications. Presents ribbons and cash awards of $20, 1st; $15, 2nd; $10, 3rd; and $5, 4th in each category. Considers all crafts except glass art; lapidary; metalsmithing; mobiles; soft sculpture; and tole painting.
Sales Tip: "If artist can send information and photos for promotion at time of entry it will be included in pre-publicity of the show. This helps the public decide ahead what is available."

BEDFORD VILLAGE ART SHOW, Rt. 1, Box 218, Bedford NY 10506. (914)234-3704. Director: Lydia Ward. Purpose: "fund raiser for cancer care. Attracts more than 10,000." Held outdoors 3rd weekend in Otober. Entries accepted until the end of September. Entry fee:

$40/8x10 space. Prejudged by 5 slides, including 1 of display. Entry fee refunded for refused work. Craftworker may sell; no commission. No kits, molds, imports.

BELL STREET ARTISTS CRAFTS FAIR, Box 211, Bellport NY 11713. (516)286-0776. Chairman, Craft Research Committee: Nancy T. Ljungqvist. Sponsor: Bell Street Artists. Estab. 1974. Annual outdoor show (in high school gym if rain) held 1 day in September.
Acceptable Work: Considers batik; candlemaking; ceramics; blown, stained and leaded glass; lapidary, leatherworking, macrame, metalsmithing, mobiles; needlecrafts; pottery; scrimshaw; soft sculpture; tole painting; weaving; spinning; woodcrafting; driftwood sculpture; cloisonne enamel and "other fine crafts." No needlepoint pictures, batik pictures or fine art. "Only items of superior quality will be accepted. Submit your finest, although not most expensive work."
Terms: Entries accepted until 6 weeks before show. Entry fee: $20/15x15 outdoor or 10x10 indoor display area. Prejudging of actual samples; entry fee due after prejudging. Work must be offered for sale; no commission. Craftworker must attend show; demonstrations OK. Registration limit: 61. Sponsor provides electricity for demonstration.
Promotion: Show is advertised by newspapers, radio, flyers, mailings and posters. Submit b&w photos plus anything relevant for publicity.

CHRISTMAS ARTS & CRAFTS SHOW, 25 Seneca St., Shortsville NY 14548. (716)289-9439. President: Ronald L. Johnson. Sponsor: Finger Lakes Craftsmen. Estab. 1975. Annual indoor show held 2 days in December at Rochester, New York. Average attendance: 10,000.
Terms: Entries accepted until show is full (sometimes early). Entry fee: $55-90/10x7 display area. Work may be offered for sale; no commission. Craftworker must attend show; demonstrations OK. Registration limit: 200. Sponsor provides 24-hour security.
Promotion: Show is advertised by TV; radio; and newspaper ($3,500 budget). Considers all crafts.

CONTEMPORARY CRAFTS SHOWCASE WITH ART AT THE BOULEVARD MALL, Box 3845, Indialantic FL 32903. (212)884-7952. President: Michael Picow. Sponsor: Prema Productions. Estab. 1977. Annual indoor show held 4 days in April at Buffalo, New York. Average attendance: 10,000.
Acceptable Work: Considers all crafts except decoupage, dollmaking, mobiles and lapidary. No commercial casts or kits, machine-made items, coin jewelry or paintings on stones. "All displays must be neat and professional looking."
Terms: Entries accepted until 4 weeks before show. Entry fee: $45/8x10 display area, $60/8x15 display area, and $80/8x20 display area. Prejudging by 35mm slides—3 of actual work and 1 of display. Entry fee refunded for refused work. Work may be offered for sale; no commission. Craftworker must attend show; demonstrations OK. Registration limit: 75. Sponsor provides electricity for demonstrations and 24-hour security.
Promotion: Show is advertised by local newspapers, radio and posters. "8x10 b&w glossy photos would be helpful" for promotional purposes.

CONTEMPORARY CRAFTS SHOWCASE WITH ART AT THE RIVERSIDE MALL, Box 3845, Indialantic FL 32903. (212)884-7952. President: Michael Picow. Sponsor: Prema Productions. Estab. 1977. Annual indoor show held 4 days in May during Mother's Day weekend at Utica, New York. Average attendance: 10,000.
Acceptable Work: Considers all crafts except decoupage, dollmaking, mobiles and lapidary. No commercial casts or kits, machine-made items, coin jewelry or paintings on stones. "All displays must be neat and professional looking."
Terms: Entries accepted until 4 weeks before show. Entry fee: $45/8x10 display area, $60/8x15 display area, and $80/8x20 display area. Prejudging by 35mm slides—3 of actual work and 1 of display. Entry fee refunded for refused work. Work may be offered for sale; no commission. Craftworker must attend show; demonstrations OK. Registration limit: 65. Sponsor provides electricity for demonstrations and 24-hour security.
Promotion: Show is advertised by local newspapers, radio and posters. "8x10 b&w glossy photos would be helpful" for promotional purposes.

CONTEMPORARY CRAFTS SHOWCASE WITH ART AT THE SHOPPINGTOWN MALL, Box 3845, Indialantic FL 32903. (212)884-7952. President: Michael Picow. Sponsor: Prema Productions. Estab. 1977. Annual indoor show held 4 days in May at Syracuse, New York. Average attendance: 10,000.
Acceptable Work: Considers all crafts except decoupage, dollmaking, mobiles and lapidary. No

commercial casts or kits, machine-made items, coin jewelry or paintings on stones. "All displays must be neat and professional looking."
Terms: Entries accepted until 4 weeks before show. Entry fee: $50/8x10 display area, $70/8x15 display area, and $90/8x20 display area. Prejudging by 35mm slides—3 of actual work and 1 of display. Entry fee refunded for refused work. Work may be offered for sale; no commission. Craftworker must attend show; demonstrations OK. Registration limit: 85. Sponsor provides electricity for demonstrations and 24-hour security.
Promotion: Show is advertised by local newspapers, radio and posters. "8x10 b&w glossy photos would be helpful" for promotional purposes.

CONTEMPORARY CRAFTS SHOWCASE WITH ART AT THE SUMMIT PARK MALL, Box 3845, Indialantic FL 32903. (212)884-7952. President: Michael Picow. Sponsor: Prema Productions. Estab. 1977. Annual indoor show held 4 days in May at Buffalo, New York. Average attendance: 10,000.
Acceptable Work: Considers all crafts except decoupage, dollmaking, mobiles and lapidary. No commercial casts or kits, machine-made items, coin jewelry or paintings on stones. "All displays must be neat and professional looking."
Terms: Entries accepted until 4 weeks before show. Entry fee: $45/8x10 display area, $60/8x15 display area, and $80/8x20 display area. Prejudging by 35mm slides—3 of actual work and 1 of display. Entry fee refunded for refused work. Work may be offered for sale; no commission. Craftworker must attend show; demonstrations OK. Registration limit: 75. Sponsor provides electricity for demonstrations and 24-hour security.
Promotion: Show is advertised by local newspapers, radio and posters. "8x10 b&w glossy photos would be helpful" for promotional purposes.

*COOPERSTOWN ANNUAL NATIONAL ART EXHIBITION, Cooperstown Art Association, 22 Main St., Cooperstown NY 13326. (607)547-9777. Exhibition Director: Olga Welch. Estab. 1928. Annual indoor prejudged show held 4 weeks in the summer. Entries accepted by agent until 6 weeks before show. Entry fee: $7.50. Maximum 1 piece per craftworker. Categories: painting; sculpture; and crafts. Considers all crafts. Presents cash awards totalling $3,000.

*CORN HILL ARTS FESTIVAL, 21 Atkinson St., Historic Corn Hill District, Rochester NY 14608. (716)546-6754. Advisor: Wayne Frank. Sponsor: Corn Hill Neighbors. Estab. 1968. Annual outdoor show held 2 days in July. Average attendance: 200,000. Entries accepted until June 15. Entry fee: $40/craftworker. Display area: 10'. Work may be offered for sale; no commission. Craftworker must attend show; demonstrations OK. Registration limit: 500. Show is advertised by newspaper; TV; radio; and Rochester's Bureau of Special Events and Tourism. Submit nonreturnable photo for publicity if you have an unusual craft. Presents $500 in cash. Considers all crafts.

CRAFT DAYS, Madison County Historical Society, 435 Main St., Oneida NY 13421. (315)363-4136. Director: John H. Braunlein. Estab. 1964. Annual outdoor show under tents held 2 days in September. Average attendance: 8,000.
Acceptable Work: Considers all crafts, except batik, decoupage, lapidary, mobiles, sculpture and soft sculpture. Must be traditional crafts and all must be handmade. No kits or machine-made items.
Terms: Entries accepted until about 4 months before show. Display area: 12x16 maximum. Prejudging by personal interview. Work may be offered for sale; no commission. Craftworker must attend show; demonstrations required. Registration limit: 120. Sponsor provides electricity for demonstrations and 24-hour security. Exhibitor handles sales and taxes.
Promotion: Show is advertised by radio, TV, and newspaper news releases. Posters and placemats are distributed in local and area restaurants and signs placed at major intersections. Submit photos and biographical data.

CRAFT FESTIVAL, Schenectady Museum, Nott Terrace Heights, Schenectady NY 12308. Chairman: Charlotte Moody. Sponsor: Designer Crafts Council of Schenectady Museum. Estab. 1971. Annual indoor show held 2 days in September. Average attendance: 5,000. Entries accepted until 3 months before show. Entry fee: $5 prejudging fee plus $35 upon acceptance. Display area: 10x10. Prejudging by slides; entry fee not refunded for refused work. Work may be offered for sale; no commission. Craftworker must attend show; demonstrations OK. Registration limit: 80-100. Sponsor provides electricity for demonstrations and 24-hour secu-

---

* Those listings preceded by an asterisk present awards for prize-winning crafts.

rity. Show is advertised by newspapers; radio; TV; and posters. Considers all crafts.

CRAFTPRODUCERS MARKETPLACE, North Hill, Readsboro VT 05350. Directors: Charley Dooley and Riki Moss. Sponsor: Craftproducers Incorporated. Annual indoor show held during the first weekend in August at Saratoga Springs, New York. Considers all crafts.
Terms: Entries accepted from mid-April to late-June. Entry fee: $80/8x10' display area. Prejudging by 5 slides. Work must be offered for sale; no commission. Craftworker must attend show; demonstrations OK. Registration limit: 50-60. Sponsors provide chairs, electricity for demonstrations ($5 fee), tables and 24-hour protection.

CRAFTS & CREATIONS, Putnam Arts Council, Box 156, Mahopac NY 10541. (914)628-3664. Chairman: Louise Wood. Estab. 1971. Annual indoor show held 2 days in November during Thanksgiving weekend. Average attendance: 1,000.
Terms: Entries accepted until filled. Entry fee: $25/8' display area. Prejudging by slides and photos; entry fee due after prejudging. Work may be offered for sale; no commission. Craftworker must attend show; demonstrations OK. Registration limit: 30. Sponsor provides chairs.
Promotion: Show is advertised by newspaper; radio; posters; and mailings. Submit publicity photos. Considers all crafts. Bestsellers: holiday gifts.

CRAFTS FAIR, First United Methodist Church, Davison St. and Atlantic Ave., Oceanside NY 11572. (516)766-9787. Committee Member: Adele Jack. Estab. 1973. Annual indoor show held 2 days in May. Average attendance: 350-400. Entries accepted until 1 week before show. Entry fee: $20/8' display area. Tables must have skirts (crepe paper). Prejudging by photos; entry fee due after prejudging. Work may be offered for sale; no commission. Craftworker must attend show; demonstrations OK. Registration limit: 30-33. Sponsor provides chairs and 24-hour security. Show is advertised by radio; magazines; and posters. Each craftworker is sent a poster to display in a prominent place. Considers all crafts.

CRAFTS IN ACTION SHOW & SALE, 8 Parkway Plaza, Canandaigue NY 14424. (716)394-0450. Manager: Ruth Brewer. Sponsor: Creative Craft Boutique. Estab. 1971. Annual outdoor show (with plaza overhang) held 3 days in July. Considers all crafts. No machine-made items.
Terms: Entries accepted until show date. Entry fee: $5/day per 5x10 or 5x12 display area. Work may be offered for sale; no commission. Craftworker needn't attend show; demonstrations OK. Registration limit: 50. Exhibitor handles sales and taxes.
Promotion: Show is advertised by newspapers, Finger Lakes Associate Calendar, *Canandaigue Shoppers Guide*, posters and sometimes radio.

CROTON CRAFTS FAIR, Box 277, Croton On Hudson NY 10520. (914)271-5302. Crafts Chairperson: Monya Brown. Sponsor: Croton Council on the Arts. Estab. 1975. Annual outdoor show held 2 days in the third week in September. Average attendance: 4,000-5,000. Entries accepted up until filled. Entry fee: $35/10x10 display area. Prejudging by 4-5 slides or photos (include 1 slide of display). Entry fee due after prejudging. Work must be offered for sale; no commission. Craftworker or representative must attend show; demonstrations "only if we agree to them." Registration limit: 100. Sponsor provides security. Considers pottery; jewelry; macrame; wood; fine arts; weaving; soft cloth work; batik; leather; stained glass; blown glass; candles; and other original crafts.
Sales Tip: "An attractive display is a huge help, also a varied price range. We suggest that all artists have inexpensive items, up to $10 plus higher priced things. Business cards are helpful and a pleasant, friendly manner as well."
Promotion: Show is advertised by posters; postcards; radio; newspaper ads and articles; a banner in the middle of the village; and large wooden signs in area. Submit b&w glossies of display or close-up of self with work to be sent to papers.

*****CURBSTONE CRAFT FESTIVAL**, 55 St. Paul St., Rochester NY 14604. (716)454-2220. Director: Jim O'Brien. Sponsor: Downtown Promotion Council of the Rochester Area Chamber of Commerce, Inc. Estab. 1973. Annual outdoor show held 3 days in June on Main St. E., Downtown Rochester, New York. Average attendance: 10,000.
Acceptable Work: Considers batik; candlemaking; ceramics; dollmaking; glass art; jewelry; leatherworking; macrame; metalsmithing; mobiles; needlecrafts; pottery; scrimshaw; sculpture; soft sculpture; weaving; and woodcrafting. No commercial kits, commercial ring settings, or commercial beads. All work must be original and of craftsman's own design.
Terms: Entries accepted until 4 weeks before show. Entry fee: $20/8x10' display area. Prejudg-

ing by photos, slides or samples. Entry fee refunded for refused work. Work must be offered for sale; no commission. Craftworker or representative must attend show; demonstrations OK. Registration limit: 250. Sponsor provides 8' table ($9 rental charge) and limited 24-hour protection. "Craftworker should provide business cards for promotional purposes."
Awards: Presents ribbons for best of show; 1st place; 2nd; and 3rd.
Profile: "The Curbstone Music Festival will be celebrated during the same time."

*DOWNTOWN SYRACUSE ARTS & CRAFTS FAIR, c/o Downtown Committee of Syracuse, 1900 State Tower Bldg., Syracuse NY 13202. (315)422-8284. Director, Public Information: Jane Joukovsky. Estab. 1969. Annual outdoor show held 3 days in the summer. Average attendance: 15,000-20,000.
Acceptable Work: Considers batik, candlemaking, ceramics, dollmaking, drawing, glass art, jewelry, leatherworking, macrame, metalsmithing, mobiles, needlecrafts, painting, pottery, scrimshaw, sculpture, soft sculpture, weaving and woodcrafting. "Not accepted are the following: objects made from commercially sold kits, dried or plastic flowers, imports, plants, velvet paintings, manufactured or kit jewelry, decoupage, ceramics cast from commercial molds, greenware, commercially produced belt buckles, cut bottles, or embellished objects. Hooks must be provided by the artist; work to be judged must be properly marked for identification and framed (when applicable) for hanging."
Terms: Entries accepted until 6 weeks before show unless space otherwise exists. Write for entry fee. Display area: 8x10. Unlimited number of general entries; only 2 entries for judging. "Entrant's work is prejudged by means of 5 slides indicating the nature and quality of work to be exhibited." Entry fee refunded for refused work. Work must be offered for sale; no commission. Craftworker or representative must attend show; demonstrations OK. Registration limit: 125. Sponsor provides display panels, free parking to first 100 entrants, insurance on exhibited work and tables.
Awards: Presents $1,000 in cash; purchase awards and ribbons.
Promotion: Show is advertised by national publications, local radio and printed media and posters. "Accepted exhibitors will be requested to send photos and biographical information for use in printed media."
Sales Tip: "Landscapes, seascapes, functional crafts, contemporary crafts, graphics and still lifes sell well."

FESTIVAL OF THE ARTS, Rm. 101A Alumni Hall, State University College at Oneonta, Oneonta NY 13820. (607)432-2070. Executive Directors: Leonard and Dorothy Ryndes. Sponsor: Upper Catskill Community Council of the Arts, Inc. Estab. 1970. Annual indoor/outdoor show held 3 days in early June. Average attendance: 30,000.
Acceptable Work: Craftworkers must be from one of the following New York counties: Chenago, Delaware, Otsego or Schoharie. Entries accepted until 2 weeks before show. Entry donation: $10/10x6. Prejudging by slides. Work may be offered for sale; 5% commission on all sales after $100. Craftworker must attend show; demonstrations encouraged. Registration limit: 450-500. Sponsor provides chairs; fencing; table; and electrical outlets on request. Categories: traditional and contemporary crafts and fine arts. Considers all crafts.

FLUSHING ART LEAGUE OUTDOOR EXHIBITION, c/o Anna M. Kraus, 43-24 160th St., Flushing NY 11358. (212)358-0388. Sponsor: The Flushing Art League. "We are incorporated to further the arts, aid the artist in any way we can." Estab. 1957. Semiannual outdoor show held 2 weekends the first 2 weekends in May and/or the second and third weekends in September. Entries accepted until show date. Entry fee: $20/10 running feet of 6' high fence. Work may be offered for sale; no commission. Craftworker must attend show; demonstrations OK if prearranged. Sponsor provides fencing. Show is advertised by newspapers; radios; TV; flyers and posters. Categories: art and crafts. Considers all crafts except wearables. Presents cash awards and ribbons for art, but no craft awards.

FULTON COUNTY STREET ARTS FESTIVAL, Fulton County Arts Council, 40 N. Main St., Gloversville NY 12078. (518)725-6248. Executive Director: Barbara H. Smith. Purpose: "to bring all of the arts together under 1 banner for the benefit of all." Estab. 1977. Annual outdoor show held 1st Saturday in June. Average attendance: 10,000. Entries accepted up until show date. Entry fee: $5/half of standard street parking place, about 9x12. Work may be offered for sale; no commission. Craftworker or representative must attend show; demonstrations encouraged. Sponsor provides limited electricity for demonstrations. Show is advertised by radio; newspaper articles and ads throughout central New York state; and posters in tourist areas. Submit any information of special interest about your craft. Considers all crafts.

Sales Tip: "People generally do not come with large amounts of cash. Items of over $50 probably will not sell that day. Some exhibitors did well in special orders though."

*GALLERY IN THE PARK, Upper Shad Rd., Pound Ridge NY 10576. (914)764-4613. Director: Anne Cook. Sponsor: Pound Ridge Lions Club. Estab. 1970. Annual outdoor show held 2 days in May. Entries accepted until show. Entry fee: $35/12 linear feet of display area. Prejudging by nonreturnable slide or photo; entry fee refunded for refused work. Work may be offered for sale; no commission. Craftworker must attend show; demonstrations OK. Registration limit: 120. Sponsor provides electricity for demonstrations when prearranged; fencing; and indoor site in case of rain. Considers sculpture; pottery; jewelry; fiber; glass; wood; and leather. Presents cash awards.

*GALLERY NORTH OUTDOOR ART SHOW, N. Country Rd., Setauket NY 11733. Contact: Sharon Cowles or Marjorie Bishop. Sponsor: Gallery North. Estab. 1965. Annual outdoor show held 2 days in July. Entry fee: $20/10' display area. Work may be offered for sale; no commission. Craftworker must attend show; demonstrations OK. Registration limit: 225. Presents $1,000 in cash prizes.
Acceptable Work: Considers batik; oil paintings; watercolor and acrylic painting graphics; ceramics; glass art; jewelry; leatherworking; metalsmithing; pottery; weavings; wall hangings; woodcrafting; graphics; and sculpture.

GARRISON ART CENTER ARTS & CRAFTS FAIR, Box 4, Garrison NY 10524. Chairman of Board: Laura S. Jones. Purpose: fundraiser. Estab. 1969. Annual outdoor show held the 3rd weekend in August. Average attendance: 10,000. Entries accepted until 8 weeks before show. Entry fee: $35/12x8 display area; only 1 artist per area. Prejudging by a minimum of 5 slides or photos and a resume. Entry fee due after prejudging. Work must be offered for sale; 10% commission. Craftworker or representative must attend show; demonstrations OK. Registration limit: 100. Sponsor provides electricity for demonstrations if notified in advance. Show is advertised by radio and newspaper in 100-mile radius, including coverage by the *New York Times*. Submit photos. 1978 show sales totalled $30,113. Considers all crafts except candlemaking and decoupage.

GERMAN ALPS FESTIVAL, Main St., Hunter NY 12442. (518)263-4141. President: Don Conover. Estab. 1976. Annual indoor/outdoor and under tent show held 17 days in summer. Average attendance: 240,000.
Acceptable Work: Considers all crafts. Categories: pure crafts (demonstration); ethnic crafts; semi-crafts (commercial); and pure commercial.
Terms: Entries accepted until 3 weeks before show. Entry fee: "craftsmen who mainly demonstrate pay nothing; others are on 10% commission and pure commercial exhibitors pay footage fee." Display area: 10x10. Prejudging by slides or photos. Work may be offered for sale. Craftworker must attend show; demonstrations OK. Registration limit: 50. Sponsor provides chairs; coverings; electricity for demonstrations; table; and 24-hour security.
Promotion: Show is advertised by brochures; newspaper stories; and magazine articles. Submit past credits; biographical material; and reviews of work to be used in press releases, articles and in festival program.

GLENS FALLS FARMER'S MARKET, Box 1453, S. Glens Falls NY 12801. (518)793-4576. Crafts Chairman: Jeannette von Linden. Estab. 1976. Outdoor show held every Saturday morning July through October at Glens Falls, New York. Average attendance: 1,000 each Saturday. Entries accepted up until show. Entry fee: $35/8' area for season; $25/4' area for season. Work may be offered for sale; no commission. Craftworker must attend show; demonstrations OK. Sponsor provides electricity for demonstrations. Show is advertised by posters; newspapers; and craft-oriented national magazines and newspapers. Considers all crafts.
Profile: "The purpose of the Glens Falls Farmer's Market is to provide an economic marketplace for area producers to sell their crops and for area craftspeople to sell their handmade wares. It offers the customer a source of quality, locally grown produce, as well as a source of unique handcrafted items. Exhibitions, demonstrations, and games are planned to encourage the whole family to come and stroll through the street."

GOLDEN HARVEST ARTS & CRAFTS SHOW & SALE, Beaver Lake Nature Center, 8477 E. Mud Lake Rd., Baldwinsville NY 13027. (315)638-2519. Show Coordinator: Lee Rentz. Sponsor: Onondaga County Department of Parks and Recreation. Estab. 1977. Annual indoor/

outdoor show held 2 days in September. Average attendance: 5,000. Show is advertised by newspapers, TV, radio, magazines and posters.
Acceptable Work: Considers all crafts, except ceramics and decoupage. No kits or dealers.
Terms: Entries accepted until 2 weeks before show. Entry fee: $10/10x10 outdoor display area; $15/10x10 indoor display area. Prejudging by slides/photos. Entry fee due after prejudging. Work may be offered for sale; no commission. "We may change our policy and take up to a 10% commission." Craftworker needn't attend show; demonstrations encouraged. Registration limit: 80. Sponsor provides electricity for demonstrations (indoors only) and fencing. Exhibitor handles sales and taxes.
Profile: "The show is part of the Golden Harvest Festival, which includes hayrides, musical entertainment, a farmer's market, craft demonstrations and guided nature walks. People will buy a variety of crafts, but the artist or craftsman should include low-priced items."

GREATER UTICA SUMMER FESTIVAL CRAFT SHOW, c/o Central New York Community Arts Council, 800 Park Ave., Utica NY 13501. (315)798-5039. Executive Director: Diane Abbey. Estab. 1977. Annual outdoor show held 3 days in July. Average attendance: 25,000.
Terms: Entries preferred 2 weeks before show, but exceptions made until show. Entry fee: $10/craftworker. Display area: 10x10. Work may be offered for sale; no commission. Craftworker must attend show; demonstrations OK.
Promotions: Show is advertised by all of the media sources in 8 counties. Submit photos of work if possible. Considers all crafts. No dealers allowed as exhibitors.

GUILD OF BOOK WORKERS EXHIBITION, 1059 3rd Ave., New York NY 10021. (212)752-0813. Contact: Exhibition Chairman. Estab. 1906. Indoor show held every 2-3 years and open to members of the Guild of Book Workers only. Considers hand bookbindings; calligraphy; and hand-decorated papers.

*****GUILDERLAND FALL ARTS FESTIVAL**, Guilderland League of Arts, Inc., Box 305, Guilderland Center NY 12085. (518)861-5338. President: Carol L. Zwicklbauer. Estab. 1974. Annual outdoor show held the first Sunday after Labor Day. Average attendance: 3,000-4,000. Presents cash prizes and certificates.
Acceptable Work: Considers all crafts. No kits. "All work must be framed and mounted. Hooks must be provided." Bestsellers: items under $5 and miniatures.
Terms: Entries accepted until 1 week before show. Entry fee: $5/3x6 display area for nonmembers. Work may be offered for sale: no commission. Prefers craftworker attends show; demonstrations OK. Sponsor provides electricity for demonstrations (if previously arranged) and fencing.
Promotion: Show is advertised by newspapers, TV, radio, posters and bulletins. Submit photos and biographies for promotional purposes.

HARVEST CRAFTS FESTIVAL, Box 1688, Westhampton Beach NY 11978. (516)325-1331. Directors: Barbara Hope and Don Gaiti. Sponsor: Creative Faires, Ltd. Estab. 1974. Annual indoor show held 3 days in November at Nassau Coliseum, Uniondale, New York. Average attendance: 25,000+.
Acceptable Work: Considers batik, candlemaking, ceramics, dollmaking, glass art, jewelry, lapidary, leatherworking, macrame, metalsmithing, mobiles, needlecrafts, pottery, scrimshaw, sculpture, soft sculpture, weaving, woodcrafting and "other unique and unusual items. No machine-made crafts, or any craft that lacks in workmanship, style or imagination."
Terms: Entries accepted until 3 weeks before show. Entry fee: $210/10x12 full or corner booth; $150/10' pie wedge booth. Prejudging by 5 slides of work, plus slide or photo of booth exhibit. Entry fee refunded for refused work. Work may be offered for sale; no commission. Craftworker must attend show; demonstrations encouraged. Registration limit: 200 selling booths. Sponsor provides electricity for demonstrations; 24-hour security; all union costs; and decorator set up (back drop).
Sales Tip: "Since we run professional shows the crafts exhibited are of high quality. We cannot state emphatically enough the importance of a good display. We furnish complete suggestion sheets to aid neophytes and inspire all to create exciting environments for themselves and the public."

*****HOLIDAY ARTS & CRAFTS FAIR**, 2205 Douglas Crescent, Utica NY 13501. Chairman: Gary McGuire. Sponsor: Upstate New York Craftsmen's Guild. Estab. 1977. Two annual indoor shows held 2 days in November and 2 days in December in at Utica, New York. Average attendance: 5,000. Entries accepted until 8 weeks before show. Entry fee: $40-45/10x6 display area. Work may be offered for sale; no commission. Craftworker must attend show; demonstrations OK. Registration limit: 100. Sponsor provides chairs; electricity for demonstrations; table; 24-hour security; set up assistance; and food discount. Show is advertised by posters; printed media; radio and TV; and personal invitations. Submit resume and description of work for publicity consideration. Considers all crafts except heshi jewelry. Presents $150 in cash prizes and ribbons. "Average reported sale price: $650; price range: $10-1,500. Nationally rated."

HOLIDAY CRAFTS FAIR, WBAI-FM, 505 8th Ave., New York NY 10018. (212)279-0707. Manager: Steve Post. Purpose: fundraiser. Estab. 1971. Annual indoor show held 2 3-day weekends in December. Average attendance: 50,000. Entry fee: $75/weekend. Prejudging. Work may be offered for sale: 15% commission. Considers all handcrafts.

*****PAULA INSEL ANNUAL EXHIBITION**, 987 3rd Ave., New York NY 10022. (212)577-5740. Director: Paula Insel. Sponsor: Galerie Paula Insel. Purpose: "the show is a vehicle for artists to expose their talents." Estab. 1975. Annual indoor show held 2 weeks in the fall. Entries accepted until 1-2 months before show. Entry fee: $8/item being displayed. Maximum 3 works/category. Work may be offered for sale; 40% commission. Craftworker needn't attend show; demonstrations OK. Sponsor provides chairs; display panels; electricity for demonstrations; and shipping costs to craftworker from show. Show is advertised by newspapers; magazines; and mailing lists. Considers batik; ceramics; glass art; macrame; mobiles; needlecrafts; pottery; enamels; sculpture; tole painting; and woodcrafting. Presents ribbons and merchandise for award-winning work.

INTERNATIONAL CRAFT SHOW, 37 W. 53rd St., New York NY 10019. (212)586-0026. Executive Director: Harry Dennis. Sponsor: New York State Craftsmen Inc. Purpose: "once a year, comprehensive, craft wholesale and retail marketplace in New York City." Estab. 1973. Annual indoor show held 1 week in spring. Average attendance: 20,000. Entries accepted up until show. Entry fee: $550-600/10x10 display area. Prejudging by individual review including slides and photos; entry fee due after prejudging. Work may be offered for sale; no commission. Craftworker must attend show; demonstrations OK. Sponsor provides booth background and 24-hour security. Show is advertised by all media including radio; TV; newspapers; and magazines. Submit 8x10 b&w glossy or slides. Considers all crafts. Bestsellers: 50c bookmark to $5,000 bed.

*****KENAN CRAFT FESTIVAL**, (formerly 100 American Craftsmen Craft Festival), 433 Locust St., Lockport NY 14094. (716)433-2617. Arts and Education Director: John D. O'Hern. Sponsor: Kenan Center, Inc. Purpose: "to offer highest quality crafts; provide craftsmen to

Held in July for 3 days, the New England Craft Expo is a popular time for show goers to get together for celebration. Sponsored by American Craft Expositions Inc., 25,000 people visit the booths at this Topsfield, Massachusetts show. To be considered as an exhibitor, write to Denise Barile or Rudy Kowalezyk at Farmington, Connecticut.

exchange ideas; and to show new directions in craft techniques and materials." Estab. 1970. Annual indoor show held 3 days in June. Average attendance: 12,000. Entries accepted until 4 months before show. Entry fee: $45/10x10 display area. Prejudging by slides; $3 jurying fee; entry fee due after prejudging. Work may be offered for sale; no commission. Craftworker must attend show; demonstrations OK. Registration limit: 100. Sponsor provides chairs; electricity for demonstrations; table; 24-hour security; and manages credit card booth for 3% of sales. Show is advertised by all media. Considers all crafts. Presents cash awards totalling $150 and ribbons.

*LEWISTON COUNCIL ON THE ARTS, INC., LEWISTON CRAFT SHOW, Box 1, Lewiston NY 14092. Sponsor: Lewiston Council on the Arts, Inc. Purpose: "to further and develop understanding of the various crafts and art forms in this portion of the state." Estab. 1971. Annual outdoor show (with tents) held 3rd weekend in June. Average attendance: 5,000-7,000. Entries accepted until 1 week before show or until filled. Entry fee: $25/tent; $15, outside. Prejudging by slides or photos. Work may be offered for sale; no commission. Craftworker must attend show; demonstrations preferred. Sponsor provides some arrangements for electricity. Show is advertised by posters; magazines; newspapers; handbills; and interviews on TV and radio. Considers all crafts. Show will be judged. Awards ribbons.

*LILAC FESTIVAL DECORATED EGG SHOW, 16 Old Forge Lane, Pittsford NY 14534. (716)385-3332. Director: Ronald Guidone. Estab. 1978. Annual indoor show held 2 days in May at Rochester, New York. Entries accepted until 4 weeks before show. Entry fee: $15/artist; $40/dealer. Display area: 6x2' tables. Work may be offered for sale; no commission. Craftworker must attend show; demonstrations OK. Registration limit: 65. Sponsor provides chairs; electricity for demonstration; table; and night security. Egg decorating seminars are held the day after the show. Show is advertised by TV; magazines; radio; and newspapers. Presents awards of ribbons and grand trophy for best of show. Considers decorated real eggs only.

LOWER ADIRONDACK REGIONAL ARTS COUNCIL ARTS & CRAFTS FESTIVAL, Box 659. Glens Falls NY 12801. Festival Co-chairman: Joan Reid Gealt. Estab. 1972. Annual outdoor show held 2 days in June. Average attendance: 10,000.
Terms: Entries accepted until 6 weeks before show. Entry fee: $158/10x10 display area plus $2 LARAC membership fee. Work may be offered for sale; no commission. Craftworker must attend show; demonstrations OK. Registration limit: 225. Sponsor provides electricity for demonstrations and limited water.
Promotion: Show is advertised by Warren County Department of Publicity and Tourism and local newspapers. Submit promotional material. Considers all crafts.

NEW YORK CITY BLUEGRASS & OLD-TIME COUNTRY MUSIC BAND CONTEST & CRAFTS FAIR, South Street Seaport, Fulton St. and East River, New York NY 10028. (212)427-1488. Crafts Coordinator: Gail Schiller. Producer: Doug Tuchman. Sponsor: Bluegrass Club of New York. Estab. 1973. Annual outdoor show held the Saturday and Sunday of the second weekend of August. Average attendance: 20,000-25,000.
Acceptable Work: Considers all crafts including instrument making. No kits, machine-made crafts, leather crafts using skins from endangered species, importers, retailers of other people's crafts, and distributors. "Also, each exhibit space is limited to the display of 1 craft (i.e., a jeweler could not also display candles). Exhibitors may not share exhibit space."
Terms: Entries accepted until spaces are filled. Entry fee: $40/10x10 display area. Prejudging by slides/photos and references. Entry fee refunded for refused work. Work must be offered for sale; no commission. Craftworker must attend show; demonstrations OK. Registration limit: 50. Sponsor provides assistance in setting up and free admission to the contest each evening.
Promotion: Show is advertised by newspapers, radio and TV in metropolitan NYC, and large direct mailings. "Photos sent us will be used as part of promotional mailngs to the press."
Profile: "The South Street Seaport is an historic site and permanent berth of several tall ships. Admission is free to the Crafts Fair."

NEW YORK RENAISSANCE FESTIVAL, Box 1688, Westhampton Beach NY 11978. (516)325-1331. Promoters: Barbara Hope or Don Gaiti. Sponsor: Creative Faires, Ltd. Estab. 1978. Annual outdoor show held six consecutive weekends from July-September at Sterling Forest Gardens, Tuxedo, New York. Average attendance: 100,000+.
Acceptable Work: Considers all original crafts except tole painting and decoupage. "No kits, machine-made crafts, or any craft that lacks in workmanship, style or imagination."
Terms: Entries accepted until 4 weeks before show. Entry fee: $125 for 1st 3 weekends, $135 for

2nd 3 weekends, $225 for all 6 weekends. Display area: 15x15. Prejudging by 5 slides of work and 1 slide of display; entry fee refunded for refused work. Work may be offered for sale; no commission. Craftworker must attend show; demonstrations OK. Registration limit: 135 booths. Sponsor provides 24-hour security.
Profile: Renaissance theme requires all exhibitors to be in Renaissance garb and provide rustic looking booth display. Camping provided nearby. One week prior to show allotted for booth set up.

*NEW YORK STATE CRAFTS, HOME ARTS & FINE ARTS COMPETITION, New York State Fair Grounds, Syracuse NY 13209. (315)487-7741. Director, Art and Home Center: Elizabeth J. Crowley. Sponsor: New York State Fair. Estab. 1950. Annual indoor show held 10 days in late summer. Average attendance: 350,000.
Acceptable Work: Considers batik; glass art; jewelry; leatherworking needlecrafts; pottery; sculpture; weaving; and woodcrafting. Strictly a competition; only prize winners on display.
Terms: Entries accepted until 3 weeks before show. Entry fee: $5. Submit up to 10 crafts in each division. Maximum 2 pieces per category; 6 total. Prejudging. Entry fee not refunded for refused work. Work may be offered for sale; 25% commission. Craftworker needn't attend show; demonstrations permitted if prearranged.
Awards: Presents cash awards of $1,680, crafts: $2,300 home art; and ribbons. Categories: fine arts (paintings); graphics and sculpture; crafts (pottery); rugs; wall hangings; metal; wood; weaving; and leatherwork.

NORTH COUNTRY ARTS & CRAFTS, Northville NY 12134. Acting President: Corinne Sherman. Annual outdoor show held 2 days in July. Average attendance: 5,000. Entries accepted up until show, space permitting. Entry fee: $15/12x15 display area. Work may be offered for sale; no commission. Craftworker must attend show; demonstrations welcome. Show is advertised by newspapers; radio; and posters. Considers all crafts. Write for additional information.

NORTHEAST CRAFT FAIR, Box 10, New Paltz NY 12561. (914)255-0039. President: Carol Sedestrom. Sponsor: American Craft Enterprises, Inc. Purpose: "to provide craftspeople in the Northeast an exposition of high quality in which to exhibit and sell their work; to provide buyers a market place to purchase quality handmade items at a time of year to accommodate summer and fall buying schedule; to encourage craftspeople from various areas and diverse traditions to come together to stimulate the interchange of ideas and enthusiasm; and to offer the general public an opportunity to better understand the American craft movement." Estab. 1965. Annual indoor/outdoor show (with 3 large tents) held 5 days (2 trade; 3 public) in June at Rhinebeck, New York. Average attendance: 40,000. Entries accepted until mid-January. Booth fee: $125, inside; $100, tent; and $60, outside. Display area: 10x10. Prejudging by "color slides of the type of work planned for exhibit. Slides will be considered solely on the merits of the work pictured, not upon any other qualifications of the craftsperson who produced the work. Submit 5 slides of the type of work you plan on exhibiting at the show. Slides must be 2x2 including cardboard or plastic mount. $5 jurying fee." Space rental fee due after prejudging. Work must be offered for sale; no commission. Craftworker must attend show; demonstrations OK. Exhibition limit: about 500. Sponsor provides electricity for demonstrations and 24-hour security. Considers all crafts including handmade musical instruments. 1978 show sales totalled "over $2,500,000."

NORTHERN NEW YORK CRAFTS FESTIVAL, Ballard Mill Center for the Arts, Malone NY 12953. (518)483-4016 or 483-5190. Chairman: Paul J. McMahon. Sponsors: Ballard Mill Center and Adirondack Region Craft Professionals. Estab. 1976. Annual outdoor and limited indoor show held the Saturday and Sunday after July 4. Average attendance: 1,500. Juried by 5 color slides due by May 15. Jury fee: $3. Entry fee if accepted: $15 for outdoor space for demonstrating craftsperson, $20 for non-demonstrating craftsperson for both outdoor and indoor space. Display area: 10x10, larger if needed. Work may be offered for sale; no commission. Craftworker or representative must attend show; demonstrations encouraged. Sponsor provides electricity and night security.
Promotion: Show is advertised by news releases throughout New York state, Quebec, Ontario, and Vermont; mailings to craft shops and organizations; and posters throughout the area.

*OLD SARATOGA HISTORICAL ASSOCIATION ART SHOW, Brown's Point, Rt. 6 Burgoyne Rd., Saratoga Springs NY 12866. Chairperson: Kate Leone. Show consultant: Armond Brown. Estab. 1967. Annual outdoor show held 2nd Sunday in August (3rd Sunday in August raindate). on Schuyler House lawns in Schuylerville, New York. Entries accepted up until show. Entry fee: $5/craftworker. Work may be offered for sale; 10% commission. Craftworker must attend show; demonstrations encouraged. Craftworkers must supply own display racks or table. Show is advertised by newspapers; radio; TV; and posters. Presents cash awards and ribbons. Considers all crafts including quilting; knitting; and crotcheting.

PALMYRA CANALTOWN DAYS, Box 64, Palmyra NY 14522. Craft Chairman: Bruce Wideman. Purpose: to relive the days when the Erie Canal was an important part of upstate New York. Estab. 1966. Annual outdoor show held 2 days in September. Average attendance: 20,000-25,000. Entries accepted until 1 week before show. Entry fee: $8/10x10 display area. Work may be offered for sale; no commission. Craftworker must attend show; demonstrations encouraged. Registration limit: 100. Show is advertised by radio and newspapers. Considers all crafts.

***PARK ART FESTIVAL,** c/o Harry Davis, 39 N. Church St., Cortland NY 13045. (607)756-8215. Program Director: Harry N. Davis. Sponsor: Cortland Art League. Estab. 1968. Annual outdoor show held 2 days Father's Day weekend. Average attendance: 1,000. Entries accepted until 1 week before show. Entry fee: $10/10x10 display area; $2 to enter judging for purchase award prizes. Work may be offered for sale. Craftworker must attend show; demonstrations OK. Sponsor provides fencing. Show is advertised by all media. Considers all crafts.

PHELPS ANNUAL SAURKRAUT FESTIVAL, c/o Cris Haag, Rt. 2, Phelps NY 14532. (315)548-3856. Estab. 1966. Annual indoor show held the first Saturday in August. Average attendance: 5,000. Entries accepted until early July or until filled. Entry fee: $8/6x12 display area. Work may be offered for sale; no commission. Craftworker must attend show; demonstrations OK. Registration limit: 30-35. Sponsor provides electricity for demonstrations. Show is advertised by TV; radio; newspapers; and posters. Considers all crafts.

PINKSTERFEST SUMMER 'MINIFEST,' 75 New Scotland Ave., Arts Office, Albany NY 12208. Director: Pat Devane. Sponsor: Albany City Arts Office. Estab. 1974. Semiannual outdoor show held 1 day in May and 1 day in summer. Average attendance: 25,000. Entries accepted until 1 week before show. No entry fee. Prejudging by slides or photos. Work may be offered for sale; no commission. Craftworker must attend show; demonstrations OK. Registration limit: 200. Show is advertised by newspapers; TV; radio; posters; and flyers. Considers all crafts.

PLEASURE FAIRE OF THE RENAISSANCE & SUMMER MARKETPLACE, Rt. 2, Farden Rd., Sterling NY 13156. (315)947-5782. Managers: Gerald A. and Virginia L. Young. Estab. 1977. Annual outdoor show held 8 weekends from mid-July through first weekend in September. Entries accepted until 4 weeks before opening day; exceptions are made for unusual circumstances. Entry fee: $25 for entire season. Exhibitors build their own permanent or semi-permanent booths in keeping with Renaissance theme. Prejudging by slides; photos; or personal visit in advance with examples of work. Entry fee due after prejudging. Work may be offered for sale; 10% commission. Craftworker or representative must attend show; demonstrations encouraged. Show is advertised by posters; newspaper ads; press releases; and local TV talk shows.
Acceptable Work: Considers batik; candlemaking; ceramics; decoupage; dollmaking; glass art; jewelry; lapidary; leatherworking; macrame; metalsmithing; mobiles; needlecrafts; pottery; sculpture; soft sculpture; weaving; woodcrafting; block printing; scrimshaw; dried flowers; and musical instruments. "Work must be representative in subject matter and medium of that produced in the Renaissance period (1450-1750). Exhibitors must provide and appear in Renaissance costume during Faire hours."
Profile: "The Renaissance Faire, a gay and colorful reproduction of the English world trade faires of the 16th century, has been created to combine history, beauty, culture, and pleasure into one important recreational activity in central New York. Comprising all the elements of old English faires—marketable fine arts and handcrafts; unusual food and drink; live theatre; music and dance; and a natural forest location—the Faire has been designed as a place where beautiful people can do beautiful things in a beautiful setting."

QUAKER ARTS FESTIVAL, Box 202, Orchard Park NY 14127. Chairman: Leonard Berkowitz. Sponsor: Orchard Park Jaycees. Estab. 1963. Annual outdoor show held 2 days in September. Held indoors if weather is inclement. Average attendance: 20,000. Considers all crafts. Entries accepted until show date. Entry fee: $20/20x10 display area. Work may be offered for sale; no commission. Craftworker needn't attend show; demonstrations OK. Sponsor provides chairs, display panels, electricity for demonstrations and fencing. Exhibitor handles sales and taxes. Presents $2,000+ in cash prizes. Show is advertised by newspapers, billboards and radio.

ROCKLAND ARTS DAY, Box 267, Spring Valley NY 10977. (914)352-5777. Executive Director: Bette Uris. Sponsor: Arts Council of Rockland. Estab. 1972. Annual indoor show held 1 day in October. Average attendance: 3,000. Entries accepted until 3 weeks before show. Entry fee: $15/10x10 display space. Prejudging by 5 35mm slides of representative works; entry fee refunded for refused work. Work may be offered for sale; no commission. Craftworker or representative must attend show. Registration limit: 100. Categories: crafts; fine arts; performances; children's theatre; and ethnic foods. Considers all crafts.
Promotion: Show is advertised by publicity in all media; advertising in newspapers; the art council's monthly tabloid; posters; flyers; and direct mail. "Anything useful for publicity will be appreciated."

SPRING EASTER ARTS & CRAFTS SHOW, 25 Seneca St., Shortsville NY 14548. (716)289-9439. President: Ronald L. Johnson. Sponsor: Finger Lakes Craftsmen. Estab. 1970. Annual indoor show held 2 days in the early spring at Rochester, New York. Average attendance: 10,000. Entries accepted until show is full (sometimes early). Entry fee: $55-90/10x7 display area. Work may be offered for sale; no commission. Craftworker must attend show; demonstrations OK. Registration limit: 200. Sponsor provides 24-hour security. Show is advertised by TV; radio; and newspapers ($3,500 budget). Considers all crafts.

SUMMER INDOOR ARTS & CRAFTS SHOW, 25 Seneca St., Shortsville NY 14548. (716)289-9439. President: Ronald L. Johnson. Sponsor: Finger Lakes Craftsmen. Estab. 1975. Annual indoor show held 2 days in July at Rochester, New York. Average attendance: 10,000. Entries accepted until show is full (sometimes early). Entry fee: $55-90/10x7 display area. Work may be offered for sale; no commission. Craftworker must attend show; demonstrations OK. Registration limit: 200. Sponsor provides 24-hour security. Show is advertised by TV; radio; and newspapers ($3,500 budget). Considers all crafts.

TAMA COUNTY FAIR, Tregre and Miller Associates, Inc., 261 3rd Ave., New York NY 10003. (212)677-7774. Contact: Paul Miller or Jeanne Tregre. Sponsor: 3rd Avenue Merchants Association. Purpose: community fundraiser. Estab. 1976. Annual show held 1 day in the fall. Entries accepted until 2 weeks before show. Entry fee: $50/10x12 display area. Work may be offered for sale; no commission. Craftworker or representative must attend show; demonstrations OK. Show is advertised by TV; radio; newspapers; magazines; and trade publications. Considers all crafts.

THANKSGIVING WEEKEND CHRISTMAS ARTS & CRAFTS SHOW, 25 Seneca St., Shortsville NY 14548. (716)289-9439. President: Ronald L. Johnson. Sponsor: Finger Lakes Craftsmen. Estab. 1970. Annual indoor show held 3 days during Thanksgiving weekend at Rochester, New York. Average attendance: 15,000. Entries accepted until show is full (sometimes early). Entry fee: $75-110. Work may be offered for sale; no commission. Craftworker must attend show; demonstrations OK. Registration limit: 200. Sponsor provides 24-hour security. Show is advertised by TV; radio; newspaper; and $3,500 paid advertising. Considers all crafts.

***VILLAGE ARTISTS' & CRAFTSMEN'S ART & CRAFT FAIR**, Box 292, Hamilton NY 13346. Corresponding Secretary: Janice Moreland. Estab. 1974. Annual indoor/outdoor show held 2 days in July. Show takes place in buildings of Americana Village and in 3 large tents on the Village Green. Average attendance: 6,000-7,000. Presents $100 for Best In Show, $75 for Second Prize, $50 for Third Prize, and ribbons for above.
Acceptable Work: Considers batik, ceramics, glass art, jewelry, leatherworking, macrame, metalsmithing, mobiles, needlecrafts, pottery, scrimshaw, sculpture, soft sculpture, weaving and woodcrafting. No kits, dried or pressed flowers, seed and pods arrangements, cut bottles, or embellished items (painted barnboards, boxes, stones, shells, buttons).
Terms: Entries accepted mid-May. Entry fee: $30/6x9 display area; $5/electrical outlet in indoor space; $20/outdoor area. (No electricity in outdoor spaces.) Prejudging by 5 slides. Fee refunded for refused work. All work must be offered for sale; no commission. Craftworker

---

* Those listings preceded by an asterisk present awards for prize-winning crafts.

must attend show; demonstrations by invitation only. Registration limit: approximately 100. Sponsor provides electricity for demonstrations ($5 fee) and 24-hour security.
Promotion: Show is advertised by local newspapers, radio and TV; national craft magazines and periodicals. Craftworker should provide b&w glossy prints, if available.

*WATERFRONT ART FESTIVAL, 21 Hidden Creek Circle, Pittsford NY 14534. (716)624-4220, (716)381-8772, (315)554-3042. Director: Adele Elmer. Purpose: "to provide an outstanding opportunity for artists and craftspeople to sell at a top quality show and to provide to the public a cultural and educational experience including musical entertainment totally free." Estab. 1974. Annual outdoor show held 3 days in August at Canandaigua Lake, New York. Average attendance: 60,000. Entries accepted until 3 weeks before show. Entry fee: $36/10x6 display area. Prejudging by 3 slides; entry fee refunded for refused work. Work should be offered for sale; no commission. Craftworker must attend show; demonstrations encouraged. Registration limit: 150. Sponsor provides electricity for demonstrations; fencing; and 24-hour security. Show is advertised by radio; newspaper display ads; news releases; signs; and cable TV. Submit b&w glossies of self at work or of specific pieces of work. Presents 4 craft cash awards of $50 each; 1 best of show craft award of $100; ribbons; and certificates. Considers batik; ceramics; jewelry; leatherworking; macrame; metalsmithing; pottery; sculpture; soft sculpture; weaving; woodcrafting; blown glass; and blacksmithing.
Profile: "This show has become a tradition. Artists and craftsmen come from all over US to participate. Early registration is strongly urged."

*WESTBURY ANNUAL OUTDOOR ART & CRAFTS FESTIVAL, Greater Westbury Arts Council, Inc., 600 Old Country Rd., Rm. 306, Garden City NY 11530. (516)741-6760. Executive Director: Roberta Oborne. Estab. 1974. Annual outdoor show held 2 days in June at Westbury, Long Island, New York. Average attendance: 1,000-2,000.
Acceptable Work: Considers all crafts. Bestsellers: "stained glass and pewter work seem to be becoming more popular."
Terms: Entries accepted until 4 weeks before show. Entry fee: $25 (refundable) + $2 prejudging fee/12x12 display area. Maximum 2 entries per category for prejudging. Prejudging by (5) slides only; entry fee due after prejudging. Work may be offered for sale; no commission. Craftworker must attend show; demonstrations OK. Registration limit: 80. Sponsor provides electricity for demonstrations and fencing.
Awards: Presents $100 best in show and ribbons.
Promotion: Show is advertised by press releases; periodicals; radio; direct mail; posters; and flyers.

WESTFIELD ARTS & CRAFTS FESTIVAL, Box 145, Westfield NY 14787. (716)326-2614. Chairman: Linda C. Dunn. Sponsor: Chamber of Commerce. "Our show is strictly held to offer any artist or craftsman the opportunity to show and sell. We feel that if they feel proud of their works we have no right to refuse, therefore no prejudging. This also means that everyone takes their chances. If they do well, fine; if not, they haven't lost much!" Estab. 1971. Annual outdoor show held the last Friday and Saturday in July. Average attendance: 10,000. Entries accepted until 2 weeks before show. Entry fee: $10, if paid in advance; $15, if paid the day of the show. Work may be offered for sale; no commission. Prefers craftworker attends show; demonstrations encouraged. Registration limit: 225. Sponsor provides electricity for demonstrations. Show is advertised by radio; newspapers; and billboards. Submit brief resume and photo (photo will not be returned) for publicity consideration. Considers all handcrafts.

North Carolina

ARTS ALIVE FESTIVAL, Box 744, Mocksville NC 27028. (704)634-3112. President: Martha Kontos. Sponsor: David County Arts Council. Estab. 1975. Annual outdoor show held 1 day in September. Average attendance: 10,000. Entries accepted up until show date. Entry fee: $10/craftworker. Work may be offered for sale; no commission. Craftworker must attend show; demonstrations OK. Considers all crafts.
Promotion: Show is advertised by newspapers; radio; brochures; and pamphlets. Submit any pamphlets or brochures available; description of craft-making methods; and information for ordering during the year to be used for publicity.

*ARTS & CRAFTS FESTIVAL OF SOUTHEASTERN NORTH CAROLINA, Rt. 2, Box 940, Elizabethtown NC 28337. (919)588-4898. Executive Director: Ann A. Hood. Sponsor: Southeastern North Carolina Arts Council. Estab. 1966. Annual indoor/outdoor show (in gym and on campus) held 2 days in the spring on the Boys Homes Campus at Lake Waccamaw, North Carolina. Average attendance: 10,000.

Acceptable Work: Considers all crafts, including cornshuck crafts and pineneedle crafts. Must be work of craftworker from one of the following southeastern North Carolina counties: Bladen, Brunswick, Columbus, Cumberland, Duplin, New Hanover, Pender or Robeson.
Terms: Entries accepted until 4 weeks before show. Entry fee: $5/ craftworker's year's membership to the Council. Maximum 2 entries/category in the visual arts show. Entry to craft show by invitation only. Work may be offered for sale; 10% commission. Craftworker must attend show; demonstrations mandatory. Registration limit: 200. Sponsor provides electricity for demonstrations; 24-hour security; receipt books; name tags; complimentary coffee and relief during show time; and free listing in rosters and calendars throughout US.
Awards: Presents $75, $45 and $30 cash awards for adults; $20, $10 and $5 cash awards for students; $800 in purchase prizes; and ribbons. "Stress originality and imagination."
Sales Tip: "There is a good market here for the $5-100 range of crafts, and the $50-200 range of artwork." 1978 craft sales totalled $3,700; artworks totalled $2,500.
Promotion: Show is advertised by national, regional, state and local calendars; news releases; TV; radio; brochures; and posters. "Show chairman will contact individuals for publicity information if needed."

AUTUMN LEAVES FESTIVAL, Box 913, Mt. Airy NC 27030. (919)786-6116. Executive Vice President: Jim Grimes. Purpose: "for the entertainment of those who attend; and to increase tourism." Estab. 1967. Annual indoor/outdoor show held 3 days in October. Average attendance: 200,000.
Terms: Entries accepted until 3 weeks before show. Entry fee: $25/10x12 display area. Prejudging by slides, photos, or actual art; entry fee due after prejudging. Work may be offered for sale; no commission. Craftworker must attend show; demonstrations OK. Registration limit: 60. Sponsor provides electricity for demonstrations and 24-hour security. Considers all crafts.
Promotion: Show is advertised by radio; TV; newspapers; and state and regional publications. Submit photo and resume for newspaper publicity; or craftwork for TV promotion.

CABARRUS COUNTY AGRICULTURAL FAIR ARTS & CRAFTS SHOW, Box 563, Concord NC 28025. (704)782-0621 or 786-7221. General Manager: Clyde Propst Jr. Fair estab. 1953; craft portion estab. 1972. Annual indoor show held 1 week in September. Average attendance: 110,000. Entries accepted until filled. No entry fee (but $50 deposit required to reserve a booth; refunded at end of show). Display area: 34 8x8 booth spaces with 10' aisles. Work may be offered for sale; no commission. Craftworker must attend show; demonstration required. Sponsor provides electricity for demonstrations and 24-hour security. Considers all crafts.

THE CAROLINA CRAFTSMENS' CHRISTMAS CLASSIC—CHARLOTTE, 3603 Old Battleground Rd., Greensboro NC 27410. (919)288-1933. Executive Director: Clyde Gilmore. Estab. 1977. Annual indoor show held 2 days in December at Charlotte. Presents variable purchase awards and plaques.
Acceptable Work: Considers all crafts, except ceramics. No kits or molds. Categories: fine arts; selected crafts.
Terms: Entry fee and size of display area variable. Prejudging by photos/slides and newspaper articles. Entry fee due after prejudging. Work may be offered for sale; no commission. Craftworker must attend show; demonstrations OK. Sponsor provides chairs, curtained booth space and 24-hour security.

THE CAROLINA CRAFTSMENS' CHRISTMAS CLASSIC—GREENSBORO, 3603 Old Battleground Rd., Greensboro NC 27410. (919)288-1933. Executive Director: Clyde Gilmore. Estab. 1977. Annual indoor show held 3 days in November. Presents variable purchase awards and plaques.
Acceptable Work: Considers all crafts, except ceramics. No kits or molds. Categories: fine arts; selected crafts.
Terms: Entry fee and size of display area variable. Prejudging by photos/slides and newspaper articles. Entry fee due after prejudging. Work may be offered for sale; no commission. Craftworker must attend show; demonstrations OK. Sponsor provides chairs, curtained booth space and 24-hour security.

***DURHAM ART GUILD ANNUAL JURIED EXHIBIT,** 810 W. Proctor St., Durham NC 27707. Contact: James C. McIntyre. Annual show held in the spring. Entry fee: $8. Maximum 2 entries per artist. Work may be offered for sale; 30% commission. Considers sculpture. No work requiring special display devices. Presents $1,700 in cash, and $1,000 in purchase prizes.

Crated works must be sent prepaid express. Parcel post entries not accepted.

FOLK SCHOOL FALL FESTIVAL, John C. Campbell Folk School, Brasstown NC 28902. (704)837-2775. Festival Coordinator: Kay Rockwood. Estab. 1974. Annual outdoor show held 2 days during the first weekend in October. "In case of rain the show is moved under shelter in the outdoor pavillion and main school building." Average attendance: 2,000.
Acceptable Work: Considers all crafts, except decoupage. No kits or mold ceramics. "We limit our show to quality crafts, which is not difficult as this area is a center for professional craftsmen. We emphasize tradional Appalachian skills (woodworking, carving, blacksmithing, pottery, weaving, vegetable dyeing and spinning, basketry and lapidary). We also have metal workers (silver and copper) and copper enameling."
Terms: Entries accepted until 4 weeks before show. Entry fee: $5/10x10 display area. "Since the area is wooded, spaces are irregular." Prejudging by 3-man jury by slides/photos or samples. Entry fee refunded for refused work. Work must be offered for sale; 10% commission. Craftworker must attend show; demonstrations encouraged. Registration limit: 45. Sponsor provides electricity for demonstrations and 24-hour security. Craftworker handles sales.
Promotion: Show is advertised by brochures (mailed and distributed), radio, TV, periodical and newspaper public service announcements and articles, calendar listings, paid newspaper ads, posters, tablecards and word-of-mouth. "We find the latter to be our most effective method of attracting new friends to our festival. Craftworker should provide a b&w photo and some biographical information for an article in craftworker's hometown newspaper. Also, the name of the paper."
Sales Tip: "Articles which sell for $5-25 sell best. However, as we now draw more and more people from Atlanta, Asheville, Chattanooga and Knoxville, higher priced items are selling better." Total sales (1978): $6,000+.

THE GUILD FAIR OF THE SOUTHERN HIGHLANDS, Box 9545, Asheville NC 28805. (704)298-7928. Director: Robert W. Gray. Sponsor: Southern Highland Handicraft Guild. Estab. 1948. Semiannual indoor show held 5 days beginning the 3rd Tuesday in July; and 4 days during the third week in October. Displayed in 2 full floors of the Asheville Civic Auditorium. Average attendance: 20,000 (in July) and 12,000-15,000 (in October).
Acceptable Work: Must be from a Guild member. Considers all crafts, except decoupage and tole painting. "Both traditional and contemporary work is done and sold by the Guild members." No kits.
Terms: No entry fee. "Work is prejudged for membership in the Guild by the Standards Committee and the Board of Trustees. Actual work must be submitted." Work may be offered for sale; 20% commission. Craftworker must attend show; demonstrations encouraged. Sponsor provides chairs, coverings, display panels, electricity for demonstrations, insurance on exhibited work, insurance on work shipped to artist, shipping costs to artist from show, tables, 24-hour security and total booth set up. Exhibitor and/or volunteer provided by the Guild handles sales and taxes. "Accounting for sales taxes and credit card sales is all done by the Guild staff."
Promotion: Show is advertised by newspapers, magazines, radio, TV, billboards and tent cards in restaurants and motels.

MT. MITCHELL CRAFTSMENS FAIR, Box 175, Burnsville NC 28714. (704)682-7413. Sponsor: Yancey County Chamber of Commerce. "The promotion of mountain crafts is the major purpose in the creation of this fair." Estab. 1956. Annual outdoor show (with covered booths) held the first Friday and Saturday in August. Average attendance: 7,000. Entries accepted until 4 weeks before show. Entry fee: $10 registration/artist. Display area: 8x10. Prejudging by slides; entry fee refunded for refused work. Work may be offered for sale; 10% commission. Craftworker must attend show; demonstrations OK. Registration limit: 130. Sponsor provides coverings and electricity for demonstrations. Show is advertised by newspapers and magazines. Considers batik; candlemaking; ceramics; dollmaking; glass art; jewelry; leatherworking; macrame; metalsmithing; needlecrafts; pottery; sculpture; weaving; and woodcrafting.

*****NORTH CAROLINA ARTISTS EXHIBITION**, North Carolina Museum of Art, Raleigh NC 27611. Head, Collections Care and Preparation: Benjamin F. Williams. Estab. 1937. Annual indoor show. Average attendance: 10,000. Entries accepted until 2-4 weeks before show. Entry fee: $5/item. Maximum 2 entries/craftworker. Prejudging by actual entries presented to a 3-man, out-of-state jury of professionals in the art field. No entry fees refunded for refused work. Work may be offered for sale; 30% commission. Craftworker needn't attend show; no demonstrations. Insurance on exhibited work; table; handles sales; and 24-hour security. Show is advertised by museum news releases; calendar; the news media; and art magazines. Considers all crafts. Maximum size: 80''. Presents cash and purchase prizes; honorable mentions; and medal awards. "Open only to North Carolina residents, natives of the state, and to nonresidents who have lived in North Carolina for at least 5 years."

*PIEDMONT CRAFTS EXHIBITION, Box 6011, Charlotte NC 28207. (704)334-9723. Assistant Curator of Exhibitions: Jane Kessler. Sponsor: Mint Museum of Art. Estab. 1976. Biennial indoor show held 6 weeks in the late winter/early spring. Entries accepted until 5 weeks before show. Entry fee: $7 for up to 4 entries. Maximum 2 entries per craftworker accepted. Prejudging; no entry fees refunded for refused work. Work may be offered for sale; 30% commission. Open to residents of Alabama, Florida, Georgia, Kentucky, Louisiana, Mississippi, North and South Carolina, Tennessee, Virginia and West Virginia. Considers all crafts. Presents approximately $4,500 in cash and purchase prizes.

SOUTHEASTERN-NORTHGATE ART SHOW, 1922 Hollywood St., Winston-Salem NC 27107. (919)723-8788. Director: Nancy Goslen. Sponsor: Southeastern Art Shows. Estab. 1975. Annual indoor show held 3 days in January at Durham, North Carolina.
Acceptable Work: Considers batik; ceramics; glass art; macrame; mobiles; pottery; sculpture; soft sculpture; weaving and woodcrafting.
Terms: Entries accepted until 6 weeks before show. Entry fee: $45-55/craftworkers. Display area: 8-16'. Prejudging by slides or photos; entry fee refunded for refused work. Work may be offered for sale; no commission. Craftworker must attend show; demonstrations OK. Registration limit: 20-25.
Promotion: Show is advertised by newspaper; radio; and direct mail. Submit glossy photos and resume. "Some exhibitors sold $1,000-1,200 during show."

SOUTHERN CHRISTMAS SHOW, 1945 Randolph Rd., Charlotte NC 28207. (704)376-6594. President: Robert E. Zimmerman. Sponsor: Southern Shows, Inc. "We are consumer and trade show managers. Our revenue is strictly from ticket sales and booth rental." Estab. 1967. Annual indoor show held 9 days in November at the Charlotte Merchandise Mart. Entry fee: $165/8x12 display area; $313.50/8x24 booth; $478.50/8x36; or $1,170/8x48 booth. Work may be offered for sale; no commission. "Craftworker's presence is required to qualify for craft rate. Booth must be manned at all times." Demonstrations encouraged. Sponsor provides chairs; prefabricated pegboard; electricity for demonstrations; table; and 24-hour security. Categories: Olde Towne ("exhibitors in Olde Towne are required to provide for visitors a special feature, visually pleasing and in Olde Towne tradition, or an educational feature, with historical significance"); Art and Crafts; Commercial (gifts, food, holiday merchandise exhibited by companies for merchandising and/or retail sales); and Bazaar (church and other nonprofit organizations qualify for space in this area. All items sold must be homemade or handmade). Considers all crafts. Bestsellers: "Christmas items."
Promotion: Show is advertised by newspaper, radio and TV advertising—mostly local, but some regional; national trade magazines and regional publications; newspaper and TV/radio interviews; and other public relations activities handled by a full-time director. "Submit biographical/background material on you, your craft and your business, along with b&w 8x10 photos of you with your craft."

SOUTHERN LIVING SHOW, 1945 Randolph Rd., Charlotte NC 28207. (704)376-6597. President: Robert E. Zimmerman. Sponsor: Southern Living Magazine. "We are consumer and trade show managers. Our revenue is strictly from ticket sales and booth rental." Estab. 1959. Annual outdoor show held 9 days the last week of February and the first week of March at the Charlotte Merchandise Mart. Average attendance: 100,000. Entries accepted until show is filled. Entry fee: $165/8x12 display area; $313/8x24 display booth; $478/8x36 booth; or $594/8x48 area. Prejudging by slides. Work may be offered for sale; no commission. "Craftworker's presence is required to qualify for craft rate. Booth must be manned at all times." Demonstrations encouraged. Sponsor provides chairs; display panels; table; 24-hour security; electricity at a fee; and liability insurance. "Show is 70% horticulture and home products. Limited area devoted to crafts." Considers all crafts. Bestsellers: "the more original, unusual, the better."
Promotion: Show is advertised by newspaper; radio; and TV advertising—mostly local, but some regional; national trade magazines and regional publications; newspaper and TV/radio interviews; and other public relations activities handled by a full-time director. "Submit biographical/background material on you, your craft and your business, along with b&w 8x10 photos of you with your craft."

*SUNBONNET FESTIVAL, Rt. 3, Box 142, Yadkinville NC 27055. (919)679-2941. Executive Director: Bill Casstevens. Sponsor: Yadkin Arts Council. Estab. 1975. Annual outdoor show (with some tents, awnings and booths) held 2 days in August. Average attendance: 5,000-6,000. Entries accepted until 1 week before show. Entry fee: $5/4 entries plus $25/booth. Maximum 4 entries per category or 8 total. Prejudging "by experts brought in from outside the county." No entry fees refunded for refused work. Work may be offered for sale; 20% commission on juried show only. Craftworker must attend show; demonstrations OK. Registration limit: 35 booths; 100 craftworkers. Sponsor provides electricity for demonstrations; table; and 24-hour security. Considers all crafts.
Awards: Presents $75 1st, $50 2nd, 2 $25 3rd, and 3 $5 honorable mention awards; and $150 in purchase prizes. "Our judges tend to be experts in their field. The purchase prize is awarded by collaboration of judges and the Arts Council. The show is so varied that any quality work can win."
Promotion: Show is advertised by TV; radio; newspapers; posters; and direct mail campaigns. Submit photos and biographical information for press releases.

SUNDAY-ON-THE-SQUARE, Arts Council of Fayetteville/Cumberland County, Inc., Box 318, Fayetteville NC 28302. (919)323-1776. Assistant Director: Carolyn C. Carlson. Estab. 1974. Annual indoor/outdoor show held 1 day in the spring. Average attendance: 15,000. Entries accepted until 1 week before show. Entry fee: $20/display area determined by request. Work may be offered for sale; no commission. Craftworker must attend show; demonstrations OK. Sponsor provides electricity for demonstrations. Show is advertised by TV; radio; newspapers; and regional and national magazines. Considers all crafts.

*TRIANGLE FESTIVAL OF CRAFTS, 810 W. Proctor St., Durham NC 27707. Executive Director: James C. McIntyre. Purpose: "to present professional designer crafts to the community and to provide a market for sale of professional crafts." Estab. 1966. Annual indoor show held 3 days in spring. Average attendance: 10,000. Entries accepted until 6 weeks before show. Entry fee: $10/craftworker. Display area: 10x4. Prejudging by 3 pieces of work; entry fee due after prejudging. Work may be offered for sale; 20% commission. Craftworker must attend show; demonstrations OK. Registration limit: 60. Sponsor provides chairs; electricity for demonstrations; fencing; table; and 24-hour security. Show is advertised by radio; TV; news media; and posters. Submit photos. Presents purchase awards totalling $300-500 and the AR Cole Award for Best Pottery, ribbon. Considers all crafts.

VILLAGE ART & CRAFT FAIR, c/o New Morning Gallery, 3½ Kitchen Place, Asheville NC 28803. (704)274-2831. Director: John Cram. Estab. 1972. Annual outdoor show held 2 days in August. Average attendance: 10,000.
Acceptable Work: Considers batik; candlemaking; ceramics; dollmaking; glass art; jewelry; lapidary; leatherworking; macrame; metalsmithing; pottery; sculpture; soft sculpture; weaving; and woodcrafting.
Terms: Entries accepted until 2 weeks before show. Entry fee: $65/8x10 display area. Prejudging. "Artists and craftsmen at great distances usually submit slides or photos; regional and local participants may have their work juried at the gallery." Work must be offered for sale; no commission. Craftworker must attend show; demonstrations welcomed. Registration limit: 125. Sponsor provides limited electricity for demonstrations.
Promotion: Show is advertised by chamber of commerce; radio; newspapers; posters; and flyers.
Profile: "The fair is held on the church grounds of All Souls Episcopal Church. It is a charming tree-covered setting for which many of the repeat craftsmen have commented as being one of the nicest settings and atmosphere for a fair. We also provide music all day of a complementary nature. The event is held the same weekend as the Mountain Dance and Folk Festival which generates a lot of fresh and interested buyers into the Asheville market."
Sales Tip: "We recommend a broad selection of work, high and low prices; major works often attract attention, but sales will come from the lower price items as a whole."

North Dakota

MINOT ART ASSOCIATION ART FAIR, Box 325, Minot ND 58701. (701)838-4445. Director: Beth Kjelson. Estab. 1975. Annual outdoor show held 1 day in September. Average attendance: 500. Entries accepted until 1 week before show. Entry fee: $20. Display area: 12x12. Work may be offered for sale; no commission. Craftworker must attend show; demonstrations OK. Registration limit: 50. Show is advertised by radio; flyers; and calendar of events. Considers all crafts except mold-type ceramics.

MINOT ART GALLERY ARTFEST, Box 325, Minot ND 58701. (701)838-4445. Director: Beth Kjelson. Estab. 1975. Annual indoor show held 3 days in March. Average attendance: 1000. Entries accepted until 1 week before show. Entry fee: $20/12x12 display area. Work may be offered for sale; no commission. Craftworker must attend show; demonstrations OK. Registration limit: 60. Show is advertised by radio; brochure; and calendar of events. Considers all crafts except candlemaking; mold-type ceramics; and dollmaking.

*** NORTH DAKOTA ART EXHIBITION**, Box 325, Minot Art Gallery, Minot ND 58701. (701)838-4445. Director: Beth Kjelson. Sponsor: Minot Art Association. Estab. 1976. Annual indoor show held the month of March. Average attendance: 1,000. Entries accepted until 1 week before show. Entry fee: $5/2 entries. Maximum 2 entries per craftworker. Prejudging; no entry fees refunded for refused work. Work may be offered for sale; 30% commission. Registration limit: 50 craftworkers from North Dakota, Minnesota, Montana, South Dakota, and members of the Art Association. Considers all original crafts. Presents cash and purchase prizes.

RED RIVER STREET FAIR, Box 962, Fargo ND 58102. (701)237-3721. Arts Coordinator: Jay Gage. Sponsor: Downtown Business Association. Estab. 1977. Annual outdoor show held 3 days in July. Average attendance: 60,000. Entries accepted until 5 weeks before show. Entry fee: $20/artist. Display area: 15x15. Prejudging by 3 35mm slides. SASE. Entry fee refunded for refused work. Work may be offered for sale; no commission. Craftworker must attend show; demonstrations OK. Sponsor provides electricity for demonstrations; and light hospitality. Categories: public sales/display—painting; drawing; sculpture; fibers; wood; metal; jewelry; leather; poetry/literature; glass; clay; plastics; and folk arts. Demonstrations OK in quilting; painting; pottery; woodcarving; jewelry; blacksmithing; dulcimer; spinning; and weaving. Considers all crafts including folk toys; musical instrument construction; and basketry. Use of good design concepts in display presentation; no clutter. Work clearly labeled and priced. Work should fulfill definition of finished status. No propping of works on non-booth display surfaces.
Sales Tip: "Larger sales volume occurs under $80 level; buying does occur to $500 level. Viewing public purchases in all areas; does not separate crafts and fine arts categories. Utility has a strong appeal."
Promotion: Show is advertised by state-wide newspapers; shopping newspapers; tourism journals; community and public TV-radio; brochures; and posters. Artists are reached by local; state; regional; and national publications. Submit unique information or photos; local artists are recruited for TV promotions.

SHEYENNE VALLEY ARTS & CRAFTS FESTIVAL, Ft. Ransom ND 58033. Sponsor: Sheyenne Valley Arts and Crafts Association. Purpose: "to provide an opportunity for artists and craftsmen to display their work." Emphasis is given to encouraging local persons to participate. Estab. 1966. Annual indoor/outdoor show held the last weekend in September. Average attendance: 2,000-3,000. Entries accepted until 2 weeks before show. Entry fee: $6/3x3 display area, plus $3 annual membership fee. Work may be offered for sale; no commission. Craftworker must attend show; demonstrations OK. Registration limit: 75-100. Sponsor provides chairs; coverings; fencing; and table. Show is advertised by radio; TV; and other mass media. Considers all crafts.

Ohio

APPALACHIAN FESTIVAL, 1015 Vine St., Rm. 304, Cincinnati OH 45202. Sponsor: Appalachian Community Development Association. Purpose: "to provide an Appalachian identity focus; to assist Appalachian regional craft group and individuals with sales in a metropolitan market; and to raise funds for community projects." Estab. 1971. Annual indoor show held 5 days in spring. Average attendance: 25,000-30,000. Entries accepted until 8 weeks before show. Entry fee: $35/10x12 display area. Prejudging by photos or slides. Work may be offered for sale; 10x commission. Craftworker must attend show; demonstrations OK. Registration limit: 110. Sponsor provides chairs; display panels; electricity for demonstrations; table; 24-hour security; housing; and 2 meals at show. Show is advertised by an advertising agency; focus is at both national and local level. Submit autobiographic information; photos; and, if possible, names of "prime buyers" for publicity. Considers only Appalachian traditional crafts made by craftworkers working in the Appalachian region. 1978 show sales totalled $120,000.

***AREA ARTISTS ANNUAL**, 524 Wick Ave., Youngstown OH 44502. (216)743-1711. Sponsor:

Butler Institute of American Art. Annual indoor show held 3 weeks in November. Entries accepted until 3 weeks before show. Entry fee: $1/item. Maximum 3 pieces per category; 9 total. Work may be offered for sale; 10% commission. Craftworker needn't attend show; no demonstrations. Considers all crafts. "Open to artists within a 40 mile radius of Youngstown, including former residents. Label works on back with name, address, title, medium and price, if for sale. No hooks or wires. Entries must be delivered and removed by hand. Rejects may be picked up after the show opens. There will be a storage charge of $1/week for each item not picked up by February." Presents cash and purchase awards.

This ceramic chicken fountain, made by Aileen Hyne, was a popular item at the University of Michigan Christmas Art Fair at Ann Arbor, Michigan. To increase sales, craftsmen should be aware of good presentations and attractive displays, says Celeste Melis, director of the show. Many of the customers find it a good time to search for Christmas presents.

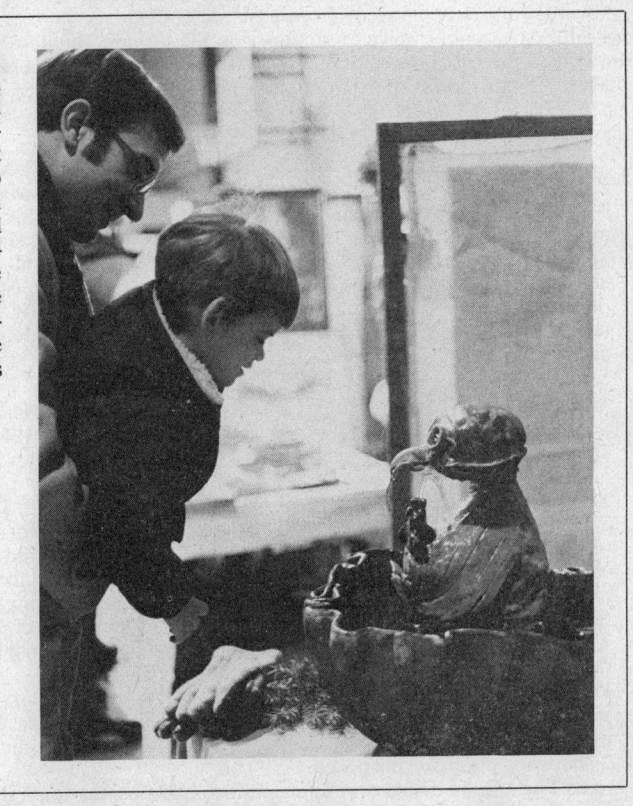

ART IN THE PARK, 142 Riverbend Dr., Dayton OH 45405. (513)225-5433. Director: Pat Shoop-Lowry. Sponsor: City of Dayton Division of Recreation and Riverbend Arts Council. Estab. 1967. Annual outdoor show held Saturday and Sunday of Memorial Day weekend. Average attendance: 15,000-20,000. Closing date for entry: 3 weeks before show. Entry fee: $20/craftworker. Craftworker must submit 4 slides per category entered. Entry fee refunded for refused work. Crafts may be offered for sale; no commission. "Out-of-state artists do exhibit in our show, but we prefer to promote area artists and we call some artists from the previous year who had interesting exhibits." Craftworker must attend show. "Demonstrating is stressed as it makes for a more interesting show. We have a yearly outdoor raku firing demonstration. There is a student and instructor show plus excellent entertainment." Registration limit: 125.
Acceptable Work: Considers batik; leatherworking; metalsmithing; pottery; weavings; wall hangings; woodcrafting; handmade jewelry; sculpture using casting or construction methods; enameling; lapidary; macrame; stained glass; graphics; drawings; paintings; and handmade instruments such as dulcimers. "We strive for a fine arts or fine arts type craft show. One-of-a-kind items."

*ARTISAN FAIR, BOSTON MILLS, Box 173, Peninsula OH 44264. (216)657-2807. Director: Don Getz. Sponsor: Junior Women's Civic Club of Akron and the *Cleveland Plain Dealer* Charities. Purpose: to present top quality craftwork to a very art conscious group of buyers. Estab. 1976. Annual indoor/outdoor (large tents) show held 4 days Labor Day weekend.

Average attendance: 10,000. Entries accepted until mid-July. Entry fee: $35-75, depending on type of display area. Display area: 10x10 lawn space; 10x10 tent spaces; and 5x15 indoor spaces. Prejudging by 5 slides; $5 screening fee. Entry fee refunded for refused work. Work must be offered for sale; no commission. Craftworker must attend show; demonstrations recommended. Registration limit: 200. Sponsor provides electricity for demonstrations; and 24-hour security. Show is advertised by newspapers; TV; radio; and posters. Considers all crafts except decoupage; dollmaking; needlecrafts; and tole painting. All works must be tagged with prices.
Awards: Presents cash awards of $250 for best of show; $100, 2nd; $50, 3rd; and certificates. Awards jury is composed of professional craftsmen.
Profile: The public pays an addmission fee to view this fair and conditioned to expecting a quality exhibit of outstanding crafts. The artisan must bring his best works to be competitive. Most "bread and butter" items are definitely out of place here. 1978 show sales totalled $100,000 for 130 exhibitors.

*ARTS & CRAFTS; FINE ARTS; HOBBY CRAFTS; COUNTRY CRAFTS, 47 N. 4th St., Zanesville OH 43701. (614)452-7571. Chairperson: Alice Mauk. Sponsor: Zanesville Area Chamber of Commerce. Estab. 1973. Annual outdoor show held 3 days in June. Average attendance: 200,000. Entries accepted until 10 weeks before show. Entry fee: $45/8x10 display area plus $5 prejudging fee. Work may be offered for sale; no commission. Craftworker must attend show; demonstrations OK. Registration limit: 138. Sponsor provides electricity for demonstrations and 24-hour security. Show is advertised by ads through Ohio; leaflets; and statewide coverage. Presents cash awards and ribbons. Categories: fine arts; country crafts; and creative crafts. Considers all crafts.

*ARTSAFFAIR, 630 S. 3rd St., Columbus OH 43206. (614)244-2606. Festival Coordinator: Jan Schmidt. Sponsor: Greater Columbus Arts Council. Estab. 1960. Annual outdoor show held 3 days in June. Average attendance: 80,000. Considers all crafts except decoupage and tole painting. No molds or manufactured art work.
Terms: Entries accepted until 8 weeks before show. Jury fee: $2. Entry fee: $50/10x10 display area. Prejudging by 5 slides/photos accompanied by entry form and brief resume. Slides and photos should cover all types of work which would be offered for sale and should be marked with name, media and size of work. Jury fee not refunded for refused work. Work must be offered for sale; no commission. Craftworker must attend show; demonstrations OK. Registration limit: 100. Sponsor provides electricity for demonstrations and night security.
Awards: Presents cash awards for Best Display. "The display should be attractive, well thought out and neat."
Promotion: Show is advertised by all local media; TV, radio, newspapers (in both large and small communities throughout Ohio), posters and billboards. Printed flyers mailed to 30,000 individuals in the Columbus area. Submit brief resume with slides; Festival Committee retains 2 slides for publicity purposes.
Sales Tip: "Good display is important to good sales. Our past shows show that the public buys from every media shown; ceramics are very good. Fibers do not always go well if the weather is hot."

*BOSTON MILLS INVITATIONAL ART FESTIVAL, Box 173, Peninsula OH 44264. (216)657-2807. Director: Don Getz. Sponsor: Akron Society of Artists and *Cleveland Plain Dealer* Charities. Purpose: "to expose the buying public to the best art and crafts available in this part of the country." Estab. 1971. Annual indoor/outdoor (large building and large tents) show held 4 days in July (July 4th weekend). Average attendance: 14,000. Entries accepted until 2 months before show. Entry fee: $30/4x4 table, limit 2; $45/10x10 open tent spaces, limit 2; and $40/10x10 open lawn space, limit 2. Entry fee refunded for refused work. Prejudging by 5 slides; $5 screening fee. Selection jury comprised of professional artists and craftsmen. Entry fee refunded for refused work. Work must be offered for sale; no commission. Craftworker must attend show; demonstrations OK. Registration limit: 80-100. Sponsor provides electricity for demonstrations; and 24-hour security. Show is advertised by newspapers; TV; radio; posters; and direct mail.
Acceptable Work: Considers batik; ceramics; glass art; lapidary; macrame; metalsmithing; mobiles; pottery; sculpture; and weaving. All works must be tagged with prices.
Awards: Presents cash awards of $250 for best of show; $100, 1st in crafts; $50, 2nd in crafts;

---

* *Those listings preceded by an asterisk present awards for prize-winning crafts.*

certificates; and purchase awards. Awards jury is composed of professional artists and craftsmen.
Sales Tip: "This is a buying public as they pay an admission to see exhibit. They purchase well in all price ranges as they realize this has always been a quality exhibit." 1978 show sales totalled $195,000 for 190 exhibitors.

***CAIN PARK ARTS FESTIVAL**, 2953 Mayfield Rd., Cleveland Hts. OH 44118. (216)321-0100. Superintendent of Parks and Recreation: Spencer Caress. Sponsor: Cleveland Heights Parks and Recreation. Estab. 1978. Annual outdoor show (indoors in case of rain) held 2 days in July. Average attendance: 12,000. Considers all original crafts. Presents cash awards of $200, $100 and $50.
Terms: Entries accepted until 3 weeks before show. Entry fee: $20/artist. Display area: 12x12'. Entries prejudged by slides. Entry fee refunded for refused work. Work may be offered for sale; no commission. Craftworker must attend show; demonstrations OK. Registration limit: 75. Sponsor provides 24-hour security; tables and chairs may be rented.

***CEDAR POINTS' CRAFTS SHOW**, Merchandise Department, Cedar Point Inc., Sandusky OH 44870. (419)626-0830, ext. 2271. Crafts Manager: Gene Goff. Estab. 1973. Annual outdoor show (indoor space available in case of rain) held the last week in July. Average attendance: 170,634. Entries accepted until 4 weeks before show. No entry fee. Display area: 10x10. Prejudging by slides or photos sent with application. Work may be offered for sale; 20-30% commission. Craftworker must attend show; demonstrations OK. Registration limit: 50-100. Sponsor provides chairs; covering; electricity for demonstrations; fencing; table; 24-hour security; and night storage. Show is advertised by TV; radio; magazines; newspapers; posters; and billboards. Considers batik; candlemaking; ceramics; decoupage; dollmaking; and jewelry. 1978 show sales totalled $41,660.

***CERAMIC, SCULPTURE & CRAFT SHOW**, 524 Wick Ave., Youngstown OH 44502. (216)743-1711. Assistant to the Directors: Cissy Cochran. Sponsor: Butler Institute of American Art. Annual indoor show held from first non-holiday Sunday in January to last Sunday in February. Entries accepted until 4 weeks before show. Entry fee: $3.50/classification. Maximum 3 pieces per artist per 4 categories. Work may be offered for sale; 10% commission. Presents cash and purchase awards totalling $1,500. Categories: ceramics; sculpture; enamel jewelry; and crafts. Considers all crafts including quilting and clothing.

COLUMBUS ART-CRAFT-HOBBY-MINIATURE FAIR, 1100 Brandywine Blvd., Box 2188, Zanesville OH 43701. (614)452-4541. Show Director: Walter E. Offinger, Jr. Annual indoor show held 2 days in October at Columbus, Ohio. Average attendance: 10,000. Entries accepted until 1 month before show. Entry fee: $100. Work may be offered for sale; no commission. Craftworker or representative must attend show; demonstrations OK. Registration limit: 250. Sponsor provides two 6' tables and 2 chairs/10x10 space. Show is advertised by direct mail; newspapers; radio; TV; and craft publications. Considers all crafts.

COLUMBUS SPRING ART FAIR, 1725 Weldon, Ann Arbor MI 48103. (313)662-4918. Show Director: Audree Levy. Sponsor: American Cancer Society. Estab. 1977. Annual indoor show held 2 days in March at Columbus, Ohio. Average attendance: 7,000-10,000.
Acceptable Work: Considers all crafts except decoupage, needlecrafts and tole painting. Fine art crafts welcome. No kits or machine-made crafts.
Terms: Entries accepted until 4 weeks before show. Entry fee: $110/10x12' display area. Prejudging by slides and resume. Entry fee due after prejudging. Work must be offered for sale; no commission. Craftworker must attend show; some demonstrations OK. Registration limit: 130. Sponsor provides electricity for demonstrations and 24-hour security.
Promotion: Show is advertised by newspapers, radio, TV and postcards. Provide resume and b&w photos for promotional purposes.

COSHOCTON CANAL FESTIVAL, Box 266, Coshocton OH 43812. (614)622-5411. Coshocton Area Chamber of Commerce, Executive Manager: John O'Reilly. Estab. 1970. Annual outdoor show held 3 days in August. Average attendance: 100,000. Entries accepted until 1 week before show. Entry fee $25/10' frontal space; $10/each additional 5'. Work may be offered for sale; no commission. Craftworker needn't attend show; demonstrations OK. Registration limit: 50-60. Sponsor provides electricity for demonstrations and 24-hour security. Show is advertised by radio; newspapers; magazines; and periodicals. Considers all crafts.

BOB EVANS FARM FESTIVAL, Box 330, Rio Grande, OH 45674. (614)245-5305. Festival Chairman: George A. Wolfe, Ph.D. Purpose: "to demonstrate and display heritage crafts once common to our early ancestors. Estab. 1971. Annual outdoor festival held during the second full weekend in October on the Bob Evans Farm in Rio Grande, Ohio. Average attendance: 120,000. Entries accepted until 12 weeks before show. Display area: 12x12 in a craft tent, barn or field. Works may be offered for sale; no commission; $25 booth display charge. Craftworker must attend show and demonstrate. Registration limit: 60 for craft tents; as space allows for field demonstrations. Sponsor provides electricity for demonstrations and 24-hour security. Show is advertised by regional television, newspapers and magazines. All crafts are selected on the basis of keeping with the festival's rural heritage theme, such as soap-making, shingle making, basket weaving and spinning.

FESTIVAL OF THE FISH, 5488 Liberty Ave., Vermilion OH 44089. (216)967-4477. Chairman: Herb Feakins. Sponsor: Vermilion Chamber of Commerce. Annual outdoor show (large tent for some displays) held 4 days the third week in June. Average attendance: 100,000. Entries accepted until show. Work may be offered for sale; no commission. Craftworker must attend show; demonstrations OK. Sponsor provides electricity for demonstrations and 24-hour security. Show is advertised by Ohio Festivals and Events; Lake Erie Firelands Tourist Council; radio; and newspapers. Submit photos for publicity. Considers all crafts. "In Vermilion anything nautical usually sells well."

FUNCTIONAL CERAMICS, Art Center Museum, The College of Wooster, Wooster OH 44691. (216)264-1234, ext. 388. Show Coordinator: Phyllis Clark. Purpose: "to make people aware of the excellent functional ceramic work being done today and to give the practicing functional potters a chance to show their work in a creditable show without all the funky stuff taking precedent; and to give functional potters the recognition they deserve for the work of merit." Estab. 1974. Annual invitational indoor show held 3 weeks in the spring. Average attendance: 1,000. Maximum 10 pieces per craftworker. Prejudging by slides or photos. Work may be offered for sale; 20% commission. Craftworker needn't attend show; demonstrations at times. Registration limit: 20-40. Sponsor provides insurance on exhibited work; insurance on work shipped to artist; and all of the display. Considers ceramics and pottery. Maximum size: less than 100 pounds. "Pots are to be numbered and priced and a matching identification list is required to accompany the pots."
Sales Tip: "Our public is aware of good functional work and will not buy inferior or campy products."
Promotion: "We have had excellent coverage by *Ceramic Monthly* magazine; local news media; state monthly magazines; mailers; and by the potters themselves. We need the biographical material on the artist and a photo of him to include in the exhibition after he is accepted."

GREAT LAKES MALL, 2918 Martel Dr., Dayton OH 45420. (513)254-2900. Director: Clarence Freeland. Annual indoor show held 11 days in October-November at Mentor (near Cleveland). Closing date for entry: 1 week before show. Entry fee: $95. Prejudging. Work may be offered for sale; no commission. Craftworker must attend show; demonstrations OK. Sponsor provides 10x10 display area. Considers all crafts.

*****INDIAN SUMMER ARTS & CRAFTS FESTIVAL**, Marietta College, Marietta OH 45750. (614)373-8027. Director: Arthur Howard Winer. Sponsor: Indian Summer Festival, Inc. Purpose: "to provide artists and crafters with an opportunity to exhibit and sell their work and to educate the general public to quality craftsmanship. Each participant is asked to assist by demonstrating and conversing with the viewing public." Estab. 1955. Annual indoor show held 2½ days during the 3rd weekend in September. Average attendance: 15,000. Entries accepted until 2½ months before show. Entry fee: $35/10x10 display area. Invited country craftworkers are required to demonstrate. Prejudging by 35mm slides. Total entry fee refunded for rejected work. Work may be offered for sale; no commission. Craftworker or representative must attend show; demonstrations encouraged. Registration limit: 125. Sponsor provides display panels; electricity for demonstrations; table ($2.50 rental fee); and 24-hour security. Show is advertised in a 200 mile radius by brochures; posters; press packs; press releases; radio; and TV. Submit b&w photos of self at work if accepted. Considers all crafts. Presents ribbons of craftsmanship.

INVITATIONAL COLUMBUS SPRING ART FAIR, 1725 Weldon, Ann Arbor MI 48103. Show Director: Audree Levy. Sponsor: American Cancer Society. Estab. 1977. Annual indoor show held 2 days in March at Columbus, Ohio. Average attendance: 10,000. Entries accepted until 2 months before show. Entry fee: $110/10x12 display area. Prejudging by 3 slides and resume. SASE. Entry fee due after prejudging. Work may be offered for sale; no commission. Craftworker must attend show; some demonstrations OK. Registration limit: 100. Show director provides 24-hour security. Show is advertised by TV; radio; and newspapers. Submit b&w photo and resume. Considers all crafts except decoupage; needlecrafts; and tole painting.

*MARIETTA COLLEGE CRAFTS NATIONAL, Marietta College, Art Department, Marietta OH 45750. (614)373-4643. Director: Arthur Howard Winer. Purpose: "to display and reward the creative efforts of artists and craftspersons in the USA." Estab. 1972. Annual indoor show held 30 days October-November. Average attendance: 5,000. Entries accepted until 6 weeks before show. $10 jurying fee. Write for prospectus. Prejudging by slides. Work may be offered for sale; 25% commission. Craftworker needn't attend show; no demonstrations. Sponsor provides insurance on exhibited work; 24-hour security; and exhibition set-up. Accepted artists should send hanging instructions. Show is advertised by 3,500 posters; 4,000 catalogs; 15,000 prospectuses; 12,000 news releases; radio; and TV. Accepted artists send photos of work for promotion. Considers all crafts. Presents cash awards of $3,500; purchase awards of $1,500; and special awards.

*THE MARIETTA NATIONAL, Marietta College Department of Art, Marietta OH 45750. (614)373-4643. Director: Arthur Howard Winer. Purpose: "to display and reward the creative efforts of painters and sculptors in US." Estab. 1967. Annual indoor show held 6 weeks April-May. Entries accepted until 2 months before show. Entry fee: $10/artist. Maximum 3 pieces/artist. Prejudging by slides. Work may be offered for sale; 25% commission. Artist needn't attend show; no demonstrations. Show is advertised by listings in art and craft magazines; press releases; posters; radio; and TV. Write for a prospectus. Considers sculpture in all media. Presents $1,000 painting, $1,000 sculpture awards and $1,500 purchase awards.

THE MASSILLON MUSEUM SIDEWALK SHOW, 212 Lincoln Way E., Massillon OH 44646. (216)833-4061. Director: Mary M. Merwin. Sponsor: Woman's Board of Members of the Museum, Inc. Purpose: "to promote the artist and make his work available for purchase to the public." Estab. 1961. Annual indoor/outdoor show held 3 days in June. Average attendance: 2,000. Entries accepted until 3 days before show. Entry fee: $3/craftworker. Maximum 25 pieces per craftworker. Work may be offered for sale; 20% commission. Craftworker needn't attend show; demonstrations OK. Sponsor provides chairs; electricity for demonstrations; insurance on exhibited work; and table. Categories: paintings; prints; drawings; photographs; and crafts. Considers all crafts.

*MAY ARTS & CRAFTS EXHIBITION, 620 Military Road, Zanesville OH 43701. (614)452-0741. Director: Dr. Charles Dietz. Sponsor: Zanesville Art Center. Estab. 1952. Annual indoor show held throughout month of May. Average attendance: 3,000. Show is advertised by radio, TV, press and bulletins.
Acceptable Work: Original painting, drawing, prints, ceramics, photography. Considers all crafts. No kits. "Items must be ready for display."
Terms: Entries accepted until 2 weeks before show. Entry fee: $5/artist. Display area: 12 galleries, 12 display cases. Maximum 3 entries/category; maximum 6 entries total. Prejudging. Entry fee not refunded for refused work. Work may be offered for sale; 15% commission. Craftworker needn't attend show; no demonstrations. Sponsor provides locked plate glass display cases and 24-hour security.
Awards: Presents $400+ in cash awards, various ribbons and honorable mentions. Also, purchases some works. "Items must be original (i.e., created in the last 3 years), never before exhibited at ZAC and entrant must live within a radius of 100 miles."

*MAY SHOW, The Cleveland Museum of Art, Cleveland OH 44106. Associate Curator: Tom Hinson. Annual indoor show held the month of April. Entries accepted until 2 months before show. Maximum 2 pieces/craftworker. Prejudging by slides. "2-dimensional works should be represented by 2 35mm slides, 2x2 mounts; 1 an overall view, the other a detail. 3-dimensional works should be represented by 3 35mm slides, 2x2 mounts; 1 of the views should show an indication of scale. The artist's name, title, media and dimensions must be marked on each slide. On the front of each slide the top of the work should be indicated and the entry number in upper right." SASE. Work may be offered for sale; 10% commission. Sponsor will carry cost of unpacking work. "All entrants will receive a preview invitation. All accepted artists will be sent 1 complimentary catalog copy." Presents 4 $1,000 cash awards.

Acceptable Work: Considers glass art; jewelry; metalsmithing; enamels; pottery; and furniture. Will only accept work "by artists who now live, work, or were born in the following Ohio counties: Ashland; Ashtabula; Cuyahoga; Erie; Geauga; Huron; Lake; Lorain; Mahoning; Medina; Portage; Summit; or Trumbull. Artist must be 18 or older. All silver objects should indicate whether sterling silver or silver plate was used. Clay objects must be fired.

MILLCREEK MALL, 2918 Martel Dr., Dayton OH 45420. (513)254-2900. Director: Clarence Freeland. Annual indoor show held 1 week in August-September and 1 week in April at Erie, Ohio. Closing date for entry: 1 week before show. Entry fee: $75. Display area: 10x10. Prejudging. Work may be offered for sale; no commission. Craftworker must attend show; demonstrations OK. Considers all crafts.

*****MONTGOMERY KIWANIS SIDEWALK ART SHOW,** 9399 Shelly Lane, Cincinnati OH 45242. (513)793-4390. Chairman: Harry Henderly. Sponsor: Montgomery Kiwanis Club. Estab. 1955. Annual outdoor show held the next to the last Sunday in September. Average attendance: 5,000-10,000. Entries accepted until show date. Entry fee: $15/adult entry; $1/youth entry. Work may be offered for sale; no commission. Craftworker must attend show; demonstrations OK. Considers some crafts.
Awards: Presents $485, cash prizes; $300, youth scholarship; $100 bicycle; 3 grand prizes and 60 1st, 2nd, 3rd and honorable mention ribbons. Judges are local artists and art teachers.

*****OHIO ARTISTS & CRAFTSMEN SHOW,** 212 Lincoln Way E., Massillon OH 44646. (216)833-4061. Director: Mary Merwin. Sponsor: The Massillon Museum. Purpose: "to give outstanding craftsmen an opportunity to show their work and also to expose the public to the work of Ohio craftsmen." Estab. 1937. Biennial indoor show held 2 months, July-August during even-numbered years. Average attendance: 2,500. Entries accepted until 3 weeks before show. Entry fee: $3/craftworker. Maximum 4 pieces per craftworker. Prejudging; no entry fees refunded for refused work. Work may be offered for sale; 10% commission. Craftworker needn't attend show; no demonstrations. Sponsor provides insurance on exhibited work and 24-hour security. Show is advertised by radio; newspapers through Ohio; and magazines. Considers batik; ceramics; glass art; jewelry; metalsmithing; mobiles; pottery; sculpture; and soft sculpture. Presents purchase awards and prizes totalling $1,500.

OUTDOOR ARTS FESTIVAL, School of Fine Arts, 38660 Mentor Ave., Willoughby OH 44094. (216)951-7500. Exhibit Coordinator: D. Foster. Purpose: "to offer a show and sell place for creative practicing artists and craftsmen. Estab. 1972. Annual outdoor show held 3 days in July. Average attendance: 10,000. Entries accepted up to 2½ months prior to festival dates. Entry fee charged. Prejudging by slides and photos; entry fee refunded for refused work. Work may be offered for sale; no commission. Craftworker must attend show; demonstrations encouraged. Sponsor provides electricity for demonstrations and 24-hour security. Considers all media.
Promotion: "All television, radio stations and newspapers receive news releases regarding this event and there is a community-wide distribution of flyers. The festival is advertised statewide through the news media, Ohio Arts Council and the Ohio Artists and Craftsmen Association." Submit 8x10 b&w glossies of self involved with work; brief paragraph on background; and name of newspaper serving your area.

RICHMOND MALL, 2918 Martel Dr., Dayton OH 45420. (513)254-2900. Director: Clarence Freeland. Annual indoor show held 1 week in October and 1 week in April at Cleveland, Ohio. Closing date for entry: 1 week before show. Entry fee: $75. Display area: 10x10. Prejudging by 3 slides or photos. Work may be offered for sale; no commission. Craftworker must attend show; demonstrations OK. Considers all crafts.

*****SHOW OF THE CRAFT GUILD OF GREATER CINCINNATI,** 6018 Ridge Ave., Cincinnati OH 45213. (513)351-3463. Newsletter Editor: Mary Klein. Purpose: "educational, to acquaint the public with the original work being done today within a 50-mile radius of Cincinnati." Estab. 1966. Annual indoor show held 4 weeks March-April. Average attendance: 5,000. Entries accepted until 2 weeks before show. Maximum 3 pieces per craftworker. Prejudging by actual work. Work may be offered for sale; 20% commission. Craftworker needn't attend show; no demonstrations. Show is advertised by radio; newspapers; posters; and mailings. Considers all crafts. Awards cash prizes.

SOUTHERN PARK MALL, 2918 Martel Dr., Dayton OH 45420. (513)254-2900. Director:

Clarence Freeland. Indoor show held 1 week in June at Youngstown, Ohio. Closing date for entry: 1 week before show. Entry fee: $75. Prejudging. Work may be offered for sale; no commission. Craftworker must attend show; demonstrations OK. Sponsor provides 10x10 display area. Considers all crafts.

*SPRING SHOW, Memorial Hall, Box 1948, Lima OH 45802. Contact: Director. Annual show. Entry fee: $4, students; $5, Lima Art Association members; $6, non-members. Maximum 3 entries. Open to artists living within 75 miles of Lima, Ohio. Presents over $1,400 in awards, including special awards for watercolors and fiber arts.

SQUARE FAIR, Box 1124, Lima OH 45805. (419)225-6156. Executive Director: Dean R. Gladden. Sponsor: Lima Area Arts Council. Purpose: "to allow artists a chance to display and sell works and to enhance the downtown area." Estab. 1973. Annual outdoor show held 2 days in August. Average attendance: 10,000. Entries accepted until 3 weeks before show. Entry fee: $10/display area. Work may be offered for sale; no commission. Craftworker should attend show; demonstrations OK. Sponsor provides electricity for demonstrations. Show is advertised by radio; TV; and news media. Considers all crafts.

*SUMMERFAIR INC., Box 3277, Cincinnati, OH 45201. Contact: Director. Annual outdoor exhibit held the first weekend in June. Closing date: April. Prejudging by slides. Write for an application. Considers a variety of media; varied and general. Offers $3,500 in prizes.

SUMMIT MALL, 2918 Martel Dr., Dayton OH 45420. (513)254-2900. Director: Clarence Freeland. Annual indoor show held 1 week in October and 10 days in June at Akron, Ohio. Closing date for entry: 1 week before show. Entry fee: $65. Prejudging. Work may be offered for sale; no commission. Craftworker must attend show; demonstrations OK. Sponsor provides 10x10 display area. Considers all crafts.

E.J. THOMAS CHRISTMAS ART & CRAFTS SHOW, 4871 Brecksville Rd., Richfield OH 44286. (216)659-3318. Director: Carol Raab. Sponsor: R&R Promotions. Purpose: "to provide a selling outlet for professional and semi-professional and qualifying amateurs, and to bring a quality show to the public." Estab. 1977. Annual indoor show held 3 days in December at Akron, Ohio. Average attendance: 12,000-15,000. Entries accepted until 4 weeks before show. Entry fee: $90-150/10x10 display area. Prejudging by slides and photos; entry fee refunded for refused work. Work may be offered for sale; no commission. Craftworker must attend show; demonstrations OK. Registration limit: 100. Sponsor provides electricity for demonstrations and 24-hour security; tables and chairs may be rented. Show is advertised by TV; radio; newspapers; magazines; posters; flyers; promotional gimmicks; and press releases. Submit pictures and promotional description of work and self. Considers all crafts.

*TOLEDO AREA ARTISTS EXHIBITION, The Toledo Museum of Art, Box 1013, Toledo OH 43697. (419)255-8000. Sponsor: Toledo Museum of Art and Toledo Federation of Art Societies. Estab. 1918. Annual indoor show held 4-6 weeks in spring. Show is advertised by area newspapers, art publications and prospectus.
Acceptable Work: Considers oil, synthetic, mixed media, watercolor, drawings, prints, photography, metalwork, enameling, woodworking, gouache, glass, sculpture, mosaic tile, pottery, porcelain, jewelry and textiles. "Original work only. No copies in whole or in part from work of another. Work on paper must be framed under glass or Plexiglas. Wires and hangers must be removed from pictures; however, metal frames must have metal hanging clips attached. Ceramics must be fired. Woven yardage must be rolled on cardboard tubes."
Terms: Entry fee: $10/artist. Maximum 3 entries per craftworker. Prejudging by actual work. Entry fee not refunded for refused work. Work may be offered for sale; 15% commission. Craftworker needn't attend show; no demonstrations.
Awards: Presents cash awards for Best of Show; 5 1st, 5 2nd, and 5 3rd place cash awards; various purchase awards by Toledo Federation of Art Societies; the Molly Morpeth Canaday Award ($100); Roulet Medal for best painting, graphic or sculpture; and Craft Club of Toledo Gold Medal.

*TOLEDO FESTIVAL OF THE ARTS, Box 7401, Toledo OH 43615. (419)536-8365. Contact: Beverlee Anderson. Sponsor: Arts Commission of Greater Toledo; Crosby Gardens Division of Forestry; Toledo Artists Club; and Garden Club Forum. Estab. 1965. Annual outdoor show held 2 days in June. Average attendance: 80,000.
Acceptable Work: Considers all crafts except candlemaking; decoupage; dollmaking; needlecrafts; and tole painting.

Terms: Entries accepted until 1 week before show. Entry fee: $40/booth; $10/table; and $10/1 side of easel. Display area: booth, 10x8; table, 2x8; and easel, 4x6. Prejudging by photos, slides and actual work. Entry fee refunded for refused work. Work may be offered for sale; no commission. Craftworker must attend show; demonstrations OK. Registration limit: 350. Sponsor provides coverings with booths; electricity for demonstrations if notified before; and 24-hour security.
Awards: Presents cash awards of $25 for each 1st place winner; $500 for purchase for permanent collection; and ribbons for 1st, 2nd, 3rd, and honorable mention. "Winners are chosen for the overall quality of their work not for specific pieces."
Promotion: Show is advertised by radio; TV; newspapers; magazines; and posters. Submit resume.

*WESTERVILLE MUSICAL & ARTS FESTIVAL, 5 W. College Ave., Westerville OH 43081. (614)882-8917. Executive Secretary: Jan Strausser. Sponsor: Westerville Area Chamber of Commerce. Purpose: "as a celebration of the arts; to continue development of all the arts throughout the area; recognizing that this development is vitally important to the growth of both the individual and the community." Estab. 1974. Annual outdoor show held 2 days in July. Average attendance: 30,000. Entries accepted until mid May. Entry fee: $35. Display area: 12'. Prejudging by slides or photos; entry fee refunded for refused work. Work may be offered for sale; no commission. Craftworker must attend show; demonstrations OK. Registration limit: 150. Sponsor provides electricity for demonstrations. Show is advertised by TV; radio; newspapers; other periodicals; and flyers. Photos may be requested for publicity. Considers all crafts. Presents $1,600 in cash awards and ribbons.

*WESTLAND ARTS & CRAFTS SHOW, 4273 Westland Mall, Columbus OH 43228. Contact: Frank McGwier. Annual show. Sponsor: Westland Shopping Center. Entry fee: $20, demonstrators less. One exhibitor per space (10x10). Art racks available. Original work only. No commission. Awards for original demonstrated work only.

WONDERFUL WORLD OF OHIO MART, Stan Hywet Hall, 714 N. Portage Path, Akron OH 44303. (216)836-5533. Director of Public Relations: Louise Goodman. Sponsor: Women's Auxiliary Board, Stan Hywet Hall Foundation, Inc. Purpose: fundraiser. Estab. 1967. Annual indoor/outdoor show (with some tents) held 4 days in October. Average attendance: 20,000. Entries accepted 7 months before show. Entry fee: $85-100, depending on location. Display area: approximately 8x10. Prejudging by work samples; entry fee due after prejudging. Work must be offered for sale. Craftworker must attend show; demonstrations requested. Registration limit: 70. Sponsor provides chairs; table; 24-hour security; and booth space is marked off. 1978 show sales totalled $90,000. Considers all crafts.
Promotion: Show is advertised by the public relations director of Stan Hywet Hall Foundation, using radio; TV; newspapers; magazines; and brochures distributed to all visitors to Stan Hywet Hall for some 2-3 months prior to the Mart. Submit biographical material (questionnaire provided) and b&w photos suitable for newspaper reproduction.

WOODVILLE MALL, 2918 Martel Dr., Dayton OH 45420. (513)254-2900. Director: Clarence Freeland. Annual indoor show held in Toledo 1 week in October and 1 week in May. Closing date for entry: 1 week before show. Entry fee: $65. Display area: 10x10. Prejudging. Work may be offered for sale; no commission. Craftworker must attend show; demonstrations OK. Considers all crafts.

YANKEE PEDDLER FESTIVAL, 4046 State Rd., Medina OH 44256. (216)239-2554. Contact: Frank Cajka. Estab. 1973. Annual outdoor show held 3 weekends in September at Canal Fulton, Ohio. Average attendance: 60,000. Considers all crafts of 1776-1825 period.
Terms: Entries accepted until 2 months before show. Entry fee: $100/10x10 display area. Prejudging by photos or slides; entry fee due after prejudging. Work may be offered for sale; no commission. Craftworker must attend show; demonstrations required. Registration limit: 150. Sponsor provides 24-hour security.
Promotion: Show is advertised by TV; radio; newspaper; brochures; and bus tour companies. Submit photos acceptable for promotion in your vicinity.

*ZANE SQUARE ARTS & CRAFTS FESTIVAL, 203 Kresge Bldg., c/o Lancaster Area Chamber of Commerce, Lancaster OH 43130. (614)653-8251. Secretary: Charlene Rowley. Sponsor: Downtown Business Association of Lancaster, Ohio. Annual show held 3 days in August. Average attendance: 3,000-5,000.

Acceptable Work: Considers all crafts. No kits or molds. "Dealers, distributors and groups may not enter."
Terms: Entries accepted until 4 weeks before show. "If space is available, we will accept late entries if they have exhibited in this show in previous years. Late entries cannot be promised listing in the program." Entry fee: $10/10x10 display area. Display area may not be shared. Prejudging by 5-6 color slides/transparencies; include SASE. Entry fee refunded for refused work. Work may be offered for sale; no commission. Craftworker needn't attend show; demonstrations encouraged. Sponsor provides 4x6 display panels (on a first come, first serve basis), electricity for demonstrations and free parking. Exhibitor handles own sales.
Awards: Presents $75 in cash for first prize and $50 in cash for second prize in each category. "A public vote is taken and the exhibitor receiving the most popular votes receives a ribbon and $25."
Promotion: Show is advertised by the Ohio Arts Council through newspapers, TV, the Ohio Arts & Crafts Guild and radio.

Oklahoma

AMERICAN INDIAN ARTS COLLECTION/GALLERY, Box 525, Shawnee OK 74801. (405)273-0184. Manager: Enoch Kelly Haney. Estab. 1976. Annual indoor show held 30 days in May and October. Average attendance: 1,500. Considers ceramics, jewelry, pottery and sculpture.
Terms: Invitational show. No entry fee. Minimum of 5 items/category. Work may be offered for sale; 35-40% commission. Craftworker must attend show; no demonstrations. Registration limit: 6. Sponsor provides chairs, display panels, table and 24-hour security.
Promotion: Show is advertised by national magazines, newspapers, TV and invitations. Send resume for promotional purposes.

AMERICAN INDIAN EXPOSITION, Box 908, Anadarko OK 73005. Sponsor: American Indians. Estab. 1931. Annual indoor/outdoor show held the third week in August. Must be American Indian to enter.

ANTIQUE, QUILT & CRAFT SHOW, c/o Mrs. J.C. Pond, Box 127, Medford OK 73759. (405)393-2888. Sponsor: Grant County Historical Society. Estab. 1974. Annual indoor show held 1 day the third weekend in April. Average attendance: 300-400. Entries accepted until show date. No entry fee. Work may be offered for sale; no commission. Craftworker must attend show; demonstrations OK. Sponsor provides chairs; electricity for demonstrations; and 24-hour security. Considers all crafts.

*****ART IN THE PARK FESTIVAL**, Box 972, 115 W. Fifth, Elk City OK 73644. (405)225-0207. Executive Director: Helen L. Brown. Sponsor: Chamber of Commerce. Estab. 1974. Annual outdoor show held 1 day during the third Saturday in September. Average attendance: 1,000-2,000.
Acceptable Work: Considers all crafts. No kits or machine-made crafts. "All exhibitors must furnish hooks, etc., for display. Each work should be clearly marked with selling price or a 'not for sale' sign."
Terms: Entries accepted until 1 week before show. "If we have spots available, we take entries till deadline of show date." Entry fee: $10/artist panel; $8.50/4x8 table. Work may be offered for sale; no commission. Craftworker must attend show; demonstrations OK. Sponsor provides display panels, electricity for demonstrations and table. Exhibitor handles sales and taxes.
Awards: Presents cash awards in varied divisions; 50 purchase awards from art patrons; and Best in Show, 1st, 2nd and 3rd place ribbons. "Entries must not have won first prize or cash awards in a previous Elk City Open Air Arts and Crafts Festival. Artists are eligible for only 1 prize in each category."
Promotion: Show is advertised by TV, radio, newspapers and personal letters to artists and craftworkers.
Profile: "Art in the Park is a part of a large festival—The Cattle Trails Festival—which has many activities going at the same time. It usually draws a large crowd and the people usually have a grand time. Since we are in the western part of the state, it seems that western art sells best."

ARTS AND CRAFTS SHOW, Chamber of Commerce Memorial Hall, Kingfisher OK 73750. (405)375-4445. Manager, Chamber of Commerce: Richard C. Stetler. Estab. 1977. Annual indoor show held 3 days in November. Average attendance: 4,000. Considers all crafts. No manufactured or machine-made articles.

Terms: Entries accepted until 1 week before show. Entry fee: $15/8x8 table. Prejudging by actual work. Entry fee not refunded for refused work. Work must be offered for sale; no commission. Craftworker must attend show; demonstrations OK. Registration limit: 95. Sponsor provides chairs pegboard display panels, electricity for demonstrations, table and 24-hour security. Exhibitor handles sales and taxes.
Promotion: Show is advertised by the Chamber of Commerce through newspapers, both locally and state-wide, and letters of invitation. Send samples of work for promotional purposes.

AZALEA ARTS & CRAFTS SHOW & SALE, Box 1705, Muskogee OK 74401. (918)682-0588 or 682-5108. Director and Sponsor: Marie Cannarsa. Estab. 1969. Annual indoor/outdoor show held 2 days in April. Average attendance: 200,000. Considers all crafts.
Terms: Entries accepted until 1 week before show. Entry fee: $15/8x6 minimum display area. Work may be offered for sale; no commission. Craftworker can attend show; demonstrations OK. Sponsor provides electricity for demonstrations.

CHEROKEE STRIP ARTS FESTIVAL, Box 69, Perry OK 73077. (405)336-9912. Chairman: Mrs. Henry Nolte. Estab. 1974. Annual indoor show held 2 days in the fall. Considers all handcrafted items.
Terms: Write for entry deadlines. Entry fee: $10-12 for 8-foot space. Work may be offered for sale; no commission. Craftworker must attend show; demonstrations OK. Registration limit: 65. Chairs, display panels, electricity for demonstrations, table, night security and hooks available for additional fee.
Promotion: Show is advertised by newspaper, TV and posters. "Send pictures and short history of you and your work for newspaper promotion."

DRUMRIGHT ART & CRAFT SHOW, 430 S. Morrow, Drumright OK 74030. (918)352-3129. Chairman: Geraldine Dockery. Sponsor: Drumright Historical Society. Estab. 1964. Annual indoor show held 3 days during the first weekend of October. Average attendance: 3,000-4,000. Considers all handmade crafts. Entries accepted until 2 weeks before show. Entry fee: $10/5' wall space; $5/5x8 table space; $4/5x8 cowbarn spaces. Work must be offered for sale; no commission. Craftworker must attend show; demonstrations OK. Sponsor provides electricity for demonstrations, night watchman and tables ($5 rental fee).

FIREHOUSE CHRISTMAS FESTIVAL, 444 S. Flood, Norman OK 73069. (405)329-4523. Executive Director: Callie Whitney. Sponsor: Norman Firehouse Art Center, Inc. Estab. 1971. Annual indoor show held 3 days in December. Average attendance: 3,000.
Acceptable Work: Considers batik, candlemaking, jewelry, leatherworking, metalsmithing, needlecrafts, pottery, sculpture, soft sculpture, weaving and woodcrafting. No kits, molds or imports.
Terms: Entries accepted until show date. Entry fee: $20/artist. Display area: 8x8. Prejudging by 3 slides/photos or 3 pieces of work. Entry fee due after prejudging; refunded for refused work. Work must be offered for sale; no commission. Craftworker must attend show; demonstrations OK. Registration limit: 100. Sponsor provides electricity for demonstrations, tables and chairs (for rental fee), and 24-hour security. Exhibitor handles sales and taxes.
Promotion: Show is advertised by press releases to 34 area papers, 4-5 articles with pictures in the local paper, billboards, radio and TV spots, banners, restaurant cards, posters and 2 mailings of 1,500 each.

FREE ART FAIR, c/o Mrs. J.C. Pond, Box 127, Medford OK 73759. (405)393-2888. Sponsor: The Medford Progress Club. Estab. 1966. Annual indoor show held the second weekend in November. Average attendance: 300-400. Entries accepted until show date. No entry fee. Work may be offered for sale; no commission. Craftworker must attend show; demonstrations OK. Sponsor provides chairs; electricity for demonstrations; and 24-hour security. Considers all crafts.

*HOBART ARTS AND CRAFTS FESTIVAL, Box 768, Hobart OK 73651. (405)726-2553. Manager: Marie Muse. Sponsor: Hobart Chamber of Commerce. Estab. 1967. Annual outdoor show held 1 day in May. Average attendance: 1,000. Show is advertised by newspaper, radio, TV and flyers.
Acceptable Work: Considers all crafts. "Artist must provide everything necessary for presentation. We will reserve space. If anything special is required, it should be noted on the entry blank." Bestsellers: $20-40.
Terms: Entries accepted until 1 week before show. Entry fee: $9/4x8 panel; $7/display space.

Work may be offered for sale; no commission. Craftworker must attend show; demonstrations OK. Sponsor provides electricity for demonstrations and hostesses during the day for short breaks. Exhibitor handles sales; no taxes.
Awards: Presents cash awards; approximately 75 purchase awards; and ribbons for all placings.

INDIAN SUMMER ARTS & CRAFTS SHOW & SALE, 641 Cincinnati, Muskogee OK 74401. (918)682-6602, ext. 42. Director, Parks & Recreation: Henry Bresser. Sponsor: Muskogee Azalea Festival Corporation. Estab. 1973. Annual outdoor show held 2 days in October. Considers all crafts. No kits.
Terms: Entries accepted until show date. Entry fee: $10/10x10 display area for 1 day; $15 for both days. Work may be offered for sale; no commission. Craftworker needn't attend show; demonstrations OK. Sponsor provides electricity for demonstrations and fencing.
Promotion: Show is advertised by Beals Advertising Agency in Fort Smith, Arkansas; and local and state TV, radio and news agencies.

LAKE EUFAULA ARTS & CRAFTS SHOW, Rt. 4, Box 168, Eufaula OK 74432. (918)689-7751. Contact: Mary Pinney. Sponsor: Lake Eufaula Association. Estab. 1978. Annual indoor show held 3 days in November at a point halfway between Eufaula and Checotah.
Acceptable Work: Considers all crafts, except mobiles. "All items must be handmade or executed by the displaying craftsman."
Terms: Entries accepted until 2 weeks before show. Entry fee: $20/7x10 display area. Work may be offered for sale; no commission. Craftworker must attend show; demonstrations OK. Registration limit: 75. Sponsor provides chairs, electricity for demonstrations and table. Exhibitor handles sales and taxes.
Promotion: Show is advertised state wide by newspapers, television, radio and flyers. Craftworker should provide pictures for promotional purposes.

LAWTON FORT SILL ANNUAL ART SHOW, Lawton Fort Sill Art Council, 1610 NW 75th St., Lawton OK 73505. Contact: Barbara Ainsworth. Annual exhibition for all media. No commission. Hand-deliver entries.

*****LEEDEY ARTS AND CRAFTS FESTIVAL**, Box 6, Leedey OK 73654. (405)488-3531. Festival Chairman: LaKeta Nichols. Sponsor: Leedey Chamber of Commerce and the Oklahoma Arts & Humanities Council. Estab. 1976. Annual outdoor show held 1 day in April. Average attendance: 800-1,000. Considers all crafts. Presents cash, purchase and ribbon awards.
Terms: Entries accepted until 1 week before show. Entry fee: $8/4x8 foot panels. Work may be offered for sale; no commission. Craftworker or representative must attend show; demonstrations encouraged. Sponsor provides display panels, electricity for demonstrations, people to help set up and dismantle displays, and people to relieve exhibit during lunch break.
Promotion: Show is advertised by mailers, radio, newspaper, and listings in the Oklahoma Arts and Humanities Council Catalogue. "If craftworker provides publicity, it may be used in the newspaper for promotion of the Festival."

MARIETTA ARTS & CRAFTS SHOW, c/o Versey R. Renick, Marietta OK 73448. Sponsor: Arts & Crafts Guild, Love County Homemakers Group and Love County Chamber of Commerce. Estab. 1965. Annual indoor show held 3 days in fall. Considers all crafts handmade by craftworker. Work may be offered for sale; no commission. Craftworker or representative must attend show; demonstrations OK. Sponsor provides chairs, electricity for demonstrations and table.

MID-SUMMER NIGHT'S FAIR, 444 S. Flood, Norman OK 73069. (405)329-4523. Executive Director: Callie Whitney. Sponsor: Norman Firehouse Art Center, Inc. Estab. 1977. Annual outdoor show held 1 evening in July. Average attendance: 2,000-3,000.
Acceptable Work: Considers batik, candlemaking, jewelry, leatherworking, metalsmithing, mobiles, pottery, sculpture, soft sculpture, weaving and woodcrafting. No kits, molds or imports.
Terms: Entries accepted until 1 week before show. Entry fee: $15/artist. Display area: 8x8. Prejudging by 3 slides/photos or 3 pieces of work. Entry fee due after prejudging; refunded for refused work. Work must be offered for sale; no commission. Craftworker must attend show; demonstrations OK. Registration limit: 100. Sponsor provides fencing and lights. Exhibitor handles sales and taxes.
Promotion: Show is advertised by press releases to 34 local papers, 4-5 articles with pictures,

billboards, posters, radio, TV, banners, restaurant cards, and 2 mailings of 1,500 each.

NEWKIRK ARTS & CRAFTS FAIR, Newkirk Chamber of Commerce, Newkirk OK 74647. (405)362-2155. Chairman of the Board: Lester French. Estab. 1968. Annual indoor show held 2 days in October. Average attendance: 3,000. Considers all crafts.
Terms: Entries accepted until full ("usually about September 15"). Entry fee: $10/6x6 display area with backscreen; $5/6' table space. Work must be offered for sale; no commission. Craftworker or representative must attend show; demonstrations OK. Registration limit: 105 exhibit spaces. Sponsor provides chairs, coverings, display panels, electricity for demonstrations, table and 24-hour security.
Promotion: Show is advertised by newspaper stories, paid ads and radio.
Sales Tip: Items that sell well include: "handcrafted jewelry, pottery, woodworking, toys, dried arrangements, metalworking, ceramics, macrame, quilts, afghans and calendars of events. Some individuals earn as much as $500 a day, others $50, depending on appeal of items and salesmanship of individual."

*NESCATUNGA ARTS FESTIVAL, Box 551, Alva OK 73717. (405)327-2693. Contact: Bill Naberhaus. Sponsor: Nescatunga Arts & Humanities Council. Annual outdoor show held 1 Saturday in June. Considers all crafts.
Terms: Entries accepted until show. Entry fee: $7.50/craftworker. Display area: 4x10 panel or "area on the courthouse lawn." Work may be offered for sale; no commission. Craftworker must attend show; demonstrations OK. Sponsor provides display panels.
Awards: Presents $115 in cash awards to craft division and rosette ribbon for best display of crafts.

O'BRIEN ARTS & CRAFTS SHOW, 6230 N. Birmingham, Tulsa OK 74130. (918)425-6719; 425-4655. Activities Director: Henry McGriff. Sponsor: Tulsa County Parks Department. Estab. 1968. Annual indoor show held 3 days during the second weekend of September. Average attendance: 3,000. Considers all handmade crafts. Presents trophy for Best Display and Greatest Distance Travel Award. Show is advertised by publications, TV, radio, newspapes and calendars of events.
Terms; Entries accepted until 2 weeks before show. Entry fee: $10/8x6 display area. Work may be offered for sale; 10% commission. Craftworker must attend show; demonstrations OK. "If demonstration is dangerous, exhibitor must obtain permission from the show director, and provide safety features." Registration limit: 120. Sponsor provides chairs, electricity for demonstrations, 24-hour security, and coffee and donuts in the morning; recommends accomodations. Exhibitor handles sales. "At the close of the show, the exhibitor turns in only 10% of sales to the show director. O'Brien will, in turn, pay approximate sales tax."

*OKLAHOMA CITY FESTIVAL OF THE ARTS, 3014 Paseo, Oklahoma City OK 73103. (405)521-1426. Festival Coordinator: Jackie Jones. Sponsor: Arts Council of Oklahoma City. Estab. 1967. Annual outdoor show (with panels covered by tents) held 6 days (crafts only 2) the last week in April. Considers all crafts. Awards several thousand dollars in purchase prizes.
Terms: Entries accepted until about 3 months before show date. Entry fee: $50/6x8 display panal. Prejudging by 10 slides or 2 pieces of actual work. Work must be offered for sale; 20% commission. Craftworkers must attend show; demonstrations OK. Sponsor provides coverings, display panels, electricity for demonstrations and 24-hour security.
Promotion: Show is advertised "in local newspapers; some advertising in national magazines; plus recommendations as 'thing to do' in publications such as TWA travel magazine. Public service radio and TV spots, plus broadcast of leading talk show from festival grounds is also used."
Sales Tip: "Have as wide a range of sizes and prices as possible. Also, the artist's attitude to public is a major factor in sales. Crafts are extremely popular with the buyers at this show, but the competition in the crafts area is putting an emphasis on creativity and uniqueness of work as well as quality of technical expertise." Total sales of art (1978): $350,000.

OLD FORT GIBSON INDIAN TERRITORY ARTS & CRAFTS SHOW, Box 1705, Muskogee OK 74401. (918)682-0588 or 682-5108. Director: Marie Cannarsa. Estab. 1964. Annual show held 2 days in August at Fort Gibson, Oklahoma. Average attendance: 10,000. Considers all crafts. "No dirty pictures or types."
Terms: Entries accepted until show date. Entry fee: $10/10x10 display area; cash payment prior

---

* Those listings preceded by an asterisk present awards for prize-winning crafts.

to set-up. Work may be offered for sale; no commission. Craftworker can attend show; demonstrations OK.

OSAGE HILLS ARTS & CRAFTS SHOW & SALE, 1801 N. McKinley, Sand Springs OK 74063. (918)245-8751 (ext. 68). Superintendant of Recreation: Patty Boyd. Sponsor: Sand Springs Parks and Recreation Department. Estab. 1972. Annual indoor show held 2 days in spring. Average attendance: 3,000. Considers all crafts. No kits or mass-produced crafts.
Terms: Entries accepted until day before show date. Entry fee charged;6x8 display area. Work must be offered for sale; no commission. Craftworker must attend show; demonstrations OK. Registration limit: 50. Sponsor provides chairs, display panels ($2 rental fee), electricity for demonstrations, table and 24-hour security. Exhibitor handles sales. Master Charge and Visa may be used.
Promotion: Show is advertised by TV, newspapers, radio, newsletter and magazines. Promotional material "not required but would probably help."

SHEPHERD MALL CRAFT SHOW, c/o Oklahoma Museum of Art, 7316 Nichols Rd., Oklahoma City OK 73120. (405)840-2759. Director of Education: Margaret Flansburg. Annual indoor show held 3 days in June. Average attendance: 120,000.
Acceptable Work: Considers all crafts. Must fit on a 4x8' panel or on table.
Terms: Entries accepted until 4 eeks before show. Entry fee: $25/museum members; $40 for nonmembers (museum membership costs $15). Prejudging; entry fee refunded for refused work. Work must be offered for sale; no commission. Craftworker must attend show ("works may not be shipped; artist must be in attendance and so would bring works himself"). "Artists are encouraged to demonstrate—times for demonstrations are given to artists when accepted." Sponsor provides display panels. Craftworker handles sales.
Awards: Presents cash prize of $200 and award of merit ribbon. "We have 1-3 jurors selected from local museums or university art staffs. Works are judged on technical accomplishments, originality and thematic development."

STARVING ARTIST ART SHOW, 5002 S. Fulton Ave., Tulsa OK 74135. (918)663-4174. Coordinators: Keith Pratt and Sam Wilson. Sponsor: YMCA Camp Takatoka. Estab. 1974. Annual indoor show held 1 day in April. Average attendance: 5,000-10,000.
Acceptable Work: Considers candlemaking, jewelry, metalsmithing, pottery, scrimshaw, sculpture, soft sculpture and woodcrafting. No copies and reproductions; molds or kits; paper flowers, leather goods or jewelry assembled from manufactured parts; stuffed animals; crocheted, knit or cloth bazaar-type items; decoupage; lamps, furniture or any flea market type items. "All works must be the original work of the exhibitor. No single item may be sold for more than $35."
Terms: Entries accepted until show date. Entry fee: $25/10x10 display area. Prejudging by slides/photos. Entry fee refunded for refused work. Work must be offered for sale; 10% commission. Craftworker must attend show; demonstrations OK. Exhibitors handle sales and taxes.
Promotion: Show is advertised by flyers (distributed by entrants), radio, newspaper, TV, local magazines, in-house publications and various mailings.
Sales Tip: The crowd we appeal to is primarily younger couples and people just moving into a new apartment or home looking for accent pieces.

Oregon

ALBANY HOLIDAY MARKET, c/o Creative Arts Guild, Box 841, Albany OR 97321. (503)928-2815. Executive Director: Corrine Woodman. Estab. 1976. Annual indoor show held 3 Saturdays between Thanksgiving and Christmas. Average attendance: 10,000.
Terms: Entries accepted until show. Entry fee: $8/day/7x7 display area. Work may be offered for sale; no commission. Craftworker needn't attend show (but is responsible for own sales); no demonstrations. Registration limit: 45. Considers all crafts.
Promotion: Market is advertised by public service announcements; paid advertising; posters; signs; and newspaper articles and photos.

ALBANY SPRING ARTS FESTIVAL, Box 841, Albany OR 97321. (503)928-2815. Director: Corrine Woodman. Sponsor: Creative Arts Guild. Estab. 1969. Annual indoor/outdoor show held 2 days in early May. Average attendance: 20,000. Entries accepted until 1 week before show. No entry fee. Maximum 2 entries per craftworker. Work may be offered for sale; 20% commission. Demonstrations OK. Considers all crafts by residents.

CHRISTMAS CRAFT FAIR, Rt. 2, Box 87C, Pendleton OR 97801. (503)276-4237. Chairperson: Loree Tucker-McKenna. Sponsor: Pendleton Arts Council. Estab. 1971. Annual indoor show held 2 days in November, Friday and Saturday following Thanksgiving. Average attendance: 600-1,000. Entries accepted until show filled. Entry fee: $1/booth. Display area: 10' wide but exceptions made if work larger. Work may be offered for sale; 10% commission plus a donation of at least 1 craft item to the Silent Auction. Craftworker or representative must attend show; demonstrations encouraged. Registration limit: 30. Sponsor provides chairs; electricity for demonstrations; table and 24-hour security. 1978 show sales totalled over $3,500. Considers all crafts including hand-made Christmas decorations.

COOS ART MUSEUM CRAFT SHOW, 515 Market Ave., Coos Bay OR 97420. (503)267-3901. Director: Maggie Karl. Purpose: "to show contemporary crafts to southwestern Oregon." Annual indoor show held 1 month in July. Entries accepted until 4 weeks before show. Entry fee: $5/craftworker. Maximum 2 entries/category. Prejudging. No entry fees refunded for refused work. Work may be offered for sale; 25% commission. Craftworker needn't attend show; demonstration OK. Sponsor provides chairs; coverings; display panels; electricity for demonstrations; insurance on exhibited work; table; museum staff handles sales; and 24-hour security. Considers all crafts; functional only. "The craftperson provides his own presentation for his/her work."

*MULTNOMAH COUNTY FAIR, Box 17364, Portland OR 97217. (503)285-7756. Manager: Sam L. Philip. Annual indoor/outdoor show held 10 days beginning in July at Portland, Oregon. Average attendance: 140,000. Considers all crafts. Write for premium book for requirements. Presents ribbons. Entries accepted until 2 weeks before show. Entry fee: $200/10x10 display area. Work may be offered for sale; no commission. Craftworker needn't attend show; demonstrations OK. Sponsor provides chairs (rental fee), display panels, electricity for demonstrations, table (rental fee) and 24-hour security. Show is advertised by radio, TV and newspapers.

NEHALEM ARTS FESTIVAL, Rt. 1, Box 193, Nehalem OR 97131. (503)368-5711. Director: Carey Tate. Sponsor: Nehalem Bay Merchants Association. Purpose: "the show is held for the artist to promote art sales." Estab. 1973. Annual outdoor show held 2 days in July. Average attendance: 2,000. Entries accepted until 2 weeks before show. No entry fee. Work may be offered for sale; no commission. Craftworker must attend show; demonstrations OK. Show is advertised by flyers; newspaper advertising; and state tour guides. Registration limit: 50. Categories: paintings; sculpture; ceramics; leather; weaving; jewelry; and miscellaneous crafts. Considers all crafts.

SATURDAY MARKET, Box 427, Eugene OR 97440. (503)686-8885. Contact: Manager. Sponsor: Saturday Market (a nonprofit corporation). Estab. 1970. Outdoor show held every Saturday from May-December. Entries accepted until market day; spaces assigned by lottery. Entry fee: "$3 first time; then 10% of gross income of preceding time." Display area: 8x8. Work may be offered for sale; no commission. Craftworker must attend show; demonstrations OK. Registration limit: 220. Considers all crafts "that are gathered from natural materials, or made or grown by the vendor (or a household family member)."

WORLD SHOWS, Box 339, Stanton CA 90680. (714)995-7509. Partners: Don, Virginia or Gale. Estab. 1977. Annual shows held 40 days in November-December at various Sears' stores throughout Oregon. Considers all crafts.
Terms: Entries accepted until show date. Entry fee: $96 for insurance. Display area: 4x6' to 10x12'. Prejudging by phone or mail. Entry fee due after prejudging; fee refunded for refused work. Craftworker must offer work for sale; 30% commission. Craftworker must attend show; demonstrations OK. Registration limit: 1-5 per store (57 stores). Sponsor provides electricity for demonstrations.
Profile: "These are concessions in high traffic areas of Sears' stores. Show is promoted by Sears' advertising. Craftworker must provide an appropriate sign and a good-looking display."

Pennsylvania

ANTIQUE SALE & FLEA MARKET, 323 E. Main St., Waynesboro PA 17268. (717) 762-6512. Coordinator: Frances H. Miller. Sponsor: Chamber of Commerce. Estab. 1972. Annual outdoor show held the 2nd Saturday of June on the sidewalks of dwntown Waynesboro. Average attendance: 10,000. Entries accepted until all spaces are filled. Entry fee: $17/22' parking space.

University Artists and Craftsmen Guild Summer Arts Festival at Ann Arbor, Michigan. There is a three-year waiting list of 200 craftworkers wanting to display in the summer show. It's no wonder. The show grosses over $1 million, an average of $1,500 per artist.

APPLE HARVEST FESTIVAL, Box 38, Biglerville PA 17307. Arts and Crafts Chairman: Jeanette Taylor. Sponsor: Upper Adams Jaycees. Purpose: fundraising. Estab. 1964. Annual outdoor show (most of festival is outdoors; limited number of indoor spaces available; some buildings have open sides) held 2 weekends in October at Arendtsville, Pennsylvania. Average attendance: 40,000-80,000. Entries accepted until 4 weeks before show. Entry fee: $30/weekend, inside booth; $20/weekend, outside booth. Display area: 10x10. Juried by photos, slides, or descriptive resumes of the items. "Photos, descriptions and price ranges must be supplied before application will be sent to exhibitor. SASE must accompany any slides that are to be returned. Decisions of the jurors are final." Entry fee due after prejudging. Work may be offered for sale; no commission. Craftworker must attend show; demonstrations encouraged. Registration limit: 85, indoor; 150, outdoor. Sponsor provides electricity for demonstrations and 24-hour security. Show is advertised by brochures; news releases; radio; and TV. Submit photographs of your work for publicity. Considers all crafts.

ARTS & CRAFTS IN LONG'S PARK, Box 5153, Lancaster PA 17601. Contact: Dick Faulkner. Sponsor: Long's Park Amphitheater Foundation and Dick Falkner. Estab. 1979. Annual outdoor show held 3 days during Labor Day Weekend.
Acceptable Work: Considers all original crafts. No kits or molds. All work must be that of exhibiting artist.
Terms: Entry fee: $40/booth. Prejudging by 4 2¼x2¼ slides. Work may be offered for sale; no commission. Craftworker must attend show; demonstrations OK.

CENTRAL PENNSYLVANIA FESTIVAL OF THE ARTS SIDEWALK SALE, Box 1023, State College PA 16801. Estab. 1966. Annual outdoor show held 4 days in July. Average attendance: 150,000-175,000. Considers all crafts except decoupage.
Terms: Entries accepted until 5 months before show date. Entry fee: $50/10x4 or 10x6 display

areas. Prejudging by 3 slides per each category entered; $5 nonrefundable jury fee. Entry fee refunded for refused work. Work must be offered for sale; no commission. Craftworker must attend show. Registration limit: 400. Sponsor provides fencing.
Promotion: Show is advertised by local radio; TV; newspapers (Philadelphia, Pittsburgh and Harrisburg); and Pennsylvania Tourist Bureau. 1977 show sales totalled $400,000. Categories: ceramics; fibers; glass; jewelry; leather; metal; paintings and graphics; photographs; wood; wax; and other.

*CENTRE SQUARE ART FAIR, Downtown Improvement Group, Inc. and Community Art League, Easton PA 18042. (215)258-2281, 253-1487. Estab. 1965. Annual outdoor show held 1 day in September. Considers all original crafts. Entries accepted until 2 weeks before show. Entry fee: $7/10' display area. Work may be offered for sale; no commission. Craftworker must attend show; demonstrations OK. Presents cash awards of $700 and ribbons for 1st, 2nd, and 3rd.

CHERRIES JUBILEE CRAFT SHOW, Box 516, Kimberton PA 19442. (215)933-7563. Sponsor: Virginia Graham. Estab. 1976. Annual indoor colonial craft fair held 3 days in February (George Washington holiday weekend) in Valley Forge, Pennsylvania. Average attendance: 1,500-2,000.
Acceptable Work: Considers candlemaking; ceramics; decoupage; dollmaking; leatherworking; macrame; metalsmithing; needlecrafts; pottery; tole painting; weaving; and woodcrafting. "We prefer traditional or colonial crafts."
Terms: Entries accepted until 2 weeks before show. Entry fee: $30/10x6 display area. Prejudging by previous shows; entry fee refunded for refused work. Work may be offered for sale; no commission. Craftworker must attend show and wear colonial attire; demonstrations encouraged. Registration limit: 60. Sponsor provides chairs; electricity for demonstrations; tables; and individual requests within reason.
Promotion: Show is advertised by Montgomery County Tourist Bureau; newspaper ads; pamphlets; TV; radio; flyers; and press releases. Submit glossies and write-up to put in PR work and brochure.

*CHRISTMAS CRAFT FAIR & SALE, 111 Chapel Rd., NewHope PA 18938. (215)862-2374. Public Relations: Emil W. Peters. Sponsor: Bucks County Guild of Craftsmen. Estab. 1960. Annual indoor show held 3 days during the 3rd weekend of November at Wrightstown, Pennsylvania. Average attendance: 15,000-18,000. Considers all crafts. No kits, automatic machine work, assemblages of commercial parts, or molds.
Terms: Must be Guild member to exhibit. Entry fee: $5/craftsman. Display area: 10x7 (more if demonstating). Prejudging at monthly meetings by Standards Committee. Entry fee due after prejudging. Work must be offered for sale; 15% commission. Craftworker must attend show; demonstrations OK. Registration limit: 115. Sponsor provides electricity for demonstrations and overnight security. Exhibitor handles sales. "At the end of the show, the Guild collects commission plus the sales tax from each member."
Awards: Presents cash awards for Best of Show, 2nd and 3rd places and for 3 best dislays. Also presents ribbons for 1st, 2nd and 3rd in each category. Maximum 1 entry/craftsman for award competition. "Always submit that item which you feel represents your very best effort. If you are doubtful of the piece, do not submit."
Promotion: Show is advertised by craft magazines; feature stores and news releases (within a 50-mile radius); TV and radio interviews; placecards in shopping areas; flyers in motels, restaurants and other public meeting places; mailings by members and various agencies; and display ads in newspapers. "Promotional material and photos are always welcome for review and possible use—but they must be current."
Sales Tip: "Be neat, congenial and enthusiastic. If practical, let people handle the merchandise. A museum-type display does not encourage sales—it's only nice to look at. Be free with honest information. Don't disturb a person examining your work, but be ready to assist. Offer a pleasant comment when they leave; remember, they may be back later." 1978 sales totaled slightly over $26,000.

*CLOTHESLINE EXHIBIT, Box 376, Waynesboro PA 17268. (717)597-4376. Vice President: Ann Brown. Sponsor: Waynesboro Studio Club. Purpose: "to bring arts and crafts to general public, also gives local artists and craftsmen a chance to compete. Each year the quality of show has improved." Estab. 1951. Annual outdoor show (indoors if rain) held 1st Saturday in June. Average attendance: 1,200. Entries accepted until 3 weeks before show. Entry fee: $10/artist. For judging maximum 5 pieces per artist; no limit for display and sale. Prejudging by

actual work; "no work refused unless copies or kits." Work may be offered for sale; no commission. Craftworker must attend show; demonstrations OK. No registration limit. Sponsor provides electricity for demonstrations if inside and fencing outside. "Exhibit at own risk." Show is advertised by 6 newspapers; 8 radio stations; printed catalog; and TV. Submit with entry form any additional information you would like to include for promotional purposes. Considers all crafts.
Awards: Presents ribbons for 1st, 2nd, 3rd and honorable mention for each category. "Cash awards vary from year to year; merchants and businesses contribute."

CRAFT DAY, 323 E. Main St., Box 512, Waynesboro PA 17268. (717)762-6512. Manager: FrancesH. Miller. Sponsor: Retail Bureau, Waynesboro Chamber of Commerce. Estab. 1975. Annual outdoor show held 1 day in September. Average attendance: several thousand. Considers all crafts. Show is advertised by newspaper and radio.
Terms: Entries accepted until show date. Entry fee: $5/artist. Display area: 1 parking space, approximately 22'. Work may be offered for sale; no commission. Craftworker needn't attend show; demonstrations OK. Registration limit: 100. Exhibitor handles sales and taxes. "If they do not have a tax license, the Pennsylvania Sales Tax Bureau will assign them a temporary number."

*****CRAFT EXHIBITION OF THE CENTRAL PENNSYLVANIA FESTIVAL OF THE ARTS,** Box 1023, State College PA 16801. Estab. 1966. Annual indoor show held 1 week in July at University Park, Pennsylvania. Prejudged. Presents cash awards of $2,000.

DEVON CRAFT FAIR, c/o National Crafts Ltd., Gapland MD 21736. (301)432-8438. Director: Noel Clark. Estab. 1979. Annual indoor/outdoor retail show held 2 days in September at Devon, Pennsylvania. Considers all crafts.
Terms: Entries accepted until 3 months before show. Entry fee: $80-100/booth, plus $3 application fee. Display area: 8x10, inside; 15x15, outside. Prejudging by 5 35mm color slides; no application fees refunded for refused work. Work must be offered for sale; no commission. Craftworker must attend show; demonstrations OK. Registration limit: 250 booths. Sponsor provides 24-hour security.
Promotion: Show is advertised by radio, newspapers, periodicals, posters and flyers.

*****EGGORAMA,** Egg Shell Craft, 66 E. Union Blvd., Bethlehem PA 18018. Contact: Mary Ellen Ellington or Peter Evans. Indoor exhibition held in Allentown PA. Entry fee: craftsman, $25/table; dealer, $40/table (6' table). Entries accepted until show date if not filled. No commission. Craftworker or representative must attend show. Considers all media in egg shell decoration. Presents best of show and ribbons in each category.

A FAIR IN THE PARK, Arts and Crafts Center of Pittsburgh, Pittsburgh PA 15232. (412)361-0873. Contact: Chairman. Sponsor: Craftsmen's Guild of Pittsburgh. Purpose: "to give the artist exposure to the public and to educate the public on what is good quality art. Also to give the artists the opportunity to learn from each other." Estab. 1969. Annual 3 day outdoor show held in September. Average attendance: 40,000. Entries accepted until 6 weeks before show. Entry fee: $40/artist. Display area: 10x10. Entries prejudged by slides; entry fee refunded for refused work. Work may be offered for sale; no commission. Craftworker must attend show; demonstrations recommended. Registration limit: 125. Sponsor provides electricity for demonstrations and 24-hour security. 1978 show sales totalled over $70,000. Considers all crafts except decoupage; lapidary; mobiles; and tole painting.
Promotion: Show is advertised by "a good publicity campaign in magazines; newspapers; TV; and radio spots. In 1977 we started having a live radio show broadcasted from the fair grounds and will repeat this."

*****FALL CRAFT MARKET AT PARK CITY MALL,** Box 5153, Lancaster PA 17601. Sponsor: Conestoga Valley Chapter, Pennsylvania Guild of Craftsmen. Purpose: fundraising. Estab. 1973. Annual indoor show held 3 days in November. Average attendance: 60,000. Entries accepted until 6 weeks before show. No entry fee. "Show open only to members of the Pennsylvania Guild of Craftsmen." Maximum 1 item per category per artist. Display area: 10x15. Prejudging by 4 slides for new craftworkers; floor jurying from past shows. Work may be offered for sale; 20% commission, $100 maximum. Craftworker must attend show; demonstrations required 20% of showtime. Registration limit: 90. Sponsor provides electricity for demonstrations and some security. Show is advertised by billboards; newspaper; posters; radio; and TV interview shows. Submit b&w photos of self at work for publicity. Presents purchase awards of $200. 1977 show sales totalled approximately $40,000. Considers all crafts except mobiles; kits and assemblage. Bestsellers: glass; leather; and pottery.

FALL FOLIAGE FESTIVAL, Bedford PA 15522. (814)847-2282. Co-chairman: Mrs. Robert Barnhart. Estab. 1964. Annual indoor/outdoor show held 2 weekends in October. Average attendance: 10,000. Entries accepted until 1 week before show. Entry fee: per weekend $10/10-12' of sidewalk. Work may be offered for sale; no commission. Craftworker needn't attend show; demonstrations OK. "Craftsmen are responsible for their own belongings. Items are displayed on town sidewalks. Must be torn down each evening." Show is advertised by radio; TV; and newspapers. Considers all crafts. Bestsellers: not more than $15 items.

FORT ARMSTRONG FOLK FESTIVAL, 325 Market St., Kittanning PA 16201. (412)548-4118. President: Dr. William E. Martin. Purpose: "to preserve the crafts of a past gone era for the benefit of our children." Estab. 1971. Annual outdoor show (some picnic shelter; may bring tents) held 5 days in August. Average attendance: 40,000-50,000. Entries accepted until 4 weeks before show; "we reserve a certain number of spaces up to show time for unusual and worthy crafts." Entry fee: $35-40/12x12 display area (includes lighting and plugs 100 volt hookups); plus $15 for special 220 volt electric hookup. Prejudging by slides; photos; promotional material; references; and other shows. Entry fee refunded for refused work. Work may be offered for sale; no commission. Craftworker must attend show; demonstrations encouraged. Registration limit: 70-90. Sponsor provides roping; and limited security. Show is advertised by flyers; 40 newspapers; brochures; Pittsburgh TV; local cable TV; and radio. Submit all background information for newspaper release. Considers all crafts; especially ones relating to the colonial era.

GRAND IRISH JUBILEE, 123 S. Main St., Mahanoy City PA 17948. (717)773-2284. Manager: Frank Guinan. Purpose: "to advance interest in Irish customs; music; dancing; and personality." Estab. 1975. Annual outdoor show (with closed buildings) held 4 days in September at Barnesville, Pennsylvania. Average attendance: 15,000. Entries accepted until 1 week before show. Work may be offered for sale; 10% commission. Craftworker must attend show; demonstrations OK. Registration limit: 20. Sponsor provides electricity for demonstrations. Show is advertised by brochures; newspapers; ethnic radio programs and publications; radio; and TV. Submit photos for promotion. Considers batik; candlemaking; ceramics; glass art; leatherworking; pottery; weaving; woodcrafting; Irish themes; and resulting products.

*****GREATER HARRISBURG OUTDOOR ARTS FESTIVAL**, Box 770, Harrisburg PA 17108. (717)238-5184. Contact: Director of Harrisburg Arts Council. Sponsor: Greater Harrisburg Arts Council. Estab. 1967. Annual outdoor show held 3 days during Memorial Day weekend. Average attendance: 100,000. Entry fee: $5/day per booth or $15/3 days. Maximum 2 entries per craftworker. Work may be offered for sale; no commission. Craftworker must attend show; demonstrations OK. Considers batik; candlemaking; pottery; decoupage; glass art; jewelry; leatherworking; metalsmithing; needlecrafts; soft sculpture; tole painting; weaving; and quilting.

GREATER HARRISBURG JURIED ARTS FESTIVAL, Box 770, Harrisburg PA 17108. (717)238-5184. Contact: Director of Harrisburg Arts Council. Sponsor: Greater Harrisburg Arts Council. Estab. 1967. Annual outdoor show held 3 days during Memorial Day weekend. Average attendance: 100,000. Entry fee: $10/craftworker. Maximum 3 pieces per craftworker for juried show. Craftworker must attend show. Registration limit: 150. Considers all forms of sculpture, stone, wood, metal, print making.

HAINES TOWNSHIP DUTCH FALL FESTIVAL, c/o Jack Smith, Rt. 45, Aaronsburg PA 16820. (814)349-5280. Purpose: "this festival was held for the Bicentennial. It was so successful and worthwhile the townspeople wanted to continue it." Estab. 1976. Annual outdoor show held 2 days in October. Average attendance: 8,000. Entries accepted until 2 weeks before show. Work may be offered for sale; no commission. Craftworker must attend show; demonstrations preferred. "We provide a large exhibit space in front of each single home on Main Street and will assist in getting items that perhaps craftworker could not bring." Sponsor provides 24-hour security. Show is advertised by newspaper; radio; and TV. Submit b&w photos. Considers all crafts.

THE HANNA'S TOWN FOLK FESTIVAL, Westmoreland County Historical Society, 221 N. Main St., Greensburg PA 15601. (412)836-1800. Festival Chairman: Arlene Kendra. Sponsor:

Elizabeth Hanna Guild of the Westmoreland County Historical Society. Estab. 1976. Annual outdoor show (some canopies available) held the last Sunday of July at Hanna's Town. Average attendance: 8,000-10,000.
Acceptable Work: Considers candlemaking; dollmaking; metalsmithing; tole painting. Especially needs colonial crafts and early Americana such as pewter. Bestsellers: "Generally things that can be easily carried in hand."
Terms: Entries accepted until 3 weeks before show. Entry fee: $15/16x10 display area. Prejudging by slides or photos; entry fee due after prejudging. Work may be offered for sale; no commission. Craftworker must attend show; demonstrations required. Registration limit: 30.
Promotion: "Show is advertised by 20 newspapers; news releases to 43 newspapers; radio announcements to 27 radio stations; publicity pictures in advance in local newspapers; information distributed by travel bureaus; listing in brochures; events calendars in several local magazines; posters; and yearly events handbill." Submit photo and resume.
Profile: "For this one day a year we attempt to recreate a modern version of life on the frontier. For those whose craft can't be sold we pay for their demonstration. We are particularly looking for a broom maker and hornsmith. This is educational and historical and in keeping with the theme of our organization."

HAZLETON CREATIVE ARTS FESTIVAL SIDEWALK SALE, c/o Greater Hazleton Chamber of Commerce, Hazleton PA 18201. (717)455-1508. Public Relations Chairman: Alice Laputka. Sponsor: Greater Hazleton Fine Arts Council. Purpose: "to encourage appreciation of original art and crafts; exposure for artists; cultural experience for local and regional residents." Estab. 1975. Annual outdoor show (indoors in case of rain) held 2 days in May at area Penn State University Campus. Average attendance: 12,000-13,000. Entries accepted until 3 weeks before show. Entry fee: $5/day; $9/both days. Display area: 10'. Work may be offered for sale; no commission. Craftworker must attend show; demonstrations OK. Registration limit: 100. Sponsor provides electricity for demonstrations; fencing; minimal insurance on exhibited work; and 24-hour security. Show is advertised by regional and local newspapers; regional and local radio; regional TV; posters; street banner; and leaflets. Considers all crafts.

HEAD HOUSE CRAFTS FAIR, 328 Bourse Bldg., Philadelphia PA 19106. Publicist: Mary Dolan. Sponsor: Head House Craftsmen's Association. Purpose: "to bring quality crafts to the people of Philadelphia in a pleasant, outside atmosphere for their summer weekend pleasure; to provide a marketplace for quality craftspeople to sell their wares." Estab. 1968. Annual outdoor show (arcade) held 12 consecutive weekends June-August. Entries accepted until 6 weeks before show. Entry fee: $30/weekend. Display area: 6x10. Prejudging by actual work. Work may be offered for sale; no commission. Craftworker must attend show; demonstrations encouraged. Registration limit: 50. Sponsor provides display panels; electricity for demonstrations; table; and 24-hour security. Considers all crafts. Bestsellers: "items not normally available in area stores."
Promotion: "A professional advertising and public relations firm is employed for the 3 month period each year. We use local newspapers; posters; door stuffers; personal appearances on TV by craftspeople; and public service spots on radio and TV." Submit b&w photos of work and biographical sketch by mail.

HOLIDAY CRAFT STORE, Box 335, Langhorne PA 19047. (215)757-3782. Program Coordinator: Jane-Rae Millard. Sponsor: YWCA of Bucks County. Estab. 1976. Annual indoor show held 1 day in November. Average attendance: 300-350. Considers all crafts.
Terms: Entries accepted until day before show. Entry fee: $2/artist. Work may be offered for sale; 20% commission. Craftworker need't attend show; no demonstrations. Sponsor provides chairs, some display panels as necessary, and table. Volunteers handle sales; no taxes.
Promotion: Show is advertised by local papers, posters and mailings to members. "A news release of specialty items to YWCA would be helpful in our promotion."

*****JENKINTOWN FESTIVAL OF THE ARTS**, c/o Jenkintown Library, York and Vista Rds., Jenkintown PA 19046. (215)884-0593. Chairman: Margaret Chalfant. Purpose: fundraiser. Annual outdoor show held the second Sunday in June. Average attendance: 25,000. Entries accepted until 4 weeks before show. Entry fee: $20/15x20 display area. Prejudging by actual work or 4 slides; entry fee refunded for refused work. Work may be offered for sale; no commission. Craftworker needn't attend show; demonstrations OK. Sponsor "rents racks for those who don't have their own display apparatus." Show is advertised by radio; TV; magazines; newspapers; and posters. Presents ribbon awards. Considers all original crafts.

*JURIED CRAFT EXHIBITION, Box 1023, State College PA 16801. Sponsor: Central Pennsylvania Festival of the Arts. Estab. 1966. Annual indoor show held in July. Average attendance: 100,000. Applications for entry due mid-April. Entry fee: $8/2 items. Maximum 3 items per exhibitor. Work may be offered for sale. Craftworker needn't attend show; no demonstrations. Sponsor provides display panels, cases and 24-hour security. Show is hung on the campus of the Pennsylvania State University. Presents $2,000 in prizes plus purchase awards. Considers ceramics; fibers; metals; wood and glass.

*JURIED CRAFTS EXHIBITION OF THE CENTRAL PENNSYLVANIA FESTIVAL OF THE ARTS, Box 1023, State College PA 16801. Managing Director: Lurene Frantz. Estab. 1966. Annual indoor show held in the summer. Average attendance: 9,000. Entries accepted until 3 months before show. Entry fee: $8/1-2 entries. Maximum 3 entries per craftworker. Prejudging by slide; no entry fees refunded for refused work. Work may be offered for sale. Show is hung on the campus of the Pennsylvania State University. Considers ceramics; glass; metals; fibers; and wood. Presents $2,000 in cash prizes.

JURIED CRAFT SHOW, c/o Greater Hazleton Chamber of Commerce, Hazleton PA 18201. (717)455-1508. Public Relations Chairman: Alice Laputka. Estab. 1975. Annual indoor show held 2 days in May during the Hazleton Creative Arts Festival Sidewalk Sale. Average attendance: 12,000-13,000. Presents cash awards in each category.
Acceptable Work: Categories include metal, fiber, clay, wood, glass and multi-media.
Terms: Entries accepted until 3 weeks before show; mailed entries are accepted. Entry fee: $3/item; limit of 5/craftworker. Work may be offered for sale; no commission. Craftworker needn't attend show; demonstrations OK. Sponsor provides electricity for demonstrations, fencing, minimal insurance on exhibited work and 24-hour security. Write for information.

KEYSTONE COUNTRY FESTIVAL, 1107 12th St., Altoona PA 16601. (814)943-8151. Director: Jim Caporuscio. Estab. 1974. Annual indoor/outdoor show held 2 days the weekend after Labor Day in a Victorian amusement park. Average attendance: 95,000/two days.
Acceptable Work: Considers all quality handcrafts and primitive or historic pieces. "No dope paraphernalia."
Terms: Entry fee: $30/lineal foot. Phone or write for more information. Registration limit: 300.

KUTZTOWN FOLK FESTIVAL, College Blvd. & Vine, Kutztown PA 19530. (215)683-8707. Director: Mark R. Eaby. Sponsor: Pennsylvania Folklife Society in cooperation with Ursinus College. Estab. 1948. Annual indoor/outdoor show held 8 days in July (over the weekend of the 4th). Average attendance: 150,000 paid visitors. "Only quilts are competitive."
Acceptable Work: Considers all crafts expect batik, decoupage, lapidary, and soft sculpture. "Work must have some tie-in with Pennsylvania Dutch culture."
Terms: "Craftsperson must be interviewed by manager of Kutztown Festival at Kutztown (by appointment) and samples of work must be presented. Call or write for appointment." No entry fee. Prejudging. Work must be offered for sale; commission varies with sales. Craftworker must attend show; demonstrations OK. Registration limit: 300. Sponsor provides chairs, coverings, display panels, electricity for demonstrations, fencing, table, 24-hour security, and business office of festival handles sales tax.
Profile: The purpose of the show is to demonstrate and display the lore and folkways of the Pennsylvania Dutch. Proceeds go to Ursinus College for scholarships and general educational purposes. Gate admission is $4 for adults and $1 for children under 12. Activities include a country auction, a stage show, a balloon ascension, demonstrations of various crafts such as cigar making, rug weaving, hex signs. There are also children's games and a farmer's market, butchering demonstrations, a country kitchen and other set-ups representative of Pennsylvania Dutch culture.
Promotion: Show is adveritised by public service TV and radio, newspapers, and feature stories in national publications.

LEHIGH VALLEY MALL ARTS FESTIVAL, Rt. 1, Box 153J, Auburn NH 03032. (603)483-2742. President: Jinx Harris. Estab. 1977. Annual indoor show held 4 days in July at Allentown, Pennsylvania. Average attendance: 50,000. Entries accepted until 1 week before show or until filled. Entry fee: $40/8x4 display area. Prejudging by slides or photos if not in a previous show. Work may be offered for sale; no commission. Craftworker must attend show; demonstrations OK. Registration limit: 50. Sponsor provides electricity for demonstrations and 24-hour security. Show is advertised by radio; TV; and newspaper. Considers all crafts except ceramics; decoupage under $25; lapidary; and strung bead jewelry.

LEWISBURG CRAFT FAIR, Box 532, Lewisburg PA 17837. (717)524-7006. Director: David Bussard. Sponsor: Winfield House. Estab. 1973. Annual indoor show held 3 days in October. Average attendance: 7,500. Entries accepted until 3 months before show. Entry fee: $45/9x7 display area. Prejudging by slides and samples; entry fee due after prejudging. Work may be offered for sale; no commission. Craftworker must attend show; demonstrations OK. Registration limit: 75. Sponsor provides electricity for demonstrations. Show is advertised by all available media. Considers all crafts except ceramics; decoupage; and needlecrafts.

*****THE MANNINGS NATIONAL JURIED SHOW**, Rt. 2, East Berlin PA 17301. (717)624-2223. Director: Harry E. Manning. Sponsor: The Mannings Creative Crafts. Purpose: "to promote and encourage handweavers and fiber craftsmen; to give a market to these people who have no exposure to the buying public." Annual indoor show held 3 weeks April-May. Average attendance: 1,200. Entries accepted until 2 weeks before show. Entry fee: $5/item. Maximum 1 item per craftworker. Prejudging by actual work. Work may be offered for sale; 20% commission. Craftworker needn't attend show; no demonstrations. Registration limit: 300. Sponsor provides display panels and insurance on exhibited work. Show is advertised by *Shuttle, Spindle and Dyepot*, magazine of the Handweaver's Guild of America; mailing list; newspapers; and other weaving publications. Submit complete description of technique and material used. Presents cash awards of $2,500. 1977 show sales totalled $1,000. Considers only handweaving and macrame. Maximum size: 4x8; "exceptions to this would be coverlets; blankets; etc. which could be displayed folded."

MAXWELL HOUSE MINIATURE SHOW & SALE, Box 653, Edinboro PA 16412. (814)734-4594. Contact: Pam Maxwell. Estab. 1976. Annual indoor show held 2 days in October. Average attendance: 2,000.
Acceptable Work: Considers dollhouse miniatures only; "any form of dollhouses, furniture, miniature items used in or for a house." Maximum size of works: 1"-1' scale.
Terms: Entries accepted until 1 week before show. Entry fee: $20/6' table, some wall space available. Work may be offered for sale; no commission. Craftworker must attend show; demonstrations OK. Registration limit: 25. Sponsor provides chairs; covering; electricity for demonstrations; table; and 24-hour security.
Promotion: Show is advertised by TV; radio; newspaper; trade magazines; mailing list; and posters. "We advertise in a 100-mile radius which includes Buffalo, Pittsburgh and Cleveland."
Sales Tip: "We have new collectors; they want inexpensive items. We have serious collectors; they want high quality original work."

MIFFLIN COUNTY GOOSE DAY CELEBRATION, 13 S. Dorcas St., Lewistown PA 17044. (717)248-6713. Executive Director: Anita Wasilko. Sponsor: Mifflin County Festival Association. Estab. 1973. Annual outdoor show held September 29-October 2. Average attendance: 22,000. Work may be offered for sale; no commission. Craftworker must attend show; demonstrations OK. Sponsor provides fencing. Show is advertised by brochures; calendar of events; travel shows; news releases; and paid ads. Submit photos and resume for publicity. Considers all crafts.

*****MIFFLIN-JUNIATA ARTS FESTIVAL**, 507 Lindbergh Way, Lewistown PA 17044. (717)248-0582. Chairman of Arts and Crafts Exhibit: Thiry Olbrich. Purpose: "to bring cultural arts to community." Estab. 1967. Annual outdoor show held 1 day in May. Average attendance: 10,000-20,000. Entries accepted until 10 days before show. Display area: 10x10. Work may be offered for sale; 10% commission. Craftworker must attend show; demonstration OK. Sponsor provides electricity for demonstrations; fencing; picnic table; and camping area. Show is advertised by newspaper; radio; TV community spots; brochures; and various listings. Presents ribbon awards. Considers all crafts.

MONROEVILLE MALL ARTS FESTIVAL, Rt. 1, Box 153J, Auburn NH 03032. (603)483-2742. President: Jinx Harris. Estab. 1972. Annual indoor show held 5 days in February at Monroeville, Pennsylvania. Average attendance: 150,000. Entries accepted until 1 week before show or until filled. Entry fee: $40/8x4 display area. Prejudging by slides or photos if not in a previous show. Work may be offered for sale; no commission. Craftworker must attend show; demonstrations OK. Registration limit: 50. Sponsor provides electricity for demonstrations and 24-hour security. Show is advertised by radio; TV; and newspapers. Considers all crafts except ceramics; decoupage under $25; lapidary; and strung bead jewelry.

MONROEVILLE MALL CHILDREN'S HOUR SHOW, Rt. 1, Box 153J, Auburn NH 03032. (603)483-2742. President: Jinx Harris. Estab. 1976. Annual indoor show held 5 days in August at Pittsburgh, Pennsylvania. Average attendance: 150,000. Entries accepted until 1 week before show or until filled. Entry fee: $40/8x4 display area. Prejudging by slides or photos if not in a previous show. Work may be offered for sale; no commission. Craftworker must attend show; demonstrations OK. Registration limit: 75. Sponsor provides electricity for demonstrations and 24-hour security. Show is advertised by radio; TV; and newspapers. Considers all child-oriented crafts except ceramics; decoupage under $5; lapidary; and strung bead jewelry.

MONTGOMERY MALL CRAFT & SCULPTURE SHOW, Rt. 1, Box 153J, Auburn NH 03032. (603)483-2742. President: Jinx Harris. Estab. 1977. Annual indoor show held 4 days in April at Montgomeryville, Pennsylvania. Average attendance: 75,000. Entries accepted until 1 week before show or until filled. Entry fee: $40/8x4 display area. Prejudging by slides or photos if not in a previous show. Work may be offered for sale; no commission. Craftworker must attend show; demonstrations OK. Registration limit: 110. Sponsor provides electricity for demonstrations and 24-hour security. Show is advertised by radio; TV; and newspapers. Considers all crafts except ceramics; decoupage under $25; lapidary; and strung bead jewelry.

MOUNTAIN CRAFT DAYS, Rt. 2, Somerset PA 15501. (814)445-6077. Director: Elizabeth M. Haupt. Sponsor: Somerset Historical and Genealogical Society Inc. Purpose: "to enable visitors to see authentic representations of the early crafts as practiced by our pioneer ancestors." Estab. 1971. Annual outdoor show (with tents and wood slab shelters) held 3 days in September. Average attendance: 18,000. Entries accepted until 1 month before show. Work may be offered for sale; 10% commission. Craftworker must attend show; demonstrations required. Sponsor provides 2 chairs; 1 table; and 24-hour security. Show is advertised by radio; TV; newspaper; and brochures. Considers candlemaking; ceramics; leatherworking; metalsmithing; pottery; tole painting; weavings; woodcrafting; and crafts pertaining to the pioneer period.

NESHAMINY MALL ARTS FESTIVAL, Rt. 1, Box 153J, Auburn NH 03032. (603)483-2742. President: Jinx Harris. Estab. 1970. Annual indoor show held 4 days in April at Cornwell Heights, Pennsylvania. Average attendance: 150,000. Entries accepted until 1 week before show or until filled. Entry fee: $40/8x4 display area. Prejudging by slides or photos if not in a previous show. Work may be offered for sale; no commission. Craftworker must attend show; demonstrations OK. Registration limit: 50. Sponsor provides electricity for demonstrations and 24-hour security. Show is advertised by radio; TV; and newspapers. Considers all crafts except ceramics; decoupage under $25; lapidary; and strung bead jewelry.

NESHAMINY MALL PROFESSIONAL CRAFT & SCULPTURE SHOW, Rt. 1, Box 153J, Auburn NH 03032. (603)483-2742. President: Jinx Harris. Estab. 1973. Annual indoor show held 4 days in August at Cornwells Heights, Pennsylvania. Average attendance: 100,000. Entries accepted until 1 week before show or until filled. Entry fee: $40/8x4 display area. Prejudging by slides or photos if not in a previous show. Work may be offered for sale; no commission. Craftworker must attend show; demonstrations OK. Registration limit: 120. Sponsor provides electricity for demonstrations and 24-hour security. Show is advertised by radio; TV; and newspapers. Considers all crafts except ceramics; decoupage under $25; lapidary; and strung bead jewelry.

NORTHERN APPALACHIAN FESTIVAL, Box 1771, Bedford PA 15522. (814)623-1771. Festival General Chairman: Wendy Cox. Sponsor: Bedford Heritage Commission and Bedford Tourist & Resort Bureau. Estab. 1974. Annual outdoor show (semi-enclosed with full roofs, barns at fairgrounds) held 2 days Memorial Day weekend. Average attendance: 3,000. Considers all crafts.
Terms: Entries accepted until show or until spaces filled. Entry fee: $20/10x10 display area. Work may be offered for sale; no commission. Craftworker must attend show; demonstrations a must. Sponsor provides electricity for demonstrations; water; food stands; and security during show.
Promotion: Show is advertised by TV shows and coverage; local radio stations and newspaper media in 8 counties; 2 magazines; and coverage in metropolitan areas in newspapers (through the Pennsylvania Festival Association). Submit b&w photos for newspaper; color photos and/or slides for TV (nonreturnable); and resume.

Profile: Show includes "crafts, special displays of historical nature and of the Armed Forces, homemade foods, music, square dancing demonstrations, a mini show, wagon rides, a pony pull, pet shows, adult dance, concerts, an antique auto show, a flea market, special guests and a parade. The festival strives to promote the *family* atmosphere through added activities aimed at all members of the family. Each year one or more new activities are added retaining many of the annual popular ones."

PEDDLER'S VILLAGE APPLE FESTIVAL, Rts. 202 and 263, Box 218, Lahaska PA 18931. (215)794-7055. Advertising/PR Director: Carla Coutts. Sponsor: Peddler's Village. Estab. 1970. Annual outdoor show held 2 days the first weekend in November. Average daily attendance: 6,000.
Acceptable Work: Considers batik, candlemaking, dollmaking, glass art, jewelry, leatherworking, macrame, metalsmithing, needlecrafts, pottery, scrimshaw, sculpture, soft sculpture, tole painting, weaving, woodcrafting and all colonial crafts. Specialty food vendors $50 entry fee. "Well-priced, well-made unique items only."
Terms: "Send photos, SASE and letter anytime to Peddler's Village Crafts Committee for invitation." Entry fee: $20. Work may be offered for sale; no commission. Craftworker must attend show; demonstrations required. Registration limit: 100. Sponsor provides electricity for demonstrations, coffee, and breakfast cakes during early set-up hours, publicity in newspapers and TV. Craftworker handles sales tax.

PEDDLER'S VILLAGE CHRISTMAS FESTIVAL, Rts. 202 and 263, Box 218, Lahaska PA 18931. (215)794-7055. Advertising/PR Director: Carla Coutts. Sponsor: Peddler's Village. Estab. 1977. Annual outdoor show held the first Saturday in December. Average attendance: 2,000.
Acceptable Work: Considers all crafts, Christmas items only.
Terms: "Send photos, SASE and letter anytime to Peddler's Village for invitation." Entry fee: $15. Work may be offered for sale; no commission. Craftworker must attend show; demonstrations required. Sponsor provides electricity for demonstrations.

PEDDLER'S VILLAGE STRAWBERRY FESTIVAL & MAY FAIR, Rt. 202 & 263, Box 218, Lahaska PA 18931. (215)794-7055. Advertising/PR Director: Carla Coutts. Estab: 1964. Annual outdoor show held 2 days the first weekend in May. See Peddler's Village Apple Festival.

*****PENNSYLVANIA GUILD OF CRAFTSMEN'S MARKET,** Box 618, Bedford PA 15522. (814)623-1857. Executive Director: Lyn Jackson. Estab. 1947. Annual show held 1 day wholesale and 3 days retail in August at Lancaster, Pennsylvania. Prejudging. Registration limit: 200. Presents awards. Considers all quality crafts.

*****PENNSYLVANIA MAPLE FESTIVAL,** Box 222, Meyersdale PA 15552. (814)634-0213. Director: Doris B. Clapper. Estab. 1958. Annual indoor show held 9 days in March. Average attendance: 25,000-40,000. Considers all crafts.
Terms: Entries accepted until 1 week before show. Entry fee: $15/10x8. Prejudging by photos. Entry fee refunded for refused work. Work may be offered for sale; 15% commission. Craftworker must attend show; demonstrations encouraged. Registration limit: 50. Sponsor provides chairs; electricity for demonstrations; fencing; table; and 24-hour security.
Awards: Presents cash awards of $96 for quilts.
Promotion: Show is advertised by radio; TV; newspaper; brochures; magazines; AAA magazines; and tours. Submit photos.

*****THE PHILADELPHIA CRAFT SHOW,** Women's Committee, Philadelphia Museum of Art, Box 7646, Philadelphia PA 19101. (215)232-1171. Co-chairmen: Nancy McNeil and Mary Lee Lowry. Estab. 1977. Annual indoor show held 3 days in November. Average attendance: 15,000. Total sales (1977): $102,000.
Acceptable Work: Considers all crafts except painting, photography, graphics, dried flower arrangements, pressed flowers, seed and pod decorations, cut bottles and embellished objects such as painted boxes, weathered boards, stones, shells, buttons, decorated furniture or kits.
Terms: Entries accepted until mid May. Booth fee: $125/10x10 display area; $5 prejudging fee. Prejudging by 5 slides. All work may be offered for sale; no commission. Craftworker must attend show; no demonstrations. Registration limit: 106. Sponsor provides electricity for booth and security during non-show hours.

---

* Those listings preceded by an asterisk present awards for prize-winning crafts.

Awards: Presents $250 Booth Award, and $1,000 1st Prize, 2 $500 2nd Prize, and 3 $250 3rd Prize.
Promotion: Show is advertised by TV, radio, and extensive mailings of flyers and newsletters sent to galleries, art institutions, schools and private individuals. Submit slides and biographical material. Photos of local artists taken by newspapers.

*PHILLIPS MILL COMMUNITY ASSOCIATION ART EXHIBITION, Phillips Mill Community Association, New Hope PA 18938. (215)862-5880. Publicity Director: Jan Cherry. Estab. 1929. Annual show held 1 month in fall. Average attendance: 2,000. Total sales (1978): approximately $6,000.
Acceptable Work: Considers sculpture and matted woodcuts. "Frames and screw eyes for all hanging art must be provided."
Terms: Entries accepted until 2 weeks before show. Entry fee: $5/item. Maximum 5 pieces per craftworker. Prejudging by 2 members of PMCA. Entry fee not refunded for refused work. Work must be offered for sale; 25% commission. Craftworker needn't attend show; demonstrations OK. Registration limit: approximately 111 out of 525 submitted. Sponsor provides display panels, electricity for demonstrations and insurance on exhibited work. Members of the PMCA handle sales and taxes.
Awards: Presents $1,300 in cash awards. "All artists entering this exhibition must be from within a 25 mile radius of New Hope. Their specific art pieces must not have been entered at the Mill previously."
Promotion: Show is advertised by radio, news releases, newspaper, magazine ads and posters. "Include biographical material for promotional purposes, if desired."

RED CROSS CRAFT MARKET, Box 88, Allenwood PA 17810. Show Director: Fred Brown. Sponsor: Lycoming County Red Cross. Purpose: to be a marketplace for creative American handcrafts. Estab. 1977. Annual indoor show held 2 days in April at Williamsport, Pennsylvania. Average attendance: 10,000. Entries accepted until 4 weeks before show or until filled. Entry fee: $45/10x10 display area, 1 exhibitor; $65/10x10 display area, 2 exhibitors (limit 2 per space). Prejudging by 4 35mm slides; entry fee refunded for refused work. Work may be offered for sale; no commission. Craftworker must attend show; demonstrations OK. Registration limit: 100. Sponsor provides electricity for demonstrations and 24-hour security. Show is advertised by radio; newspaper; billboards; posters; and flyers. Submit b&w glossies and background information.

SHIPPENSBURG FAIR CRAFTS-ARTS SHOW & SALE, c/o Rose Dillner, Blythstead, Shippensburg PA 17257. (717)532-8155. Chairman: Rose Dillner. Sponsor: Shippensburg Bi-County Fair. Estab. 1969. Annual outdoor show (demonstrating craftsmen under tents) held 1 day in July.
Acceptable Work: Considers all crafts; especially interested in early primitive crafts. Maximum size: 10x10 unless permission is obtained.
Terms: Entries accepted until 3 weeks before show. No fee for demonstrating craftsmen. Non-demonstrating craftworkers will be in open-air section $10/20' display area. Work may be offered for sale; no commission. Craftworker must attend show; show is basically demonstrating show. Registration limit: 125. Sponsor provides coverings and electricity for demonstrating craftworkers only.

SOUTH HILLS VILLAGE ARTS FESTIVAL, Rt. 1, Box 153J, Auburn NH 03032. (603)483-2742. President: Jinx Harris. Estab. 1972. Annual indoor show held 4 days in March at Pittsburgh, Pennsylvania. Average attendance: 75,000. Entries accepted until 1 week before show or until filled. Entry fee: $40/8x4 display area. Prejudging by slides or photos if not in a previous show. Work may be offered for sale; no commission. Craftworker must attend show; demonstrations OK. Registration limit: 60. Sponsor provides electricity for demonstrations and 24-hour security. Show is advertised by radio; TV; and newspapers. Considers all crafts except ceramics; decoupage under $25; lapidary; and strung bead jewelry.

SOUTH HILLS VILLAGE CHILDREN'S SHOW, Rt. 1, Box 153J, Auburn NH 03032. (603)483-2742. President: Jinx Harris. Estab. 1977. Annual indoor show held 4 days in July at Pittsburgh, Pennsylvania. Average attendance: 75,000. Entries accepted until 1 week before show or until filled. Entry fee: $40/8x4 display area. Prejudging by slides or photos if not in a previous show. Work may be offered for sale; no commission. Craftworker must attend show; demonstrations OK. Registration limit: 75. Sponsor provides electricity for demonstrations and 24-hour security. Show is advertised by radio; TV; and newspapers. Considers all child-oriented crafts except ceramics; decoupage under $5; lapidary; and strung bead jewelry.

SOUTH HILLS VILLAGE PROFESSIONAL ARTS FESTIVAL, Rt. 1, Box 153J, Auburn NH 03032. (603)483-2742. President: Jinx Harris. Estab. 1972. Annual indoor show held 4 days in October at Pittsburgh, Pennsylvania. Average attendance: 85,000. Entries accepted until 1 week before show or until filled. Entry fee: $40/8x4 display area. Prejudging by slides or photos if not in a previous show. Work may be offered for sale; no commission. Craftworker must attend show; demonstrations OK. Sponsor provides electricity for demonstrations and 24-hour security. Show is advertised by radio; TV; and newspapers. Considers all crafts except ceramics; decoupage under $25; lapidary; and strung bead jewelry.

SPRING ARTS FESTIVAL, Johnstown Area Arts Council, Box 402, Johnstown PA 15907. (814)536-1333. Executive Secretary: Maryanne Larison. Purpose: "a chance to exhibit and sell craft to about 25,000 people." Estab. 1963. Average attendance: 25,000. Annual indoor show held 3 days in April. Entries accepted until 4 weeks before show. Entry fee: $25/10x10 display area. Prejudging by slides; photos; or actual work. Work may be offered for sale; no commission. Craftworker must attend show; demonstrations required. Considers all crafts.

*****SPRING CRAFT FAIR & SALE**, 111 Chapel Rd., New Hope PA 18938. (215)862-2374. Public Relations: Emil W. Peters. Sponsor: Bucks County Guild of Craftsmen. Estab. 1960. Annual indoor show held 3 days the third weekend of June at Wrightstown, Pennsylvania. Average attendance: 10,000-13,000. Considers all crafts.
Terms: Exhibitors must become Guild members. Work is prejudged at monthly Standards Committee meetings. "Only submit that item which you feel represents your very best effort. If you are doubtful of the piece, do not submit it." $5 entry fee/craftworker. Display area: 10x7, "slightly more if needed to demonstrate." Work must be offered for sale; 15% commission. Sponsor provides electricity for demonstrations and overnight security.
Awards: Presents cash and ribbon awards for Best of Show and 1st, 2nd and 3rd place awards in each category. Only 1 piece/craftworker may be entered into competition.
Sales Tip: "Be neat, congenial and enthusiastic. Don't overprice, but don't underprice either. Don't disturb a person examining your work, but be ready to assist. Offer a pleasant comment when they leave, always remember they may come back later. Don't feel that your expertise is your secret. Be free with your information." 1978 sales totaled slightly over $26,000.
Promotion: Show is advertised by listings in craft magazines; feature stories and news releases in news media in 50-mile radius; TV and radio interviews; placards in shopping areas; flyers in motels, restaurants and other public meeting places; and mailings by members and various agencies.

*****SPRING CRAFT MARKET AT PARK CITY MALL**, Box 5153, Lancaster PA 17601. Sponsor: Conestoga Valley Chapter, Pennsylvania Guild of Craftsmen. Purpose: fundraising. Estab. 1974. Annual indoor show held 3 days in May. Average attendance: 40,000. Entries accepted until 6 weeks before show. "Show open only to members of the Pennsylvania Guild of Craftsmen." Display area: 10x15. Maximum 1 item per category per artist. Prejudging by 4 slides for new craftsmen; floor jurying from past shows. Entry fee due after prejudging. Work may be offered for sale; demonstrations required 20% of showtime. Registration limit: 90. Sponsor provides electricity for demonstrations and some security. Show is advertised by billboards; newspaper; posters; radio; and TV interview shows. Submit b&w photos of self at work. Presents cash awards of $200. 1977 show sales totalled $40,000. Considers batik; candlemaking; ceramics; glass art; jewelry; lapidary; leatherworking; macrame; metalsmithing; pottery; sculpture; soft sculpture; tole painting; weaving; and woodcrafting. Bestsellers: glass; leather; and pottery.

*****SPRING SHOW**, 338 W. 6th St., Erie PA 16507. (814)459-5477. Executive Director: John L. Vanco. Sponsor: Erie Art Center. Purpose: "annual presentation of the best regional art." Estab. 1898. Annual indoor show held 2 months April-May. Average attendance: 2,500.
Acceptable Work: Considers batik; ceramic sculpture; mobiles; sculpture; and soft sculpture. Maximum size: 60" and 100 pounds.
Terms: Entries accepted until 1 month before show. Entry fee: $3/item. Display area: 1,000 square feet. Maximum 2 pieces per craftworker. Work may be offered for sale; 25% commission. Craftworker needn't attend show; no demonstrations. Registration limit: 60-70. Sponsor provides insurance on exhibited work and 24-hour security. 1978 show sales totalled $3,500.
Awards: Presents cash awards of $1,000 and purchase awards of $3,000.
Promotion: Show is advertised regionally through newspaper; TV; radio; and direct mail.

SPRINGFIELD MALL CHILDREN'S HOUR SHOW, Rt. 1, Box 153J, Auburn NH 03032. (603)483-2742. President: Jinx Harris. Estab. 1977. Annual indoor show held 4 days in February at Springfield, Pennsylvania. Average attendance: 60,000. Entries accepted until 1 week before show or until filled. Entry fee: $40/8x4 display area. Prejudging by slides or photos if not in a previous show. Work may be offered for sale; no commission. Craftworker must attend show; demonstrations OK. Registration limit: 60. Sponsor provides electricity for demonstrations and 24-hour security. Show is advertised by radio; TV; and newspapers. Considers all child-oriented crafts except ceramics; decoupage under $5; lapidary; and strung bead jewelry.

SPRINGFIELD MALL CRAFT & SCULPTURE SHOW, Rt. 1, Box 153J, Auburn NH 03032. (603)483-2742. President: Jinx Harris. Estab. 1975. Annual indoor show held 4 days in September at Springfield, Pennsylvania. Average attendance: 55,000. Entries accepted until 1 week before show or until filled. Entry fee: $40/8x4 display area. Prejudging by slides or photos if not in a previous show. Work may be offered for sale; no commission. Craftworker must attend show; demonstrations OK. Sponsor provides electricity for demonstrations and 24-hour security. Show is advertised by radio; TV; and newspaper. Considers all crafts except ceramics; decoupage under $25; lapidary; and strung bead jewelry.

SPRINGS FOLK FESTIVAL, Box 134, Springs PA 15562. Chairman Crafts Committee: John Hepler. Sponsor: Springs Historical Society and Penn Alps, Inc. Purpose: "to revive and preserve the arts and crafts of the area by providing a market for craftsmen and demonstrating and teaching pioneer and contemporary arts and crafts." Estab. 1957. Annual outdoor show (with some shelters and building) held 2 days in October. Average attendance: 10,000-12,000. Entries accepted until 2 months before show; will fill cancellations. Display area: 8x8. Prejudging by slides; photos; or actual work. Work may be offered for sale; 15% commission. Craftworker must attend show; demonstrations required. Registration limit: 100. Sponsor provides display panels; electricity for demonstrations; table; 24-hour security; and roof. Show is advertised by newspaper ads; radio; travel magazines; and folders.
Acceptable Work: Considers candlemaking, dollmaking, glass art, leatherworking, metalsmithing, needlecrafts, pottery, sculpture, tole painting, weaving, woodcrafting and other types of Early American crafts of Appalachia.

*****STITCHERY '80**, c/o Clare Hoffman, Registrar, 1200 Heberton St., Pittsburgh PA 15206. (412)362-2720. Sponsor: Embroiderers' Guild of Pittsburgh, Inc. Estab. 1959. Biennial indoor show held 3 weeks in the spring. Next show scheduled for April 22-May 13, 1979. Average attendance: 2,500. Slide submissions for jury date due January 17, 1979. Entry fee: $10 for maximum 3 entries per craftworker. Prejudging by 3 slides of each piece entered; no entry fees refunded for refused work. Work may be offered for sale; 30% commission. Craftworker needn't attend show; no demonstrations. Sponsor provides $100 deductible insurance on exhibited work and 24-hour security. Show is advertised by the press; educational radio and TV; publications in arts; etc. Considers soft sculpture and "work including the embellishment of a surface or area with fiber and needle." Presents 2 $100 and 1 $500 cash awards; $1,000 purchase award fund; and other prizes as available.

*****THREE RIVERS ARTS FESTIVAL**, 4400 Forbes Ave., Pittsburgh PA 15213. (412)687-7014. Executive Director: John Jay. Sponsor: Carnegie Institute. Purpose: "to showcase the work of artists and performers in western Pennsylvania." Estab. 1960. Annual indoor/outdoor show held 10 days, May-June. Average attendance: 200,000. Entries accepted until 2 months before show. Rental fee: $100, each 5 day period; $75, second 5 days/4x8 display area. Maximum 3 pieces per exhibit. Prejudging by slides; $7 jurying fee. Work must be offered for sale; no commission in attended space; 25% commission in exhibit space. Craftworker needn't attend unless entering attended portion of show; limited demonstrations. Registration limit: 175. Show is advertised by all media. Submit publicity card attached to entry form. Presents cash and purchase awards. Considers all crafts except candlemaking; decoupage; dollmaking; lapidary; mobiles; and tole painting.

WAYNESBORO'S CRAFT DAY, 323 E. Main St., Box 512, Waynesboro PA 17268. Coordinator: Frances H. Miller. Sponsor: Chamber of Commerce. Estab. 1975. Annual outdoor show held 1 day in September. Entries accepted until show. Entry fee: $5/1 parking space, approximately 22'. Work may be offered for sale; no commission. Craftworker needn't attend show; demonstrations OK. Registration limit: 120. Show is advertised by newspaper and radio. Considers all crafts.

Rhode Island

CRAFTS MARKETPLACE, Rainbow Enterprises, 58 Dixon St., PeaceDale RI 02883. (401)789-8260. Contact: Andrea Kotula. Estab. 1973. Annual outdoor show held 3 days in July at Newport, Rhode Island. Entry fee: $45. Considers all crafts.

EARTHWORKS, 1819 Kingston Rd., Kingston RI 02881. Contact: Helme House, Ceramics Workshop. Sponsor: South County Art Association. Annual indoor show held 6 days in May. Acceptable Work: Considers original clay work. "All wall pieces should be properly strung and ready for hanging. The gallery walls will not safely support any piece weighing more than 15-20 pounds."
Terms: Open to Rhode Island craftworkers only. Entries must be brought to Helme House on a day to be specified approximately 2 weeks before show. Entry fee: $300/item. Maximum 6 entries/craftworker. Entry fee not refunded for refused work. Prejudging. Work may be offered for sale; 15% commission. Entries not marked for sale must be so marked. Taxes are collected and paid by the South County Art Association. Write for information.
Awards: Presents $100 cash for 1st place, $75 for 2nd place, $50 for 3rd place, and $25 for 4th place; and honorable mentions.

The Cooperstown National Art Exhibition, Cooperstown, New York, which just recently celebrated its 50th anniversary exhibition is held for four weeks during the summer. Awards are presented for the three categories in which the show is divided—paintings, sculpture and crafts.

*****SOUTH COUNTY ART ANNUAL**, 1319 Kingston Rd., Kingston RI 02881. Contact: Helme House. Sponsor: South County Art Association. Annual indoor show held the second and third weeks in April. Entry fee: $3/item. Maximum 2 entries per artist. Work may be offered for sale; 15% commission. Work must be hand-delivered. Considers sculpture. Presents $250 in cash prizes.

THE USQUEPAUGH JOHNNY CAKE FESTIVAL, Box 221, West Kingston RI 02892. (401)783-4054. Manager: Herb Arnold. Sponsor: Johnny Cake Festival Committee. Estab. 1974. Annual outdoor show held 2 days during late October. Average attendance: 10,000. Entries accepted until 4 weeks before show. Entry fee: $15/8x8 display area. Work may be offered for sale; no commission. Craftworker must attend show and demonstrate. Sponsor provides electricity for a $5 fee. Show is advertised by posters throughout the county and ads in Providence papers. Considers all crafts.

Sales Tip: "Our craft show is primarily a selling show. We advise craftspeople to promote their items for holiday gift giving as this is the last outdoor show in Rhode Island before the holiday season. Also, for an additional $15, the craftsperson can place an ad in the festival program which can be used like a business card to promote their Christmas mall shows."

Profile: "The Usquepaugh Johnny Cake Festival is essentially a village street fair with parades, antique auto show, petting zoo and animal rides, band concerts and various homemade foods (most especially johnny cakes which are a native Rhode Island food of the Indians). There are Indian dancing demonstrations and crafts as well as commercial crafts."

WARWICK MALL CHILDREN'S HOUR SHOW, Rt. 1, Box 153J, Auburn NH 03032. (603)483-2742. President: Jinx Harris. Estab. 1977. Annual indoor show held 4 days in April at Warwick, Rhode Island. Average attendance: 50,000.

Acceptable Work: Considers all child-oriented crafts except ceramics; decoupage under $5; lapidary; and strung bead jewelry.

Terms: Entries accepted until 1 week before show or until filled. Entry fee: $40/8x4' display area. Prejudging by slides or photos if not in a previous show. Work may be offered for sale; no commission. Craftworker must attend show; demonstrations OK. Registration limit: 60. Sponsor provides electricity for demonstrations and 24-hour security.

WARWICK MALL PROFESSIONAL CRAFT & SCULPTURE SHOW, Rt. 1, Box 153J, Auburn NH 03032. (603)483-2742. President: Jinx Harris. Estab. 1971. Annual indoor show held 4 days in October at Warwick, Rhode Island. Average attendance: 60,000. Entries accepted until 1 week before show or until filled. Entry fee: $40/8x4 display area. Prejudging by slides or photos if not in a previous show. Work may be offered for sale; no commission. Craftworker must attend show; demonstrations OK. Registration limit: 100. Sponsor provides electricity for demonstrations and 24-hour security. Show is advertised by radio; TV; and newspapers. Considers all crafts except ceramics; decoupage under $25; lapidary; and strung bead jewelry.

*****WESTERLY ART FESTIVAL**, 159 Main St., Westerly RI 02891. Secretary, Diane B. Howard. Sponsor: Westerly-Pawcatuck Area Chamber of Commerce. Purpose: "The Westerly Art Festival is held as a community project. All funds are maintained in a separate fund and used exclusively for the Art Festival." Estab. 1967. Annual outdoor show held 2 days in July. Average attendance: "several thousand." Entries accepted until show. Entry fee: $15/fine artist; $20 for applied art; and $1 for students. Prejudging of applied art only; by slides, photos or samples of work. Entry fee refunded for refused work. Work may be offered for sale; no commission. Craftworker or representative must attend show; demonstrations OK. Registration limit: 50 for applied art; no limit on fine art exhibitors. Sponsor provides fencing for students; 24-hour security; coffee and donuts; and pages to help loading and unloading. Categories: graphic art; b&w rendering; sculpture; photography; paintings; batik; and applied art.

Acceptable Work: Considers batik hangings; ceramics (but no greenware); glass art; jewelry; lapidary; leatherworking; macrame; metalsmithing; mobiles; needlecrafts; pottery; sculpture; tole painting; weaving; woodcrafting; and decoupage if designs are done by the artist.

Awards: Presents $50 cash prize for "Best-in-Show," purchase awards and ribbons.

WICKFORD ART FESTIVAL, Box 124, North Kingston RI 02852. (401)295-5944. Chairman: Alice Ryan. Sponsor: Wickford Art Association. Estab. 1960. Annual outdoor show held 3 days in July. Entries accepted until 4 weeks before show. Entry fee: $25 for 1-3 days. Maximum 25 entries per craftworker. Work may be offered for sale; no commission. Craftworker must attend show; demonstrations OK. Considers ceramics; leatherworking; macrame; metalsmithing; pottery; sculpture; tole painting, and woodcrafting.

South Carolina

THE CAROLINA CRAFTSMEN'S CHIRSTMAS CLASSIC, 3603 Old Battleground Rd., Greensboro NC 27410. (919)288-1933. Executive Director: Clyde Gilmore. Estab. 1976. Annual indoor show held 2 days in November at Columbia, South Carolina. Considers all original crafts. Presents purchase prizes and plaques.

Terms: Write for information on registration deadlines and fees. Prejudging by slides, photos and/or newspaper articles about the craftworker; entry fee due after prejudging. Work may be offered for sale; no commission. Craftworker must attend show; demonstrations OK. Sponsor provides chairs, curtained booth space and 24-hour security.

CHRISTMAS CRAFT & ART SHOW, Box 1177, Aiken SC 29801. Contact: M. F. Facciolo. Sponsor: Aiken Recreation Department. Estab. 1970. Annual indoor show held in December. Average attendance: 10,000. Entry fee: $15. Display area: 5x8. All media OK. Work may be offered for sale; no commission. Craftworker must attend show.

DILLON COUNTY ARTS & CRAFTS FESTIVAL, Dillon County Chamber of Commerce, Dillon SC 29536. (803)774-8551. Secretary: Pansy Courtney. Estab. 1975. Annual outdoor show (under tents and tarpaulins) held 2 days in April. The show "could be moved to nearby buildings if the weather is very bad." Average attendance: 6,000-8,000.
Acceptable Work: Considers all crafts. "We would prefer strictly original work. Anything for hanging must be ready to be hung."
Terms: Entries accepted until show date, or 2 weeks before show to be placed on program. Entry fee: $5/20x20 average display area. Work may be offered for sale; 10% commission. Craftworker or representative must attend show; demonstrations encouraged. Sponsor provides coverings (occasionally), electricity for demonstrations, 24-hour security and assistance in setting up. Treasurer handles sales and taxes.
Promotion: Show is advertised by TV, radio, newspapers, mailings and calendar of events. Promotional material is optional. "If the craftworker has something very unusual, we could use it as a newspaper writeup in our pre-show publicity."
Sales Tip: "Customers buy jewelry, ceramics, things made of pine cones and wood, and leather crafts. They really like 'gew gaws' (like carved seagulls on wood or carved owls)."
Profile: "We are a young organization and can't offer cash prizes as yet. Hope to be able to do so in a year or so."

***FALL FIESTA OF THE ARTS**, Sumter Cultural Commission, County Courthouse, Sumter SC 29150. (803)773-1581. Executive secretary: Martha Greenway. Estab. 1977. Annual outdoor show held 3 days in the fall. Average attendance: 5,000-10,000. Considers all crafts.
Terms: Entries accepted until 1 week before show. Entry fee: $15/exhibitor. Display area: 10x12. Work may be offered for sale; no commission. Craftworker must attend show; demonstrations OK. Registration limit: 25. Sponsor provides electricity for demonstrations and 24-hour security.
Awards: Presents $525 in 3 categories and $500 in purchase prizes. Prizes based on quality workmanship and imaginative approach to craft.
Promotion: Show is advertised by state department of tourism, newspapers, posters and radio and TV. "It would be helpful to have photos of artist at work along with a brief biographical sketch. Especially emphasize anything unique or unusual."

GOPHER HILL FESTIVAL, Box 1267, Ridgeland SC 29936. (803)726-8126. Executive Vice President: Thomas H. Rhodes. Sponsor: Jasper County Chamber of Commerce. Estab. 1972. Annual outdoor show held the first Saturday in October. Average attendance: 9,000. Considers all crafts.
Terms: Entries accepted until show date. Booth fee: $10/15x20. Work may be offered for sale; 10% commission. Craftworker must attend show; demonstrations OK. Registration limit: 30. Sponsor provides electricity for demonstrations.
Promotion: Show is advertised by TV, radio, newspaper and publications. "If they would like, we would be happy to use any information sent for promotional purposes."

***HILL SKILLS**, 627 Pelham Rd., Greenville SC 29615. (803)288-4088. Manager: Rachel Pringle McKaughan. Purpose: "Hill Skills began as a tri-centennial city function to show and sell crafts made in the area. It has grown to a national show with top craftsmen from all states exhibiting. Three-quarters of the show educates by demonstration." Estab. 1970. Annual indoor show held 5 days in October. Average attendance: 20,000. Entries accepted until mid-February. Entry fee: $60/10x10 display area. Work may be offered for sale; no commission. Craftworker must attend show; demonstrations encouraged. Registration limit: 150. Sponsor provides curtains; electricity for demonstrations; and shopping bags. Considers all crafts.
Promotion: Show is advertised by billboards; posters; flyers; TV; shoppers guides; placemats; newspapers; and penny postcards. "Will select craftworkers to send items for showing on TV month before show."

HISTORIC CAMDEN CRAFTS FESTIVAL, Box 605, Camden SC 29020. (803)432-4181, 432-2525. Executive Vice President: Walter C. Sprouse Jr. Sponsor: Greater Kershaw County Chamber of Commerce. Estab. 1971. Annual outdoor show (with army tents) held 2 days in May. Average attendance: 3,000-4000. Considers all crafts.

Terms: Entries accepted until show date. Entry fee: $20/display area. Prejudging by slides/photos. Entry fee not refunded for refused work. Work must be offered for sale; no commission. Prefers craftworker to attend show; demonstrations OK. Registration limit: 50. Sponsor provides coverings, electricity for demonstrations and 24-hour security. Exhibitor handles own sales and taxes.
Promotion: Show is advertised by radio, TV, newsletter and newspapers. Submit slides/photos, samples or the actual craft for promotion.

HOLIDAY FAIR, Box 5823, Greenville SC 29606. (803)233-2562. Director: Sandra Reese. Sponsor: Textile Hall Corporation. Estab. 1971. Annual indoor show held 2 days in late November or early December. Average attendance: 28,000. Show is advertised by TV, radio, newspapers and posters.
Acceptable Work: Considers all crafts. "No commercial businesses or commercial products are permitted".
Terms: Entries accepted until show date. "Applications are accepted on a 'first come, first serve' basis; however, the show is usually sold out many months before." Entry fee: $35/12x10 booth. Work must be offered for sale; no commission. Demonstrations OK. Registration limit: approximately 417. Sponsor provides chairs, electricity for demonstrations (if requested), drape and 24-hour security. Exhibitor handles sales and taxes.

INVITATIONAL CRAFTS SHOW, The Gallery, 385 S. Spring St., Spartanburg SC 29301. (803)582-7616. Sponsor: Spartanburg County Art Association. Purpose: "to promote the area of crafts as a fine art form that is functional as well as artistic." Estab. 1970. Annual indoor show held 1 month November-December. Average attendance: 800. Entries accepted until 1 month before show. Work must be offered for sale; 33⅓% commission. Craftworker needn't attend show; demonstrations OK. Registration limit: 35. Sponsor provides insurance on exhibited work and 24-hour security. Show is advertised by newspaper; radio; posters; invitations; and TV public service announcements. Submit resume or biography and slides.
Acceptable Work: Considers batik, candlemaking; jewelry; lapidary; leatherworking; macrame; metalsmithing; needlecrafts; pottery; weaving; and woodcrafting.
Sales Tip: "This is basically a sales show with almost all work selling. It is specifically scheduled for the Christmas shopping period and special publicity is designed to attract the holiday shopper."

LEE COUNTY COTTON-PICKIN' FESTIVAL, Box 272, Bishopville SC 29010. (803)484-5302. Ex-Director: Jack Bethea. Estab. 1977. Annual indoor show held 3 days in October. Average attendance: 10,000.
Acceptable Work: Considers all original crafts. No kits or machine-made crafts.
Terms: Entries accepted until show date. Entry fee: $20/8x10' display area. Work may be offered for sale; no commission. Craftworker must attend show; demonstrations OK. Registration limit: 55. Sponsor provides electricity for demonstrations.
Promotion: Show is advertised by TV, radio, newspapers, billboards and posters. Send pictures of any special items.

LOWCOUNTRY CHRISTMAS FESTIVAL, 77 Calhoun St., Charleston SC 29401. (803)788-5269 or 884-7204. Vice President: Mrs. Nelson Garrett. Sponsor: Nelson Garretts, Inc. Estab. 1972. Annual indoor show held 4 days in November. Average attendance: 35,820. Considers all crafts.
Terms: Entries accepted until show. Entry fee: $120/10x10 display area. Work may be offered for sale; no commission. Craftworker must attend show; demonstrations encouraged. Registration limit: 68. Sponsor provides chairs, electricity for demonstrations, table and 24-hour security.
Promotion: Show is advertised by TV, radio, 12 newspapers and nonprofit groups sell advance tickets. "Our advertising budget is $18,000. Submit b&w photos and any information suitable for newspaper stories, TV, talk shows, etc."

*****RICE FESTIVAL ARTS & CRAFTS SHOW**, 104 Longleaf Dr., Walterboro SC 29488. (803)538-3424. Chairperson: Ann Gustin. Estab. 1976. Annual outdoor show held 2 days in April. Average attendance: 5,000. Considers all original crafts.
Terms: Entries accepted until 2 weeks before show. Entry fee: $15/10x10 display area. Work may be offered for sale; no commission. Craftworker must attend show; demonstrations OK. Registration limit: 75.
Promotion: Show is advertised by TV, radio, newspapers, brochures and South Carolina Arts Commission.

SANTEE-WATEREE EXPO, 302 W. Boyce St., Manning SC 29102. (803)433-8994. President: Billie S. Fleming. Sponsor: NAACP. Annual outdoor show held 1 day. Average attendance: 7,000. Considers all crafts. Entries accepted until show date. Work may be offered for sale; no commission. Craftworker must attend show; demonstrations OK. Sponsor provides chairs, coverings, electricity for demonstrations, fencing, table and 24-hour security.

*SOUTH CAROLINA ARTS COMMISSION EXHIBITION, 1800 Gervais St., Columbia SC 29201. (803)758-3442. Contact: Coordinator. Annual indoor show held 3-4 weeks in the spring. No entry fee. Prejudging by slides. Maximum 2 entries per craftworker. Work may be offered for sale; no commission. Presents $5,000 in purchase prizes.
Acceptable Work: Considers batik; ceramics; glass art; jewelry; needlecrafts; pottery; soft sculpture; weavings; wall hangings; and woodcrafting completed by South Carolina residents or craftworkers having lived at least 1 year in the state. "Works of professional quality are required since those purchased will become works in the state's art collection; therefore simple hobby crafts are not acceptable."

SOUTH CAROLINA CRAFTSMEN GUILD CRAFT FAIR AT SPOLETO, South Carolina Arts Commission, 1800 Gervais St., Columbia SC 29201. (803)758-7943. Contact: Crafts Coordinator. Estab. 1977. Annual show held during the first weekend in June at Charleston, South Carolina.
Acceptable Work: Considers batik, ceramics, glass art, jewelry, basketry, pottery, textiles and woodcrafting.
Profile: "The fair takes place in conjunction with the International Cultural event drawing a sophisticated buying public."

SOUTH CAROLINA FESTIVAL OF FLOWERS, Box 980, Greenwood SC 29646. (803)223-8431. Sponsor: Greenwood County Chamber of Commerce. Estab. 1968. Annual indoor show held 3 days in late July. Average attendance: 20,000.
Acceptable Work: Considers all crafts. No kits, machine-made work, or items purchased for resale.
Terms: Entry fee: $25/8x8 display area for craftworkers. No booth fee for artists. Maximum 5 entries/category. Work must be offered for sale; 10% commission for artists. No commission charged for craftworkers. Craftworker or a representative must attend show; demonstrations OK. Registration limit: approximately 60. Sponsor provides chairs, display panels, electricity for demonstrations (with advance notice), table and 24-hour security.
Sales: "About half the artists and craftsmen had tax numbers and report directly to State Tax Commission in 1978; the others, who paid through this office, reported sales taxes of $769.71."
Awards: Presents $300 craft juried show; $800 professional juried art show; and $100 amateur juried art show.

SOUTH CAROLINA FESTIVAL OF ROSES ARTS & CRAFTS FAIR, Drawer 328, Orangeburg SC 29115. (803)534-6821. Contact: Lynn Baumblatt, Assistant Manager, Chamber of Commerce; or Arts & Crafts Chairman. Sponsor: Greater Orangeburg Chamber of Commerce. Estab. 1972. Annual outdoor show held 2 days in May. Average attendance: 15,000. Considers all crafts. Presents ribbons.
Terms: Entries accepted until 2 weeks before show. Entry fee: $15/15x12' display area. Work may be offered for sale; no commission. Craftworker or representative must attend show; demonstrations OK. Registration limit: 80 or as much as space allows.
Profile: "The show is promoted as one of the feature activities of the South Carolina Festival of Roses which also includes: a beauty pageant, canoe races, road races, golf and tennis tournaments, a parade, and a major show or concert."

SPRING ARTS & CRAFTS FESTIVAL, Box 111, Cheraw SC 29520. Arts Coordinator: Mary G. Burr. Sponsor: Cheraw Recreation Department. Estab. 1973. Annual indoor show (with some booths outside) held 2 days in the spring. Average attendance: 5,500. Considers all handmade crafts. No kits or molds.
Terms: Entries accepted until 4 weeks before show. Entry fee: $15/single booth (8x9), $30/double. Work may be offered for sale; no commission. Craftworker must attend show; demonstrations OK. Sponsor provides chairs, electricity for demonstrations, table and 24-hour security. Exhibitor handles sales and taxes.
Promotion: Show is advertised by newspapers, TV, radio and magazines such as *Southern Living* and *Sandlapper*. "Send any informations that we could use for a feature in our local newspaper."

*SUMMERTHING ARTS FESTIVAL, 36 Artillery Dr., Sumter SC 29150. (803)773-9363. Program Coordinator: Mary Hinson. Sponsor: Sumter Parks & Recreation Dept. Estab. 1968. Annual indoor show held 2 days in July. Average attendance: 300-400. Awards 3 ribbons in each category.
Acceptable Work: Considers all crafts except candlemaking and mobiles. All art and needlework must be framed for hanging.
Terms: Entries accepted until show date. Entry fee: $10/card table-size space. Work may be offered for sale; no commission. Demonstrations OK. Sponsor provides chairs, electricity for demonstrations and 24-hour security.

*U.C.R.D. HOBBY SHOW, South St., Union SC 29379. (803)427-1208. Program Director; Kay McCutcheon. Sponsor: Union County Recreation Commission. Estab. 1972. Annual indoor show held 2 days in April. Average attendance: 2,000. Presents Best of Show, 1st, 2nd and 3rd place ribbons.
Acceptable Work: Considers all original crafts. No kits or molds. "For framed work, you must have your own means of hanging."
Terms: Entries accepted until 1 week before show. Entry fee: $10/single 8x10 space. Work may be offered for sale; no commission. Craftworker must attend show; demonstrations OK. Registration limit: 50. Sponsor provides chairs, electricity for demonstrations, table and 24-hour security. Exhibitor handles sales and taxes.
Promotion: Show is advertised by local newspaper and radio, state newspaper, TV and craft magazines. "Artists and craftsmen will furnish their own promotional display materials and these will be confined to booth area."

WHITMIRE ARTS & CRAFTS EXHIBIT, Box 164, Whitmire SC 29178. (803)694-3350. Chairman: Lila Sherrets. Sponsor: Arts Association. Estab. 1974. Annual indoor show held 1 week in February. Average attendance: 200-400. Show is advertised by newspapers.
Acceptable Work: Considers all original crafts. Bestsellers: quilts, needlework and leatherwork.
Terms: Entries accepted until show date. Entry fee: $2/artist. Prejudged by art judge. Entry fee due after prejudging. Work may be offered for sale; no commission. Craftworker needn't attend show; demonstrations OK. Sponsor provides chairs, electricity for demonstrations, table and 24-hour security. Exhibitor handles sales and taxes.

South Dakota

ABERDEEN ARTS FESTIVAL, Box 1751, Aberdeen SD 57401. (605)622-2530. Registration chairman: Beth Wray. Sponsor: Aberdeen Area Arts Council. Estab. 1976. Annual outdoor show held 2 days the third weekend in June. Average attendance: 15,000. Considers all original crafts.
Terms: Entries accepted until show. Entry fee: $20/12x12 display area ($25 after June 1). Work may be offered for sale; no commission. Craftworker must attend show; demonstration encouraged. Registration limit: 150. Electricity for demonstrations available for $10 charge.
Sales Tip: "Have an attractive display. Ceramics, glass art, jewelry, macrame, pottery, woodcraft and paintings sell very well."
Promotion: Show is advertised by radio, newspapers, brochures, posters, TV, calendar of events and newsletters. Artists are encouraged to submit biographical information and photographs of themselves with registration forms for publicity purposes.

BROOKINGS SUMMER FOLK ARTS FESTIVAL, Box 555, Brookings SD 57006. Board Member: Perry Vining. Estab. 1972. Annual outdoor show held 2 days in July. Average attendance: 15,000. Entries close in mid June. Entry fee: $20. Display area: 12x12. Work may be offered for sale; no commission. Craftworker must attend show; demonstrations OK. Registration limit: 215. Sponsor provides electricity for limited demonstrations and 24-hour security. Show is advertised by radio; TV; billboards; newspapers; posters; and brochures. Considers all crafts made by the exhibitor. "A state tax representative should be on hand to collect sales tax."

CREATIVE CRAFT SHOW N SELL, Box 430, Madison SD 57042. (605)256-4114. Co-chairmen: Esther Brandes or Sylvia Tonsager. Sponsor: Creative Crafts. Purpose: "to give local and area people who do not maintain a shop, but do crafts, an opportunity to sell these items." Estab. 1973. Annual indoor show held 1 day in November. Average attendance: 1,800.

---

* Those listings preceded by an asterisk present awards for prize-winning crafts.

Entries accepted until show date. Entry fee: $10 before November; $12 after. Display area: 8x6. Work may be offered for sale; no commission. Craftworker must attend show; demonstrations OK. Registration limit: 125. Sponsor provides electricity for demonstrations. Show is advertised by local radio and newspaper ads and public service announcements and flyers put in business windows. Considers all crafts.

FESTIVAL IN THE PARK, Vermillion Area Arts Council, Box 484, Vermillion SD 57069. (605)677-5228. Contact: Festival Chairman. Estab. 1975. Annual outdoor show held 1 day in late summer or early fall. Average attendance: 2,000. Considers all crafts.
Terms: Entries accepted until 2 weeks before show. No entry fee. Work may be offered for sale; no commission. Craftworker must attend show; only demonstrating craftspeople. Sponsor provides some electricity for demonstrations.
Promotion: Show is advertised by area newspapers, posters, flyers and mailers. "Promotional materials are not needed, but helpful."
Sales Tip: "Have an attractive display of wares. Pottery and clothing have sold well in the past."

FORT SISSETON HISTORICAL FESTIVAL AND STARR RENDEZVOUS, Box 390, Brookings SD 57006. (605)692-7171. Coordinator: Perry Vining. Sponsor: South Dakota Department of Wildlife, Parks and Forestry; South Dakota Department of Tourism; South Dakota Arts Council; and Glacial Lakes Association. Estab. 1978. Annual outdoor show held first weekend in June. Average attendance: 20,000.
Terms: Entries accepted until approximately 5 weeks before show. Entry fee: $20/12x12 display space. Prejudging by 3 slides or photos; 1 must be of display. Work may be offered for sale; no commission. Craftworker must attend show; demonstrations OK. Registration limit: by invitation and juried. Considers arts and crafts by exhibitor. Submit 3 slides or photographs of display. Sponsor provides limited electricity for demonstrations.
Promotion: Show is advertised by radio, T.V., billboards, newspapers, national magazines, posters, brochures and 3 state tourism departments and AAA.

LEMMON CHAMBER OF COMMERCE CHRISTMAS FAIR, 500 A Main Ave., Lemmon SD 57638. (605)374-5716. Executive Secretary and Manager: Elaine Dolin. Purpose: "to promote Lemmon during the holiday season." Estab. 1972. Annual indoor show held 1 day in November or December. Average attendance: 700. Entries accepted until 1 week before show (may be on a list in case there is an opening after the 1 week deadline). Entry fee: $5/6x8 display area. Work may be offered for sale; no commission. Craftworker must attend show; demonstrations OK. Registration limit: about 60. Sponsor provides electricity for demonstrations. Show is advertised by newspapers; circulars; radio; and direct mail. Considers all crafts. "Most of the crafts sold at this Fair are for Christmas gifts or personal use. So, generally gear the crafts for Christmas time."

*****NORTHWESTERN CRAFTSMEN**, South Dakota Memorial Art Center, Harvey Dunn St. at Medary Ave., Brookings SD 57007. (605)688-5423. Assistant to the Director: Rex Gulbranson. Purpose: "to promote and show craftsmen from Iowa, Minnesota, Nebraska, North Dakota and South Dakota." Estab. 1974. Entry by invitation only. No entry fee. Maximum 3 entries per craftworker. Prejudging by slides or photos. Work may be offered for sale; 20% commission. Craftworker needn't attend show; no demonstrations. Registration limit: 30-40. Sponsor provides insurance on exhibited work and on work shipped to artist from show; shipping costs to artist from show; 24-hour security; publishes a show catalog; and sales are handled by the South Dakota Memorial Art Center Shop. Show is advertised by newspaper publicity; radio; and South Dakota State University's entertainment calendar. Submit resume for publicity. Presents purchase awards. Bestsellers: items under $200.
Acceptable Work: Considers batik; ceramics; glass art; jewelry; macrame; metalsmithing; mobiles; pottery; sculpture; soft sculpture; and weavings.

*****RED CLOUD INDIAN ART SHOW**, Red Cloud Indian School, Pine Ridge SD 57770. (605)867-5491. Director: Brother C.M. Simon, S.J. Purpose: "to better acquaint people with Indian heritage and Indian art." Estab. 1968. Annual indoor show held from mid-June to mid-August. Average attendance: 4,000. Entries accepted until 3 weeks before show. No entry fee. Maximum 3 crafts/craftworker. "If entries exceed exhibit space, they are prejudged at show, and extras are put in the gift shop." All work must be offered for sale; no commission. Craftworker needn't attend show; demonstrations OK. Registration limit: 80. Sponsor provides insurance on exhibited work and on work shipped to craftworker; 24-hour security; and handles sales. Categories: oil paintings; watercolors; graphics; mixed media; and 3-dimensional. Considers sculpture. "Indian theme not necessary, but preferred." Presents $1,150 in cash prizes and $1,500 in purchase awards. Bestsellers: "good quality work, with Indian themes in the less than $200 price range."

SHORT GRASS ARTS FESTIVAL, Box 55, Pierre SD 57501. (605)224-7402. President: Jim Carter. Sponsor: Short Grass Arts Council. Purpose: "to promote the arts in this area. Also to provide a way for artisans to display and sell their work." Estab. 1973. Annual outdoor show held 2 days in the summer at Griffin Park. Average attendance: 500-1,000. Entries accepted until 3 weeks before show. Entry fee: $10/10x10 display area. Work may be offered for sale; no commission. Craftworker must attend show; demonstrations encouraged. Sponsor provides electricity for demonstrations and fencing; assumes no liability. Considers all crafts.
Sales Tip: "Pottery seems to sell well. Knitted items, especially for babies, and Western art also sell quite well. A well-designed booth seems to attract people, as well as a well thought out demonstration. Be prepared for all sorts of questions."
Promotion: Show is advertised by radio; TV; newspapers; and posters. "Send 8x10 b&w glossies of you involved with your work with information on background for promotional consideration. Feature articles in the newspaper with pictures of the artist seem to go over well."

WEST BOULEVARD SUMMER FESTIVAL, Box 2487, Rapid City SD 57709. Contact: Norm Nelson or Sandy Hudyma. Sponsor: West Boulevard Neighborhood Association. Estab. 1977. Annual outdoor show held 2 days in June. Average attendance: 3,000-5,000. Considers all original crafts.
Terms: Entries accepted until full ("probably 2-3 weeks before"). Entry fee: $20 nonrefundable. Display area: 10x10 or 12x12. Work may be offered for sale; no commisison. Craftworker must attend show; demonstrations encouraged. Sponsor provides electricity for demonstrations, some plastic for rain cover and 24-hour security.
Sales Tip: "Those who demonstrate seem to have a slight advantage. Bestsellers included wooden toys, laminated wood bowls, handwork pillows, etc. Craftspeople seemed to do better than artists."
Promotion: Show is advertised by radio, TV, posters, South Dakota tourism offices and South Dakota Arts Council. For publicity consideration, craftworkers should submit 8x10 b&w glossies useful for TV and newspaper coverage.

Tennessee

ARTS & CRAFTS MART, Standards Committee, Box 3361, Kingsport TN 37664. Sponsor: Metropolitan Sertoma Club. Annual indoor show held in the spring at Fort Henry Mall. Entries accepted until 6 weeks before show for previous entries. Entry fee: $50 for a 64 square foot booth. Send slides, resume and price list. No commission. Registration limit: 50. Sponsor provides pegboard and electricity. Considers all crafts.

ARTS & CRAFT SHOW & SALE, Box 141, Murfreesboro TN 37130. (615)893-1646 or 893-6537. Chairman: W. Harold Duncan. Sponsor: Noon Lions Club. Purpose: fundraiser. Semi-annual indoor show held 2 days in the spring and 2 days in the fall. Average attendance: 5,000/day. Applications for entry sent out to potential exhibitors 90 days prior to show. Entry fee: $10/8x10 (or larger) display area. "Prejudging by slides, unless work has been seen by a member of the committee at another show and invitation was issued"; entry fee due after prejudging. Work must be offered for sale; 10% commission. Craftworker must attend show; demonstrations OK. Registration limit: 80. Sponsor provides insurance on exhibited work; handles Visa and MasterCharge; and 24-hour security. Show is advertised by radio; newspaper; and TV. Considers all crafts except batik.

*****ARTS & CRAFTS SHOW**, Box 611, Lawrenceburg TN 38464. President: Jerry Tipper. Sponsor: Lawrence County Arts Commission. Estab. 1971. Annual indoor/outdoor show held 2 days in August. Average attendance: 20,000. Entries accepted until show date. Entry fee: $10, outdoors; $15, indoors/12x12 display area. Work may be offered for sale; no commission. Craftworker must attend show; demonstrations OK. Sponsor provides electricity for demonstrations and 24-hour security. Show is advertised by radio; magazines; billboards; and posters. Considers all crafts. Presents $10, 1st prize; and 2nd and 3rd place ribbons.

*****THE CAROLINA CRAFTSMEN'S CHRISTMAS CLASSIC**, 3603 Old Battleground Rd.,

Greensboro NC 27410. (919)288-1933. Executive Director: Clyde Gilmore. Estab. 1978. Annual indoor show held 2 days in November at Chattanooga, Tennessee. Considers all crafts. Presents purchase prizes and plaques.

Terms: Write for entry deadlines and fees. Prejudging by slides, photos and/or newspaper articles; entry fee due after prejudging. Work may be offered for sale; no commission. Craftworker must attend show; demonstrations OK. Sponsor provides chairs, curtained booth areas and 24-hour security.

*DAVID CROCKETT ARTS & CRAFTS FESTIVAL, Lawrence County Arts Commission, Box 611, Lawrenceburg TN 38464. Contact: Ardythe Craig. Annual show held in August. Entries accepted until show date. Entry fee: $10, outside; $10-15, inside. Work may be offered for sale; no commission. Considers sculpture; ceramics; leathercraft; needlecraft; metalcraft; jewelry; and lapidary. Presents cash purchase prizes and ribbons.

*DOGWOOD ARTS FESTIVAL STATE CRAFTS FAIR, Box 2506, Knoxville TN 37901. (615)523-2151, ext. 204. Assistant Director: Dan Alvis. Sponsor: The Arts Council, West Town Mall and Dogwood Arts Festival. Purpose: "to provide a market for craftsmen of Tennessee; to educate the public as to the strength of Tennessee crafts; and to augment the Dogwood Arts Festival." Entries accepted until 8 weeks before show. Entry fee: $5/10x15 display area. Prejudging by 5 slides submitted with application; no entry fees refunded for refused work. Work may be offered for sale; 10% commission. Craftworker must attend show; demonstrations OK. Registration limit: 75. Sponsor provides chairs; electricity for demonstrations; table; 24-hour security; name cards; assistance maps; unloading assistance; booth assistance; MasterCharge and Visa facilities; and show officials collect sales tax at the end of the show. Presents $500 in cash awards: $100, best of show; and 8 $50 merit awards. Bestsellers of 1979: pottery, fiber/textiles, metal, glass wood. 1979 exhibitor sales totalled $25,995.34.

Acceptable Work: Considers batik; dollmaking; stained and blown glass; jewelry; leatherworking; macrame; metalsmithing; possibly mobiles; needlecrafts; pottery; sculpture; soft sculpture; weaving; and woodcrafting. "No dried flower arrangements; pressed flowers; seed pod decorations; decorated or painted boxes; decoupage; or objects made of commercially-produced parts or paintings."

FALL COLOR CRUISE CRAFT SHOW & FOLK MUSIC FESTIVAL, 5832 Northshore Dr., Chattanooga TN 37343. Contact: Show Chairman. Sponsor: Mid-South Hobby, Crafts & Arts Association and Chattanooga Area Convention & Visitors Bureau. Estab. 1974. Annual outdoor show (in large tent) held the last 2 weekends in October. Average attendance: 25,000/weekend.

Acceptable Work: Considers all crafts. No kits, merchandise bought for resale or work shown on consignment. All must be the work of the exhibitor.

Terms: Limited to members of Mid-South Hobby, Crafts and Arts Association and a few selected prospective members. Display area: 10x10. Prejudging for prospective members by photos and interview. Entry fee refunded for refused work. SASE. Work must be offered for sale; no commission. Craftworker must attend show; demonstrations required. Registration limit: 55. Sponsor provides electricity for demonstrations and 24-hour security. Exhibitor handles sales and taxes.

Promotion: Show is advertised by newspaper, TV and radio. Provide b&w glossy photos for newspaper.

FOOTHILLS CRAFT GUILD SHOW & SALE, Box 99, Oak Ridge TN 37830. Co-director: Jude Martin. Sponsor: The Guild and Oak Ridge City Department of Recreation. Purpose: "to educate the public; to give Tennessee craftsmen a reliable outlet; to provide cash for scholarships, the guild library, monthly newsletter, poster contest and high school craft show competitions." Estab. 1968. Annual indoor show held 3 days always the first weekend in November. Average attendance: 12,000. No entry fee; but $5 membership fee. Display area: 8x8-8x16. "Write for application. Craftsman must submit 3 pieces of work; if they pass standards set by 2 standards judges, then they are voted on by board of directors; if that passes, then the work is voted on by the membership." Work may be offered for sale; 20% commission. Craftworker must attend show; demonstrations encouraged. Registration limit: 80-95. Sponsor provides chairs; electricity for demonstrations; table; volunteer relief; and 24-hour security. Presents "Chucky," an original sculpture by Chuck Caldwell, for the best-looking booth.

Acceptable Work: Considers batik; candlemaking; ceramics; dollmaking; glass art; jewelry; lapidary; leatherworking; macrame; metalsmithing; needlecrafts (stitchery); pottery; sculpture; soft sculpture; weaving; woodcrafting; basketry; brooms; wrought iron; bread dough;

quilting; needlepoint; counted thread embroidery; and pipes. No decoupage or fine arts.
Promotion: Show is advertised by newspaper articles and ads; listings in national craft magazines; posters and postcards; and TV coverage. "On sending in booth contracts, the craftworker should send photos, list name and address of their local newspapers, and answer all questions concerning publicity."

GRINDERS SWITCH ARTS & CRAFTS FAIR, 107 Huddleston St., Centerville TN 37033. (615)729-3054. Chairman: Martha Chessor. Sponsor: Hickman County Art Guild. Estab. 1974. Annual outdoor show held 2 days in June. Average attendance: 8,000. Entries accepted until show date. Entry fee: $10/12x30 display area. Work must be offered for sale; no commission. Craftworker must attend show; demonstrations encouraged. Considers all crafts.
Profile: "Displays are set up in wooded camping sites and vehicles may be kept at exhibitor's site without distraction. Overnight camping, a bath house and showers are available at $3/night."

HARDING MALL ARTS & CRAFTS SHOW, 615 South 'H' St., Lake Worth FL 33460. (305)968-9029. Contact: Jim Readey. Sponsor J.J. Readey Promotions. Semiannual indoor show held 3 days in October and May at Nashville, Tennessee.
Acceptable Work: Considers all original crafts. "A drop cloth is a must. Height of racks: 6'6" maximum"
Terms: Entries accepted until 1 week before show or until spaces are filled. Entry fee: $35/12x6' display area. No refunds after closing date, unless show is cancelled. No confirmations sent—use cancelled check as confirmation. Work may be offered for sale; no commission. Craftworker must attend show; demonstrations OK. "All artists must exhibit complete hours of the show. Anyone leaving a show before closing will be refused entrance into further shows. Supply your own racks and tables. Tables must be covered to floor on all sides. Work left up overnight is at your own risk."
Promotion: "We would appreciate glossy b&w photos for publicity releases."
Profile: Located in enclosed and air conditioned mall. "We suggest dressing appropriate to your craft."

LIONS CLUB SPRING ARTS & CRAFT SHOW, Box 141, Murfreesboro TN 37130. (615)893-1646. Co-chairman: W.H. Duncan. Semiannual indoor/outdoor show held 2 days in April and November. Average attendance: 10,000. Closing date for entry: about 30 days before show. Entry fee: $10/8x10 display area. Prejudging; display area fee refunded for refused work. Work must be offered for sale; 10% commission. Craftworker must attend show. Registration limit: 58 booths, fall; 88 booths, spring. Sponsor provides insurance during exhibit period and MasterCharge and Visa at no discount to exhibitor. Considers all crafts.

*****MIDLAND CENTER ARTS & CRAFTS FESTIVAL**, Box 237, Maryville TN 37801. Festival Director: Katie Gorman. Sponsor: Blount County Arts & Crafts Guild and Midland Merchants. "The Blount County Arts & Crafts Guild is obligated by its by-laws to provide shows annually for display and sale of art. $1 of each registration goes to scholarship (art) fund of the Blount County Arts & Crafts Guild. Remainder pays for expenses and publicity." Estab. 1977. Annual outdoor show (under covered mall) held 2 days in June at Alcoa, Tennessee. Average attendance: 30,000. Entries accepted until 2 weeks before show. Entry fee: $25/5x12 display area. Prejudging of new exhibitors by 3 slides or photos; entry fee due after prejudging. Work must be offered for sale. Craftworker must attend show; demonstrations OK if approved prior to show. Registration limit: 200. Sponsor provides electricity for demonstrations and MasterCharge and Visa facilities for a 5% charge. Presents $1,000 in purchase awards and ribbons.
Acceptable Work: Considers batik; dollmaking; jewelry; lapidary; leatherworking; macrame; metalsmithing; needlecrafts; pottery; sculpture; tole painting; weaving; and woodcrafting. No crackle art; commercial jewelry; crochet; decoupage; dip flowers; knitting; marble figures; plaster art; paper tole; or ceramics from commercial molds.
Promotion: Show is advertised by TV (48 paid spots on 3 Knoxville channels, plus 18 public service spots); radio (120 public service spots in 28 cities); newspaper (48 inches in *Knoxville News Sentinell and Journal* run in 2 editions, and 48 inches in the *Maryville Daily Times*; 500 posters; 2,000 leaflets; and 2,000 enclosures. Submit b&w photo of self with work for newspaper use. Resumes for articles are also welcome.

MID-SOUTH ARTS & CRAFTS SHOW/SALE, 5618 Fox Meadows Cove, Memphis TN (901)363-4178. Sponsor: Virginia and Bill Miller. Estab. 1971. Annual indoor show held 3 days in November at Cook Convention Center in Memphis. Average attendance: 20,000. Entries

accepted until approximately 3 months before show. Entry fee: $60/10x10 display area. Prejudging by 8x10 glossy prints or minimum 3 slides; entry fee refunded for refused work. Work may be offered for sale; no commission. Craftworker must attend show; demonstrations OK. Registration limit: 300. Sponsor provides chairs; table; and 24-hour security. Considers all crafts.
Promotion: Show is advertised in area newspapers; TV; and by radio. "Submit 8x10 glossies of exhibitor with his work and brief description of craft and individual's background."

*MID-SOUTH CRAFTS FAIR, Memphis Pink Palace Museum, 3050 Central Ave., Memphis TN 38111. (901)454-5603. Contact: Chairperson, Mid-South Crafts Fair. Estab. 1973. Annual outdoor show (with some tents) held 4 days in October. Average attendance: 20,000-25,000.
Acceptable Work: Considers batik, candlemaking, dollmaking, jewelry, lapidary, leatherworking, macrame, metalsmithing, mobiles, pottery, quilting, scrimshaw, weaving and woodcrafting.
Terms: Entries accepted until approximately 6 months before show. Entry fee: $75/10x20 grounds space; $100/10x10 tent space; $125/10x15 tent space. Prejudging fee: $7.50 nonrefundable. Prejudging by slides accompanied by SASE. Work may be offered for sale; no commission. Craftworker must attend show; demonstrations encouraged. Registration limit: about 75.
Sales Tip: "Large market for small items, especially those priced under $25. Emphasis of show is on crafts."

MISSISSIPPI RIVER CRAFT SHOW, Brooks Memorial Art Gallery, Overton Park, Memphis TN 38112. Biennial show held during odd-numbered years. Open to craftworkers residing in a state bordering on the Mississippi River.

MOTHER'S DAY SHOW—PLANTS, WOOD & PLANT RELATED ITEMS, 615 South 'H' St., Lake Worth FL 33460. (305)968-9029. Contact: Jim Readey. Sponsor J.J. Readey Promotions. Annual indoor show held 4 days in May at Hickory Hollow Mall, Nashville, Tennessee.
Acceptable Work: Considers all plants, wood and plant related items including pottery and macrame. "A drop cloth is a must. Height of racks: 6'6" maximum"
Terms: Entries accepted until 1 week before show or until spaces are filled. Entry fee: $50/12x4' display area; some larger. No refunds after closing date, unless show is cancelled. No confirmations sent—use cancelled check as confirmation. Work may be offered for sale; no commission. Craftworker must attend show; demonstrations encouraged. "All artists must exhibit complete hours of the show. Anyone leaving a show before closing will be refused entrance into further shows. Supply your own racks and tables. Tables must be covered to floor on all sides. Work left up overnight is at your own risk."
Promotion: "We would appreciate glossy b&w photos for publicity releases."
Profile: Located in enclosed and air conditioned mall. Approximately 135 stores including Sears.

NASHVILLE HOBBY & CRAFT CHRISTMAS MARKET, c/o Fred and Ruth Hicks, Rt. 1, Box 155-D, Fairview TN 37062. (615)799-0084. Estab. 1974. Annual indoor show held 2 days the first weekend in December at the Tennessee State Fairgrounds. Average attendance: 30,000. Considers all crafts. "We try to not overload a craft field."
Terms: Entries accepted until show date or filled. Entry fee: $50/10x10 display area. Work may be offered for sale; no commission. Craftworker must attend show; demonstrations OK. Registration limit: 250. Sponsor provides chairs; curtains at rear of booth; electricity for demonstrations; 1 table (extras at $3 each); and 24-hour security.
Promotion: Show is advertised by talk shows, county seat papers, trade papers, TV, FM radio and other means. "We ask exhibitors for slides of work, news articles and we have several craftspeople appear on TV."
Sales Tip: "Corner space is provided for craftspeople who demonstrate their work as long as available. The best sales seem to be made by those demonstrating. The theme is gift buying, so these items sell best."

NATIONAL CRAFTS FESTIVAL, Box 928, Pigeon Forge TN 37863. (615)453-4616. Special Events Manager: Nellie Speer. Estab. 1977. Sponsor: Silver Dollar City. Annual outdoor show (with tents and porches for covering) held 9 days in October. Average attendance: 25,000. Show is advertised by TV, radio and newspapers.
Acceptable Work: Considers candlemaking, decoupage, dollmaking, jewelry, lapidary, leatherworking, macrame, metalsmithing, needlecrafts, sculpture, tole painting, weaving and woodcrafting. "All crafts must be fitting with the 1800s theme of Silver Dollar City."

Terms: "Entries accepted when there is an available space." No entry fee. Prejudging by slides or photos with application, or personal interview preferred. Work may be offered for sale; 15% commission. Craftworker must attend show; "demonstrations required 80% of the time." Registration limit: about 50. Sponsor provides chairs; coverings; electricity; for demonstrations; table; and 24-hour security. "Sales are handled by the craftsman. Daily sales sheets must be turned in. After the sales tax is collected it may be turned into Silver Dollar City to be paid under the corporate sales tax number."
Profile: "Demonstration can be a blend of talking about your craft and actually making an item. No power tools are allowed. Any modern materials which would not have existed in the late 1800s must be disguised (Elmer's Glue can be put in a Mason jar)."

***NOON LIONS CLUB ART—CRAFT SHOW & SALE**, Box 141, Murfreesboro TN 37130. (615)893-1646. Chairman: W. Harold Duncan. Estab. 1964. Semiannual indoor/outdoor show (under metal roof) held 2 days in April and and 2 days in November. Average attendance: 10,000. Considers all original crafts.
Terms: Entries accepted until 4 weeks before show. Entry fee: $10/8x10 display area. Prejudging by slides/photos. Work must be offered for sale; 10% commission. Craftworker must attend show; demonstrations OK. Sponsor provides electricity for demonstrations, insurance on exhibited work and 24-hour security protection.
Promotion: Show is advertised by TV, radio and newspapers. Send photo and write-up for promotional purposes.
Sales Tip: "Almost no abstract sells. Sales can be made on Visa and MasterCharge with no discount to exhibitors." November shows average total of $20,000.

OLDE TYME ARTS & CRAFTS FAIRE, 615 South 'H' St., Lake Worth FL 33460. (305)968-9029. Contact: Jim Readey. Sponsor J.J. Readey Promotions. Annual indoor show held 5 days in June at Rivergate Mall, Nashville, Tennessee.
Acceptable Work: Considers leather, furniture, rug hooking, weavings, wood items, decoupage, sculpture, china painting (including jewelry), shell craft (no jewelry), egg craft (including jewelry) and woodcarving. No basketweaving, jewelry, lapidary, wax, macrame or dried flowers. "A drop cloth is a must. Height of racks: 6'6" maximum."
Terms: Entries accepted until 1 week before show or until spaces are filled. Entry fee: $60/10x10' display area. No refunds after closing date, unless show is cancelled. No confirmations sent—use cancelled check as confirmation. Prejudging by 3 slides. Work may be offered for sale; no commission. Craftworker must attend show; demonstrations OK. "All artists must exhibit complete hours of the show. Anyone leaving a show before closing will be refused entrance into further shows. Supply your own racks and tables. Tables must be covered to floor on all sides. Work left up overnight is at your own risk."
Promotion: "We would appreciate glossy b&w photos for publicity releases."
Profile: Occurs during National Fanfare Week. Located in enclosed and air conditioned mall. Anchor stores are Cain Sloan Co., Caster Knott and Penney's; mall includes 70 other stores.

***PAINTS, POTS & POTPOURRI**, Box 74, Hermitage TN 37076. (615)883-0331 or 889-2673. Arts & Crafts Chairwoman: June McCormack. Sponsor: Stones River Women's Club. Estab. 1976. Annual show held 2 days in October at Donelson, Tennessee. Considers all handmade crafts.
Terms: Entries accepted until show date. Entry fee: $15/10x10 display area. Work must be offered for sale; no commission. "We ask for 1 piece of work from each craftsman to raffle off for our club projects." Craftworker or representative must attend show; demonstrations OK. Sponsor provides electricity for demonstrations.
Awards: Presents cash award for Best In Show and 1 blue ribbon for each category.

PIKEVILLE ARTS & CRAFTS SHOW, Rt. 1, Box 314A, Pikeville TN 37367. (615)447-6280. Chairperson: Mary E. Smith. Sponsor: Black Fox Festival. Estab. 1975. Semiannual outdoor show (indoors if rain) held 2 days in May. Average attendance: about 20,000. Entries accepted until 2 weeks before show. Entry fee: $5/craftworker. Display area: 10x10. Prejudging by photo; entry fee refunded for refused work. Work may be offered for sale; 10% commission. Craftworker or representative must attend show; demonstrations OK. Registration limit: 50 (no more than 2/category). Show is advertised by TV; radio; newspapers; and trade magazines. "Submit b&w Polaroid or glossies for publicity purposes."
Acceptable Work: Considers batik; candlemaking; glass art; decoupage; lapidary; needlecrafts; mobiles; pottery; sculpture; soft sculpture; tole painting; weaving; woodcrafting; and basketwork.

RIVERGATE MALL SUMMER FESTIVAL OF ARTS & CRAFTS, 615 S. "H" St., Lake Worth FL 33460. (305)582-6133. Director: J.J. Readey. Estab. 1976. Annual indoor show held 1 week in June at Nashville, Tennessee. Attendance: 30,000. Entries accepted until 1 week before show. Entry fee: $60/10x10 display area. Prejudging by 3 slides or color photos; entry fee refunded for refused work. Work may be offered for sale; no commission. Craftworker or representative must attend show; demonstrations OK. Registration limit: 60. Sponsor provides electricity for demonstrations if requested in advance. Submit 8x10 b&w glossy photo and resume for newspaper release.
Acceptable Work: Considers batik; decoupage; dollmaking; glass art; mobiles; needlecrafts; sculpture; soft sculpture; tole painting; woodcrafting; egg craft; and china painting. "Emphasis is on old fashioned arts and crafts. Others acceptable."

*****TOWNSEND ARTS & CRAFTS FAIR**, Box 204, Townsend TN 37882. (615)448-2259. President: J. L. Wilsford. Sponsor: Nawger Nob Inc. Estab. 1974. Annual outdoor show held 3 days beginning in late June. Average attendance: 5,000-6,000 paid. Show is advertised by newspapers, magazines, radio, TV and posters.
Acceptable Work: Considers all crafts. "Items must be handcrafted; no factory-type work."
Terms: Entries accepted until 6 weeks before show. Entry fee: $20/15x20 display area. Work may be offered for sale; no commission. Craftworker must attend show; demonstrations OK. Registration limit: 100. Sponsor provides electricity for demonstrations, fencing and 24-hour security.
Sales Tip: "We are in the Great Smokey Mountains (a tourist area) so items should be small enough to pack in a car."
Awards: Presents $50 cash for 1st place; $25 for 2nd place; purchase awards for Best Craft, Best Art and Best Display. $225 worth of awards total.

TUCKALEECHEE COVE ARTS, CRAFTS & MUSIC FESTIVAL, Box 66, Townsend TN 37882. (615)448-6461. Chairman: Mary Hmielewski. Sponsor: Townsend Chamber of Commerce. Purpose: "to create an awareness of crafts, especially mountain crafts, as we are in a tourist area. Townsend is the western entrance to the Great Smoky Mountain Park." Estab. 1974. Annual outdoor show (with spaces under a large circus tent) held 3 days the last weekend in September. Average attendance: 8,000-10,000. Entry fee: $25 and you bring your own canopy. Display area: 10x10 or 12x12. Prejudging by 3 photos or slides; entry fee refunded for refused work. Work may be offered for sale; no commission. Craftworker must attend show; demonstrations OK. Sponsor provides electricity for demonstrations and night security. Show is advertised by radio and TV. Considers all crafts except decoupage; soft sculpture; crackle art; dip flowers; marble figures; plaster art; or paper tole.

TWO RIVERS MALL ARTS & CRAFTS SHOW, 615 South 'H' St., Lake Worth FL 33460. (305)968-9029. Contact: Jim Readey. Sponsor J.J. Readey Promotions. Semiannual indoor show held 4 days in June and November at Clarksville, Tennessee.
Acceptable Work: Considers all original crafts. No wax or belt buckles (except on belts). "A drop cloth is a must. Height of racks: 6'6" maximum"
Terms: Entries accepted until 1 week before show or until spaces are filled. Entry fee: $40/12x6' display area. No refunds after closing date, unless show is cancelled. No confirmations sent—use cancelled check as confirmation. Prejudging by 3 slides if have not previously shown with J.J. Ready. SASE. Work may be offered for sale; no commission. Craftworker must attend show; demonstrations OK. "All artists must exhibit complete hours of the show. Anyone leaving a show before closing will be refused entrance into further shows. Supply your own racks and tables. Tables must be covered to floor on all sides. Work left up overnight is at your own risk."
Promotion: "We would appreciate glossy b&w photos for publicity releases."
Profile: Located in enclosed and air conditioned mall. Anchor stores are Sears, Park-Belks, Walgreens, Kress; mall includes 26 other stores.

*****WEBB SCHOOL ART & CRAFT FESTIVAL**, The Webb School, Bell Buckle TN 37020. (615)275-3641. Chairman: Carol McCall. Estab. 1977. Annual outdoor show held 2 days in the fall. Average attendance: 8,000-10,000. Entries accepted until October 1. Entry fee: $15. Display area: 15x15. Prejudging by 5 slides or photos; entry fee due after prejudging. Work may be offered for sale; no commission. Craftworker must attend show; demonstrations encouraged. Registration limit: 100. Sponsor provides electricity for demonstrations. Categories: graphics; painting; sculpture; jewelry; pottery; fibers; and traditional crafts. Considers all original crafts except ceramics and decoupage.

Awards: Presents over $2,000 total awards: over $1,000, purchase; 1st, 2nd and 3rd place ribbons and cash awards in each category; and 2 best of show awards (1 in art division; 1 in craft division).
Promotion: Show is advertised by newspapers; radio; TV; posters; and postcards. "Submit b&w photo of self and work, or, preferably, self working at craft."

*THE WISHING WELL ARTS & CRAFTS FESTIVAL, c/o The Wishing Well, 7501 E. Brainerd Rd., Chattanooga TN 37421. (615)899-9496. Contact: Susanne or Bob Johnson. Estab. 1976. Annual outdoor show held 2 days in September. Entries by invitation only. Will accept photos of work for consideration. Work may be offered for sale; no commission. Considers all crafts. Presents awards."

Texas

AMERICANA DAY CELEBRATION, Box 424, Baytown TX 77520. (713)427-7477. Recreation Supervisor: Laurie Kelley. Sponsor: City of Baytown Park and Recreation Department. Estab. 1973. Annual outdoor show held 4th of July. Average attendance: 20,000. Entries accepted until about 2 weeks before show. Entry fee: $10/8x10 display area. Work may be offered for sale; no commission. Craftworker must attend show; demonstrations OK. Registration limit: 80. Show is advertised by radio; newspapers; and posters. Considers all crafts.

ART JAMBOREE, Box 1010, Corpus Christi TX 78403. (512)884-3844, Artists' Contact: Chairman. Sponsors: The Auxiliary to the Art Museum of South Texas, Kappa Alpha Theta Alum and Delta Delta Delta Alumnae. Purpose: fundraiser. Estab. 1963. Annual outdoor show held 1 day in April. Average attendance: 5,000. Entries accepted until about 3 weeks before show. Entry fee: $50/craftworker. Display area: $50/10x10 space; $35 for second person in shared space; $85/retail business. Work may be offered for sale; no commission. Craftworker must attend show; demonstrations OK. Registration limit: 200. Show is advertised by "as much advertising as we can acquire from donations; been very good in the past." Considers all crafts.

ARTS & CRAFTS FAIR, 401 N. Carancahua, Corpus Christi TX 78412. (512)882-4351. Executive Director: Jean Keas. Sponsor: YWCA and City Park and Recreation. Purpose: "This show has a long history of providing a service to the community in bringing good craftsmanship and art work to the public." Estab. 1950. Annual indoor show held 2 days in November. Considers all crafts.
Terms: Entries accepted until 3 months before show. "Applicants must get on our mailing list by May or no later than June to meet the entry deadline." Entry fee: $50 plus table costs/8x12 display area. Prejudging by slides or photos; entry fee refunded for refused work. Work may be offered for sale; no commission. Craftworker must attend show; demonstrations OK if feasible. Registration limit: 200. Sponsor provides chairs; display panels; limited electricity for demonstrations; 24-hour security; and Bank Americard/MasterCharge service.
Promotion: Show is advertised by newspaper; radio; TV; and poster campaign. Categories: art; craft; and bazaar.

*ARTS & CRAFTS FESTIVAL, Box 75, Killeen TX 76541. (817)634-2168. Arts and Crafts Chairman: John E. Carter. Sponsor: Greater Killeen Chamber of Commerce, Killeen Art Guild, and Arts and Crafts Teachers in the Killeen Independent School District. Purpose: "to stimulate an interest in original artistic endeavors both in the artist and the observer regardless of age." Estab. 1964. Annual indoor show held 3 days in April. Average attendance: 8,000. Entries accepted until 1 day before show; "exhibitors must reside within 75 miles of Killeen." Maximum 2 pieces per craftworker per category. Show is advertised by local and area media. Presents cash awards totalling $300. Considers all crafts.

*ARTS IN ACTION, Amarillo Chamber of Commerce, Amarillo Bldg., Amarillo TX 79101. (806)374-5238. Assistant Manager: F. LeRoy Tillery. Purpose: a showcase for artists and craftsmen. Estab. 1972. Annual indoor show held 2 days in November. Average attendance: 5,000. Entries accepted until 3 weeks before show; late entries accepted until full. Entry fee: $40/8x10 display area. For awards, maximum 1 piece per craftworker. Prejudging by slides or photos; entry fee refunded for refused work. Work may be offered for sale; no commission. Craftworker must attend show; demonstrations OK. Registration limit: 150. Sponsor provides chairs; display panels for extra fee; electricity for demonstrations; table; and 24-hour security. Show is advertised by local and statewide media; "we are one of 4 regional state shows." Submit publicity photo and promotional information. Presents ribbon awards for 1st; 2nd; 3rd; and honorable mention in 11 categories. Considers all crafts.

BLACK EYED PEA JAMBOREE ARTS & CRAFTS SHOW, Box 608, Athens TX 75751. (214)675-5181. Chairman: Jimmie Del Moore. Sponsor: Athens Chamber of Commerce. Estab. 1971. Annual outdoor show held 3 days in July. Average attendance: 10,000. Entries accepted until 1 week before show. Entry fee: $15/display area. Work may be offered for sale; no commission. Craftworker must attend show; no demonstrations. Registration limit: 125-150. Sponsor provides fencing for $10, and 24-hour security. Show is advertised by news media and trade magazines. Submit promotional material.

BOND'S ALLEY ART & CRAFT FAIR, Hillsboro City Library, Hillsboro TX 76645. Chairman: Scotty Cason. Purpose: fundraiser. Estab. 1965. Annual outdoor show (with tents and parachute awnings) held 2 days in June. Average attendance: 4,000-5,000. Entries accepted until May 15. Booth rental $25-60. No commission. Craftworker must attend show; demonstrations OK. Registration limit: 120. Sponsor provides coverings and display panels. Show is advertised by brochures; mailings; newspapers; TV; magazines; radio; and posters. Considers all original crafts.

BORGER FINE ARTS FESTIVAL, Box 490, Borger TX 79007. (806)274-2211. Manager: Colie Donaldson. Sponsor: Women's Division of the Borger Chamber of Commerce. Purpose: "to promote the arts and crafts and to project the hospitable attitude of our town." Estab. 1968. Annual indoor show held 3 days in October. Average attendance: 6,000. Entries accepted until 2 weeks before show. Entry fee: $5/6x10 display area. Work may be offered for sale; no commission. Craftworker or representative must attend show; demonstrations OK. Sponsor provides electricity for demonstrations; table for $5; and 24-hour security. Show is advertised by newspaper; radio; news media; and personal invitation. Submit publicity materials. Considers all crafts.

BUFFALO GAP ART FESTIVAL, Box 1858, Abilene TX 79604. (915)673-4587. Contact: Chairman. Sponsor: Abilene Fine Arts Museum. Estab. 1977. Annual outdoor show held 2 days in May at Buffalo Gap, Texas. Average attendance: 10,000. Entries accepted until 4 weeks before show. Entry fee: $35-60/display area. Prejudging. Entry fee refunded if work refused. Work may be offered for sale; no commission. Craftworker or representative must attend show; demonstrations OK. Registration limit: 100. Show is advertised by newspapers; radio; TV; newsletter; and art and crafts directories. "Any PR by the craftworker will be considered in the general promotion." Considers all crafts.

CENTRAL TEXAS ARTS & CRAFTS SALE, Box 75, Killeen TX 76541. (817)526-9551. Arts and Crafts Chairman: Frank Norvell. Sponsor: Greater Killeen Chamber of Commerce and Killeen Art Guild. Estab. 1976. Annual indoor show held the first Sunday in May. Average attendance: 5,000. Entries accepted until 7 days before show. Entry fee: $35/10x10 display area. "There is no prejudging but new exhibitors are asked to send slides or pictures of items to be sold at the time of their registration." Work may be offered for sale; no commission. Craftworker must attend show; no demonstrations. Registration limit: 50. Show is advertised by local and area media and invitations. Considers all crafts. Bestsellers: craft items indigenous to area.

*****CRAFT SHOW**, Hill Country Arts Foundation, Box 176, Ingram TX 78025. (512)367-5121. Art Chairman: Frances B. Jowdy. Estab. 1967. Biennial indoor show held 2 weeks in April or May. Average attendance: 300. Show is advertised by brochures, newspapers and magazines. **Acceptable Work:** Considers all crafts. "All works must be original and not done in a classroom."
Terms: Entries accepted until 1 week before show. Entry fee: $7 for 3 entries for members. Non-members: $10 for 3 entries. Maximum 3 items. Prejudging by personal interview with actual work. Entry fee not refunded for refused work. Work may be offered for sale; 30% commission. Craftworker needn't attend show; no demonstrations. "All hanging is done by the Hanging Committee using our own props." Hill Country Arts Foundation Art Committee staff handles sales and taxes.
Awards: Presents cash and purchase awards. "All rules of the show must be obeyed and forms filled on arrival. Objects should be attractively framed or displayed. Do not try to enter copies."

CRAFTS VILLAGE AT KERRVILLE MUSIC FESTIVALS, Box 1466, Kerrville TX 78028. (512)896-3800. President: Rod Kennedy. Sponsor: Kerrville Festivals Inc. Purpose: "to complete the festival atmosphere and provide creative people with an outlet for their work." Estab.

1973. Outdoor show (with 50 permanent craft booths) held 4 times a year for 3 days during Memorial Day weekend; 4th of July weekend; last weekend in July; and Labor Day weekend. Average attendance: 4,000. Entries accepted until 1 week before show. Entry fee: $25/8x8 display area. Work may be offered for sale; 10% commission. Craftworker must attend show; demonstrations OK. Registration limit: 50. Sponsor provides electricity for demonstrations and 24-hour security. Show is advertised by 50,000 brochures; 1,000 posters; radio advertising; and heavy publicity campaigns for each weekend. Considers all crafts. Bestsellers: work oriented toward Western motif; for last weekend in July work oriented toward Christian themes.

CREEKWALK ART & CRAFTS SHOW, Star Rt. 1, Box 178, Blanco TX 78606. (512)833-4983; 833-4558. Publicity Chairman: Janet Fisher. Director, Chamber of Commerce: Elizabeth Morgan. Sponsor: Hill Country Artists and Blanco Chamber of Commerce. Estab. 1970. Annual outdoor show held the second Sunday in October. Considers all crafts. No kits or machine-made items. Show is advertised by newspaper, radio and TV.
Terms: Entries accepted until show date or filled. Entry fee: $15/10x12 display area; larger area available for higher fee. Work may be offered for sale. Craftworker must attend show; demonstrations OK (upon special advance request).

FIESTA, 4215 University Ave., Lubbock TX 79413. (806)762-6411, ext. 363. Supervisor: Georgia Booker. Sponsor: Lubbock Garden Arts Center, Inc. Purpose: "to provide sales space for artists, craftsmen, and nonprofit organizations." Estab. 1970. Annual outdoor show held 1 day in September. Average attendance: 5,000-6,000. Entries accepted until 4 weeks before show. Entry fee: $35/5x8 display area. Work may be offered for sale; no commission. Craftworker must attend show; demonstrations OK. Sponsor provides coverings. Show is advertised by Center newsletter; local news media; and handbills. Considers all crafts.

KALEIDOSCOPE, Beaumont Art Museum, 1111 9th St., Beaumont TX 77702. (713)832-3432. Director: Betty W. Hirsch. Estab. 1974. Annual outdoor show held 2 days the 2nd weekend in May. Average attendance: 22,000. Considers all crafts except decoupage and tole painting.
Terms: Entries accepted until mid-February. Entry fee: $100/individual 8x10 display area; $60/shared 8x10 display area. Prejudging by slides; entry fee refunded for refused work. Work may be offered for sale; no commission. Craftworker must attend show.

KERMEZAAR, El Paso Museum of Art, 1211 Montana Ave., El Paso TX 79902. (915)543-3800. Chairman: Kathleen Juel. Sponsor: Members Guild, El Paso Museum of Art Association. Purpose: fundraiser. Estab. 1970. Annual indoor show held 3 days in fall. Average attendance: 10,000. Entries accepted until about 3 months before show. Entry fee: $100/8x8x11 display area. Prejudging by 3 slides; entry fee refunded for refused work. Work may be offered for sale; no commission. Craftworker must attend show; demonstrations OK. Registration limit: 130. Sponsor provides display panels and 24-hour security. "Chairs; table; electricity; and other supplies may be rented at our cost by craftworkers." Show is advertised by local and regional newspapers; magazines; billboards; flyers; radio; and TV. Submit basic biographical details.

LAGUNA GLORIA FIESTA, Box 5705, Austin TX 78763. (512)458-3035. Chairman, Artist Reservations: Lilla Ezell. Sponsor: Laguna Gloria Art Guild. Estab. 1951. Annual outdoor show (booths with sheet metal roofs) held 3 days in May. Average attendance: 35,000.
Acceptable Work: Considers all crafts. Categories: arts; crafts.
Terms: Entries accepted until 22 weeks before show. Entry fee: $120/8x8 booth ($60 if sharing). Prejudging by 3 professional artists; 3 slides representative of work. Entry fee refunded for refused work. Work may be offered for sale; no commission. Craftworker must attend show; demonstrations arranged by committee. Registration limit: 190. Sponsor provides booths with pegboard display panels and sheet metal roofs, electricity for demonstrations (if chosen), and 24-hour security. Exhibitor handles sales and taxes.
Promotion: Show is advertised by "our Public Relations staff in all media: local, state and national. Most artists bring brochures, cards, etc. to provide to the viewing public. Each may also bring a tasteful sign for their booth. This is a benefit for Laguna Gloria Museum."

LUBBOCK ARTS FESTIVAL, Box 561, Lubbock TX 79408. (806)763-4666. Executive Director: James Toland. Sponsor: Lubbock Cultural Affairs Council. Estab. 1979. Annual indoor show held 3 days in April at Lubbock Memorial Civic Center.
Acceptable Work: Considers batik, ceramics, glass art, jewelry, leatherworking, metalsmithing, mobiles, needlecrafts, pottery, scrimshaw, sculpture, tole painting, weavings and

woodcrafting. No molds; plastic or paper flowers; painted rocks or velvet; shell crafts; decoupage; kit crafts; T-shirts; candles; or beads. All jewelry and leatherworking must be handcrafted. "Artist must furnish their own tools, extension cords, tables, shelves and 1 chair/booth."
Terms: Entries accepted until 12 weeks before show. Entry fee: $50/artist. Display area: 8'x12'. "Artists must have sufficient number of work of the same caliber." Prejudging by a 20-person jury; slides representative of artists work. Entry fee due after prejudging. Craftworkers must offer their work for sale; 20% commission. Craftworker must attend show; scheduled demonstrations will be arranged. Sponsor provides display panels, electricity for demonstrations and 24-hour security. "As this is our first show, sales and sales tax will be handled by the Lubbock Arts Festival."
Promotion: Show is advertised by radio, newspapers, magazines, TV and direct mail.

LUBBOCK GARDEN & ARTS CENTER "FIESTA," 4215 University Ave., Lubbock TX 79413. (806)762-6411. Contact: Georgia Booker. Estab. 1967. Annual outdoor show held the second Saturday in September. Average attendance: 5,000-6,000. Entry fee: $35/7x7x5 booth. Craftworker must attend show; demonstrations encouraged. Registration limit: 100 booths. Considers all crafts.

*MAYFEST, 3505 W. Lancaster, Fort Worth TX 76107. (817)738-9181. Chairman: Nancy Ricker. Sponsor: Junior League of Fort Worth; Park and Recreation Department, City of Fort Worth; Streams and Valleys Committee of Fort Worth; and Tarrant County Water Control and Improvement District 1. Estab. 1973. Annual outdoor show (substantial wooden frame booths with canvas coverings) held 4 days in May. Average attendance: 200,000. Considers all crafts.
Terms: Entries accepted until 3 months before show. Entry fee: $75/gallery booth, 252 square feet covered area; $50/full booth, 84 square feet covered area; $25/half booth, 42 square feet. Prejudging by 5 slides; entry fee refunded for refused work. Work may be offered for sale; no commission. Craftworker must attend show; demonstrations encouraged. Registration limit: 50 full booths; 10 gallery booths. Sponsor provides chairs; coverings; display panels; electricity for demonstrations; table; and 24-hour security.
Awards: Presents $3,100 total in cash and purchase awards.
Promotion: Show is advertised by local news media and listing services.

*NATIONAL DRAWING & SMALL SCULPTURE SHOW, Del Mar College, Ayers at Baldwin, Corpus Christi TX 87404. (512)881-6216. Chairman: Joseph A. Cain. Estab. 1967. Annual indoor show held in the spring. Entry fee: $10 (handles entry fee plus return via parcel post, 2 entries). Prejudging of sculpture only by slides; entry fee not refunded. Sponsor provides 24-hour security. Show is advertised by art magazines. Presents cash awards of $3,000 and purchase awards of $2,000. Considers sculpture and soft sculpture. All work must conform to parcel post regulations, 84" length plus girth. One-man shows offered to award winners in sculpture and drawing.

*PARIS ART FAIR, 308 S. Main, Paris TX 75460. (214)785-5221. Executive Director: Linda Clark. Sponsor: Young Women's Christian Association. Held at Paris Junior College Campus. Purpose: "to promote art and artists in an area without a museum." Annual outdoor show held 1 day in April, usually last weekend. Average attendance: 5,000. Stall entries accepted until 2 weeks before show. Entries in competetion accepted day of show. Entry fee: $2/item for prize money, and $25/10x10 display area. Work may be offered for sale; 20% commission from competition; no commission for stall sales. Craftworker must attend show; demonstrations OK. Sponsor provides electricity for demonstrations and 24-hour security. Show is advertised by newspapers; posters; magazines; radio and TV. Presents cash awards of $100 and 16 ribbons. Considers all crafts except decoupage; lapidary; and tole painting.

PEARSALL FALL ARTS & CRAFTS FESTIVAL, 309 E. San Marcos St., Pearsall TX 78061. (512)334-2242. Manager: Dale Martin. Sponsor: Pearsall Chamber of Commerce. Estab. 1972. Annual indoor/outdoor show (with brick veranda with roof) held 2nd Saturday in October. Average attendance: 500. Entries accepted until show is filled. Entry fee: $20/craftworker. Display area: 10x10. Work may be offered for sale; no commission. Craftworker or representative must attend show; demonstrations OK. Registration limit: 50. Sponsor provides electricity for demonstrations. Show is advertised by ads in local artist magazines and crafts publications; radio; and newspapers. Considers all crafts.

---

* Those listings preceded by an asterisk present awards for prize-winning crafts.

RIVER ARTS FESTIVAL, 308 E. Hopkins St., San Marcos TX 78666. (512)392-8332. Arts/Craft Show Chairman: Mrs. Tim Hamilton. Sponsor: Heritage Association of San Marcos, Inc. and Southwest Texas State University. Estab. 1973. Annual outdoor show held last Saturday in April. Average attendance: 5,000. Entries accepted until 2 weeks before show. Entry fee: $15/craftworker. Display area: 10x10. Work may be offered for sale; no commission. Craftworker must attend show; demonstrations encouraged. Registration limit: 90. Sponsor provides electricity for demonstrations. Considers all crafts that are original and not manufactured.
Promotion: Show is advertised by Texas Travel Agency; Texas Tourist Development; TV; *Southern Living*; local and nearby newspapers; and University News Service. Submit brochures or cards on background and work.
Profile: "The Festival takes advantage of the beauty of our river, establishes rapport between the performers, mostly local amateurs and the University's music department, and the people of San Marcos and the Central Texas area. It provides a show case for the artists and craftsmen in our area. We hope to build up a festival that will be a unique experience for this part of the country. It is altogether a family festival; you might say old-fashioned in the full meaning of the word."

RUNNING WATER DRAW ARTS & CRAFTS FESTIVAL, Wayland College, Plainview TX 79072. (806)296-5521. Director: Robert Strong. Sponsor: Rotary Club of Plainview. Purpose: fundraiser. Estab. 1975. Annual indoor show held 3 days in October. Average attendance: 6,000. Entries accepted until show. Entry fee: $35/8x12 display area. Prejudging by 3 slides representative of the type of work planned to be sold; 2x2 color horizontal slides preferred. Entry fee refunded for refused work. Work may be offered for sale; 10% of first $250 sold. Craftworker must attend show; demonstrations recommended. Registration limit: 125. Sponsor provides chairs; display panels; electricity for demonstrations; insurance on exhibited work; 24-hour security; water; and booth assistance. 1977 show sales exceeded $50,000. Considers all crafts.
Promotion: Show is advertised by radio; TV; newspapers; magazines; civic club programs; and city billboard signs. Submit 2x2 color horizontal slides of the types of work to be exhibited.
Profile: "The Festival is the only 1 of its kind in this large geographic area outside of 2 large regional cities so it is well attended by surrounding towns and counties."

SALADO ART FAIR, Box 444, Salado TX 76571. Chairman: Art Fair. Sponsor: Chamber of Commerce. Estab. 1967. Annual outdoor show held the first full weekend in August along the banks of Salado Creek. Average attendance: 15,000. Entries accepted until May 15. Entry fee: $35/craftworker for a 10x10 display area; $50 if shared. Prejudging. Work must be offered for sale; no commission. Craftworker must attend show; demonstrations OK. Registration limit: 175. Sponsor provides 6x8 rack. Considers all crafts.

*****SAN ANTONIO ARTISTS' EXHIBITION**, 310 W. Ashby, San Antonio TX 78212. (512)732-6048. Chairman: Mrs. Dana Young. Sponsor: San Antonio Art League. Purpose: "to encourage the young artists in the area by allowing them to enter a competition judged by a nationally or internationally known juror and compete with their peers for awards and purchase prizes." Estab. 1929. Annual indoor show held 3 weeks in April. Average attendance: 2,000. Entries accepted in March. Entry fee: $5/entry unless Art League member. "Only artists with established current residence within 60 mile radius of San Antonio are eligible." Maximum 3 pieces per craftworker. Prejudging by actual work; entry fee not refunded for refused work. Work may be offered for sale; 30% commission. Craftworker needn't attend show; no demonstrations. Registration limit: 100. Sponsor provides 24-hour security and hangs or displays all work. Show is advertised by newspaper and radio. Presents cash awards and purchase prizes approximating $4,000. Considers all crafts except candlemaking and dollmaking.

SAN GABRIEL ARTS & CRAFTS SHOW, Box 346, Georgetown TX 78626. (512)863-2251. Manager: Vivian Wood. Sponsor: Greater Georgetown Area Chamber of Commerce. Estab. 1971. Annual indoor show held 2 days in November. Average attendance: 3,000. Entries accepted until 1 week before show or until full. Entry fee: $20/10x10 display area. Work may be offered for sale; no commission. Craftworker must attend show; demonstrations OK. Registration limit: 50-60. Sponsor provides chairs; electricity for demonstrations; table; and 24-hour security. Show is advertised by radio; TV; and newspapers. Considers all crafts.

SANTA'S TREASURE HOUSE ARTS & CRAFTS BAZAAR, Box 764, Raymondville TX 78580. (512)689-3171. Manager: Jo Bowyer. Sponsor: Raymondville Chamber of Commerce.

Estab. 1971. Annual indoor show held 1 day in December. Average attendance: 500. Entries accepted up until show. Entry fee: $10/8x8 display area. Work may be offered for sale; no commission. Craftworker needn't attend show; demonstrations OK. Registration limit: 50. Sponsor provides chairs; electricity for demonstrations; and a few tables available. Show is advertised by newspaper; public service announcements on TV and radio; and posters. Considers all crafts. Bestsellers: gift items.

SOUTHWESTERN CRAFT & HOBBY SHOW, 1100 Brandywine Blvd., Box 2188. Zanesville OH 43701. (614)452-4541. Trade Show Director: Walter E. Offinger, Jr. Sponsor: Southwestern Craft & Hobby Association. Purpose: "to bring the industry together. Open to trade buyers only." Estab. 1974. Annual indoor show held 3 days in July at Dallas Market Center. Average attendance: 4,500. Entries accepted until 1 month before show. Entry fee: $325/100 square feet. Display area: 10x10 minimum; no subletting. Work may be offered for sale; no commission. Craftworker or representative must attend show; demonstrations OK. Registration limit: 400. Sponsor provides 2 chair; nightly cleaning; ashtrays; empty crate storage during show; 6' draped table; 24-hour security; waste basket; 3' high side rails draped; 8' draped backwall; and I.D. booth sign. Show is advertised by direct mail sent to 8,000 buyers; advertising in most trade publications; and news releases to all trade publications. Considers all crafts.

SPRING ARTS & CRAFTS SALE, GKCC Box 75, Kileen TX 76541. Chairman: Frank C. Norvell. Sponsor: KIOOD Art Guild and Greater Killeen Chamber of Commerce. Estab. 1975. Annual outdoor show held the first Sunday in May. Considers all crafts.
Terms: Entry fee: $25/12x12 display area. Work must be offered for sale; no commission. Craftworker or representative must attend show; no demonstrations.

Dedicated to preserving a portion of a vanishing mountain lifestyle, the Folk School Fall Festival emphasizes traditional Appalachian skills. The show takes place in the southern Appalachian mountains near the Tennessee and Georgia borders. Sponsored by John C. Campbell Folk School, the festival lasts two days.

SPRING ART & CRAFTS SHOW & SALE, 4200 Ansley Lane, Denison TX 75020. (214)465-5647. Booth Reservation Chairperson: Mrs. John R. Summers. Sponsor: Grayson County Frontier Village, Inc. Purpose: fundraiser. Estab. 1975. Semiannual indoor show held 3 days in May, 3 days in December. Average attendance: 9,000-10,000. Work may be offered for sale; no commission. Craftworker must attend show; demonstrations OK. Registration limit: 70. Sponsor provides 24-hour security. Show is advertised by TV; radio; news media; posters; and flyers. Considers all crafts including soft goods such as crochet; embroidery; aprons; bonnets; and pot holders.

*****SPRING FLING**, 2 Eureka Circle, Wichita Falls TX 76308. (817)692-0923. Director: Larry Francell. Sponsor: Wichita Falls Museum Guild. Purpose: "to bring quality arts and crafts to the Wichita Falls area." Estab. 1971. Annual outdoor show (with covered booths) held 2 days in April. Average attendance: 15,000. Considers all crafts.
Terms: Entries accepted until 2 months before show. Entry fee: $50/craftworker. Display area: 8x8x8. Prejudging by slides; entry fee refunded for refused work. Work may be offered for sale; no commission. Craftworker must attend show; demonstrations OK. Registration limit: 75-80. Sponsor provides coverings; display panels; and 24-hour security.
Awards: Presents 5 cash awards of $100 for outstanding quality, creativity and originality; 10 $50 Gallery of Honor Recognition Awards; $500 in Museum Sales Desk Purchase awards. Categories: 2 dimensional pottery; fiber; toys; musical instruments; and jewelry.
Promotion: Show is advertised by all media and various promotional materials. Submit any promotional materials for publicity.

STARVING ARTIST ART SHOW, 508 Paseo de La Villita, San Antonio TX 78205. (512)226-3593. Chairperson: Cleo Edmunds. Sponsor: The Historic Little Church of La Villita. Purpose: "to help beginning artists get established and as a fundraiser." Estab. 1963. Annual outdoor show held 2 days in March. Average attendance: 50,000. Entries must be postmarked on February 1 or thereafter. Display area: 10' long. Work displayed must be offered for sale; 10% commission. Craftworker must attend show; demonstrations encouraged. Registration limit: 1,000. Sponsor provides electricity for demonstrations if prearranged. Show is advertised by newspapers. Considers all crafts.

STARVING ARTIST'S SALE, GKCC, Box 75, Killeen TX 76541. (817)634-3268. Chairman: John E. Carter. Sponsor: Greater Killeen Chamber of Commerce and KIOOD Art Guild. Purpose: "to provide funds for community art projects and to stimulate the interest of artists and craftsmen." Estab. 1967. Annual outdoor show held first Sunday in October. Entries accepted until 3 days before show. Entry fee: $35/12x12 display area. Work may be offered for sale; limit $35; no commission. Craftworker or representative must attend show; no demonstrations. Registration limit: 110. Show is advertised by letters; radio; TV; and newspaper. 1977 show sales totalled $10,000. Considers all crafts.

*****TEXAS AREA ARTISTS AT VALLEY VIEW CENTER**, 2040 Valley View Center, Dallas TX 75240. (214)661-2424. Marketing Director: Carol Kirchhoff. Sponsor: Texas Area Artists. Estab. 1974. Annual indoor show held 1 week in May. Average attendance: 250,000. Entries accepted until 6 weeks before show. Display area: 10x15. Work may be offered for sale; 10% commission. Craftworker must attend show; demonstrations OK. Registration limit: 50. Sponsor provides electricity for demonstrations and 24-hour security. Show is advertised by newspaper and radio. Submit explanation about craft and resume for publicity. Presents ribbon awards. Considers sculpture. "Pegboard not acceptable. Themed booths only."

TEXAS FOLKLIFE FESTIVAL, 801 S. Bowie, San Antonio TX 78205. (512)226-7651. Festival Manager: Claudia Ball. Sponsor: The Institute of Texan Cultures. Estab. 1972. Annual outdoor show held 4 days in August. Average attendance: 90,000.
Acceptable Work: Considers candlemaking; dollmaking; lapidary; leatherworking; needlecrafts; pottery; weaving; woodcrafting; and folk arts.
Terms: Entries accepted until December. Entrance is by invitation only and it is limited to Texas artists and craftspeople." Display area: multiples of 8'. Work may be offered for sale; 20% commission; artist paid a per diem in event of no sales. Craftworker must attend show; demonstrations required. Sponsor provides electricity for demonstrations; fencing; table; and 24-hour security.
Promotion: Show is advertised by news releases; radio and TV public service announcements; magazines; brochures; posters; and slide shows. Submit b&w photos of self at work.
Profile: "The Festival is an extension of the main floor exhibit of the Institute of Texan

Cultures. It shows living folkways and history of Texans who are the descendents of more than 26 ethnic and cultural groups. These ethnic demonstrations (arts, entertainment, foods) stand alongside folkcrafts, folksongs and storytellers and give the visitor a true and full taste of life in Texas."

TEXAS RENAISSANCE FESTIVAL, Rt. 2, Box 219A-1, Plantersville TX 77363. (713)356-2178. President of Festival: George Coulam. Estab. 1975. Annual outdoor show held Saturday and Sunday for 6 weekends from the last weekend in September-the first weekend in November. Average attendance: 174,000-200,000. Considers all crafts displayed in the spirit of the Renaissance.
Terms: Entries accepted until August 1. Entry fee: $150/15-20 or 22x20' area (this allows 2 craftworkers/area); $75/additional artist. Prejudging by slides, photos and/or samples; entry fee refunded for refused work. Work must be offered for sale. Craftworker must attend show; demonstrations OK. Registration limit: about 200.

*****TEXAS STATE ARTS & CRAFTS FAIR**, Box 1527, Kerrville TX 78028. (512)896-5711. Executive Director: Audie Hamilton. Sponsor: Texas Arts and Crafts Foundation. Purpose: "to showcase the vast array of handcrafted arts and crafts made by native Texans. No out of state artists are allowed to enter." Estab 1972. Annual outdoor show (with huge tents) held 3 days in May. Average attendance: 33,500. Entries accepted until 5 months before show. Entry fee: $85/8x10 covered or 16x20 outdoors display area; $100/display area with electricity. Entry limited to 2 categories. Prejudging by 3 color slides per category; entry fee due after prejudging. Work must be offered for sale; no commission. Craftworker must attend show; demonstrations encouraged. Registration limit: 200. Sponsor provides coverings; display panels; fencing; and 24-hour security. Young artist competition. Considers all crafts except decoupage and tole painting.
Promotion: Show is advertised by full-color brochures; promotional tours; TV; and radio. "We get excellent editorial coverage because we are the official Texas art event." After acceptance submit resume and b&w photo for personal news release to home paper.

THE WESTHEIMER COLONY ART FESTIVAL, 908 Westheimer, Houston TX 77006. (713)521-0133. Contact: Chairperson. Estab. 1973. Semiannual outdoor show held 2 days in April and 2 days in October. Average attendance: 400,000-500,000. Entries accepted until 4 weeks before show. Entry fee: $10 nonrefundable registration fee; $90 booth fee/100 square feet area, refundable. Prejudging by slides or photos; entry fee refunded for refused work. Work may be offered for sale; no commission. Craftworker must attend show; demonstrations OK. Sponsor provides liability insurance and police guards during show. Show is advertised by magazines; newspapers; TV; and radio. Considers all crafts.

WIMBERLEY COUNTRY ARTS & CRAFTS FAIR, Box 2182, Austin TX 78768. (512)474-6981. Executive Director: Patricia E. Francis. Sponsor: March of Dimes, Capital Area Chapter. Purpose: fundraiser. Estab. 1974. Annual outdoor show held 2 days in May. Average attendance: 10,000. Entries accepted until 3 weeks before show. Entry fee: $45/12x12 display area; $45 with electricity (110 volts). Prejudging by 3 color slides; entry fee refunded for refused work. Work may be offered for sale; donation of 1 item for auction—10% of bid proceeds kept by exhibitor. Craftworker must attend show; demonstrations OK. Registration limit: 150. Sponsor provides 24-hour security; free babysitting; and limited number of campsite accommodations. Show is advertised by radio; TV; periodicals; billboards; flyers; and posters. Submit 8x10 b&w glossies of media and self and resume. Considers all crafts.

WORLD SHOWS, Box 339, Stanton CA 90680. (714)995-7509. Partners: Don, Virginia or Gale. Estab. 1977. Annual shows held 40 days in November-December at various Sears' stores throughout Texas. Considers all crafts.
Terms: Entries accepted until show date. Entry fee: $96 for insurance. Display area: 4x6' to 10x12'. Prejudging by phone or mail. Entry fee due after prejudging; fee refunded for refused work. Craftworker must offer work for sale; 30% commission. Craftworker must attend show; demonstrations OK. Registration limit: 1-5 per store (57 stores). Sponsor provides electricity for demonstrations.
Profile: "These are concessions in high traffic areas of Sears' stores. Show is promoted by Sears' advertising. Craftworker must provide an appropriate sign and a good-looking display."

Utah

FAR COUNTRY CRAFT FAIR, Box 785, Moab UT 84532. (801)259-5029. Contact: Peggy

Page. Sponsor: Southeastern Utah Fine Arts Guild. Estab. 1973. Annual outdoor show held 2 days during Memorial Day weekend. Average attendance: 3,000-5,000. Entries accepted until show date. Entry fee: $20/10x10 display area. Work may be offered for sale; no commission. Craftworker must attend show; demonstrations OK. MasterCharge and Visa system available. Show is advertised by radio; newspapers; and flyers. Considers all crafts. Bestsellers: "lower cost items, say under $50. But sales are good in pottery, jewelry, tie dye and batik."

GREAT WEST FAIR, c/o Festival of the American West, Utah State University, UMC 14, Logan UT 84322. (801)752-4100, ext. 8421. Director: Ron Jones. Sponsor: Utah State University. Purpose: "to preserve pioneer, Indian, Spanish, and other ethnic arts of the early West near the turn of the century; to demonstrate and exhibit handmade articles; and to provide an opportunity for the public to participate." Estab. 1971. Annual outdoor show (with canopy tents, booths and tepees) held 8 days in the summer. Average attendance: 60,000. Entries accepted until 2 weeks before show. No entry fee; "we pay honorariums of $35/day to each participant." Display area: 9x9. Prejudging by "physical inspection if possible, 5 slides if not." Craftworker must attend show and demonstrate. Registration limit: 100. Sponsor provides chairs; display panels; fencing; table; 24-hour security; and "sales are handled in a special Craftworker's Store so craftsmen can concentrate on demonstrating and interesting the public in their craft."
Acceptable Work: Considers folk art such as candlemaking; dollmaking; leatherworking; metalsmithing; needlecrafts; pottery; weaving; pewter; woodcrafting; calligraphy; and blacksmithing. No modern crafts—should be turn of the century arts.
Promotion: Show is advertised by radio; TV; newspapers; magazines; and other means. "Submit photos of self working at craft. B&w glossy is optional."

*__NATIONAL APRIL ART EXHIBIT__, 126 E. 400 South, Springville UT 84663. (801)489-7305. Director: T.G. Rose. Sponsor: Springville Museum of Art. Estab. 1903. Annual indoor show held during April. Average attendance: 10,000. Entry fee: $2/work. Optional prejudging by slides; no entry fees refunded for refused work. Work may be offered for sale; 20% commission. Sponsor pays insurance for exhibited work. Considers 2-dimensional crafts. Presents up to $3,000 in cash and purchase prizes.

PARK CITY ART FESTIVAL, Box 1880, Park City UT 84060. (801)649-8882. Sponsor: Kimball Art Center/Park City Arts Council. Annual outdoor show held in August. Closing date for entry: 8-10 weeks before show. Entry fee: $15; "display fee of approximately $65-85." Art and crafts are eligible. Craftworker must attend show. All work is juried. Sponsor does not supply display equipment. Applications available in March.

*__SPRINGVILLE QUILT & FIBER SHOW__, 126 E. 400 South, Springville UT 84663. (801)489-9434. Assistant Curator: Dusty Collings. Sponsor: Springville Museum of Art. Purpose: "to stimulate better quality quilting and fiber arts in western US." Estab. 1975. Annual indoor show held the month of June. Average attendance: 7,000. Entries accepted until 2 weeks before show. Entry fee: $4/item. Maximum 2 pieces per craftworker. Prejudging by actual work; no entry fees refunded for refused work. Work may be offered for sale; 20% commission. Craftworker needn't attend show; demonstrations might be arranged. Registration limit: 70. Sponsor provides 24-hour protection. Show is advertised by radio, news, newsletter, and mailers. Presents cash awards of about $1,000 and about 15 ribbons. Considers quilts and other fiber media. "Submit work with excellent craftsmanship and original, creative design. Tabs for stapling must be sewn on top, back of quilts 24" apart and 2" down from top edge."

Vermont

AMERICANA WEEK, Norton House Museum, Wilmington VT 05363. (802)464-5102. Organizer: James Dassatti. Estab. 1967. Annual indoor/outdoor show held the last week in May.
Acceptable Work: Considers all crafts. "We prefer colonial and 19th century historical items, but will not exclude others. Those wishing to attend should have their own tables, chairs, pinups, etc.; display is up to the choice of the craftperson."
Terms: Exhibits for 2 days only. Entry fee: $5/day. Work may be offered for sale; "We prefer craftsmen dressed in 18th and 19th century clothing and will discount booth space by 1/3 for costumed craftspeople." Craftworker must attend show; demonstrations OK. Sponsor provides insurance on exhibited work.
Profile: The show "is designed to pay tribute to the spirit of a new awakening and to pay respect to what has gone on in the past. The Annual Tree Planting tells us that we can live with nature and even help to return some of the beauty we have stolen. The crafts exhibits and street fairs

remind us that man has unique talents to produce beauty and usefulness from nature's objects." Customers are usually young to middle age with middle incomes and interested in early American home crafts.

ANTIQUES & UNIQUES FESTIVAL, c/o Vermont Children's Aid Society, 72 Hungerford Terrace, Burlington VT 05401. (802)864-9883. Business Manager: Kennedy Snow. Purpose: fundraiser. Estab. 1971. Annual outdoor show held 1 Saturday in July (but never 4th of July weekend) at Craftsbury Common, Vermont. Average attendance: 2,000-3,000. Entries accepted until 1 week before show. Entry fee: $20/24x16 display area. "Screening of new entrants is done by photo, brochure or description with application; firm no-refund policy after acceptance of application." Work may be offered for sale; no commission. Craftworker must attend show; demonstrations OK. Registration limit: 105. Categories: crafts and antiques. Considers all crafts; "antique dealer booths comprise about 35% of the show."
Promotion: "Publicity releases go to newspapers, TV stations and magazines in Vermont, New York, New Hampshire, Massachusetts, Maine and Quebec. Submit pictures and description of work for newspaper articles."

ART ON THE MOUNTAIN, Box 275, Wilmington VT 05363. (802)464-8096. President: Lana Palumbo. Sponsor: Deerfield Valley Health Center Volunteers. Estab. 1964. Annual indoor show held 10 days in August. Average attendance: 4,000.
Acceptable Work: Considers all original crafts. "Items to be hung must be ready for hanging. Notification of wish to enter exceptionally large pieces requested.
Terms: Entries accepted until 2 months before show. Entry fee: $5/craftworker. Maximum 100 pieces of work/craftworker. Prejudging by slides, photos and/or personal viewing; entry fee due after prejudging. Work must be offered for sale; 20% commission. "Our staff handles all sales." Craftworker needn't attend show; demonstrations OK. Registration limit: about 60. Sponsor provides coverings, display panels, electricity for demonstrations, table, 24-hour security, and all set-up is done by Art on the Mountain staff with their display materials.

THE FOLIAGE CRAFT MARKET, Craftproducers Inc., North, Readsboro VT 05350. Contact: Charles Dooley or Riki Moss. Estab. 1974. Semiannual indoor show held 3 days on Columbus Day weekend in the base lodge of the Mount Snow ski area. Average attendance: 6,000. Entry fee: $80, +$5 for electricity. Display area: 8x10 or smaller. Prejudging by 5 slides. Work may be offered for sale; no commission. Craftworker must attend show; demonstrations OK if arranged in advance. Registration limit: 70. Sponsor provides chair; table; 24-hour security; and party. Show is advertised by radio; newspapers; flyers; and posters. Considers all crafts. 1978 August exhibitor sales totalled $60,000.

*****OLD WORLD CRAFT SHOW**, c/o Michael Holland, Star Route at Pico, Rutland VT 05701. (802)775-1939. Sponsor: Killington/Pico Rotary Club. Estab. 1972. Annual indoor show held 2-3 days in the late summer.
Acceptable Work: Considers all crafts. "We try to have no more than 3 of any 1 craft. This past show had craftsmen from Connecticut, Massachusetts, New Hampshire and Maine; but 80% are Vermonters." Bestsellers: work under $100.
Terms: Entries accepted until 4 weeks before show. Entry fee: $40/artist. Display area: 8x10. Prejudging by 5 slides or photos; entry fee due after prejudging. Work may be offered for sale; no commission. Craftworker must attend show; demonstrations OK. Registration limit: 60. Sponsor provides chairs; electricity; tables; and moving help. Awards plaque.
Promotion: Show is advertised by central Vermont radio stations; posters; flyers; and newspapers. Submit any descriptions for publicity consideration.

STRATTON ARTS FESTIVAL, Stratton Mountain VT 05155. Sponsor: Vermont Council of the Arts. Annual indoor show usually held from mid-September to mid-October. No entry fee. Work must be offered for sale; 30% commission. Sponsor provides plywood display panels and $200 deductible insurance minus commission. Ship entries UPS or deliver in person by appointment. Considers all crafts by Vermont craftworkers.

VERMONT MAPLE ART & CRAFT SHOW, Rt. 3, St. Albans VT 05478. Chairperson: Lucille Mae Callum. Purpose: "to promote the Vermont Maple Festival and the maple syrup industry." Estab. 1969. Annual indoor show held 3 days in April. Average attendance: 5,000. Write for entry specifics. Display area: 6' table. Work may be offered for sale; no commission. Craftworker must attend show; demonstrations OK. Registration limit: 60. Sponsor provides some chairs; table; and 24-hour security. Considers all crafts except lapidary; metalsmithing; mobiles; sculpture; and soft sculpture."

VERMONT PUBLIC RADIO CRAFT FAIR, Box 92, Readsboro VT 05350. (802)423-7692. Co-Directors: Charles Dooley and Riki Moss. Sponsor: Craftproducers Incorporated. Estab. 1979. Annual indoor show held 3 days in late July at Bennington, Vermont.
Acceptable Work: Considers all crafts except decoupage and tole painting. No kits, machine-made crafts, embellished found items, pressed flowers, shell jewelry or coin crafting. "Yet, if a person feels his work is exceptional in these categories, we are open to screen it."
Terms: Entries accepted until 3 months before show. Entry fee: $80/10x8' display area. Prejudging by 5 slides. Entry fee due after prejudging; entry fee refunded for refused work. Work may be offered for sale; no commission. Craftworker must attend show; demonstrations OK. Registration limit: 100. Sponsor provides chairs, electricity for demonstrations and 24-hour security.
Promotion: Show is advertised by all media. Needs photos for newspaper articles.
Tips: "The New England market in the summer is looking for sophisticated quality work. Most sales are in the $5-30 range, although expensive furnishings and other items sell. We want beautiful work, thoughtfully displayed. Good functional craftwork as well as gallery pieces."

Virginia

*****APPLE HARVEST ARTS & CRAFTS FESTIVAL**, Drawer E., Middletown VA 22601. (703)869-1120. Chairman: Dr. William H. McCoy. Sponsor: Winchester Rotary Club. Estab. 1975. Annual outdoor show held 2 days in September. Average attendance: 10,000. Considers all crafts.
Terms: Entries accepted until 3 weeks before show. Entry fee: $30/20' of running space. Prejudging by slides or photos; entry fee refunded for refused work. Work may be offered for sale; demonstrations encouraged. Registration limit: 120-150. Sponsor provides 24-hour security. Presents ribbons.
Promotion: Show is advertised by news releases in 5 states; 125 newspapers and periodicals; radio ads in Virginia, West Virginia and DC; posters; flyers and through the Virginia travel bureau. "Submit b&w glossy photos of self engaged in craft."

ARTS IN THE PARK, 1112 Sunset Ave., Richmond VA 23221. (804)353-8198. Chairman: Mrs. R. S. Lovelace III. Sponsor: Carillon Civic Association. Purpose: to promote the arts in Richmond and as a community project. Estab. 1971. Annual indoor/outdoor show held 2 days in May. Average attendance: 100,000. Entries accepted until 2 weeks before show. Entry fee: $20/10x10 display area. Work may be offered for sale; no commission. Craftworker must attend show; demonstrations OK. Show is advertised by TV; radio; newspapers; and posters. Considers all crafts except ceramics; decoupage; mobiles; and soft sculpture. Send slides and photos of work. Include SASE when requesting information.

BLACKSTONE CHAMBER OF COMMERCE ANNUAL ARTS & CRAFTS FESTIVAL, Box 295, Blackstone VA 23824. (804)292-4624. Chairperson: Mrs. J. L. Tramel. Purpose: "to further promote interest in arts and crafts in our rural locality; and to expose local artists and craftpersons to a wider range of arts and crafts." Estab. 1970. Non-profit annual indoor show held 2 days during the first weekend in October preceded by a Thursday. Average attendance: 4,000. Entries accepted until 4 weeks before show; "thereafter to fill a cancellation." Entry fee: $10 for craftworkers with sales tax numbers; other pay 5% commission of $200 of sales following show. Display area: 8x10. Prejudging "for crafters new to our show. Please send either nonreturnable color slides or photos"; application fee refunded for refused work. Craftworkers must attend 2 days of show; demonstrations encouraged. Registration limit: 80-90. Sponsor provides chairs; electricity; table; and overnight security. Considers all crafts.
Sales Tip: "Be friendly, courteous and prompt. Prices under $50 are rapid sales items; prices $100 and upward move well." 1978 exhibitor sales totalled $19,000.

*****BOARDWALK ART & CRAFT SHOW**, 2 Boundary St., Colonial Beach VA 22443. (804)224-7531. Secretary: James D. Karn. Sponsor: Colonial Beach Chamber of Commerce. Purpose: "We are in a historic part of Virginia (10 miles from Washington's birthplace) and this show is held to promote the area." Estab. 1967. Annual outdoor show held 2 days in August. Average attendance: 25,000. Entries accepted until 2 weeks before show. Entry fee: $15/craftworker. Display area: 10'. Work may be offered for sale; no commission. Craftworker must attend show; demonstrations OK. Registration limit: 200. Show is advertised by radio; newspaper; and direct mail. Presents cash awards of $400, best in show; $200, 1st; $100, 2nd; $50, 3rd; purchase awards and ribbons. Considers all crafts.

*****BUCKROE BEACH ART SHOW**, 38 Hampton Roads Ave., Hampton VA 23661.

(804)723-6162. Board Member: Herbert Goldstein. Sponsor: Peninsula Exchange Club. Purpose: fundraiser for student scholarships. Estab. 1965. Annual outdoor show held 3 days in August. Average attendance: 25,000. Entries accepted until show. Entry fee; $20/8' display area. Work may be offered for sale; no commission. Craftworker must attend show; demonstrations OK. Sponsor provides fencing. Show is advertised by newspapers; posters; and radio. Considers all crafts. Presents about $1,000 in cash prizes in all categories, and ribbons for 1st, 2nd and 3rd places.

CHRYSLER MUSEUM MAY FAIR, Olney Rd. and Mowbray Arch, Norfolk VA 23510. (804)622-1211. Librarian: Jean O. Chrysler. Sponsor: Chrysler Museum Art Reference Library Associates. Estab. 1979. Annual indoor show held 2 days in May. Average attendance: 10,000.
Acceptable Work: Considers all crafts. Bestsellers: photography, jewelry, ceramics, stained glass and macrame.
Terms: Entry fee to be announced. Work may be offered for sale; no commission. Sponsor provides fencing, table and 24-hour security.

FESTIVAL IN THE PARK OF DANVILLE, INC., Box 3300, Danville VA 24541. (804)799-5200. Contact Director. Estab. 1975. Annual outdoor show (with parachutes for art area) held 3 days in May (the weekend after Mothers Day) at Ballou Park in Danville. Average attendance: 70,000. Entries accepted until 2 months before show for crafts. Entry fee: $10/15x20 display area. Prejudging by slides; entry fee refunded for refused work. Work may be offered for sale; no commission. Craftworker must attend show; demonstrations encouraged. Sponsor provides electricity for demonstrations. Show is advertised by radio; TV; newspapers; and magazines. Considers all crafts. Presents $2,000 in cash and 1st, 2nd and 3rd place ribbons.

FOURTH OF JULY CARNIVAL, Box 162, Fredericksburg VA 22401. (703)371-4504. Executive Director: Ronald Shibley. Director: Historic Frdericksburg Foundation Inc. Purpose: fundraiser. Estab. 1975. Annual outdoor show (with canopies) held 1 day during July 4 weekend. Average attendance: 4,500-10,000. Entries accepted until 2 weeks before show. No entry fee. Work must be offered for sale; 20% commission. Prefers craftworker attends show; demonstrations encouraged. Sponsor provides electricity for demonstrations. Show is advertised by press releases to New England and mid-Atlantic newspapers. Bestsellers: items under $20. "Best mix is several low cost pieces if higher priced items are also being offered."

GREENWOOD ARTS & CRAFTS FAIR, Box 281, Greenwood VA 22943. Sponsor: Greenwood Community Center. Purpose: fundraiser to benefit Greenwood Community Center. Estab. 1968. Annual indoor/outdoor show held 2 days in September. Average attendance: 8,000. Entries accepted until July 1. Entry fee: $25-50/10x6 display area. Prejudging by slides or photos; entry fee refunded for refused work. Work may be offered for sale; no commission. Craftworker must attend show; demonstrations encouraged. Registration limit: 100. Sponsor provides chairs; electricity for demonstrations; table; and 24-hour security. Show is advertised by local TV station, radio; newspapers; posters; and flyers. Submit photos of self at work for promotion. In 1978 show "several craftworkers sold over $1,000; some over $2,000 in 1 day." Considers all crafts except ceramics and soft sculpture.

HOME CRAFTS DAY, Mountain Empire Community College, Big Stone Gap VA 24219. (703)5230-2400. Director, Continuing Education: Patricia M. Collier. Sponsor: Mountain Empire Community College. Estab. 1972. Annual indoor/outdoor show held 1 day in October. Average attendance: 5,000. Show is advertised by newspapers, pamphlets, TV and radio.
Acceptable Work: Considers leatherworking, candlemaking, dollmaking, metalsmithing, needlecrafts, weaving and woodcrafting. Only those crafts in old Appalachian tradition.
Terms: Entries accepted until 2 weeks before show. No entry fee: Display area: 10x20. Prejudging by slides, photos and/or samples. Work may be offered for sale; no commission. Craftworker must attend show; demonstrations OK. Registration limit: 50. Sponsor provides chairs, coverings, electricity for demonstrations, table and 24-hour security.

LYNCHBURG CRAFT FAIR, 2008 Langhorne Rd., Lynchburg VA 24501. (804)846-7029. Contact: Mrs. Harvey Harriss. Sponsor: Virginia Handcrafts and Lynchburg High Schools. Estab. 1970. Annual indoor show held Saturday and Sunday afternoons during the first weekend in November. Average attendance: 1,500-2,000.
Acceptable Work: Considers all crafts. No kits. "All work must be professional craftspersons' own original work."

Terms: Entries accepted until 4 weeks before show. Entry fee: $5/booth. Total display area: 144 square feet. Prejudging by slides/photos. Entry fee refunded for refused work. Work must be offered for sale; 15% commission. Craftworker must attend show; demonstrations required whenever possible. Registration limit: approximately 40. Sponsor provides chairs, electricity for demonstrations, table (if required) and 24-hour security.
Promotion: Show is advertised by newspaper, radio and posters. Submit resumes and/or photos for promotional purposes.
Sales Tip: "A large percentage should be in the range of Christmas gifts at prices up to $10. A small percentage should be in higher price ranges. Sales ranged this past year from $0-900 per craftsman."

MARKET SQUARE FAIR, Box 162, Fredericksburg VA 22401. (703)371-4504. Executive Director: Ronald E. Shibley. Sponsor: Historic Fredericksburg Foundation, Inc. Purpose: fundraiser. Estab. 1737. Annual outdoor show held second Saturday in May. Average attendance: 5,000-6,000. Entries accepted until 2 weeks before show. No entry fee. Work may be offered for sale; 20% commission. Craftworker must attend show; demonstrations encouraged. Sponsor provides electricity for demonstrations. Show is advertised by newspaper releases, radio ads, and posters. Considers all crafts. Bestsellers: items under $20.

NEW MARKET ARTS & CRAFTS SHOW, Box 506, New Market VA 22844. (703)740-3212. Contact: William H. Garber. Sponsor: New Market Arts & Crafts Club. Purpose: "to get artisans' work before the public and assist them with sales." Estab. 1961. Annual indoor/outdoor show held the last Saturday and Sunday in September. Average attendance: 2,000-5,000. Entries accepted until show date. Entry fee: 25¢/class being displayed. Work may be offered for sale; 15% commission. Craftworker needn't attend show; demonstrations OK. Sponsor provides chairs; display panels; electricity for demonstrations; and 24-hour security. Show is advertised by radio; newspapers; posters; literature in motel rooms; and signs. Considers all crafts.

NEWMARKET NORTH MALL ARTS & CRAFTS SHOW, 1219 Elmart Lane, Richmond VA 23235. (804)745-1085. Coordinator: Mary Lehner. Sponsor: Newmarket North Merchants Association. Estab. 1976. Annual indoor show held 4 days in October at Hampton, Virginia. Average attendance: 50,000-60,000. Entries accepted until 2 weeks before show (only accepts money order or certified check within 3 weeks of show). Entry fee: $50/10x10 display area. Prejudging by "at least 3 slides or photos of representative work. Also like overall picture of display with exhibitor in background, or exhibitor at work." Entry fee refunded for refused work. Work may be offered for sale; no commission. Craftworker must exhibit during store hours; demonstrations encouraged. Registration limit: 90 (usual number, about 65). Sponsor provides some A-frame panels; electricity for demonstrations; and 24-hour security.
Acceptable Work: Considers batik, candlemaking; decoupage; dollmaking; glass art; jewelry; leatherworking; macrame; metalsmithing; mobiles; needlecrafts; wheel thrown or hand-built pottery; sculpture; soft sculpture; tole painting; weaving; and woodcrafting. "A person must specialize in 1 category and list items in category to be exhibited. There is a quota on each category. A person who does some of everything upsets the quota."
Profile: Show is advertised in daily newspaper; radio spots; and in-house advertising. "Many artists keep names and addresses of former customers and send a card to arrive on first day of show to let them know they are in the show. This seems to help them very much. Exhibitors should have a name plate on their exhibit and some printed material for the patrons to pick up."

*****PORTSMOUTH NATIONAL SEAWALL ART SHOW**, c/o Parks and Recreation Dept., 430 High St., Portsmouth VA 23704. (804)393-8481. Director: Donna Morris. Sponsor: Parks and Recreation Department and Chamber of Commerce. Estab. 1970. Annual outdoor show held Memorial Day weekend. Average attendance: 20,000. Entries accepted until 4 weeks before show. Entry fee: $13/6x8 display area; $17 with wire fencing. Maximum 3 spaces per craftworker. Work may be offered for sale; no commission. Craftworker or representative must attend show; demonstrations encouraged. Registration limit: 350. No crafts accepted in advance. Considers all original crafts.
Awards: Presents $2,500, cash prizes; $2,000, purchase awards; 35 ribbons. Judging done by 3 well-known East Coast artists or art educators.

POWHATAN ARTS & CRAFT SHOW & SALE, Box 103, Powhatan VA 23139. Chairman:

---

* Those listings preceded by an asterisk present awards for prize-winning crafts.

Mrs. Robert C. Baltimore. Sponsor: Powhatan Junior Woman's Club. Purpose: fundraiser. Estab. 1976. Annual indoor show held 2 days in fall. Entries accepted up until show. Entry fee: $15, late fee $20/100 square feet display area. Tables rented for extra fee of $3 each. Work may be offered for sale; no commission. Craftworker must attend show; select demonstrations. Registration limit: 50. Sponsor provides chairs; overnight security, and name banners. Electricity limited for demonstrations; gym has good lighting. Show is advertised by newspaper ads; community service radio and TV announcements; illuminated billboards; flyers; and posters. Considers all crafts but looking for "country" type crafts. Artists do well. Bestsellers: "Christmas decorations and gifts. Children's items draw interest as well as handmade furniture. Ceramics have not proved to be a big seller."

*RICHMOND CRAFT FAIR, 7 N. 6th St., Richmond VA 23219. (804)649-0674. Director: Ruth T. Summers. Sponsor: Hand Work Shop, Inc. Purpose: fundraiser. Estab. 1976. Annual indoor show held 3 days in November. Average attendance: 7,000-10,000. Entries accepted until June 1. Entry fee: $5/slide fee plus $120 booth fee. Prejudging by 5 color slides, standard size mount. Booth fee due after prejudging. Work must be offered for sale; no commission. Craftworker must attend show; demonstrations OK. Registration limit: 122. Sponsor provides chairs; electricity for demonstrations; table; 24-hour security; and exhibitor curtains. Show is advertised by TV public service announcements and talk shows; flyers; posters; and press releases. Submit photo and resume. 1976 show sales totalled $90,000. Presents cash awards of $1,300 and purchase awards of $2,000. Categories: folk and designer crafts.
Acceptable Work: Considers designer crafts and all crafts except decoupage; dollmaking; needlecrafts; tole painting; dried flowers; seed and pod decorations; cut bottles; embellished objects such as painted waxes, weathered woods, stones, shells, buttons, and furniture; raw materials; unfinished objects; and Christmas decorations. Bestsellers: functional plus decorative, $25-40 range.

THE ROANOKE CRAFT FESTIVAL, Box 8161, Roanoke VA 24014. Coordinator: Marcia Carpenter. Sponsor: Docent Guild of the Roanoke Fine Arts Center. Purpose: fundraiser. Estab. 1971. Annual indoor show held 3 days in November. Average attendance: 11,000. Entry fees accepted until 6 months before show. Entry fee: $60-225/display area. Prejudging by slides; photos; or actual work. Work may be offered for sale; no commission. Craftworker must attend show; demonstrations OK. Registration limit: 84. Sponsor provides chairs; coverings; display panels; 24-hour security; some free housing; lounge; coffee; tea; and relief workers. Show is advertised by numerous magazines; radio; TV; posters; and newspapers. Submit promotional material only if requested. 1978 show sales totalled $93,000. Considers all crafts.

*VIRGINIA BEACH FOLK ARTS FESTIVAL, 4700 Recreation Dr., Virginia Beach VA 23451. (804)467-4884. Festival Coordinators: Bea Weigand and Nancy Soscia. Sponsor: Virginia Beach Department of Parks and Recreation. Annual outdoor show (with tent space for fiber crafts) held 2 days in May. Average attendance: 25,000-30,000. Entries accepted until 4 weeks before show. Entry fee: $10/craftworker. Prejudging by 4 35mm color slides; entry fee due after prejudging. Work may be offered for sale; no commission. Craftworker or representative must attend show; demonstrations OK. Registration limit: 115. Sponsor provides electricity for demonstrations; table; relief personnel; water for demonstrations; and tent space if needed. Presents 3 awards and merit ribbons for excellence in a craft area.
Acceptable Work: Considers batik; candlemaking; old traditional decoupage and dollmaking; glass art; jewelry; lapidary; leatherworking; macrame; needlecrafts; pottery; sculpture; soft sculpture; tole painting; weaving; woodcrafting; old world crafts; and skills handed down through the generations.
Promotion: Show is advertised by national publications; newspaper; posters; flyers; statewide craft show listings; area magazines; TV; and radio.
Profile: "The Festival is a celebration of our rural cultural heritage with sales and demonstrations of Old World crafts and skills. We try to provide a family weekend of fun with live entertainment and an opportunity to view and purchase fine handcrafted items not available on the average market. We hope to help preserve the skills and crafts of the past that are in danger of dying out."

VIRGINIA CRAFTS COUNCIL CRAFT FAIR, 116 Second St., N.E., Charlottesville VA 22901. (804)295-6360. Executive Director: Mary Maher. Purpose: "to provide member craftspeople with a good spring outlet for both wholesale and retail sales. To educate the buying public as to the nature, variety and quality of contemporary and traditional crafts." Estab. 1972. Annual indoor show held 3 days in April. Average attendance: 6,000-8,000. "Open to

All crafts are considered at the Zane Square Arts & Crafts Festival. This three-day show is held in the beautiful and historic Fountain Square area of downtown Lancaster, Ohio. Display booths, demonstrations, entertainment and a street dance are all part of the festivities.

Virginia Crafts Council members only. However, Virginia Crafts Council membership is open to all; must be a member by November 15 of preceding year to enter next year's show; not limited to Virginia residents." Entry fee: $30/10x10 display area. Prejudging by sides if not of exhibiting member status; by actual work for those of exhibiting member status. Work may be offered for sale; 15% commission on total sales over $200 and under $1,000; 10% on total sales above $1,000. Craftworker must attend show; demonstrations encouraged and paid for. Registration limit: 80-100. Sponsor provides chairs; electricity for demonstrations; table; 24-hour security; free housing with area hosts; and relief personnel. 1977 show sales totalled $42,000. Considers all crafts except painted rocks, decoupage boxes; dried flower arrangement; seed and pod decorations; cut bottles; and embellished objects.

Promotion: Show is advertised by private mailing of brochures; radio; TV; newspapers; magazines; posters across the State of Virginia and Washington DC. Submit photos and resume. "Craftsperson may supply his or her personal mailing list. Brochures will be addressed and sent to those people."

*VIRGINIA CRAFTSMEN, Virginia Museum of Fine Arts, Boulevard & Grove Ave., Richmond VA 23221. (804)257-0886. Contact: Curatorial Assistant. Biennial indoor show held 4-5 weeks in the spring. Average attendance: 35,000-45,000. Considers all quality crafts. Awards certificates of distinction. Write to be placed on mailing list.

Terms: Entries accepted until 3 months before show. Entry fee: $7.50/craftworker. Maximum 3 pieces/artist. "The works are juried before the exhibition by an expert in the field. They are not prejudged by Museum staff."Method of jurying to be announced. No entry fees refunded for refused work. If accepted for exhibition, work may be offered for sale; 25% commission. Craftworker needn't attend show; no demonstrations. Sponsor provides insurance on exhibited work and 24-hour security.

Promotion: Show is advertised by "broad circulation of entry blanks, radio, TV and newspaper coverage throughout Virginia."

YMCA ARTS & CRAFTS FAIR, 304 Squires Student Center, Blacksburg VA 24060. (703)961-6468. Fair Director: Betty C. Williams. Estab. 1970. Annual indoor show held 3 days in November. Average attendance: 12,000.

Acceptable Work: Considers batik, candlemaking, ceramics, dollmaking, glass art, jewelry, lapidary, leatherworking, macrame, metalsmithing, needlecrafts, pottery, scrimshaw, tole painting, weaving, woodcrafting and musical instruments (dulcimers, flutes, recorders). No kits, mass-produced items or decoupage.

Terms: Entries accepted until 5 months before show. Display area: 8x8. Prejudging by slides or personal interview. Work must be offered for sale; 20% commission. Craftworker must attend show; demonstrations OK. Registration limit: 100; must be from Virginia, West Virginia, North or South Carolina, Maryland, Ohio, Pennsylvania or Tennessee. Sponsor provides chairs, electricity for demonstrations, table, 24-hour security, booth sitters (for meals and breaks), rooms with local townspeople, and assistance in unloading, loading, and setting up.

"The craftspeople handle their own sales and taxes if they have a Virginia tax number. The YMCA turns in the sales tax for those without a tax number."
Promotion: Show is advertised by magazines, newspapers, radio, TV, posters and calendars of events. "Pictures and information for articles are appreciated on request."
Sales Tip: "Good display and variety encourage sales. Jewelry, leatherwork, pottery and woodworking are the bestsellers. Total sales (1978): $85,000."

Washington

ALLIED ARTS STREET FAIR, Box 573, Wenatchee WA 98801 (509)662-1213. Coordinator: Judy Mills. Sponsor: Allied Arts Council of North Central Washington. Purpose: fundraiser and to provide a place for quality craftsmen to exhibit. Estab. 1973. Annual outdoor show held 3 days in September. Average attendance: 5,000-10,000. Entries accepted until 1 week before show. Entry fee: $20/2 blocks. Prejudging by slides; photos; and descriptions. Entry fee refunded for refused work. Work may be offered for sale; no commission. Craftworker must attend show; demonstrations OK. Registration limit: 100. Sponsor provides electricity for demonstrations. Show is advertised by all media. Considers all crafts.

*****ANACORTES ARTS & CRAFTS FESTIVAL,** Box 6, Anacortes WA 98221. Chairman: Brooke Lindholm. Purpose: "to expand the cultural environment of our city and to provide exposure for the Northwest's many fine artists and craftspeople." Estab. 1960. Annual outdoor show held 2 days in August. Average attendance: 20,000. Entries for booth space accepted until about mid-May. Entries for juried show accepted until 2 weeks before show. Entry fee: $3/category in juried show; $30/10x12 display area. Maximum 2 pieces per artist per category; total 20. Prejudging by actual work; entry fee due after prejudging. Work may be offered for sale; 20% commission on sales over $125. Craftworker must attend show; demonstrations OK. Registration limit: 90. Sponsor provides electricity for demonstrations; table; 24-hour security; and some festival booths. Show is advertised by newspaper; direct mailing; posters; TV; and radio. Presents cash awards of $3,500 and purchase awards of $300-1,000, not necessarily awarded each year. 1977 show sales totalled $40,000. Considers all crafts.

ANGELES ARTS IN ACTION, Box 176, Port Angeles WA 98362. (206)457-3004. Fair Manager: Virginia DelGuzzi. Estab. 1968. Annual outdoor show held 2 days in July. Entries accepted until 4 months before show. Prejudging by slides; photos; or actual work. "Northwest artists given preference." Work may be offered for sale. Registration limit: 90. Considers jewelry, leather, candles, and macrame.

APPLE BLOSSOM FESTIVAL ARTS & CRAFTS FAIR, Box 850, Wenatchee WA 98801. (509)662-3616. Manager: Dianne Gamel. Sponsor: Washington State Apple Blossom Festival Association. Estab. 1975. Annual outdoor show held 3 days in May. Average attendance: 75,000.
Acceptable Work: Considers all crafts. Bestsellers: "items that enhance their homes—pottery; jewelry; and woods."
Terms: Entries accepted until 2 weeks before show. Entry fee: $45/10x10 display area. Prejudging by photos and descriptions; entry fee refunded for refused work. Work may be offered for sale; no commission. Craftworker must attend show; demonstrations OK. Registration limit: 120. Sponsor provides electricity for demonstrations and 24-hour limited security.
Promotion: Show is advertised by brochures; magazines; radio; and newspaper.

APPLE VALLEY STREET FAIR, Box 573, Wenatchee WA 98801. (509)662-1213. Coordinator, Allied Arts: Ann Storey. Sponsor: Allied Arts Council of North Central Washington. Estab. 1973. Annual outdoor show held 3 days in September. Considers all crafts.
Terms: Entries accepted until 2 weeks before show. Entry fee: $25/10x10 display area. Prejudging by slides and/or photos; entry fee refunded for refused work. Work may be offered for sale; no commission. Craftworker must attend show; demonstrations OK. Registration limit: 125-150. Sponsor provides electricity for demonstrations and security guard.
Sales Tip: "Offer good quality items. Pottery and jewelry seem to be the more popular items."

*****CLARK COUNTRY FAIR,** 17402 NE Delfel Rd., Ridgefield WA 98642. (206)573-1921. Manager: David A. Pittman. Purpose: "agriculture fair, geared to youth in the community, 4-H, FFA, etc." Estab. 1868. Annual show held 6 days in August at Vancouver. Average attendance: 250,000. Display area: 10x10 and up. Prejudging; no entry fees refunded for refused work. Work may be offered for sale in commercial area only; no commission. Craftworker needn't attend show; demonstrations OK. Registration limit: 100. Sponsor provides electricity for demonstrations; table; and 24-hour security. Show is advertised by news media; radio; TV; billboards; and posters. Presents cash awards and ribbons. Categories: open class; 4-H and FFA; premium awards; and commercial exhibitors. Considers all crafts.

*EDMONDS ART FESTIVAL, Box 212, Edmonds WA 98020. Contact: President. Estab. 1957. Annual indoor/outdoor show held 3 days in June. Average attendance: 60,000 plus. Entries accepted only on Friday and Saturday the week before festival. Entry fee: $3/2 entries. Maximum 2 entries per category per craftworker. Work must be offered for sale; 25% commission. Sponsor provides display equipment and insurance. Deliver and pick up work in person.
Acceptable Work: Considers batik; ceramics; dollmaking; glass art; jewelry; leatherworking; mosaics; mobiles; macrame; metalsmithing; needlecrafts; pottery; soft sculpture; weavings; wall hangings; and woodcrafting.
Awards: Presents a total of $5,600 in cash prizes for all categories. Craft portion is awarded $1,800.

FREE AIR ARTS FAIR, Box 1995, Vancouver WA 96886. (206)696-8171. Supervisor: Margaret Bostwick. Sponsor: City of Vancouver. Annual outdoor show held the 4th of July. Average attendance: 40,000-60,000. Considers all crafts.
Terms: Entries accepted until 1 week before show. Entry fee: $5/display area size as needed. Work may be offered for sale; no commission. Craftworker must attend show; demonstration OK. Registration limit: 100. Show is advertised by newspapers and TV. Individual craftworker averaged $200 in 1977 show.
Profile: "The Fair is a part of a day long community celebration that features the largest fireworks display outside of Washington DC. The artists are invited to bring families and participate in games and races; enjoy entertainment; and join with us in celebrating the 4th of July."

*NORTHWEST ARTISTS THUNDERBIRD ARTS & CRAFTS, 4210 Terrace Hgts. Rd., Yakima WA 98901. (509)453-3379. Director: Ruth Wyman Reese. Sponsor: Thunder Bird Motel. Estab. 1979. Annual indoor show held 3 days in April.
Acceptable Work: Considers all crafts. No kits, molds or imports.
Terms: Entries accepted until 2 weeks before show. Entry fee: $35/8x10 display area. Prejudging by photos. Entry fee due after prejudging. Work may be offered for sale; 15% commission. Craftworker must attend show; demonstrations encouraged. Registration limit: 30. Sponsor provides chairs, electricity for demonstrations, table and 24-hour security. "Craftworker must have a Washington tax number."
Profile: "This motel has 250 rooms and many conventions and meetings. There's a guarded room, coffee shop, large banquet room and nightly entertainment. Takima people always look for best quality. They are very aware of really good art and have money to buy."

NORTHWEST ARTISTS VALLEY MALL ARTS & CRAFTS, 4210 Terrace Hgts. Rd., Takima WA 98901. (509)453-3379. Director: Ruth Wyman Reese. Sponsor: Valley Mall. Estab. 1978. Annual indoor show held 5 days in October.
Acceptable Work: Considers all crafts. No kits, molds or imports. No Heishi jewelry.
Terms: Entries accepted until 2 weeks before show. Entry fee charged per 10x10 display area. Prejudging by photos. Entry fee due after prejudging. Work may be offered for sale; 10% commission. Craftworker must attend show; demonstrations encouraged. Registration limit: 48. Sponsor provides electricity for demonstrations and 24-hour security.
Promotion: Show is advertised by mall ads, TV, radio and papers. "Pictures of work are appreciated for publicity in newspapers."
Profile: Mall contains 3 anchor stores, 45 shops and specialty stores. Attendance is very good. Takima people always look for best quality. They are very aware of really good art and have money to buy."

SEATTLE ARTS FESTIVAL: BUMBERSHOOT, 305 Harrison St., Seattle WA 98109. (206)625-5050. Producer: Jim Royce. Sponsor: City of Seattle, Seattle Center Dept. Estab. 1971. Annual indoor/outdoor show held 3 days during Labor Day weekend. Average attendance: 180,000. Considers all crafts.
Terms: Entries accepted until June. No entry fee. Display area: 10x12. Maximum 3 pieces/craftworker. Prejudging by actual work. Work must be offered for sale; 20% commission. Craftworker must attend show; demonstrations OK. Registration limit: 65-75. Sponsor provides chairs, display panels, and electricity for demonstrations only.

Sales Tip: "Sales of crafts at Bumbershoot have, in years past, reflected the quality and originality of the work. It seems very hard to judge the buying public's taste, but I have noticed particular interest in original designs. Craftworker is responsible for having a City business license and State Tax documents, reporting sales taxes and commissions to the City and State, in addition to other government requirements such as permits or health cards in the event food is sold as a craft." 1978 gross sales for 65 exhibitors totaled just over $40,000.
Promotion: Bumbershoot is promoted in all Washington, Oregon and Idaho news services. Locally it is publicized on TV, radio, newspapers, posters and community newsletters. "If the artist has b&w photos suitable for newspaper reproductions we will use any and all we get."

SEATTLE HARVEST FESTIVAL, 832 Bancroft Way, Berkeley CA 94710. (415)548-5440. Contact: Steve Kyle, Warren Cook, or Ellen Schwartz. Sponsor: General Expositions Corporation. Estab. 1977. Annual indoor show held 3 days in November at Seattle, Washington. Entries accepted until full. Entry fee: $135/8x10 display area. Prejudging by 6 photos or slides or actual work may be brought to our office. Work must be offered for sale; no commission. Craftworker must attend show; demonstrations encouraged. Sponsor provides 500 watts electricity; backdrop drapery; side rails; 24-hour security; cleaning; motel or hotel accommodations at group rate; inexpensive trucking of booth setup and stock round-trip between other Harvest Festival Shows. Presents awards for best costumes; best designed booths; and best demonstrating booths. Show is advertised by newspaper; radio; TV; billboard; direct mailings; posters; discount coupons; news releases; and TV guest appearances. Considers all crafts.
Profile: "The Harvest Festivals are patterned after the famous country autumn fairs of the 19th century America. These fairs were held to give thanksgiving for bountiful crops and as a last celebration before the hard winter set in. Craftworkers are required to be in 19th century costume."

SIDEWALK SHOW, 89 Lee Blvd., Richland WA 99352. (509)943-9815. Chairman: Jane Kuechle. Sponsor: Allied Arts Association. Estab. 1950. Annual outdoor show held 2 days in July. Average attendance: 10,000-15,000. Closing (postmark) date for entry: 6 weeks before show. Entry fee: $15/craftworkers. Display area: 15x15. Work must be offered for sale; 15% commission. "Items $200 or less sell very well." Craftworker must attend show; demonstrations encouraged. Registration limit: 225. Sponsor provides some electricity (if pre-requested) and security. Presents $50 for best display. Considers all crafts except what might be mistaken for kit work. Write for prospectus in mid-March.

SILVERDALE'S WHALING DAYS, Box 1218, Silverdale WA 98383. Contact: Central Kitsap Chamber of Commerce. Show held in July. Average attendance: 20,000. Closing date for entry: 2 weeks before show. Entry fee: $25. Craftworker must attend show. Considers a variety of media.

*****WESTERN WASHINGTON FAIR ART SHOW**, Box 430, Puyallup WA 98371. Curator: Marcia Jartun. Annual show. Entry fee required. Limit 2 entries. Work may be offered for sale; 25% commission. Presents $1085 in prizes.
Acceptable Work: Original work completed within the past 2 years, not previously shown in the area OK. Open to Washington artists ages 18. All media except sculpture. Size limit: maximum, 6x7; minimum, 8x12".

WHISTLIN' JACK ARTS & CRAFTS, 4210 Terrace Heights Rd., Yakima WA 98901. (509)453-3379. Sponsor: Whistlin' Jack Lodge. Purpose: "this area is very popular as a tourist attraction; tourists are looking for gifts from this area." Estab. 1974. Indoor/outdoor show (depending on weather) held 5 days in July. Average attendance: 3,000-5,000. Entries accepted until 2 weeks before show. Entry fee: $35/10x10 display area. Prejudging by photos; entry fee due after prejudging. Work may be offered for sale; 10% commission. Craftworker must attend show; demonstrations encouraged. Registration limit: 30. Sponsor provides chairs; electricity for demonstrations; and free camping area. Show is advertised by all media. Submit b&w photos. Considers all crafts.

WORLD SHOWS, Box 339, Stanton CA 90680. (714)995-7509. Contact: Don, Virginia or Gale. Estab. 1977. Annual shows held 40 days in November-December at various Sears' stores throughout Washington. Considers all crafts.
Terms: Entries accepted until show date. Entry fee: $96 for insurance. Display area: 4x6' to 10x12'. Prejudging by phone or mail. Entry fee due after prejudging; fee refunded for refused work. Craftworker must offer work for sale; 30% commission. Craftworker must attend show;

demonstrations OK. Registration limit: 1-5 per store (57 stores). Sponsor provides electricity for demonstrations.
Profile: "These are concessions in high traffic areas of Sears' stores. Show is promoted by Sears' advertising. Craftworker must provide an appropriate sign and a good-looking display."

West Virginia

ALDERSON-BROADDUS COLLEGE ARTS & CRAFTS FAIR, Box 1397, A-B College, Philippi WV 26416. (304)457-1700, ext. 235. Director of Student Activities: Carl Hatfield. Estab. 1974. Annual indoor show held 1 day in October. Average attendance: 2,000. Closing date for entry: 2 weeks before show. $10 entry fee. Maximum 1 entry per craftworker. Work may be offered for sale; no commission. Considers primarily West Virginia craftworkers. Craftworker must attend show; demonstrations OK. Registration limit: 40. Sponsor provides tables. Considers all crafts.

APPALACHIAN ARTS & CRAFTS FESTIVAL, Box 1798, Beckley WV 25801. (304)252-7328. Executive Director: Robert L. McKeands. Sponsor: Beckley-Raleigh County Chamber of Commerce. Purpose: to preserve Appalachian heritage. Annual indoor/outdoor show held Labor Day Weekend. Work may be offered for sale; 15% commission. Craftworker must attend show; demonstrations OK. Sponsor provides chairs; display panels and electricity for demonstrations. Show is advertised by paid public relations company. Submit photographs for promotion. 1977 show sales totalled $60,000. Considers all crafts; "Appalachian heritage is our objective."

APPLE BUTTER FESTIVAL, 204 N. Washington St., Berkeley Springs WV 25411. (304)258-3738. Contact: Andrea Beth Peters. Sponsor: Morgan County Chamber of Commerce. Estab. 1973. Annual outdoor show held 3 days in October, the fall color season. Average attendance: 15,000-20,000. Total sales for 124 exhibitors (1978): $50,000.
Acceptable Work: Considers all crafts. "Original arts and crafts are shown in one area, those from kits or otherwise machine-made in another."
Terms: Entries accepted until 2 weeks before show. Entry fee: $25/10x10 display area. "A larger area can be arranged in advance." Prejudging by slides/photos. Either entry fee due after prejudging or is refunded for refused work. Work may be offered for sale; 10% commission (after $250). Craftworker or his/her representatives must attend show; demonstrations OK. Sponsor provides electricity for demonstrations and bathroom facilities. Exhibitor handles sales and taxes; taxes paid to tax department representative at close of Festival.
Promotion: Show is advertised by radio, newspaper, TV, posters and brochures. "Berkeley is a resort community. We have excellent cooperation from the tourist industry in our area and the metro areas of Baltimore and Washington. Some artists are asked for cooperation in providing information and photos for publicity use."

BLUE RIDGE QUILT SHOW, Box 3053, Bakerton WV 25410. (304)535-6968. Show Chairman: Alice Newton. Sponsor: Blue Ridge Quilters. Estab. 1976. Annual indoor show held 3 days in May at Harpers Ferry, West Virginia. Average attendance: 1,000.
Acceptable Work: Considers quilting, patchwork and applique. "Quilts must have a basting strip for hanging."
Terms: Entries accepted until 2 weeks before show. Work cannot be offered for sale. Craftworker needn't attend show; demonstrations by Blue Ridge Quilters only. Registration limit: 100.

BURLINGTON OLD-FASHIONED APPLE HARVEST FESTIVAL, Box 96, Burlington WV 26710. (304)289-3511. Coordinator: Kim Kubelick. Sponsor: Burlington Community and the Auxiliary of the Burlington United Methodist Home for Children and Youth, Inc. Estab. 1975. Annual outdoor show (under circus-like tents) held 3 days during the first weekend in October. Average attendance: 12,000.
Acceptable Work: Considers all crafts. No commercially manufactured goods. All equipment and props must be provided by craftworker.
Terms: Entries accepted until 2 weeks before show. Display area: 8x12, more if requested. Work may be offered for sale; 10% commission on gross sales. Craftworker must attend show; demonstrations OK. Registration limit: 40. Sponsor provides electricity for demonstrations and 24-hour security.
Promotion: Show is advertised by newspapers, TV, radio, brochures and members of the Potomac Highland Travel Council. "Photos and related copy would be appreciated, if available."

CAPITAL CITY ART & CRAFT SHOW, Box 4373, Charleston WV 25304. (304)346-3427. Exhibitor chairman: W. F. Lany Sr. Sponsor: Kanawha City Lions Club. Purpose: fundraiser. Estab. 1973. Annual indoor show held 3 days in November. Average attendance: 12,000. Entries accepted until "maximum number of booths are filled." Entry fee: $17.50/10x10 display area. Prejudging by slides or photos; entry fee due after prejudging. Work may be offered for sale; 15% commission. Craftworker must attend show; demonstrations OK. Registration limit: 130. Sponsor provides chairs; display panels; electricity for demonstrations; fencing; table; and 24-hour security. Show is advertised by radio; TV; direct mail; talk shows; banners; posters; leaflets; and newspapers. Submit resume and photos of work. 1978 show sales totalled $84,000. Considers all crafts.

*****CHRISTMAS IN SEPTEMBER FESTIVAL**, c/o The Serendipity, Shepherdstown WV 25443. Contact: Helen Myers Seeley. Purpose: "to promote the newer crafts in this, the oldest town in West Virginia which is steeped in the traditional crafts." Estab. 1977. Annual indoor show held 2 days in September. Average attendance: 1,000. Entries accepted until 1 week before show. Entry fee: $2/8' table. Work must be offered for sale; no commission. Craftworker must attend show; demonstrations "practically mandatory." Registration limit: 30. Sponsor provides chairs; electricity for demonstrations; table; 24-hour security; and poster for each display table. Show is advertised by newspaper; radio; and newsletter. Submit photo. Presents cash awards of $25, $10 and $5. Considers all crafts. "Table must be draped; where possible, work should be plastic wrapped." Most sales are less than $10.

*****EXHIBITION 280**, Huntington Galleries, Park Hills, Huntington WV 25701. (304)529-2701. Contact: Program Coordinator. Estab. 1952. Annual indoor show held 6 weeks in the spring. Average attendance: 6,000. Entries accepted until January 28. Entry fee: $10/craftworker. Maximum 3 entries per craftworker. No entry fees refunded for refused work. Work may be offered for sale; no commission. Considers all crafts completed by residents within a 280-mile radius of Huntington. Write for prospectus in summer. Presents $1,500 in cash and $2,500 in purchase prizes. Painting, sculpture and crafts held in odd numbered years; slide entries required. Photographs, drawings and prints held in even numbered years; no slide entries.

HERITAGE DAYS, Parkersburg Community College, Box 167A, Rt. 5, Parkersburg WV 26101. (304)424-8252. Chairman: Nancy Pansing. Estab. 1974. Annual indoor show held 3 days in spring. Average attendance: 8,000-9,000.
Acceptable Work: 1Considers all crafts, except decoupage and macrame. "Emphasis on heritage crafts with modern design." No kits, machine-made crafts or items using plastic (e.g., Chlorox bottles).
Terms: Entries accepted until 3 weeks before show. Entry fee: $10/8x10 display area. Prejudging by slides/photos and samples. Entry fee due after prejudging. Work must be offered for sale; no commission. Craftworker must attend show; demonstrations required. Registration limit: 50. Sponsor provides chairs, electricity for demonstrations, table, 24-hour security and lodging in faculty homes. Exhibitor handles sales and taxes.
Promotion: Show is advertised by newspapers, radio, TV, brochures, and local and national show listings. Submit upon acceptance a photo and resume for publicity.
Sales Tip: "An ability to relate to visitors, to chat easily during demonstrations helps increase sales."

HUNTINGTON DOGWOOD ARTS & CRAFTS FESTIVAL, Box 2767, Huntington WV 25727. (304)696-5940. Contact: Promotion Supervisor. Sponsor: City of Huntington and Huntington Civic Center. Purpose: to promote quality arts and crafts in the Huntington community. Annual indoor show held 5 days in May. Average attendance: 70,000. Entries accepted until 10 weeks before show. Entry fee: $30/10x10 display area. Prejudging by slides or photos; entry fee refunded for refused work. Work must be offered for sale; demonstrations required. Sponsor provides chairs; electricity for demonstrations; table; and 24-hour security. Show is advertised by billboards; radio; newspapers; professional entertainment; and general publicity. Considers all crafts.

KANAWHA COUNTY FAIR, Rt 4, Box 141-B, Charleston WV 25312. (304)984-3311. Director: Dick Waybright. Sponsor: Kanawha County 4-H Foundation. Estab. 1974. Annual indoor/outdoor show held 4 days in May at Camp Virgil Tate. Average attendance: 28,000. Considers all crafts. Entries accepted until 3 weeks before show. Entry fee: $15/6x8 display area. Work may be offered for sale; no commission. Craftworker must attend show; demonstrations OK.

Registration limit: 40. Sponsor provides coverings, electricity for demonstrations and 24-hour security. Exhibitor handles sales and taxes.

LOGAN COUNTY ARTS & CRAFTS FAIR, Box 218, Logan WV 25601. (304)752-1324. General Crafts Chairman: Theresa Dingess. Logan County Chamber of Commerce. Estab. 1972. Annual indoor show held 3 days in August. Average attendance: 5,000. Considers all crafts. No machine-made crafts.
Terms: Entries accepted until 4 weeks before show. Entry fee: $20/10x8 booth. Prejudging by slides/photos or samples. Entry fee due after prejudging. Work must be offered for sale; 15% commission. Craftworker must attend show; demonstrations OK. Registration limit: 60. Sponsor provides chairs, electricity for demonstrations, table, 24-hour security, display sitters, coffee, and help loading and unloading.

MOUNTAIN HERITAGE ARTS & CRAFTS FESTIVAL, Box 430, Charles Town WV 25414. (304)725-5514. Manager: George E. Vickers. Sponsor: Jefferson County Chamber of Commerce, Inc. Estab. 1972. Semiannual invitational outdoor show (with tents) held 3 days in June, and 3 days in September near Harpers Ferry, West Virginia. Average attendance: 32,000 paid.
Terms: Entry fee: $25/8x16 display area; $50/16x16 display area. Work may be offered for sale; 15% commission. Craftworker must attend show; demonstrations mandatory. Registration limit: 130. Sponsor provides electricity for demonstrations; 24-hour security; apple boxes and plywood for table tops and enclosure of booth; and pegboard background.
Promotion: Show is advertised by press releases; ads in newspapers, magazines and radio; billboards; brochures; and TV. Notice of prejudging and instructions upon request.

*MOUNTAIN STATE ART & CRAFT FAIR, Cedar Lakes, Ripley WV 25271. (304)372-6263. Sponsor: West Virginia Artists and Craftsmens Guild; West Virginia Department of Agriculture; Governor's Office of Economic and Community Development; Bureau of Vocational and Technical Education; West Virginia University Extension Service; and West Virginia Department of Natural Resources. Purpose: "to promote, develop and perpetuate the friendly exchange of information and sale of arts and crafts of West Virginia. In so doing we hope to acquaint the general public and visitors to the State of West Virginia with various cultural aspects of arts and crafts in our state." Estab. 1963. Annual indoor/outdoor show (exhibits are in building or under tents) held 5 days in June/July. Average attendance: 50,000. Applications accepted until 7 months before show. Display area: 6x8, 6x12, 6x16, 10x20 and 20x20 in tents; 6x8 and 6x16 in building. Prejudging by at least 5 pieces of actual work in each category. Work may be offered for sale; 15% commission. Craftworker must attend show; demonstrations required. Registration limit: 100 regular; 30 special exhibits. Sponsor provides display panels; electricity for demonstrations; table; and 24-hour security. Presents 5 awards of excellence each $100 and plaque; and letters of commendation to 5 additional craftworkers. 1977 show sales totalled $257,707.47. Considers all crafts except ceramics; decoupage; and any craft made outside of West Virginia. "This is a show for West Virginia craftsmen and artists only."

MULLENS ARTS & CRAFTS SHOW, 113 Broadway St., Mullens WV 25882. (304)294-5852. Chairman: Mrs. Gene Scott. Sponsor: Woman's Civic Club of Mullens. Estab. 1958. Annual indoor show held 3 days in October/November. Average attendance: 500+.
Acceptable Work: Considers decoupage, dollmaking, glass art, jewelry, lapidary, leatherworking, macrame, mobiles, needlecrafts, pottery, weaving, woodcrafting and other crafts that "can be exhibited indoors without danger to patrons."
Terms: Entries accepted until 1 week before show. Write for entry fee information. Work may be offered for sale; no commission. Craftworker must attend show; demonstrations OK. Sponsor provides chairs, electricity for demonstrations, table and 24-hour security.
Promotion: Show is advertised by TV, posters, radio and newspapers. "We would like to have artist's picture and resume for publicity."

OGLEBAY INSTITUTE CRAFT FESTIVAL, Oglebay Park, Wheeling WV 26003. (304)242-7700. Director, Creative Arts: Mary E. Fish. Purpose: "to promote crafts that reflect the highest standards of craftmanship by offering a specific time and place for demonstration, display and sale of work in order that the artist and viewer may reach a better mutual understanding and appreciation." Estab. 1950. Annual indoor show held 2 days in June. Average attendance: 2,700. Entries accepted until 1 week before show. Entry fee: $20/8' table and/or pegboard display area. Work may be offered for sale; no commission. Craftworker or representative must attend show; demonstrations encouraged. Registration limit: 70. Sponsor provides chairs; display panels; electricity for demonstrations; table; and 24-hour security.

1977 show sales totalled $3,012. Considers all crafts including musical instruments.
Promotion: Show is advertised by newspaper ads; hobby magazines; public service radio and TV; mail; posters placed in craft shops and interstate tourists stops within 30 miles; and state of West Virginia brochure that is distributed nationally. Submit photos and stories.

*OGLEBAY INSTITUTE UPPER OHIO VALLEY ART SHOW, Oglebay Institute, Oglebay Park, Wheeling WV 26003. (304)242-7700. Estab. 1964. Annual indoor show held 1 month in the fall. Average attendance: 1,000. Entries accepted until 1 week before show. Entry fee: $4, Institute member entry; $5, nonmember entry. Maximum 2 entries per exhibit. Work may be offered for sale; 35% commission. Open to West Virginia artists and those living within 100-mile radius of Wheeling. For insurance purposes, work must be delivered by the artist or an agent.
Acceptable Work: Considers all painting media; batik; glass art; leatherworking; metalsmithing; pottery; soft sculpture; weavings; wall hangings; and woodcrafting.
Awards: Cash awards and honorable mention ribbons. Judging panel consists of college art instructors or professional artists.

PIONEER DAY OF POCOHANTAS COUNTY, 8th St., Marlinton WV 24954. (304)799-6538. Chairperson: Louise Barlow. Purpose: "for local people to show their wares and encourage others to do the same, and to bring other craftsmen to our area." Estab. 1967. Annual indoor/outdoor show held 3 days in July. Average attendance: 10,000. Entries accepted until show. Entry fee: $1/pioneer badge. Work may be offered for sale; 10% commission. Craftworker must attend show; demonstrations OK. Sponsor provides chairs; display panels; electricity for demonstrations; table; 24-hour security; and some booths and dividers. Show is advertised by newspapers; leaflets; posters; TV; and radio. Considers all crafts.

*RHODODENDRON STATE OUTDOOR ART & CRAFT FESTIVAL, 3804 Noyes Ave. SE, Charleston WV 25304. (304)925-3364. Director: Eleanor Chandler. Estab. 1967. Annual outdoor show held the first Sunday in June. Held in rotunda if raining. Average attendance: 10,000-12,000. Considers all crafts. Entries accepted until show date; late applicants may not be listed in directory. Entry fee: $6/artist. Display area: 7x9. Work may be offered for sale; no commission. Craftworker must attend show; demonstrations OK. Sponsor provides electricity for demonstrations. Exhibitor handles sales and taxes. Presents 1 trophy, cash awards of approximately $3,000 and several purchase awards, but varies each year.

SALEM COLLEGE HERITAGE ARTS FESTIVAL, Salem College, Salem WV 26426. (304)782-5261. Chairman: Paul Plate and Robert McConnell. Estab. 1971. Annual indoor/outdoor show held 3 days in April. Average attendance: 15,000. Considers all crafts. No kits or plastics. Show is advertised by TV, radio, newspapers, and releases to colleges and organizations. Craftworker should provide promotional materials. Approximate total sales for last show: $3,790.
Terms: Entries accepted until show date. Display area: 6x10. Prejudging. Work may be offered for sale; 15% commission. Craftworker must attend show; demonstrations OK. Registration limit: 60. Sponsor provides chairs and electricity for demonstrations. Exhibitor handles sales and taxes.

SHOW & SELL, Moundsville Area Chamber of Commerce, Box 186, Moundsville WV 26041. (304)845-2773. Assistant Secretary: Jean Barger. Estab. 1976. Annual outdoor juried show (with some roofed areas) held 2 days in August. Average attendance: 20,000. Entries accepted until mid-July. Entry fee: $10/day, per space, display area equal to 1 car's parking space. Work may be offered for sale; no commission. Craftworker or representative must attend show; demonstrations encouraged. Sponsor provides electricity for demonstrations if requested in advance. Show is advertised by continuous newspaper releases; radio, TV, and newspaper ads; and bulletins. Submit photos for publicity. Considers all crafts. "This is not a luxury-buying market."

SOUTH PARKERSBURG BAND BOOSTERS CHRISTMAS ARTS & CRAFT SHOW, Rt. 1, Box 1004, 4th Ave., Parkersburg WV 26101. (304)422-8925. President: Emily Bargeloh. Purpose: fundraiser. Estab. 1972. Annual indoor show held 2 days in November. Average attendance: 2,000. Entries accepted until 4 weeks before show. Entry fee: $20/8' display area; $22.50/8' display area with table. Work may be offered for sale; no commission. Craftworker must attend show; demonstrations OK. Registration limit: 56-75. Sponsor provides chairs; electricity for demonstrations; insurance on exhibited work; and 24-hour security. Show is advertised by TV; newspapers; flyers; and posters (covered in Pennsylvania also). Submit nonreturnable photos and a brief description of work for publicity. Considers all crafts.

STONEWALL JACKSON JUBILEE, Box 956, Weston WV 26452. (304)269-4660. Manager: Madge Fultineer. Sponsor: Jubilee, Inc. Purpose: "to promote the culture and arts of the central West Virginia and Appalachian region." Estab. 1974. Annual indoor show held 3 days near Labor Day weekend. Average attendance: 10,000. Entries accepted until 3 weeks before show. Display area: 5x8 minimum. Prejudging of 1 item in each category. Work must be offered for sale; 15% commission. Craftworker must attend show; demonstrations required. Registration limit: 80-100. Sponsor provides chairs; electricity for demonstrations; fencing; limited insurance on exhibited work; table; 24-hour security; and coffee in lounge. Show is advertised by brochures; listing; radio; TV; newspaper ads and stories. Submit photographs for publicity. 1978 shows sales totalled $39,000. Considers all crafts except those made from kits. "Crafts must be representative both in style and method of creation of the Appalachian region." Bestsellers: "$5-500, should have full price range."

Wisconsin

*** ARTARAMA**, Rt. 1, Eagle River WI 54521. (715)479-8947. Chairman: Donna Schwartz. Sponsor: Chamber of Commerce. Estab. 1971. Annual outdoor show held 1 day in July. Average attendance: 2,000. Entries accepted until 1 week before show. Entry fee: $10/10' display area. Work may be offered for sale; no commission. Craftworker must attend show; demonstrations OK. Registration limit: 150. Sponsor provides electricity for demonstrations. Show is advertised by radio; newspaper; posters; and mailings. 1977 show sales totalled $20,000. Presents 6 $75 cash awards of excellence; purchase awards of $500; ribbons for honorable mention and junior awards. Categories: artwork; graphics; craft; handicraft; photography; sculpture; fiber; oils and acrylic; watercolor; pottery; and jewelry.

ARTS & CRAFTS BY THE HANDICAPPED, c/o Division of Vocational Rehabilitation, Department of Health and Social Services, 1570 E. Moreland, Waukesha WI 53186. (414)547-0171. Contact Vivian Traskowski. Annual indoor show held 3 days in October at Brookfield, Wisconsin. Open only to "the handicapped and disabled from the state of Wisconsin. New exhibitors must send chairman statement from their doctor before registration." No entry fee. Work must be offered for sale; no commission.

ARTS & CRAFTS MARKET, GSR Box 6, Medford WI 54451. President: Bob Rohrick. Sponsor: Taylor County Arts Council and University of Wisconsin, Medford. Purpose: "to give all persons a chance to show and sell whatever kind of art or craft they do." Estab. 1972. Annual indoor show held 2 days in June. Average attendance: 1,000. Entries accepted until 2 weeks before show. Entry fee: $10/5x10 display area. Work may be offered for sale; no commission. Craftworker must attend show; demonstrations OK. Registration limit: 75. Sponsor provides electricity for demonstrations and 24-hour security. Show is advertised by TV; radio; newspaper; posters; and signs. Submit description of arts and craft. Considers all crafts, excepts kits.

***BELOIT & VICINITY EXHIBITION**, Wright Art Center, Beloit College, Beloit WI 53511. (608)365-3391. Director: Marylou S. Williams. Sponsor: Wright Art Center and Beloit Art League. Estab. 1957. Annual indoor show held 4 weeks in May-June. Average attendance: 800-1,000. Entries accepted until 3 weeks before show. Entry fee: $7/entry. Maximum 1 entry per craftworker. Prejudging; no entry fees refunded for refused work. Work may be offered for sale; no commission. Sponsor provides display equipment. Deliver crafts in person. Presents $2,000 in cash and $250 in purchase prizes.
Acceptable Work: Considers batik; ceramics; glass art; soft sculpture; weavings; and wall hangings by craftworkers within driving distance of Beloit. No student work. Crafts must be ready for installation. No brackets.

BROOKFIELD SQUARE FALL FINE ART SHOW, 2150 S. 67th Place, West Allis WI 53219. (414)321-5288. Show Coordinator: Rosemary Roth. Estab. 1967. Annual indoor show held 1st weekend in November. Average attendance: "thousands."
Acceptable Work: Considers batik, ceramics, glass art, lapidary, metalsmithing, mobiles, pottery, scrimshaw, sculpture, soft sculpture, tole painting, weaving, woodcrafting and collage. "Work is not acceptable if made from commercial stencils, patterns, molds, etc. No two

---

Those listings preceded by an asterisk present awards for prize-winning crafts.

of a kind crafts. Nothing mass-produced. All artwork that the artist had had commercially reproduced from original work that is included in his display must be labeled as such."
Terms: "Show is invitational, which means interested artists must be screened beforehand at least 5 months in advance of each show." Entry fee: $35/8x10 display area (due after prejudging). Prejudging by photos accompanied by SASE. Work must be offered for sale; no commission. Craftworker must attend show; demonstrations OK. Sponsor provides electricity for demonstrations and 24-hour security.
Promotion: Show is advertised by radio and TV and special monthly flyer sent to newspaper subscribers. "We ask specific persons for a photo of themselves at work for newspaper, along with a brief resume for publicity."

BROOKFIELD SQUARE SUMMERTIME ART & CRAFT SHOW, 2150 S. 67th Place, West Allis WI 53219. (414)321-5288. Show Coordinator: Rosemary Roth. Estab. 1967. Annual indoor show held 3 days in July. Average attendance: "thousands."
Acceptable Work: Considers batik, ceramics, glass art, lapidary, metalsmithing, mobiles, pottery, scrimshaw, sculpture, soft sculpture, tole painting, weaving, woodcrafting and collage. "Work is not acceptable if made from commercial stencils, patterns, molds, etc. No two of a kind crafts. Nothing mass-produced. All artwork that the artist had had commercially reproduced from original work that is included in his display must be labeled as such."
Terms: "Show is invitational, which means interested artists must be screened beforehand at least 5 months in advance of each show." Entry fee: $35/8x10 display area (due after prejudging). Prejudging by photos accompanied by SASE. Work must be offered for sale; no commission. Craftworker must attend show; demonstrations OK. Sponsor provides electricity for demonstrations and 24-hour security.
Promotion: Show is advertised by radio and TV and special monthly flyer sent to newspaper subscribers. "We ask specific persons for a photo of themselves at work for newspapers, along with a brief resume for publicity."

***CEDAR CREEK FESTIVAL OF ARTS & CRAFTS**, Box 205, Cedarburg WI 53012. Festival Co-Director: Judy Nader and Shari Brown. Sponsor: Cedarburg Junior Woman's Club. Purpose: "to promote art in our community and let the public see good art from Midwest artists." Estab. 1975. Annual indoor show held 1 day in spring. Average attendance: 1,000. Entries accepted until "early December". Entry fee: $20/12x10 display area. Prejudging by 5 slides and resume; entry fee refunded for refused work. Work must be offered for sale; no commission. Craftworker or representative must attend show; demonstrations OK. Registration limit: 50. Sponsor provides chairs; electricity for demonstrations where possible; table; lunch; lounge; and set-up help. Show is advertised by TV; radio; publicity articles in local newspapers and *Milwaukee Journal* and *Milwaukee Sentinal*; and news releases to college art departments. Presents cash awards and ribbons. Considers batik; ceramics; glass art; jewelry; leatherworking; macrame; metalsmithing; needlecrafts; pottery; sculpture; weaving; and woodcrafting.

CLINTONVILLE ART FAIR, 415 Meyer St., Marion WI 54950. (715)754-5320. President: Floramae Buhr. Sponsor: Clintonville Arts & Crafts Club. Estab. 1975. Annual outdoor show (indoors in case of rain) held the fourth Sunday in June at Clintonville, Wisconsin. Average attendance: 1,500.
Acceptable Work: Considers all crafts except ceramics, decoupage and dollmaking. No commercial molds, patterns or kits. All work must be original designs and executed by the craftperson. Bestsellers: under $100.
Terms: Entries accepted until 1 week before show. Entry fee: $9/15' of snow fence; 10' indoor space if raining. Work may be offered for sale; no commission. Craftworker must attend show; demonstrations OK. Registration limit: 90. Sponsor provides electricity for demonstrations, fencing and free coffee and roll in the morning.
Awards: Presents cash and purchase awards totalling $1000+. "Judges have usually been university art professors or equally qualified persons.

***CRAFT FAIR**, Box 234, Park Plaza Shopping Center, Oshkosh WI 54902. (414)233-5051, ext. 344. Promotion Director: Joey Beth Bauer. Semiannual indoor show held 3 days in spring and fall. Average attendance: 25,000. Entries accepted up to 2 weeks before show. Entry fee: $30/6x12 display area. Prejudging for new entrants by slides or photos; entry fee refunded for refused work. Work may be offered for sale; no commission. Craftworker must attend show; demonstrations encouraged. Registration limit: 45. Sponsor provides eletricity for demonstrations ($5 fee). Show is advertised by radio and newspaper. Submit information on your craft. Presents awards based on working demonstrations. Considers all crafts except jewelry and lapidary.

DANE COUNTY HUMANE SOCIETY ANIMAL ART FAIR, 2250 Pennsylvania Ave., Madison WI 53704. (608)249-6656. Contact: Deborah Morgan. Purpose: fundraiser. Estab. 1977. Annual outdoor show held 2 days in August. Average attendance: 6,000-8,000. Entries accepted until 6 weeks before show. Display area: 15x10. Prejudging by slides or photos. $15 entry fee. Craftworker must attend show; demonstrations OK. Registration limit: 75. Show is advertised by public service announcements; newspaper; and flyers. Submit photo of craft to be displayed. Considers all crafts that relate to animals, wild or domestic subject matter.

A DETAILED LOOK, NATIONAL METALSMITHING & JEWELRY INVITATIONAL, Art Department, University of Wisconsin, 800 W. Main St., Whitewater WI 53190. Contact: Kelley Morris. Purpose: "to provide a 'detailed look' at current metalsmithing and jewelry concepts for local; regional; and national visitors; faculty; and students." Estab. 1978. Annual indoor show held 2-3 weeks in fall. "This is an invitation only show. Not competitive, and no call for work."

FESTIVAL OF ARTS, Box 1763, Wausau WI 54401. Contact: Peggie Mallery. Estab. 1969. Annual outdoor show held 2 days in September. Average attendance: 15,000.
Acceptable Work: Considers ceramics, glass art, jewelry, metalsmithing, pottery, sculpture, soft sculpture, weaving and woodcrafting. "We only accept *original* works of visual art—the closest we get to 'crafts' is in the areas of leatherwork and woodcrafting."
Terms: Write for entry deadlines. Entry fee: $20/exhibitor. Display area: 6x10. Prejudging by slides; entry fee due after prejudging. Work must be offered for sale; no commission. Craftworker must attend show; no demonstrations. Registration limit: 125. Sponsor provides chairs and 24-hour security.
Awards: Presents $150 in cash awards in 7 categories, $200 Best of Show award and $600 in purchase prizes.

FOLK ART FAIR, 95 N. Moorland Rd., Brookfield Square WI 53005. Show Coordinator: Rosemary Roth. Sponsor: Brookfield Square Merchants' Association. Purpose: to revive an interest in the old crafts. Estab. 1978. Annual indoor show held 3 days in August. Entries accepted until 4 weeks before show. Entry fee: $25/display area. Prejudging by photo or slide of several pieces of craft and 1 photo of entire display. Entry fee due after prejudging. Work may be offered for sale; no commission. Craftworker must attend show; demonstrations encouraged. Registration limit: 75-100. Sponsor provides electricity for demonstrations and 24-hour security. Show is advertised by newspaper and radio. Submit 8x10 glossy of self involved in work and resume. Considers candlemaking; dollmaking; leatherworking; macrame; metalsmithing; needlecrafts; pottery; sculpture; soft sculpture; tole painting; weaving; woodcrafting; and all folk art.

*****FOND DU LAC ARTISTS ASSOCIATION ANNUAL ARTS & CRAFTS FAIR**, Rt. 3, Box 444, Fond Dulac WI 54935. (414)921-1209. President: John Delfeld. Purpose: to bring good art and craftsmanship to the community. Estab. 1967. Annual indoor/outdoor show held 2 days in June. Average attendance: 2,000. Entries accepted until 4 weeks before show. Write for entry fee and forms. Work may be offered for sale; no commission. Craftworker or representative must attend show; demonstrations OK. Sponsor provides limited amount of chairs; display booths; electricity for demonstrations; out of doors fencing; limited amount of tables; and 24-hour security. Show is advertised by local and area radio spots and talk shows; TV; newspapers; and posters. Presents purchase awards of over $1,200 and ribbons. Considers all crafts except soft sculpture.

GAYS MILLS PACE CLUB ARTS & CRAFTS FAIR, Pace Club, Gays Mills WI 54631. Contact: Mrs. Karen Ambrose. Semiannual indoor/outdoor show held 1 day in May and September. Average attendance: 1,000. Entries accepted until filled. Entry fee: $10/10x5 display area. Work may be offered for sale; no commission. Craftworker must attend show; demonstrations encouraged. Registration limit: 75-100. Considers all crafts.

*****GREAT RIVER FESTIVAL OF TRADITIONAL MUSIC & CRAFTS**, c/o Pump House, 119 King St., LaCrosse WI 54601. Co-chairwoman, Crafts: Barbara Starner. Purpose: "to enrich the area's experience and education in traditional music and crafts. Also to provide a sales market for traditional crafts. We emphasize demonstrations." Estab. 1976. Annual outdoor show (inside in case of rain) held 2 days over Labor Day Weekend on University of Wisconsin-La Crosse Campus. Average attendance: 5,000. Entries accepted until 2 weeks before show. Entry fee: $20/display area as large as needed. Prejudging by 3 slides unless accepted last year,

then immediate acceptance; no entry fees refunded for refused work. Work may be offered for sale; no commission. Craftworker must attend show; demonstrations OK. No registration limit. Sponsor provides chairs and tables; electricity for demonstrations; fencing; table; and 24-hour security. Committee tries to find area housing if desired by craftspeople. Presents cash awards of $800-1,000; table fee also allows passes to evening concerts; "all table-area fees are turned into prizes for crafts."
Acceptable Work: Considers batik; candlemaking; ceramics; rosemalling; dollmaking; glass arts; jewelry; leatherworking; macrame; metalsmithing; mobiles; needlecrafts; pottery; sculpture; tole painting; weaving; carving; boat making; folk instruments; puppets and marionettes; dollhouses; eggs; lacemaking; wrought iron; tin smithing; papercutting; and quilting. Bestsellers: ceramics; jewelry; minature dollhouse furniture.
Promotion: Show is advertised by posters; ads in 40 area newspapers; series of feature articles in local newspapers; TV; radio; and articles in area magazines. Submit b&w glossy of self at work and any feature article material.

*HOLLAND DAY ART FAIR "ON THE GREEN", Cedar Grove WI 53013. Contact: Mrs. Robert Klein or Mrs. Carl Winkelhorst. Annual outdoor show held the last Saturday in July. Average attendance: 10,000. Entries accepted until July 23. Entry fee: $8/10x10 display area. Craftworker must attend show. Work may be offered for sale; no commission. Considers all crafts. Presents trophies and ribbons.

HOLLY DAY FAIR, N97 W21763 White Horse Dr., Colgate WI 53017. (414)251-3858. Cochairman: Lonnette Richards. Sponsor: Germantown Jr. Woman's Club. Purpose: fundraiser. Estab. 1977. Annual indoor show held 1 day in November. Average attendance: 1,000. Entries accepted until 10 weeks before show. Entry fee: $12/10x6 display area. Work may be offered for sale; no commission. Craftworkers must attend show; demonstrations OK. Registration limit: 90. Sponsor provides electricity for demonstrations if requested. Show is advertised by newspaper articles; posters; flyers; signs; and newspaper ads. Considers all crafts.

INDIAN HEAD ART FAIR, Wisconsin Indian Head Country, Inc., 3015 E. Clairemont Ave., Eau Claire WI 54701. Show Director: Jean Johnson. Annual show held in March. Entry fee: $15/12x5 display area; limit 2 spaces/exhibitor. Entries accepted until January for previous exhibitors; February for new exhibitors. Prejudging of new exhibitors by representation of work and current resume. Work may be offered for sale; 10% commission charged on total gross sales exceeding $100. Demonstrations OK. Considers woodcuts; jewelry (gold, silver, copper, semi-precious stones); wood carving and turning; batik; leather; pottery; and wood, metal and clay sculpture.

JANESVILLE MALL ARTS & CRAFTS SHOW, Box 61, Rome IL 61562. (309)274-3001. Coordinator: Judy Kelley. Sponsor: Janesville Mall Merchants Association. Triannual indoor show held 3 days in March, August and November at Janesville, Wisconsin. Average attendance: 10,000-20,000.
Acceptable Work: Considers glass art; jewelry; metalsmithing; pottery; sculpture; tole painting; weaving; and woodcrafting.
Terms: Entries accepted until 2 weeks before show. Entry fee: $35-40/12x6' display area. Prejudging by 2 slides or photos. SASE. Entry fee refunded for refused work. Work may be offered for sale; no commission. Craftworker must attend show; demonstrations OK. Registration limit: 55. Sponsor provides electricity for demonstrations. Show is advertised by radio and newspapers. Submit b&w glossies.

*KENOSHA ART FAIR, Kenosha Public Museum, 5608 10th Ave., Kenosha WI 53140. Annual show. Sponsor: Friends of the Kenosha Public Museum. Entry fee: $10/12' fencing. Work must be offered for sale; no commission. Considers all crafts.
Awards: Presents $650 in cash prizes; "Honorary Awards"; $200 museum purchase prize; purchase pledges; and pledger's choice award.

KETTLE MORAINE ART & CRAFTS, 730 N. 14th St., Sheboygan WI 53081. (414)458-6561. Chairman: Karen Lewandoske. Purpose: to provide an outlet for the work of craftsmen and artists. Estab. 1973. Annual indoor show held 1 day in November at West Bend, Wisconsin. Average attendance: 5,000. Entries accepted until 1 week before show; "show usually filled 1 month before show." Entry fee: $9/8x5 display area. Work may be offered for sale; no commission. Craftworker must attend show; demonstrations OK. Registration limit: 85. Sponsor provides chairs and electricity for demonstrations. Show is advertised by radio and newspapers. Considers all crafts.

KETTLE MORAINE CHRISTMAS FAIR, 730 N. 14th St., Sheboygan WI 53081. (414)458-6561. Chairman: Karen Lewandoske. Purpose: to provide an outlet for the work of craftsmen and artist. Estab. 1973. Annual indoor show held 1 day in November at West Bend, Wisconsin. Average attendance: 5,000. Entries accepted until 1 week before show; "show usually filled 1 month before show." Entry fee: $9/8x5 display area. Work may be offered for sale; no commission. Craftworker must attend show; demonstrations OK. Registration limit: 85. Sponsor provides chairs; and electricity for demonstrations. Show is advertised by radio and newspapers. Considers all crafts.

KING RICHARD'S FAIRE—A RETURN TO THE RENAISSANCE, 12420 128th St., Kenosha WI 53142. (312)689-2800. (414)396-4385. General Manager: Robert F. Rogers. Sponsor: Greathall of Illinois, Limited. Purpose: "to provide the most unusual and exciting art and craft marketplace in the Midwest." Estab. 1973. Outdoor show held 13 days on July and August weekends at Bristol, Wisconsin. Entries accepted until 3 weeks before show. Entry fee: $225/before January 15th; $250/by April 15th; $275/after April 15th. Display area: 20' frontage, unlimited depth. Prejudging by prints; slides; or actual work. Entry fee refunded for refused work. Work may be offered for sale; no commission. Craftworker must attend show; demonstrations OK. Registration limit: 175. Sponsor provides electricity for demonstrations; fencing; and 24-hour security. Presents cash awards for best demonstration; best shop; and best costume. Considers any craft practiced during the Renaissance Period. "All craftsmen must be costumed in attire of the period."
Promotion: Show is advertised by 12 month campaign provided by PR firm featuring paid TV spots in Milwaukee and Chicago markets; complete radio and newspaper blitz in Chicago, Milwaukee and outlying areas.

*****MAIN ST. ART FAIR**, Box 720, Black River Falls WI 54615. (715)284-2238. Director: Mary Busching. Sponsor: Black River Child Care Center. Estab. 1977. Outdoor show (indoors if rains) held 1 Saturday in August. Average attendance: 1000+. Considers all crafts.
Terms: Entries accepted until 1 week before show. Entry fee: $10/6x12 display area. Work may be offered for sale; no commission. Craftworker must attend show; demonstrations OK. Registration limit: 60. Exhibitor handles sales and taxes.
Promotion: Show is advertised by local newspapers, posters and public service announcements on the radio and TV.

*****MONUMENT SQUARE ART FAIR**, 223 6th St., Racine WI 53403. (414)633-5332 or 633-3215. Secretary-Treasurer: Mrs. John R. Hackl. Sponsor: AAUW Racine Branch; Downtown Association of Racine; Junior Woman's Club; Racine Art Association; Racine Art Guild; Racine Department of Park and Recreation; and Woman's Club of Racine. Purpose: "to bring the best in art to Racine." Estab. 1963. Annual invitational indoor/outdoor show held 2 days in June. Average attendance: 18,000. Entry fee: $25/12x5 display area. Prelimary juring required; held first Saturday in Janaury. Send 10 slides or bring in 3 pieces of work; slides marked as to size, media, and craftworker's name. SASE. All work exhibited must be for sale. Demonstrations encouraged. Sponsor provides limited number of chairs; snow fencing outside; limited electricity inside for demonstrations; and 24-hour security. Show is advertised by newspapers; radio; TV; and public announcement and talk programs. Presents cash awards of $1,000 and ribbons. 1978 show sales totalled $57,500. "Gift certificates for sale all during the year and program of purchase pledges." Considers batik; ceramics; glass; jewelry; leatherworking; macrame; metalsmithing; needlecrafts; pottery; sculpture; soft sculpture; weaving; and woodcrafting.

MUSCODA ARTS & CRAFTS FAIR, Box 246, Muscoda WI 53573. (708)739-3679. Chairman: Rita Storms. Sponsor: Art Fair Committee. Estab. 1971. Annual indoor/outdoor show held 2 days in August. Average attendance: 2,000. Entries accepted until 1 week before show; $7 late entry fee. Entry fee: $6/10' display area. Work may be offered for sale; no commission. Craftworker or representative must attend show; demonstrations OK. Sponsor provides chairs; electricity for demonstrations; and 24-hour security. 1978 show sales totalled $4,800. Considers all crafts.

NEW HOLSTEIN KIWANIS ARTS & CRAFTS FAIR, Box 29, New Holstein WI 53061. (414)898-5766 business, 898-5232 home. Chairman: Lee J. Tikalsky. Purpose: fundraiser and to bring arts and crafts to the community. Estab. 1973. Annual outdoor show (with shelter and pavilion available in case of rain) held 1 day in September. Entries accepted until 1 week before show. Entry fee: $5/10x15 display area. Work may be offered for sale; no commission. Craftworker must attend show; demonstrations encouraged. Sponsor provides electricity for demonstrations and fencing. Show is advertised by radio; TV; listings in area newspapers and advertisers (100 mile radius); and listings with arts and crafts associations. Considers all crafts.

*NORTHEASTERN WISCONSIN ART ANNUAL, 129 S. Jefferson St., Green Bay WI 54301. Curator of Art, Neville Public Museum: James W. Kreiter. Annual show usually held in the late fall. Entry fee: $2/entry. Maximum 5 entries per artist. Open to residents (ages 18) of the following Wisconsin counties: Brown, Calumet, Door, Fond du Lac, Kewaunee, Manitowoc, Marinette, Oconto, Outagamie, Shawano, Sheboygan, Waupaca and Winnebago. Work must be offered for sale, under $400. No commission. Work must be hand-delivered. Sponsor insures exhibited items for ⅓ of the sale price. No 2-dimensional work over 5x5; no 3-dimensional work over 150 lbs. Considers all work. Presents 3 $200 purchase prizes; ribbons; and entrance into a 4-person exhibition.

OLD CRAFT DAY, Box 131, Fond du Lac WI 54935. (414)922-6390. Chairman: Roland Martin. Sponsor: Fond du Lac County Historical Society. Estab. 1973. Annual indoor/outdoor show held the Sunday after the 4th of July at Galloway Village. "The show is held outdoors if weather permits. Some crafts are put indoors if preferred." Average attendance: 1,300. Considers all crafts.
Terms: Entries accepted until 4 weeks before show. Display area: 3x6 table; more upon request. Work may be offered for sale; no commission. Craftworker must attend show; demonstrations required. Registration limit: about 100; 3 craftworkers/category. Sponsor provides chairs, electricity for demonstrations and table.
Promotion: Show is advertised by state newspaper and radio; local advertising; and listings in publications of interest to historic places.
Profile: Located in a historic village which includes a 30-room restored Victorian house, a gristmill, a 100-year old church, a log cabin home, a depot with caboose, as well as other restored buildings of the late 1800s.

OLDE JAIL HOUSE CRAFT FAIR, 300 Bernard St., Hurley WI 54534. (715)561-2445. Coordinator: Charlene Newhouse. Co-Chairman: Marge Tezak. Estab. 1977. Annual outdoor show (indoors if inclement weather) held 1 day in June. Average attendance: 1,000-2,000.
Acceptable Work: Considers all crafts. "Smaller items, especially medium priced, do well."
Terms: Entries accepted until show date. Entry fee: $10/display area or 10% commission on sold items. Work may be offered for sale. Craftworker must attend show; demonstrations preferred. Registration limit: 20. Sponsor provides electricity for demonstrations.
Profile: "We open the North Country Heritage Festival which runs for 1 week. All advertising is put out by 2 counties to promote the week. We're followed the next day by a juried art show in a neighboring city.

*OUTDOOR ARTS FESTIVAL, Box 204, Watertown WI 53094. Corresponding Secretary: Sandra Pirkel. Estab. 1965. Annual outdoor show held 1 day in August. Entries accepted until show date. Entry fee: $5/display area. Work may be offered for sale; 10% commission. Craftworker must attend show; demonstrations encouraged. Considers all original, fine crafts. Presents $700 in purchase prizes and ribbons.

*OUTDOOR ARTS FESTIVAL, John Michael Kohler Arts Center, 608 New York Avenue, Sheboygan WI 53081. (414)458-6144. Director: R.D. Kohler. Estab. 1971. Annual outdoor show held 2 days in mid-July. Held indoors if raining. Average attendance: 22,000.
Acceptable Work: Considers ceramics, blown glass and stained jewelry, leatherwork, metalwork, needlecrafts, pottery, scrimshaw, sculpture, soft sculpture, fiber and woodwork. No kits, commercial molds or imitations. "All work must be of original design and execution."
Terms: Entries accepted until 8 weeks before show. Entry fee: $25/artist. Display area: minimum 10x12. Prejudging by 35mm slides. Entry fee refunded for refused work. Work must be offered for sale; no commission. Craftworkers encouraged to be present; demonstrations OK (if arranged prior to show). Registration limit: 135. Sponsor provides electricity for demonstrations and free buffet supper. Exhibitor handles sales and taxes.
Awards: Presents $1,000+ in cash awards; and a variety of purchase prizes. "Awards are based on the total work displayed, not on 1 piece."
Promotion: Show is advertised by news media, posters, flyers, and complete on-the-spot coverage by 2 radio stations during the entire festival. Craftworker should provide resume for promotional purposes.

PALMYRA P.T.O. HOLIDAY BAZAAR, c/o Carol Meech. Helenville WI 53137.

(414)495-8695. General Chairman: Carol Meech. Sponsor: Palmyra Parent Teacher Organization. Estab. 1972. Annual indoor show held the third Saturday of November at Palmyra. Average attendance: 5,000 plus. Considers all crafts.
Terms: Entries accepted until all 100 spaces are filled, usually by mid-June. Entry fee: $15/10x10 display area. Work must be offered for sale; no commission. Craftworker needn't attend show; demonstrations OK. Registration limit: about 100. Sponsor provides chairs, electricity for demonstrations and table ($4 rental charge). "Boy Scouts help load, unload and run errands. There's a lunch stand with free coffee before departure and a coat and package check and a nursery for children of shoppers." Exhibitor handles sales and taxes.
Promotion: Show is advertised by 300+ posters, TV appearances, radio interviews, 50 newspaper articles and ads, radio and TV announcements, calendar events, publicity photos, local display boards and newsletters sent to all the residents in the school district.

RACINE CHRISTMAS GIFT MARKET, 420 Main St., Racine WI 53402. (414)637-4471. Director: Daniel Thekan. Purpose: to bring artists and their patrons together before Christmas. Estab. 1971. Annual indoor show held 1 day in December. Average attendance: 1,500. Entries accepted up until show date or until filled. Entry fee: $15/80 square feet of display area. Prejudging by slides; entry fee due after prejudging. Work may be offered for sale; no commission. Craftworker needn't attend show; demonstrations OK. Registration limit: 145. Sponsor provides chairs; electricity for demonstrations; and table. Show is advertised by radio and newspapers. Considers all crafts. Bestsellers: items that will make good Christmas gifts.

***RURAL REMBRAND ANNUAL ART SHOW**, Rt. 1, Box 159, Neshkoro WI 54960. (414)293-4328. Secretary: Lydia Dettmann. Estab. 1950. Annual indoor show held 3rd Sunday in July at Waushara County Fair Grounds. Average attendance: 500-700. Considers all crafts. Awards ribbons.
Terms: Entries accepted until 2 weeks before show. Entry fee: $3/4 paintings and/or crafts. Work may be offered for sale; no commission. "Items cannot leave show until closing. This is not a selling show." Craftworker needn't attend show; demonstrations OK. Sponsor provides space to hang work.

SANTAVILLE ARTS & CRAFTS FAIR, Waukesha County Technical Institute, 800 Main St., Pewaukee WI 53072. (414)691-3200, ext. 313. Contact: Janet Birch or Barbara Ollhoff. Sponsor: Fashion Unlimited Club. Purpose: fundraiser. Estab. 1973. Annual indoor show held 2 days the weekend prior to Thanksgiving. Average attendance: 4,000. Entries accepted until 3 months before show. Entry fee: $25/9x6 display area. Prejudging by photos; entry fee refunded for refused work. Work may be offered for sale; no commission. Must donate 1 item for door prize. Craftworker must attend show; demonstrations OK. Registration limit: 115. Sponsor provides chairs; limited electricity for demonstrations; and table. Show is advertised by newspapers; radio; TV; and posters. Considers all crafts and Christmas decorations. Bestsellers: smaller items for Christmas gifts and decorations.

***SAUK COUNTY ART FESTIVAL**, Box 222, Baraboo WI 53913.21 (608)356-5013. President: Robert Griffith. Sponsor: Sauk County Art Association. Purpose: to promote art and as a fundraiser.1 Estab. 1964. Annual outdoor show held 2 days in August. Average attendance: 5,000. Entries accepted until 1 week before show. Entry fee: $12/10' display area. Work may be offered for sale; no commission. Craftworker or representative must attend show; no demonstrations. Registration limit: 175. Show is advertised by TV; radio; and newspapers. 1977 show sales totalled $21,000. Presents purchase awards. Considers candlemaking; dollmaking; glass art; jewelry; lapidary; leatherworking; macrame; metalsmithing; pottery; tole painting; weaving; and woodcrafting.

***SHAWANO ARTS & CRAFTS FAIR**, Shawano County Art Council, Box 213, Shawano WI 54166. Chairman: Ruth A. Gehr. Purpose: "to promote and develop public interest in fine art and crafts; and to enable the exhibitor to market his product." Estab. 1969. Annual outdoor show held 4th Sunday in July at Shawano, Wisconsin. Average attendance: 3,000-4,000. Entries accepted until 2 weeks before show or until spaces are filled. Entry fee: $15/12' display area. Work may be offered for sale; no commission. Craftworker must attend show; demonstrations OK. Registration limit: 120. Sponsor provides fencing. Show is advertised by various arts and crafts listings; area and local newspapers, including Milwaukee paper. Presents cash awards; purchase awards; and ribbons. Considers all crafts.

SIDEWALK ART & CRAFT FAIR, Box 512, Marinette WI 54143. (715)735-6681. Contact: Kim

Merholtz. Sponsor: Marinette Area Chamber of Commerce. Estab. 1977. Annual outdoor show held the last Friday of June, July and August. Considers all crafts. No machine-made crafts. Show is advertised by newspaper, radio and listings in the Midwest 'things to do' lists.
Terms: Entries accepted until show date. Entry fee: $5/6' display area. Work must be offered for sale; no commission. Craftworker needn't attend show; demonstrations OK.

SUMMERFEST, 200 N. Harbor Dr., Milwaukee WI 53202. Contact: Pat Rowe. Estab. 1967. Annual outdoor show held 11 days in June-July. Average attendance: 750,000. Closing date for entry: January 1. Entry fee: $1,000. Work may be offered for sale; no commission. Registration limit: 24. Considers all crafts.

*SUTTENDE MAI ARTS & CRAFTS, 1513 Williams Dr., Stoughton WI 53589. (608)873-5288. Chairwoman: Ann Sawyer. Estab. 1966. Annual outdoor show (with indoor facilities available in case of rain) held 2 days in May. Average attendance: 60,000-100,000. Presents cash and purchase awards and ribbons.
Acceptable Work: Considers batik, painting, glass art, jewelry, lapidary, leatherworking, macrame, metalsmithing, needlecrafts, pottery, scrimshaw, sculpture, soft sculpture, tole painting, weaving and woodcrafting. No poured ceramics.
Terms: Entries accepted until 4 weeks before show. Entry fee: $15/12x12 display area. Prejudging by slides/photos; entry fee refunded for refused work. Work must be offered for sale; no commission. Craftworker must attend show; demonstrations OK. Registration limit: 135-140. Sponsor provides electricity for demonstrations, fencing and coffee and donuts.

Ron Simon, an award-winning metal sculptor from Cuyahoga Falls, Ohio, is a regular exhibitor at the Boston Mills Artisan Fair at Peninsula, Ohio. This exhibit is held under small canopies and large tents at the ski resort, which is closed during the summer months.

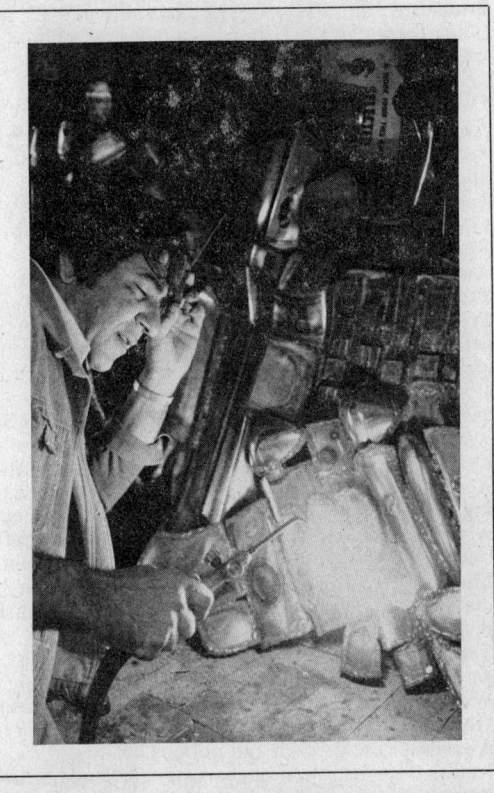

VILLAGE MALL FINE ART & CRAFT SHOW, 2150 S. 67th Place, West Allis WI 53219. (414)321-5288. Contact: Rosemary Roth. Sponsor: Merchants' Association. Estab. 1974. Annual indoor show held 2 days in December at Menonomee Falls, Wisconsin.
Acceptable Work: Considers batik, ceramics, glass art, lapidary, metalsmithing, mobiles, pottery, scrimshaw, sculpture, soft sculpture, tole painting, weaving, woodcrafting and collage. "Work is not acceptable if made from commercial stencils, patterns, molds, etc. No two of a kind crafts. Nothing mass-produced. All artwork that the artist had had commercially

reproduced from original work that is included in his display must be labeled as such."
Terms: "Show is invitational, which means interested artists must be screened beforehand at least 5 months in advance of each show." Entry fee: $12/8x10 display area (due after prejudging). Prejudging by photos accompanied by SASE. Work must be offered for sale; no commission. Craftworker must attend show; demonstrations OK. Sponsor provides electricity for demonstrations and 24-hour security.
Promotion: Show is advertised by radio and TV and special monthly flyer sent to newspaper subscribers. "We ask specific persons for a photo of themselves at work for newspaper, along with a brief resume for publicity."

VILLAGE MALL FINE ART & CRAFT SPRING SHOW, 2150 S. 67th Place, West Allis WI 53219. (414)321-5288. Contact: Rosemary Roth. Sponsor: Merchants' Association. Estab. 1974. Annual indoor show held 2 days in the spring at Menonomee Falls, Wisconsin.
Acceptable Work: Considers batik, ceramics, glass art, lapidary, metalsmithing, mobiles, pottery, scrimshaw, sculpture, soft sculpture, tole painting, weaving, woodcrafting and collage. "Work is not acceptable if made from commercial stencils, patterns, molds, etc. No two of a kind crafts. Nothing mass-produced. All artwork that the artist had had commercially reproduced from original work that is included in his display must be labeled as such."
Terms: "Show is invitational, which means interested artists must be screened beforehand at least 5 months in advance of each show." Entry fee: $35/8x10 display area (due after prejudging). Prejudging by photos accompanied by SASE. Work must be offered for sale; no commission. Craftworker must attend show; demonstrations OK. Sponsor provides electricity for demonstrations and 24-hour security.
Promotion: Show is advertised by radio and TV and special monthly flyer sent to newspaper subscribers. "We ask specific persons for a photo of themselves at work for newspaper, along with a brief resume for publicity."

*VOLKSFEST OF THE ARTS, Box 2, Waunakee WI 53597. (608)849-5534. President: Colette Koltes. Coordinator: D.J. Chalgren. Sponsor: Waunakee Art Council. Purpose: fundraiser. Estab. 1975. Annual outdoor show held 2 days in July. Average attendance: 7,000. Considers all crafts.
Terms: Entries accepted until 2 weeks before show. Entry fee: $20/12x12 display area. Work may be offered for sale; no commission. Craftworker must attend show; demonstrations OK. Registration limit: 75.
Awards: Presents cash awards; purchase prizes; and ribbons.
Promotion: Show is advertised by state and local newspapers; local TV; and radio.
Profile: "This affair honors Waunakee's German background. It is the only German festival of arts in Wisconsin and as far as we know the only in surrounding states. Other events of the day include folk entertainment; German beer garden; kinder parade; and German foods."

*WISCONSIN DESIGNER CRAFTSMEN MORNING GLORY FAIR, 2742 N. 95th St., Milwaukee WI 53222. (414)774-6861. Fair Spokesman: Leslie J. Brockel. Estab. 1975. Annual outdoor show held 2 days in August. Average attendance: 8,000-10,000.
Acceptable Work: Considers batik, ceramics, fine blown glass, jewelry, lapidary, leatherworking, macrame, metalsmithing, mobiles, needlecrafts, pottery, sculpture, soft sculpture, weaving, woodcrafting and other high quality crafts. "Anything not original is forbidden. No toaster-cover, 'craftsy' junk is permitted. We want crafts of the same level of workmanship as fine art (i.e., professional, high technical quality, original creative work of definite artistic distinction and artistic merit.) Pieces must be finished properly, ready to be hung or otherwise displayed—ready to be sold, to be taken home by the purchaser."
Terms: Entries accepted up to 6 weeks before fair). Entry fee: $20/craftworker. Show is set in a garden setting with no set space sizes. Prejudging by slides; $5 nonreturnable prejudging fee. Work must be offered for sale; no commission. Craftworker must attend show; demonstrations OK. Registration limit: 55-70. Participation limited to craftsmen who reside in Wisconsin.
Awards: Presents cash and ribbons awards. "We would stress that high quality be evident, as well as demonstration of creative excellence, in order to qualify as a possible award winner."
Promotion: Show is advertised by mailers, newspaper notices, advertisements, radio and posters.
Sales: "Good quality, moderately-priced work sells itself." 1978 sales totaled about $8,000.

*WO-ZHA-WA DAYS ART FAIR, Box 183, Wisconsin Dells WI 53965. (608)254-8594. President: Cheryl Wenker. Sponsor: Wisconsin Dells Art Association. Purpose: to promote art in the community and a fundraiser. Estab. 1973. Annual outdoor show held 2 days in September.

Average attendance: 2,000-3,000. Entries accepted up until show. Entry fee: $15/10x10 display area. Work may be offered for sale; no commission. Craftworker must attend show; demonstrations OK. Show is advertised by various craft and art show listings; local and state newspapers; radio; and TV interviews. Presents cash awards of $365; purchase awards of $1,000, and ribbons for 1st and 2nd place in each category. Considers all crafts except ceramics.

Canada

BOW RIVER FOLK ARTS FAIRE, No. 300, 223 12th Ave. SW, Calgary, Alberta, Canada T2R 0G9. (403)265-5123. Manager: Gabor Varsany. Sponsor: Prairie Front Workshops. Estab. 1974. Annual outdoor show held 4 days Labor Day weekend. Average attendance: 15,000. Considers crafts handmade by the exhibitor only. Presents booth building prizes of $200, $100 and $50.
Terms: Entries accepted until June 30, jurying July 1-2, replies mailed July 4. Entry fee: $200/15x15 display area, plus $50 refundable clean-up deposit. Prejudging by samples, slides or photos of latest works (even if you exhibited previously in Bow River). If sharing a display area, samples, slides or photos of work of all those exhibiting should be sent. Work may be offered for sale; no commission. Craftworker must attend show; demonstrations OK. Registration limit: 35 spaces. Sponsor provides free camping with sauna and showers 1 mile from Faire site; cafe with discounts for craftspeople; nightly security; and electricity for $30 (craftworker supplies cords). No building materials provided, but there is a lumber yard across the street from the Faire site.

*****CAMBRIDGE TEXTILE FESTIVAL**, 215 Queen St. W., Cambridge (Hespeler), Ontario Canada. (519)658-9311. Contact: Mrs. A. Dawson. Annual indoor show held 2 days in June. Average attendance: 20,000. Show is advertised by radio, TV and newspapers. Considers all crafts. No importers.
Terms: Entries accepted until 4 weeks before show (for the quilt and sewing competition). Entry fee: $25/table for 2 days; $1/item for sewing competition; $10/item for quilt competition. Total display area: size of standard hockey ring. Work may be offered for sale; no commission. Craftworker needn't attend show; demonstrations OK. Sponsor provides electricity for demonstrations, insurance on exhibited work, insurance on work shipped to artist, shipping costs to artists from show (only in competitions), table and 24-hour security. A tax number must be obtained from the local office.
Awards: Presents $500 for best quilt; $100 for best quilt in each category; $100 for best display; and cash awards for sewing competitions. "Make it appeal to the unrestricted eye. If a noncraftperson finds your display attractive, a craftperson will really appreciate it."
Sales Tip: "Anything under $10 which is well-made and has good color and design sells easily. Quilts require a little more thought and must be unusual."

*****THE CANADIAN CRAFT SHOW LTD.**, 458 St. Clements Ave., Toronto, Ontario Canada M5N 1M1. (416)489-9711. Contact: Martin Rumack. Purpose: "to provide an all-Canadian Christmas season craft and art show, gathering fine artisans from across Canada to sell (retail) their own works." Estab. 1975. Annual indoor show held 1 week in late November or early December. Average attendance: 50,000. Entry payment deadline is 2 months before show. Entry fee; $400/10x10 display area. Prejudging by slides, photos, samples and/or personal interviews; entry fee refunded for refused work. Work may be offered for sale; no commission. Craftworker must attend show; demonstrations encouraged. Registration limit: 270. Sponsor provides display panels; electricity for demonstrations; 24-hour security; plastic shopping bags; and Visa and MasterCharge facilities. Show is advertised by flyers; posters; listings; interviews on radio, TV, and in magazines; back of city buses; printed shopping bags; and paid ads on radio, newspapers and magazines. Considers all crafts handmade in Canada. Awards 4 $75 cash prizes.

CHRISTMAS CRAFT FAIRE, No. 300, 223 12th Ave. SW, Calgary, Alberta, Canada T2R 0G9. (403)265-5123. Manager: Gabor Varsany. Sponsor: Prairie Front Workshops. Estab. 1974. Annual indoor show held 4 days in December. Considers most crafts. "Best booth wins a turkey, goose or 25 pounds of soybeans."
Terms: Entries accepted until approximately 5 weeks before show. Entry fee: $150 with no commission for 10x10 full booth; $80 with no commission for 5x10 half booth; $10 plus 30% commission for consignment "Olde Curiousity Shoppe." Prejudging of all work by slides, photos or samples of work. Work must be offered for sale. Craftworker must attend show; demonstrations OK. Registration limit: 40 booths. Sponsor provides table and chairs; electricity (but craftworker must provide cords, plugs and lighting); and a discount food booth.

CHRISTMAS CRAFT MARKET, Box 3355, Halifax, Nova Scotia Canada B3J 3J1. Sponsor: Nova Scotia Designer Craftsmen. Annual indoor show held 3 days in November. Average attendance: 10,000. Presents $50 for best booth.
Acceptable Work: Considers batik; candlemaking; dollmaking; glass art; jewelry; leatherworking; macrame; metalsmithing; mobiles; needlecrafts; pottery; tole painting; weaving; and woodcrafting. "Skill with materials must be exhibited."
Terms: Entries accepted until approximately 2 months before show. Entry fee: $65/6' frontage display area. Prejudging 2 times/year by slides, photos or actual work. Work may be offered for sale; no commission. Craftworker must attend show; demonstrations OK. Registration limit: 100 local craftworkers only. Sponsor provides chairs; lounge area with coffee and tea; information booth; table; and 24-hour security.

ELMIRA MAPLE SYRUP FESTIVAL CRAFTS EXHIBITION & SALE, 5 First St. E., Elmira, Ontario CANADA. (519)669-2605. Chairman, Crafts Committee: Linda Drudge. Sponsor: Elmira and Woolwich Chambers of Commerce. Estab. 1965. Annual indoor show held 1 day in April. Average attendance: 50,000. Considers all handmade crafts.
Term: Entries accepted until 4 weeks before show. Entry fee: $15/8x4 display area. Prejudging by slides and photos. Entry fee due after prejudging. Work may be offered for sale; 10% commission. Craftworker must attend show; demonstrations preferred. Registration limit: 50. Sponsor provides chairs, electricity for demonstrations, liability insurance, table and 24-hour security.
Profile: Takes place during the Elmira Maple Syrup Festival. Food served, antiques sold and entertainment provided. All commission goes to charity.

***FAIR NOVEMBER**, c/o University Centre Programming Office, University of Guelph, Guelph, Ontario Canada N1G 2W1. (519)824-4120, ext. 3902. Assistant Programming Officer: Diana McClure. Purpose: "Fair November is an expose and sale of Canadian crafts. Artists are chosen from across Canada but primarily from Ontario. The purpose of the show is to educate the public and provide a broader base for understanding and appreciating crafts." Estab. 1974. Annual indoor show held 2 days in November. Average attendance: 15,000. Entries needed for jury show 3 months prior to show. Entry fee: $20/artist. Display area: 12 running feet. Prejudging by slides; photos; and references from reputable people in crafts; entry fee due after prejudging. Work may be offered for sale; 15% commission. Craftsman must attend show; demonstrations OK. Registration limit: 70. Sponsor provides chairs; display panels whenever possible; electricity for demonstrations; insurance on exhibited work; table; and 24-hour security protection. Categories: fiber; metal; clay; wood; and miscellaneous.
Acceptable Work: Considers all crafts except decoupage; mobiles; sculpture; soft sculpture; and tole painting.
Awards: Presents $250, cash; ribbons; and "if a piece is considered excellent, it is purchased by the University." Categories for jurying: craftsmanship; use of media; design; originality; and execution. Show sales for Fair November 1978 were around $50,000.
Promotion: Show is advertised by posters; flyers; newspaper; and radio ads. "Six weeks prior to the show we attempt to arrange short stories in the local newspaper and interviews on the radio to discuss some of the upcoming exhibitions. We ask that many of our artisans send us any pertinent information they have such as reviews and critiques of their work."

***FESTIVAL OF FRIENDS**, 21 Augusta, Hamilton, Ontario, Canada L8N 1P1. (416)525-6644. Director: William Powell or Con Furey. Sponsor: Hamilton-Wentworth Creative Arts. Estab. 1976. Annual outdoor show held 3 days during the second weekend in August at Gage Park. Average attendance: 200,000. Presents $3,000-4,000 in purchase prizes. Sales totals unknown but "most craftsmen are sold out and one artist turned $11,200."
Acceptable Work: Considers all crafts, except decoupage, lapidary, scrimshaw and tole painting. No bead strings, assemblages or kits. "All pieces must be 'consumer ready' and with no dangerous elements—lead-free glazes, child proof toys."
Terms: Entries accepted until 3 weeks before show. Entry fee: $75/8x10; maximum 2 spaces. Prejudging by slides/photos. Entry fee refunded for refused work. Work must be offered for sale; no commission. Craftworker must attend show; demonstrations OK. Sponsor provides chairs (rental fee), some electricity for demonstrations, credit card services, fencing, and table (rental fee). Exhibitor handles sales and taxes.
Promotion: Show is advertised by radio, TV, newspapers, and national and international magazines. "Artist should provide some resume and photos for program purposes."

---

* Those listings preceded by an asterisk present awards for prize-winning crafts.

FESTIVAL OF THE ARTS MARKET, Box 3355, Halifax, Nova Scotia Canada B3J 3J1. Sponsor: Nova Scotia Designer Craftsmen. Purpose: "to promote the appreciation and sale of fine craftwork." Annual indoor show held 3 days in August. Average attendance: 10,000. Entries accepted until approximately 2 months before show. Entry fee: $50/4x6 display area. Prejudging 2 times/year by slides, photos or actual work. Work may be offered for sale; no commission. Craftworker must attend show; no demonstrations. Registration limit: 100 Nova Scotia craftworkers only. Sponsor provides chairs; information booth; table; and 24-hour security. Show is advertised by posters; radio; TV; newspapers; and word of mouth. Presents $50 for best booth.
Acceptable Work: Considers batik, candlemaking; dollmaking; glass art; jewelry; leatherworking; macrame; metalsmithing; mobiles; needlecrafts; pottery; tole painting; weaving; and woodcrafting. "No beaded wire jewelry. Skill with materials must be exhibited."

*****FOLK ARTS FESTIVAL MOLSON'S CRAFT SHOW**, 185 Bunting Rd., St. Catharines, Ontario Canada L2M 3Y2. (416)685-6587. Program Director: St. Catherine's Craft Guild. Sponsor: Folk Arts Council and Molson's. Estab. 1975. Annual indoor show held 2 days in June. Presents cash awards and ribbons.
Acceptable Work: Considers batik, pottery, quilting, glass art, jewelry, textile arts, leatherworking, macrame, pottery, sculpture, weaving and woodcrafting. "All coverings for tables of booths must meet fire regulations. Must provide own hooks for hanging."
Terms: Entries accepted until 3 weeks before show. Entry fee: $15/artist; $10/display area. Prejudging by 3 35mm slides of work and 1 slide of booth display. Entry fee non-refundable for refused work. Work may be offered for sale; no commission. Craftworker must attend show; demonstrations OK if in accordance to fire regulations. Registration limit: 40. Sponsor provides chairs, electricity for demonstrations, table, and reception for presentation of awards. Exhibitor handles sales and taxes.
Promotion: Show is advertised by radio, newspapers, promotional brochures, calendar of events and magazines. "It is promoted jointly as part of a 2-week Folk Arts Festival." Small write-up of craftworker should be provided.
Sales Tip: "Have articles priced reasonably where public can view without asking. Sales vary from medium to high depending on price and the way work is exhibited. If artists could have cards readily available, it would help. We are often asked for contacts throughout the year for purchases.

*****OTTAWA CHRISTMAS CRAFT SALE**, Box 5709, Station F, Ottawa, Ontario Canada. 226-1633. Directors: Dan and Barbara Gamble. Sponsor: Gamble Craft Productions Ltd. Purpose: "to help Canadian craftspeople make a full-time living at crafts by providing them with a secure annual market where they know they will do well." Canadian craftworkers only. Estab. 1975. Annual indoor show held 9 days in early December. Average attendance: 60,000. Entries accepted until May 1. Entry fee: $450/100 square feet. Booths available for half of show at $250/100 square feet. Prejudging by slides and photos (minimum of 5, maximum of 10); and resume; entry fee due after prejudging. Work may be offered for sale; no commission. Craftworker must attend show; demonstrations OK. Registration limit: 167 booths. Sponsor provides chairs; display curtains; electricity; 24-hour security; advertising; exhibitor's lounge; 24 page program with biography of all exhibitors; and booth identification. Considers all crafts except commercially molded ceramics, commercially cast jewelry, no kits. Awards 3 cash awards of $300.
Promotion: $18,000 advertising campaign for 1979 show; and b&w photos are appreciated for publicity.

ROCKHOUND ROUND-UP, Box 297, Parrsboro, Nova Scotia Canada B0M 1S0. Chairperson: Marilyn Smith. Sponsor: Chamber of Commerce. Purpose: "to bring people to our area; to promote the lapidary and craftsmen; to teach local people how to do new arts." Estab. 1966. Annual indoor show held 3 days in August. Attendance: 2,500-3,000. Entries accepted until 4 weeks before show. Entry fee: $40/7'3"x3' table; or 10% of sales for demonstrators. Prejudging by slides and photos plus written description of work; registration fee refunded for refused work. Work may be offered for sale; 10% commission. Craftworker must attend show; demonstrations OK. Registration limit: 10-15. Sponsor provides chairs; coverings on tables; display panels; electricity for demonstrations; night watchman; water; canteen facilities; and table. Categories: mineral and gem (rough and finished); and crafts. Considers all crafts. "Macrame must be exhibited demonstrating the purpose it is used for." Presents plaques for best displays.
Sales Tip: "Reasonably-priced items sell best. I have found when work is demonstrated there is

more interest. Dealer handles sales—we collect provincial hospital taxes from them."
Promotion: Show is advertised in newspapers in Halifax, Amherst, Parrsboro, and Springhill; on radio; rock magazines; and flyers. "If craftworkers have any speciality they should tell use so we can promote. If they will demonstrate we should know also."

ST. JOHN'S OUTREACH—ARTS, CRAFTS & ANTIQUES SALE, 135 Dunn St., Oakville, Ontario, Canada. Craft Convenor: Judith M. Graham. Sponsor: St. John's United Church Outreach Committee. Estab. 1967. Annual indoor show held 1 day in October. Average attendance: 2,000. Considers all crafts.
Terms: Entries accepted until spaces are filled, usually 5 months before show. Entry fee: $10/craftworker. Display area: 5-10 feet. Prejudging by actual work, photos or slides. Work may be offered for sale; 20% commission. Craftworker must attend show; demonstrations OK. Registration limit: 35-37 craftworkers. Sponsor provides chairs, display panels, electricity for demonstrations, table and 24-hour security.

*THANKSGIVING FESTIVAL & CRAFT SHOW, Box 460, Fonthill, Ontario, Canada L0S 1E0. (416)892-2621. Supervisor of Education of Planning: Niagara Peninsula Conservative Authority. Estab. 1976. Annual indoor/outdoor show (in large barn and under large tents) held 3 days in October during Canadian Thanksgiving Weekend at Vineland, Ontario. Average attendance: 8,000. Considers all crafts. Show is advertised by news releases, word of mouth, tourist promotion agencies, posters, and radio and TV appearances.
Terms: Entry fee: $25/10x10 display area. Prejudging to ensure broad selection. Work may be offered for sale; no commission. Demonstrations encouraged. Sponsor provides electricity for demonstrations, table and 24-hour security. Exhibitor handles sales and taxes.
Awards: Presents $25, $15 and $10 cash awards, and ribbons. "Prizes in the past have been based on artistic presentation of craft items offered for sale."
Profile: Festival includes old time music, square dancing, grist mill with fresh whole wheat flour for sale, historic buildings (some operating), Sunday afternoon service in a 1864 church, cider mill and hot spiced cider, a shingle mill, autumn colors, Twenty Mile Creek with 2 waterfalls, and food and refreshments.

WINNIPEG FOLK FESTIVAL, 171 Lilac St., Winnipeg, Manitoba Canada R3M 1S1. (204)284-9840. Contact: Rosalie Goldstein. "The arts and crafts area is part of a folk music festival, which also has a dance area. The purpose of the festival is two-fold—we wish to help maintain the health of folk traditions and, at the same time, many people are being reintroduced to their roots." Estab. 1974. Annual outdoor show (with some tents) held 3 days in July at Birds Hill Provincial Park. Average attendance: 25,000. Entries accepted until 6 weeks before show. Entry fee: $75/10x10 display area. Work may be offered for sale; no commission. Craftworker must attend show; demonstrations essential. Registration limit: 32. Sponsor provides 2 chairs; coverings; table; and 24-hour security.
Acceptable Work: Considers all crafts. "The arts and crafts area at the Festival is called the Handmade Village. All crafts are to be handmade, or original in design. We tend to stay away from commercial ventures—we prefer to lend support to those artists and craftsmen who have few commercial outlets. We require that the artist/craftsmen take a large amount of pride in their work. We appreciate the craftsman having a piece of work in various stages of completion in order that the consumer will have a chance to see the different steps involved. Only 1 craftsperson is allowed per craft. That is we will only have 1 potter, 1 leatherworker, etc. The artist is responsible for an attractive display suitable for promotion of his particular craft."
Promotion: "The festival is promoted by posters in 19 cities in North America; also by a brochure going out to a mailing list of 3,000 people; as well as local TV, radio and billboard ads. Newspaper ads are placed in Manitoban papers as well as folk music magazines such as *Folkscene* and *Come For to Sing*."

Puerto Rico

*PAULA INSEL ANNUAL EXHIBITION, 39 Los Meros, Ponce, Puerto Rico 00731. (809)844-8478. Director: Paula Insel. Sponsor: Galerie Paula Insel. Purpose: "the show is a vehicle for artists to expose their talents." Estab. 1956. Annual indoor show held 2 weeks in the spring. Entries accepted until 1-2 months before show. Entry fee: $8/item being displayed. Maximum 3 works/category. Work may be offered for sale; 40% commission. Craftworker needn't attend show; demonstrations OK. Sponsor provides chairs; display panels and electricity for demonstrations. Show is advertised by newspapers; magazines; and mailing lists. Considers batik; ceramics; glass art; macrame; mobiles; needlecrafts; pottery; enamels; sculpture; tole painting; and woodcrafting. Presents ribbons and merchandise for award-winning work.

Apprenticeships

If you find yourself wanting to begin a career in the crafts field, but not knowing which way to turn, you may want to consider working on a one-to-one basis with an experienced craftworker. The individuals and groups in this section are willing to work with interested beginners to teach the creative and marketing skills that help talented individuals become professional craftworkers.

STEVE ALBAIR, 425 N. McArthur St., Macomb IL 61455. Works 30-45 hours a week in metalwork (jewelry). Promotes and works through galleries and is involved with fashion. "Will work with those interested in design elements strictly on an individual basis because my work is in limited editions or are one-of-a-kind pieces that extend the range of 'jewelry' as an art form and have limited marketability. I will accept an apprentice for a 3 month period."

ALETTA, Leonard Rd., Shutesbury MA 01072. (413)256-0174. Works 35-45 hours a week in ceramics: stoneware and flameware. Sells from own studio; sells at shows; consigns work at shops/galleries; sells work outright to shops. Will work with 1 apprentice on a 3 month trial period, stay for 1 year total. Applicaions should be *written* in a letter of application. Work for approximately 20 hours per week. Studio space available.

FARIS ABDULLAH ASHKAR, Box 274, Swannonoa NC 28778. (704)686-5353. Works 15-20 hours a week in wood (Arabic calligraphy, chandeliers, cabinetmaking, model building); macrame materials (plant hangers, sculpture, wall hangings); cloth (clothing design and execution); and design concepts for a variety of media. Sells from own studio; sells at shows; consigns work at shops/galleries; sells work outright to shops; and sells at craft fairs. "Will negotiate with prospective apprentice concerning what he wants to learn."

"B. RUGGED", c/o Susanna Cuyler, 214 Mulberry St., New York NY 10012. (212)226-2933. Works in nonwoven fabric; hooked and knotted wall rugs and rug clothing. Sells from own studio; consigns work at shops/galleries; sells work to interior design firms; and works on direct commission. Interested in hearing from craftworkers looking for apprenticeships. Will take "1-2 fast worker apprentices with originality and enthusiasm. Would work in a casual workshop relationship. I am working on a tape and a brochure to teach and illustrate my method of rugmaking." Inquiries welcome.

KEN & KATHLEEN DALTON, Box 95, Coker Creek TN 37314. (715)261-2157. Works 40-60 hours a week in white oak, bark, vine, and handspun wood basketry and wood carving. Sells from own studio; sells at shows; and sells work outright to shops. Interested in hearing from craftworkers looking for apprenticeships.

WILLIAM R. DERREVERE, 1347 E. 19th St., Tulsa OK 74120. (918)749-6032. Works 30-40 hours a week in jewelry and metalsmithing. Sells from own studio; sells at shows; and consigns work at shops/galleries. "If an individual enjoys the way I work (being concerned with form, surfaces, and manipulation of materials) then I would be interested in working with such an individual. The length of time would depend upon the individual and what they want to learn and how fast they pick up new ideas. Fees and payments would depend upon the person's situation. The main concern would be learning and sharing information, not capital gains."

LYNN EARNEST, Box 884, Palerno WV, Griffithsville WV 26541. (304)524-7578. Works 4-8 hours a day in batik. Sells from own studio; sells at shows (exhibits one-person or more); and sells some work outright to shops. Will accept apprentice for 6-9 months. MFA instruction. Can obtain college credit. Must pay for room and board and hours of instruction. Studio use.

JUDITH FIRME, 4033 Glenbrook Dr., Arlington TX 76015. (817)467-1612. Works 40 hours a week in spinning; weaving; and fiber arts. Sells from own studio; sells at shows; sells work outright to shops/galleries; sells work to interior design firms; and does special commission work. "My students pay a fee of $5/2 hour sessions. An apprentice may provide work instead of money being exchanged. A letter of application should be sent with name, address, phone, and prior experience with the media involved.

JOEL GODSTON, 87 Meadowgate, Wethersfield CT 06109. (203)563-4335. Works up to 10 hours a week in metal (welding); mosiac (glass); and wood. Sells at shows; consigns work at shops/galleries; and sells work outright at shops. "I've never conducted an apprentice program but feel it could be a summer project of 2-3 months, 1-2 times a week for 2-4 hours on a 1 to 1 basis."

HAMPSHIRE PEWTER COMPANY, Rt. 28, Wolfeboro NH 03894. (603)569-4944. Works in handcast "queens metal" pewter. Specializes in pewter holloware and museum reproductions. Sells from own studio and through jewelry and department stores. "We operate the only program certified by the US Department of Labor for the training of Master Pewterers." Veterans Administration approved. Interested in 2 apprentices.
Terms: Apprentices must be accepted by a Master Pewterer within the shop. In preparation, the cadidate will be given 15 minutes of preliminary instruction and one hour of actual work. If the candidate shows promise and if there is an opening, candidate becomes a paid apprentice working at minimum wage for two years.

GRETE BODOGAARD HEIKES, Rt. 1, Box 20, Vermillion SD 57079. (605)624-3056. Works 30 hours a week in fiber. Sells from own studio; sells at shows; and works by commission. "During 1979 I had 2 apprentices from the University of South Dakota, plus one in the summer. They got paid by the hour with money or other items like meat, eggs, etc."

DAVID HOFFMAN, 1601 Trumansburg Rd., Ithaca NY 14850. Works 60 hours a week in wood. Sells from own studio and at shows; consigns work and sells outright to shops/galleries; and designs custom furniture and interiors. Will work with up to 3 apprentices for 1-6 month periods. "Payment negotiated on basis of experience. Make application by letter."

PHYLLIS JOHNS, Cobble Brook Pottery, 136 Cobble Rd., Kent CT 06757. Works 30 hours/week in stoneware. Sells in own retail shop, at shows and wholesale. Will work with one apprentice. Interested applicants for apprenticeship should apply in writing.

FRANK ANDREW KIRBUS, 6256 Highland Rd., Highland Heights OH 44143. (216)442-3211. Works in metal, mobiles and plastics (liquid and solid). Sells from own studio; consigns work at shops/galleries; lectures and conducts workshops in mobiles, metal sculpture and plastics (liquid and solid); and sells work outright to shops. Will work with apprentice. Write for more information.

JOYCE YAMAMOTO KLEPP—SANSEI POTTERY, 1049 Grand Ave., St. Paul MN 55105. (612)224-7159. Works in stoneware and porcelain clay producing functional items. Sells from own studio; sells at shows; sells work outright to shops; and sells work to interior design firms. Will sponsor 1 apprentice/year with previous production experience. Write for information.

EDNA MASON, 3707 Beatly Rd. SW, Huntsville AL 35805. Works in quilting. Sells from home through mail orders. "I would like to help others learn quilting but have to work. I do quilts in my spare time. I couldn't pay anyone to learn under me and couldn't furnish room and board. I am just a working person who has to earn a living myself. If anyone wants to write to me about quilting, enclose a stamp for a reply."

KAREL MIKOLAS, Rt. 3, Studio 131, Slatington PA 18080. Works 40-50 hours a week in glass in combination with other materials (sculpture). Specializes in architectural glass. Sells from own studio; consigns work at shops/galleries; and works on commission. Will work with apprentice on individually-arranged basis.

GARY W. MILLER-GOLDSMITH, 6 Watrous Lane, Milford CT 06460. (203)878-1112. Works 55 hours a week in gold; silver; and precious stones. Sells from own studio; consigns work at shops/galleries; and sells work outright to shops. Will work with apprentice "ages 14-25 on a 7 year program, 4 year program, 8 hour day, 5 day week, $4,000/year payable quarterly in advance with job placement."

NORTH CAROLINA DEPARTMENT OF CULTURAL RESOURCES, Summer Intern Program, North Carolina Arts Council, Raleigh NC 27611. Offers 3 summer internships in arts administration. Must have 4 year college degree, strong administrative and business abilities, and wide knowledge and appreciation of the arts. Preference will be given to North Carolina residents or those with close ties to the state. Also desirable is the ability to accept employment in September if positions should be available. Write for applicaton; application deadline is March 1.

NORTHERN KINGDOM PRINTWORKS, 44 Central St., Bangor ME 04401. (207)942-7245. Works 50-70 hours a week in silk screen printing; art prints; cards; and artistic T-shirts. Sells at shows; consigns work at galleries; and sells work outright to shops. Will work with apprentice on unstructured basis. Studio is small. Pay or fee is negotiable.

ALBERT PALEY, 335 Aberdeen St., Rochester NY 14619. (716)328-7533, 654-8244 (studio). Works 40 hours a week in jewelry (gold, silver, stones) and blacksmithing (architectural metal work and sculpture). Sells from own studio; sells at exhibitions; sells work outright to shops' and sells work to interior design firms. "In the past I have had 3 NEA Master-Apprenticeship Grants in my blacksmithing studio. All worked extremely well for me and apprentices. Please contact."

JERRY PORTER, 141 Harvington Dr., Rochester NY 14617. (716)271-0327. Works in silver and copper jewelry (necklaces, earrings, bracelets, rings) and sculpture. Sells at shows and sells work outright to shops. Will work with 2 apprentices who have a basic craft background. "Experience in almost any media helps." Previously sponsored 2 apprentices (6 months each) teaching them jewelry and sculpture basics and advanced work. "Housing is provided. Apprentice is paid on a piece work basis after 1 week. Apply with a brief summary of experience and desires."

ANNA SALIBELLO, Jockey Hollow Rd., Bernardsville NJ 07924. (201)766-3577. Works 20-40 hours a week in low fire whiteware and in salt glazed ceramics. Sells from own studio; sells at shows; and sells work outright to shops. Will work with 1 apprentice for 1 year minimum time. "No money to be exchanged; payment is made by agreed upon exchange of work time for free use of studio; clay; kiln; glazes; and lessons. Application by mail preferred but phone acceptable as a preliminary."

C. R. SCHIEFER, 5270 Low Gap Rd., Martinsville IN 46151. (317)342-6211. Works full time in stone sculpture, limestone and marble. Sells from own studio; sells at shows; sells work outright to shops; and sells some work to interior design firms. "I have no formal apprentice program but I have allowed some men/women to live with me for a week or so for work provided and let them work alongside me to learn the use of an air hammer with limestone and to learn sanding; cutting; and finishing work."

CHARLES C. SCOTT, Box 213, 934 Mineral Rd., Glenville WV 26351. (304)462-7186. Works 30 hours a week in pottery (stoneware and porcelain); painting; and photography. Sells from own studio; sells at shows; sells work outright to shops; and displays at competitive art exhibitions and one-man shows. Will work with pottery apprentice. "The apprentice should have the basic skills of throwing functional pottery and the desire to further his skills and to learn the operation of a pottery shop; to market; and to exhibit and demonstrate his craft at fairs. He would be required to assist in summer pottery workshops at my studio. The studio has 1,250 square feet which includes living accommodations for 2 people. The shop has 3 potter's wheels, 2 Gilmore looms; some machinery; and a blacksmith shop in another building. I would accept 1 apprentice, a young married couple, or 2 persons who are of high moral character. Living accommodations would be provided in exchange for work. Length of stay would be commensurate with the desire of learning. There would be a profit sharing of all wares made and sold by the apprentice. Applicants should send letter; slides; and resume for screening. Applicants considered must have personal interview."

KAREN SHULER, Baker St., McClellanville SC 29458. Works in stoneware and porcelain producing dinnerware, distinctive cookware and teapots. Sells from own studio; sells at shows; and sells through artists' cooperative. Interested in hearing from craftworkers looking for apprenticeships. "Several local adults and children have exchanged lessons for labor, a few hours/week—a casual arrangement. Apprentice must be thorough, conscientious, dependable, observant and have a lively imagination. I'm more interested in attitude than training, although carpentry and other handyman skills are a definite advantage. I provide no housing or payment. It is a simple trade, measured in hours or by the job, of labor for lessons. An apprenticeship would have to involve a minimum of my time—3 hours per week maximum."

ALLAN J. SINDLER, N. Brailsford Rd., Camden SC 29020. (803)432-4865 or 425-2750. Works in concrete, stone and wood producing sculpture (primarily large outdoor pieces). Sells from own studio; sells at shows; consigns work at shops; sells work outright to shops; and works on direct commission. Will work with 1 apprentice/summer for 3-4 weeks. Room and board provided.

JOHN SKARE, Box 51, Bricelyn MN 56014. (507)653-4571. Works in fibers producing woven wall hangings and sculptural forms (knotting and wrapping). Sells at shows; consigns work at shops; sells from studio; and sells work outright to shops. Will work with 1 apprentice in summers. Craftworker must have a "strong interest in fiber, but experience isn't necessary. Must have good work habits (3 job references), be willing to live with and be a part of my family (1 child), have a Christian background and be over 18. Living accomodations are provided in exchange for work. A 40-hour week includes: idea research and drawing, reading fiber books and periodicals, selecting and buying yarns, developing weaving and related skills, and helping market work at art/craft fairs. 50% of the profits are shared on all items made and sold by the apprentice." Craftworker starts with 3 month probation period; may stay longer if work is satisfactory. "Make an application by letter or in person. A personal interview is a must to be considered."
Profile: "My studio and home are located in the old creamery building. My spare time is spent working on the creamery building and gardening."

STANLEY SPRECHER, 477 Abbottsford, Philadelphia PA 19144. (215)438-6390. Works 24-40 hours a week in metal craft (manufactures costume jewelry). Sells from own studio; sells at shows; consigns work at shops/galleries; and works in craft with mentally disturbed, blind and handicapped people. Will work with 10 apprentices (teenager and up and handicapped people) at 1 time if in Philadelphia area. Fees would depend on what medium, hours, and equipment.

SPRING STREET ENAMELS GALLERY, c/o Joan Itzcovitz, 171 Spring St., New York NY 10012. (212)431-8151. Works in enameling producing jewelry, wall pieces, boxes, bowls and sculpture. Uses enameling techniques of limoges, cloisonne, champleve and basse taille. Sells from own studio/gallery. Will work with several apprentices. "The workshop is separated from the gallery by a wall of burlap. The public is invited to see the operation." Send resume, slides or call for appointment.

KAAREN L. STONER, Box 1447, Orient WA 99160. Works 45-60 hours a week (depending upon season and fair schedules) in ceramics (functional pottery). Sells from own studio and shows; consigns work and sells outright at shops/galleries; and sponsors private pot selling parties. Will work with 1 apprentice at any given time for "any span of time from 1 month to a year or more, mostly depending upon the needs of the apprentice. Some experience necessary; at least 1 or 2 college courses or equivalent experience, and must have basic throwing skills." No payment, so apprentice must be able to support self. Free housing available. Write, explaining background and reasons for wanting to be an apprentice.
Profile: "I have been making a living by producing and selling crafts for the past 10 years—even put myself through a private university graduate school selling pots."

SUNFLOWER STUDIO APPRENTICESHIP PROGRAM, c/o Constance La Lena, 2851 Road B½, Grand Junction CO 81501. (303)242-3883. Works in fibers producing handwoven textiles of traditional 18th and early 19th century design, period costumes, designer fabrics and commissioned architectural pieces. "The program requires a minimum 1-2 year time commitment from the apprentice and involves a 2-step program. Step 1 is an intensive program of skill development through formal instruction and actual weaving experience at the studio. In a live-in situation, the apprentice is exposed to all aspects of running a professional production studio. A full 40-hour week is spent in the studio; in addition, the apprentice is expected to spend a small amount of time assisting in household chores. Step 2 is a period during which the apprentice is actually established in his/her own weaving studio and provided with the financial security of contract weaving for Sunflower Studio, while being given assistance in the personal development of his/her own work. We do not require any cash outlay for the program until the apprentice has acquired sufficient earning power as a weaver to pay back the loan for equipping his/her own personal studio. Write for information."
Profile: "The studio is housed in a 2-story carriage barn which has been remodeled to include weaving and dyeing studios, office and shipping facilities and a showroom.

L.B. WALKER, Box 464 Laurel Ave., Kingston NJ 08528. Works in fiber producing yarns and garments "from our own sheep's wool". Sells from own studio/shop; through mail order catalog; at juried shows; and sells work outright to shops. Previous apprentices—college students (receiving credit) and high school students (part of work/study program or senior projects), both of which were sponsored by the schools. 1-1 relationship with apprentice. "I actually prefer to train the people myself. I look for dedication and enthusiasm in an apprentice rather than experience. The apprentice must choose 1 skill to learn (e.g., spinning, dyeing, etc.); time is too short to teach all the skills in 3 months. The apprentice must provide own housing. I need a 3 month minimum commitment, 3-4 days/week. Any less time would be of no benefit to them. As my apprentices are treated like private students, I must receive tuition to compensate for the long hours I spend with them."

WARP & WEFT WEAVERS, c/o Linda Agar, Elm St., Stockbridge MA 01262. (413)298-3379. Works in fabrics producing wall hangings clothing and lampshades. Sells from own studio/shop. Interested in hearing from craftworkers looking for apprenticeships. Visit by appointment only.

NANCILEE WYDRA, 9 Franklin St., Newark NJ 07102. (201)621-8583 (studio). Home address: Rt. 2, Box 371, Newton NJ 07102. (201)383-8754. Works in sterling silver and 14k gold producing one-of-a-kind neckpieces and production rings and earrings. Sells at shows; sells work outright to shops; and sells from own store in Washington DC. Will work with 1 apprentice. Must have jewelry background working both in wax and metal. "I also will train a person without a great deal of experience, but with sufficient talent. I work full-time at my studio except when traveling on the show circuit. I would provide living accommodations and a small salary in exchange for 4 days/week in the studio. During the other times the apprentice shall have use of my studio. I will *consider* summer-only apprentice, but prefer a longer arrangement. Apply by letter."
Profile: "I have a full scale shop and studio with all the heavy equipment which most jewelers do not have, including casting equipment and a stamping machine. I have had 3 apprentices in the past 5 years. The first 2 worked together during their last year in high school (which had an extensive jewelry program). My last apprentice just left for her own business. She had worked 2½ years living outside the studio on a piece work basis."

Glossary

Artists-in-Schools Program. Funded by the National Endowment for the Arts and administered by individual states, the program offers visual and performing artists salaried residencies at colleges and universities.

Commission. Percentage of retail price taken by a sponsor/salesperson (go between) on work sold.

Consignment. Arrangement by which the craftworker leaves work with a retailer and does not get paid for the work until it is sold. A commission is almost always charged for this service.

Exclusive Representation. Requirement that a craftworker's work appear in only one gallery/shop within a defined geographical area.

Prejudging. Process by which a committee or designated individual reviews one's work prior to acceptance. (Frequently called jurying.)

Purchase Prize. Awarded for an entry which has been purchased by the sponsor of a competition.

Retail Price. Amount of money charged to the ultimate consumer by the retailer.

Retailer. Person or outlet that sells goods to the ultimate consumer. Retailers in this book include shops, galleries, museums and department stores.

Royalty. An agreed percentage paid by the salesperson to the craftworker for each copy of his/her work sold.

Wholesaler. Person or outlet which sells work in large amounts to retailers or jobbers rather than directly to consumers.

Index

A

Abacus Gallery 173
Academy of the Arts 503
Acadia Corporation, The 173
Acadia Gifts 371
Acadian Crafts Association 173
Accents 157
Acorn Gallery 80
Act 1, Gallery 291
Ada Gifts & Crafts 308
Adamsco, Inc. 49
Added Touch, The (see Pacesetter Gifts 96)
ADI (Ashworth Designs, Inc.) 22
ADI Gallery (McAllister, San Francisco) 80
ADI Gallery (Pier 39, San Francisco) 80
Adirondack Folkwares 254
Adirondack Region Craft Professionals (see Northern New York Crafts Festival 560)
Adirondack Store 254
Adrian College 30
Adult Toys 465
Adventures in Crafts Decoupage Sale & Exhibit 550
After the Gold Rush 80
Agricultural Hall of Fame 157
Agricultural Heritage Museum 339
Alameda County Fair 423
Alaska Ceramic Supply, Inc. 68
Alaska Four Seasons Gallery 69
Alaska Native Arts & Crafts 69
Albair, Steve 643
Albany Arts Festival 461
Albany Holiday Market 581
Albany Park Arts & Crafts Fair 466

Albany Spring Arts Festival 581
Albatross Gallery 106
Albatross, The 136
Alberta Crafts (see The Calgary Cabin—Alberta Crafts 395)
Albright-Knox Art Gallery—The Gallery Shop 254
Alderson-Broaddus College 31
Alderson-Broaddus College Arts & Crafts Fair 626
Alena Jewelers—Designers 115
Aletta 643
Alexandria Bicentennial Museum Shop 371
Alex's Imports 309
Alford House 149
Algonac Art Fair 513
Ali Baba (see Echoes 190)
Alianza 187
All Arts Festival 507
All By Hand 254
All Crafts Fair 513
Allanstand 291
Allard's Flathead Indian Trading Post, Doug 227
Allen Country Store & Gift Shop, Ebenezar 358
Allen Gift Shoppe, Ethan 359
Allens' Creations Inc. Frame & Art Gallery 335
Allentown Outdoor Art Festival 550
Alley Rat, The 383
Alliance Museum Shop, The 149
Allied Arts Association (see Sidewalk Show 625)
Allied Arts Council of North Central

Washington (see Allied Arts Street Fair 623, Apple Valley Street Fair 623)
Allied Arts Street Fair 623
Alpena Art Show 514
Alpha Double Plus 377
Alrod Enterprises 168
Altamonte Mall 448
Amanda's 216
Amarillo Art Center Sales Gallery 347
Amateur Stained Glass Competition 423
American Artists & Artisans 466
American Cancer Society (see Columbus Spring Art Fair 571, Invitational Columbus Spring Art Fair 572)
American Celebration, An 482
American Concern for Artistry and Craftsmanship (see American Crafts Festival 551)
American Craft Enterprises, Inc. (see Pacific States Crafts Fair 431, Berlin Craft Expositions 440, Farmington Crafts Expo 441, Hartford Christmas Craft Expo I and II 443, Baltimore Craft Expo 503, Winter Market of American Crafts 507, Boston Christmas Craft Expo 508, New England Craft Expo 512, Northeast Craft Fair 560)
American Crafts Festival 551
American Designer Crafts Association (see Museum Shop of the Arkansas Arts Center 76)
American Indian Arts Collection/Gallery 577
American Indian Exposition 577
American International College 31
American Miniatures 49
American Museum of Quilts & Related Arts 81
American Society of Artists, Inc. 136 (see American Artists & Artisans 466, Artists & Artisans at Work 467, Arts & Crafts in Action 467, Autumn Fest of Arts & Crafts 467, Ethnic/Folk Fest of Arts & Crafts 471, Fall Festival of Arts 472, Holiday Festival of Arts & Crafts 475, Ice House Arts Festival 475, Mid-Summer Festival of Arts & Crafts 477, Oak Park Village Mall Art & Craft Festival 478, Spring Arts Festival 480, Spring Fest of Arts & Crafts 480, Water Tower Art & Craft Festival 481, Your Adventures in Art 482)
American Society of Interior Designers (see ASID International Exposition of Designer Sources 551)
Amish Farm Market 136
Anacortes Arts & Crafts Festival 623
Anderson County Arts Council 335
Anderson Fine Arts Center 149
Anderson Gallery 371
Andersonville Festival Art Fair 466
Angeles Arts in Action 623
Angelique Jewelry 49

Animal Crackers 123
Ann Arbor Art Association 201
Ann Arbor Street Art Fair, The 514
Annapolis Arts Festival 503
Anthony Gallery, The 255
Antique, Quilt & Craft Show 577
Antique Sale & Flea Market 582
Antique Show & Collectors Flea Market 533
Anyart Contemporary Arts Center 334
Anything Goes 255
Anything Goes: The Craft Gallery 300
Apollos Art 161
Appalachia: American Mountain Crafts & Culture 81
Appalachian Arts & Crafts 161
Appalachian Arts & Crafts Festival 626
Appalachian Festival 568
Appalachian House 115
Appalachiana 182
Apple Barrel, The 384
Apple Basket, The 309
Apple Blossom Festival Arts & Crafts Fair 623
Apple Butter Festival 626
Apple Harvest Festival 583
Apple Valley Street Fair 623
Aquinas College 31
Arabia's Art Gallery 384
Arachne 298
Arc En Ciel Stained Glass, Ltd. 256
Arcosanti Festival 416
Area Artists Annual 568
Arethusa Crafts 393
"Arizona Crafts" 416
Ark, The 216
Arkansas Arts Center Art Rental—Purchase Gallery 75
Arkansas Arts Center, The (see Delta Art Exhibition 419, Prints, Drawings & Crafts Exhibition 422, Toys Designed by Artists Exhibition 423)
Arkansas Arts, Crafts & Design Fair 418
Arkansas River Valley Arts & Crafts Fair & Sale 418
Arkwright & His Friends, The 136
Arrow Rock Craft Festival 533
Arrowcraft Shop & Gallery 342
Art Adventures 256
Art Affaire, The (see Mud in Your Eye Pottery Studio 95)
Art Association of Columbus (see Calico Fair 532)
Art Barn, The 387
Art Box, The 157
Art Center Museum (see Functional Ceramics 572)
Art Center, The 348
Art Center 387
Art Centre of New Jersey, The 542
Art Crate, Inc. (Minnesota) 211

Art Crate, Inc. (Wisconsin) 387
Art Enterprise (see Down Town Fulton Show 427, Down Town Novato Center 427, Monterey County Fair 430, Santa Cruz County Fair 432, Sonoma County Fair 433)
Art Festival in the Village, The 449
Art Gallery of Ontario, Gallery Shop 394
Art Gallery, The (see Wings West Gallery 230)
Art Glass Alcove, The 201
Art Go Round 514
Art Guild Burlington, Inc. (see Snake Alley Art Fair 493)
Art in the Barn 466
Art in the Park (Clarinda, Iowa) 489
Art in the Park (Clinton, Iowa) 489
Art in the Park (Fort Dodge, Iowa) 489
Art in the Park (Kansas) 494
"Art in the Park" (Michigan) 514
Art in the Park (Mississippi) 531
Art in the Park (New York) 551
Art in the Park (Ohio) 569
Art in the Park Festival 577
Art in the Park Trade Fair 424
Art, Inc. 69
Art Independent Gallery 387
Art Institute of Boston (see MacIvor Reddie Gallery 195)
Art Latitude 256
Art Lease & Sales Gallery 235
Art Mart (see Studio Wefan 409)
Art Merchant, The 314
Art on the Green—Artisans in Action 464
Art on the Green—Juried Show 464
Art on the Rocks (Alabama) 413
Art on the Rocks (Michigan) 514
Art Palette, The 384
Art Plus Association (see Wonderful World of Crafts 481)
Art Sales & Rental Society 394
Art Shop & Studio of J. Van Hoesen, The 69
Art Shoppe & Gallery, The 309
Art Unlimited 227
Artarama 630
Artesans Gallery 318
Arthritis Art Committee 500
Artifactory, The 232
Artifacts Galleries Ltd. 227
Artique Ltd. 70
Artisan Fair, Boston Mills 569
Artisan House 256
Artisan Shop & Gallery 137
Artisans' Alley, Inc. 81
Artisan's Cooperative (Center Street, Nantucket Island, Massachusetts) 187
Artisan's Cooperative (Straight Wharf, Nantucket Island, Massachusetts) 187
Artisan's Cooperative (Ardmore, Pennsylvania) 319

Artisan's Cooperative (Philadelphia) 319
Artisan's Cooperative/Cooperative Craft Marketing Center 318
Artisans Corner 115
Artisan's Gallery (Boston) 187
Artisan's Gallery (Michigan) 201
Artisans Gallery (Pennsylvania) 319
Artisans Gallery Ltd., The 256
Artisans' Market Place, The 394
Artisan's Studio 394
Artisan's Workshop 232
Artist Co-op (see Lake Tahoe Art & Craft Fair 429)
Artist Exhibition & Registry Series 137
Artistree 300
Artists Alpine Holiday 437
Artists & Artisans at Work 467
Artists' Co-op Gallery 245
Artists in Action (see Belle of the Bend 490)
Artists in Wood 137
Artists' Market 116
Art-on-the-Lake Show 413
Artpark Store 257
Arts Alive Festival 563
Arts & Crafts by the Handicapped 630
Arts & Crafts Fair (Connecticut) 439
Arts & Crafts Fair (Kansas) 494
Arts & Crafts Fair (Michigan) 515
Arts & Crafts Fair of the Southwest 549
Arts & Crafts Fall Festival Show & Sale 534
Arts & Crafts Festival (Connecticut) 440
Arts & Crafts Festival (Florida) 449
Arts & Crafts Festival (Kentucky) 497
Arts & Crafts Festival (Minnesota) 527
Arts & Crafts Festival of Southeastern North Carolina 563
Arts & Crafts; Fine Arts; Hobby Crafts; Country Crafts 570
Arts & Crafts in Action 467
Arts & Crafts in Long's Park 583
Arts & Crafts in the Park 482
Arts & Crafts Market 630
Arts & Crafts on the Village Green 527
Arts & Crafts Outdoor Exhibit 515
Arts & Crafts Show (Iowa) 489
Arts & Crafts Show (Michigan) 515
Arts and Crafts Show (Oklahoma) 577
Arts & Crafts Unlimited 202
Arts Commission of Greater Toledo (see Toledo Festival of the Arts 575)
Arts Council of Fayetteville (see Sunday-on-the-Square 567)
Arts Council of Spartanburg County, Inc., The 335
Arts Crafts Show 465
Arts Festival of Atlanta 461
Arts Fete 516
Arts Guild Winter Festival, The 424
Arts International, Ltd. 137
Arts 'n Crafts by the Sea 424

Arts/Objects 182
Arts Potpourri in the Park 449
Artsaffair 570
Artspace, Ltd. 387
Artwear 257
Artworks 257
Artworks, Inc. 387
Artworks, The 70
Ashkar, Faris Abdullah 643
Ashtabula Arts Center 300
ASID International Exposition of Designer Sources 551
Association of Artists and Craftsmen of Porter County (see Chesterton Art & Craft Fair 482)
Atikokan Centennial Museum 394
Atlantic City Art Center (see Indian Summer Art Show 545)
Auburn Mall Arts 'n Crafts Expo 508
Aufrichtig's Pottery and Jewelry Shop 116
August Competition—Exhibition 534
Austin University, Stephen F. 31
Autumn Art Festival 551
Autumn Craft Festival 503
Autumn Fest of Arts & Crafts 467
Autumn Leaves 131
Autumn Leaves Festival 564
Averett College 31
Avila College 31
Ayn's Shuttle Shop 187
Ayottes' Designery 233
Azalea Arts & Crafts Show & Sale 578
Aztec Corporation 50

B

"B. Rugged" 643
B.C. Headache 137
Baker, William R. 22
Bakery Square Gallery 161
Baldwin Pottery Inc. 257
Ball State University 31 (also see Drawing & Small Sculpture Show 483)
Ballard Mill Center (see Northern New York Crafts Festival 560)
Ballard Mill Center for the Arts (see The Mill Gallery 277)
Baltimore Craft Expo 503
Baltimore Museum of Art 183
Banana Box at Ybor Square, The 124
Banff Center, The 395
Bank Building Corp. of America 22
Banks Haley Gallery—The Gallery Shop 131
Barbara's Tole Shoppe 75
Bare Wall Gallery 319
Barn Gallery & Frame Shop 216
Barnes Galleries, Ltd. 257
Barrington Art Fair 467
Barron Fibre Creations, Barbara 257
Barroncraft Co. 395
Bartel Interior Design 81

Barter Day 531
Bates & Son, C.J. 50
Batesville Annual Art Mart 532
Baumgarten's 50
Bay Area Art Association (see Waterfront Art Fair 527)
Bay Studio Crafts 173
Bayly Museum Shop, University of Virginia 371
Bazaar Del Mundo Gallery 81
Bea Hive, The 235
Beach Plum Tree, The 258
Beadery, The 50
Bearpaw Leather Shop 235
Beatricia & the Kid 319
Beaumont Art Museum Sales Gallery 348
Beautiful Things (Scotch Plains, New Jersey) 235
Beautiful Things (Summit, New Jersey) 236
Beautiful Woods Inc. 258
Beaux Arts Gift Shop of Fresno Arts Center 82
Beckerhoff in Stowe, Ltd. 356
Becky's Country Nook 183
Becky's Crafts 50
Bedford/Downing Glass 258
Bedford Village Art Show 551
Bee Skep, The 258
Bell Street Artists Crafts Fair 552
Bella Vista Arts & Crafts Festival 419
Bellardo Ltd. 258
Belle of the Bend 490
Bellfort Frame & Art Center 348
Belmar Editions Ltd. 50
Beloit & Vicinity Exhibition 630
Belvidere Mall Fall Festival of Crafts 467
Belvidere Mall Starving "American" Arts & Crafts Fair 468
Benchmark Gallery 162
Bencsik Gallery 381
Bennett Folk Festival, Sue 497
Bennett Spring Hillbilly Days 534
Benson Gallery 258
Bentley College 31
Bergen, Wesley 259
Bergstrom Museum Shop, The 387
Bering Straits Eskimo Arts & Craft 70
Berkshire Crafts Fair, The 508
Berlin Craft Expo 440
Bernat & Sons Co., Emile 50
Bernier Studio 234
Berry College 32
Berry Patch Arts & Crafts Festival, The 461
Bersted's Hobby Craft Inc. 52
Beverly Hills "Affaire in the Gardens" Art Show 424
Beyond Expression, Inc. 259
BFM Gallery, Ltd. 259
BGI Crafts International 52
Big Thicket Museum 348

Bird House Enterprises 52
Bird in the Hand, Inc. 320
Bishop Museum 133
Bissell Craft Fair 534
Bits & Pieces, Inc. 216
Bitterroot Pottery 227
Bittersweet Farm 116
Black Expo & Bazaar 440
Blackbear's Great Plains Studio 157
Black's Art Glass Studio 348
Bloom 'n Crafts 516
Bloomingdale Women's Club Festival of Fine Arts 468
Bloomington Fine Arts Museum (see Friends of Art Bookstall 151)
Bloomington's Fourth Street Festival of the Arts & Crafts 482
Blue Delft Co. Inc. 52
Blue Door Gallery/Gift Shop 245
Blue Door Too Gallery 106
Blue Duck, The 392
Blue Grass Art and Hobby Center 154
Blue Heron Gift Shop 395
Blue Mountain Designs 259
Blue Onion 236
Blue Ridge Hearthside Crafts 291
Blue Ridge Quilt Show 626
Blue Sky Gallery, The 320
Boca Raton Mall Arts & Crafts Show 449
Bogalusa Chamber of Commerce Arts, Crafts & Antique Mart 498
Bohemian, The 336
Boise Gallery of Art 135
Bonneville Gallery 377
Booger Hollow Novelty Co. 75
Booktique, The 299
Boston Athenaeum Gallery 188
Boston Baked Beads 174, 188
Boston Christmas Craft Expo 508
Boston Mills Invitational Art Festival 570
Boston Spring Crafts Expo 508
Bosworth Handcrafts 259
Bounty Shop 124
Bourbon County Arts & Crafts & Antique Show 494
Boutz Family Glassblowers 342
Bow River Folk Arts Faire 639
Bowdoin College 32
Boye Needle Co. 52
Boynton Beach Annual Festival of the Arts 449
Bradford College 32
Brandywine Arts Festival 447
Breckenridge Galleries, Inc. 107
Brevard Mall Festival of Arts & Crafts 450
Bridgewater State College 32
Bridgton Art Show 501
Brigham City Museum & Gallery 354
Bristol Art League (see Bristol Mum Festival Art Show 440)

Bristol Mum Festival Art Show 440
Brockman Gallery Productions 82
Brody Miniatures, Molly 116
Brookfield Square Fall Fine Art Show 630
Brookfield Square Merchants Association (see Folk Art Fair 632)
Brookfield Square Summertime Art & Craft Show 631
Brookline Art Society (see Fall Arts & Crafts Market 510)
Brooklyn Artists Rose Festival, Fine Arts & Crafts Show & Sale 516
Brooklyn Center Community Center 211
Brooklyn Museum Gallery Shop 260
Brookneal Department Store 372
Brookside Museum 260
Brown County Craft Guild Gallery, The 149
Brown Studio, Ken 52
Bucks County Guild of Craftsmen (see Christmas Craft Fair & Sale 584, Spring Craft Fair & Show 593)
Burgett's Myrtlewood Shops 314
Burkid's 202
Burlington Mall Children's Hour Show 509
Burlington Mall Professional Craft & Sculpture Show 509
Burlington Old-Fashioned Apple Harvest Festival 626
Bushwacker Arts & Crafts Festival 534
Busyfingers Gift Shop 356
Butler Institute of American Art (see Ceramic, Sculpture & Craft Show 571)
Butterfly, The 336
Buy Arts for Christmas Show 425
By Hand Fine Craft Gallery 236
Byrds Floral 309

C

C.R.A.F.T. 549
Cabarrus County Agricultural Fair Arts & Crafts Show 564
Cabin Craft Shoppes 388
Cabin Creek Quilts (Cabin Creek, West Virginia) 384
Cabin Creek Quilts (Charleston, West Virginia) 384
Cable Cookhouse 395
Cabot's Old Indian Pueblo Museum 82
Cadillac Festival of the Arts 516
Cain Park Arts Festival 571
Cal-Accessories Co., Inc. 52
Caledonia Cobbler, The 356
Calgary Cabin—Alberta Crafts, The 395
Calico Art Festival 425
Calico Cat, Inc. 183
Calico Dollhouse, The 52
Calico Fair 532
Calico Kitten, The 292
California Artists & Craftsmens Guild 82

California Clothing Co. 216
California Country Furniture 82
California Crafts 426
California Craftsman, The 426
California State Polytechnic University (see Ink & Clay 429)
California 3-Dimensional Regional Exhibit & Competition 426
Cambridge Textile Festival 639
Campbell Folk School, John C. 292 (also see Folk School Fall Festival 565)
Campbell River & District Museum 396
Campus Martius Museum 300
Canaan Craftsmen's Christmas Fair 541
Canaan's Music and Crafts Festival 541
Canadian Craft Show Ltd., The 639
Canadian Crafts Gift Shop 396
Candle in the Night, A 356
Candleriggs Craft Shop, The 396
Candlewic Company 320
Candling Mill, The 211
Candy Stick Studio Art Gallery 82
Cannon Shop 377
Canton Flea Market Arts & Crafts Show, The 532
Canton Gallery, Inc. 260
Canyon Gallery Two 83
Cape Henlopen Craft Fair & Folk Life Festival 447
Cape May County Art League Boardwalk Art Show 542
Capital City Art & Craft Show 627
Capital Expo Arts & Crafts Invitational 497
Capital Expo Fine Art & Crafts Show 497
Capital Woodcarvers Association Show 426
Capitol Art Gallery 202
Caravan Gallery, Ltd. 309
Carbon County Arts Guild (see Christmas Fair & Bazaar 539)
Carbondale Mountain Fair 437
Cardinal China Company 52
Cards & Shards 188
Caribou Fall Arts & Crafts Festival 502
Caribou Sidewalk Arts & Crafts Festival 502
Carmel Work Center Shop 83
Carnegie Institute (see Three Rivers Arts Festival 594)
Carolina Arts Gallery 292
Carolina Craftsmen's Christmas Classic, The 596
Carolina Craftsmen's Christmas Classic—Charlotte, The 564
Carolina Craftsmen's Christmas Classic—Greensboro, The 564
Carolina Craftsmen's Christmas Classic—Louisville, The 497
Carolina Craftsmen's Christmas Classic—Montgomery, The 413
Carolina Mountain Arts & Crafts 292
Carolista Jewelry Designers 292

Carousel Crafts Company 53
Carriage Barn, The 357
Carroll Sidewalk Art Show 490
Carroll-Condit Galleries 260
Casa de Colores 245
Casa Del Sol 314
Case Trading Post—Wheelwright Museum 246
Cass County Log Cabin Festival 534
Castle Gallery 227
Catawba College 32
Cat's Cradle 188
Cave House, The 372
Cedar Chest, The 392
Cedar Creek Festival of Arts & Crafts 631
Cedar Point, Inc. 300
Cedar Point's Crafts Show 571
Celebration of the Arts 426
Center for the Textile Arts (see Fiberworks 89)
Center of Modern Art, Inc., The 124
Center of the History of American Needlework 320
Center Shop, The 292
Central Madison Council 388
Central Pennsylvania Festival of the Arts (see Juried Craft Exhibition 588)
Central Pennsylvania Festival of the Arts Sidewalk Sale 583
Centre Square Art Fair 584
Centro Artes Populares 411
Century Gallery, Inc. 162
Ceramic Hut 348
Ceramic, Sculpture & Craft Show 571
Ceramics Workshop (see Earthworks 595)
Cermak Road Business Association (see Spring Arts & Crafts Fair 480)
Cezar 168
Chalaka Arts and Crafts Festival 414
Changing Scene, The 388
Chaparral 348
Chapman Galleries Ltd. 397
Charles Town Factory Outlet Complex 261
Charlevoix Waterfront Art Fair 517
Chase Gallery, Gail 377
Chase Galleries, Ltd., Merrill 137
Chatauqua of the Arts 482
Chatham College 32
Chatham Festival of the Arts 509
Cherokee Strip Arts Festival 578
Cherokee Strip Living Museum 158
Cherries Jubilee Craft Show 584
Cherry Creek Festival of the Arts 437
Cherry Hill Mall Arts Festival 542
Cherry Hill Mall Craft & Sculpture Show 543
Cherry Hill Mall Professional Craft & Sculpture Show 543
Chesapeake Bay Maritime Museum Shop 183

Chesterton Art & Craft Fair 482
Chicago State University 32
Chickasaw Council House Museum 309
Childrens Educational Toys 354
Chillicothe Art & Craft Show 468
Chitimacha Craft 168
Chmielewski Gallery 320
Chocolate & Vanilla Ltd. 53
Chocolate Soup, The 261
Choice Incorporated 83
Christian Book Center (see Little Bit of Heaven 345)
Christina's 261
Christmas Art & Craft Sale 427
Christmas Arts & Crafts (Abilene, Kansas) 494
Christmas Arts & Crafts (Topeka, Kansas) 494
Christmas Arts & Crafts Show 552
Christmas Arts Festival 440
Christmas Craft & Art Show 597
Christmas Craft and Hobby Show 517
Christmas Craft Bazaar 535
Christmas Craft Fair 582
Christmas Craft Fair, The 502
Christmas Craft Fair & Sale 584
Christmas Craft Faire (Canada) 639
Christmas Craft Faire (see University of California at Davis 42)
Christmas Craft Market 640
Christmas Elves, The 397
Christmas Fair and Bazaar 539
Christmas Fair at Project Arts Center, The 509
Christmas Gift & Hobby Show 483
Christmas in September Festival 627
Christmas Show 465
Christmas Stocking Craft Show 441
Chuck's Gallery 228
Cincinnati Museum of Natural History Collectors Shop 301
Citrus County Art League (see Citrus County Festival of the Arts 450)
Citrus County Festival of the Arts 450
Civic Fine Arts Association Museum Shop 339
Clamshell, The 397
Clapper Publishing Co., Inc. 53
Clark Country Fair 623
Classical Glass 202
Clay & Fiber Gallery 246
Clay Crafts Community 261
Clay Gallery, The 202
Clay Place Gallery, The 321
Clay Pot, The 261
Clear Light Studio 262
Clemson University 33
Cleveland Historical Society (see Pioneer Craft Festival 422)
Cleveland Museum of Art, The (see May Show 573)
Clinton Historical Museum Village 236 (also see Craft Day in the Park 543)
Clintonville Art Fair 631
Cloth & Clay, Inc. 397
Clothesline Exhibit 584
Clouds 262
Coast Gallery 83
Coast Guard Festival Crafts Fair 517
Coastland Center Invitational Winter Festival of Art 450
Cobble Brook Pottery (see Phyllis Johns 644)
Cob-Web Hall 71
Coffee Cantata 84
Coffeetrees at Stewart's 162
Cohn Co., M.M. 75
Colby College 33
Colby Craft Fair (see Colby College 33)
Cold Hollow Cider Press 357
Collage Boutique 398
Collage, The 299
Collection, The 321
Collector's Corner, Huntington Galleries 384
Collector's Gallery 162
Collectors' Showroom 137
College of New Rochelle 33
College of Wooster, The 33 (also see Functional Ceramics 572)
Colonial Craftsmen, Inc 53
Colonial Vermont, Inc. 357
Colorado Renaissance Festival 438
Colorado River Indian Tribes Museum 71
Columbia Art Gallery 314
Columbia Mall Professional Arts Festival 503
Columbus Art-Craft-Hobby-Miniature Fair 571
Columbus Arts League (see Fair on the Square 484)
Columbus Museum of Art (see Designer Craftsman Shop 302)
Columbus Spring Art Fair 571
Common Ground Artists Co-operative 84
Common Place 149
Commonwheel Artists Cooperative 107
Community Art Gallery 377
Community Craft Cooperative 342
Community Crafts & Arts Co-op, Inc. 388
Company Store, The 84
Complex, The 343
Comstock Lode, The 138
Concordia Christmas Craft Show (see Concordia Teachers College 33)
Concordia Teachers College 33
Confederation Centre of the Arts (see Gallery Gift Shop 400)
Confluence Gallery 107
Connecticut Craft Professionals, Inc. (see Spring Market 446)
Conner Prairie Pioneer Settlement (see Conner Trading Post 150)

Conner Trading Post 150
Connoisseur Studio 53
Consortium for Children's Services 262
Contemporary Art Glass Gallery 262
Contemporary Art Workshop 138
Contemporary Arts Center of Hawaii 133
Contemporary Craft Exhibition 448
Contemporary Crafts Association 314
Contemporary Crafts Showcase With Art at the Boulevard Mall 552
Contemporary Crafts Showcase With Art at the Riverside Mall 552
Contemporary Crafts Showcase With Art at the Shoppingtown Mall 552)
Contemporary Crafts Showcase With Art the the Summit Park Mall 553
Contemporary Crafts Showcase With Art at the Worcester Center 509
Contemporary Craftsmen, The 246
Contemporary Gallery 349
Contemporary Quilt, The 138
Contemporary Stained Glass & The Creative Arts 301
Conversation Piece 133
Cool Moose, The 174
Coon Holler 150
Cooper & French, Ltd. 334
Cooperative Artisanale de Cheticamp Ltee. 398
Cooperstown Annual National Art Exhibition 553
Coos Art Museum 315
Coos Art Museum Craft Show 582
Copper Country Gallery 517
Copper King Mansion 228
Coqui Galleries 117
Coral Gables Miracle Mile Sidewalk Art Show 450
Corcoran Gallery of Art, The (see The Corcoran Shop 381)
Corcoran Shop, The 381
Corn Hill Arts Festival 553
Cornell University 33
Cornerhouse Gallery & Frame 154
Cornerstone Crafts 343
Corning Glass Center 262
Cornwall Crafts 357
Cortland Art League (see Park Art Festival 561)
Cosanti Foundation (see Arcosanti Festival 416
Coshocton Canal Festival 571
Cottage Crafts of Vermont 357
Cottage Studio Ltd., The 398
Cottonbrook Gallery 358
Cottonlandia Foundation 215
Cottonpatch Inc. (see Village Craftsman 154)
Council Bluffs Old-Time Country Music Contest & Pioneer Exposition 490
Country Cottage, The 293

Country Craft Boutique 217
Country Crafts 388
Country Craftsmen, The 378
Country Fair & Auction 468
Country Fair Mall Art & Craft Show 468
Country Gallery, The 263
Country Joy 150
Country Roads 461
Country Shop 336
Countryside Mall Arts & Selected Crafts Fair 469
Countryside Mall Fall Festival of Selected Crafts 469
Countryside Mall Starving "American" Arts & Crafts 469
Countryside Village Art Fair 539
Countrywide Crafts 84
County Bazaar 117
Courthouse Arts Festival 504
Couturier Galerie (see International Guest Exhibition of Painting, Sculpture & Graphics 443)
Coweta Festivals, Inc. (see Powers' Crossroads Country Fair & Art Festival 464)
Cox AIA Architect, Carl 22
Cox, Maria Radoslovich 23
Coyne Galleries, Elaine 131
Coyote Den, The 392
Craft Adventure 509
Craft Alliance Gallery 217 (also see August Competition—Exhibition 534)
Craft Alliance, The 168
Craft & Folk Art Museum 84
Craft Barn, The 263
Craft Basket, The 188
Craft Carnival V 517
Craft Center 189
Craft Center Fair 510
Craft Clocks & Gifts 138
Craft Connection, Ltd. 138
Craft Cranny, The 344
Craft Day 585
Craft Day in the Park 543
Craft Days 553
Craft Designs Unlimited 263
Craft Exhibition of the Central Pennsylvania Festival of the Arts 585
Craft Fair 631
Craft Fair (Connecticut) 441, 631
Craft Fair (Andover, Massachusetts) 510
Craft Fair (Boxborough, Massachusetts) 510
Craft Fair at Riverfront 483
Craft Festival 553
Craft Gallery 469
Craft Gallery, Ltd., The 184
Craft Gallery of the Ontario Crafts Council, The 398
Craft Gallery, The 85
Craft Industries 349

Index

Craft Place 217
Craft Products Companies (Elmhurst, Illinois) 138
Craft Products Companies (St. Charles, Illinois) 138
Craft Seller, The 358
Craft Shop Crafts Fair 470
Craft Store 321
Craft Street, Inc. 85
Craft Studio of Takoma Park, The 184
Crafters' Gallery 372
Craftily Yours 189
Craftproducers Incorporated (see Craftproducers Marketplace 450, 554, Sarasota Spring Festival of Craft 457)
Crafts 544
Crafts & Creations 554
Crafts & Things 125
Crafts Barn, The 263
Crafts End 117
Crafts Fair 554
Crafts in Action Show & Sale 554
Crafts Incredible, Inc. 158
Crafts Ltd. 53
Crafts Marketplace 595
Craftsman's Gallery Ltd., The 263
Craftsman's Gallery of Carmel (Carmel, California) 85
Craftsman's Gallery of Carmel (San Francisco) 85
Craftsmen Corner, Inc. 264
Craftsmen of Chelsea Court 381
Craftsmen Two 236
Craftsmen's Fair 541
Craftsmen's Fair at Delaware Art Museum 448
Craftworks, Inc. 237
Crafty Fox, The
Cranbrook Academy of Art Museum Bookstore 202
Cranbrook Institute of Science 203
Create Your Own, Inc. 53
Creation Art & Craft Center 301
Creations & Crafts Co. 264
Creative Art Gallery 125
Creative Artists Group (see Marysville Mall Art & Craft Show 540, Peach Tree Mall 431)
Creative Arts Guild (see Albany Holiday Market 581, Albany Spring Arts Festival 581)
Creative Arts Guild, Inc. (see Firehouse Arts & Crafts Festival 462)
Creative Arts League of Sacramento (see California Craftsman 426)
Creative Arts Studio 389
Creative Clutter by Vergene 301
Creative Conspiracy 125
Creative Corners 85
Creative Craft Boutique (see Crafts in Action Show & Sale 554)
Creative Crafts 544
Creative Crafts (Federal Way, Washington) 378
Creative Crafts (Olympia, Washington) 378
Creative Crafts (Vancouver, Washington) 378
Creative Faires, Ltd. (see Super Crafts Sunday 547, Harvest Crafts Festival 557, New York Renaissance Festival 559)
Creative Gift Studio, Inc. 139
Creative Hands (Florida) 125
Creative Hands (Pennsylvania) 321
Creative Treasures Artisans' Cooperative 301
Creative Women's Collective 264
Creatively Yours Studio 139
Cresco Art & Craft Fair 490
Crested Butte Festival of the Arts 438
Crewel Elephant, The 107
Critters & Cohorts 470
Crocker Art Museum (see California Craftsman 426)
Croft House Gift Shop, The 399
Croft, The 398
Cross Canada Crafts 399
Cross County Mall Art & Craft Show 470
Crossfire Gallery 134
Crossroads Museum of Art, The 162
Croton Crafts Fair 554
Crowley's Ridge Area Folk Trade 75
Crutcher AIA & Associates, Judith Wolf 23
Cuelenaere Library, John M. 399
Cumberland County Fair 544
Cumberland Valley Exhibition 504
Curbstone Craft Festival 554
Current Crafts 117
Curt, Denise (see Meet the Artists—Chapel Square Mall 443, Meet the Artists—Milford Green 443, Meet the Artists—Olde Mystic Village 444, Meet the Artists—Meriden Square Mall 444)
Curwood Festival Arts & Crafts Market 518
Custom Handweavers 86
Custom House 217
Custom House of Needle Arts & Design, Inc. 53
Custom-Foam Crafts, Inc. 54

D

Dacotah Prairie Museum 339
Dakin Farm 358
Dakota State College 33
Dallas Museum of Fine Arts Museum Shop 349
Dalton, Ken & Kathleen 643
Damron Hall 264
Dancing Deer, The 174
Dandelion 2 322
Dane County Humane Society Animal Art Fair 632
Danforth Museum Shop 189

Danish Festival Arts & Crafts Show 518
Danville Museum of Fine Arts & History Shop, The 372
Dar Gift Shop 215
Darlene's House of Gifts 155
Darline's Antiques & Needlecraft 217
David 86
David County Arts Council (see Arts Alive Festival 563)
Daviess Martin County Art Festival 483
Davis & Elkins College 34
Davis Art Center (see Christmas Art & Craft Sale 427)
Dawntreader 372
Day & Associates Landscape Architects & Planners ASLA, A. Dewitt 23
Day in the Country, A 470
Daytona Beach Museum of Arts and Sciences (see Halifax Art Festival 453)
De Saisset Art Gallery & Museum Gallery Shop 86
De Vargas Arts & Crafts Fair 246
De Vargas Summer Arts & Crafts Show 549
Deadwood Gulch Art Gallery 340
Decatur Civic Chorus Annual Arts & Crafts Fair 462
Decorative Things, DBA Things, Inc. 358
Dedham Mall Arts 'n Crafts Expo 510
Deepwood Crafts Gallery 322
Deerfield Commons Arts & Selected Crafts Fair 470
Deerfield Commons Spring Festival of Selected Crafts 470
Del Mano Gallery (Los Angeles) 86
Del Mano Gallery (Pasadena, California) 86
Del Mar College 34
Del Sol, Inc. 246
Deland Outdoor Art Festival 451
Delaware Art Museum (see Contemporary Craft Exhibition 448, Craftsmen's Fair at Delaware Art Museum 448, Wilmington Craft Fair 448)
Delaware Museum of Natural History 122
Delta Art Exhibition 419
Denver Museum of Natural History Gift Shop 107
Department of Tourism, City of Petersburg 373
Departure, The 71
Deptford Mall Patriots Art Brigade 544
Derrevere, William R. 643
Deshane Miniature Galleries 54
Design Division-Regency/Century Greetings 54
Design Group 3 24
Designer Crafts Council of Schenectady Museum (see Craft Festival 553)
Designer Craftsman Shop 302
Designs in Silver, Etcetera 264
Detailed Look, National Metalsmithing & Jewelry Invitational, A 632
Detroit Artists Market 203
Devon Craft Fair 585
Dewey-Kofron Gallery 247
Dexterity, Ltd. 237
Dezign House III 24
DFC Gallery, Division of Designers Furniture Center International 265
Dickinson County Council for the Arts (see Midwest Arts & Crafts Show 522)
Different Drummer, A 125
Different Drummer 189
Dillon County Arts & Crafts Festival 597
Dinjii Zhuu Enjit Museum 70
"Discover Ravinia Day" 471
Discovery Art Galleries 237
Discovery Center 126
Divided House, Inc. 190
Dodge House Art Gallery 190
Doll House, Inc., The 131
Doll House Master 54
Dollhouse Factory, The 237
Dollhouse Furniture & Accessories Shop 238
Dollhouse World 302
Door Knob, Inc., The 349
Doubletree Gallery 238
Douglas Gallery, Inc., The 117
Douglass College (see New Jersey Folk Festival 546)
Doust Art Galleries (Arbordale Rd., Syracuse, New York) 265
Doust Art Galleries (Warren Street, Syracuse, New York) 265
Dovetail 87
Down East Craftsman (see Midtown Professional Art & Craft Fair 529)
Down Home 87
Down on the Farm, Ltd. 118
Down Town Fulton Show 427
Down Town Novato Center 427
Downtown Bay City Sidewalk Days 518
Downtown Syracuse Arts & Crafts Fair 555
Drawing & Small Sculpture Show 483
Dream Masters, A Gallery of Fantasy & Science Fiction Art 88
Drumm Studios & Gallery, Don 302
Drumright Art & Craft Show 578
Drutt Gallery, Helen 322
Ducks Unlimited National Wildlife Art Show 535
Dulcimer Shoppe, The 75
Duluth Folk Festival 528
Dundee Arts & Crafts Club (see Arts & Crafts Outdoor Exhibit 515)
Dundee Arts and Crafts Club Outdoor Exhibit 518
Dunlap Co., The 350
Duquesne University 34
Durham Art Guild Annual Juried Exhibit 564

Dyeco 139

E

Eagle Creek Arts & Folk Music Festival 484
Eagle Gallery, Clara M. 162
Earnest, Lynn 643
Earth & Fire Ceramic Studio & Gallery 238
Earth Glass Studio, Inc. 139
Earth Muse 399
Earth to Stone 158
Earthcraft 265
Earthworks 595
Earthworks & Artisans 265
Earthworks, Inc. 381
Earthworks Pottery 265
East Grand Forks Arts & Crafts 528
East Tennessee Crafts Inc. 344
Eastern Illinois University (see Festival 472)
Eastern Maine Crafts Co-op 174
Eastern New Mexico University (see Peanut Valley Festival 549)
Eastern States Exposition (see Craft Adventure 509)
Eastfield Mall Arts Festival 510
Echelon Mall Arts Festival 544
Echelon Mall Children's Hour Show 545
Echoes 190
Edens Plaza Arts & Craft Fair 471
Edgemont Yarn Service, Inc. 163
Edmond Scientific Co. 54
Edmonds Art Festival 624
Egg & the Eye, The (see Craft & Folk Art Museum 84)
Egg Shell Craft (see Eggorama 585)
Eggorama 585
Eight Hands at the Farm Women's Market, The 184
8-State Annual 497
El Diablo Forge Guild (see Forge Patio Art Gallerie, Association 89)
El Diez Y Seis De Septiembre 438
El Gingo 247
El Paso Museum of Art Gift Shop 350
El Rincon 247
Elder Craftsmen of Philadelphia 322
Elder Craftsmen, The (New York) 266
Electrum Festival of the Arts 539
Electrum Jewelry 266
Elements, The (Connecticut) 118
Elements, The (New York) 266
Ellicott B&O R.R. Station Museum 184
Elliot Designs Jewelry 190
Elmhurst Festival Crafts Fair 471
Elmira Maple Syrup Festival Crafts Exhibition & Sale 640
Elpa Marketing Industries, Inc. (see Thorens Music Boxes 63)
Elvehjem Museum of Art 389
Embroiderers' Guild of Pittsburgh, Inc. (see Stitchery '80 594)
Emergency Workshop 163
Emerson Arts & Crafts Fair 518
Emerson Gallery 88
Emporium 228
Emporium, The 322
Enchanted Doll House, The 359
Encounter, The 108
Endion Station 211
Enlightened Sights Stained Glass 88
Epsilon Omega Arts & Craft Show 471
Erie Art Center (see Spring Show 593)
Especially Maine 175
Essex Institute Museum Shop 191
Etgen Fine Jewelry, Beth & Bill 55
Ethnic/Folk Fest of Arts & Crafts 471
Euclid Leather Loft 218
Evans Farm Country Store 373
Evanston Art Center (see Olde Town Gallery 145)
Evansville Arts & Education Council (see Craft Fair at Riverfront 483, Walkway Festival 488)
Evansville Museum of Arts and Science (see Mid-States Craft Exhibition 487)
Eva's Interiors 24, 139
Everhart Museum Sales Shop 323
Everson Museum 266
Everyday People 323
Everything Creative by Susie Sells 140
Exhibition 280 627
Exhibitors Gallery 336

F

Fair in the Fields 528
Fair in the Park, A 585
Fair November 640
Fair on the Square 484
Fair, The 299
Fairbanks Museum & Planetarium, The 359
Faith Workshop 385
Fall Art Show 518
Fall Arts & Crafts Market 510
Fall Arts Fair 528
Fall Craft Market at Park City Mall 585
Fall Festival of Arts 472
Fall Fiesta of the Arts 597
Fall Foliage Festival 586
Fall for Art 451
Fall National Craft Fest 535
Fallfest (see Septemberfest 415)
Family & Friends 88
Famous French Gallery 72
Fanshawe Pioneer Village 399
Fantasy Creations 24
Farmer Hodge's Roadside Stand & Country Christmas Shop 359
Farmer—Mann Interiors, Inc. 24
Farmer's Daughter, The 218
Farmington Crafts Expo 441

Farmington Valley Arts Center, Inc. 118
Farnsworth Library & Art Museum, William A. 175
Faunce Jewelers, Brian 191
Favell Museum of Western Art & Indian Artifacts 315
Favorite Things 185
Fayerweather Craft Center 334
Feast of the Hunter's Moon 484
Federal Establishment, The 360
Feldman Fine Arts, Arthur L. 302
Felician College 34
Felician College Arts & Crafts Fair 472
Fell's Point Fun Festival 504
Ferrous Frolics (see Iron County Museum 206)
Ferrum Craft Shop 373
Festival 472
Festival Arts & Crafts Fair 417
Festival Arts & Crafts Show 484
Festival in the Park 414
Festival of Art 451
Festival of Art in the Park 491
Festival of Arts (Connecticut) 441
Festival of Arts (Wisconsin) 632
Festival of Arts & Crafts 427
Festival of Friends 640
Festival of Frostburg 504
Festival of the Arts (California) 427
Festival of the Arts (Florida) 451
Festival of the Arts (New York) 555
Festival of the Arts Market 641
Festival of the Fish 572
Festival of the Forks 519
Fiber & Print Works, The 89
Fiber Show 427
Fiberforms & Pots 267
Fiberworks (New York) 140
Fiberworks (California) 89
Fiberworks Gallery, The 229
Fibrations Weaving Studio & Gallery 126
Fibrec, Inc. 55
Fibre-Form Products, Inc. 55
Fiesta 484
Fiesta de las Artes 428
Fiesta in the Park 451
Fife & Drum Gift Shoppe (Chestertown, New York) 267
Fife & Drum Gift Shoppe (Lake George, New York) 267
Fifth Avenue Gallery 378
57th Street Art Fair 472
Filley Department Store, George 350
Finck, Stowell & Frolichstein, Inc. 25
Fine Arts Center of Clinton 140
Fine Arts Center of Kershaw County, Inc. 337
Fine Arts Museum (see Friends of Art Bookstall 151)
Fine Arts Museum of the South, The (see Outdoor Arts & Crafts Fair 415)
Finger Lakes Craftsmen (see Christmas Arts & Crafts Show 552, Spring Easter Arts & Crafts Show 562, Summer Indoor Arts & Crafts Show 562, Thanksgiving Weekend Christmas Arts & Crafts Show 562)
Fire on the Mountain Glass Shop (see Sonora Christmas Fair 434)
Fire Works, The 140
Firehouse Arts & Crafts Festival 462
Firehouse Christmas Festival 578
Firme, Judith 643
First Impressions 373
First National Bank 389
First Sunday in the Park 428
Fisher & Spillman 25
Fisher Gallery, Inc., Huguette 203
Fitchburg State College Campus Center 34
Fitzgerald Enterprises, Inc. 55
Five Ninety Three 72
Flannel Festival 519
Flathead Valley Art Festival 539
Flight Breakfast May Fest 491
Florida Folk Festival 452
Florida Forest Festival Arts & Crafts Show & Sale 452
Florida Technological University (see University of Central Florida 43)
Flo-Sculpt Studios, Inc. 55
Floyd County Museum 151
Flushing Art League Outdoor Exhibition 555
Fly By Night 238
Focus Crafts & Furnishings, Inc. 267
Fogg, F.B. 151
Folk Art Fair 632
Folk Art Show 476
Folk Arts & Music Festival 485
Folk Arts Fair 519
Folk Arts Festival Molson's Craft Show 641
Folk Music & Crafts Festival 535
Folk School Fall Festival 565
Folklorica 191
Following Sea 134
Fond du Lac Artists Association Annual Arts & Crafts Fair 632
Fontana Gallery 324
Foothills Art Center 108 (also see Threads Unlimited 439)
Forge Patio Art Gallerie, Association 89
Forms and Foliage, Ltd. 267
Fort Armstrong Folk Festival 586
Fort Delaware—Museum of Colonial History 268
Fort Dodge Area Fine Arts Council (see Art in the Park 489)
Fort Edmonton Park 400
Fort Lewis Military Museum (see Cannon Shop 377
Fort Pitt Museum Gift Shop 324
Fort Quiatenon Blockhouse Trading Post 151

Fort Wayne Museum of Art Gift Shop 151
Fort Worth Museum of Science & History—Gift Shop 350
Foster Museum, The Ralph 218
Founders Weekend 519
Fountain Square Plaza Starving "American" Arts & Crafts Fair 472
Fourth of July Celebration & Open Air Crafts Fair 452
Fourth Street Artists Gallery, Inc. 155
Fowler House Museum (see Tippecanoe County Historical Association, Fowler House Museum 153)
Fox River Grove Lions Arts & Crafts 474
Fraemar Enterprises Ltd. 400
Frame Factory, The 324
Framingham State College 34
Francis Park Art & Craft Show & Ethnic Food Fair 474
Franco-American Festival 502
Frankenmuth Bavarian Festival 519
Frankenmuth Historical Museum 203
Frankfort Waterfront Art Fair 519
Franklin Gallery, The 72
Franklin Street Mall 126
Fran's Miniatures 140
Frederick Craft Fair 504
Fredericksburg Gallery of Art 373
Fredonia Arts Council, Inc. 158
Free Air Arts Fair 624
Free Art Fair 578
Free Library of Philadelphia (see Friends of the Free Library Gift Shop 324)
Freeland, Clarence (see Great Lakes Mall 572, Millcreek Mall 574, Richmond Mall 574, Summit Mall 575)
Freeport Art Museum 141
French Art Colony 303
Friends & Company 360
Friends of Art Bookstall 151
Friends of the Free Library Gift Shop 324
Friends of the Middle Border Museum 340
Friends of the Museum, Inc. 126
Friends of the Plains Art Museum (see Red River Annual 530)
Frishman Gallery, Daniel 191
Frog Tool Co., Ltd. 141
From the Hands of Man 238
Front Room, The 72
Fulton County Street Arts Festival 555
Fun Festival 419
Functional Ceramics 572

G

Gadsden Art Association (see Art on the Rocks 413)
Gainesville Mall Arts & Crafts Show 452
Galerie de Tours 89
Galerie Internationale 268
Galerie Paula Insel 268
Gales Creek Enterprises of Oregon Limited 315
Galleria Internazionale, Ltd. 203
Galleries, Ltd., The 192
Gallery 8 89
Gallery 18 123
Gallery 84 Inc. 268
Gallery 500 324
Gallery Gift Shop 400
Gallery House Sol 400
Gallery in the Park 556
Gallery K 381
Gallery Nimba 378
Gallery North 268
Gallery North Outdoor Art Show 556
Gallery of Contemporary Metalsmithing 268
Gallery of Miniatures, Inc. 164
Gallery of World Art Inc. 192
Gallery on Main Street, The 303
Gallery on the Park 185
Gallery One 204
Gallery 187 239
Gallery Place 268
Gallery Shop at the Jamaica Arts Center, The 269
Gallery Shop, The (Michigan) 204
Gallery Shop, The (Utah) 354
Gallery Shop, The (Canada) 401
Gallery 10 Ltd. 382
Gallery, The (Illinois) 141
Gallery, The (Kentucky) 164
Gallery, The (Ohio) 303
Gallery, The (South Carolina) 337 (also see Invitational Crafts Show 598)
Gallery 3 (Arizona) 72
Gallery III (Tennessee) 344
Gallery 3 (Virginia) 373
Gallery 2W0 239
Gallery Yolanda 141
Gallo Manufacturing Co. 55
Gamble Craft Productions Ltd. (see Ottawa Christmas Craft Sale 641)
Gamekeeper, Inc., The 175
Garendo Gallery 90
Garret Galleries, The 192
Garret, The 340
Garrison Art Center Arts & Crafts Fair 556
Gasparilla Sidewalk Art Festival 453
Gateway Gallery of Arts & Crafts 218
Gathering, The 219
Gays Mills Pace Club Arts & Crafts Fair 632
Gazebo, Ltd., The 310
Gazehound Crafts, The (see Main Street USA Antiques 165
Gem Accessories & Gifts, Ltd. 55
General Exposition Corporation (see Seattle Harvest Festival 625)
Geneva's Gift Shoppe 155
Gentle Side of Life, The 204
Georgia Jubilee 462

Georgia Mountain Arts Association 131
Georgia Mountain Fair 462
Geppetto's 344
German Alps Festival 556
German American Day 505
Gibson House Museum 401
Gift Festival 428
Gift Haus 269
Gift Horse of Sturbridge, Inc., The 192
Gifts Unique 90
Gila River Arts & Crafts 72
Gilcrease Museum Gift Shop 310
Gillary Gallery 269
Gillingham and Sons, F.H. 360
Ginger Jar Ceramics 310
Gingerbread House, The 67
Gingham Goose 219
Glad Hand 90
Glass Blowers of Gatlinburg 344
Glass Factory, The 90
Glass Lantern Ltd., The 108
Glass Workbench, Inc., The 219
Glassblowing Shoppe 141
Glassmasters Guild 269
Glastonbury Art Guild (see On the Green 445)
Glens Falls Farmer's Market 556
Glenview Art Fair 474
Glooscaps Trading Post 401
Glynn Art Association (see Golden Isles Arts Festival 462)
Go Fly a Kite Inc. 55
Godston, Joel 644
Gold & Silversmiths of Vail, The 108
Gold Coast Art Fair 474
Gold Hill Art Festival 540
Gold Hill Pottery and Art Gallery (see Gold Hill Art Festival 540)
Gold Mill Outdoor Craft Fair 474
Golden Apple—Keene Craft Center 234
Golden Door Gallery 324
Golden Harvest Arts & Crafts Show & Sale 556
Golden Hobby Shop 303
Golden Isles Arts Festival 462
Golden Kite, The 303
Golden Pheasant, The 360
Golden Toad, The 234
Golden West Ceramic Show 428
Goldenbells Festival Art & Craft Market 441
Goldmann's & Sons, A. 389
Goldsboro Art Center 293
Goldsmith Shop, The 324
Goldstein Architect, P.C., Perry B. 25
Good Stuff Gifts 360
Gopher Hill Festival 597
Goundie House Museum Shop 325
Gourley's Olde Shoppe 152
Gra Wun Jewelers, Ltd. 73
Grabill Country Fair 485

Graham Gallery 269
Grand Irish Jubilee 586
Grand Prairie Festival of Arts 419
Grand Teton Lodge Co. 393
Grandma's Folly 219
Grandmother's Trunk 192
Granite State Ceramic Show 541
Granny's Attic 155
Granny's Closet 293
Graphic Ideas 55
Grass Hut Oddities 310
Grass Roots 211
Grassroots Handcrafts 123
Gray Gallery, Inc., Lenore 334
Great American Craft Shows, The 540
Great Chase, The 185
Great Danbury State Arts & Crafts Fair 442
Great Gulfcoast Festival 453
Great Lakes Mall 572
Great River Festival of Traditional Music & Crafts 632
Great River Roads Craft Fair, The 532
Greater Birmingham Arts Alliance, The 68
Greater Columbus Arts Council (see Artsaffair 570)
Greater Harrisburg Juried Arts Festival 586
Greater Harrisburg Outdoor Arts Festival 586
Greater Hartford Civic & Arts Festival 442
Greater Utica Summer Festival Craft Show 557
Greater Vernon Jaycees Crafts Fair 442
Greathall of Illinois (see King Richard's—A Return to the Renaissance 634)
Green Country Art Center 310
Green Flash, The 126
Green Hill Art Gallery, Inc. 293
Green Mountain Stained Glass 361
Green Mountain Sugar House 361
Green River 109
Green Spring Farm Gallery 374
Greenbrier Valley Artisans' Guild 385
Greenburg Publishing Co. 56
Greene Co., Eric H. 56
Green-field Galleries 350
Greenmont Guild Hall 361
Greenup Old Fashioned Days Arts & Crafts Show 498
Group Showing of American Artists 453
Grove House, Inc. 127
Grove North, Inc. 127
Gruzen & Partners 25
Gryphon Galleries, Ltd. 109
Guild Crafts 294
Guild Fair of the Southern Highlands, The 565
Guild Gallery (Kentucky) 164
Guild Gallery (Virginia) 374
Guild of Book Workers Exhibition 557
Guild of Shaker Crafts, Inc. 204

Index **665**

Guild of Strawbery Banke, Inc., The 234
Guild Store, The 90
Guilderland Fall Arts Festival 557
Guilford Handcraft Center 118 (also see Guilford Handcrafts Exposition 442)
Guilford Handcrafts Exposition 442

H

H.O.M.E. Fair 502
Habitat Galleries, Inc. 205
Hackley Art Museum (see Regional 523)
Hager Frontier Craft Day, Jonathan 505
Hahn Gallery Inc., The 325
Haines Township Dutch Fall Festival 586
Half Moon Bay Art & Pumpkin Festival 429
Halfpenny Playhouse, The (see West Hudson Community Arts Festival 547)
Halifax Art Festival 453
Halifax Historical Society, Inc. 127
Hallie's West Gallery 90
Hamilton Art Dealer, Martina 26
Hamilton-Wentworth Creative Arts (see Festival of Friends 640)
Hamlet, The 303
Hammond Gallery & Silver Shop, The 269
Hampshire Pewter Company 644
Hand & Eye, Inc., The 134
Hand & the Spirit Crafts Gallery, Inc., The 73
Hand Feats 239
Hand Made USA, Inc. 350
Hand Made USA, Inc. (Montana) 229
Hand Made USA, Inc. (New Mexico) 247
Hand Maiden 247
Hand of the Craftsman 270
Hand Work Shop, Inc. 374
Handcrafter, The 193
Handcrafters Gallery 175
Handmade 270
Hands of Man 185
Handscapes 193
Handworks 193, 270, 325
Hanna's Town Folk Festival, The 586
Hanover Square Gallery 271
Happy Hangups 91
Happy Peasant Gallery 393
Harbour Town Crafts 337
Harpswell House Gallery 175
Harris, Jinx (see Columbia Mall Professional Arts Festival 503, Burlington Mall Children's Hour Show 509, Burlington Mall Professional Crafts & Sculpture Show 509, Natick Mall Children's Hour Show 511, Natick Mall Craft & Sculpture Show 511, Mall of New Hampshire Professional Craft & Sculpture Show 541, Cherry Hill Mall Arts Festival 542, Cherry Hill Mall Craft & Sculpture Show 543, Cherry Hill Mall Professional Craft & Sculpture Show 543, Echelon Mall Arts Festival 544, Echelon Mall Children's Hour Show 545, Moorestown Mall Arts Festival 545, Moorestown Mall Children's Hour Show 545, Moorestown Mall Craft & Sculpture Show 545, Quaker Bridge Mall Arts Festival 547, Quaker Bridge Mall Children's Hour Show 547, Willowbrook Mall Art Show 548, Willowbrook Mall Children's Hour Show 548, Willowbrook Mall Fiber Fair 548, Willowbrook Mall Wooden Way Show 548, Woodbridge Center Craft & Sculpture Show 548, Lehigh Valley Mall Arts Festival 588, Monroeville Mall Arts Festival 589, Monroeville Mall Children's Hour Show 590, Montgomery Mall Craft & Sculpture Show 590, Neshaminy Mall Arts Festival 590, Neshaminy Mall Professional Craft & Sculpture Show 590, South Hills Village Arts Festival 592, South Hills Village Children's Show 592, Springfield Mall Children's Hour Show 594, Springfield Mall Craft & Sculpture Show 594, Warwick Mall Children's Hour Show 596, Warwick Mall Professional Craft & Sculpture Show 596)
Hartford Christmas Craft Expo I and II 443
Hartstone, Inc. 56
Harvest Arts & Crafts Fair 417
Harvest Crafts Festival 557
Hatcher Square Arts & Crafts Show 463
Hattie's Stained Glass & Gifts 340
Haven House 271
Hawkins House 361
Hayloft, The 389
Hays Arts & Crafts Fair 494
Hazleton Creative Arts Festival Sidewalk Sale 587
Head House Crafts Fair 587
Head House Craftsmen's Association (see Head House Crafts Fair 587)
Headley-Whitney Museum 164
Heard Museum Guild (see Indian Artists & Craftsmen of North America 417)
Heart of the Artichoke, The 212
Hector National Exhibition Centre 401
Heikes, Grete Bodogaard 644
Helena Arts Council (see Electrum Festival of the Arts 539)
Hellroarin' Gallery 229
Helme House (see Earthworks 595, South County Art Annual 595)
Hempwill-Wells Co. 351
Henry & Associates, Inc., D.E. 56
Hen's Nest, The 127
Here Comes the Sun 271
Heritage Days 627
Heritage Gallery Ltd. 401
Heritage House 325
Heritage Metalcraft, Inc. 175

Heron Point Gallery 176
Herron Stained Glass Studios 326
Hide 'n' Freak Leather Workshop & Crafts Bazaar 91
High Point Glass & Decorative Co. 26
High Point Museum Craft Shop 294
High Street of Boston 194
Highland House 169
Highlands & Islands Imports, Inc. 56
Hill Skills 597
Hill-Looney, Inc. 56
Hills Indian Crafts 401
Hillside Selected Crafts Festival 474
Hillside Shopping Center Starving "American" Arts & Crafts Fair 474
Hired Hand, The 271
Historic Camden Crafts Festival 597
Historic Hoosier Hills Antique Collectors and Hand Craftsmen's Guild (see Gourley's Olde Shoppe 152)
Historic Hoosier Hills Guild Festival 485
Historical Association of Southern Florida, Inc. 127
Hobart and William Smith Colleges 35
Hobart Arts and Crafts Festival 578
Hobbit House 176
Hockaday Center for the Arts (see Flathead Valley Art Festival 539)
Hoffman, David 644
Hogback Mountain Gift Shop, Inc. 362
Holden Arboretum, The 304
Hole in the Wall Gallery, The 326
Holiday Arts & Crafts Fair 557
Holiday Craft Store 587
Holiday Crafts Fair 558
Holiday Fair 598
Holiday Festival of Arts & Crafts 475
Holiday Gift Show 520
Holland Day Art Fair "On the Green" 633
Holly Day Fair 633
Holly Holiday Art & Craft Show 520
Holly Woodworking 272
Holston Mountain Art & Crafts Co-op (see The Cave House 372)
H-O-M-E, Inc. 176
Homeplace 132
Honeycomb, The 212
Hood College 35
Hoonah Arts Fair 415
Hoot Owl, The 205
Hopi Arts & Crafts Cooperative Guild 73
Hopi Craftsmen (see Museum of Northern Arizona 74)
Horizon Gallery 91
Horner Museum Gift Area 315
Horse Feathers 272
Horse feathers West 240
Hospitality House Arts & Crafts Fair 419
Hot Spring County Art & Craft Show & Sale 419

Hot Springs Arts & Crafts Show 420
Hotel Gift Shop 402
Houby Festival Arts & Craft Fair 475
House & Table 248
House of Alexander 374
House of Bernard 240
House of Crafts 402
House of Fine Art, Inc. 128 (also see Group Showing of American Artists 453)
House of Gifts & Crafts 311
House of Glass 337
Howard Art Galleries, Inc. 142
Howard Galleries, Ltd. 128
Huachuca Historical Society 73
Hubbuch In Kentucky 26
Hudson Valley Art Association, Inc., The 443
Huff's Hang-Ups 304
Hunt Stained Glass Supply Ltd., E.D.R.
Hunter Museum of Art 344
Huntington Dogwood Arts & Crafts Festival 627
Huntington Galleries (see Exhibition 280 627, Collectors Corner, Huntington Galleries 384)
Huntress Stained Glass 248
Huron City Museums 205
Huronia Handcrafted Gifts 402

I

I.S.L.E. Laboratories, Inc. 56
I & We 326
Ice House Arts Festival 475
Idea Factory 169
Idea, The 194
Illinois Railway Museum 142
Image Gallery 194
Image, The 91
In Things 92
Incorporated Galleries 272
Indian Artists & Craftsmen of North America 417
Indian Craft Shop 382
Indian Crafts Festival & Pioneer Fair 414
Indian Head Art Fair 633
Indian Hills Trading Co. 206
Indian Museum of the Carolinas 294
Indian Summer Art Show 545
Indian Summer Arts & Crafts Festival 572
Indian Summer Arts & Crafts Show & Sale 579
Indiana Artist-Craftsmen, Inc. (see Talbot Street Art Fair 488)
Indiana University of Pennsylvania (see Kipp Gallery 327)
Indianapolis Museum of Art (see The Alliance Museum Shop 149)
Industry Productions of California Incorporated (see Professional Arts, Crafts & Indoor Plants Show 431)
Ink & Clay 429

Index **667**

Insel Annual Exhibition, Paula (New York City) 558
Insel Annual Exhibition, Paula (Puerto Rico) 642
Institute of American Indian Arts Museum 248
Instituto de Cultura Puertorriquena (see Centro Artes Populares 411)
International Art Gallery (New York) 272
International Art Gallery (Pennsylvania) 326
International Craft Show 558
International Festival 520
International Folk Festival 545
International Guest Exhibition of Painting, Sculptures & Graphics 443
International Handcraft & Supply 92
International Institute (see Folk Arts Fair 519, International Festival 520)
Intrarc Planning Corp. 26
Intuition 240
Invitational Ann Arbor Spring Art Fair 520
Invitational Ann Arbor Winter Art Fair 520
Invitational Columbus Spring Art Fair 572
Invitational Craft Fair 536
Invitational Crafts Show 598
Iowa City/Johnson County Arts Council (see Paper/Fiber 493)
Iris 92
Iron County Museum 206
Island Art Center 132
Island Art Fair 520
Island Crafts 403
Island Store, The 176
Island's Imports 56
Islandview Handcraft Shop 403
Iszard Co., S.F. 272
Ithaca House Gallery 272
It's a Small World 142
I-Yee-Quee Gift Shop 92

J

J. Bob Creations 152
J.D. Enterprises 57
Jacksonville Art Museum Shop 128
Jacqu Min Inc. 57
Jaffrey & Chase, Ltd. 176
Jamaica Trading Co. 362
Jane-Gray Shoppe 177
Janesville Mall Art & Craft Show 475, 633
Jan's Gallery 156
Jay Country Store, The 362
Jeannine's Ceramics 142
Jeffersonville Arts & Crafts Festival 485
Jellybeans 248
Jenkintown Festival of the Arts 587
Jenkintown Library (see Jenkintown Festival of the Arts 587)
Jewellry Workshop & Gallery 273
Jewish Community Center's Craft Sale 505
Jewish Museum Shop 273

Joanne's Antique and Gift Shoppe 355
Jo-Han Models, Inc. 57
Johnny Appleseed Day 429
Johns, Phyllis 644
Johnson Gallery, Helen 351
Johnson Miniatures, Jean 240
Johnstown Area Arts Council (see Spring Arts Festival 593)
Joilet Ceramic Arts & Crafts, Inc. 142
Jorice Designs, Inc. 273
Journeyman, Inc. 194
Jove/Daniels/Busby 26
Joy Enterprises 57
J-P's Gallery 273
J-S Wood Products, Inc. 57
Jugtown Pottery 294
Julie: Artisans' Gallery 273
Junction City Art in the Park 495
Jung & Cloyes, AIA 26
Juniata College 35
Juried Craft Exhibition 588
Juried Craft Show 588
Juried Crafts Exhibition of the Central Pennsylvania Festival of the Arts 588
Just Accessories, Inc. 57, 274

K

K&L Co. 57
Kaffe Klatter Krafts & Art Fair 528
Kagan Studio & Gallery, Richard 326
Kaill Fine Crafts 71
Kalamazoo Nature Center 206
Kalamazoo Valley Art Association (see Milham Park Art Fair 522)
Kalico Korner 212
Kalkaska Arts & Crafts Festival 520
Kamm's Brewery Arts & Crafts Festival 485
Kanawha County Fair 627
Kansas City Art Institute (see Renaissance Festival 537)
Kansas Heritage Center 159
Kata Gallery 274
Kathy's Craft Shop 403
Kats 315
Katy-Did, The 169
Kauri Shell Gallery 92
Kay's Aloha Art Gallery 134
Kazoo School Mayfaire 521
Keatington Art Festival 521
Keene State College 35
Kelley, Judy (see Chillicothe Art & Craft Show 468, Country Fair Mall Art & Craft Show 468, Cross County Mall Art & Craft Show 470, Janesville Mall Art & Craft Show 475, the Mall At Cherry Vale & Craft Show 476, Sandburg Mall Art & Craft Show 480, Janesville Mall Arts & Crafts Show 633)
Kelly & Historical Museum Gift Shop, Emmett 158Kenan Craft Festival 558

Kennedy Brothers Woodenware 362
Kenosha Art Fair 633
Kenosha Public Museum (see Kenosha Art Fair 633)
Kent State University 35
Kentuck Arts & Crafts Festival 414
Kentucky Guild of Artists & Craftsmen, Inc. 164 (also see Guild Gallery 164)
Kentucky Guild of Artists & Craftsmen's Fair 498
Kentucky Hills Industries, Inc. 165
Kerns Art Center, Maude I. 315
Kettle Moraine Art & Crafts 633
Kettle Moraine Christmas Fair 634
Key Biscayne Art Festival 454
Keystone Country Festival 588
Kiddy Kraft Klub Craft Show (see Bersted's Hobby Craft Inc. 52)
Kiln Room, The 294
Kimball Art Center 355
King Richard's Faire—A Return to the Renaissance 634
Kingdom Come Swappin' Meetin' 498
King's College 36
Kinston Arts Council 295
Kipp Gallery 327
Kirbus, Frank Andrew 644
Kirkland Art Center 274
Kishwaukee Valley Art League Spring Art & Craft Fair 475
Kittery Art Association Sidewalk Sale 502
Kiva: Artisan's Gallery, The 274
Kiwanis Art Fiesta (see Town and Country Village—Kiwanis Art Fiesta 435)
Klein Art Gallery 92
Klepp—Sansei Pottery, Joyce Yamamoto 644
Knob Alley 311
Knock on Wood 274
Knotty Pine, The 374
Knox Campbell Galleries 73
Knox College 36
Koehnline Gallery 142
Kohler Arts Center, John Michael 389
Kondos Art Galleries, Peter J. 390
Kornbluth Gallery 241
Kottler Galleries, Lynn 274
Kouts Annual Arts & Crafts Show 485
Kruger Gallery 275
Kutztown Folk Festival 588

L

La Galeria 73
La Galerie Rouge 275
La Have River Trading Co. 403
La Paloma Gallery 248
La Posada Gift Shop 249
La Roche College 36
La Salle College 36
Lady Bug Shop, The 304
Ladycliff College 36

Lafayette Natural History Museum & Planetarium (see Le Magasin 169)
Lafayette Park Art Fair 521
Lake Eufaula Arts & Crafts Show 579
Lake Odessa Arts Commission (see "Art in the Park" 514)
Lake of Ozarks Arts & Crafts Show & Sale 536
Lake Superior Art Association (see Art on the Rocks 514)
Lake Tahoe Art & Craft Fair 429
Lakeside Gallery School of Art 135
Lakewood Sales/Rental Gallery 143
Lakewinds Gallery 206
Lakewood Community College (see Fair in the Fields 528)
Lambda Rising 382
Lamoureux Inc. 57
Lamp Post Craft Shop, The 177
Langdon Bridge Crafts 363
Langman Gallery 327
Lansing Art Gallery 207
Lapeer Fine Arts Council (see Art Go Round 514)
Las Novedades 249
L'Atelier Gallery of Arts and Crafts 241
Laughing Bear's Adventures in Noble Metals 109
Laughing Gypsy 355
Laurentian University 36
Laurentian University Museum & Arts Centre 404
Lawrence Gallery 316
Lawrence University 36
Lawton Fort Sill Annual Art Show 579
Le Blanc Handcraft 404
Le Magasin 169
League of New Hampshire Craftsmen (Concord, New Hampshire) 234
League of New Hampshire Craftsmen (Wolfeboro, New Hampshire) 235
League of New Hampshire Craftsmen, Hanover Shop 235
Lea's Hallmark Shop 311
Leather Etc., Inc. 132
Leathercrafter, The 345
Leaves 'n' Weaves 207
Lebanon County Historical Society Museum Store 327
Lebowitz Designs, Jack 275
Ledge Craft Lane (see Island Art Fair 520)
Lee County Cotton-Pickin' Festival 598
Lee Shop, The 275
Lee Sidewalk Arts & Crafts Show 454
Leedey Arts and Crafts Festival 579
Left Bank Gallery (see Fall Art Show 518)
Left Bank, The 177
Legacy, Ltd., The 378
Lehigh Valley Mall Arts Festival 588
Leisure Time Publishing & Craft Products,

Inc. 57
Leverett Craftsmen & Artists, Inc. 195
Lewisburg Craft Fair 589
Lewiston Council on the Arts, Inc., Lewiston Craft Show 559
Lewittes Design Gallery, Esther 93
Liberty Gifts 393
Life-Like Products Inc. 57
Light Opera 93
Lighthouse Gallery, Inc. 128
Lilac Festival Decorated Egg Show 559
Lima Area Arts Council (see Square Fair 575)
Lim's Art Gallery 404
Lincoln Center for the Performing Arts (see American Crafts Festival 551)
Lincoln University 37
Lion's Valley Stoneware Ltd. 57
Little Art Gallery 295
Little Bit of Heaven 345
Little Gallery & Things Original, The 304
Littleton Gallery 195
Lively Arts Festival, The (California) 429
Lively Arts Festival (see Art in the Park 531)
Livery Stable 345
Living Desert Reserve 93
Livonia Arts & Crafts Festival 521
Loch Haven Art Center Shop 128
Lock 21 Antique & Handcrafts 404
Lodi Grape Festival & National Wine Show (see Gift Festival 428)
Log House Sales Room 165
Logan County Arts & Crafts Festival 628
Lollie Shop, The 68
London Venturers Co. 195
Long Beach Museum of Art Bookshop/Gallery 93
Longhouse Museum, The 275
Longpre Gallery 93
Looking Glass, Inc., The 363
Loom Room, Inc. 170
Loom Room, The 143
Looms, The 390
Loon Mountain Arts & Crafts Show 541
Loon's Nest, The 404
Los Angeles County Museum of Art, Museum Shop 93
Los Arboles Artisans Coop (see Mama's Art-a-Fair 430)
Louisiana Crafts Council 170
Louisville School of Art Gallery 165
Love-Built Toys & Crafts 58
Loveland's Annual Arts & Crafts Festival 438
Lowcountry Christmas Festival 598
Lower Adirondack Regional Arts Council Arts & Crafts Festival 559
Loyola University 37
Lubec Crafts Council, Inc., The 178
Ludington Arts & Crafts Fair 521

Lumbertown USA 212
Luminere Creations, Inc. 275
Luta Studios 119
Lutheran Brotherhood—Lutheran Center Gallery 212
Lynwood Ltd. 405

M

Mabee-Gerrer Museum, The 311
Mabou Village Gallery 405
MacAlester College 37
McCall's at Old City Park 351
McClendon's Art Factory 219
McCloskey and Associates 26
McCormick Interior Design Inc., Margaret 27
MacIvor Reddie Gallery 195
McKendree Collaborative 207
McLaughlin Gallery, Robert (see The Shop Downstairs 409)
Maco Crafts, Inc. 295
Mad Money Boutique 213
Mad Monk, The 276
Made in Iowa Shop 156
"Made in the Ozarks" Arts & Crafts Show 536
Madison Art Center Gallery Shop 390
Magi, The 170
Magic Mushroom Gallery, The 229
Magnes Museum Gift Shop, Judah 94
Magnolia Sidewalk Arts Festival 420
Magnus Crafts Corporation 58
Maher Antiques & Gifts, Camille 171
Mail Train, The 351
Main Line Center of the Arts 327
Main St. Art Fair 634
Main Street Craft Cooperative 241
Main Street Department Store 276
Main Street Gallery Shop 156
Main Street USA Antiques 165
Maine Craft Store 178
Maine Scene, The 276
Mall of New Hampshire Professional Craft & Sculpture Show 541
Maltwood Art Museum & Gallery 405
Mama's Art-a-Fair 430
Man Clothing & Jewelry Co. 385
Manchester Institute of Arts & Sciences (see The Yuletide Fair 542)
Manhattan College 37
Manistee World of Arts & Crafts 521
Mannings Creative Crafts, The (see The Mannings National Juried Show 589)
Mannings National Juried Show, The 589
Many Hands Creative Arts Cooperative 94
Maple Hill Pottery Craft Gallery 178
Mapleshade Pottery 327
Marathon County Historical Society 390
Marathon East Art Center 170
Mari Galleries of Westchester, Ltd. 276

Marietta Arts & Crafts Show 579
Marietta College 37 (also see Indian Summer Arts & Crafts Festival 572)
Marietta College Crafts National 573
Marietta National, The 573
Marinaccio Doll House Furniture & Accessories, Mary Anne 241
Marine Museum Gift Shop 276
Marion College 37
Mark of the Potter, Inc. 132
Market Square Fair 620
Market, The 249
Marketplace, Inc., The 178
Marks Studio/Gallery 207 (also see Classical Glass 202)
Marlborough Creative Arts Festival 443
Marson Ltd. 185
Martin Schweig Gallery 224
Martis Jr., Architects, James A. 27
Maryland Historical Society Museum Shop 186
Marymount College 37
Marysville Mall Art & Craft Show 540
Mason, Edna 644
Massachusetts Audubon Society Gift Shop 196
Massillon Museum Sidewalk Sale, The 573
Massillon Museum, The 304 (also see The Massillon Museum Sidewalk Sale 573, Ohio Artists & Craftsmen Show 574)
Mathis Gallery 390
Matsqui-Sumas-Abbotsford Museum 405
Mattatuck Community College (see Spring Crafts Fair 446)
Maxwell House Miniature Show and Sale 589 (also see Maxwell House Miniatures 58)
Maxwell House Miniatures 58
Maxwell Museum Gift Shop 249
May Arts & Crafts Exhibition 573
May Show 573
Me Enterprises 58
Meadowcroft Village 327
Meadowfound Galley 109
Meet the Artists—Chapel Square Mall 443
Meet the Artists—Meriden Square Mall 444
Meet the Artists—Milford Green 444
Meet the Artists—Olde Mystic Village 444
Mel Mar Shops 75
Melange 536
Melting Point Glassworks & Pottery, The 249
Mendocino Art Center Gallery 94
Mendocino Art Center Summer Art Fair 430
Mercer Museum Shop 328
Merchants Association (see Countryside Mall Arts & Selected Crafts Fair 469)
Meridian Museum of Art Bi-State Show 533
Merkel's Department Store 277
Merritt Square Festival of Arts & Crafts 454
Merry Jane's Country Shoppe 277

Metro Arts Center 165
Meuniers 277
Michigan State University 37
Michigan State University Museum Gift Emporium 207
Micmac Indian Village 405
Middlesex County College (see International Folk Festival 545)
Midland Art Fair 522
Midland Crafters, Inc. 295
Midnight Sun, The 382
Mid-Summer Night's Fair 579
Midtown Professional Art & Craft Fair 529
Midwest Arts & Crafts Show 522
Mifflin County Goose Day Celebration 589
Mifflin-Juniata Arts Festival 589
Mikasa 58
Mikolas, Karel 644
Milan Art Fair 522
Milford Oyster Festival 445
Milford Pottery, The 304
Milham Park Art Fair 522
Milk Co., The 94
Mill Gallery, The 277
Mill Valley Arts Guild (see Fiber Show 427)
Millcreek Mall 574
Miller Gallery 305
Miller—Goldsmith, Gary W. 644
Miller's Thumb, The 363
Million Pines Arts & Crafts Festival 463
Milwaukee Art Center Wisconsin Gallery 390
Mindscape Gallery & Studio, Inc. 144 (also see Adult Toys 465, Critters & Cohorts 470)
Mini Gallery 390
Mini Gallery, The Newark Museum, The 241
Mini Mundus Shop 277
Miniature Reflections 58
Minis By Me 58
Minneapolis Aquatennial Nicollet Mall Art Fair & Marketplace 529
Minnesota Crafts Festival 529
Minnesota Landscape Arboretum Gift Shop 213
Minnesota State Fair 529
Minot Art Association (see North Dakota Art Exhibition 568)
Minot Art Association Art Fair 567
Minot Art Gallery 299
Minot Art Gallery Artfest 568
Mint Museum of Art (Piedmont Crafts Exhibition 566)
Mintz Company, Stephen A. 58
Miryam's Farm 328
Miss Boutique Inc. 58
Missouri State Fair 536
Mizpah Art Gallery 378
Monroeville Mall Arts Festival 589
Monroeville Mall Children's Hour Show 590

Index

Monterey County Fair 430
Monterey Peninsula Museum of Art (see The California Craftsman 426)
Montgomery Kiwanis Sidewalk Art Show 574
Montgomery Mall Craft & Sculpture Show 590
Montreal Military & Maritime Museum, The 406
Monument Square Art Fair 634
Moorestown Mall Arts Festival 545
Moorestown Mall Children's Hour Show 545
Moorestown Mall Craft & Sculpture Show 545
Moravian College 37
Moreau Gallery Three 152
Morgan Loom Factory 58
Morgie's 220
Morris Museum Shop 242
Morristown Craftmarket 546
Moser's Dried Flower Barn 208
Mossy Creek Pottery & Gallery 316
Mosteller's Inc. 328
Mostly Handmade, Inc. 144
Mother Lode Art Show 430
Mount Dora Art Festival 454
Mt. Mitchell Craftsmens Fair 565
Mount Vernon College 38
Mountain Aire 430
Mountain Craft Days 590
Mountain Craft Shop 385
Mountain Empire Community College 38
Mountain Heritage Arts & Crafts Festival 628
Mountain State Art & Craft Fair 628
Mountain Valley Gifts 109
Mountain Weaver 94
Muckle's Ridge Festival 414
Mud Dauber's Nest, The 133
Mud in Your Eye Pottery Studio 95
Mueller's Wrought Iron Shop 144
Mullens Arts & Crafts Show 628
Multiple Sclerosis (see Adventures in Crafts Decoupage Sale & Exhibit 550)
Multnomah County Fair 582
Muriel Originals 208
Murry State University 38
Muscoda Arts & Crafts Fair 634
Museo de la Fundacion Arqueologica de Puerto Rico 412
Museum of Afro American History 196
Museum of Anthropology Sales Desk, University of Missouri-Columbia 220
Museum of Appalachia 345
Museum of Art & Archaeology, University of Missouri 220
Museum of Arts & History Shop & Rental Gallery 208
Museum of Arts & Sciences 129
Museum of Fine Arts Shop 129

Museum of Holography Bookstore 278
Museum of International Folk Art (see New Mexico Crafts Biennial 549, Southwest Crafts Biennial 550)
Museum of Native American Cultures 379
Museum of Natural History—Museum Shop, The 159
Museum of New Mexico (see New Mexico Crafts Biennial 549, Southwest Crafts Biennial 550)
Museum of Northern Arizona 74
Museum of Northern British Columbia, Museum Art Gallery 406
Museum of the Arts Gift Shop 129
Museum Ship Valley Camp 208
Museum Shop at the International Folk Art Museum, The 249
Museum Shop, Bowdoin College Museum of Art 179
Museum Shop of the Arkansas Arts Center 76
Museum Shop—Palace of the Governor 250
Museum Shop, Portland Art Museum 316
Museum Shop, The (Indiana) 152
Museum Shop, The (San Francisco) 95
Museum Shop, The (Texas) 351
Museum Shop, Philadelphia Museum of Art 328
Mushroom Gallery, The 379
Musical Museum, The 278
Muskogee Azalea Festival Corporation (see Indian Summer Arts & Crafts Show & Sale 579)
My House Gallery 95
My Sister 279
Mystic River Guild, The 119
Mystic Seaport Museum Store 119

N

Nancy's Corner 311
Nappi, AIA, Anthony T. 27
Naranjo's American Indian Arts 352
Nashco Products, Inc. 60
Natcol Crafts, Inc. 60
National Carvers Museum 110
National Crafts Ltd. (see Rocky Mountain Craft Fair 439, Devon Craft Fair 585)
National Exhibition 546
National Postal Museum 406
National Trust for Historic Preservation (see Preservation Shops 382)
Native Arts & Crafts Festival 537
Natural Leather 279
Natural Selection 144
Navajo Craftsmen (see Museum of Northern Arizona 74)
Navajo Nation Fair 417
NCAA Juried Show 445
Necessities, Inc. 295
Needle in the Haystacker, Inc. 60

Needle Nook, The 95
Nehalem Arts Festival 582
Nelson Leather Co. 76
Nescatunga Arts Festival 580
Neshaminy Mall Arts Festival 590
Neshaminy Mall Professional Craft & Sculpture Show 590
Neville Public Museum (see Northeastern Wisconsin Art Annual 635)
Neville-Sargent Gallery 144
New Brunswick Museum Shop, The 406
New England Painting & Sculpture Exhibition 445
New Hampshire Arts Festival 541
New Hampshire College 38
New Harmony Gallery of Contemporary Art 152
New Holstein Kiwanis Arts & Crafts Fair 634
New Jersey Designer-Craftsmen (see Morristown Craftmarket 546)
New Jersey Folk Festival 546
New Market Arts & Crafts Show 620
New Mexico Art League 250
New Mexico Arts & Crafts Fair 549
New Mexico Crafts Biennial 549
New Morning Gallery 296 (also see Village Art & Craft Fair 567)
New Salem Mountain Festival 463
New Visions Gallery, Inc. 390
New World Resource & Supply Co. 95
New York City Bluegrass & Old-Time Country Music Band Contest & Crafts Fair 559
New York Exchange for Woman's Work 279
New York Renaissance Festival 559
New York State Crafts, Home Arts & Fine Arts Competition 560
New York State Craftsmen Incorporated (see International Craft Show 558)
New York State Fair (see New York State Crafts, Home Arts & Fine Arts Competition 560)
Newkirk Arts & Crafts Fair 580
Newmarket North Mall Arts & Crafts Show 620
Newton County Arts & Crafts Show 420
Nicholas Press 60
Niddy Noddy, The 279
9 Artisans, Inc. 279
Nonpareil 145
Norman Firehouse Art Center, Inc. (see Firehouse Christmas Festival 578, Mid-Summer Night's Fair 579)
Normandale College Gallery 213
North American Model Enterprises Inc. 60
North Carolina Artists Exhibition 565
North Carolina Department of Cultural Resources 644
North Carolina League of Creative Arts & Crafts, Inc. 296

North Carolina Museum of Art (see North Carolina Artists Exhibition 565)
North Carolina Museum of Art—The Museum Store 296
North Country Arts & Crafts 560
North Country Arts & Crafts Store, Inc. 279
North Dakota Art Exhibition 568
North Park College 38
North Point Pier 96
North St. Paul Jaycee Women's Art and Crafts Fair 530
North Shore Art Fair 530
North Star Arts & Crafts Festival 530
North View Gallery 280
Northeast Craft Fair 560
Northeastern Wisconsin Art Annual 635
Northern Appalachian Festival 590
Northern Kingdom Printworks 645
Northern New York Crafts Festival 560
Northfield Arts Guild (see Fall Arts Fair 528)
Northfield Looms 60
Northfork Indian Shop 312
Northland Store Inc. 406
Northridge Gallery & School of Art 96
Northwest Alabama Arts & Crafts Festival 414
Northwest Artists Thunderbird Arts & Crafts 624
Northwest Artists Valley Mall Arts & Crafts 624
Northwest Craft Center 379
Northwest Gallery 296
Northwestern Connecticut Art Association (see NCAA Juried Show 445)
Northwestern Michigan College 38 (also see Traverse Bay Outdoor Art Fair 525)
Norton House Museum 363
Nova Scotia Designer Craftsmen (see Festival of the Arts Market 641)
Nuckols—Greely Interiors 27

Oak Grove Country Fair 463
Oakton Community College 38
Oates Gallery 345
O'Brien Arts & Crafts Show 580
OCA Crafts Co. 60
Ocean Beach Park Arts & Crafts Show 445
Ocean City Arts Center (see Crafts 544)
Octagon Art Center Shop, The 156
Octagon Shop 145
Octoberfest Art Craft & Antique Show & Sale 430
Of Cabbages & Kings 280
Offray & Son Inc., C.M. 60
Oglebay Institute Craft Festival 628
Oglebay Institute Upper Ohio Valley Art Show 629
Ohio Artists & Craftsmen Show 574

Index **673**

Ohio State University 38
Ojai Crafts Festival 431
Okefenokee Festival Arts & Craft Show 463
Oklahoma Arts & Humanities Council (see Leedey Arts and Crafts Festival 579)
Oklahoma City Festival of the Arts 580
Oklahoma Indian Arts & Crafts Co-operative 312
Oklahoma Museum of Art (see Shepherd Mall Craft Show 581)
Oktoberfest 420
Old Avon Village Arts & Crafts Show 445
Old Bedford Village 329
Old Bronte Post Office Gallery, The 407
Old Cabin Crafts Society (see The Calgary Cabin—Alberta Crafts 395)
Old Country Store & Museum 220
Old Craft Day 635
Old Fashioned Day Arts & Crafts Fair 420
Old Fort Gibson Indian Territory Arts & Crafts Show 580
Old Home Day 541
Old Market Craftsmen's Guild 231
Old Mill Craft Shop 364
Old Mill Crafts 220
Old Mill Village 329
Old Saratoga Historical Association Art Show 560
Old Sash Mill 96
Old Slave Mart Museum & Gallery 338
Old Woodstock School House (see Windmill Craft Coop Association 410)
Olde England Framing 375
Olde Jail House Craft Fair 635
Olde Town Gallery 145
Olde Tyme Crafts and Arts 454
Oleary Library & Museum Association 407
Omaha Summer Arts Festival (Arts Festival on the Mall) 540
Omega Pottery Shop 221
On the Green 445
100 American Craftsmen Craft Festival (see Kenan Craft Festival 558)
120 in the Shade 208
One Manz Family Arts & Crafts 221
1 of a Kind 250
One Step Up Gifts 166
Only Originals 242
Opelika Arts Festival 415
Open Door Art Shop, The 329
Open Door Enterprises, Inc. 60
Orange Ox 364
Orange Park Mall Festival of Art 454
Orange Park Mall Winter Craft Show 456
Orchard Crafts 407
Orchard Yarn & Thread Co. Inc. 61
Oregon Electric Railway Historical Society 316
Oregon Historical Society 317
Oregon Institute of Technology 38

Oregon School of Arts & Crafts 39
Oregon School of Arts & Crafts Gift Gallery & Craft Supply Store, The 317
Orlando Gallery 96
Osage Hills Arts & Crafts Show & Sale 581
Osceola Art Festival 456
Other Delights 407
Ottawa Christmas Craft Sale 641
Ottumwa Heights College 39
Ouachita Council on Aging 171
Ouachita County Arts & Crafts Fair 421
Ouray County Arts Association (see Artists Alpine Holiday 437)
Outdoor Arts & Crafts Fair 415
Outdoor Arts Festival (Ohio) 574
Outdoor Arts Festival (Sheboygan, Wisconsin) 635
Outdoor Arts Festival (Watertown, Wisconsin) 635
Outdoor Crafts Festival 456
Overly Museum, W.H. 340
Overly-Raker Village 329
Owattonna Arts Center (see September Fest 530)
Owensboro Area Museum 166
Owensboro Museum of Fine Art 166
Owl's Nest Gift Shop, The 364
Owl's Nest, The 250
Own Your Own Art Show 438
Oxford Gallery 280
Ozark Art Fest 537
Ozark Craft Festival 537
Ozark Folk Center Sales Shop, The 76
Ozark Foothills Craft Guild 76 (also see Sugar Creek Craft Shop 78, Sylamore Creek Craft Shop 79, Ozark Foothills Craft Guild Spring Show & Sale 421, Ozark Frontier Trail Festival & Craft Show 421)
Ozark Foothills Craft Guild Spring Show & Sale 421
Ozark Frontier Trail Festival & Craft Show 421
Ozark Market Basket 221
Ozarks Arts & Crafts Fair 421
Ozark's Ceramic Corner 78

P

Pacesetter Gifts 96
Pacific Arts & Crafts 431
Pacific Basin School of Textile Arts 96
Pacific Center of Arts & Crafts 379
Pacific States Crafts Fair 431
Paddlewicker 196
Paley, Albert 645
Palm Springs Desert Museum Shop 96
Palmer Park Fine Arts Festival, The 523
Palmyra Canaltown Days 561
Palmyra P.T.O. Holiday Bazaar 635
Panache 110

Papercraft Corp. 61
Paraffinalia 280
Paramount Arts Center 166
Paris Gibson Square (see Emporium 228)
Park Art Festival 561
Park Shore Plaza Festival of Arts & Crafts 456
Parksburg Art Center 385
Parkersburg Community College (see Heritage Days 627)
Parkway Craft Center 297
Parlour, The 352
Patriots Art Brigade 546
Pennsylvania Folklife Society (see Kutztown Folk Festival 588)
Partridge, Irene "Rae" (see Belvidere Mall Fall Festival of Crafts 467, Belvidere Mall Starving "American" Arts & Crafts Fair 468, Countryside Mall Arts & Selected Crafts Fair 469, Countryside Mall Fall Festival of Selected Crafts 469, Countryside Mall Starving "American" Arts & Crafts 469, Deerfield Commons Arts & Selected Crafts Fair 470, Deerfield Commons Spring Festival of Selected Crafts 470)
Pascos, The 179
Past & Present 242
Pastimes Alive (see Colorado Renaissance Festival 438)
Patchwork 221
Patchwork Factory, Inc., The 305
Patchwork Parlor 159
Patriots Art Festival 456
Patterson's Corner 221
Patty's Place 379
Paula's Place 242
Pavilion, The 74
Peaceable Kingdom, The 209
Peach Tree Mall 431
Peanut Patch, The 375
Peanut Valley Festival 549
Pearson Handicrafts, Hazel 61
Peddler's Cart Gallery 250
Peddlers Cellar, The 242
Peddler's Shop, The 330
Peddlers, The 213
Peddler's Village Apple Festival 591
Peddler's Village Christmas Festival 591
Peddler's Village Strawberry Festival & May Fair 591
Pedestal, The 280
Pendleton Arts Council (see Christmas Craft Fair 582)
Pendleton Shop, The 74
Penguin's Pantry, The 281
Penn Museum Shop, William 330
Pennsylvania Guild of Craftsmen (see Fall Craft Market at Park City Mall 585, Spring Craft Market at Park City Mall 593)
Pennsylvania Guild of Craftsmen's Market 591
Pennsylvania Maple Festival 591
Pensacola Arts Council (see Great Gulfcoast Festival 453)
Pensacola Museum of Art 129
Peoples & Cultures Shop-in-the-Flats 305
Peoria Art Guild 145
Pepperdine University 39
Pera's Summer Resort 305
Perceptions, Inc. 196
Performers' Outlet 281
Persimmon Seed, The 312
Peters Valley 243
Peters Valley Craftsmen (see National Exhibition 546)
Petersham Craft Center & Craft Shop 197
Peyton Originals 119
Phelps Annual Saurkraut Festival 561
Philadelphia Art Alliance, The 330
Philadelphia Craft Show, The 591
Philadelphia Museum of Art (see Museum Shop, Philadelphia Museum of Art 328, Philadelphia Craft Show, The 591)
Phillips Mill Community Association Art Exhibition 592
Phoebus 338
Phoenix Art Museum Shop 74
Phoenix Gallery 281
Phoenix Shop 97
Pickard Gallery, Ben M. 312
Pickwick Place 222
Picuris Pueblo Museum Center 251
Piedmont Crafts Exhibition 566
Piedmont Craftsmen, Inc. 297
Pierre National Bank, The 341
Pik Place, The 391
Pinchpenny Gallery 281
Pine Tree Kiln 179
Pink Corral Gift Shop 393
Pink Petunia, The 129
Pinksterfest summer 'Minifest' 561
Pioneer Craft Festival 422
Pioneer Day of Pocohantas County 629
Pioneer Shoppe, The 171
Pippin Apple Jewelry 364
Pittsburg State University 39
Placer County Museum 97
Placerville Arts Association (see Mother Lode Art Show 430)
Places des Arts 407
Plains Art Museum 213
Plaza Arts & Crafts Show 549
Pleasure Faire of the Renaissance & Summer Marketplace 561
Plebian, The 97
Plum Dandy 179
Plum Nelly Shop, The 346
Polk Street Fair 431

Pomfret Shop, The 365
Pompanoosuc Mills 365
Ponchatoula Country Market, Inc. 171
Poor Richard's Gallery 197
Popovi Da Indian Arts & Crafts 251
Porter, Jerry 645
Portland Art Museum (see Museum Shop, Portland Art Museum 316)
Portside Craft Fair 523
Portsmouth National Seawall Art Show 620
Pot Shop/Art Gallery, The 156
Pot-pour-ri 61
Pot-Pourri Gallery of American Crafts 281
Potpourri Inc. 305
Pots 'n Stuff 229
Potter's Guild of Balto, Inc. 186
Potters Studio 97
Pottery & South 4th 282
Pottery Northwest 379
Powers' Crossroads Country Fair & Art Festival 464
Powhatan Arts & Crafts Show & Sale 620
Praire Flower Crafts 159
Prairie Front Workshop (see Bow River Arts Faire 639, Christmas Craft Faire 639)
Prairie House 146
Prairie Peoples Handicraft Market, Inc. 341
Prairie Textures 408
Prater's Mill Country Fair 464
Prema Productions (see Contemporary Crafts Showcase With Art at the Worcester Center 509, Contemporary Crafts Showcase With Art at the Boulevard Mall 552, Contemporary Crafts Showcase With Art at the Riverside Mall 552, Contemporary Crafts Showcase With Art at the Shoppingtown Mall 552, Contemporary Crafts Showcase With Art at the Summit Park Mall 553)
Preservation Shops 382
Prestige Galleries, Inc.
Pricketts Fort Memorial Foundation, Inc. 385
Priehs Department Store 209
Primitives & Contemporaries 251
Prints, Drawings & Crafts Exhibition 422
Prism Crescents 97
Professional Arts, Crafts & Indoor Plants Show 431
Promenades Shopping Center Festival of Arts & Crafts, The 456
Pug Mill Gallery, The 110
Pumpkin Patch, The (Maine) 180
Pumpkin Patch, The (Pennsylvania) 330
Putnam Arts Council (see Crafts & Creations 554)
Pyramid Shop, The 330

Q

Quaigh Design Centre, Inc. 365
Quaigh Designs 197

Quaint Corners 305
Quaker Arts Festival 561
Quaker Bridge Mall Arts Festival 547
Quaker Bridge Mall Children's Hour Show 547
Qualla Arts & Crafts Mutual, Inc. 297
Queens College 39
Queens Museum, The 282
Quest For Handcrafts, The 119
Quill Art, Inc. 62
Quilt Country Enterprises, Inc. 222
Quilt Craft 146
Quilter's Haven 346
Quiltery, The 331
Quimby Country 365
Quivira Shop 251

R

Raach's Plaza Gallery Inc. 222
Racine Art Association (see Monument Square Art Fair 634)
Racine Art Association of Wustum Museum of Fine Arts (see Mini Gallery 390)
Racine Art Guild (see Monument Square Art Fair 634)
Racine Christmas Gift Market 636
Raggedy Ann Antique Doll & Toy Museum 243
Rag-Time Artistry 153
Rainbow Enterprises (see Crafts Marketplace 595)
Rainbow, The 97
Rainbow Tree, Inc. 412
Rainbow West Batiks 62
Rainbow's End 282
Raintree Book & Art Shop 282
Raku, The (Claremont, California) 98
Raku, The (Santa Barbara, California) 98
Ralston Museum & Art Center Gift Shop, J.K. 230
Ralston Museum & Art Center Juried Exhibit, J.K. 539
Ramnad Corporation—D/B/A Pink Flamingo 146
Rare Discovery Collectables 134
Readey, J.J. (see Boca Raton Mall Arts & Crafts Show 449, Coastland Center Invitational Winter Festival of Art 450, Festival of Art 451, Gainesville Mall Arts & Crafts Show 452, Merritt Square Festival of Arts & Crafts 454, Olde Tyme Crafts and Arts 454, Orange Park Mall Festival of Art 454, Orange Park Mall Winter Craft Show 456, Park Shore Plaza Festival of Arts & Crafts 456, The Promenades Shopping Center Festival of Arts & Crafts 456, Tomato—Snook Festival 459, Hatcher Square Arts & Crafts Show 463, West Georgia Commons Mall Arts & Crafts Show 464)

Red Cloud Coop Arts & Crafts 341
Red Cock Craftsmen's Outlet, The 317
Red Cross Craft Market 592
Red Cupboard, The 366
Red Oak, The 146
Red River Annual 530
Red River Street Fair 568
Red Store & Ashery, The 366
Reed City Derby Days 523
Reedcraft Weavers 209
Reeder's Alley & Co. 230
Reflections Art Gallery 209
Regional 523
Regional Craftsmen's Fair 542
Renaissance Festival 537
Replica Sea Craft Studios 62
Return 251
Reyna Indian Shop, Tony 252
Rhode Island Association of Craftsmen (see Slater Mill Museum Shop 334)
Rhododendron State Outdoor Art & Craft Festival 629
Rice Festival Arts & Crafts Show 598
Richmond Craft Fair 621
Richmond Mall 574
Ricker Blacksmith Shop 180
Ridgeway Gallery 346
Ringling Museum's Annual Crafts Festival (see Outdoor Crafts Festival 456)
Ris Galleries, William (New Jersey) 243
Ris Galleries, William (Camp Hill, Pennsylvania) 331
Ris Galleries, William (Hershey, Pennsylvania) 331
River Gallery 317
Riverbend Arts Council (see Art in the Park 569)
Riverfront Market Day 415
Riverside Art Center & Museum 99 (also see Buy Arts for Christmas Show 425)
Riverside Downtown Saturday Market 432
Roach Galleries, J. 222
Roads Galleries 282
Roanoke Craft Festival, The 621
Robinsons' Red Door Gallery 99
Rock 'N Chair Productions (see Mountain Aire 430)
Rockhound Round-Up 641
Rockland Arts Day 562
Rocky Mountain Craft Fair 439
Rocky Mountain Gallery & Gift Shop, The 110
Rocky Mountain Park Co. 111
Rome Historical Society Ft. Stanwix Museum 283
Ronbach Shop 391
Rooftop Gallery 129
Roscoe Craft Center 283
Roseville Arts Center 99
Rosser's Arts & Crafts Center 341

Rothenberg Associates, Abraham 27
Rountree Gallery, Inc. 172
Royal Oak Outdoor Air Fair 523
Rubaiyat Crafts Gallery 408
Rubidoux Arts & Crafts Fair, Joseph 537
Rug Crafters 99
Rumpelstiltskin 297
Rural Rembrand Annual Art Show 636
Rustic Shoppe, The 99
Ruybalid's Indian Shop & Santa Fe Arts & Crafts 252

S

S&A Ceramics 147
Sacramento Regional Arts Council (see Festival of the Arts 427)
Saginaw West Side Art Festival 523
St. Andrews Presbyterian College 39
St. Augustine Arts & Crafts Council (see Arts & Crafts Festival 449)
St. Charles Artists Guild 222
St. Clair Art Fair 524
St. Cloud State University 39
St. Francis College (Indiana) 40
St. Francis College (Pennsylvania) 40
St. John's Outreach Arts, Crafts, & Antiques Sale 642
St. Joseph Art Association's Outdoor Art Fair 524
St. Joseph College 40
St. Joseph College Arts & Crafts Fair 446
St. Louis Art Museum—Museum Shop 222
St. Mary of the Woods College 40
St. Mary's College 40 (also see Moreau Gallery Three 152)
St. Mary's College of Maryland 40
Salem College Heritage Arts Festival 629
Salibello, Anna 645
Saline County Craft Fair 423
Salisbury Manor 283
Salt Lake Art Center (see The Gallery Shop 354)
Samara 366
San Francisco Annual Arts Festival 432
San Jose Art Center Gallery 100
San Jose Art League (see California 3-Dimensional Regional Exhibit & Competition 426)
San Jose Christmas Gift Show & Sale 432
San Mateo County Fair Crafts Exhibition 432
Sandeen's Scandinavian Gift & Art Shop 214
Sandie's Showcase 352
Sandpiper, The 243
Sanford-Seminole Art Association (see Fall for Art 451)
Sanibel Shell Fair 457
Santa Barbara Museum of Natural History 100
Santa Clara Valley Quilt Association (see

Index 677

American Museum of Quilts & Related Arts 81)
Santa Cruz County Fair 432
Santa Fe Community College 41 (also see Spring Arts Festival 458)
Santa Fe Festival of the Arts 550
Santa Monica Art Show 432
Santa-Cali-Gon Days 538
Santa's Christmas Gift Show 433
Santa's Land 366
Santaville Arts & Crafts Fair 636
Sarasota Spring Festival of Craft 457
Saturday Market 582
Saugatuck Douglas Art Fair 524
Sauk County Art Festival 636
Sault Summer Arts Festival 524
Sawdust Fine Arts and Crafts Festival 433
Scandesigin, Inc. 306
Scarborough Gallery of Arts & Crafts 283
Schacht—Johnson Associates, Inc. 27
Schaden Unlimited Productions, Jon 78
Schelu Artisans 252
Schenectady Museum (see Craft Festival 553)
Schiefer, C.R. 645
School On the Hill 408
Schuylkill County Council for the Arts 331
Schwab's Pipes 'n Stuff 166
Scott, Charles C. 645
Scottsdale Arts Festival 417
Scottsdale Center for the Arts (see Scottsdale Arts Festival 417)
Scubco 331
Sea Chest, The 180
Sea Crafters, The 180
Sea Gallery 100
Sea, The 100
Sears, Roebuck and Co. (see World Shows 437, 439, 540, 582, 625)
Seas National 457
Seattle Arts Festival: Bumbershoot 624
Seattle Harvest Festival 625
Sebastian-Moore Gallery 111
Second Hand Rose 159
Seidel Shops, Betty 332
Selexor Displays Inc. 62
Self Expressions 112
Senior Citizen Arts & Crafts Coop 385
Senior Citizens Handcraft Shoppe 160
September Fest 530
Septemberfest 415
Seraph 382
Serendipity 215
Serendipity Arts and Crafts Shop 386
Serendipity Galleries 346
Serendipity, The (see Christmas in September Festival 627)
Serenity Leather & Crafts 197
Serkin Co., L.J. 366
Sermon-Anderson, Inc. 224

7 Lively Arts Festival, Incorporated, Art Show 457
Seven Springs Crafts Shop 78
Seventeenth Colony House 306
Shadetree Antiques 172
Shaker Lakes Regional Nature Center 306
Shaker Museum, The 283
Shalako Shop, Inc. 252
Shawano Arts & Crafts Fair 636
Shawnee Arts & Interiors 312
Shaw-Rimmington Gallery 408
Shepherd Mall Craft Show 581
Sheri's House of Crafts 147
Sherman Corporate Art, Liza 28
Sherrymike Pottery/Gallery 180
Shetani Gallery 408
Sheyenne Valley Arts & Crafts Festival 568
Shiawassee Arts Council (see Curwood Festival Arts & Crafts Market 518)
Shippensburg Fair Crafts-Arts Show & Sale 592
Shippensburg State College 41
Shiva, Inc. 62
Sholem Aleichem Institute Art Show & Sale 524
Shoop, Charles E. 332
Shop, Adirondack Lakes Center for the Arts, The 284
Shop, Albany Institute of History & Art, The 284
Shop at the Inn, The 367
Shop Downstairs, The 409
Shop—Guilford Handcraft Center, The 120
Shop of the Rainbow Man, Inc. 252
Shop of the Southwest 352
Shop, The (California) 100
Shop, The (West Virginia) 386
Shops for Pappagallo (Acton, Massachusetts) 197
Shops for Pappagallo (Faneuil Hall Marketplace, Boston) 197
Shops for Pappagallo (Newbury Street, Boston) 197
Shops for Pappagallo (Newton, Massachusetts) 197
Shorebirds 101
Show & Sell 629
Show of Hands, A 284
Show of the Craft Guild of Greater Cincinnati 574
Shuler, Karen 645
Side Street, The 147
Sidewalk Art & Craft Fair 636
Sidewalk Arts & Crafts Fair 530
Sidewalk Show 625
Sierra Nevada Museum of Art Shop 232
Sign of the Acorn 160
Sign of the Copper Lantern, The 209
Silk Purse & the Sow's Ear, The 367
Silo, The 120

Silver Dollar City, Inc. 224
Silverado Country Fair 433
Silverdale's Whaling Days 625
Silvermine Guild of Artists (see Christmas Arts Festival 440, New England Painting & Sculpture Exhibition 445)
Silvers-Mi-Thing 101
Silverworks, The 120
Simonds Studio, M. (see Earthworks & Artisans 265)
Simple Gifts Inc. 284
Simply Natural 284
Sindler, Allan J. 646
Skagway Artists Coop 71
Skare, John 646
Sketch Box, The 352
Skin Trade, The 367
Skull Creek Craft Shop 338
Skylight Gallery 380
Slater Memorial Museum 446
Slater Mill Museum Shop 334
Smith College, William 41
Smith Interiors, Dixon 28, 172
Smith Silversmith Shop, C. Leslie 332
Smith-Mason Gallery Museum 383
Smithsonian Museum Shops 383
Smull Gallery, A.D. 383
Sneak Box Studio, The 197
Snell Ltd., Judith 62
Snowmass Arts & Crafts Fair 439
Society of Arts & Crafts, The 198
Society of Connecticut Craftsmen 120
Society of the Arts' Annual Festival of the Arts "Arti Gras" 457
Soft Touch, Ltd., The 367
Sol Del Rio 352
Solstia, Inc. (see Winterworks 416)
Some Place 101
Somerset Invitational 525
Something Special in Sierra City 101
Something to Crow About 101
Sonnenberg Gardens, Garden Gifts 285
Sonoma County Fair 433
Sonora Christmas Fair 434
Sonrise Design 409
Sophienburg Museum Shop 353
Source Gallery 102
South County Art Annual 595
South County Art Association (see Earthworks 595, South County Art Annual 595)
South County Crafts Show & Sale 538
South Dakota Memorial Art Center Shop 342
South Dakota State University 41 (also see Agricultural Heritage Museum 339, South Dakota Memorial Art Center Shop 342)
South Florida Fairs & Expositions, Inc. 458
South Hills Village Arts Festival 592
South Hills Village Children's Show 592

South Hills Village Professional Arts Festival 593
South Lake Festival of the Arts 434
South Parkersburg Band Boosters Christmas Arts & Craft Show 629
Southeast Missouri Council on the Arts (see Christmas Craft Bazaar 535)
Southeastern Missouri State University 41
Southeastern-Northgate Art Show 566
Southern California Exposition 434
Southern California Powwow 434
Southern Christmas Show 566
Southern Highland Handicraft Guild (see Guild Crafts 294, Piedmont Craftsmen, Inc. 297)
Southern Illinois University (Edwardsville, Illinois) (see Craft Shop Crafts Fair 470)
Southern Illinois University (Carbondale, Illinois) 41
Southern Living Magazine (see Southern Living Show 566)
Southern Living Show 566
Southern Park Mall 574
Southern Shows, Inc. (see Southern Christmas Show 566)
Southern Tier Arts Association Inc. (see Art in the Park 551)
Southland Art Show 434
Southold Historical Society Museum 285
Southwest Arts, Inc. (see De Vargas Summer Arts & Crafts Show 549)
Southwest Crafts Biennial 550
Southwest Georgia Art Association (see Albany Arts Festival 461)
Southwestern Association on Indian Affairs (see Swaia Indian Market 550)
Spartanburg County Art Association (see Invitational Crafts Show 598)
Spectra Productions (see Arts Crafts Show 465, Christmas Show 465)
Spectrum of American Artists & Craftsmen, Inc., The (Brewster, Massachusetts) 199
Spectrum of American Artists & Craftsmen, Inc., The (Hyannis, Massachusetts) 199
Spectrum of American Artists & Craftsmen, Inc., The (Nantucket, Massachusetts) 199
Spectrum of American Artists & Craftsmen, Inc., The (Rhode Island) 335
Speed Art Museum Shop, J.B. 166
Sperry Univac Plant (see Charles Town Factory Outlet Complex 261)
Spertus Museum of Judaica, Museum Store 147
Spillikin Corners at Magic Mountain 102
Spin It-Weave It 102
Spinnerin Yarn Co., Inc. 62
Spirit Tree, The 306
Sports Art 172
Sportsman's Gallery 353
Spot Arts & Crafts Shop 285

Sprecher, Stanley 646
Spring Arts Festival (Florida) 458
Spring Arts Festival (Pennsylvania) 593
Spring Arts Potpourri in the Park 458
Spring Craft Fair & Sale 593
Spring Craft Market at Park City Mall 593
Spring Crafts Fair 446
Spring Easter Arts & Crafts Show 562
Spring Market 446
Spring National Crafts Festival 538
Spring Show (Ohio) 575
Spring Show (Pennsylvania) 593
Spring Street Enamels Gallery 285, 646
Spring Street Pottery, The 78
Springfield Art Association 147
Springfield Art Museum (see Invitational Craft Fair 536)
Springfield Mall Children's Hour Show 594
Springfield Mall Craft & Sculpture Show 594
Springs Folk Festival 594
Spurgeon Mercantile Co. 147
Square Fair 575
Sragow Ltd., Ellen 286
Stained Glass Associates 297
Stanley, Architects, Duffy B. 28
Starving Artist Art Show 581
State Historical Society of Wisconsin—Museum Store, The 391
State University College at Oneonta (see Festival of the Arts 555)
Station Gallery 153
Steeple Artworks 409
Stencil-Magic 62
Stephens County Historical Museum 313
Sterling/Drake Publishers, Inc. 62
Stitchery '80 594
Stitchery, Inc., The 63
Stone Mountain Crafts, Inc. 298
Stone Soldier Pottery 368
Stone Village Art Center (see The Clay Gallery 202)
Stoner, Kaaren L. 646
Stonewall Jackson House, The 375
Stonewall Jackson Jubilee 630
Store, Arkansas Territorial Restoration, The 78
Store Ltd., The 186
Store, The 332
Storehouse 298
Storehouse, Inc. (Apple Valley Rd., Atlanta) 133
Storehouse, Inc. (Buckhead, Atlanta) 133
Storehouse, Inc. (Northlake, Atlanta) 133
Storehouse, Inc. (Sandy Springs, Atlanta) 133
Storehouse, Inc. (Tennessee) 346
Storehouse, Inc. (Austin, Texas) 353
Storehouse, Inc. (Carillon Plaza, Dallas, Texas) 353
Storehouse, Inc. (Preston Center Plaza, Dallas, Texas) 353

Storehouse, Inc. (Champion Forrest Plaza, Houston, Texas) 353
Storehouse, Inc. (Greenspoint Mall, Houston, Texas) 353
Storehouse, Inc. (Sharpstown Center, Houston, Texas) 353
Storehouse, Inc. (South Post Oak Road, Houston, Texas) 353
Storehouse, Inc. (Town & Country Village, Houston, Texas) 353
Storehouse, Inc. (San Pedro Avenue, San Antonio, Texas) 353
Storrowton Village Museum 199
Story Book Crafts 306
Strasburg Museum 375
Strawberry Walrus, The 129
Streets of Taos 252
Strong Craft Gallery (Connecticut) 121
Strong Craft Gallery (Maine) 181
Students' Museum 346
Studio Gallery, The 253
Studio of Natural Arts 210
Studio S Gallery 347
Studio 7 102
Studio Suenaga 103
Studio, The (California) 102
Studio, The (New York) 286
Studio Wefan 409
Studio West—Encintas 103
Stuff & Things 386
Stuffed Stocking, The 224
Sturgis Newcomers' Club Arts & Crafts Fair 525
Suburban Fine Arts Center 147
Suffolk Marine Museum Gift Shop 286
Sugar Creek Craft Shop 78
Suggin Folklife Art Show 423
Summer Craft Show & Bazaar 446
Summer in the City 465
Summer Indoor Arts & Crafts Show 562
Summer Mall Art Show 547
Summerfair Inc. 575
Summerfest 637
Summit Mall 575
Sumter Cultural Commission (see Fall Fiesta of the Arts 597)
Sun Circle Crafts Gallery 232
Sun Shop, The 332
Sun Sign 112
Sun Valley Center's Invitational Arts & Crafts Festival 465
Sunbonnet Festival 567
Sunbow Gallery 317
Sunbury Shores Arts & Nature Centre 410
Sunday-on-the-Square 567
Sunflower Shop 210
Sunflower Studio Apprenticeship Program 646
Sunnyvalle Creative Arts Center 103
Sunrise 181

Sunrise of Santa Fe 253
Sunrise Shops 386
Sunshine Factory, The 121
Sunshine Gallery, The 286
Sunshine Shoppe, The 243
Sunshine Snowy Day 368
Sunshine Unlimited, Inc. 148
Sunwise Leather Co. 79
Suny College of Enviromental Science & Forestry 42
Super Crafts Sunday 547
Suprises in Store 130
Suttende Arts & Crafts 637
Sutter Street Art Festival 435
Sutter's Mill 199
Sutton-Hoo Goldsmith 112
Suwannee River Crafts Show-Sale 458
Suzuki Gallery 286
SWAIA Indian Market 550
Swamp John's 181
Sweet Earth Shop 103
Sylamore Creek Craft Shop 79
Symmography, Inc. 63
Syndicate, The (Dallas, Texas) 353
Synechia Arts Center Inc. 286
Synergy 307
Szoradi, AIA, Charles 28

T

Talbot Flower & Gift 313
Talent Tree, The 160
Talents & Co. Art Gallery 313
Tama County Fair 562
Tanana Valley Fair Mosquito Market 416
Tanana Valley State Craft Market 416
Taos Festival of the Arts 550
Tapestry 112
Tapestry Associates 29
Tarbox Gallery 103
Tarkio College 42
Tarpon Springs Arts & Crafts Show 458
Tawas Bay Waterfront Art Fair 525
Taylor-London's Old Curiousity Shop 355
Teasel Crafts 333
Tehachapi Mountain Festival Art Faire 435
Temple Mound Museum 130
Temple of Good Things 104
Terra-Cotta, Inc. 199
Texas Christian University 42
Tex-Craft Co. Inc. 63
Textiles by Design 104
Textured Yarn Arts, Inc. 63
Thanksgiving Festival & Craft Show 642
Thanksgiving Folk-Craft Festival 435
Thanksgiving Weekend Christmas Arts & Crafts Show 562
Theatre by the Sea Street Fair 542
Thendara Studio Gallery 121
Things for Living 113
Thistledown Gallery 244

Thomas Christmas Art & Crafts Show, E.J. 575
Thompson Gallery, The 74
Thorens Music Boxes 63
Thought Form & Fantasy 307
Threads Unlimited 439
Three Bags Full—Toys 368
Three Crowns, The 287
Three Rivers Arts Festival 594
3 Rooms Up 214
3's Company Gallery, Ltd. 410
Thumb Fun Amusement Park 391
Tidepool Gallery (California) 104
Tidepool Gallery (Maine) 214
Tifanee Tree, The (Bethesda, Maryland) 186
Tifanee Tree, The (Chevy Chase, Maryland) (see The Great Chase 185)
Tifanee Tree, The (Washington DC) 383
Tilles Park Arts & Crafts Fair 538
Tippecanoe County Historical Association, Fowler House Museum
Titusville Art League Annual Show 459
Tivoli Fair 525
Toledo Area Artists Exhibition 575
Toledo Artists Club (see Toledo Festival of the Arts 575)
Toledo Federation of Art Societies (see Toledo Area Artists Exhibition 575)
Toledo Festival of the Arts 575
Toledo Museum of Art (see Toledo Area Artists Exhibition 575)
Tom Sawyer Dioramas & Aunt Polly's Handcrafts 223
Tomar 307
Tomato—Snook Festival 459
Tomlinson Craft Collection, The 186
Tomtegard, Inc., Scandinavian Design Interiors 181
Tool & Talent—Handcrafts of Distinction 244
Topeka Public Library Gallery of Fine Arts 160
Touch of Glass, Stained Glass Studio, A 393
Touch of Whimsy, A 287
Tower Gallery 148
Towle Company, E.J. 64
Town & Country Gallery 230
Town and Country Village—Kiwanis Art Fiesta 435
Toy Chest & Handcarved Circus, The 153
Toy Chest, The 368
Toy Factory, The 410
Toy Store, Inc., The 369
Toymakers Shop 224
Toys Designed by Artists Exhibition 423
Trade Path, The 298
Trading Company, The 253
Tranquil Things 369
Traverse Bay Outdoor Art Fair 525
Treasured Timbers 130
Treehouse, The Holden Arboretum, The 308

Index 681

Tregre and Miller Associates, Inc. (see Tama County Fair 562)
Treskunoff Studio, Inc., The 121
Triangle Festival of Crafts 567
Trillium Fine Crafts 369
Trilogy Gallery Inc. 154
Trimble Court Artisans 114
Trinity College 42
Triton Museum of Art 104
Truckee Art Guild (see Truckee Outdoor Arts & Crafts Fair 436)
Truckee Outdoor Arts & Crafts Fair 436
Tucker Tower Museum 313
Tucson Festival Arts & Crafts Fair 418
Tucson Museum of Art (see "Arizona Crafts" 416)
"Tuesday's Child" Art Gallery 135
Tullahoma Fine Arts Center 347
Turtle, The 339
Tuttles Seashore Shell House 130
Twelmeyer Galleries 391
Twenty Four Collection, The 130
Twenty-nine Palms Artists Guild (see Southland Art Show 434)
26 East Art Center, Inc. 314
Two Flags Festival Outdoor Show 418
2 + 2 Ltd. Gallery 172
Two Rivers Gallery/Roberson Center for the Arts & Sciences 287

U

U.F.O. & Plants 135
Uncommon, The 287
Unfinished Universe, The 167
Unicorn 369
Unicorn City Corporation, The 288
Union College 42
Union Street Spring Festival & Crafts Fair 436
Unique Shop 375
Unique, The 114
Universal Galleries, Inc. 244
University Artists & Craftsmen Guild Christmas Art Fair 526
University Artists & Craftsmen Guild Fall Art Fair 526
University Artists & Craftsmen Guild Spring Arts Festival 526
University Artists & Craftsmen Guild Summer Arts Festival 526
University Gallery of Chicago State University, The 148
University of Alabama 42
University of California at Davis 42
University of California at Riverside 43
University of Central Arkansas 43
University of Central Florida 43
University of Georgia 43
University of Guelph (see Fair November 640)
University of Iowa 43
University of Kentucky 44
University of Maine at Farmington 44
University of Maryland 44
University of Massachusetts at Boston 44
University of Michigan 44
University of Missouri-Columbia 45
University of Nebraska at Lincoln 45
University of New Mexico (see Maxwell Museum Gift Shop 249)
University of North Carolina at Chapel Hill 45
University of North Carolina at Greensboro 45
University of North Dakota Art Galleries 299
University of Pennsylvania (see The Pyramid Shop 330)
University of Santa Clara (see De Saisset Art Gallery & Museum—Gallery Shop 86)
University of Santa Clara 45
University of South Dakota 45 (also see W.H. Overly Museum 340)
University of Southern California 45
University of Southern California Craft Center 436
University of Southern Colorado (see Own Your Own Art Show 438)
University of Southern Louisiana Union Craft Shop 173
University of the Pacific 46
University of Victoria 46 (also see Maltwood Art Museum & Gallery 405)
University of Virginia 46
University of Wisconsin (see Detailed Look, National Metalsmithing & Jewelry Invitational 632)
University of Wisconsin at Oshkosh 46
University of Wisconsin at Stevens Point 46
Unusual Shop, The 224
Up in Central Park Art Fair 527
Up North Handcrafts/Lady Slipper Designs 214
Upper Echelon 104
Upstairs 148
Upstairs Gallery, The 167
Upstairs Pottery 121
Upstairs Pottery & Crafts 167
Upstate New York Craftsmen's Guild (see Holiday Arts & Crafts Fair 557)
Uptown Art Fair 530
Urban Development Co. 29
Uriah Heeps 114
Ursuline Gallery at the Southwest Craft Center, The 354
Usquepaugh Johnny Cake Festival, The 595
USS Alabama Battleship 68
Utexiqual Products, Div. 64

V

Valley Art Center, Inc. 380

Valley Art Gallery 104
Valley Craft Guild Christmas Show 436
Valley, The 215
Valur Boutique Ltd. 167
Van Cline & Davenport Ltd. 244
Van Doren Gallery 105
Vancouver Aquarium (see The Clamshell 397)
Venice Place Arts Center 105
Verde Valley Art Gallery, Inc. 74
Vermont Crafts Market, Inc. 370
Vermont Historical Society 370
Vermont State Craft Center at Windsor House 370
Vero Art Club Gallery (see Vero Beach Art Club Winter Art Show 459)
Vero Beach Art Club Winter Art Show 459
Very Special Art Show, A 436
Verzyl Gallery 288
Vesta Glass, Inc. 64
Vestibule Shop 135
Victorian Craft Festival 531
Victorian House, The 79
Victorian Stable, The 182
Village Art & Craft Fair 567
Village Artists' & Craftsmen's Art & Craft Fair 562
Village Crafts 347
Village Crafts & Curios 288
Village Craftsman 154
Village Craftsmen 298
Village Green Craft Shop (see East Tennesssee Crafts Inc. 344)
Village Leather Shop, The 187
Village Mall Fine Art & Craft Show 637
Village Mall Fine Art & Craft Spring Show 638
Village Miniatures 225
Village Silversmith, The 288
Virginia Beach Folk Arts Festival 621
Virginia Commonwealth University 46 (also see Anderson Gallery 371)
Virginia Crafts Council Crafts Fair 621
Virginia Craftsmen 622
Virginia Handcrafts, Inc. 376
Virginia Museum-Council Sales Shop 376
Virginia Museum of Fine Arts (see Virginia Craftsmen 622)
Virginia Polytechnic Institute & State University Art Gallery 376
Vlada 199
Volksfest of the Arts 638
Voltaire's Shop & Gallery 121
Vortex Stained Glass Studios 200

W

Walker, L.B. 647
Wall Gallery, The 244
Walnut Creek Civic Arts Gallery 105
Walnut Street Theatre Gallery, The 333

Walrus Factory, Inc. 64
Walt Disney World (see The Arts Festival in the Village 449)
Walthers Inc., William K. 64
Ward, Lydia (see Bedford Village Art Show 551)
Ward-Nasse Gallery 288
Ward's University Bookstore (St. Cloud State University 39)
Ware Gallery, Gifts 123
Ware Gallery 123
Warp & Weft Weavers 647
Warren Festival of Arts 527
Warwick Mall Children's Hour Show 596
Warwick Mall Professional Craft & Sculpture Show 596
Washington Art Association 122
Washington County Museum of Fine Arts 187
Water Wheel, The 114
Waterfront Art Fair 527
Waterfront Art Festival 563
Watkins, Inc. 354
Waunakee Art Council (see Volksfest of the Arts 638)
Wax-Beyman Associates 29
Way Ahead Boutique 370
Wayne County Historical Museum 154
Waynesboro Studio Club (see Clothesline Exhibit 584)
Waynesboro's Craft Day 594
Weavers Guild Fiber Fair 531
Weavers' Store, The 225
Weaving Place Ltd., The 288
Weaving Workshop 148
Web, Inc., The 130
Webb & Parsons 122
Weber Galleries 289
Wee Little Shoppe 392
Wee Littles in Hobby City 105
Wee Spinnaker, The 200
Weed Lady & Other Wondrous Wares & Gingham Gallery, The (Bellevue, Washington) 380
Weed Lady & Other Wondrous Wares & Gingham Gallery, The (Edmonds, Washington) 380
Weissner Designs, Inc., Helene 29
Welcome Rood Studio 335
Well Fancy This 333
Wells College 46
West Georgia Commons Mall Arts & Crafts Show 464
West Hartford Spring Arts & Crafts Fair 446
West Hudson Community Arts Festival 547
West Nebraska Arts Center 231
West Plains Council on the Arts (see Folk Music & Crafts Festival 535)
West Shore Art League (see Ludington Arts & Crafts Fair 521)

West Texas Museum Association (see The Museum Shop 351)
West Virginia Artists and Craftsmen Guild (see Mountain State Art & Craft Fair 628)
West Yellowstone Museum 230
Westbury Annual Outdoor Art & Crafts Festival 563
Westerly Art Festival 596
Western Heritage Gallery 230
Western Kentucky University 46
Western Maryland College 47
Western Washington Fair Art Show 625
Western Woodcarvings 342
Westerville Musical & Arts Festival 576
Westfield Arts & Crafts Festival 563
Westlake Gallery Ltd. 289
Westland Arts & Crafts Show 576
Weston Bowl Mill 371
Westport Creative Arts Festival 447
Westport Handcrafts Fair 447
Westwood Clay National 436
Wewoka Trading Post 314
Whale's Tale 245
Wharf Shop, The 182 (also see The Lubec Crafts Council, Inc. 178)
Whatsmenot? 253
Wheaton Village 245
Wheelbarrow, The 289
Wheelhouse, The 225
Wheelwright Museum, The 253
Whichcraft 105
Whickerbill Contemporary 114
Whiff 'N Pouff 347
Whifferdill, The 392
Whiffletree, The 318
Whimsey Craftshop & Gallery, The 289
Whistlin' Jack Arts & Crafts 625
White Bear Arts Council (see Fair in the Fields 528)
White Bird Gallery 318
White Buffalo Gallery 160
White Elephant Galleries, The 68
White Oak Pottery 79
White River Valley Arts & Crafts Fair 538
White Unicorn Gallery 290
Whitworth College 47
Wholly Cow 105
Why Not 1 122
Wicker Garden, Inc., The 290
Wickersham & Sons, Inc. 105
Wickford Art Festival 596
Widen Gallery, Ross 308
Wiita Decorator Crafts, Inc., Betty 64
Wild Flower, The 225
Wild Oats 225
Wild Rose Studio 114
Wild Weft, The 210
Wilderness Road Clockworks 226
Wilkes College 47
Wilkes Gallery, Inc. 290

Williamsburg Art Gallery 376
Will-o-the-Wick, Ltd. 290
Willowbrook Mall Art Show 548
Willowbrook Mall Children's Hour Show 548
Willowbrook Mall Fiber Fair 548
Willowbrook Mall Wooden Way Show 548
Wilmington Craft Fair 448
Wind & Sun Creations 210
Windmill Craft Coop Association 410
Window on Main Street 290
Windsong House Ltd. 411
Windsor Gallery 215
Windward Crafts 68
Winfield House (see Lewisburg Craft Fair 589)
Winfield House 333
Winge, AIA, Cleveland A. 29
Wings West Gallery 230
Winnipeg Folk Festival 642
Winona County Historical Society Museum Shop, The 215
Winona Trading Post 253
Winslow I-40 Expo 418
Winston Salem State University 47
Winter Artas & Crafts Fair 418
Winter Park Mall Craft Show 459
Winter Park Sidewalk Art Festival 459
Winterthur Museum Bookstore & Gift Shop 123
Winterworks 416
Winthrop Gallery 154
Wisconsin Dells Art Association (see Wo-Zha-Wa Days Art Fair 638)
Wisconsin Designer Craftsmen Morning Glory Fair 638
Wistariahurst Museum 200
Witte Museum Shop 354
Womencrafts, Inc. 200
Wonderful Things, Inc. 201
Wonderful World of Ohio Mart 576
Wondrous Things, Inc. 291
Wood Islands Handcraft Coop 411
Wood 'N' Wool Gift Shop 411
Wood Shop, The 380
Woodbridge Center Craft & Sculpture Show 548
Woodchop 376
Woodland Workshop 211
Woodmere Museum Shop 333
Wood-n-Thread 80
Woodring Craft 64
Woodville Mall 576
Woodville Museum of Southern Decorative Arts 216
Wool-Art 80
Woolmark, The 105
Wooly Llama 318
Worcester Art Museum 201
Worcester Polytechnic Institute 47
Worcester State College 47

Works Craft Gallery, The 334
Works Gallery East, Inc., The 291
World Shows 437, 439, 540, 582, 625
Worlds Fair 226
Worlds of Wildlife 106
Worthington Historical Society Gift Shop 308
Woven Images 226
Wo-Zha-Wa Days Art Fair 638
Wright Art Center (see Beloit & Vicinity Exhibition 630)
Wudtke, Watson, Davis, Inc. 29
Wydra, Nancilee 647

X

X-Acto 66
Xavier University 47

Y

YAAF Exhibition of Fine Art 447
Yadkin Arts Council (see Sunbonnet Festival 567)
Yakima Valley Museum Shop 380
Yaley Enterprises 66
Yancey County Country Store 298
Yankee Artisan 182
Yankee Peddler Country Crafts 226
Yankee Peddler Festival 576
Yarn Bazaar 376
Ybor Square Christmas Crafts Carnival 460
Ybor Square Fall Arts & Crafts Fiesta 460
Ybor Square Spring Arts & Crafts Fiesta 460
Ybor Square Summer Crafts Carnival 461
Ye Olde Huff N Puff 66
Ye Wise Owl Shoppe Ltd. 411
Yeatts Gallery, J.M. 376
Yellow Daisy Festival 464
Yellow Door, The 245
Yellowstone Art Center 231
Yen Nan Gallery 167
Yesteryear Toy Company, Inc. 386
YMCA Arts & Crafts Fair 622
Young Artist Association of Fairfield (see YAAF Exhibition of Fine Art 447)
Young Gallery 106
Yuletide Fair, The 542
Yuma Art Center 74

Z

Zane Square Arts & Crafts Festival 576
Zanesville Art Center (see May Arts & Crafts Exhibition 573)
Zara Gallery 106
Zeeland Arts Festival 527
Zero Wampum 335
Zjay Gallery 354

Books of Interest From Writer's Digest

Artist's Market, edited by Cathy Bruce and Betsy Wones. Contains over 3,000 commercial art buyers. Listings tell you who to contact and where, pay rates, special requirements and more. 432 pp. $10.95.

The Beginning Writer's Answer Book, edited by Kirk Polking, Jean Chimsky, and Rose Adkins. "What is a query letter?" "If I use a pen name, how can I cash the check?" These are among 567 questions most frequently asked by beginning writers—and expertly answered in this down-to-earth handbook. Cross-indexed. 270 pp. $8.95.

How to be a Successful Housewife/Writer, by Elaine Fantle Shimberg. The art of being a successful housewife/writer. 256 pp. $10.95.

The Cartoonist's and Gag Writer's Handbook, by Jack Markow. Longtime cartoonist with thousands of sales, reveals the secrets of successful cartooning—step by step. Richly illustrated. 157 pp. $8.95.

A Complete Guide to Marketing Magazine Articles, by Duane Newcomb. "Anyone who can write a clear sentence can learn to write and sell articles on a consistent basis." says Newcomb (who has published well over 3,000 articles). Here's how. 248 pp. $7.95.

The Confession Writer's Handbook, by Florence K. Palmer. A stylish and informative guide to getting started and getting ahead in the confessions. How to start a confession and carry it through. How to take an insignificant event and make it significant. 171 pp. $7.95.

The Craft of Interviewing, by John Brady. Everything you always wanted to know about asking questions, but were afraid to ask—from an experienced interviewer and editor of *Writer's Digest*. The most comprehensive guide to interviewing on the market. 244 pp. $9.95.

Craftworker's Market, edited by Lynne Lapin. Over 3,500 places for you to sell and exhibit your work. Listings include names and addresses, payment rates, special requirements and other information you need to sell your crafts. 696 pp. $11.95.

The Creative Writer, edited by Aron Mathieu. This book opens the door to the real world of publishing. Inspiration, techniques, and ideas, plus inside tips from Maugham, Caldwell, Purdy, others. 416 pp. $8.95.

The Greeting Card Writer's Handbook, by H. Joseph Chadwick. A former greeting card editor tells you what editors look for in inspirational verse...how to write humor...what to write about for conventional, studio and juvenile cards. Extra: a renewable list of greeting card markets. Will be greeted by any freelancer. 268 pp. $8.95.

A Guide to Writing History, by Doris Ricker Marston. How to track down Big Foot—or your family Civil War letters, or your hometown's last century—for publication and profit. A timely handbook for history buffs and writers. 258 pp. $8.50.

Handbook of Short Story Writing, edited by Frank A. Dickson and Sandra Smythe. You provide the pencil, paper, and sweat—and this book will provide the expert guidance. Features include James Hilton on creating a lovable character; R.V. Cassill on plotting a short story. 238 pp. $9.95.

Law and the Writer, edited by Kirk Polking and Leonard S. Meranus. Don't let legal hassles slow down your progress as a writer. Now you can find good counsel on libel, invasion of privacy, fair use, taxes, contracts, social security, and more—all in one volume. 249 pp. $9.95.

Magazine Writing: The Inside Angle, by Art Spikol. Successful editor and writer reveals inside secrets of getting your mss. published. 288 pp. $10.95.

Magazine Writing Today, by Jerome E. Kelley. If you sometimes feel like a mouse in a maze of magazines, with a fat manuscript check at the end of the line, don't fret. Kelley tells you how to get a piece of the action. Covers ideas, research, interviewing, organization, the writing process, and ways to get photos. Plus advice on getting started. 220 pp. $9.95.

Mystery Writer's Handbook, by the Mystery Writers of America. A howtheydunit to the whodunit, newly written and revised by members of the Mystery Writers of America. Includes the four elements essential to the classic mystery. A comprehensive handbook that takes the mystery out of mystery writing. 273 pp. $8.95.

1001 Article Ideas, by Frank A. Dickson. A compendium of ideas plus formulas to generate more of your own! 256 pp. $10.95.

Writing for Regional Publications, by Brian Vachon. How to write for this growing market. 256 pp. $10.95.

One Way to Write Your Novel, by Dick Perry. For Perry, a novel is 200 pages. Or, two pages a day for 100 days. You can start and finish your novel, with the help of this step-by-step guide taking you from blank sheet to polished page. 138 pp. $8.95.

Photographer's Market, edited by Melissa Milar. Contains what you need to know to be a successful freelance photographer. Names, addresses, photo requirements, and payment rates for 3,000 markets. 624 pp. $12.95.

The Poet and the Poem, by Judson Jerome. A rare journey into the night of the poem—the mechanics, the mystery, the craft and sullen art. Written by the most widely read authority on poetry in America, and a major contemporary poet in his own right. 400 pp. $11.95.

Sell Copy, by Webster Kuswa. Tells the secrets of successful business writing. How to write it. How to sell it. How to buy it. 224 pp. $11.95.

Songwriter's Market, edited by William Brohaugh. Lists 2,000 places where you can sell your songs. Included are the people and companies who work daily with songwriters and musicians. Features names and addresses, pay rates and other valuable information you need to sell your work. 432 pp. $10.95.

Stalking the Feature Story, by William Ruehlmann. Besides a nose for news, the newspaper feature writer needs an ear for dialog and an eye for detail. He must also be adept at handling off-the-record remarks, organization, grammar, and the investigative story. Here's the "scoop" on newspaper feature writing. 314 pp. $9.95.

Successful Outdoor Writing, by Jack Samson. Longtime editor of *Field & Stream* covers this market in depth. Illustrated. 288 pp. $11.95.

A Treasury of Tips for Writers, edited by Marvin Weisbord. Everything from Vance Packard's system of organizing notes to tips on how to get research done free, by 86 magazine writers. 174 pp. $7.95.

Writer's Digest. The world's leading magazine for writers. Monthly issues include timely interviews, columns, tips to keep writers informed on where and how to sell their work. One year subscription, $15.

The Writer's Digest Diary. Plan your year in it, note appointments, log manuscript sales, be prepared for the IRS. It will become a permanent annual record of writing activity. Durable cloth cover. 144 pp. $8.95.

Writer's Market, edited by William Brohaugh. The freelancer's bible, containing 4,500 places to sell what you write. Includes the name, address and phone number of the buyer, a description of material wanted and rates of payment. 912 pp. $14.95.

The Writer's Resource Guide, edited by William Brohaugh. Over 2,000 research sources for information on anything you write about. 488 pp. $11.95.

Writer's Yearbook, edited by John Brady. This large annual magazine contains how-to-articles, interviews and special features, along with analyses of 500 major markets for writers. 128 pp. $2.50.

Writing and Selling Non-Fiction, by Hayes B. Jacobs. Explores with style and know-how the book market, organization and research, finding new markets, interviewing, humor, agents, writer's fatigue and more. 317 pp. $10.95.

Writing and Selling Science Fiction, compiled by the Science Fiction Writers of America. A comprehensive handbook to an exciting but oft-misunderstood genre. Eleven articles by top-flight sf writers on markets, characters, dialog, "crazy" ideas, world-building, alien-building, money and more. 197 pp. $8.95.

Writing for Children and Teen-agers, by Lee Wyndham. Author of over 50 children's books shares her secrets for selling to this large, lucrative market. Features: the 12-point recipe for plotting, and the Ten Commandments for Writers. 253 pp. $9.95.

Writing Popular Fiction, by Dean R. Koontz. How to write mysteries, suspense, thrillers, science fiction, Gothic romances, adult fantasy, Westerns and erotica. Here's an inside guide to lively fiction, by a lively novelist. 232 pp. $8.95.

Writing the Novel: From Plot to Print, by Lawrence Block. Practical advice on how to write any kind of novel. 256 pp. $10.95.

(1-2 books, add $1.00 postage and handling; 3 or more, additional 25¢ each. Allow 30 days for delivery. Prices subject to change without notice.)
Writer's Digest Books, Dept. B, 9933 Alliance Road, Cincinnati, Ohio 45242